IFIP Advances in Information and Communication Technology 409

IFIP – The International Federation for Information Processing

IFIP was founded in 1960 under the auspices of UNESCO, following the First World Computer Congress held in Paris the previous year. An umbrella organization for societies working in information processing, IFIP's aim is two-fold: to support information processing within ist member countries and to encourage technology transfer to developing nations. As ist mission statement clearly states,

> IFIP's mission is to be the leading, truly international, apolitical organization which encourages and assists in the development, exploitation and application of information technology for the benefit of all people.

IFIP is a non-profitmaking organization, run almost solely by 2500 volunteers. It operates through a number of technical committees, which organize events and publications. IFIP's events range from an international congress to local seminars, but the most important are:

- The IFIP World Computer Congress, held every second year;
- Open conferences;
- Working conferences.

The flagship event is the IFIP World Computer Congress, at which both invited and contributed papers are presented. Contributed papers are rigorously refereed and the rejection rate is high.

As with the Congress, participation in the open conferences is open to all and papers may be invited or submitted. Again, submitted papers are stringently refereed.

The working conferences are structured differently. They are usually run by a working group and attendance is small and by invitation only. Their purpose is to create an atmosphere conducive to innovation and development. Refereeing is less rigorous and papers are subjected to extensive group discussion.

Publications arising from IFIP events vary. The papers presented at the IFIP World Computer Congress and at open conferences are published as conference proceedings, while the results of the working conferences are often published as collections of selected and edited papers.

Any national society whose primary activity is in information may apply to become a full member of IFIP, although full membership is restricted to one society per country. Full members are entitled to vote at the annual General Assembly, National societies preferring a less committed involvement may apply for associate or corresponding membership. Associate members enjoy the same benefits as full members, but without voting rights. Corresponding members are not represented in IFIP bodies. Affiliated membership is open to non-national societies, and individual and honorary membership schemes are also offered.

Alain Bernard
Louis Rivest
Debasish Dutta (Eds.)

Product Lifecycle Management for Society

10th IFIP WG 5.1 International Conference, PLM 2013
Nantes, France, July 6-10, 2013
Proceedings

Springer

Volume Editors

Alain Bernard
École Centrale de Nantes, IRCCyN - IS3P UMR CNRS 6597
1, rue de la Noë, BP 92101, 44321 Nantes Cedex 3, France
E-mail: alain.bernard@irccyn.ec-nantes.fr

Louis Rivest
École de Technologie Supérieure
Département de Génie de la Production Automatisée
1100 rue Notre-Dame Ouest, Montréal, QC H3C 1K3, Canada
E-mail: louis.rivest@etsmtl.ca

Debasish Dutta
University of Illinois, Graduate College
204 Coble Hall, 891 S. Wright Street, Champaign, IL 61820, USA
E-mail: ddutta@illinois.edu

ISSN 1868-4238 e-ISSN 1868-422X
ISBN 978-3-642-41500-5 e-ISBN 978-3-642-41501-2
DOI 10.1007/978-3-642-41501-2
Springer Heidelberg New York Dordrecht London

Library of Congress Control Number: 2013950270

CR Subject Classification (1998): K.6.1, K.4, J.7, J.6, D.2, H.4, I.2, I.6

Typesetting: Camera-ready by author, data conversion by Scientific Publishing Services, Chennai, India

Printed on acid-free paper

Springer is part of Springer Science+Business Media (www.springer.com)

Foreword

Since 2003, **PLM International Conference** (PLM IC) brings together researchers, developers, and users of **Product Lifecycle Management** (PLM), an integrated business approach to the collaborative creation, management, and dissemination of engineering data throughout the extended enterprises that create, manufacture, and operate engineered products and systems.

The conference aims to involve all stakeholders in the broad concept of PLM, hoping to shape the future of this field and advance the science and practice of enterprise development. From its inception, PLM IC has been the official conference of the **International Journal of Product Lifecycle Management's** Editorial Board (IJPLM, `www.inderscience.com/ijplm`). In 2009, PLM IC became the official conference of the **IFIP Working Group WG 5.1** "Global product development for the whole lifecycle" (`www.ifip-wg51.org`).

PLM13 was the 10th International Conference on Product Lifecycle Management. This year, the conference's overall theme was **PLM for society**.

With the help of the advisory board, the International Program Committee, the Organizing Committee, and not discounting the support of all our sponsors, the event offered a wide range from scientific presentations to technical demonstrations and industry visits to some of Nantes' leading high tech companies (such as Airbus, STX Europe and Euriware). The conference also offered an active social program with participants enjoying La Cité, the castle and the cruise on the Erdre River.

PLM for society was explored through a series of **topics,** which also formed the format of the proceedings:

- PLM for sustainability, traceability, and performance,
- PLM infrastructure and implementation processes,
- Capture and reuse of product and process information,
- PLM and knowledge management,
- Enterprise systems integration,
- PLM and influence of/from social networks,
- PLM maturity and improvement concepts,
- PLM and collaborative product development,
- PLM virtual and simulation environments,
- Special session on BIM (Building Information Modeling).

One-hundred and eighteen abstracts were submitted and ninety-one papers proposed to the reviewers. Sixty-three papers were selected for presentation during the conference and are included in this proceedings book.

Six excellent keynotes, both from academia and industry, have contributed to open discussions amongst participants. Two of them are published in this book.

The industry day was dedicated to PLM as envisioned by industry: its program was dedicated to papers from industry representatives. Five of them form the industrial papers chapter of this book.

As the last step of scientific and technical knowledge diffusion in the field of PLM, this proceedings book is the synthesis publication of the material shared with the attendees during PLM13.

August 2013

Prof. Alain Bernard
Prof. Louis Rivest

Organization

Conference Chair

Dutta, Debasish	University of Illinois at Urbana-Champaign, USA

Steering Committee

Bouras, Abdelaziz	University Lumière Lyon2, France
Fukuda, Shuichi	Keio University, Japan
Gurumoorthy, Balan	Indian Institute of Science, India
McMahonm, Chris	University of Bristol, UK
Pels, Henk Jan	Technische Universiteit Eindhoven, The Netherlands
Thoben, Klaus-Dieter	BIBA, University of Bremen, Germany

Program Chairs

Bernard, Alain	Ecole Centrale de Nantes, France
Rivest, Louis	ETS Montréal, Canada

Program Committee Members

Abderrazak, El Ouafi	UQAR, Canada
Amor, Robert	University of Auckland, New Zealand
Bandinelli, Romeo	University of Florence, Italy
Bernard, Alain	Ecole Centrale de Nantes, France
Bilalis, Nikolaos	Technical University of Crete, Greece
Bouras, Abdelaziz	Université Lumière Lyon 2, France
Breit, Manfred	Univ. of Applied Sciences and Arts Northwestern FHNW, Switzerland
Chakpitak, Nopasit	Chiang Mai University, Thailand
Corney, Jonathan	University of Strathclyde, UK
Cugini, Umberto	Politecnico di Milano, Italy
Cuillière, Jean-Christophe	UQTR, Canada
Culley, Steve	Bath University, UK
Demoly, Frédéric	Université de Technologie de Belfort-Montbéliard, France

Do, Namchul	Gyeongsang National University, South Korea
Dutta, Debasish	University of Illinois at Urbana-Champaign, USA
ElMaraghy, Waguih	University of Windsor, Canada
Eynard, Benoit	Université de Technologie de Compiègne, France
Foufou, Sebti	Qatar University, Qatar
Fukuda, Shuichi	Keio University, Japan
Gakwaya, Augustin	Université de Laval, Canada
Garetti, Marco	Politecnico di Milano, Italy
Germani, Michele	Università Politecnica delle Marche, Italy
Ghie, Walid	UQAT, Canada
Gomes, Samuel	Belfort-Montbéliard University of Technology UTBM, France
Gu, Ning	University of Newcastle, Australia
Gurumoorthy, Balan	Indian Institute of Science, India
Hartman, Nathan William	Purdue University, USA
Henry, Sébastien	Université Lumière Lyon 2, France
Hong, Paul C.	University of Toledo, USA
Huang, George	University of Hong-Kong, Hong Kong
Huet, Greg	Ecole Polytechnique Montreal et Bombardier Aéronautique, Canada
Jamshidi, Jafar	University of Coventry, UK
Kärkkäinen, Hannu	Tampere University of Technology, Finland
Keraron, Yves	KRCF, France
Kiritsis, Dimitris	EPFL Lausanne, Switzerland
Lamouri, Samir	Arts et Metiers ParisTech, France
Laroche, Florent	Ecole Centrale de Nantes, France
Le Duigou, Julien	Université de Technologie de Compiègne, France
Lee, Sang Hun	Kookmin University, South Korea
Li, Jiping	Dalian Polytechnic University, China
Lim, Jong Gyun	Samsung Electronics Co., South Korea
Louhichi, Borhen	ETS Montréal, Canada
Lu, Wen	National University of Singapore, Singapore
Malak, Richard	Texas A&M University, USA
Malmqvist, Johan L.	Chalmers University of Technology, Sweden
Maranzana, Nicolas	Arts et Métiers ParisTech, France
McKay, Alison	University of Leeds, UK
McMahon, Chris	University of Bristol, UK

Miller, Craig L.	Purdue University, USA
Mitchell, John	BuildingSmart Company and University of New South Wales, Australia
Monticolo, Davy	Belfort-Montbéliard University of Technology UTBM, France
Naduthodi, Haris	Government Engineering College Thrissur, India
Nassehi, Aydin	University of Bath, UK
Nicolle, Christophe	Université de Bourgogne, France
Noël, Frederic	Grenoble-INP, France
Noh, Sang Do	Sungkyunkwan University, South Korea
Nongaillard, Antoine	Université Lumière Lyon 2, France
Ouertani, Mohamed Zied	University of Cambridge, UK
Paredis, Chris	Georgia Institute of Technology, USA
Park, Youngwon	University of Tokyo, Japan
Parlikad, Ajith	Cambridge University, UK
Pellerin, Robert	Ecole Polytechnique de Montréal, Canada
Pels, Henk Jan	Technische Universiteit Eindhoven, The Netherlands
Perry, Nicolas	Arts et Métiers ParisTech, France
Reeveerakul, Napaporn	Chiang Mai University, Thailand
Rivest, Louis	ETS Montréal, Canada
Robin, Vincent	University Bordeaux 1, France
Roucoules, Lionel	Arts et Métiers ParisTech, France
Sapidis, Nickolas	University of Western Macedonia, Greece
Schabacker, Michael	Otto von Guericke University Magdeburg, Germany
Segonds, Frederic	Arts et Metiers ParisTech, France
Silventoinen, Anneli	Lappeenranta University of Technology, Finland
Singh, Vishal	Aalto University, Finland
Smirnov, Alexander	SPIIRAS, Russia
Song, Bin	Singapore Institute of Manufacturing Technology, Singapore
Srinivasan, Vijay	NIST, USA
Sriram, Ram	NIST, USA
Terzi, Sergio	University of Bergamo, Italy
Thoben, Klaus-Dieter	BIBA, University of Bremen, Germany
Thomson, Vincent	McGill University, Canada
Tiwari, Ashutish	Cranfield University, UK
Troussier, Nadège	Université de Technologie de Troyes, France

Uotila, Tuomo	LUT, Finland
Vajna, Sandor	Magdeburg University, Germany
Vieira, Darli	UQTR, Canada
Whyte, Jennifer	University of Reading, UK
Witherell, Paul	NIST, USA
Young, Bob	Loughborough University, UK
Zeng, Yong	Concordia University, Canada
Zhang, Linda	IESEG School of Management, France
Zhang, Yufeng	Cambridge University, UK

Chair of the Organizing Committee

Alain Bernard	Ecole Centrale de Nantes, France

organised by

sponsorded by

supported by

Table of Contents

Keynotes

PLM for Sustainability, Traceability and Performance

PLM Infrastructure and Implementation Processes

Capture and Reuse of Product and Process Information

PLM and Knowledge Management

Enterprise Systems Integration

PLM and Influence of/from Social Networks

PLM Maturity and Improvement Concepts

PLM and Collaborative Product Development

PLM Virtual and Simulation Environments

Special Session: BIM

Industrial Papers

Product Lifecycle Management in an Open Industry Framework

Shuichi Fukuda

Keio University, SDM, 4-1-1, Hiyoshi, Kohoku-ku, Yokohama, Kanagawa, 223-8526, Japan
shufukuda@gmail.com
Stanford University, Stanford, CA, 94305, USA
shufukuda@cdr.stanford.edu

Abstract. The basic concept of "an Open Industry Framework" is proposed. Current industry framework is closed and industries are making their efforts to produce best quality products in their own particular field. This is because current industries developed on the basis of their inventions. But quickly increasing diversification and frequent and extensive changes are calling for an open framework. In this new framework, industries operate on the basis of Parallel Distributed Processing model. They process multiple tasks in parallel among different types of industries. To achieve such a goal, modular production is called for but current ones are not fully integrated between design and manufacturing. We have to develop a module system which integrates design and manufacturing and which can be shared across industries. When such a system is developed, industries will be divided into two groups. One is subsystem suppliers and the other is system integrators. The subsystem here works in the same way as Lego pieces. Such a framework will enable to distribute production activities to local factories according to their capabilities so that it will increase local employment and their buying power. And we do not have to carry heavy final product over a long distance. Thus, an Open Industry Framework will reduce time to market, cost and energy consumption considerably and industries can be more flexible and adaptive and can satisfy the basic needs of customers.

Keywords: open Industry framework, parallel distributed processing, different types of industries, modular production, basic needs.

1 Introduction

It is pointed out that the current industries are operating too much independently and that much closer collaboration and sometimes their integration are needed to respond to quickly diversifying needs of our customers.

If we note the non-physical nature of knowledge and experience, a great amount of information can be shared among different industrial sectors and far greater reduction in time to market, cost and energy consumption can be achieved.

If we use computer science terms, what we have been pursuing up to now is to introduce concurrent processing, i.e., to process multiple tasks in parallel on a single

A. Bernard, L. Rivest, and D. Dutta (Eds.): PLM 2013, IFIP AICT 409, pp. 1–9, 2013.

processor, i.e., in a single industry. Concurrent Engineering is a typical example. But if we process these tasks by distributing them among multiple processors, i.e., among different types of industries, then time to solution or in industrial terms, time to market can be greatly reduced. Therefore, we have to change our product development from concurrent processing style to parallel distributed processing one.

Parallel distributed processing (PDP) product development will change our industry framework from the traditional closed style to open one. Knowledge and experience will be an open source for different types of industries.

Such an Open Industry Framework will be composed of two groups: One is intermediate product producing industries and the other is final product producing industries, i.e., subsystem suppliers and system integrators.

System integrators select modules and assemble them into a final product to truly meet the needs and preferences of customers. Subsystem suppliers can produce their intermediate products in mass and they can supply them to many different types of final product industries. And subsystem suppliers can be divided into several tiers according to their capabilities. The developing countries where knowledge and experience are still not enough to produce complex subsystems can produce simpler ones. Such appropriate assignment of roles would help increase local employment and their buying power.

Such intermediate products or subsystems may be compared to Lego pieces. Lego pieces vary only in shape but these subsystems vary in a wide variety of attributes to cover the whole gamut of choices for system integrators.

2 Modular Production

To achieve such a goal, we have to introduce modular production. But current modular design or modular manufacturing focus their attention on design or manufacturing alone and they are not too much integrated. We have to develop modules which can be accessed easily either from design or from manufacturing. In short, it must be able to retrieve the best or better modules from any perspective.

This can be expressed in another way. Current industries are operating in a sequential processing manner and if we use computer processing terms, the way they are operating is forward chaining or data- or technology-driven. (Figure 1).

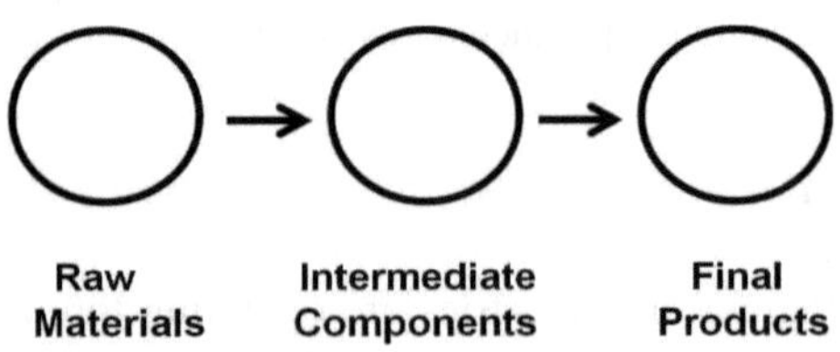

Fig. 1. Current sequential product development

But if we divide industries to subsystem suppliers and system integrators, then system integrators have to find the best or better combination of subsystems easily. Therefore, we have to make our industry framework not only open but also flexible and easily accessible.

Therefore, modules in an Open Industry Framework must be a versatile tool for many different applications, but their characteristics or features must be clearly identifiable with the specifications of system integrators.

The current industries focus on particular final products and operate independently. But if we focus on intermediate components, there is much common knowledge which can be shared across different industries. Therefore, if we change our focus from final products to intermediate components, then our product development will be such as shown in Figure 2.

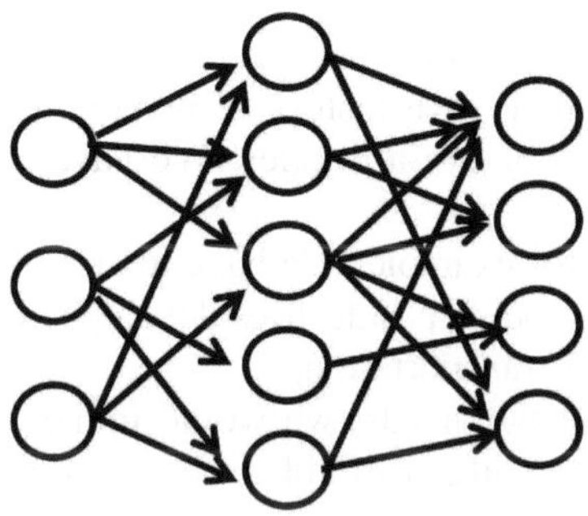

Fig. 2. Parallel Distributed Processing (PDP) Model

We can develop final products by combining different pieces of intermediate components just as we do in playing Lego or to express it in French, in Bricolage style. Lego, however, is just a combination of shapes, but in this case we have to consider many attributes at the same time. But the basic idea is the same as Lego.

This is nothing but a Neural Network. It is interesting to note that a neural network not only represents our brain activities, but it also is analog-based. Such a Neural Network based product development will bring forth greater flexibility and adaptability and allows multi-modal or cross-modal product developments. If we recall a Neural Network used to be called Parallel Distributed Processing (PDP), it will be easily understood that greater reduction of time, cost and energy consumption and greater increase of productivity can be expected.

Modules in the traditional industry framework focused on efficiency but modules in an Open Industry Framework focus on interchangeability or wide applicability. Therefore, modules in an open industry framework also work better for MRO (Maintenance, Repair and Overhaul/Operations) because we can collect data more precisely module by module so that they facilitate introduction of PHM (Prognostics and Health Management) system and makes system health management easier.

3 Supplier Relationship Management

Current SRM (Supplier Relationship Management) focuses on relations among a group of suppliers to one industry. It discusses how a tree structure composed of a group of suppliers at the lower nodes and a final product industry or user at the top node can work well. The "Open Supplier Relationship Management" discussed here is a network.

4 Basic Needs

Another important point which must be stressed here is the importance of looking back to the basic needs of customers rather than to keep on going forward on the track of past history of inventions [1], [2]

The Industrial Revolution brought about specialization of industries and current industries developed based upon their own history of inventions. In old days, most of the enterprises are more or less jack-of-all-trades. We have to make our industries more flexible and adaptive.

Take transportation industry for example. We have to change vehicles for land, air and water, because car, airplane and ship industries developed by expanding the technologies invented for a particular transportation.

But if we come back to our basic needs, we would immediately realize what we want is to travel comfortably and without troubles. No one wants to change vehicles. We do so because we have to. Thus, most of current industries are technology-driven. They say customers' voices are important. But these customers mean the users of their products developed by their own technologies [3].

We have to note that B to B relations are nothing other than S to C (Supplier to Customer) relations. Customers, no matter whether they are end-users or business enterprises, would like to select industries as they like in order to meet their needs and preferences. However, customers have no other choices than to select among the samples offered by the final product industries. They are supposed to be passive consumers.

But customers have their dreams and they would like to make their dreams come true. If we look back into the very old days, man produced tools to realize their dreams. Tools are nothing but tools, but what man really wanted was to make his dream come true. Why man is called Home Faber is because he makes tools to realize their dreams. Animals can use natural objects as tools. But they do not manufacture tools to realize their dreams. Man can look into the future. But animals live for now [4]. Homo Faber is not trying to develop a better tool, but what he is trying is to make his dream come true and in order to realize that, he produces a tool.

But current industries are making efforts to produce better tools and seem to forget why they are offering such tools or what their customers really want.

Let us consider Brazil. She is so big that there are air taxis. But even if you can use an air taxi and you can land where you want, you cannot go any further, if a car is not available there. So integration of airplane and car is a necessity in Brazil. Such requirements vary from country to country, from region to region and from person to person. What is important is to satisfy such basic needs or requirements. They are not asking us to produce a better airplane.

Thus, we have to re-organize industries to satisfy the true needs or demands of our customers. We have been discussing how we can meet diversifying needs, but these discussions are focused on one particular industry and more often than not with particular final product in mind. We have not really look back to the basic needs of our customers. Our final goal is to make their dreams come true. It is not to provide our customers with the best quality products or tools.

5 Integration of Design and Manufacturing into a Module

Then, how can we make our industry framework flexible and adaptive enough to meet such basic requirements. As discussed before, it is to introduce modular design and manufacturing. But current modular design and modular manufacturing are developed separately and not integrated enough and what is most lacking is that the current product development is forward chaining or technology driven. If we are going to realize such an Open Industry Framework, we have to change it so that it also enables backward chaining or needs- or goal-driven processing. Or we should say we have to change it from one way to both ways. Then, how can we integrate design and manufacturing together into a module to achieve such a goal?

6 An Illustrative Example

Let us take AWS (American Welding Society) standard for example. AWS standardizes welding procedures in terms of system components or sub-assemblies such as a box for example (Figure 3).

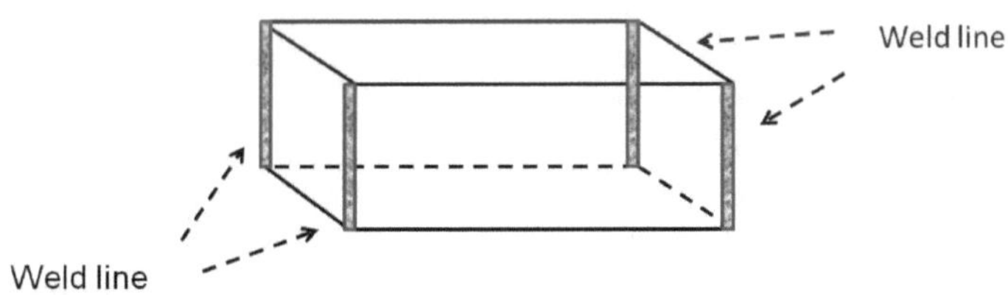

Fig. 3. AWS Standard

Ship design is fundamentally based on boxes and boxes are used in many other areas such as cars, trains, ships, houses, containers, etc. If we introduce such a box type design, it would facilitate integrating car, plane and ships into one. This standard is for welding, but such standardization would greatly facilitate integrating design and manufacturing. And it would make introduction of robots much easier.

And if we use such a method as DSM (Design Structure Matrix) [5] by paying close attention to the integration of design and manufacturing as illustrated here, such modules proposed here will be developed.

7 Concurrent Engineering (CE)

CE proved how effective it is to integrate design and manufacturing knowledge and experience [6], [7]. The success of CE can be attributed to the fact that it noted the non-physical nature of our knowledge. Since knowledge and experience are non-physical so we can pack them in a much smaller box than physical elements (Figure 4).

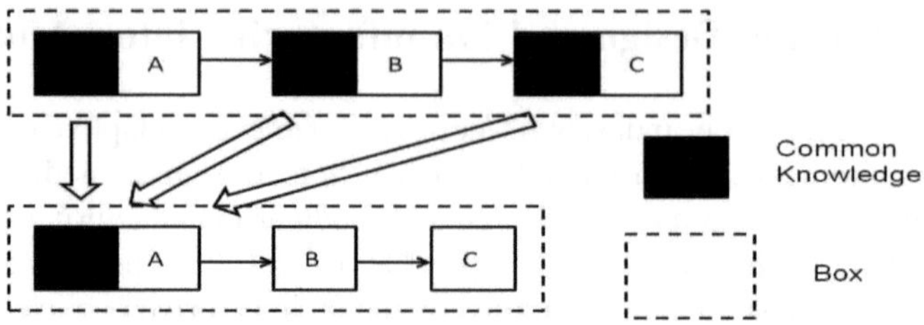

Fig. 4. Concurrent Engineering as a packing problem

7.1 Traditional CE: Reduction of Time

Traditional CE focused its attention on how we can reduce time to market because it was originally developed for military competition, although later it was expanded to industry sectors. Thus, reduction of time to realize a product was mandatory. Reduction of time to market is also welcomed by industry, because they are fighting another war on the market. And this reduction meant nothing other than increase of productivity. Increasing productivity was becoming more and more difficult. But if we note knowledge is non-physical, we were able to increase productivity remarkably. Thus, CE spread very quickly and widely.

The advantage of CE is not reduction of time to market alone. DARPA Initiative in Concurrent Engineering (DICE) project [8] spreads the name of CE, but what DICE tried to achieve is to develop a competitive weapon, when you find out your enemy is developing a better weapon. Then, you have to develop a equally capable weapon until your enemy realize it. So reduction of time to realization is crucial. But we have to remember that we have to achieve this goal with the current resources. So how we can make our product development flexible and adaptive enough with current resources was what CE pursued.

The idea of CE presumably comes from Concurrent Processing (CP) in Computer Science. What we should note is that CP is to process multiple tasks in parallel, but on a single processor. If we regard one industry as one processor, CE is exactly the same as CP.

7.2 New Role of CE: Reduction of Energy

But today CE is not so much appreciated by industry as it was. Why? This is because customers' requirements are diversifying very quickly and extensively today. Yesterday, industry could survive by mass production. So CE yesterday had much to offer for industry. But today industry has to customize their products to meet the diverse requirements of their customers.

Another emerging issue of importance is the lack of energy. Industry has to reduce energy consumption. But we should remember energy reduction is very important for industry from the first. Energy saving is important for keeping the world green, but apart from that, reduction of energy consumption is nothing other than cost reduction. The more we can reduce cost by reducing energy consumption, the more profit we can obtain. Then, how can we adapt CE to such changing situations?

7.3 Expanding CE into 2 Dimensions of Time and Space

If we recall that CE solved a packing problem with attention paid to the non-physical nature of knowledge, we could find our solution. CE yesterday only solved one dimensional problem. It solved the problem with respect to time. But if we expand CE into 2 dimensions, i.e. time and space, then we can adapt CE to the current situations.

Thus, CE today will be illustrated as shown in Figure 6. The core idea of sharing knowledge is the same. In fact, if we expand CE from one dimension to two dimensions, the reduction of space would be greater so that we could pack processes in much smaller box (Figure 5).

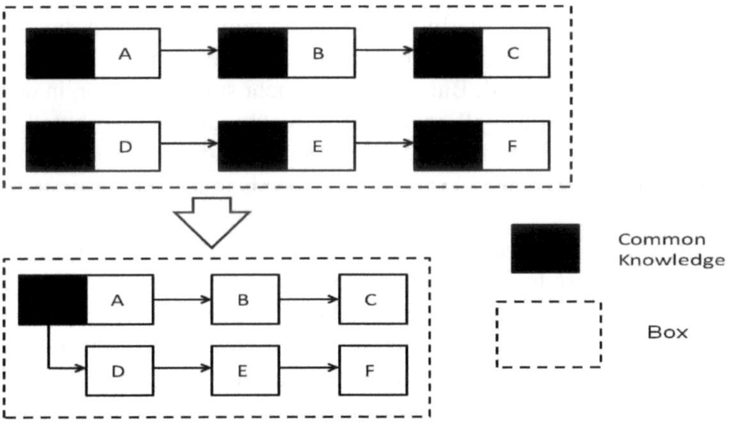

Fig. 5. Concurrent Engineering in two dimensions

8 From Concurrent Processing to Parallel Distributed Processing

In CS area, it was soon found out that we can reduce time considerably if we use multiple processors. This leads to Parallel Distributed Processing (PDP) on multiple processors. If we use PDP, then the time to solve can be reduced remarkably.

So if we come back to our original discussion about industry framework, we can reduce time to market very remarkably if we distribute our tasks among multiple industries. Of course, reduction of time is nothing other than reduction of cost and energy consumption. So, collaboration among industries will bring forth much greater benefits for those involved.

Modularization of design and manufacturing will expedite such industry-wide collaboration. But such modules should be something like Lego pieces. Current modules focus on efficiency, but they must enable a versatile selection for the customers. Although customers do not select and combine them into a final product by themselves and system integrators carry out such jobs for them, the recent remarkable progress of digital manufacturing such as 3D printers, etc, will visualize customers' dreams more easily and clearly so the integrators can understand what kind of products they really want and integrators can work together with them to find appropriate elements and combine them into the final product their customers expect.

9 Benefits of an Open Industry Framework

Integrated design and manufacturing subsystem standardization will lead to true glocalization. Components can be purchased from factories near the market and assembled locally. Local people can assemble them into a final product to meet their needs and to their preferences. And it will reduce the necessity to transport heavy final products over a long distance. If some components cannot be procured near the market, we can import them from nearby countries or regions. The energy, time and trouble to transport such components to the market can be minimized.

Current economy is centralized. But such component standardization in design and manufacturing across industries will open a door to autonomous distributed economy system. Then, far greater reduction of energy and much improved productivity will be achieved. Furthermore, it will meet local people's needs to a T and bring much greater satisfaction to them.

And it should also be stressed that final product industries do not have to stick to particular types of final products as they are doing now. What they need is an ability to integrate various elements into a final product so they can be very flexible and adaptive. They do not have to worry about their stocks any more. Subsystem suppliers are happy too. They do not have to worry because they can supply their subsystems to far wider range of integrators or customers.

Therefore, an Open Industry Framework proposed here will bring forth Win-Win relations for all.

References

[1] Fukuda, S.: Emotional Engineering, vol. 1. Springer (2011)
[2] Fukuda, S.: Emotional Engineering, vol. 2. Springer (2013)
[3] Fukuda, S.: Concurrent Engineering in a New Perspective: Heading for Seamless Engineering. In: Stjepandic, J., Rock, G., Bil, C. (eds.) Concurrent Engineering Approaches for Sustainable Product Development in a Multi-Disciplinary Environment, vol. 1, pp. 15–26. Springer (2013)

[4] What Will Our Consciousness about the Future, Which is Specific to Human Bring to Us? In: Applied Brain Science Symposium, Institute of Science of Survival (2010) (in Japanese)
[5] Eppinger, S.D., Browning, T.R.: Design Structure Matrix Methods and Applications (Engineering Systems). MIT Press (2012)
[6] Sriram, R., Logcher, R., Fukuda, S.: Computer-aided Cooperative Product Development. Springer (1991)
[7] Frey, D.D., Fukuda, S., Rock, G. (eds.): Improving Complex Systems Today. Springer (2011)
[8] http://www.dtic.mil/dtic/tr/fulltext/u2/a226394.pdf

Proposal for the Conceptual Design of Aeronautical Final Assembly Lines Based on the Industrial Digital Mock-Up Concept

Fernando Mas[1], Alejandro Gómez[2], José Luis Menéndez[1], and José Ríos[2]

[1] AIRBUS, Av. García Morato s/n, 41011, Sevilla, Spain
fernando.mas@airbus.com
[2] Universidad Politécnica de Madrid, José Gutiérrez Abascal 2, 28006 Madrid, Spain
jose.rios@upm.es

Abstract. The design of a Final Assembly Line (FAL) is carry out in the product industrialization activity. The phase dealing with the definition of conceptual solutions is characterized by depending heavily on the personnel experience and being time-consuming. To enhance such process, it is proposed a development of a knowledge based software application to assist designers in the definition of scenarios and to generate conceptual FAL alternatives. Both the scenario and the generated FAL solution are part of the industrialization digital mock-up (IDMU). A commercial software application used in the aircraft programmes and supporting the IDMU concepts of: Product, Process and Resource; was selected to implement a software prototype. This communication presents the adopted methodological approach and the architecture of the developed application.

Keywords: aeronautical final assembly line conceptual design, industrial Digital Mock-Up, PLM systems.

1 Introduction

The design of a Final Assembly Line (FAL) can be decomposed into three assembly line design phases: concept, definition and development. The FAL design is part of the product industrialization activity. Such industrialization activity can be decomposed into three main sub-activities: “create conceptual assembly process”, “define assembly process” and “develop detailed assembly process”. Each of these activities is carried out in its corresponding assembly line design phases: concept, definition, and development [1].

Requirements are under definition during the conceptual design phase of an aeronautical FAL. For instance: work share, work load distribution, factory locations, production processes and technologies, main machinery and tooling. During the conceptual phase, designers require defining FAL alternatives with different values for the input requirements. A set of values for the input requirements defines a scenario and allows executing ‘what-if’ analyses [2]. A Project Management Office (PMO) is responsible to define the scenarios.

A. Bernard, L. Rivest, and D. Dutta (Eds.): PLM 2013, IFIP AICT 409, pp. 10–19, 2013.

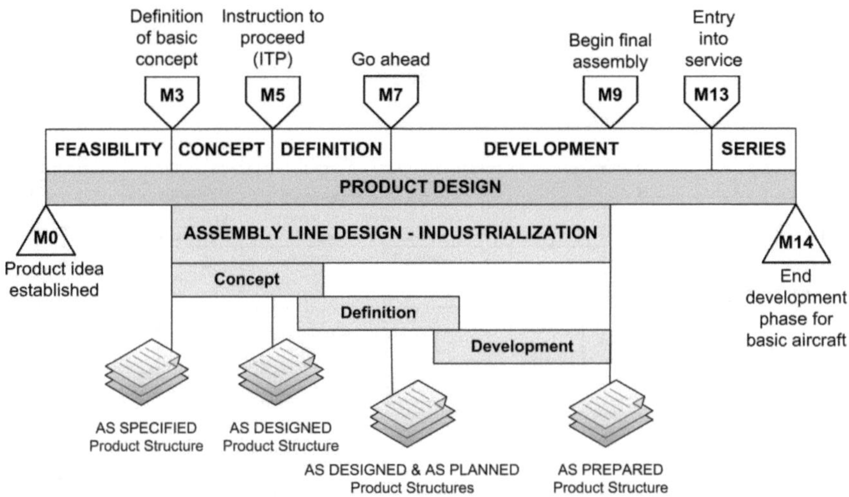

Fig. 1. AIRBUS Product lifecycle and development milestones

The design of the whole plane, and its corresponding subassemblies, evolves along the design process, four types of product definition structures are created along the lifecycle: '*as specified*' (M3), '*as designed*' (M5), '*as designed & as planned*' (M7), and '*as prepared*' (M9) [3]. The design of a FAL is shifted from the product lifecycle, starts in M3 and ends in M9 (Fig. 1).The conceptual functional aircraft definition, mainly the product configurations 'as design' and 'as planned', is responsibility of the Design Engineering (DE) in collaboration with the Manufacturing Engineering (ME). Based on the product configuration and the scenario, the ME is responsible to execute the case and to define the digital mock up of the industrialization solutions or FAL alternatives. As a result, the 'as prepared' product structure is created. The final decision is responsibility of the PMO. Both the scenario and the FAL design are part of the Industrialization Digital Mock-Up (IDMU). An IDMU comprises product, processes and resources information, both geometrical and technological [4]. PLM systems are the tool to create, manage and support any digital mock-up related to products, processes and resources [4-6] (Fig. 2).

At the conceptual phase, the process of generating industrialization solutions depends heavily on the personnel experience and it is time-consuming. Consequently, manufacturing engineers can only check a simplified set of cases to generate and submit early manufacturing processes and resource requirements. In order to enhance such process, it was decided to investigate the development of a software application to assist designers in the definition of scenarios and to generate FAL alternatives at the conceptual stage. The development had to be carried out within the framework of a commercial PLM/CAX system used in the aircraft programs (Catia/Delmia v5) (Fig. 2).

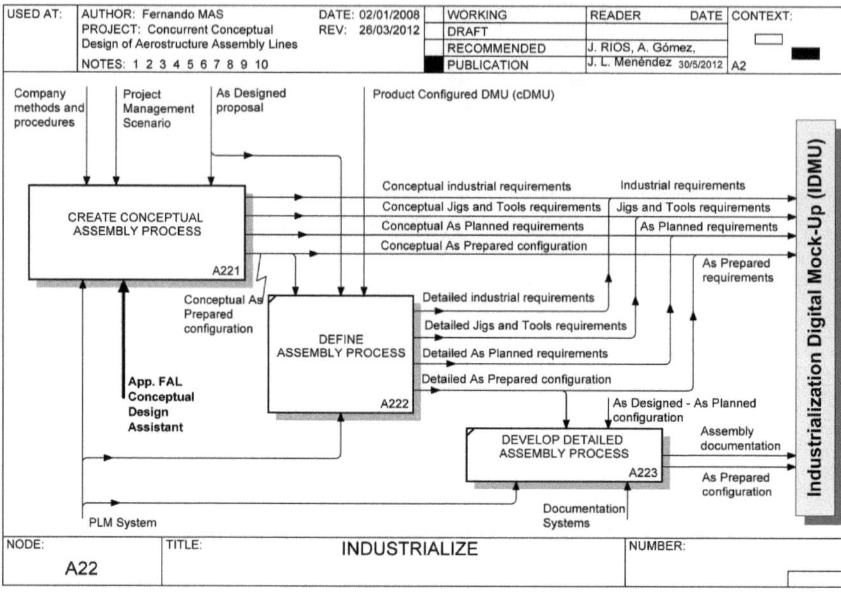

Fig. 2. IDEF0 Context diagram for the Application FAL Conceptual Design Assistant

This communication presents the methodological approach followed along the development process and the architecture of the developed application. In the next section, the methodological approach adopted in the work and the models, created to support the development of the application, are briefly presented.

2 Methodological Approach and Developed Models

Rather than relying on experience and rules of thumb, the literature shows the need to develop formal models of manufacturing systems for analysis and decision making [7-8]. The literature shows also that the development of aid tools, to assist in the design of process and aircraft assembly lines, is a topic of interest. An example is the development of an aid tool, based on the definition of an assembly graph, which allows the specification of several alternatives for processes and factory layouts, in a way that they can be compared within a CAD environment and transferred into a simulation software tool for task scheduling analysis [9].

The development of a software application, to assist designers in the definition of scenarios and to generate FAL alternatives at the conceptual stage could not be identified in the literature. Such development requires capturing and reusing product and process knowledge in an integrated way. IDEF0 (Integrated DEFinition for function modeling) and UML (Unified Modeling Language) were selected to define the methodological approach adopted in this work and the resulting models.

The first task was a literature review to analyze both the product design process on engineering design and the assembly line design process described in textbooks. While most textbooks on engineering design provide a similar general structure for the design process with three main phases: Conceptual Design, System level or Embodiment Design and Detail Design; textbooks on assembly line design rather than providing a systematic process, provide a general view of the elements involved in the assembly line design and tend to focus on the assembly line balancing task [1]. The second review task was the creation of an 'as is' IDEF0 process model based on the industrial practices from previous aircraft projects. From the analysis of such 'as is' model two main elements were identified: process improvements actions and activities that could benefit from the development of software utilities [4]. Based on these two inputs, a 'to be' IDEF0 process model focused on the Industrialize activity was defined. The process model shows the activities to conduct, the flow of information and helps to identify the concepts and knowledge involved in the aircraft FAL conceptual design process [1, 10].

The next step was to develop a knowledge model using UML. The knowledge modeling of aircraft assembly lines requires reviewing works dealing with modeling of assembly information, processes and lines [1]. From such review was concluded that the semantic concepts involved in the conceptual design phase of an aircraft assembly line were not fully taken into account in the identified models. Models presented in the literature provide three main views: product, process and line balancing. The modeling of the conceptual phase demanded to integrate and to extend concepts from the three views, particularly from the process view. The proposed conceptual model was divided into three interrelated sections or knowledge units: Product, Processes and Resources; that together constitute the IDMU [1]. The product section comprises the concepts to define the joints to be assembled and, both the functional (as designed) and the industrial (as planned and as prepared) views. The process section comprises the concepts, in terms of technology, sequencing and resources, to define a procedure to assemble each joint defined in the product section. Technology, sequencing and resources are collected in the work station concept, and work stations are grouped into the assembly line concept. The resources section comprises the concepts to define three main types of resources: jigs and tools, industrial means and human resources.

To implement the developed IDMU model, classes were mapped into elements of the commercial software (Catia/Delmia v5), where the IDMU is created. Catia/Delmia v5 provides the PPR structure (Process-Product-Resource) to support the IDMU concept. The model is implemented by means of Catia v5 macros in VBA language that use the Catia v5 Application Programming Interface (API). A process document (.CATProcess) integrates three lists corresponding to: Product, Process and Resource. A component is the basic class in the product knowledge unit (KU). A component is defined in a file of type CATPart and corresponds to the lowest level in a product tree. There are three product trees to represent the three product views: as designed, as planned and as prepared. Each product tree has its corresponding nodes:

functional_nodes, industrial_nodes and as_prepared_nodes. The classes AsPlanned and AsPrepared were defined to generate the corresponding product structures. Each product structure is defined in a file of type CATProduct. The nodes of a product tree can point to a CATProduct file (intermediate elements) or to a CATPart file (lowest level individual element). The joint class is linked to a CATProduct file. The joint class has a link to the Basic_assembly_process class. An object of the Basic_assembly_process class is defined in a CATProcess file. Fig. 3 shows the mapping of the proposed model into classes defined in CATIA (shadowed) and the corresponding type of files where instances are stored.

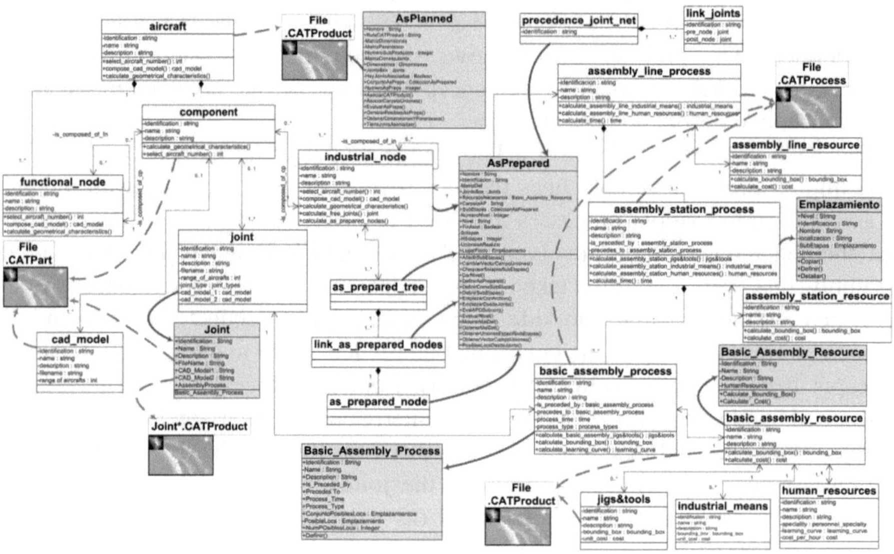

Fig. 3. Mapping of the developed UML class model into Catia v5 concepts

3 Results: FAL Conceptual Design Assistant Tool Prototype

The main result is an assistant tool, integrated within Catia v5, which helps designers to generate FAL alternatives by defining scenarios. The application generates technological information integrated within an IDMU supported by the commercial PLM system. The current development implements the three main elements: product, processes and resources. A very simple aircraft model was created and used to test the application. The results obtained in the executed case studies relate to requirements for: space, transport, resources, industrial means and cost; and allow validating the conceptual approach adopted in the research. Fig. 4 shows the main tasks supported by the assistant tool prototype, such tasks are executed within the activity 'Create Conceptual Assembly Process' A221 (see Fig. 2).

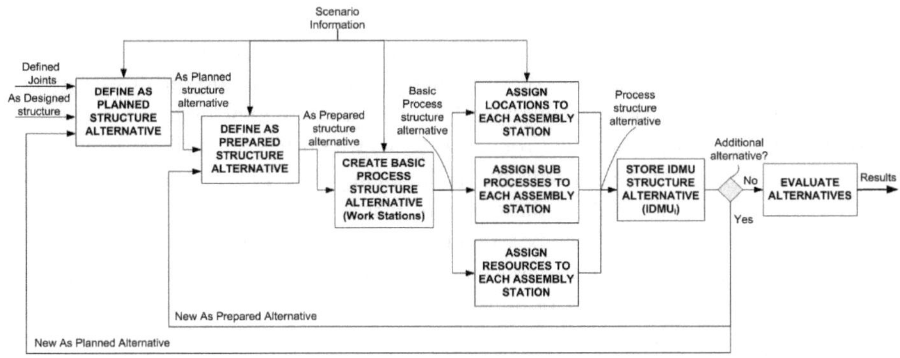

Fig. 4. Architecture of the FAL conceptual design assistant tool prototype

Defining an assembly process alternative, as proposed in the assistant application (Fig. 4), requires using the scenario information and involves fixing an assembly sequence, establishing sub-assemblies associated to the sub-stages of the process, locating them into real industrial plants belonging to the set of available company's facilities, adding sub processes depending on the type of joint to be executed (e.g.: fuselage join-up) and assigning the resources to be used (e.g.: NC machine, overhead crane).

An assembly sequence comprises defining the order of execution of the required 'Joints'. Such ordering provides a hierarchical precedence structure with possible parallel branches; that is the 'As Prepared' product model view. Along the execution of the application, the user defines the sequence by selecting the different joints in inverse order of execution from last to first. After selecting each joint, the user can select its predecessors.

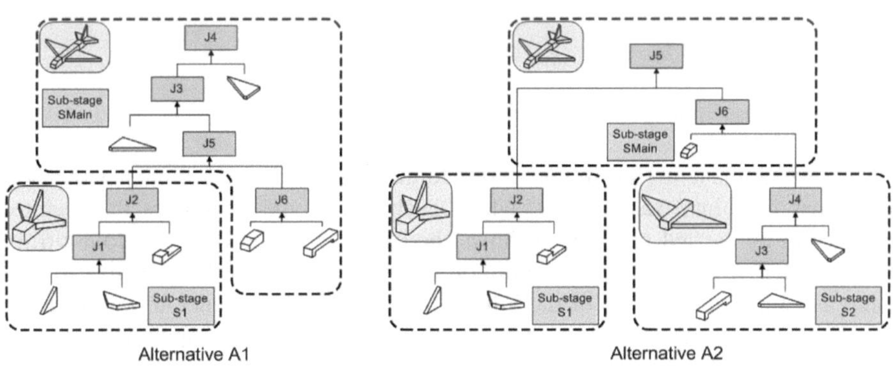

Fig. 5. Example of two alternatives for the 'as planned' and 'as prepared' structures

Once the sequence is defined, sub-stages must be defined. Each one must contain a number of executions of joints and is related with a sub-assembly or set of components depending on the position of the involved joints within the sequence. Each sub-stage is an industrial node. Fig.5 shows two examples of assembly process alternatives. Alternative A1 comprises two sub-stages, called S1 and SMain. Joints J1 and

J2 are executed at S1, and the rest of the joints, at SMain. S1 and SMain will be located in different industrial plants. Locating sub-stages is controlled by a constraint: the user can select exclusively industrial plants where the assembly processes involved in the sub-stage can be made (scenario information). Each joint object is related with an instance of class *BasicAssemblyProcess* (Fig. 3), which has an attribute related to the possible plants where can be carried out. In the example of Fig. 5, alternative A1, sub-stage S1 can only be located in those plants where joints J1 and J2 (actually their associated assembly processes) can be executed. Feasible locations for each sub-stage are shown to the user in this step of the assistant application execution. A detailed discussion of a case study, executed with a prior version of the assistant tool, where the product knowledge unit was implemented, is presented in Gómez et al. [11].

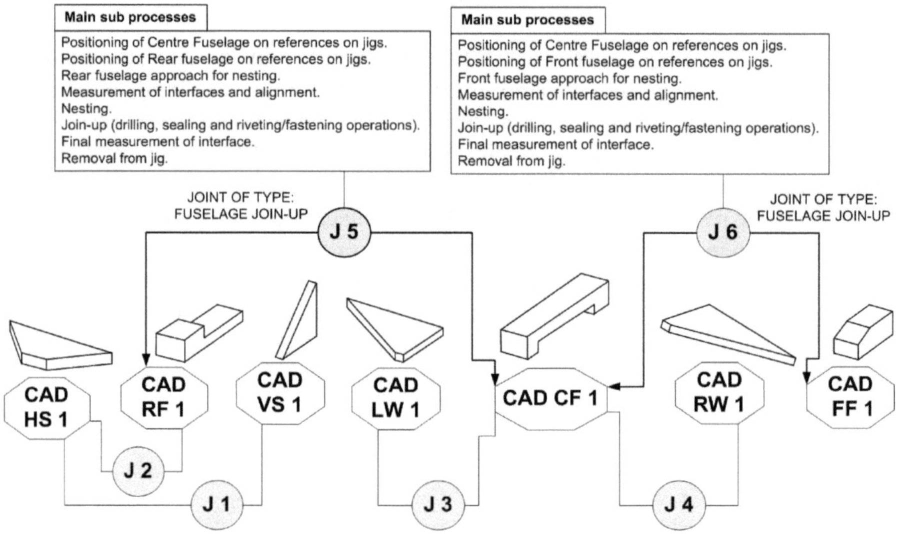

Fig. 6. Main sub processes to be carried out to execute a joint of type Fuselage Join-Up

The next step is to assign sub processes to the work stations. A library with a set of basic types of joints was defined, where each basic type comprises the main sub processes to be carried out. Fig. 6 shows the example of the Fuselage Join-Up joint type. For each work station, depending on the type of joints to be executed in it, the design assistant, making use of the joint sub process library, generates automatically the main level of sub processes to be carried out and the corresponding nodes are created in the Process List structure provided by Catia/Delmia v5.

The last step in the configuration of the process structure alternative is the assignment of resources. The assistant tool provides a list of possible resources to the designer. Each resource has a set of basic attributes for its basic definition (e.g.: bounding_box, capacity, cost). The designer has to select the resource type, input the value for each attribute and select the process node where the resource will be used. The assistant tool will generate a node in the Resources List structure provided by Catia/Delmia v5. The geometric definition of the resource is out of scope of this work and it will have to be created separately.

At this stage, a conceptual structure of a possible FAL solution is defined. Since an 'as designed' product structure may have more than one 'as planned' alternative. The 'as planned' structure is defined by grouping components into different sub-assemblies which represent industrial nodes in the real process. And an 'as planned' structure may have more than one 'as prepared' structure. The 'as prepared' structure is created by sequencing the execution of the joints to get the sub-assemblies defined at the 'as planned' structure. Once the first possible process structure (i.e.: FAL alternative) is created, the designer is requested to select if more alternatives need to be evaluated.

The evaluation of FAL alternatives defined at the conceptual phase relates to estimate: space requirements, transportation requirements, cost, and operation time. Space requirements for a specific assembly plant are bigger when a higher number of joints must be executed in it, due to the increase on the number of components to be processed. Transport requirements depend on the distance between the chosen locations and the dimensions of the intermediate products to be transported. The whole assembly process cost and operation time is strongly related with the resources to be used and the transport requirements, the space utilization has also a high impact in the final cost. In the last part of the assistant, each FAL alternative is evaluated according to the five criteria: dimensions, resources requirements, transport requirements, time and cost. The coding needed to implement the resources requirements evaluation is currently in progress.

To execute the evaluation of alternatives, three main generic utilities were developed: the tree structure analyzer, the component dimensions calculator, and the node properties calculator. The product tree analyzer captures the Components Tree Structure of a CATProduct file. The function was programmed with a recursive algorithm which is valid for any product structure. This utility allows capturing information about the product model view structures, which are represented by CATProducts files. This utility could be adapted to analyze a resource structure.

The component dimensions calculator determines the dimensions of a product. Dimensions of each component are calculated by defining parallel planes and checking if the part is cut by them. If that condition is false, the distance between planes is reduced. The loop is executed until precision required is achieved. Dimensions of an assembly are calculated by using the dimensions, the relative positions and the orientations of each of its components. This utility is linked with the industrial facilities space requirements and the space evaluation for transportation.

The node properties calculator allows finding a property in the components or defining it if it is not found. It also calculates the value of the property in all the nodes of the product tree by using the utility to capture its structure and applying an adding upward algorithm. This utility is used to calculate the cost at each node of the product tree. Fig. 7 shows the assistant user interface when linking a resource to a process node, and the PPR trees created by the assistant when executing one of the cases showed in Fig. 5.

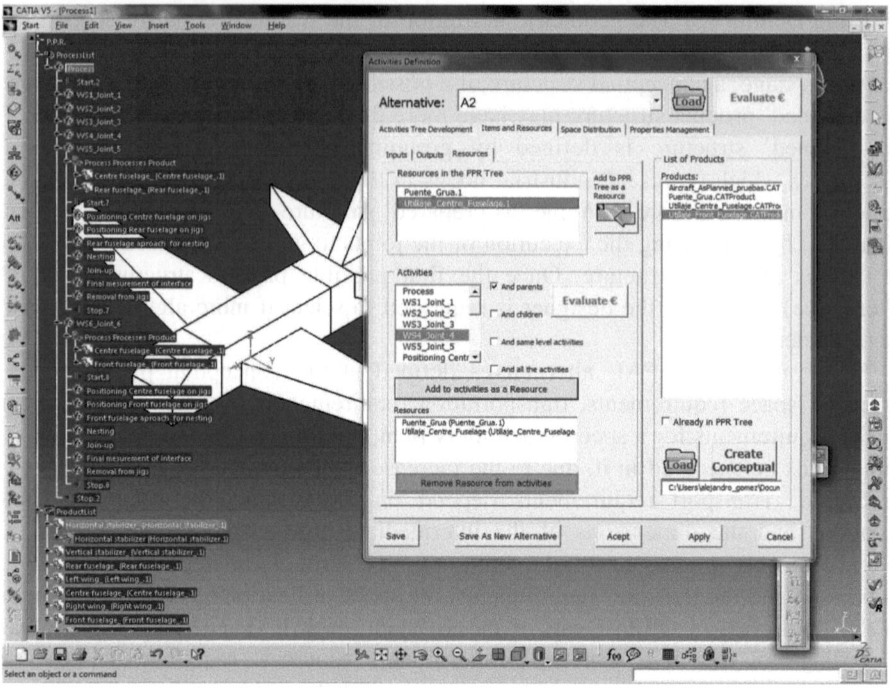

Fig. 7. Assistant user interface example: activity definition window and resource linking

Conclusions

This paper presents a proposal to assist designers during the conceptual design of an aircraft final assembly line. The approach is based on the definition of an Industrial Digital Mock-Up (IDMU). To create the IDMU an ad-hoc assistant tool was modelled, developed and integrated within a commercial software system (Catia/Delmia v5). The assistant tool allows defining different alternatives and evaluating them in terms of: dimensions, resources requirements, transport requirements, time and cost. Although, the resources requirements evaluation is currently under development, the current prototype confirmed the feasibility of the approach. The reader is referred to Gómez et al. [11] for a detailed discussion of a case study executed with a prior version of the assistant tool, where the product knowledge unit was implemented.

Although the evaluation of the alternatives is conducted at the industrialization conceptual phase, when products are still preliminarily defined, the evaluation of different scenarios allows creating estimates that help designers during the decision making process.

In addition to the already mentioned fully implementation of the resource knowledge model, future work aims an automatic process planning capability in the form of an algorithm to create the 'as prepared' alternatives from the information defined in the 'as planned' structure, the joints to execute and the assembly process information.

Acknowledgments. The authors would like to thank the AIRBUS Military colleagues for their contribution during the development of this work.

References

1. Mas, F., Ríos, J., Menéndez, J.L., Gómez, A.: A process-oriented approach to modeling the conceptual design of aircraft assembly lines. Intl. J. of Advanced Mfg. Technology 62 (2012)
2. Mas, F., Ríos, J., Menéndez, J.L.: Scenario for concurrent conceptual assembly line design: a case study. In: AIP Conf. Proc., 4th Mfg. Eng. Soc. Intl. Conf., MESIC 2011, vol. 1431, pp. 625–632 (2011)
3. Pardessus, T.: Concurrent engineering development and practices for aircraft design at Airbus. In: Proc. of the 24th ICAS Conf., Yokohama, Japan (2004)
4. Menéndez, J.L., Mas, F., Serván, J., Ríos, J.: Virtual Verification of an Aircraft Final Assembly Line Industrialization: An industrial case. Key Engineering Materials 502, 139–144 (2012)
5. Delpiano, M., Fabbri, M., Garda, C., Valfré, E.: Virtual Development and Integration of Advanced Aerospace Systems: Alenia Aeronautics Experience. RTO AVT Symposium, Paris, RTO-MP-089 (2002)
6. Van Wijk, D., et al.: Integrated Design and PLM Applications in Aeronautics Product Development. In: Proc. of the 19th CIRP Design Conf. – Competitive Design, Cranfield University, pp. 128–133 (2009)
7. Fowler, J.W., Rose, O.: Grand Challenges in Modeling and Simulation of Complex Manufacturing Systems. Simulation 80, 469–476 (2004)
8. Butterfield, J., Crosby, S., Curran, R., Price, M., Armstrong, C.G., Raghunathan, S., McAleenan, D., Gibson, C.: Optimization of aircraft fuselage assembly process using digital manufacturing. J. of Computing Information Science Engineering 7, 269–275 (2007)
9. Anselmetti, B., Fricero, B.: Aid tool for the design of process and aircraft assembly lines. Aerospace Science and Technology 23, 387–398 (2012)
10. Mas, F., Ríos, J., Menéndez, J.L., Hernández, J.C., Vizán, A.: Concurrent conceptual design of aero-structure assembly lines. In: Proceedings of the 14th Intl. Conf. on Concurrent Enterprising (ICE), Lisbon, Portugal, pp. 783–790 (2008)
11. Gómez, A., Mas, F., Menéndez, J.L., Ríos, J.: Development to assist in the creation of product development structures. In: Proc. of the 29th Intl. Manufacturing Conference (IMC29), Belfast, UK (August 2012)

Product Portfolio Management: An Analysis of a Large Medical Device Company

Aidan O'Connor[1] and Kathryn Cormican[2]

[1] NDEC, Dublin City University, Dublin, Ireland
[2] College of Engineering & Informatics, National University of Ireland, Galway, Ireland
Kathryn.Cormican@nuigalway.ie

Abstract. This paper focuses on product portfolio management in a large multinational medical device organization. The contribution of this research is to provide insights into the nature, composition and decision making processes of product portfolios in a real world setting. The research is important because portfolio management decisions have a significant impact and influence the performance at each stage in the product life cycle. Results of the study indicate that portfolio management is a complex process in general but particularly challenging when dealing with technology development projects or innovative new products as unchartered waters are difficult to assess. We found that there are challenges with transparency and that stakeholders need fact based and information driven decisions. There is a need for better up front planning and systems to guide the process. Consistent criteria should be used to select and prioritize projects to facilitate better comparative ranking and allow for balanced portfolios, as well better resource distribution. However we also found that these criteria may change depending on the stage in the lifecycle.

Keywords: Product Portfolio Management, New Product Development, Medical Device Industry, Best Practice.

1 Introduction

The mechanisms for introducing new medical device products are now more complex than ever due to long development cycles, expensive technology development, and lengthy regulatory pathways. Systematic structures and processes are required to select, prioritize and manage new projects in order to ensure that the right projects are chosen and that scarce resources are effectively distributed throughout the development lifecycle [1]. Portfolio management can be defined as a formalized method to select, support and manage a collection of projects that share and compete for the same resources and are carried out under the sponsorship or management of an organization [2], [3]. Product portfolio management is complex and fraught with challenges in practice. For example, research suggests that formalized systems are often not in place [4]. Indeed where systems are in place they often lack rigor and in many cases the system does not clearly align with the organization's strategy; the criteria for assessment are poorly defined and decision making is sporadic and inconsistent [5], [6].

A. Bernard, L. Rivest, and D. Dutta (Eds.): PLM 2013, IFIP AICT 409, pp. 20–28, 2013.

The goal of this study is to analyze product portfolio management in a large medical device company. A detailed case study was undertaken in order to understand the nature and composition of new technology and new product portfolios. To do this we analyzed the type of projects; the value of projects and the amount of minor projects in the portfolio. We also wanted to better understand the decision making processes. Therefore we investigated whether structured processes are in place; how they have evolved in recent years; the nature of the gating system (i.e. the number of gates and scoring criteria throughout the lifecycle (start, middle and end); when and why projects are terminated and how resources are allocated.

2 Product Portfolio Management

According to Cooper et al [7] portfolio management "*is a dynamic decision making process*", where an organizations' list of technology development and new product development projects is continuously reviewed, revised and renewed. In this process, new projects are "*evaluated, selected, and prioritized; existing projects may be accelerated, killed, or de-prioritized; and resources are allocated and reallocated to the active projects*" [8]. The portfolio decision making process is characterized by uncertain and changing information, dynamic opportunities, multiple goals and strategic considerations, interdependence among projects, and multiple decision-makers and locations. According to Martinsuo and Lehtonen [3] "*The objective of project portfolio management [is] to maximize the value of the portfolio in terms of company objectives, to achieve a balance of projects in terms of strategically important parameters, or to ensure strategic direction of projects*". Portfolio management also allows for an effective allocation of resources among on-going projects and helps to minimize competing for a small pool of resources [1]. A synthesis of the literature in the area reveals that effective portfolio management should include the following performance goals [1], [5], [6], [8], [9], [10], [11], [12].

- To have the right number of projects in the portfolio for the resources available.
- To avoid pipeline gridlock in the portfolio undertaking projects on time and in a time-efficient manner.
- To have a portfolio of profitable, high return projects with solid commercial prospects.
- To have a balanced portfolio i.e. long term versus short term, high risk versus low risk, and across markets and technologies.
- To have a portfolio of projects that is aligned with the business's strategy.
- To have a portfolio where spending breakdown mirrors the business's strategy and strategic priorities.

3 Research Methodology

A detailed case study was employed in a leading medical device manufacturer in Ireland utilizing a mixed method research approach. In keeping with the organization's requests for anonymity, the identity of the organization and the participants is not disclosed. All participants were directly involved in the new product or new technology development process which feeds the project portfolio and are directly involved in the process for accepting or rejecting projects. Informants included project managers; program managers; senior researchers; managers and directors or senior leaders. The subjects selected were proportional and representative of their sub-population. The research comprised of initial open-ended interviews to identify key themes from the outset. This was followed by a detailed structured survey. Validation interviews then took place to verify initial findings and provide more in-depth analysis. Quantitative data was analyzed using excel, SPSS, and Minitab software. The output was presented as frequency analysis, histograms plots, boxplots, ANOVA, and ANOM plots. The qualitative analysis was broken down in two stages. First, the initial coding broke up the data into components relating to actions and meanings. The data was analyzed using three methods: open coding, axial coding, and selective coding. Open coding is the process by which data is broken down analytically [13]. The common attributes were linked together to form categories. In axial coding, categories were related to their subcategories through conditions, strategy, context, and consequence. Selective coding unifies all categories around a core category.

4 Findings

4.1 Project Portfolio Structure

Findings from our analysis reveal that product portfolios are well balanced as they contain a mix of small, medium, and large projects at the time of capture and the median lies between seven and nine projects. Data was collected about the value of the products in the portfolio. We found that a good mix of both high and low value projects existed in the portfolios. Interestingly, the majority of the portfolios contained at least one high value "*blockbuster*" or "*superstar*" project. The number of minor projects (i.e. limited scope, capital, and financial return) within the portfolio is an important metric. We found that the median percentage of minor projects lies somewhere between 20% and 40%.

4.2 Level of Innovation in the Portfolio

We attempted to establish the type and level of innovation with the portfolios. The lowest occurrence project type (13%) was "*Revolutionary or Breakthrough*". The next was "*Evolutionary or Derivative*" (40%). The remaining 47% was "*Platform-Next Generation*" projects. In order to better understand the link between technology development projects and new product development projects and the impact of this in the portfolio, we probed whether there was a specific technology which had led to new product development within the portfolio. The vast majority of participants agreed that technology development leads to new product development in the project portfolio. One informant noted that "*the company runs a formal technology development program in order to develop novel technology platforms that can be commercialized across a broad range of products through the formal new product development process*" while another stated that *"technology was developed at an academic level for 5 years; pilot plant established internally and then finally migrated to production system"*.

4.3 Portfolio Management Process

The results reveal that the majority of product portfolios had a structured management process in place. However, our study found that a notable change occurred in the decision-making processes within the last five years. Processes were changed in order to ensure better consistency and to avoid conflicting messages and prioritization of projects across divisions and business units: "*Project ratings and justifications were not consistent among business units or project leaders making it hard to compare projects*." Better streamlining and strategic alignment was also a motivating factor to alter the decision-making processes. The overall aim was to limit the number of projects and prioritize high value ones for the project portfolio: "*There has been a reduction in the number of projects to allow more focus on the high priority ones. Streamlining of project/investment selection based on company strategy and alignment with current economic climate and future state factors*." Many project managers felt the need for more defined structures for both technology development and product development projects that has formulized gating systems to facilitate better control on the projects: "*A fully procedural system for new development projects was rolled out and gating items identified and formalized for acceptance/rejection within/into the portfolio.*"

4.4 Gating Process

There are a high number of gates active in the new product development process. These projects had about 11 gates but a standard deviation of 3.5, which may highlight some inconsistency in the response. There are, on average, 10 gates for new technology development projects, but the standard deviation is 8.0. These results are significant, showing a wide distribution of gate numbers within the technology development process.

4.5 Scoring Criteria

In order to evaluate the best criteria that can be used to evaluate a projects successful inclusion in the portfolio we asked participants to rank a series of criterion chosen from the literature. These include: development timeline; strategic market penetration; cost of goods sold (COG); product complexity; next generation platform; adequate resources available; blockbuster product; return on investment; capital costs and level of project risk. Each criterion was ranked in order of perceived importance from 1–10, where 1 represents the highest priority and 10 the lowest (see Figure 1). The results show a spread of data within each criterion. However market penetration was deemed the most important factor. The other criterion show varying rank levels, which makes determination of the next level of priority difficult to assess.

In order to assess the next priority level, mean variation and ranks are analyzed relative to each other. The P-values for both Bartlett's and Levene's (F-Test) in the test for equal variance on all the factors shows P-values in excess of 0.05 (0.730 and 0.454 respectively) which supports the hypothesis that there is no statistical difference in variation across all factors. An analysis of means (ANOM) highlights a shift between differing factors. This suggests that "*market penetration*" was the highest priority. The median level of priorities were "*blockbuster product*", "*cost of goods (COG's)*", "*development time*", "*next generation platform*", "*project risk*", and "*short return on investment (ROI)*". The lowest priority criterions were "*capital costs*", "*product complexity*" and "*resource availability*".

We then attempted to identify the best criteria to measure the health of the project within the formal review process over the project lifecycle i.e. once approval was granted to initiate the project and officially make it part of the portfolio. We found that "*alignment to the portfolio strategy*", "*return on investment*", and the "*technical feasibility or challenge*" were important criteria. Other key criteria that were identified include: alignment with the business strategy; product advantage; technical feasibility; target market penetration; likelihood of success and risk versus return.

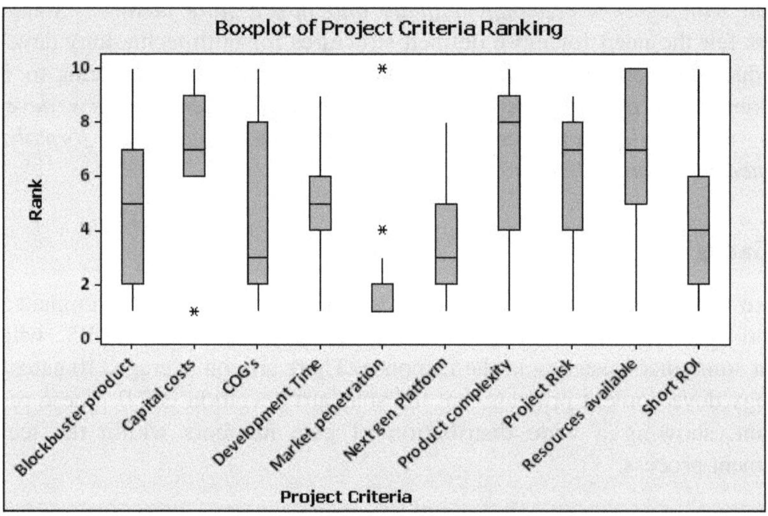

Fig. 1. Project Selection Criteria

In order to ascertain what criteria should be used to evaluate the successful launch of any new product participants were asked to rank a series of criterion chosen from the literature. These include: on time launch; market demand; requirements met for cost of goods sold (COG); return on investment (ROI) achieved; project resourced adequately; project managed well (from plan to assess phases) and blockbuster product. The ranking ranged from 1–10. The results showed a spread of data within each of the criterions. Based on visual factors, it can be deduced that achieving ROI is the most significant factor for product launch (see Figure 2). The other criteria showed varying rank levels, and so further analysis was required.

An analysis of the means variation and means rank relative to each other were conducted. A test for equal variance on all the factors was calculated. The P-values for both Bartlett's and Levene's (F-Test) shows P-values in excess of 0.05 (0.247 and 0.402 respectively). This supports the hypothesis that there is no statistical difference in variation across all factors. An analysis of means found that "*achieved ROI*" is the highest priority. The next level of priorities are identified as "*blockbuster product*", "*market demand*", "*product met COG's*", "*on time launch*" and "*project managed effectively*" as occupying the median of the ranking. The lowest priority criterion was "*resourced adequately*".

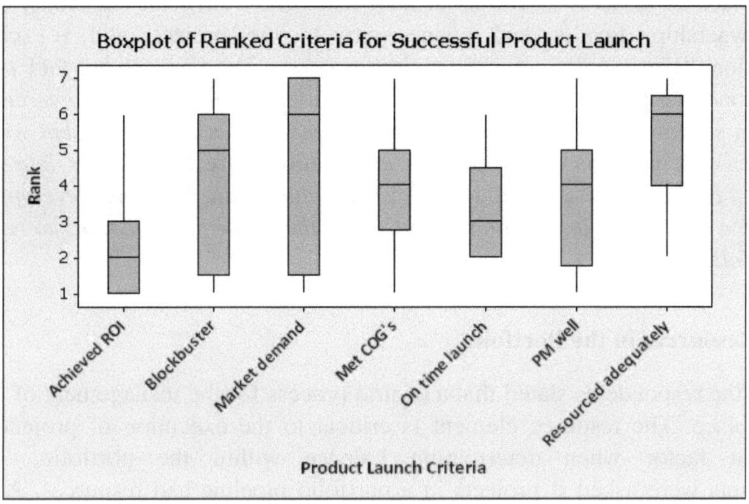

Fig. 2. Successful Product Launch Criteria

4.6 Project Termination

We tried to uncover what the main reasons were for terminating a project in the portfolio prior to final development or market launch. Changing business priorities was cited as a significant reason for projects stopping within the portfolio. One respondent notes that "*the main reason projects are stopped is because of shifting business trends....*" Often other projects took priority and resources were reallocated. According to one informant, "*resources in either product development or operations [were] transferred to other projects.*" Other contributory factors for terminating projects include the inability to realize key technology potential and a poor understanding of market requirements. High costs are cited as a reoccurring problem throughout the analysis. The cost to develop new technologies increase or unforeseen costs arise. Sometimes the product cannot compete with a product currently on the market. Also, the marketing of a new technology may take too long to recoup the costs incurred. Markets also erode which has an impact on recouping costs.

The development of new technologies and innovative products is a risky endeavor and the level of risk has a major impact on decisions to terminate a product in the portfolio. For example, a more complicated regulatory path or other notified body requests may add significant project risk, resulting in a No Go decision. The changing market environment is having a significant impact on how business strategy is developed. The economic downturn affects growth, making it difficult to launch new products, especially ones with higher premiums: "*External environment changes and projections for growth alter accordingly; new or niche products are more likely taken up during booming economic conditions.*"

The main reasons for projects stopping late in the development process is a result of (a) a lack of systems and tools to help make these difficult decisions, (b) strong team ownership, loyalty and connectivity to the project, and (c) change in expectation: "*You usually get a sense that programs are off track but lack the formal decision making tool to guide the teams.*" Also, "*teams feel they can overcome many obstacles so they won't back down from challenges even if they present with risks.*" Other reasons, such as poor up front expectations, are blamed for late decision-making: "*Expectations upfront set the scene which adjust during development and can have a significant impact on the benefits of the project thus leading to rejection at the portfolio level.*"

4.7 Resources in the Portfolio

Most of the respondents stated that a central process for the management of resources was in place. The resource element is critical to the execution of projects and an important factor when determining balance within the portfolio. Therefore participants were asked if projects in a portfolio pipeline had resources. A majority concluded there was an imbalance regarding resources within the portfolio. We explored this further and some key categories emerged. These included the conflict between functional priorities and project priorities "*It is always hard to get a perfect balance due to so many departments working on a project. Sometimes priority of project for the company makes the managers prioritize the project for the team members.*" The projects may start with fewer resources than required until a defined execution plan with a resource map is in place: "*Early research project resources tend to be limited, until potential for ROI is identified; it takes careful management of what is available ... Projects are predominantly started with inadequate resources.*"

While insufficient resources were found to impact on the success of projects so too did inappropriate appropriate resources. We found that poor skills and limited capability often result in the poor execution of projects: "*It's not an issue on the headcount number but in the capability or competency of those resources. A new team with little experience will take longer to do tasks therefore may feel under resourced.*" We also found that high-value projects have a very high probability of being resourced, although careful allocation of seasoned staff is required to ensure adequate capability and competency within the team structure: "*If the business case is strong enough the resources will be found.*"

4.8 Potential Improvements

Participants identified some challenges with transparency towards stakeholders. The use of facts and data to drive decisions is logical and transparent: *"It is not quantified and hence not highlighted if a department is falling behind in their tasks..."* Additionally, the use of the global resource network could eliminate the impact of imbalanced portfolios in particular divisions. This network could remove the low-value elements existing in each division's portfolio. One participant proposed having *"divisions compete for resources so that the top return is picked not just the top for that division."* Another emphasized the need for *"agreement to have a globally funded product development team that only spends money where there is the most Return on Investment".*

Greater up-front planning is always desired but not always achieved. Change in the market environment can have a significant impact on the success of new product launch: *"It is critical to ensure that the project portfolio aligns with the business strategy and is constantly monitored in the context of the ever-changing business environment in order to ensure that appropriate projects are supported and projects that are no longer relevant are stopped."* The final improvement category is Increase Formal Reviews. The responses considered greater project health checks as a pruning operation to encourage better and timelier decision-making: *"More regular checks on the health of the overall portfolio and if we're on track to meet strategic objectives."*

5 Conclusion

Portfolio management is an effective method for organizations to manage their projects through their development lifecycles, provided ranking, priority, gating, and consistent approaches are taken into consideration. However, there are some challenges which can be overcome by implementation of new processes and a shift in culture. Our study found that a balanced portfolio is integral to resource availability and risk management. However to achieve this, greater uniformity in the system of scoring and ranking of projects is needed. In other words a robust review gating system is required throughout the development lifecycle. Without a unilateral process, differences of approach can occur within the organizations sub-structures.

References

1. Heising, W.: The integration of ideation and project portfolio management - A key factor for sustainable success. International Journal of Project Management 30(5), 582–595 (2012)
2. Jonas, D.: Empowering project portfolio managers: How management involvement impacts project portfolio management performance. International Journal of Project Management 28(8), 818–831 (2010)
3. Martinsuo, M., Lehtonen, P.: Role of single-project management in achieving portfolio management efficiency. International Journal of Project Management 25(1), 56–65 (2007)

4. Barczak, G., Griffin, A., Kahn, K.: Trends and Drivers of Success in NPD Practices: Results of the 2003 PDMA Best Practices Study. Journal of Product Innovation Management 26(1), 3–23 (2009)
5. Augusto, P., Miguel, C.: Portfolio management and new product development implementation: A case study in a manufacturing firm. International Journal of Quality & Reliability Management 25(1), 10–23 (2008)
6. Killen, C., Hunt, R., Kleinschmidt, E.: Project portfolio management for product innovation. International Journal of Quality & Reliability Management 25(1), 24–38 (2008)
7. Cooper, R., Edgett, S., Kleinschmidt, E.: Portfolio Management in New Product Development - Lessons from the leaders II. Research Technology Management 40(6), 43–52 (1997)
8. Cooper, R., Edgett, S., Kleinschmidt, E.: Portfolio management for new product development: results of an industry practices study. R&D Management 31(4), 361–380 (2001)
9. Petit, Y.: Project portfolios in dynamic environments: Organizing for uncertainty. International Journal of Project Management 30(5), 539–553 (2012)
10. Meskendahl, S.: The influence of business strategy on project portfolio management and its success - A conceptual framework. International Journal of Project Management 28(8), 807–817 (2010)
11. van Oorschot, K., Sengupta, K., Akkermans, H., van Wassenhove, L.: Get Fat Fast: Surviving Stage-Gate® in NPD. Journal of Product Innovation Management 27(6), 828–839 (2010)
12. Grönlund, J., Sjödin, D., Frishammar, J.: Open Innovation and the Stage-Gate Process: A revised model for new product development. California Management Review 52(3), 106–131 (2010)
13. Corbin, J.M., Strauss, A.L.: Basics of qualitative research: Techniques and procedures for developing grounded theory. SAGE publications, London (1998)

A Few Guidelines for a Good Usage of PLM Software

Mickaël David

LEMNA, IEMN-IAE, University of Nantes, France
mickael.david@univ-nantes.fr

Abstract. Softwares providers offer PLM solutions to support the homonym organizational approach, especially during New Product Development (NPD) process. However these tools are not a panacea. This communication takes its theoretical and methodological foundations in management science. We seek to understand how managers can influence the users so they make a good use of their PLM tool. We analyze the case of a car manufacturer that has purchased a PLM software eight years ago. Our qualitative approach has allowed us to highlighting the importance of managerial action and regulation for an efficient use of PLM tools. On a theoretical level, we use the PLM features in line with Grieves to determine the informational integration effectiveness permitted by the tool. We propose some extensions to the sociomaterial typology of agencies recognized in Information Systems literature. Finally, we propose some managerial guidelines for a good use of PLM tools.

Keywords: PLM Tools, NPD Process, Informational Integration, Agency, Rules of use.

1 Introduction

Many industrial companies have to produce more and more complex goods, while optimizing development costs and reducing time to market [1]. A major concern in this sector is being able to handle the various facets of a product (manufacturing, logistics, recycling...) in a comprehensive manner as soon as its design phase. However, the New Product Development (NPD) process is distributed among different organizational functions, and regularly inter-organizational [2]. Informational integration including sharing of updated documents is thus critique.

IT vendors offer packaged Product Lifecycle Management (PLM) solutions to meet this challenge [3]. The Literature recognizes three functional subsystems within these solutions: 1°) Organizational Memory System (OMS) with storage, classification and research features; 2°) Project and Resources Management System (PRMS), with workflow, monitoring and milestones features, and 3°) Collaborative Work System (CWS), with viewer features and management of files by their status [4], [5].

However these softwares sold in the market are not a panacea, their potential must be activated [6]. In management science, many researchers consider the organizational performance as an emergent, technical and social, construction [7]. In this communication, we seek to understand the construction of a performing use of

A. Bernard, L. Rivest, and D. Dutta (Eds.): PLM 2013, IFIP AICT 409, pp. 29–38, 2013.

the PLM softwares (i.e. here, a use permitting to improve the informational integration of NPD process). To do this, we have to identify the different causes enacting the idiosyncratic usage of the PLM software in an organization (see 3.1). We are not trying to determine what a good tool is but what a good use of this PLM tool is. Finally, we wish to be able to propose guidelines for a good use of PLM tools.

2 State-of-the-Art

The potential of these complex softwares must be activated during the implementation project. A "fit" between the users' practices (and others organizational specificities) and the IT solution must be created [8], [9]. However, a perfect fit seems impossible to obtain. The user's practices are too different and conflicting between them and with the organizational interest. This irreducible "misfit" is called "imposition"[8].

This potential of the software must be also activated by a good use of this solution. The term "infusion" of the technology is generally used to denote the complete appropriation of the tool spirit by users [10], which leads them to propose new developments of the solution or new virtuous uses of the existing solution [6]. A collective appropriation of the software (i.e the users' capacity to effectively use the solution's functionalities when it's necessary, and only when it's useful) is an important asset for an organization [5]. This appropriation need to be managed [11]. In this vein, workaround phenomena and resistance to use the tool are not necessary blamed. They can result from a second type of misfit called "deficiency"[8]. These phenomena can be the premise of the invention by users of new virtuous uses which are not foreseen by the solution designers [12], [13].

3 Construction of Our Analytical Model

Our analytical model is composed of a typology of causes of the IT use (independent variables) and of an informational integration model (dependent variable).

3.1 The Causes of the Idiosyncratic Use of a PLM Tool

We mobilize the concept of agency from the structurationist paradigm as it has been regularly used to answer this issue of the idiosyncratic use of PLM tools [7], [14]. Agency is conceptualized as a spatiotemporally located expression of a material or social structure influencing determination of actual action, in this case the use of the tool. Leonardi [14] makes a distinction between material agency and human agency. We separate the individual form of human agency and its organizational form represented by prescribed or emergent collective rules of use (Fig. 2).

We make again two distinctions in order to refine our analytical model: first, on the subject of these organizational rules between NPD process and PLM tool use; second, between intrinsic material agency (resulting from the basic structure of the tool) and extrinsic material agency (resulting from tool parameter settings wanted by the organization, and therefore which is a transfiguration of an organizational agency to a material agency).

Regulations are then captured by the organizational agency (NDP or PLM) and by the extrinsic material agency of the PLM tool. The intrinsic material agency and the individual agency allow us to put into perspective the need of managerial rules (by increasing it or decreasing it).

3.2 Informational Integration Per Se

Informational integration is often inferred from consequences presumed to cause (including coordination [15]), but it is rarely grasping per se [16]. Inspired by the characteristics of PLM tool, Grieves proposes six characteristics of product information integration: correspondence, singularity, traceability, differentiated availability, cohesion of representations and reflexivity [17]. These characteristics are consistent with the four phases of organizational memory generally used in the literature [18] as well as with the Patnayakuni, Ruppel et Rai's model of informational integration [16]. However, the characteristics of PLM tool have two advantages over the current informational integration model: the consideration of the acquisition phase and the consideration of the notion of parsimony by the differentiated availability of items (Fig. 1).

CHARACTERISTICS OF PLM (Grieves 2006)	ORGANIZATIONAL MEMORY (Walsh and Ungson 1991)	INFORMATIONAL INTEGRATION MODEL (Patnayakuni, Ruppel and Rai 2006)
CORRESPONDENCE	ACQUISITION	N/A
SINGULARITY		
TRACEABILITY	STORAGE	EASY ACCESSIBILITY
N/A	DIFFUSION	INFORMATION PORTABILITY
DIFFERENTIATED AVAILABILITY		N/A
COHESION OF REPRESENTATIONS		NO LOSS OF SEMANTIC INFORMATION
REFLECTIVITY	USE	COMMUNICATION OF MODIFICATIONS

Fig. 1. Comparison of informational integration models (adapted from references)

- The information acquisition must be comprehensive. The correspondence*[1] is required between the information richness contained in PLM tool and the complexity of reality. The information acquisition must also be non-redundant. A singularity* of objects for the same information facilitates their updating.
- The information storing represents an informational integration with past tasks/phases. This integration is characterized by an easy accessibility to historical data design#, especially permitted by their traceability*.

[1] * Items from Grieves [17], # items from Patnayakuni, Ruppel et Rai [16].

- The information diffusion must be efficient. Under condition of information portability#, only the information needed must be presented at user, and in a relevant way. The availability is differentiated* by the user's interest. However, this personalization should not prevent the cohesion of virtual representations* and it should preserve the coherence of the logical model#. The aim is mutual understanding of different trades without loss of semantic information#.
- Finally, informational integration implies that any change to the environment captured by the system is communicated# in order to produce the necessary consequences about its use (the reflectivity* in the Grieves' terminology).

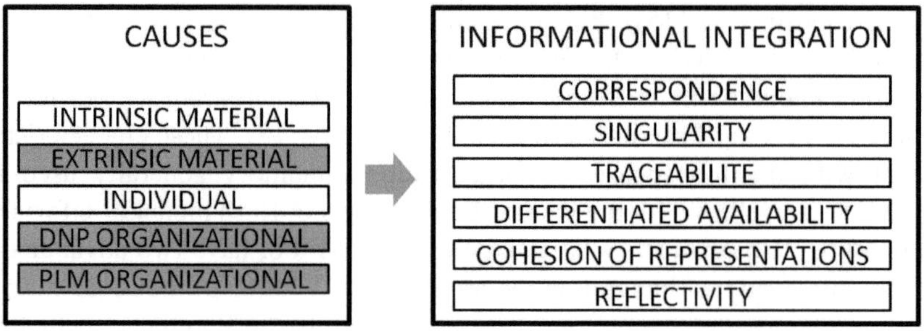

Fig. 2. Our analytical model (the three shaded variables are the managerial variables)

4 The Results of the Case Studied

The case is a car manufacturer SME that designs, manufactures and assembles kits. The design and methods office is divided into four products families. There are forty PLM tool users; half of them work in the design and methods office.

The solution has been implemented between 2002 and 2004 by a phased deployment is Smarteam of Dassault Systemes. The available PLM functionalities are limited compared to functionalities offered on the market (no workflow, no project monitoring). In addition, the junction with the enterprise system is not carried out. Then, the PLM tool is used as an electronic documents management server offering some collaborative features. The results will be presented successively depending on the informational integration model (Fig. 2).

4.1 Information Acquisition

The correspondence (or completeness) is examined in width and breadth.

The principle of formalization is inherent to design office work; the individual agency and the NPD organizational agency are congruent. The PLM functionalities (interfaced with CAD software) lead Smarteam to almost exclusively support technical information on product, such as CAD or DXF (Drawing eXchange Format) files, plans, test and accreditation reports; an intrinsic material agency supports the correspondence of this information with reality.

With regards to the information depth, the expected level of product detail by major car manufacturers is greater than that expected by this enterprise for its product on own-brand. Major car manufacturers require their parts are fully defined. However, a part's product on own-brand is described in order to provide ease of assembly. Thus there is a NDP organizational agency on a more or less important detail degree of CAD files.

These agencies coincide for that product information has a good correspondence with reality, both in width and breadth (less for the products on own-brand).

The information singularity is in particular obtained by the absence of multiple individual agencies. There is only one designer per team because the design and methods office is divided into products families (NPD organizational agency). In these conditions the PLM tool becomes the single source of product information without difficulties (as wanted by the organization) through its shared server and its indexed incrementing of files (intrinsic material agency). However, interoperability problems sometimes require records in various formats and/or on different servers (adverse intrinsic material agency).

The acquisition phase of product information meets the correspondence criterion and meets relatively well the singularity criterion. This effectiveness is enabled by the overall convergence of various organizational, material and individual agencies. However, the information singularity appears to be the result both of the reduced structure of the organization and of the intrinsic properties of the tool.

4.2 Information Storage

The documentary retrieval and the traceability are only partially effective. The documentary ontology of PLM tool (extrinsic material agency) supports generally the various attributes of product information. The users dispose of search unique keys as plan number for example.

However, designers are allowed to create their own folder in the tool directory tree (no extrinsic material agency). Thus, designers are free to organize the project folder as they want, to store anything they want in this folder, but especially they are free to name their files the way they want (individual agency/absence of PLM organizational agency). Eight years after the implementation of PLM tool, this absence of standardization of PLM use rules leads to time-consuming consequences. The designers have difficulty to retrieval a document if they are not the creator of it or if the document is "stored" in a folder which they are not accustomed. The peripheral users, such as those of manufacturing workshop or warehouse, use only the search keys and refuse a visual search in the directory tree without being leading by a designer by phone. Documents such as procedures have not attributes offering specific search keys. They are therefore particularly susceptible to problems resulting from the weak structuring of the directory tree. In addition, the NDP organizational agency promotes an accounting perspective on the project perimeter: a project is an annual expenditure commitment. Then there are as many folders as calendar years for a same technical project. This causes an expansion of the directory tree increasing the difficulty of visual search.

Storage and retrieval are therefore only partially effective (because it is sometimes laborious) despite the various features offered by PLM tool (intrinsic material agencies). It seems that the company has relied too much on the intrinsic properties of the tool. Despite the small size of the company, several users work on the same project and must access to the same documents. This common tool requires common rules of use (i.e. standards that counteract the multiplicity of individual patterns of use) especially in structuring of directory tree and in description of items.

4.3 Information Diffusion

Differentiated availability is only partially effective too. We analyze it with two points of view: static and dynamic.

Only documents having the last index are available for manufacturing workshop. However, despite the structuring of organization by products families, everyone has access to the folders of others products families. User profiles are not fully utilized (partial extrinsic material agency). In a dynamic point of view, the PLM tool does not contain workflow functionality (not intrinsic material agency). The information transfer by PLM tool is mainly pulled by manufacturing workshop or quality department. The designer (individual agency) is the pilot of the design and he pushes the information when he needs it, especially for prototyping. A procedure of electronic diffusion of technical notes via email (with a link to the document in Smarteam) has recently been implemented (PLM organizational agency). For some, the e-mail inbox provides a more efficient search engine than the one of Smarteam.

The partial formalization of the availability is based on the individual responsibility. In the retrieval case, the users have to differentiate useful information and in the filing case, they have to find the appropriate location storage of the document.

Cohesion of virtual representations (not mental) calls several objects of representation: the directory tree, the product geometry or the technical domain of product. The directory tree of a project is the same regardless of the user, so there are no distinct representations. However, we have seen, the directory tree is subject to the accountant constraint (adverse PLM organizational agency). Then the geometric vision of object in 2D (plan) is automatically generated from the CAD file (favorable intrinsic material agency). Finally, the electrical design is not integrated in mechanical CAD files because the CAD softwares (respectively Electra and Catia) are not interfaced (adverse intrinsic material agency). Due to the weak coupling of these two technical areas, the electrical design is realized according to the CAD file after mechanical design (adverse NPD organizational agency).

In information diffusion phase, the criterions of differentiated availability and of representations cohesion are only partially effective. Differentiated availability is only permitted by individual efforts and the pressure exerted by individuals to build better practices of PLM use. Regarding to cohesion of representations, only one between the plan and the CAD file seems to be sought by the organization.

4.4 Information Use

The criterion of information reflectivity translates into an automatic mechanism by the tool: an alert for updating of all products using a part/item which has just been modified (intrinsic material agency). This constraint of tool is not always respected because the added value of the operation is too weak compared to the time required to do it. This is legitimized by the collective criterion of weak impact on the product manufacturing. A NPD organizational agency counteracts the intrinsic material agency for time consuming tasks. Products having a long life-series have therefore a large number of inconsistency markers between the different versions of the parts and assemblies. In addition, the absence of intrinsic material agency regarding the technical integration of PLM tool with ERP tool does not permit to draw all consequences in terms of use cases and nomenclatures.

4.5 Summary of the Results

The figure 3 summarizes the results.

- The intrinsic material agency - the inherent properties of the tool - contributes to the effectiveness of informational integration in its various phases. However in this case, this contribution is lower on the last phases because there is neither workflow nor integration of CAD softwares and nor integration with ERP.
- The individual agency - the will of the individuals - has an ambivalent contribution: it generates a heterogeneity of practices (singularity, storage and retrieval), but it is also at the initiative of adaptive and palliative behaviors to functional deficiencies of the tool (storage, search and retrieval, differentiated availability).
- The extrinsic material agency - the parameter settings of the tool - does not seem necessary for the acquisition or use phases. However, it is necessary to optimizing the directory tree, the ontological structure of the database and the differentiated access to information by the individuals' digital profile.
- The PLM organizational agency – the rules of PLM tool use – is important for enforcing shared use practices of the tool (singularity), especially for imposing the filling of attributes and naming files standards and standards of structuring of directory tree (storage and documentary retrieval).
- The NPD organizational agency – the rules related to the NPD process - defines the degree of correspondence and the updating degree of parts (reflectivity). It regulates the information needing by structuring the project teams (singularity) and it defines the scope of project and related product information (storage and documentary retrieval).

	Acquisition		Storage	Diffusion		Use
	Correspondence	Singularity	Traçability and Retrieval	Availability discerned	Representations cohesion	Reflectivity
Intrinsic Material Agency	⬆	⇧	⬆		⇩	⇧
Individual Agency	⇧		⬇	⬆		
Extrinsic Material Agency			⇧	⇧		
PLM Organizational Agency		⬆		⇧	⬇	
NPD Organizational Agency	⬆	⬆	⬇		⇩	⬇
Effectiveness	✖	✖	✕	✕	✕	✕

The three shaded boxes correspond to the measurement of regulations.

⬆ UNEQUIVOCAL SUPPORT ⬇ UNEQUIVOCAL BRAKE ✖ STRONG EFFECTIVENESS

⇧ EQUIVOCAL SUPPORT ⇩ EQUIVOCAL BRAKE ✕ WEAK EFFECTIVENESS

Fig. 3. Summary of the results

5 Discussion

After eight years of using the solution, information retrieval is more difficult. Informational saturation is a risk in the medium term. The company has opted for a weak formalization and standardization of PLM uses to increase the chances of acceptance of tool by users. The daily users have integrated the underlying logic of the tool and they have gradually created virtuous uses. For instance, they use this for constituting a catalog of standard parts or for sharing documents formalizing information on the project progress or on manufacturing workshop's constraints.

It is necessary to exceed the ambivalent character of the regulation by distinguishing between aspects of the usage of PLM software that require strict rules of use and those for which users' leeway is preferable in order to activate the potential of PLM software. The leeway given to users to create, to organize their folders and to store any document (if the required documents are present) into the PLM tool seems to be a good management practice, especially for appropriation of the tool by users. However, this implies strict rules for naming files and filling of their attributes in order that retrieval functionalities can effectively operate. The consequences are that is also necessary to ensure the adaptation of the ontological structure of the tool to new uses and to formalize tasks for ensuring the maintenance of the information content of the tool.

6 Conclusion

This communication takes its theoretical and methodological foundations in management science. By a qualitative approach, we study how users are influenced when they use the tool and what is the performance of this use in terms of informational integration. We have developed a model to assess the informational integration; it must also be validated by more systematic studies. Although they must to check them on other cases, this case study allows us to consider a few managerial guidelines for optimize the use of the solution.

- The technical integration of the PLM software with CAD and ERP softwares must be wanted because it is necessary for enabled various functionalities of PLM software.
- The modeling of (changing) practices and informational environment of the NDP process should be accurate, inserted and updated in parameter setting in the tool.
- Some usage rules must be put in place (the filling of attributes, the naming of files and the structuring of the directory tree). It is important to not formalize the contents of the tool in order to let users set up their own personal space and uses it to develop virtuous usages of the tool.
- These tools are not able to forget; it's important to formalize tasks for ensuring the maintenance of the information contained in the tool.

References

[1] Hatchuel, A., Weil, B.: Design-oriented organizations. In: 6th International Product Development Management Conference (1999)

[2] Merminod, V., Rowe, F.: How does PLM technology support knowledge transfer and translation in new product development? Transparency and Boundary Spanners in an International Context. Information and Organization 22(4), 295–322 (2012)

[3] Ameri, F., Dutta, D.: Product lifecycle management: closing the knowledge loops. Computer-Aided Design & Applications 2(5), 577–590 (2005)

[4] Nambisan, S.: Information Systems as a Reference Discipline for New Product Development. MIS Quarterly 27(1), 1–18 (2003)

[5] Pavlou, P.A., El Sawy, O.A.: From IT leveraging competence to competitive advantage in turbulent environments: The case of new product development. Information Systems Research 17(3), 198–227 (2006)

[6] Leonardi, P.M.: Activating the Informational Capabilities of Information Technology for Organizational Change. Organization Science 18(5), 813–831 (2007)

[7] Desanctis, G., Poole, M.S.: Capturing the Complexity in Advanced Technology Use: Adaptive Structuration Theory. Organization Science 5(2), 121–148 (1994)

[8] Strong, D.M., Volkoff, O.: Understanding Organization-Enterprise System Fit: A Path To Theorizing the Information Technology Artifact. MIS Quarterly 34(4), 731–756 (2010)

[9] Garetti, M., Terzi, S., Bertacci, N., Brianza, M.: Organisational change and knowledge management in PLM implementation. International Journal of Product Lifecycle Management 1(1), 43–51 (2005)

[10] Cooper, R.B., Zmud, R.W.: Information Technology Implementation Research: A Technological Diffusion Approach. Management Science 36(2), 123–139 (1990)

[11] Jasperson, J., Carter, P.E., Zmud, R.W.: A comprehensive conceptualization of post-adoptive behaviors associated with information technology enabled work systems. MIS Quarterly 29(3), 525–557 (2005)

[12] Ferneley, E.H., Sobreperez, P.: Resist, comply or workaround? An examination of different facets of user engagement with information systems. European Journal of Information Systems 15(4), 345–356 (2006)
[13] Boudreau, M.-C., Robey, D.: Enacting Integrated Information Technology: A Human Agency Perspective. Organization Science 16(1), 3–18 (2005)
[14] Leonardi, P.M.: When Flexible Routines Meet Flexible Technologies: Affordance, Constraint, and the Imbrication of Human and Material Agencies. MIS Quarterly 35(1), 147–167 (2011)
[15] Hoopes, D.G., Postrel, S.: Shared knowledge, "glitches," and product development performance. Strategic Management Journal 20(9), 837–865 (1999)
[16] Patnayakuni, R., Ruppel, C.P., Rai, A.: Managing the Complementarity of Knowledge Integration and Process Formalization for Systems Development Performance. Journal of the Association for Information Systems 7(8), 545–567 (2006)
[17] Grieves, M.: Product lifecycle management: driving the next generation of lean thinking. McGraw-Hill, New York (2006)
[18] Walsh, J.P., Ungson, G.R.: Organizational Memory. Academy of Management Review 16(1), 57–91 (1991)

Components Margins through the Product Lifecycle

Claudia Eckert[1], Chris Earl[1], Safaa Lebjioui[1], and Ola Isaksson[2]

[1] The Open University, Milton Keynes, Walton Hall, MK6 7AA, UK
[2] GKN Aerospace Engine Systems Sweden, SE-461 81 Trollhättan, Sweden

Abstract. Engineering change is ubiquitous throughout the product lifecycle to meet new requirements or deal with emerging problems in the product.. Components have a certain capacity to buffer the impact of changes before they pass changes on to other components. These buffers are margins on the components which exceed the current requirements. Typically these margins are designed into a product at the beginning and eroded in the course of the design process or during future upgrades. Fundamental design decisions are being taken based on an understanding of the margins available when considering design alternatives. This paper argues that the knowledge and understanding of these margins is the key to managing engineering changes through the product lifecycle. By tracking key product margins a company can assess when an engineering change could lead to costly knock-on effects.

1 Introduction

Design is an iterative process. Many decisions have to be revisited and changed throughout the design process. This often involves changes to components that are considered finished. However, engineering change is not confined to design processes. It occurs through the entire life cycle of the product. Fricke et al. (2000) estimate that 30% of all work arises from changes of one form or another. Changes arise either from external factors, such as new requirements or advances in technology or are the result of other changes or problems with the state of the design. A change only needs to be made, if the existing design cannot meet the new requirements.

Most components or systems have the ability to absorb some degree of change. This arises from incorporating margins. These are added by different stakeholders for a variety of reasons. However how these margins are introduced and how they work in design have not been addressed in a unified manner in the context of managing change. After a discussion of relevant literature the paper introduces the concept of margins, defines key terms and types, and shows ways to model margins. The paper is set in the context of recent studies on engineering change such as Eckert et al. (2004) and Pasqual & de Weck (2011). It addresses the role of margins at different phases of product development and through product lifecycle.

2 Background

One way to avoid problems with engineering design changes, is incorporating flexibility and adaptability into a products in the first place. This section provides a brief overview of the literature on design for flexibility and engineering change.

A. Bernard, L. Rivest, and D. Dutta (Eds.): PLM 2013, IFIP AICT 409, pp. 39–47, 2013.

2.1 Design for Flexibility

Product flexibility can be defined as "the *degree of responsiveness (or adaptability) for any future change in a product design"* (Ross and Hastings, 2005). Qureshi et al. (2006) propose 17 different strategies to achieve flexibility in a product, grouped into four types: a modular approach, a special approach, an interface decoupling approach and an adjustability approach based on the principle of TRIZ (e.g. Altshuller, 1998), Martin & Ishii (2002)). The 17th of Qureshi et al's strategic principles, referred to enabling "the device to respond to minor changes, by controlling the tuning of design parameters". Both Qureshi et al. (2006) and Muir Wood et al. (2010) advocate assessing the flexibility of a product by systematically anticipating and rating the potential changes to 'future proof' the design. Ross and Hastings (2005) advocate assessing the changeability of a system by mapping out the tradespace, i.e. the range of possible parameter values that provides potential solutions. Where the design sits within this tradespace, defines the product margins.

2.2 Engineering Change

Changes are ubiquitous through the product lifecycle of a design (see Figure 1 and Eckert et al. 2007 for a more detailed discussion). Almost all complex products are designed by modification from an existing product, so that engineering change starts right at the beginning of design processes and continues.throughout the process as adaptations are made to existing components until parts of the designs are frozen. The process of preparing a product for manufacturing typically also leads to frequent changes. Once a base product is produced, orders are placed for other versions of the product or requests are received for customisation. This may be covered by options from a defined set of configurations, but change to the underlying design might also be required. Products in operation and use are subject to changes through product upgrades.

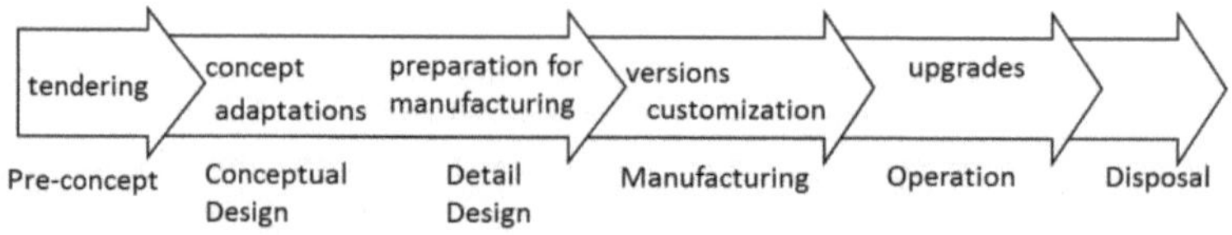

Fig. 1. Changes throughout the product life cycles

Engineering change has been looked at from several perspectives. Jarratt et al. (2012) present a review. The processes of handling change and the challenges that arise from change propagation are similar regardless of the cause of the change or the phase of the design project (Eckert et al., 2004). The impact of changes is not limited to the product itself, but can affect the rest of the organisation through shared resources and interlinked processes (Ariyo et al. 2006; Shankar et al. 2012). Change is difficult to predict, because it is inherently not deterministic, and involves people making decision about how to respond to the need for change (Earl et al. 2005). Various tools have been developed to assist predicting the impact of change, through anticipating changes (Cohan et al. 2000), probabilistic links (Clarkson et al., 2004) and network analysis (Pasqual & de Weck, 2011).

2.3 The State of Components

Whether a change in one component (or system) will propagate to another component, depends both on the exact nature of the change and the current state of the component that is being changed. Each proposed change can be expressed as changes to one or more parameter of the component. Various parameters are associated with each component .These can become critical in the sense that small required changes (or combinations of changes) initiate significant changes in behaviour in components with linked parameters (Figure 2).

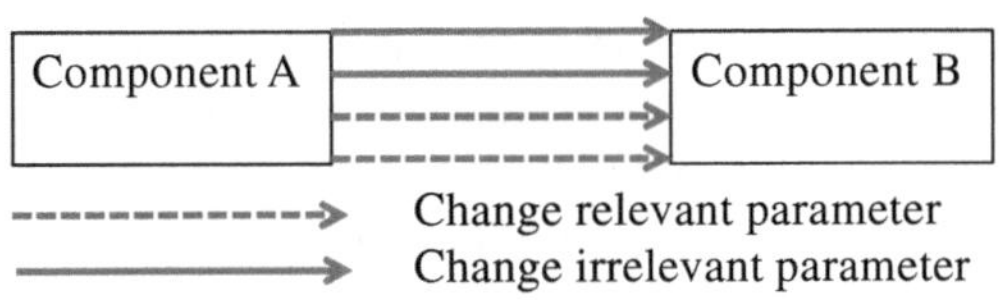

Fig. 2. Parameter links between components

Eckert et al (2004) argue that components either act as (i) change *absorbers*, receiving change without passing it on, (ii) change *carriers* passing the same degree of change on as they have received, or (iii) change *multipliers*, which pass more changes on to others parts of the system, which in turn will need to be redesigned.

Change becomes problematic when change absorbers turn into change carriers or change multipliers and critical when changes cause an avalanche creating more and more potential changes. Often the changes can be brought under control given sufficient design resources and time, but companies might need to abandon these projects. From the perspective of an individual change, there might be several knock-on effects. Some can be dealt with directly and others require detailed analysis. This leads to ripple effects. Pasqual & de Weck (2011) studied change requests for a complex product over many years, observing ripple patterns, with the number of change requests increasing towards deadlines.

3 A Generic Model of Margins

Margins occur in many guises through the lifecycle of a product. This section introduces a base definition before relating margins to other phenomena. For the purpose of this paper we define a margin as: *"the extent to which a parameter value exceeds what it needs to meet its functional requirements regardless of the motivation for which the margin was included".*

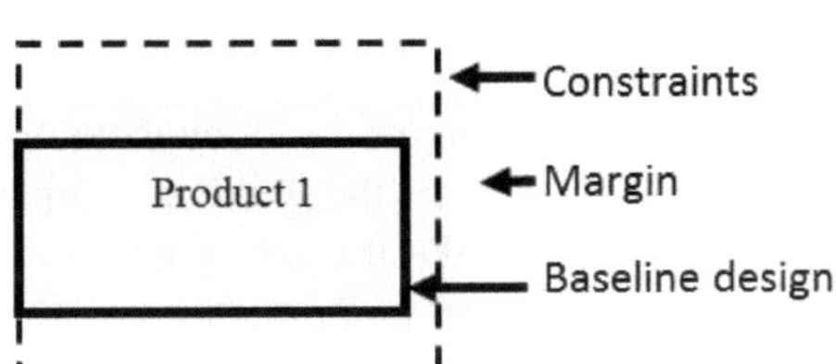

Fig. 3. Requirements, margins and constraints

Figure 3 illustrates the relationship between the base line parameters (heavy black outline) that are required and the actual component parameters (the grey shape with margins in several parameters). In addition the component might be subject to constraints. Note that the margined product exceeds constraints in the figure and is a non-viable design. Viable margined products sit within constraints.

Each component or subsystem of a product can be conceptualized along three dimensions: form (internal structure and configuration of features), function and material. By form we are referring both to external shape and internal (possibly micro) structure. The component carries out a specified function in the product, which is usually described in terms of performance parameters and other target parameters reflecting the component's role in the product. For the third dimension, a component is constructed from a particular material or combination of materials with their own inherent properties. The combination of these three dimensions creates a working component, and the parameters arising from each of the three dimensions are required to describe the component. Parameters in each dimension have their own type of margin, Individual parameters can be traded off against each other across the three categories (Figure 4) and margins allow this tradeoff.. The closer a component gets to its margins the less flexibility it has to absorb a change and make tradeoffs (Figure 5).

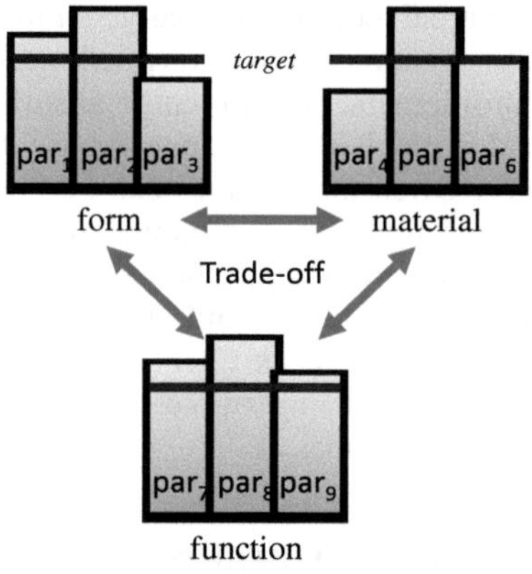

Fig. 4. Trade-offs among form, function and material

Margins do not only reside with individual components, but also apply to subsystems and systems in a way that is not deduced from the margins on specific parameters of individual components. These system margins on system parameters, allow changes in response to changes in other system parameters or in the operating conditions and uses of the product. The margins to absorb different operating conditions and uses does not relate to the margins of individual components in a linear and predictable way. For example a change in the ambient temperature in operation can require direct changes to the product, like the introduction of isolation material, but can also affect the behaviour of individual components, e.g. through heat expansion.

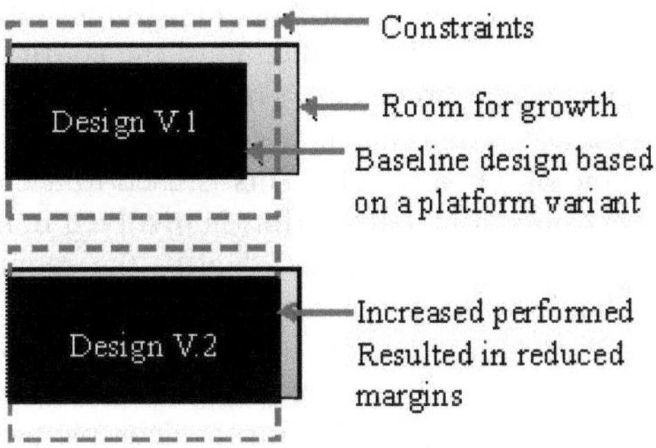

Fig. 5. Reduced margins for change

Changes can rarely be addressed in isolation and display complex interactions. For example a component might expand in the heat while at the same time the isolation material takes up some of the expansion space. The challenge lies in identifying these interlinking changes and managing them together in a coordinated way. Giffen et al. (2008) map out the relationship of change requests illustrating both how change requests to specific components are repeatedly rejected and how changes to specific components multiplies repeatedly across the system. A particular challenge arises when the same margins is affected by seemingly unconnected changes carried out in parallel.

4 Margins across the Product Lifecycle

Product margins need to be considered even before a specific design process starts. As companies aim to control the amount of innovation required for a new product (Suh et al., 2008) and assess the risk associated with the planned innovations (Suh et al., 2010), they need to plan when major changes to the design are to be carried out and therefore where margins are required. This helps avoid unplanned changes. It requires a detailed understanding of the dependency between components and systems, to estimate when knock-on changes are likely to force significant redesign and thereby unplanned innovation. The is complemented by a deliberate design for flexibility approach (see Ollinger an Stahovich 2001).

Planning product changes over longer periods of time is particularly critical in the context of platform design, as the margins of each component are different with regards to different products in the platform, as illustrated in Figure 6.

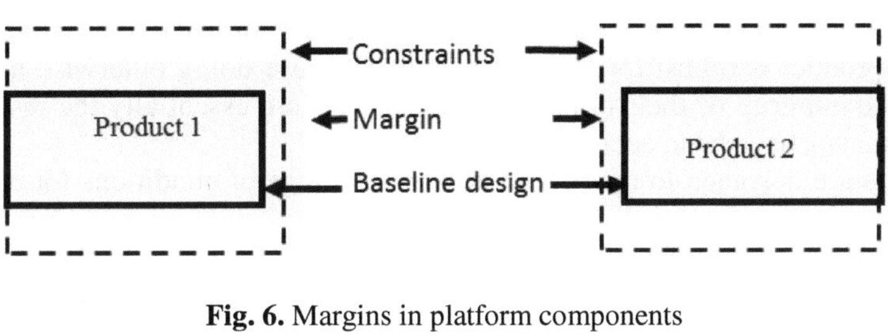

Fig. 6. Margins in platform components

Margins are added or identified in the product in different forms through the design process, as illustrated in Figure 7. The evaluation of the starting design stands at the beginning of many 'new' design processes. This evaluation can refer to the existing test data as well as use and warranty data, which allows the designers to understand the actual parameter value of a component. This is used to access which components need to be redesigned and thus how much effort is involved in the new design. At the beginning of the design process companies identify the requirements for different parameters and often plan in *room for growth*, i.e. parameter margins which accommodate further changes to the requirements for an emerging design or design changes in future generations or upgrades. These margins are used up as the design process progresses, often without the company having a clear picture of the margins still available on a component. This is particularly an issue when multiple components need to make use of the same margin and the designers may not be aware of their colleagues' decisions.

During the design process, testing begins with the aim of assessing whether a product can meet its requirements, rather than understanding exactly the extent of margins exist in a component. In some cases companies test products to destruction and thereby determine the actual margins on components. Virtual testing, i.e. computer simulation of test conditions on analysis models can also reveal the actual component margins. Test results require a certain degree of post-processing to ascertain the parameter margins. This appears to takes place rarely.

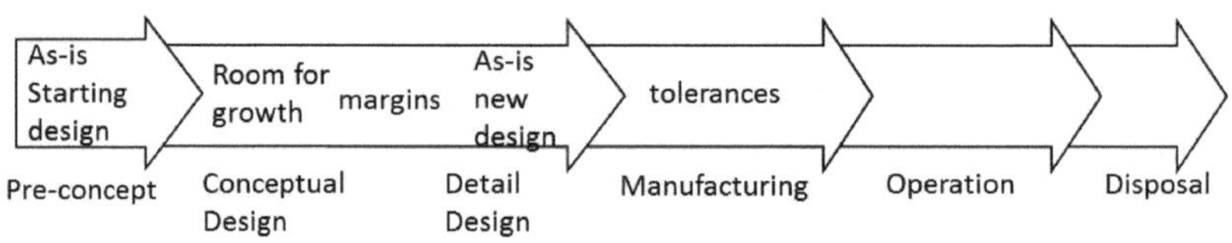

Fig. 7. Margins throughout the product life cycles

Margins are often thought of as *tolerances* or associated boundaries designed into a component to accommodate variability in manufacturing and assembly. This is typically the angle on margins picked up in robust design, which is concerned with assuring the quality of a specific product in service (see Chen et al. 1996). To reduce the risk of product failure in service it is necessary to understand the manufacturing variabilities or set them as hard requirements for suppliers. Products also require safety margins to cater for extreme working environments, for example cold weather and the potential misuse of the product by customers. To a certain extent this can be covered by certifying a product for a specified range of conditions and behaviours or by imposing warranty conditions on the product. However companies still want to be sure that their product is robust to potential misuse, because doing otherwise might compromise the integrity of their brand. Design margins are essentially the residue when these tolerances have been accommodated.

Products are designed to operate under a given range of conditions for a target life time, which is specified in the product warranty. In practice products are often used for different purposes than intended or for a much longer period than anticipated. How products behave after the end of their target life also plays an important part in brand reputation. In the past products have often exceeded their target life by many years, because the products were overdesigned with large margins and the excess cost could be passed on to customers. As mathematical analysis tools have been improving, companies now have a handle on these excess margins and can optimise the products for a particular situation. Optimised products are both cheaper and have better performance, but are more susceptible to negative effects of engineering change, as they have lower, or potentially no, margins to absorb change.

To date, consideration of margins does not systematically capture or analyse margins. However, the information to do so exists to some extent in companies. Those responsible for the last changes affecting a particular margin, usually have a good understanding that a margin could become critical, but on the other hand do not have a means to flag this up. To capture margins systematically companies would need to capture the results from testing with regards to margins. If a test fails, companies it is necessary to determine exactly what contributed to the failure, i.e. which margin was exceeded. To gain a more detailed understanding the companies would need to engage in physical (or virtual) destructive testing.

5 Example

The design of a rear turbine structural frame for an aircraft jet engine clearly displays the problem with design margins (Eckert et al. 2012). The function of the component is partially to ensure mechanical load transfer, structural stability and integrity of the turbine section, whilst contributing to aerodynamic performance (low drag and gas-flow control) of the gas passing through the section. Weight and cost targets are important, so the final design solution typically follows a design optimization effort.

The margins on the metal temperature are critical. Making the turbine frame out of a well known and understood material may be a cost efficient way to produce, but has a narrow upper boundary of allowable metal operating temperature, Since the performance of the new engine is often expected to be higher than that of previous designs, the gas temperature may increase. The margin to ensure structural integrity using the well known material consequently reduces and may vanish entirely.

The design team then faces several design options: (A) use another material, capable of withstanding the new gas temperature, which might be more expensive, and costly to produce and maintain. (B) alter the actual design, e.g. to select a cooled version of the turbine frame, and maintain the "simpler" material.

Comparing (A) and (B) reveal different behaviour from a design margins point of view. Alternative (A) can be made without too much interaction with other parts of the engine system, but still has a definite upper bound in thermal resistance and the material itself may be quite expensive. Alternative (B) impacts the engine system design to use cooling air (expensive), but uses a known and less costly material. From a margins point of view the upper boundary of thermal resistance may be less definite. If the gas temperature turns out to be higher that first expected – the solution may be possible to manage without changing material.

In reality change in conditions happens throughout the development process. Preconditions such as operating design gas temperature are uncertain, and often subject to change. Alternative (A) may initially seem to be a wise choice, whereas alternative (B) is more adjustable from a design perspective.

This simple – yet realistic – example reveals several aspects of margins.

1. The need to represent margins of principally different design alternatives (material up-grade vs. alternative cooled design solution).
2. The need to manage dependencies between design components (the turbine frame) in a system (the jet engine)
3. The need to strategically analyse and predict consequences of change in loads and pre-requisites.

The third aspect is crucial to make informed design decisions, and requires that the underlying design information actually contain information about margins. Today, the analytical ability to make such design simulation is limited, and often handled qualitatively using FMEA and FMECA type approaches for risk analysis.

6 Conclusions

Margins play important roles in engineering change processes under different guises, which, although related, are typically considered and modelled separately. These roles include:

- helping to predict the knock-on effects of changes;
- assessing uncertainty concerning the properties and behaviour of the product and conditions of its use;
- evaluating flexibility regarding the use, manufacture and assembly of the product;
- tolerancing for manufacturing and assembly and the robustness implications.
- Building in adaptability for future products

To manage margins efficiently, the ability to model margins and eventually assess consequences of changes, first requires a sound understanding and adequate representation of underlying margins. Further, the relations and couplings between design components and system with regards to margins needs to be identifiable.

Further research is currently being conducted in several case studies on product planning and platform development to (a) see how industry is handling margins in practice and (b) explore the role of margin models in change predication. The goal of this research is describe margins in a suitable language and model margins in a way that can be linked to existing product representations. The objective is to use margins directly in change prediction.

References

Altshuller, G.: 40 Principles: TRIZ Keys to Technical Innovation. In: Shulak, L., Rodman, S. (eds.), Technical Innovation Center, Worcester (1998)

Ariyo, O.O., Eckert, C.M., Clarkson, P.J.: Unpleasant surprises in the design of complex products: why do changes propagate? In: ASME (IDETC/CIE), Philadelphia, pp. 1057–1064 (2006)

Chen, W., Allen, J.K., Tsui, K.L., Mistree, F.: A Procedure for Robust Design: Minimizing Variations Caused by Noise Factors and Control Factors. Journal of Mechanical Design, Transactions of the ASME 118, 478–485 (1996)

Clarkson, P.J., Simons, C., Eckert, C.: Predicting Change Propagation in Complex Design. Journal of Mechanical Design 126(5), 788–797 (2004)

Cohen, T., Navathe, S., Fulton, R.: C-FAR: Change Favorable Representation. Computer Aided Design (2000)

Earl, C.F., Eckert, C.M., Clarkson, P.J.: Predictability of Change in Engineering: a Complexity View. In: Proceedings of ASME (DTM), Long Beach, USA (2005)

Eckert, C.M., Earl, C.F., Isaksson, O.: Product Property Margins: An underlying critical problem of engineering design. In: Proceedings of TMCE 2012 (2012)

Eckert, C.M., Jowers, I., Clarkson, P.J.: Knowledge requirements over long product lifecycles. In: 16th Int. Conference on Engineering Design (ICED 2007), Paris, France, pp. 913–914 (2007)

Eckert, C.M., Clarkson, P.J., Zanker, W.: Change and customisation in complex engineering domains. Research in Engineering Design 15(1), 1–21 (2004)

Fricke, E., Gebhard, B., Negele, H., Igenbergs, E.: Coping with changes: causes, findings and strategies. System Engineering 3(4), 169–179 (2000)

Giffin, M., de Weck, O., Bounova, G., Keller, R., Eckert, C.M., Clarkson, P.J.: Change propagation analysis in complex technical systems. Journal of Mechanical Design 131(8) (2009)

Jarrett, T., Eckert, C.M., Caldwell, N., Clarkson, P.J.: Planning Development Processes for Complex Products. Research in Engineering Design 22(2), 103–124 (2011) ISSN: 0934-9839

Martin, M.V., Ishii, K.: Design for Variety: Developing Standardized and Modularized Product Platform Architectures. Research in Engineering Design 13(4), 213–235 (2002)

Muir Wood, A.P., Moultrie, J., Eckert, C.M.: Product Form Evolution. In: Silva, A., Simoes, R. (eds.) Handbook of Research on Trends in Product Design and Development: Technological and Organizational Perspectives. IGI Global (2010)

Ollinger, G.A., Stahovich, T.F.: ReDesignIT – A Model-Based Tool for Managing Design Changes. Journal of Mechanical Design 126(2) (2001)

Pasqual, M., de Weck, O.: Multilayer Network Model for Analysis and Management of Change Propagation. In: International Conference on Engineering Design, ICED 2011 (2011)

Qureshi, A., Murphy, J.T., Kuchinsky, B., Seepersad, C.C.C., Wood, K.L., Jensen, D.D.: Principles of Product Flexibility. In: ASME International Design Engineering Technical Conference, Philadelphia, PA (September 2006)

Ross, A.M., Hastings, D.E.: The Tradespace Exploration Paradigm. In: INCOSE International Symposium, Rochester, NY (July 2005)

Shankar, P., Morkos, B., Summers, J.: Reasons for change propagation: a case study in an automotive OEM. Research in Engineering Design 23(4), 291–303 (2012)

Suh, E., Furst, M.R., Mihalyov, K.J., de Weck, O.L.: Technology infusion: An assessment framework and case study. In: ASME 2008 DETC Computers and Information in Engineering Conf., DETC 2008, New York, August 3-6, DETC2008-49860 (2008)

Suh, E., Furst, M.R., Mihalyov, K.J., de Weck, O.: Technology Infusion for Complex Systems: A Framework and Case Study. Systems Engineering 10(1), 1–25 (2010)

System Modeling: A Foundation for Costing Through-Life Availability Provision

Ettore Settanni, Nils E. Thenent, and Linda B. Newnes

Department of Mechanical Engineering, University of Bath, United Kingdom
E.Settanni@bath.ac.uk

Abstract. Under performance-guaranteeing contracts, such as availability-based contracts, the Original Equipment Manufacturers (OEMs) have become increasingly concerned with understanding and managing the cost of their commitment to deliver specific results to customer through-life. However, current approaches to cost estimating hardly offer more than sheer claims of the existence of a link between cost and organizational performance – no matter whether products, services or product-service-systems (PSS) are at stake. This paper presents an intermediate step towards a computational structure explicitly linking cost and performance for PSS. A PSS is represented formally as a system combining assets and activities delivering the results OEMs are committed to through-life. Inter-temporal aspects of PSS provision which typically define the successful delivery of an asset's availability are taken into account. Network formalism and principles derived from Input-Output Analysis are employed to base PSS cost estimation on a representation of a PSS as a 'system'.

Keywords: Product-Service-System, Availability contracts, Through-life costing, Systems, Input-Output Analysis, Defence aerospace.

1 Introduction

Availability-based contracts that provide incentives to guarantee the usability of engineering systems are seen as a desirable alternative to purchasing individual items and then supplementing them with support arrangements [1]. An Original Equipment Manufacturer (OEM) – if not a third party service provider – takes responsibility for all or most of the cost of delivering a result to the customer by means of a combination of assets and through-life activities commonly referred to as Product Service Systems (PSS) [2].

An in-depth analysis of the Through-life Costing (TLC) literature has highlighted the methodological challenges arising from PSSs [3]. To summarize, the current approaches to estimate the cost of PSS deal with one cost object at a time, i.e. one product or service characterized by a set of features, and assume that all the relevant costs directly relate to it. They fail to recognize that 1) the results delivered by a PSS are not just designed into an individual end-item. Rather, performance is attained

A. Bernard, L. Rivest, and D. Dutta (Eds.): PLM 2013, IFIP AICT 409, pp. 48–57, 2013.

through the actions a business undertakes, their effectiveness and efficiency; and 2) in the presence of multiple deliverables within certain organizational boundaries, the consequence of a series of decisions taken independently is not necessarily the sum of the effects of each individual decision, and may not result in an immediately observable change in cash flows.

This research illustrates an intermediate step towards a computational structure for costing PSS concerned with the formalized system representation in TLC. Unlike product-by-product analysis incumbent in TLC, performance is rendered in terms of undertaken actions, their purposes, the output delivered and necessary preconditions. In this way, performance and cost can be linked in the flow of work through an organizational system, and dealt with simultaneously. In the remainder of this paper, the need for a 'system' approach is discussed first. Then, the principles for obtaining a mathematically treatable representation of the system investigated that can be used for PSS costing are detailed. Additional steps from system representation to PSS costing are left to further research.

2 Need for a 'System' Approach

The concept of PSS embeds that of 'system'. A system is a combination of interacting elements organized to achieve one or more stated purposes. Within a PSS the relevant system is what delivers the results OEMs are committed to as an outcome of a specific combination of assets and through-life activities. Examples include complex engineering services such as providing the availability of aircraft or major aircraft sub-systems [4].

For the purpose of cost estimation a system – even a PSS – tends to be entirely characterized in terms of the architecture and properties of the physical entities needed to carry out the system's functions. Less attention is paid to another domain, called the 'process' domain, which is essential when trying to understand certain system behaviors. It concerns the actions or operations performed within or by the system and their mutual relationships [5]. System-thinking and process-thinking are indeed intertwined [6]. This is evident especially for service processes [7], and PSS [8]. Also, a formalized system representation often relies on process representation techniques – including IDEF0, UML and Petri Networks to mention but a few [9]. Ma et al. [10] summarize the advantages and disadvantages for a variety of such representation techniques with a service operations outlook. In the field of cost estimation a system approach is often claimed. However, it is not the case that formal system representation and modeling always play an explicit role in the cost analysis (see [11]). In the absence of a formalized system approach, priority is given to chasing accurate cost estimates in the same way as 'goodness of fit' is chased in forecasting uncontrollable external events [12] (see for example [13]).

Linking system/process-thinking and cost becomes more important if the aim in cost estimation is to improve cost consciousness i.e., consciousness of the cost implications of the actions taken [14]. When cost consciousness is at stake, cost is no longer deemed an intrinsic property of e.g., a product or service. Rather, it is an "emergent property" of the context in which products or services are designed and delivered [15]. Hence, the primary rationale for developing a cost model becomes to translate the interrelated consequences of changes occurring in such a context into cost metrics, through a consistent and transparent representation of that context.

Causal understanding has to precede the estimate of costs. The development of such an understanding rests on the representation of the quantitative flow of goods and services delivered by organizations, whereas money serves as a meta-language merely providing a value representation of that flow [16]. Based on the flow of goods and services the virtual cost flow paths within stated organizational boundaries can be determined [17].

Research on system/process-thinking in TLC is rather sparse. Only a few TLC studies conceptually identify a system through means-ends relationships between the operations or activities performed within or by that system [18, 19]. Applications include defense aerospace [20], and PSS [21]. In most cases, however, there is lack of published detail on how the links and mutual dependencies between the operations or activities constituting the system affect the computation of cost. To overcome these limitations, TLC can be based on a technological model of the enterprise or supply chain, implemented through the formalism of Input Output Analysis (IOA) [22].

A technological model is a model which relates to the notion of technological knowledge as detailed process understanding [23]. IOA has been originally meant to represent economic systems such as whole national economies. However, IOA can also handle particularly intricate technical-economic systems consisting of mutually interconnected stages, such as production-inventory systems [24], thus making it potentially suitable for modeling such a PSS as the provision of availability. The theory of IOA owes greatly to Nobel Laureate Wassilly Leontief, whose belief that "...partial analysis cannot provide a sufficiently broad basis for fundamental understanding", coexisted with that that uncritical enthusiasm for formidable mathematical formulation is too often prone to concealing lack of substantive content. IOA guarantees a balance between formalization, which is important for general validity to be proved mathematically, and computability, which is important for relevance to be proved empirically [25].

3 A System Representation for PSS Cost Estimation

Prior to estimating cost an understanding of the causal relationships has to be developed. This is a matter of formally representing a PSS as a 'system' i.e., identifying the boundaries and scope of the analysis; and within those boundaries the actions taken, their dependencies, the input resources required and the outputs delivered by each action. Inputs and outputs leading to the outcome(s) the system is meant to achieve can be "goods" (products or services) or "bads" (by-products or 'waste') [17].

For illustrative purposes, consider a hypothetical PSS delivering the availability of end-items such as military aircraft (A/C) [26], or A/C LRUs (Line Replaceable Units). As an example, Fig. 1 illustrates a range of outcomes that such a PSS may deliver in the case of a Multi-functional Display (MfD), and where this research stands. Focus is on the sustainment of end-items (the provision of which remains outside the system boundaries), the aim of which is guaranteeing they are in operable and committable state for certain missions (also outside the system boundaries) over a certain time-span.

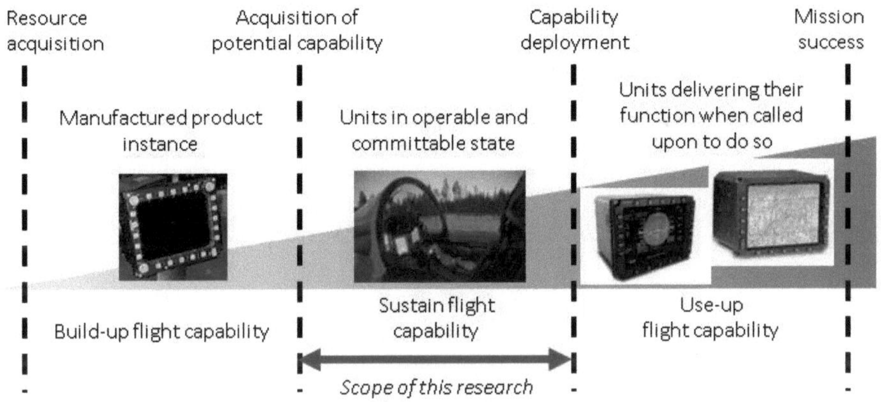

Fig. 1. Example of PSS deliverables for MfD availability

Fig. 2 shows the structure of the main end-item involved in the PSS. Proceeding clockwise, it shows the structure of the sustaining operations delivering the availability of such an item in terms of means-ends – or supply-demand – relationships using IDEF0. At this stage, the aim is to provide a structured representation of the modeled system without committing to a specific modeling language (e.g, SysML etc.).

First, a single-block context diagram defines the boundaries and scope of the system studied. Outside the boundaries are the exogenous factors i.e., those factors the provision of which is not deemed controllable, and hence left outside the analysis. Not only goods and services may be acquired from outside the system boundaries, but also conditions may be externally imposed on the system functioning, and the system's functions may be delivered outside its boundary. Then, the context diagram is detailed progressively through child diagrams. All the items involved, as well as the flows between the activities the PSS consists of, can be expressed in terms of a common, fictitious metric called 'capability units' – *c.u*.

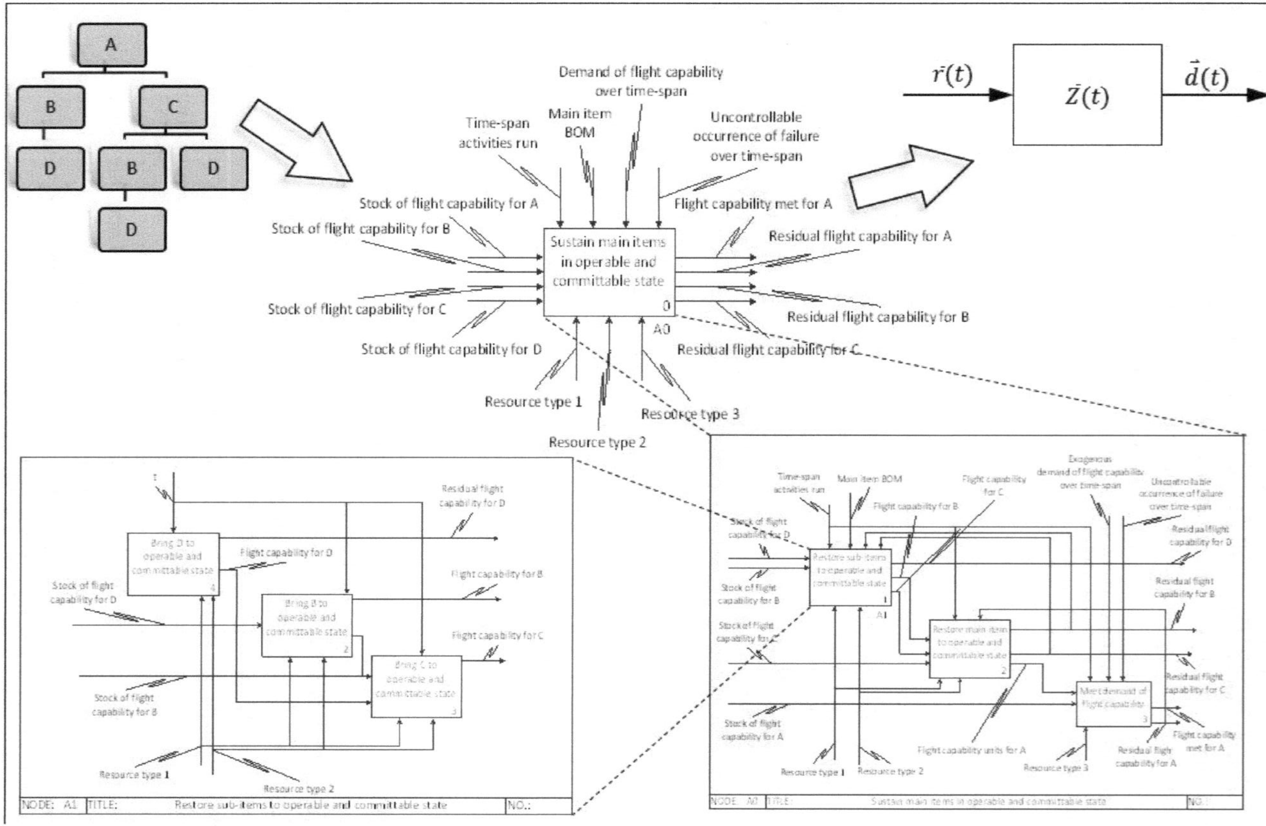

Fig. 2. From product structure, through an IDEF0 PSS representation, to time dimension

Capability units may be thought of as flyable hours (sorties, cycles etc.) equivalent to a top-level item (whole A/C or LRU) or sub-items. For example, a fleet of two A/C each of which has a life-cycle capability of flying 2 missions worth 25c.u. can be pooled as an initial "stock" of 100c.u. at time "zero". If a mission having duration 1 time unit is called at time 1, and nothing goes wrong the stock is depleted of 25c.u. leaving a residual capability of 75c.u. A failure occurrence (assumed here to be a completely uncontrollable event) when the mission is called again, would deplete the stock of capability of 50c.u. instead (i.e., one grounded A/C and one spare A/C flying the mission). In this sense, a failure acts like an additional (although wasteful) "demand" of capability. Shortage of capability triggers activities generating more capability units – e.g., by restoring the main item or sub-items into an operable and committable stage.

Although each activity has its lead time, activities are not time-phased in an IDEF0 blueprint. The latter can be thought of as a "picture" of a system taken using a conveniently long "exposure time", which corresponds to the system's total active period i.e., the time-span these activities run. In the presence of non-zero lead times, however, activities must be triggered a number of time units in advance of the time a certain demand of flight capabilities occurs. To introduce this dynamics, an Input-Output based production-inventory system for multi-indenture items [24] is adapted to the PSS of interest. The model is modified so that 1) it fits a specific framework for IOA known as "supply-use"; and 2) dynamics is induced similarly to the time-distributed systems' activities approach in IOA [27]. Only discrete time is of interest here.

Let n be the number of activities the PSS is composed of. Let θ_j be the lead time for the j-th activity $(j = 1 \dots n)$. Let τ be the total active period's length. For each discrete time t $(0 < t \leq \tau)$ the relevant system can be described in terms of the following multi-period balance of quantities:

$$\mathbf{r}(t-1) + \mathbf{V}_t(0)\mathbf{s}(t) = \sum_p \mathbf{U}_{t-p}(p)\mathbf{s}(t-p) + \mathbf{y}_t + \mathbf{r}(t) \tag{1}$$

where p is the time lag $(-\theta \leq p \leq 0,\ \theta = max\{\theta_j\})$, and $t-p$ is the delivery time $(0 < (t-p) \leq \tau)$.

The $n \times n$ time-distributed "*use*" matrix $\mathbf{U}_{t-p}(p) \equiv \left[u_{ij}(t) \cdot \delta_{\theta_j,-p}\right]_{n\times n}$ records for each activity j its direct requirements of input i $(i = 1 \dots n)$ supplied by another activity within the system $|p|$ time units prior to the delivery time $t-p$ i.e., at time t. The corresponding quantity $u_{ij}(t)$ is then multiplied by the Kroneker symbol taking values $\delta_{\theta_j,-p} = 1$ if $\theta_j = -p$ and 0 otherwise. The $n \times n$ time-distributed "*supply*" matrix $\mathbf{V}_t(0) \equiv \left[v_{ij}(t)\right]_{n\times n}$ records for each activity j its gross output of i delivered at time t. By assumption, an activity's output is entirely delivered θ_j time units ahead the fulfillment of the necessary preconditions (e.g., the provision of inputs). These matrices recording supply and use flows can be combined to give the system's net output as follows:

$$\begin{cases} \mathbf{Z}_t(0) = [\mathbf{V}_t(0) - \mathbf{U}_t(0)] & \text{for } p = 0 \\ \mathbf{Z}_t(-p) = [-\mathbf{U}_{t-p}(p)] & \text{for } -\theta \leq p < 0 \end{cases}$$

The $n \times 1$ vectors $\mathbf{r}(t-1)$ and $\mathbf{r}(t)$ are, respectively, the beginning and final inventories of each activity's outputs at time *t*. For $t = 1$ the values of the beginning inventory $\mathbf{r}(0)$ are known and serve as initial conditions. The $n \times 1$ vectors $\mathbf{s}(t-p)$ and $\mathbf{s}(t)$ are the unknown activity levels at each delivery time, and at each time *t* respectively. Finally, the $n \times 1$ vector $\mathbf{y}_t$ is the demand of system's outcomes imposed exogenously at each time *t*. In our case it should be further distinguished into 'good' demand of units in operable and committable state, and 'bad' demand due to e.g., failures: $\mathbf{y}_t = \mathbf{y}_t^G + \mathbf{y}_t^F$. Equation (1) is developed for $t = 1 \dots \tau$. Let $\mathbf{I}$ be an $n \times n$ identity matrix and $\mathbf{0}$ a null matrix of appropriate dimensions:

$$\begin{bmatrix} \mathbf{Z}_1(0) & \mathbf{Z}_1(1) & \cdots & \mathbf{Z}_1(t-1) & \cdots & \mathbf{Z}_1(\tau-1) & -\mathbf{I} & & & & & \\ & \mathbf{Z}_2(0) & \cdots & \mathbf{Z}_1(t-2) & \cdots & \mathbf{Z}_1(\tau-2) & \mathbf{I} & -\mathbf{I} & & & \mathbf{0} & \\ & & \ddots & \vdots & & \vdots & & \ddots & \ddots & & & \\ & & & \mathbf{Z}_t(0) & & \mathbf{Z}_1(\tau-t) & & & \mathbf{I} & -\mathbf{I} & & \\ & \mathbf{0} & & & \ddots & \vdots & & & & \ddots & \ddots & \\ & & & & & \mathbf{Z}_\tau(0) & & \mathbf{0} & & & \mathbf{I} & -\mathbf{I} \end{bmatrix} \begin{bmatrix} \mathbf{s}(1) \\ \mathbf{s}(2) \\ \vdots \\ \mathbf{s}(t) \\ \vdots \\ \mathbf{s}(\tau) \\ \mathbf{r}(1) \\ \mathbf{r}(2) \\ \vdots \\ \mathbf{r}(t) \\ \vdots \\ \mathbf{r}(\tau) \end{bmatrix} = \begin{bmatrix} \mathbf{y}_1 - \mathbf{r}(0) \\ \mathbf{y}_2 \\ \vdots \\ \mathbf{y}_t \\ \vdots \\ \mathbf{y}_\tau \end{bmatrix}$$

or, in compact terms:

$$[\mathbf{Z} \quad \mathbf{\Phi}] \begin{bmatrix} \mathbf{s} \\ \mathbf{r} \end{bmatrix} = \mathbf{d} \tag{2}$$

The problem becomes finding the elements of $\mathbf{s}$ as the minimum nonnegative integers such that the entries of $\mathbf{r}$ are non-negative:

$$\begin{aligned} &\text{minimize } z = \mathbf{1} \cdot \mathbf{s}(1) + \cdots + \mathbf{1} \cdot \mathbf{s}(\tau) + \mathbf{0} \cdot \mathbf{r}(1) + \cdots + \mathbf{0} \cdot \mathbf{r}(\tau) \\ &\text{subject to:} \\ &\begin{bmatrix} \mathbf{Z} & \mathbf{\Phi} \\ \mathbf{F} & \mathbf{0} \end{bmatrix} \begin{bmatrix} \mathbf{s} \\ \mathbf{r} \end{bmatrix} = \begin{bmatrix} \mathbf{d} \\ \mathbf{0} \end{bmatrix} \\ &\text{s} = \text{integer} \\ &\mathbf{s} \geq \mathbf{0}; \mathbf{r} \geq \mathbf{0} \end{aligned}$$

where $\mathbf{1}$ is a unity vector of appropriate dimension. $\mathbf{F}$ is a matrix of the same size as $\mathbf{Z}$, which contains a set of constraints. These constraints are such that an activity *j* cannot deliver its output unless there is time for doing so. For $t = 1 \dots \theta$ diagonal matrix $\mathbf{D}_t \equiv [d_{jj}]$ is defined such that $d_{jj} = 1$ if $\theta_j \leq t - 1$ and zero otherwise. Hence: $\mathbf{F} = \begin{bmatrix} \mathbf{Z}_1(0) \cdot \mathbf{D}_1 & \cdots & \mathbf{0} & \\ \vdots & \ddots & \vdots & \mathbf{0} \\ \mathbf{0} & \dots & \mathbf{Z}_\theta(0) \cdot \mathbf{D}_\theta & \end{bmatrix}$

Alternative approaches to the multistage, mixed-integer linear programming used here (e.g. [24]) can be more effective for the mathematically literate, yet less practical to implement e.g., using spreadsheets. The algorithm can be applied to the example in Fig 2. The example features a PSS consisting of four activities ($n = 4$). Each activity brings either the main-item (A) or the sub-items it is made of (B, C, D) into an operable and committable state. Assuming for simplicity the use matrix remains constant over time $[u_{ij}(t)]_{n \times n} = [u_{ij}]_{n \times n}$ and so does the supply matrix

$[v_{ij}(t)]_{n\times n} = [v_{ij}]_{n\times n}$ the following hypothetical numerical values (all expressed in *c.u.*) are assumed:

$$[u_{ij}]_{n\times n} = \begin{matrix} & A & B & C & D \\ A \\ B \\ C \\ D \end{matrix}\begin{bmatrix} 0 & 0 & 0 & 0 \\ 800 & 0 & 0 & 0 \\ 400 & 600 & 0 & 0 \\ 0 & 1200 & 1700 & 0 \end{bmatrix}; \qquad [v_{ij}]_{n\times n} = \begin{matrix} A \\ B \\ C \\ D \end{matrix}\begin{bmatrix} 200 & 0 & 0 & 0 \\ 0 & 600 & 0 & 0 \\ 0 & 0 & 850 & 0 \\ 0 & 0 & 0 & 900 \end{bmatrix}$$

The beginning inventories for each item in terms (all expressed in *c.u.*) are $\mathrm{r}(0) = [170 \quad 920 \quad 2650 \quad 4800]^T$. (Superscript T means matrix or vector transposition). Finally, the hypothetical values for the lead times of each activity (expressed in discrete time units) are $[\theta_j]_{1\times n} = [2 \quad 1 \quad 3 \quad 2]$. Fig. 3 shows the values for activity levels **s** and capability stock levels **r** given the exogenous demand for flight capability (including "bad" one i.e., due to thing going wrong) shown at the bottom (for the main item only), over a discrete time-span ($\tau = 8$).

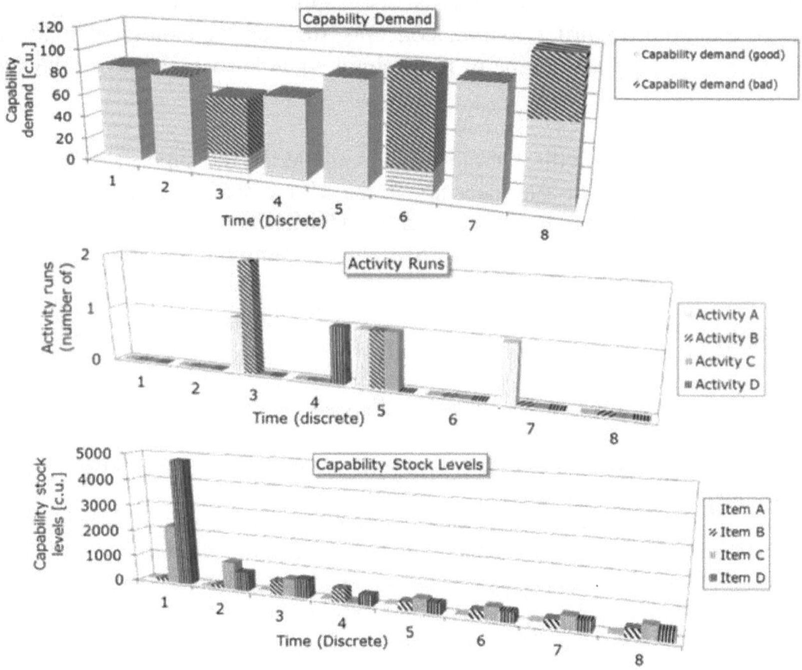

Fig. 3. Inter-temporal behavior of hypothetical PSS: main aspects

4 Conclusion and Need for Future Work

This research lays the foundation of an original, formalized system representation for use as a preliminary step for PSS costing. It draws on principles developed in disciplines like IOA and inventory modeling, which are not taken into account in current approaches to PSS cost estimation. The insights associated with a rigorous and transparent quantitative approach to model PSS as 'systems' are meant to support the improvement of *cost consciousness*.

The approach developed here requires a distinction between what can, or has to be included within the system's boundaries, and what is deemed exogenous to the system and hence uncontrollable. The focus on the provision of flight capability and the introduction of *c.u.* as fictitious units represents an assumption. However, it has allowed to show how the principles of inventory modeling which are well-developed for products apply to more generic "functional units", suitable for representing the intermediate and final results delivered by a PSS. The approach that has been illustrated here is in generic form, and is taking a deterministic standpoint. Topics of co-production and inefficiencies/waste generation have been left aside.

These aspects can be taken into account as the basic model presented here grows into a costing model consistent with the Input-Output technological approach to TLC suggested in the field of sustainability management by [22]. Further work is necessary to address potentials and limitation of the proposed model through its application to an industrial context. Future research must also address what needs to be known about a PSS, for example, in order to link concepts such as technological maturity and obsolescence to changes over time of the technological knowledge about the system's inputs and outputs.

Acknowledgments. The authors gratefully acknowledge the support provided by the Department of Mechanical Engineering at the University of Bath, the Innovative electronics Manufacturing Research Centre (IeMRC) and the Engineering and Physical Sciences Research Council (EPSRC) for funding the research.

References

1. Meier, H., Roy, R., Seliger, G.: Industrial Product-Service Systems—IPS2. CIRP Ann.-Manuf. Technol. 59, 607–627 (2010)
2. Tukker, A., Tischner, U.: Product-services as a research field: past, present and future. J. Clean. Prod. 14, 1552–1556 (2006)
3. Settanni, E., Newnes, L.B., Parry, G.C., Goh, Y.M.: A conceptual model to address the methodological challenges of costing through-life availability. Working paper (2011)
4. Ng, I.C.L., Parry, G.C., Wild, P., McFarlane, D., Tasker, P. (eds.): Complex engineering service systems. Concepts and research. Springer, Berlin (2011)
5. Bartolomei, J.E., Hastings, D.E., de Neufville, R., Rhodes, D.H.: Engineering Systems Multiple-Domain Matrix: An organizing framework for modeling large-scale complex systems. Syst. Engin. 15, 41–61 (2012)
6. Emblemsvåg, J., Bras, B.: Process thinking — a new paradigm for science and engineering. Futures 32, 635–654 (2000)
7. Batista, L., Smart, A., Maull, R.: The systemic perspective of service processes: underlying theory, architecture and approach. Production Planning & Control 19, 535–544 (2008)

8. Kim, Y.S., Lee, S.W., Koh, D.C.: Representing product-service systems with product and service elements. In: Howard, T.J., McAloone, T.C., Hansen, C.T. (eds.) Proceedings of the 18th International Conference on Engineering Design (2011)
9. Aguilar-Saven, R.S.: Business process modelling: Review and framework. Int. J. Prod. Econ. 90, 129–149 (2004)
10. Ma, Q., Tseng, M.M., Yen, B.: A generic model and design representation technique of service products. Technovation 22, 15–39 (2002)
11. Valerdi, R.: Heuristics for Systems Engineering Cost Estimation. IEEE Systems Journal 5, 91–98 (2011)
12. Makridakis, S.G., Wheelwright, S.C., Hyndman, R.J.: Forecasting Methods and applications, 3rd edn. John Wiley & Sons, New York (1998)
13. Roy, R.: Cost engineering: why, what and how? Decision Engineering Report Series, Cranfield University (2003)
14. Lindholm, A., Suomala, P.: Learning by costing: Sharpening cost image through life cycle costing? Int. J. Prod. Perform. Manag. 56, 651–672 (2007)
15. Field, F., Kirchain, R., Roth, R.: Process cost modeling: Strategic engineering and economic evaluation of materials technologies. JOM-J. Min. Met. Mat. S. 59, 21–32 (2007)
16. van der Merwe, A.: Management accounting philosophy II: The cornerstones of restoration. Cost Management 21, 26–33 (2007)
17. Möller, A.: Material and Energy Flow-Based Cost Accounting. Chem. Eng. Technol. 33, 567–572 (2010)
18. Emblemsvåg, J.: Life-cycle costing. Using activity-based costing and Monte Carlo methods to manage future costs and risks. Wiley, Hoboken (2003)
19. Mévellec, P., Perry, N.: Whole life-cycle costs: a new approach. International Journal of Product Lifecycle Management 1, 400–414 (2006)
20. Davis, N., Jones, J., Warrington, L.: A framework for documenting and analyzing life-cycle costs using a simple network based representation. In: Proceedings of the Reliability and Maintainability Symposium, pp. 232–236 (2003)
21. Kimita, K.: Cost evaluation method for service design based on Activity Based Costing. In: Proceedings of the 7th International Conference on Manufacturing Research (2009)
22. Settanni, E., Tassielli, G., Notarnicola, B.: An Input–Output technological model of Life Cycle Costing: computational aspects and implementation issues in a generalised supply chain perspective. In: Burritt, R., et al. (eds.) Environmental Management Accounting and Supply Chain Management, pp. 55–109. Springer, Dordrecht (2011)
23. Bohn, R.E.: Measuring and Managing Technological Knowledge. Sloan Manage. Rev. 36, 61–73 (1994)
24. Grubbstrom, R.W., Tang, O.: An Overview of Input-Output Analysis Applied to Production-Inventory Systems. Economic Systems Research 12, 3–25 (2000)
25. Augusztinovics, M.: What Input-Output is about. Structural Change and Economic Dynamics 6, 271–277 (1995)
26. Hollick, L.J.: Achieving shared accountability for operational availability attainment. In: Proceedings of the Reliability and Maintainability Symposium, pp. 247–252 (2009)
27. ten Raa, T.: The economics of input-output analysis. Cambridge University Press, Cambridge (2005)

Product Life Cycle Data Management: A Cross-Sectoral Review

Gary Ford, Tom Bartley, Joel Igba, Alison Turner, and Chris McMahon

Faculty of Engineering, University of Bristol, UK
{cegnf,tom.bartley,ji0905,am0249,chris.mcmahon}@bristol.ac.uk

Abstract. The paper explores data management in the product life cycle of three engineering domains – civil/construction, marine and wind energy – each with distinct but potentially common issues. The approach has been to assess issues within each domain against the life cycle stages defined in ISO 15288 "Systems and software engineering - System life cycle processes", i.e., Concept, Development, Utilisation, Support and Retirement. These were then assimilated and comparisons drawn to identify common problems and areas that appear particular to the do-main. The paper presents a position statement, taken from the experience of practitioners in each of the relevant sectors; the purpose is to understand if there may be opportunities for cross-sectoral learning.

Keywords: Information management, Lifecycle, Civil, Marine, Wind.

1 Introduction

The management of engineering data for the operation and maintenance of large complex artefacts such as ships, buildings and power generation systems is very challenging owing to the long life spans, multiplicity of stakeholders, diversity of data types and complexity of interactions in the artefacts and supporting systems. This paper explores these challenges and in particular makes a cross-sectoral analysis of issues across three distinct engineering domains: construction and civil engineering, marine (UK Defence) and renewable energy (offshore wind). Initial comparison of the domains would indicate a number of similarities, e.g., complexity, capital investment, but none-the-less significant differences exist, in business/engineering maturity and structure of the supporting industry, which have strong implications for data management approaches in each domain.

The purpose of the paper was to explore opportunities for engineering communities to share good practice with others and identify issues which are still to be resolved across all engineering sectors.

2 Background

The three sectors under study are construction/civil engineering, marine and wind energy. Each is characterised by large, long-lived artefacts and by distributed operations, but there are differences, especially in the nature of the industries.

A. Bernard, L. Rivest, and D. Dutta (Eds.): PLM 2013, IFIP AICT 409, pp. 58–67, 2013.

Within civil engineering/construction, Egan's [1] 1998 report highlights the disjointed and adversarial nature of the industry. Designs are often created by multiple companies, and construction and operation may be performed by entirely different organisations with little input to upstream decision making. To counter this, in the UK the Government (along with major clients worldwide) has adopted a Building Information Modelling (BIM) strategy which mandates a life cycle approach to the production of project information on public projects by 2016 [2]. BIM is the construction industry's response to Product Lifecycle Management (PLM), in which a federated database is developed to serve an asset from "*cradle to cradle*" [3].

Marine engineering/construction within UK Defence currently constitutes 3 of the 4 major Ministry of Defence (MOD) projects, e.g. the Queen Elizabeth class aircraft carrier with capital expenditure in 2012/13 of £9.1 billion. However, the operation and maintenance cost of a warship will typically be twice the cost of acquisition [4]. Data management within the marine domain experiences issues similar to construction, e.g., ships designed and built by multiple companies and operationally maintained by another set of organisations, but national security, nuclear engineering and weapons systems are important additional factors, creating a complex data management environment.

The wind energy resources will have a large role to play in meeting renewable energy targets but to be competitive the Cost of Energy (COE) produced from them must be competitive. Hence there is need for innovation and improvements in the sector with reliability and COE as the major drivers. In wind power higher than expected costs of Operations & Maintenance (O&M) is a particular issue [5]. Reducing the cost of O&M triggers the need for a more comprehensive and integrated through-life service and maintenance management approach [6]. Data management is an important step towards optimising O&M activities and reducing COE [7].

As an example of the challenges involved in the operational support of very long-lived artefacts for which much information is pre-digital we have studied the Clifton Suspension Bridge (CSB) in Bristol which first opened in 1864. The bridge is managed by the Clifton Suspension Bridge Trust (CSBT) which finances all maintenance, conservation and operating costs through tolls. The Trust owns a range of information dating from the 1830's including the original bridge design in addition to operations, management and maintenance details for the bridge. There also exist many technical investigations, reports and general interest material that also form part of the CSBT's collection.

3 Systems Engineering Life Cycle

A number of standards exist that can be used to assist in managing the construction and operation of a system. The selection and adoption of a life cycle will be dependent upon a number of factors, e.g., definition of requirements, anticipated complexity, urgency, proof of concept, etc. Given the size, cost and complexity of a typical civil engineering project/maritime vessel the design and construction will normally adhere to a life cycle typical of ISO 15288 [8] which defines discrete stages to form a system life cycle, i.e., Concept, Development, Production, Utilisation/Support and Retirement. This review selected ISO 15288 as a current Systems Engineering standard recognised by The International Council on Systems Engineering for a structured comparison of the life cycle stages for each of the selected artefacts. Each ISO 15288 stage details a number of deliverables and purpose, e.g., Concept ~ "*develop preliminary system requirements and a feasible design solution*". The ISO standard, originally intended for Systems Engineering was modified in 2008 to include software engineering. Some major technical projects carried out to maintain or improve an asset may be viewed as having life cycles of their own embedded within the whole system life cycle.

The utilisation/support stage of the life cycle includes both operation and maintenance and these are the activities that typically cost an organisation most out of the entire life cycle. In some cases up to 70% of the total cost of ownership of an asset is consumed at this stage [9].

4 Data Management within Each Domain

Civil Engineering/Construction: BIM has become the accepted term for a new paradigm in the production and management of a built asset's information through design, construction and operations with a view to achieving transformational change [10]. Because the industry has traditionally been slow at adopting new technologies the adoption of BIM is mainly a client-led initiative. Whilst there is an established understanding of how BIM will be implemented there are many technical and cultural challenges to overcome and there are few examples of effective life cycle information management. The Institution of Civil Engineers has identified many case studies where BIM processes have been used effectively in distinct sectors or part of the construction life cycle [11].

An important factor for some clients in specifying the use of BIM is that it can enable better Facilities Management [12]. The Construction Operations Building Information Exchange (COBie), a subset of the Industry Foundation Classes (IFC) standard, has been developed to aid handover of as-built in-formation about an asset in human readable format (spreadsheets) [13]. COBie structures information hierarchically describing the facility's objects and systems and includes service schedules and maintenance requirements and can then be used to interface with Computer Aided Facilities Management applications and used throughout the life of the asset. There are issues in having too much data in that it becomes inaccessible and there is complexity in the number of soft-ware packages which need to interact [14].

There are many issues to be resolved before BIM is fully functional. The con-struction industry has large quantities of legacy data. Where data does exist it is often very difficult to find and likely to not to be in a digital format. Model interoperability also remains an issue [15]. The buildings sector is very mature at producing 3D models and the IFC standard is becoming mature enough for widespread use. However, as yet for the linear asset sectors (e.g. highways, railways) the standard is not yet comprehensive enough.

Marine: Warships are complex integrated systems, and may be viewed as systems of systems, e.g. a submarine contains in excess of 100 integrated systems which are linked structurally, mechanically, electrically, hydraulically and pneumatically. PLM of a warship/submarine thus requires a comprehensive systems approach from initial concept through to disposal necessitating the integration of numerous complex systems delivering a synergistic, flexible, maintainable, reliable and available cost effective weapon platform. To support such an approach the UK MOD has developed an Acquisitions Operating Framework [16] that decomposes the full acquisition life cycle into 6 distinct stages: Concept, Assessment, Demonstration, Manufacture, In-Service and Disposal (CADMID).

Assessment and Demonstration map onto the Development stage of the ISO 15288 life cycle and In-Service maps to Utilisation and Support.

The development of a warship/submarine entails a number of specific engineering tasks that correlate to and overlap with the CADMID life cycle, e.g. design survey, design synthesis, design assessment, system design, etc. [17]. Each stage within the life cycle specifies data or physical outputs, e.g. User Requirements Document and Through Life Management Plan (TLMP) for the Concept stage, System Requirements Document, refined TLMP and detailed plans for Assessment and combination of prototyping and engineering evaluation of the evolving design and its maturity for Demonstration stage.

To aid independent assessment of major defence programmes, a formal gate process is used to assess the maturity of the design. This includes definition of the Support Solution (for in-service) and its data requirements against the Support So-lution Envelope and ISO 10303 for PLM. In addition, a warship may receive a number of upgrades to enhance its capability or extend its life. Each will constitute a discrete CADMID life cycle.

The complete lifespan of a naval vessel may be extremely long. The new Ford-class aircraft carriers of the USA are designed for a 50-year lifespan. The data associated with such a lifespan are considerable and issues include multiplicity of formats stored in multiple locations and hardware systems, owned by many organisations and with much of the data security classified in addition to being commercially sensitive. Records maintained by naval vessels are often more complex and onerous than commercial vessels, e.g., quality control: material certification, surveyed material condition, high value/sensitive equipment, and legislative requirements for operation (Lloyds Shipping, Nuclear Inspectorate). This is particularly relevant with respect to nuclear power plant.

The "*In-Service*" stage of the project will not only encompass capability enhancements of the artefact but also preventive and corrective maintenance. Royal Navy data indicating the "*material state*" of an artefact is stored in a considerable number of sources, including the Unit Maintenance Management System (a work management scheduling application utilising Reliability Centred Maintenance as the maintenance methodology), Operational Defects system (that records defects that degrade the operational capability of a vessel), engineering logs (paper-based logs detailing defects, fuel usage, engine hours run, equipment temperatures, fire main pressure,...), financial reports (planned and actual expenditure of maintenance undertaken), test/trials specifications and stores usage reports.

The data sources may be combined to formulate a material state assessment; however, the integrity and accuracy of the sources vary. They may exhibit fuzziness, incompleteness and randomness. For example, trials teams' reports lag the operational environment/system condition; financial reports may reflect the hours available rather than the actual work undertaken rather, test specifications reflect what has been achieved rather than a perspective of the system condition/performance. There is also an issue of trust in the data since the management of the data sources may vary between vessels and classes of vessel.

Wind Energy: The first wind farms were built in the UK in the 1980's [18] with a typical design life of between 20 to 30 years [5] which suggests most early turbines are reaching the end of their design life. A number of wind turbines may suffer from early failure, however, this may still be considered acceptable within the overall design of the artefact. The life cycle stages of Concept, Design, Production, Utilisation, Support and Retirement apply equally in the wind energy industry, which has adopted and incorporated computer aided tools for design and data management from its infancy. As noted by Guo [19] and Hameed [20] the main life cycle stage where data management issues persist is during Utilisation/Support. This is because of the gaps that currently exist in the ability to capture, feedback and re-use in-service information of wind power plants.

5 Product Lifecycle Management Data Issues

Tables 1, 2 and 3 show data management issues at the different life cycle stages for civil/construction, marine and wind sectors respectively.

Table 1. Data Management Issues: Civil/Construction Sector

Life cycle stage	Issues (especially concerning long-lived assets)
Concept	With an ageing infrastructure, similar projects may have been undertaken previously; hence, a search of historical information is essential. For ageing assets search/retrieval of legacy data is often difficult and tacit knowledge is used.
Development	Development of design solutions relies on legacy data to understand what has been done in the past or to validate calculations or models. There are issues with finding relevant data and it is not always known whether it even exists. During the development stage much data can be generated, and in some cases almost all data is kept regardless of value. Data may not be in a digital format and it may be stored in locations that require special provisions. There are interoperability issues owing to data and organisational diversity. .
Production	Issues arise in capturing details of work undertaken and how. The "as-built" dataset is often incomplete or has errors, without checking every drawing and document this is difficult to manage. There is no formal process for storing configuration data or the required data format. This can result in data that is less useable in the future and may require time to convert or digitise.
Utilisation/ Support	Conversion and interpretation of original data is challenging for example because original drawings are in "imperial" units, modern materials are SI units. Inspections and regular risk assessment are part of ongoing asset management and may generate substantial quantities of data in various formats. Issues include data capture, format and storage and whether information can be found when needed. In some cases the data that is collected may never be used, conversely data that has not been recorded would be useful. Data quality is an issue; any data used must be checked first as errors have been found in calculations, drawings and surveys. Many different people may have worked on the asset over many years which raises issues with respect to retrieval, classification and terminology. Some data about the asset may be very old and need preservation. Digitisation may be needed to aid access and to prevent excessive handling of originals
Retirement	A long term storage policy is required for retired assets, especially for culturally significant artefacts. To enable the safe retirement of infrastructure, information relating to how it was built, the as-built structure and materials used may be required.

Table 2. Data Management Issues: Marine (Defence) Sector

Life cycle stage	Issues
Concept	Documenting and agreeing user requirements is challenging given the numerous operational, human factors, safety, environmental, security and other issues identified by stakeholders, e.g. operational capability/ restrictions, potential future changes, constraints on capability such as legislation, policy, timescale. The process of defining user and system requirements for complex naval systems has resulted in "the addition of costly, and often unneeded, requirements to the Department's most expensive platforms" [21].
Development	The engineering task, Contract Design is the process within this stage; the process will produce a number of detailed specifications the builder can utilise, e.g., Performance specification, System specification, Sub-system specifications, Equipment specifications, Material specifications, Standards, Acceptance criteria and methods, Costs, Build Programme, Delivery date.
Production	The construction of a naval vessel generates a very large volume of design and construction records including "as fitted" documentation of the artefact. It is not uncommon as a consequence of "supplier changes, changing needs and technologies and in-service engineering changes, [that] no two ships are identical when delivered or remain static after delivery." [22]. Configuration management is essential to maintaining a record of the artefact. Test specifications: a precise record of the design is essential when defining test specifications. They are maintained not only by the builder but also the operators, and there are quality issues in their collection
Utilisation/ Support	Configuration Management (CM) records may be incomplete/inaccurate and as a consequence effective operations and maintenance may be an issue. Failure to maintain satisfactory CM records has the potential for significant impact. Material state: data to ascertain the material state for maintenance is multifarious and requires fusing and analysis. Furthermore, the management/ administration of the numerous data sources is subject to variations with respect to operational commitment, on-board management and data configuration. Test specifications and results as a consequence of maintenance and upkeep are created and maintained to verify the installation and performance of the numerous onboard systems. Test specifications are maintained not only by the shipyard but also the operating navy.
Retirement	Configuration Management: records may be incomplete/inaccurate because of changes in legislative policy and/or hazards not envisaged at the time of construction raising potential issues regarding the disposal of controlled materials. Consultation documentation regarding the disposal of nuclear submarines [23] and the handling of radioactive waste is an issue. Sales literature: a vessel may be sold for further use as a warship, artificial reef, recycling, etc. hence a "detailed" sales brochure may be produced for prospective buyers, e.g., "Commercial sale of Type 22 frigates" [24]. Drawings, documentation, etc., associated with a "retired" vessel will be archived for reference in potential future designs, lessons learnt etc.

Table 3. Data Management Issues: Wind Energy Sector

Life cycle stage	Issues
Concept Development Production	There are institutional barriers that hinder communication during design of wind turbines [19] which lead to issues with data access and ownership. During product development, issues arise with respect to data transparency and availability, whereby components and subsystems are produced by multiple suppliers unwilling to share design information for confidentiality reasons [5]. There are also issues with ownership of key design information especially when several sub-suppliers are involved in designing and delivering parts of a system while trying to preserve their Intellectual Property. The use of legacy data for product development purposes may be problematic, because the wind sector is still relatively young with little historical data and because of poor data accumulation during the in-service stage of early turbines.
Utilisation/ Support	Data management issues during utilisation include data capture, access, technological level, data availability, data quality, database management etc. [20] discuss in detail the challenges in collecting reliability and maintainability data of offshore wind turbines, and assert the need for a common shared database such as the Offshore Reliability Database used in the oil and gas industry. Some researchers and laboratories have started to capture field data, but in-service data collection may be difficult owing to access issues especially in the case of offshore turbines and onshore turbines erected on harsh terrains. Technicians may not complete maintenance records within the turbine due to safety concerns, space limitations, etc. thus record keeping may comprise on-site photographs and off-site report completion. Consequently there may be a "time lag" between inspection and reporting, and data may lack definition and quality. Assessing availability/reliability data is often difficult, exacerbated by confidentiality, data collection methods, e.g., hand-written and computer-written report sheets raising issues with respect to inconsistency of data source format. Some failures of turbines have been gathered without details of the failure mode. There is inconsistency in file formats and problems with interoperability due to the use of both hand-written and computer based field data collection. Such issues make it difficult for data to be reused for new designs. .
Retirement	Although a number of wind turbines have been decommissioned as a consequence of catastrophic failure and early installed turbines are just reaching their end of life there is limited experience or evidence that would support any claims of data management issues during the retirement stage of wind turbines. .

6 Cross-Sectoral Comparison

Mapping the "information management" issues given in the previous section to these engineering processes the areas of potential concern identified in Table 4.

The largest number of issues relate to "Civil", potentially as a consequence of the age of structures, construction techniques, material, legacy data and complexity of the support function. In all domains information management issues are related to the

Table 4. Analysis of Information Management Issues. Note (1) Owing to limited maturity of wind technology, issues associated with "Retirement" are excluded.

Data operation	**ISO 15288 Stage.** Note C ~ Civil, M ~ Marine (Defence), W ~ Wind														
	Concept			**Development**			**Production**			**Utilisation/ Support**			**Retirement**		
	C	**M**	**W**	**C**	**M**	**W**	**C**	**M**	**W**	**C**	**M**	**W**	**C**	**M**	**W[1]**
Generate	x			x			x			x			x		
Collect	x		x	x		x	x	x	x	x	x	x	x		
Transform	x	x	x	x	x		x	x	x	x	x	x	x		
Retain										x	x	x			
Retrieve	x	x	x	x	x	x	x	x	x	x	x	x	x	x	
Disseminate	x	x	x		x	x		x	x		x	x		x	
Dispose	x			x			x			x			x		

maturity of the technology and the availability, accuracy and volume of data. The Marine domain is assisted by a controlled and defined system engineering environment, and the considerable history and experience of ship design and maintenance, but data dissemination of sensitive data is an issue.

Collecting data is an issue for all domains. This may be due to the availability of data/stakeholders, and volume and accuracy of data. Issues may also arise as a consequence of the physical environment. Data retrieval although an issue in each domain exhibits differences in application, e.g., Civil ~ large volume of legacy data including historical paper records, Marine/Wind ~ numerous locations and data held by multifarious organisations. Utilisation/Support identifies the largest number of issues, i.e., collating, processing, retaining and retrieving data potentially as result of the volume of data, availability of data / stakeholder, time constraints.

7 Conclusion and Proposals for Future Work

Engineering domains have similar data management issues but it is important to consider the circumstances in each domain to understand the full range of issues that may apply. In particular, very long lived artefacts have special requirements especially artefact such as the CSB which has a distinctive requirement "*to pre-serve [...] in perpetuity*", not simply as a monument but as a fully functioning bridge. The large volume of CSB data which includes historical records exacerbates the data management issues. Special issues may also arise, however, when issues of national security or commercial confidentiality are present, as shown by our study of the marine sector and wind energy respectively. For all of the sectors studied the greatest number of issues, and hence perhaps the greatest potential for improvement, arise in data management for the utilisation/support stage. Technology may ease the burden of data collection by means of remote sensing, hand held devices, etc. allowing data to be more readily transformed. Engineers and management may subsequently utilise/apply data mining techniques to retrieve, interpret and exploit data as a real resource/tool.

Future work should start by clarifying the issues highlighted into specific workflow issues and expanding the study to encompass a larger number of case studies. The stages of the life cycle could be grouped into pre-utilisation (concept, development and production), utilisation/support and retirement. Grouping the stages may provide a clearer understanding of the cross-sectoral nature of issues but suffer from a loss of granularity as a consequence; finally, data/information transfer between stages may also be studied as a potential area of weakness.

Acknowledgments. The work reported was supported by the Bristol/Bath Industrial Doctorate Centre in Systems, funded by EPSRC grant EP/G037353/1.

References

1. Egan, J.: Rethinking Construction: Report of Construction Task Force. HMSO, London (1998)
2. Government Construction Strategy, `http://www.gov.uk/government/publications/government-construction-strategy`
3. Smith, M.: BIM in Construction - Building Information Modelling (2011), `http://www.thenbs.com/topics/bim/articles/bimInConstruction.asp`
4. Harris, F.: Total Ownership Cost. American Society of Naval Engineers Day 2011, Arlington, Virginia, February 10-11, p. 3 (2011)
5. Musial, W., Butterfield, S., McNiff, B.: Improving wind turbine gearbox reliability. In: Proceedings of the European Wind Energy Conference (2007)
6. Igba, J., Alemzadeh, K., Anyanwu-Ebo, I., Gibbons, P., Friis, J.: A Systems Approach Towards Reliability-Centred Maintenance of Wind Turbines. Procedia Computer Science 16, 814–823 (2013)
7. Fischer, K., Besnard, F., Bertling, L.: Reliability-centered maintenance for wind turbines based on statistical analysis and practical experience. IEEE Transactions on Energy Conversion 27(1), 184–195 (2012)
8. Systems and Software Engineering - System Life Cycle Processes. International Organization for Standardization (2013), `http://www.iso.org/iso`
9. Koronios, A., Nastasie, D., Chanana, V., Haider, A.: Integration Through Standards–An Overview of International Standards For Engineering Asset Management. In: Fourth International Conference on Condition Monitoring, Harrogate, United Kingdom (2007)
10. Venugopal, M., Eastman, C.M., Sacks, R., Teizer, J.: Semantics of model views for information exchanges using the industry foundation class schema. Advanced Engineering Informatics 26(2), 411–428 (2012)
11. BIM 2012. London (2012), `http://www.ice.org.uk/News-Public-Affairs/ICE-News/ICE-BIM-2012-report`
12. Arayici, Y., Onyenobi, T., Egbu, C.: Building Information Modelling for Facilities Management (FM). International Journal of 3-D Information Modeling 1(1), 55–73 (2012)
13. Nisbet, N.: COBie-UK-2012. AEC3 UK Ltd. (2012)

14. Anderson, A., Masters, A., Dossick, C.S., Neff, G.: Construction to Operations Exchange: Challenges of Implementing COBie and BIM in a Large Owner Organization. In: Construction Research Congress, pp. 688–697, ASCE (2012)
15. Grilo, A., Jardim-Goncalves, R.: Value Proposition on Interoperability of BIM and Collaborative Working Environments. Automation in Construction 19(5), 522–530 (2010)
16. Acquisition Operating Framework, http://www.aof.mod.uk/index.htm
17. Warship Engineering Management Guide. Defence Equipment & Support (December 2007)
18. Tavner, P.J., Xiang, J., Spinato, F.: Reliability Analysis for Wind Turbines. Wind Energy 10(1), 1–18 (2007)
19. Guo, H., Watson, S., Tavner, P., Xiang, J.: Reliability Analysis for Wind Turbines with Incomplete Failure Data Collected from after the Date of Initial Installation. Reliability Engineering and System Safety 94(6), 1057–1063 (2009)
20. Hameed, Z., Vatn, J., Heggset, J.: Challenges In The Reliability And Maintainability Data Collection for Offshore Wind Turbines. Renewable Energy 36(8), 2154–2165 (2011)
21. National Defense Authorization Act Fiscal Year 2006. The Committee on Armed Services House of Representatives (2006), http://www.gpo.gov/fdsys/pkg/CRPT-109hrpt89/html/CRPT-109hrpt89.htm
22. Hall, W.P., Richards, G., Sarelius, C., Kilpatrick, B.: Organizational Management of Project and Technical Knowledge over Fleet Lifecycles. Engineering Asset Management, 767–778 (2006)
23. Submarine Dismantling Project, http://www.gov.uk/government/organisations/ministry-of-defence/series/submarine-dismantling-project
24. Commercial Sale of Type 22 Frigates, http://www.gov.uk/commercial-sale-of-type-22-frigates

Toward a Reference Architecture for Archival Systems

Raphael Barbau[12], Joshua Lubell[2], Sudarsan Rachuri[2], and Sebti Foufou[31]

[1] Le2i, Université de Bourgogne,BP 47870, 21078 Dijon, France
[2] National Institute of Standards and Technology, Gaithersburg, MD 20899, USA
[3] CSE Department, CENG, Qatar University, Doha, Qatar

Abstract. Long-term preservation of product data is imperative for many organizations. A product data archive should be designed to ensure information accessibility and understanding over time. Approaches such as the Open Archival Information System (OAIS) Reference Model and the Audit and Certification of Trustworthy Digital Repositories (ACTDR) provide a framework for conceptually describing and evaluating archives. These approaches are generic and do not focus on particular contexts or content types. Enterprise architecture provides a way to describe systems in their potentially complex environments.

This paper proposes a holistic approach to formally describe the architecture and the environment of archival systems. This approach relies on the formal representation of the preservation terminology, including OAIS concepts, using the Department of Defense Architecture Framework (DoDAF). The approach covers the various interactions of other business functions with the archive, and the information models necessary to ensure preservation and accessibility. This approach is a step toward a reference architecture for the formal description of archival systems.

1 Introduction

A large amount of digital information is produced and consumed every day. Although most of this information is for immediate consumption, many organizations have an interest in long-term preservation[1]. The main motivations for preserving information are reusing existing knowledge, or keeping proofs of past events. Besides typical digital data management, specific information and activities are needed to ensure data's long-term preservation and accessibility[2, 3]. These information objects and activities are part of a dedicated entity: the archive. Design of an archive is a key factor in successful preservation, especially when complex information and activities are involved. Product data preservation is a good example of such complexity.

A complex product may be composed of numerous systems and parts. For each part, various product data may be produced from conception to disposal. Product data may be formally represented through large and complex information models. The metadata necessary to organize, interpret, or prove the authenticity

A. Bernard, L. Rivest, and D. Dutta (Eds.): PLM 2013, IFIP AICT 409, pp. 68–77, 2013.

of the information may also be complex. Finally, the interactions between the different product data repositories and the archive may be complex, and may involve many different stakeholders at different product lifecycle stages. One issue of this complexity is that the production and the consumption of preserved information is usually part of business functions not dedicated to preservation. This means that the archive has to be well integrated within the organization.

Some efforts address product data preservation by proposing alternative representations for the content [4, 5]. This paper focuses more on the infrastructure aspect of product data preservation, and more particularly on the computer systems involved in the preservation: the archival systems.

The design of archival systems should include the information, activities, systems, and other concepts needed to carry out the preservation mission. In the most complex situations, a product models archival system may have to communicate with different data sources (e.g. Product Data Management, Enterprise Resource Planning, Maintenance and Repair Operations, etc.). Communications among systems, activities, and information have to be well defined and interrelated in a consistent way. The objective of this paper is to propose a way to formally describe these elements.

The modeling of systems and their environment in the context of an enterprise is addressed by Enterprise Architecture (EA). EA establishes a link between the missions of an organization and their implementations. EA typically supports the description of systems, services, activities, information, and constraints within an organization. In our case, EA can be leveraged to detail how the preservation strategy is implemented.

Different efforts have attempted to determine the common elements that constitute archival systems. The Reference Model for an Open Archival Information System (OAIS RM) [6] is a mature conceptual framework for describing and comparing archives. It defines a common terminology for information preservation, especially from the information and functional perspectives. The OAIS RM has been adopted in various product data preservation efforts[7, 8]. However, its models are generic and conceptual: they are not meant to be directly implemented, but rather to serve as guidance for preservers to develop their own solutions.

This paper presents an approach that combines the concepts and terminology defined in the OAIS RM with those used in EA to allow formal description of archival system architectures. By using a formal description, the preservation concepts are explicitly referred to, which increases the understanding of the design, ensures consistency among the various elements described, and ultimately leads to an implementation of high quality. This approach is a first step towards the definition of a generic reference architecture to guide and constrain the description of archival systems.

This paper is organized as follows. Section 2 presents background information on preservation and enterprise architecture. Section 3 presents the approach for combining the OAIS RM and EA to enable the description of an archival system. Finally, Section 4 presents our conclusions.

2 Background on Digital Preservation and Enterprise Architecture

This section provides background information about the conceptualization, development, and certification of archival systems. It also introduces enterprise architecture, and particularly the Department of Defense Architecture Framework used in our approach.

2.1 Conceptual Frameworks and Certification of Archival Systems

Reference Model for an Open Archival Information System (OAIS RM), also known as ISO 14721, proposes a conceptual framework for describing and comparing archives[6]. It defines the terminology related to information preservation, including the types of information required to ensure preservation and accessibility of the content, and the main functions that an archive should support.

The OAIS RM defines the different kinds of information in an archive. This information, composed of content and metadata, is encapsulated in information packages. The Submission Information Package (SIP) refers to what the producer sends to the OAIS. The Archival Information Package (AIP) refers to what the archive stores. The Dissemination Information Package (DIP) refers to what the archive delivers to the consumer. Preservation Description Information (PDI) refers to information added to the content to ensure its preservation. Descriptive Information (DI) is a subset of PDI used to locate the desired information.

The OAIS RM describes the main functions of an archive (see Figure 1). The Ingest function receives the SIPs, and generates AIPs to be sent to Archival Storage, and DI to be sent to Data Management. The Data Management function sends some DI to the Access function when needed, and the Archival Storage function sends the desired AIP to the Access function. Then, the Access function returns a DIP to the consumers. The Preservation Planning function monitors the environment of the OAIS. The Administration function, directed by the management, establishes the overall preservation strategy of the OAIS. Each function is further decomposed into smaller functions in the OAIS RM.

Both information and functions are presented in a conceptual and generic way: they are not tied to a particular domain or implementation method. Actual solutions need to be tailored to the specific preserved content and to the context of the preservation. Also, the OAIS RM does not make the distinction between functions done by humans and functions performed by computers. However, it is unclear how to formally incorporate this terminology within actual archival system designs.

Audit and Certification of Trustworthy Digital Repositories (ACTDR)[9] is a standard for the certification of an OAIS. It addresses organizational aspects that are not considered in the OAIS RM, and it gives more details about what is expected from the archive. The certification concerns three different areas: the organizational infrastructure, the digital object management and the infrastructure and security risk management. Each area is composed of requirements and examples of how to demonstrate that the organization meets that requirement.

2.2 Introduction to Enterprise Architecture and Its Use for Information Preservation

Our approach to design archival systems is to rely on enterprise architecture. EA is the discipline of formally describing an enterprise, in particular the systems that compose it. An enterprise can be defined as an organization or a subset of an organization. EA describes how the objectives of an enterprise are realized through systems, services, and activities [10]. EA provides an abstract view that makes it easier to understand how the enterprise works, and how the systems are integrated. The actual description of an enterprise or of one of its parts is called architectural description.

Using EA for representing systems requires two components: a method that provides the steps in the development of the architecture, and the tools to concretely describe this architecture, for example by providing a metamodel. Different Enterprise Architecture Frameworks (EAFs) propose varying approaches to describe enterprises, and sometimes they focus on the aspect they judge the most important. For example, The Open Group Architecture Framework (TOGAF) [11] is an EAF well known for its Architectural Development Method. TOGAF has not incorporated a metamodel until recently. On the other hand, the Ministry of Defence Architecture Framework (MODAF)[12] and the US Department of Defense Architecture Framework (DoDAF)[13] focus on defining a metamodel and a set of views to formally represent architectural descriptions. Other EAF include the Generalized Enterprise Reference Architecture and Methodology (GERAM), developed by the IFIP-IFAC Task Force [14], and included as an Appendix of ISO15704:2000 [15] is a generalized EAF for enterprise integration and business process engineering. GERAM defines all the components required for use in enterprise engineering. Other well-known reference architectures are the Purdue Enterprise Reference Architecture (PERA)[16], and CIMOSA[17].

Becker et al. presented a reference architecture approach for archives, which emphasized the development process rather than the description of the actual implementations[18]. Becker et al.'s approach was to highlight the different recommendations and standards that need to be considered during the design of

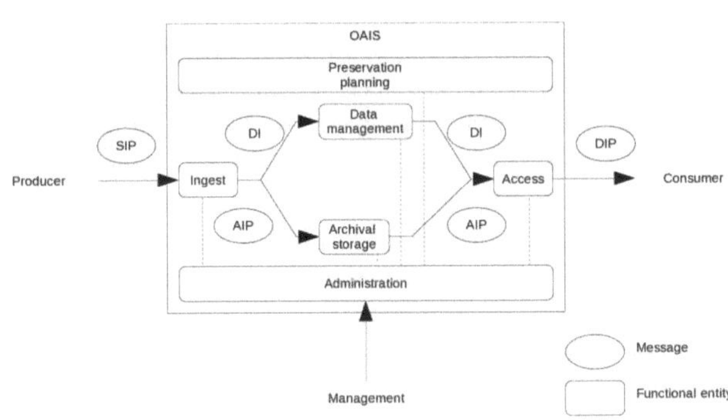

Fig. 1. OAIS Functional Model

the archive. Becker et al. took into account preservation recommendations and information technology standards related to risk management, data quality, or security. However, they did not address the formal description of the archival system architecture.

This paper presents an approach that focuses on the formal description of archival system architectures. Our approach consists of 1) formally representing the preservation terminology to be used in architectural descriptions, and 2) defining a set of views to describe important aspects of an archival system. We rely on DoDAF to provide the core enterprise architecture concepts to which preservation concepts relate. DoDAF provides a metamodel made of generic concepts, which don't include domain-specific concepts such as preservation concepts[13]. A formal description offers several benefits: 1) the preservation concepts are explicitly referred to, which increases the understanding of the design, 2) the same preservation concepts can be reused across multiple descriptions, 3) the different elements of the description can be consistently described and reused under different perspectives, and 4) parts of the formal description can lead to software implementation using a model-driven architecture approach.

The DoDAF metamodel is implemented as an extension of the Unified Modeling Language (UML)[19] in the Unified Profile for DoDAF/MODAF (UPDM) [20]. UPDM makes it possible to develop architectural descriptions with generic UML modeling tools. DoDAF concepts are implemented as stereotypes, and views are implemented as UML diagrams.

3 Approach to the Architectural Description of Archives

The approach presented in this paper relies on enterprise architecture to describe archival systems, to formally describe the interactions involving the archival system, and the functions performed by this system. Although the approach does not focus on a particular content type, it can be used to represent, in a coherent fashion, the complex interactions and information models involved in product data preservation. The intent is to provide a high-level description of the archival system, which can then drive the actual software implementation of the whole system.

This approach, depicted in Figure 2, is split into two parts. The first part extends the metamodel defined in DoDAF to incorporate a new archival vocabulary derived from the OAIS RM. The expanded terminology can then be used to represent archival system elements in architectural descriptions. The second part selects DoDAF views to represent specific aspects of the preservation solution. These views can serve as ACTDR evidence to demonstrate the ability of the archival system to preserve information. The approach, which is referred to as Reference Architecture for Archival System, can serve to guide and constrain architectural descriptions of archival systems. Note that a complete archival system description would go beyond what is in the scope of our approach, so other views may be used to address other aspects.

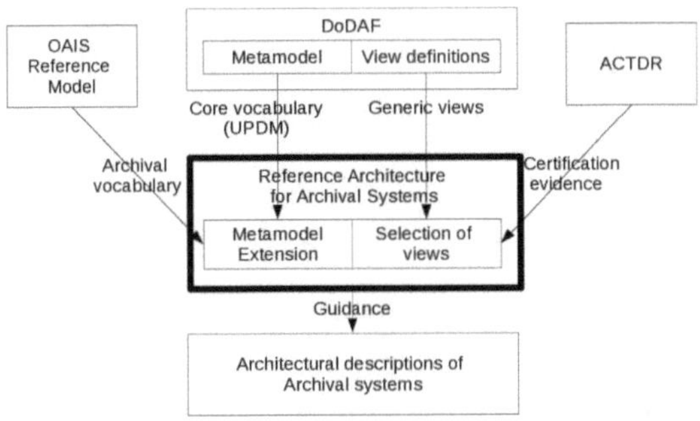

Fig. 2. Presentation of the approach

3.1 Representation of Preservation Concepts

DoDAF provides a generic, formal vocabulary to describe architectures, and the OAIS RM provides an informal, specific vocabulary to describe archival systems. Our approach combines both to allow a formal description of archival systems using enterprise architecture, and by incorporating the preservation terminology. Only the terminology related to the archival system and the interactions between this system and the environment are considered. Preservation functions such as customer monitoring or technology monitoring are present in the OAIS RM, but they are not in the scope of our approach. While these functions can be represented using DoDAF, we focus on the interactions between the archival system and the other business functions.

The OAIS RM describes archives in a conceptual and technology-independent manner, while DoDAF describes concrete implementations within an organization. So, more preservation concepts can be inferred by determining what DoDAF concepts would be used in an archival system description.

The approach uses UPDM, an implementation of DoDAF as a UML profile, which allows using the DoDAF terminology in UML tools. We will provide a conceptual description of the approach, as opposed to a detailed implementation.

The core terminology of DoDAF used in our approach is presented in Figure 3. The Figure shows how the different enterprise architecture concepts relate to each other. A *System* provides *Services*, and performs *Functions*. A *Node* performs *Activities*. Both *Functions* and *Activities* involve *Information*. A *Standard* can apply to *Information*, and *Constraints* can apply to *Information* or *Activities*.

3.2 Adapting the DoDAF Concepts for Preservation

The following paragraphs present some of the preservation concepts considered in our approach. The objective is to provide a way to formally describe the preserved content, the information packages, the representation information, the

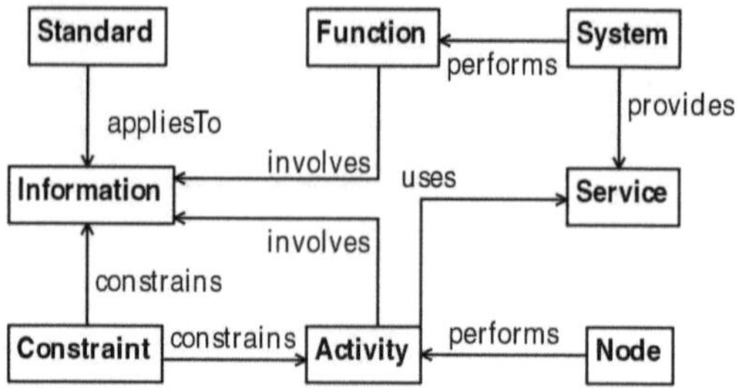

Fig. 3. DoDAF concepts used in the approach

preservation description information, the operational nodes, the activities, the system functions, the constraints, and the standards. The preservation concepts are written in italics.

Content and Information Packages. Content and information packages are OAIS concepts relating to information that is exchanged during preservation-related activities. Content is the information that is meant to be preserved. Information packages encapsulate content information as well as additional information required to ensure a long-term preservation and accessibility. The SIP, AIP, and DIP represent the information packages respectively as they are received, preserved, and disseminated. In UPDM, the concept *ExchangeElement* represents a resource exchanged during an activity, so both content and information packages are defined as the following specializations of *ExchangeElement*: *SubmissionInformationPackage*, *ArchivalInformationPackage*, *DisseminationInformationPackage*, and *Content*.

In the context of product data preservation, the *SubmissionInformationPackage*, the *ArchivalInformationPackage*, and the *DisseminationInformationPackage* represent the container of product data during ingest, retention, and dissemination activities respectively. A *Content* may represent the actual product data, or a piece of information that corresponds to the target of the preservation.

Representation Information and Presentation Description Information. Within information packages, the OAIS RM defines Preservation Description Information (PDI) and representation information that can be attached to the content. Representation information represents information that gives more meaning to the data: it could be everything that allows computers or humans to interpret the data, such as format specifications, software, or dictionaries. PDI is further detailed in four categories. Reference information identifies the content. Provenance information describes the content history. Fixity information represents the information used to check that the content is not altered. Finally, Context information provides the relationships between a content and the other various contents.

In the context of product data preservation, some of the preservation description information can be extracted from Product Data Management (PDM) or Product Lifecycle Management (PLM) systems, such as identifiers, creators, or relationships among product data.

Nodes. Producers and consumers can also be seen as *nodes* instead of physical persons. A *node* is a logical abstraction, meaning that it may correspond to people or systems. The following specializations of nodes are added *Producer*, *Consumer*, *Preserver*, and *Archive*.

In the context of product data preservation, *Producer* may correspond to the data source from which the product data originate (e.g., PDM systems), *Archive* abstracts the physical realization of the archival system, and *Consumer* may correspond to where the product data is used over time. *Preserver* can represent the persons in charge of the preservation of product data.

Activities. Three kinds of activities can be identified: the interaction between the archive and the producers, consumers, and management constitute respectively ingest, access, and management activities. In addition, the activities that are within the OAIS are also defined, in particular the preservation activities that include update and disposal of the preserved content. All of these activities are defined as specialization of *OperationalActivities* in UPDM: *IngestActivity*, *PreservationActivity*, and *AccessActivity*.

In the context of product data preservation, *IngestActivity* may represent the activities of taking product data from their original place, preparing a *SubmissionInformationPackage*, and sending it to the archive. *PreservationActivity* may represent the activities undertaken for preserving the product data over time by accessing the archival system. *AccessActivity* may represent the activities that request product data from the archive.

Services. Services constitute another concept that is important in the implementation of archival systems. Nowadays many software development approaches rely on a Service-Oriented Architecture. UPDM supports this approach by defining the notion of *service*. *IngestServices* are the services exposed to the producers for the ingest. *ManagementServices* are the services exposed to the preservers to make sure the content stays interpretable. *AccessServices* are the services exposed to the consumers for accessing the preserved content.

System Functions. The OAIS RM defines various functions that an OAIS performs. Two kinds of functions can actually be differentiated: those intended to be performed by humans, and those intended to be performed by computers. UPDM makes the distinction between these two types, and calls them respectively *OperationalActivities* and *Functions*. The *Functions* that are likely to be implemented by systems are the following: *IngestFunction* ingests the content, *ManagementFunction* manages the preserved content, and *AccessFunctions* makes the preserved content accessible.

4 Conclusion

This paper discussed an approach to formally describe the information and activities related to archival systems. This approach relies on the DoDAF enterprise architecture framework, and it uses a preservation terminology inspired by the Reference Model for an Open Archival Information System to describe the main elements of the archival system. Using this approach, the preservation concepts defined in the OAIS RM can be referred to within archival system designs. DoDAF also provides a way to consistently define and interrelate the different elements that constitute an archival system. This approach can lead to the definition of a comprehensive reference architecture for archival systems. A caveat is that to maximize the approach's usefulness, the entire enterprise should be described using DoDAF.

This approach is generic enough to be used in many different preservation cases, including product data preservation. The long-term access of product data is essential for product lifecycle management, especially in the case of products with a long life. This approach can be demonstrated by describing a product data ingest, to show the activities and information involved in the ingest. The ingest activity can be formally described according to the OAIS RM terminology, showing for example the transfer from PDM systems to the archive. From the information perspective, the content and the metadata can also be formally defined.

Disclaimer. No approval or endorsement of any commercial product by NIST is intended or implied. Certain commercial software are identified in this report to facilitate better understanding. Such identification does not imply recommendations or endorsement by NIST nor does it imply the software identified are necessarily the best available for the purpose.

References

[1] Beagrie, N.: Digital curation for science, digital libraries, and individuals. International Journal of Digital Curation 1(1), 3–16 (2006)
[2] Kuipers, T., Hoeven, J.V.D.: Insight into digital preservation of research output in europe – survey report (2009)
[3] Blue Ribbon Task Force. Sustainable Economics for a Digital Planet: Ensuring Long-term Access to Digital Information (2010)
[4] Patel, M., Ball, A., Ding, L.: Strategies for the curation of cad engineering models. International Journal of Digital Curation 4(1), 84–97 (2009) ISSN 1746-8256
[5] Regli, W.C., Grauer, M., Kopena, J.B.: A framework for preservable geometry-centric artifacts. In: 2009 SIAM/ACM Joint Conference on Geometric and Physical Modeling, pp. 67–78. ACM, New York (2009) ISBN 978-1-60558-711-0, doi:`http://doi.acm.org/10.1145/1629255.1629265`
[6] International Organization for Standardization. ISO 14721:2012, Space data and information transfer systems – Open archival information system (OAIS) – Reference model (2012)
[7] ASD-STAN. LOTAR - LOng Term Archiving and Retrieval of digital technical product documentation such as 3D, CAD and PDM data
[8] Verband der Automobilindustrie e. V. VDA 4958: Long-Term Archiving of digital Product Data, which are not based on technical drawings. Technical report, Verband der Automobilindustrie e. V. (2005)
[9] Consultative Committee for Space Data Systems. Audit and Certification of Trustworthy Digital Repositories (October 2009)

[10] Bernard, S.A.: An introduction to enterprise architecture. AuthorHouse (2005)
[11] The Open Group (ed.): TOGAF Version 9.1, Enterprise Edition. Van Haren Publishing (2011)
[12] Ministry of Defence Architecture Framework (MODAF) 1.2
[13] Department of Defense Architecture Framework (DoDAF) 2.0
[14] IFIP-IFAC Task Force. IFIP-IFAC task force on architectures for integrating manufacturing activities and enterprises. In: IFIP Newsletter/IFAC Newsletter (1993)
[15] International Organization for Standardization. ISO/IS 15704:2000, industrial automation systems requirements for enterprise reference architectures and methodologies (2000)
[16] Williams, T.J.: The Purdue enterprise reference architecture. Computers in Industry 24(2-3), 141–158 (1994)
[17] A CIMOSA presentation of an integrated product design review framework. Int. J. Computer Integrated Manufacturing 84(4), 260–278 (2005)
[18] Becker, C., Antunes, G., Barateiro, J., Vieira, R., Borbinha, J.: Modeling digital preservation capabilities in enterprise architecture. In: 12th Annual International Conference on Digital Government Research (dg. o 2011), College Park, MD, USA, June 12-15 (2011)
[19] Unified Modeling Language (UML) 2.0
[20] Unified Profile for the Department of Defense Architecture Framework (DoDAF) and the Ministry of Defence Architecture Framework (MODAF)

Examining the Use of Model-Based Work Instructions in the Aviation Maintenance Environment

Nathan W. Hartman[1] and Timothy D. Ropp[2]

[1] Purdue University, West Lafayette, IN USA
nhartman@purdue.edu
[2] Purdue University, West Lafayette, IN USA
tropp@purdue.edu

Abstract. A fundamental tenet of product lifecycle management (PLM) environments is the use of high-fidelity, 3D product models. The capability to create models with high degrees of fidelity to the physical world has driven companies to extract as much benefit and use from these digital assets as possible throughout the design, production, and support stages of the lifecycle. This is particularly apparent in the aviation industry where aircraft lifecycles routinely reach 80 years or longer. As the aviation industry migrates to the use of 3D model-based communications mechanisms in lieu of 2D drawings, multiple factors will impact the use of digital model-based work instructions, including the device, the form of the product model data, and levels of detail in geometry and interactivity. This paper will present a series of short studies conducted over the last three years using novice university students and expert university staff aircraft mechanics to evaluate the use of model-based work instructions in a general aviation maintenance environment. The results indicate that varying levels of detail and levels of interactivity have an effect on number of errors, time on task, and mental workload.

Keywords: product lifecycle management, aviation maintenance, model-based product definition, model-based work instructions, user experience, mobile computing, undergraduate research.

1 Introduction

The U.S. Federal Aviation Administration's (FAA) Next Generation Air Transportation System (NextGen), which transforms the U.S. national airspace system [1,2], has rapidly advanced the evolution of intelligent, networked aircraft and their sophisticated sustainment and support systems. This technology shift places tremendous pressure on aircraft maintenance and engineering organizations, as well as the individual technician, who require more access to detailed product information pipelines to work on more advanced and integrated air vehicle systems, minimize downtime, and meet unyielding air worthiness and quality requirements. This requires innovative data support systems integrated with product data definitions delivered to the point of maintenance. While electronic signoff and networked maintenance data capabilities currently exist within the aircraft maintenance industry [3,4], model based work instructions are neither widespread

A. Bernard, L. Rivest, and D. Dutta (Eds.): PLM 2013, IFIP AICT 409, pp. 78–89, 2013.

nor standardized; however, they are being realized more and more as key tools for the 21st century technician's use. Despite the tremendous computerized capabilities of modern aircraft and existing electronic maintenance networks containing aircraft technical manuals and diagrams, maintenance job tasks are still largely accomplished and tracked using manual methods such as job task "signoff" on paper-based work instructions in larger proportion than complete electronic systems [5].

It has been noted that properly applied visualization and component presentation of technical or complex systems is critical for improving daily maintenance tasks in both efficiency and accuracy [6]. Specifically, use of high fidelity model images on demand at the point of maintenance (for example a 3D image of a wing tip fairing installation) has been noted to result in less rework or missed steps. By leveraging a model-based product definition, MRO technicians would have access to the most relevant product geometry and accompanying metadata [7,8,9,10]. Moreover, in an estimate of the financial cost of maintenance errors to industry, Markou & Kalimat [11] concluded the worldwide maintenance expenditure to be $45.2B in 2008. Maintenance expenses represent approximately 10%-15% of an airline's operational cost.

This paper describes a series of experiments conducted in the context of a senior-level undergraduate research course at Purdue University. These studies involve the use of undergraduate students in an Aeronautical Engineering Technology program (novices) and University staff mechanics (experts) charged with the maintenance and support of the University's fleet of aircraft. All product data was acquired through the use of scanning and modeling technologies, and the accompanying technical documentation for the University's Boeing 727-200 records.

2 Experiment Frameworks

These pilot studies examined three critical characteristics associated with aircraft Maintenance, Repair and Overhaul (MRO) environments – time on task, error rate, and mental workload. As aerospace vehicle developers and maintenance firms leverage 3D assets beyond design and into assembly and service of the product it is important to decipher how these variables impact safety, airworthiness, and stability of the air vehicle.

Research frameworks in this study evolved on a number of dimensions. The first study examined differences between typical paper-based work instructions versus a non-interactive 3D animation of the same procedure. The study progressed to a comparison between non-interactive and interactive 3D graphics (as well as paper-based instructions). The third study used on 3D graphics (interactive and non-interactive), included variance in devices used to display the work instructions. The fourth study addressed varying levels of detail within the 3D model-based presentations as a way to influence the experimental variables and the computing capability on the devices used. Mobile devices and tablets have become increasingly popular, in the design, manufacturing and MRO space to disseminate technical data. Much work remains to assess their effectiveness in this environment as compared to traditional computers and flat-panel monitors used in the same way. Studies 3 and 4 began to assess these issues. A summary of the studies is included in Table 1.

As is the case with many tasks, differences in experts and novices data interpretation is essential to understand if aviation maintenance is to become more efficient and more accurate. Experts and novices in Purdue University's Aviation Technology department participated in the experiments. Study participants with more experience began to combine and omit assembly steps in the test procedure, indicative of expert behavior in a specific domain [12]. Experts in the study were FAA certified Purdue Aviation Technician staff with at least ten years of experience. According to Ericsson [13], ten years of experience is accepted in many industries. The novices consisted of Aeronautical Engineering Technology students with classroom and laboratory experience, but have yet to acquire an FAA certification. The NASA-TLX (Task Load Index) was used in the post-questionnaire in an effort to make connections between modality of the work instructions and the mental work load exerted by the participant [14]. Figures 1-4 show the various aircraft subassemblies used in these studies, with a brief description of how each one was used.

Table 1. Summary of Research Study Frameworks

Research Study Frameworks

	Experience Level	Group size	Device Type	Mode (2D or 3D)	Interactivity
Study 1	Novice Expert	8 8	Laptop, tablet	2D paper, 3D digital	2D paper, continuous loop video
Study 2	Novice Expert	9 7	Laptop, tablet	2D paper, 3D digital	2D paper, 3D non-interactive, 3D interactive
Study 3	Novice	28	Desktop computer, iPad	3D digital	3D non-interactive, 3D interactive
Study 4	Novice	35	Desktop	3D digital	High LOD vs. Low, LOD; continuous loop presentation vs. step-wise presentation

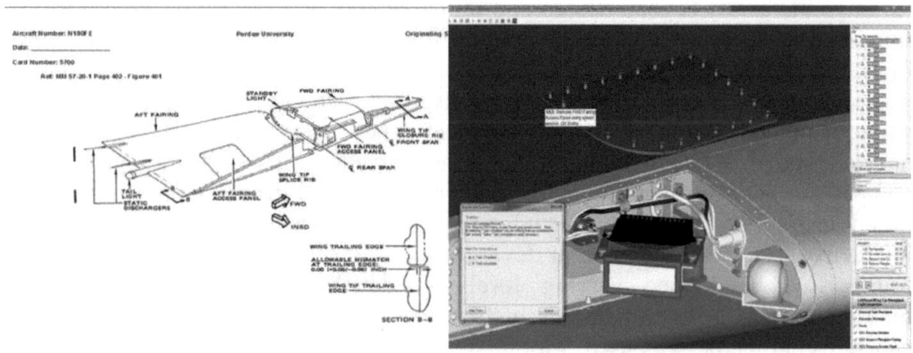

Fig. 1. Left wing-tip fairing position light from Boeing 727-200Assembly instructions from 2D and 3D job task card

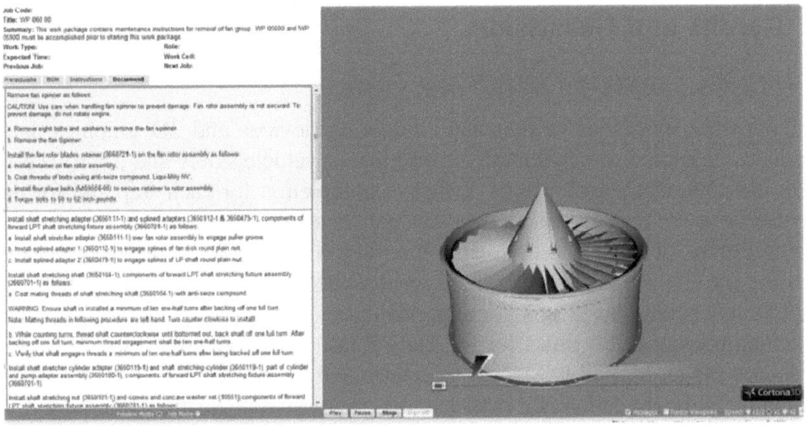

Fig. 2. Front Fan Assembly of F-109 Engine. Comparing 3D interactive (NGRAIN), 3D static (Cortona 3D), and 2D (paper) Job Task Cards.

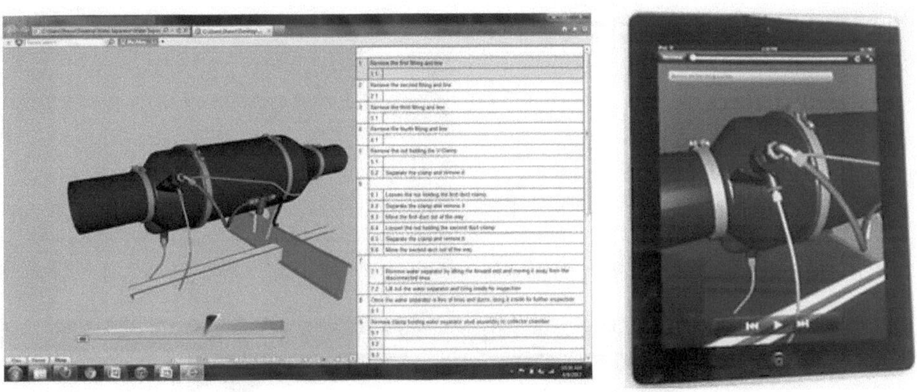

Fig. 3. Water separator unit on Boeing 727-200. Comparing Mobile and Stationary Job Task Cards

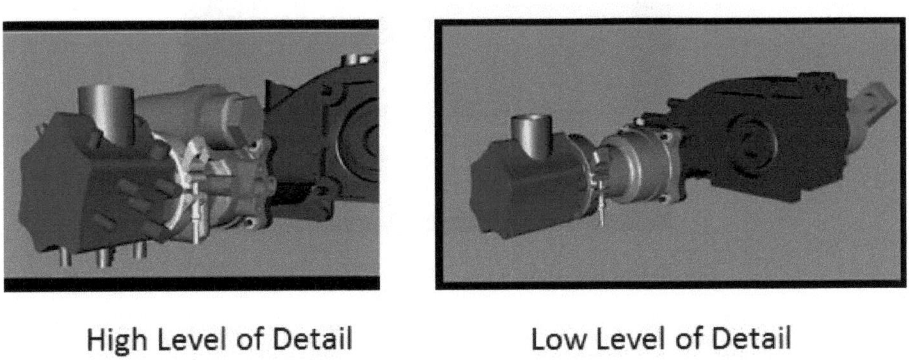

Fig. 4. Fuel Pump and Gear Box from F-109 Engine. Comparing High and Low Levels of Detail and Interactivity of the CAD Assembly Work Instructions.

3 Results and Discussion

Study 1: Comparing 2D and 3D Job Task Cards

Leveraging the capabilities of personal computing devices and 3D graphics data could help reduce common errors potentially impacting air vehicle safety and improve efficiency of aviation maintenance technicians. Times to completion for each step and for the overall process between test groups showed no statistically significant difference. However, completion times of those subjects using the 3D job task card showed less variance than those using the 2D job task card. These results differed from those in an industrial case study [15]. After removing results determined to be outliers, range between the minimum and maximum completion times for the 2D job task card was three times that of the 3D job task card range. Mental workload, as determined by the NASA TLX, also showed no statistically significant difference between test groups. Statistically significant difference between test groups ($p<.05$; $p=.033$) was found in the total number of procedural and assembly errors made by participants. The group using the 2D job task card made twice as many errors as the group using the 3D job task card (Figure 5).

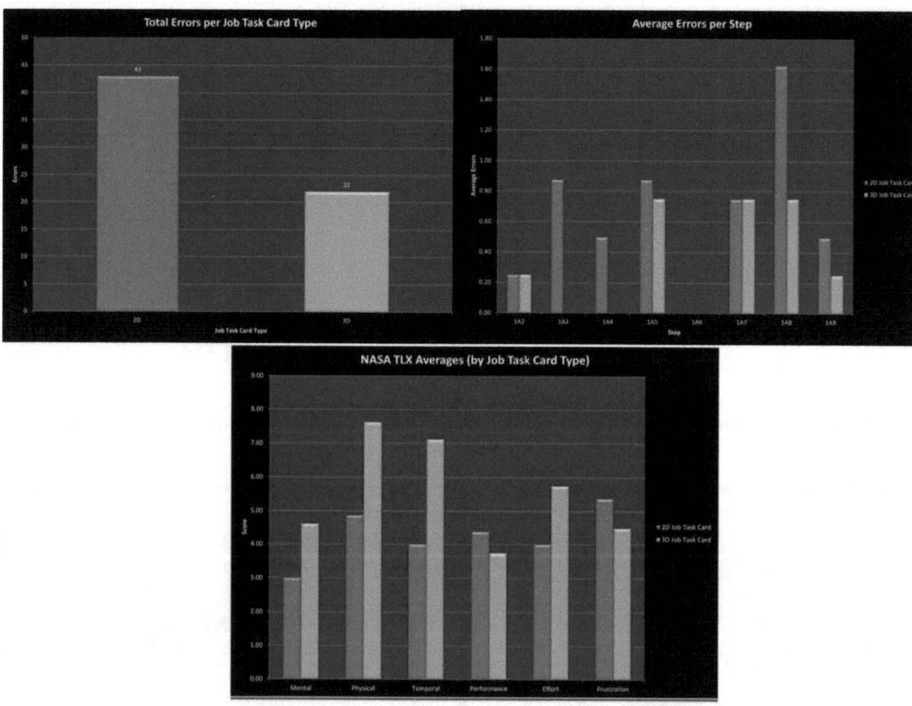

Fig. 5. Results from 2D vs. 3D Task Card Comparisons

Study 2: Comparing 3D interactive (NGRAIN), 3D static (Cortona 3D), and 2D (paper) Job Task Cards

There were 16 participants total in the study, 7 of which were experts and 9 were novice. Due to the small sample size, results were analyzed using a non-parametric method called the Kruskal-Wallis test. A p-value of .05 was used to evaluate statistical significance. The average time for experts was higher than that of the novices, although statistically insignificant. Between types of work instructions (paper, 3D interactive, 3D non-interactive), there was no significant difference in time; however, paper was found to be slightly faster than 3D static, and 3D static was marginally faster than 3D interactive in both experts and novices (Figure 6).

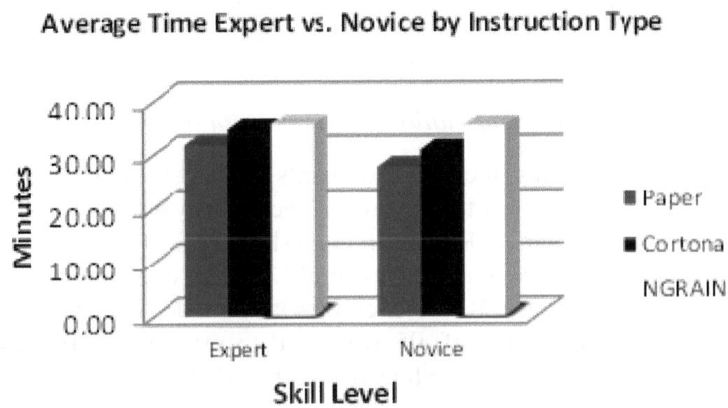

Fig. 6. Time on Task between Experts and Novices

As expected, the average number of errors for experts was lower than for novices. The experts made more errors on the 3D interactive mode than any other type of work instructions; whereas the average number of errors on the 3D static mode for novices was slightly higher than the other types of work instructions, although statistically insignificant. The majority of the NASA-TLX results were also found to be statistically insignificant. Modality of the work instructions significantly affected how the novice participants felt they had performed the task. Performance of novice participants using 3D static work instructions was significantly lower than those using 3D interactive and paper (Figure 7).

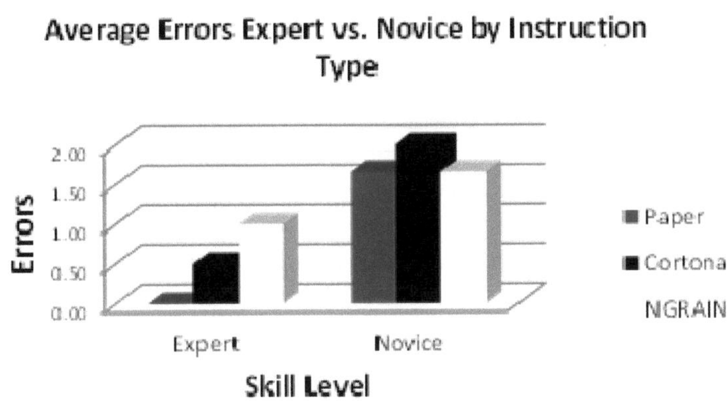

Fig. 7. Number of Errors between Experts and Novices

In the post questionnaire, participants were asked to comment on the method they were tested on. In summary, most of the participants felt the 3D work instructions were more effective than the 2D work instructions. One novice technician stated, “There was less room for error, as you have to verify completion of each and every step” in reference to the NGRAIN product. In contrast, one of the experts said that NGRAIN was “too slow for mind function” because he prefers to read through the entire task first rather than do it step by step. In addition, several of the participants, experts and novices alike, indicated graphics helped clarify the text instructions if they were unclear. One comment about the 2D paper work instructions was that it needed more pictures.

Study 3: Comparing Mobile and Stationary versions of a 3D Job Task Card

As with the previous studies, the 28 participants in this study were junior- or senior-level undergraduate students in the Aviation Technology program, with an emphasis in their studies of Maintenance, Repair and Overhaul (MRO) skills and system safety. The results of the study were analyzed using ANCOVA due to the selection methods and sample sizes. See Figure 10 for a comparison of the data between mobile and stationary platforms. A p-value of .05 was used to establish statistical significance. The average time for completion when using the iPad was found to be faster than using the computer by more than two minutes. The p-value found for this difference was .0565. This showed the difference in time for completion was just shy of statistical significance. Eight errors were made throughout the testing process for the iPad participants and one for those using the computer. The p-value for these differences was .028. This value showed the amount of errors made was statistically significant indicating iPad users had more errors. Finally, the difference in mental workload scores yielded a p-value of .3638. This value showed that there was no statistical significance in mental workload when comparing the computer and iPad task cards. See Figure 8.

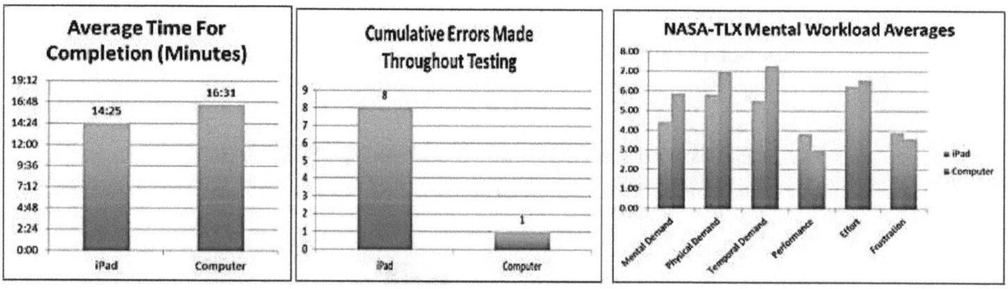

Fig. 8. Comparison of Data for Mobile and Stationary Platforms

Study 4: Comparing Level of Detail and Presentation Mode for Graphics in the Work Instruction

Results comparing levels of detail are presented first. The first was mental workload measured by assessing the NASA TLX test. The largest difference was in the temporal demand section with low level of detail being 5.3% higher than high level of detail. While analyzing the data, it was predicted that providing a simple disassembly contributed to the low mental workload. Evaluation revealed a t-value of .318, indicating the difference in mental workload was not significant. Figure 9 shows mental workload data from the level of detail comparison.

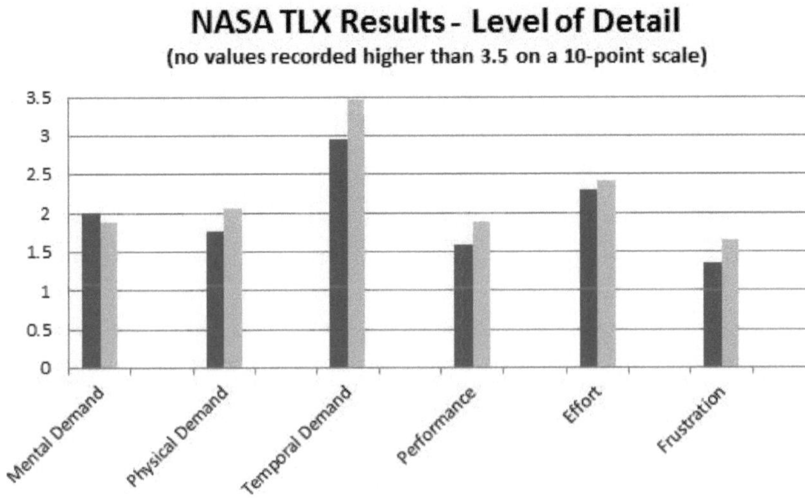

Fig. 9. NASA-TLX Results for Level of Detail Comparison

The second variable tested was time on task, assessed by starting the timer as soon as test subjects began viewing the work instruction and stopped when test subjects stated they were finished. Subjects were required to verbally express when they were finished to confirm they fully understood the beginning and end of the work instruction. The difference for average time on task was minimal as high level of detail took 5:37.2 and low level of detail took 5:30.8. The t-value found for difference in time on task was .142, indicating no statistical significance and the null hypothesis cannot be rejected. The third variable tested was number of errors. After testing was complete, five errors for high level of detail and five errors for low level of detail were recorded. The t-value for difference in number of errors was .142. This indicated the difference in number of errors was not statistically significant, and the null hypothesis cannot be rejected.

The NASA TLX was utilized to measure mental workload variable for the delivery method similar to level of detail. The largest difference was in the temporal demand section with animation being 9.1% higher than screen capture. Figure 10 shows the results of this analysis. After analysis, it is likely a short disassembly process contributed to the low mental workload. Test subjects retained nearly all information by viewing only one time. The t-value was 1.985, indicating that the difference in mental workload (NASA TLX) was not significant. Number of errors was another variable tested. Four errors for the animation and six errors for the screen capture were recorded. The t-value was .442. The final variable tested was time on task. The procedure was done in the same manner, with little discrepancy noted between animation and screen capture. Dynamic animation averaged 5:41.1 and screen capture averaged 5:27.3. The t-value found for difference in time was .214, indicating once again no statistical significance and the null hypothesis cannot be rejected.

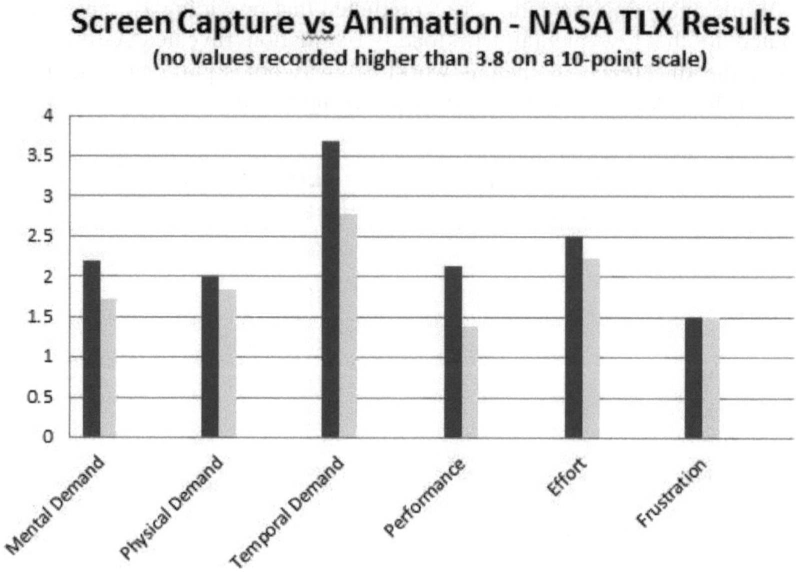

Fig. 10. NASA-TLX Results for Dynamic Presentation of Work Instructions

4 Summary

In Study 1, the original intent was to integrate a maintenance job task card into a digital 3D environment assessing performance impact on maintenance technicians. While test subject performance was measured by time to completion, sum of errors made, and mental workload, the only result acquired from experimentation with statistical significance was the total amount of errors made between the two job task card forms. Moreover, these errors are considered human error. According to Rankin & Allen [16], 20% - 30% of engine in flight shutdowns are caused by maintenance error and can cost an estimated $500,000 per shutdown. Reducing the amount of human error in aviation maintenance processes can allow companies to realize tremendous cost savings. Considering that maintenance expenses make up 10%-15% of airline operational costs [11], a reduction in maintenance expenses would allow airlines to allocate resources elsewhere.

Study 2 involved the comparison of 3D interactive, 3D static, and 2D paper forms of the work instructions. Study 3 also involved the comparison of expert and novice mechanics. Novice technicians had a broader computer background than the experts, including CAD experience and familiarity with CAD interfaces. 3D interactive and non-interactive maintenance manuals were positively received by both expert and novice technicians, with Cortona being the most popular. They expressed the helpfulness of the 3D graphics and animation verbally and during the questionnaire. Despite this, there was one very puzzling result pertaining to 3D interactive work instructions and experts.

The number of errors committed by expert technicians was much higher than expected. It was believed that, since NGRAIN requires the user to stop and confirm each step was completed, users would commit fewer errors than they would with the paper based or non-interactive manual. A possible explanation for this result could be the experts' use of chunking [12]. Since experts have been shown to gather task information together and cluster it as they go, it is likely many of them read the steps provided in NGRAIN, skipping the completion checks, and clustered the tasks together in a way they saw fit. In most instances of expertise, experts display a high ability to perform tasks almost without thinking about them by mixing procedural and declarative knowledge in strategic ways. If these maintenance experts had used the paper-based methods for a long time, it is highly likely that a level of automaticity had developed in their mental processing of the information. Anything that interrupted that level of performance (i.e., the introduction of a 3D mode for viewing work instructions) would likely result in a performance decrement.

The two alternatives used 3D graphics and animations providing visual communication of the task at hand to accompany the basic written instructions. The two products developed included an NGRAIN animation and a 3D PDF document. Participant feedback showed preference for 3D graphics-based support documentation of the newly developed job task cards. Participants agreed that task visualization was a tremendous instructional help. In Study 3, mobile and stationary model-based instructions were investigated. The iPad is still a fairly new technology, and a number of subjects mentioned more familiarity using laptops for productivity and iPads for entertainment. This may explain why so many errors were made. Portions of the NASA-TLX mental workload suggested this as well.

Study 4 examined multiple areas –delivery platform, form of the product model data, and levels of detail in geometry and interactivity – and gathered data on number of errors, time on task, and mental workload. If integration of model-based work instructions in aviation maintenance is to be useful, industry must address challenges with infrastructure and computing architecture, the level of graphics preparation needed, human information processing, and deployment platforms. There were no significant statistical differences between the high and low level of detail work instructions. These results are contrary to the initial hypothesis and research. The research indicated that removing unnecessary visual information provided the potential for improved learner efficiency and reduced cognitive load [17].

Similarly, animation based work instructions yielded no statistically significant results when compared to screen captures. These results were also contrary to initial predictions [18]. Most test subjects had experience working with similar assemblies resulting in high mechanical reasoning abilities. Subjective comments from test subjects imply both delivery methods have positives and negatives. Some subjects felt step by step clicking was an advantage, allowing for slower comprehension and feeling "more in control" of the work instruction. A negative expressed was the inability to see the parts come apart. This is where the animation work instruction gained more approval. Test subjects in favor of animation favored ability to see dynamic movement of parts occur. They said, "This improved understanding of how the parts went together and came apart." It is evident that both methods have advantages and disadvantages. The challenge for the future is developing a process that effectively uses the correct method in each situation.

Study 4 did not find statistically significant differences in regards to a specific delivery method or level of detail. In order to test as many subjects as possible, the work instructions were condensed. Allowing assessment of all 34 available test subjects, but results were very similar between subjects. This could suggest that simple maintenance procedures and tasks are minimally affected by the delivery method and level of detail. Industry professionals and data suggest that component complexity and assembly frequency are critical factors impacting work instructions. Additionally, certain regulatory guidelines require assembly technicians to have both hands available to be engaged in work while performing a task, thereby rendering them unable to hold a tablet or other mobile device while working. Future work should concentrate on interaction between variables associated with geometric level of detail and specific display modalities, as well as the positioning of the computing device in the assembly work environment.

Acknowledgements. The authors would like to acknowledge the following research student team members involved in this study: Bret Angel, Gilbert Bracey, Anthony Butcher, Zachary Carnahan, Nathan Christopher, Kelsey Crowe, Nick Delcore, Bret Gastineau, Brandon Hall, Matt Harris, Andrew Klaassen, Patrick McGuire, Ian Pack, Matthew Pizzatto, John Pourcho, Josh Rathke, Nick Rohe, Shawn Ruemler, Joshua Schliessman, Samantha Schreiber, Jacob Seeley, Stephen Trimboli, and Athan Valaskatgis,

References

1. FAA – JPDO, Federal Aviation Administration – Joint Planning and Development Office (FAA-JPDO). "Safety Culture Improvement Guide" V.1.0. Paper number 08-010. p. 22 (2008)
2. Federal Aviation Administration, FAA NextGen Implementation Plan (2010)
3. ATE&M, Online maintenance tools: Online help for aircraft operations and maintenance staff. Aircraft Technology and Engineering Maintenance (ATE&M), (102), p. 70 (October-November 2009)
4. Boeing (2010). Boeing Commercial Aviation Services website. Maintenance Services page. Airplane Health Management: Managing Information to Improve Operational Decision Making (2010), `http://www.boeing.com/commercial/ams/mss/brochures/airplane_health.html` (retrieved October 18)
5. Block, E.E., Ropp, T.D., Speca, T.P.: Implementing digital technologies and network systems into aircraft maintenance. In: Proceedings of the 1st International Conference on Aviation Information Technology in Engineering and Management, New Orleans, LA, March 22-24 (2010)
6. Kim, S., Woo, I., Maciejewski, R., Ebert, D.S., Ropp, T.D., Thomas, K.: Evaluating the effectiveness of visualization techniques for schematic diagrams in maintenance tasks. In: Proceedings of the 7th Symposium on Applied Perception in Graphics and Visualization, Session: displays and visualization, Los Angeles, California, pp. 33–40 (2010) ISBN:978-1-4503-0248-7
7. Hartman, N., Rosche, P., Fischer, K.: A framework for evaluating collaborative product representations in product lifecycle workflows. In: Rivest, L., Bouras, A., Louhichi, B. (eds.) PLM 2012. IFIP AICT, vol. 388, pp. 424–434. Springer, Heidelberg (2012)

8. Lubell, J., Hartman, N.W., Cheney, D.: Model-based engineering standardization and validation. NISTIR 7796, National Institute of Standards and Technology (2011), http://www.nist.gov/manuscript-publication-search.cfm?pub_id=908106
9. Versprille, K.: Model-based Definition for the Masses, Collaborative Product Development Associates (2008), http://www.righthemisphere.com/_base/static/img/whitepapers/2_cpda_rh_wp.pdf (retrieved January 27, 2013)
10. Quintana, V., Rivest, L., Pellerin, R., Venne, F., Kheddouci, F.: Will model-based definition replace engineering drawings throughout the product lifecycle? A global perspective from aerospace industry. Computers in Industry 61(5), 497–508 (2010)
11. Markou, C., Kalimat, T.: IATA Airline Maintenance Costs An Executive Commentary (May 2010), http://www.iata.org/workgroups/Documents/MCTF/Form41_2010Report_2010.10.27.pdf (retrieved)
12. Egan, D.E., Schwartz, B.J.: Chunking in recall of symbolic drawings. Memory and Cognition 7(2), 149–158 (1979)
13. Ericsson, A.K., Prietula, M.J., Cokely, E.T.: The making of an expert. Harvard Business Review (June 7, 2007), http://www.coachingmanagement.nl/The%20Making%20of%20an%20Expert.pdf (retrieved)
14. NASA, NASA TLX: Task Load Index (2006), http://human-factors.arc.nasa.gov/groups/TLX/paperpencil.html (retrieved)
15. NGRAIN, Field Case study: Leveraging ngrain-enabled IETMs for Performance Support (2009), http://www.ngrain.com/pdfs/CaseStudy-20Leveraging NGRAIN-enabledIETMsforPerformanceSupport(CanadianAirForce).pdf (retrieved)
16. Rankin, W., Hibit, R., Allen, J., Sargent, R.: Development and evaluation of maintenance error decision aid (MEDA) process. International Journal of Industrial Ergonomics 26, 261–276 (2000)
17. Allen, C.: The effects of visual complexity on cognitive load as influenced by field dependency and spatial ability. New York University (2011), http://gradworks.umi.com/3478262.pdf
18. Boucheix, J., Schneider, E.: Static and animated presentations in learning dynamic mechanical systems. Learning and Instruction 19, 112–127 (2009), http://elsevier.com/locate/learinstruc (retrieved)

Enhancing the Flow of Information in the PLM by Using Numerical DSMs – An Industrial Case Study

Thomas Luft[1], Johanna Bochmann[2], and Sandro Wartzack[1]

[1] Friedrich-Alexander-University of Erlangen-Nuremberg, Chair of Engineering Design, Martensstrasse 9, 91058 Erlangen, Germany
[2] Siemens AG, Energy Sector, Energy Service Division, Frankenstrasse 70-80, 90461 Nuremberg, Germany
luft@mfk.fau.de

Abstract. This paper proposes a methodology to enhance the information flow in the product life cycle through the example of the product development process. The methodology refines the existing approaches of revealing indirect dependencies with a multiple domain matrix by introducing the numerical derived design structure matrix as indicator of quantifying indirect dependencies between process steps, information and people. These dependencies are quantified by the pieces of information causing the indirect linkage. The subsequent analysis is narrowed down to the content level of information to identify the root causes. This methodology has been successfully tested in an industrial case study. As a result, this paper helps to manage the complexity in the PLM by making the linkages caused by the information flow visible to improve collaborative product development.

Keywords: Collaborative product development, information management, process management, design structure matrix, multiple domain matrix, case study.

1 Motivation and Objectives

The successful development of modern products is becoming increasingly difficult for companies because they are faced with many challenges such as the consideration of a variety of customer requirements, the compliance with Design for X rules regarding different issues that occur in different product life cycle phases as well as the increasing need of collaboration of diverse engineering disciplines in the product development process (PDP). This leads to a steadily growing complexity of the relationships and interactions between the following three important domains: 'process steps', 'people/departments' and 'information'.

Due to these complexities, it comes to a lack of information exchange between the departments and consequently to delayed product development processes. One reason is that it is often not known how people (within the meaning of roles) are connected to each other based on the information they generate or receive [5]. The other reason is that it is seldom understood how process steps are connected to each other based on

A. Bernard, L. Rivest, and D. Dutta (Eds.): PLM 2013, IFIP AICT 409, pp. 90–99, 2013.

the information being generated or used during a process step [5]. Thereby, the term information covers the 'knowledge and information objects' (KaI-object) according to Luft [6]. Therefore, not only the direct dependencies but also the indirect dependencies between these three domains create problems within the development of modern products.

Subsequently, the information flow between the affected employees and every single step of the development process has to be analyzed and enhanced in order to realize an improved flow of information [8]. The main objective of this paper is to provide a methodology which allows revealing and quantifying indirect dependencies between different departments (domain people) and different process steps (domain process) based on the exchanged information or KaI-objects (domain information), since these are not obvious as the direct dependencies. In order to do this, a Multiple Domain Matrix (MDM) that consists of several Design Structure Matrices (DSM) and Domain Mapping Matrices (DMM) is created. On this basis, the calculation of the so called numerical derived Design Structure Matrix (nd-DSM), which is introduced and presented in this paper, is possible. The nd-DSM allows besides the identification also the quantification of indirect dependencies. Thereafter, an analysis strategy is proposed in order to improve the information flow in the PDP. Using this methodology in an industrial case study, the authors show that not only the transparency of the dependencies between the three domains increases but also the flow of information in the collaborative product development process can be improved significantly.

2 State of the Art and Related Work

The current state of science as well as the relevant work regarding the objective pursued is described in this chapter. The PDP can be considered as a complex system of different subsystems which can be also called as domains [5]. The modeling of the entire system allows understanding the complexity of it by considering the different domains of interest (e.g. process steps, people, information) and the relationship between the respective elements [2]. The linkage of different elements of a certain subsystem can be modeled by the DSM developed by Steward [9]. The DSM is an intra-domain square matrix showing the direct dependencies of elements to each other, which are belonging to the same domain (figure 1). However, the DSM cannot represent the dependency between elements of different domains (e.g. certain information cannot be assigned to a process step).

In contrast, the DMM is an inter-domain matrix that reflects the direct dependencies between the elements of two different domains and is also considered as a cause-effect-matrix [9]. Thereby, the rows represent the elements of one domain while the columns show the elements of the other domain. Both types of matrices represent only direct dependencies, which become visible, e.g. by analyzing the product structure or by mapping the development process steps (figure 1). In the following the IR/FAD (input in the rows/feedback above the diagonal) convention according to Eppinger is applied to read the following matrices [4].

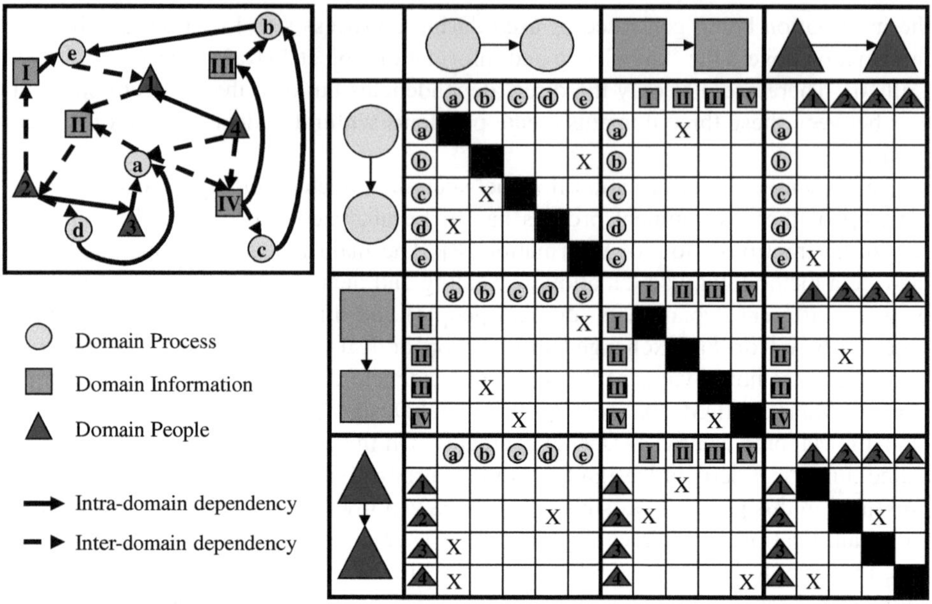

Fig. 1. Dependencies between the elements of the different domains in a MDM [cf. 5]

Maurer developed the MDM being a square matrix, which shows the direct dependencies within a single domain (DSM) and between different domains (DMM) [5] (figure 1). Consequently, the MDM consists of DSMs and DMMs. Nevertheless, for improving the PDP it is also important to understand and to analyze indirect dependencies. An indirect dependency is caused through the linkage of two elements of certain domain via one or more elements of another domain. As shown in figure 1 at the top on the left, person (2) is indirectly dependent on person (1) because person (1) generates a KaI-object (II) (e.g. a piece of information) and the other person (2) uses it, even though they are not directly linked (e.g. by belonging to the same department). The indirect dependencies are apparent from derived DSMs, which are the result of a matrix multiplication of different matrices of the MDM.

For enhancing the information flow in the PDP, the following question needs to be answered: How are the different departments as well as process steps indirectly dependent on each other based on the exchanged information [5]? However, the above mentioned matrices only display the existence of a dependency by setting a cross or the binary value '1'. This means no further information is available how strong the dependency is and therefore they are called binary matrices.

In literature several approaches (e.g. [3], [7] and [9]) exist to weight the dependency of elements of a certain domain by using numerical DSMs. While a binary DSM only indicates a relationship between elements by '0' and '1', a numerical DSM has the numerical value of the number of elements causing the dependency. Consequently, the advantage of numerical DSMs is that more information is given about the relationship between two elements. Numerical DSMs already considered in research [3], [7] and [9] to be only applicable in a flow-directed environment by weighing the marks, which are indicating, for example, a rework loop in activity based DSMs.

However, all previous methods are based on a subjective assessment of the dependency and, moreover, the self-dependency is considered in none of these approaches. For this reason a methodology is proposed in the following, which allows to quantify the strength of indirect dependencies and to analyze these on a content level as well as to identify self-dependencies.

3 Methodology

The methodology for enhancing the flow of information between the participating departments in the PDP consists of three phases. The first phase is the identification of the problem area, followed by the modeling of the development process and finally the analysis of it. All steps can be done with usual spreadsheet software (e.g. Excel) and Matlab. So, no expensive and difficult-to-use software application is necessary.

First of all, the problem area of the PDP needs to be identified. Hereby, it is recommended to conduct explanatory interviews with the affected departments along the process chain of the PDP to get background knowledge about the holistic process. Besides the different pieces of information, the process steps themselves as well as the involved departments which exchange information throughout the process have to be investigated. So, a detailed analysis of the three relevant domains 'process', 'information' and 'people' needs to be carried out in order to enhance the information flow. As a first step, the process is mapped by using event-driven process chain (EPC) which is a type of flowchart and is in particular used for business process modeling. With the EPC the flow of activities of the process is modeled as functions which starts and ends with an event. Thus, the entire PDP is shown in its logical sequence.

Once the whole process is mapped with all its activities, the focus is on the information flow because the information exchange between the departments with their respective staff is seen as an enabler for a successful PDP. Therefore, according to Behncke, four different levels have to be taken into account [1]: The 'transmitter-receiver level' describes the communication between the departments, the second level 'content level' focuses on which information is exchanged whereas the 'information carrier level' considers how the information is transmitted between sender and receiver; the fourth level 'target level' is not in focus of this methodology because an evaluation and a categorization of information are not absolutely necessary.

Each process step within the workflow is analyzed from these three perspectives of an information flow. For this purpose, a so called information flow matrix (IFM), which is depicted in figure 2, is built up. The process step itself is marked by the activity (function of the EPC-diagram) and the organizational unit carrying out the process step (executer). For each process step the information input and output is determined. The focus is not only put on the transmitter-receiver relationship (first level or brown colored) but also on the content of the information (second level or orange colored) and carrier of it (third level or blue colored). Moreover, the fourth level 'storage of information' helps to identify whether the information stays at the same place. Finally, the perspective 'information type' is also considered (cf. [6]).

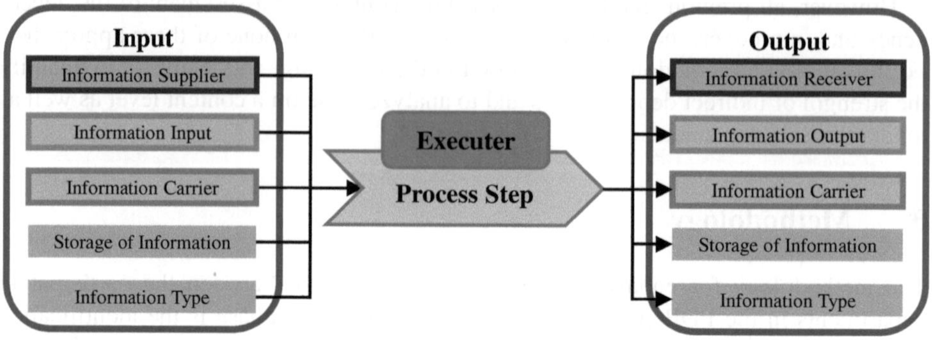

Fig. 2. Structure of the Information Flow Matrix

Since the process, information and people perspective is covered by the IFM, it is used as the basis for building up the MDM. Hereby, all elements of every domain are listed in the columns and in the rows of the MDM. It helps to use the pivot-function in Excel in order to prevent double entries in the MDM because some elements, especially of the domains information and people, exist more than once in the IFM. Therefore, three Pivot-tables are created of the specific rows (information input and output, executer, process step) of the IFM. The rows 'information input' and 'information output' are combined into one row. So, all elements of the domains are directly transferred to the rows and columns of the MDM.

Afterwards, all DMM fields need to be filled out with information from the IFM. It has to be ensured that the IR/FAD convention is used in order to fill in the correct data. The first DMM ($DMM_{Process \rightarrow Information\ Output}$) indicates which process step generates which information output. The $DMM_{Process \rightarrow People}$ shows the executer of each process step. This DMM is the transposed one to $DMM_{People \rightarrow Process}$ and therefore only one of the two DMMs need to be filled out. The entries of one of the two DMMs can be transferred to the opposed DMM by using the function 'paste' of the transposed values in Excel. The third $DMM_{Information\ Input \rightarrow People}$ shows which information the executer of the process step(s) needs in order to conduct the process step. Hereby, it is useful to insert the information process step by process step because the executer of a certain process step needs a certain information input. The $DMM_{People \rightarrow Information\ Output}$ considers the information output, which is generated by a certain executer. As in the opposed $DMM_{Information\ Input \rightarrow People}$ it is helpful to do this process step wise. The $DMM_{Information\ Input \rightarrow Process}$ focuses on the information input needed for a certain process step [5].

It is important to set the number '1' instead of a cross in the fields of the DMMs in which a dependency exists in order to use the matrix for further analysis. Sometimes information is used several times by the same executer and in these cases it is assumed that the information is still available for the executer. Consequently, the entered figure is not increased. The empty fields, which are representing non-existing relationships, can be filled out easily with '0' by using the 'replaced-by'-function in Excel. The result is a binary MDM with the respective DMMs.

Once the MDM is filled out, the indirect dependencies can be determined. In accordance with the initially mentioned objective are two issues in the focus of this contribution (cf. [5]):

- How are people (or departments) connected based on the information they generate or receive?
- How are process steps connected to each other based on the information being generated or used during a process step?

For each dependency a separate matrix multiplication needs to be done. The DMMs are multiplied with each other in order to receive the nd-DSMs, which quantify the strength of the indirect dependency. It is recommended to conduct the matrix multiplication with the software Matlab to avoid the limitation of the array size of the matrices in Excel. For the first issue, the dependencies between people, equation 1 is applied while the second equitation 2 is needed for answering the second question about the dependency of the process steps. The formula for the matrix multiplication is written down in equation 3. Matrix A (a_{ij}) is a (m, n)-matrix and is multiplied with the (n, l)-Matrix B (b_{jk}). The product of this multiplication is matrix C (c_{ik}) with the array size (m, l).

$$\text{nd-DSM}_{\text{People}} = \text{DMM}_{\text{People}\rightarrow\text{Information Output}} \times \text{DMM}_{\text{Information Input}\rightarrow\text{People}} \tag{1}$$

$$\text{nd-DSM}_{\text{Process}} = \text{DMM}_{\text{Process}\rightarrow\text{Information Output}} \times \text{DMM}_{\text{Information Input}\rightarrow\text{Process}} \tag{2}$$

$$A \cdot B = (a_{ij}) \cdot (b_{jk}) = (c_{ik}) \quad \text{with} \quad c_{ik} = \sum_{j=1}^{n} a_{ij} \cdot b_{jk} \tag{3}$$

In order to get a better overview, these two nd-DSMs are entered into the MDM on the place of the original DSMs. This is only possible because the direct dependencies between elements of the same domain are not respected in this case. In cases of considering also direct dependencies, it is important to store the nd-DSMs in a separate matrix instead of overwriting the original DSMs (figure 3).

The multiplication of the blue (or marked) row with the blue (or marked) column results in the (pink) colored people-people-matrix. The department d_2 delivers three information (i_2, i_3, i_7) as an output while the department d_3 needs only two of them (i_2, i_7); besides three other information (i_1, i_4, i_6) as input. Hence, a dependency exists only if a certain piece of information (e.g. i_2) is generated by a department (e.g. d_2) and this one is required by another department (d_3). If the information (e.g. i_3) is not used (multiplication with zero), there is no dependency. The sum of the dependencies is corresponding to the number of information of which the departments or process steps are dependent. This allows giving a quantitative analysis about the strength of dependency, which is objective through the actual number of information (figure 3).

By considering the linkage of two different elements, both ways of dependencies with their weightings has to be considered in detail. As depicted in figure 3 at the bottom on the right (and schematically on the left), the element d_3 provides element d_2 four different pieces of information while d_2 only provides two pieces of information to d_3 (figure 3). This assumes the existence of different weighted dependencies. This weighted dependency based on the exchanged information can be expressed formally as follows: The element d_i of the domain d is dependent on the element d_j of the same domain based on x different pieces of information. So, the information-generating element has to be before the information-receiving element. Thus, a sequential analysis of the diverse functions within the process is possible and can be used for process improvements as well as serves as a basis for concurrent engineering.

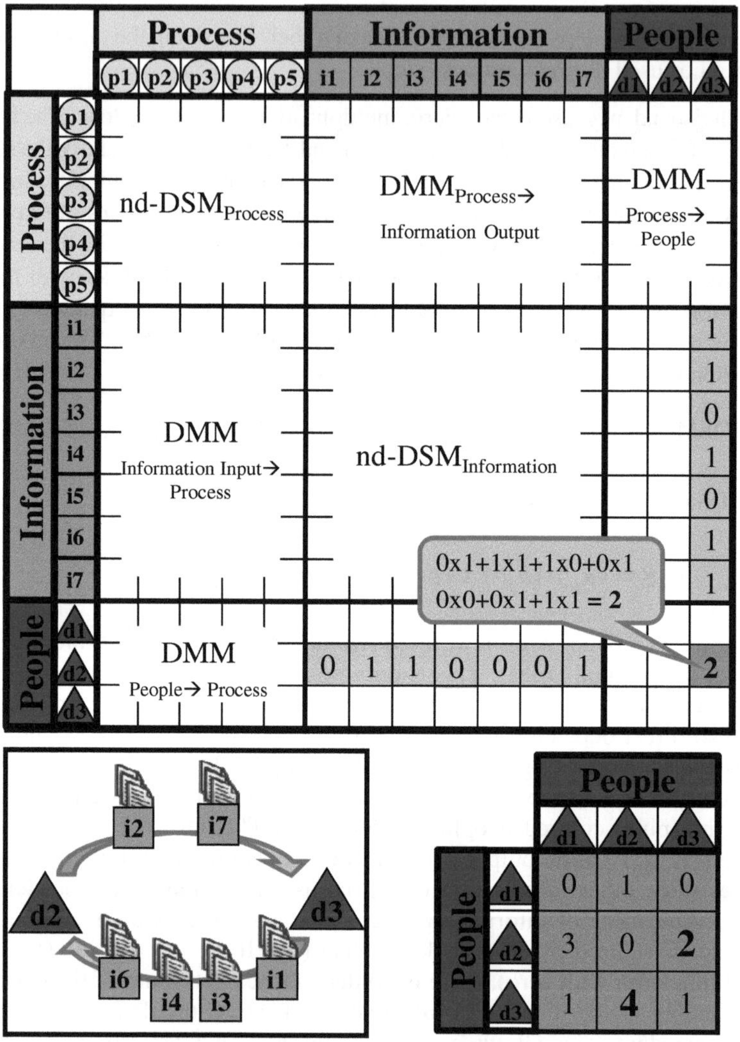

Fig. 3. The calculation of the nd-DSMPeople (simplified extract)

The analysis is done on a content level by looking on each individual KaI-object itself. Hereby, the knowledge about the process background is important in order to categorize the type of the different indirect dependencies. By considering both directions of a dependency, three different types of a mutual dependency are possible. These are summarized and elucidated briefly in figure 4.

Graphical representation	Type	Example
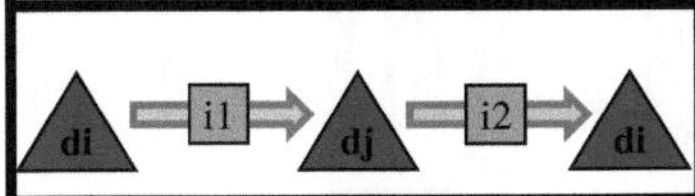	No mutual dependency on the same information.	Information i1 generated by di is needed by dj in order to generate information i2 which is needed by di.
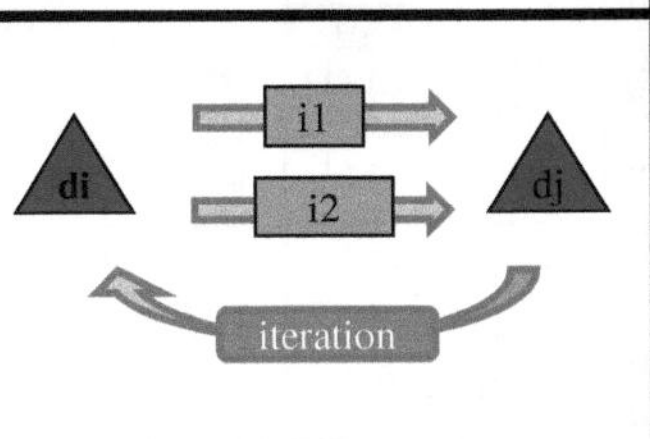	1) Negative iteration with rework due to wrong or missing information. 2) Positive iteration with a positive effect on the product development regarding the product's degree of maturity.	1) Information i1 coming from di to dj is not sufficient. A request is sent from dj to di regarding information i1. Di provides an improved or new information i2. 2) Information i1 coming from di is needed by dj. The information i1 is revised from dj due to e.g. new insights and sent back to di. Di provides an improved information i2 based on the revision by dj.
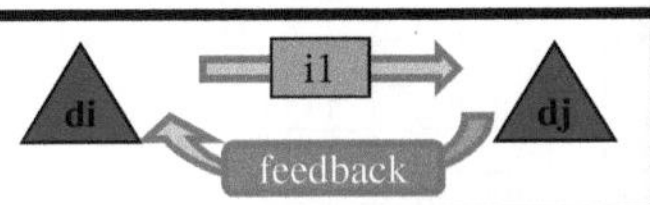	Feedback loop with no effect on the current development	Information i1 generated by di is needed by dj. Dj sends a feedback (e.g. that i1 is okay) back to di regarding information i1, which does not effect the current development.

Fig. 4. Types of mutual dependencies

Besides analyzing both directions of dependencies, this methodology allows also the quantification of the self-dependency of elements. This is possible with the nd-DSMs as shown in figure 3, but only one direction of dependency can be considered because the information generating elements is at the same time the information receiving element. The self-dependency is shown by a value equal or greater one in the diagonal of the nd-DSMs. The self-dependency should not be out of focus because it shows that lots of information is generated and used by the element itself. The MDM with its nd-DSMs as shown in figure 3 can be used for analyzing the pieces of information that are responsible for the self-dependency. The self-dependencies are an indicator whether internal structure of certain elements needs to be set-up (especially if the figure in the diagonal is high) or whether they have to be evaluated regarding their efficiency.

4 Case Study

This methodology has been evaluated through its application in an industrial case study (development of a repair method for a certain expendable part of a gas turbine). The development process was mapped by the EPC-methodic in several workshops. It consists of 56 different process steps, includes 155 KaI-objects and 15 units (departments), which are executing the process steps, are identified by the IFM.

Based on the IFM, the MDM (226 elements) with its respective DMMs are built up. For this manual transferring, two days were needed in this case. Hence, a macro for speeding up the set-up is recommended. The pieces of information causing the indirect dependencies were calculated by the mentioned equations. Using Matlab, the multiplication of the matrices takes only a few seconds. This results in the nd-DSMs which are showing the strength of the indirect and self-dependencies between the different process steps and the involved departments.

The nd-DSM_{People} of the industrial case study is illustrated in figure 5. The department d_{12}, for example, generates 38 pieces of information which are needed later in the process by the department itself. This reveals the demand for an identification and optimization of the internal information flow within this department.

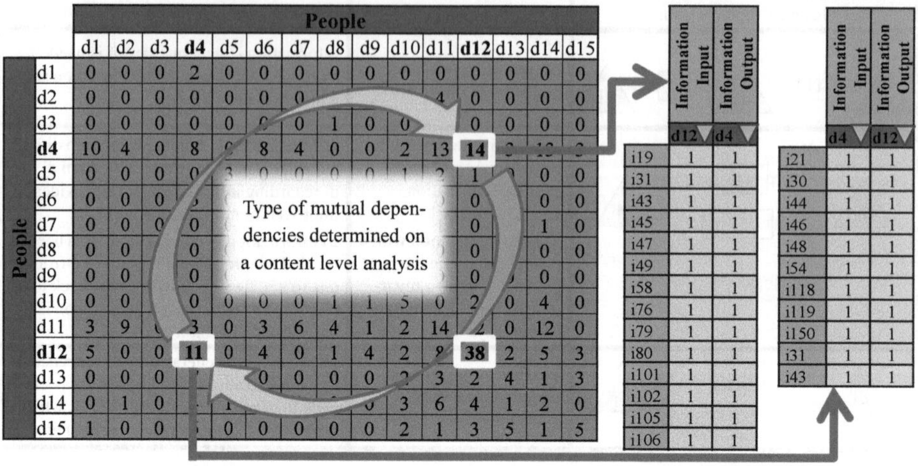

Fig. 5. The nd-DSM$_{People}$ together with the information dependency between d12 and d4

Besides this, the nd-DSM emphasizes the strength of the indirect dependencies by quantifying the pieces of information which cause the dependency. This quantitative information can be seen as advantage compared to the binary derived DSM proposed by Maurer [5]. High figures in the nd-DSM indicate elements being critical in product development. These have to be picked out for the content-level-analysis of the indirect dependencies by focusing on the KaI-objects itself [6].

In the shown industrial case, the information flow between the elements e.g. d_{12} and d_4 is of importance to understand their linkage. The department d_4 delivers fourteen pieces of information to d_{12} while eleven pieces of information are provided by d_{12} to d_4. To define the type of a mutual dependency between these elements, the content level of the pieces of information needs to be analyzed in detail. For this analysis, the two corresponding DMMs from the MDM, for example, $DMM_{Information \rightarrow People}$ and $DMM_{People \rightarrow Information}$, are used. The original, binary DMMs make it possible to use a filter for indicating whether a certain piece of information belongs to the element of interest. After transposing of the $DMM_{People \rightarrow Information}$, both DMMs are copied into a new sheet. So, the matrices have the elements of the domain people in columns and the information in rows. By selecting 'auto-filter', the two elements of interest are linked through one KaI-object. If the filter is set to '1' for d_4, only the KaI-objects are shown which are generated as an output by d_4. By setting the filter for d_{12} to '1', only the information gets visible that are generated as output by d_4 and used by d_{12} as input (as shown in figure 5 on the right). Afterwards, the type of mutual dependency can be determined by looking at the content level. The detailed knowledge about the KaI-objects causing the dependency enables enhancing the collaboration between the involved people since the information flow is the basis for cooperation.

5 Conclusion and Further Research

The proposed methodology allows identifying the pieces of information causing the indirect dependencies between two elements by quantifying it as a numerical value in the nd-DSMs what differs from existing approaches. One advantage is hereby that the analysis is narrowed down to the content level of the information. After identifying the case of mutual dependencies, this leads to an easier analyzing strategy and serves as a basis for improving the information flow between departments along the PDP. This allows developers to enhance the information exchange and to improve the coordination and collaboration in the PDP. The practical suitability of this approach was evaluated and successfully proven in an industrial case study.

The introduction of weighting factors might be of interest in order to differentiate between the importances of certain information. Furthermore, it would be also interesting to provide a guideline for classifying information in several levels to define different collaboration environments during the PDP because different people are interested in different information. This leads to further research topics.

Acknowledgment. Part of the work presented was supported by the German Research Foundation (DFG) within the research project "Product-oriented process management – iteration management based on a property-based product maturity".

References

1. Behncke, F., Gabriel, F., Langer, S., Heppler, C., Lindemann, U., Karl, F., Pohl, J., Schindler, S., Reinhart, G., Zaeh, M.: Analysis of information flows at interfaces between strategic product planning, product development and production planning to support process management. A literature based approach. In: Proceedings of the IEEE International Conference in Systems, Man and Cybernetics, Anchorage (2011)
2. Browning, T.R.: Applying the design structure matrix to system decomposition and integration problems. IEEE Transactions on Engineering Management 48, 292–306 (2001)
3. Browning, T.R., Eppinger, S.D.: Modeling Impacts of Process Architecture on Cost and Schedule Risk in Product Development. IEEE Transaction on Engineering Management 49, 428–442 (2002)
4. Eppinger, S.D., Browning, T.R.: Design Structure Matrix Methods and Applications. The MIT Press, Cambridge (2012)
5. Lindemann, U., Maurer, M., Braun, T.: Structural Complexity Management - An Approach for the Field of Product Design. Springer, Berlin (2009)
6. Luft, T., Wartzack, S.: Requirement analysis for contextual management and supply of process- and design knowledge – a case study. In: Proceedings of the 12th International Design Conference, Dubrovnik (2012)
7. Pimmler, T.U., Eppinger, S.D.: Integration Analysis of Product Decompositions. In: Proceedings of the ASME Design Theory and Methodology Conference, Minneapolis (1994)
8. Sandkuhl, K.: Improving Engineering Change Management with Information Demand Patterns. In: Proceedings of 8th International Conference on PLM, Eindhoven (2011)
9. Steward, D.V.: Design structure system: A method for managing the design of complex sytems. IEEE Transaction on Engineering Management 28, 71–74 (1981)

A Sustainability Lifecycle Assessment of Products and Services for the Extended Enterprise Evolution

Margherita Peruzzini, Michele Germani, and Eugenia Marilungo

Università Politecnica delle Marche, via Brecce Bianche 12, 60131 Ancona
{m.peruzzini,m.germani,e.marilungo}@univpm.it

Abstract. Recently numerous companies are moving from products to services to create new business opportunities and increase the value perceived by the customers thanks to an extended value creation network. The research challenge is to support traditional manufacturing enterprises evaluating the shift from products to services as far as sustainability is concerned. While product sustainability can be assessed by several tools, the impacts of PSS (Product-Service Systems) are almost unexplored. This paper adopts a holistic approach to assess sustainability by estimating three main impacts: environmental, economical and social. The methodology is illustrated by means of an industrial case study focusing on washing machines; it analyses the traditional scenario based on tangible product selling with a vertical supply-chain, and an innovative PSS scenario proposing washing as a service within an extended network. Data comparison highlights the achievable benefits of PSS on sustainability.

Keywords: Sustainability, Lifecycle Design, Extended Enterprise, PSS (Product-Service System).

1 Introduction

Numerous manufacturing enterprises are challenged by the transition from a traditional product-oriented model to a new extended service-oriented one, which can be realized by Product-Service Systems (PSS) [1]. This trend mainly consists of adding a wide range of services to increase the value perceived by the customers and better satisfy their needs. In manufacturing industry, PSS are almost realized by technical services (e.g. maintenance, user training, retrofitting and product monitoring, etc.). They usually imply high cost reduction, new market potentials and higher profit margins, and they can significantly influence performances and sustainability. In order to achieve these benefits with low impact, PSS require creating new relationships between different stakeholders to fully exploit the virtual enterprise capabilities. As a consequence, the interrelations between products and non-physical services are complex to model: different lifecycles must be adopted and properly indicators considered.

In this context, the research aims to support the extended enterprise in PSS ideation and design embracing sustainability principles. The paper proposes a methodology for a holistic assessment of both manufacturing product and technical services according

A. Bernard, L. Rivest, and D. Dutta (Eds.): PLM 2013, IFIP AICT 409, pp. 100–109, 2013.

to main sustainability factors. It combines LifeCycle Assessment (LCA), LifeCycle Costing (LCC) and Social LifeCycle Assessment (SLCA), and finally obtains a unique Sustainability Assessment value (SA). Such an analysis can be carried out until the preliminary design stages in order to envisage the environmental, economical and social impacts of different solutions; impacts can be analysed separately or in a global way. The method validity is demonstrated by an industrial case study focusing on washing machines, which compares the sustainability of traditional product (where washing machine is sold as usual) and PSS (where the user only pays for the washing cycles as a service).

2 Background on PSS and Sustainability Performance

Although the existing numerous definitions, it's possible to gather some common aspects of services [2]. A product-service consists of proposing a mix of tangible products and intangible services designed and combined to increase the value for customers [3]. Value creation can be provided through an extended business network involving different stakeholders, which concur to create the services. Product-service idea starts from the concept of extended product [4], where intangible services are incorporated into a core product to add value. In particular, Product+Service refers to a contemporary offer of product and services, while Product2Service refers to selling only the services. The term PSS usually includes the tangible product, the related services, the enterprise network and the infrastructures needed [5]. In manufacturing applications PSS are almost based on technical services [6]. Technical services are characterized by: supporting the product use, having a concurrent lifetime to the product to which they relate, and interacting with the customers. Technical services offer some advantages from manufacturers: low-cost, quick diversification, creation of wider market offer, shorter time-to-market, and higher sustainability [7].

Sustainability is nowadays accepted as a guiding principle for achieving highly competitive solutions and creating added value. Actually, the modern sustainability thinking considers three dimensions: environment, economy, and social wellbeing [8]. From the economical viewpoint, services can create new market potentials and higher profit margins, and can contribute to higher productivity by means of reduced investment costs along the lifetime as well as reduced operating costs for the final users [9]. From an ecological viewpoint, product-services can be more efficient thanks to a more conscious product usage, an increased resource productivity and a close loop-chain manufacturing as reported by some examples [9, 10]. Finally, PSS can be also socially advanced, as services are able to build up and secure knowledge intensive jobs and can contribute to a more geographically balanced wellbeing distribution [11]. However, the biggest challenge is carrying out a reliable sustainability assessment for PSS.

As far as product sustainability is concerned, it has been demonstrated that lifecycle approaches offer a structured methodology to proceed with comparative analysis [12]. LifeCycle Assessment (LCA) and LifeCycle Costing (LCC) enable the achievement of eco-efficiency solutions [10, 13], while SLCA can estimate the social impact in terms of Quality Adjusted Life Years [14, 15]. Nevertheless they are generally applied to physical products.

About service analysis, several methods have been recently proposed to manage PSS (from modularization-focused approach, to stochastic and behaviour-focused approach, until lifecycle-focused methods) [16]. However, some of them are very theoretical and hard to implement in practice, while others are too specific and have a limited applicability. None of them provide a concrete sustainability evaluation to be applied in manufacturing cases on both PSS and traditional products.

3 Methodology for an Integrated Sustainability Assessment

The proposed methodology is based on lifecycle modelling and analysis to measure environmental, economical and social impacts, and finally perform a global Sustainability Assessment (SA) by coupling separated analysis. Such an approach has three main advantages: it well address technical services as it exploits the lifecycle approach; it can be adopted until the preliminary design stages to support decision-making and objectively compare and validate the technicians' choices; and it can be easily applied to both product and services to compare alternative scenarios, evaluating the consumed resources and choosing the solution with the lower impact. Furthermore, it adopts the basic concepts of the benchmarking methods: defining reliable metrics to assess and compare different design solutions. Such an approach has been already used for other purposes [17-18], but not for product-services.

The method steps are:

Step 1. Lifecycle modelling: it is based on a detailed functional analysis and the assessment of all the systems/subsystems at different lifecycle stages. Modelling comprehends the core product, the technological infrastructure and the services. Products are modelled according to LifeCycle Design (LCD) approaches, so the main stages are: ideation, design, manufacturing, use, and end-of-life. Services modelling follows the ISO 15704 (2000) suggestions and considers the following main stages: ideation, design, implementation, operation and final disposal;

Step 2. Use scenario definition: it consists of identifying the user profiles, describing the users' behaviours and defining the lifetime to be considered;

Step 3. Lifecycle analysis: each system is analysed separately by LCA, LCC and SLCA to find out the separated impacts. Analyses are fully consistent as they share the same product/service model, but each of them focuses on different aspects: LCA on environmental resources and ecosystem, LCC on total costs by considering the company, the consumer and the dismissing consortium viewpoints, and SLCA on human resources and human health. Step 3 is described in more details in section 3.1;

Step 4. Global sustainability assessment (SA): for each analysed scenario, the three calculated indexes are normalized and then summed to obtain a unique assessing value SA:

$$LCA + LCC + SLCA = SA \tag{1}$$

Step 4 is fully explained in section 3.2.

The proposed methodology is schematized in Figure 1. Product and PSS analyses run in parallel and converge in some points. Sustainability assessment focuses only on the operative phases; indeed, the impacts of ideation and design stages is limited and they are similar for product and PSS, so they can be neglected. The method procedure is pragmatic and can be straightforwardly carried out in different manufacturing contexts, since data can be easily inferred investigating product/service BOM (Bill Of Material), production documents, use data and disposal practices. Such method extends a recent work about PSS where the analysis lacked of normalization [10]. It can be also implemented by a collaborative platform supporting an extended enterprise [19] to evolve the network from product to services.

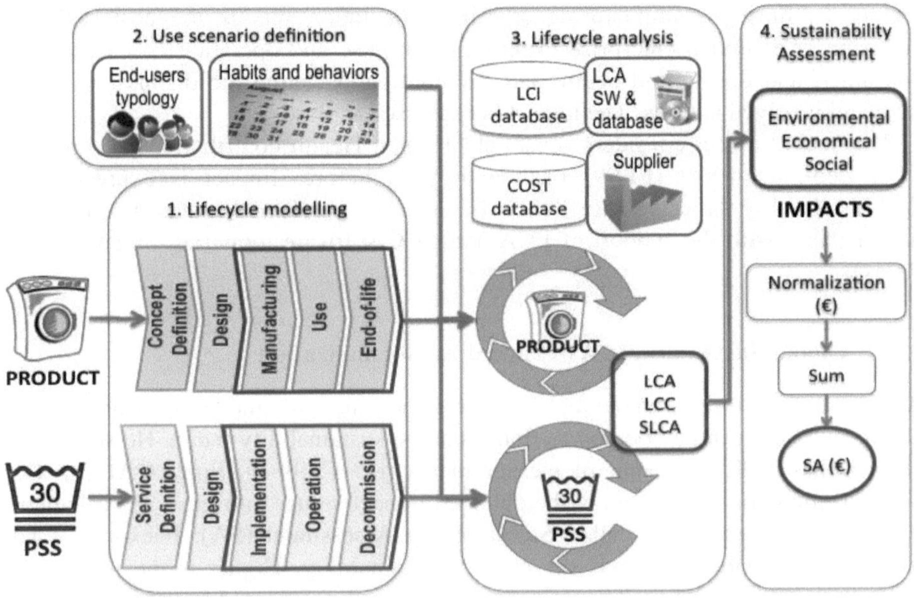

Fig. 1. Methodology for Product and PSS sustainability assessment

3.1 Lifecycle Analysis and Sustainability Impacts

The lifecycle analysis considers all significant data referring to the analysed phases for product (Manufacturing, Use, End-of-life) and service (Implementation, Operation, Decommission). The analysis follows LCA approach [13]. Firstly, all data about raw materials extraction, processing, assembling and transportation as well as the use and operational data and the end-of-life information need to be collected according to the functional model of each specific case. Then, the impacts are estimated for each lifecycle phase and a global value is defined. Such an approach allows comparing different alternative cases by considering the global impact; the comparison can be also focused on a specific identified phase.

The environmental impact is calculated by LCA Eco-Indicator99 (EI-99) methodology [20], considering Ecosystem Quality impact and Resources consumption. The <unit of measurement is EI-99 point (Pt).

The economical evaluation considers the same functional model and adopts the Equivalent Annual Cash Flow technique (EA) to transform a generic cash flow distribution into an equivalent annual distribution by cost actualization according to (1):

$$EA = P\frac{(i+1)^n * i}{(i+1)^n - 1} \quad (2)$$

where *n* is the lifetime years' number, *i* is the generic discount rate (for example *3%*), and *P* is the value during the all lifetime. The obtained cost impact considers all system costs: during manufacturing and implementation phases the costs relate to company or extended enterprise expense, during use and operation cost refer to the consumer, and during end-of-life and decommission charge the dismissing consortium and involved entities. The impact is expressed in Euro.

The social impact considers separately Human Health contributions according to LCA Eco-Indicator99 (EI-99) methodology as before. Impact is expressed into QALYs (Quality Adjusted Life Years). Such values can be calculated by creating ad hoc analyses with the support of LCA and LCC software tools (i.e. SimaPro, Gabi, Relex).

3.2 Global Sustainability Assessment by Normalization

All the three analyses are coherent with the same functional model; it assures that the obtained results can be coupled to find a unique sustainability index. However, each analysis has a different unit of measurements (i.e. EI-99 Pt, Euro, QALYs). Data normalization allows translating the obtained impact values into Euro and calculating a unique monetary value called Sustainability Assessment (SA). It expresses how each analysed solution affects the overall sustainability. Higher is the impact, and lower is the sustainability. The normalization procedure adopted in the proposed method is described in Table 1. The adopted formulas are based on European average data for having a consistent redefinition.

Table 1. Normalization procedure

IMPACT CATEGORY	Original meas. unit	Normalization formulas	Normalized meas. unit
Environmental Impact	EI-99 Pt	Pt -> PDFm2yr -> $(PDFm2yr) * 1{,}4 = Euro$ Pt -> MJ -> $MJ * \frac{0{,}00411}{lifetime} = Euro$	Euro
Economical Impact	Euro	-	Euro
Social Impact	QALY	$1\ QALYs * 74.000 = Euro$	Euro

PDFm2yr = Potentially Disappeared Fraction of species per square meter per year, MJ = Mega Joule, QALYs = Quality Adjusted Life Years

4 Industrial Case Study: Washing as a Service

4.1 Product and PSS Case Studies

The case study has been realized in collaboration with an Italian company producing household appliances and home care device. The company is actually organized in a vertical supply-chain and adopts a product-oriented development process. Collaboration with partners and suppliers is limited to design innovation and reduction of production time and cost. The case study focuses on washing machine product (WM) and its evolution towards the creating of a new PSS to better satisfy the market needs.

The product case study considers the tangible good as an assembly of numerous components, which enables washing clothes. The consumer pays the product at the beginning (about 460,00 €) and than pays for the consumed resources (clean water, electric energy and detergents) according to a traditional model. The PSS case study refers to selling a Product2Service solution where the customer pays only for the service while the WM is given for free. The user pays a service rate consisting of two parts: a "payXuse" fee at each washing cycle effectively done (0,45 €/cycle) and a discounted rate for the consumed resources (water and energy) fixed in collaboration with the energy suppliers. Compared to the traditional case, the product is enhanced with some additional components able to connect the WM to Internet and allow remote monitoring. Furthermore, the ecosystem is more complex as it is made up of multiple partners: the producer company, the energy supplier, the water supplier, a service provider who is responsible for service activation and delivery, and some local technical partners, which deliver the WM at home and control its status.

4.2 User Profile and Use Scenarios

For both Product and PSS cases, three scenarios are investigated. They consider the most representative European lifestyle according to a recent market analysis carried out by the producer company's marketing department. The identified user profiles are:

- *House Manager* (HM): it is an expert user, generally a woman, spending a lot of time at home (e.g. housewife or retired), who takes care house management and family issues in a special way. HM is characterized by a medium number of cycle per week (4,3 cycles/week) with optimized loading;
- *Efficiency Seeker* (ES): it is a user, generally a senior man or a young woman, with an active social life and an efficient, fast and pragmatic house management. ES is characterized by an high number of cycle per week (5,8 cycles/week) with low loading;
- *Delegator* (D): it is a young user, girl or boy, who pays a limited attention to the house care in general due to an intense workload or other causes. D is characterized by a limited number of cycles per week (3,9 cycles/week) with medium/high loading.

The use scenarios considers the three user profiles according to the average number of cycle per week and a variable lifetime that varies from 1 to 10 years, for both product and PSS.

4.3 Product and PSS Sustainability Assessment

The proposed method (see Fig. 1) is applied to compare the different use scenarios for both product and PSS designed solutions.

As far as traditional product is concerned, the *Manufacturing phase analysis* considers all the components used for production and assembly, and data are organized according to the main product functional entities (e.g. oscillating group, balancing and suspensions, electrical components, hydraulics, aesthetics, cabinet). A 5% cut-off is applied to neglect those parts that have a limited impact. The *Use phase analysis* considers the habits of the investigated user profiles (HM, ES, D) during the lifetime (1-10 years). As suggested by real data monitoring and statistical data from the producer company's technical departments, a realistic decrease of the washing machine performance corresponding to efficiency losses is estimated. Performance decrease is expressed by a cut percentage according to the number of the executed cycles (5% reduction after 500 cycles, 10% reduction after 1000 cycles, 20% reduction over 2000 cycles). Costs are generated by resource consumptions and are considered with the relative prices: electric energy (0,2 €/kWh), water (0,0011 €/lt), detergents (2,5 €/lt), softener (1,4 €/lt), calcium remover (0,33 €/cycle). In the *End-of-Life phase analysis*, LCA follows European Directive on Electric Equipment Waste (WEEE) for managing the product components, which indicate the percentage for recycling (55 %), reuse (10 %) and landfill (35 %).

As far as the PSS assessment is concerned, the *Implementation phase analysis* considers product as well as the product analysis, but comprehends also the additional components and the system infrastructure. The approach is similar to the product scenario. Furthermore, a new cost item is represented by the "*service expense*", which considers the call-centre services, the personnel employed there and the wiring network. The *Operation phase analysis* considers higher performances due to a continuous control of the machine status and real-time monitoring and assistance (i.e. PSS machine is monitored and parts can be substituted in advance to guarantee a high quality performance for the entire lifetime). The *Decommission phase analysis* differs from product because the manufacturer directly manages product disposal and the extended enterprise manages the service decommission. Data about percentage of recycling, reuse and landfill are taken from the producer company and the dismantling consortium.

4.4 Results and Comparative Analysis

Table 2 shows the obtained results for both product and PSS, focusing on a 10-year lifetime. It contains the values derived from the separated analysis as well as the global Sustainability Assessment (SA), which is calculated after normalization. For each user profile, SA expresses the total impact as it sums all the contributions. It is worth to notice that, for a period of 10 years, PSS is more convenient for any user profile, regardless to the user habits. Furthermore, data can be investigated also over the years to better understand whether and how PSS advantages evolve during the lifetime.

Table 2. Lifecycle analysis results (LCA + LCC + SLCA)

	PRODUCT			PSS		
10-years lifetime	**HM**	**ES**	**D**	**HM**	**ES**	**D**
Env. Impact (Pt)	6,00E+02	7,72E+02	6,44E+02	4,57E+02	6,08E+02	5,02E+02
Eco. Impact (€)	€ 5.994,32	€ 6.688,50	€ 6.071,67	€ 4.544,01	€ 5.577,53	€ 4.513,08
Soc. Impact (QALY)	1,00E-02	1,29E-02	1,05E-02	6,64E-03	9,14E-03	7,09E-03
GLOBAL SA (€)	**€ 6.849,99**	**€ 7.772,95**	**€ 6.955,65**	**€ 5.118,80**	**€ 6.355,90**	**€ 5.120,02**

Figure 2 shows the SA trend over the years in respect with the user classes: the product impact is constantly higher, but ES users are more charged. Services have always less impact, even if the advantages are greater along in years. Moreover, PSS is particularly good for HM and D users, especially after 5 years. Interesting analyses can be also carried out about some specific aspects: indexes can be separately mapped over the years to compare product and PSS relatively to one specific contribution.

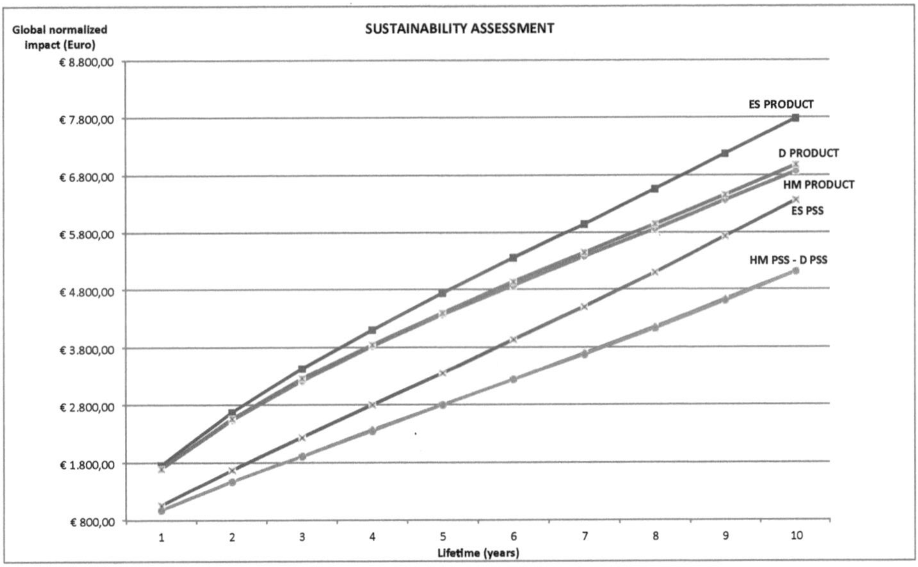

Fig. 2. Global Sustainability assessment over the years (normalized value)

Finally, figure 3 shows the cost analysis along 10-years lifetime, considering both the company expenses and the consumer rates. Company costs are lower than the consumer ones and slightly in growth in both cases; finally, PSS is marginally more expensive. Contrariwise, the consumer perspective is very interesting: washing as a service is always cheaper than traditional product and the benefits for consumers are greater and steady in growth over the years.

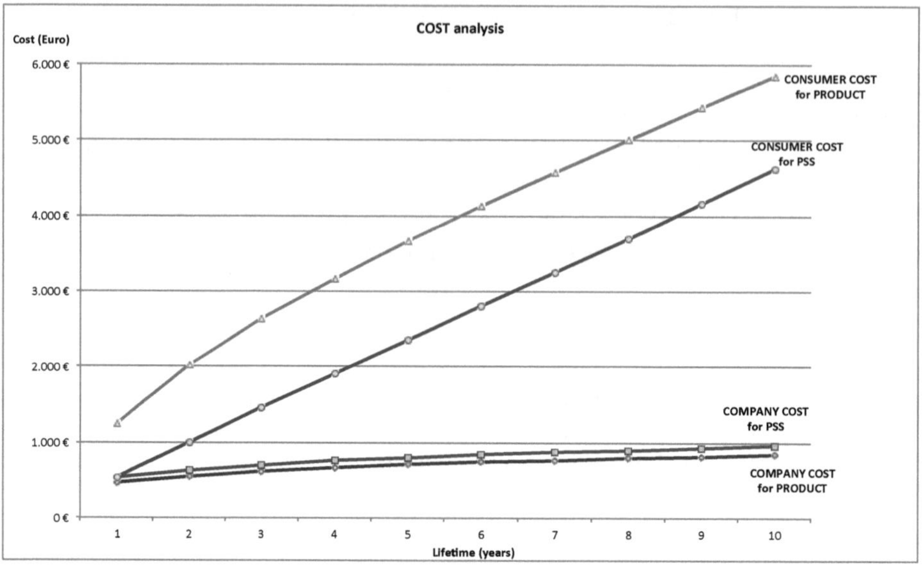

Fig. 3. Comparative cost analysis (company cost and consumer expense during the lifetime)

5 Conclusions

The paper proposes a methodology to assess PSS sustainability and compare with traditional product solutions. The method validity is demonstrated by an experimental case study focusing on washing as a service and exploring the benefits in respect with the traditional product. Both scenarios are modelled according to lifecycle design approaches and investigated in terms of environmental, economic and social impacts. Experimentation demonstrates the reliability of such a method to easily assess sustainability of both products and services and compare different organizational assets. The paper extends the latest research in product-service and proposes a concrete application of a sustainability assessment method to support decision-making during the design or optimization phases within the extended enterprise.

References

1. Goedkoop, M.J., Van Halen, C.J.G., Riele, H.R.M., Rommens, P.J.M.: Product-Service Systems – Ecological and Economic Basic. PWC, The Hague (1999)
2. Balin, S., Giard, V.: A process oriented approach to service concepts. In: 8ème Conférence Internationale de Génie Industriel, Tarbes, France (2009)
3. Furrer, O.: Le rôle stratégique des "services autour des produits". Revue Française de Gestion (113), 98–108 (2007)
4. Thoben, K.D., Jagdev, H., Eschenbaecher, J.: Extended Products: Evolving Traditional Product Concepts. In: Proc. 7th International Conference on Concurrent Enterprising, Bremen (2001)

5. SUSPRONET final report: `http://www.suspronet.org/`
6. Mont, O.K.: Clarifying the concept of Product-Service System. Journal of Cleaner Production 10(3), 237–245 (2002)
7. Aurich, J.C., Fuchs, C., Wagenknecht, C.: Life Cycle oriented design of technical Product-Service Systems. Journal of Cleaner Production 14, 1480–1494 (2006)
8. Adams, W.M.: The Future of Sustainability: Re-thinking Environment and Development in the Twenty-first Century. Report of the IUCN Renowned Thinkers Meeting (2006)
9. Baines, T.S., Lightfoot, H., Evans, S., Neely, A., Greenough, R., Peppard, J., Roy, R., Shehab, E., Braganza, A., Tiwari, A., Alcock, J.R., Angus, J.P., Bastl, M., Cousens, A., Irving, P., Johnson, M., Kingston, J., Lockett, H., Martinez, V., Michele, P., Tranfield, D., Walton, I.M., Wilson, H.: State of the art in Product-Service System. Journal of Engineering Manufacture 221, 1543–1552 (2007)
10. Favi, C., Peruzzini, M., Germani, M.: A lifecycle design approach to analyse the eco-sustainability of industrial products and product-service systems. In: Marjanovic, Storga, Pavkovic, Bojcetic (eds.) Proc. of International Design Conference DESIGN 2012, pp. 879–888 (2012)
11. Stahel, W.: The Utilization-Focused Service Economy, Resource Efficiency and Product-Life Extension. In: Allenby, B., Richard, D. (eds.) The Greening of Industrial Ecosystem, pp. 178–190. National Academy Press, Washington, DC (1994)
12. Jeswiet, J.: A definition for life cycle engineering. In: Proc. 36th International Seminar on Manufacturing Systems, Saarbrucken, Germany (2003)
13. ISO 14040, Environmental Management - Life Cycle Assessment - Principles and Framework (2006), ISO 14044, Environmental Management - Life Cycle Assessment - Requirements and Guidelines (2006)
14. Weidema, B.: The integration of economic and social aspects in life cycle impact assessment. Int. J. Life Cycle Assess. 11(1), 89–96 (2006)
15. Norris, G.A.: Integrating Life Cycle Cost Analysis and LCA. Int. J. LCA Assess. 6(2), 118–120 (2001)
16. Garetti, M., Rosa, P., Terzi, S.: Life Cycle Simulation for the design of Product–Service Systems. Computers in Industry 63, 361–369 (2012)
17. Germani, M., Mengoni, M., Peruzzini, M.: Metrics-based Approach for VR Technology Evaluation in Styling Product Design. In: ASME 2009 International Design Engineering Technical Conferences & Computers and Information in Engineering Conference, DETC/CIE (2009)
18. Germani, M., Mengoni, M., Peruzzini, M.: A benchmarking method to investigate co-design virtual environments for enhancing industrial collaboration. In: ASME World Conference on Innovative VR 2010 (2010)
19. Germani, M., Mandolini, M., Mengoni, M., Peruzzini, M.: Collaborative design system for supporting dynamic virtual enterprises. In: Camarinha-Matos, L.M., Boucher, X., Afsarmanesh, H. (eds.) PRO-VE 2010. IFIP AICT, vol. 336, pp. 577–584. Springer, Heidelberg (2010)
20. Goedkoop, M., Effting, S., Collignon, M.: The Eco-indicator 99 – A damage oriented method for Life Cycle Impact Assessment. Manual for Designers, 2nd edn. (2000)

Knowledge Management for Complex Product Development

Framework and Implementation

Alexander Smirnov[1], Alexey Kashevnik[1], Nikolay Teslya[1], Nikolay Shilov[1], Andreas Oroszi[2], Mario Sinko[2], Michael Humpf[2], and Jens Arneving[2]

[1] St.Petersburg Institute for Informatics and Automaton of the Russian Academy of Sciences (SPIIRAS)
39, 14 line, 199178, St.Petersburg, Russia
{smir,alexey,teslya,nick}@iias.spb.su
[2] Festo AG & Co. KG,
Plieninger Straße 50, Ostfildern-Scharnhausen, 73760, Germany
{oro,sni,hump,arv}@de.festo.com

Abstract. Complex product development process in global companies usually consists of several stages involving different software systems and numerous users from various departments and centers. Automation of this process assumes changes in company's workflows, data models and software systems used. As a result, implementation of such changes in large companies faces a lot of difficulties because business process cannot be stopped to switch between old and new workflows, old and new software systems, etc. The paper represents an ongoing long-term project aimed at knowledge management for multi-level complex product development at Festo AG&Co KG. It is based on the central product ontology describing product classification, their properties and configuration & compatibility restrictions. The developed system complex significantly simplifies and speeds up the process of product development and maintenance.

Keywords: product knowledge management, product design, complex product configuration.

1 Introduction

Current trends in the worldwide economy and increasing competition require companies to propose not only new products but whole integrated solutions to their customers. Such solutions might consist of multiple physical devices as well as services. One of the consequences of this is appearance of "complex products", which consist of other products (both regular products and complex products) and often include software units using different services.

Another strategy that brings companies and their customers in a closer collaboration is innovation democratisation. This is a relatively new term standing for involvement of customers into the process of designing and creating new products

A. Bernard, L. Rivest, and D. Dutta (Eds.): PLM 2013, IFIP AICT 409, pp. 110–119, 2013.

and services. This makes it possible for companies to better meet needs of their customers. (Hippel, 2006)

Modularisation is one of the keys to carry out mass customisation and innovation democratization strategies with low cost (Egan, 2004; Sharda and Voß, 2005). Module is a result of disassembling functions and architecture of the product. It can provide the end-products in wider scope while decreasing diversification in product components.

In this situation the previously developed PLM mechanisms and workflows supporting products from the design phase to putting them to the market and further has appeared to be inefficient. As a result, there was a need to design new, knowledge-based workflows and supporting software systems to increase efficiency of designing and maintaining new product ranges. Knowledge-based PLM is currently a critical and strategic issue (Bernard and Tichkievitch, 2008) and the company recognizes this (e.g., Smirnov and Shilov, 2011).

However, implementation of such changes in large companies faces many difficulties because business process cannot be stopped to switch between old and new workflows, old and new software systems have to be supported at the same time, the range of products, which are already in the markets, has to be maintained in parallel with new products, etc. Another problem is that it is difficult to estimate in advance which solutions and workflow would be efficient and convenient for the employees. Hence, just following existing PLM implementation guidelines is not possible (also confirmed by Bokinge and Malmqvist, 2012), and this process has to be and iterative and interactive.

The paper represents an ongoing long-term project aimed at knowledge management for multi-level complex product development at Festo AG&Co KG company that has more than 300 000 customers in 176 countries supported by more than 52 companies worldwide with more than 250 branch offices and authorized agencies in further 36 countries.

Fig. 1 represents the developed multi-level knowledge management concept for complex product development, which is the core of the described project. The black rectangles have been already implemented and the appropriate tools are indicated (grey areas).

The major product ontology is in the center of the model. It is used to solve the problem of knowledge heterogeneity and enables interoperability between heterogeneous information sources due to provision of their common semantics and terminology (Uschold and Grüninger, 1996). It describes all the products (produced and to be produced) and their features (existing and possible). This ontology is supported by two tools addressed in sec. 2: NOC (New Order Code) and CONCode ("old code", CON is a prefix based on the reverse acronym of New Order Code). Building a knowledge map that connects this ontology to different knowledge sources of the company is yet to be addressed.

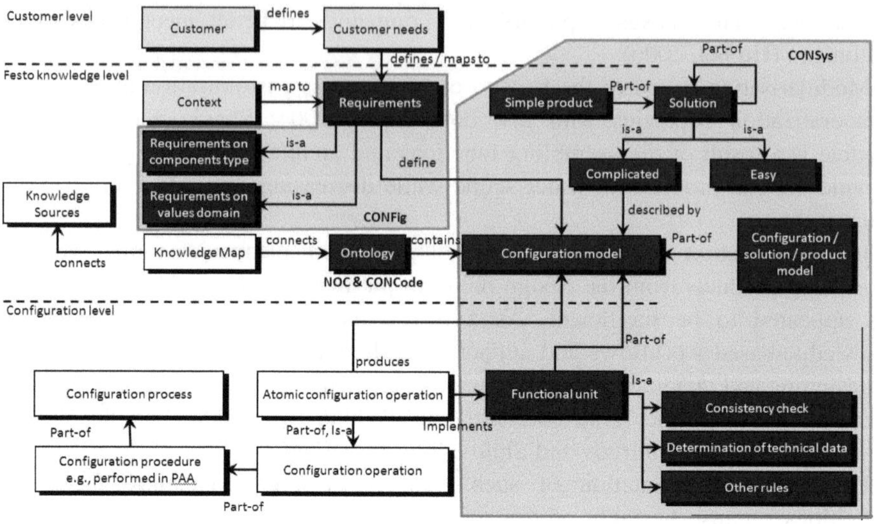

Fig. 1. Multi-level knowledge management for complex product development

The configuration level has also been addressed only partially so far. The tool called CONSys (SYStems of products) supports creation of configuration models of complex products and solutions (sec. 3). Configuration models include their structures as well as different rules responsible for complex product consistency checks, technical data calculation, etc. The support of the configuration process design (the left lower part of the figure) has not been implemented yet.

Based on the built configuration model the process of complex product or solution configuration in accordance with given requirements can be automated. This is done via the tool called CONFig (CONFIGuration) addressed in sec. 4. So far this tool supports the configuration process in terms used within the company (Festo knowledge level). In reality, the customers are used to operate different terminology (Customer level), which doesn't correspond "one to one" to that used within the company. Besides, customers from different industries can also operate different terms. As a result, there is a need to create configuration tools that can map customers' requirements to those used in the company taking into account the context (customer's industry segment, history of customer's orders, etc.). This is the goal of the future research.

2 Product Ontology

The developed approach is based on the idea that knowledge can be represented by two levels. The first level describes the structure of knowledge. Knowledge represented by the second level is an instantiation of the first level knowledge; this knowledge holds object instances.

The knowledge of the first level (structural knowledge) is described by a common ontology of the company's product families (classes). Ontologies provide a common way of knowledge representation for its further processing. They have shown their usability for this type of tasks (e.g., Bradfield et al., 2007; Chan and Yu, 2007; Patil et al., 2005)

The first step to implementation of the approach is creation of the ontology. This operation was done automatically based on existing documents and defined rules of the model building. The resulting ontology consists of more than 1000 classes organized into a 4 level taxonomy, which is based on the VDMA classification (Verband Deutscher Maschinen- und Anlagenbau, German Engineering Federation, VDMA, 2013). Taxonomical relationships support inheritance that makes it possible to define more common attributes for higher level classes and inherit them for lower level subclasses. The same taxonomy is used in the company's PDM and ERP systems.

For each product family (class) a set of properties (attributes) is defined, and for each property its possible values and their codes are defined as well. The lexicon of properties is ontology-wide, and as a result the values can be reused for different families. Application of the common single ontology provides for the consistency of the product codes and makes it possible to reflect incorporated changes in the codes instantly.

The ontology is multilingual. Each class and attribute can be assigned names in different languages so that specialists from different countries could work simultaneously preserving consistency of the ontology.

The selectable properties can be communicated to the customers with so called configuration solutions or product selectors. These tools can be used in electronic catalogues and online shop systems. As a result, a new product codification scheme based on product families and characteristics has been developed (Oroszi et al., 2009). For companies with wide assortments of products (more than 30 000 – 40 000 products of approx. 700 types, with various configuration possibilities) it is very important to ensure that customers can easily navigate among them. This is an important task for customer communication management because well defined and understandable product identification is mandatory for ensuring good corporate look for the company (Baumeister, 2002; Fjermestad and Romano, 2002; Piller and Schaller, 2002). The system should be organised in such a way that would ensure the uniqueness of the code and its validity. The resulting code is supplied into the company's PDM and ERP system.

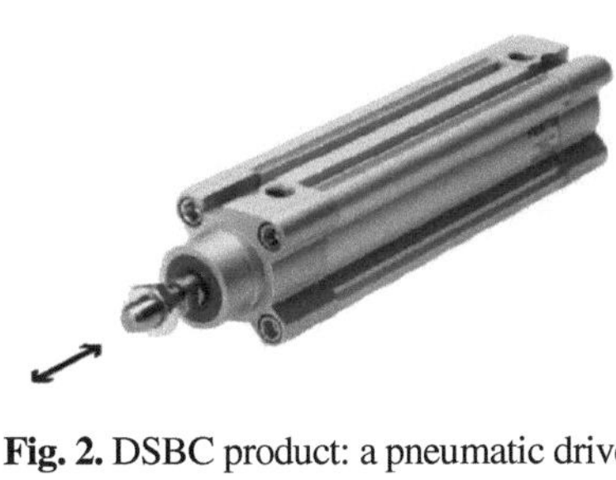

Fig. 2. DSBC product: a pneumatic drive

The described above ontology provides rules for the codification system in the following way. For each class a number of attributes is assigned in a certain sequence. This sequence of attributes forms a template for codes of products belonging to the appropriate product family. For each product the properties are replaced with codes of their values corresponding to the particular product to generate its code.

For example, the DSBC series is a family of pneumatic drives with a single moving rod (Fig. 2). There are 35 different properties with each between 4 to 10 values. Customer and engineers can select from these properties and values. Some combinations of different properties and values are not allowed because they are technically impossible.

Typical properties of the DSBC series are "locking in end positions" and "special antifriction features". Their possible values are presented in Table 1.

Given code template consisting of a delimiter and the above two properties, the following codes can be built:

- Standard (no locking, no antifriction features): DSBC
- "Extend / retract" (locking in both directions) and no antifriction features: DSBC-E1
- "Extend / retract" and "Low friction": DSBC-E1L

Fig. 3 represents a fragment of the real code scheme for the DSBC series. Inheritance of more common properties from higher, more abstract classes ensures that for different branches of the classification the sequence of common properties will be the same that simplifies the code interpretation.

After finding the desired product based on its properties, the set of selected properties is translated into a product code based on the existing code scheme of its class (product type). After transmitting the product code to the company, the customer receives an order confirmation listing selected product properties. The confirmation is generated with the company's ERP system, which uses code schemes to translate product codes into the properties of product.

Table 1. Compatibility table

Value Code	Value Name	Description
Locking in end positions		
	Without (Standard)	the most common choice, no locking in end positions
E1	Extend / Retract	locking is applied in both directions of movement
E2	Extend	locking is applied in the direction of extension
E3	Retract	locking is applied in the direction of retraction
Special antifriction features		
	None / Normal type	the most common choice, no special antifriction features
L	Low friction	product with reduced friction
S	Slow speed	product oriented to slow movement

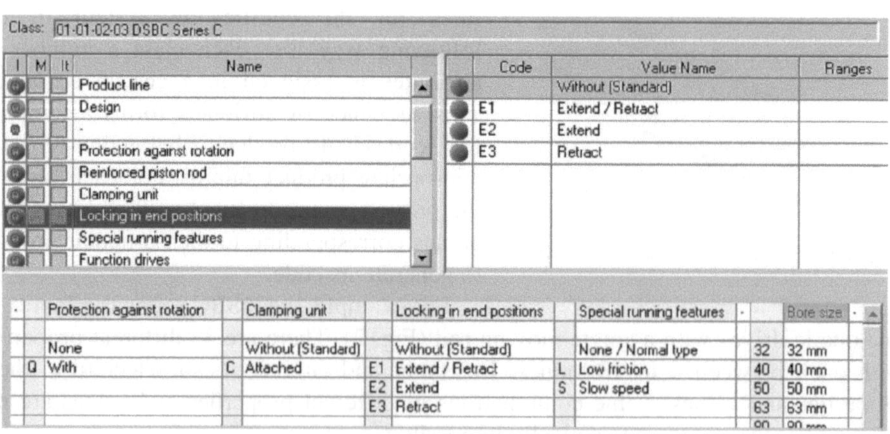

Fig. 3. Code scheme for the DSBC series (a fragment)

3 Complex Product Configuration Rules

As it was already mentioned, today, the customers tend to buy complete customized solutions (referred to as "complex products") consisting of numerous products, rather than separate products. Before, the complex products were configured by experts based on the customer requirements. Today, this process requires automation. However, inter-product relationships are very challenging. For example, the most common use case is the relationship between a main product and an accessory product. While both products are derived from different complex products there are dependencies which assign a correct accessory to a configured main product. The dependencies are related to the products' individual properties and values. E.g., "1x3/2 or 2x3/2-way valve" cannot be installed on a valve terminal if its size is "Size 10, deviating flow rate 1". The depth of product-accessory relationships is not limited, so accessory-of-accessory combinations have also to be taken into account. The relationships can be very complex when it comes to define the actual location and orientation of interfaces and mounting points between products.

Complex product description consists of two major parts: product components and rules. Complex product components can be the following: simple products, other complex products, and application data. The set of characteristics of the complex product is a union of characteristics of its components. The rules of the complex products are union of the rules of its components plus extra rules. Application data is an auxiliary component, which is used for introduction of some additional characteristics and requirements to the product (for example, operating temperatures, certification, electrical connection, etc.). They affect availability and compatibility of certain components and features via defined rules.

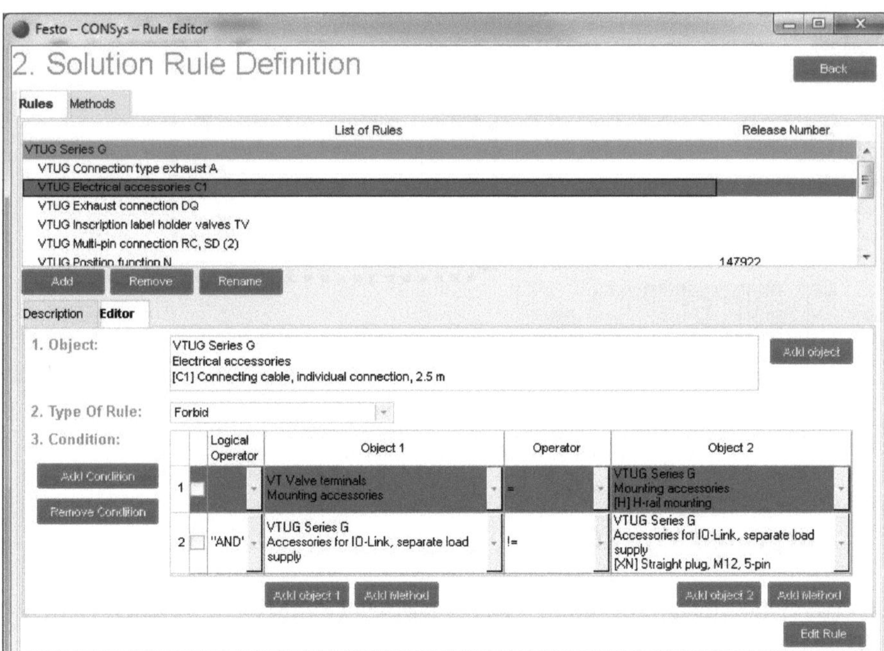

Fig. 4. Solution rules example

Some example rules are shown in Fig. 4. The figure represents a valve terminal (VTUG) and compatibility of electrical accessories option C1 (individual connecting cable) with mounting accessories (compatible only with H-rail mounting) and accessories for input-output link (not compatible with 5 pin straight plug M12). These rules are stored in the database and can be later used during configuration of the valve terminal for certain requirements.

4 Product Configuration

When the configuration model is finished it is proposed to the customers so that they could configure required products and solutions themselves or with assistance of product managers.

An example configuration interface is presented in Fig. 5. The figure represents the mentioned above valve terminal VTUG with an electrical control module CTEU. The user can choose values (from drop down lists, outlined in Fig. 5 with bold dotted line) for different properties (rows in the table). Depending on the choices other properties either selected automatically, disabled or become hidden. This is done on the basis of the rules described during the complex product definition. The rules are processed "on the fly", i.e. as soon as the user chooses a value, all other values are checked for consistency immediately.

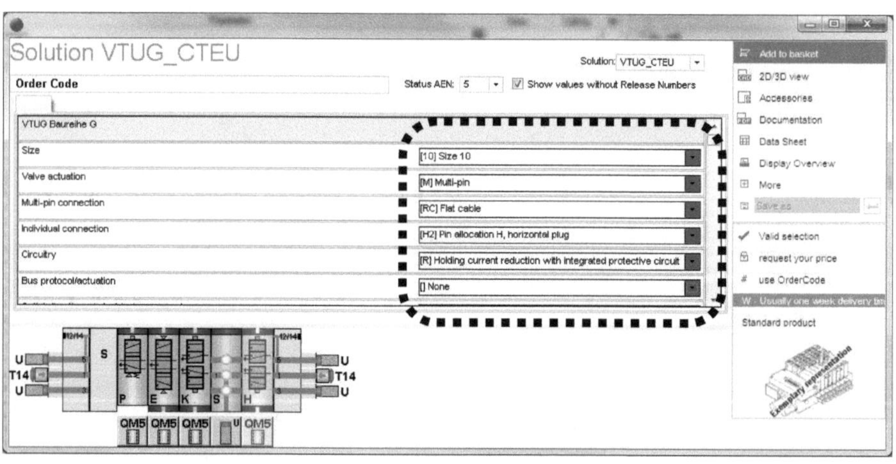

Fig. 5. Product configuration interface: an example

5 Integrated Workflow

So far developed integrated knowledge management workflow is presented in Fig. 6. At the first stage the major product ontology is filled with generic classifications of products and their components. This is done via two tools (NOC and CONCode) since recently developed order code scheme differs from that used before. However, since multiple customers are used to operate with the old classification it has to be maintained.

At the next stage the product managers and modelers design new products and solutions based on existing products and components (the CONSys tool). If a new product or component is needed, its implementation can be requested from the order code structure team. Together with new products and solutions, the appropriate rules and conditions are designed as well (e.g., acceptable load, size, compatibility constraints, etc.).

When the configuration model is finished it is proposed to the customers so that they could configure required products and solutions themselves or with assistance of product managers (the CONFig tool).

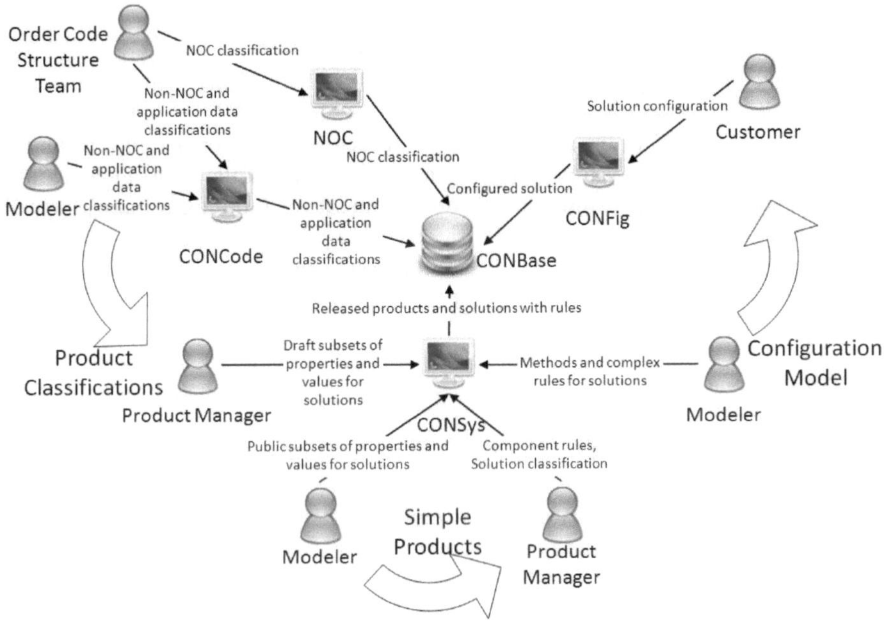

Fig. 6. Integrated workflow

6 Conclusion

The paper presents a long-term ongoing project aimed at introduction of product knowledge management for different stages of its lifecycle. The systems significantly simplify and speed up the process of product development. The technical options presented by the product manager and developer are converted into order-relevant options. As most of the characteristics can be used again, only new options must be discussed and entered in the system. Besides this, the error risk has been significantly reduced.

The major advantages of the developed systems are: systematic order codes for all products; machine readability; quick orientation for selecting right products and services; security when selecting and ordering products and services.

One other advantage is the reusability of the data. The structured data are used in other processes such as:

- Automatically creating master data in SAP models;
- Automatically creating data for the configuration models and services;
- Automatically generating an ordering sheet for the print documentation (this ordering sheet was generated earlier with high expenditure manually);
- Automatically generating a product and service list which is needed in the complete process implementing new products.

Acknowledgments. The research presented is motivated by a joint project between SPIIRAS and Festo AG&Co KG. Some parts of the work have been sponsored by grants # 12-07-00298-a, # 12-07-00302-a of the Russian Foundation for Basic Research, project # 213 of the research program "Intelligent information technologies, mathematical modelling, system analysis and automation" of the Russian Academy of Sciences, and project 2.2 "Methodology development for building group information and recommendation systems" of the basic research program "Intelligent information technologies, system analysis and automation" of the Nanotechnology and Information technology Department of the Russian Academy of Sciences.

References

Baumeister, H.: Customer relationship management for SMEs. In: Proceedings of the 2nd Annual Conference eBusiness and eWork e2002, Prague, Czech Republic (2002)

Bokinge, M., Malmqvist, J.: PLM implementation guidelines – relevance and application in practice: a discussion of findings from a retrospective case study. International Journal of Product Lifecycle Management 6(1), 79–98 (2012)

Bernard, A., Tichkievich, S. (eds.): Methods and Tools for Effective Knowledge Life-Cycle-Management, 588.p. Springer (2008)

Bradfield, D.J., Gao, J.X., Soltan, H.: A Metaknowledge Approach to Facilitate Knowledge Sharing in the Global Product Development Process. Computer-Aided Design & Applications 4(1-4), 519–528 (2007)

Chan, E.C.K., Yu, K.M.: A framework of ontology-enabled product knowledge management. International Journal of Product Development 4(3/4), 241–254 (2007)

Egan, M.: Implementing a Successful Modular Design. In: Proceedings of the 7th Workshop on Product Structuring – Product Platform Development, pp. 49–58 (2004)

Fjermestad, J., Romano Jr., N.C.: An Integrative Implementation Framework for Electronic Customer Relationship Management: Revisiting the General Principles of Usability and Resistance. In: Proceedings of the 36th Hawaii International Conference on System Sciences (HICSS 2003), Big Island, HI, USA (2003) ISBN 0-7695-1874-5 - Track 7

Von Hippel, E.: Democratizing innovation, p. 208. The MIT Press, Cambridge (2006)

Oroszi, A., Jung, T., Smirnov, A., Shilov, N., Kashevnik, A.: Ontology-Driven Codification for Discrete and Modular Products. Int. J. of Product Development 8(2), 162–177 (2009)

Patil, L., Dutta, D., Sriram, R.: Ontology-based exchange of product data semantics. IEEE Transactions on Automation Science and Engineering 2(3), 213–225 (2005) ISSN: 1545-5955

Piller, F., Schaller, C.: Individualization Based Collaborative Customer Relationship Management: Motives, Structures, and Modes of Collaboration for Mass Customization and CRM. Working Paper No. 29 of the Dept. of General and Industrial Management, Technische Universität München ISSN 0942-5098, http://www.mass-customization.de/download//TUM-AIBWP029.pdf (May 2002, 2004)

Sharda, R., Voß, S.: Information and Management Systems for Product Customization. Integrated Series in Information Systems, 270. p. Springer (2005); (ISBN 978-0-387-23347-5 (Print) 978-0-387-23348-2 (Online)

Smirnov, A., Shilov, N.: Collaborative Recommendation Systems for PLM: Approach and Technological Framework. In: Proc. of the 8th International Product Lifecycle Management Conference, PLM 2011, Eindhoven, The Netherlands (2011)

Uschold, M., Grüninger, M.: Ontologies: Principles, methods and applications. Knowledge Engineering Review 11(2), 93–155 (1996)

VDMA, German Engineering Federation (2013), http://www.vdma.org/en_GB/

Uniting Lifecycle Information – From Items to Assets, from Concepts to Practice

Marja Lintala[1] and Pierre Bonnal[2]

[1] Karlsruhe Institute of Technology, Institute for Information Management in Engineering, Karlsruhe, Germany
[2] CERN, European Organization for Nuclear Research, Genève, Switzerland
marja.lintala@kit.edu, pierre.bonnal@cern.ch

Abstract. Many products have become more and more complex and tailor-made. Consequently, product data is an extremely important factor to ensure the success and the sustainability of a product. Large and complex products, systems or facilities were managed in the past without the enhanced information technology systems available nowadays. Among some successful products or systems, one can cite space programs such as the NASA Apollo program or the particle accelerators built as from the 1950s such as that of CERN, Geneva, Switzerland, which serves as a case study for this paper. Some of the products developed in these eras are still in operation. Projects and practitioner approaches were developed and are still under development to address the problem of migrating data, produced with different technologies, to today's technologies. For instance, the ISO 10303 standard—also known as the STEP standard (Standard for the Exchange of Product Data)—provides the means to transfer CAD data between systems. But only little attention has been drawn to providing reliable means for integrating the information from different lifecycle phases together. This paper aims to draw attention to the issues raised by the use of different terminologies and systems in different lifecycle phases, in particular the concept of item during conception and development phase, and the concept of asset during that of operations and maintenance and some problems that this may bring.

Keywords: Item, Asset, Product Lifecycle Management, Change Management, CERN.

1 Introduction

In our constantly changing world, even consumer products have become more and more complex and tailor-made. So it is no wonder that industrial products and systems are increasingly engineered. On the other hand, regulations such as laws, directives and standards are being constantly updated and are becoming stricter and more constraining. For example, in the European Union (EU) and European Economic Area (EEA), Machinery Directive 2006/EC/42 [1] valid as from December 2009 and the related standards dedicate more and more room to safety features. In this quickly evolving environment, product information management throughout the entire lifecycle has become an extremely important factor to ensure the success of a product.

A. Bernard, L. Rivest, and D. Dutta (Eds.): PLM 2013, IFIP AICT 409, pp. 120–129, 2013.

Just a few decades ago, large and complex products, systems and facilities were conceived, developed, operated and maintained simply with paper archived in filing cabinets. With the advent of microcomputers, files and folders took over. Documents were managed manually and data exchange, in the modern sense, was the manual transportation of documents or later documents in a digital format such as floppy disks [2]. Nowadays, information systems that embed word-processed and CAD data are widely used, especially when the products are complex. Information systems, such as those used in PLM (Product Lifecycle Management), are no longer only technically focused, but take into account the entire product lifecycle and enable the collaboration of various business units from development to service [2].

In products with a long life, and with a great amount of history, information may have been produced with different technologies for different product lifecycle purposes. For instance, the Proton Synchrotron (PS) particle accelerator in CERN (European Organization for Nuclear Research, Geneva, Switzerland) built in the 1950s is fifty years later still a key component of CERN's accelerator complex. Operations and maintenance of scientific facilities such as that of the PS rely on information originating from various sources: paper documents in filing cabinets, some files still on microcomputers, but also documents in shared access on CERN's several electronic data and document management systems. The in-formation also relates to different lifecycle phases: 2D drawings, engineering specifications, design reports, manufacturing and assembly procedures and records prepared or released in the conception and development phase; and operations and maintenance documentation such as operations and maintenance manuals, procedures and control reports released in the operation and maintaining phase.

Methods for solving the problem of integrating information from different tools, for instance different CAD software, have gained attention over time. Standards such as the ISO 10303—also known as the STEP standard (Standard for the Exchange of Product Data) [3]—have been developed. Approaches for product architectures, such as modular or integral architecture [4], and for creating a customer demand adaptable product [5], also emerged. However, these methods concentrate on the design phase of the whole product lifecycle, and hence, adding product information from different lifecycle phases needs more attention. The aim of this paper is to draw attention on the issues that arise out of the use of different terminologies and also information systems in different lifecycle and some problems that this may bring.

2 Lifecycle Management

The importance of coherency and the integrity of data are widely recognized, because it avoids a loss of time. This 'loss of time' consists of searching and waiting for data, data translations, working with wrong data and recreating the existing knowledge as described in [6]. The Product Lifecycle Management (PLM) approach addresses streamlining the product and related processes, and in-formation flows throughout the product's lifecycle [6]. The aim of PLM is to pro-vide a continuous and transparent flow of digital information within the lifecycle [2]. However, as it is pointed out in [6], the underlying concept in PLM is knowledge management.

Knowledge is according to [7] 'learned information'. Information on the other hand is 'interpreted data' and data 'syntactic entities' [7]. The relationship between these three key concepts have been discussed in previous research, for in-stance in [7], [8]. An extensive amount of research about information and knowledge management in the context of PLM is also available, for instance [6], [9–11].

Tacit knowledge usually is subjective, cognitive and a result of experimental learning (knowledge that is still in the mind of the person) [6][12]. While tacit knowledge is formed into explicit, knowledge becomes more objective, rational and technical knowledge, (knowledge, that can be relatively easily saved, processed and shared, and that is well documented and accessible) [6], [12]. In this phase technological solutions have an active role [6].

The technological enablers for PLM are the different ICT tools used during the life of the product. Consequently, PLM can be described as multilayered and multisystem architecture [9]. From this ICT point-of-view, Garetti et al. [10] use 'connective tissue' to describe the role of PLM, for instance, the connection from design software to production and supply chain software in the extended enterprise [10]. The reason for this metaphor is that at the moment there is no comprehensive and well-accepted commercial PLM tool [9]. It is therefore appropriate to refer to PLM in ICT terms as a 'system of systems' [9]. Single systems are deficient without synthesis with other systems. In management sciences the system approach focuses on the whole, not on the separate parts, hence the relationships (interactions and compatibility) between the parts are important for the total sys-tem performance [13].

A philosophical view of PLM is to close the knowledge loops of the solutions enable creating, transforming and sharing the knowledge throughout the product lifecycle [6]. In order to close the knowledge loops, the interactions and compatibility of the IT solutions, integrations are needed. Integration of different software solutions such as CAD (Computer Aided Design), PDM (Product Data Management), ERP (Enterprise Resource Planning), and CRM (Customer Relationship Management) started some years ago [10]. The integration of the different software solutions is important in ensuring the information flow without any gaps between. However, less attention has been paid to the integration of operation and maintenance tools, i.e. the so-called asset management system.

Change management is also an important function of any PLM frame-work. There are systems that provide means for managing changes, but in practice there are still problems with assessing the scope of the change [14]. Changes, especially in complex engineering domains, can be 'initiated', such as front-end new requirements or new innovative solutions [15]. In addition, changes can be 'emergent', such as problems occurring in different lifecycle processes such as testing [15]. As observed by Eckert et al. [15], even if the changes can in both cases be handled the same way, their causes are different. It is important that changes, whatever their origin, are handled and managed systematically and effectively. Particular attention should be paid to change management while the product is in operations; during corrective or preventive maintenance interventions for instance. As highlighted by Ulrich [4], products frequently undergo changes such as upgrades, add-ons, adaptations, wear, flexibility in use and even consumption.

3 Background – Use Case

The case study for this research is, as mentioned, a large-scale and complex scientific facility: that of CERN located across the French-Swiss border, in the vicinity of

Geneva, Switzerland. CERN is an international research center dedicated to experimental particle physics [16]. CERN equipment consists of accelerators, detectors and computing centers, which are substantially conceived in-house and partially manufactured, assembled and installed with the support of industrial firms.

As in many large-scale organizations, CERN has introduced and sometimes also developed different in-house means for keeping track of the equipment and their associated information. This need was enforced by the fact that several of CERN's facilities are subject to ionizing radiation and it is especially important to operate and maintain this equipment with a high degree of reliability and of traceability, and to accurately keep track of all pertinent information associated to equipment throughout its lifecycle.

The accelerator facility at CERN consists of many highly technological assets, but also of more common infrastructures such as industrial buildings and fully-equipped underground civil works. Technological assets include equipment from different decades. For instance, the PS mentioned above is from the 1950s, while that of the Large Hadron Collider (LHC), a 27-km circumference superconducting accelerator, was built in the late 1990s and early 2000s, and commissioned in 2008.

The LHC relies on superconducting magnets (see figure 1), altogether 1232 main dipoles in two variants 1104 dipoles in the arcs and 128 dipoles in the so-called dispersion suppressor (DS) regions of the tunnel [17]. The LHC is not a perfect circle; it is made of eight arcs and of eight long straight sections (LSS) linked by16 DS sections [17]. Even if they count fewer components, LSS and DS are more demanding from an engineering point of view [17]. While the variants of the main cryodipole magnets share the same basic design, they may differ slightly in that they were manufactured by three different manufacturers [17].

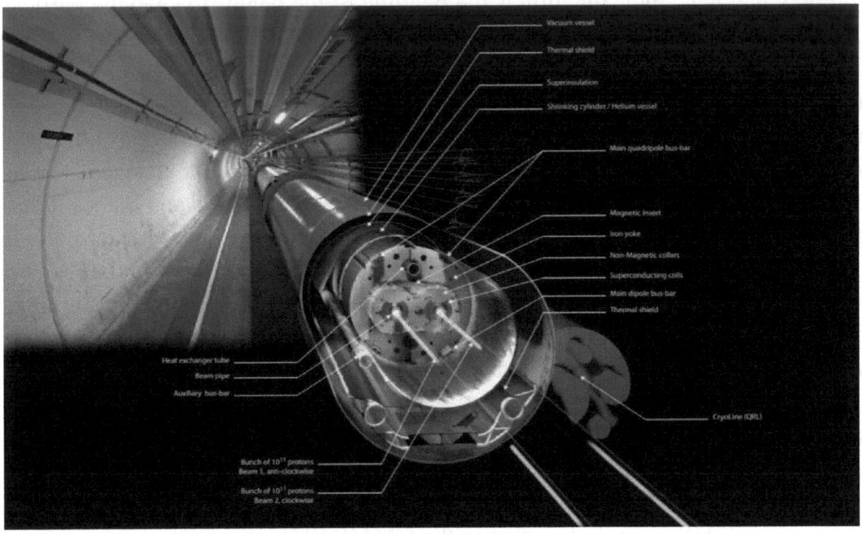

Fig. 1. Cross section of an LHC dipole in the tunnel. © 2011 CERN [18]

4 Items to Assets

When equipment such as the superconducting cryodipole magnets in the LHC are designed, the CERN's design offices use the term 'item' to qualify and to identify the object being conceived. Items are in general any independent objects that have an identity [19]. Moreover, through items, for example products, product modules and components are identified, encoded and named in a systematic and standardized way [20].

At CERN, the LHC design information is managed through several systems: the still-in-use so-called CDD (CERN Drawing Directory, Oracle-base system developed for archiving 2D-CAD data), more recently CATIA® SmarTeam for handling 3D mock-ups and the CERN EDMS (Engineering & Equipment Data Management Service). The typical characteristic of this early phase of the product lifecycle is that the objects are not yet tangible; they do not have yet a physical existence.

When design is ready and approved, the physical instances required are manufactured and assembled based on items. One item can lead to the manufacture and assembly of a one of a kind product. This is, for instance, the case of the LHC detectors, or in many instances the case of the 1232 units in two variants of the LHC cryodipole magnets described in section 3.

After their manufacture and assembly, either done in-house in one of CERN's many machine shops and workshops, or outsourced to specialized industrial firms through procurement contracts or to partner institutes through partnership agreements, the assets are finally installed and commissioned to achieve the function they were aimed at, the facilities can move to operations and maintenance. In the case of LHC cryodipole magnets, their function is the bending of the beams to keep the particles on an orbital trajectory.

Figure 2 describes the materialization of the intangible items used in the design of tangible assets used in operations and maintenance. This figure conveys the fact that conceptually our world is made of intangible objects, i.e. that do not have intrinsically a physical existence, and of tangible objects that have a physical existence. The model uses the well-know V-model (for example, [21], [22]) as a basis and places items and assets on the different branches of the V. Items can be broken down into sub-items and described accordingly along the descending left branch of the V-model; assets are integrated along the right branch of the V-model. In between is the materialization process. The materialization process aims to transform items into assets; out of one item, one to several assets can be materialized (the link 1 item to 1...n assets).

At CERN the LHC asset information is also managed through several systems mainly the CERN EDMS (Engineering & Equipment Data Management Service) or the CERN CMMS (Computerized Maintenance Management System). This asset information can be stored as electronic files such as maintenance control records stored in the EDMS, or stored as data in the CMMS [23].

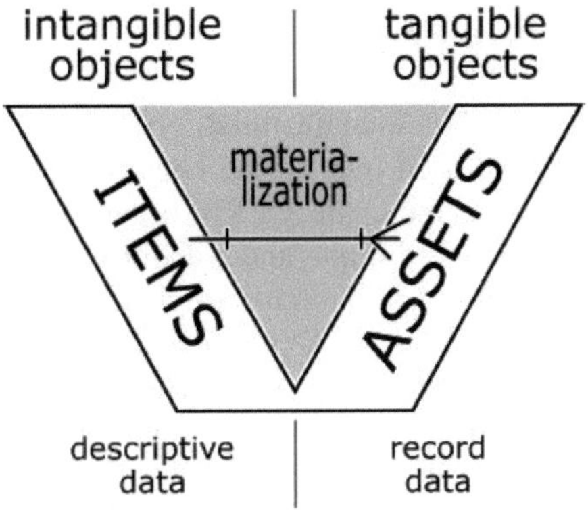

Fig. 2. V-model of materializing items to assets

As a general principle, equipment is manufactured and assembled based on engineering information developed at item level. However, a vast amount of information is also produced while operating and maintaining the equipment. If this information is generic, i.e. applicable to all instances of an asset, then it shall be at item level. If this information is specific to a given instance of equipment, then the asset shall be the repository for this information. Figure 3, adapted from basic quality management practices shows the categorization of different types of information. It is also of interest to notice that the information is different according to the phases of life of a product [23]. Information associated with an item shall typically be at 'descriptive level' i.e. level 3 in the quality assurance hierarchy of documents, while an asset's information shall be at 'records level' i.e. level 4 (see figures 2 and 3).

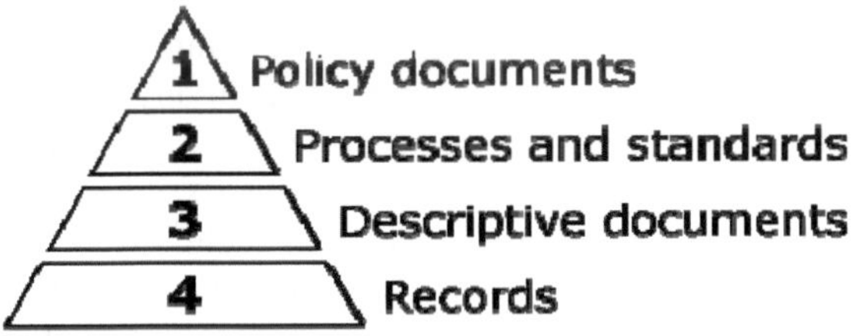

Fig. 3. Document hierarchies in CERN adapted from [23]

As described above, during the life of equipment at CERN there is a transfer from one terminology to another, but also transfer from one system of information systems (SmarTeam, CDD and EDMS) to another (EDMS and CMMS). The terms and systems mentioned here do not cover all of those in use at CERN, but are a simplification for the use in this paper. For instance following (sometimes synonymous) terms are in use: item, equipment, part, system, asset, functional position, slot and location. It becomes evident that if there is no link between the terminology and the information systems, there will be problems when the need to proceed to some modifications to the original design will appear. It is then of prime importance to keep the information coherent throughout the whole lifecycle of the equipment.

5 From Concepts to Practice

When the items have been manufactured, installed and commissioned, the materialized equipment is handed over to the operation and maintenance phase. For the sake of operational efficiency, the CERN organizational structure is made of different sectors, departments groups and sections. For instance, the so-called Accelerator and Technology (A&T) sector groups three departments, namely the Beams, Engineering and Technology Departments. Further down, the Engineering Department take care of particular part of the equipment, systems and facilities by means of specialized groups: e.g. Cooling and Ventilation Group, Electrical Engineering Group, Handling Engineering Group, Beam Instrumentation Group or Cryogenics Group to cite just a few. Finally through their sections, the groups provide services such as the operational maintenance of the equipment for which they have responsibility. The problem with such an organizational approach is that transverse processes such as maintenance operations, whether they are corrective or preventive, are performed in different departments and groups and rather independently.

In the handover process, an item is transformed into one or several assets. Figure 4 shows that after materialization items and assets may have independent lifecycles, but necessarily interdependent ones: design activities belong to the item lifecycle. Materialization is an activity that 'bridges' both lifecycle, i.e. that initiates an asset instance of an item. After materialization, an item in design may be subject to changes. There are many challenges in the change implementation, regardless of cause or type [24]. In the generic engineering change process introduced in Jarratt et al. [25], the first step is an engineering change request, which determines reason, priority and type of a change in addition to components and systems that are likely to be affected.

Changes to items, propagates to versioning or revising the item. Unfortunately, as pointed out in [26], the terminologies are not fixed. In any case, the meaning is that the item is changed in a matter that it will replace the original item [19], [26]. When changes are made as revisions, an important issue to keep in mind is the rules for revisions. The ISO 11442 standard dedicated to technical product documentation management [27] provides insights into revision rules for documents to reflect design changes. The revision rules also affect the identification of the components. The following passage of ISO 11442 [27] shall be kept in mind:

> "Technical changes with requirement for interchangeability between the old and the new version. The form, fit and function of the component is not affected, and consequently the identification number is retained." [27]

This raises the question of interchangeability: while an item design evolves, how to guarantee that the results of its evolution are compatible with the requirements of its corresponding assets that are in use?

Sometimes items are changed in such a manner that this rule does not apply and the original item is not replaced. This process produces variants. Variants are parallel options for items [19], [26]. Items may evolve, while their corresponding assets are kept physically unchanged (see figure 4). A problem may arise when the need to replace or modify an asset appears. Shall the replaced or repaired asset be based on version 1 of the item (that may have an obsolete status) or on version 2 (that is the latest released version of the asset)? It is noteworthy that the figure 4 is meant to be a discussion opener for the topic.

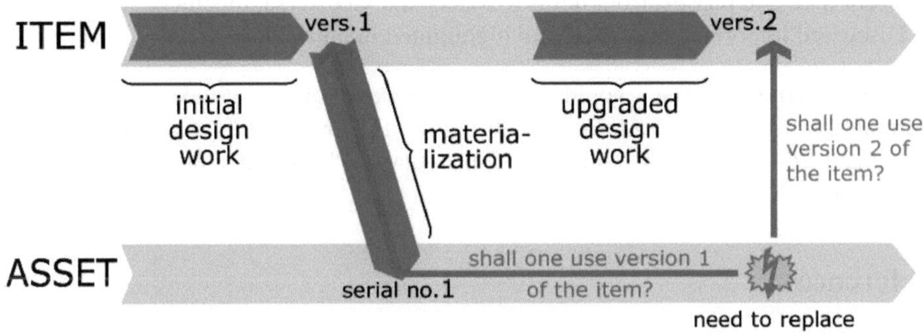

Fig. 4. Item and Asset Lifecycles

Another point of view on the information flow is backwards from assets to items. While modifying items the versioning and creation of variants are well defined procedures (e.g. [19], [26]), whereas describing what will happen in the item level when an asset is modified is to the best of our knowledge not well described. However, the modification of the description of an asset should be reflected at item level by creating a variant to receive this descriptive information.

6 Summary and Conclusions

In a complex and tailor-made environment, with the long life of equipment, it is extremely important to put emphasis on managing product information. The characteristics of the information such as that produced in different lifecycle phases and different period of time also bring their own flavour to the problems. In this paper we have raised and discussed a few issues: possible misunderstanding due to different

Table 1. The challenges discussed

Challenge	Description
Concepts vs. Practice	In system design objects are still intangible, while in operation and maintenance the objects are tangible with a physical existence. In the materialization process one intangible object is transformed into one or several tangible objects and the link shall be maintained.
Terminology	Different terminology is used in different lifecycle phases. Problems may occur, when changing from term to term, and in the interfaces.
Different lifecycles	Different objects (i.e. items and assets) may have different lifecycles. In the need of modification or replacement there is a need for 'bridging' the different lifecycles.

terminologies used over the lifecycle; and additional misunderstanding due an insufficient distinction between the key concepts of item and asset.

Throughout its whole lifecycle, a product is prone to change [25]. Engineering changes is a largely noticed issue in industry, but also an active research area of academia [25]. The paper also draws attention integrating the information from different lifecycle phases, from items to assets and vice versa, together.

Discussed important challenges are highlighted in table 1.

Acknowledgments. We would like to express our gratitude for European Commission Marie Curie Actions for providing funding for this research (FP7 grant agreement 264336). We would also like to thank PURESAFE-project consortium, especially CERN for their insight.

References

[1] European Commission, Directive 2006/42/EC of the European Parliament and of the Council of 17 May 2006 on machinery, and amending Directive 95/16/EC (2006)

[2] Technology monitoring 1|02 Product Lifecycle Management, Berliner Kreis – Wissenschaftliches Forum für Produktentwicklung e.V. WGP – Wissenschaftliche Gesellschaft für Produktionstechnik (September 2002), `http://www.berliner-kreis.de`, `http://www.wgp.de`

[3] ISO 10303, Industrial automation systems and integration - Product data representation and exchange (ISO 10303)

[4] Ulrich, K.: The role of product architecture in the manufacturing firm. Research Policy 24(3), 419–440 (1995)

[5] Maurer, M., Lindemann, U.: Individualized Product Design by Evolutionary Algorithms. In: Khosla, R., Howlett, R.J., Jain, L.C. (eds.) KES 2005. LNCS (LNAI), vol. 3683, pp. 1359–1365. Springer, Heidelberg (2005)

[6] Ameri, F., Dutta, D.: Product lifecycle management: Closing the knowledge loops. Computer-Aided Design and Applications 2(5), 577–590 (2005)

[7] Aamodt, A., Nygård, M.: Different roles and mutual dependencies of data, information, and knowledge — An AI perspective on their integration. Data & Knowledge Engineering 16(3), 191–222 (1995)

[8] Tuomi, I.: Data is more than knowledge: implications of the reversed knowledge hierarchy for knowledge management and organizational memory. In: Proceedings of the 32nd Annual Hawaii International Conference on Systems Sciences, HICSS-32, Track1, 12. p (1999)

[9] Terzi, S., Bouras, A., Dutta, D., Garetti, M., Kiritsis, D.: Product lifecycle management – from its history to its new role. International Journal of Product Lifecycle Management 4(4), 360–389 (2010)

[10] Garetti, M., Terzi, S., Bertacci, N., Brianza, M.: Organisational change and knowledge management in PLM implementation. International Journal of Product Lifecycle Management 1(1), 43–51 (2005)

[11] Abramovici, M.: Future Trends in Product Lifecycle Management (PLM). In: Krause, F.-L. (ed.) The Future of Product Development, pp. 665–674. Springer, Heidelberg (2007)

[12] Gupta, B., Iyer, L.S., Aronson, J.E.: Knowledge management: practices and challenges. Industrial Management & Data Systems 100(1), 17–21 (2000)

[13] Ackoff, R.L.: Towards a System of Systems Concepts. Management Science 17(11), 661–671 (1971)
[14] Ahmad, N., Wynn, D.C., Clarkson, P.J.: Change impact on a product and its redesign process: a tool for knowledge capture and reuse. Res. Eng. Design, 1–26 (2012), doi:10.1007/s00163-012-0139-8
[15] Eckert, C., Clarkson, P.J., Zanker, W.: Change and customisation in complex engineering domains. Research in Engineering Design 15(1), 1–21 (2004)
[16] Research at CERN: a gateway to the Universe, `http://public.web.cern.ch/public/en/Research/Research-en.html` (acessed: November 28, 2012)
[17] Evans, L., Bryant, P.: LHC Machine. Journal of Instrumentation 3(08), SO8001 (2008)
[18] Brice, M.: Cross section of an LHC dipole in the tunnel. CERN Document Server (July 07, 2011), `http://cds.cern.ch/record/1365795` (accessed: February 02, 2013)
[19] Peltonen, H., Martio, A., Sulonen, R.: PDM: tuotetiedon hallinta. Edita. IT Press (2002)
[20] Sääksvuori, A., Immonen, A.: Product Lifecycle Management, 3rd edn. Springer, Berlin, Heidelberg (2008)
[21] Sage, A.P., Rouse, W.B.: Handbook of Systems Engineering and Management, 2nd edn. John Wiley & Sons, Inc., Hoboken (2009)
[22] Hull, E., Jackson, K., Dick, J.: Requirements Engineering, 2nd edn. Springer (2004)
[23] Bonnal, P., Delamare, C., Mugnier, C., Pace, M., Perinic, G., Pilon, R., Rühl, I., Van Uytvink, E., Zaharieva, Z.: Maintenance Management Project Concept Report. CERN EDMS No. 1173942 (June 2012) (restricted Access)
[24] Clarkson, P.J., Simons, C.S., Eckert, C.M.: Predicting change propagation in complex design. In: Proceedings of the 13th International Conference on Design Theory and Methodology, Part of (DETC 2001) (September 12, 2001), `http://publications.eng.cam.ac.uk/328560/` (accessed: December 14, 2012)
[25] Jarratt, T.A.W., Eckert, C.M., Caldwell, N.H.M., Clarkson, P.J.: Engineering change: an overview and perspective on the literature. Res. Eng. Design 22(2), 103–124 (2011)
[26] Schichtel, M.: Produktdatenmodellierung in der Praxis. Carl Hanser Verlag, München (2002)
[27] ISO 11442, Technical product documentation - Document management (ISO 11442:2006)

Integrated Platform from CAD to CNC: A Survey

Christophe Danjou, Julien Le Duigou, and Benoît Eynard

Mechanical Engineering Systems Department, Université de Technologie de Compiègne,
Mechanical laboratory Roberval UMR UTC/CNRS 7337,
CS 60319, 60203 Compiègne cedex, France
{christophe.danjou,julien.le-duigou,benoit.eynard}@utc.fr

Abstract. Nowadays, interoperability is essential to ensure the Product Lifecycle Management (PLM). However there are still some barriers to interoperability both technical and scientific which inhibit exchanges between the different information systems. This exchange can occur at different levels. In this paper the first one deals with exchanging and sharing information during the industrialization stage on the chain CAD-CAM-CNC. The second level developed concerns the chain of information systems materialized by the link between PDM-MPM-ERP. This paper identifies first the locks to interoperability and then explores the work done on those links with an interoperability point of view in order to remove the barriers identified.

Keywords: Interoperability, Integrated Design and Manufacturing, CAD-CAM-CNC.

1 Introduction

Face to the globalization and the growing competition concerning product costs, companies must constantly increase their productivity. In a “Rapid-development” context, companies have to improve their industrialization ability. In fact, they must industrialize their products and processes with an increasing speed, lower costs and maintaining a high level of quality.

French FUI project called ANGEL (Atelier Numérique coGnitif intEropérable et agiLe) will focus on the capitalization of cuts know-how in order to improve the competitiveness of enterprises in developing tools and methods to retrieve information from the numerical-control machine-tool. To achieve the information flow bi-directionality (capitalization and control of machines), the systems must be able to exchange information and to use these information.

Defining interoperability as the exchange of information between systems and the use of their functionality, interoperability can be a solution to treat the continuity of digital flow. It also ensures capitalization of technical know-how linking the different stages from the design to manufacturing.

The next section deals with interoperability state of the art and existing solutions to enhance it. Third section analyses papers which deals about the information exchange

A. Bernard, L. Rivest, and D. Dutta (Eds.): PLM 2013, IFIP AICT 409, pp. 130–139, 2013.

and share in order to show the link between the different industrialization stages. The fourth section concludes this paper and gives our research framework concerning the integrated platforms interoperability.

2 State of the Art

2.1 Interoperability Definition

According to Kosanke [1] a careful chosen web search produces 22 definitions of interoperability. Following the interpretation and the people who use it, the term interoperability can make different senses. This explains why a large number of definitions can be found in the literature. IEEE [2] defines interoperability as "the ability of two or more systems or components to exchange information and to use the information that has been exchanged". ATHENA [3] and INTEROP NoE [4] projects define interoperability for enterprises. In this case, interoperability is the ability of interaction between companies or at least between parts of them. Vernadat [5] defines interoperability as the "ability to communicate with peer systems and access their functionality". This definition highlights the need to exchange functionalities. But here we will use Wegner's [6] definition which describe interoperability as "The ability of two systems (or more) to communicate, cooperate and exchange services and data, thus despite the differences in languages, implementations, executive environments and abstraction models". ANGEL project will focus on the industrialization phase interoperability between the different CAX systems and Information Systems.

2.2 Interoperability Levels

According to EIF [7] there exist three levels of interoperability: Technical level, Semantic level and Organizational level. A system is interoperable if and only if it satisfies the three levels of interoperability at every moment. The technical level ensures the continuity of the information flow through tools and technological solutions. The semantic one ensures the information sharing and services to keep the semantics flow. The organizational level deals with the processes, users and those involved in the operation of the system [8]. Most articles in the literature tend to satisfy the technical and semantic levels. However organizational level barriers are less treated in the literature because of they are associated human kind problems.

2.2.1 Technical Level

To implement interoperability between two systems, two solutions are possible: the integration point by point or the "Enterprise Application Interface" interoperability oriented [9].

In the point-to-point strategy, the number of translators is $(n^2-n)/2$ for the direct translation. It seems obvious that such architecture is not feasible given the number of translators to develop but also for all maintenance costs necessary to ensure the proper functioning of the system [10]. In contrast to the point-to-point strategy the mediator strategy has been developed and appears to be promising [11]. With this architecture there is a greater agility of information systems and a lower cost of interface. With an architecture based on a mediator, the number of relations is equal to the number of systems in architecture, considering mediator as a bidirectional translator.

According to Booth [12], service oriented architecture (SOA) is another way to ensure interoperability. Web services provide a means to interoperate between applications regardless of platform or environment in which they are executed. Combining SOA and mediator, we obtain the model developed by Paviot [8]. This model is shown in Figure 1 with a service-oriented information mediator. Such a mediator must fulfill three basic functions defined by Bénaben [13]: Data conversion and provision, Application Management and Collaborative processes orchestration. However, this system based on the mediator may have some disadvantages developed by Zimmerman [14]. In fact, he points that a mediator failure will cause the entire system failure. In addition, if the semantic flow is too large, the mediator may be a bottleneck and may limit the semantic flow. The SOA and the mediator appear as a serious solution to interoperability for the industrialization phase. There are also mediators of mediators which can help systems to translate its own information before sending it to the all system.

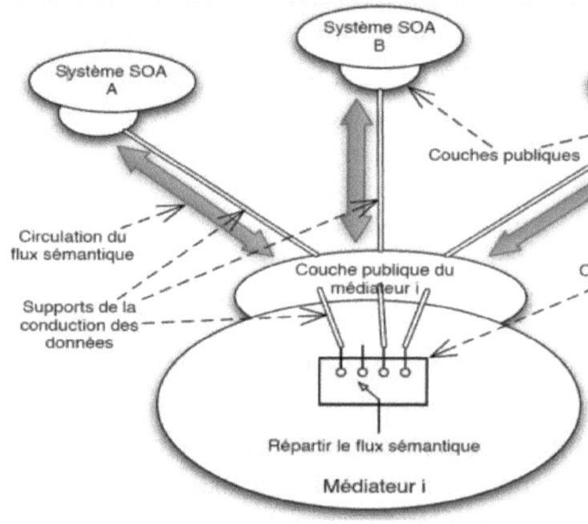

Fig. 1. Mediator distribution function of multiscale mediation [12]

2.2.2 Semantic Level

According to the standard ISO 14258 there are three different approaches to achieve semantic interoperability: Integration, Unification and Federation.

The integration is based on the existence of a common format for all models. Unification is based on a high level common format. Finally, the federation is based on the use of ontologies and Semantic Web standards in order to have automated transfers and routing of information between heterogeneous applications.

Many works use unifying approach [8], [15] which gets more flexible and more dynamics aspects than integration approach as seen before. It is necessary to translate data from one system to another so that there is the possibility of information exchange. To achieve interoperability through unifying approach, it is possible to use standards such as STEP standard [16]. The STEP standard is an open and normalized standard that aims to promote the data exchange in a format which is understandable and shared by all. According to [17], the STEP standard provides a neutral, a sustainable and a scalable data exchange format. In the last years, STEP-NC, a new standard format with enriched data has been developed in order to improve the systems interoperability [18] by integrating processing data. Moreover, according to the NIST [19] the standard can potentially save up to a billion dollars a year by reducing the costs of interoperability in sectors such as automotive, aerospace and shipbuilding. The STEP standard has positioned itself as a viable alternative to product-oriented interoperability. The concept of product-oriented interoperability was introduced by Baïna and describes the ability for a company to manage, share and exchange product information for more transparency for the user [9]. In the same way the PPO Model uses a SOA architecture for placing the model at the center of expertise that revolve around. This expertise can be related to the product (consultancies and methods expert for example) but may also be related to organizational, policy aspects, etc... However, unification imposes to totally appropriate information models of each system due to the meta-data use.

The federation is based on ontologies or web-services. "An ontology is a vocabulary of such terms (names of relations, functions, individuals), defined in a form that is both human and machine readable" [20]. More broadly an ontology is the structured set of terms and concepts representing the meaning of an information field, whether as a meta-data namespace or the elements of a knowledge field. Besides ontologies the federation is also based on the semantic web standards which provide additional necessary information to understand. So that simplifies the programming and maintenance of knowledge based on web services architecture [21], [22]. According to Mellor [23] and the OMG that develops Model-Driven Engineering (MDE), ontologies are also solutions for the implementation of Model-Driven architecture (MDA) which is based on four ontological levels [24]. Hence the MDA provides a basis to enhance formalization of trade and obtain solutions to achieve interoperability through a unifying approach. To develop the interoperability between the different stages of the industrialization, it is necessary to use the same language for all the systems. This is why unification can be an approach for semantic interoperability. Moreover, federative approach can be used for interoperability between information systems and each industrialization stages. Finally, the interoperability between information systems can be seen as integration because they must exchange data and functionalities. As Kosanke says [1], interoperability cannot exist in a single approach, but certainly as an aggregation of three approaches in order to conserve the semantic flow.

2.2.3 Organizational Level

According to Vernadat [25], the organizational aspects of interoperability define the objectives, ensure coherence and process coordination. It is the ability to make collaboration between different structures and organizations if they wish to exchange information, although they may have different structures and different internal processes. In addition, process must be managed by placing users at the heart of the problem [26]. It is necessary to focus on functional aspect of the system to be as accessible as possible. Work on the human-machine interface systems is necessary for organizational interoperability. To achieve interoperability at the organizational level certain barriers must be removed [27]: Definition of responsibility (who is responsible for what?), Definition of authority (who is authorized to do what?) and Incompatibility of organization structures (matrix vs. hierarchical ones). In fact, once these three barriers are treated, it is possible to define the information exchange process and the information use.

In this part, it appears that interoperability deals with different level in order to ensure the data exchange, the data use and the functionalities use of other systems. The interoperability of the industrialization phase must be established through the three different interoperability levels in order to match the integration continuum.

3 Interoperability for Industrialization

This section exposes the study of the link between the different industrialization phases. We look at these links in "interoperability" terms to determine the interoperability levels and the methods used. The integrated design/industrialization platforms contain various expert software (CAD, Simulation, CAM ...) and different systems to support these expertises (PDM (Product Data Management), MPM (Manufacturing Process Management), ERP (Enterprise Resource Planning Information), MES (Manufacturing Execution System)). In the chain of industrialization three types of links are identified:

- The Design / Simulation link covering links between CAD software, Simulation and PDM
- The Design / Manufacturing link covering links between CAD, CAM, PDM, MPM, ERP and MES
- The Design / Assembly link covering the same software links and information systems as above, but taking into account a different expertise (assembly and non-manufacturing)

3.1 Design / Simulation Link

The design / simulation can help designers to make technology choices for their designs through the information from the simulation. In fact with the bidirectionality of the design / simulation chain, validation of the design may result from a smaller number of exchanges between the design and simulation as a result of increased knowledge capitalization. Reducing the number of round trips between the numerical model and simulation design, development time are reduced consequently the development cost are reduced too. Nguyen Van [28] defines architecture with collaborations loops between design and simulation. Via this architecture he ensures the preservation of the semantic link using STEP standard. To save this link Assouroko [29] connect every ontologies thanks to the RelationShip Manager principle (RsM). Li [30] defines ontologies in order to enrich the data and information exchange with Annotation. According to Barbau [31], OntoSTEP provides an OWL representation for EXPRESS data, which allows the creation of semantically enriched product models. Catalano [32] also uses Ontologies to develop a new model called Product Design Ontology which allow to index information on the CAD model. Troussier [33] uses the dependencies that exist between the information contained in the notes of calculation" to ensure interoperability. In the same way, Etienne [34] develop a PPO Kernel in order to create interoperability between the CAD expert tool. Valilai [35] have develop the INFELT STEP platform which make possible the interoperability between CAD and Simulation systems. Similarly, Nassehi [36] has developed a “universal CNC manufacturing platform” with interfaces which allow to connect CADs and simulation systems. According to Jun [37] closed-loop PLM focuses on tracking and managing the information on the whole product lifecycle, with information feedback. Pratt [38] and Newman [39] define the exchanges CAD-Simulation allowed through STEP and STEP-NC standard. Biahmou [40] develops a translator called CAMAT (CATIA-MATLAB Translator) insuring the interoperability between Design and Simulation. According to Tan [41] Product Service System which places the simulation for design is a new organizational interoperability.

3.2 Design / Manufacturing Link

The capitalization of knowledge from the machine tool enables an optimized design for manufacturing. Moreover, if a problem is corrected directly on the CNC interoperability between design and manufacturing can propagate upstream changes. Harik [42] develop a tool for the Usiquick project which enriches the CAD model in order to define the machining program and tool path. Valilai [35] with the INFELT platform allows the interoperability between CAD and CAM systems. Delplace [43] developed an automated cell to promote the casting process full integration. Newman [39] defines the CAD-CAM exchanges through STEP-NC standard. Nassehi [36] has developed interfaces to connect CAD and CAM systems on the ”universal platform”. Martin [44] developed a tool based on the Visual Basic language to create a "mediator" for all the APIs to ensure the link between design and foundry manufacturing. Similarly Paviot [8], uses mediator to link ontologies. At the same time, he develops a model based on "semantic tags", which deals with the interoperability semantic level. Le Duigou [45] deals with interoperability between design and manufacturing defining a generic data model. He first uses a unifying approach then he uses the integration to complete his data model thus ensuring the semantic flow. According to Kuo [46], based on artificial intelligence, the intelligent DFX systems help the designer to make choices thanks an experience data basis. As seen before, closed-loop PLM [37] ensures technical interoperability between design and Manufacturing. Through the UbiDM (design and manufacturing via ubiquitous computing technology), Suh [47] allow the transfer of data from the different Lifecycle stages. Tan [41] deals with the organizational interoperability between design and Manufacturing.

3.3 Design / Assembly Link

The link between design and assembly essentially helps the designer in the technical choices process. Demoly [48] defines a Multi-Views Oriented assembly model (MUVOA) which aims to ensure the link between design and assembly. It also treats the organizations problems. Mantripragada [49] develops a tool called Assembly Oriented Design (AOD) which decomposes each assembly into sub-assembly informing designers the way to realize a system. The NIST [50] has developed the Core Product Model which treats the link between Design and Assembly. Jun [37] ensures technical interoperability for the link design/Assembly.

3.4 Synthesis

In order to analyze this literature review, the three levels of interoperability seen previously are used: Semantical level, Technical level and Organizational level. From these elements, the literature review can be summarized in a double-entry table to classify the different jobs in the category that corresponds to it. The results of this analysis are presented in Table 1.

Table 1: Synthesis of the literature survey

	Technical Level	Semantic Level	Organizational Level
Design / Simulation link	[33]; [35]; [36]; [37]; [40]	[28]; [29]; [30]; [31]; [32]; [38]; [39]	[41]
Design / Manufacturing link	[8]; [35]; [36]; [37]; [42]; [43]; [44]; [46]; [47]	[8]; [39]; [45]	[41]
Design / Assembly link	[37]; [46]; [49]	[45]; [48]; [50]	[41]; [48]

Literature extensively addresses the barriers related to technical and semantic levels. However barriers related to organizational level as associated human nature problems are less treated in the literature [51]. On the technical level, SOA systems and mediators are mainly used. On the semantic level, federative approach and ontologies are the most exploited.

4 Conclusion and Future Work

As explained in Xu work [52], STEP-NC can wear through its rich data format, much information that can be integrated in the digital flow CAD-CAM-CN. In opposition to the multi-interfaces needs [53] this standard let compile all the information from the design, simulation and manufacturing. STEP-NC format provides bidirectional digital flow because it allows feedback from the manufacturing and simulation stages to the design.

Given the state of the work already completed for interoperability between design and simulation phases [54], it appears that interoperability between PDM / MPM / ERP / MES has been little addressed. Indeed, MPM appears as an essential element for lifecycle management of production lines. According to [55], the MPM is the only software able to provide a link between the early phases such as CAD and PDM, and downstream applications, such as ERP and MES.

This paper presents the state of the art of the various interoperability levels. Three interoperability levels (semantic, technical and organizational) exist and we have seen the different approaches to overcome interoperability barriers. We will use OntoSTEP-NC - an ontology based on STEP-NC format for CAD-CAM-CNC chain - as a basis to support ontology for MPM model. OntoSTEP-NC seems a possible way to improve the design / industrialization chain interoperability. This axis will be studied in our future work.

Acknowledgments. This work is done in the French FUI project ANGEL. We also thank all consortium partners for their contribution during the development of ideas and concepts proposed in this paper.

References

[1] Kosanke, K.: ISO Standards for Interoperability: a comparison. In: Proceedings of the 1st International Conference on Interoperability of Enterprise Software and Applications, pp. 55–64 (2005)
[2] IEEE, IEEE (Institute of Electrical and Electronics Engineers): Standard Computer Dictionary-A Compilation of IEEE Standard Computer Glossaries (1990)
[3] ATHENA, Document Deliverable D.A1.1.1, Project A1: Enterprise Modelling in the Context of Collaborative Enterprises ATHENA, EU IP- Project - No 507849 (2004)
[4] INTEROP, Knowledge map of research in interoperability in the INTEROP NoE, Deliverable D1.1, EU-NoE Project IST-508 011 (2004), `http://www.interop.noe.org`
[5] Vernadat, F.: Enterprise Modelling and Integration: principles and applications. Chapman & Hall (1996) ISBN 0 412 60550 3
[6] Wegner, P.: Interoperability. ACM Computing Surveys (CSUR) 28(1), 285–287 (1996)
[7] EIF: European Interoperability Framework. White Pages, pp. 1–40 (2004)
[8] Paviot, T.: Méthodologie de résolution des problèmes d'interopérabilité dans le domaine du Product Lifecycle Management. Thèse de doctorat de l'Ecole Centrale Paris (2010)
[9] Paviot, T., Cheutet, V., Lamouri, S.: Design and logistics IT federation through Product Lifecycle Support standard. In: PLM 2009, Bath, UK, July 6-8 (2009)
[10] Guyot, E., Ducellier, G., Eynard, B., Girard, P., Gallet, T.: Product data and digital mock-up exchange based on PLM. In: Proceedings of PLM 2007, Milano, Italy, July 11-13 (2007)
[11] Wiederhold, G.: Mediators in the Architecture of Future Information Systems Gio Wiederhold. The IEEE Computer Magazine 25(3), 1–38 (1992)
[12] Booth, D., Haas, H., McCabe, F., Newcomer, E., Champion, M., Ferris, C., Orhcard, D.: Web Services Architecture. W3C Working Group, W3C Working Group Note (2004)
[13] Bénaben, F., Touzi, J., Rajsiri, V., Truptil, S.: Mediation Information System Design in a Collaborative SOA Context through a MDD Approach. In: MDISIS 2008, Montpellier, France, June 16 (2008)
[14] Zimmermann, A., Krötzsch, M., Euzenat, J., Hitzler, P.: Formalizing Ontology Alignment and its Operations with Category Theory. In: Formal Ontology in Information Systems, pp. 277–288 (2006)
[15] Tursi, A., Panetto, H., Morel, G., Dassisti, M.: Ontological approach for products-centric information system interoperability in networked manufacturing enterprises. Annual Reviews in Control 33(2), 238–245 (2009)
[16] Lee, S.-H., Jeong, Y.-S.: A system integration framework through development of ISO 10303-based product model for steel bridges. Automation in Construction 15(2), 212–228 (2006)
[17] Rachuri, S., Subrahmanian, E., Bouras, A., Fenves, S.J., Foufou, S., Sriram, R.D.: Information sharing and exchange in the context of product lifecycle management: Role of standards. Computer-Aided Design 40(7), 789–800 (2008)

[18] Laguionie, R., Rauch, M., Hascoet, J.: Toolpaths programming in an intelligent STEP-NC manufacturing context. Journal of Machine Engineering 8(1), 33–43 (2008)
[19] Gallaher, M.P., O'Connor, A., Phelps, T.: Economic Impact Assessment of the International Standard for the Exchange of Product Model Data (STEP) in Transportation Equipment Industries. NIST Report (2002)
[20] Gruber, T.R.: Ontolingua: A Mechanism to Support Portable Ontologies. KSL 91-66 581(1), 1–61 (1992)
[21] Benjamins, V.R., Contreras, J., Corcho, O., Gómez-Pérez, A.: Six Challenges for the Semantic Web. Challenges 1(1), 1–15 (2001)
[22] Matthews, B., Brickley, D., Dodds, L.: Semantic Web Technologies. JISC Technology and Standards Watch (2005)
[23] Mellor, S.J., Uhl, A., Weise, D.: Model-Driven Architecture Models and Metamodels. OMG white paper, pp. 290–297 (2000)
[24] Naumenko, A., Wegmann, A.: Two approaches in system modeling and their illustrations with mda and RM-ODP. In: ICEIS, Angers, France, April 23-26 (2003)
[25] Vernadat, F.: Technical, semantic and organizational issues of enterprise interoperability and networking. Annual Reviews in Control 34(1), 139–144 (2010)
[26] EIF.: European Interoperability Framework for pan-European eGovernment Services. In: Interoperable Delivery of European eGovernment Services to Public Administrations (2004)
[27] Chen, D., Doumeingts, G., Vernadat, F.: Architectures for enterprise integration and interoperability: Past, present and future. Computers in Industry 59(7), 647–659 (2008)
[28] Nguyen Van, T.: System engineering for collaborating data management systems: Application to design/simulation loop, PhD thesis from Ecole Centrale Paris (2006)
[29] Assouroko, I., Ducellier, G., Eynard, B., Boutinaud, P.D.: Semantic-based approach for the integration of product design and numerical simulation. In: PLM 2011, Eindhoven, Netherland, July 11-13 (2011)
[30] Li, C., Mcmahon, C., Newnes, L., Liu, Y.: Ontology-Based Annotation in PLM Systems. In: International Conference on Product Lifecycle Management (2010)
[31] Barbau, R., Krima, S., Rachuri, S., Narayanan, A., Fiorentini, X., Foufou, S., Sriram, R.D.: OntoSTEP: Enriching product model data using ontologies. Computer-Aided Design 44(6), 575–590 (2012)
[32] Catalano, C.E., Camossi, E., Ferrandes, R., Cheutet, V., Sevilmis, N.: A product design ontology for enhancing shape processing in design workflows. Journal of Intelligent Manufacturing 20(5), 553–567 (2008)
[33] Troussier, N.: A Way to Identify and Manage the Knowledge Provided by Mechanical Simulations in Engineering Design. Computing and Information Systems 7(3), 79–84 (2000)
[34] Etienne, A., Guyot, E., Van Wijk, D., Roucoules, L.: Specifications and Development of Interoperability Solution dedicated to Multiple Expertise Collaboration in a Design Framewor. International Journal of Computer Integrated Manufacturing, 1–14 (2011)
[35] Valilai, O., Houshmand, M.: INFELT STEP: An integrated and interoperable platform for collaborative CAD/CAPP/CAM/CNC machining systems based on STEP standard. International Journal of Computer Integrated Manufacturing 23(11), 1097–1117 (2010)
[36] Nassehi, A., Newman, S.T., Xu, X.W., Rosso, R.S.U.: Toward interoperable CNC manufacturing. International Journal of Computer Integrated Manufacturing 21(2), 222–230 (2008)
[37] Jun, H.-B., Kiritsis, D., Xirouchakis, P.: Research issues on closed-loop PLM. Computers in Industry 58(8-9), 855–868 (2007)
[38] Pratt, M.J.: ISO 10303: the STEP Standard for Product data Exchange and its capabilities. International Journal Product Lifecycle Management 1(1), 86–94 (2005)

[39] Newman, S.T., Nassehi, A., Xu, X.W., Rosso, R.S.U., Wang, L., Yusof, Y., Ali, L., Liu, R., Zheng, L.Y., Kumar, S., Vichare, P., Dhokia, V.: Strategic advantages of interoperability for global manufacturing using CNC technology. Robotics and Computer-Integrated Manufacturing 24(6), 699–708 (2008)
[40] Biahmou, A., Fröhlich, A., Stjepandic, J.: Improving Interoperability in Mechatronic Product Developement. In: PLM 2010, Bremen, Germany, July 12-14 (2010)
[41] Tan, A.R., Matzen, D., McAloone, T.C., Evans, S.: Strategies for designing and developing services for manufacturing firms. CIRP Journal of Manufacturing Science and Technology 3(2), 90–97 (2010)
[42] Harik, R., Capponi, V., Lombard, M., Ris, G.: Enhanced functions supporting process planning for aircraft structural parts. Computational Engineering in Systems Applications (2006)
[43] Bernard, A., Delplace, J.-C., Perry, N., Gabriel, S.: Integration of CAD and rapid manufacturing for sand casting optimisation. Rapid Prototyping Journal 9(5), 327–333 (2003)
[44] Martin, L., Moraru, G., Véron, P.: Development of an integrated tool for the foundry industry. In: 6th International Conference on Engineering, Design and Manufacturing in Mechanical (IDMME), Grenoble, France, May 17-19 (2006)
[45] Le Duigou, J., Bernard, A., Perry, N.: Framework for Product Lifecycle Management integration in Small and Medium Enterprises networks. Computer-Aided Design 8(1) (2012)
[46] Kuo, T., Huang, S., Zhang, H.: Design for manufacture and design for 'X': concepts, applications, and perspectives. Computers & Industrial Engineering 41(3), 241–260 (2001)
[47] Suh, S.-H., Shin, S.-J., Yoon, J.-S., Um, J.-M.: UbiDM: A new paradigm for product design and manufacturing via ubiquitous computing technology. International Journal of Computer Integrated Manufacturing 21(5), 540–549 (2008)
[48] Demoly, F., Toussaint, L., Eynard, B., Kiritsis, D., Gomes, S.: Geometric skeleton computation enabling concurrent product engineering and assembly sequence planning. Computer-Aided Design 43(12), 1654–1673 (2011)
[49] Mantripragada, R.: Assembly oriented design: concepts algorithms and computational tools. Thesis (Ph. D.)– Massachusetts Institute of Technology (1998)
[50] Fenves, S.J., Foufou, S., Bock, C., Sriram, R.D.: CPM: A Core Model for Product Data. Journal of Computing and Information Science in Engineering 8(1), 1–14 (2008)
[51] Chen, D.: Enterprise interoperability framework. In: Proceedings of Entrerpise Modelling and Ontologies for Interoperability, Luxembourg, June 5-6 (2006)
[52] Xu, X.W., Wang, H., Mao, J., Newman, S.T., Kramer, T.R., Proctor, F.M., Michaloski, J.L.: STEP-compliant NC research: the search for intelligent CAD/CAPP/CAM/CNC integration. International Journal of Production Research 43(17), 3703–3743 (2005)
[53] Van Houten, F.: Manufacturing interfaces. CIRP Annals - Manufacturing Technology 41(2), 699–710 (1992)
[54] Paviot, T.: MultiCAD/MultiPDM integration framework. PLM 2008, Seoul, Korea (July 2008)
[55] Elheni-Daldoul, D., Le Duigou, J., Eynard, B., Hajri-Gabouj, S.: Enterprise information systems' interoperability: Focus on PLM challenges. In: Emmanouilidis, C., Taisch, M., Kiritsis, D. (eds.) APMS 2012, Part II. IFIP AICT, vol. 398, pp. 184–191. Springer, Heidelberg (2013)

Repositories and Interoperability Standards

Hondjack Dehainsala[1] and Philippe Perdriau[2]

[1] AREVA, France as Interoperability Expert
[2] EURIWARE, France as PLM project manager
hondjack.dehainsala@areava.com,
philippe.perdriau@euriware.fr

Abstract. Enterprise have needs for interoperability and exchange data interact with repositories; some standards exists and news are come in, particularly those related to the life cycle of facilities and plants. Technical and functional principles have been implemented in an interoperability platform built to meet these needs and to be open to the different standards (existing and news).

PLM tools for repository management are inadequate for handling exchanges in that they consider only the development of point-to-point tools or data copying, and that current exchange standards are also about point-to-point tools and do not really meet the needs of engineering companies and facility operators. This deficiency has led the community to focus on new standards based on Semantic Web technologies (in particular ISO15926) [8] which make these repositories and other authoring tools interoperable with one another.

Feedback is given on the inclusion of this standard, its implementation and deployment.

Keywords: PLM, Plants, ISO15926, Iring, Exchange Process, Interoperability, Semantic-Web, AIRE.

1 The Need to Interoperate and the Expected Functions

1.1 Functions Integrated into the Repositories

The term PLM is taken to mean all processes, activities and functions used to manage and configure data, documents, files and information during the cycle [7] of a product or facility. Presently only functions and data are considered.

PLMs are widely deployed in manufacturing industries [7] and are starting to be in companies involved in the design, construction, operation, maintenance and decommissioning of facilities. However, in this latter context special features appear that are particularly linked to the eco-system engaged on projects and to the nature of the objects and design processes of continuous-process industries.

1.2 Purpose of This Document

The purpose of this paper is to analyze the features and tools for data exchange and between systems to make them interoperable, given, to use the definition outlined by Wikipedia, that interoperability is the ability of a product or system, whose interfaces

A. Bernard, L. Rivest, and D. Dutta (Eds.): PLM 2013, IFIP AICT 409, pp. 140–148, 2013.

are fully known, to work with other existing or future products or systems with unrestricted access or implementation; the creation of a specific tool to make A and B communicate does not make A and B interoperable.

The main question is: do we need interoperability with PLM tools and why?

After that, we consider the characteristic of exchange standards and why the news standards like ISO15926 are based on new technology as the semantic Web.

We conclude with our feedback from a platform development and from first tests in interoperability.

1.3 Special Cases in the Design, Construction and Maintenance of Petrochemical, Chemical and Nuclear Power Process Facilities

In these situations, the eco-system of the stakeholders involved is not known in advance from one project to another, which distinguishes this context from those commonly encountered in other sectors. It is assembled and dismantled for each operation: partners one day are competitors the next and suppliers' cultural differences are important, as the projects are mainly international with the contractual obligation to employ local businesses.

Operators ultimately recover the documentation (data, study, construction, inspection and commissioning documents) models, files and requirements, and classify and integrate them into their own operational systems or archiving.

Facilities comprise a large number of objects (of the order of one million compared, for example, with a car which has only a few thousand).

At this stage, the following observation can be made:

- The exchanges between systems are numerous, very diverse and need to be controlled and secured [2]
  - If we consider that out of the million objects referenced in a facility, 10% are subject to a collaborative process with the outside world and that this process requires 3-5 exchanges of partial or complete information, this makes about 1000 exchanges per day at the peak, with about a hundred stakeholders.
- A single repository shared with several stakeholders is not a good idea, in addition to the fact that it is very complex to set up (especially if it is needed throughout the duration of a project, because it may be completed only after the end of the project).

A functional architecture should therefore be chosen, suited to the needs of each entity and to its responsibilities, but open and interoperable with other systems.

Example: interoperability need for an operator
An operator uses different business views of the various systems and equipment items

- *For example, a technological view per equipment family*
- *A maintenance view for equipment maintenance and monitoring activities*
- *An operational view for control and supervision systems*
- *A project view related to carrying out technical modifications*

The PLM can produce different business views (trees and data), and present structures identical to the internal breakdown of the various tools in the information system. The same object can then be seen by the different tools while retaining the overall consistency, as shown in the diagram below.

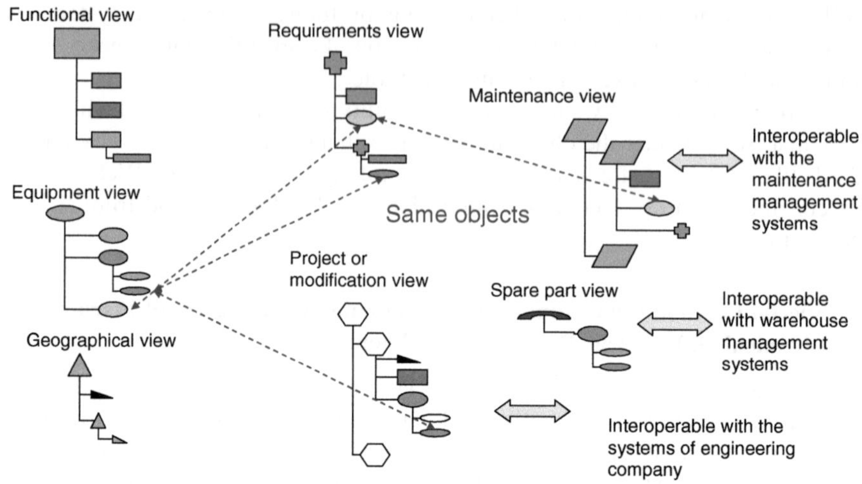

Fig. 1. Interoperability needs for an operator

The interoperability functions are then used to synchronize the systems, but it is also necessary to control the process of dissemination and integration between the source and the various targets.

1.4 Exchange Needs with Others: How to Achieve This

The previous sections show the diversity of exchange needs in both engineering projects and facility modification activities. There are structured into 4 categories:

1) Exchanges with suppliers

- Supplies input data to subcontractors
- Information back from supplier to populate the engineering databases
- Creation of collaborative catalogues

2) Coordination between non-integrated specialties

- Synchronizing data (periodic or with milestones) between unconnected systems

3) Exchanges within a consortium

- Controlling and synchronizing data (periodic or with milestones) between unconnected systems

4) Providing data to a third-party

- Periodic or with milestones = handover
- Populating operating and maintenance systems

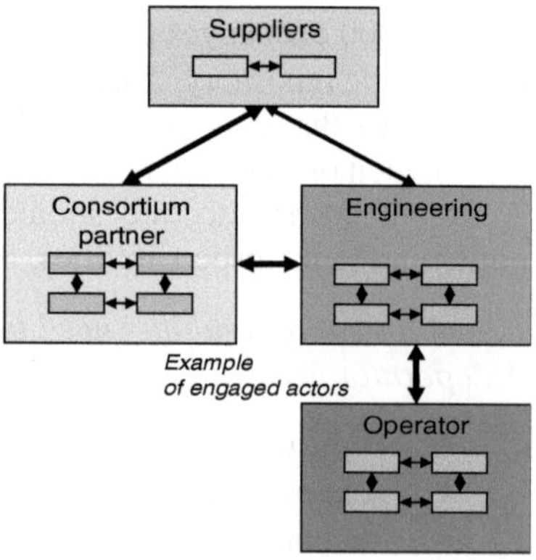

Fig. 2. Exchanges between Plant actors

While some exchanges consist of synchronizing information, it is standard practice they are supported by the publishing processes on the one hand and integration processes on the other. It is recommended to filter and check the data to be made accessible, control the quality of the data received and see the changes; the tools must be able to deal with the exchange safely, both for the value of data and for a data set or the whole of a facility, either in sync mode or via formalized transmissions.

The lack of interoperability between these stakeholders is a source of costs (4 % according to [1]) which may be important in absolute terms in major contracts and may be even more so in relative terms for modifications to facilities, even if they are less costly.

In conclusion, interoperability functions are complementary functions that are found in PLM tools. The development of tools, **based on exchange standards**, connected to PLMs, but also to other sources of information, helps to streamline information systems and optimizes project processes. Only adopting a standard shared by the eco-system is able to solve the problem.

2 Exchange or Interoperability Standards and New Technologies

Exchange standards (ISO10303, ISO15926, for example) have similar characteristics:

1. An expression language of a data model
2. A data model representing a concept,
3. A dictionary describing types of reference objects and their characteristics,
4. Means to exchange and access information.

The choice of the exchange standard is based on the characteristics of the data model and the contents of the dictionary.

The usage of a standard by a company differs according to the disciplines (civil engineering, equipment, I & C, requirements), that these often refer the same information and that the consistency of information published or integrated becomes very difficult to maintain.

The ISO15926 standard (also called iRing) developed and maintained by the association PCA (POASC CAESAR ASSOCIATION) under the authority of the FIATECH (in relation with standardization bodies, in particular TC184/SC4) proposes a significant change in the approach in terms of both modelling and technology.

In terms of modelling, the following notable points can be distinguished:

1. The model is based on the overall classification if each element satisfies the inclusion criteria in its category and on class specialization for a subclass to inherit the properties of the parent class; relationships between classes can be also categorized.
2. This fairly complex modelling is intended to be described in the language of the Semantic Web, i.e. OWL (Ontology Web Language).
3. Objects and object attributes are identified by URIs (Uniform Resource Identifier) and allow sharing by means of web navigation.

4. The ISO15926 standard, based on the notion of roles (defining attributes of a class) that can be instantiated on an object, enables representation to be simplified while remaining under the control of the principles set out in the general model.
5. Each company makes a mapping between the data model of its business application with the data model of ISO15926, its dictionary (private or public) and its roles (templates).

In terms of technology, using the Semantic Web [3] provides the following benefits:

1. Based on a general purpose, non-specific communication standard for technical data: this makes it possible to use distributed technological layers.
   - So OWL modelling can be handled by existing tools inherent in this technology.
2. Using rules, this handling makes it possible to combine different concepts (domains) insofar as a relationship can be expressed to relate these concepts.

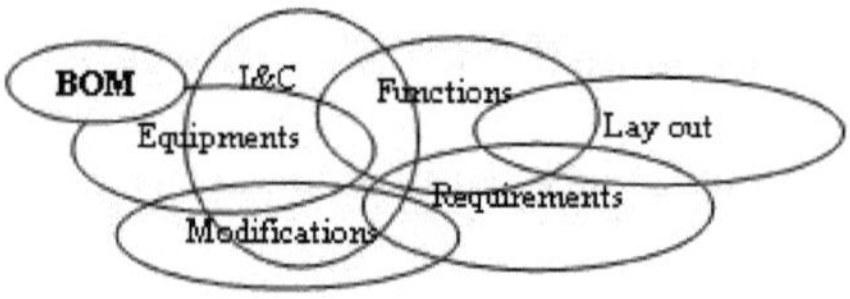

Fig. 3. Example of adding different concepts

The dictionary of standard ISO15926 (RDL) today contains the characteristics of objects contained in the facility: equipment (heat exchangers, columns, etc.), components (pumps, valves, motors, etc.) which make it possible to describe a technical tree of physical objects. It is also possible to describe an abstract object tree as a functional tree.

However exchanging this data is insufficient, particularly in the management of critical facilities and it is recommended that they should be accompanied by exchanges concerning the related requirements (e.g. requirements about the equipment). Semantic Web technologies allow this association and make it possible to implement it more efficiently than the simultaneous implementation of different protocols (AP221, AP227 and AP233) of ISO 10303..

3. Constraints (such as those formulated in STEP Express language) can then be added to the OWL model. These constraints, expressed as additional rules, can be enriched by each stakeholder without having to be uniquely defined in the standard.
4. The general use of URIs allows the construction of dictionaries at normative for the all concepts, sector or private level.
5. The exchange of information can be done in OWL files which include both data and the data model. We can then speak of knowledge transfer.
6. The notion of façade (RDF = Resource Description Framework) makes it possible to make data searchable via the Internet accessible using a suitable query system (SPARQL language). This language enables the concepts of the OWL data model in order to access the required information.

Another point to consider is that the exchanges are supported by the processes of each entity. In contractual terms, the exchanges must be traced and accompanied by a document possibly associated with an electronic signature of compliance.

The ISO15926 standard supports all its promises, the question being to find the most effective tools and see how they can be deployed in practice. This has been explained and experimented as set out in Part 3 of this document.

In conclusion, the new information technologies, especially the Semantic Web are able to provide innovation in achieving exchange standards: they allow exchanges that are internal and external to the Company and are more flexible to implement. They also allow different contexts to be aggregated. The emerging ISO15926 standards based on these technologies is potentially able to take up a key position (especially in process industries) and must therefore be investigated and equipped while maintaining a broad view of possible extensions and technical and contractual implementation constraints.

3 Experience Feedback from Industrial Implementation

The AIRE platform (AREVA Interoperabilty Rich Environment or AREVA IRING Environment following the redesignation of ISO15926 by the IRING brand) was developed to experiment and industrialize the above principles.

Technologically, this platform has been designed to:

- Be compliant with the Semantic Web technology,
- Implement all parts of ISO15926[1],
- Take into account the constraints related to data privacy and cyber security.

And in functional terms, it has been designed to:

- Be open to taking into consideration the exchange of data from multiple domains either by extension of the Part 2 model of ISO15926 and the RDL dictionary, Part 4, or by integrating other standards (e.g. - ISA, BIM/IFC, STEP).
- Support the information publishing process, filtering information to be published[2], creation and management of publication spaces according to data and recipients[3].
- Produce reports accompanying the publication of such information in order to meet contractual requirements.
- Support the information integration process with evaluation of changes between two successive integrations and performance of integrity checks[4].
- Produce examination and integration reports to meet contractual requirements.
- Allow queries on data published by means of query generators.
- Exchange data sets by producing OWL files (on XML layer) making data and data model consistent with each other.

---

[1] It's mandatory to share data thru internet way, to extend the ISO15926 data model with new concepts and dictionary.

[2] To avoid publication of internal data that the company have to protect if these data are also stored in the application with the data that the company must publish.

[3] To separate information regarding recipient need to have the data.

[4] To control data with company rules before integration in the target tool.

- Produce private RDLs and check correspondence (mapping) between source data and the RDLs (those maintained by certification bodies PCA/JORD and private RDLs generated) within a collaborative dialogue between two third-party partners. This check focuses on the completeness of the mapping and on the practical checks on the basis of test data before running the exchanges.
- Manage master data with alerting in case of modification of these data
- Take into account the exchange of attribute data, schematic data and ultimately 3D data and their changes (version or time effectiveness).

To demonstrate its capability, several connectors are made with off-the-shelf packages so as to build some real feedback on tool integration.

This has made it possible to validate the source integration methodology and to develop transactions and man-machine interfaces related to the above process: exchanges are prepared in AIRE but are directly carried out in the interfaces of these tools which therefore become interoperable.

3.1 Source Integration Methodology

The founding principle of the AIRE methodology (using the work described in [4]) is a) to transpose the data model of the application into an interface (source or target) and perform data transfer (import or export) in the formalism of the Semantic Web: b) construction of ontology of the application and c) execution of technical interface functions. This action gives a mirror of the data application in RDF format (in the form of subject-predicate-object triples) of both the data model and data directly manipulated by an OWL reasoner tool (into which the ontology of the standard has previously been loaded).

This is done once and for all for each application. The import and export functions can then be realized by the same way.

3.2 Exchange Transformation Methodology in the Standard

The second step is then to link the dictionary elements to the elements of the data model of the application. This is called "mapping" and is handled within a module of AIRE, the "configuration editor" which can question the public RDLs maintained by the PCA) or create private RDLs (at the level of the company, a group of companies or a business sector)[5].

This operation is performed once per application and per standard. However, it needs to have a validation process to ensure that the mapping made is understood by the other parties: and the "configuration editor" can do this in collaborative mode with a third party, independently of whether the latter has the AIRE platform or not.

[5] RDL = Reference Data Library = the dictionary of the standard.

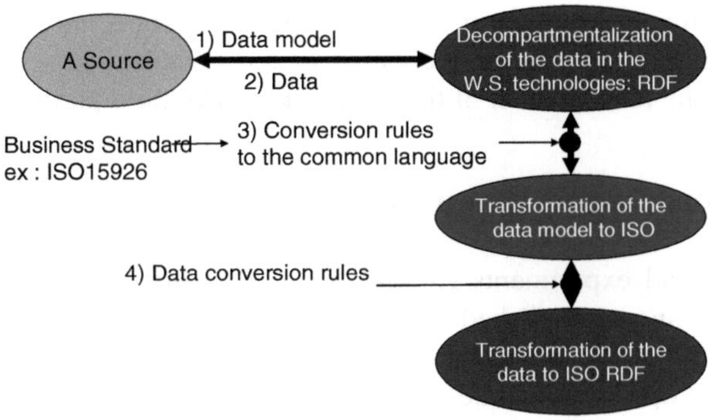

Fig. 4. Transformation principle

The configuration editor then generates a certain number of rules that are added to the ontology of the standard (here Part 2 of the ISO15926 standard) making it possible to link the dictionary (Part 4) and the roles (Part 7).

These rules are then carried out to publish or integrate the application data in interaction with the formalisms of the standard. This formalism can be expressed in the language of the Semantic Web (through RDF facades or OWL exports as is the case for ISO 15926), but can be expressed in other formats (XML based for example such as PROTEUS/XMPLANT or as AEX).

3.3 Validation and Certification

The AIRE solution has been validated with blind exchanges with a third party as part of a handover process. This experiment has improved functionality and means that the solution can be presented for certification by the PCA (POSC CAESAR ASSOCIATION).

3.4 Feedback

Firstly, the inclusion of a new standard in the company takes time that should not be underestimated. It seems important that the company should build case studies, depending on its activity and its own feedback, and clearly identify its levers, whether these be technical, technological, business or commercial.

In the case of the developments and experiments made, the flexibility provided by the Semantic Web is confirmed without significant performance degradation due to this flexibility.

One difficulty that should not be underestimated is related to communication of the standard and its implementation especially in the presentation of findings from the experiments: if it is too technical, it will seem very complicated and will alarm decision-makers; if this complexity is hidden, it becomes too easy or simplistic and states the obvious. It is therefore necessary to refer to difficulties encountered daily by the company which requires prior acceptance of these problems.

Finally, the implementation of these interoperability tools introduces new tasks and new roles or may even require adaptation of the organization within the Company, particularly in the management of these interfaces with third parties.

4 Conclusion and Extensions

Developments and experiments carried out as part of the R&D project led to the construction of an accomplished solution, benefiting both from the advantages of a solid base, and also from business transactions deriving from a group with both engineering and operation/maintenance of complex systems services.

It has also been shown that interoperability should be seen as a specific function with specialized stakeholders defining models and mappings, and organizing exchange flows.

This solution is integrated into the PLM repositories, which thereby have an additional interoperability function, and prevents/reduces manual copying of information or the implementation of specific point-to-point developments as well as the risk of errors and related cost overruns.

The choice of technological solutions and their design is essential in order to accompany these changes without calling them into question. The Semantic Web technologies and their implementation flexibility allow us to meet these goals by drastically reducing the costs and risks: they live up to their promises.

References

[1] NEI Nuclear Asset Management Community of Practice Report: The Standard Nuclear Performance Model - A Process Management Approach - Revision 4 et INPO AP929 Configuration Management Process Description
[2] Etude NIST (NIST GCR 04-867: Cost Analysis of Inadequate Interoperability in the U.S. Capital Facilities Industry) published in 2004 for an assessment of such costs (2004)
[3] Document " introduction to ISO15926" published by Fiatech in October 2011 for a description of the standard, its history and a detailed argument for this change
[4] Berners-Lee, T., Hendler, J., Lassila, O.: The Semantic Web. Scientific American 284(5), 34–43 (2001)
[5] Bellatreche, L., Pierra, G., Xuan, D.N., Hondjack, D., Ameur, Y.A.: An a Priori Approach for Automatic Integration of Heterogeneous and Autonomous Databases. In: Galindo, F., Takizawa, M., Traunmüller, R. (eds.) DEXA 2004. LNCS, vol. 3180, pp. 475–485. Springer, Heidelberg (2004)
[6] Topbraid, Editor of a toolbox for the Semantic Web, http://www.topquadrant.com/resources/documentation.html#tbc
[7] Teijgeler, H.: The Process Industries and the ISO 15926 Semantic Web, http://www.infowebml.ws/intro/paper.htm
[8] Le Duigou, J., Bernard, A., Perry, N., Delplace, J.C.: Generic PLM system for SMEs: Application to an equipment manufacturer. IJPLM (2012)
[9] Matsokis, A.: An Ontology-Based Approach for Closed-Loop Product Lifecycle Management, Thesis (2010), http://infoscience.epfl.ch/record/150273/files/EPFL_TH4823.pdf

Developing a PLM Framework: A Case Study Application in an Energy Company

Angelo Corallo[1], Mariangela Lazoi[1], Antonio Margarito[1], and Davide Pinna[2]

[1] Dipartimento di Ingegneria dell'Innovazione, Università del Salento, Italy
[2] Ansaldo Energia, Italy
mariangela.lazoi@unisalento.it

Abstract. Product lifecycle management has to be related to a business approach that requires IT solutions and also organizational changes in order to produce the desired effects. Different aspects (product data, people, processes, organization, IT technologies) needs to be integrated together for the achievement of a competitive advantage for the company. PLM needs of operational tools that can support the implementation of the theoretical principles. In particular, as extensively studied in the literature, company needs frameworks to refer for guiding the implementation of PLM initiatives and to support improvement actions. Based on an action research, the paper wants to describe the development and application of a PLM framework in Ansaldo Energia, an Italian leader energy company. The framework is product-centred and focused on processes and related IT systems. It allows to diffuse knowledge and culture on products lifecycle inside the company. Indications for the framework development in the ARIS Software AG are also provided.

Keywords: PLM, framework, lifecycle phases, processes, configuration management, IT systems.

1 Introduction

PLM means an integrated management of technological, methodological and strategic issues along the whole product lifecycle [1],[2]. A product data is not created and used only in a specific activity but it is linked to the whole set of data that are created and used during its lifecycle [3]. Having this awareness, inefficiencies related to waste of time, energy and resources can be avoided. Many companies refer to the PLM considering only the IT side and ignoring the organizational impact [4]. If it is underestimated, wrong investments and long time for IT deployment can arise. The understanding of these issues is not immediate. It needs a cultural change [5] based on a consciousness and knowledge of the impacts and relations among the whole product lifecycle elements.

Several scholars have developed models and frameworks on PLM (e.g. [6], [7], [8]) and have analyzed the industrial case studies (e.g. [9], [10]) to evaluate their validity. The available works don't explore the context of an energy company and don't propose a PLM framework and a corresponding methodology for process representation.

A. Bernard, L. Rivest, and D. Dutta (Eds.): PLM 2013, IFIP AICT 409, pp. 149–158, 2013.

Therefore, based on an action research between University and Industry, the paper explore a case study on PLM features and relations in Ansaldo Energia, an Italian leading energy company. A PLM framework is proposed and validated in the paper. The aim is to generate a pragmatic view around PLM for company working for complex product development in high-technological sectors, such as energy one. structure processes, activities, data and IT tools related to a specific product lifecycle are highlighted and represented in an organic and integrated structure. The proposed framework has been used by the company to diffuse a PLM culture and knowledge.

2 Background

A wide set of PLM model is available in scientific papers as a result of both theoretical and industrial research. The most comprehensive models in literature present a holistic PLM vision describing the complexity of PLM and harmonizing all its aspects in a limited set of key dimensions.

Budde et al. [7] include in their framework four elements important for the development and the implementation of PLM: strategy, process, product structure and IT-architecture. According to the author the challenge is not the selection of single solutions, but the integration of different tools and systems in the holistic implementation. Budde's model has been discussed by Silventoinen et al. [8], who add a fifth element, people and culture, in order to emphasize the importance of organizational culture and human factor in PLM implementation. Interrelation between key dimensions are defined both in Budde et al. [7] and Silventoinen et al. [8].

Others authors have proposed models that identify PLM main components. In Schuh et al. [6], the central point consists of a set of lifecycle oriented business process reference models which vary according to a group of company's characteristics. The centrality of business processes and product data are also the distinctive element of the PLM model defined by Abramovici [11]. He proposes a model that includes methods, models and IT tools for managing product information, engineering processes and applications along the different phases of the product lifecycle [11]. PLM is also analyzed by Rangan et al [5] that define just the broad scope of PLM specifying eight key dimensions: Business Drivers, Transformation Drivers, Domain Model, Generic Product Lifecycle, PLM tools, Implementation Drivers and Deployment Transition.

The role of processes in PLM is relevant as described in someone of the previous framework (e.g. [6]; [7]). Through processes, products evolve along the lifecycle and feedbacks (e.g. lesson learned and best practice) are diffused among the organizational practices. Different researchers have studied the relevance of processes in the product lifecycle. Messaadia et al [12] have explored the System Engineering processes to model PLM and concluded that this approach is complimentary to PLM to address the systems technology. Etienne et al [13] have proposed a interoperability platform based on product processes organizations. Schulte [14] instead has proposed a methodology to better integrate the customers' requirements of actual or attended products in the PLM functions, processes and metadata. As highlighted by Rangan et al [5], PLM processes need further exploration and a "cultural change management" is required in order to optimize organizational processes rather than individual benefits.

In literature, several case studies analyze the company practices in the PLM field. In the study of Golovatchev et al. [10], a telecommunication industry is explored and a PLM-process management approach is proposed and validated. This approach is suitable for complex products composed by several elements each-one characterized by a proper lifecycle. Some case studies have a technological focus such as the work of An Chiang & Trappey [15] in which a PLM system implementation in LCD industry is described through the proposal of a conceptual architecture of PLM. Focusing on companies working in complex sectors, there are specific case studies analyzing the aerospace and automotive sectors. For the aerospace sector, relevant studies are: 1) Alemanni et al. [9], which propose a KPI framework to test the adoption of a PLM tool, validated in an aerospace and defence company and 2) Lee et al. [16], which discuss two case studies from the aviation MRO companies in Singapore that stress the high potentiality of PLM applications. In the automotive sector, the study of Tang & Qian [17] needs a citation: it illustrates the PLM implementation among an OEM and its suppliers highlighting practices and characteristics.

Therefore, several researchers have argued both on the PLM representation in framework and models and on the relevance of PLM as a business approach integrating different companies' perspectives. In a high quantity of studies, the role of processes is clearly highlighted and included in the PLM treatments as a central element. Furthermore, to support the wide relevance of PLM for the companies practices several case studies are available that discuss and make relevant the strategic role of PLM both as a technology and as a business approach in different industrial sectors. None of the analyzed cases study in literature are focused on the energy sectors but best practices and lesson learned can be grasped and extended. This element is relevant to highlight the uniqueness of case study research focused on a specific object.

Additionally, in literature it doesn't exist an holistic PLM framework described with a methodology for process representation that support and allow a further extension and replication.

Finally, several are the enterprise architecture frameworks (i.e. Zachman Framework [18], CBM [19], DCOR [20], APQC [21], CMMI [22]) that treat the representation and integration of different organizational dimensions in a unique framework. This enterprise architecture framework however miss of a focus on the product and on its lifecycle. For example, configuration management aspects are not treated as a whole. Suggestions of linkages among elements and the use of standardized item name (e.g. such as for APQC) have been considered and integrated in the research results.

3 Research Design

3.1 Research Method

Based on the previous literature background, the paper wants to describe the development and application of a PLM framework, product-centred and focused on processes and involved IT systems, in an energy company. The main research question that the paper wants to address is: How to represent a PLM framework for complex products in order to diffuse a PLM culture and share features and insights of a product lifecycle?

This question has emerged as aim of an action research in which University of Salento was involved with its partner company Ansaldo Energia in the MindSh@re community of Finmeccanica. The paper presents an industrial case study based on the results of the carried out action research.

A case study is particularly appropriate to study contemporary events and non-controllable units of analysis [23]. The case study is thus guided by the pragmatism knowledge claim: it is problem-centric and the attention is therefore placed on the problem and how to solve it in a real organizational setting [24]. Multiple sources of evidences have been used to increase the case study's construct validity [23]: the direct researchers' observations and interviews with key users. Most of the information was collected through a set of interviews to key company referents. They are a convenience sample since are involved in the phases of product lifecycle as manager or responsible [25]. For each phase, a key informant have been involved and information have been shared and collected with its collaboration. An open-ended questionnaire has been administered at each key informant to better stimulate perspectives, views and opinions sharing among the participants [24]. The key informants have reviewed the case study report and validated the main findings and conclusions. Data and information of the PLM framework have been represented using the software ARIS Business Architect 7.1. This software is suitable to create, analyze, manage and administer an enterprise process architecture.

3.2 Research Context

Ansaldo Energia (AEN) is a Finmeccanica Group company and is the Italian largest supplier, installer and service provider for power generation plants and components. AEN is a manufacturing company working in the production of gas turbines, steam turbines and generators (hydro and air-cooled generators) dedicated to energy production. Depending on the contract type, AEN provides a variety of system configurations ranging from the simple supply of machines to the design, implementation and management of the entire plant.

AEN considers the PLM as essential and strategic to manage information, processes and resources that support the product along its lifecycle, from the conceptualization to the design, from the manufacturing to the sell, until the maintenance.

4 Results

4.1 The PLM Framework

Each time a company's product is designed, physically realized, delivered to a customer and, in some cases, also maintained and disposed, its lifecycle is put into effect requiring several resources and impacting on different organizational dimensions.

The structure of the proposed PLM Framework is composed by four blocks and related relational levels. The four blocks are: Block A - PLM Definition and Foundation; Block B - PLM Phases and Processes; Block C - PLM Configuration Management Views; Block D - PLM IT Architecture.

The PLM Framework can be developed for each product typology in the company. Each product has its own phases of lifecycle led by the processes execution. During the activities done in the processes, the product data evolve and are represented in the configuration management (CM) views. IT tools are used in the processes and make available the CM Data.

Each block is designed to be detailed for including further relevant information. A specification of detail levels with the corresponding ARIS models is available:

- Block A: 1) Company's products (as Product-Tree), 2) Structure of Products (as Product-Tree) and 3) Structure of Products Component(as Product-Tree).
- Block B: 1) Synthesis of company's products lifecycle (as Value-added Chain Diagram), 2) Product Lifecycle Phases (as Value-added Chain Diagram), 3) Processes for a specific Product Lifecycle Phase (as Value-added Chain Diagram), 4) Process Activities for a specific Product Lifecycle Phase (as EPC column display) and 5) Detail of IT systems, inputs, outputs and organizational units for an activity (as Functional Allocation Diagram)
- Block C: 1) Sets of Configuration Management Views for company's products (as Value-added Chain Diagram), 2) Product Configuration Management Views (as Value-added Chain Diagram) and 3) Metadata, software and activities for the Configuration Management View of a given Product (as UML Class Diagram).
- Block D: 1) Sets of IT systems for company's products (as EPC), 2) Product IT Systems (as Entry Diagram) and 3) Details (available modules, integrations and supported activities) of the IT system for a given Product (as Entry Diagram).

About the first two levels of the lask block, IT systems are specified as isolated entities that are used for different aims and in different moments of the life-cycle. In the third level "Details", instead, the integration among the different IT systems are specified, if it is present. Generally, in the practice of the companies is almost impossible to observe that all the software tools used along the lifecycle of a product are directly integrated without the need of re-working or uploading among different systems. This evidence justify the chosen block structure.

4.2 The Application in AEN

The gas turbine has been chosen as test-case for the application of the PLM Framework. It is a core product for AEN and is considered as a "single equipment" that can be expanded including also the whole plant or the maintenance services.

According to analyzed AEN practices, the following lifecycle phases have been defined:

- Plan: a product life cycle starts with the definition of the company strategic plan that include research and business initiatives.
- Concept Development: incremental or radical innovation activities on existing products are carry out to satisfy the needs of a specific customer or to increase and improve the company products portfolio.
- Product Design: when a job order is received, product changes and installation details are designed.
- Manufacturing: it is comprehensive of all the industrialization activities, including two fundamental moments the productive process design and the effective production.
- Sell & Distribution: the realized product is delivered and installed at the customer site.
- Service: when the product is operative in its site, a set of maintenance activities are executed based on the agreement conditions.
- Disposal: an AEN product lifecycle is very long but if established by agreement, at the end of its lifecycle, it can be retired and its recyclable and un-recyclable components adequately managed.

The Lifecycle Phases are characterized by Technical Processes [26] based on technical activities executed in the lifecycle for realizing the customers desired products. The Lifecycle Phases with their Technical Processes are supported by Project Processes [26] that allow to manage resources and assets allocated to a project. Among them, in the specific case of AEN, the Tollgate Process and the Product Configuration Management Process are highlighted.

For each lifecycle phase, the Technical processes have been identified (e.g. Figure 1) and for each process, the activities, IT systems and data have been modeled using the EPC (Event Process Chain) standard. A Function Allocation Diagram (FAD) have been created for the activities with more than one input, output or IT system. Such activities have been extracted from the process and the related features have been assigned.

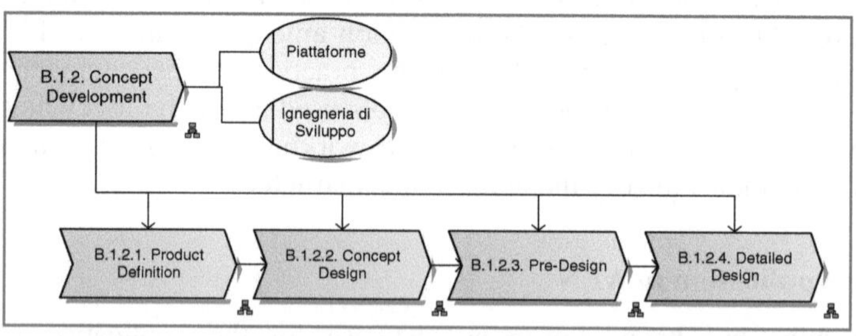

Fig. 1. Processes of Gas Turbine Concept Development phase

The configuration management views recognized and managed in AEN are As Designed, As Planned and As Delivered. A CM View is a visualization of data in a specific moment of the lifecycle allocated for specific tasks. Such data are available on information systems and represents the product features. Therefore, for the aim of the Framework, the CM views have been broken up in their meta-data (e.g. Figure 2). IT systems in which are available, and activities in which are created, have been also specified.

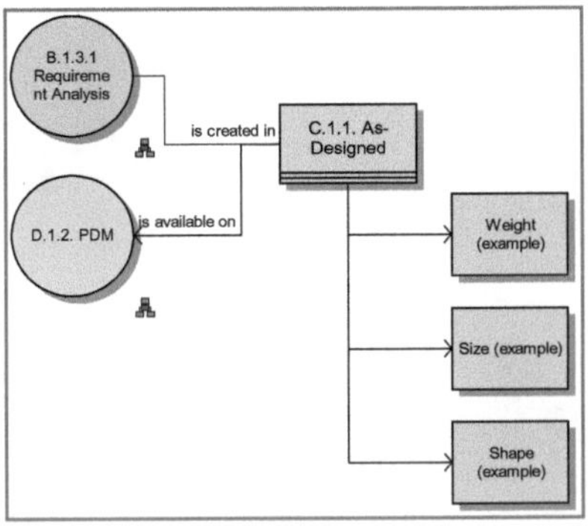

Fig. 2. Detail of As-Designed View (for privacy issues, meta-data are reported as example)

In AEN, several IT systems are used to manage and execute processes and to store configuration management data. A type classification is: Product Lifecycle Management (PLM) System, Product Data Management (PDM) System, Computer Aided Design (CAD) System, Computer Aided Engineering (CAE) System, Computer Aided Manufacturing (CAM) System, Project Management System, Enterprise Resources Planning (ERP) System, Legacy Software, Optimization Software and the Materials Database (DB). AEN has both a PLM and PDM System, this last one is mainly used as Document Management System in some processes. For each IT system, a map has been realized with available modules, supported activities and integration with others tools.

The analysis done for product data, processes, configuration management views and IT systems along the gas turbine lifecycle, is summarized in the following figure that represents the high level of the PLM framework for AEN.

The Framework is easy to navigate by simply clicking on the selected item both in the ARIS software and in a web format (html) that can be integrated in companies' portals. The use of the software ARIS Business Architect 7.1 have allowed to satisfied the need of a better traceability, integration and representation of the Framework elements thanks to the availability of several models suitable for each block's element. Furthermore, the Framework elements are structured in folders guaranteeing an easier consultation and exploration.

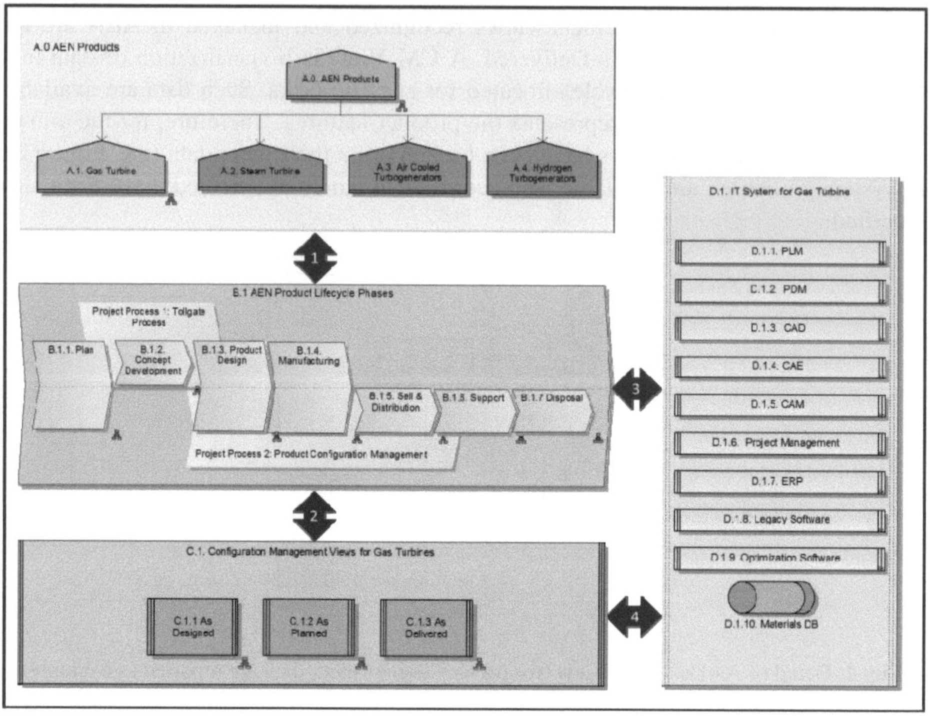

Fig. 3. PLM Framework for Gas Turbine in AEN

5 Discussion and Conclusion

In the study, the context of the company Ansaldo Energia has been explored and structured around a PLM framework suitable to represent in an integrated scenario product data, processes, configuration views and IT systems. The study results provide an evidence from a real company practices in the PLM field and suggest the adoption of a PLM framework detailed using the software ARIS Business Architect. In the paper, indications on the selected ARIS models for the representation of the Framework are also provided that can be used to replicate the framework in others contexts.

In the PLM Framework, the lifecycle is represented as an integrated framework in which data, processes and IT systems co-exist and are linked. The main field of application of the PLM Framework is to create a reference for the PLM issues inside the company. It can be used for documentation purposes inside the company in order to diffuse a PLM culture and knowledge among the employees. In this manner, the employees are stimulated to think to their job as a small part of a wider set of activities that impact on the whole product lifecycle performance.

The PLM Framework can also be useful in performance measurement of processes and IT inside a company or among different companies, as it provides a reference to assess performances on a wider scope, covering the whole product lifecycle, instead of providing measurements of individual elements separated from the whole context. Furthermore, representing IT and processes for different products, it allows to compare the different company scenarios and can support the design of improvements and rationalise initiatives.

Such a tool, as correlates all the different parts, allows a more accurate assessment of the effort and of the impacts that a change in the company (e.g. a change to a process, an update of an IT system, etc.) can have in terms of cost and/or performance over the entire lifecycle. It can be used to better manage the change management process.

Future research will be dedicated to better formalize the PLM framework methodology and apply it to other organizational contexts within Ansaldo Energia and in other companies as well.

References

[1] Garetti, M., Terzi, S., Bertacci, N., Brianza, M.: Organisational change and knowledge management in PLM implementation. International Journal of Product Lifecycle Management 1(1), 43–51 (2005)
[2] Grieves, M.: Product Lifecycle Management: Driving the Next Generation of Lean Thinking. McGraw-Hill, New York (2006)
[3] Ameri, F., Dutta, D.: Product Lifecycle Management: Closing the Knowledge Loops. Computer-Aided Design & Applications 2(5), 577–590 (2005)
[4] Batenburg, R., Helms, R.W., Versendaal, J.: PLM roadmap: stepwise PLM implementation based on the concepts of maturity and alignment. International Journal of Product Lifecycle Management 1(4), 333–351 (2006)
[5] Rangan, R.M., Rohde, S.M., Peak, R., Chadha, B., Bliznakov, P.: Streamlining Product Lifecycle Processes: A Survey of Product Lifecycle Management Implementations, Directions, and Challenges. Journal of Computing and Information Science in Engineering 5(3), 227–237 (2005)
[6] Schuh, G., Rozenfeld, H., Assmus, D., Zancul, E.: Process oriented framework to support PLM implementation. Computers in Industry 59(2-3), 210–218 (2008)
[7] Budde, O., Schuh, G., Uam, J.: Holistic PLM Model – Deduction of a Holistic PLM-Model from the General Dimensions of an Integrated Management. In: International Conference on Product Lifecycle Management, Bremen, Germany (2010)
[8] Silventoinen, A., Pels, H.J., Kärkkäinen, H., Lampela, H.: Holistic PLM Model. In: 8th International Conference on Product Lifecycle Management, Eindhoven, Netherlands (2011)
[9] Alemanni, M., Grimaldi, A., Tornincasa, S., Vezzetti, E.: Key performance indicators for PLM benefits evaluation: The Alcatel Alenia Space case study. Computers in Industry 59(8), 833–841 (2008)
[10] Golovatchev, J.D., Budde, O., Hong, C.: Integrated PLM-process-approach for the development and management of telecommunications products in a multi-lifecycle environment. International Journal of Manufacturing Technology and Management 19(3), 224–237 (2010)

[11] Abramovici, M.: Future trends in product lifecycle management (PLM). In: Krause, F.-L. (ed.) The Future of Product Development, pp. 665–674. Springer, Berlin (2007)
[12] Messaadia, M., Jamal, M.H., Sahraoui, A.E.K.: Systems Engineering Processes Deployment for PLM. In: International Conference on Product Lifecycle Management, Lyon, France (2005)
[13] Etienne, A., Guyot, E., Van Wijk, D., Roucoules, L.: Specifications and development of interoperability solution dedicated to multiple expertise collaboration in a design framework. International Journal of Product Lifecycle Management 5(2), 272–294 (2011)
[14] Schulte, S.: Customer centric PLM: integrating customers' feedback into product data and lifecycle processes. International Journal of Product Lifecycle Management 3(4), 295–307 (2009)
[15] Chiang, T.A., Trappey, A.: Development of value chain collaborative model for product lifecycle management and its LCD industry adoption. International Journal of Production Economics 109(1-2), 90–104 (2007)
[16] Lee, S.G., Ma, Y.-S., Thimm, G.L., Verstraeten, J.: Product lifecycle management in aviation maintenance, repair and overhaul. Computers in Industry 59(2-3), 296–303 (2008)
[17] Tang, D., Qian, X.: Product lifecycle management for automotive development focusing on supplier integration. Computer in Industry 59(2-3), 288–295 (2008)
[18] Zachman International, The Zachman framework (2006), http://www.zachman.com/ (accessed on November 16, 2012)
[19] IBM Consulting Services, A component-based approach to strategic change (2011), http://www-935.ibm.com/services/uk/igs/html/cbm-bizmodel.html (accessed on November 16, 2012)
[20] Supply-Chain Council, Supply Chain Council Website (2008), http://supply-chain.org/ (accessed on November 28, 2011)
[21] APQC, APQC Process Classification Framework Website (2011), http://www.apqc.org/process-classification-framework (accessed on November 16, 2012)
[22] CMMI Product Team, CMMI for Development, Version 1.3 (2010), http://www.sei.cmu.edu/reports/10tr033.pdf (accessed on November 16, 2012)
[23] Yin, R.K.: Case Study Research: Design and Methods. Sage, Thousand Oaks (2003)
[24] Creswell, J.W.: Research Design: Qualitative, Quantitative, and Mixed Methods Approaches. Sage Publications, Thousand Oaks (2008)
[25] Bryman, A., Bell, E.: Business Research Methods. Oxford University Press, Oxford (2007)
[26] ISO/IEC 15288, Systems and software engineering — System life cycle processes, ISO/IEC-IEEE (2008)

A Framework for PLM Model Design

Onur Yildiz[1,3], Philippe Pernelle[2], Lilia Gzara[3], and Michel Tollenaere[3]

[1] Audros technology, 41 rue de la cite F-69003 Lyon, France
[2] University of Lyon 1, DISP, F-69621 Villeurbanne Cedex, France
[3] INP Grenoble, Laboratory G-SCOP, F-38000 Grenoble, France
oyildiz@audros.fr,
philippe.pernelle@univ-lyon1.fr,
{lilia.gzara,michel.tollenaere}@grenoble-inp.fr

Abstract. In this article we focus on the implementation of business model in PLM sytems. PLM may be an information system that can natively implement business model without any specific development. This implementation is a crucial step in any project deployment of these information systems. Its also an important step during their evolution. However, the lack of standards and methodologies does not simplify the design and reconfiguration. This paper proposes a modeling approach in PLM systems based on MDA approach. In this context, we propose different levels of modeling (CIM / PIM / PSM) as well as rule mechanisms based on constraints (OCL). This approach is being prototyping by the framework realization based on Eclipse.

1 Introduction

Information system design for industrial enterprises requires finding a good compromise between the standardization of functionalities from the main components (ERP, PLM...) and the specific development. PLM systems are sufficiently generic to propose models adapted to companies specific needs without an additional development. However, the initial implementation of such systems and its multiple reconfigurations are never easy to implement. There are several reasons for this :

- Lack of standard : There is no standard methodology which covers all the scope (from metamodel to PLM implementation). The existing models (or metamodels) [1] [2] [3] [4] [5] [6] [7] are restricted to a context (business domain context, exchange data context, mechanical context...).
- Costs of providing : Enterprises are often required to be assisted by an external consultant (editor or integrators). Furthermore, internal cost (development, configuration, maintenance) [8] is more important than software license cost.
- Consistency control : As example, in the case of an initial deployment, the need to manage CAD data is limited by CAD software constraints. The model design (Part, Sub Assembly, CAD Drawing) will have to be validated by this constraints in order not to create structural inconsistency. Another

A. Bernard, L. Rivest, and D. Dutta (Eds.): PLM 2013, IFIP AICT 409, pp. 159–169, 2013.

example, to adapt itself to their market, companies are often brought to modify their models. Yet, in most cases, the company is not able to identify the impacts of these modifications as problems of consistency or side effects. Currently, companies do not have the tools (or methods) to enable them to generate and modify their PLM business model by ensuring the overall consistent of data and processes.

So, creation or modification steps of the models imply to set up a methodological approach allowing to create or to maintain the system in a structural and functional coherence. In this paper we propose a coherent and global approach for design [9] and adaptation of structured models within PLM systems [10]. This approach is built around an MDA approach (Model Driven Architecture) and based on the design of models under constraints. Indeed, MDE (Model Driven Engineering) [11] allows, by various processing steps and constraint additions, to create one robust data model, with no inconsistency.

In the first section we present MDA concepts and modelling proposals according to MDA levels. We also also specify the typology of constraints applied to these models. In the second section we present a framework that allows the proposed approach as well as an implementation example.

2 MDA Approach for PLM

2.1 From Business Logic to Implementation PLM Platform

MDA is an approach based on MDE (Model Driven Engineering) proposed by the OMG (Object Management Group) [12] [13] which uses the concepts of MOF (Meta Object Facility) [14] and UML (Unified Modeling Language) as modeling tools. This approach is based on several levels of models (or metamodels) and mechanisms of transformation of these models [3]. It enables to make models operational, to transform a source model into another target model of the same system but on a different level. We can identify two types of transformations :

- Endogenous transformation from the same meta-model, the source model and the target are in conformity with the same meta-model. In this case, we can use two transformations : Model-to-model or model-to-code.
- Exogenic transformation starting from different meta-models, the source model and the target are not in conformity with the same meta-model.

In line with MDA, models transformations starts with business concepts and ends with executable code . This is very close to the modeling needs within PLM systems. Indeed, modeling in PLM systems is a recurring issue that should be asked at different steps of a PLM project :

- During the deployment phase of a PLM system in a specific business context: It is to model the objects which are managed in the PLM with the businness concepts in the area of activity of the company.
- During collaborative exchanges between companies: It is to model the combination of semantic concepts used in each company.

- During necessary adaptations to economic context or business: It is to enable the reconfiguration of models while ensuring structural and behavioral consistency of existing model.

The fundamental principle of MDA is the separation between business logic and implementation logic around three levels

- CIM level : It characterizes the design business of the highest level of abstraction independent of any system implementation. It defines the vocabulary resources shared with other models. The technical independence of this model enables it to keep all its interest over time and is changed only if the model of a company needs change.
- PIM level : It is independent of any technical platform and does not contain information on technologies that will be used to deploy the application. PIM models represent a partial view of an CIM and they describe the system, but do not show the details of their use on the platform.
- PSM level : It depends on the used platform (used for code generation). There are several levels of PSM. The first, derived from the transformation of a PIM. The others are obtained by successive transformations. These enable to obtain the code in a specific language. In our context, the PSM level stops at an execution level within a PLM system.

In the following paragraphs, we present models (and metamodel) for a framework based on MDA.

Metamodel for CIM. The purpose of our metamodel (fig. 1) is to define the key concepts that will be used by models (PIM). These concepts should be independent of PLM system. They are used to characterize the compliance models of lower level. The elements proposed in the metamodel allows to identify structural and behavioral invariant concepts that must be used by a PLM system.

Model for PIM. The PIM is a level of modeling which has to enable implementing business concepts within a PLM system. In the context, the modeling is not unique and can evolve in time. The business concepts defining the models of this level characterize a contextual business terminology. Here the contextual meaning implies a low level of invariance for two reasons :

- Concepts treated are very specific for industrial sector and the concepts used involve a certain ambiguity.
- Concepts treated are evolving over time.

Template for PSM. Specific business model identified in the previous level finally have to be to implemented in a PLM platform. The level of implementation is different depending on the systems. In our case, the PIM concepts transformation does not produce executable code. Indeed, our approach is intended to be used in a context of PLM (or reconfiguration definition). the execution platform is implicitly a PLM system and generated elements are in fact elements that will

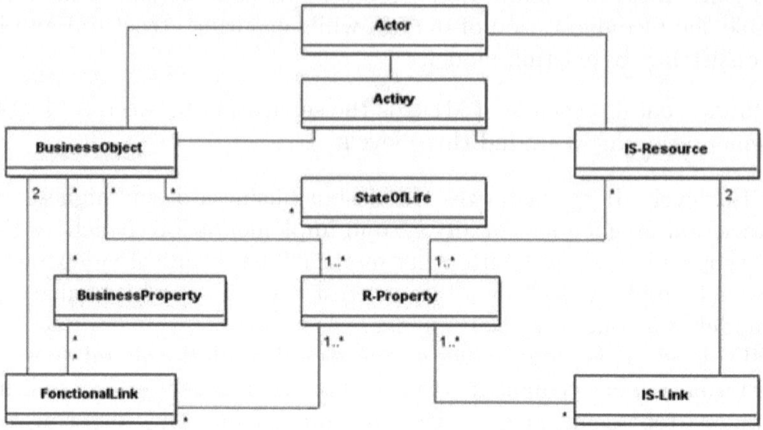

Fig. 1. Metamodel for CIM level

be instantiated in the basics of PLM by the application server. The purpose of PDM (platform description model) is precisely to describe the templates for the models transformation (from PIM to PSM).

2.2 Constraints-Based Approach

Relations (associations, composition...) proposed initially by UML are not enough to characterize business specificities. UML 2 proposes an extension of these relations by the definition of constraints. A constraint represents a boolean-valued expression which can be attached to any UML element. It generally indicates a limitation, or gives further information onto a model. They are used in most cases to specify invariants on the meta classify. An invariant expresses a predicative constraint on an object, or a group objects, which must be permanently respected (regardless its state). So, to define constraints of modeling and according to the expression of constraints in data modeling, it is possible to use :

- Pre-conditions and post-conditions on operations.
- Constraints on the value returned by an operation.
- Derivation rules of attributes.
- Description of targets for messages and actions.
- Conditions in dynamic diagrams.
- Type Invariants for stereotypes (particular to describe UML semantics).

These constraints complete existing diagrams and allow to return more precise relations and without ambiguities. To model constraints on our models, we chose to use OCL constraints (Object Constraint Language) [15]. OCL 2.0 was integrated into the definition of UML 2.0 in 2003. It is in accordance with UML 2 and with the MOF 2.0. Features brought by the integration of constraints OCL are the following ones:

- Model storage with their constraints.
- Syntactic and semantic validation of the constraints
- Code generation to verify the constraints in the execution.

To be able to automate the maximum of checks, it is necessary to define constraints at every level (CIM / PIM / PSM). For that purpose, we propose the following typology of constraints :

Conformity constraints: They have to guarantee the conformity of a business model and PLM models regarding to their higher levels.

Business constraints: These constraints enable to express, on the models, business rules on classes or relations.

Support constraints: These constraints are characteristic to the PLM system implementation. These are constraints on the concepts of PLM (uniqueness, traceability...).

Consistence constraints: These constraints are used to characterize the rules relating to the system dynamics.

This figure (Fig. 2) describes our modeling approach in the PLM systems context.

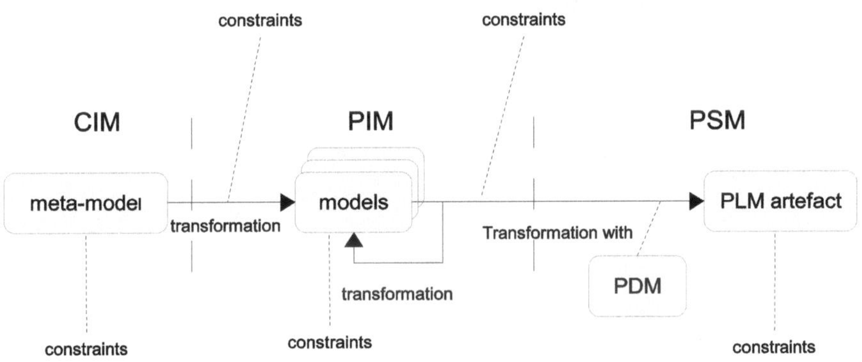

Fig. 2. Global MDA approach for PLM

3 Design of a Framework for PLM

3.1 Description of Framework

Our proposed approach with MDA is supported by a framework which is going to operate transformation models and checks of the constraints. This framework is realised relying on Eclipse Modelling Framework (EMF) [16] [17] [18] based metamodeling facilities. EMF is an implementation of the MOF particularly adapted to the applications based on a model of structured data, which is the case for PLM systems. In the Eclipse environment, EMF enables the implementation of DSL (Domain Specific Language). Furthermore, the genericity of Eclipse plugins allows leaning on EMF to propose inherited corresponding mechanisms in the models presented in section 2. So, we propose designer wizards to help him in his choices. We propose three wizards' levels.

- The first level correspond to the definition of rules of the business concepts. At this level, the designer must identify his main business concepts and the relationships between them. He must also characterize the conformity constraints by associating each of its concepts with elements of the CIM metamodels. This wizard enables to define a first PIM model.
- The second type of wizard enables to enrich or to specialize a PIM model with standard business concepts. For instance, you can complete a model with everyday objects : Documents, CAD objects, Engineering Change Request (ECR), Engineering Change Order (ECO)... This wizard enables to help the designer to produce a PIM model adjusted to his needs.
- The third wizard enables to configure the templates that will produce the elements in the target platform.

Thus, we propose a framework that helps the designer in the process of MDA modeling. The wizards (Fig.3) can not completely characterize the models. The other modeling elements (constraints) are made from a specific view of Eclipse.

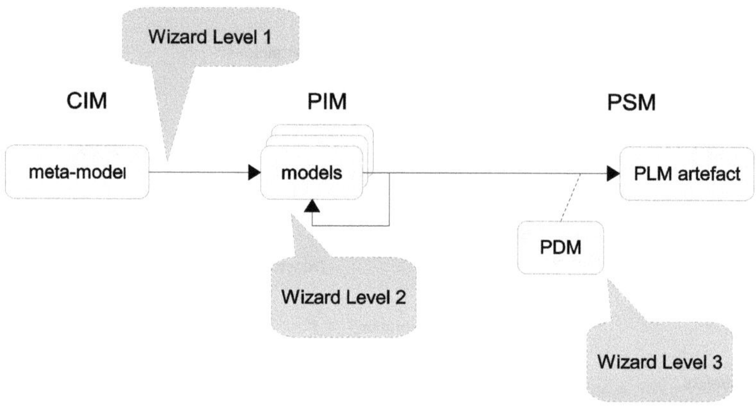

Fig. 3. Wizards for helping designer

In the next section, we present an example of using this approach with the PLM system.

3.2 Industrial Example for SMEs/SMIs

Our industrial example leans on the PLM system Audros. This system is used in of numerous domains by SMEs/SMIs. In this frame, we suggested realizing a version adapted to SMEs/SMIs in the field of the mechanics.

A PIM Model for SMEs/SMIs. The objective of this mechanics model is to propose a minimalist model that works for an SME. It must contain :

- Useful objects, define from the main client data models (part, product, drawing, document, CAD documents, BOM...).
- Standard viewpoints (design, engineering , manufacturing...).
- Standard change management (ECR, ECO...).

For enterprises working with CAD documents, a PIM model is given by the following diagram (Fig. 4). In this model, the metamodel concepts are represented by stereotypes (UML2).

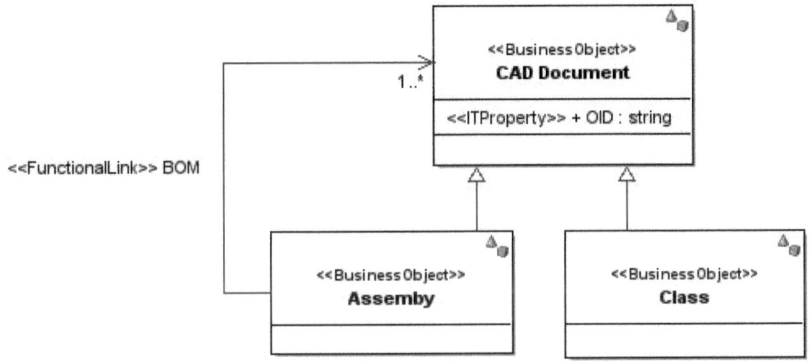

Fig. 4. Extract from PIM model - CAD Document

Another case is the viewpoint notion that is present in all PLM systems and that allows to characterize the access rights on the business objects (Fig.5).

The following diagram (fig. 6) shows an extract from the mechanics's PIM model.

At this level the model is not dependent on the Audros platform, compliance is checked by the metamodel and constraints.

Constraints. The constraints enable to characterize the verification rules at each modeling level. Some constraints are implicit. For instance, the relationships (composition, aggregation...) defined on the metamodel implies to be veriefied in the PIM models to ensure compliance. The explicit rules have been defined on different modeling levels. In table 1, we present some extracts rules defined for the mechanical model in SMEs.

Rule 1. This rule characterizes that in PLM system, every object has a unique reference and its creation is temporalized and is not anonymous.

Rule 2. This rule characterizes a consistence constraint in process management. A process that changes the life cycle of an object must concern at least one object.

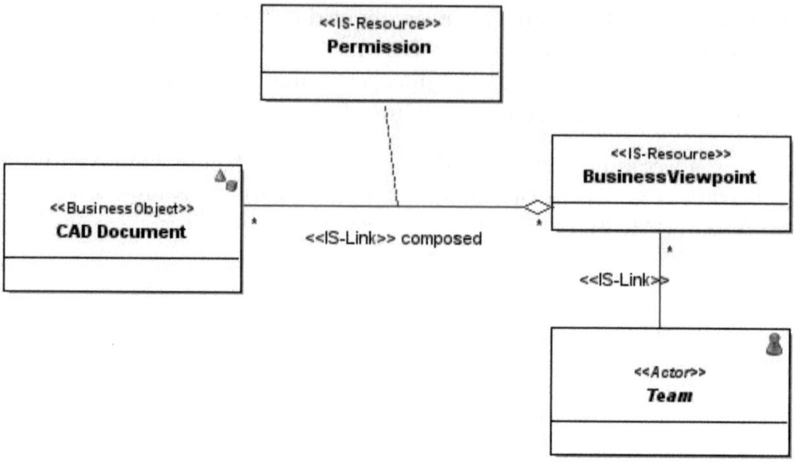

Fig. 5. Extract from PIM model - ViewPoint

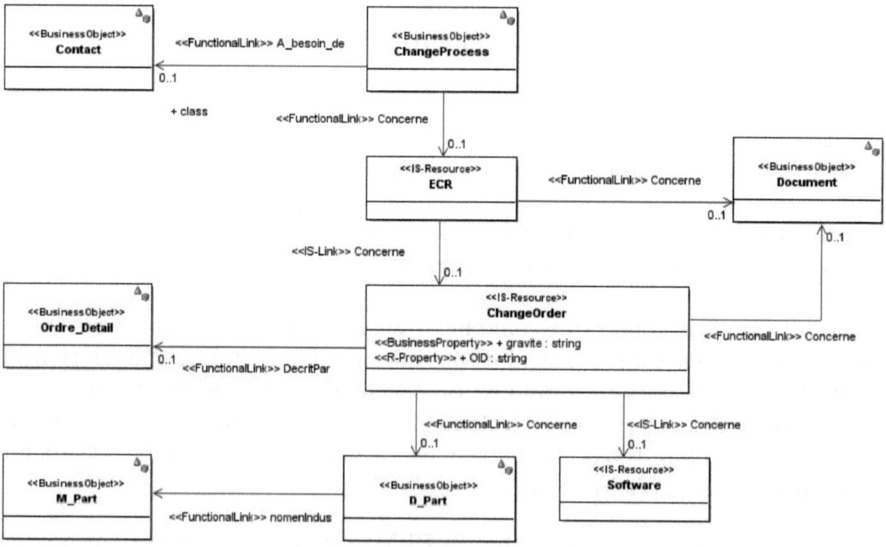

Fig. 6. Extract from PIM model

Table 1. Example of constraints

Type	Ref. Rule	Ref. OCL	Constraint description
Support constraint	rule 1		Any business object must have at least one attribute system.
Consistence constraint	rule 2		Check the existence of a link between a process and at least another object in the data model (otherwise it will be impossible to create a process instance).
Business constraint	rule 3		The BOM link (bom-link type 'BOM ') enables to connect CAD objects. The ends only contain (father, son) : ASM → PRT, ASM → ASM, ASMPRT → ASMPRT, ASM → ASMPRT, ASMPRT → ASM, ASMPRT → PRT.
-		OCL-1.1	The CAD link (cad-link type 'CAD') enables to define dependancies between CAD objects other than BOM link. The ends only contain (father, son) : ASM → ASM, ASM → PRT, PRT → PRT, ASMPRT → ASMPRT, ASM → ASMPRT, ASMPRT → ASM, ASMPRT → PRT. The DRAWING link (draw-link type 'DOC') enables to describe the models referenced by the CAD drawing. The ends only contain (father, son) : DRW → ASM, DRW → PRT, DRW → ASMPRT, DRW → PLT. The DOCBOM link (docBom-link type 'DOCBOM') enables to group different components of BOM. The ends only contain : Same definition that 'DOC' and 'BOM'.

Rule 3. This rule characterizes a business constraint related to the use of a CAD system.

The different examples below show some constraint definitions with OCL.

Listing 1.1. Exemple Constraint OCL-1

```
context c : cad-link FonctionnalLink
inv : c.link_type = 'CAO'
and (c.father.type = 'ASM' or
      c.father.type='ASMPRT' or c.father.type='PRT')
and (c.son.type = 'ASM' or
      c.son.type='PRT' or c.son.type='ASMPRT')
```

4 Conclusion

In this paper a Framework prototype based on Eclipse was proposed which goal is to enable companies to model their business concept in a PLM system. In this approach, Framework enables to model the main business concepts, according to the different levels. So, the constraint definition can complete the modeling by adding global consistence rules. Thanks to the collaboration with Audros (PLM editor), we built a prototype that implements our metamodel. Although incomplete, we used this metamodel to generate standard modeling elements of a mechanical company. The next step will be the definition of transformation rules to automate model generation.

Acknowledgments. We would like to thank ANRT (Association Nationale de la Recherche et de la Technologie) and Audros Technology for the support in these research.

References

1. Sudarsan, R., Fenves, S., Sriram, R.: A product information modeling framework for product lifecycle management. Computer Aided Design 37(13) (2005)
2. Eynard, B., Gallet, T., Roucoules, L., Ducellier, G.: Pdm system implementation based on uml. Mathematics and Computers in Simulation 70(5-6), 330–342 (2006)
3. Bach, J.C., Crégut, X., Moreau, P.E., Pantel, M.: Model transformations with tom. In: DTA - 12th Workshop on Language Descriptions, Tools and Applications - 2012, Tallinn, Estonie. ACM (2012)
4. Chettaoui, H.: Interoperabilite entre modeles heterogenes en conception cooperative par des approches d'Ingenierie dirige par les modeles. PhD thesis, Institut polytechnique de Grenoble (2008)
5. Srinivasan, V.: STEP in the context of Product Data Management. In: Advanced Design and Manufacturing Based on STEP. Springer (2009)
6. Le Duigou, J., Bernard, A., Perry, N., Delplace, J.C.: Generic plm system for smes: Application to an equipment manufacturer. International Journal of Product Lifecycle Management, IJPLM (April 2012)
7. Iraqi-Houssaini, M., Kleiner, M., Roucoules, L.: Model-Based (Mechanical) Product Design. In: Whittle, J., Clark, T., Kühne, T. (eds.) MODELS 2011. LNCS, vol. 6981, pp. 548–562. Springer, Heidelberg (2011)
8. Elkadiri, S., Pernelle, P., Delattre, M., Bouras, A.: Collaborative process control: Observation of tracks generated by plm system. In: Proceedings of the International Conference on Advances in Production Management Systems, APMS 2008, Espoo, Finlande (September 2008)
9. Turki, S.: Ingénierie système guidée par les modèles: Application du standard IEEE 15288, de l'architecture MDA et du langage SysML à la conception des systèmes mécatroniques. These, Université du Sud Toulon Var (October 2008)
10. Yildiz, O., Gzara, L., Pernelle, P., Tollenaere, M.: An MDA approach for PLM system design. In: Emmanouilidis, C., Taisch, M., Kiritsis, D. (eds.) APMS 2012, Part II. IFIP AICT, vol. 398, pp. 216–223. Springer, Heidelberg (2013)
11. Bézivin, J.: Model Driven Engineering: An Emerging Technical Space. In: Lämmel, R., Saraiva, J., Visser, J. (eds.) GTTSE 2005. LNCS, vol. 4143, pp. 36–64. Springer, Heidelberg (2006)

12. OMG: OMG model driven architecture (2001), http://www.omg.org/mda/
13. France, R.B., Ghosh, S., Dinh-Trong, T., Solberg, A.: Model-driven development using uml 2.0: Promises and pitfalls. IEEE Computer 39(2) (2006)
14. OMG: Meta object facility (mof) (2011), http://www.omg.org/spec/MOF/2.4.1/
15. OMG (2006), http://www.omg.org/spec/OCL/2.0/
16. Eclipse-Foundation: Eclipse modeling project, http://www.eclipse.org/modeling/
17. Steinberg, D., Budinsky, F., Merks, E., Paternostro, M.: Eclipse Modeling Framework. Pearson Education (2008)
18. Bézivin, J., Kurtev, I.: Model-based technology integration with the technical space concept. In: Metainformatics Symposium 2005, Esbjerg, Denmark (November 2005)

Proactive Engineering and PLM: Current Status and Research Challenges

Frédéric Demoly[1,⋆], Henk Jan Pels[2], and Samuel Gomes[1]

[1] IRTES-M3M, UTBM, 90010 Belfort Cedex, France
{frederic.demoly,samuel.gomes}@utbm.fr
[2] Technische Universiteit Eindhoven, Eindhoven, The Netherlands
h.j.pels@tue.nl

Abstract. This paper discusses about the evolution of Product Lifecycle Management (PLM) through the introduction of an emerging vision in engineering design, proactive engineering. Over the last two decades, engineering design has seen some relevant approaches covering sequential engineering and then concurrent engineering (CE). Indeed, this shift was required to encompass knowledge integration issue into product design stages. This has led to relevant approaches such as design for X, parametric design, PLM-based approaches, decision-making support and ontology-based approaches to name a few. Proactive engineering can be considered as an emerging engineering framework which integrates as early as possible lifecycle knowledge and technological constraints in product design and manage those knowledge in an integrated and harmonious manner. The fact of using lifecycle process knowledge as design context demands therefore the definition of downstream processes before defining he product geometry so as to overcome current limitations in CE oriented PLM approaches. Hence, with such stakes, understanding and awareness becomes crucial in PLM in order to deliver well-balanced products.

Keywords: Product Lifecycle Management; Proactive engineering, Qualitative description, Understanding, Awareness in design.

1 Introduction

Nowadays companies need to be more competitive (externally focused) and productive and efficient (internally focused) to deliver personalizable products which are lifecycle-friendly oriented [1]. Over the last decades, engineering design has incrementally shifted to different engineering paradigms in order to overcome industrial stakes and research challenges, especially the optimisation of product development lead time and knowledge integration in product design [2–4]. This has led to successful methods enabling the promotion of Concurrent Engineering (CE) philosophy and Product Lifecycle Management (PLM) vision [5]. Nevertheless, product design still required a more efficient verification and validation

⋆ Corresponding author.

A. Bernard, L. Rivest, and D. Dutta (Eds.): PLM 2013, IFIP AICT 409, pp. 170–181, 2013.

procedure regarding lifecycle stages expectations [6], and suitable and anticipatory contexts for designers based on process procedural knowledge [7, 8]. Currently, the concurrent consideration of lifecycle constraints and knowledge does not provide enough awareness and understanding for stakeholders, especially for designers [1]. The traditional "pass the torch" (in other words: "over the wall" issue) exchange procedure over lifecycle phases and involved actors is still a critical step with some barriers [9]. This can be understood as the lack of rationale, intents, logic on product design decisions and its impact on downstream processes, and the need of appropriate product representations in line with stakeholders' viewpoints and concerns [10]. This statement can be confirmed regarding the current concurrent product design process as well as the associated PLM processes. The proposed work does not describe a comprehensive state-of-the-art review in engineering design and PLM – as successfully realised in [3, 5] –, but particularly addresses its current limitations to fully integrated lifecycle phases and related constraints and knowledge in product design. Hence this paper discusses the required evolution of PLM – as initiated in [11] – through the introduction of proactive engineering as an emerging paradigm in engineering design. Over the last two decades, engineering design has seen some relevant approaches covering sequential engineering and then CE [12]. Indeed, this shift was required to encompass the knowledge integration issue into product design stages. This has led to relevant approaches such as design for X (DFX) [13], parametric design, PLM-based approaches, decision-making support and ontology-based approaches [14] to name a few. Proactive engineering can be considered as an emerging engineering framework which integrates as early as possible lifecycle knowledge – described in a formal manner for example – and technological constraints in product design and manage this knowledge in an integrated and harmonious manner [15, 1, 16]. The fact of using lifecycle process knowledge in design context [7] demands therefore the definition of downstream processes (i.e. lifecycle sequence planning) before defining he product detailed geometry, so as to overcome current limitations in CE oriented PLM approaches. Therefore with such stakes, understanding and awareness aspects become crucial in PLM in order to deliver well-balanced products (i.e. products fulfilling lifecycle constraints and knowledge in a harmonious and consistent manner), while considering X planning definition where X stands for manufacturing, assembly, disassembly, maintenance, transport, etc. In such a way, traditional DFX approaches need to be turned back towards "X sequence planning for design".

Following this original point of view, the paper highlights in Section 2 the current stakes in the CE paradigm with the recent birth of proactive engineering. Then, Section 3 presents the remaining challenges and emerging needs in PLM regarding this novel paradigm. Finally, Section 4 addresses the description of a proactive design framework within PLM. The final outcome of this proposal is to propose a novel shift in both product design and PLM, and give new directions for further research activities in these fields.

2 Current Stakes in Concurrent Engineering

At a critical place, the product design phase requires the consideration and integration of all constraints and knowledge (business processes, business terms, expert rules, job experience, etc.) of product lifecycle phases. This implies to embrace a large amount of rules which increases the work complexity of product architects and designers [6], and consequently increases computational complexity of the design phase [10]. Over the past two decades, this issue has been tackled by shifting from sequential engineering to CE, therefore facilitating the integration of specific concerns (i.e. manufacturing knowledge, assembly knowledge, etc.) into product detailed design stages with the support of expert systems and inference engines [12]. It can be noticed that this shift has generated potential gains by using heuristics rules with associated quantitative engineering data [17, 18]. Thus a set of relevant design for X (DFX) and design to X (DTX) components were proposed [12, 19]. These approaches can be understood in a way that DFX components gather numerous rules and constraints and DTX components concern properties values to be checked [20]. Literature has provided numerous published research works in the above-listed fields, among them Design For Assembly (DFA) seems to be the most investigated component in DFX. These approaches can be considered as semi-generative and based on heuristics and geometrics rules in order to tackle current difficulties in the management of the product structure complexity and related product modelling [17]. Recent research efforts in proactive DFA (also called assembly oriented design) have proven that the early generation of admissible assembly sequences during conceptual design stages can be created in order to provide an appropriate contextual support for assembly design and modelling phases [17, 18], even for the geometric definition in a top-down manner [21]. Other DFX approaches are still described while using assessment techniques in order to evaluate the current product design according to specific rules and constraints [22]. Relevant future trends in decision-based DFX can also be found in [13]. Moreover, the combinatorial complexity of processing knowledge and rules and the need of agility in design has been partially covered by knowledge-based engineering (KBE) techniques and applications in detailed design stage [23].

Today, the CE philosophy has reached its limit or at least has some pending issues, and some key points can be introduced to argue this statement. As such, the current CE-based approaches do not provide enough reasoning layer for a full understanding and awareness of product architects and designers. Indeed, designers need to reason and understand the context in which the design is carried out, that is why a qualitative description layer would be an added value [24]. Knowledge from lifecycle processes is not yet considered as design aid but as verification and validation procedure in the detailed design stage [6]. This fact demonstrates that lifecycle knowledge has to be considered in a way that aids designers from preliminary design stage, therefore improving designer's awareness and anticipation [25]. In such a way, it is important to address a proactive vision of the product development by considering downstream processes as early as possible in product design. Thus awareness and understanding will be promoted to product/process architects and designers. This can be done with relevant data input and some specific layers which may introduce qualitative context based on formal description. Here qualitative context may include formal description of engineering intents and knowledge such as explained in [24]. Another relevant aspect is the way of knowledge reuse, if lifecycle context in design is required, it therefore demands an appropriate injection process of knowledge. An interesting research effort towards knowledge on-demand procedures based on context capturing would provide benefits in design phase [7, 3, 27].

As a synthesis, current stakes in engineering can be represented in Figure 1, where engineering shifts from sequential to CE and CE to proactive engineering are shown. In the past, sequential engineering meant the execution of engineering tasks without overlapping and information exchange were made possible with quantitative data. Based on this process, CE has provided gains in Beginning-Of-Life (BOL) by overlapping detailed design stage with manufacturing planning and then assembly planning, etc. This was enabled with the support of heuristic rules and parameters to be considered in design. More recently, proactive engineering aims to fully overlap engineering phases based on minimum design information, on which manufacturing and assembly planning can be generated and considered to define a qualitative context for designers as early as possible in the preliminary design stage. As result, with such emerging paradigm, product development lead time becomes more optimised and more efficient by improving understanding and awareness of designers decisions, and promoting knowledge activation and injection in design in an appropriate manner.

3 Remaining Challenges and Emerging Needs in PLM

If proactive engineering is designing products for optimal performance over its lifecycle, then it needs a consistent PLM strategy since PLM is about managing knowledge on the product and all its lifecycle processes in order to optimise product lifecycle benefits and minimise product lifecycle cost [28, 29]. In the PLM context a suitable definition of knowledge is that of [30, 31]: K = I .E.S.A, where K stands for Knowledge, I for Information, S for Skill, E for Experience and A for Attitude. This definition takes the pragmatical view that knowledge is what enables a person (or a machine) to perform a task. If two different persons execute the same task with different performance in terms of cost, time and quality, than the difference is explained by different knowledge. To perform a task a certain skill is needed. Skill is obtained by teaching (from documents or by imitation). The more often the task is repeated, the more the performance increases. This is the Experience factor. In most cases the execution of a task requires some choices or decisions to be taken. More information enables better decisions and thus better task performance. Finally, the person may have skill, experience and information; if he is not motivated there will be little or no result.

The product lifecycle encompasses many different processes that require many tasks to be executed like design, manufacturing, assembly, installation, operation, maintenance, refurbishing and demolition. Product lifecycle performance

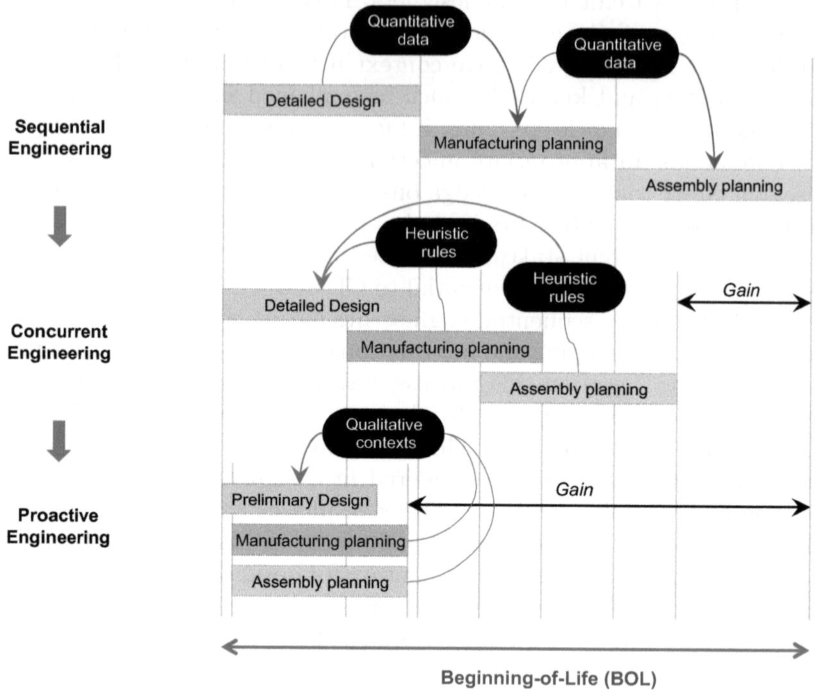

Fig. 1. Towards a new engineering shift: proactive engineering

depends by definition on the knowledge applied in all those tasks. Like the core function of ERP (Enterprise Resource Planning) is to make all resources available to perform a particular tasks when and where it is to be executed, the core function of PLM is make the proper knowledge available in each resource. Product development creates and documents the knowledge. Human resources organizes the hiring and training to acquire skill and should record the experience. Information systems organize the availability of information and management takes care for Attitude. Knowledge is increasingly dynamic so a main competitive capability (internally focused) is to get new knowledge faster in operation in all lifecycle processes.

Three flows of knowledge can be distinguished. The first is from new technology to be implemented in reliable product design. The second is from new customer needs to be implemented in a product serving that customer. The third is from new knowledge on possible process improvement from the field into new knowledge available in the resources executing those processes. This third one is the object of proactive engineering, i.e. observe product behaviour in different lifecycle processes, generate ideas for improvements (or sequence planning) and implement those ideas (i.e. as contextual information) in new product and process designs. Currently in most cases the flow of knowledge from real life processes to product development is very slow and narrow. An important reason is that by the time the downstream processes like maintenance are starting, product development is already working on the next product generation. When knowledge flows faster along the three axes mentioned above, this problem will get smaller.

PLM has basically three ways of improving product development performance: 1) eliminate non value adding activities from the process to reduce cost, 2) reduce waiting times in knowledge flows in order to reduce time to operation and 3) stimulate reuse of knowledge in order to increase quality, efficiency and anticipation. The last one is the most powerful to improve product lifecycle value. Reuse in design is achieved first by reusing existing components and modules, but second by parameterizing the design (via rules and parameters). The effect is that the knowledge for a class of specific product types is abstracted to the level of a single product family via a consistent configuration of rules and parameters. Then product and process specifications for specific products can be derived – cheap, fast and reliable – by feeding parameter values into the product family models.

In the context of proactive engineering product families are important because family specifications have a longer lifetime, change slower, that those of individual products. This means that experience with process families can be collected and used while the product family is still alive, thus enabling faster learning of process designers. Another important PLM feature for proactive design is enabling concurrent engineering, meaning that downstream processes are designed concurrently with the product. Both the new product and the new process are to be designed as a limited set of changes to and existing product and its processes. Most component (families) are to be reused without change, while only specific components and processes may be redesigned. Thus the knowledge in the stable part can be reused, has a longer life, more repetitive application so the knowledge can be of much better quality. Not only for the resource applying the knowledge repetition is important to create experience, also for the knowledge creation process it holds that to each repetition of application gives a possibility to learn and improve the specification of the skill.

As a result, current PLM vision requires evolution towards the effective and consistent management of knowledge [11], the improvement of knowledge reuse from downstream processes in product design and the appropriate knowledge representation and reasoning [32]. Among knowledge types, PLM still requires the consideration and the qualitative and formal description of design intents with declarative knowledge (know-what), rationale with causal knowledge (Know-Why), process intents with procedural knowledge (Know-How) and temporal knowledge (Know-When) so as to increase awareness and understanding of information and knowledge flows [33]. Computational layers should also be introduced in order to facilitate information and knowledge processing between each engineering phases. In this context, mediator-based applications [34], hub-based applications, context-aware and context-sensitive applications, and knowledge on-demand mechanisms [35] with the support of reasoning features and agents [36] would provide an interesting "peacemaker" for existing PLM ecosystems. The peacemaker concept here will ensure the closed-loop of information and knowledge flows [37] and promotion of information irrigation with semantic federation [38] for various abstraction levels of information [39].

Figure 2 presents a summary of the main existing PLM systems (grey boxes) and applications (white boxes) covering the product lifecycle and associated to specific content (i.e. what, how, when and where). This map is composed of PLM systems which manages spatial and temporal information related to the product and its lifecycle processes (i.e. Product Data Management – PDM, Manufacturing Process Management – MPM and ERP), and applications which defines and optimizes product and process definitions. Hub and bridge applications have not been represented since these applications remains too specific regarding current research efforts. Here “what” is about technical entities and engineering data related to the product, “how” is about processes and functions, “when” addresses temporal events, and “where” denotes places and networks such as initiated in the Zachman's framework [40]. The “why” part (i.e. rationale and motivation) is not addressed yet, or at least not commonly agreed yet by the PLM community. This figure also highlights some overlaps along the lifecycle phases axis and some gaps about the content orientation axis. A critical feature is the lack of connection between content types, where continuity, logic and associated reasoning mechanisms of information and knowledge flows are currently missing in PLM ecosystems, especially in BOL phase. Indeed, current information exchange procedures are not sufficient to understand stakeholders' intents. Hence there is an opportunity to improve current position of PLM systems in order to promote proactive engineering by introducing new reasoning and computing layers on semantics and logics aspects in a central manner.

4 Towards a Proactive Design Framework within PLM

Proactive design implies that not only knowledge about the product technology, but knowledge about all lifecycle processes is used in optimizing the design of not only the product, but also that of all lifecycle processes. It means that each designers in the product lifecycle must have access to knowledge from all other designers. In such a way, The proposed proactive design framework, presented in Figure 3, introduces some new knowledge processing mechanisms in order to link “what” with “how” and “when” contents of PLM in a way that considers “X sequence planning for design” (DFX is actually turned back). The breakthrough lies in the understanding of design and process contexts and related designer's intents, and the description and instantiation of knowledge on-demand for its appropriate injection (i.e. accurate reuse) in the design process. As a result, the proposed framework, which provide a novel “why” layer for processing and controlling information and knowledge flows between product design and lifecycle sequence planning, can be deployed as follows:

Step 1. Generation of lifecycle (manufacturing, assembly, etc.) sequence planning. Based on preliminary product design input (e.g. bill of material, part-to-part relationships, etc.), it is then possible to generate admissible lifecycle

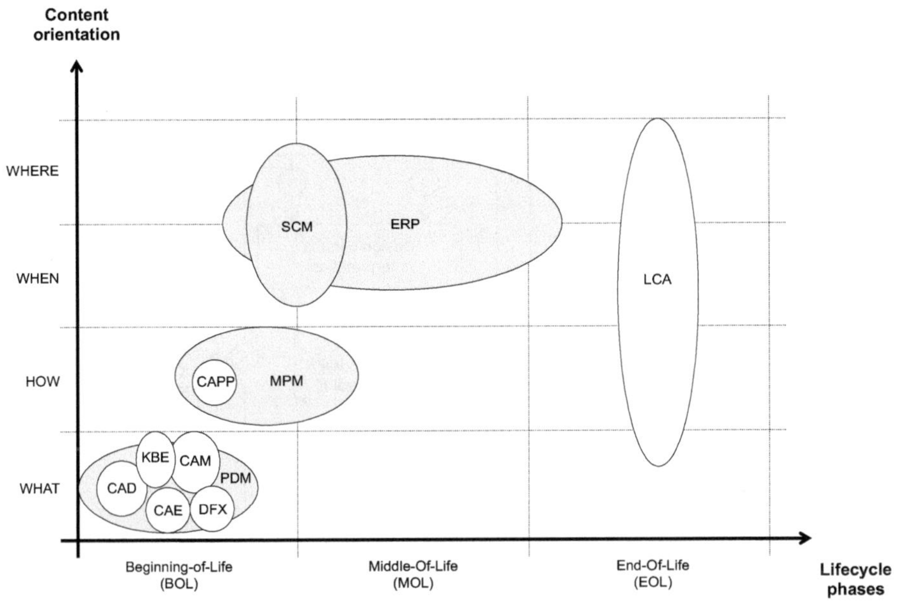

Fig. 2. Map of existing PLM systems and applications along lifecycle phases and content orientation

sequence planning (e.g. assembly sequence planning), on which a good one can be identified based on process planner experience [17, 18].

Step 2. Product structuring. The early-defined assembly sequence for example can be consistently considered in product design for product structuring. The same reasoning procedure can be done via the definition of the manufacturing sequence for part features structuring.

Step 3 & 3'. Knowledge on-demand in design. This action is required and active all along the design process, from conceptual to detailed design stages. At any time, it should be possible to interpret the designer's context (in CAD modelling for example) in a way to understand and capture its design intents with surroundings engineering data related to the product. Here the captured intents are then described with declarative knowledge (knowing what).

Step 4 & 4'. Knowledge on-demand in process planning. Similar to the previous step, the interpretation of process context is also needed at any time in order to describe planner's intents with procedural knowledge (knowing how) and temporal knowledge (knowing when).

Step 5. Knowledge consistency checking. This step links declarative knowledge with procedural and temporal knowledge by introducing causal knowledge (i.e. rationale). In such a way, knowledge about "what" and "how" can be described and linked so as to check knowledge consistency with logical inferences.

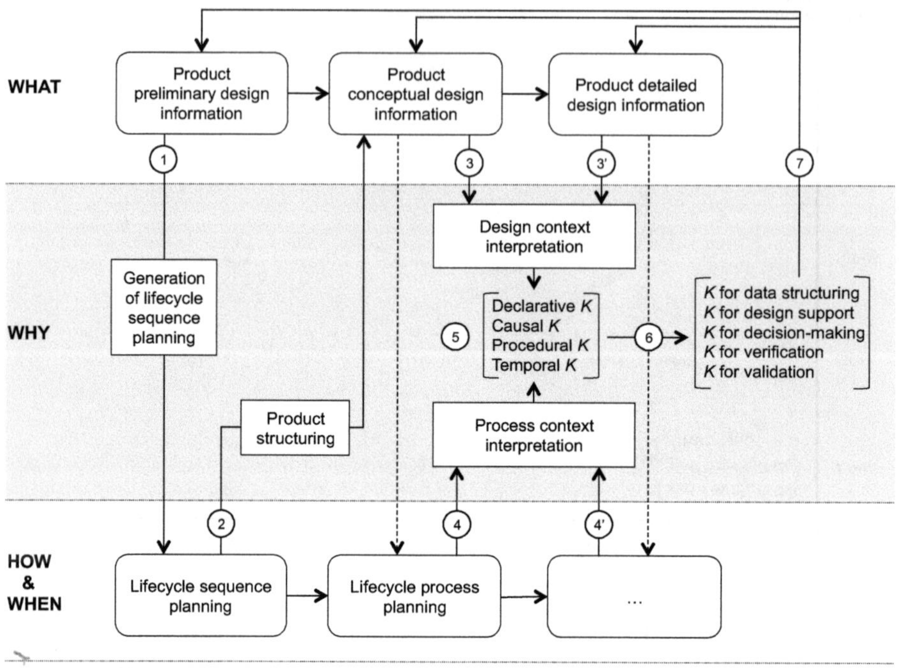

Fig. 3. Proactive design framework (K stands for Knowledge)

Step 6. Knowledge activation and instantiation. Based on the previous descriptive knowledge and the captured contexts, the needed knowledge is activated and instantiated towards the context purpose (i.e. data structuring, design support, decision-making, verification and validation).

Step 7. Knowledge injection in design. Finally, once activated, the knowledge is injected in the appropriate format (i.e. qualitative description) to the right person at the right place in the design process.

5 Conclusions and Future Works

This paper has highlighted current stakes and limits in concurrent engineering towards the need of a proactive engineering vision in consistency with PLM emerging needs. The authors have presented how traditional approaches can be turned back (e.g. DFX methods) by considering lifecycle sequence planning for design so as to promote awareness and understanding in design. Built on this, a novel proactive design framework within PLM has been proposed in order to link "what" with "how" and "when" contents by introducing an emerging "why" layer, where contexts and intents are described with qualitative knowledge (i.e. declarative, procedural , temporal and causal knowledge). This framework provides knowledge on-demand mechanisms and some consistency checking procedures in order to facilitate the knowledge injection process in product design.

Hence future works will address each step of the proposed framework with specific mechanisms and algorithms. In addition, a PLM implementation will be conducted in order to introduce the missing "why" layer for linking existing PLM components (information systems and applications) in BOL phase.

References

1. Demoly, F., Deniaud, S., Gomes, S.: Towards an harmonious and integrated management approach for lifecycle planning. In: Emmanouilidis, C., Taisch, M., Kiritsis, D. (eds.) APMS 2013, Part II. IFIP AICT, vol. 398, pp. 208–215. Springer, Heidelberg (2013)
2. Sapuan, S.M., Osman, M.R., Nukman, Y.: State of the art of the concurrent engineering technique in the automotive industry. Journal of Engineering Design 17(2), 143–157 (2006)
3. Liu, S., Boyle, I.M.: Engineering design: perspectives, challenges, and recent advances. Journal of Engineering Design 20(1), 7–19 (2009)
4. Demoly, F., Yan, X.-T., Eynard, B., Gomes, S., Kiritsis, D.: Integrated product relationships management: a model to enable concurrent product design and assembly sequence planning. Journal of Engineering Design 23(7), 544–561 (2012)
5. Liu, W., Zeng, Y., Matlez, M., Brisson, D.: Product lifecycle management: a review. In: ASME International Design Engineering Technical Conferences (IDETC) and Computers and Information in Engineering Conference, DETC 2009-86983, San Diego, August 30-September 2 (2009)
6. Maropoulos, P.G., Ceglarek, D.: Design verification and validation in product lifecycle. CIRP Annals - Manufacturing Technology 59(2), 740–759 (2010)
7. Hong, J., Suh, E.-H., Kim, J., Kim, S.: Context-aware system for proactive personalized service based on context history. Expert Systems with Applications 36, 7448–7457 (2009)
8. Song, B., Jiang, Z.: Proactive search enabled context-sensitive knowledge supply situated in computer-aided engineering. Advanced Engineering Informatics 27, 66–75 (2013)
9. Derrick, J., Wehrheim, H.: Model transformations across views. Science of Computer Programming 75, 192–210 (2010)
10. Kusiak, A., Salustri, F.A.: Computational intelligence in product design engineering: review and trends. Transactions on Systems, Man, and Cybernetics 37(5), 766–778 (2007)
11. Ameri, F., Dutta, D.: Product Lifecycle Management: Closing the Knowledge Loops. Computer-aided Design & Applications 2(5), 577–590 (2005)
12. Huang, G.Q., Lee, S.W., Mak, K.L.: Web-based product and process data modeling in concurrent "design for X". Robotics and Computer-Integrated Manufacturing 15, 53–63 (1999)
13. Holt, R., Barnes, C.: Towards an integrated approach to "Design for X": an agenda for decision-based DFX research. Research in Engineering Design 21, 123–136 (2010)
14. Matsokis, A., Kiritsis, D.: An ontology-based approach for Product Lifecycle Management. Computers in Industry 61(8), 787–797 (2010)
15. Dencker, K., Fasth, A., Stahre, J., Martensson, L., Lundholm, T., Akillioglu, H.: Proactive assembly systems-realising the potential of human collaboration with automation. Annual Reviews in Control 33, 230–237 (2009)

16. Wu, J.-W., Tseng, J.C.R., Yu, W.-D., Yang, J.-B., Lee, S.-M., Tsai, W.-N.: An integrated proactive knowledge model for enhancing engineering services. Automation in Construction 24, 81–88 (2012)
17. Demoly, F., Yan, X.-T., Eynard, B., Rivest, L., Gomes, S.: An Assembly oriented design framework for product structure engineering and assembly sequence planning. Robotics and Computer-Integrated Manufacturing 27(1), 33–46 (2011)
18. Demoly, F., Troussier, N., Eynard, B., Falgarone, H., Fricero, B., Gomes, S.: Proactive assembly oriented design approach based on the deployment of functional requirements. Journal of Computing Information and Science in Engineering 11(1), 014501-1 (2011)
19. Kuo, T.C., Huang, S.H.H., Zhang, H.C.: Design for manufacture and design for X: concepts, applications, and perspectives. Computers & Industrial Engineering 41(3), 241–260 (2001)
20. Kimura, F., Matoba, Y., Mitsui, K.: Designing Product Reliability based on Total Product Lifecycle Modelling. CIRP Annals - Manufacturing Technology 56(1), 163–166 (2007)
21. Demoly, F., Toussaint, L., Eynard, B., Kiritsis, D., Gomes, S.: Geometric skeleton computation enabling concurrent product engineering and assembly sequence planning. Computer-Aided Design 43(12), 1654–1673 (2011)
22. Lambert, A.J.D., Gupta, S.M.: Disassembly modeling for assembly, maintenance, reuse and recycling (resource management). CRC Press (2004) ISBN-10: 1574443348
23. Myung, S., Han, S.: Knowledge-based parametric design of mechanical products based on configuration design method. Expert Systems with Applications 21(2), 99–107 (2001)
24. Demoly, F., Matsokis, A., Kiritsis, D.: A mereotopological product relationship description approach for assembly oriented design. Robotics and Computer-Integrated Manufacturing 28(6), 681–693 (2012)
25. Zamenopoulos, T., Alexiou, K.: Towards an anticipatory view of design. Design Studies 28, 411–436 (2007)
26. Liu, Z., Xiao, J., Huang, Y.: Proactive product quality control: An integrated product and process control approach to MIMO systems. Chemical Engineering Journal 149, 435–446 (2009)
27. Nevo, D., Benbasat, I., Wand, Y.: The knowledge demands of expertise seekers in two different contexts: knowledge allocation versus knowledge retrieval. Decision Support Systems 53(3), 482–489 (2012)
28. Stark, J., et al.: Product Lifecycle Management - Paradigm for 21st century. Springer, Berlin (2004)
29. Terzi, S., Bouras, A., Dutta, D., Garetti, M., Kiritsis, D.: Product lifecycle management - from its history to its new role. International Journal of Product Lifecycle Management 4(4), 360–389 (2010)
30. Song, X.M., van der Bij, J.D., Weggeman, M.C.D.P.: Determinants of the level of knowledge application: a knowledge-based and information-processing perspective. Journal of Product Innovation Management 22(5), 430–444 (2005)
31. Song, X.M., van der Bij, J.D., Weggeman, M.C.D.P.: Factors for improving the level of knowledge generation in new product development. R&D Management 36(2), 173–187 (2006)
32. Chandrasegaran, S.K., Ramani, K., Sriram, R.D., Horvath, I., Bernard, A., Harik, R.F., Gao, W.: The evolution, challenges, and future of knowledge representation in product design systems. Computer-Aided Design 45(2), 204–228 (2013)

33. Kim, K.-Y., Kim, Y.S.: Causal design knowledge: Alternative representation method for product development knowledge management. Computer-Aided Design 43(9), 1137–1153 (2011)
34. Madhusudan, T.: An Intelligent Mediator-Based Framework for Enterprise Application Integration. Journal of Computing and Information Science in Engineering 4, 294–304 (2005)
35. Lee, H.J., Kim, J.H.: Mining knowledge demands from information flow. Expert Systems with Applications 39(8), 6799–6806 (2012)
36. Fan, X., Yen, J., Volz, R.A.: A theoretical framework on proactive information exchange in agent teamwork. Artificial Intelligence 169, 23–97 (2005)
37. Jun, H.-B., Kiritsis, D., Xirouchakis, P.: Research issues on closed-loop PLM. Computers in Industry 58, 855–868 (2007)
38. Fabian, B., Kunz, S., Konnegen, M., Müller, S., Günther, O.: Access control for semantic data federations in industrial product-lifecycle management. Computers in Industry 63, 930–940 (2012)
39. Helms, R.W.: Product Data Management as enabler for Concurrent Engineering. Thesis (PhD). Eindhoven University of Technology, The Netherlands (2002)
40. Zachman, J.A.: A Framework for Information Systems Architecture. IBM Systems Journal 26(3), 276–292 (1987)
41. Feng, G., Cui, D., Wang, C., Yu, J.: Integrated data management in complex product collaborative design. Computers in Industry 60, 48–63 (2009)

Established Mass Customization in Highly Customized Cabins of Passenger Transport Systems

Felix Schulz[1], Lars Wolter[2], Turgay Coruh[3], Haygazun Hayka[1], and Rainer Stark[1,2]

[1] Fraunhofer IPK Berlin, Germany
[2] Technical University Berlin, Germany
[3] Airbus Operations GmbH, Germany
felix.schulz@ipk.fraunhofer.de

Abstract. Mass customization is an approach that provides methodologies for the development of customized products while still profiting from the benefits of mass production such as economies of scale. Today, mass customization approaches have found their way into different industries such as clothes and furniture but also, to some extent and named differently, into more complex products like cars. Products like busses, trains, or aircrafts are not particularly known for applying similar approaches. They deal with complex systems that are highly regulated by legal requirements and thus seem to be restricted with respect to their possible degree of customization. This paper presents results from a study that was conducted in order to analyze applied practices in these industries. One of the goals of the study was to detect limitations of today's mass customization approaches that prevent an easy applicability. Configuration and customization approaches in the airplane cabin design, in the bus and in the train industry were investigated and compared. Finally, shortcomings in the applied practices and in the supporting solutions were identified and suggestions for improvements were formulated.

Keywords: Mass Customization, Configuration.

1 Introduction

This paper illustrates that the branches bus, train, and aircraft manufacturing industry are facing challenges that are comparable to problems addressed by mass customization approaches. Furthermore, it will be explained that common approaches for the investigated branches are not sufficient, due to multiple reasons. This information shall be used in order to derive suggestions for improvement of the current approaches. This enables an application of methods for more customizable complex products.

The outcome of this paper can be used for enhancing the use of mass customization strategies for industries that offer products with a higher degree of customizability.

2 State of the Art in Mass Customization

In order to discuss needs regarding configuration management in the investigated field it is necessary to define a uniform terminology used throughout this paper.

A. Bernard, L. Rivest, and D. Dutta (Eds.): PLM 2013, IFIP AICT 409, pp. 182–193, 2013.

This terminology is coming from general language within the investigated branches and was extended and consolidated by the authors for better understanding. First of all, configurable and highly customizable products – like buses and trains– usually only exist as virtual products during the offering of the product. By contrast, products that are offered in a pick-to-order business model do already physically exist during the ordering process. It is, therefore, necessary to differentiate between a *product*, a *product line* and a physically existing *product instance*. The product instance is the configured product to meet the individual needs by customization or using a set of configuration options. Further differentiation is necessary between *configuring within a closed catalogue of options*, common in the automobile industry, and *open configuration* which allows the creation of more customer-specified options. For the latter case the customer defines requirements in so called Customer Special Requests (CSR) that describe a single feature or combination of feature which is not in any catalogue of the company.

The general approach for mass customization is used for products that are configurable without having CSRs. This is true for computers, shoes, cars and many other products. It is not the case for products like busses, trains, airplanes and ships. Therefore, the general methods that handle mass customization are mainly applicable to the first kind of products. The increased need of producing large numbers of CSR driven products may make it desirable to use mass customization methods during their development.

There are no consolidated typical characteristics of mass customization. Several sources mention different aspects or so called mass customization characteristics. Kumar deals with mass customization, its relation to business strategy and its demand within a company's supply chain and management [1]. According to that, mass customization is characterized or usually associated with a *customer co-design process*, a *finite solution space*, and normally *low production cost per unit*.

Moser identifies the strategic considerations companies follow when pursuing the mass customization concept and differentiate the existing types of mass customization in his research [2]. In industry studies he detected that one characteristic is that in mass customization there exists intensive *customer integration*. According to Wikström [3], an *application of product configuration systems* is necessary to compose a mass customized product. The consumer decision-making process is often a complicated process. Bettman writes about this increased decision-making effort in his study [4]. Petruzellis addresses this problem in his studies about bundling of configurable product items [5]. A decision-making process is influenced by enormous number of criteria like decision-making strategy, individual's character, kind of presentation of alternatives and options. Therefore companies need to reduce choice complexity as demanded by Petruzzellis and Chatterjee [5], [6]. An *employment of product modularity* is usually seen in companies that use the mass customization approach, which is a basic principle to modularize product architectures. A broad *product variant management* is claimed to be necessary. Furthermore it is necessary to establish a *central production and logistics planning* as well as a *management of mass and individual production*. Mäkipää describes this with: "customization strategies often require a high technology production environment" [7]. A special *management of flexible organization processes* is required to achieve a flexible production environment. Also a *process documentation and IT support* is required

Mäkipää and Mertanen identify similar elements in their study about the application-level of mass customization approaches within the Finnish industry [7], [8]. These elements are a *customer integration and relationship management*, a high focus on *product development*, *manufacturing resource planning and procurement*, *after sales*, special *management*, and *other factors* like organizational commitment and creativity. The contents of these topics are more or less comparable to the contents of the studies mentioned before. All referenced sources offer a comparable view on mass customization. Moser and Mäkipää offer more comparable aspects. Kumar offers a more reduced view on mass customization. This is due to the facts that he does not analyze the business change management required for mass customization.

It shows that there is a shared understanding of mass customization among researchers although there is no consolidated definition.

The tool landscape from the engineering perspective consists of multiple IT tools [7], [8] and can be clustered as shown in Figure 1. The IT systems used for configuration management are mostly depending on the user's role. Product (line) development is used to execute product data management (PDM) systems. Enterprise resource planning (ERP) systems arise from the need of production and manufacturing and as they manage the enterprise's resources they are closely linked to sales. Therefore today's ERP systems offer increasingly more functionalities for product configuration and to synchronize orders with production. Customer relationship management (CRM) systems are just as ERP systems not in the focus of this investigation and are usually sales-oriented. It is fair to say that each IT-Tool has its right to exist, because it is able to deal with the special requirements existing in each domain and no system is able to substitute all other systems. Therefore an integration of all the systems is achieved by having some kind of PLM infrastructure which more or less connects the different IT systems as found out in an expert survey ("Delphi-Studie 2020") about future PLM systems [9]. Aside from the infrastructure various data systems like IMDS for hazardous or dangerous materials are used throughout the whole lifecycle. Stark summarizes aspects of virtual product development in automotive industry. He mentions for example, that the demand for IT tools and methods in automotive industry is larger than it is in software development [10]. Consequently, during the whole lifecycle, it will be necessary to constantly bridge between a variety of information databases and authoring systems to handle patchwork solutions. Müller et al conducted a study about deficits and potentials of today's collaborative product development [11]. It shows that there is a rising demand for transparency within different IT systems to increase information logistics and project management.

Most of the product configuration tasks during product planning and development are handled by PDM systems. Modern PDM Systems offer different tools for configuration management and are normally linked to CAD authoring systems where geometric parameters are processed. Although all the systems mentioned are

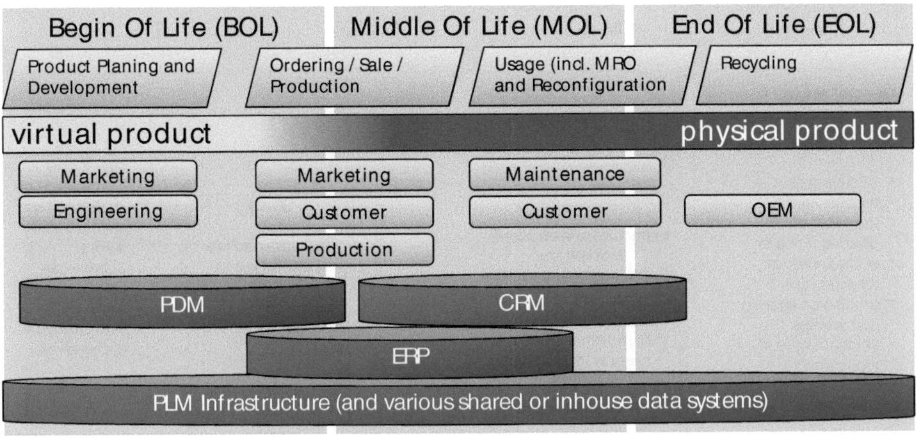

Fig. 1. Phases of product lifecycle, roles and range of influence of IT systems within lifecycle

specialized for engineering, there are different approaches to deal with product variation. One approach is to enrich the items with configuration meta data. The other approach is to establish logical links between items and possible variants. Further problem is that systems prefer to use their own standards for models and interfaces.

Using this flexible set of methods and tools the mass customization approach might be transferred to products using multiple CSRs during their ordering process. Different industries take slightly different approaches in realizing mass customization with a bit of fully individual customization wishes. To gain this knowledge, different industries have been analyzed during this study regarding their customization approaches focusing on the interior design.

3 Research Approach and Data Ascertainment

The study is carried out in three main phases. The overall approach is inspired by the first phases of the Six Sigma approach for problem solving. It is named DMAIC [1] as it consists of the phases to define the problem, measure the relevant measurement parameters, analyze the results of the measurement, improve a solution, and control the success of the improved solution. Since the purpose of this study does not include the improvement of a specific solution, the main phases considered are the definition and the measurement phase. An outlook on the improvement phase is given as the result of the study is used to give recommendations and improvement possibilities. Figure 2 shows the structure of the study.

The use of the Six Sigma DMAIC approach is on purpose limited to the concept and the use of the main generic phases. Six Sigma analysis tools are not used in this study. The initial definition phase investigates customization practice and the description of terms and solutions from a research point of view. Additional prescriptive studies where used to gather information about the industries using contacts of the Fraunhofer IPK.

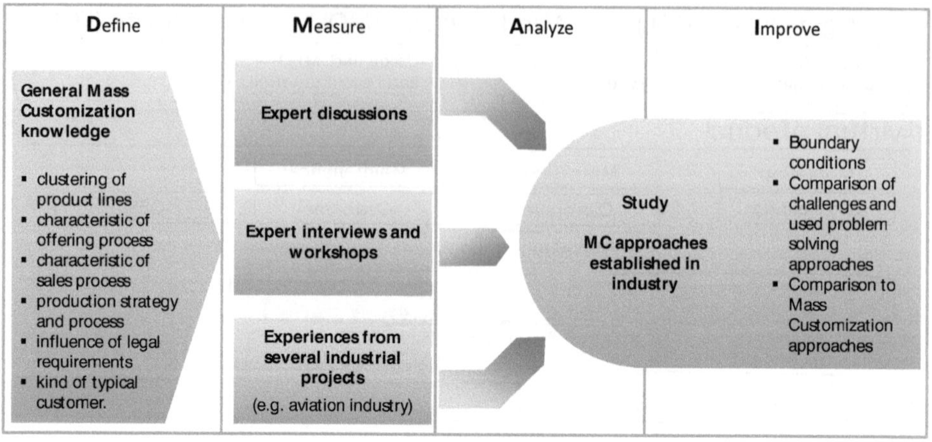

Fig. 2. The conduction of the study about mass customization (MC) approaches established in industry inspired by the DMAIC Approach

During the measurement phase multiple descriptive studies where performed and analyzed in an iterative manner. These studies included a small pre survey, telephone interviews and in depth workshops with experts from different companies of the bus and train industries. The workshops deepened the results from some of the telephone interviews. The interviewed experts were employees from different companies from automotive, train, and aircraft industry working as product managers, sales managers, development engineers, or IT managers. Three major results have been derived from this preliminary analysis: knowledge about the mass customization approaches established in the bus and train industries, the problems these industries are facing, and possible common solution approaches to solve these problems.

In addition, two expert discussions in 2011 and 2012 were set up during execution of the study and are discussed in Detail in chapter 5.

4 Investigated Industries – General Overview

Since the objective of this paper is to compare and to identify the applied practices of bus and train industries with respect to the cabin customization, there is the need to describe those two industries. Additional knowledge about automobile and aircraft industry extends this comparison. Knowledge about configuration approach and customizing practice within these branches is not cabin-specific as these branches were not core areas of the investigation.

The focus on cabin customization results from the complexity in this area. Customers purchasing a product commonly have very special wishes for the interior as it represents their company. Most of the cabins also introduce repeating elements and structures that allow a lot of automation during the configuration. This kind of flexibility between open configurable areas and closed configuration options together with the general understanding of the different cabin elements makes the cabin a perfect example and the study also applicable to other areas of product development.

A difference exists concerning the type of the customer. Whereas typical buyers of coaches are often smaller private carrying companies, public transport busses and trains are almost exclusively sold in tendering procedures. In this case, the buyers are companies or governmental institutions. Airplanes are often sold either to airlines or to leasing companies. Caused by kind of typical customers, the characteristics of offering process are different, as well.

As this overview between the industries bus and train and the comparison to automotive and aircraft industry shows, different business models and different production philosophies are in use but the industries are still comparable, especially when looking at the cabin interior. The expected similarities between these industries are therefore validated and hints for detailed investigations are identified.

4.1 Bus Industry

The development of busses is following an engineer-to-order approach and differs in time from several weeks for coaches to several months for city busses. Customization of busses is standard. There are two different segments of busses, which should be differentiated. The first segment is "city busses". The second segment is "coaches" which are usually used for long distance travelling. From an engineering perspective, there are differences in terms of floor height and customization degree. City busses typically are ordered in tendering procedures and widely specified by customers such as regional operators (cities). As these operators often maintain busses in own workshops, they have broad requirements concerning maintenance, repair and overhaul (MRO), such as colors of specific cables, use of switch connector fuses and so on. Furthermore highly specified requirements concerning corporate design, ticket machine interfaces, seats, handles, stop-buttons, and so on are common. Design parameters for those elements include number, model, position constraints like seat pitch, colors, materials, and so on. These busses are typically ordered in higher take rates than long distance coaches. City busses for instance may be ordered in series of five to 20 (in few cases approx. 80) busses.

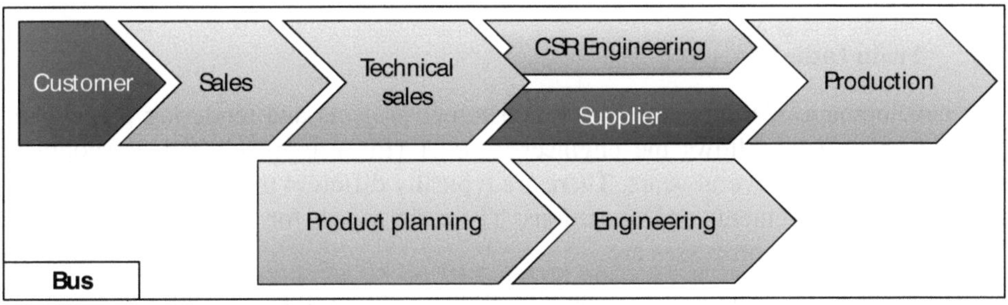

Fig. 3. Abstract bus development process. Ordering of busses happens in the upper horizontal lane. Non-CSR Engineering handles productline development and specific customer wishes.

Long distance coaches do have less customization although offering higher degrees of comfort, advanced designs (in the sense of styling) and media features. One reason is the customer segment, which mainly consists of operators with smaller fleets. Coaches are typically ordered in single items; in few cases series of 5 same items are ordered.

The development process is standardized and well structured. An abstracted view is presented in figure 3. According to a configuration, the top level product structure and bill of material become defined and are filled with design solutions during the engineering process. The product structure is a flat, 3 levels deep in average, structure for every product line defining the modules that each bus consists of on the first level. Products are configured within this 150%-structure to reach 100%-structure. Design solutions from former projects are adapted to the requirements of the new project and considered like "standard components" in a serial development process. More challenging requirements (special customer requests, CSR) are treated separately with regular customer interaction and more engineering time in parallel to the serialized standard process which is also common to the automotive industry. Usually numbers of CSRs within coaches are in one-digit levels. City buses usually have hundreds of CSRs. Special customer requests that have been realized as design solutions become part of the standard module catalogue if promising for later projects.

The design of coaches and city busses is based on platforms and modules. Validation of module fit to customized configurations is necessary during the design process and performed each time particularly. The investigated cases provide a reference that there are different degrees of competence in companies to validate possible customized configurations already during the offering process. In one case, the validation was quick because extended design verification and validation against the standard catalogue is carried out more extensively while developing design solutions for specific customer request. This raises effort the first time but pays off in case of high take rates in later projects.

Systematization of IT tool chains is established and continuously evolved, because the development process and the parts and document management (product data management) is common for all projects.

4.2 Train Industry

The development of trains is driven by customer projects and tendering procedures. Train development follows the engineer-to-order (EtO) approach and development time can take up to several years. There are typically different train types that are built for different requirements and operations. The main aspect for the customization and development project processes are:

- Train type: high velocity train, intercity trains, region trains, and city trains
- Customer type: large customers, small operators
- Role in the supply chain: (contractor / tenderer, supplier)
- Dependencies of railroad network (different tracks and electrical power supply)

- Performance parameters: speed, acceleration, transportation capacity
- Design parameters to be mentioned (min. curve radius, envelop curve, and track gauge)

High velocity trains, regionally operated trains as well as trams do have significant differences in terms of customer requirements and design. In general, the design of trains is driven by customer-driven functional and style requirements, national requirements, regional requirements (e.g. height of station platforms) and performance requirements.

Trains are produced in small series between 10 and 40 trains (in single cases up to 200 trains), each having several coaches. Production (assembly) may happen in the assembly lines of the main contractor, but also at lines of suppliers. For instance, SIEMENS and Bombardier assemble trains of the same ordering process in their assembly lines in case of collaboration.

Depending on the train platform or modularization strategy, the degree of customization and configuration differs. In the investigated cases, selected trains are based on platform and module concepts. In the one case, it was applied to a regional train. The idea was to allow a dedicated flexibility of cabin design, but with controlled low inner variance. The instantiation of the design allowed outer variance constrained by configuration rules. Even options for train reconfiguration in operation (quick seat changes) and in longer cycles (door changes) were scoped within the design. In the other case, a high velocity train was designed with a platform concept integrating "black box modules" applied to zones.

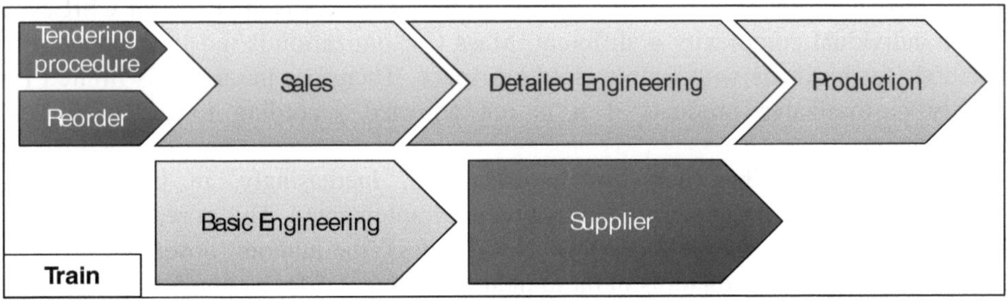

Fig. 4. Abstract representation of the train development process

The development process is comparable to the development process of plant engineering. An abstracted view is presented in figure 4. A basic design is developed independently to conceptualize a train and to implement new technology. The customization and instantiation is then happening in customer projects, mostly organized in tendering projects. The train manufacturer can participate in a tendering by specifying a train towards the customer requirements published in the tendering procedure. If a train manufacturer has questions about the requirements, his question will be answered and the question and answer are visible for all applicants. Customer contact after ordering the train is normal, but larger changes are not possible due to the initially defined requirements. If those requirements are changed, other applicants can later complain about the process.

After contracting, the detail design is performed based on the offered specification. Components and systems are developed with suppliers and accepted by the customer. Within the detail engineering, a common approach is to "copy" best-fit former projects and to use product structures and train components that fit best to the current project. Developed components can become available in new "standard catalogues" for later projects. The general product structure is more or less oriented at stakeholders but not used for customer-specific product configuration as trains are usually individually developed and sold in projects. Nevertheless, train manufacturers use to establish intern product configurators to raise the amount of reusability.

The configuration of seats, handles and buttons etc. is not constrained by fully defined configuration rules. In each development project, the cabin configuration is validated and designs are verified particularly. One reason is for instance security regulations and the particular use case (rail track, number of expected travelers, etc.). Another reason is the enormous count of variance caused by combination of existing design parameters like number of seats, kind of seat ("model"), required seat pitch, colors / materials, interfaces, and so on.

5 Comparison of Investigated Industries and Mass Customization

As seen in chapter 4 the need for mass customized highly complex products is given in the bus and train industry. Common for all the industries is the need for CSR even if the individual complexity is different. Mass Customization is mostly seen to offer methods for products with a finite solution space. Therefore the usage is limited for highly customizable products if it is not adjusted according to the industries' requirements.

Chapter 4 describes that bus industry and, increasingly, in train industry configuration tools for customer interaction are implemented. This is reasonable from a mass customization's point of view. Nevertheless, the authors' observation shows that today's configuration tools in these industries do not offer a complete coverage of the solution space. Even if the customers have different requirements for the configuration of trains and busses or even differing expectations for ordering travel coaches or city busses, a common configuration backend is needed. This configuration backend is required to supply either the customer or a sales person with the ability to create a suitable configuration including special requests with minimal costs.

The investigated industries do obviously use the concept of product modularity to gain benefits. Busses are divided into different zones within their layout which can more or less be configured separately. Trains incorporate black box modules with fully defined interfaces to enable configuration regarding power requirements for example. Variant management is hardly to divide from modularity.

During the expert discussions the Fraunhofer IPK put together engineers from those different industries to discuss common problems and possible solutions for some or all industries. This expert discussion was focusing on product complexity. Its objective was to define product complexity, to find causes of product complexity, and to discuss ideas for management of product complexity.

Complexity from the point of view of the participant experts was seen to have an intensive relationship with number of product's elements, number of involved parties and breadth of project or product in general. To handle that complexity powerful models are necessary which are able to simply derive different views. The ATA chapters (Air Transport Association) used in the aircraft industry as a common documentation standard were seen to be an applicable way to ensure completeness and unambiguousness. Additionally, experts mentioned that there is a need for standard interfaces to bill of materials, PDM, ERP, MES as well as all the other domain-independent systems in the IT landscape with assured interoperability. In that context the questions that asks for the centralization of solutions is seen to be important. Those questions include how much every site should be able to establish their own local solutions. They also handle the question regarding the required steering mechanisms (production sites, customers, validation).

During a second expert discussion the Fraunhofer IPK focused on product customization. Therefore, causes and methods for managing product customization were discussed. The expert group was divided into two groups.

The first group discussed ideas for IT solution that provides "help" for customization. The discussed solution was called generic product structure. This solution was seen to be able to model project-specific "100% product structures" by project-related reduction of elements of a "150% product structure". The expected benefits were seen to provide the ability of trace linking to requirements management. This would allow evaluation of single solutions (functional, geometrical, and other aspects) and other beneficial functions.

The second group of experts discussed current and future challenges for product customization in general and solution approaches. Today's challenges were seen to be extended in future, namely customer-specific customization. Additionally, the extension of legal requirements and demographic change produce new requirements. Additionally legal requirements by the European Union and other institutions are seen to come up. Aim of the second group discussion was to gain knowledge about future challenges, together with a prioritization to address those challenges in the most useful order. Therefore the progress of these challenges have been evaluated and where supplemented with currently evolving and possible future challenges.

These expert discussions show that current and future requirements of highly individualized products are met by the aims of mass customization. Additionally, they show that methods and tools used within these industries need to be improved to apply mass customization to highly individualized, complex goods, and that improvements are on their way.

6 Conclusion

This paper presents current methods and tools used for product development, sales, and production of mass-customized complex products with a high level of individualization. The results of an analysis of the bus and train industry yielded insights on typical industry requirements relevant for mass customization. It turned out that there is a need for open configurable areas in the product models since products like busses and trains must offer open solution spaces. Furthermore, a reduced use of configuration rules is required. Currently, the effort of developing and maintaining configuration rules exceeds the benefits of using configuration rules in some cases. This is why general mass customization methods are usually not implemented in the analyzed businesses in complete accordance with their description in literature. Instead, the analysis revealed that methods of mass customization are indeed implemented partially in the analyzed industries. Obviously, the benefits offered by mass customization are already recognized as potentials for highly customizable products. Solutions today are used in different levels.

Therefore, there exists a need for sophisticated structuring methods supported by intelligent tools to handle the complexity in the development of mass individualized products. Important is the above mentioned differentiation between configurable parts of a product and parts which are open for customer-specific requirements. Today's mass customization approaches do not cover parts of a product that are totally free to customize. An extended mass customizing approach which includes the option of open configuration is needed. Knowledge based engineering and model based systems engineering as well as other approaches seem to be promising in this context. An investigation of the applicability of such approaches should thus be done in following studies.

The presented approaches might also be valid and applicable to other branches and industrial products, such as plant engineering. In other industries there seems to be a stronger focus on technical aspects while esthetic aspects play a minor role. Such deviant demands of other industries should be analyzed in further studies. This paper delivers a starting point for the development of solutions for an extended mass customization approach mentioned before and the planning of further studies.

References

1. Kumar, A., Piller, F.T., Reismann, A., et al.: A Prioritization Algorithm for Configuration Scheduling in Mass Customization Environment. In: Mass Customization & Personalization Conference (2007)
2. Moser, K.: Mass Customization Strategies. In: Mass Customization & Personalization Conference (2007)
3. Wikström, S.: Value creation by company-consumer interaction. Journal of Marketing Management 12(5), 359–374 (1996)
4. Bettman, J.R., Johnson, E.J., Payne, J.W.: A Componentional Analysis of Cognitive Effort in Choice. In: Organizational Behavior and Human Decision Processes, vol. 45, pp. 111–139 (1990)

5. Petruzzellis, L., Somma, E.: Bundling, Mass Customization and Competition under Consumption Uncertainity. In: Mass Customization & Personalization Conference (2007)
6. Chatterjee, S., Heath, T.B.: Conflict and Loss Aversion in Multiattribute Choice: The Effects of Trade-off Size and Reference Dependence on Decision Difficulty. In: Organizational Behavior and Human Decision Processes, vol. 67, pp. 144–155 (June 1996)
7. Mäkipää, M., Ahoniemi, L., Mertanen, M., et al.: The state of art of mass customization practices in Finnish technology industries – Preliminary results of multiple case study of 40 companies. In: Mass Customization & Personalization Conference (2007)
8. Mertanen, M., Sievänen, M.: A Practical Approach to Mass Customization – Lessons Lerned from Finnish Machine Construction. In: Mass Customization & Personalization Conference (2007)
9. Abramovici, M., Bellalouna, F., Neubach, M.: Delphi-Studie 2020 – Experteneinschätzung zur zukünftigen Entwicklung des Product Lifecycle Managements. Industrie Management (3) (2010)
10. Stark, R., Hayka, H., Israel, J.H., Kim, M., Müller, P., Völlinger, U.: Virtuelle Produktentstehung in der Automobilindustrie. Informatik Spektrum 34(1), 20–28 (2010)
11. Müller, P., Pasch, F., Drewinski, R., Hayka, H.: Kollaborative Produktentwicklung und digitale Werkzeuge, Defizite Heute – Potenziale Morgen. Fraunhofer IPK, CONTACT Software, VDI e.V., Berlin, Bremen, Düsseldorf (2013); Publisher: Stark, R., Drewinski, R., Hayka, H., Bredenbender, H.
12. Hahn, G.J., Doganaksoy, N., Hoerl, R.: The Evolution of Six Sigma. Quality Engineering 12(3), 317–326 (2000)

PLM and Classification Society Management in Marine Manufacturing Companies

Niko Ville Salonen

Rolls-Royce Marine AS
niko.salonen@rolls-royce.com

1 Introduction

This study was started after 'Systems thinking and systems engineering' program arranged in Finland by group of technical universities and educational learning centre, Edutech, during 2011-2012. The program inspired to think could system modelling techniques give new ways of solving, proving and improving operational strategies and models in conjunction with PLM/ERP systems, Integrated Production Systems (IPS) in combination with more general techniques of UML modelling and other types of use case and data flow map presentation methods, and by using improvement tools such as lean six sigma 'toolbox'.

This study concentrates to identify specific Marine industry specific engineer to order based classification society management requirements and processes, which are known, but create extensive landscape of various certification processes influencing operational management of design, manufacturing, procurement and financial transactions, including invoicing and cost control to manufacturers like Rolls-Royce. This study focuses on modelling of different certification processes for configurable project specific products.

This study illustrated the same need and missing functionality from component manufacturer's point of view as Ehrler et al. (2007) [4] describes for classification society Germanischer Lloyd (GL), that currently these requirements are not sufficiently addressed by state of the art PDM/PLM software tools and solutions. Classification societies have to manage product oriented structures (as designed, as built), associated analysis and simulation data (FEM, CFD) and manifold relationships to external part catalogues and material databases Additionally, the underlying information model has to be extensible and adaptable during production use in order to satisfy short term requirements from different certification projects.

The outcome of this study is setting a framework of studies carried out currently and in next coming 1-2 years trying to describe specifically manufacturer's business processes to meet the requirements from the classification society's, project management's and engineering change management's process point of view including the engineering to order logistical planning requirements for marine products. All these requirements are generic to all products, which are to be certified.

The key question for PLM from this study is could system modelling of dynamic systems give new ways of solving product lifecycle management system development issues by introducing modelling techniques to enable simulations to prove and select

A. Bernard, L. Rivest, and D. Dutta (Eds.): PLM 2013, IFIP AICT 409, pp. 194–209, 2013.

best option from possible technical architectures. The elements identified in this study should be compared with ISE information model AP239, Product Life Cycle Support (PLCS), known officially as ISO10303-239:2012 [5], is an international standard for the definition and exchange of product data needed for the long-term support of very complex products, such as ships. This model is again linked to various information models, including STEP geometry definition standards.

2 Approach

The approach used in this study is based on 13 years of experience working in marine manufacturing industry. During this time, first working with classification society processes in engineering at Rolls-Royce, in Finland. Later work has included developing different PDM/PLM solutions in local engineering organisations and during the last 3 years in central Rolls-Royce Marine PLM team enabling new methods and systems to comply with the varying classification society rules from the perspective of Rolls-Royce Marine delivering more than 150 different product types to thousands of customers.

The approach is taking account current ISO standards and commercial PDM/PLM/ERP tool capabilities, and articles and papers written within Marine industry conferences and organisations like ISSC. Statistical information from current IPS systems is supporting the practical knowledge. The conclusions are based on abstraction of true artefacts into concept generalisation.

3 Classification Societies [6]

It is important to understand the relation between product manufacturers using different PLM/IPS systems and marine industry Classification Societies.

A classification society is a non-governmental organization that establishes and maintains technical standards for the construction and operation of ships and offshore structures. The society will also validate that construction is according to these standards and carry out regular surveys in service to ensure compliance with the standards. To avoid liability, they explicitly take no responsibility for the safety, fitness for purpose, or seaworthiness of the ship.

Classification societies set technical rules, confirm that designs and calculations meet these rules, survey ships and structures during the process of construction and commissioning, and periodically survey vessels to ensure that they continue to meet the rules. Classification societies are also responsible for classing oil platforms, other offshore structures, and submarines. This survey process covers diesel engines, important shipboard pumps and other vital machinery.

Classification surveyors inspect ships to make sure that the ship, its components and machinery are built and maintained according to the standards required for their class.

Today there are a number of classification societies, the largest of which are Det Norske Veritas, Lloyd's Register, Germanischer Lloyd, Nippon Kaiji Kyokai, RINA and the American Bureau of Shipping.

Marine vessels and structures are classified according to the soundness of their structure and design for the purpose of the vessel. The classification rules are designed to ensure an acceptable degree of stability, safety, environmental impact, etc.

All nations require that ships and other marine structures flying their flag meet certain standards; in most cases these standards are deemed to be met if the ship has the relevant certificate from a member of the IACS or EMSA. Certificates issued by the classification society on behalf of the flag country are also required for pumps, engines, and other equipment vital to the ship's function. Equipment under certain sizes is usually excluded from these certificate requirements.

In particular, classification societies may be authorised to inspect ships, oil rigs, submarines, and other marine structures and issue certificates on behalf of the state under whose flag the ships are registered.

As well as providing classification and certification services, the larger societies also conduct research at their own research facilities in order to improve the effectiveness of their rules and to investigate the safety of new innovations in shipbuilding.

There are more than 50 marine classification organizations worldwide. [6]

4 Principle Certification Requirements for Component Manufacturer

The principle certification requirements defined by the IACS include two main requirements that can be extracted and implied how product manufacturers need to comply in general terms against specific classification rules. The rest of requirements are focused more on ship building principle certification requirements. Classification process for key component supplier, manufacturer consists of:

A. A technical review of the design plans and related documents for a new vessel to verify compliance with the applicable Rules; [2]
B. Attendance by a Classification Society surveyor(s) at the relevant production facilities that provide key components such as the steel, engine, generators and castings to verify that the component conforms to the applicable Rule requirements; [2]

Generalizing above IACS certification rules and adding the requirement for material traceability

Classification Certification Requirements for Manufacturer are

- Satisfy international classification rules and documentation requirements in Marine industry products
- Satisfy material quality and traceability of every certified component

5 Design Certification Models

Design certification is one part of certification process. The IACS definition A. above describes the final requirement for design to be certified. The most used model as the IACS implies is the project specific "*case by case*" certificated design certification model.

Unfortunately the review process is not tuned from information flow and process point of view to level that customer delivery time requirement is always met. The demanding addition in ship building industry is the engineer to order process, which in reality means that all requirements are not defined before the design process starts and in many cases even the manufacturing must be started before all requirements are fully known. This means that customer detail requirements are changing during the delivery process. For configurable marine products the definition of "product design plan for new vessel" is even more challenging as the vessel, generally 'application' changes the rules against the product.

Therefore classification societies have various design certification models to support and improve management of delivery time. The next more generic is *"product (design) type certification"*, which is in some classification societies named as *"design appraisal"* (incl. Lloyd's Register). The next level of approval is *"design type certification"*. Some classification societies also have *"special agreements"*, which two are mentioned below.

Special agreement (DNV) [7]:

In order to support efforts on reduced delivery time and to ensure efficient and correct certification processes, DNV consider it beneficial to establish General Certification Agreements (GCA) between manufacturers and DNV.

In such agreements the daily procedures for efficient processes for design approval and surveys will be laid down. Information and documentation needed and required by the two parties may also be defined and be part of such agreements.

Further, the agreement will also normally include commitments on transfer and sharing of information and experiences that are considered beneficial for the manufacturer and DNV. [7]

There are also concepts of certifying the entire PLM/IPS system in cases where products can be fully 'configured to order'. Then the certification is done against the PLM/IPS systems and configuration rules within the system. In these cases the management focuses in the robustness of the system rules and to the change management of these rules. This level of certification is extremely difficult to obtain as the next sections will identify from the fact how much the processes vary. This type of certification is also business risk for the manufacturer as the system management becomes controlled also externally and the entire business knowledge is tight to the systems, and dynamical business changes or business strategy changes can not be easily adapted and systems modified.

6 Component and Materials Certification Models

Component and materials certification is the second part of certification process. The purpose of this process is to ensure the quality and traceability of used materials and components.

This model contains again classification specific variations, but elements are based on international standards like the *"standard inspection documents"*, which is defined from ISO 10474 [8] (previous EN 10204-91) and EN 10204:2004 [10]. Classification societies have own definitions and names for these, but manufacturers refer usually to the ISO standards.

The material certification process starts from the combination of application and product specific rules. Some critical components require certification of material. These are identified from the basis of criticality of operability and safety of the application (vessel). Classification rules define specific inspection document types [7] for each component or functional component category, for example main propulsion shaft line components (including shafts, gears, bearings, clutches, couplings, propellers etc.).

The actual material certification process requires specific *"samples"* and *"test reports"* performed and documented by defined authority, which again can vary, and finally including *"material inspection"*, also having element of options which party can perform the inspection.

Certified components and materials can be traced by unique item codes or by item serialization. Serialization has been more used and rational way of managing item data in ERP systems. Materials are serialized *"by lot"* and components requiring certificate *"by unit"* or *"by lot"*. By lot means the material is traced to a level of raw material batch. By unit means that the component is traced to level of every unit produced.

Most used component/material certification is *"case by case"* certification as is for design approval. Manufactures and classification societies are trying to improve the process performance in different ways. One of these methods is by *"group certification"*, which is not fully standardized approach from the fact that sharing the certification is not improving classification society's individual profitability of their business. From customer's, ship builder's and manufacturer's perspective this would be excellent way of improving the process as it increases flexibility to use certified materials and components. This is another topic for the financial management and dynamic systems modelling of the classification society management.

More used classification society specific process model for manufacturing is called *"type approved manufacturing process"*, which is defined as part of *"type approval"* in some classification societies (incl. Lloyd's Register). In DNV this approval model is called Manufacturing Survey Arrangement (MSA) [7] in Lloyd's Register of Shipping type approval term is used for overall approval of design and manufacturing, and *'design appraisal'* is the term used for design certification.

In general classification society type approval requires companies to be certified with ISO 9001. This rule applies to all type approvals.

7 Product Certification Process

Product certification is the top level certification that links the product to the actual application, ship, oil rig or submarine. Type approved components or products must always be still documented against the application and classification societies will review that the type approvals are compliant within the application and usage of product in it. However, when configuration management of product is done properly within the limits of the type approvals, manufacturer can process the product certification efficiently by extracting and collecting the documentation from the PLM/IPS system.

"Manufacturer's declaration" is the first principle assurance of compliance from the manufacturer, that each installed product will be according the specific classification society rules.

The product certification process usually includes system and assembly level testing. The classification society inspects onsite that the specific serialised manufactured product and certified documentation is according the rules for specific application. When product and documentation is according specific rules the inspector will issue unit certification and product is ready to be installed to the application (vessel etc.).

From manufacturer point of view the product is now ready to be shipped to shipyard to be installed to the specific application. This study does not include the classification processes in the shipyard. This process includes also the sea trials, but this level certification is against the entire application and main aspects of manufacturer classification processes have been performed before this lifecycle phase.

8 Financial Invoicing and Costing Models

Financial aspects of classification society management are not part of scope of this study, however it is important part of overall evaluation of classification society management and even more important for understanding and improving using dynamic system modelling and simulation methods.

The complexity of classification processes makes recording and managing cost difficult based from two different aspects. As the rules itself are complex and variable, so are the financial transaction models. First point is that invoicing is not standardized among classification societies and there are several agents causing additional variation to the cost collection and invoicing process. This again means that manufacturers can not record accurate classification process cost and often even invoices against specific items in ERP systems. Very often the cost is recorded for the delivery project or even worse on yearly basis. Defining standard costing models and processes for financial invoicing and costing must be part of future study to be able model and simulate the system dynamics.

9 Current Product Life Cycle Standards for Marine and Classification Societies

The standard exchange ship Product Data Model is STEP (ISO 10303). This Application Protocol shares some modules with the AP239 devoted to Product Life

Cycle Support (PLCS) that was published on 2005 and latest 2012. AP233 is the standard for Systems Engineering Data Representation. The objective is to provide the functionality defined in the shipbuilding application protocols using a combination of STEP AP239, AP214, and reference data libraries.

DNV has presented a product model specifying a standardized vessel description for class work (Vindøy, 2008) [3] based on ISO 15926 and DNV's own "ships functional" classification hierarchy.

Classification society approval processes in shipbuilding introduce additional and specific requirements for information management systems to be used in the ship design process. ISO 10474 [8] defines the inspection documentation requirements adopted with modifications to classification societies. ISO 9001 is quality standard that most marine product manufacturers have adopted also to support ways to improve the classification society certification processes.

Different engineering change management approaches which form the basis of these functions in PDM systems are listed. The most relevant ones are: Quality management - Guidelines for configuration management (ISO 10007), Institute of Configuration Management (CMII), Workflow Management Coalition (WfMC) and the ISO 10303 Standard for the Exchange of Product Model Data (STEP).

10 Product Lifecycle View of Certification Processes

Below a simple component based certification process (Figure 1.) is described in SIPOC (Supplier – Input – Process – Output – Customer) process model. The process is also the most often used *"case by case"* classification (meaning all documentation and process is re-used and each step in the process is performed again and again for each delivery project for specific customer). Any dynamics (including feedbacks, other loops, delays etc.) are not considered in the SIPOC model. The SIPOC does not either consider the original design requirements that have been identified against the product definition.

The SIPOC process figure's key elements are creating design documentation that is reviewed by classification society authority and stamped as approved. Then the manufacturing process is inspected based on rules and against the approved design documentation (the meeting point of design and physical product).

This process is performed to all components defined requiring certification by the specific classification society rules. Final product/system (Unit) inspection is collecting all related approved documents and product certification is given to the equipment.

This process is followed for every product delivered to customers. There are two very specific differences compared to other businesses (car, aero manufacturing): Rules change based on specific classification society (and there is several as mentioned in the chapter Classification Societies) and the other difference is that final inspection is done by specific classification society inspector for every sold unit.

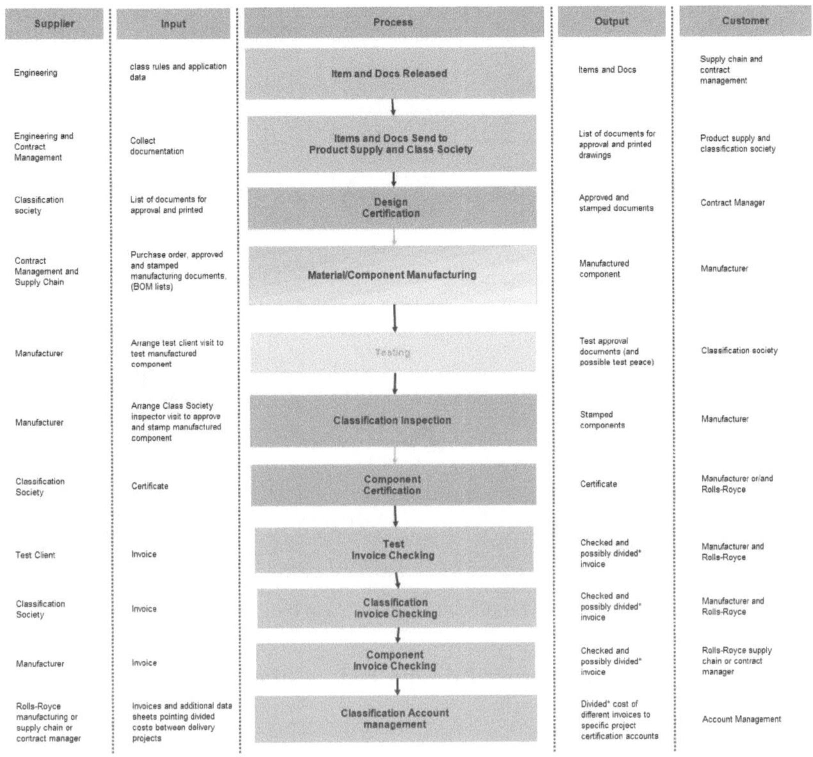

Fig. 1. SIPOC for *'case by case'* classification process without any dynamics

When manufacturer is operating by *"case by case"* basis and using manufacturing suppliers the flow of information, material and people can be illustrated as in figure 2. This figure shows also the 'happy path' without any additional loops, which may occur in the process.

The link from certificate management to the supplier or to internal production is critical flow connection point of documentation information to physical product flow. These connection points and the dynamic flow of information and components/material is causing that *"case by case"* certification does not work, main reason for dynamics is that both flows contain variations of loops and delays.

There have been situations, where classification societies request the documentation package of the entire product to be sent only when fully complete, which again fights against the ETO process principles. It is fully understandable from classification society point of view, that it would be easier to review the documentation as one fully defined package rather than one evolving package of documentation to obtain the product approval. However the business requirements do not make this easy or practical.

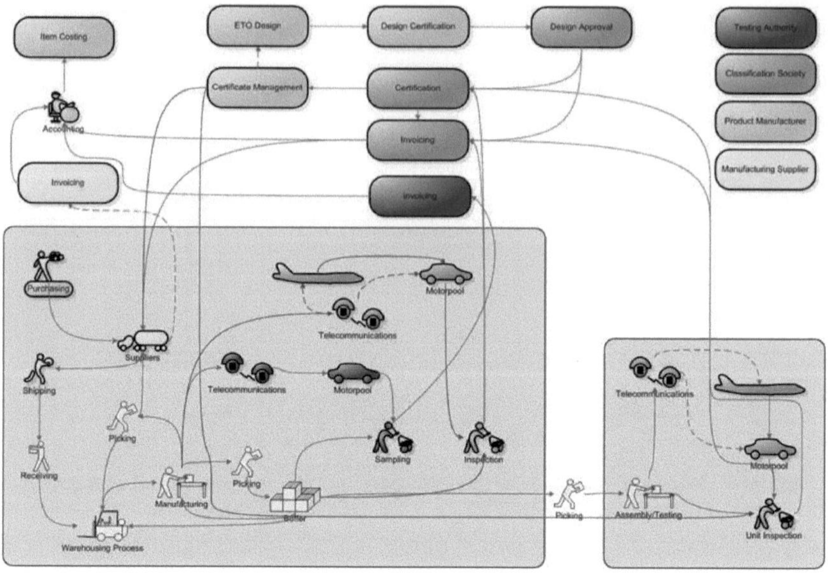

Fig. 2. Information and material flow in 'case by case' delivery process

In comparison for type approved design and certified manufacturing process the flow is presented in figure 3.

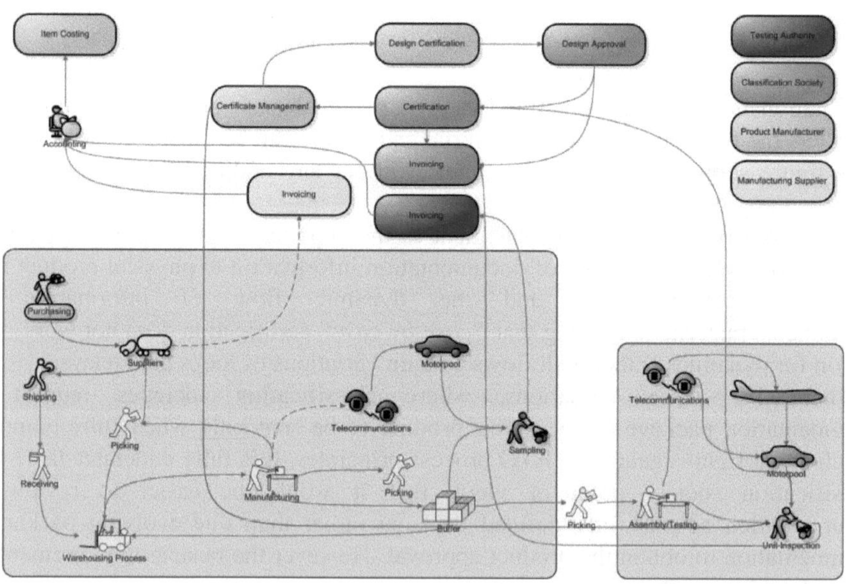

Fig. 3. Information and material flow of type approved and manufacturing approved process

The situation of *"design type approved"* documentation information flow in figure 3 would show in stock flow model differences from *"case by case"*. The difference is, the design certification is already obtained and the data can flow through the purchase order or production order process information flow and not as separate information flow. Obtaining the Product (Unit) level design approval is easier as the package of documentation can be provided early on the process.

11 Theoretical Link between PLM and Classification Society Management

The theoretical relation between PLM and Classification Society management can be identified by systems thinking (including many systems engineering principles) and information science levels. Operations management theories could be linked also between PLM and Classification Society, but are out-scoped as systems thinking and information science are deeper principles that this study concentrates.

Using definitions: openness, purposefulness, multidimensionality, emergent properties and counterintuitive from Jamshid Gharajedaghi's, 'Systems thinking, managing chaos and complexity' book [11], the link between systems definitions and certification process can be achieved.

The certification of component within an application has direct correlation to open systems principles, where the certification requirements can be understood only in the context of the environment, the ship and product located in specific function. The certification changes additionally between classification societies, but these differences can not be reasoned directly, but can be seen as variation or immaturity of understanding systems.

Purposefulness can be seen of understanding why certification is happening. The value-guided system can be identified in this study by challenging the current models, especially the 'case by case' certification process based on understanding the what, how and why of the system, classification society management.

The plurality or multidimensionality of classification society management and certification process can be identified in function, structure and process levels. The system ship-product-component and certification process has several functions, for ship owner it is means to manage the insurance cost, secure the quality of product, for classification society it is means to earn money and improve global safety of sailing ships, and for component manufacturer it can secure easy entry to market and help identifying principle rules that shall be complied when designing and manufacturing products to commercial marine ships. The plurality of structure for certification required components and an entire product structure are closely linked between the PLM and Classification Society certification process. The plurality and 'equifinality': a final state can be reached from same initial conditions by number of routes. Certification processes can be seen from the differentiating from causality by ability to certify the product with various certification methods.

Emergent properties of classification society certification management could be the overall satisfaction of all parties in the certification process, ship owner, shipyard, classification society, manufacturer and others. This satisfaction will evolve the systems behaviour over time.

Counterintuitive behaviour can also be seen part of classification society management. Only taking one example is component manufacturer's overall cost management. The cost structure and behaviour of certified components for many manufacturers can not understand if there is not enough knowledge how the system behaves with various dynamical relations. This can lead to mistakes from 'assuming' that changing one parameter of the system would lead to positive reaction, but actually result can be opposite, negative increase of overall cost.

Systems engineering and it specific area of requirement management is core part of PLM principles and also PLM systems. The classification society rules are requirements and very much structured requirements.

Information and library science's classification, collection, manipulation, storage of information is field, which is basement for researching computer science, database systems and overlaying PLM applications. Turning the conceptual certification process and information principles identified in this study will eventually lead to defining information architectures, information management and information retrieval concepts for the PLM (IPS) systems.

12 Principle Impacts to PLM and Entire IPS

Previous classification rules, including design, component/material and product certification creates complex process and data model requirements to manufacturing company, especially when same product is certified to different classification societies and product is used in different applications (ships, oil rigs etc.) or/and having different usage models.

The engineering principle of form, fit and function (FFF) definition can be jeopardized by this if items contain data of classification society specifics. From engineering perspective keeping product definition purely compliant to FFF reduces enormous numbers of variants of items. From engineering point of view and from management point of view isolating the item definition purely into FFF, means that the item (raw material, component, assembly or product) must be maintained as such trough it's whole lifecycle from cradle to grave. To the question how the requirements can be met without jeopardizing true FFF item definition is explained next.

The classification rules for manufacturer can be identified as requirements same way as actual customer requirements are defined. The requirements can be divided to into categories described earlier. The requirements are also assigned to different lifecycle phases of the product. Common requirement and domain is that requirements are including the application domain, which creates need for conditional requirements from manufacturer point of view manufacturer wants to use the product in different applications. For configurable products this creates more complex data model requirement as there can be configurable modular products as the product (unit) level product definition is very generic. As described in earlier study [9] the "*unit concept*" model can be used as the representative item against the requirements, before actual delivery specific item is created.

Based on statistical study in azimuth thrusters the same component can have different certification models (documentation and process requirements) already in the generic product structure (also called as 150% BOM) definitions. The variation can increase when generic product is configured to physical product structure definition (100% BOM). This fact and the previous application and unit level definition based metadata combined define the abstraction into *"conditional occurrence tree based requirements"*. This means that the specific component occurrence can have conditional requirement against the classification society management process.

The application domain requirements can be identified for design, some for documentation during product design, some specific for application engineering phase, some for actual manufacturing processes (inspection, sampling and testing, certification), which again all can contain documentation needs and keeping records. The requirements can be pointing to different certification types based on application or usage in application. Managing documentation specific for each application (engineer to order delivery project) for specific system/component/material creates own data model requirements.

Example of azimuth thruster's product structure and conditional requirements is shown in figures 4. and 5. In figure 4, azimuth thruster's (unit) structure is having parent application (vessel "Tug") and the azimuth thruster is containing one branch of configurable modular product structure. The parent child structure has deep sub-module structure, which are also configurable and the lowest level components have sub structure of pre-fabrication components and finally raw materials.

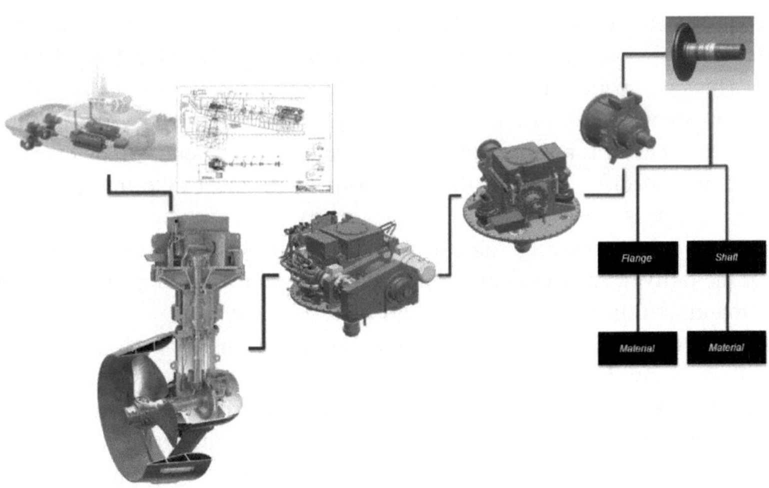

Fig. 4. Example of Azimuth Thruster product structure, installed in a harbour tug

In figure 5, azimuth thruster (unit) structure and the parent application (vessel "Tug") have extractions of metadata, shown in green arrows. The actual requirements are linked as previously defined not against the components (Shaft and raw materials), but against the occurrence of the components. The conditional rules are illustrated with IF-AND clauses. The red arrows mean positive outcome "Yes" and yellow are negative outcome "No". The black arrows are conclusion links "To Obtain", which can link between requirements, representing the sequencing, or to artefacts (documents), which will be received or created by the manufacturer.

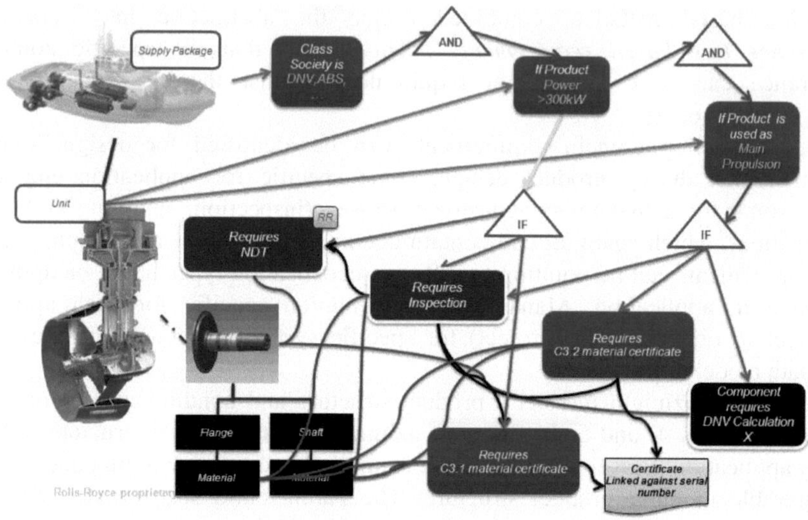

Fig. 5. Example of conditional requirements against the shaft

The requirements (rules) themselves are also moving target for manufacturer. The rules are revised and classification societies identify the effective date for each version. This is specifically the Rules effective dates, which are defined by classification society. The rule is linked to requirement defined by the manufacturing company. One reason for separating the rule and requirement is that many rules are not precise and specific and manufacturer sometimes must take interpretation of the rule. This happens also in real cases, when different inspectors from same classification society interpret rules differently. This type situation can be recovered from, but the delivery process can be impacted by delay and loops of communication between manufacturing company and classification society.

Businesses can not react as fast even classification societies identify the rule change dates early in advance. Manufacturers main focus is bringing value to customers, which means the customer requirements drive the changes in products. The regulations must be complied, but the phasing of design changes do not match.

Marine manufacturers work according the ship building project principles and timelines. The sales phase and contracts are long processes and the commitment to customer requirements need freezing classification society requirements in certain point to be able to deliver product in time according contract. This means that item definition and the class society requirement relation has also effective date.

Linking requirements based on classification rules from top application to low level components and materials need conditional requirements as the rules are not standardized. The product and application relation and application performance characteristics make some requirements not valid or not active. The difference of not valid and not active is quite different by means of data model if the item definition is kept intact. The linking of the requirement can be done to several items and the validity of the requirement is conditional of the combination of characteristics.

In IPS landscape the active requirements and only active (delivery specific product configuration) must be transferred to resource planning system for manufacturing integration to inform supplier or internal manufacturing of the testing and inspection and certification requirements. Again avoiding multiplying actual FFF items creates specific need to manage the information until As Built configuration has been created. There can be several methods how the information of requirements can be transformed to documentation package objects and processes and how the information is transferred to ERP systems. These models are often company specific models not described in this study.

13 Thinking of Dynamic System Models

Static modelling as done in this study is not enough to develop integrated production systems (IPS) and select the optimal operations strategies. One of the key questions developing and maintaining these systems is overall IT cost against the achieved business benefit.

The classification society management process has many feedback loops and delays all influenced by different certification models or combination of models used by the business. Understanding the dynamics and simulating the options can first of all improve the decision making of certification strategies, but also what IPS functions should be developed and which order.

Defining the relations of other manufacturers is required for the dynamic business system model. From modelling the dynamics the behaviours and sensitivity analysis could indicate and help PLM and IPS developers to understand what system configurations must be in place to create solution to include flexibilities for business environment changes in short term and in long term.

14 Conclusions

This study defined the principles of classification society rules for a product or component manufacturer in marine business sector. Different certification processes were identified and described and single component classification certification process and, data and material flow models for *'case by case'* and *'type approved'* were illustrated.

The classification society rules define conditional requirements against the product definition and production process definition. These requirements are linked from the top level application (vessel) and product (unit or concept unit) through to lowest level of components and materials. The documentation requirements are from the original designs or design templates to the application engineering phase documentation for specific application. The rules vary also in the manufacturing phase, requiring different traceability levels for item to various testing and inspection requirements, including documentation.

The item traceability with related documentation for specific application starts from delivery project. In configure to order and engineering to order type business, highest level structure items can be used to carry documentation for the child items, however this is not optimal solution for learning and lean organization. Adding folder type objects or manufacturer's internal serialized objects having traceability to enabling addition of documentation against the FFF items improves the information capture and use or re-use of existing data improves.

Without question various system configurations can be developed to facilitate solutions for the IPS applications to manage classification society data, data flow and processes as explained above. As the classification societies are not working in standard models (requirements nor financial operations) manufacturers must base their PLM and ERP strategies on their own product portfolio and positioning in the market sector creating flexible solutions. Unfortunately this creates more complex unique technical solutions for each manufacturer. This influences selection what operational strategies and system development strategies should be taken to simplify and optimise the operations to improve internal processes and reduce overall cost of classification society management.

15 Discussion and Further Work

This study has recognized several improvements what IACS could focus on. Standardizing the rules of classification societies and including rules for standardizing financial management, especially invoicing of the classification certification process. It is understandable that this type of improvements require long time and involvement of international standards like ISO, major insurance companies and entire shipping community, including ship owners, ship operators, shipyards and the logistical chain to raw material producers. Some of topics have been raised already in the European Union organisations.

This study brought up need for studying the financial invoicing and costing models of the classification society certification process based on the fact that the cost of classification society management is business critical parameter. This study has also been completed, but official papers or articles have not been published. More important for manufacturers is to model, analyse and understand the system behaviours and ways to control and optimise the overall performance of the company. The types of dynamics, which have been presented in this study, are also being modelled and later simulated with tools like Vensim [1]. This study is still ongoing.

References

[1] http://vensim.com/

[2] IACS, http://www.iacs.org.uk/document/public/explained/CLASS_KEY_ROLE.pdf

[3] Vindøy, V.: A Functionally Oriented Vessel Data Model Used as Basis for Classification. In: COMPIT 2008 (2008)
[4] http://www.prostep.org/fileadmin/user_upload/ProSTEPiViP/Events/Symposium-2006/Programm/V20_Presentation_Grafe_Ehrler_Final.pdf
[5] ISO10303-239: Industrial automation systems and integration - Product data representation and exchange, Part 239: Application protocol: Product life cycle support (2012)
[6] Wikipedia, http://en.wikipedia.org/wiki/Classification_society
[7] DNV, http://exchange.dnv.com/publishing/stdcert/Standard1-1.pdf
[8] ISO10474; Standard inspection documents
[9] Dynamic product structure configuration of superimposed part structure solutions, Niko Ville Salonen. International Journal of Interactive Design and Manufacturing, doi:10.1007/s12008-007-0009-1
[10] EN 10204:2004; Metallic materials. Types of inspection documents
[11] Gharajedaghi, J.: Systems thinking: managing chaos and complexity, 3rd edn., ISBN 978-0-12-385915-0

Improving Digital Engineering Tools in Complex Product Development by Means of an Adequate Monitoring of Research Projects

Iris de Fontaines[1,2], Didier Lefeuve[1], Guy Prudhomme[2], and Michel Tollenaere[2]

[1] Eurocopter France, Aéroport MP 13725 Marignane Cedex France
[2] Laboratoire G-SCOP, Grenoble INP, Université Grenoble 1, CNRS UMR5272
46 Ave. Félix Viallet 38031 Grenoble
{iris.de-fontaines,didier.lefeuve}@eurocopter.com,
guy.prudhomme@g-scop.inpg.fr, michel.tollenaere@inpg.fr

Abstract. Complex products development relies on established and tested processes that embed software applications in collaborative PLM systems. Many efforts are performed by companies to improve their development process by means of research projects. However the transfer of research results into industrial processes implies a high level of risk. The maturity assessment and the proof of usage are two criteria that help decreasing the risky transition. Technology Readiness Level (TRL) methodology and usage scenarios are tools which provide evidence associated to those two criteria. In this paper, a methodology is proposed to guide stakeholders in the development of usage scenario in the frame of TRL methodology. Thanks to the proposed methodology, at the end of the research project, the proof of usage and the maturity of engineering technology products are validated and could support their industrialization.

Keywords: technology transfer, PLM process improvement, research steering, maturity, TRL, scenarios, proof of usage, BPMN.

Introduction

PLM provides enhanced tools and methods to perform design and engineering in industry or service activities. Thus PLM is focused on engineering data management, CAD data handling, engineering document management, different natures of bill of materials; it supports the main engineering processes, like authoring, data creation, engineering changes, assessment and approvals between different departments or companies. It is expected from PLM systems to control access rights to the data as read-only, RW, print, via roles of actors within an organization or in an extended enterprise. In the recent decades, improvements in engineering methods have been mainly brought by means of massive introduction of digital engineering [1]. Thus digital engineering is an important part of R&D efforts in large-scale companies, with digital mockup, multi physics simulations, optimization, virtual reality and support to PLM processes (changes, extended enterprising, data exchange…).

A. Bernard, L. Rivest, and D. Dutta (Eds.): PLM 2013, IFIP AICT 409, pp. 210–219, 2013.

Aerospace industry develops very complex products, because of the multiple kinds of technology involved (materials, electronics, control…) and the accurate tools in use to assess and optimize the behavior of an aircraft [2]. R&D departments from the major aerospace companies are massively involved in the improvements of both the technologies embedded in the products (airplanes, helicopters, launchers, satellites, drones) and also the methods and tools (PLM tools) in use for the development process itself. From a sustainable business perspective, both innovative R&D results are required, the first ones to deliver best in class products to the customers, while the seconds aim at reducing time to market, developing more customized products and optimizing human design resources production. This paper focuses on that latter kind of research results, namely R&D propositions for methods and tools improvements that tend to improve PLM tools seen as a support to digital engineering processes.

Managing research and innovation implies managing some kinds off risks. Indeed new technologies produced by research project ought to be developed and deployed inside industrial projects. Therefore, research processes should allow studying and anticipating all related impacts and disturbance that might occur when a new technology is inserted in industrial projects. The technology insertion relies on a multidisciplinary decision that implies discussions, contradictions and arguments. Actors of these multidisciplinary teams are invited to decide on a go/no-go way based on the maturity of the new technologies. *But how could a "piece of technology" be defined as mature? How could the research process be steered in order to answer maturity requirements'?*

In the field of product technology (aircraft system and components), the maturity is assessed thanks to the technology readiness level (TRL) methodology during R&T projects. Let's remind that this paper deals with the field of method and tools (M&T). Using TRL methodology in the field of engineering methods and tools opens the following issues: *is this TRL methodology transferable for such kind of products?* Methods and Tools have not only to show a high level of efficiency from a scientific and technical point of view, but they also have to be usable by stakeholders. In other words, the proof of usage of such method and tools has to be realized as soon as possible. New resources have to be proposed in order to adapt the TRL methodology to this field and to include and assess the proof of usage in research process. *Which resources could been associated to the TRL methodology, and how to better anticipate the proof of usage of new technology product? Finally how to qualify those resources?*

The study was realized in Eurocopter Company, the manufacturer of helicopters from EADS Company. An action research methodology was applied in order to propose answers to the research issue. As an actor of the research process but also of the industrial process, the researcher analyzed the as-is situation of the technology transfer. The analysis pointed ways of improvement, solved by the integration of scenario inside the TRL methodology. A scenario methodology was developed, and then evaluated on a case study.

The first part of the article explains the major concepts used as the TRL methodology, the proof of usage and the scenario. The second step presents a new approach for assessing M&T maturity and proof of usage. The third part validates the approach on a Eurocopter case study.

1 Definition and Concepts

1.1 Maturity of a Technology Product

Research projects aim, in one hand, to study new technology products and, on the other hand, to reduce risks and uncertainties associated to their future integration into industrial projects. The Technology Readiness Level (TRL) methodology, developed by the NASA [3], is the tool presently in use for assessing technology product maturity. A TRL is a key milestone where the transition from each TRL requires a review to ensure that specific criteria have been considered, completed and validated. The methodology is built around nine levels of readiness [4], rapidly described in Figure 1. From our experience, TRL 6 is a critical level. Indeed it represents the first level of applied research.

However, the TRL methodology is initially developed for space technical products and our study focuses on engineering technology products (processes, tools and methods dedicated to designers and engineers). Is the NASA TRL methodology and criteria adaptable to engineering technology product? Indeed aircraft and engineering technology products transfer success do not depends on the same criteria. Engineering products need to be adopted by future users. The concept of usage needs to be integrated inside the TRL methodology.

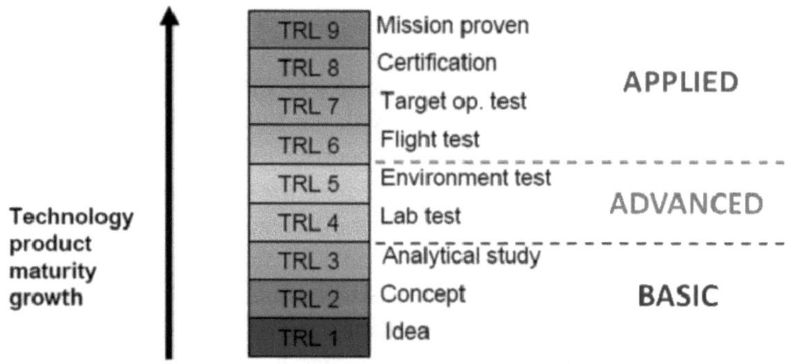

Fig. 1. TRL scale

1.2 The Proof of Usage

Engineering technology products are dedicated to designers and are used during aircraft development programs. We distinguish a current way of working, the AS-IS situation where technical and business issues are identified.

The integration and use of new engineering technology products in a new way of working, the TO-BE situation [5], reduce and/or solve those issues.

Users interact with new technology products and the success of user/technology products interactions depends on the success of technology product integration in their functional environment. Therefore requirements and functionalities of technology products have to be co-studied with final users in order to anticipate their future usage in TO-BE situation. Furthermore the success of user/technology products interactions depends on users. As [6] points out, a prescribe usage is different of a real one. *The success of user/engineering technology product interactions is called the proof of usage.* It is validated and verified into a TO-BE situation. The Figure 2 illustrates relationships between technology products and AS-IS/TO-BE situations.

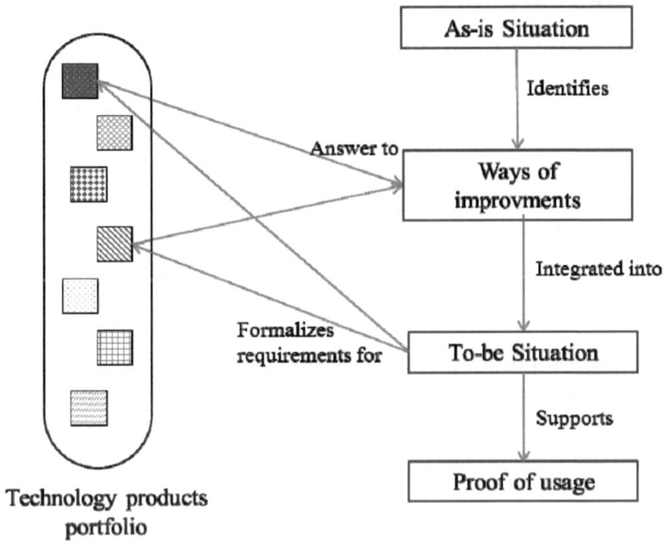

Fig. 2. Relationships between Technology Products, AS-IS/TO-BE situations and Proof of usage

1.3 Scenarios

Scenarios are used in different scientific communities as human computer interaction (HCI), software engineering, information systems, requirement engineering and as strategic management community. All those communities have different definitions of scenarios and use them with different goals. [7] and [8] have written two complete papers about scenarios in those different communities. Furthermore, [8] proposes a global and shared definition of a scenario:

"A scenario is a description of the world, in a context and for a purpose, focusing on task interaction. It is intended as a means of communication among stakeholders, and to contain requirements engineering from one or more viewpoints"

The final aim of a scenario is to explore and anticipate a future usage of a product or system [6]. Therefore *scenario is a pertinent tool for assessing the proof of usage.* Description, context, task are items that define usage scenario. In the context of requirement engineering, [7] proposes a classification framework based on four views: form, content, purpose and lifecycle; themselves qualified by facets and attributes.

Technology products aim to improve a current situation characterized into an AS-IS scenario. The integration of new technology products is realized into a new way of working, the TO-BE scenario.

2 A New Approach for Assessing Engineering Tools Maturity during Research Projects

The aim is to assess the maturity of engineering technology products during R&T projects in order to anticipate development phases.

It has been seen that the TRL methodology contributes to monitor and assess the technology products maturity but seems not sufficient in the case of engineering products. It is proposed to integrate the concept of proof of usage as new criteria of TRL methodology. *The proof of usage proves the coherency and validates the user/technology products interactions.* Proof of usage is validated thanks to analysis of scenarios.

A new approach is proposed in order to associate proof of usage and scenario with technology readiness levels. The methodology, illustrated in Figure 3, is applied between TRL3 and TRL6. The AS-IS scenario is defined when TRL 3 is assessed and it is not modified all along the process.

– *Phase 1: Analysis of usage scenarios*

First Step: Creation and analysis of the AS-IS scenario based on scenario framework [7]: it is a diagnostic step which describes how stakeholders work and collaborate today in order to answer technical and business issues. Based on the AS-IS scenario, ways of improvement are identified

Second Step: Description of TO-BE scenario based on scenario framework: it is a picture of an improved AS-IS scenario which implies the use of new technology products. New technology product answers previous ways of improvement. Users have to plan new processes, new ways of working. In particular, they do not have to be afraid of change [9].

– *Phase 2: Technology product requirements and prototypes*

First Step: Based on TO-BE scenario: actors are able to formalize technology product requirements (characteristics, architecture, performance, integration, interfaces).

Second Step: Rapid prototyping of technology products: most of the time technology products are already developed thanks to research project but they have to be adapted to the previous identified requirements.

– *Phase 3: Prototypes and requirements validation and TRL assessment*

First Step: Execution of the TO-BE scenario in the TRL associated environment:

At TRL4, critical components are developed and tested with simplified data in a laboratory environment

At TRL5, the whole system is developed and tested with simplified data

At TRL6, the whole system is tested with real data

Second step: Validation of the adequacy and coherency between the TO-BE scenario developed and the initial requirements. If technology products are not validated, iteration is realized on requirements-prototype steps.

The maturity is assessed thanks to the TRL questionnaire, based on evidence provided by the TO-BE scenario. Associated to the proof of usage, a work has been done on the TRL questionnaire in order to adapt maturity criteria to engineering technology products. For confidentiality restrictions, the questionnaire and proposed criteria could not be shared.

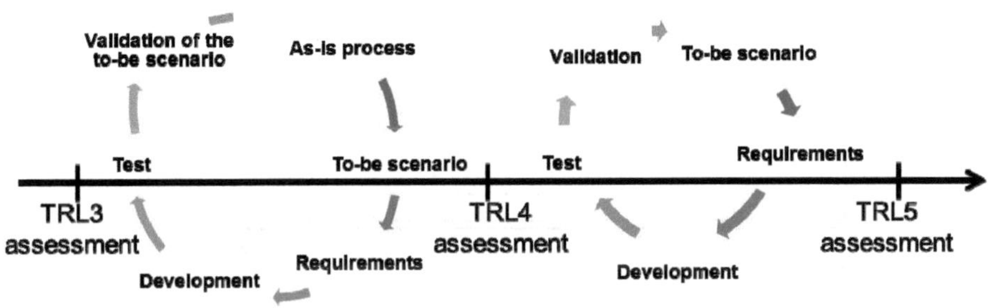

Fig. 3. Description of the two interlocked processes: TRL linear process and cycle usage scenario process

3 Validation of the New Approach on a Case Study

An application of the new approach on engineering technology products in Eurocopter Company is described in this part.

3.1 Construction and Analysis of AS-IS Scenario

Two issues are treated in the scenario:

- A technical issue consisting in the thermal integration of helicopter engine into its compartment. Ventilations have to be designed on the compartment in order to ensure the cooling of the engine.
- A business issue consisting in ensuring a collaborative work between involved actors. The actors work with non-interoperable tools in different firms.

The two issues were identified by users during interviews and are described in a narrative text. The case was studied in the frame of a European research project named CRESCENDO [10].

The AS-IS scenario describes all activities and data exchanges currently implemented for answering previous issues: the verification and validation of ventilation design of the engine compartment. The scenario was modelled collaboratively between involved actors. A business process model was built by one of the actors, progressively thanks to interviews and reviews with others actors. Because of confidentiality restriction, the business model could not been shared. A high-level process, represented in Figure 4, is rather proposed.

Four actors are represented: the engine manufacturer, the CAD designer of the design office, the aerodynamic engineer and the thermal engineer. Ten main information flows leaning on activities, each of them modelled by an arrow, are identified. A narrative text, joined to the process modelling, explains the different steps.

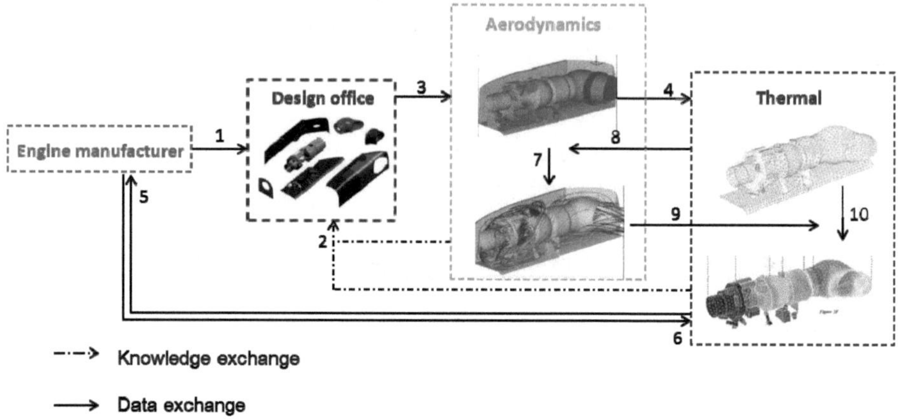

Fig. 4. Business model of the AS-IS scenario

3.2 TO-BE Scenario: Technology Products Requirements and Prototypes Validation

Thanks to the AS-IS scenario, ways of improvement are identified:

- new tools for tracing and storing all data and knowledge exchanged
- new working method in order to facilitate the meshing step but also in order to reduce the number of model data set up and calculation
- new modelling and simulation workflow

Those improvements are translated into four technology products, integrated inside a TO-BE scenario, illustrated on Figure 5. Major improvements concern the calculation workflow and data management. It was proposed to realize automated coupling between aerodynamic and thermal disciplines.

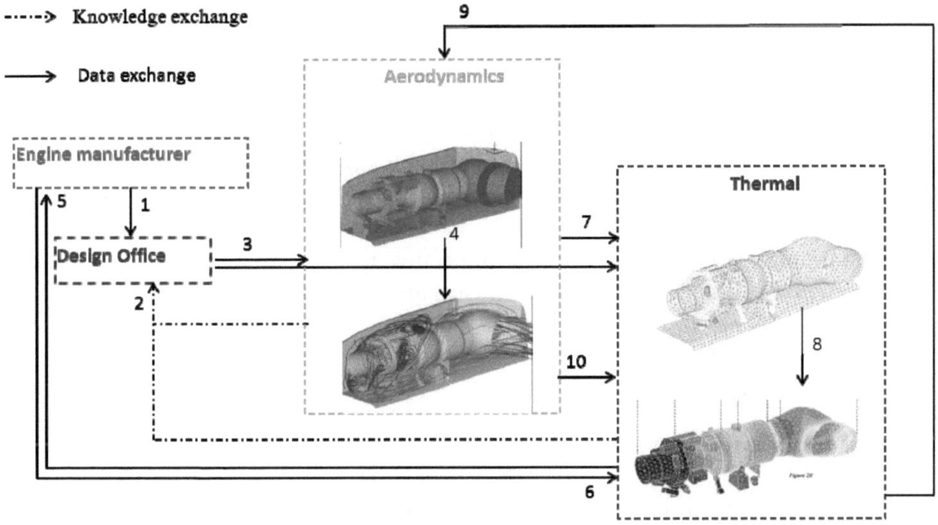

Fig. 5. Business model of the TO-BE scenario

Table 1 summarizes the four technology products.

Table 1. Technology products to develop in the TO-BE process of the usage scenario

TP	Technology product	Action solved
TP1	Collaborative calculation workflow	Iterative automate calculation workflow
TP2	New tools and methods for model set-up and calculation	A benchmark is realized in order to find the best tool for each thermal and aerodynamic discipline with the best interoperability
TP3	Surrogate model of the engine	Improvement and better precision of the engine behavior
TP4	Data management	Data management in order to trace and store all knowledge, parameters and data exchange all along the TO-BE process.

The TO-BE scenario illustrates all the interactions between the technology products themselves and with the firm ecosystem. The analysis of this TO-BE scenario contributes to the formalization of technology product requirements and to their development. Then developed technology products that means prototypes, are tested in the TO-BE scenario. Thanks to the execution, two aspects are verified and validated:

- the global result of TO-BE scenario and so the TO-BE scenario
- the technology products characteristics and ability to answer to user's expectations

3.3 Maturity Assessment in a Perspective of Technology Transfer

Final step is to assess the maturity of technology products. A TRL review is organised and all criteria are discussed. The TRL targeted implies conditions of execution of the TO-BE scenario, which means on previous step.

For a TRL4, TO-BE scenario is executed with simplified conditions (light CADs, local environment, few users). The success of TO-BE scenario validates the proof of usage.

Furthermore, the TO-BE scenario illustrates technology product requirements, environment and interactions. Thus, the scenario is an appropriate tool that allows assessing the technical maturity and the proof of usage of engineering technology product.

Conclusion and Perspectives

This paper focuses on the monitoring of research results, namely R&D propositions for methods and tools improvements that tend to improve PLM tools seen as a support to digital engineering processes. The TRL methodology is used during research project for assessing technology product maturity. Proposition is done to improve this methodology in the case of engineering technology product. A new criterion is defined: the proof of usage. It translates the success of the interaction between users and technology. Associated to the proof of usage, scenarios are developed. Two typologies are defined: AS-IS and TO-BE scenarios. Scenario supports the proof of usage assessment. Scenarios are co-developed with impacted stakeholders and are modeled under Business Process Model Notation (BPMN). Thanks to models, TRL criteria are assessed and justified: technology requirements, interfaces, performance, and applications. Furthermore stakeholders can forecast usage related technology products.

However, several TO-BE scenarios could be proposed. Additional works have to be realized on this issue. How could we choose between several TO-BE scenarios? How to evaluate them?

A global approach is proposed in order to monitor research project advancement from TRL3 to TRL6. The validation of TRL6 is the key for technology transfer in development phase. Current approach covers "technologic and business aspects" thanks to the maturity and proof of usage but what about "financial aspects"? Does the proof of usage justify the investment? In practice the multidisciplinary decision at the transition is also based on a business case. Technology products have to prove their added-value. The concept of proof of value [11] has to be defined and integrated in the methodology proposed in part 2.

References

[1] Terzi, S., Bouras, A., Dutta, D., Garetti, M., Kiritsis, D.: Product lifecycle management – from its history to its new role. Int. J. of Product Lifecycle Management 4(4), 360–389 (2010)

[2] Etienne, A., Guyot, E., Van Wijk, D.V., Roucoules, L.: Specifications and development of interoperability solution dedicated to multiple expertise collaboration in a design framework. Int. J. of Product Lifecycle Management 5(2/3/4), 272–294 (2011)
[3] Department of Defense, Technology Readiness Assessment (TRA) Guidance (2011)
[4] Mankins, J.C.: Technology readiness level, pp. 4–8 (1995)
[5] Cornu, C.: Vers un guide méthodologique pour la définition, la prise en compte des exigences et de contraintes d'interopérabilité et le déploiement de processus d'ingénierie système dans une entreprise multi-sites, Ecole Nationale Supérieure des Mines de Paris (2012)
[6] Pascal, A., Rouby, E.: Construire des scénarios d'aide à la conception de solutions TIC: une approche cognitivo-structurationniste. Le cas KMP. In: SdC 2006 (2006)
[7] Rolland, C., Ben Achour, C., Cauvet, C., Ralyté, J., Sutcliffe, A., Maiden, N., Jarke, M., Haumer, P., Pohl, K., Dubois, E., Heymans, P.: A proposal for a scenario classification framework. Requirements Engineering 3(1), 23–47 (1998)
[8] Jarke, M., Carroll, J.M.: Scenario Management: An Interdisciplinary Approach. Requirements Engineering, 1–31 (1999)
[9] Bergsjo, D., Catic, A., Malmqvist, J.: Implementing a service-oriented PLM architecture focusing on support for engineering change management. Int. J. of Product Lifecycle Management 3(4), 335–355 (2008)
[10] CRESCENDO, CRESCENDO EU Project
[11] Yannou, B.: Which research in design creativity and innovation? Let us not forget the reality of companies. Journal of Design Creativity and Innovation (2012)

A Product Model to Capture and Reuse Ecodesign Knowledge

Miriam Kozemjakin da Silva, Emmanuel Guyot, Sébastien Remy, and Tatiana Reyes

Université de Technologie de Troyes, Troyes, France
{kozemjam,emmanuel.guyot,sebastien.remy,
tatiana.reyes_carrillo}@utt.fr

Abstract. Ecodesign is the improvement of the environmental performance of products or services throughout their whole lifecycle. Because there is less design freedom in the late stages of the design process, it is assumed that if the environmental constraint is introduced early, the designers would develop a product that would have a better environmental performance. Thus, case-based reasoning is proposed as a strategy to incorporate ecodesign early in the design process.

The paper shows the investigation about the different possibilities of capturing information during the product development process. The idealized model to capture information called Core Product Model extension for environmental evaluation (CPMe³) is presented. This formal model would allow capturing the data from the whole product's lifecycle with a link to the environmental evaluation.

Keywords: Ecodesign, knowledge capture, lifecycle thinking, product model.

1 Introduction

The environmental performance of products is emerging as a new constraint for designers. This is a complex constraint due to multiple indicators (e.g. global warming, toxicity and water depletion) and to the need of a lifecycle view, i.e. a perspective of consequences of the design decisions. There is then, an effort to make ecodesign tools that would help designers to improve the environmental performance of products.

Life cycle assessment (LCA) is one of the most used environmental evaluation tools. This tool requires an advanced stage of design to evaluate the product with reduced uncertainty. The problem is that, as seen in figure 1, as more advanced in design, fewer are the possibilities of the designer to influence the product's environmental performance [1]. This implies that the designer has access to the product's environmental evaluation when it is too late to make significant changes to the product. To summarize, "the goal during the design process is to learn as much about the evolving product as early as possible in the design process because during early phases changes are least expensive" [2].

A. Bernard, L. Rivest, and D. Dutta (Eds.): PLM 2013, IFIP AICT 409, pp. 220–228, 2013.

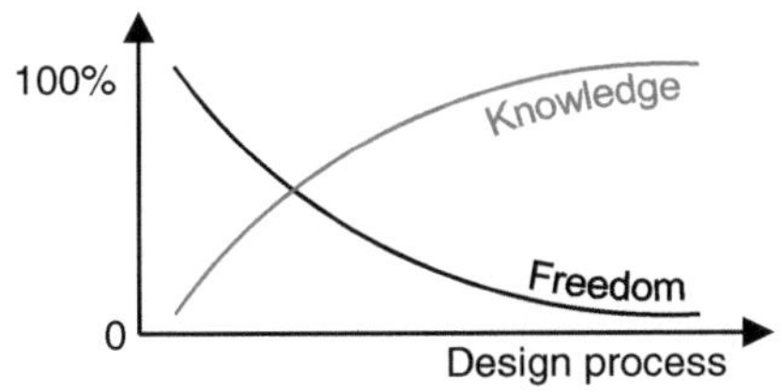

Fig. 1. Design paradox. The designer's freedom to make changes to the product versus the knowledge about the design problem (adapted from [2]).

There are several approaches that have been developed to act in early stages of design, for example, guidelines and checklists [3]. This approaches present generic conclusions and need constant updates to guide decision making in a good direction. Hence, the authors approach is to improve efficiency of ecodesign, by helping engineering designers to make better-informed decisions, learning from past designed products.

1.1 Literature Review

Research in cases-reuse for ecodesign (i.e. the estimation of environmental impact of a new product, early in design, based on products with similar characteristics) has been done by Jeong et al. [4]. The authors introduced a case-based reasoning (CBR) with environmental evaluation purposes. CBR is an artificial intelligence technique that imitates the human behavior for problem solving, i.e. finding similar cases in the past and adapting it for solving a new problem [5]. The case is, here, stored within a database structured using the product model FBSe (function-behavior-structure-environment). After, similarity is analyzed between the new product and the products' cases stored in a casebase; finally analogy is used to estimate the impact of the new product.

Moreover, Devanathan [6] conduct LCA into teardown benchmarked products giving an impact to the bill of materials (BOM). Then, the authors relate the BOM to product's functions. Next, those functions are related to customer and environmental requirements (QFD). The redesign is then focused on the functions impacts to support conceptual design and concept selection. Here, the called "working knowledge model" is also centred on the product. The structure FBS is found again, enriched by Objective, Constraint, Attributes and Requirements.

Another approach dependent on the analysis of past designs, presented by Dick et al. [7] and Ostad-Ahmad-Ghorabi et al. [8], is parametric ecodesign. The idea is to "establish a coupling between functional requirements (FR) or design parameters (DP) that product developers have at hand in early design phases and the environmental impact (EI) of the product" [7].

Finally, Bohm et al. [9] have used a design repository of environmental evaluated products to automatically generate virtual concepts. Once more, the repository is structured around product entities, mainly the BOM.

1.2 Case-reuse in Ecodesign

The approach proposed by the authors is based on the capture of information about the product during its whole lifecycle and the use of it in the next product's generation. In other words, a design process in the form of a decision chain is stored. Analyzing this memory could allow designers to see the cause-effect link, where the cause is the decision and its effect on the environmental impact. Next, if during the development of a new product, a similar set of decisions has to be taken, the designer can look at its consequences throughout the entire life of the previous product. Doing so, the user is able to evaluate the consequences of this same decision on the current product. The designer concludes, then, about the options that should be reconsidered for having less environmental impact in the next product's generation.

The research showed in the literature review share close motivation to this work when enabling designers to compare the product that is being designed to previous products in order to evaluate its environmental impact. Nevertheless, this research aims to go further by addressing the following specifications:

- The lifecycle view aspect. On the form of a network of decisions linked to the environmental impact. Because life cycle view is the heart of ecodesign practice;
- The reasoning behind the decisions of the product development process and the context of the product's design (design rationale). Because design rationale has interesting assets to information reuse: "design rationale can offer designers useful information about how previous designs evolved and the context in which such evolution happened" [10];
- The dependency on the designer's interpretation, meaning that it is out of our interest to replace the designer interpretation by automatic generation of LCA results or automatic generation of design concepts. Because the knowledge reuse can be source of inspiration and reflection [11];
- The capture and retrieval system is adapted to casual users. Because designers and environmental specialists are not computer system experts;

The focus of this paper is on investigating how to capture design information so that it could be reused with ecodesign purposes. In section 2, based on literature review, the possibilities seen of knowledge capture and reuse techniques are shown and discussed. Section 3 describes the core product model extension for environmental evaluation (CPMe³). Finally, discussions and conclusions are addressed in section 4.

2 Knowledge Reuse Scenarios

The ability to reuse design information is dependent on capture, representation and retrieval mechanisms. The design information is extracted from the design process. It is widely assumed that design is an unstructured and informal process, which produces many data. These data are included in many types of file formats (e.g. email, reports and conversations). It is also important to understand that neither the mind of the designer, nor the process of design, follows a specific structure or sequence [12].

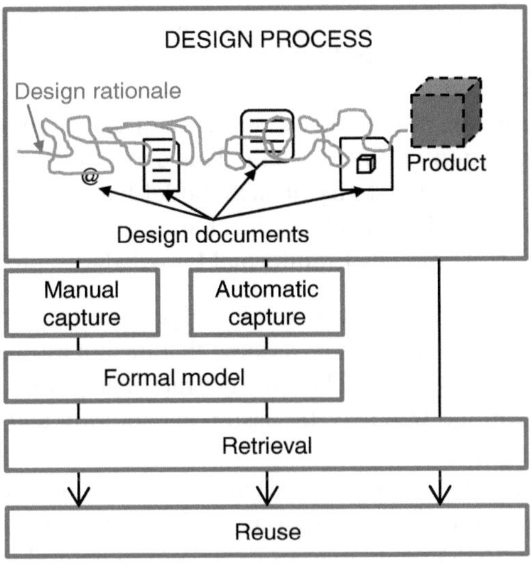

Fig. 2. The knowledge reuse possibilities

From the design process, three scenarios are seen for reusing knowledge, as illustrated in figure 2. In the first scenario, design information is manually captured and structured to a formal model. In the second one, the information is automatically captured and structured to a formal model. In the third one, the information is retrieved and presented without any treatment.

From the three scenarios presented, only those that require a formal model are going to be considered, because:

- it is less likely that disorganized design information would be reused, it would require a lot of time for reinterpretation;
- the retrieving phase would lose in effectiveness;
- it would imply storing a large amount of data, which would mostly not going to be necessary;

Also, as presented in section 1.1, the related work that have been presented have chosen to use a structure, a product model, as a formal model to capture and store design information.

Next section is about an overview of some technologies for capturing the product development process information.

2.1 Knowledge Capture

The mechanisms for capturing the design process, as seen before, are either automatic or manual.

Manual capture means that someone will have to formalize the process by inputting data to some structured format. A product model, for example, is a format that enables structuring the design by centring on product data during the product development process. Among all the product models, the widely mentioned Core Product Model from the NIST (National Institute of Standards and Technology) is presented in section 3.

The main inconvenience of manual capture is the heavy human involvement to interpret and load information into the system. This extra time required from designers is the main reason for the unpopularity of such model-based approach [13].

Therefore, there is a need to develop a mechanism to *automate* the data capturing process. For instance, technologies for informal knowledge capture are presented by:

- Liang et al. [14], that use text-mining algorithm to process design rationale documentation. The authors assume that design rationale is documented in natural language (text). Then, design rationale points are automatically extracted from the free text: the issue, the solution and the artifact information.
- Habernal et al. [15] use semantic search system with a natural language interface. The authors believe that as modern search engines are approaching the ability to deal with queries expressed in natural language, full support of natural language interfaces seems to be the next step in the development of future systems.
- Ahmed [16] performed an empirical study to identify a visible indexing structure for the reuse of design knowledge that is captured from many formats. The author states that "indexing design knowledge is one method to support the retrieval of knowledge from a system".

These technologies are not exhaustive and the human-computer interaction field is full of promising solutions. Gruber [17] states that intelligent systems can acquire knowledge by being programmed or modeled that way, or by machine learning from data and information in the world (like Google®). The author foresees machines looking for data without being told to and machines learning from us. A more comprehensive review of knowledge representation in product design is done by Chandrasegaran et al. [12].

Summarizing, there is a clear tradeoff between the effort in capturing the design process, the effectiveness of retrieving it and the convenience for reusing it.

Automatic capture of the design process is certainly suitable for reducing user input work. Nevertheless, two main advantages are seen for doing manual capture: first, a formalization that is done manually reduces the expertise required for implementing the knowledge system; second, filling out the formal model acts as a reminder of what kind of information to input. Besides, the impact of knowledge reuse for ecodesign is the main purpose of this research, the means for doing it being a technical issue.

In the following section, an ideal formal product model is proposed. It is a generic model that can be used to structure information-capture in further case-studies, at first manually. It will also provide technical feedback that would help further information system development.

3 CPMe³ Product Model

Product model assists product development process. It deals with information representation, capture, exchange and classification in different levels of abstraction. There are many product models available in literature. The NIST (National Institute of Standards and Technology) worked on a product model to capture the full engineering context to support Product lifecycle management (PLM) [18]. Core product model (CPM) is open, non-proprietary, generic, extensible and UML (Unified modeling language) based [19].

The contribution of CPM is on covering the design process information. The main classes of the model, as seen in figure 3, are: **Artifact**, represents any physical entity in a product (e.g. part and assembly); **Feature**, artifact's form that has a function; **Form**, geometry and material; **Function**, the intended behaviour; **Behaviour**, how the Form fulfils the Function. Moreover, **OAMFeature** is a specialisation of **Feature**, from the Open Assembly Model extension [18], to support the product structure, i.e. the relation between assemblies and parts.

The created extension to support LCA is based on systems thinking, similar to the modelling logic of LCA software Gabi [20] and Umberto [21].

The heart of the model is the link between **Flow**, **Process**, **ProcessPlan**, **Product** and **Artifact** (see grey classes on figure 3). The environmental impact is given for a **Flow**, so the impact of a **Process** is the sum of the impacts of the **Flows**. Consequently, the impact of a series of processes (**ProcessPlan**) is the sum of each **Process'** impact. Finally, the impact of a **Product** is the sum of the impacts of the **ProcessPlan**. The **Product** then, inherits the classes from CPM by being connected to **Artifact**.

The other part of the model describes the lifecycle aspects. A **Flow** is classified by its **nature** that is specialized in: material goods like **Part**, **Assembly** and **Consummable&tools**; immaterial goods like **Energy** or even a **Substance** (i.e. a single type of matter consisting of uniform units).

The class **ProcessPlan** can be found in the CPM extension Manufacturing Process Planning Information Model [22]. Nevertheless, the meaning here is wider, it shows the sequence of manufacturing operations and equally the logistics between them. This idea of mixing **Processes** to tell the history of the product is valid for all the **ProcessPlans**, for example, we could find **Manufacturing** in the **UseScenario**, as a maintenance process or at the **EOLscenario** (end-of-life) for disassembling the product.

The phases that are only hypothesized, called scenarios can also be described as a sequence of processes. The two phases considered scenarios are use and end-of-life because they take place after-sales and usually companies have less information about them. **EOL Process** covers the reuse and waste: recycle (waste materials reprocessed into products), energy recovery (waste recover as a combustion fuel or composting) and disposal (landfill or incineration). Finally, **Use** is related to the consumptions of the product during the use phase, like the disposable coffee filter for a coffee machine.

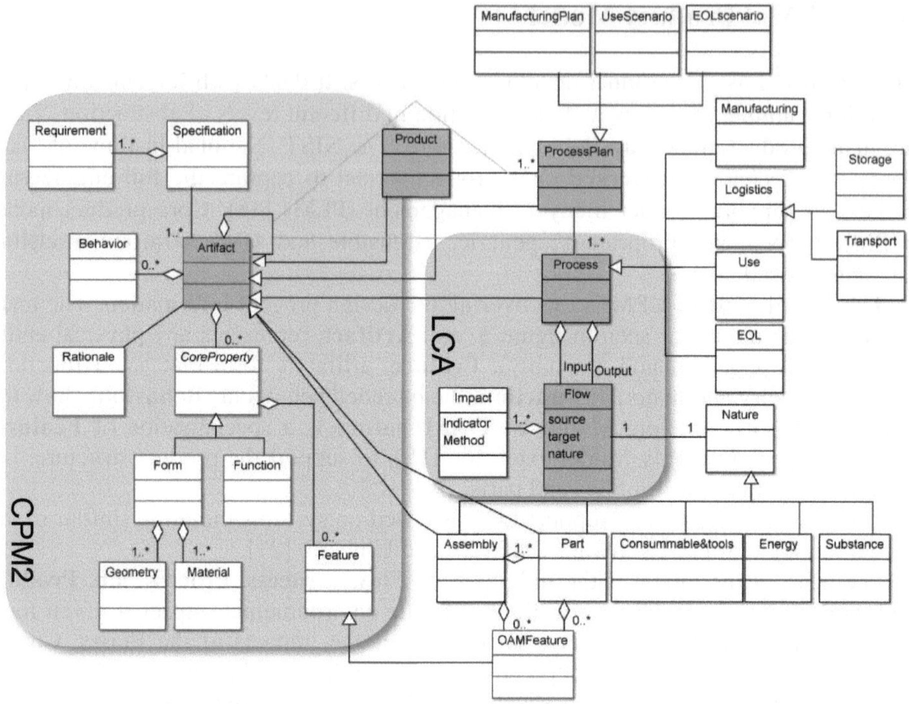

Fig. 3. The CPMe³ extension to support ecodesign

This model is created to support the knowledge capture. Here, this implementation would be done during the lifecycle of the product, allowing environmental evaluation purposes. People involved in the product development process should complete the model as they make decisions.

Thus, the foreseeable implementation of the CPMe^3 would be similar to a "top-down" PLM approach. In such an approach, considering the case of a bike, the main **Artifact** in the model, the **Product,** is the bike itself. Then, as the design process goes on, the structure of components, **Part** and **Assembly**, known as Bill Of Materials (BOM), appear in the model. All the **Artifacts** are linked to technical data using the CPM product model and linked to **Processes** of the lifecycle phases.

It is hard to find a product development project with enough documentation to completely instantiate CPMe^3. It is also understood that the actual use of PLM in companies does not have the necessary level of data capture and exchange for doing environmental evaluation; and that implementing CPMe^3 would depend on a shift on the way things are done in companies. Research has been done towards changing information management so that it would integrate environmental aspects, for instance: by facilitating the interaction of experts [23] and by gathering and making available lifecycle information [24]. CPMe^3 is then seen as a generic idealization.

4 Conclusion

As stated in the introduction of this communication, the aim of this research is to capture knowledge during the design process of a product in order to reuse it to improve the environmental impact of new products.

It is assumed, in section 1 and 2, that a formal model is needed to capture and store design information from the design process in order to be able to properly reuse it. The challenge of representing the product development process is approached with an extension of the Core Product Model from the NIST.

CPMe³, if implemented, would structure data from the product development linking it to the environmental evaluation dimension. It would give interoperability between the two dimensions (design and environmental evaluation).

Further research is going to be made on the interface, in which product design process representation is better suited for application in the context of knowledge reuse, for applying a CBR methodology. Nevertheless, the CPMe³ conceptual model contributes as a background on which data is needed to describe the product development process.

Acknowledgements. This research is funded by the Fonds Unique Interministériel (Single Interministerial Fund) and the Champagne-Ardenne Region of France, by the Finather3 project.

References

1. Dewulf, W.: A pro-active approach to ecodesign: framework and tools (2003)
2. Ullman, D.G.: The mechanical design process. McGraw-Hill (1997)
3. Luttropp, C., Lagerstedt, J.: EcoDesign and the Ten Golden Rules: generic advice for merging environmental aspects into product development. Journal of Cleaner Production 14, 1396–1408 (2006)
4. Jeong, M., Suh, H., Morrison, J.R.: A Framework for Stepwise Life Cycle Assessment during Product Design with Case-Based Reasoning. In: 6th Annual IEEE Conference on Automation Science and Engineering, pp. 118–123 (2010)
5. Watson, I.: Applying case-based reasoning: techniques for enterprise systems. Morgan Kaufmann (1998)
6. Devanathan, S., Koushik, P., Zhao, F., Ramani, K.: Integration of sustainability into early design through working knowledge model and visual tools. In: Proceedings of the 2009 International Manufacturing Science and Engineering Conference, pp. 1–10 (2009)
7. Dick, M., Dewulf, W., Birkhofer, H., Duflou, J.: Estimating the environmental impacts of similar products. In: International Design Conference, Dubrovnik, pp. 1–6 (2004)
8. Ostad-Ahmad-Ghorabi, H.: Parametric ecodesign - An integrative approach for implementing ecodesign into decesive early design stages. In: Proceedings of the 10th International Design Conference, DESIGN 2008, Dubrovnik, Croatia, pp. 1327–1334 (2008)
9. Bohm, M.R., Haapala, K.R., Poppa, K., Stone, R.B., Tumer, I.Y.: Integrating Life Cycle Assessment into the conceptual phase of design using a design repository. Journal of Mechanical Design 132 (2010)

10. Wang, H., Johnson, A.L., Bracewell, R.H.: The retrieval of structured design rationale for the re-use of design knowledge with an integrated representation. Advanced Engineering Informatics 26, 251–266 (2012)
11. Guo, Y., Peng, Y., Hu, J.: Research on high creative application of case-based reasoning system on engineering design. Computers in Industry 64, 90–103 (2012)
12. Chandrasegaran, S.K., Ramani, K., Sriram, R.D., Horváth, I., Bernard, A., Harik, R.F., Gao, W.: The evolution, challenges, and future of knowledge representation in product design systems. Computer-Aided Design 45, 204–228 (2013)
13. Tang, A., Babar, M.A., Gorton, I., Han, J.: A Survey of the Use and Documentation of Architecture Design Rationale. In: 5th Working IEEE/IFIP Conference on Software Architecture (WICSA 2005), pp. 89–98 (2005)
14. Liang, Y., Liu, Y., Kwong, C.K., Lee, W.B.: Learning the "Whys": Discovering design rationale using text mining — An algorithm perspective. Computer-Aided Design 44, 916–930 (2012)
15. Habernal, I., Konopík, M.: SWSNL: Semantic Web Search Using Natural Language. Expert Systems with Applications (2013)
16. Ahmed, S.: Encouraging reuse of design knowledge: a method to index knowledge. Design Studies 26, 565–592 (2005)
17. Gruber, T.R.: Nature, nurture, and knowledge acquisition. International Journal of Human-Computer Studies 71, 191–194 (2013)
18. Sudarsan, R., Fenves, S.J., Sriram, R.D., Wang, F.: A product information modeling framework for product lifecycle management. Computer-Aided Design 37, 1399–1411 (2005)
19. Fenves, S.J., Foufou, S., Bock, C., Sriram, R.D.: CPM2: A Core Model for Product Data. Journal of Computing and Information Science in Engineering 8 (2008)
20. GaBi Software, `http://www.gabi-software.com`
21. Umberto: know the flow, `http://www.umberto.de`
22. Marchetta, M.G., Mayer, F., Forradellas, R.Q.: A reference framework following a proactive approach for Product Lifecycle Management. Computers in Industry 62, 672–683 (2011)
23. Rio, M., Reyes, T., Roucoules, L.: Toward proactive (eco)design process: modeling information transformations among designers activities. Journal of Cleaner Production 39, 105–116 (2013)
24. Lejon, E., Lundin, M., Jeppsson, P., Näsström, M.: Integrating Information in Product Development. In: CIRP LCE, Singapore (2013)

Capitalizing Data, Information and Knowledge on Mechanical Experiments through Ontologies*

Vincent Cheutet, Patrice Leclaire, Tony Da Silva Botelho, and Geneviève Inglebert

LISMMA (EA 2336) / SUPMECA,
3 rue Fernand Hainaut,
93400 Saint-Ouen, France
vincent.cheutet@supmeca.fr

Abstract. Experiments in a laboratory or a company, either physical or virtual, generate a large amount of data and information (raw data, consolidated results, experimental conditions, etc.) that has to be managed in order to preserve and enhance the knowledge and the expertise of the organization, especially when turn-over happens. If simulation data management has been especially explored and standardized (STEP AP 209 for instance), experimental data did not create the same interests and only standard data management tools are proposed. In this paper, we propose an ontology to capitalize such information and knowledge, with an efficient reuse objective. This ontology, for which specific taxonomies have been defined according to the relevant literature of the domain, is illustrated on a set of data on previous experimental campaigns, corresponding to two kinds of mechanical experiments: tribology tests and material characterization tests.

Keywords: Ontology, experimental data and information, knowledge management.

1 Introduction

In the current context of digitalization of the product design process and the reduction of physical mock-up usage, having knowledge on properties and behaviors of material components and systems is of prior interest for companies. Even if material science is a well-established one with a large community, material innovation and new usages imply an important turn-over of knowledge and so specific needs in competency and knowledge capitalization. Moreover, the design process is faster if accurate and reliable materials data are made quickly available. Paper reports on such material data and experiments, although tidy and available, are not so efficient if compared with modern data storage techniques, in particular because the data classification is not standardized from one report to the other and these data tend to be considered as "dead" because it is difficult to reuse raw data for new analyses.

If management of digital simulation data and knowledge has been largely explored (Kibamba *et al.*, 2009) (Buda *et al.*, 2011) and standardized (STEP AP 209 for instance), experimental data did not create the same interests and only standard tools are proposed, like Granta MI[1] for material information management or classical content management software tool for experimental data. To overcome this research

* Corresponding author.
[1] http://www.grantadesign.com/products/mi/

A. Bernard, L. Rivest, and D. Dutta (Eds.): PLM 2013, IFIP AICT 409, pp. 229–238, 2013.

gap, ontology is a promising approach, allowing both the capitalization of data and information and the capture of certain domain knowledge.

The paper is structured as follows. Section 2 analyzes the domain of material experiments in laboratory, and in particular what has been proposed to structure data and information in this domain. Section 3 focuses on data and information modeling, especially by ontology. Section 4 describes the proposed approaches and how the demonstrator has been tested. Section 5 discusses the results of the experimentation.

2 Modeling a Mechanical Experiment

An experiment can be generically defined as a campaign of tests realized on several machines by different operators and with different experimental protocols, in order to validate a certain objective and deliver a set of deliverables.

Several types of mechanical experiments exist, like tensile, torsional or flexural testing, metal fatigue, creep etc. (Lemaitre *et al.*, 2009). To illustrate our approach, we selected the field of tribology, involving all contact, friction, wear and lubrication phenomena for its multi-physic, multi-domain characteristics, and complexity of situations and experimental data (Fig. 1). This choice is motivated by our laboratory, which is dedicated to engineering of complex systems with teams working on nearly all the fields involved in design and production of complex systems. More than fifty years of parallel development of experimental apparatus and models have enlightened the need to structure experimental data and basic lines to do it. In this context and due to the accumulated experience in the considered laboratory (Pieuchot *et al.*, 1969), (Gras & Courtel, 1973) (Lemaire-Caron *et al.*, 2009), several aspects have to be detailed.

First of all, tribology implies a set of operational variables: local geometry of the contact, external loading, kinematics of the contact, surfaces roughness and environment (including lubrication). On each of our test machines, some of them have been settled, the others varying in a more or less wide range. In this field, experimental scattering is a main feature observed which guided us toward some statistic models (fatigue or roughness influenced evolutions).

Fig. 1. Pin-on-disc under thermo-regulated lubrication test machine with some examples of results

Design of each of the test machines was guided by the contact mode and range of loading, kinematics and environment encountered in the industrial applications which retained our interest; according to the natural scattering of results, having the best knowledge of what happens during the test is a mandatory need: this implies to use single contact, with a precise measurement of load, displacements and possibly temperatures and accelerations.

3 Ontology for Data, Information and Knowledge Modeling

In order to model DIK (Data, Information and Knowledge), ontologies are currently recognised to be a powerful instrument. An ontology can be defined as a formal specification of a shared conceptualization of a domain (Gruber, 1993). Born from artificial intelligence community, ontologies are used in the semantic web to model knowledge objects of a certain domain, by associating to them a structure of semantic network plus an inference engine. Currently, it is possible to find them in the design community, when databases are too restricted to model linked information, especially in the "PLM 2.0" perspective. Ontologies are used to capture information, to assist on-line collaboration by proposing a common understanding, dais of communication and knowledge exchanges between different collaborators of a product development process (Giménez *et al.*, 2008), (Matsokis & Kiritsis, 2011).

After a large increase of works in this domain the last years, several papers propose a state-of-art in this domain (Liu & Lim, 2010), (Fortineau *et al.*, 2011), each proving a large diversity of ontology usage in design, like knowledge management systems specialized for a particular point of view (Xie & Shen, 2006) to interoperability of information systems (Ishak, 2010).

Moreover, ontology development is known to be a dynamic process and a literature exists to ensure a consistent ontology evolution (Sure & Tempich, 2004). This property is especially interesting here, since the mechanical experiment domain is still evolving.

More than the ontology by itself, the methodology to obtain such shared understanding of the domain is of prior interest for the different actors implied in the process. As a matter of fact, providing an effective methodology for creating ontological models is a crucial issue, especially since there is a lack of a general methodology for creating ontologies (Nanda *et al.*, 2006). In various domains, some methodologies for creating ontologies have been developed, like METHONTOLOGY for chemistry applications (Fernandez-Lopez *et al.*, 1999), Toronto Virtual Enterprise (TOVE) with a scenario-based methodology (Gruninger & Fox, 1995) or the On-To-Knowledge methodology (Staab *et al.*, 2001). In software engineering, (De Nicola *et al.*, 2009) proposes the UPON methodology, as an adaptation of the Unified Software Development Process or Unified Process (UP) for ONtology building.

According to our context and knowledge, we chose the On-To-Knowledge methodology, which includes the identification of goals that should be achieved by knowledge management tools and is based on an analysis of usage scenarios (Staab *et al.*, 2001). As a consequence, an ontology developed with such methodology does not provide an exhaustive conceptualization, but ensures the consistency between the needs of the domain expert and the ontological model. The steps proposed by the methodology are:

- *kick-off*, where ontology requirements are captured and specified, Competency Questions (CQs) are identified, potentially reusable ontologies are studied and a first draft version of the ontology is built;
- *refinement*, where a mature and application-oriented ontology is produced;
- *evaluation*, where the requirements and competency questions are checked, and the ontology is tested in the application environment;
- and *ontology maintenance*.

In order to model the ontology, we use the Protégé software[2] and the OWL-DL language.

4 DIK Modeling of an Experiment

The objectives of the ontology are first to model the crucial data and information related to each experimental projects and secondly to make explicit the specific knowledge of the laboratory on the experiments. A part of such knowledge is used to define the crucial data and information, but the other part allows to model specific restrictions or axioms inside the ontology.

For the kick-off phase, we integrate both experts from the domain, i.e. professors of our laboratory scientifically known for the experience in the tribology domain, and some "naïve" people that should use such ontology, i.e. young PhD students of the tribology research group. From such phase, we define a set of CQs that lead us to the definition of the ontology in the refinement phase.

4.1 Ontology Model

The ontology is decomposed in two different facets. We model the generic and common concepts of the domain in the core ontology and we add all specific instances of projects and tests in the instance ontology.

Fig. 2 presents a partial model of the crucial data and information generated and used during an experiment, with the main classes and object properties between classes. In this figure, the plain arrows represent the *isA* property with the adequate direction (i.e. a ***tribologyTest*** is a certain type of ***Test***) whereas the dot arrows represent the other type of semantic object properties (e.g. a ***Test*** *isRealisedOn* a ***TestMachine***).

---

[2] Version 4.1, available at `http://protege.stanford.edu/`

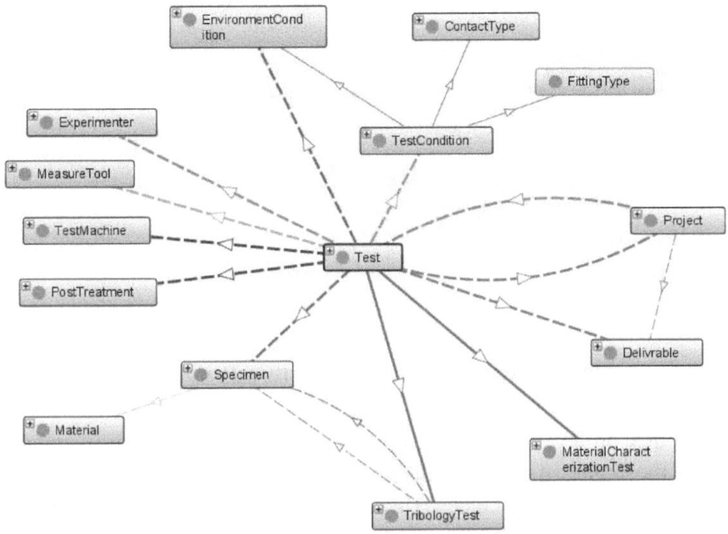

Fig. 2. Core ontology model of the experiment, with main classes and object properties represented

The ***Test*** class is the central element of the ontology. So an experiment is a project constituted of several tests. Each test is realized on a specific context: machine, experimenter, measurement tools, post-treatment chain, that are each modeled as instances in consistency classes. It is realized on one specimen for material characterization test or two specimens for tribology test, with adequate conditions, either in terms of environment (for example: ambient temperature or cryo-test, atmosphere or under neutral gas) or in terms of load (nature and intensity of force for instance). These conditions are defined by specific values of data properties when being digitally differentiable (like the sliding speed for a tribology test) or by instances when being chosen between a list of predefined concept (like the contact type).

Specific taxonomies have also been defined for the classes ***Test***, ***Material***, ***TestMachine***, ***MeasureTool*** and ***PostTreatment***, based on the literature in the domain (Gras 2008), (Ashby 2010).

Several object properties are more detailed, always with the idea of fasten and simplify the queries of the ontology:

- the relations between the two classes ***Project*** and ***Test*** are defined as inverse ones: in the CQs defined, one can ask the ontology either for a project that contains tests with specific conditions or for tests that have been performed for a specific project, without a too complex syntax,
- the relations between the classes ***Test*** and ***Specimen*** are defined as a taxonomy, with adapted semantics (fig. 3): *isPerformedOn*, generally linking a ***Test*** instance to a ***Specimen*** one, is specialized through functional two sub-properties, linking a ***TribologyTest*** instance to a ***Specimen*** one. Such modeling allows to define that if a test is generally performed on one or several specimens, there are exactly 2 specimens in the case of a tribology test, one considered as the large surface, the other one as the small surface.

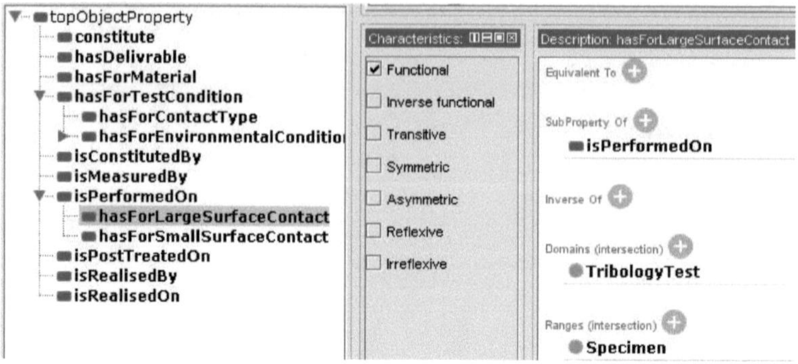

Fig. 3. Taxonomy of object property isPerformedOn

Fig.4 illustrates an example of ***Test*** instance with its connection either with core instances (like the name of the considered ***TestMachine*** instance *LowSpeedAlternative-Tribometer*) and specific instances (like the ***Specimen*** instance *EADS42.11GHL_ Disk1*).

4.2 Experiments of the Model

Once the ontology created and the instances added, two types of experiments have been performed. The first one validates the consistency of the ontology, either at the class level or at the instance one.

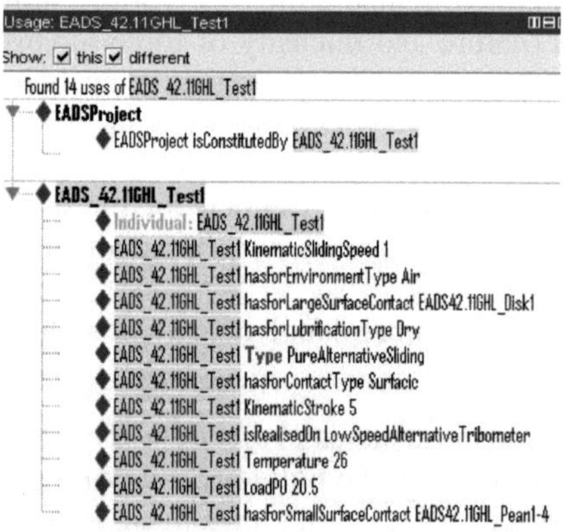

Fig. 4. Example of instance insertion inside the ontology

The second validation considered the match of the ontology to the CQs defined in the On-To-Knowledge process. The ontology is questioned through the DL Query widget of Protégé by using the Manchester OWL syntax[3]. In the example (Fig. 5), two queries have been defined:

[3] http://www.co-ode.org/resources/reference/manchester_syntax/

1. on the left, which are the projects with at least one test that has been realized on a particular machine,
2. on the right, which are the projects with at least one test that has been performed with a load greater than a specific value.

To ease the addition of instances of each tribology project without a complex training on ontology for the experimenters, a specific interface has been developed on Microsoft Excel (Fig. 6). The characteristics of the project is defined and we use the properties of the OWL language (close to XML and interpreted by a parser inside Protégé) to add, at the end of the instance OWL file, the new elements.

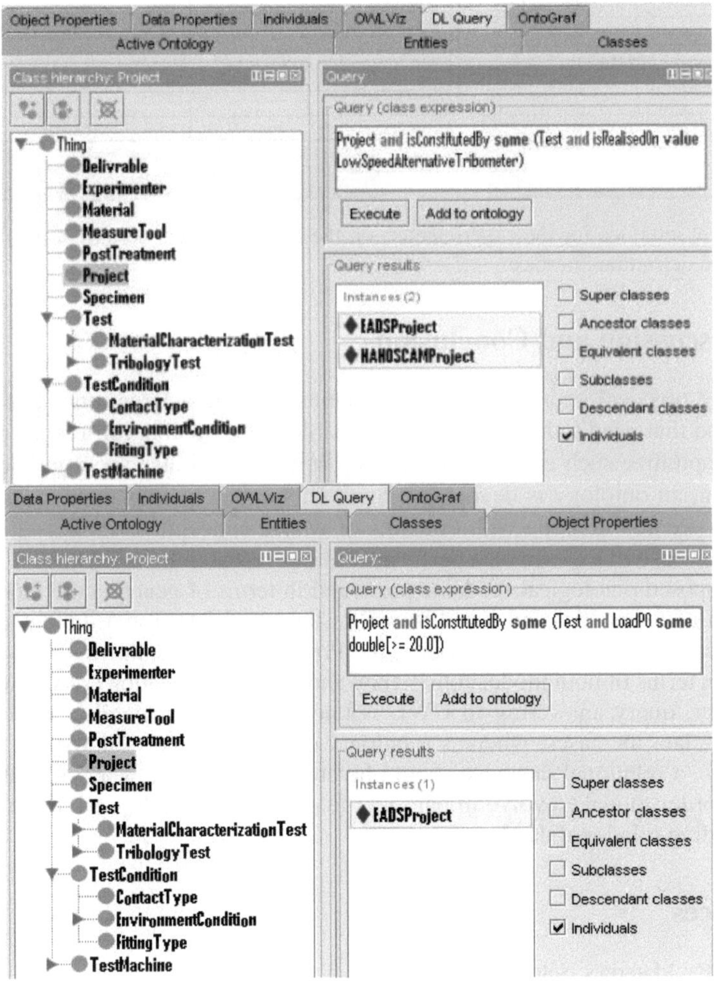

Fig. 5. Queries of the ontology

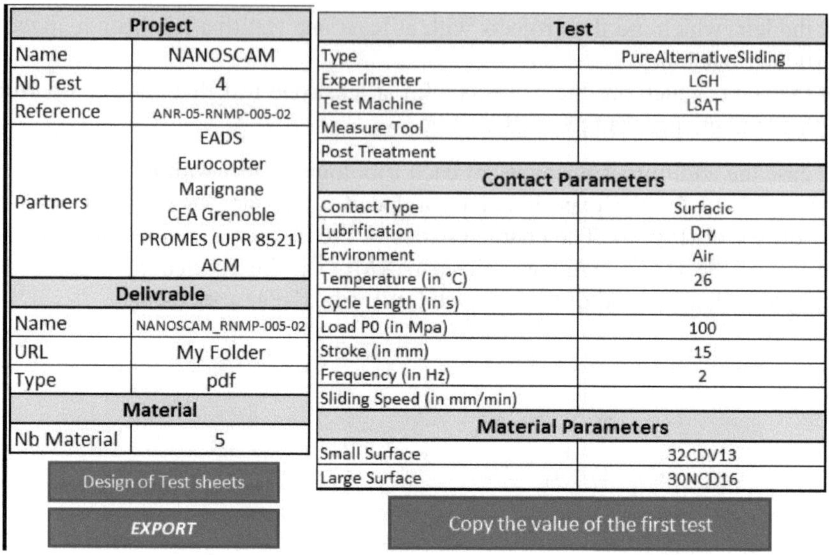

Fig. 6. Excel interface for the experimenter: on the left the project definition interface, on the right the test definition interface

5 Discussion and Conclusion

Performing physical and/or digital experiments provide a large amount of data and information that need to be organized, accessible and available for a reuse purpose. In order to capitalize such crucial data and information, and also specific knowledge of the domain, an ontology is developed. Such choice can be explained by the fact that ontologies are able to cope with domains of whose conceptualization is still moving, which is the case of experiments performed in our research laboratory.

The proposed ontological model is presented in terms of generic core model and domain specific taxonomies and tested on real instances of data from tribology and material characterization tests domains. Using the Protégé software allows us to validate this ontology in terms of both model consistency and expert expectation consistency.

However, query answering in OWL is known to have scalability issue while the number of data increases, whereas relational databases cope well with it. Thus, as a perspective, a relational database should be created, using the work of (Kupfer *et al.*, 2006), in order to make evolve in parallel the ontological model and the implemented corresponding relational database.

References

Ashby, M.F.: Materials Selection in Mechanical Design, 4th edn. Butterworth, Heinemann (2010)

Buda, A., Makkonen, P., Derroisne, R., Cheutet, V.: PDM suitability study for CAE data management. In: 8th International Conference on Product Lifecycle Management, PLM 2011, Eindhoven, Netherlands (2011)

Da Silva Botelho, T., Progri, R., Inglebert, G., Robbe-Valloire, F.: Analytical and experimental elastoplastic spherical indentations of a layered half-space. Mechanics of Materials 40, 771–779 (2008)

De Nicola, A., Missikoff, M., Navigli, R.: A software engineering approach to ontology building. Information Systems 34(2), 258–275 (2009)

Fernandez-Lopez, L., Gomez-Perez, A., Sierra, J.: Building a chemical ontology using Methontology and the ontology design environment. IEEE Intelligent Systems 14(1), 37–46 (1999)

Fortineau, V., Paviot, T., Lamouri, S., Thomazo, M.: Utilisation d'ontologies pour le PLM: Etat de l'art. In: Proceedings of 7ième Conférence Internationale Conception & Production Intégrées, CPI 2011, Oujda, Maroc (2011)

Giménez, D., Vegetti, M., Leone, H., Henning, G.: PRoduct ONTOlogy: Defining product-related concepts for logistics planning activities. Computers in Industry 59(2-3), 231–241 (2008)

Gras, R.: Tribologie, Principes et solutions industrielles. Collection Technique et Ingénierie, Ed. Dunod/L'usine Nouvelle (2008)

Gras, R., Courtel, R.: Frottement à haute température du titane et de l'alliage TA6V. Wear 26(1), 1–26 (1973)

Gruber, T.: A translation approach to portable ontology specification. Knowledge Acquisition 5, 199–220 (1993)

Gruninger, M., Fox, M.S.: Methodology for the design and evaluation of ontologies. In: Proceedings of International Joint Conference on Artificial Intelligence, Montreal, Canada (1995)

Ishak, K.: Integration of semantic interoperability in a distributed architecture for multi-site planning. Ph.D. thesis, University of Toulouse, France (2010)

Kibamba, Y., Gallet, T., Eynard, B., Troussier, N., Derigent, W.: PLM - digital engineering and numerical simulation for collaborative product development. In: International Conference on Research into Design, ICoRD 2009, Bangalore, India (2009)

Kupfer, A., Eckstein, S., Stormann, B., Neumann, K., Mathiak, B.: Methods for a synchronised evolution of databases and associated ontologies. Frontiers in Artificial Intelligence and Applications 155, 89–102 (2007)

Lemaire-Caron, I., Isac, N., Quillien, M., Da Silva Botelho, T., Gras, R., Ganne, T.: Coatings for Ti6Al4V in cryogenic space engine applications. Int. J. of Engineering Systems Modelling and Simulation 1(4), 253–261 (2009)

Lemaitre, J., Chaboche, J.L., Benallal, A., Desmorat, R.: Mécanique des matériaux solides, 3ème edn. Dunod (2009)

Liu, Y., Lim, S.: Using ontology for design information and knowledge management: a critical review. In: Proceedings of 20th CIRP Design Conference, Nantes, France (2010)

Matsokis, A., Kiritsis, D.: Ontology applications in PLM. International Journal of Product Lifecycle Management 5(1), 84–97 (2011)

Nanda, J., Simpson, T., Kumara, S., Shooter, S.: A methodology for product family ontology development using formal concept analysis and web ontology language. Journal of Computing and Information Science in Engineering 6(2), 103–113 (2006)

Pieuchot, A., Blouet, J., Gras, R., Alfred, M., Courtel, R.: Méthodologie et classement des essais de frottement et de leurs résultats. Mécanique Matériau Electricité (1969)

Staab, S., Studer, R., Schnurr, H.P., Sure, Y.: Knowledge processes and ontologies. IEEE Intelligent Systems 16(1), 26–34 (2001)

Sure, Y., Tempich, C.: State of the art in ontology engineering methodologies. SEKT informal deliverable 7.1.2, Institute AIFB, University of Karlsruhe (2004)

Xie, H., Shen, W.: Ontology as a mechanism for application integration and knowledge sharing in collaborative design: a review. In: Proceedings of International Conference on Computer-Supported Cooperative Work in Design, Nanjing, China (2006)

Knowledge-Based Lifecycle Management Approach for Product Service Systems (PSS)

Michael Abramovici, Youssef Aidi, and Hoang Bao Dang

Chair of IT in Mechanical Engineering, Ruhr-University Bochum, Germany
{Michael.Abramovici,Youssef.Aidi,Bao.Dang}@itm.rub.de

Abstract. Product Service Systems (PSS) are new industrial offerings which integrate a product and related services into a customer-specific bundle and offer the customer an overall solution to a specific issue. The lifecycle of PSS is characterized by merged product and service structures and a close interaction among the provider, the suppliers, and the customer, not only in the development phase but especially during the operation of PSS. Therefore a lifecycle management approach for PSS has to merge both the virtual and real (operational) lifecycle of PSS. To reach that goal operational knowledge about a PSS instance must be gathered, aggregated, managed, and used by enhanced lifecycle management methods in order to support providers, suppliers, and customers by developing, delivering and operating PSS. The paper in hand presents a knowledge-based lifecycle management approach for PSS, which considers an ontological representation of PSS knowledge and 3 knowledge-based lifecycle methods to make engineering processes adaptive, to provide the involved actors with the appropriate PSS knowledge and support the stakeholders in their decision making processes. The components of this approach have been identified as key lifecycle management methods for managing PSS. They are still being developed within the collaborative research center TR29 funded by the German Research Foundation (DFG), who investigate the overall engineering of PSS.

1 Introduction

Due to emerging global markets, companies must develop suitable products that meet the regional requirements of various customers in each country, and face the rapid technological development, unpredictable social and political changes, as well as compliance. The reaction of the industry to these discerning demands is new overall offerings called Product Service Systems (PSS). PSS are defined as "an integrated industrial product and service offering that delivers value in use" [1]. At the core of this approach is the increase in provider and customer benefits through the integration of products and services. This definition puts emphasis on *value in use*. Instead of spending money on the product as a mere physical artifact, the customer nowadays wants to pay for the use of the product and its resulting value to reduce inherent risks. Compared to traditional products, and driven by growing customer pressure due to newly emerging availability and result-oriented business models, the PSS provider is

A. Bernard, L. Rivest, and D. Dutta (Eds.): PLM 2013, IFIP AICT 409, pp. 239–248, 2013.

responsible both for developing and delivering PSS [3]. In Contrast to common PLM solutions PLM approach for managing products a PSS lifecycle Management has to deal with merged product and service structures and focus more on the operation phase where a close interaction among the provider, service suppliers, and customers is required. Within the Collaborative Research Center TR29 funded by the German Research Foundation (DFG), a lifecycle management approach has been developed which is presented in this paper. Based on own surveys carried out [2][4], three key knowledge-intensive processes have been identified that constitute the core PSS lifecycle methods: Adaptive change processes, use information feedback processes and decision processes. The realization of those processes is based first on an ontological approach for the integration and management of PSS information and on an open service-oriented architecture for a loose integration in the existing IT environment.

2 Requirement to a PSS Lifecycle Management and Challenges

Over the last decade, Product Lifecycle Management (PLM) has become the central management approach of engineering processes and data, and it has been used as a company-wide integration platform. Current PLM solutions are focused mainly on the support of administrative information flow processes (e.g. release and change management) within the development phase. The solutions offer data models and methods which are used for the lifecycle management of product classes or families of similar products and reflect the provider's perspective on the lifecycle. A variety of research works are currently ongoing to extend the PLM approach and cover after sales phases like the closed loop PLM approach [13] but without taking into account the management of service components. The development and management of services, however, have only been considered by few methods like Service Blue Printing [5] or Service CAD [6]. An overall lifecycle management approach that supports the integrated engineering of products and services and considers the properties of PSS engineering is still required.

Depending on the PSS business model the PSS provider also becomes responsible for the operation and later phases of the PSS lifecycle, which increases both revenue and risks. In order to keep up the performance of the PSS offering, single PSS instances are changing continuously during the delivery phase [7]. Hence, providers must be able to adapt their PSS to unpredictable boundary condition changes swiftly, and therefore require adaptive change management that does not define change processes a priori. In order to make the appropriate improvements by reducing risks, the involved actors must carry out different analysis activities. Hence, they must be informed in detail about the real lifecycle of the concerned PSS instance. Thus a feedback flow of PSS use information must be established, which merges information of the real PSS lifecycle from the operation phase with information of thc virtual PSS lifecycle in the development phase. Stakeholders on tactical and strategic enterprise levels are confronted with high risk decisions (e.g. the definition of the PSS business model). They need a powerful decision support system that gathers different technical and financial information from different sources and aggregates it for comprehensive analysis.

3 Overall PSS Lifecycle Management Approach

Based on the requirements defined and own surveys, an overall PSS lifecycle management approach has been developed within the collaborative research center TR29 funded by the German Research Foundation (DFG). This approach is based on the established PLM approach and introduces the knowledge component as a key factor to offer the required support for managing PSS engineering. It proposes three knowledge-based assistants which address the requirements mentioned above and an ontological information modeling approach (cf. Fig. 1).

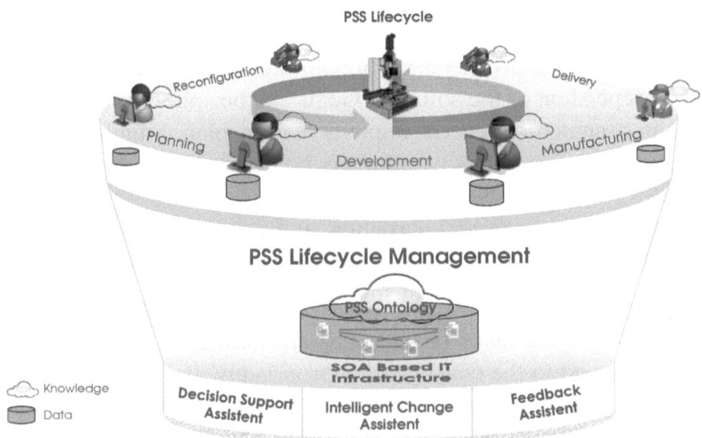

Fig. 1. Concept for the knowledge-based, overall PSS Lifecycle Management

The intelligent Change Assistant which responds to the non-deterministic properties of PSS change processes. The use information feedback assistant has been introduced, which generates and leads use knowledge from the operating phase back into the development phase, for continuous improvement of the offered PSS. And a decision support assistant supporting tactical and strategic decision makers. Furthermore, an ontological approach has been introduced to map specific PSS ontologies onto existing ontologies. To reduce the complexity of data and system integration, the proposed approach follows an SOA paradigm.

In the following sections, the components of the PSS lifecycle management approach are investigated.

3.1 Intelligent Change Assistant

A PSS provider must be able to adapt PSS offerings to quickly respond to unforeseeable changes in the environment throughout the lifecycle, which are caused by various drivers [8]. Hence, a prompt reaction to these unpredictable changes along the overall lifecycle of PSS has a significant impact on the economic success of a company and her network partners [9]. Each PSS change process can be unique. Different technical, organizational, and financial circumstances, the relationships and mutual influence of product and service components [8] in particular, influence how the change goal can be reach. In contrast to existing deterministic and firmly planned, current Engineering Change Management processes, the PSS Change Management aim is a goal-oriented real-time definition of executable change process activities and their execution priorities depending on change contents, context, objectives, and current conditions [2] (e.g. continuous real-time plan-and-execute rather than static plan-and-execute). This approach allows a prompt configuration and immediate start-up [10] while taking into consideration the great uncertainties that arise in the development and delivery phases during the execution of PSS change processes. An example of an adaptive PSS Change Assistant of that kind has been developed based on a new goal-oriented process management approach defined by Daimler AG and Whitestein Technologies [11].

- First and foremost, the processes are to capture and characterize the defined business goal, independent of the solution. Goals can be split into further sub goals.
- Each goal is assigned a generic implementation plan, which merely consists of independent tasks or activities without any predefined execution sequence or priorities.
- The specifications of tasks and activities, and the order in which they are carried out are determined during process execution, in real time, and depending on the main process issues and the current situation (rules) of the process.

Within the process, the tasks or activities are defined as intelligent agents. They represent the right road to the (sub) goal, appropriately, independently, and subject to the rules [12] (cf. Fig. 2). These rules are represented in the PSS Change Ontology, which describes the change activities and their interaction under different circumstances. Through reasoning of the PSS Change Ontology the PSS Change Assistant defines possible activity chains and permanently checks the achievement of the phase goals. In case of trouble alternative activities can be found and the change process can be adjusted to the new circumstances.

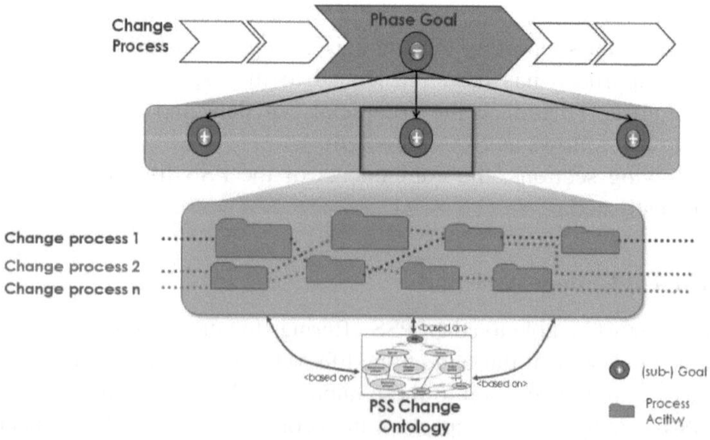

Fig. 2. Goal-oriented process modeling

3.2 PSS Feedback Assistant

To comply with the PSS contract, the PSS provider has to provide any required service to ensure the delivery of the promised value of the product use. Furthermore continuous and effective improvements can enhance the PSS performance, which increases both customer and provider proceeds. The availability of product use data creates new opportunities by generating product use knowledge as a feedback for PSS developers and PSS operation planners. The offering of PSS enables the PSS provider to have access to and control over any product use and service process data. Technical progress in embedded micro-sensors facilitates a continuous systematic acquisition of product use data for the control and planning of the machine operation and maintenance processes [13] [14]. At present, the improved design of new product generations only uses isolated and unsystematic feedback from customers, retailers, or service partners, which mainly refers to warranty cases, complaints, or product recalls [15]. As product use information is not exploited systematically, new product generations are still suboptimal or over-engineered [14] [16]. The PSS Feedback Assistant (cf. Fig. 3) considers the exploitation of a large amount of individual, similar PSS components data to aggregate using Extract, Transformation and Loading (ETL) methods [14]. This is a necessary step to provide crucial knowledge to the product developer later on [17]. The assistant considers the following design-relevant information:

- product instance use information, like use incidents (i.e. failures, breakdowns, cracks, leaks), operational parameters (i.e. operation duration and cycles, rotation speed, temperature, vibrations), or resource consumption (i.e. energy, materials)
- product instance workspace information, like parent assembly or neighbor influencing parts
- product service data (i.e. repair, maintenance, overhaul events, replacement of parts)
- product user/operator data (i.e. personnel data, qualifications, workload) [15]

Based on the central database, the following methods have been realized [14]:

- Analysis methods provide statistical data analysis methods, e.g. for overlooking key indicators, generating use profiles and their visualizations.
- Diagnostic methods provide knowledge-based methods (Bayesian Networks) to detect causes of failure. A Bayesian Network is a probabilistic graphical model that represents a set of variables and their probabilistic dependencies. [18].

These methods support developers within a PSS change process in choosing the appropriate PSS configuration alternative. The modularity of PSS leads to more than one possible solution, and various criteria must be met in decision-making, which alternatively guarantee the desired performance under real boundary conditions.

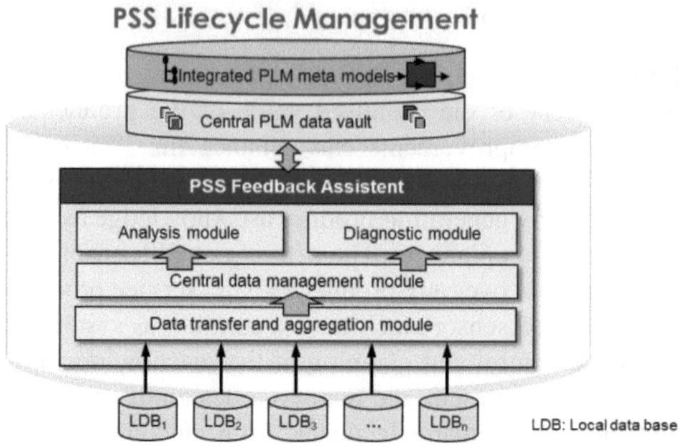

Fig. 3. Concept for the PSS Feedback Assistant

3.3 PSS Executive Decision Assistant

The increasing interdisciplinary of modern products and the introduction of product service offerings (PSS), as well as the related close interactions among providers, suppliers, and customers, pose new challenges to managers and decision makers [19]. On one average day, decision makers like managers are involved in a variety of tasks such as meetings, appointments, business negotiations, and report-reading [20]. Their experience cannot be fully used to manage such interdisciplinary and highly complex decision processes. First, the most technical aspects of products and characteristics of engineering processes influence the economic end result. On the other hand, the required information within the decision processes is distributed on many systems, and there is no transparency about its origin. Furthermore, current commercial systems like Business Intelligence solutions mostly focus on financial information and business operations, and thus cannot fully meet the requirements of decision makers in modern companies [21]. The employed applications (such as ERP, SCM, CRM, PLM, etc.) at tactical and strategic levels contain a high amount of valuable data and information for decision making at the respective level. However, only few provide specific modules to meet the information demand of decision makers and managers. These modules can also analyze the data stored in the single system.

The PSS Executive Decision Assistant supports decision makers on tactical and strategic level through gathering any required data within their decision processes from different data sources at provider, customer, and supplier level. That data is analyzed and aggregated to provide a holistic and transparent PSS Key Performance Indicator [22] (cf. Fig. 4).

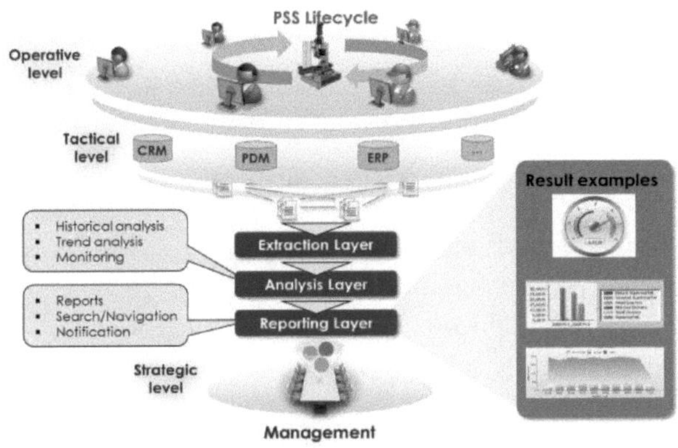

Fig. 4. Concept for the PSS Executive Decision Support Assistent

The following functions are required:

- **Extraction** to gather data from different internal and external sources involved in the whole lifecycle such as ERP, SCM, etc.
- **Analysis** by means of mathematical methods and based on existing internal and external data to make trend analyses and forecasts, which are used as valuable references for future decisions.
- **Reporting** to automatically provide decision makers with the right reports at the right time, according to their issues at the appropriate decision level and respective situation. That way, unnecessary reports are avoided and the time to prepare the reports is greatly shortened.

3.4 The Ontological Approach of PSS Lifecycle Management

One of the most important goals of the PLM concept and the PSS-LM concept is the integration of different domain-specific systems. Throughout the lifecycle of PSS, different partners are involved. Some of them may be part of the PSS network right from the start while others join in at later points of the PSS use. This poses the challenge to supply all partners with relevant information and to integrate their systems accordingly, so that information can be gathered and exchanged efficiently. As the partner's systems and IT infrastructure are diverse and may change during PSS use, a system-independent approach is required.

To integrate information from different sources of this dynamic PSS network and to support the above-mentioned intelligent assistants, an 'over-the-top' integration concept (cf. Fig. 5) has been developed that extends the semantic aspect of normal relational PLM databases. This concept enables coping with the challenges of flexible data model extensibility and management of implicit knowledge. Furthermore, this knowledge-based approach includes a PSS ontology that integrates PSS-relevant data

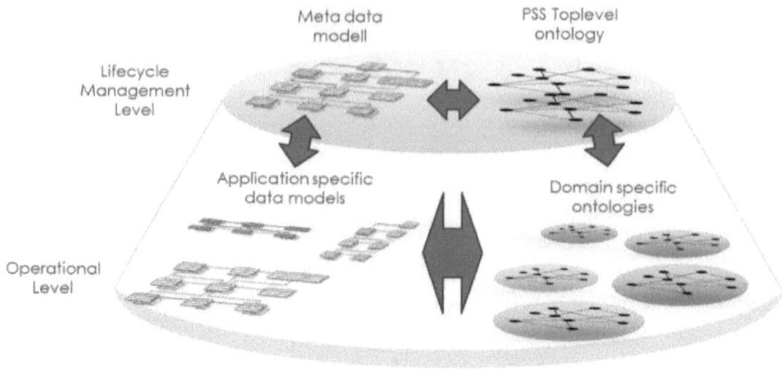

Fig. 5: 'Over-the-top' integration concept

via predefined rules and axioms. There are two relevant layers in the PSS ontology: The first layer describes eleven important PSS concepts and the relationships among them (i.e. product, service, product-service module, PSS, requirement, business models, resource, needs, functions, support information, and PSS-specific knowledge). This is called a 'PSS top-level ontology'. A comprehensive description of the eleven PSS ontology concepts can be found in a previous publication [23]. The web ontology language OWL 2 DL has been used to describe the PSS top domain ontology, as it is easily extensible and backward compatible. The description of the relations serves as a basis for the integration of domain-specific ontologies and systems from operative levels. In order to connect to other ontologies or to extend the PSS ontology, a mapping method has been developed. This method considers the four key components of the ontology concept (class including subclasses, relation including axioms, instances, and properties) as well as the influential role of the knowledge engineer. The relationships between the four key components are analyzed to determine whether a class of ontology 1 can be mapped onto another class, instance, or properties of ontology 2, and thus determine the required relations or axioms. In order to archive and maintain the concepts/classes and relationships among them, graph database technology is used as it offers the ability to work efficiently with relationships. Moreover, the mapping method integrates data from heterogeneous sources in order to discover implicit knowledge. The knowledge engineer can manipulate the results of the mapping process. The second layer contains other ontologies, which are of importance in order to execute intelligent PLM-extended methods (e.g. adaptive change management, SOA Service Management with Function-As-Service Ontology – FAS Ontology). By means of the PSS ontology, new semantic information is provided that is based on information stemming from domain-specific data sources and generated by predefined rules and axioms.

4 Conclusion

The overall PSS Lifecycle Management is the central approach for the integration of PSS engineering data, processes, IT tools, and actors involved in the entire lifecycle, both on the provider's and the customer's sides. The outlined approach takes into account the main development stream driven by different economic and technological drivers. The flexible SOA-based IT infrastructure and the ontological approach for PSS knowledge exploration provide a suitable platform for the described knowledge-based assistants. That way, PSS use information can be lead back to earlier engineering phases. In order to make change processes more efficient, the adaptive PSS Change Assistant provides a real-time generation of change workflows considering current constraints. In addition, decision makers on tactical and strategic levels are supported by PSS Executive Decision Support which collects enterprise data from different sources and aggregates it for a high transparency of PSS lifecycle processes.

References

[1] Datta, P.P., Roy, R.: Cost Modelling Techniques for Availability Type Service Support Contracts: A Literature Review and Empirical Study. In: Proceedings of the 1st CIRP IPS^2 Conference, Cranfield, UK, pp. 216–223 (2009)

[2] Abramovici, M., Aidi, Y.: Next Generation Product Lifecycle Management (PLM). In: Proceedings of the 5th International Conference on Integrated Systems Design and Technology, Mallorca, Spain (2012)

[3] Mont, O.: Clarifying the concept of product-service systems. Journal of Cleaner Production 10(3), 237–245 (2002)

[4] Abramovici, M., Schulte, S.: Study "Benefit of PLM – The Potential Benefits of Product Lifecycle Management in the Automotive Industry". ITM Ruhr-University Bochum, IBM BSC, Detroit (2007)

[5] Arai, T., Shimomura, Y.: Service CAD System-Evaluation and Quantification. CIRP Annals - Manufacturing Technology 1, 463–466 (2005)

[6] Shostack, G.L.: Service Design in the Operating Environment. In: Developing New Services, Chicago (1984)

[7] Främling, K., Chong, B.B., Brusey, J.: Globally unique product identifiers – requirements and solutions to product lifecycle management. In: Proceedings of the 12th IFAC Symposium on Information Control Problems in Manufacturing (INCOM), Saint-Etienne, France, pp. 47–51 (2006)

[8] Abramovici, M., Bellalouna, F., Goebel, J.C.: Adaptive change management for industrial product service systems (IPS^2). In: Proceedings of the TMCE 2010, Ancona, Italy (2010)

[9] Brown, J., Boucher, M.: Engineering Change Management 2.0: Better Business Decisions from Intelligent Change Management (2007)

[10] Kernland, M., Hoeffleur, O., Felber, M.: The Agility Challenge in Business Process Management. Product Data Journal 1/2008, 40–42 (2008)

[11] Burmeister, B., Arnold, M., Copaciu, F., Rimmassa, G.: BDI-Agents for Agile Goal-Oriented Business Processes. In: Proceedings of the 7th International Conference on Autonomous Agents and Multiagent Systems (AAMAS), Estorial, Portugal (2008)

[12] Roa, A.S., Geogreff, M.P.: BDI Agents: From Theory to Practice. In: Proceedings of the 1st International Conference on Multi-Agent Systems, San Francisco, USA (1995)

[13] Dimitris, K.: Closed-loop PLM for intelligent products in the era of the Internet of things. Computer-Aided Design 43, 479–501 (2011)

[14] Abramovici, M., Lindner, A., Walde, F., Fathi, M., Dienst, S.: Decision support for improving the design of hydraulic systems by leading feedback into product development. In: Proceedings of the 18th International Conference on Engineering Design 2011 (ICED 2011), Kopenhagen, Denmark, August 15-18, vol. 9, pp. 1–10 (2011)
[15] Abramovici, M., Lindner, A., Krause, F.L.: Providing Product Use Knowledge for the Design of Improved Product Generations. CIRP Annals - Manufacturing Technology 60(1), 211–214 (2011)
[16] Abramovici, M., Neubach, M., Fathi, M., Holland, A.: Knowledge-based Feedback of product Use Information into Product Development. In: Proceedings of the 17th International Conference on Engineering Design (ICED), Stanford, CA, USA, vol. 8, pp. 227–238 (2009)
[17] Meier, H.: Ganzheitliches, regelbasiertes Verfügbarkeitsmanagement von Produktionssystemen (VeraPro). Apprimus Verlag, Aachen (2009) ISBN: 978-3-940565-99-0
[18] Abramovici, M., Neubach, M., Fathi, M., Holland, A.: Competing Fusion for Bayesian Applications. In: Proceedings of the 12th International Conference on Information Processing and Management of Uncertainty in Knowledge-Based Systems, Málaga, Spain (2008)
[19] Abramovici, M., Michele, J., Neubach, M.: Erweiterung des PLM-Ansatzes Für Hybride Leistungsb ündel. In: ZWF, vol. 103, pp. 619–621. Carl Hanser Verlag (2008)
[20] Wang, S.Z.: Research on Executive Information System (EIS) for Enterprises. Jianton Unversity Xi'an, Doctoral Thesis (1999)
[21] Leidner, D., Elam, J.: Executive Information Systems: Their Impact on Executive Decision Making. Journal of Management Information Systems 10, 139–155 (1994)
[22] Abramovici, M., Jin, F.: A New Method for Monitoring Industrial Product-Service System based on DSC and AHP. In: Proceedings of ICEIS 2011, Beijing, China (2011)
[23] Michael, M., Bellalouna, F., Schulze, M., Spura, C.: Metadata Reference Model for IPS^2 Lifecycle Management. In: Proceedings of the 1st CIRP IPS^2 Conference, Cranfield, UK, pp. 268–272 (2009)

Challenges in Knowledge Management for Structuring Systems

Vincent Cheutet*, Marc Zolghadri, Florent Couffin, Patrice Leclaire, Roberta Costa Affonso, and Caroline Bourcier

LISMMA/SUPMECA,
3 rue Fernand Hainaut,
93400 Saint-Ouen, France
vincent.cheutet@supmeca.fr

Abstract. Structuring Systems can be defined as systems, designed, installed, used and maintained within their operational environment for an extremely long duration, answering to the fundamental needs of the society. Examples of such systems are water systems, transport or electricity network. Due to their nature, these systems are characterized to be highly complex, according to the general system theory. In this context, the classical Knowledge Management (KM) approaches are not suited, due to the nature and origins of some data, information and knowledge, the complexity of partner networks that are interacting around the systems, the evolution history of such systems, etc. In this article, we present the main challenges for KM in Structuring Systems, especially in terms of knowledge traceability and heritage from one hand, and knowledge preservation at another one.

Keywords :tructuring systems, knowledge management, traceability, heritage.

1 Introduction

In recent years, companies showed a growing interest in Data, Information and Knowledge Management (DIKM) to ensure their competitiveness. (Tsuchiya, 1993) introduces a distinction between *datum*, *information* and *knowledge*: "Although terms "datum", "information" and "knowledge" are often used interchangeably, there exists a clear distinction among them. When datum is sense-given through interpretative framework, it becomes information, and when information is sense-read through interpretative framework, it becomes knowledge". In companies and research literature, DIKM is classically separated in two main domains: on one hand, *data and information management* realised by information system, and on the other, *knowledge management*.

Various papers have contributed to improve comprehension of the specific characteristics of knowledge (Bernard and Tichkiewitch, 2008). The concept of *Knowledge Capitalization* appeared since 1990 in an objective of preserving and enhancing the

* Corresponding author.

A. Bernard, L. Rivest, and D. Dutta (Eds.): PLM 2013, IFIP AICT 409, pp. 249–258, 2013.

know-how acquired in an organization. It can be described by the model proposed by (Grundstein 2012), composed of five facets (Fig. 1): *locate* the knowledge, *preserve* the knowledge, *enhance* the knowledge, *actualize* the knowledge, and *manage* the interactions between the 4 preceding facets.

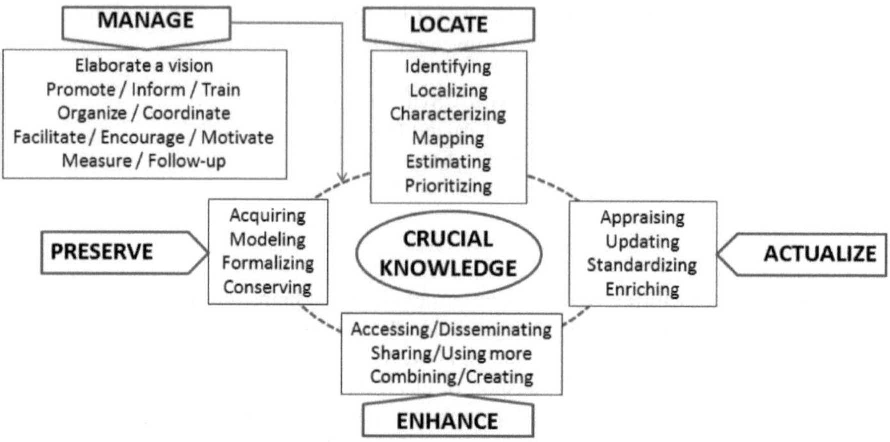

Fig. 1. The problem of knowledge capitalization in company (Grundstein, 2012)

Knowledge Management (KM) is defined as the management of activities and processes aiming at increasing the creation and usage of knowledge inside an organisation. The valorisation of knowledge satisfies an economic issue at stake for both society (UNESCO, 2005) as well as companies. As a consequence, a large literature exists on different domains. Nevertheless, most of KM works have been developed for companies specialised in design, production and control of industrial products or complex systems. Structuring Systems (Zolghadri *et al.*, 2013), like water systems or transport networks, are systems that currently require a new vision of knowledge management suited to their characteristics.

The article is constructed as follow. After a brief state-of-art in Section 2 on main research contributions in KM, Section 3 defines and characterizes Structuring Systems. Based on these two analyses, Section 4 enlightens the main challenges in KM for Structuring Systems.

2 Knowledge Management State-of-the-Art

To satisfy the issues at stake in the valorisation of knowledge, there are two main approach strategies: approaches focussing on the reification of knowledge and those focussing on individuals as holders of knowledge. (McMahon *et al.*, 2004) summarises the various terms relative to these approaches as: "commodity view", "codification" and "object view" for the first and "community view", "personalisation" and "process view" for the second.

Personalisation approaches cover the various knowledge transformation mechanisms as applied within an individual or between individuals when they are freely expressed and lead to solutions oriented towards practices communities (Amin and Roberts, 2008) as well as CSCW-type (Computer-Supported Collaborative Work) tools (Lewkowicz and Zacklad, 2001).

Codification approaches cover the elicitation of knowledge in a controllable form beyond the actual individual and are, for the most part, based on information and communication technology (Chen and Huang, 2012). This explicit knowledge desynchronised from the interpretative framework of individuals then takes on a dual information/knowledge status. The simple documents, codified in line with the interpretative framework of the individuals who will read them, will be a source of knowledge for them similar to that of the people who wrote these documents. In this case, it becomes possible to consider these documents as knowledge. Otherwise, it will be information source of knowledge. Moreover, the information embedded in expert systems constitutes the intrinsic knowledge of these systems inasmuch as they are able to use it to reason, via their own interpretative patterns.

In his analysis of the literature produced between 1995 and 2002 on the technology and applications covered by knowledge management, Liao (2003) identified seven technical areas, which (Louis-Sidney *et al.*, 2012) proposes to combine as follows:

- framework(1) and modelling (2),
- artificial intelligence (KBS(3) and expert systems (4)),
- databases (5), data mining(6) and information and communication technology (ICT) (7) (e.g. the Internet, Extranets and wireless web..).

The technical fields covering the tools made directly available to product designers to carry out their redesign activities, supporting the codified knowledge, are those of artificial intelligence for a very formal approach, and databases, data mining and ICT where less formal codification approaches are used.

(Chandrasegaran *et al.*, 2013) reviews current research works in Knowledge representation and capture in product design and concludes by this sentence: "*Although much progress has been made as outlined in the current paper, we are yet to see wide spread use of knowledge-aided systems in the industry*". (Verhagen *et al.*, 2012) reviews current research works in Knowledge-Based Engineering, and points out in particular the needs in improving methodologies to support KBE development project, and in developing knowledge traceability.

Moreover none of the research contributions elicited in these two articles tackles the specific context of Structuring Systems.

3 Structuring Systems

In this paper, Structuring Systems are defined as systems, designed, installed, used and maintained within its operational environment for an extremely long duration, answering to the fundamental needs of the society (Zolghadri *et al.*, 2013).

As a special type of systems, a Structuring System shares with general systems some fundamental properties such as:

- it is composed of subsystems,
- these subsystems are interconnected,
- they have dependencies with their environment within which they have various exchanges. This environment is composed not only of other structuring systems but other kind of systems.

Moreover, compared with other types of systems, the Structuring Systems have a very long utilization duration, disproportionately higher than the other phases. To take concrete examples of these systems, we can name the water supply systems, energy networks (electricity), transport networks (road, rail, inland waterways), the sites of highly hazardous waste and / or toxic (nuclear, chemical, etc.).

Let us now qualify these services thanks to three criteria: (1) Number of users, (2) Usage frequency, and (3) Usage duration. A product or system provides its services to either one individual customer or a more or less large group of customers. The frequency of usage and also the duration of the service usage by customers could vary from one kind of service to another. These three criteria allow to structure the space of the services offered by a product or a system (Fig. 2).

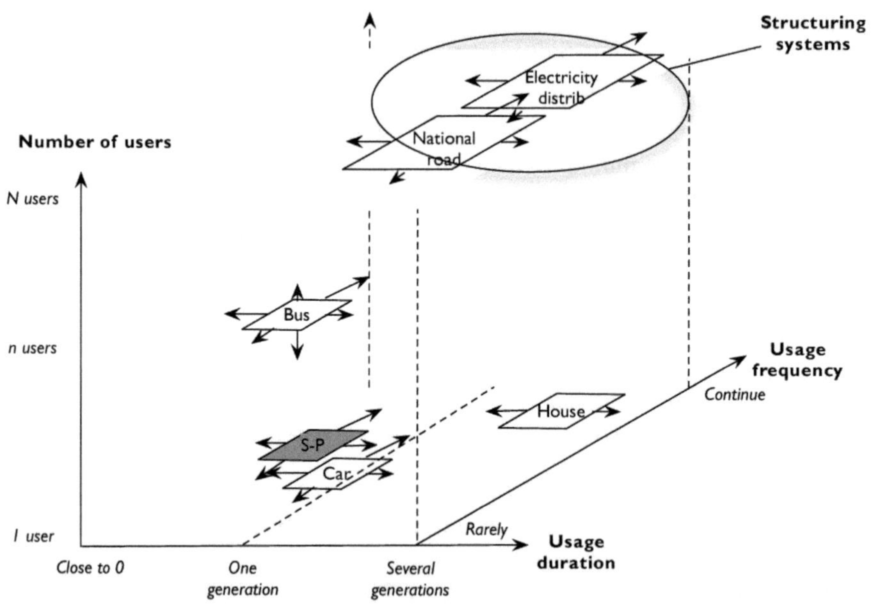

Fig. 2. The usage space of a product or a system

According to this usage space, we suggest a very first sub-space where the structuring systems are gathered and a very first definition of such systems is the following: "*A structuring system is as a complex system which offers its services for a very long period of time covering more than one generation of human being. A structuring system is a heritage of its users*".

Other dimensions of the structuring systems' characterisation reveal some properties that allow to understand them in a better way:

- these systems are made of a large number of inter-connected sub-systems forming a complex network,
- mainly they correspond to the public utility organizations, and their highest-level decision-makers are the public authorities that are accountable of their decisions to citizens,
- they are firmly connected to other Structuring Systems but use a myriad of products (computers, cars, etc.),
- their operation phase duration is much longer than any other phase of their lifecycle,
- they are in perpetual evolution and one can hardly define their end-of-life,
- they are continuously partially re-designed and refurbished, and continuously maintained.

We can qualify these systems as *structuring* because they have such deep influences on the society, economy and their eco-systems that they become the main drivers of their evolution (Berion *et al.*, 2007). They play a crucial role in the organisation of actors and their relationships. This is to say that structuring systems structure themselves, eco-systems in which they are implemented but also other systems with which they are connected. The structuring systems express, control and drive the "heavy trends" of the eco-system. These systems are the concretisation of the main political and societal inspiration of a country that goes much further than other kind of design decisions.

From the previous definition, Structuring Systems have several principles that are typical of such systems:

- *continuous answer to evolving needs*: since consumers' needs evolve not only according to the general evolution of science and technologies but also thanks to the evolution of their own awareness (see (Tillman, 2001) for the water needs evolution for instance), Structuring Systems have the obligation of service continuity and they are so reconfigured or changed partially to cope with the evolving needs,
- *incipience-germination-coalescence*: the existing Structuring Systems have been and are still obtained thanks to this iterative threefold process (Fig.3),
- *functional, structural and technological continuity*: due to non service break and long-life principles, these systems are inherited and partial evolution of such systems have to ensure continuity with their history, at the three levels,
- *durable impacts on and from the environment*: some impacts can be tangible in the short term (population movement after the construction of a new bridge) while others may be observed slowly, e.g. the change of the industrial landscape after the construction of transportation infrastructure (Berion *et al.*, 2007).

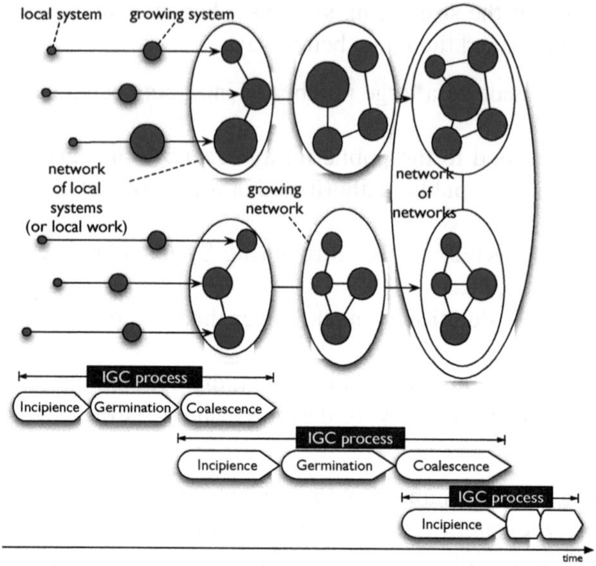

Fig. 3. Iterative process for Structuring Systems: incipience-germination-coalescence

Structuring Systems cover durable needs of users. In this case, the local and national public authorities are the main decision-makers and strategy definers. Nevertheless, private actors are often involved in almost all of the lifecycle's phases. Public and private financing organisations are also those partners that allow a structuring system to be launched, used and maintained. We can model the connections among all these actors by the model represented in Fig. 4.

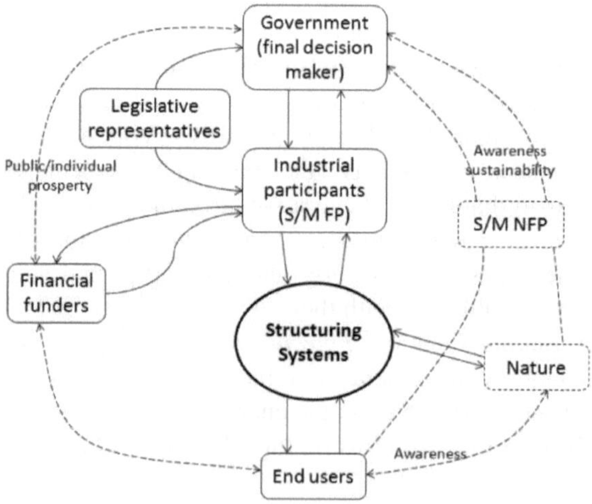

Fig. 4. Influences among stakeholders and a Structuring System

KM approaches have been partially deployed in several Structuring Systems, specifically at each system. The major contributions are related to knowledge-based engineering, with the development of knowledge-based systems to support decision processes associated to these structuring systems, potentially by simulating human expertise during the problem solving process, either for the water domain (Wukovits et al., 2003), (Chau, 2007), (Garrido-Baserba *et al.*, 2012), or the urban planning one (Rubenstein-Montano, 2000). In particular, (Davis, 2000) details a specification that identifies the types of data, knowledge, and internal and external factors likely to be of relevance in a full decision-support tool (Fig. 5), proving the diversity of partners implied in the decision process and the complexity of knowledge management required to support such process.

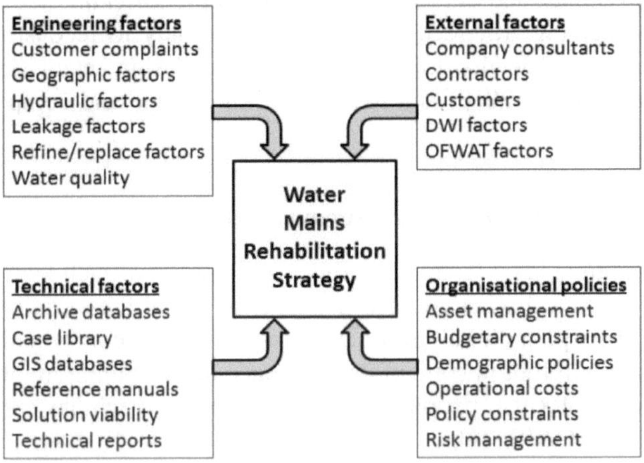

Fig. 5. Influences to be captured in a complete decision-support tool (Davis, 2000)

4 Challenges in KM for Structuring Systems

The previous sections have enlightened two characteristics of Structuring Systems: they are continuously evolving, and innovation is an important aspect. These two dimensions are deeply connected to the knowledge existing on them.

Nevertheless, several issues attached to Structuring Systems make KM more complex and current approaches in this domain are not suited. If the model in five facets can still be used, each facet should be re-imagined in the context of Structuring Systems.

4.1 Locate Knowledge for Structuring Systems

Structuring Systems, due to their nature, are inherited from a long history, and their architecture is so the result of past decisions that may be lost at that time. (Kujinga and Jonker, 2006) illustrates on the example of water governance transformation in Zimbabwe how the knowledge diffusion process is as non-easy and non-intuitive as expected. As a consequence, locate knowledge generated and used during this history is a complex task, with two main dimensions.

The first dimension is related to the large scale of actors that may contribute and/or interact with structuring systems. In this case, specific knowledge capture approaches are needed, for instance by analyzing either knowledge co-production between different partners (Hordijk and Baud, 2006), (Edelenbos *et al.*, 2011), or cognitive biases from human expertise in the domain (Scholten *et al.*, 2012), (Taylor and de Loë, 2012).

The second dimension is more associated to time scale and especially the inheritance of such systems. In this case, knowledge may have disappeared and locate such knowledge is more associated to the archaeology discipline (Bernard & Proust, 2013). To help this archaeology task, even if a methodology to support such process is still required, several approaches and tools may be of prior interest:

- extraction of information and knowledge from ancient texts, like the approaches proposed by (Gomez and Segami, 2007) or by (Buitelaar *et al.*, 2008),
- Reverse Engineering, where the objective is not only to reconstruct a complete model of a piece, but also to capture the initial design intent (Huang and Tai, 2000), (Durupt *et al.*, 2010) and reconstruct knowledge and competencies implemented at the origin.

4.2 Preserve Knowledge for Structuring Systems

Since their usage time is far from being finished, to preserve such knowledge requires specific preservation techniques, called Long Term Digital Preservation (NLA, 2003), with the mean of keeping digital information so that the same information can be used at some point in the future in spite of obsolescence of everything involved: hardware, software, processes, format, people, etc. Such LTDP approach has contributed to the definition of the OAIS (Open Archival Information System) Standard (ISO 14721:2012).

In the domain of product development (and especially aeronautics), several approaches have been proposed for digital preservation of data and information attached, like the LOTAR project (LOTAR, 2013).

Nevertheless, the main interest of such projects is until now to preserve only data or information attached to the products, like digital geometric data (Regli *et al.*, 2011). In our case, preserving technical and organisational knowledge, especially the one attached to any decision process that may be crucial in 150 years for instance, needs further research.

4.3 Enhance and Actualise Knowledge for Structuring Systems

As previously said, Structuring Systems are characterized by a large diversity of stakeholders that are contributing and/or interacting all over the usage time of such systems. Decisions and so knowledge are distributed in organisations that can be considered as short-lived ones compared to the service non-end time of Structuring Systems.

A change of paradigm is so needed for Knowledge Management and the facets "Enhance" and "Actualise" in particular, to attached knowledge not to the organisation that creates knowledge but to the systems by itself.

References

Amin, A., Roberts, J.: Knowing in action: Beyond communities of practice. Research Policy 37(2), 353–369 (2008)

Berion, P.: The construction of a major transport infrastructure and its initial territorial impacts; the case of the A39 motorway between Dole and Bourg-en-Bresse. Géocarrefour 77(1), 7–20 (2002)

Bernard, A., Proust, C.: Ancient Scientific Sources and Teaching Contexts: Problems and Perspectives. Springer (2013)

Bernard, A., Tichkiewitch, S.: Methods and tools for effective knowledge life-cycle management. Springer (2008)

Buitelaar, P., Cimiano, P., Frank, A., Hartung, M., Racioppa, S.: Ontology-based information extraction and integration from heterogeneous data sources. International Journal of Human-Computer Studies 66(11), 759–788 (2008)

Chandrasegaran, S.K., Ramani, K., Sriram, R.D., Horváth, I., Bernard, A., Harik, R.F., Gao, W.: The evolution, challenges, and future of knowledge representation in product design systems. Computer-Aided Design 45(2), 204–228 (2013)

Chau, K.W.: An ontology-based knowledge management system for flow and water quality modelling. Advances in Engineering Software 38(3), 172–181 (2007)

Chen, Y.Y., Huang, H.L.: Knowledge management fit and its implications for business performance: A profile deviation analysis. Knowledge-Based Systems 27, 262–270 (2012)

Committee on National Security Systems, National information assurance glossary (2010), http://www.cnss.gov/Assets/pdf/cnssi_4009.pdf (accessed January 15, 2013)

Davis, D.: Agent-based decision-support framework for water supply infrastructure rehabilitation and development. Computers, Environment and Urban Systems 24(3), 173–190 (2000)

Durupt, A., Remy, S., Ducellier, G.: Knowledge Based Reverse Engineering—An Approach for Reverse Engineering of a Mechanical Part. Journal of Computing and Information Science in Engineering 10(4) (2010)

Edelenbos, J., van Buuren, A., van Schie, N.: Co-producing knowledge: joint knowledge production between experts, bureaucrats and stakeholders in Dutch water management projects. Environmental Science & Policy 14(6), 675–684 (2011)

Garrido-Baserba, M., Reif, R., Hernández, F., Poch, M.: Implementation of a knowledge-based methodology in a decision support system for the design of suitable wastewater treatment process flow diagrams. Journal of Environmental Management 112, 384–391 (2012)

Gomez, F., Segami, C.: Semantic interpretation and knowledge extraction. Knowledge-Based Systems 20(1), 51–60 (2007)

Grundstein, M.: Three postulates that change knowledge management paradigm. In: Hou, H.-T. (ed.) New Research on Knowledge Management Models and Methods, ch. 1 (2012)

Hordijk, M., Baud, I.: The role of research and knowledge generation in collective action and urban governance: How can researchers act as catalysts? Habitat International 30(3), 668–689 (2006)

Huang, M.C., Tai, C.C.: The pre-processing of data points for curve fitting in reverse engineering. The International Journal of Advanced Manufacturing Technology 16, 635–642 (2000)

ISO 14721:2012 Space data and information transfer systems – Open archival information system (OAIS) – Reference model

Kujinga, K., Jonker, L.: An analysis of stakeholder knowledge about water governance transformation in Zimbabwe. Physics and Chemistry of the Earth 31(15-16), 690–698 (2006)

Lewkowicz, M., Zacklad, M.: Une nouvelle forme de gestion des connaissances basée sur la structuration des intéractions collectives. In: Zacklad, M., Grundstein, M. (eds.) Ingénierie et Capitalisation des Connaissances, ch. 3, pp. 49–64. Hermès Sciences Publication (2001)

Liao, S.H.: Knowledge management technologies and applications-literature review from 1995 to 2002. Expert Systems with Applications 25(2), 155–164 (2003)

LOTAR, LOng Term Archiving and Retrieval (2013), http://www.lotar-international.org/

Louis-Sidney, L., Cheutet, V., Lamouri, S., Puron, O., Mezza, A.: A conceptual model for the implementation of IKOES in automotive industry. Engineering Applications of Artificial Intelligence 5(5), 1090–1101 (2012)

McMahon, C., Lowe, A., Culley, S.: Knowledge management in engineering design: personalization and codification. Journal of Engineering Design 15(4), 307–325 (2004)

National Library of Australia, Guidelines for the Preservation of Digital Heritage. UNESCO (2003)

Regli, W.C., Kopena, J.B., Grauer, M.: On the long-term retention of geometry-centric digital engineering artifacts. Computer-Aided Design 43(7), 820–837 (2011)

Rubenstein-Montano, B.: A survey of knowledge-based information systems for urban planning: moving towards knowledge management. Computers, Environment and Urban Systems 24(3), 155–172 (2000)

Scholten, L., Scheidegger, A., Reichert, P., Maurer, M.: Combining expert knowledge and local data for improved service life modeling of water supply networks. Environmental Modelling & Software (2012), doi:10.1016/j.envsoft.2012.11.013

Taylor, B., de Loë, R.C.: Conceptualizations of local knowledge in collaborative environmental governance. Geoforum 43(6), 1207–1217 (2012)

Tillman, D.: Stakeholder analysis in water supply systems. Swiss Federal Institute of Technology, PhD (2001)

Tsuchiya, S.: Improving Knowledge Creation Ability through Organizational Learning. In: Proceedings of ISMICK, Compiègne, France (1993)

UNESCO, Towards Knowledge Societies (2005), http://www.unesco.org/new/en/unesco/resources/online-materials/publications/unesdoc-database/ (accessed January 15, 2013)

Verhagen, W.J.C., Bermell-Garcia, P., van Dijk, R.E.C., Curran, R.: A critical review of Knowledge-Based Engineering: An identification of research challenges. Advanced Engineering Informatics 26(1), 5–15 (2012)

Wukovits, W., Harasek, M., Friedl, A.: A knowledge based system to support the process selection during waste water treatment. Resources, Conservation and Recycling 37(3), 205–215 (2003)

Zolghadri, M., Couffin, F., Cheutet, V., Bourcier, C., Costa Affonso, R., Leclaire, P.: Structuring Systems. LISMMA technical report (2013)

Knowledge Management in E-commerce Mass Customization

Yang Xu, Jing Xu, and Alain Bernard

Department of Information Management, Peking University, Beijing, China
College of Mechanical Engineering, Yangzhou University, Yangzhou, China
IRCCyN, Ecole Centrale de Nantes, Nantes, France

Abstract. Mass customization is one of the leading strategies in satisfying customers and assuring companies survival in today's markets. From the point of view of lifecycle management, it includes knowledge of customer requirement, customer preference, raw material purchasing, customization manufacturing process, product price which reflects satisfaction of both sides of bargain. This paper proposes a knowledge management model in E-commerce mass customization, which is consisted of three parts: the customer information gathering model, the purchasing and manufacturing model and the pricing model. The modeling process and further analysis show that the model efficiently integrates different knowledge in mass customization lifecycle and can serve as a useful platform in E-commerce.

Keywords : Knowledge management, Mass customization, modeling.

1 Introduction

In this era characterized by constantly changing environment, rapid technology progress and fierce market competition, knowledge is recognized as a manageable key resource for enterprises to survive and develop (Grover and Davenport, 2001; Bernard and Tichkiewitch, 2008). Knowledge, also known as intellectual capital, has been regarded as one of the sustainable assets, so people are paying more and more attention in knowledge management issues (Xu et al., 2011). Knowledge can add value to products/services so as to help enterprise make profit, and knowledge management aims at figuring out how to add value as much as possible within a given cost (Xu and Bernard, 2010). Although the strategic value of knowledge is clear, in most cases people have not mastered the art of managing knowledge. Thus, it is quite useful to make a profound study on knowledge management in a given business model, for example, mass customization.

Mass customization (MC) is usually referred as a term as an oxymoron of mass production and customized goods (Kaplan and Haenlein, 2006), and it has become an undisputable reality that MC is one of the leading strategies in satisfying customers and assuring companies survival in today's markets (Daaboul et al., 2011). Mass

A. Bernard, L. Rivest, and D. Dutta (Eds.): PLM 2013, IFIP AICT 409, pp. 259–267, 2013.

customization makes high value-added products/services, and enhances profitability by reducing the costs of production and logistics and better satisfying the customer personalized requirements (Jian et al., 2003; Grenci and Watts, 2007). When an enterprise is able to offer personalized or customized products, customer is then involved in the product design process, which may increase the value of the product – customer perceived value (CPV) (Gautam and Singh, 2008). One of the most distinguished features of mass customization is to provide customers with the possibility to co-design products/services according to their personalized preferences and interests. Providing customers with the ability to co-design products/services based on their own preferences has been considered one of the most distinctive features of mass customization (Ogawa and Piller, 2006). Products/services can be considered to be an integration of different modules, and different features of these modules can satisfy customers' needs and provide value. From this point of view, mass customization can be regarded as a method to provide customers with a choice menu based on market segmentation (Fogliatto and da Silveira, 2008).

Implementing mass customization in pure traditional manufacturing industrial is quite difficult, so it is usually integrated with information technology (IT) systems to form E-commerce solutions. E-commerce can provide the linkage to capture external information and it is regarded as a possible solution for mass customization (Helms et al., 2008). E-commerce uses computer and networks to do business, such as buy and sell products/services, transmit information, etc. With the rapid progress of information technology, people are award of the fact that when a business model is created, built and applied properly, E-commerce would facilitate mass customization in many aspects (Turowski, 2002; Helander and Jiao, 2002). Meanwhile, E-commerce based on the rapid progress of advanced Information and Communication Technologies (ICT) should be linked with effective knowledge management strategies. Knowledge gained and managed via e-business can enhance customer relationship management, supply chain management, product development, etc. (Fahey et al., 2001)

In order to better explain the proposed theoretical model, this paper takes mass customization on food menu in E-commerce as example. With the rapid growth of people' requirement on food, people do not only care about nutrition and safety issues but also need more customized menu. There exists "special supplied food" which can be ordered by customers to fit their personalized requirements, but they are quite expensive because there is a lack of mass production. Scale effect is one of the primary means to reduce costs (Easton and Sommers, 2003), so mass customization should be applied to balance the two sides of scale effect and customized requirements. As a result, the main problem to be solved is that, to what extent the benefit brought by customization can compensate the increased cost caused by quantity reduction, in other words, what to customize and how to customize.

This paper mainly focuses on knowledge management issues in E-commerce mass customization and proposed a model for real case implementation.

2 Modeling Process

Mass customization is applied by more and more enterprises to attract customers and make more profits. A survey based on market investigation (Xu et al., 2012) shows that customers are willing to pay about 50% more to get a customized diet menu (different collocations of the food materials, to what extent the food is cooked, flavors, etc. can be determined by customers) rather than homogeneous fast food supply. Another results got from the investigation is that customers are willing to pay more for personalized requirements but they would like to pay extra fees as little as possible. Consequently, an obvious conclusion can be made: enterprises which can apply mass customization to provide customized product and/or service with a lower price will win in the fierce market competition.

The integrated model is consists of three parts: the customer information gathering model, the purchasing and manufacturing model and the pricing model. Figure 1 shows the framework of the mass customization lifecycle management model.

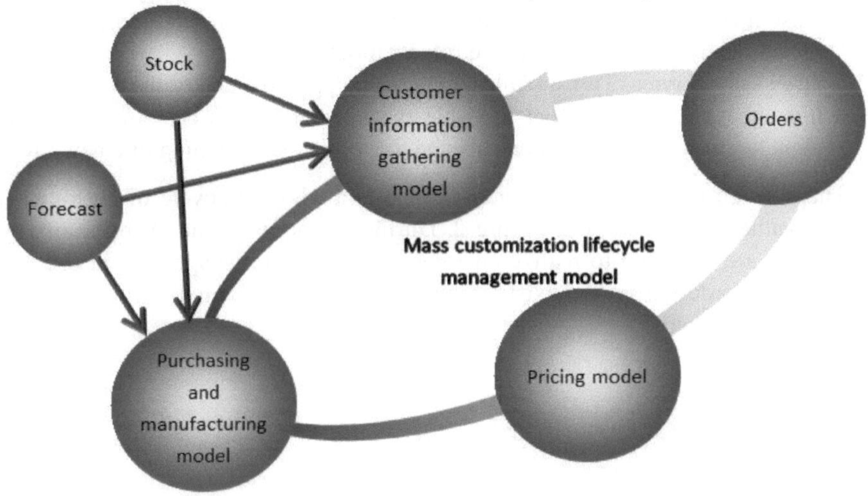

Fig. 1. Framework of the mass customization lifecycle management model

3 Customer Information Gathering Model

In the phase of customer information gathering, seven modules are constructed as follows.

1) Information announcement on the official website. The company announces the types of food that it will accept to be ordered in the next time period, for example, in the next month. Customers may choose one or some of them according to their preferences, determine possible attributes of the food they will order, and illustrate customized package. This module may integrate official website announcement, channel marketing, email pushing, etc.
2) Customer account management. Each customer may have an account, which will be a base of the customer's information. This module may include registration, login, logout, edit, administrator management, etc.
3) Customized design by the customer himself/herself. Customers choose the foods they need for their menu according to the choices given by the company website,

and determine the possible combination. For example, if a customer choices milk as a part of the menu, he may determine its value: sugar percentage, fat percentage, etc. In order to control the complexity of customization, attribute values can be restricted if needed, for example, for the possible value of fat percentage of milk, only whole milk, skim milk and half skim milk are available.

4) Weight assignment. The customer should assign different weight values to each customized choice according to their preference. To facilitate later processes, the sum of all weight values is 1. These weights reflect the priorities of customers' preferences.
5) Customer order processing. This module will be discussed in detail in the following sections.
6) Customer feedback. This module enables customers to give some feedbacks to the company, which are valuable information.
7) After sales service. This module can be regarded as the end of the mass customization lifecycle. Like product lifecycle management, mass customization management has also an end, but it can also be treated as the beginning of a new lifecycle.

These seven modules fundamentally consists a whole lifecycle of customer information gathering process, c.f. Figure 2. During its implementation in the real world, companies are expected to realize customer relationship management in order to encourage new orders from the existing customers, so as to form a virtuous lifecycle of mass customization.

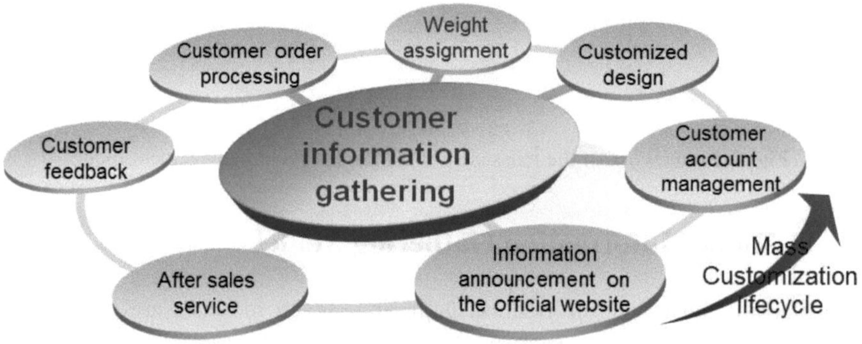

Fig. 2. Customer information gathering sub-model

4 Purchasing and Manufacturing Model

In the phase of purchasing and processing, three modules are constructed as follows.

1) Purchasing general components based on prediction. General components refer to foods in their original status, such as pure milk with any skimming treatment. General components are obtained directly from raw materials. In this phase, the purchasing amount are forecasted based on existing stock, order data of the same period in the past years, etc.

2) Purchasing customized components based on customer orders. After receiving orders from customers, the company will purchase customized components.
3) Semi-manufactured food processing. Semi-manufactured foods are made according to the customer order and purchased material. For example, 100L of calcium-fortified milk are produced with pure milk (purchased in phase 1) and calcium additive (purchased in phase 2). The amount of semi-manufactured food is determined by orders.
4) Customized manufacturing process. After producing all kinds of semi-manufactured food, the company assembles them for a customized menu ordered by customers.

Figure 3 shows the purchasing and manufacturing sub-model.

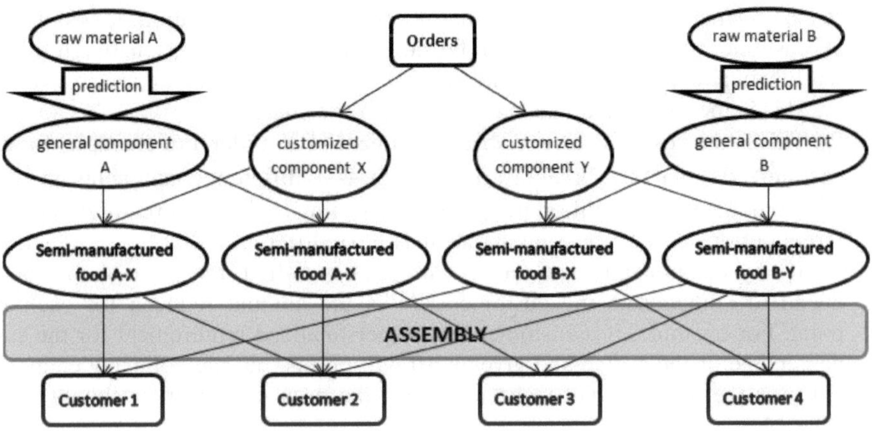

Fig. 3. Purchasing and manufacturing sub-model

5 Pricing Model

Pricing issue is crucial for mass customization (Aron et al., 2006). Unsuitable pricing strategy will prevent companies to gain their maximum profit and customers are not willing to pay an unreasonable price for the customized goods either. In our model, four parts form the pricing strategy for the customized orders:

1) The fundamental price. This part is determined by the minimum costs of all raw materials.
2) Price for customization. Customization needs extra cost compared to homogeneous order.
3) Price reduction to compensate the unaccomplished parts of the customized order. When the customers required a customized order and are willing to pay a high price, they deserve a complete product/service. If the company could not accomplish the task, they should be punished. In other words, the

company should take the risk brought by mass customization as well as the profit brought by it.

4) Extra cost caused by order revision. Customers may not be satisfied with their order or the price matching their order. As customer orders have impacts on the mass customization process, such as purchasing processes and the pricing processes, some costs will happen each time a customer order is processed. As a result, for the customer side, they should undertake a higher price if they adjust their customized orders.

Here are some parameters used in the pricing sub-model.

- α_i $(1 \le i \le c, \sum_{i=1}^{c} \alpha_i = 100)$. This is the will point that customers assigned to each customized need. c is the number of customized needs. It is reasonable that when the customer has a high requirement in some aspects, he/she should reduce his/her expectations in some others. Mass customization does not mean all customer requirements have to be satisfied, which is unreasonable in the real world where everything has a budget.
- L_i. This is the lowest purchasing cost of each raw material.
- P_{ij}. This is the cost of each possible component of an order. For example, for a customized order for a breakfast menu, there is i different components and the ith component has j different options. According to different requirements, different options of a given components may have different costs.
- M. If any customized requirement cannot be satisfied, the price should be reduced to compensate the customers. M is the amount reduced for each will point. For example, if a customer has an personalized requirement for the sugar percentage of the coffee and gives it 10 will points, but the company cannot satisfy (or feel it worth not to be satisfied), the price of the order should reduce $10 \times M$.
- N. This is the number of order matching round. For example, when a customer proposes a customized order for the first time, $N = 1$. If the customer is not satisfied and choose to adjust the order for a second round, $N = 2$.
- F. If the customer adjusts his/her customized order, there will be an additional cost, which is F. For example, when the customer adjusts his/her order and resubmits it for the Nth time, there is an addition of $(N-1)F$ on the price he/she will pay.
- X_i. This is a 0-1 variable, which is used to judge whether a given customized requirement has been realized.

$$X_i = \begin{cases} 1, \textit{the } i^{th} \textit{ customized requirement has been realized} \\ 0, \textit{the } i^{th} \textit{ customized requirement hasn't been realized} \end{cases}$$

- r. This is the expected interest of the customized order. r can be obtained by statistical and/or forecasting method using historical data of the company.

As a result, the customized price is calculated as follows.

$$\text{Price} = \left[\sum_{i=1}^{C} L_i + \sum_{i=1}^{C} (P_{ij} - L_i) \cdot X_i\right](1 + r) - \sum_{i=1}^{C} (1 - x_i) \cdot \alpha_i \cdot M + (N - 1) \cdot F$$

Pricing procedure is shown in Figure 4.

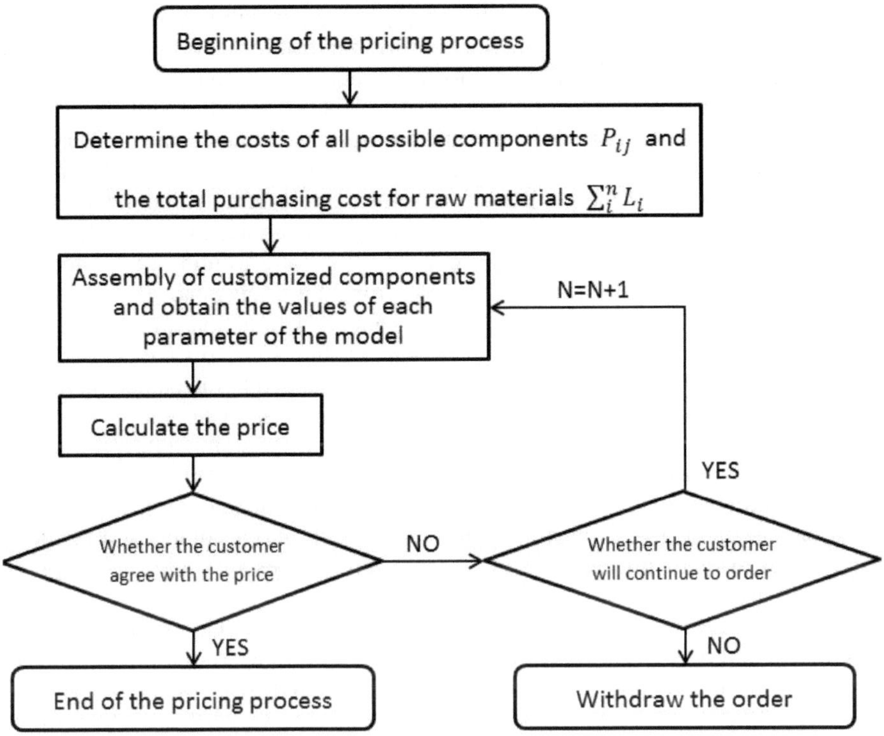

Fig. 4. Pricing procedure

Figure 4 shows that the pricing procedure firstly figures out the lowest cost of all raw materials used for the order, i.e. L_i. The addition of L_i is the fundamental price of the order. Then, in the assembly process, the model records what is actually used to form the menu order and thus determine all parameters to calculate the price. Using the proposed calculation equation, the price is calculated. At the same time, the difference between the menu provided and the original order of the customer is sending back to the customer, and ask the customer whether he/she agrees with the menu provided and the correspondent price. If the customer agrees, the procedure arrives to a happy ending. If the customer does not agree and does not want to continue the order, the order will be canceled automatically. If the customer does not agree with the menu provided and its price, but would like to make a customized order for a second round, the parameter N will be adjusted to $N + 1$, and a new process will begin.

6 Discussions

One of the key issues in the proposed E-commerce mass customization model is how to design the choice menu for the customer. Customization does not mean to satisfy all customer requirements without any constraint. Not only the production cost or manufacturing activities should be controlled, but the customer requirements should also be controlled. In other words, customization in our model does not refer to original creativity of customer, and the range of customization is controlled by the company, so as to make the E-commerce platform realizable and efficient. The design of customized choice menu should take former orders into account and consider current stock situation as well. Once a customer order is processed, it will have impacts on the following purchasing activities and the design of choice menu. During the modeling process, the purchasing of general components is determined by the forecasting and the stock, and the purchasing of semi-manufactured components is determined by orders. In fact, orders reflect to what extent the choice menu satisfy customer satisfaction. As not all customer requirements are satisfied, online choice menu can be adjusted according to the feedback reports from the pricing model. Furthermore, the design of choice menu should also take current stock situation into account, so as to reduce the stock. For example, if the company has some overstock beefsteaks, some options providing menu with beefsteak could be added to the choice menu, so as to increase the probability of consumption of those overstock materials.

Another crucial issue processed by the model is how to customize the product price. According to the model, production costs of each order are not the same, so as for the purchasing strategies. The pricing model takes the fundamental costs, costs for customization and the degree of customization satisfaction into account. As a result, different choices made by different customers at different times vary a lot, so the product prices are customized.

In order to increase the impacts of customers' preference and control customers' requirements in a reasonable range, customers are required to weight to their different options during the customer information gathering model. On one hand, companies may have a deeper understanding of customers' preferences which can help companies to adjust their commercial activities; on the other hand, customers' preferences are better respected. For example, if an important preference (given a relatively high weight) of a customer cannot be satisfied, more compensation are given to the customer by reducing the customized price.

7 Conclusions

This paper has proposed a knowledge management model in E-commerce mass customization. The proposed model is consisted of three parts, the customer information gathering model, the purchasing and manufacturing model and the pricing model. The model integrates knowledge about customers' requirements and preferences, customization processes and product prices, so as to provide reasonable products/service with a suitable price. The model also analyzes knowledge management issues in mass customization from the point of view of lifecycle management, from information gathering, material purchasing, customization manufacturing and feedbacks. In this integrated process, not only the company but also customers are involved, especially performed in the pricing model.

Further research opportunities could include more consideration on customer relationship management and supply chain management so as to integrate more knowledge related to the mass customization lifecycle.

Acknowledgement. This work is supported by the National Social Science Foundation of China (No. 13CTQ022) and the National Natural Science Foundation of China (No. 51205344).

References

Aron, R., Sundararajan, A., Viswanathan, S.: Intelligent agents in electronic markets for information goods: customization, preference revelation and pricing. Decision Support Systems 41, 764–786 (2006)

Bernard, A., Tichkiewitch, S.: Methods and tools for effective knowledge lifecycle management. Springer, Berlin (2008)

Daaboul, J., DaCunha, C., Bernard, A., Laroche, F.: Design for mass customization: Product variety VS process variety. CIRP Annals – Manufacturing Technology 60, 169–174 (2011)

Easton, P.D., Sommers, G.A.: Scale and the Scale Effect in Market-based Accounting Research. Journal of Business Finance & Accounting 30(1-2), 25–56 (2003)

Fahey, L., Srivastava, R., Sharon, J.S., Smith, D.E.: Linking e-business and operating processes: the role of knowledge management. IBM Systems Journal 40(4), 889–907 (2001)

Fogliatto, F.S., da Silveira, G.J.C.: Mass customization: A method for market segmentation and choice menu design. International Journal of Production Economics 111, 606–622 (2008)

Gautam, N., Singh, N.: Lean product development: maximizing the customer perceived value through design change (redesign). International Journal of Production Economics 114, 313–332 (2008)

Grenci, R.T., Watts, C.A.: Maximizing customer value via mass customized e-consumer services. Business Horizons 50(2), 123–132 (2007)

Grover, V., Davenport, T.H.: General perspectives on KM: fostering a research agenda. Journal of Management Information Systems 18(1), 5–21 (2001)

Helander, M.G., Jiao, J.: Research on E-product development (ePD) for mass customization. Technovation 22, 717–724 (2002)

Helms, M.M., Ahmadi, M., Jih, W.J.K., Ettkin, L.P.: Technologies in support of mass customization strategy: Exploring the linkages between e-commerce and knowledge management. Computers in Industry 59, 351–363 (2008)

Jiao, J., Ma, Q., Tseng, M.M.: Towards high value-added products and services: mass customization and beyond. Technovation 23, 809–821 (2003)

Kaplan, A.M., Haenlein, M.: Toward a parsimonious definition of traditional and electronic mass customization. The Journal of Product Innovation Management 23, 168–179 (2006)

Ogawa, S., Piller, F.T.: Reducing the risks of new product development. MIT Sloan Management Review 47(2), 65–71 (2006)

Turowski, K.: Agent-based e-commerce in case of mass customization. International Journal of Production Economics 75, 69–81 (2002)

Xu, J., Houssin, R., Caillaud, E., Gardoni, M.: Fostering continuous innovation in design with an integrated knowledge management approach. Computers in Industry 62, 423–436 (2011)

Xu, Y., Bernard, A.: Quantifying the value of knowledge within the context of product development. Knowledge-Based Systems 24(1), 166–175 (2011)

Xu, Y., et al.: A survey on mass customization in restaurant industry. Technical report, Peking University (2012)

A Knowledge Based Collaborative Platform for the Design and Deployment of Manufacturing Systems

George Pintzos, Loukas Rentzos, Konstantinos Efthymiou,
Nikolaos Papakostas, and George Chryssolouris*

Laboratory for Manufacturing Systems and Automation, Department of Mechanical Engineering and Aeronautics, University of Patras, 26500 Patras, Greece
xrisol@lms.mech.upatras.gr

Abstract .he PLM systems do not provide any link to actual performance indicators, related to cost, time, and quality parameters. This paper describes a collaboration platform, based on a semantic core that expresses knowledge about Products, Processes and Resources. The platform is internet based, connecting engineers in the extended enterprise with shopfloor personnel. The concept is based both on a series of distinct components and elements comprising the knowledge base, and on a set of software agents. The latter are interfaced with a set of Computer Aided (CAx) systems and provide decision support capabilities for the design of a production line.

Keywords. Collaboration platform, Production design, Ontology.

1 Introduction

Most industrial sectors strive to find methods to reduce costs, time-to-market as well as to improve quality and expand market opportunities [1]. Production line design and development can be regarded as one of the most challenging decision-making processes, since it is affected by numerous design factors and criteria. Furthermore, it involves collaborative work carried out by several engineers such as process, industrial, and manufacturing equipment engineers [2]. Thus, different models, methods, techniques and technologies have been researched and developed to aid engineers in managing the complexity of production line design and development. Khan and Day in 2002, introduced a knowledge-based conceptual design methodology for single, multi- and mixed-product assembly lines; this methodology, based upon a selection of a suitable assembly systems can decide on suitable cycle times, parallel work station requirements, and parallel line implementation achieving an economical number of work stations [3]. Several system analysis methods were developed for assisting engineers with the optimization of their design, namely in [4, 5] where dynamic programming algorithms and Taylor series expansions were used in order to determine values such as the number of machines for each station and analyse the average steady-state throughput of cyclic production lines, respectively. Two noticeable

* Corresponding author.

A. Bernard, L. Rivest, and D. Dutta (Eds.): PLM 2013, IFIP AICT 409, pp. 268–276, 2013.

examples of integrated simulation models, in production design processes, comprise a method of the simulation tools being used as modules for JIT manufacturing design [6] and an integration framework of analytic and simulation tools for the assembly line design [7]. A later approach has discussed the implementation of a web-based workflow management system for integrated production engineering, where the workflow of a production engineering project could be configured within a BPEL Engine layer [8].

These simulation tools can demonstrate the behaviour of production lines, before their implementation, and contribute to a reduction in the development lead-time. However, they are subject to the availability of detailed engineering information, before useful simulation models for analysis can be developed. Consequently, these tools are usually utilized during the final stages of the design process in order for the configurations of design solutions, already planned in detail, to be verified [2], whereas analytical methods are applied during the conceptual design stage, when design solution outlines are constructed [12]. Furthermore, these design methodologies do not consider the collaborative aspect of the design and the development processes, meaning that similarly to the product development process, the production line design process is a very knowledge-intensive and collaborative task that involves different stakeholders and knowledge bearers [9]. While knowledge-intensive collaboration has emerged as a promising discipline for dealing with the modelling and decision-making processes, in distributed product design systems, the same cannot be said for the design of manufacturing systems and production lines [10]. However, with the advent of the Internet, software frameworks will continue being developed for improving the ability to represent, capture and reuse design knowledge [11].

2 Platform Architecture

The proposed platform is expanded into four main domains; the Execution, the Workflow, the Interface and the Knowledge domain (Figure 1). The Knowledge and Workflow domains include the so-called "Knowledge base", which is a semantic description of the acquired knowledge and workflow structure of production design processes, comprising production data structures as well as information about the production parameters. Further details concerning the Knowledge domain will be given in the next section.

The Execution domain includes software agents and applications that directly assist the production design participants in performing various tasks, with reference to project execution and project management. The latter is supported by separate agents (Workflow agents), which inform engineers of their task (e.g. regarding the location of necessary input data files) on the basis of a project's latest progress and keep track of it (through the Workflow domain). The execution of tasks is supported by specific agents that, depending on the expected results of a task, provide links to either web-services working as tools for specific steps (e.g. for line balancing, cycle time calculation) or translation services, regarding the possible incompatibility of file formats (e.g. translation of proprietary file formats to open standard formats, such as PLCopen or STEP).

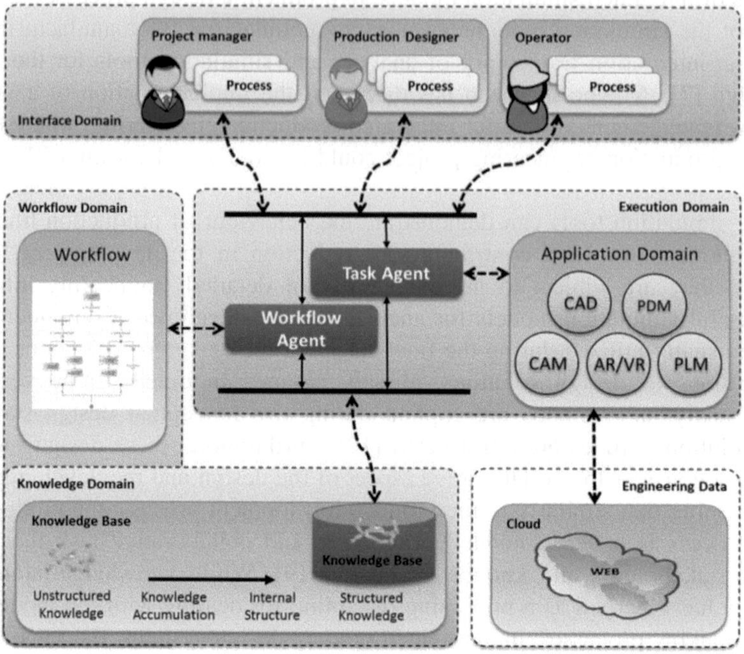

Fig. 1. Specific domains of the proposed platform

The Engineering data represent a cloud service in the form of an Infrastructure as a Service (IaaS) that includes a common database. It is connected to the knowledge repository and the physical data repositories placed in each stakeholder's facilities. When data have to be shared, the Workflow agents use the Project management information model, in the Knowledge base, for the calculation of the access rights that either provide the relevant link to the file or not. Finally, the interface domain includes all the necessary interfaces among the SW agents, the web-based services and the production design participants that work in the various projects.

3 Knowledge Structure in the Extended Engineering

The structure of the information and consequently the formation of knowledge, as regards production design and deployment, was realised with the use of an ontology modelling and it was based on two main requirements:

- The model that will be used should have a very definite set of concepts including the relations between the concepts.
- The concepts should be as generic as possible in order to satisfy possible differences within the organisations in extended engineering.

These requirements are somewhat contradictory, since the greater the depiction of concepts, the lower the generic character of the model. Therefore, the modelling was performed on the basis of cases created by industry partners that served as Original

Equipment Manufacturers (OEM), production system Integrators and parts/ equipment suppliers.

3.1 Product-Process-Resource Model and Relevant Files

The Product, Process and Resource views are common terms in PLM systems and represent the different views that engineers have on CAx files during the production design execution. In the proposed platform, the first sets of concepts of the Product-Process-Resource (PPR) include the modelling of the actual digital, production planning related data. The main concepts here are Product, Process and Resource. The modelling of these concepts derives from the higher level structures of relevant files, used by commercial CAx products and STEP Part 21, at the extent of their being considered consistent with each other. The selection of the CAx tools was based on questionnaires, delivered both to OEMs and SMEs, as well as a production system integrator. The lower levels of the structures were not used since there were inconsistencies between the different CAx products' file structures. In cases that information from the lower levels of a file's structure needs to be extracted, e.g. for the identification of process times from a CAM file, this can be done through the parsing of files or the direct input by the user of the relevant attribute values through a Graphical User Interface.

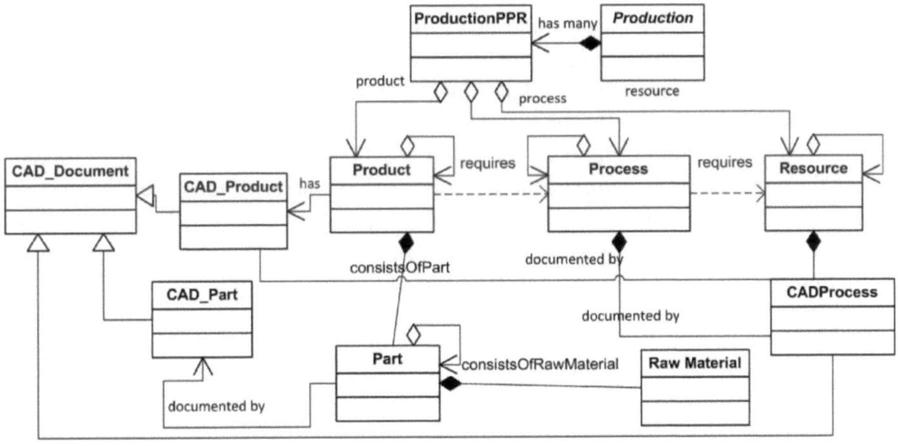

Fig. 2. Product-Process-Resource model

The product data have their own structure that links them to the part data with a simple object relation. The processes can also be depicted as a CAx file, while the resource files are also described as product data through a simple "*has*" relation. The relevant data objects are not only CAx files. Therefore, a special concept named *DesignDataObject,* was defined as shown in the figure below. The specific components of this concept represent documents, spreadsheets and files, relevant to one or more tasks of the design process and the creation of various documentations.

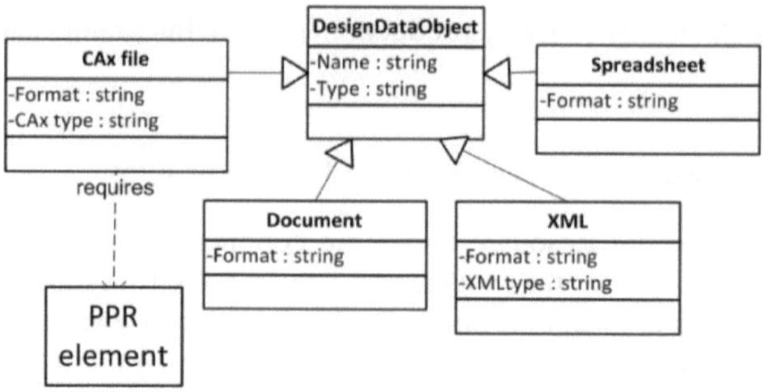

Fig. 3. Design data objects' structure

The specific concept also includes XML files that can be manufacturing related, such as machine controller programs (e.g. PLCopen XML format) or they can express process sequences or even support business processes such as tendering (selection of suppliers).

3.2 Workflow and Human Resources

This section describes the main concepts that are related to project workflow management and human resources. The term *human resources* here is used to describing the relevant actors participating in the design of a production system. The main concept, regarding project workflow management, is the *Project Element*, which has as subclasses the project, the phases and tasks of a certain project. The project individuals coming from the *Project* subclass serve as a reference that lasts throughout the design and deployment phases. The data attributes can be filled in through a web-application that works by means of collecting all the initial specifications for the design project (e.g. by an OEM to the Integrator). Each project element is linked to another through relations, namely the *hasTask* or *hasPhase*. When a new project concept is created, the individuals of the *Phase* concept are already set: Planning Process/ Layout, Planning of tools and equipment, Line balancing, Specification of tools & equipment, Purchasing of equipment, Realisation/Ramp up.

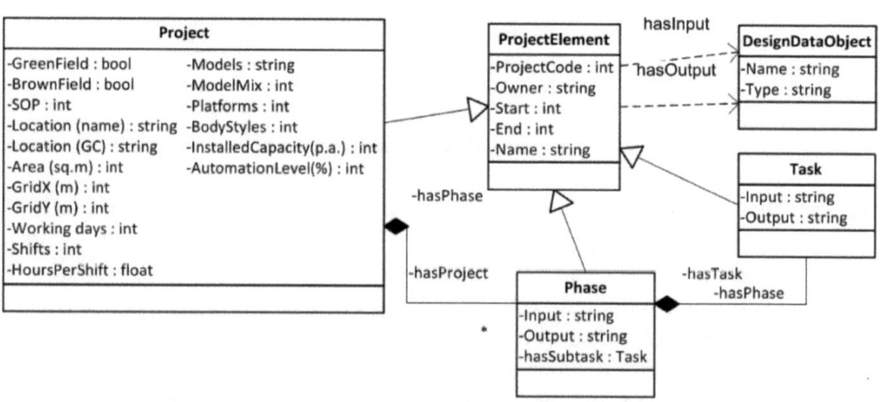

Fig. 4. Project elements' concept

The tasks of each phase can also be copied from the previous versions on the basis of similarity measurements, regarding the initial specifications of the project. Each Project element is linked to one or more Design data object(s) (described in the previous section) through relations such as *hasInput* and *hasOutput*. Therefore, the workflow also represents a data flow in the sense of certain files, required as input or output from each phase.

As regards human resources, the main concept connecting people to tasks is that of the *Role* (Figure 5). Each person is inserted into the platform as an *Actor*, a concept which includes information with reference to a person's experience and background. At each time instance of the project, the information about a person's involvement in the project is described. Furthermore, the most relevant people that can fit in a role can be identified by simple queries that can be performed by SW agents. In the following section, the technological implementation that allows the mapping and the data exchange between the central ontology and the local data bases of the project's stakeholders is presented.

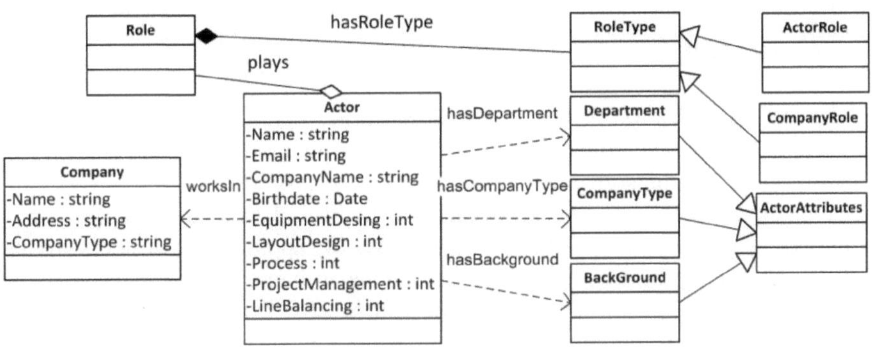

Fig. 5. Human resource model

4 Knowledge Base Mapping

Although the models presented fulfil the requirements of the end users, the elements that represent the actual files, used by engineers, should be somehow linked to the locations of the actual data. This section describes the way that the ontology elements' structure described in section 3.1 can be mapped to the local database structures of the

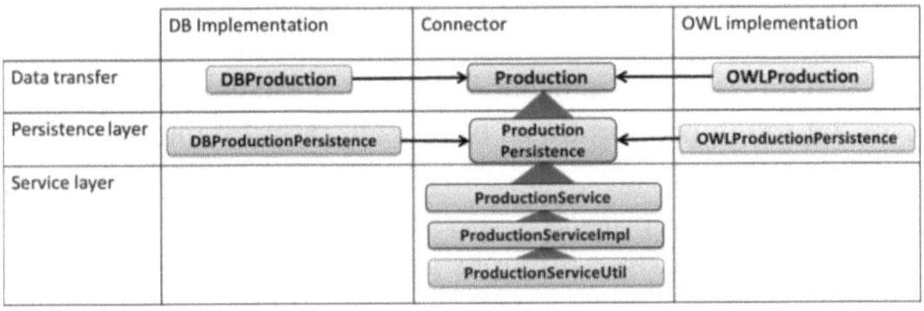

Fig. 6. Knowledge base mapping

various stakeholders, participating in a collaborative project. The knowledge base mapping refers to the linking of the corresponding elements and the data exchange between the central ontology and the local data bases of the project stakeholders.

The implementation is made through a middle step (Figure 6, Connector), in the Jena framework (Java). Via Jena, all the relevant ontology objects can be linked to the corresponding files in local data repositories. The persistence layer is the main link between the different objects, while the service layer is where different web-services and agents can interact with the ontology model and in the course of it with the relevant data attributes, files etc. Since the ontology describes a number of projects (complete and on-going), the relevant concepts are not used as they are, but are automatically recreated each time that a new project is set up. These concepts are included in separate OWL files, connected to the main ontology through uniform resource identifiers (URIs). This helps boost the editing, reading and reasoning functionalities of the model. The re-instantiated concepts include all the PPR models as well as the relevant tasks, roles etc.

5 Case Study

In order for the utilization of the proposed platform to be demonstrated, a case study is presented below. The actors belong to a system integrator that has been commissioned by an OEM to design a new line.

One of the platform's main functionalities is the use of web-based applications that can interact with the ontology. In this case study, the application considers the initial rough line balancing from an assembly line that has to be performed at the initial steps of the line balancing phase. The application can be provided as a link to the relevant actor that has the corresponding role. The application reads the ontology of the project and calculates the cycle time using data from the project's instance (individual). More specifically, the application automatically uses capacity, working days, shifts and working time per shift values (see Figure 4) and provides the value of the cycle time. Then, the user is requested to input the number of processes, including their expected times as well as any alternatives that derive from the use of different equipment. This can be done through a common web-based interface, where the information from the engineer is sent to the application through XML (Figure 7). Finally, the application forwards the results, which the user can either accept or try using different data, or even inform the relevant actors that the setup has to change (change request). In this case, the platform agents can inform the other participants of the change requests, by reasoning through the *hasInput* and *hasOutput* semantic relationships for the identification of the tasks that provide the input to this task, the relevant *Roles* and subsequently, the *Actors*.

Since, the initial rough process times have been inserted into the line's description, another actor can use the semantic repository available in order to identify appropriate equipment for the rest of the processes (e.g. electric screwdrivers). The platform uses a semantic Rule that groups from previous projects processes similar to the ones that

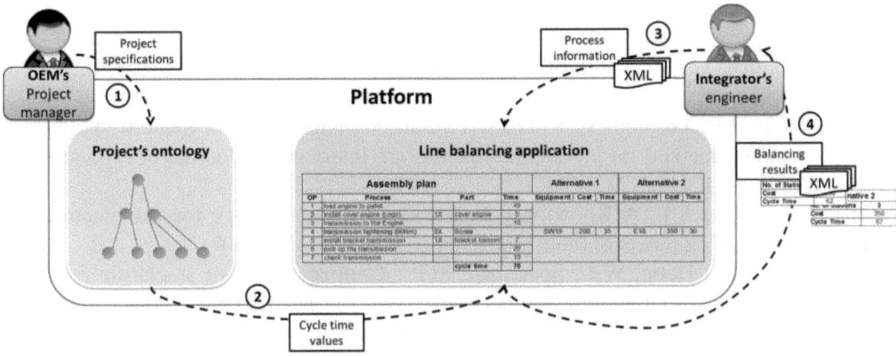

Fig. 7. Rough line balancing using the platform components

the user has defined based on their name (e.g. transmission tightening), the type (e.g. manual) along with their corresponding duration. After the grouping, a query that provides the resources belonging to the similar processes is executed. The engineer can now select the equipment that can be reused in the new project and automatically, the project's data including the line's cost are updated in the repository.

6 Conclusions

In this paper, there is a presentation of a collaborative platform that uses an ontology model for the description of different engineering files, business processes and human resources. The ontology serves as a communication layer between the different organisations, within extended engineering and can be handled by different SW agents as well as by engineering related web-based applications. The ontology is used not only as a representation of the engineering processes but also as a description and a mapping between engineering and business processes, which can be regarded as an extension of the current PLM approaches to production design. It is anticipated that this approach will enable the boosting of collaborative processes, including project management and data exchange between different stakeholders. Furthermore, the ontology can be used for the storage of knowledge with reference to certain business and engineering processes that can be identified by SW agents in new projects. Possible challenges that should be addressed in the future are the access rights management, concerning files shared by different companies as well as the support for the exchange of open standards by commercial CAx tools. Moreover, ontology related technologies need to be further evolved as regards their integration with various database technologies. Incorporating human-centred interface technologies, such as Augmented and Virtual Reality into the platform and expanding the business processes could be two very interesting paths to be explored in a future study.

Acknowledgments. This study was partially supported by the IP project Know4Car/ FoF-ICT-2011.7.4 - 284602, funded by the European Commission in the 7th Framework Programme.

References

[1] Chryssolouris, G.: Manufacturing Systems: Theory and Practice, 3rd edn. Springer, New York (2006)

[2] Yoshimura, M., Yoshida, S., Konishi, Y., Izui, K., Nishiwaki, S., Inamori, Y., et al.: A rapid analysis method for production line design. International Journal of Production Research 44(6), 1171–1192 (2006)

[3] Khan, A., Day, A.J.: A Knowledge Based Design Methodology for manufacturing assembly lines. Computers & Industrial Engineering, 441–467 (2002)

[4] Donohue, K.L., Hopp, W.J., Spearman, M.L.: Optimal design of stochastic production lines: a dynamic programming approach. IIE Transactions, 891–903 (2002)

[5] Han, M.-S., Park, D.-J.: Performance analysis and optimization of cyclic production lines. IIE Transactions, 411–422 (2002)

[6] Martínez, F., Bedia, L.: Modular simulation tool for modelling JIT manufacturing. International Journal of Production Research, 1529–1547 (2002)

[7] Hsieh, T.S.-J.: Hybrid analytic and simulation models for assembly line design and production planning. Simulation Modelling Practice & Theory, 87–108 (2002)

[8] Alexopoulos, K., Makris, S., Xanthakis, V., Chryssolouris, G.: A Web-Services oriented workflow management system for integrated production engineering. In: Proc. of the 43rd CIRP Int. Conf. on Manuf. Sys., p. 351 (2010)

[9] Wang, L., Keshavarzmanesh, S., Feng, H.-Y., Buchal, R.O.: Assembly process planning and its future in collaborative manufacturing: a review. The International Journal of Advanced Manufacturing Technology, 132–144 (2009)

[10] Zha, X.F., Dub, H.: Knowledge-intensive collaborative design modeling and support. Part I: Review, distributed models and framework. Computers in Industry, 39–55 (2006)

[11] Chandrasegaran, S.K., Ramani, K., Sriram, R.D., Horváth, I., Bernard, A., Harik, R.F., Gao, W.: The evolution, challenges, and future of knowledge representation in product design systems. Computer-Aided Design, 204–228 (2013)

[12] Daaboul, J., Cunha, C.-D., Bernard, A., Laroche, F.: Design for mass customization: Product variety vs. process variety. CIRP Annals - Manufacturing Technology 60, 169–174 (2011)

A Knowledge Management Approach through Product Lifecycle Management Implementation: An Industrial Case Study

Ricardo Mejía-Gutiérrez, Carolina Marroquín, and Juan David Giraldo-Gomez

Design Engineering Research Group (GRID), Universidad EAFIT. Medellín, Colombia
rmejiag@eafit.edu.co

Abstract. During new product development, knowledge must be exchanged across organizational, geographical, cultural, and language barriers [1]. Emerging technologies such as Product Lifecycle Management (PLM) combined with Business Process Modelling (BPM) tools provide means to enable collaboration among distributed participants specifically in the product design process. In this paper, an alternative approach for planning and development of projects that requires knowledge management and information integration in small and medium enterprises, is presented. A case study in the Architecture Engineering and Construction (AEC) industry is performed and, as a result, the methodology is applied to support the design and construction of waste treatment plants. Finally, the design of the proposed approach is presented including how engineering processes were identified, analyzed and improved through BPM and PLM.

Keywords: Product Lifecycle Management, Business Process Modelling, Knowledge Management, Industrial implementation.

1 Introduction

Increasing market demands has forced companies to take into account Knowledge Management (KM) during the complete product lifecycle [2] but they present issues such as disjointed processes and lacking in automation. In addition, organizations are trying to get their senior engineers to write more significant guidelines, best practices and design manuals [3] in order to preserve company´s knowledge and know-how, but as it should be exchanged, it creates high potential to failure [4]. On the other hand, there is a need to combine human-based and computer-based methods and tools for KM and Product Lifecycle Management (PLM) [5]. However, computer-based tools for KM only improve part of the knowledge exchange in a company, being necessary to implement methodologies that not only allows access to knowledge, but integrates PLM, Business Process Modelling (BPM) and Business Process Re-Engineering (BPR).

PLM aims to maximize the value of current and future products for both customers and stakeholders [6], but companies will fail to exploit PLM advantages, without a correct understanding of PLM. It is necessary to incorporate business process understanding, in order to fully implement a PLM strategy. With this purpose, an integrated

A. Bernard, L. Rivest, and D. Dutta (Eds.): PLM 2013, IFIP AICT 409, pp. 277–286, 2013.

approach is presented for project design and development applied in a Small and Medium Enterprise (SME) from the Architecture Engineering and Construction (AEC) sector, using a novel PLM implementation strategy and considering mechanisms that offer high potential for developing countries. The case study aims to impact knowledge capture and transfer and project efficiency in the company´s New Product Development (NPD) process [1].

2 Background

KM is an organizational strategy that seeks to structure, formalize and define the proper manner to capitalize, manage and exploit the intellectual assets of an organization [7][8]. The understanding of knowledge as a company resource has become of great interest in recent years [9][10]. The ability to constantly harness company knowledge creates competitive advantages for organizations due to the increase of high quality developments and efficient processes performance. In a project base, task oriented industry such as the AEC case, these benefits are achieved through the proper use of tools, methods and techniques to capture, re-use and produce knowledge as a result of constant project analysis and feedback.

The multidisciplinary groups involved in design, construction and assembly activities demand efficient planning, programming and execution under low margin profits and strict time constrains demanded by clients. Usually the knowledge captured is related to the consolidation of lessons learned after project conclusion and during post project evaluation [11]. Although this information may be stored, it is usually ruled out in new developments due to the lack of effective frameworks for knowledge reuse and communication. As a result corporative knowledge is not suitable for real use.

The engineering process planning can be restructured through the use of BPR. This method seeks to improve process efficiency, reduce project development cycles and include the extended enterprise into the company's perception. It is achieved through the definition of the initial AS-IS and TO-BE analysis of the company's process (step 1), the new solution is physically built (step 2) and then tested in a pilot environment before the final implementation (step 3) [12]. Allowing access to knowledge requires integration of BPM with methods and tools such as PLM that incorporate an understanding of business processes and facilitate knowledge transfer.

Product Lifecycle Management (PLM) is a strategy developed to manage the product life cycle, from generating an idea, concept description, business analyzes, product design, solution architecture and technical implementation, to the successful entrance to the market, service, maintenance and innovative product improvement, through the management of intellectual capital that is generated around it, in the extended enterprise, by integrating people, processes and resources supported by an organizational culture that can be supported on a technological platform [13][14][15][6].

PLM has been proposed to be used as a KM tool [16][17], as it offers the possibility of capturing domain specific knowledge, such as product development and fabrication knowledge [3].

3 PLM Implementation Methodology

The proposed methodology is an alternate approach for design and development of projects that requires KM and information integration in SME. The implementation team decides to use two different approaches towards knowledge capture, distribution and communication. (1) The use of IT tools may be an option to capture implicit knowledge manage it, communicate it and re-use it. (2) The use of people-centered techniques such as interviews and group sessions may contribute to the implicit knowledge capture and facilitate the communication of tacit knowledge.

In the AEC industry engineering, knowledge is mainly generated from: (1) technical specifications that define and constraint the work subject, (2) technological knowledge, (3) knowledge that is generated during the project's development, and (4) re-use of engineering performed on similar projects already completed.

To capture both implicit and tacit knowledge a close understanding of the processes and the operational information is necessary. An integration of a loosely coupled PLM environment is proposed to support the design and construction processes. PLM includes processes, organization (people), information, tools and software [18]. Each of these elements is approached in different ways:

- Processes are modelled through workflows or Work-Breakdown-Structure (WBS). Workflows define a sequence of activities that must be performed in a specific order. Here we aim to model internal knowledge representation of the operational processes that conforms the core business.
- Organization is approached involving the entire organizational structure from technical engineers to CEO and managers.
- Information is captured in documents, which are digitally stored allowing speeding up the search and retrieval processes.
- Tools and software are considered, especially, open source tools that minimize costs, licenses fees and deployment time. It is important to clarify that the software in this project is a decision-making supporting tool.

PLM is used to communicate knowledge throughout the organization and during all the stages where a product is involved. The status of each document is reflected during its entire lifecycle. This means that each document, and thus, the information and knowledge gathered, is accessible at any time, allowing not only knowledge generation through document creation, but also knowledge transmission. As a result, data, information, and knowledge are integrated within the PLM. One important aspect is that information is centralized, thus, having an overview of the whole process and facilitating the access to knowledge.

Finally, PLM is used in knowledge communication integrating information storage/retrieving, decision-making support and organization involvement during the core business processes. The previously exposed elements may be integrated through four stages: 1) *Discerning knowledge*: In order to capture the existent knowledge, people centered methodologies such as interviews and works sessions must be executed. These methods allow the proper understanding of the aspects involved in the knowledge usage to achieve a successful project development. 2) *Consolidation*: Involves the understanding and analysis of AS-IS processes and the creation of an improved TO-BE process through BPR methodology. In addition, the use of BPM tools implies the integration of the process captured information in a graphic model that facilitates the understanding of engineering processes; such representation improves the visualization and logical analysis of all concepts and factors involved in the process providing suggestions and improvements to the AS-IS processes. 3) *Transformation*: The BPM models were implemented in the PLM software using workflows and WBS, along with the related working methods applied in the company. This open source technology results the perfect means to store and manage the integrated Knowledge Information and Data (KID) regarding product design, manufacturing process and production capabilities, specifically for collaborative process planning tasks[19]. 4) *Use*: Although the software provides the means to communicate information, it only becomes knowledge through usage. The creation of forms and instructive documents to store the information should carry a common standard so they can be found and retrieved.

PLM is used as the main mechanism for knowledge transfer, i.e. project members can share common representations (e.g. CAD drawings and 3D visualizations) facilitating cohesion and tight coupling [20].

4 Case Study

The presented methodology has been applied within an ACE SME to support the design and construction of waste treatment plants. Identified difficulties regarding the low profit margins of the project developments seem to focus attention on improving project profitability. Also, constant difficulties regarding delivery time constrains demanded by customers were reported. Moreover, the company did not have standardized processes or better practices implementation. The increased need for KM methods came from the constant re-work done by engineers, the repetitive mistakes unsolved by the absent historical information and the willingness to gather all the exclusive implicit knowledge that provide them with competitive advantages.

Considering the company's investment constrains, ARAS PLM Open source software [21][22] was chosen to promote the distribution and communication of knowledge between project members. Also to determine a KM approach, the necessity of understanding the working methods and the engineering activity sequences involved in the company's processes was a priority. The implementation of a BPR method and Aris express BPM tool [23] were chosen to create the process models.

The knowledge capture resulted in the complete definition of the AS-IS model. It comprises the core engineering process of the organization and the identification of the complete operational information regarding approvals, interactions, role profiles and current documents. The findings were presented in a process model generated with ARIS Express using Event-driven Process Chain (EPC) diagrams. Each stage was detailed and analyzed in order to (1) ensure activity sequences coherency, with their associated subsequent events (2) fill the gaps with possible best practices and (3) eliminate those activities that had no value in the process. In addition, the complete operational information regarding approvals, interactions, role profiles and current documents was identified (see Fig 1).

The application of BPR methodology has foreseen five core AS-IS processes in waste treatment plant design. Two of them are related to design activities and three of them are related to the execution of construction an assembly. Learning occurs in every day operations or in specific critical events of these stages. The results gathered from the BPM modelling were submitted for analysis in order to find weaknesses and mistakes in the sequence of activities generated for each process and create a new model (TO-BE). This analysis was done through the evaluation of activity value, criticality, cost, time and complexity. The results show that:

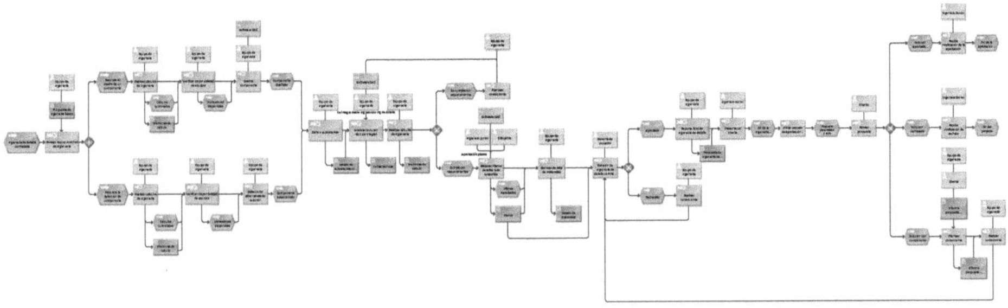

Fig. 1. EPC diagram

- Although the process was suitable, some of the identified activities were not correctly performed or done at all, interrupting the proper performance of the projects. There was not existing information to ensure how many times were done and how many times were neglected due to the lack of historical performance indicators.
- Out of the 92 identified activities only 34 had consistent records, meaning that 64% of the process occurred without keeping any associated documents. Moreover, the small amount of resulting records, lack of information standards and conventions, and the company had no instructive documents or manuals indicating the proper execution of complex tasks to ensure successful outcomes of the activities. The revisions were often made by engineers, the participation of other roles such as lawyers, accountants and commercial agents was absent from the decision making process even when the legal and cost related decisions were crucial to ensure delivery within requirements, hence the planning process may be inconsistent and the construction an assembly stages may present multiple corrective actions.

The PLM implementation identified six core TO-BE engineer processes for Project development in the AEC industry. Three processes belong to the design stage; two belong to the construction stage, a delivery process occur at the end of each process as well. The use of EPC diagrams allowed the business unit members to define the activity sequences, the responsible roles; the events and the inputs and outputs necessary to develop the activities. The diagrams prove to be efficient in providing visualization and understanding on processes regardless of the participant's knowledge area. The BPR methods proved to be particularly compatible with the needs of the PLM software. Most of the methods outcomes supported the PLM software modules. The identification of roles, participants, events, items and, state of those items within the core processes were suitable to customize the PLM modules.

The deployment of the PLM software involved the following steps: (1) selection of the tool, in this case, Aras Innovator was selected due to its free availability as an open source software that is based on a service-oriented architecture. (2) Process modelling: For each process identified with BPM, a workflow was defined and modelled in Aras innovator including the activities, assignees and tasks. For each workflow, the lifecycle and permissions of each item were defined. (3) Modules implementation: Different modules were used in the implementation such as project scheduling and document management. The result is a data structure represented in PLM that let users associate members with activities, components and documents. Additionally, a structure expressed through variety of relationships such as project structure, activity structure and data structure was created (see Fig 2). (4) KM: mechanisms to assist in searches were defined, adding value to existing knowledge and data collected. Also, mechanisms for finding, collecting, aggregating and displaying information were defined (e.g. forms).

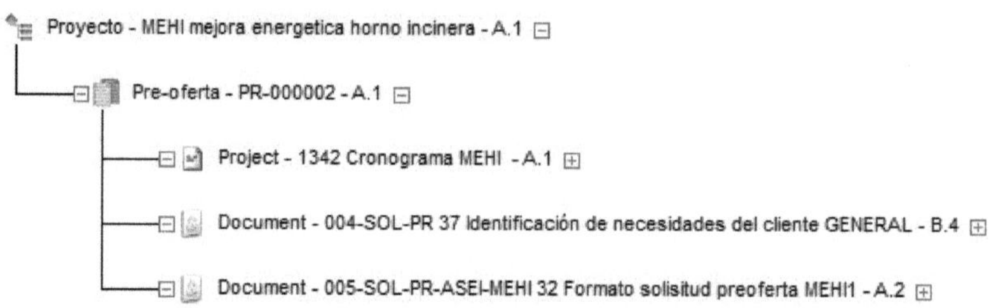

Fig. 2. Structure of a project

The autoclaving project (AYSA) began in February first 2013 with a Pre-Offer process. The objective of this process is to respond to a project request. This particular process included the participation of a project manager responsible of supervising a senior engineer and a junior engineer. It also involved some other roles of the company such as environmental engineer and a lawyer intervention due to the contractual responsibilities in which the customer and the company were involved. The workflow was initiated as soon as the project manager received an official request, accordingly, a set of automated activities were set in motion in the explained order (1) request reception (2) request evaluation, i.e. rejection or approval of request (3) request development (4) request final evaluation (5) request delivery to customer as shown in Fig 3.

The request was approved by an internal committee meeting and the project manager sent the approved decision through the software automatically enabling the activity of "request development", the senior engineer created the project schedule with its assignments as shown in Fig 4. The project schedule module was set with 35 activities, a notification alert was immediately sent to each project member with its corresponding assigned activity and the time range given to notify the activity completion.

The completion is mandatory, if a project member fails to fulfill the activity in the system the project will fall behind and so will the activities linked to it. Thus, the project schedule shows a real time execution of the project activities. Soon the engineers

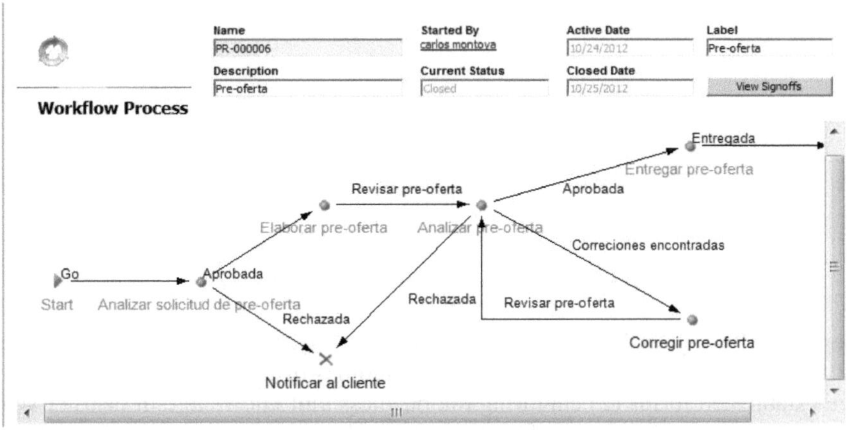

Fig. 3. Process implementation in PLM

started to focus on the deadlines of the automated activities and the visualization of the project advance, making their own initiatives to ensure the activity completion.

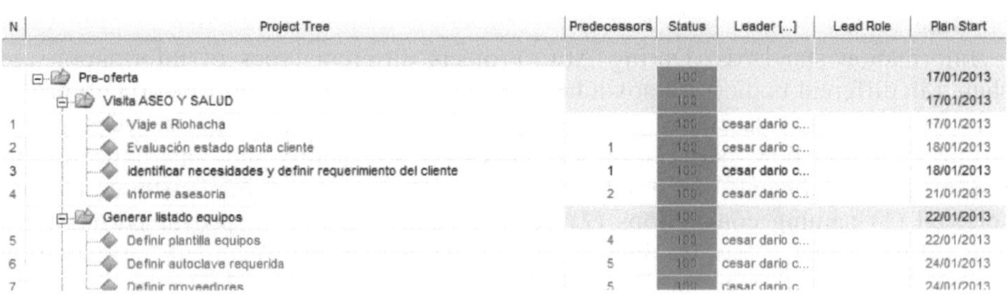

N	Project Tree	Predecessors	Status	Leader [...]	Lead Role	Plan Start
	Pre-oferta		100			17/01/2013
	Visita ASEO Y SALUD		100			17/01/2013
1	Viaje a Riohacha		100	cesar dario c...		17/01/2013
2	Evaluación estado planta cliente	1	100	cesar dario c...		18/01/2013
3	identificar necesidades y definir requerimiento del cliente	1	100	cesar dario c...		18/01/2013
4	Informe asesoria	2	100	cesar dario c...		21/01/2013
	Generar listado equipos		100			22/01/2013
5	Definir plantilla equipos	4	100	cesar dario c...		22/01/2013
6	Definir autoclave requerida	5	100	cesar dario c...		24/01/2013
7	Definir proveedores	5	100	cesar dario c...		24/01/2013

Fig. 4. AYSA project completion

The project manager changed his working methods to include daily check-outs on the project advance. A total of 33 documents were created 100% of them were properly named. The solution was delivered to the customer after being approved by consensus. The Pre-Offer was successfully closed after 46 days Fig 5, all process records remain in the PLM software accessible to all business unit members but restricted for modification due to the closed state of the process. The familiarization with the software took at list 3 month of usage, 40 training hours and 180 follow up hours were spend during 6 months to ensure optimal usage of the software.

The workflow and project activities are linked to the capture, transfer and use of knowledge. A great deal of information must be managed in the business process. Before the implementation the business unit members had addressed a number of issues regarding information management. The methodology and objectives suggested for the implementation solve the pending issues; BPR methods provide a clear understanding of the information flow and the interactions between participants. The findings were customized in the PLM software as follows:

Workflow History Report

Item: PR-000005 AYSA | Pre-oferta | Current Status is: Closed
Started By: cesar dario cock lara | Started On: 01/02/2013 11:54:53 a.m. | Completed On: 20/03/2013 11:46:53 a.m.

Activity	State	Assigned To	Completed By	How Voted	When	Comments
Recibir solicitud	Closed	cesar dario cock lara	cesar dario cock lara	Analizar	01/02/2013 12:27:49 p.m.	Se programa comité para enterarios de la visita a la empresa Aseo y Salud
Analizar solicitud	Closed	Gerentes de Proyectos	carlos montoya	Delegate	01/02/2013 12:34:00 p.m.	
Analizar solicitud	Closed	cesar dario cock lara	cesar dario cock lara	Aprobada	01/02/2013 03:29:03 p.m.	
Elaborar pre-oferta	Closed	cesar dario cock lara	cesar dario cock lara	Revisar pre-oferta	19/03/2013 02:48:52 p.m.	
Analizar pre-oferta	Closed	Gerentes de Proyectos	carlos montoya	Delegate	19/03/2013 05:17:42 p.m.	
Analizar pre-oferta	Closed	cesar dario cock lara	cesar dario cock lara	Aprobada	20/03/2013 11:46:26 a.m.	
Entregar pre-oferta	Closed	cesar dario cock lara	cesar dario cock lara	Entregada	20/03/2013 11:46:53 a.m.	

Fig. 5. Workflow history report

Support information: The engineering activities often required regulatory proceeds; there was also interest on (1) ensuring the outcomes of the activities through the use of pre-established forms (2) capturing the business unit knowledge in instructive documents. The recompilation of information proved to be a long term task. 11 libraries were suggested for creation, 64% of those were created during the 11 months agreed for the implementation. The business unit members created 16 instructive documents, 39 forms, 3 Check list. Ensuring 100% supportive documents a 100% of knowledge capture for autoclaving plant design and construction, and providing a 64% improvement in project records compared to previous developed project within PLM strategy on place.

Information standards: During AEC projects different types of information are shared in different bodies of known how. From customer needs information, to protocols for equipment assembly and testing, information consistency is necessary to ensure the interactions between project stages and the quality and compliance of engineering developments. In order to control information the implementation team selected (1) naming conventions (2) version control and (3) approval permissions. The software kept a few versions of each development and recorded the evolution through a change history, in which each responsible person is also pointed out improving change management and document traceability. Information search went from hours to minutes. The projects developed previously in the business unit had no control over developments, the scenario in which the project manager was completely blind of project advance and information resulted in delays, overwork and non-compliance with customer requirements, issues that usually end in contractual difficulties and non profitable projects. The new scenario supported with PLM customized software provides real time information and demands deliverable revisions before presenting a solution to a client. The participants have at hand all the information of the evolution of the project for consulting and validation.

The information however is more efficiently used if classified in an autonomous way as an indicator. Direct information may be extracted from it percentage of detected failures and project metrics are still unavailable for measurement due to the long term developments of the industry.

5 Conclusions

PLM strategy and BPR methodology were successfully integrated inside the engineering unit of an AEC industry. The corporative knowledge was captured and the engineering processes were identified, analyzed and improved through BPR methodology, also the use of BPM tools allowed the visual understanding of process components and interactions and provides an organized way to properly introduce the combine elements into the PLM software modules.

The standardization of working methods and document management procedures and conventions allowed the creation of a common language for the multi-project team. In addition, proper distribution and communication of knowledge were executed through the PLM collaborative configuration. The integration resulted in proper capture, storage, distribution and communication of knowledge throughout the organization. Although the PLM Software prove to be an asserted IT tool to store, distribute and communicate explicit knowledge, it is also evident that the tacit knowledge shared between interviews and work sessions performed to discern engineering process in this case study, enhanced the personal knowledge of each company member. Strategies to share this tacit knowledge must be also implemented in the company to capitalize the experience of the employees in their combine working areas.

In this paper, an implementation methodology for new product development was shown. This approach uses emerging technologies such as PLM and BPM combined with KM that help reduce communication glitches among project members. BPR was used to identify best practices and processes that would enable companies to increase their control over product development and defining key project milestones and deliverables. PLM systems can contribute in different ways, such as retention of the knowledge, enhancement of project and process reuse and quality improvement through standardization [3].

Acknowledgements. This research has been by the Colombian Administrative Department of Science and Technology (Colciencias) trough grant number 1216-502-27393. The research team also acknowledges the company´s engineering staff for their commitment to the project.

References

1. Merminod, V., Rowe, F.: How does PLM technology support knowledge transfer and translation in new product development? Transparency and boundary spanners in an international context. Information and Organization 22(4), 295–322 (2012)
2. Kiritsis, D., Nguyen, V.K., Stark, J.: How closed-loop PLM improves Knowledge Management over the complete product lifecycle and enables the factory of the future. International Journal of Product Lifecycle Management 3(1), 54–77 (2008)
3. Briggs, H.C.: Knowledge management in the engineering design environment. In: 47th AIAA/ASME/ASCE/AHS/ASC Structures, Structural Dynamics, and Materials Conference, Newport, Rhode Island, May 1-4 (2006)
4. Bjørn, P., Ngwenyama, O.: Virtual team collaboration: building shared meaning, resolving breakdowns and creating translucence. Information Systems Journal 19(3), 227–253 (2008)

5. Probst, G., Raub, S., Romhardt, K.: Knowledge Management. Utilization of Company's most Valuable Resource (Wissen managen. Wie Unternehmen ihre wertvollste Ressource optimal nutzen). 2. Aufl. Frankfurt Allgemeine Zeitung GmbH. Gabler Verlag, Frankfurt/Main, Wiesbaden (1998)
6. Stark, J.: Product lifecycle management: 21st century paradigm for product realisation. Springer (2011)
7. Carrillo, P., Chinowsky, P.: Exploiting knowledge management: The engineering and construction perspective. Journal of Management in Engineering 22(1), 2–10 (2006)
8. Webb, S.P.: Knowledge management: linchpin of change. ASLIB the Association for Information Management, London (1998)
9. Forcada, M.N., Fuertes Casals, A., Gangolells Solanellas, M., Casals Casanova, M., Macarulla Martí, M.: Knowledge management perceptions in construction and design companies (2012)
10. Hamid, Z.A., Kamar, K.A.M., Kissi, J., Dainty, A., Liu, A., Chun, C.K., ...Ling, F.Y.Y.: Construction Innovation: Information, Process, Management. Construction Innovation 12(1), 4–10 (2012)
11. Orange, G., Burke, A., Boam, J.: The facilitation of cross organisational learning and knowledge management to foster partnering within the UK construction industry. Paper Presented at the Proc., 8th European Conf. on Information Systems (2000)
12. Bertoni, M., Bordegoni, M., Cugini, U., Regazzoni, D., Rizzi, C.: PLM paradigm: How to lead BPR within the Product Development field. Computers in Industry 60(7), 476–484 (2009)
13. CIMDATA, PLM - Empowering the Future of Business. CIM Data Report (2002)
14. Grieves, M.: Product lifecycle management: driving the next generation of lean thinking. McGraw-Hill (2006)
15. Pol, G., Merlo, C., Legardeur, J., Jared, G.: Implementation of collaborative design processes into PLM systems. International Journal of Product Lifecycle Management 3(4), 279–294 (2008)
16. Gecevska, V., Buchmeister, B., Anisic, Z., Lalic, B.: Product lifecycle management with knowledge management as strategic approach for innovative enterprise environment
17. Raza, M., Kirkham, T., Harrison, R., Reul, Q.: Knowledge Based Flexible and Integrated PLM System at Ford. Journal of Information & Systems Management 1(1), 8–16 (2011)
18. Ameri, F., Dutta, D.: Product lifecycle management: closing the knowledge loops. Computer-Aided Design & Applications 2(5), 577–590 (2005)
19. Siller, H., Estruch, A., Vila, C., Abellan, J., Romero, F.: Modeling workflow activities for collaborative process planning with product lifecycle management tools. Journal of Intelligent Manufacturing 19(6), 689–700 (2008)
20. Yoo, Y., Boland, R.J., Lyytinen, K.: From organization design to organization designing. Organization Science 17(2), 215–229 (2006)
21. Arascorp, Advanced PLM Solutions Next Generation PLM Platform (2011), http://www.aras.com/getting-started/white-papers.aspx (May 18, 2012)
22. ArasCorp, Aras website (2012), http://www.aras.com/ (December 13, 2012)
23. Software AG, Aris express (2012), http://www.ariscommunity.com/aris-express (August 12, 2012)

Proposal of a Knowledge-Based Engineering Methodology for Mass Customization

Kiyan Vadoudi[1] and Sergio Terzi[2]

[1] Politecnico di Milano, Milano, Italy
[2] University of Bergamo, Bergamo, Italy
kiyan.vadoudi@mail.polimi.it, sergio.terzi@unibg.it

Abstract. The proposed methodology aims to tackle Mass Customization (MC) from a knowledge management perspective and attempts to propose a systematic framework to implement and modify the process of MC, based on best practice with storing the data as experiences, customer behaviors and data related to a specific product family. This process is the result of providing support and appropriate automation of repetitive and routine design tasks to perform multi-disciplinary activities. The forces of the proposed methodology are its ease to use, providing a consistency process of developing and maintaining Knowledge-Based Engineering (KBE) methodology for implementing MC and reduction in lead-time and cost in the design process. A first tentative application made in the apparel industry of the methodology is also reported.

Keywords: Knowledge management, Knowledge-Based Engineering, Mass Customization.

1 Introduction

In today's rapidly changing and globalizing markets the traditional mass production paradigm is not possible to support high variety of customer needs. In this context, Mass Customization (MC) [1],[2] appeared as a new paradigm representing the trend towards the production of highly variant products under mass production time and cost conditions. Key enablers for implementing a MC strategy [3], from one side are advanced manufacturing systems – which allows the provision of customer-individual products using flexible production processes – and on the other side is the availability of rapid design and development processes for creating highly product and service variants.

In this context, this paper proposes a methodology to tackle MC from a knowledge management perspective for reducing lead-times and costs in the design process. A first tentative application made in the apparel industry is also reported.

2 State of the Art

The nature of MC occurs in the product and service and the challenge is the ability to realize and capture hidden market niches and subsequently develop technical

A. Bernard, L. Rivest, and D. Dutta (Eds.): PLM 2013, IFIP AICT 409, pp. 287–294, 2013.

capabilities to meet the different types of needs for target customers. Understanding the latent market niches requires the exploration of customer needs. To encapsulate the needs of target customer groups means to imitate existing or potential competitors in quality, cost and quick response. Thus, the requirements of MC depend on a balance of three elements: (i) time-to-market / quick responsiveness, (ii) variety / customization and (iii) economy of scale for volume production efficiency [4].

The main stress of design for MC is to elevate the practice of designing individual products to design product families [4]. A product family is a set of products derived from a common platform which includes a set of variables, features or components that remain constant in a product platform / module and from product to product [5]. A modular design approach gives the capability to rapidly create a large number of product variants, generating a lot of diversified knowledge in short times.

For keeping the MC constrains, design knowledge should be managed in an efficient way, avoiding redundant design tasks and supporting the process of the knowledge creation, management, extraction and re-use. Knowledge management has a long history and related to World War II in order to build the fighter planes. That time, observes shown that building of second airplane took less time and less defects than the first one and this understanding about process of production was beginning to appear the concept of knowledge management. By the mid-1980s, the importance of knowledge as a competitive asset was apparent and by increasing the importance of organization's knowledge [6],[7], the concern emerged about dealing by growing up by the amount of available knowledge in organization.

The computer technology that cooperated so heavily to superabundance of information started to become part of the solution, in a variety of domains. nowledge-Based Engineering (KBE) is a combination of object-oriented programming, artificial intelligence, and computer aided design [8] in order to capture product and process information to allow businesses to model engineering processes, and then use the model to automate all or part of the process.

A number of methodologies are available to support the development of KBE applications and systems [9]. By far the most famous of these is the *Methodology and software tools Oriented to Knowledge-based engineering Applications*, or MOKA methodology [10],[11]. This methodology consists of six life-cycle steps (*Identify*, *Justify*, *Capture*, *Formalize*, *Activate* and *Delivery*), and it is supported by informal and formal models to take a project from beginning towards industrialization and actual use. KNOMAD (*Knowledge Nurture for Optimal Multidisciplinary Analysis and Design*) is another methodology to address the identified shortcomings of KBE [12], consisting of six steps: *Knowledge Capture*, *Normalization*, *Organization*, *Modeling*, *Analysis* and *Delivery*.

3 The Proposed Methodology

The global competitions in industries change manufactures' view in terms of contact with customer from a seller point of view to a buyer. Both changes from companies' side and changes in customers' needs, result in a drastic increase in the number of product variants and costs of production. Through these changes, companies are trying to stay in competitive atmosphere through making a modeled system for their production processes by introducing the platform concept [13], which changed production concept from no customizable products to modular products. Moreover, by recent development of IT technologies the possibility of using software-based product configuration systems [14] increased. These systems are supporting the process of customized product development by using the modules based on the customer's requirements. The proposed methodology uses the platform concept and tries to transfer the logic of no customizable products to the modular products in order to support different individual needs.

The proposed methodology includes seven steps (Fig.1) and each step is characterized from several subclasses to introduce the methodology as a general framework to implement for the process of MC.

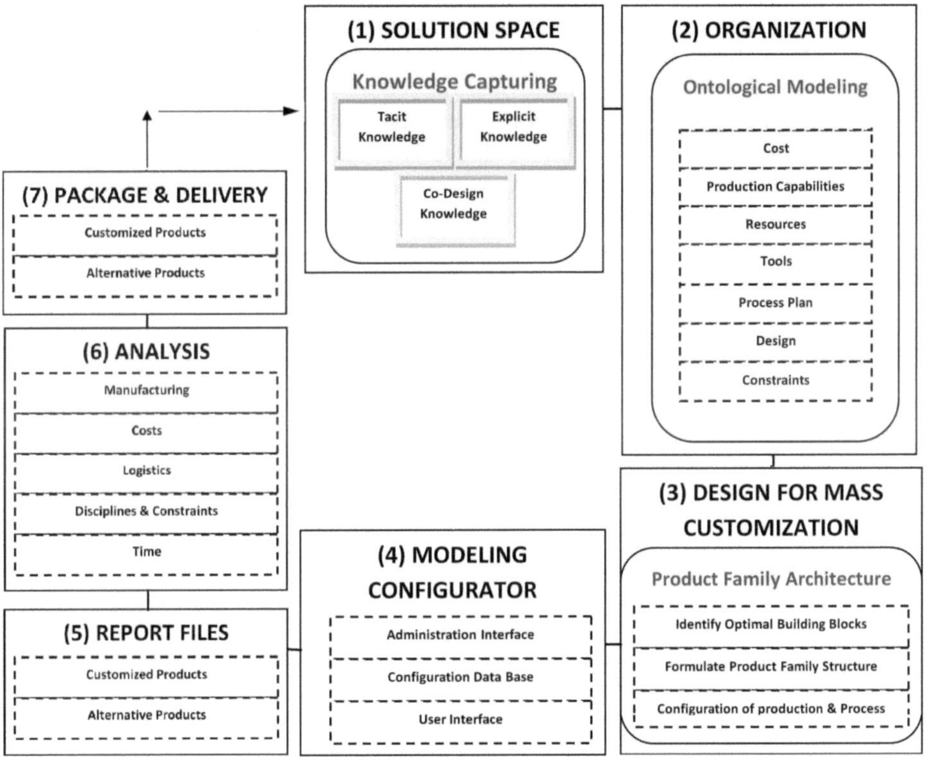

Fig. 1. Seven steps of Knowledge-Based engineering methodology in Mass Customization

The first step (*Solution Space*) includes the identification of the objectives, scope and assumptions about a specific project and the definition of the required knowledge sources. This phase includes three different types of knowledge: (i) *tacit knowledge*, (ii) *explicit knowledge* and (iii) *co-design knowledge* (the collaboration between customers and company):

- *Tacit knowledge*: most of the knowledge used in the design and development process is tacit [15]. Tacit knowledge typically is developed by trial and error in practices and intuitions. Judgment, values, beliefs, assumptions and subjective insights are examples of this knowledge.
  Explicit knowledge: this type of knowledge can be generally written down or otherwise documented (through print, electronic methods and other formal means), and then shared [16].
- *Co-design knowledge*: this knowledge is related to customer needs and co-design experiences, coming from customers' emotional connection with the product and purchasing process. *Physio*, *Socio*, *Psycho* and *Ideo* are four types of pleasure associated with products [17]. *Physio* pleasure related to the body and it is the feedback from sensory organs such as touch, taste, smell, etc. *Socio* pleasure is the result of connection with individual or groups that gives the feedback about owners view in society. *Psycho* pleasure is the emotional reaction result from cognitive interaction, and finally *Ideo* pleasure is taste, moral values and personal aspirations that define how people would like to be.

Solution Space acts as a container for these three types of knowledge, to be used in the process of MC. Each type of knowledge is extracted through the process that is using in the first three steps of MOKA methodology (*Identify*, *Justify* and *Capture*). In previous KBE methodologies, the knowledge container has included only tacit and explicit knowledge, while the proposed methodology adds the third co-design knowledge (Fig. 2) to consider changes in customer needs.

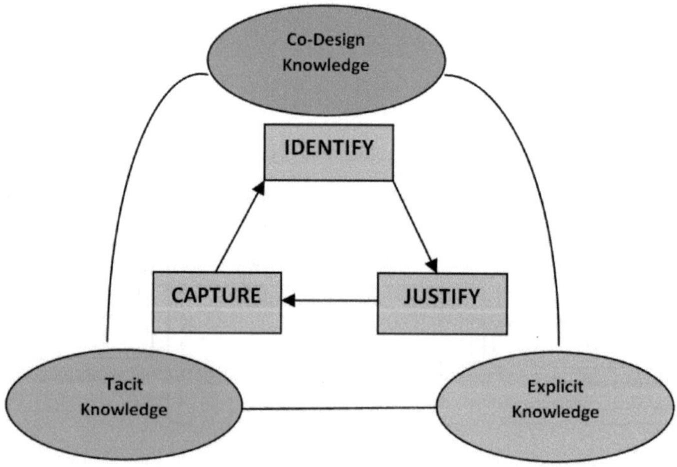

Fig. 2. Details about step one (Solution Space)

The second step (*Organization*) is a necessary step about knowledge utilization and organization in the process of modeling and analysis. The knowledge extracted through the first step should be provided in a way to give possibility to stakeholders to automatically access and retrieve the necessary knowledge. To do this, ontology can be used. Ontology forms a formalized knowledge structure through the use of concept definitions and interrelationships as expressed in axioms to support the instantiation of captured knowledge within the structure [12].

The third step is called *Design for Mass Customization*. To support customized product, a product family platform is required to characterize the different needs of customer by the process of Product Family Architecture (PFA). PFA means the underlying architecture of firm's product platform that various product can derived from basic product designs in order to satisfy different types of customer needs [13]. A good PFA provides a generic architecture to keep the variant forms of the same solution based on individual customer needs within a coherent framework and a good PFA development depends to the appropriate formulation of building blocks with paying attention to functional, behavioral and structural perspectives. Building block has two kinds of meaning, first a type of building blocks through modularity that means to decompose a system to modules and second for each module, various instances that shows certain similarity. Before starting to find the optimal building blocks, the information about current and future customs need should be evaluate to find the repeatability in design and fulfillment.

The fourth step of the methodology is *Modeling Configurator*. When a product line falls into catalog products, then a simple configurator is the best condition tool to minimize risk by accurate assessments of costs and profits about specific production before a project starts [18]. Generally, the framework of these configurators consists of an administration interface, a configuration database and an user interface. After the modeling step, the results from configurator must be published as a *Report File* to show the specification of finalized product in terms of technology, processes of production and functions. We can identify two kinds of report files: (i) data related to customized products(ii) data about alternative configuration models. The sixth step is the *Analysis*. There are different approaches to analyze the reports files and through them, DEE (Design Engineering Engine, [19]) could be a proper source for this section. The DEE methodology employs report files that contain the set of product and process models in order to use in detailed analysis modules. These modules calculate the design implications on a per-discipline basis. Manufacturability, disciplines and constraints, cost and logistics are four areas to analyze the models. The last step (*Package & Delivery*) of the methodology starts with a check for the solutions about customize, alternative and pure products versus the requirements specified at the beginning of the design process. If this study is accepted, the detailed analysis results and resource implication about three kinds of products could be delivered. The first step of proposed methodology in the process of knowledge capturing is a combination with three steps of MOKA methodology and the first step of KNOMAD methodology, but the sources of knowledge are different. In addition, the second step some similarities with the *Formalize* step in MOKA and the third step in KNOMAD. Furthermore, the *Analysis* step has some similarities with the fifth and the sixth steps of KNOMAD. Finally, step seven *Package & Delivery* is similar to MOKA steps *Package* and *Activate*.

4 Application Case

The following application case provides a practical implementation of the proposed methodology in apparel industry. The purpose is to validate the first step of the proposed methodology through providing three kinds of knowledge related to apparel industry to deal fast as possible with changes in consumers' needs and habits. Data are collected through two approaches. From one side analyzing various configurators that are using by different companies and from other side by a survey, which was answered by users and experts. *Fine Cotton*, *Nur Berlin*, *Custom Panties*, *Blume* and *Diejeans* are five companies selected to extract knowledge through their configurators with some clear differentiations to represent better the concept of knowledge extraction. The specific objective of this study is to identify the fundamental variables in apparel industry and use them to develop the building blocks, which are essential for the third step of the methodology.

In apparel industry there are different features such as material, body measurement, color, size, pocket shape for each product that are acting as various blocks. Assembling of these blocks with paying attention to the importance and consequences of each block in the process of configuration gives customized products. For example, based upon the analysis of five shirt manufactures' configurators, blocks are divided in two general categories as *Fit* and *Style* and each of these categories is divided to five blocks. In order to receive the most customized products, it is very important to implement the configuration process with all blocks that are prepared in each category. By the data extracted through survey about apparel characterizes, 81% of respondents believed that size range is the first and most important constraint about cloths and as a second constrain 73% answered fabric is important for them and only 58% believed that style is important. Diversity of colors by 37%, functionality 31% and weight 8% are in next grades. After this, the identified knowledge should be justified. Justification process has done paying attention to the sequence of block in terms of importance and use.

In this case, block *Size* is selected for justification process. One of the significant problems in apparel industry is the diversity of people sizes because of many different ethnic groups. Usually homogeneous populations are much easier to supply. For example in some countries such as Japan and Korea, only dozen sizes of people's apparel are typically needed. By comparison, people's clothing is developed and sold in categories for misses, juniors and petites with about eight to twelve sizes in each category. In addition to the issue of diversity, there are more issues such as the intermarriage and lifestyle changes, including eating habits and general fitness that producer should care about them. Product developers and buyers must be knowledgeable about the target population of the geographic area to which they market if they are to produce apparel that will fit their target customers. Sizing problem is common to all categories of clothing, including men's, women's and children's. For example in women's body measurements, the variations between the mature and general populations tended to occur only in the location and distribution of weight and shape. This separation of women body's shapes (in four domains) is the result of justification process and helps to reach accurate building blocks.

However, with paying attention to the point that body's size depends to ethnic groups, it should precise more. The next step will solve this problem to reach the final knowledge that exactly makes the nature of building blocks. These final blocks will be uses in step *Design for Mass Customization.*

5 Conclusions

Because of the MC's nature, it is important to find important factors of customization for different industries to realize and capture knowledge from hidden market niches and subsequently develops technical capabilities to meet the different types of needs for target customers. The proposed methodology has some advantages, both in terms of MC and KBE:

- In the proposed methodology, the process will repeat in a lifecycle mood and this opportunity will facilitate to find the optimal building blocks that plays critical role in design for MC.
- MC process starts with finding the customers individual needs and ending with fulfillment process targeting each particular customer. The proposed methodology also includes this important challenge about MC through step four.
- The most important step is knowledge re-use process. After the knowledge captured from internal and external sources, the knowledge will be used to model product family structure. In the process of modeling, sometime the product family will not change and this is exactly the time for reuse of previous captured knowledge.

The proposed methodology has some limitations and further researches are need:

- The validation process could be improved with more application.
- The development of the methodology should implement also other aspect of Mass Customization such as sale, cost, logistics etc.

References

1. Pine, B., Davis, S.: The New Frontier in Business Competition. Harvard Business School Press (1999) ISBN 0-87584-372-7
2. Felfernig, A.: Standardized Configuration Knowledge Representations as Technological Foundation for Mass Customization, University Klagenfurt (2007)
3. Ackoff, R.L.: From Data to Wisdom. Journal of Applies Systems Analysis 16, 3–9 (1989)
4. Ulrich, P.V., Anderson-Connell, L.J., Wu, W.: Consumer Co-Design of Apparel for Mass Customization. Journal of Fashion Marketing and Management 7, 98–412 (2003)
5. Meyer, M.H., Lehnerd, A.P.: The Power of Product Platforms, New York (1997)
6. Polanyi, M.: The logic of Tacit Inference. In: Grene, M. (ed.), pp. 138–158. University of Chicago Press, Chicago (1969)
7. Pan, S.L., Scarborough, H.: Knowledge Management in Practice, An Exploratory Case Study. Technology Analysis & Strategic Management 11(3) (1999)

8. Gupta, J., Sharma, S., Hsu, J.: Creating Knowledge Based Organizations (2004) ISBN 1-59140-162-3
9. Sandberg, M.: Knowledge Based Engineering In product Development, Department of Applied Physics and Mechanical Engineering, Lulea University of Technology (2003) ISSN 1402-1536
10. Stokes, M. (ed.): Managing Engineering Knowledge-MOKA. In: Methodology for Knowledge Based Engineering Application. ASME Press
11. Callot, M., Kneebone, S., Oldham, K., Murton, A., Brimble, R.: MOKA – A Methodology for Developing Knowledge Based Engineering Apllications (1998)
12. Curran, R., Verhagen, W.J.C., Van Tooren, M.J.L., Van der Laan, T.H.: A multidisciplinary Implementation Methodology for Knowledge-based Engineering, KNOMAD. Expert Systems with Applications, 7336–7350 (2010)
13. Kamali, N., Loker, S.: Mass customization: on-line consumer involvement in product design. Journal of ComputerMediated Communication 7(4) (2002)
14. Xuan, F.Z., Ram, D.S.: Platform-Based Product Design and Development, A Knowledge Intensive Support Approach. Manufacturing System Integration Division National Institute of Standards and Technology, Gaithersburg, MD 2089, USA (2006)
15. Blecker, T., Abdelkafi, N., Kreuter, G., Friedrich, G.: Product Configuration Systems, University of Klagenfurt, Universitätsstrasse 65-67, A 9020 Klagenfurt, Austria (2004)
16. Fulton, J., Pal, S.: Leveraging Tacit Knowledge in The New Product Development Process. ASAC, Toronto, Ontario (2005)
17. Sanchez, R.: "Tacit Knowledge" versus "Explicit Knowledge", Approaches to Knowledge Management Practice, Department of Industrial Economics and Strategy (2006)
18. Cooper, S., Fan, I., Li, G.: A Best Practice Guide – Achieving Competitive Advantage through Knowledge-based Engineering, Department of Trade and Industry, UK (1999)
19. La Rocca, G., Van Tooren, M.J.L.: Enabling Distributed Multidisciplinary Design of Complex Products, A Knowledge Based Engineering Approach. Journal of Design Research 5(3), 333–352 (2007)

Unified Taxonomy for Reference Ontology of Shape Features in Product Model

Ravi Kumar Gupta[1,2] and Balan Gurumoorthy[1]

[1] CPDM, Indian Institute of Science, Bangalore –560012, India
[2] Deptt. of Mechanical Engg., National Institute of Technology, Silchar – 788010, India
{rkg,bgm}@cpdm.iisc.ernet.in

Abstract. This paper presents a unified taxonomy of shape features. Such taxonomy is required to construct ontologies to address heterogeneity in product/shape models. Literature provides separate classifications for volumetric, deformation and free-form surface features. The unified taxonomy proposed allows classification, representation and extraction of shape features in a product model. The novelty of the taxonomy is that the classification is based purely on shape entities and therefore it is possible to automatically extract the features from any shape model. This enables the use of this taxonomy to build reference ontology.

Keywords: Product information exchange, Shape feature taxonomy, volumetric feature, Deformation feature, Free-form surface feature.

1 Introduction

In product development cycle, several applications and engineering domains come into play making the ability to exchange of product data with semantics very critical. With product development happening in multiple locations with multiple computer-based tools, automatic exchange of meaning associated with product data between these tools and domains becomes important.

Ontologies have been proposed to address the issue of interoperability as they are a 'shared and common understanding of a domain that can be communicated between people and computers' [1]. A first step in constructing an ontology is the identification of scope of the ontology [2] followed by definition of formal taxonomies in the different concepts/themes that constitute the ontology [3]. These taxonomies are then linked by forming relationships between concepts across the different taxonomies. Shape entities are one of the critical concepts in any product or engineering ontology. Presently either STEP AP or vocabularies from popular CAD packages are used [3].

This paper presents a unified taxonomy of shape features to enable interoperability of heterogeneous shape models encountered during the product lifecycle.

A. Bernard, L. Rivest, and D. Dutta (Eds.): PLM 2013, IFIP AICT 409, pp. 295–307, 2013.

Shape features in a product model are (i) volumetric, (ii) deformation and (iii) free-form surface features (FFSFs). Volumetric features are the features that are associated with addition or subtraction of volume i.e. manufacturing features, design features by volume addition and/or subtraction operations. Deformation features, on the other hand, are not associated with addition or subtraction of volume but are created by deformation of material as features in sheet-metal part or by forming of material as features in injection molded part. Free-form surface features (FFSFs) are the features that modify a free-form surface in a part model.

Paper [4] has reviewed shape features extraction techniques. Nalluri [5], Han [6], Subramani [7] and Bok and Mansor [8] have reviewed shape features taxonomies for volumetric features. Liu et al., [9], Sunil and Pande [10], Gupta and Gurumoorthy [11] and Kannan and Shunmugam [12] have reviewed shape features taxonomies for sheet metal features. Pernot et al., [13], Gupta and Gurumoorthy [14] and Bok and Mansor [8] have reviewed shape features taxonomies for free-form surface features. Table 1 summarises shape features considered in the classification schemes reported in the literature. The shape features which are not handled by these classification schemes are also presented in the table. Many classification and representation schemes for representation of features and feature extraction have been developed for volumetric features. There are some approaches for deformation features [9], [10], [11], [12], [15] and free-form surface features [14], [16], [17]. Current art in feature technology does not handle the different classes of features mentioned above in a single framework to arrive at a unified representation and taxonomy.

Current art in feature technology has separate classifications for volumetric, deformation and free-form surface features. A product has all these features and therefore it is very much required to have single taxonomy for all the shape features. The paper presents unified taxonomy which allows classification, representation and extraction of shape features in a product model. This can be used for establishing semantic equivalences of shape features across heterogeneous shape models using the ontology based on this taxonomy as a reference ontology.

Table 1. Comparison of shape feature classification schemes in literature

Research Work	*Classification scheme*	*Purpose*	*Shape features covered*	*Remarks*
Wilson and Pratt [18]	Taxonomy of features for solid modeling	Taxonomy for feature based modeling into solid modeling system	Volumetric features	Does not handle FFSFs and deformation features. Formal representation of volumetric features is not presented.
Nalluri [5]	Classification of volumetric features as DIF Features	Feature based modeling of form features	Volumetric features	Does not handle FFSFs and deformation features.
Poldermann and Horváth [19]	Classification of Freeform surface features	Surface-based design	FFSFs	Does not handle volumetric and deformation features. Formal representation of FFSFs is not presented.
Lipson and Shpitalni [15]	Features in sheet metal products	Euler operators for sheet metal products has been defined	Deformation features	Does not handle volumetric features and FFSFs.
Fontana, et al., [16]	Free Form Feature Taxonomy	Free Form Feature for aesthetic design	FFSFs	Does not handle volumetric and deformation features. Parameters are different for different features.
Liu et al., [9]	Features in sheet-metal parts	Recognizing deformation features in sheet-metal parts.	Deformation features	Does not handle volumetric features and FFSFs.
Sunil and Pande [10]	Taxonomy of features in sheet-metal parts	A method to recognize features from sheet-metal parts represented in STL format.	Deformation features	Does not handle volumetric features and FFSFs. For each sheet-metal feature, different rule has to be defined to identify the feature.
Gupta and Gurumoorthy [20]	Classification of volumetric features	Semantic interoperability of shape model containing volumetric features only	Volumetric features	Does not handle FFSFs and deformation features.
Gupta and Gurumoorthy [11]	Classification of deformation features	Semantic interoperability of shape model containing deformation features only.	Deformation features	Does not handle volumetric features and FFSFs.
Kannan and Shunmugam [12]	Classification for sheet-metal features	Manufacturing feature classification for sheet-metal features.	Deformation features	Does not handle volumetric features and FFSFs.
Gupta and Gurumoorthy [14]	Classification of free-form surface features	Automatic extraction of free-form surface features (FFSFs) in a part model	FFSFs	Does not handle volumetric and deformation features.
Tan et al.,[21]	Taxonomy of Hole form feature	Development of feature recognition system for CAD/CAM integration for Hole form feature in a part model	Hole form feature in a solid model (STEP file) is recognized and further classified as Through and Blind	Does not handle FFSFs and deformation features. Recognition of complex hole features and other features such as slots, pockets, bosses, step and ribs are considered as future research.

2 Shape Features in Part Model

A part model may have volumetric features, Deformation features and FFSFs as shown in Fig. 1. The FFSFs may be on a face of the model or on a face of volumetric feature. Example of a solid part model with volumetric features and FFSFs is shown in Fig. 1(a). Examples of volume feature, deformation features and FFSFs in a sheet-metal part are shown in Fig. 1 (b).

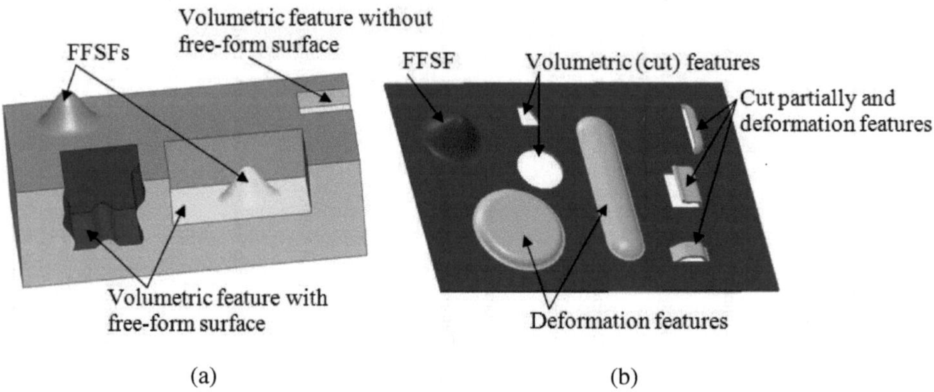

Fig. 1. Example of Shape features in part model

Shape feature is defined as a set of faces (or a face) with distinct topological and geometrical characteristics. The shape features in a product model are classified as follows:

1. Volumetric features (features created by addition or subtraction of volume),
2. Deformation features (features created by deformation of material (as in sheet-metal parts) or forming of material (as in injection molded parts of constant thickness)) – associated with constant thickness sections,
3. Free-form surface features (feature on a single face of the part model).

2.1 Volumetric Features

A volumetric feature is defined as a set of faces with distinct topological and geometrical characteristics and is created by the addition or subtraction of a sweep solid from an arbitrary solid [5]. The faces of the volume (solid-piece) that is added or removed are classified as shell-faces and end-faces. The faces that form the closed shell are classified as shell-faces and the faces which close the ends of the shell are classified as end-faces as shown in Fig. 2. Addition or subtraction of the solid-piece leaves an impression (feature) on the base-solid. The faces in the impression which do not exist in the base-solid before the addition or subtraction operation are classified as created faces (newly created faces). The faces in the base-solid, which are modified by the addition or subtraction operation and are shared by the solid-piece and the base-solid, are classified as shared faces (modified faces) as shown in Fig. 2.

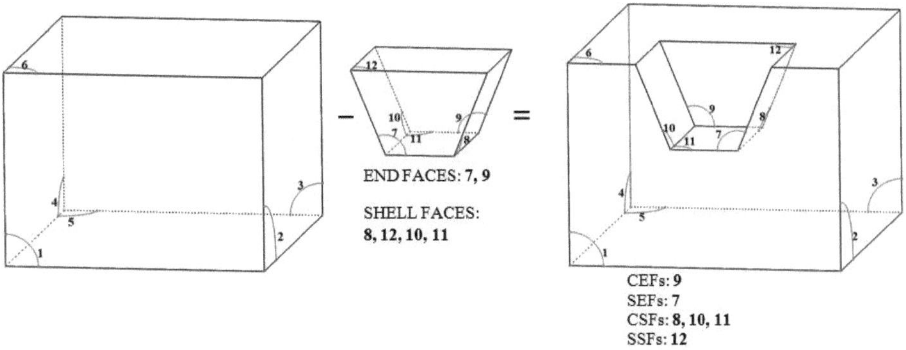

Fig. 2. Classification of feature faces for volumetric feature

The faces in the final solid associated with an individual feature are classified as follows:

Created Shell Faces (CSFs) - newly created faces in the base-solid corresponding to the shell-face of the solid-piece.

Shared Shell Faces (SSFs) - already existing faces in the base-solid corresponding to the shell-face of the solid-piece.

Created End Faces (CEFs) - newly created faces in the base-solid corresponding to the end-face of the solid-piece.

Shared End Faces (SEFs) - already existing faces in the base-solid corresponding to the end-face of the solid-piece. One shared end face of a feature can coincide with more than one face in the base-solid.

The representation of a feature in terms of these four types of faces and the characteristic relationship among them is called the Domain Independent Form Feature (DIFF) model. A classification of volumetric features based on the above classification of faces is summarized in Fig. 3.

2.2 Free-Form Surface Features

These features can be formed either by manipulating a free-form surface or realized during the construction of a free-form surface. The criteria for classification are based on the topology and geometry of the surface with the feature and do not rely on any domain knowledge.

The presence of a feature on a free-form surface is indicated by a distinct change in the geometric characteristics of the surface. The separating curve is the curve on the surface where this distinct change occurs so that the portion of the surface on one side of the separating curve forms the feature. This bound portion of the base surface that forms the feature is referred to as the influence region. The separating curve can be a closed or an open curve; if the separating curve is open, it will bound the feature on the surface along with a portion of the boundary curves of the base surface.

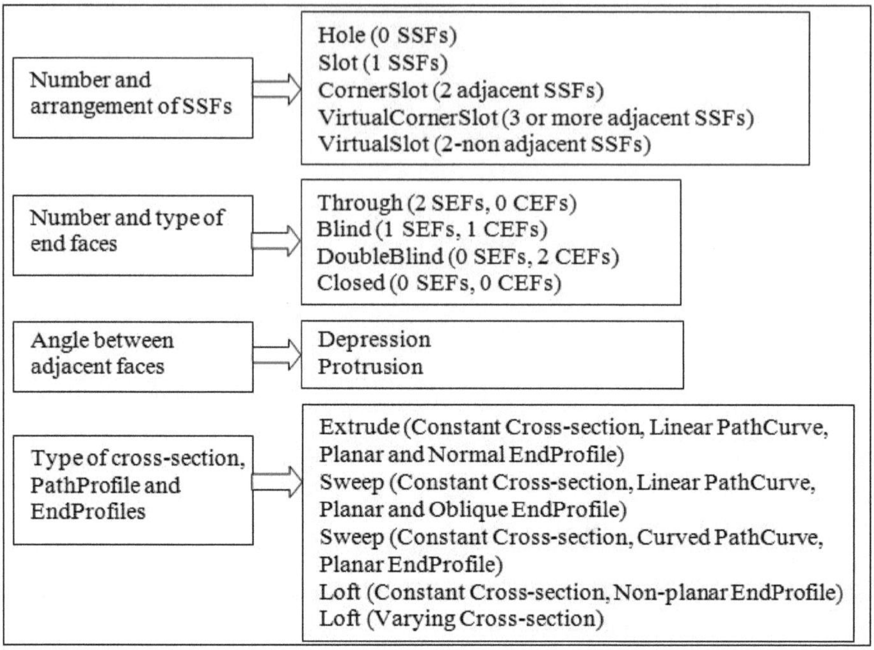

Fig. 3. Hierarchy of classification criteria in feature definition of volumetric features

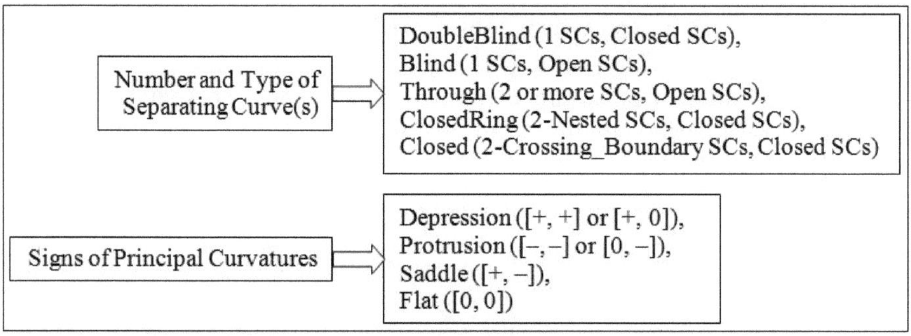

Fig. 4. Hierarchy of classification criteria in feature definition of FFSFs

The separating curve, its interaction with the base surface boundary and the influence region provide the criteria for classifying FFSFs. An FFSF is classified based on its type and nature. The type of an FFSF is defined in terms of the number of separating curves and the interaction of the separating curve(s) with the base surface boundary. The nature of an FFSF is decided by a combination of the signs of the principal curvatures in the influence region (the region enclosed by the separating curve). The principal curvature can be + (concave), - (convex) or 0 (neutral, flat). The number and type of separating curve(s) and the nature of principal curvatures in the influence region of each feature constitutes the DIFF model for FFSFs. The classification of FFSFs based on the above is summarized in Fig. 4.

2.3 Deformation Features

Deformation features are present in constant thickness part models, as a result of deformation of material (as in sheet-metal parts) or forming of material (as in injection molded parts of constant thickness)), also referred to as constant thickness features [9].

These features are created by beading, bending, forming, folding, turning, joggling, embossing, lancing or louver operation. Example of sheet-metal deformation features are depicted in Fig. 5.

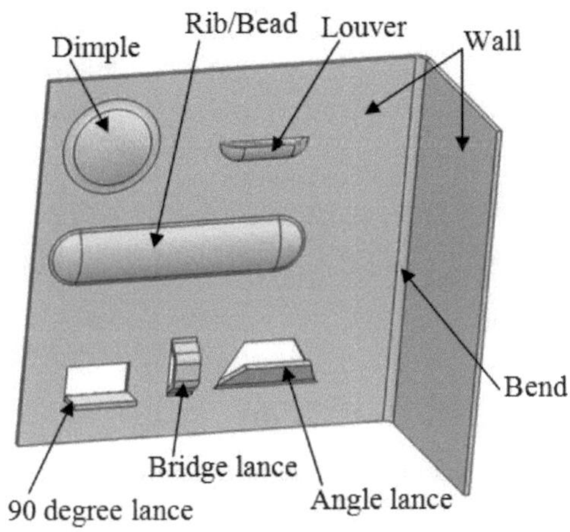

Fig. 5. Deformation features in constant thickness part

The faces in the object associated with an individual "deformation feature" are classified as follows:

Created End Faces (CEFs) – End faces in a deformation feature that are also created faces are termed as created end faces. The CEFs are further classified as **Created Wall End Faces (CWEFs)** and **Created Bend End Faces (CBEFs)** depending upon the basic deformation feature type responsible for its creation, as shown in Fig. 6(a). CBEFs are non-planar whereas CWEFs are planar.

Shared Shell Faces (SSFs) – If a shell face in a feature is a shared face then the shell face is classified as *shared shell face (SSF).* Examples of shared shell faces are shown in Fig. 6. The SSFs are further classified as **BSSFs** (Boundary SSFs) or **ISSFs** (Interior SSFs) based on whether the SSF of a feature is boundary shell face or interior shell face.

Created Shell Faces (CSFs) – If a shell face in a feature is created face then the shell face is classified as *created shell face* (CSFs) as shown in Fig. 6(a). The CSFs are further classified as **BCSFs** (Boundary CSFs) or **ICSFs** (Interior CSFs) based on whether the CSF of a feature is boundary shell face or interior shell face.

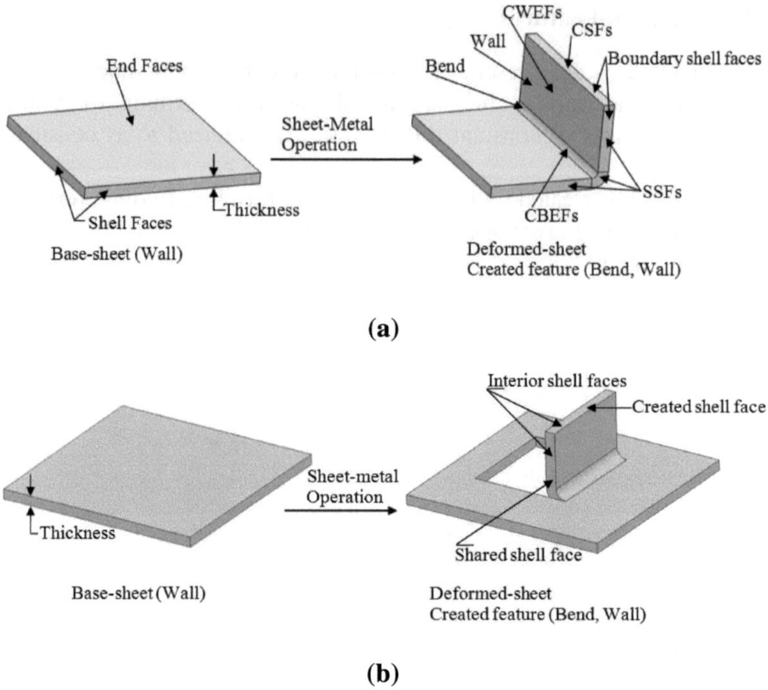

Fig. 6. Classification of feature faces for deformation features

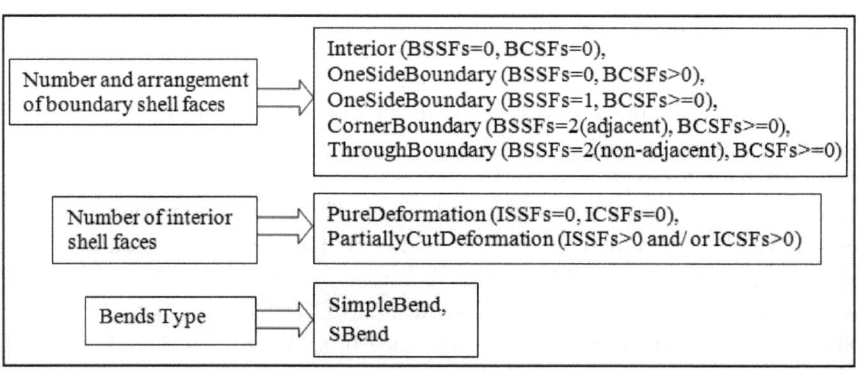

Fig. 7. Hierarchy of classification criteria in feature definition of deformation features

All features are therefore defined in terms of these six types of faces (CWEFs, CBEFs, BSSFs, ISSFs, BCSFs, ICSFs). Deformation features are represented by these six types of faces and the characteristic relationship between them in the DIFF model. The classification of deformation features based on the above classification of faces is shown in Fig. 7.

3 Taxonomy for Shape Features

Based on the above classifications, for each of the three types of features, a common hierarchy of classification has been defined as shown in Fig. 8. The generic content captures information regarding general class of the feature whereas the non-generic content captures content pertaining to defining a particular instance of that general class of the feature. For the feature in Fig. 2 for instance, the generic content would pertain to the feature being a blind slot while the non-generic content would contain the detail that it is a V-shaped slot. Parameters used for classifying and defining a shape feature in the DIFF model are extracted from the geometric and topology information available in product model [5], [11], [14].

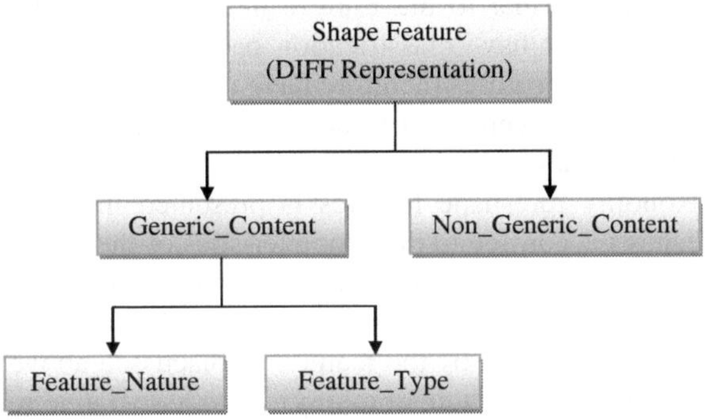

Fig. 8. Class structure of every shape feature in the DIFF model

Parameters with their possible values used for defining shape feature are shown in Figs. 3, 4 and 7 for volumetric features, free-form surface features and deformation features, respectively. These parameters are used for reasoning about shape features and are grouped under class 'Generic_Content'. These parameters are further classified and grouped as

(i) Feature_Type of a shape feature in the taxonomy is classified and represented based on the interactions of the feature with the boundary elements of the base solid/surface. Parameters associated with class 'Feature_Type' to classify shape features are based on number and arrangement of faces in a feature for volumetric and deformation features, and, number and type of separating curves in a feature for FFSFs. The differences in parameters are because of dimensionality as volumetric and deformation features are associated with volume whereas FFSFs are associated with surface.

(ii) Parameters associated with class 'Feature_Nature' to classify shape features are based on curvature characteristics in a feature. Feature_Nature of a shape feature in the taxonomy is classified and represented based on the curvature variations across entities (faces, edges) in the feature.

In the case of FFSFs, the feature is part of a base surface which has boundary edges as base surface boundary. So the interactions of the separating curves(s) with the base surface boundary curves are used to classify and define type of FFSFs, whereas volumetric and deformation features are part of base solid/sheet which has boundary faces as base solid/sheet boundary. So the interactions of the faces in the feature with faces in the base solid/sheet are used to classify and define the type of these features.

The feature type of a FFSF is based on a single attribute – namely the type of interaction between the separating curve and the boundary curve of the base surface. The feature type of deformation and volumetric features, on the other hand is decided by two attributes. These are (i) Number and arrangement of boundary shell faces, and (ii) Interior shell faces for deformation features, and (i) Number and arrangement of shell faces, and (ii) Number and type of end faces for volumetric features. The volumetric features are further classified based on the variations of cross-sectional shape and PathCurve in the feature. As the cross-sectional shape is constant and PathCurve is linear and normal to the EndProfile in a deformation feature, so the deformation features do not have classification based on cross-sectional shape and PathCurve. The volumetric features therefore have one more type of classification for the feature type as "Loft, Sweep and Extrude" based on the variations of the cross-sectional shape and PathCurve.

The unified taxonomy for shape features is presented in Fig. 9. The taxonomy classifies shape features according to the characteristics of the parameters in the DIFF model which makes definition of a shape feature simple, consistent and amenable to automated reasoning. The number of branches for each class of feature varies with the dimensionality of space occupied by the feature, as discussed above. The proposed is referred to as a taxonomy (and not an ontology) as no associative relations across the branches or with other entities are captured [2].

4 Discussion

The classification schemes presented in papers [5], [7], [18], [20], [21] classify volumetric features in a part model. Deformation and freeform surface features are not discussed in these papers. The classification schemes [13], [14], [16], [17], [22], [23] do not have procedures to include volumetric and deformation features in their taxonomies. The classification schemes presented in papers [9], [10], [11], [12], [15] have classified sheet-metal features in a sheet-metal part model. The proposed unified taxonomy has all shape features in a part model, classified under single classification and representation scheme, and can be used for automated reasoning.

The reasoning module for finding semantic equivalences for exchanging volumetric features has been discussed in paper [20]. A reasoning module for finding semantic equivalences for all type of shape features and automatic construction of the product model using semantically equivalent shape features in a target application is in the development stage. The primary requirement for the reasoning module is to have unified taxonomy with formal representation for all shape features in a product model. The developed unified taxonomy with formal representation for all shape features has been presented in this paper and can be used for automated reasoning in the reasoning module.

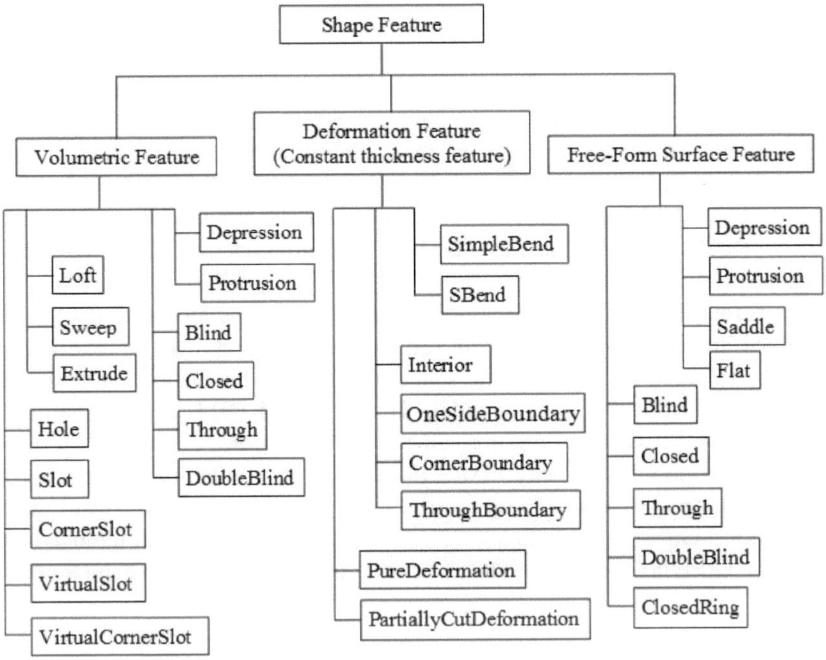

Fig. 9. Unified taxonomy for classification of shape features

The work presented in this paper brings volumetric, deformation and free-form surface features in product models under a single classification and representation. The taxonomy is unified because the basis for classification is similar (coarse at the top – nature, type and, fine at the bottom – through hole, blind slot). Classification of features in this taxonomy is concise (the maximum number of branches at any level is four and there are only three levels. As the features are classified based on the arrangement of faces/curves, the classification is purely based on form (geometry and topology) and therefore consistent. Completeness of the classification is harder to argue. At present the only claim that can be made is that the classification scheme does capture all the features that are in use in product models. Secondary features that are seen in some taxonomies are not separately classified here as, most secondary features such as fillet or blend can be modeled as a volumetric feature. The taxonomy therefore is application independent and amenable to automated reasoning.

The definition and classification thus far has been with respect to single features. In real parts features will interact and intersect. However, intersecting or interacting features do not cause a problem as long as the application does not require the interacting features to be handled as a single feature. The feature extraction routines can identify the DIF features that constitute the overlapping or interacting feature. Subsequently, the individual feature can be processed or manipulated. However, if the interacting features have to be handled as a single feature then the mapping from the DIFF based classification scheme to the application domain has to be addressed

The classification and representation of shape features are based on faces and curves, and, a characteristic arrangement amongst them. As mentioned above, this representation uses only geometric and topological entities that are explicitly available in the shape model. Recognising these features and extracting their DIFF model automatically from a shape model is therefore feasible [5], [11], [14]. The proposed taxonomy can therefore be used to develop reference ontology for handling heterogeneity in shape models. This is because the DIFF model can be extracted from the shape model and can be used as a basis to compare different feature models of the same shape.

For any other domain specific feature, the geometry associated with the feature can be obtained unambiguously and the DIFF representation can be extracted. The parameters, required to represent a shape feature in the DIFF, can therefore be obtained from B-rep of a shape model. The extracted DIFF representation of the feature can now be used for finding semantically matching entities in the ontology based on the proposed taxonomy. Extraction of feature semantic, as understood by a target application for a matching entity, can also be obtained from the DIFF representation. Ongoing work is addressing the development of a reference ontology based on the DIFF taxonomy to enable semantic interoperability of shape models.

5 Conclusion

Unified taxonomy has been developed to represent, classify and extract shape features under three main classes namely, volumetric features, deformation features and free-form surface features. This taxonomy is based on the Domain Independent Form Feature (DIFF) model to represent features. Parameters in the model are geometric and topological entities available in the shape model. DIFF model of the features can therefore be automatically extracted and the features in the model are classified. The unified taxonomy is proposed as a candidate for use in defining reference ontology to handle heterogeneous shape models.

References

1. Fensel, D.: Ontologies: A silver bullet for knowledge management and electronic commerce. Springer, Berlin (2003)
2. Stevens, R., Goble, C., Bechhofer, S.: Ontology-based knowledge representation for bioinformatics. Briefings in Bioinformatics 1(4), 398–414 (2000)
3. Li, Z., Raskin, V., Ramani, K.: Developing engineering ontology for information retrieval. Trans. of ASME Journal of Computing and Information Science in Engineering 8 (2008)
4. Yang, M., Kpalma, K., Ronsin, J.: A survey of shape feature extraction techniques. In: Yin, P.-Y. (ed.) Pattern Recognition, pp. 43–90 (2008)
5. Nalluri, S.R.P.R.: Form feature generating model for feature technology. Ph.D. Thesis, Indian Institute of Science, Department of Mechanical Engineering, Bangalore, India (1994)
6. Han, J.: Survey of feature research. Technical Report IRIS-96-346, Institute for Robotics and Intelligent systems, USC, USA (1996)

7. Subramani, S.: Feature mapping, associativity and exchange for feature-based product modeling. Ph.D. Thesis, Indian Institute of Science, Department of Mechanical Engineering, Bangalore, India (2005)
8. Bok, A.Y., Mansor, M.S.A.: Generative regular-freeform surface recognition for generating material removal volume from stock model. Computers & Industrial Engineering 64, 162–178 (2013)
9. Liu, Z.J., Li, J.J., Wang, Y.L., Li, C.Y., Xiao, X.Z.: Automatically extracting sheet-metal features from solid model. Journal of Zhejiang University Science 5, 1456–1465 (2004)
10. Sunil, V.B., Pande, S.S.: Automatic recognition of features from freeform surface CAD models. Computer-Aided Design 40, 502–517 (2008)
11. Gupta, R.K., Gurumoorthy, B.: Extending feature based semantic interoperability for sheet-metal product development. In: Proceedings of International Conference on Trends in Product Lifecycle Modeling, Simulation and Synthesis, PLMSS 2008, Bangalore, India, pp. 236–246 (2008)
12. Kannan, T.R., Shunmugam, M.S.: Processing of 3D sheet metal components in STEP AP-203 format. Part I: feature recognition system. International Journal of Production Research 47, 941–964 (2009)
13. Pernot, J.P., Falcidieno, B., Giannini, F., Léon, J.C.: Incorporating free-form features in aesthetic and engineering product design: State-of-the-art report. Computers in Industry 59, 626–637 (2008)
14. Gupta, R.K., Gurumoorthy, B.: Automatic extraction of free-form surface features (FFSFs). Computer-Aided Design 44, 99–112 (2012)
15. Lipson, H., Shpitalni, M.: On the topology of sheet metal parts. Trans. of ASME Journal of Mechanical Design 120, 10–16 (1998)
16. Fontana, M., Giannini, F., Meirana, M.: A free form feature taxonomy. In: Brunet, P., Scopigno, R. (eds.) Proceedings of Eurographics 1999, Computer Graphics Forum, vol. 18, pp. 107–118 (1999)
17. Nyirenda, P.J., Bronsvoort, W.F., Langerak, T.R., Song, Y., Vergeest, J.S.M.: A generic taxonomy for defining freeform feature classes. Computer-Aided Design & Applications 2, 497–506 (2005)
18. Wilson, P.R., Pratt, M.J.: A taxonomy of features for solid modeling. Geometric Modeling for CAD Applications, 125–136 (1988)
19. Poldermann, B., Horváth, I.: Surface-based design based on parameterized surface features. In: Horváth, I., Varadi, K. (eds.) Proceedings of the International Symposium on Tools and Methods for Concurrent Engineering 1996, pp. 432–446. Institute of Machine Design, Budapest (1996)
20. Gupta, R.K., Gurumoorthy, B.: A feature-based framework for semantic interoperability of product models. SV - Journal of Mechanical Engineering 54, 446–457 (2008)
21. Tan, C.F., Kher, V.K., Ismail, N.: Design of a feature recognition systems for CAD/CAM integration. World Applied Sciences Journal 21(8), 1162–1166 (2013)
22. Nyirenda, P.J., Bronsvoort, W.F.: Numeric and curve parameters for freeform surface feature models. Computer-Aided Design 40, 839–851 (2008)
23. Nyirenda, P.J., Mulbagal, M., Bronsvoort, W.F.: Definition of Freeform Surface Feature Classes. Computer-Aided Design & Applications 3, 665–674 (2006)

Deployment of Knowledge Management in a PLM Environment: A Software Integrator Case Study

Sébastien Nila [1], Frédéric Segonds [1], Nicolas Maranzana [1], and Dorothée Crepe [2]

[1]Arts et MetiersParisTech, LCPI,
151 bd de l'Hôpital, 75013 Paris, France
Sebastien.nila@gmail.com, {frederic.segonds, nicolas.maranzana}@ensam.eu
[2] Keonys 308 Bureaux de la Colline, 92210Saint-Cloud, France
Dorothee.crepe@keonys.com

Abstract. The past years have seen growing investments in the area of PLM by several industries. In today's industrial production, PLM is an essential tool to cope with the challenges of more demanding global competition and ever-shortening product lifecycles. Complex products require collaboration of large specialist networks. Knowledge Management (KM) can be apprehended in two manners: the defensive manner builds the stock of knowledge to face the departures of personnel, or, the offensive manner sees in the knowledge development an advisability to generate new products. The link between PLM and KM is interesting as it can help answering "on field" problems. In this paper we first make a state of the art of knowledge and KM in a PLM context. Then we propose a methodology to deploy KM in the particular case of a software integrator. Finally, we propose an experimental protocol that will allow us to improve a tool demonstrator in an agile way.

Keywords: PLM, Knowledge Management, methodology, software integrator.

1 Introduction

PLM systems are nowadays widely used in engineering design. The economic context forces industries to achieve more and more ambitious projects with ever shortening time and money. On the other side, knowledge is the most important thing in a company, and is mainly stored in the employees' mind, as illustrated in Figure 1, extracted from (Segonds 2011).It seems worth remembering that most of the knowledge can't be stored on a computer, because it is the fruit of Human. Design choices made are often implicit and very few are archived in any software. This kind of knowledge is, at the moment, difficult to store and manage. The progressive integration of KM in PLM systems is means to improve knowledge spread.

In this paper, we first make a state of the art of knowledge and KM in a PLM context. Then we propose a methodology to deploy KM in the particular case of a

A. Bernard, L. Rivest, and D. Dutta (Eds.): PLM 2013, IFIP AICT 409, pp. 308–316, 2013.

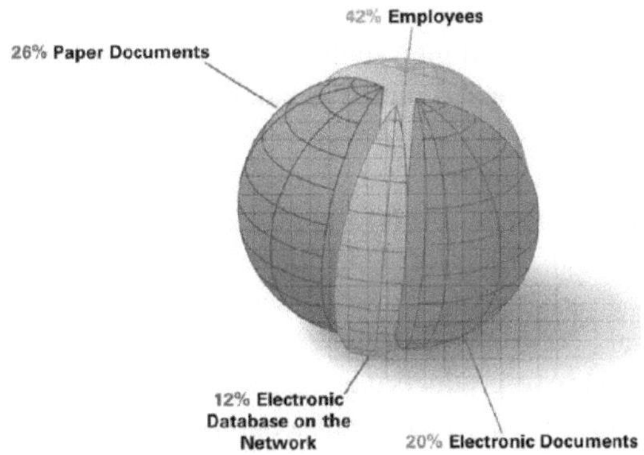

Fig. 1. distribution of knowledgeinproduct design, extracted from (Segonds, 2011)

software integrator. Finally, we propose an experimental protocol that will allow us to improve a tool demonstrator in an agile way.

2 PLM Context and Associated Challenges

2.1 Evolution of Design Methodologies and Dedicated Software Tools

In a context marked by increasing competition, businesses must suit their organization to the demands of their customers. In this context, the reduced duration of development cycles and the increasing complexity of mechanical systems force businesses to involve actors from various professional and cultural backgrounds in collaborative projects. The organization of design teams has also had to adapt to these changes in the industrial context.

Figure 2 illustrates the changing patterns in the formation of new product development teams as these moved to greater collaboration and virtuality.

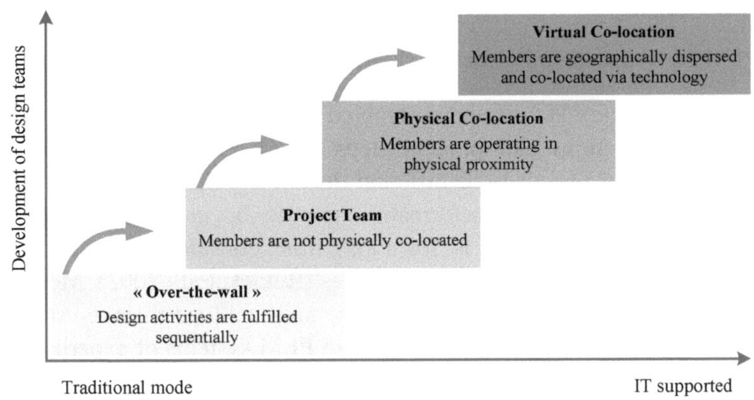

Fig. 2. Changes in design teams adapted from (Sharifi et al., 2001)

Obviously, these industrial evolutions have been supported by evolutions in work methods and in the associated digital tools, such as PLM solutions. At the same time, research is actively being carried out to develop methodologies and technologies to support geographically dispersed teamsin order to facilitate product development processes (Dodgson et al.,2006). The objective is to organize collaborative work based on the rapid evolution of information technologies. Research works and commercial systems have appeared to provide solutions for collaborative and distributed product development, and the practical applications are getting more and more mature (Li et al., 2006).

In an attempt to improve productsand reduce costs and time to market, concurrent engineering (Solhenius, 1992) or lifecycle engineering has emerged as an effective approach to address these issues in a competitive global market (Asiedu et al.,1998).Influenced by the NTIC development, global economic challenges, and decentralized structures, the objectives and scope of Product Data Management technology (PDM) have changed. Thus, in the early 2000s, PLM emerged as a solution to adapt industrial design to the demands of globalization. Indeed, as PLM addresses the entire lifecycle of the product, it has a cross-functional nature and deals closely with the way a company runs (Garetti et al., 2005). Collaborative design has been the subject of numerous studies. With the development of PDM, PLM and associated workflows, software firms have proposed solutions to the everyday problems of engineering design departments (versioning of documents, naming etc.). The PLM approach can be viewed as a trend toward a full integration of all software tools taking part in design and operational activities during a product life cycle (Garetti et al., 2005; Donati et al. 2010). Therefore, PLM software packages need product data management system; synchronous and asynchronous, local and remote collaboration tools; and if necessary, a digital infrastructure allowing exchanges between software programs.These systems are distributed technological information systems for archiving, administrating and providing all product or facility related information in required quality and at the right time and place (Ameriet al., 2005): they are nowadays real key points for companies businesses.

2.2 PLM Systems: Key Points for Business

A product is a complex "fabricated-assembled" element, comprising a large number of components, functions and process steps (Clark et al., 1991). To be or stay competitive, anindustry needs to be different than others (Danneels, 2002), that's why most of industries are in a transformation step to be more responsiveness about customers and competitors. PLM is, for a long time, considered as a key for business and the transformation of engineering processes (Rekieket al., 2002). Moreover, PLM solutions are efficient tools to store knowledge and facilitate their re-use. In the next section, we will discuss about the integration in PLM systems of expertises generated all along projects, also known as knowledge.

3 Knowledge Management and PLM

3.1 Knowledge Management

According to Wiig (1997), knowledge is information combined with experience, context, interpretation and thinking. It is a high value form of information that is ready to apply to decisions and actions. Simply put, knowledge can be defined as the integration of ideas, experience, skills that have the potential to create value for a business by informing decisions and improving performance. In this view, knowledge is a key enabler to organizational success. However, in order to be useful, knowledgemust be available, accurate, effective and accessible.

In NewProduct Development (NPD), there is an implicit distributed interaction among different actors.As we enter the knowledge society, ownership of knowledge and information as a source of competitive advantage is becoming increasingly important. In other words, organizations depend more on the development, use and distribution of knowledge based competencies. Consequently, organizations are focus more attention to the concept of managing their knowledge base in order to increase competitive advantage, through effective decision making and innovation (Nonaka et al., 1995; Davenport et al., 1996; Sveiby et al., 1997).

Knowledge is a key resource that must be managed if improvement efforts are to succeed and businesses are to remain competitive in a networked environment (Gunasekaran, 1999). Indeed, it is a big adds value for organizations to capitalize on knowledge sources by trying to predict how the new product will perform in an unknown context. From the social perspective, the challenge consists in sharing knowledge and interconnecting people that are imagining these future conditions.

Managing knowledge is about creating an environment in continuous creation, aggregation, use and reuse of both organizational and personalknowledge in the pursuit of new business value. KM can be considered as a systematic and organized attempt to use knowledge within a company to transform its ability to generate, store and use knowledge in order to improve performance. In short, the leading purpose of KM is to make knowledge accessible and reusable to the organization.

As PLM, KMhas a true add value. As we will discuss in next chapter (4), these two methods (and dedicated tools)can be combined in order to deliver knowledge all along the lifecyle of a product.

3.2 PLM and KM Integration

Currently, there is alack of studies on information flows needed acrossproduct lifecycle operations.Thus, the unavailability of explicit flows leads to a certain degree of inefficiency in performing lifecycle operations. Methods dedicated to efficiently represent, control and search information flows are critical. KM requires the identification of information flows and their efficient management, which can play an important role in analyzing and taking decisions during the product lifecycle (Jun et al., 2012).As Ouertani et al. (2011) mentioned, querying and sharing product knowledge is becoming a key issue in enterprise. Hence, the success of PLM and KM integration lies in identifying what kind of information are available in the other phase, and how we can use them in order to streamline business processes.

An emergent challenge consists in providing a context-driven access to federated information and knowledge, fostering cross-discipline collaborations between actors to improve quality in product development. In the next section, we will try to address this challenge by proposing a methodology to deploy KM in PLM environment.

4 Proposition of a Methodologyto Deploy KMin PLM Environment

4.1 Industrial Context: The Keonys Company

The context and problem of identifying and thereafter representing, analyzing and managing information and knowledge in an organization has always been very crucial to achieve business goals in an efficient and flexible way. Particularly in a PLM context, the issue of information overload is growing in importance. Among the existing integrators, Keonys the European leader in the integration of PLM solutions is in constant development, both in its workforce as its revenue and services offered to customers. In the same way the company's knowledge, defined as expertise and know-how, is in growth and is divided in different branches of the group in Europe.In this growing environment, Keonys is looking for a way to capitalize on the knowledge of the company and arrange them in different ways in order to define Best Practices.

The purpose of this paper is to propose a methodology which can answer the needs of development of Keonysthrough the integration of KM in PLM environment. It includes several points, from the categorization of company knowledge to the identification of an adapted Knowledge Based Engineering System (Sriram, 2006).In the next section, we describe the proposed methodology.

4.2 Proposed Methodology to Deploy KM in PLM Context

Agile methodology is an alternative to traditional project management, typically used in software development. It helps teams respond to unpredictability through incremental, iterative work cadences, known as sprints. Agile methodologies are an alternative to waterfall, or traditional sequential development.

Agile development methodology provides opportunities to assess the direction of a project throughout the development lifecycle. This is achieved through regular cadences of work, known as sprints or iterations, at the end of which teams must present a potentially shippable product increment. By focusing on the repetition of abbreviated work cycles as well as the functional product they yield, agile methodology is described as "iterative" and "incremental." In waterfall, development teams only have one chance to get each aspect of a project right. In an agile paradigm, every aspect of development, requirements, design, is continually revisited throughout the lifecycle.

The main advantage is its flexibility during the development. This method is oriented on code development and ensures an adapted implementation of the functionalities. It tends to improve how software and process are developed. Segonds (2011) developed a generic model based on a collaborative environment by integrating an agile development method. We base on this model to develop a methodology attempting to integrate KM approach seen in the state of art (Figure 3).

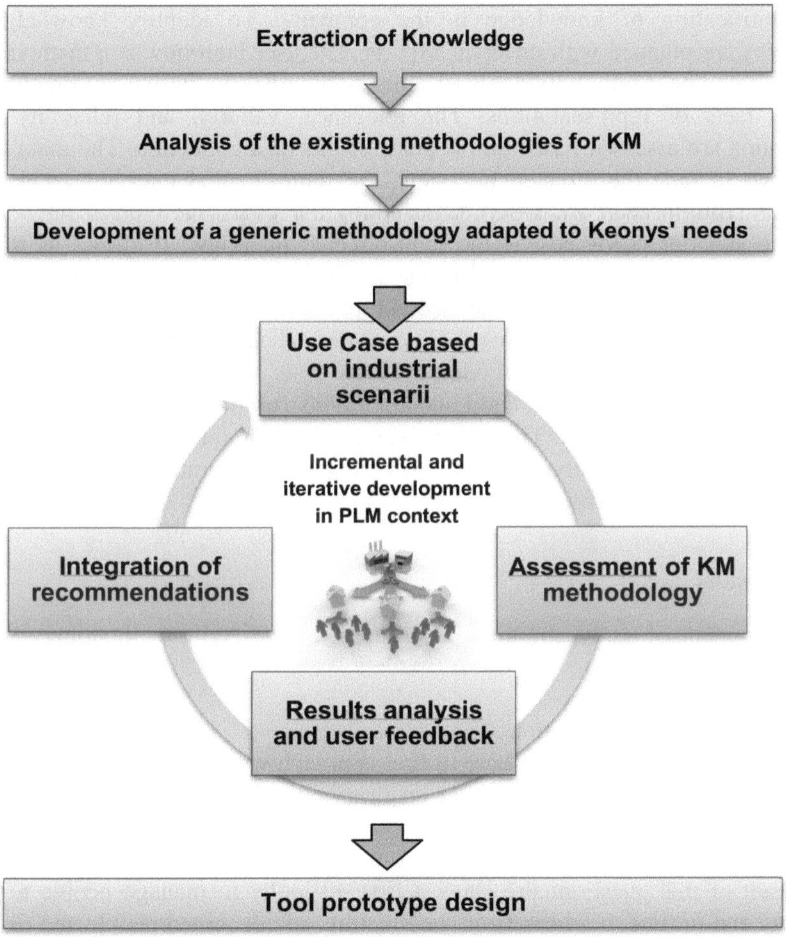

Fig. 3. PLM interface model design with KM integration and agile development, adapted from Segonds (2011)

Considering the case of Keonys, this company is oriented in a standardization development strategy, they want to create generic application in PLM tools to make an add value and to be different from their competitors.The group is separated in different work places. This method is a good way to develop a prototype tool adapted to the way of work of this company. With the consulting activity, it's difficult to group all developers in the same moment to adapt a methodology. The incremental and iterative development help to develop the methodology in asynchronous time.

4.3 Experimental Knowledge Extraction and Methodology Test

The first phase of the proposed methodology is one of the most important as it allows the identification of knowledge in the company. To identify knowledge, user interviews are planned with different experts. The user interview is a method used to collect oral data from individuals or groups in order to derive information from specific facts or representations. The relevance, validity, and reliability of this information are assessed based on the goals of this data collection. The main types of interviews include the directed interview, the semi-directed interview, and the free interview (Blomberg et al., 1993). Considering our goals, the type of interview that seems to suit our needs best is the semi-directed interview. It allows us to collect precise data in a reasonable length of time and fosters a genuine dialogue between the interviewer and interviewee. The second phase is the analysis of the existing methodologies of KM to inventory functionalities. Then, in order to test the reliability and validate the proposed methodology, user tests will be run with experts and novices. According to Nielsen and Laudauer (1993), no more than ten participants are needed for a usability tests. The recommendations made during the tests will help us to develop a tool prototype in an incremental and iterative way to fulfill the requirements expressed by the users.

4.4 Results

At this moment of study, the three first phases of the Agile methodology has been treated.

4.4.1 Knowledge Extraction

For the extraction knowledge phase, a first approach was to target people who are in charge of developing activities. After an overview of the company we selected ten employees in three different entities, a questionnaire was created for a first approach. The questionnaire goals is to refer project, industry, type of development, time spent. The result of this questionnaire show a first difficulty to manage people to answer correctly and in time, it comes from the volatility of concerned people and from their manager to push them. The data collected with the questionnaire is well organised and structured. Every project referenced is followed by the development code, use instruction and setup instruction. This first approach is a good way to get direct or phone contact and speak more easily to developer if there is missing explanation or missing data in the questionnaire. After this step all developmentwas tested and analysed to add new information's like usability, adaptability, pertinence. All information collected by questionnaire, interviews, test and analysis helped to categorize data and put priorities.

The second phase of the methodology is to analyse existing KM methodology in the company. There is four main tools using KM (Opportunity Review Business, Enterprise Resource Planning, Service Request, Intranet). These tools serves the company to capitalize data and information in an end to end way, from the opportunity to the billing. After a deep analyse of these tools, there is not the possibility to use one of them or a part of one of them to answer to Keonys needs concerning the development activity.

5 Conclusion

This article proposes to integrate KM approach to improve PLM systems. The state of art demonstrates that evolutions in design methodologies and dedicated software tools have promoted PLM and KM as key points for companies businesses. The presented methodology combines agile software development in PLM context. KM will allow us to provide a tool prototype dedicated to Keonys company. The extension of this method to others companies could increase user's satisfaction and, as a consequence, the efficiency of the company through the use of KM integrated in PLM environments.

References

1. Ameri, F., Dutta, D.: Product Lifecycle Management: Closing the Knowledge Loops. Computer-Aided Design & Applications 2(5), 577–590 (2005)
2. Asiedu, Y., Gu, P.: Product life cycle cost analysis: State of the art review. International Journal of Production Research (1998)
3. Awazu, Y., Baloh, P., Desouza, K.C., Wecht, C.H., Kim, J., Jha, S.: Information communication technologies open up innovation. Research-Technology Management 52(1), 51–58 (2009)
4. Blomberg, J., Giacomi, J., Mosher, A., Swenton-Wall, P.: Ethnographic field methods and their relation to design. In: Schuler, D., Namioka, A. (eds.) Participatory Design: Principles and Practices, pp. 123–156. Lawrence Erlbaum Associates, Mahwah (1993)
5. Brem, A., Voigt, K.I.: Integration of market pull and technology push in the corporate front end and innovation management–insights from the German software industry. Technovation 29(5), 351–367 (2009)
6. Davenport, T.H., Jarvenpaa, S.L., Beers, M.C.: Improving knowledge work processes. Sloan Management Review 37(4), 53–65 (1996)
7. Donati, T., Bricogne, M., Eynard, B.: PLM platform: integrated support of the entreprise digital chain for Collaborative Product Development. In: 7th International Conference on Product Lifecycle Management, Bremen, Germany (2010)
8. Garetti, M., Terzi, S., Bertacci, N., Brianza, M.: Organisational change and knowledge management in PLM implementation. International Journal of Product Lifecycle Management 1(1), 43 (2005)
9. Gunasekaran, A.: Agile manufacturing: a framework for research and development. International Journal of Production Economics 62(1-2), 87–105 (1999)
10. Jun, H.-B., Kiritsis, D.: Several aspects of information flows in PLM. In: Rivest, L., Bouras, A., Louhichi, B. (eds.) PLM 2012. IFIP AICT, vol. 388, pp. 14–24. Springer, Heidelberg (2012)

11. Khurana, A., Rosenthal, S.R.: Towards holistic "front ends" in new product development. Journal of Product Innovation Management 15(1), 57–74 (1998)
12. Kim, J., Wilemon, D.: Strategic issues in managing innovation's fuzzy front-end. European Journal of Innovation Management 5(1), 27–39 (2002)
13. Li, D., Qiu, M.: State-of-the-art technologies and methodologies for collaborative product development systems. International Journal of Production Research 44(13) (2006)
14. Milicic, A., Perdikakis, A., El Kadiri, S., Kiritsis, D., Ivanov, P.: Towards the Definition of Domain Concepts and Knowledge through the Application of the User Story Mapping Method. In: Rivest, L., Bouras, A., Louhichi, B. (eds.) PLM 2012. IFIP AICT, vol. 388, pp. 58–69. Springer, Heidelberg (2012)
15. Navarro, R., Cloonan, J., Dubois, R., Tiwari, A.: Improving efficiency in Product Lifecycle Management implementation projects by applying lean principles. In: International Conference on Product Lifecyle Management, Eindhoven, Netherlands (2011)
16. Nonaka, I., Takeuchi, H.: The knowledge-creating company: How Japanese companies create the dynamics of innovation. Oxford University Press, USA (1995)
17. Ouertani, M.J., Baina, S., Gzara, L., Morei, G.: Traceability and management of dispersed product knowledge during design and manufacturing. Computer-Aided Design 43(5), 546–562 (2011)
18. Rekiek, B., Dolgui, A., Delchambre, A., Bratcu, A.: State of art of optimization methods for assembly line design. Annual Reviews in Control 26(2), 163–174 (2002)
19. Saaksvuori, A., Immonen, A.: Product Management Lifecycle. Springer (2008)
20. Segonds, F.: Contribution to the integration of a collaborative design environment in the early stages of design, PhD thesis, Arts et Metiers ParisTech (2011)
21. Sharifi, S., Pawar, K.S.: Product Development Strategies for Agility. In: Agile Manufacturing: The 21st Century Competitive Strategy, pp. 175–197 (2001)
22. Sohlenius, G.: Concurrent Engineering. Annals of CIRP 41, 645–655 (1992)
23. Sriram, R.D.: Artificial intelligence in engineering: Personal reflections. Advanced Engineering Informatics 20(1), 3–5 (2006)
24. Sveiby, K.E.: The new organizational wealth: Managing & measuring knowledge-based assets. Berrett-Koehler Pub. (1997)
25. Tayaran, E., Schiffauerova, A.: The Role of Internal and External Sources of Knowledge in the Product Lifecycle in Biotechnology Sector. In: Rivest, L., Bouras, A., Louhichi, B. (eds.) PLM 2012. IFIP AICT, vol. 388, pp. 46–57. Springer, Heidelberg (2012)
26. Utterback, J., Suarez, F.: Innovation, competition, and industry structure. Research Policy 22(1), 1–21 (1993)
27. Van der Velden, C., Bil, C., Yu, X., Smith, A.: An intelligent system for automatic layout routing in aerospace design. Innovations in Systems and Software Engineering 3(2), 117–128 (2007)
28. Wiig, K.M.: Knowledge management: where did it come from and where will it go? Expert Systems with Applications 13(1), 1–14 (1997)

Co-working for Knowledge Management in Cultural Heritage: Towards a PLM for Museum

Benjamin Hervy[1,2,3], Florent Laroche[1], Alain Bernard[1], and Jean-Louis Kerouanton[2]

[1] IRCCYN, LUNAM Université, Ecole Centrale de Nantes, France
[2] Centre François Viète, LUNAM Université, Université de Nantes, France
[3] Château des ducs de Bretagne, Musée d'histoire de Nantes, France
Benjamin.Hervy@irccyn.ec-nantes.fr

Abstract. Dealing with historical knowledge implies specific approaches. Then, modeling it and the different know-hows involved is a complex task. Indeed, patrimonial objects are historical witnesses whose life cycle is hard to handle. In this paper, we discuss possibilities of managing such heterogeneous content through a PLM system dedicated to historical knowledge and museum. Based on previous research in the field of ancient advanced archaeology, we demonstrate our process through an industrial research and development project with a history museum.

Keywords: Knowledge management, Cultural Heritage, PLM, Museum, DHRM.

1 Introduction

Museum is filled with knowledge treasures and specific, specialised know-how. Many professional domains are involved. Either they are heterogeneous, they work together for a common goal: preserve and promote cultural heritage. In this paper, we propose a dualistic approach in order to capitalise available knowledge related to patrimonial objects. Thanks to systemic analysis methods and tools, we try to identify the lacks of such approaches when dealing with heritage objects as a product knowledge management. In addition, we discuss the importance of human-centered approach for historical comprehension of non-explicit phenomena (political influences, historical sources contexts). To demonstrate our methodology, we present a research and development project done thanks to the collaboration between Nantes history museum, a research center in history of sciences and techniques (Centre François Viète) and IRCCyN laboratory. This project tends to promote an historical wooden model of Nantes harbour in 1900 with historical knowledge and virtual engineering tools.

First, we discuss on usability of engineering tools and methods for heritage knowledge capitalisation. Enterprise modeling such as PLM operating system provides efficient ways to capture information for co-working (FBS, ISO standards). But we identify a significant lack about long-term evolution of objects: patrimonial objects are concerned by this issue. As we cannot imagine what promoting system

A. Bernard, L. Rivest, and D. Dutta (Eds.): PLM 2013, IFIP AICT 409, pp. 317–325, 2013.

will be used in the future, we have to identify and to link significant data and knowledge provided by experts (historians, museum curators, etc.). This will allow museum to challenge the huge amount of knowledge they host for a better collection management. It will also improve cultural promotion and innovation thanks to digital projects. Indeed, if we look at the number of such projects all over the world, it is significantly increasing.

Then we demonstrate our scientific proposition with the results of a 5-years research and development project. It is led by Nantes history museum (France) and concerns two of their collection objects: wooden models of two parts of Nantes city in early 1900's. Many professional domains were involved such as historians, engineers (computers, mechanics, automatics), and museum professionals. They worked together in order to gather information, link it and design the final museography application. The result leads into a virtual augmented reality system based on the real object. The system is web-connected and allows the knowledge database to be enriched both by experts and general public. The content includes geographical, semantic information and historical links between points of interest. We capitalise both geographical areas (buildings, streets), for which we can store evolution during time and heterogeneous semantic information like people, historical events and so on.

Finally we discuss on challenges that can be handle by our method, especially the way that it can be extended to the whole museum through all the objects' collection. The way the system was designed allows us to connect other museum objects together, through historical links, and also to add know-how knowledge from museum activities. Thus, we imagine designing a PLM for museum that would store the whole processes of object acquisition, protection and promotion.

2 Industrial Knowledge Management for Cultural Heritage

Models and methods for knowledge management in industry offer many advantages but present lacks when dealing with historical information. MKSM/MASK, REX, KOD, KALAM are mainly related to industrial knowledge (nuclear, factory), but give significant clues for effective knowledge management. This would give advices when taking into account communities of practice. In addition, product-process oriented models, implemented for product design management [5] also give interesting trails as a systemic and functional approach. As far as digital documents are concerned, we also have to explore such approach for effective document and archive management [4]. Yet, we need to confront these approaches to historical and cultural heritage needs.

Singularities in cultural heritage come from temporal characteristics (long-time span analysis) and retro-analysis. Usually, knowledge management methods focus on existing knowledge in enterprise modeling.

Yet, a tool for historical knowledge management can take benefit from industrial knowledge management methods. Simply because industrials methods are in most cases reproducible, these should be considered useful. Some tools are already used in the field of history sciences such as archaeology, but they are related to specific knowledge (e.g. GIS). What we aim to do is to gather historical knowledge from different experts' fields as it would be in enterprise models.

New ways of knowledge management yet appear to place humans as a critical factor when dealing with knowledge management [9]. In cultural industry, such approach is more common, and lead to interesting results [7]. We then aim to provide a methodology, inspired by historians' research approach, very close to these methods. That means we have to deal with heterogeneous information and develop an approach mainly based on people's knowledge.

The Digital Heritage Reference Model [6] (DHRM: methodology based on Product-Process approach but dedicated to historical knowledge) has been designed to answer this problematic. The main idea is to combine different "schemes", capitalising heterogeneous knowledge, allowing us to understand and to model one idea under different points of view (internal, external, technical, socio-economic, political aspects).

According to this approach, we now explore ways to implement and to validate DHRM on practical use cases. This brings new problematic, especially about knowledge extraction modes and historical information visualisation [3].

3 Industrial Use-Case of an Interactive Knowledge-Based System: Augmented Historical Mock-Up

3.1 Context of the Project

In 2008, Nantes history museum started a research and development project about a wooden model, exposed inside the museum. This mock-up, designed in 1899 for the "Exposition Universelle of 1900" (world's fair held in Paris) by Paul Duchesne, represents Nantes harbour in the very end of nineteenth century. It is a great historical object, due to its size – 9.20 meters long and 1.85 meters wide, but also due to the geographical area it represents (approximately 7 square kilometers). As for now, museum visitors cannot interact with the mock-up, nor get any historical information about it (except those provided by the museum label).

The goal of the project is to design an interactive system, connected to a database in order to provide information to visitors. Database would host both experts' contributions and general public material: photographs, postcards, etc.

3.2 An Historical Information System

We then designed an information system, according to what we discuss in section 2. This would allow us to manage heterogeneous historical contents, and other materials coming from the process of "advanced industrial archaeology" described in [6].

A glimpse of the data structure is given on Fig. 1. The information system can store both semantic and geometric data. We can therefore store the whole structure of an object (for example a factory) from a macroscopic to a microscopic point of view (Fig. 2). The system also provides links, or relationships that represent historians' knowledge. Visualisation of such knowledge is somehow a complex task, both from

Fig. 1. Glimpse of the historical data structure

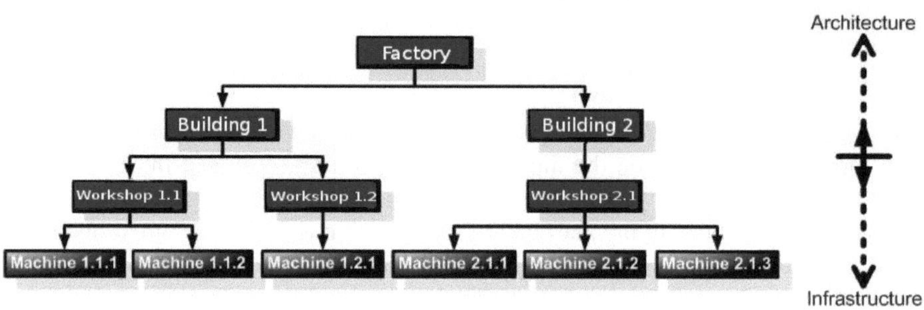

Fig. 2. Example of multi-dimensional levels of old industrial objects

ergonomics and computer programming points of view. At this point of the paper, it is important to notice that many skills are involved when dealing with cultural heritage capitalisation.

Based on this concept-knowledge space, we now want to identify historians' knowledge-mining modes. That means identifying ways the system will interact with historians whether they want to consult or to fill information.

3.3 Knowledge Visualisation

The proposed system (Fig. 3) is composed of a knowledge database, the historical object, and some visualisation devices: touch-screens and video-projectors. In fact, due to the process we applied in the project, we can now imagine any other interactive application: virtual worlds, augmented reality, web application, or any other future fruit of imagination… The system is scalable, and free from technology evolution, contrary to most of museum promoting systems. Scalability is provided by semi-automatic processes, whether it concerns 3D model acquisition and treatment (automatic semantic recognition algorithms) or content updates of visualisation applications.

In addition to this visualisation application, the system can be enriched (currently through web-client software) by experts and general public. This is a significant aspect because we cannot ensure that the whole knowledge related to the object was capitalised in the first iteration. We thus allow the system to capitalise future knowledge. The use of such promotion applications would generate new knowledge for example that the system has to take into account for its new knowledge reference basis. We also have in mind to improve the system in a way that it can assist researchers in their work. For example, it may be able to provide decision help while doing some research on particular historical subject.

Fig. 3. Augmented historical mock-up

4 Our Proposition: Towards a PLM for Museum

According to the results of our demonstrating system, we can imagine reproducing the process on other patrimonial objects and extending the process to the whole museum collection. Indeed, as done in contemporary industry, patrimonial objects are concerned by PLM paradigm. From preservation to promotion, many actors are involved, and so is the related knowledge. During these steps - museum lifecycle – several processes and resources are engaged.

The challenge now is to introduce this methodology in a PLM system for museum, allowing the different business areas to work together for better management of historical knowledge (Fig. 4).

4.1 Historical Knowledge Management and Museography Issues

As discussed before, when capitalising historical knowledge, we need to involve working areas that do not usually communicate. That leads to new processes of cooperation in the design of products and services [1]:

- Products as implementation of cultural mediation devices, which in turn may become heritage objects.
- Services when creating new heritage preservation processes: 3D scanning, structuring documentary corpus…

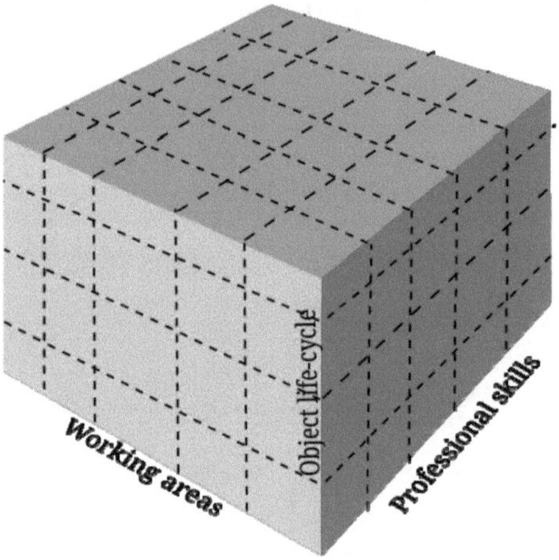

Fig. 4. Co-working on patrimonial objects

Interdisciplinary Aspects. An overview of the skills needed has been given in the preceding sections of this document. However, let's detail it a bit further:

- Expertise on contemporary engineering tools. These tools will be used for the capitalisation phase external data, but also for structuring information. Indeed, the concepts involved may be different depending on the scope (archives, museums, libraries, industry, etc.). This kind of expertise includes mostly engineering skills: experts in modeling and 3D scanning, and IT engineers.
- Expertise on the manipulated objects (mostly conservatives)
- Expertise in object's contemporary period that leads to an understanding of the object's environment. Mostly historians, historians of science and technology, and archivists for the corpus of documents. These skills are also required for translation of object's contemporary semantics in a current comprehensible language (contemporary to heritage capitalisation stage). Here we see the importance of communication among businesses that usually do not communicate. In fact, each business adopts a vocabulary related to its field of activity. From this point of view, we can assert that different occupations as historians, engineers, conservators, computer are able, under the banner of the common concern of preserving heritage to communicate and work together. This can probably be explained by the common goal, but also by a shared passion that

is a community's heritage. Indeed, and this is easily conceivable, heritage and history of a group (in the ethnological sense of the term) is a common root. This can also be seen through the craze that is observed among students working on a subject of their history, yet coming from all sides (engineering schools, universities, etc.).

- Expertise on the development and dissemination of information. This includes occupations related to cultural mediation, ergonomists, psychologists, cognitive scientists, or all occupations related to science communication, and data visualisation. This field is therefore also involved in automation or computer programming.

4.2 Management of Museum Collections and Associated Knowledge

The museum management complexity is as important as for any business. The main difference comes from the nature of manipulated objects. Indeed, the life cycle of products is remarkably different from those in the contemporary design process: the accumulation of knowledge is made retrospectively. It should be used to understand the object's life, influence he has had in a given space-time, and influence of the space-time evolution of the object, described by J.L Ermine in [2]. Therefore, the goal is not related to manufacturing process optimisation. However, the tools developed in the field of engineering are designed to be reproducibles. Then, a reproducible method for capitalisation and modeling of historical knowledge would be an answer to many problems. As an example, it would allow the establishment of a reading grid for cultural heritage preservation as recommended by UNESCO [8].

Another significant difference comes from the multi-dimensionality of the concerned knowledge. The phenomenon of reverse capitalisation requires a crossing of objects' life cycles and links between multi-dimensional information.

This is why the implementation of DHRM introduces a slightly different definition of the product life cycle as the one usually used in a current industry. Involved concepts and knowledge capitalisation contexts are differents.

Currently, the management of museum collection is provided by dedicated software (usually a specific Database Management System for museum) associated with a thesaurus. These DBMS are often under proprietary license, which prevent from efficient interoperability and implies specific skills. However, only people related to the administration of collections (museum curators, conservators, system administrator, research associates) work on the museum collection database. Indeed, cultural mediators, although the first link between visitors and museum collection objects exposed cannot interact with the collection management system. The information contained in the database is also often codified in a well specified and structured thesaurus. Knowledge of technical teams involved in the maintenance of cultural promotion systems are not taken into account in the system except for some characteristics such as illuminance maximum rate.

In the case of temporary exhibitions, whose aim is to expose heritage objects related to a particular theme, some objects are provided by donors. However, some of these objects are merely loaned and other data are permanently leaved to the museum.

It also frequently happens that many museums work together and proceed to exchanges from their own collections to meet the general discourse of the exhibition. However, only objects definitely bequeathed to the museum are then being digitised and loaded into the collections management system (through an historical sheet). Even if the exhibition is stored in the database as an event and linked to exhibited objects, the whole process of the exhibit design and discourse is not capitalised.

Thus, accumulation of knowledge in the sense we have explained in this paper would move towards a knowledge management tool museum, both for collections but also for people working in museum. Moreover, interaction and multi-disciplinarity is evident in the museum world where skills are extremely varied and heterogeneous. Yet, they work toward a common goal: preservation and promotion of cultural heritage. It is therefore a source of knowledge that just waits to be transmitted from generation to generation.

5 Conclusion

Trying to handle historical knowledge with industrial knowledge management methods is a great challenge. Both researchers and museum experts would take benefit from a global information system dedicated to cultural heritage. Yet, such methods are still incompatible when dealing with ancient objects. Moreover, the way of thinking usually used in industry and enterprise research is very new to history.

The approach detailed in this paper may allow researchers in history fields (archaeologists, historians, historians of science…) to develop new issues that would be underlined by the system (e.g. comparison of historical sources or intuitions analysis). To do so, we now have to identify which ways the system would use to communicate with semantically different working areas.

Another challenge we point out is the management of knowledge inside museum. Most of the knowledge from cultural heritage is hosted by such institutions (like libraries or archives). Designing museographic discourses involve many professional skills (designers, curators, and technical staff) and need accurate vision of knowledge provided by museum collection. In fact, many of exhibited heritage objects are linked through this discourse. Specific information system being able to host incremental knowledge related to museum collection would support museum activities, heritage preservation and cultural promotion.

Finally, what we aim to do is to make every community of practice involved in this heritage capitalisation process to take benefit on from each other. Industrial knowledge management should take inspiration from these works in order to improve innovation and design processes.

References

1. Boujut, J.F., Jeantet, A.: Les entités de coopération dans les nouvelles organisations de la conception. Revue Performances Humaines & Techniques 96, 38–44 (1998)
2. Ermine, J.L., Pauget, B., Beretti, A., Tortorici, G.: Histoire et ingénierie des connaissances. Paper Presented at the Colloque Sources et Ressources Pour les Sciences Sociales, Paris, 20 p. (2004)

3. Hervy, B., Laroche, F., Kerouanton, J.L., Bernard, A.: Advanced virtual reality visualisation system based on a meta-model dedicated to historical knowledge. In: Proceedings of the 3rd IEEE International Conference on Cognitive Infocommunications, Kosice, Slovakia, December 2-5, pp. 225–230 (2012)
4. Keraron, Y., Bernard, A., Bachimont, B.: Annotations to improve the using and the updating of digital technical publications. Research in Engineering Design 20(3), 157–170 (2009)
5. Labrousse, M., Bernard, A.: FBS-PPRE, an enterprise knowledge lifecycle model. In: Bernard, A., Tichkiewitch, S. (eds.) Methods and Tools for Effective Knowledge, pp. 285–305. Springer (2008)
6. Laroche, F., Bernard, A., Cotte, M.: Advanced Industrial Archaeology: A new reverse-engineering process for contextualizing and digitizing ancient technical objects. Virtual and Physical Prototyping 3(2), 105–122 (2008)
7. Laroche, F., Jeanjean, A.: Le paradigme de l'ingénieur dans un imaginaire ubiquitaire. Keynote of International Conference "Rencontres Jules Verne", Nantes, November 22-23 (2012)
8. UNESCO: Operational Guidelines for the Implementation of the World Heritage Convention (1977-2012), http://whc.unesco.org/en/guidelines/
9. Zobrist, J.F.: La belle histoire de Favi: l'entreprise qui croit que l'homme est bon. Humanités & Organisations (2010)

A Reference Architecture for an Enterprise Knowledge Infrastructure

Daniel Fitzpatrick, François Coallier, and Sylvie Ratté

École de Technologie supérieure, Montréal, QC Canada
Daniel.fitzpatrick@etsmtl.net

Abstract. With the emergence of social media, data available for market analytics has grown significantly, especially in the context of product lifecycle value analysis. Existing architecture frameworks do not support knowledge management, required to process massive amount of market data, or 'big data'. In order to perform product lifecycle value analysis, product managers need to access, in a seamless manner, data from several domains from systems within the organization and from external sources such as social media, government and industry sites, to name a few. The structured and integrated data must then be transformed into information, or contextualized data, and ultimately into actionable information or knowledge. To achieve this objective, this paper proposes an innovative approach, the Reference Architecture of an Enterprise Knowledge Infrastructure (RA-EKI) that provides a holistic approach to manage the complete knowledge lifecycle.

Keywords: Knowledge management, multi-domain ontology, data integration, product lifecycle management, enterprise architecture.

1 Introduction

Product Lifecycle Management (PLM) reveals itself as a crucial business-enabling paradigm. It supports the business effort to ensure efficiency and consistency in the entire product lifecycle. Interoperability between PLM, Customer Relationship Management (CRM), Enterprise Resource Planning (ERP) and Manufacturing Execution Systems (MES) is also required to provide better process efficiency and customer satisfaction. These information systems need to be integrated in order to satisfy data quality requirements[1].

Within and between each of these systems, knowledge has become a strategic asset to the enterprise. It increases the innovative capability and core resource utilization, such as people and assembly lines[2]. It also favors knowledge reuse, helps improving workers efficiency and safety. Many obstacles still hinder the generalized adoption of cross-enterprise knowledge management in the PLM paradigm. Current PLM business process definition, product information model and information treatment approaches lack the required agnostic and holistic quality to support industry independent solution patterns[3]. The difficulty in extracting information stored in several

A. Bernard, L. Rivest, and D. Dutta (Eds.): PLM 2013, IFIP AICT 409, pp. 326–335, 2013.

types of formats such as image, video and audio constitutes an important hurdle to the enterprises' progress. Such a heterogeneous information environment conceals crucial knowledge. Locating and retrieving such knowledge imposes costly processes and specialized human resources[4].

These many constraints may explain the great level of difficulty currently experienced by the organizations to adapt their PLM processes, and others, so that they can be more agile, flexible and adaptive to the rapidly changing market conditions[5, 6].

This research project intends to provide a Reference Architecture for an Enterprise Knowledge Infrastructure (RA-EKI), inspired form The Open Group Architecture Framework's TOGAF Reference Architecture - Information Integration Infrastructure (RA-III) to address these shortcomings. RA-EKI proposes a set of generic applications and a multi-domain ontology at its center. A description of the inductive research method used to elicit ontology patterns in this project can be found in [3]. RA-EKI's fundamental purpose is to deal with the issue of being data rich and knowledge poor, to be inundated with massive quantity of data but with limited capability to convert it into valuable knowledge.

The next section provides an insight on related projects that propose various ontology-based architecture approaches. Section 3 provides an overview of RA-EKI and a more detailed perspective on RA-EKI's generic applications. Section 4 covers a use case on the use of RA-EKI in support of product value analysis and section 5 concludes the paper.

2 Related Work

As presented in [1], data quality constitutes one of the purposes of knowledge management models. Since enterprise knowledge is often unearthed from corporate data, data quality plays an important role in the presented models. Certain models extend their coverage of PLM and reach out to other process-centric paradigms such as Manufacturing Execution Systems (MES) [1, 7], Enterprise Resource Planning (ERP) [1] and Customer Relationship Management (CRM) [8], forming a synergy that would increase even more the potential of sustainable growth in revenue, profitability and market share.

Proposed methods use various semantic exchange mechanisms such as mediation web services[1, 9], Service-Oriented Architecture (SOA) semantic services[6, 9], intelligent agents[2, 10], Extraction, Transformation and Load (ETL)[4, 11] and Enterprise Application Integration (EAI) message broadcasting [5] to resolve the syntactic and semantic heterogeneity between the systems.

The reference models, such as SCOR [8] and VFDM [7] put forward knowledge management infrastructure functions that handle the transformation of raw data to refined knowledge. Table 1 synthesizes these knowledge management functions as described in the cited literature.

Table 1. Knowledge management functions

Functions	Description
Data Quality	A mediation approach to resolve syntactic and semantic heterogeneities between business processes [1].
Knowledge extraction	Applications can extract information from unstructured and semi-structured data, Information is grouped and ultimately forms unit of knowledge. The applications annotate text files using W3C standards for XML, adding rich meta-information[2, 6, 9].
Knowledge structuring	Knowledge is structured after extraction from data into knowledge representation formats such as RDF triples[4, 6].
Knowledge storage	Archiving enterprise knowledge in a way to facilitate retrieval. Relational database and XML document technologies are used[2, 12].
Knowledge access	The treatment of queries to access stored knowledge. This can be accomplished through query processors or with the use of knowledge dashboards [4, 6, 12].
Intelligent agents	Applications dedicated to specific tasks such as supporting transactions between business entities[2, 10].
Process definition	An ontology-based design-time application that assists the enterprise to create or modify business processes with the use of generic process template and process modeling such as BPMN[5].
Data integration	Applications that map data from heterogeneous sources to a global schema and allowing to be restructured as contextualized data, or information, to be circulated and processed for knowledge extraction[3, 6, 13].
Natural Language Processing (NLP)	An problem solving method that uses stored knowledge to convert unstructured data in a form of text to structured data and information[6, 14].

The knowledge management models utilize various ontology approaches to provide a formal vocabulary to their semantic applications. Most models use widely known ontologies such as STEP, CPM, Onto-PDM and TOVE [1, 2, 7, 8]. With these ontologies and others built from within the projects, the models cover many concepts considered unrelated to PLM such as customer data. The pervasiveness of data subjects as explained in [15] highlights the changing nature of not only PLM but all of the other process-centric paradigms as well. The cited papers enunciated a significant set of concepts, such as: customer demographic data, orders, invoices, complaints, transactions, contracts, material orders, market information, new legislations affecting regulatory compliance, etc.

3 Description of RA-EKI

3.1 Overview

RA-EKI, as illustrated in figure 1, comprises a set of processes, a collection of orthogonally linked ontologies and databases to process unstructured, semi-structured and structured data. Further processing converts data into information and ultimately into knowledge. A more detail description of RA-EKI ontology structure can be found in [3]. Furthermore, since the inductive phase of the research is on-going, the final findings of the ontology structure including the multi-domain ontology will be the subject of future publications. Data can be extracted from within the organization, such as from structured databases, documents, emails, etc., and from external sources such as social networks, customer and government sites, etc. RA-EKI is described in greater depth in the next section. RA-EKI's applications may be implemented as agents or in other forms. Furthermore, although this paper covers RA-EKI with a warehouse style core database, this reference architecture may be implemented without a persistent central database, relying solely on mediated services or a hybrid configuration using both approaches.

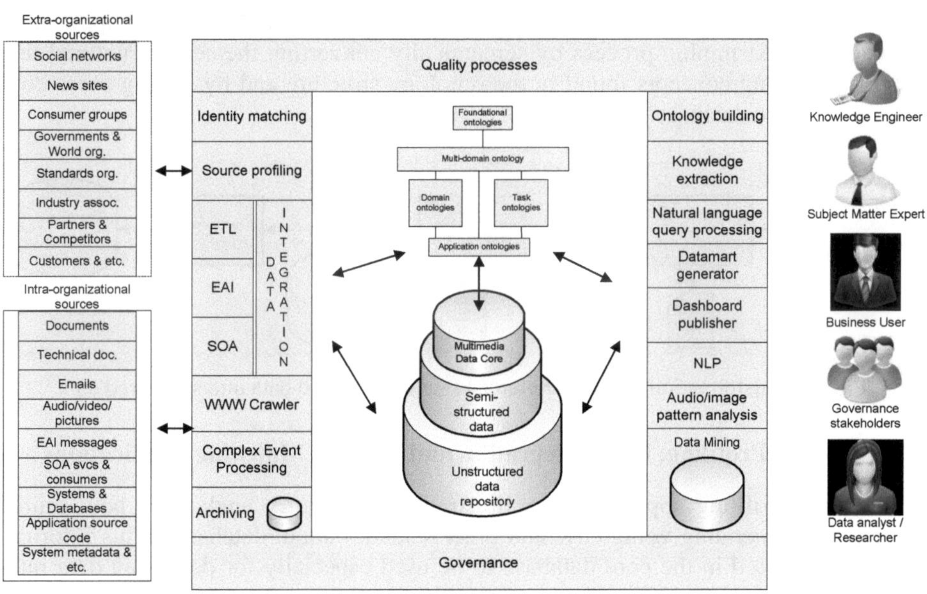

Fig. 1. Reference Architecture of an enterprise knowledge infrastructure (RA-EKI)

3.2 Description of RA-EKI`s Applications

3.2.1 Transformation of Unstructured Data and Semi-structured to Structured Data

The data transformation applications, as an assembly line, progressively convert unorganized, massive amount of symbols into structured data, as illustrated in figure 2. There are three data structures used for storage: the unstructured data repository, the semi-structured database and the multimedia database core. The unstructured data repository contains raw text XML files pre-processed and summarily annotated by the crawler application. The semi-structured database contains refined XML text files processed by the NLP part 1 application with syntactic transformation. The core database, contains structured data and multimedia material. Along with the ontology structure, the core database is RA-EKI's central data structure. This database is structured semantically in line with the multi-domain ontology. Assertions are stored in RDF triples and incorporated in an object relational database such as the core database for performance reasons[16].

The crawler application, using a decay concept and genetic programming as proposed by [17], and following search goals stored in the core database, navigates through the web and detects internet material of interest. The crawler extracts HTML pages, per example, and pre-processes them by removing unnecessary items such promotional hyperlinks. The crawler annotates the raw XML file with meta-information such as author, location and time, thus providing a useful context for downstream applications[17].

The NLP part 1 application performs syntactic, morphological and lexical analysis on the raw data and provides a sentence structure to the text. Nouns, verbs and other sentence items are tagged and meta-information is added. The NLP part 2 application finalizes the text mining process by semantically converting the semi-structured text and by extracting concepts found in the ontology structure and by storing these concepts in the core database.[14, 18].

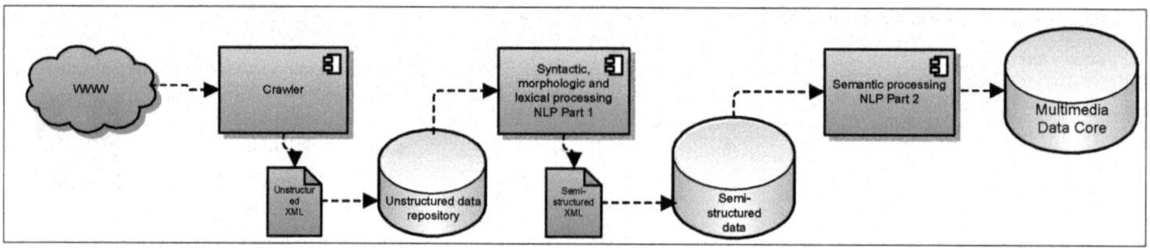

Fig. 2. Transformation of unstructured and semi-structured data into structured data

3.3 Source Profiling, Data Integration and Identity Matching Applications

The Source profiling application, as illustrated in figure 3, analyzes a new source database by generating volumetric and other statistics about databases. This information is then stored in the core database to be used especially for designing data integration mappings. It also provides an assessment on data quality issues.

The ontology-driven data integration applications convert in run time data from a heterogeneous source to a global schema that follows the same conceptualization as the multi-domain ontology and the core database. The three approaches used are EAI message broadcasting [5], SOA [6, 9, 10] and ETL [11, 19]. Although the underlying technologies are different, the fundamental mechanism remains the same. Mapping rules are also added to translate data from a heterogeneous source databases to the target global schema, represented in the ontology structure and core database. The mapping rules ensure that the source data are translated into the syntactic and semantic structures of RA-EKI's ontologies and core database. The same process is reversed when data is sent back to the source system either using SOA services or EAI message broadcasting. Current research issues can also be found notably in [13] about data integration in the context of knowledge management. Finally, the identity matching application is used in the attempt to associate objects, people and organizations per example, originating from different source databases but being potentially the same individual.

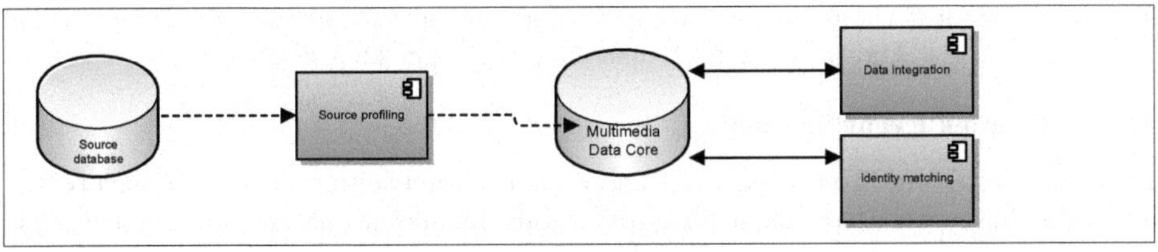

Fig. 3. Source profiling, data integration and identity matching applications

3.4 Transformation of Structured Data into Information

As highlighted by [4] and illustrated in figure 4, one of the more efficient and popular mean to distribute information consists in pulling decontextualized data from RA-EKI's core database and then re-contextualizing the data in the form of a user-friendly dashboard. The dashboard publisher is ontology based in RA-EKI. The datamart generator uses corporate objectives, critical success factors, key performance indicators and other performance monitoring requirements that are stored in the ontology structure and the core database. A requirements ontology-driven datamart generator may reduce the time for delivering a datamart[20].

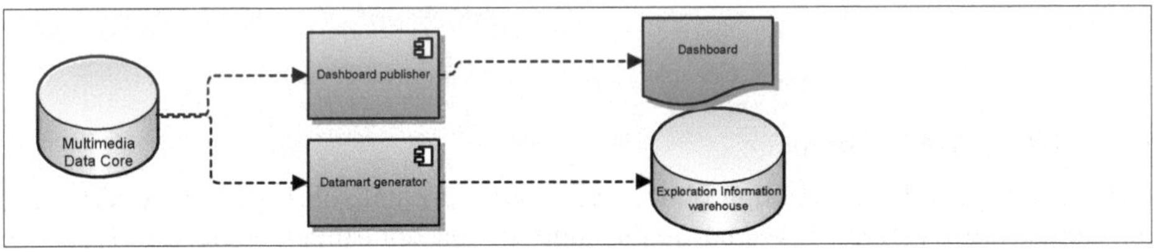

Fig. 4. Transformation of structured data into information

3.5 Transformation of Information into Knowledge

The data mining application, ironically, extracts knowledge not data. Through predictive and descriptive modeling, this design-time ontology-based application leverages the data scientist's skills and expertise to produce knowledge that can be encapsulated in a XML variant, a Predictive Model Markup Language (PMML). PMML is a standard adopted by most database technology manufacturers to facilitate the development and deployment of algorithms developed using data mining techniques. Research is currently conducted to perform ontology-driven knowledge extraction from PMML files[21]. RA-EKI knowledge extraction application stores extracted knowledge into the core database in transit to the downstream ontology building application. Various ontology-building methods are proposed in [4, 6, 16]. See figure 5 for the transformation of information into knowledge.

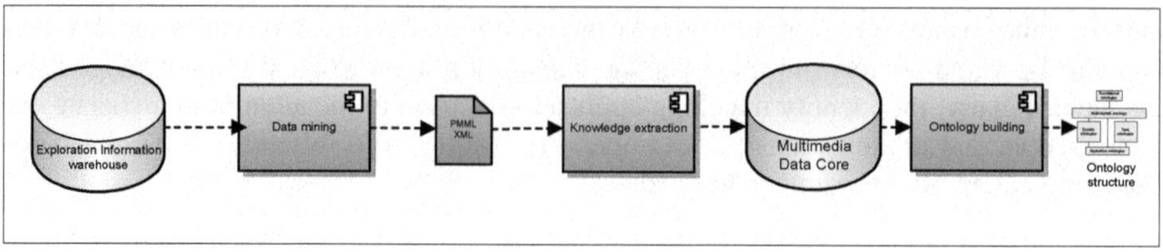

Fig. 5. Transformation of information into knowledge

3.6 Complex Event Processing

The Complex Event Processing (CEP) application, represented in figure 6, scans RA-EKI's databases on a continual basis. As these databases can be populated in right time, some data, such as those related to events, can be summarily analyzed by the CEP application. The ontology-driven CEP application attempts to detect any event of significance for the enterprise, guided by a set of prioritized subjects stored in the core database. This application may broadcast an alert through an EAI message, SOA service or using email services. The authors in [22] also describe an event ontology, an application and technology architectures dedicated to a CEP application. In RA-EKI, the CEP application shares with the other applications the same ontology structure and core database. The CEP application also stores the event in the core database.

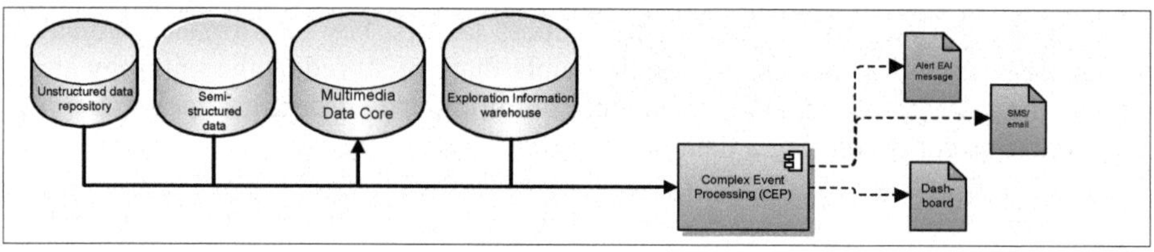

Fig. 6. Complex Event Processing (CEP)

3.7 Other Applications

The other applications, although playing equally important roles, will be covered in a subsequent publication. The data quality application contributes significantly to the overall capacity of RA-EKI to meet its challenges. The Archiving application effectively stores historical versions of data, information and knowledge that can be used by other application. Challenging research issues associated with multimedia mining are being addressed notably by [23].

4 Uses Case in Product Lifecycle Value Analysis

The following use case, outlined in table 2, illustrates the capacity of the RA-EKI model to provide assistance in performing product lifecycle value analysis by enhancing the process to transform massive amount of data into useful knowledge.[15] The use case formulates a competency question, describes the workflow used by ontology-driven components of the RA-EKI described, maps the concepts specific to the case against abstract concepts of RA-EKI's multi-domain ontology and core database, and identifies the sought benefits.

As indicated in[24], product design, that include product lifecycle value analysis, constitute one of the crucial stages in the entire product lifecycle. It often lacks procedural rigor and can progress through trial and error because of the complexity at hand. Furthermore, the massive amount of data affects product development, forcing the designers to spend a significant amount of time manipulating data in order to harvest crucial knowledge that may influence the product's commercial success.

Table 2. Use case in product lifecycle value analysis

Competency question:	"What are the factors that may influence the financial, customer and environmental value of the new product currently under development?"
RA-EKI workflow summary:	• The crawler detects government, social media and competitor sites, notably, in all countries or regions considered for the market. The crawler will pre-process acquired text in removing unnecessary items, annotate the text and generating annotation tokens to be stored in the core database; • The NLP function further annotates unstructured text and extracts structured data from internal documents, competitor web sites, social media texts with relevant material for sentiment analysis, government regulatory documents, past similar product recall events, etc.; • Imaging and voice-recognition functions also annotate pictures (similar products...) and voice recording from customer service centers' logs[23]; • The data mining support function allows the data analysts and researchers to develop targeting models to detect correlations and potential causalities that may influence the future product's market success; • The datamart generator, based on an goal oriented approach from [20], can produced in a semi-supervised mode, datamarts to provide a rich set of information to the product designers and to the product management governance stakeholders. • The knowledge extraction and integration functions pulls new semantic material from the core database and converts it into subsumed concepts, in a semi-supervised mode, in the ontology structure.[25]
Abstract concept mappings	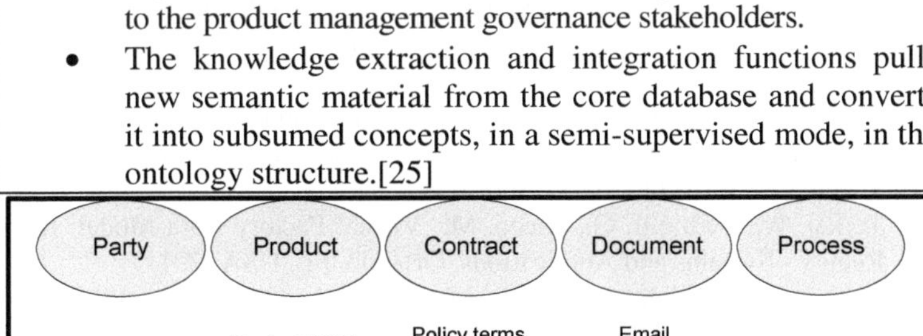
Benefits sought:	1. Provide the product designers and managers a 360-degree perspective on a new product to maximize its value and competitive position on the market. 2. Mitigate the risks by leveraging on lessons learned.

5 Conclusion

A significant number of publications have addressed the challenge of developing integrative ontologies to assist in the various stages of the product lifecycle management, and notably, in product lifecycle values analysis. This paper proposes a reference architecture, the RA-EKI, as the foundation of a comprehensive knowledge management that would allow a full cycle unstructured data to knowledge and know-how. The final results of this current project will constitute the foundation for future research involving the development of an implementation of the RA-EKI in the form of a prototype in laboratory settings and ultimately in a trial process to be performed the industry.

References

1. Khedher, A., Henry, S., Bouras, A.: Quality improvement of product data exchanged between engineering and production through the integration of dedicated information systems. In: 11th Biennial Conference on Engineering Systems Design and Analysis, Nantes, France (2012)
2. Marchetta, M., Mayer, F., Forradellas, R.: A reference framework following a proactive approach for Product Lifecycle Management. Computers in Industry 62(7), 672–683 (2011)
3. Fitzpatrick, D., Coallier, F., Ratté, S.: A holistic approach for the architecture and design of an ontology-based data integration capability in product master data management. In: Rivest, L., Bouras, A., Louhichi, B. (eds.) PLM 2012. IFIP AICT, vol. 388, pp. 559–568. Springer, Heidelberg (2012)
4. Mazumdar, S., Varga, A., Lanfranchi, V., Petrelli, D., Ciravegna, F.: A Knowledge Dashboard for Manufacturing Industries. In: García-Castro, R., Fensel, D., Antoniou, G. (eds.) ESWC 2011 Workshops. LNCS, vol. 7117, pp. 112–124. Springer, Heidelberg (2012)
5. Han, K., Park, J.: Process-centered knowledge model and enterprise ontology for the development of knowledge management system. Expert Systems with Applications 36(4), 7441–7447 (2009)
6. Raza, M., Harrison, R.: Information Modeling and Knowledge Management Approach to Reconfiguring Manufacturing Enterprises. International Journal of Advanced Information Technology (IJAIT) 1(3), 1–20 (2011)
7. Terkaj, W., Pedrielli, G., Sacco, M.: Virtual Factory Data Model. In: Virtual and Mixed Reality - Systems and Applications, Orlando, FL, USA (2011)
8. Lu, Y., et al.: Ontology Alignment for Networked Enterprises Information Systems Interoperability in Supply Chain Environment. International Journal of Computer Integrated Manufacturing 26(1-2), 140–151 (2013)
9. Yusuf, J., et al.: Extensive Overview of an Ontology-based Architecture for Accessing Multi-format Information for Disaster Management. In: International Conference on Information Retrieval & Knowledge Management (CAMP), Kuala Lumpur (2012)
10. Wang, X., Wang, T., Wang, G.: Service-oriented architecture for ontologies supporting multi-agent system negotiations in virtual enterprise. J. Intell. Manuf. 23, 1331–1349 (2012)

11. Thames, J., Eck, O., Schaefer, D.: A Semantic Association Hardware AcCeleration System for Integrated Product Data Management. Journal of Computing and Information Science in Engineering 12 (September 2012)
12. Liu, X., Yang, G.: Research of Ontology-based coal Enterprise Knowledge Management Model system. Applied Mechanics and Materials 40-41(625), 625–630 (2011)
13. Calvanese, D., De Giacomo, G., Lembo, D., Lenzerini, M., Rosati, R.: Conceptual modeling for data integration. In: Borgida, A.T., Chaudhri, V.K., Giorgini, P., Yu, E.S. (eds.) Mylopoulos Festschrift. LNCS, vol. 5600, pp. 173–197. Springer, Heidelberg (2009)
14. Feldman, R., Sanger, J.: The text mining handbook: Advanced approaches in analyzing unstructured data 2007, 410 p. Cambridge University Press (2007)
15. Terzi, S., et al.: Product lifecycle management - from its history to its new role. International Journal of Product Lifecycle Management 4(4), 360–389 (2010)
16. Khouri, S., Bellatreche, L.: DWOBS: Data Warehouse Design from Ontology-Based Sources. In: Yu, J.X., Kim, M.H., Unland, R. (eds.) DASFAA 2011, Part II. LNCS, vol. 6588, pp. 438–441. Springer, Heidelberg (2011)
17. Bazarganigilani, M., Syed, A., Burki, S.: Focused Web Crawling Using Decay Concept and Genetic Programming. International Journal of Data Mining & Knowledge Management Process (IJDKP) 1(1), 1–12 (2011)
18. Wimalasuriya, D.C., Dou, D.: Ontology-based information extraction: An introduction and a survey of current approaches. Journal of Information Science 36(3), 306–323 (2010)
19. Maynard, D., Saggion, H., Yankova, M., Bontcheva, K., Peters, W.: Natural language technology for information integration in business intelligence. In: Abramowicz, W. (ed.) BIS 2007. LNCS, vol. 4439, pp. 366–380. Springer, Heidelberg (2007)
20. Ta'a, A., Abdullah, M.: Goal-ontology approach for modeling and designing ETL processes. In: World Conference on Information Technology, pp. 942–948. Elsevier (2011)
21. Sottara, D., et al.: Enhancing a production rule engine with predictive models using PMML. In: PMML 2011 Proceedings of the 2011 Workshop on Predictive Markup Language Modeling (2011)
22. Schaaf, M., et al.: Semantic Complex Event Processing. Recent Researches in Applied Information Science, 38–43 (2012)
23. Perner, P.: Learning an ontology for visual tasks. In: Salerno, E., Çetin, A.E., Salvetti, O. (eds.) MUSCLE 2011. LNCS, vol. 7252, pp. 1–16. Springer, Heidelberg (2012)
24. Chandrasegaran, S.K., et al.: The evolution, challenges, and future of knowledge representation in product design systems. Computer-aided Design 45(2), 204–228 (2012)
25. Bissay, A., et al.: Knowledge integration through a PLM approach. In: 15th International Conference on New Technologies and Products in Machine Manufacturing Technologies, Sucuava, Romania (2009)

A Case Study on the Integration of GPS Concepts in a PLM Based Industrial Context

Francesco Ricci[1], Joel Sauza Bedolla[1], Javier Martinez Gomez[1,2], Suela Ruffa[1], Manuela De Maddis[1], and Paolo Chiabert[1]

[1] Politecnico di Torino, C.so Duca degli Abruzzi 24, Torino 10129, Italy
[2] Universidad Industrial de Santander, Calle 9 Cra.27, Bucaramanga, Colombia

Abstract. The innovative principles of the Geometrical Product Specification and Verification "GPS" framework promise a breakthrough in the management of geometry-related information and will lead to effective product management based on the concept of uncertainty minimization. GPS standards define a technical language completely based on mathematics to achieve these objectives and, for this reason, only major companies are able to cope with it. This paper presents a new methodological and software tool developed for integrating GPS principles into Product Lifecycle Management (PLM). It captures and structures the information gravitating around product geometry and finally encapsulates GPS principles into a user-friendly platform suitable for enterprises of any scale. This work also represents the first complete application of GPS standards to a product lifecycle, which is useful for training in the field.

1 Introduction

The work of the ISO Technical Committee 213 (ISO/TC-213) on Geometrical Product Specification and Verification (GPS) started in 1992 to modernize and improve on more than fifty years of industrial drawing and tolerancing practice consolidated in GD&T (Geometric Dimensioning and Tolerancing) standards [1]. The aim of TC-213 is to provide tools (the GPS technical language) for the economic management of variability in products and processes. GPS maintains the basic symbols of GD&T and introduces an operation-based representation of geometrical specification and verification procedures. It then uses the concept of uncertainty to quantify the system efficiency and identify the process areas on which to focus investments or reduce costs.

Since the GPS language is completely based on mathematics, the user's first impression is usually that it is more geared to academics than to industry. Hence, GPS principles need to be encapsulated into user-friendly applications that can be integrated into companies' Product Data Management (PDM) systems. GPS ensures the unambiguous declaration of the products geometrical requirements. However, the way this information is created, modified and exchanged is not within its declared bounds.

Nevertheless the GPS approach prepares the ground for a Product Lifecycle Management (PLM) system to assess and minimize the uncertainty generated at different steps of a product lifecycle. PLM is a strategic business approach that integrates all

A. Bernard, L. Rivest, and D. Dutta (Eds.): PLM 2013, IFIP AICT 409, pp. 336–345, 2013.

the information related to the company's products and activities, throughout the different phases of a product lifecycle, and allows its sharing within and between organizations [2,3]. Its aim is to ensure the fast, easy and trouble-free finding, refining, distribution and reutilization of the data required for daily operations [4].

Nowadays, GPS language is still in a state of dynamic change and continuous improvement [5]. While the main framework has already been drawn, innovative principles are still being studied by ISO experts, academics and industry [6]. At the same time, work is being done to integrate these new principles in the PDM practices. This paper is concerned both with tools, to deliver softwares able to handle the new kind of geometrical information, and with training, to spread the concepts on which GPS relies. This paper briefly presents the results that the Great 2020[1] research project achieved on this topic. An experimental case study is used to explore all the process areas involved in GPS (see Fig. 1.a) with particular attention to the implementation of uncertainty-based product management. In particular, a flatness requirement (the datum feature A of the workpiece shown in Fig. 1.b) is considered, realizing the first full application of a set of GPS standards (technically called "chain of standards" [6]).

2 The Novelty of GPS Standards

The GPS project was born to enhance the GD&T language, preserving the semantics of geometrical tolerances while adding more prescriptions aimed at guiding the verification procedures. These prescriptions are not provided aside the tolerance cartouche, but become part of the tolerance semantics: they are embedded in it by means of a detailed operation-based description, which sets clear limits for interpretation and becomes a guideline for proper verification [7]. However, even if specifications have all the attributes to fully prescribe the verification strategy, in the GPS fundaments there

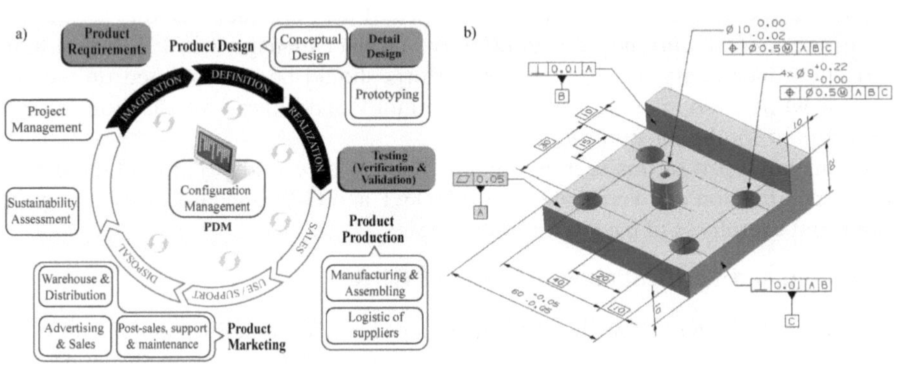

Fig. 1. a) Highlight of the stages of product lifecycle (in black) and process areas that are interested by the GPS standards (in gray) and b) the case study used to explore them

[1] The GREAT 2020 research project, funded by the Piedmont Region, involved the Polytechnic of Turin and several large, medium, and small Italian enterprises operating in the aerospace and aeronautic field, both as designers and manufacturers.

is the awareness that some uncertainty arises anytime the product information is exchanged between two parties or when it comes to cope with the limitations of real measuring instruments.

The GPS language looks at products on a perspective that is broader than that of GD&T, going further the mere definition of geometrical specifications and compliance verification [8]. The final aim of a workpiece is to perform a function (on its own or in the assembly of a more complex machine), therefore a proper assessment of its quality has to consider the consistency of the actual workpiece geometry with the functionality it is designed and demanded to satisfy. Though it may seem to be a nuance, this is a breakthrough point with respect to GD&T.

GPS gives birth to a series of uncertainty contributions that join the consolidated concept of *measurement uncertainty* [9] (innovatively divided into the components of *method uncertainty* and *implementation uncertainty*) in order to consider also the completeness and unambiguity of specifications (*specification uncertainty*), the capability to state the compliance of geometry with respect to the geometrical specifications (*compliance uncertainty*) and the adequacy of the geometrical specification to guarantee the functional needs (*correlation uncertainty*) [10]. All these uncertainty contributions participate in the *total uncertainty*, which describes the adequacy of the actual (measured) feature to guarantee the intended workpiece functionality, according to the scheme presented in Fig. 2.

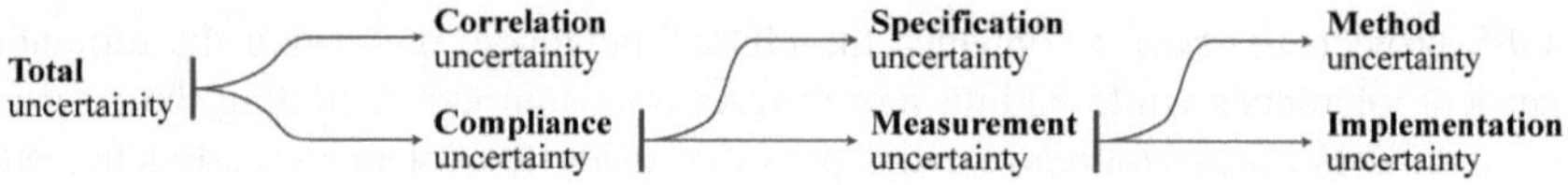

Fig. 2. Composition scheme for the GPS uncertainty contributions

The different terms of uncertainty introduced by GPS are powerful estimators of the quality of each stage of product development, starting from the first phase of design until the verification prior to delivery. Hence, if they are quantitatively estimated, they can become the currency for an effective product management [6]. E.g. a high specification uncertainty means that more efforts should be concentrated on the design phase while a too high measurement uncertainty underlines a verification process that is too poor for the job purpose.

The remaining part of this section uses the flatness case study to present the differences of specification and verification with GD&T and GPS standards, explaining the meaning and usefulness of each term of uncertainty.

Specification and Verification at the Time of GD&T

GD&T standards, born in 1966 [11], had been shaped to cope with the requirements of an industry led by the automotive and aeronautic/aerospace fields, hence, with the need to guarantee interchangeability within increasingly larger assemblies in a context strongly characterized by mass production. A set of symbols, the *geometrical tolerances,* was designed to control the geometry of components and guarantee the functional requirements of single workpieces as well as the assembly requirements (design for assembly). The semantic of these symbols is very clear and soundly defined from a geometrical and mathematical point of view (see the example of a flatness specification depicted in Fig. 3.a). However, it can be quite cumbersome when dealing with verification issues.

While the GD&T standards were defined, the economy of mass production, and the relative simplicity of most of specifications, allowed the realization of functional gauges that easily reproduced the envelope principle and the verification of mating conditions [12]. GD&T was born in symbiosis with these tools, and few recommendations were sufficient to guide most of the verification processes [13]. Particularly, the verification strategy for a flatness specification would require a measurement setup like the one shown in Fig. 3.b. Here the flatness error, whose values should be lower than the flatness tolerance for the feature to be acceptable, is represented by the maximum travel registered by the dial gauge.

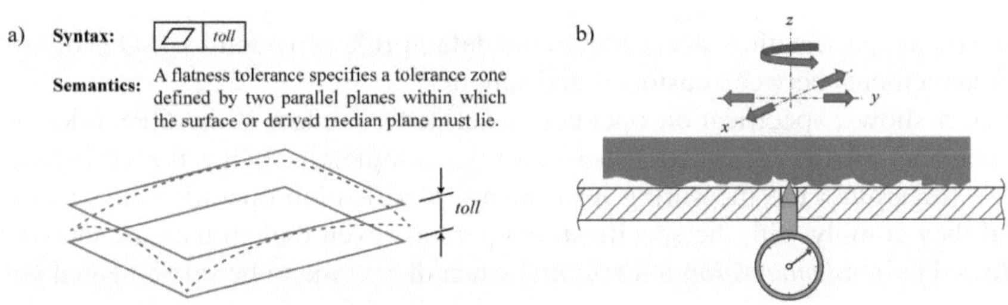

Fig. 3. a) Syntax and semantics of a flatness specification and b) measurement setup suggested by the GD&T standards for its verification

Nowadays the shift towards mass customization, the increased complexity of components, and the demand for precision features constrain the evolution of measuring equipments towards greater flexibility. The best mix of flexibility and accuracy, in this field, is represented by Coordinate Measuring Machines (CMM); instruments that have literally revolutionized the way of thinking about and taking measurements [14]. The characteristics of this revolution, and the aids provided by the GPS language to cope with the issues of the new measurement philosophy, are analyzed thoroughly in the next section.

Specification and Verification Based on GPS

The GPS language is based on seven operations that can be combined in operators to define geometrical specifications and verification procedures. According to the *duality principle* [11], these operations are defined by the designer on the skin model (a mental representation that is used to imagine the deviations from the nominal geometry that could be introduced by manufacturing processes), registered in the tolerance callout, and then replicated by the metrologist during verification procedures on the real workpiece. A graphical example of the operations necessary for defining and verifying a flatness specification (tolerance) is given in Fig. 4. Particularly each operation is completely addressed by the tolerance callout and consists of:

1) **Partition:** isolation of the feature to which the specification refers to.
2) **Extraction:** acquisition of the information necessary to define the feature characteristics. In the case of Fig. 4, it is a measurement where the distance between sampling points is minor than 0.357 mm in order to comply with the filter cut-off wavelength [15]).

3) **Filtration:** elaboration of measurement results in order to separate the content of deviation to which the specification refers to. Only the error components with a wavelength greater than 2.5 mm are to be considered for the assessment of the flatness deviation.
4) **Association:** a nominal flatness feature is fitted to the filtered measurement points according to the specified association criterion (Minimum Zone).
5) **Evaluation:** operation that returns the value of flatness deviation as the maximum distance of the filtered measurement points from the associated nominal feature.

After the verification operator has been implemented, the compliance with specifications can be assessed by comparing the results of the evaluation operation against the geometrical specification, according to the default rule provided by ISO [16] or to different agreements between customer and supplier.

As Fig. 5 shows, specification operator is defined complete if the GPS tolerance callout contains all the information necessary to completely define the verification procedure (regardless the measuring instrument). Verification operations are labeled *perfect* if they comply with the specification operator (even though they are unavoidably affected by *implementation uncertainty*, when they come to be implemented with a real measuring instrument) and *simplified* if they intentionally introduce some deviation (deviations add *method uncertainty*). If the specification is not complete, as for a GD&T geometric tolerance, every choice for the verification operations implies *specification uncertainty* as, for example, a metrologist that is using a CMM do not exactly know how many points to sample or the association criterion he should use to analyze them. With some examples presented here we can improve the understanding of verification operators and GPS uncertainties, however we recommend the ISO/TS 17450-2 [10] for a thorough reading.

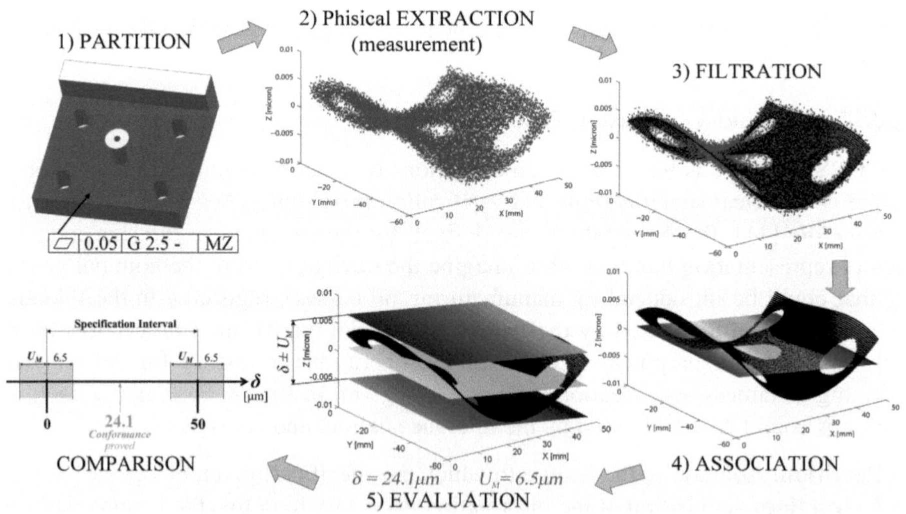

Fig. 4. Operations that define a verification operator fully compliant with specifications

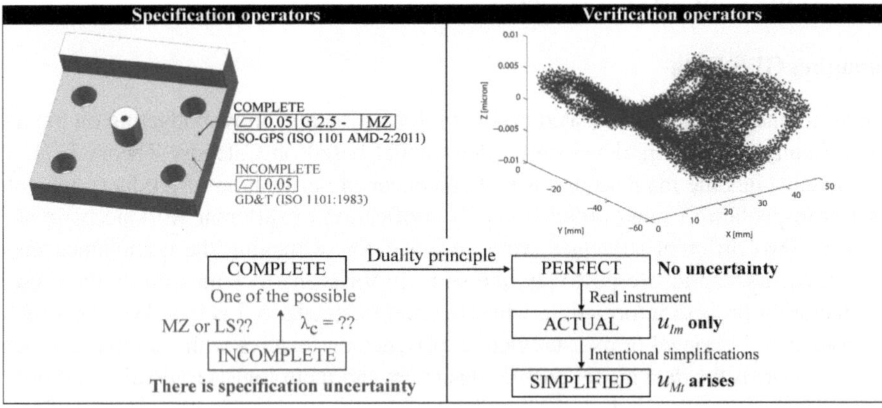

Fig. 5. GPS specification and verification operators with uncertainty contributions

For example, Fig. 6 shows the effect of association criteria on the assessment of flatness error. Two different criteria can be used according to GPS standards: Least Squares (LS) and Minimum Zone (MZ). The former always estimates an error larger than the latter, in this particular case 5 μm larger. Hence, if the LS method is used instead of the required MZ, the 5 μm difference shall be accounted as method uncertainty. On the other hand, if the specification is incomplete and does not explicitly require a particular association criterion, the same 5 μm difference shall be accounted as specification uncertainty whichever criterion is used.

The number of sampling points used to inspect the measurand, and their spatial distribution on the surface, can be a source of uncertainty too. If the reduction of sampling points is intentional, its effect should be accounted as method uncertainty, otherwise (e.g. the cutoff wavelength is not indicated in the tolerance callout as the specification is not complete) it should be accounted as specification uncertainty.

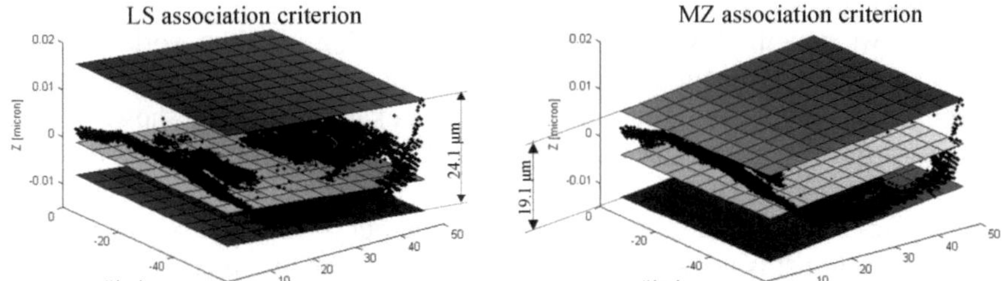

Fig. 6. Analysis of a cloud of measurement points with the LS and MZ association criteria. LS overestimates the flatness error of 5μm.

3 Achieving a GPS Based PLM

Managing GPS Data

In order to integrate all GPS-related product information and allow budgeting on the basis of uncertainty the authors developed a data model based on Category Theory [17]. The data model suites the main scenarios that can occur in verification of products geometry: 1) serial inspection of mass productions, 2) verification of different workpieces in small numbers. Two different strategies were designed for estimating the compliance uncertainty in each scenario. Respectively, the strategy for scenario 1 maximizes the reuse of manufacturing process information, while the one for scenario 2 is based on the structuring, storage and retrieval of measurement experience on features with a similar geometry. In both scenarios the data model enables designers and metrologists to predict (not only to assess) the uncertainties and costs associated with a given specification plus verification strategy; thus to use it for design purposes too. For a thorough presentation, reader refers to [18]. The data model was hence implemented into an object oriented programming language to obtain the *VerificationManager* software demonstrator. Until now it handles flatness features only, but can be expanded to the specification and verification of other geometrical features thanks to its general approach.

Integrating GPS into PLM

One of the main aims of the research project has been achieved by renewing the PLM system of each company involved, orienting it toward the GPS philosophy in order to allow the integration of instruments such as the *VerificationManager*. Amongst the different methodological approaches and modeling languages used for understanding and representing complex organization systems, *visual representation* was chosen for its capacity to show what lies within, to clarify relations, answer questions, and understand things that cannot be captured so readily in other forms [17]. We therefore developed a formal Visualization Model (VM) of enterprise processes that offers a graphic representation of the main elements of a product lifecycle (processes, people, tools, and information) involved in GPS and makes it possible to address them on an overall level [18].

Fig. 7 shows how the VM works. Particularly, starting from the workflow of GPS-related design and verification activities, that is shown in Fig. 7.a, a Decomposition Diagram (DD) is prepared for each activity. As an example, the DD shown in Fig. 7.b breaks down the "Measurement planning" into 5 simpler operations. Besides collecting simpler operations, DDs define the skills and tools that the metrologist shall use, the input items he will receive and the expected output documents. Notice that, at this level, the metrologist is not a person but a role that can be interpreted by a single person rather than a team. Fig. 7.c shows an example of output document obtained with the *VerificationManager*: a forecast of the uncertainties and cost of the verification strategy the metrologist is planning. A similar graphical representation, which for the sake of brevity is not reported here, describes each activity of the workflow.

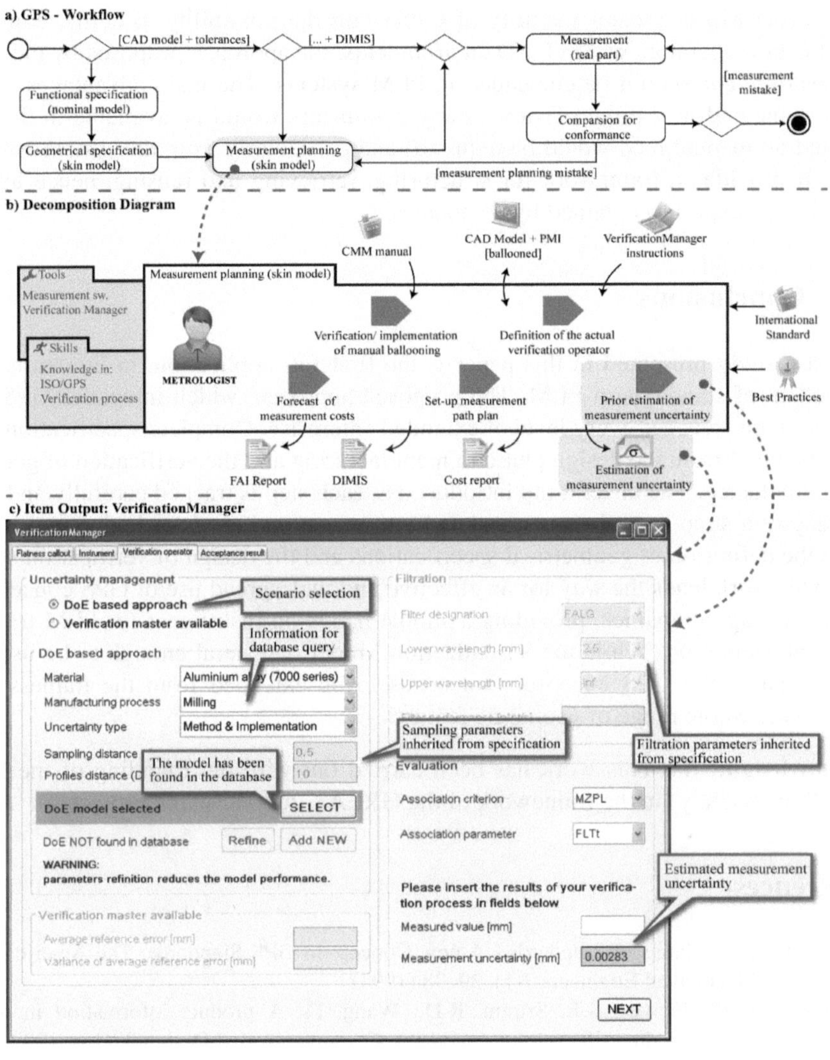

Fig. 7. VM of a GPS-based PLM: a) Workflow of design and verification activities; b) DD of one of the workflow activities: "Measurement planning"; c) Example of output item: "Estimation of the measurement uncertainty" using the *VerificationManager* tool

From the point of view of software implementation, at the state of the art, the *VerificationManager* is just a demonstrator and needs to be manually fed by users to work. Basically it needs to collect information about the complete specification operator and the actual verification operator (considering also the environment, the measurement strategy, the instrument at hand, etc.) to correctly assess the scenario, within those resumed in Fig. 5, and retrieve and elaborate the proper data for estimating the compliance uncertainty and the associated costs.

In a scenario of greater maturity of GPS, with the possibility to define complete specification operators within CAD environments, the approach proposed by the *VerificationManager* should be embedded in PLM systems. The main advantages would be from the end-user point of view (many parameters would be available in the system and no manual feed would be required) and particularly from the system point of view. It provides a framework for structuring, retrieving and reusing, hence adding value to, the experience gained by companies.

4 Conclusions

The case study presented in this paper is the first full application, in literature, of a GPS chain of standards in PLM. The proposed approach, which integrates GPS into PLM systems, reaches every level of extended enterprise. Complete specifications can be transmitted from the design phase to manufacturing and the verification of geometrical compliance. The uncertainty introduced at each step is tracked carefully and used as a decision support tool (it is translated into a cost and used for budgeting) to improve the definition of geometrical specifications and the design of verification strategies. This work leads the way for an effective and widespread use of GPS concepts in manufacturing companies, providing a simple hands-on instrument for PLM training and implementation. While the Visualization Model is general enough to be used by any company, the GPS encapsulation needs to be extended from the flatness case study to the whole range of geometric features.

Acknowledgments. This work has been carried out with the founding of the Piedmont Region (Italy) in the framework of the GREAT 2020 research project.

References

1. Bennich, P.: Chains of Standards - A new Concept in GPS Standards. The American Society of Mechanical Engineers 7(1), 29–38 (1994)
2. Sudarsan, R., Fenves, S.J., Sriram, R.D., Wang, F.: A product information modeling framework for product lifecycle management. Computer-Aided Design 37(13), 1399–1411 (2005), doi:10.1016/j.cad.2005.02.010
3. CIMdata PLM Market Trends & Evolution. CIMdata, Paris, France (2009)
4. Saaksvuori, A., Immonen, A.: Product Lifecycle Management, 3rd edn. Springer (2008)
5. Humienny, Z.: State of art in standardization in GPS area. CIRP Journal of Manufacturing Science and Technology 2(1), 1–7 (2009), doi:10.1016/j.cirpj.2009.06.007
6. ISO, Geometrical product specifications (GPS) - Masterplan. ISO/TR 14638. ISO, Geneve (1995)
7. ISO, Geometrical product specifications (GPS) - General concepts - Part 1: Model for geometrical specification and verification. ISO/TS 17450-1. ISO, Geneve (2005)
8. Srinivasan, V.: An Integrated View of Geometrical Product Specification and Verification. In: 7th CIRP Seminar on Computer-Aided Tolerancing, April 24 (2001)
9. ISO/IEC, Guide to the Expression of Uncertainty in Measurement (GUM: 1995). Guide 98-3. BIPM, IEC, IFCC, ISO, IUPAP, IUPAC, OIML (2008)

10. ISO, Geometrical product specifications (GPS) - General concepts - Part 2: Basic tenets, specifications, operators and Uncertainties. ISO/TS 17450-2. ISO, Geneve (2002)
11. ISO, Geometrical product specification (GPS) – Fundamentals – Concepts, principles and rules ISO 8015. ISO, Geneve (2011)
12. Chiabert, P., Lombardi, F., Orlando, M.: Benefits of geometric dimensioning and tolerancing. Journal of Materials Processing Technology 78(1-3), 29–35 (1998), doi:10.1016/s0924-0136(97)00459-7
13. ISO, ISO system of limits and fits - Part 2: Inspection of plain workpieces. ISO/R 1938. ISO, Geneve (1971)
14. Weckenmann, A., Knauer, M., Kunzmann, H.: The Influence of Measurement Strategy on the Uncertainty of CMM-Measurements. Annals of the CIRP 47(1), 451–454 (1998)
15. ISO, Geometrical product specifications (GPS) - Straightness - Part 2: Specification operators. ISO/TS 12780-2. ISO, Geneve (2003)
16. ISO, Geometrical product specifications (GPS) - Inspection by measurement of workpieces and measuring equipment – Part 1: Decision rules for proving conformance or non-conformance with specifications. ISO 14253-1. ISO, Geneve (1999)
17. Friendly, M.: Milestones in the history of thematic cartography, statistical graphics, and data visualization. Engineering 9(2) (2009)
18. Chiabert, P., Lombardi, F., Sauza Bedolla, J., Martinez Gomez, J.: Visualization Model for Product Lifecycle Management Annals of Faculty Engineering Hunedoara, vol. 11 (1) (2013)

Product Lifecycle Management Adoption versus Lifecycle Orientation: Evidences from Italian Companies

Monica Rossi[1], Dario Riboldi[1], Daniele Cerri[1], Sergio Terzi[2], and Marco Garetti[1]

[1] Politecnico di Milano, Milan, Italy
[2] Università degli Studi di Bergamo, Bergamo, Italy
{monica.rossi,daniele.cerri,marco.garetti}@polimi.it,
dario.riboldi@mail.polimi.it,
sergio.terzi@unibg.it

Abstract. The present paper shows some of the results coming from an Italian research initiative in the field of PLM. Aim of this initiative – partly supported by the Linked Design European project – is to conduct an empirical research on the main drivers and issues related with the implementation of PLM in industries. In particular, the relationship between "PLM adopter" and "lifecycle-oriented" companies is discussed in this paper.

Keywords: Product Lifecycle Management, Lifecycle orientation, Empirical research.

1 Introduction

What is PLM (Product Lifecycle Management)? How do enterprises intend these "lifecycle issues"? Are companies buying PLM suites also becoming "lifecycle-oriented"? These questions are often discussed at industrial level and some practitioners are struggling on them. The practical experience shows how PLM and its IT tools are more and more diffused in industries, even if a general confusion is still affecting the PLM concept itself. This issue is not new and it has its origin on the first days of the PLM market, when many acronyms were created to address the same issue. This confusion is in some way due to the same market opportunities that PLM has created in the last years: tons of vendors, consultants, practitioners are using the PLM acronym to present their methods, make their offers and sell their solutions, even if – at least sometimes – they support just a small slice of "lifecycle".

Within PLM, the term lifecycle has a central role, not only from a mere graphical point of view. Each product has a lifecycle: it is created, produced, delivered, used, maintained, retired, dismissed, etc. Several issues are pushing companies to consider the lifecycle of their products: for example, customers call for more reliable solutions, as well as the society asks for greener and less-polluting systems, while regulations demand to track all the history of an equipment, etc. In this, ideally, PLM aims to track, trace, store, manage, share all the knowledge generated along an artifact lifecycle, from its creation, design, development, to its production, distribution, till its

A. Bernard, L. Rivest, and D. Dutta (Eds.): PLM 2013, IFIP AICT 409, pp. 346–355, 2013.

utilization, dismantling, etc. In the real world, so far PLM has been limited to activities related with the design and development of a product, generally realized along the innovation process of manufacturing companies. In some way, it is possible to observe how the "lifecycle management concept" is still far from the real application of "PLM systems". Aim of this paper is exactly to arise this issue: are companies adopting PLM also lifecycle-oriented?

This paper comes from a research initiative currently on going in Italy, the so-called GeCo Observatory, which is collecting industrial experiences and case studies related to the PLM concept. The GeCo Observatory also works within the wider context of a European project, Linked Design, which aims to create the next generation of PLM solutions. The paper is organized as follow: section 2 gives an overview on the PLM concept, section 3 shows the results of the empirical research done in the Italian market, while section 4 debates the main results and concludes the paper.

2 Definition of PLM

Different issues contribute to the definition of PLM. First, PLM is the activity of managing product across the lifecycle, a kind of new model for managing company's processes in a more integrated and efficient lifecycle-oriented way [5]. For supporting this lifecycle perspective, information management is mandatory: PLM aims to post the right information, at the right moment, in the right place for an efficient capitalization of intellectual capital of a company [1]. Comprehensively, PLM is a business concept that leads the usage of all the information connected to the product in the organization [6]. Because of this holistic nature, the concept of PLM in an organization comprehends also IT aspects of it. Although IT is not sufficient to describe the entire concept, PLM is mainly based on IT implementations for the integration of people, processes, data, and information. In its IT essence, PLM is an extension of old PDM (Product Data Management) platforms that try to overcome the PDM boundaries, from the management of design data to – ideally – the planning and control of all the processes along the whole lifecycle. PLM IT systems have the purpose to connect engineering and design software to the other suites of manufacturing and supply chain in the organization [2] and generate a common view for all the product stakeholders.

As it is known, in the market there is thousands of IT solutions tagged as "PLM-ready", from CAD systems to web-based vaults. In the last year, PLM acronym has been added to the catalogue of many vendors, selling FEM solutions as well ERP suites. Today, the PLM IT market is made by a plethora of providers and many companies are nowadays adopting a PLM IT system, or part of it, in their business. But are these "PLM adopters" also "lifecycle-oriented companies"? Does really the PLM concept come first than the PLM IT system? These shiny questions arose in the mind of the authors and some answers are presented in the next paragraph.

3 Empirical Research

This research is part of a broader empirical study conducted by the researchers of the GeCo Observatory, an Italian initiative supported also by the Linked Design European project. The main research aims at investigating how manufacturing companies are structuring and managing their product design, development and engineering processes. The research is conducted with direct interviews made with technical directors, using a reference semi-structured questionnaire. This paper refers specifically to the questions and the collected data dealing with the company lifecycle consciousness and the adoption of PLM tools. 103 companies, coming from different sectors, compose the analyzed sample for this paper. 49 of them are typical Small and Medium Enterprises (SMEs), while 54 are bigger companies. The reference questionnaire adopted in the research is based on a CMMI maturity model [4], which describes and analyzes the design and engineering processes of a company according to three main dimensions (Organization, Process and Knowledge Management). Each dimension is divided in sub-dimensions. Each dimension is measured in terms of maturity of a specific practice, from a minimum value to a maximum one. The list of practices and their maturity have been created according to the literature, but for the purposes of this paper, it is not here detailed (see [4] for details). A subset of questions chosen from the main questionnaire was coupled to better represent the existence of a company attitude towards lifecycle consciousness (lifecycle-oriented), and the presence of PLM systems (PLM-adopter). These two dimensions are analyzed in detail in the next sections.

3.1 Lifecycle Orientation

The first dimension is called "Lifecycle Orientation", corresponding to the broader concept of product lifecycle introduced above. Each company provided an evaluation about how lifecycle phases are considered in taking design decisions. This evaluation is based on 5 steps, from 0 (not considered) to 4 (very high consideration). Generally, more persons answered to this question for each case and the resulting average was used as reference.

Lifecycle is defined in 3 main phases: Beginning of Life (BOL), Middle of Life (MOL) and End of Life (EOL). Data were collected using a more detailed lifecycle model, which identifies the following sub-phases:

- BOL: (i) Design and Industrialization, (ii) Manufacturing, (iii) Assembly, (iv) Testing, (v) Packaging and Warehousing,
- MOL: (i) Delivery and Distribution, (ii) Usage by the customer, (iii) Maintenance and After-sale Services provision,
- EOL: (i) Check, Re-Use, Updating, Revamping, and (ii) Disassembly, Recycling and Disposal.

Figure 1 shows the Lifecycle Orientation of the sample. BOL and MOL phases are normally well considered (a part sub-phases related with logistic and distribution tasks) during the design process, while EOL phase is barely considered.

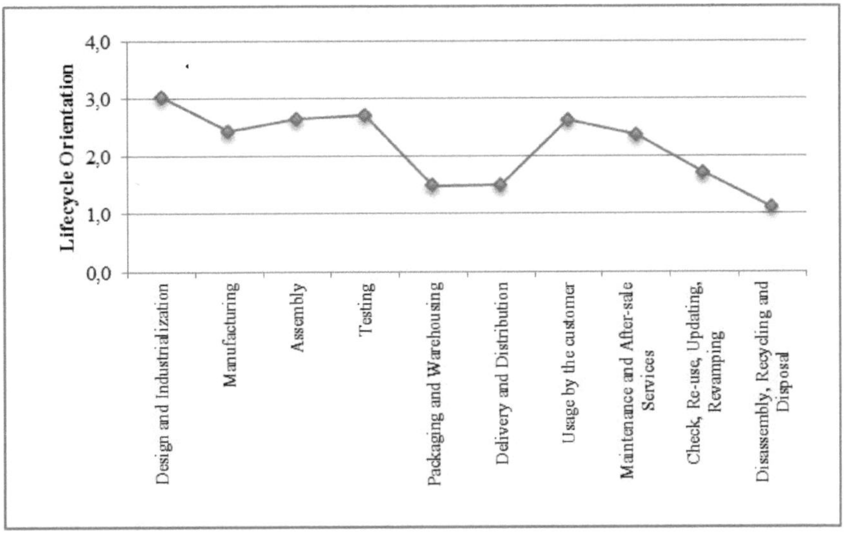

Fig. 1. Lifecycle Orientation of the sample

The degree of Lifecycle Orientation could be discussed according to two main affecting variables: (i) how the customer is involved in the design process of the company, and (ii) how the company structures itself to reply to the market demand. For the first variable, the analysis defines three positions:

- Companies not involving the customer in their design process. These companies serve the market with a detailed catalogue of solutions, not allowing relevant modifications / personalization.
- Companies involving partly representative customers in their design process, for providing them some levels of customization.
- Companies involving deeply the customer in their design process, providing highly personalized solutions.

According to this variable, Figure 2 shows that higher the possibility of product customization – consequently higher the involvement of the customer in the process – higher the consciousness of the downstream phases of the process at the beginning of the lifecycle is. Generally, companies that work with the possibility of product personalization have a higher average of Lifecycle Orientation. The second variable classifies a company according to the se-called CODP (Customer Order Decoupling Point), the logical point in the development process where the possibility of a company to control the growth of the variety of finished goods ends. Generally, this point is used to classify companies according to how they respond to their customers' demand. Possible positions are: ETO (Engineering To Order), MTO (Make To

Order), ATO (Assembly To Order), and MTS (Make To Stock). As Figure 3 shows, xTO companies (in particular ETO) have a higher consideration of downstream phases due to the customers' possibility to create their product from the upstream phases of the chain.

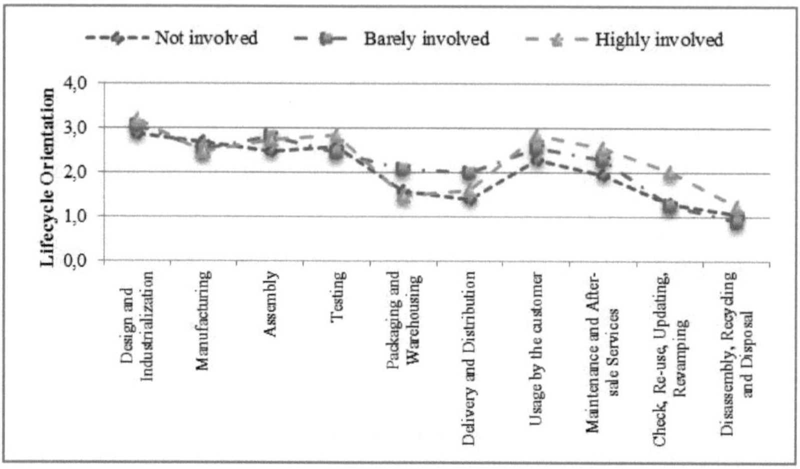

Fig. 2. Lifecycle Orientation of the sample, according to the degree of involvement of the customer in the design process

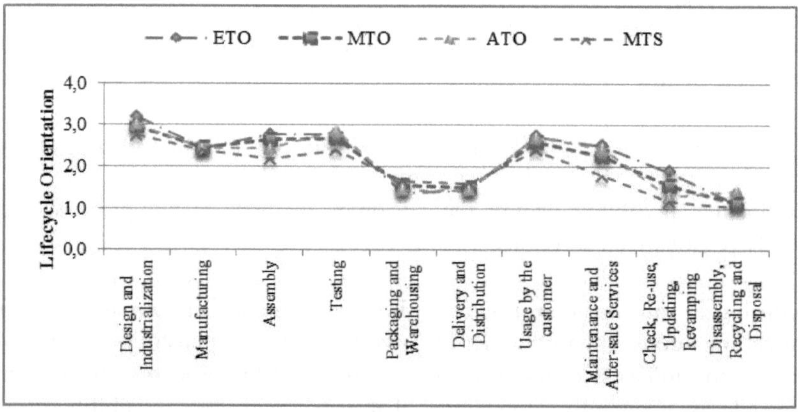

Fig. 3. Lifecycle Orientation of the sample, according to how the company replies to the market demand

3.2 PLM Adoption

A similar analysis has been conducted for the so-called "PLM Adoption" variable. For each single case, a deep analysis on the installed IT tools and platforms and their utilization has been performed. At the end, 59 companies among 103 were defined as "PLM adopters". These companies installed a PLM comprehensive platform for supporting the collaboration among different actors of the development process and they are using it for managing most of the explicit knowledge generated within.

A very interesting issue deals with the attitude of a company to reuse and retrieve knowledge from previous projects and experiences and the adoption of PLM IT systems. In the questionnaire, this analysis is made thought a complex variable which measures a maturity index (measured from 0 to 4): higher the index is, higher the knowledge reuse along the development process is. Figure 4 shows the results: PLM adopters re-use much more knowledge than companies without PLM. Figure 4 shows also how the index changes in the different stages of the design phase, from initial concept formulation, to detailed design, till final industrialization. This analysis confirms how PLM IT solutions are physically supporting the management of the enterprise knowledge. This happens independently from the type of industry, as well as from the type of company.

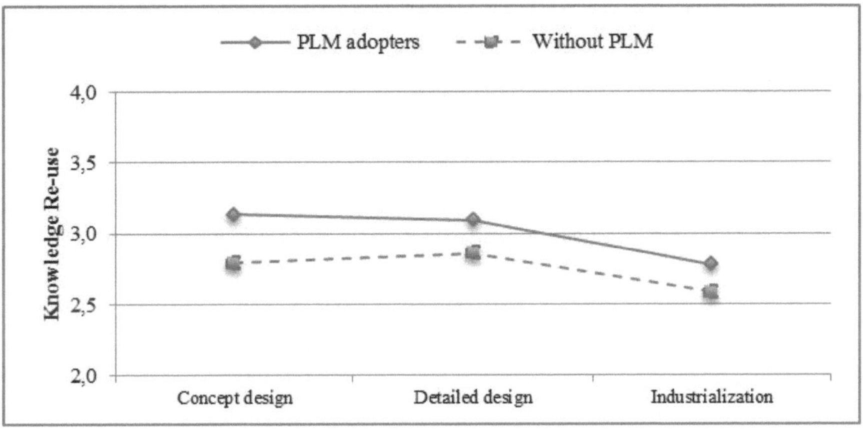

Fig. 4. Knowledge re-use versus PLM Adoption

Figure 5 represents the impact of lifecycle phases during the early stage of the process comparing PLM adopters and companies without PLM. Y-axis is the same of Figure 1, 2 and 3 (Lifecycle Orientation). It is evident how Lifecycle Orientation has a direct link with PLM Adoption. In average, PLM adopters show a higher consideration of the lifecycle, generally 15% more than companies without PLM, even if the general trend of the lifecycle consciousness of the whole sample is still confirmed. The small improvement of Lifecycle Orientation is provided by the utilization of PLM systems, which generally bring better organization and discipline in the development process of the company, supporting a more holistic view on the whole lifecycle. The data of the sample could support the evidence that companies with a high lifecycle consideration can better exploit it with a complete and conscious use of a PLM system. This evidence could be partly confirmed making a cross analysis of the previously presented variables. Figure 2 and 3 showed sensitively how more customer-oriented companies have higher consideration of the product lifecycle: being focused on their customers' request, they need to provide products with more reliable lifecycles. Then, Figure 6 and Figure 7 show how customer-oriented companies adopting PLM systems are more lifecycle-oriented that the same type of companies without PLM.

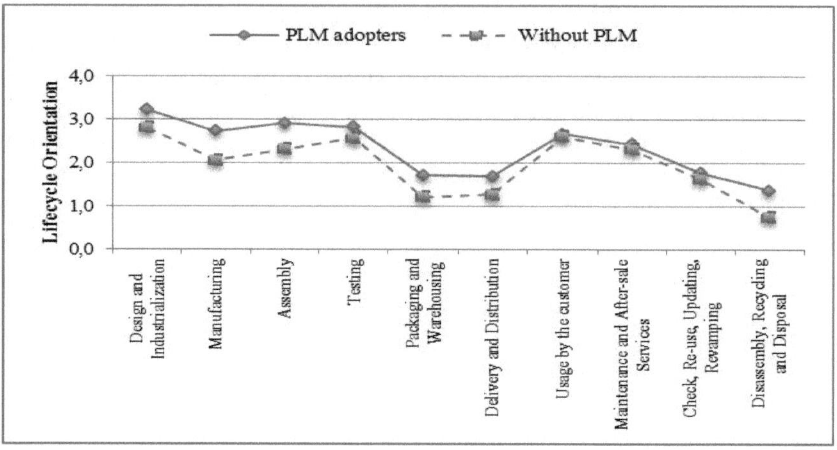

Fig. 5. Lifecycle Orientation versus PLM Adoption

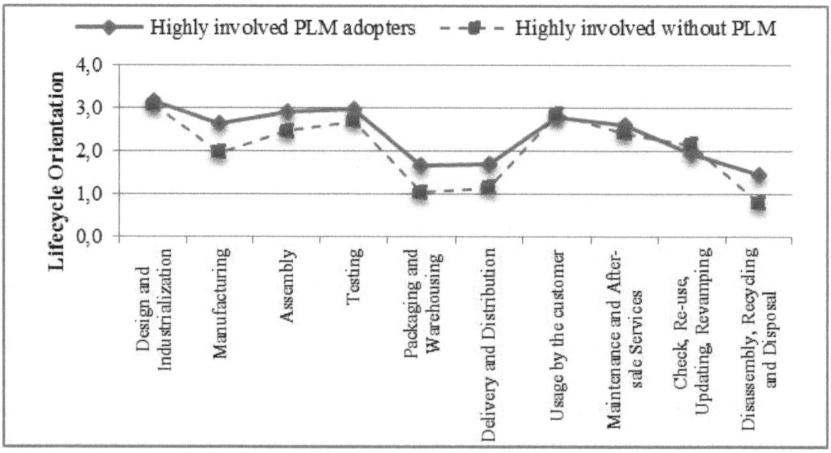

Fig. 6. Lifecycle Orientation of companies highly involving customers in the design process versus PLM Adoption

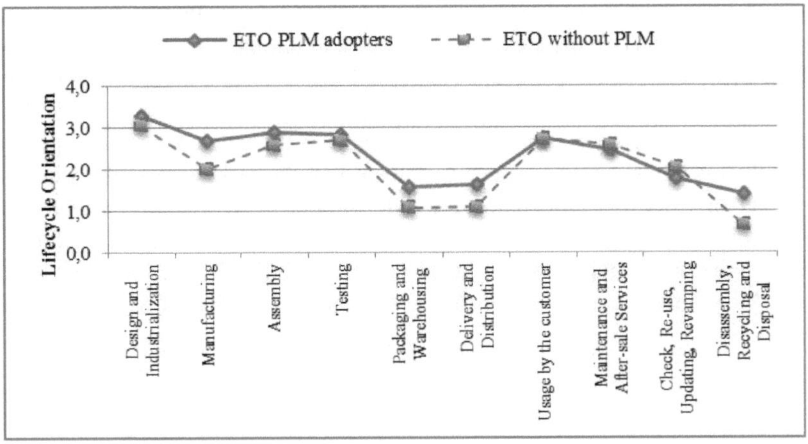

Fig. 7. Lifecycle Orientation of ETO companies versus PLM Adoption

4 Conclusions

PLM acronym has a wide definition, intrinsically linked with the usage of IT solutions along the ideal product lifecycle. The fact that the PLM acronym is today used and known is already a good result, after that for years a plethora of acronyms and terms have been proposed by vendors, consultants and academics to address similar issues.

Said this, it might be noticed that the use of PLM acronym is not an easy task. In some way, it is possible to argue that the same PLM acronym could generate a kind of confusion in a listener/reader, due to the double meaning that it embodies. The first meaning concerns with the fact that lifecycle phases might be more and more considered in developing a product, and PLM aims to support this. The second refers to the industrial need of managing efficiently the huge amount of data distributed among different functions and actors and dispersed in a plethora of IT solutions, and again PLM aims to do this. PLM has in itself a kind of dichotomy: it is a concept, and it deals with IT.

In the market, there are some lifecycle-oriented companies, which make their design decisions considering the impacts on the lifecycle of their products (how it will be produced, how it will be used, how it will be maintained, etc.). At the same time, in the market there are companies using IT solutions for defining and managing the lifecycle knowledge of their product (or part of it).

In this paper, we have investigated these two dimensions in real companies: Lifecycle Orientation and PLM Adoption. Data showed how Lifecycle Orientation is a matter of customer-orientation: more a company is focused on the needs of its customer more a company is lifecycle-oriented. The adoption of PLM IT solutions is intrinsically a matter of knowledge management. IT systems support the creation and the re-use of knowledge, permitting a better management of design and development processes. Crossing these two dimensions, some interesting results appeared: in average, PLM adopters are more lifecycle-oriented than companies without PLM IT solutions. We cannot say the opposite: not all the lifecycle-oriented companies are also PLM adopters. Figure 8 maps the global Lifecycle Orientation of the sample with the PLM Adoption. The first variable is defined as the total area covered by the curve of Lifecycle Orientation of each specific case (analytically it is the integral of the curve). This figure shows how several companies with a high level of Lifecycle Orientation are still without PLM systems in their practices. There are some clusters of companies, which could be explained in terms of time (not all the lifecycle-oriented companies have already installed a PLM system) and/or in terms of needs (PLM systems are installed for managing product knowledge, without any lifecycle reason).

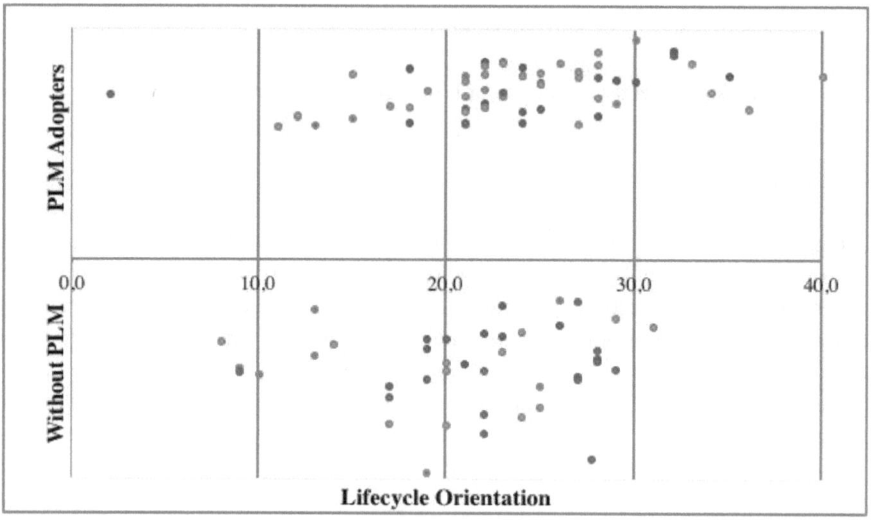

Fig. 8. PLM Adoption and Lifecycle Orientation of the sample (each dot is a company, while the different colors mean companies' dimension)

The performed research has tons of limits. It has been carried on only 103 cases and only in Italy. Not all the performed analysis have been presented, and many of the possible analysis were not performed, not-having adequate data. However, the authors believe that this discussion will arise again in the future of PLM, being intimately part of it.

Acknowledgments. This work was partly funded by the European Commission through the Linked Design Project (FP7-2011-NMP-ICT-FoF, www.linkeddesign.eu). The GeCo Observatory was also partly funded by some PLM vendors. The authors wish to acknowledge their gratitude and appreciation to all the partners and supporters for their contributions. Moreover, the authors wish to thank the reviewers of PLM13 for their valuable comments.

References

1. Ameri, F., Dutta, D.: Product Lifecycle Management: Closing the Knowledge Loops. Computer-Aided Design & Applications 2(5), 577–590 (2005)
2. Garetti, M., Terzi, S., Bertacci, N., Brianza, M.: Organisational change and knowledge management in PLM implementation. Int. J. of Product Lifecycle Management 1(1), 43–51 (2005)
3. GeCo Observatory, http://www.osservatorio-geco.it
4. Rossi, M., Terzi, S., Garetti, M.: Proposal of an Assessment Model for New Product Development. In: Emmanouilidis, C., Taisch, M., Kiritsis, D. (eds.) APMS 2012. IFIP AICT, vol. 397, pp. 383–390. Springer, Heidelberg (2013)
5. Terzi, S., Bouras, A., Dutta, D., Garetti, M., Kiritsis, D.: Product lifecycle management – from its history to its new role. Int. J. of Product Lifecycle Management 4(4), 360–389 (2010)
6. Silventoinen, A., Pels, H.J., Kärkkäinen, H., Lampela, H.: Towards future PLM maturity assessment dimensions. In: PLM 2011 - The IFIP WG 5.1 Global Product Development for the Whole Lifecycle, 8th International Conference on Product Lifecycle Management, Eindhoven, The Netherlands, July 11-13 (2011)

The Role of Enterprise Social Media in the Development of Aerospace Industry Best Practices

Nancy Doumit[1], Greg Huet[2], and Clément Fortin[1]

[1] Department of Mechanical Engineering, École Polytechnique of Montreal, Canada
{nancy.doumit,clement.fortin}@polymtl.ca
[2] Department of Automated Production Engineering, École de Technologie Supérieure, Montreal, Canada
Gregory.Huet@etsmtl.ca

Abstract. This paper presents a new approach for the development of best practices in the aerospace industry through social media. A survey and semi-structured interviews used on a smaller sample suggest that integrating social media to formal organizational structures around a community of practice could indeed be employed to facilitate knowledge and experience sharing between established experts and participants. Finally, this paper also explores the extension of this framework to complement more formal and structured information processes typically managed by PLM solutions to better support the development of best practices via communities of practice. In this case, a complementary link between best practices under development in a community of practice and the design solution being developed in the Digital Mock-Up is presented.

1 Introduction

Best practices as clarified by Szulanski (1996) are a "replication of an internal practice that is performed in a superior way to internal alternated practices and known alternatives outside the company. The practice refers to the organization routine use of knowledge and often has tacit component embedded". The widespread terminology of "best" practice however can easily lead to confusion; it is not so much a universal practice, but rather a localized one related to a specific context. Methodologies and tools in engineering are typically based on a set of theoretical foundations but many are then adapted in their practical formulation in order to meet the specific needs of their implementation context. A common illustration of this would be the use of the House of Quality methodology in different companies. Although the general framework does not vary, each firm will adapt the tool to suit the specific objectives of its implementation. These "in house" adaptations or variants are typically documented in the form of best practices (Cristiano et al. 2000). In order to generate and validate this type of corporate knowledge, companies rely on experienced users to rationalize, document, and disseminate best practices using a network of colleagues and following a standard verification and validation process. Although best practices

A. Bernard, L. Rivest, and D. Dutta (Eds.): PLM 2013, IFIP AICT 409, pp. 356–364, 2013.

are quite obviously a core item of corporate knowledge, their production is time consuming and their use across projects and departments can be erratic. This research targets improved approaches to best practice development in aerospace, more specifically the study explores how enterprise social media could be used to improve best practice sharing within a community of practice. The data is based on an industrial case study from which qualitative aspects have been analyzed. The observations and conclusions reported in the paper are grounded on information gathered from interviews and process maps. Before presenting the results of the case study, the current role and perceived value of social media in the enterprise is reviewed.

2 Social Media in the Enterprise

In the context of the enterprise and from a systems perspective, social media poses interesting challenges. Indeed, enterprise social networking activities through internet based social software suggest a number of different scenarios that in some cases involve radical transformations with respect to the borders of the enterprise system and its environment. To some extent, many of these "new" collaboration scenarios have always existed but through informal and often secretive mechanisms; the support offered by social software and the internet has quite simply extended communication modes and collaborative knowledge sources that could not have been imagined even a decade ago.

Should social media be bounded by the borders of the enterprise? Wouldn't this limit the collaborative knowledge potential that social networking brings to the table? Are some departments or teams at risk of jeopardizing their decisional influence with respect to operational processes?

As these question suggest, most of the concerns related to the deployment of social software in the enterprise are related to information security and quality; the communication and collaboration potential of this new medium characterized by its informal and spontaneous attributes is counterbalanced by a risk of Intellectual Property leakage. Moreover, policies in place imply that all information shared, whether it is be through formal or informal communication processes, is subjected to governmental aviation authority regulations (EASA, FAA, etc.). From a judicial perspective, social media are considered an extension of electronically stored information —ESI— (Carlisle 2012) and the same tracking rules apply to any information/document shared on this kind of platform. Businesses are therefore obliged to develop guidelines, policies and procedures to safeguard from legal action. In this paper, the integration of social computing in the enterprise is viewed in a context which avoids these organizational dilemmas. The role of enterprise social media in the development of aerospace industry best practices is studied in a specific environment where the networking activities take place within the boundaries of a firm.

2.1 Use of Social Media to Support Communities of Practice

Over the last two decades, a new recognized group structure – Communities of Practice – has emerged to complement the existing formal work breakdown structures that divide a company, e.g. departments, functions or Integrated Product Teams. According to Wenger and Sydner (2000) Communities of Practice (CoP) can be defined as "groups of people informally bound together by shared expertise and passion for a joint enterprise". A CoP is therefore characterized by a domain, a group of people (the community), and shared practices. The domain is typically an expertise that is practiced by a number of individuals engaged in sharing the knowledge and experiences through joint activities and discussions. In an enterprise context, CoPs are consolidated through five means: mutual engagement, interpersonal relationships, joint enterprise, identity acquisition and shared repertory (Wenger 1999).

With the various collaborative features proposed by social software, technology now plays an important role in the establishment and vitality of CoPs. They enable the virtual exchange of information between collocated and distributed communities, also known as Virtual Communities of Practice, i.e. " CoPs supported by information and communication technologies" (Annabi et al. 2012).

Social media rely on a number of collective participation tools such as blogs (individual authorship) or wikis (group authorship) to capture and distribute information. McAfee (2006) proposes an interesting classification of the types of activities that can be supported by social software in the context of the enterprise under the acronym "SLATES" (Search, Links, Authoring, Tags, Extensions and Signals).

3 Improving Best Practices through Social Media

The field study on best practices carried out by the authors encompasses two specific investigations: a study of the company's current processes and semi structured interviews. Results from these two investigations are reported in this paper. It is important to note that the notions of "best practices" in this study are essentially related to the following types of contents:

- Design aspects that needed to be taken into consideration during the preliminary design phase. (e.g.: Maintenance and accessibility criteria)
- The types of analysis required. (e.g.: Pressure drop analysis)
- Design evaluation criteria and preferred tool to meet those criteria. (e.g.: Nominal clearance between systems)
- Procedures specific to the department under study. (e.g.: Parts release)

3.1 Process Based Analysis

In this section, the descriptive study of a best practice development process aims at providing the reader with an illustrated reference of the actual approach taken by the company without the use of a social media. The data used to build the best practice development process presented in Fig. 1 was based on existing documentation and a work session with various experts in the department to validate the map.

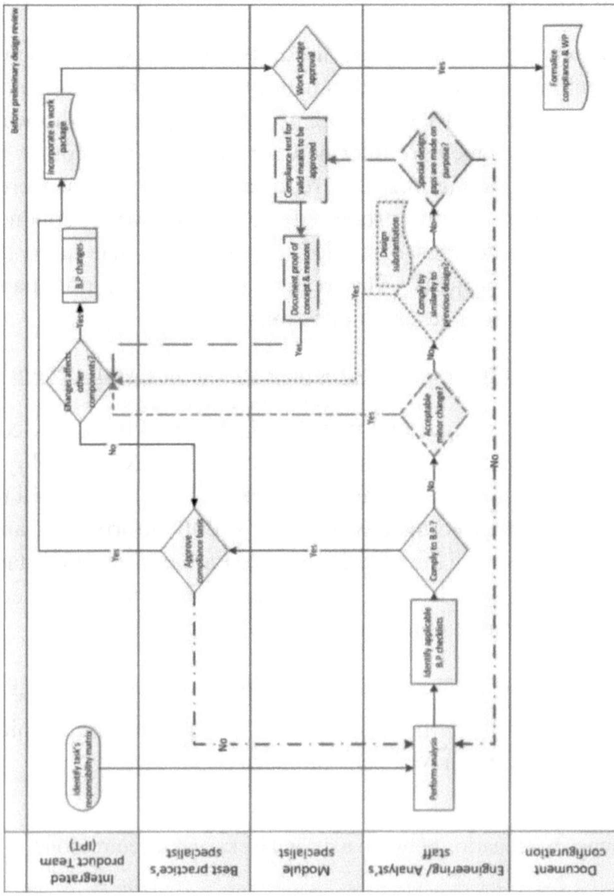

Fig. 1. Best practice development process in an aerospace company

The process highlights a long validation process of the best practice's check list. It is very sequential and activities are therefore executed through a linear flow path up to the validation gate. It is important to note that information is not shared among the different roles for feedback unless the designer has collected a minimum required set of proof of compliance. This is a rather inefficient approach as external parties have generally more objectivity to identify missing information. Furthermore the close supervision of an expert would help point to similarities in previous designs. The information is only shared late in the process hence exposing the best practice development to greater rework.

3.2 Interview Analysis

The preliminary process analysis was used to build a semi structured interview focusing on current best practice development process in the company. An initial list of participants was suggested by the company. Most engineers who were interviewed also recommended colleagues to interview or referred to another department or discipline. In this study the authors only reported interviews that were conducted in one specific department. Semi structured interviews were conducted with ten engineers with different degrees of seniority working in the same department but sometimes on different projects. The results presented in this paper have been summarized according to four research questions.

Question 1: When do you refer to best practices to validate your design activities?

The experienced engineers suggested that they had a working knowledge of the best practices and therefore hardly ever consult the documents. New employees (2 years of experience or less) are not always aware of the existence of a best practice for a given design task and for them finding any kind of useful information and guidance is already a challenge in itself. This case highlighted a basic yet important requirement for best practice distribution: when a design task is initiated, the users must have a reminder of the corresponding company best practices.

Question 2: What happens when a given design task ignores an existing best practice?

If the design does not follow the best practice's guideline, five typical cases were raised by the participants and have been summarized in table 1.

Table 1. Discrepancy scenarios between a design tasks and its corresponding best practice

Discrepancy	Typical mitigation
Case 1: The process or methodology used is similar to the best practice	The designer must detail a "proof of similarity" with previous designs. The proof is verified by best practice specialists before approval
Case 2: The results do not affect safety and do not impact other components.	The designer must flag the component so that this result cannot be used as a proof of similarity on future designs
Case 3: The divergence with the best practice has been endorsed by the IPT	A request for approval from the best practices specialist must be sought. A revision of the corresponding process based best practice will often be initiated.
Case 4 : A request for change of best practice is required	The formal change management process is engaged very much like a design change on a released part. Many different actors are involved in this prolonged amendment process.
Case 5 : All cases above are rejected	The design must be entirely revised to meet best practice requirements

Question 3: What would be your suggestions in terms of tools to improve best practice dissemination?

"Message boards with very specific topics. Currently we write memos to summarize the knowledge but they are not generally categorized. Organizing them into a coherent structure would certainly help in finding relevant data.".

"Efficient search engine and better indexing, the ability to write and properly control non-technical data is what we need".

A forum under a question/answer format could ease the clarification of a specific requirement or interpretation of an analysis. Since several companies have already their internal wikis, the majority of interviewees agreed on adding a wiki platform to share definitions and know how; "currently, only one person can work on a document at any one time. The only way around this is to use shared worksheets on public drives" more specifically some asked for "wiki pages". People expressed also their need to have a list of people outside the team with their expertise to know who they must contact.

The scope of the interview was wider than just best practice development and aimed at measuring the interest of using social media around a community of practice to facilitate knowledge and experience sharing between established employees. Fourteen engineers answered the questions.

Of all the respondents, only one had heard about an existing community of practice in another department. A short review on CoPs was therefore programmed as a training activity for the department._For the purpose of this study, only the results concerning the features of social software are presented. Figure 2 summarizes the results for each category of feature.

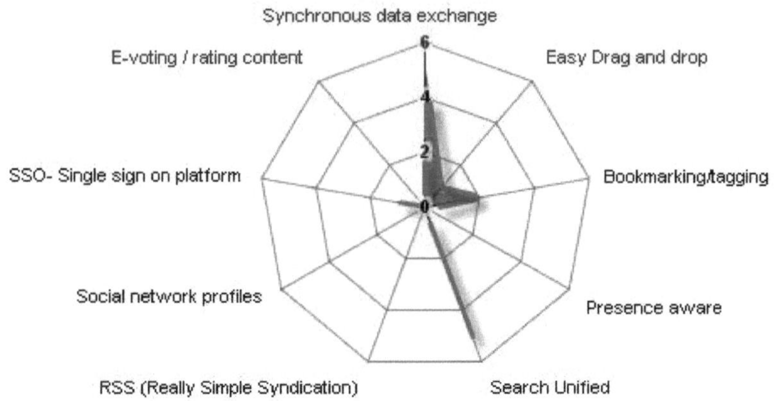

Fig. 2. Social media features relevant to engineering day to day work

This analysis confirmed what had been said during the interviews. Indeed, users need to edit documents at the same time while having a unified search (36 %). Engineers first want to solve their current barriers in information sharing; once a single platform (7%) answers their needs in term of co-authoring (36%) and tagging (14%) they might need extra features to enhance the collaboration process.

3.3 Future State: Developing Best Practices Using Social Media

In this prescribed scenario, engineers can openly join any engineering community or can be requested to join one for the purpose of a specific project. The community exists as long as the design is not in production or there is interest to keep it (indicating the existence of a key knowledge domain).

As a first interaction, designers would make use of the "discussion" type features such as a question/answer (Q/A) forum to get insight about the job to do. As shown in Figure 3, the essential contribution of the design focused virtual community of practice is to facilitate the problem definition phase, i.e. when designers make hypotheses and look for constraints related to the perceived tasks (typically found in company best practices). Thanks to the virtual CoP, knowledge is gradually and collaboratively explored with the inputs from at least the following key participants: moderator, best practice specialist, subject expert, security/legal representative.

Based on the investigations reported in the previous sections of this paper, the authors prescribed a preliminary best practice development process integrating social media. A generic version of this process is illustrated in figure 3.

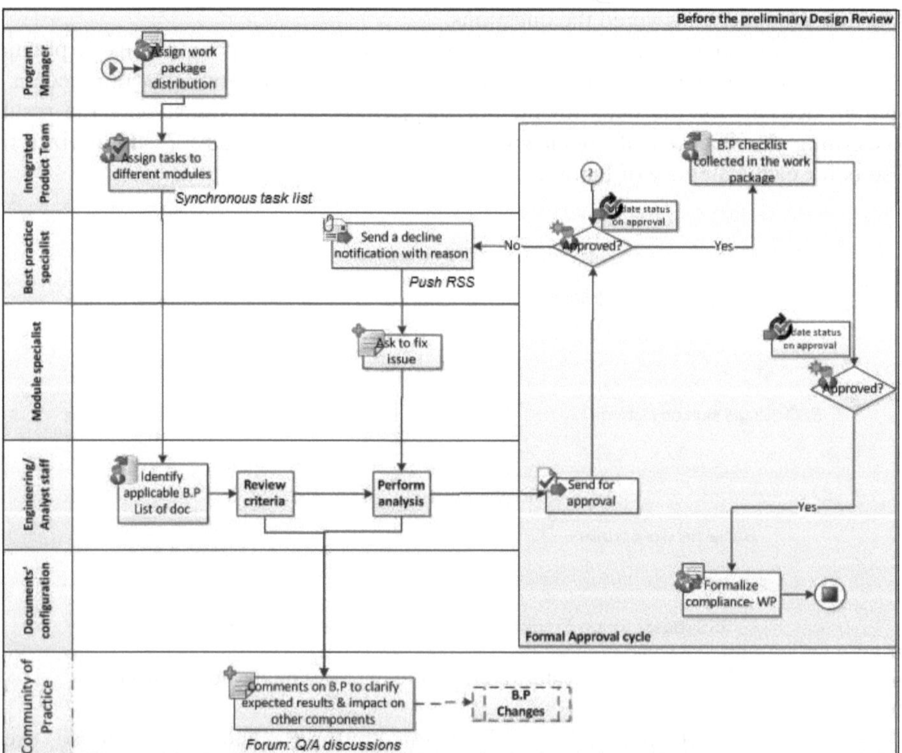

Fig. 3. Prescribed best practice development

4 The Potential Role of PLM and Future State

With the advent of Social PLM (Brown 2012), the aforementioned benefits of social software could be integrated to a more secure information platform used by a number of engineering designers. Hence, information about a product and the related know how could be exchanged in a continuous workflow and once formalized would then be pushed to a single secure location in the PLM. Distributed information on social media would follow a maturity curve up to a certain level of confidence where the information is formalized and attached to the controlled product structure. Social tools could be extended to support some formal data as the maturity of the data evolves.

Since the focus of ongoing research is on the best practice definition and refinement, a correlation with the above proposition can be made with the current study: knowledge about a specific component could be shared among CoPs based on the best practices as knowledge references, then formalized and linked to the product structure as it reaches a certain maturity level.

For the aerospace case study, this framework can be achieved using two different approaches: either two separate platforms (PLM and Social Media) or imbedded social functionalities within the PLM software. In the case where both platforms a separated, the social networking advantages are made available to the entire company and focused on knowledge sharing at large; indeed, PLM remains more of a specialist tool and as such does not propose the same user friendliness nor does it really extend to the entire enterprise (Huet et al. 2012). On the other hand, imbedded social features propose a unified platform to engineers. Both approaches need nonetheless to be pursued as social media is now well documented to offer the unique advantage of converting collaborative tacit knowledge into explicit information (Panahi et al. 2012).

Even though using social media to support virtual CoPs has been successfully demonstrated (Michaelides et al. 2010), there are few reported studies on the use of virtual CoPs to share engineering design knowledge. Further work needs to be done to ensure the validity of the proposition and as such this paper should be regarded as a work in progress. The research is now set to focus on establishing the detailed requirements for the customization of enterprise social software in the company with the constraints of complementing the use of a large PLM platform.

References

Annabi, H., McGann, S.T., Pels, S., Arnold, P., Rivinus, C.: Guidelines to align communities of practice with business objectives: An application of social media. In: 45th Hawaii International Conference on System Sciences (HICSS), Maui, Hawaii, pp. 3869–3878. IEEE (January 2012)

Brown, J.: Social Business Collaboration and the Product Lifecycle: Combining the Collaborative Power of Social Media with PLM. Tech-Clarity, Inc., http://www.tech-clarity.com/documents/Tech-Clarity_IssueinFocus_Social_Business_PLM.pdf (accessed January 1, 2012)

Carlisle, D.: Legal issues for business use of social media. Available via ARMA International, http://www.arma.org/r1/news/newswire/2012/06/27/legal-issues-for-business-use-of-social-media (accessed November 12, 2012)
Cristiano, J.J., Liker, J.K., White, C.C.: Customer-driven product development through quallity function deployment in the U.S and Japan, vol. 17, pp. 286–308 (2000)
Giles, J.: Internet encyclopaedias go head to head. Nature 438(7070), 900–901 (2005), doi:10.1038/438900a
Hoffmann, E.: Defining information: An analysis of the information content of documents. Information Processing & Management 16(6), 291–304 (1982), doi:10.1016/S0306-4573(80)80011-2
Huet, G., Zeng, Y., Fortin, C.: Theoretical foundations supporting the implementation of complementary information structures across the life of a product. In: ASME 2012 11th Biennial Conference on Engineering Systems Design and Analysis, Nantes, France, July 2 (2012)
Kaplan, A.M., Haenlein, M.: Users of the world, unite! The challenges and opportunities of Social Media. Business Horizon 53(1), 59–68 (2010), doi:10.1016/j.bushor.2009.09.003
Young, M.J., Salerno, J., Liu, H.: Social computing and behavioral modeling. Springer, US (2009), doi:10.1007/978-1-4419-0056-2
McAfee, A.: Enterprise 2.0: The dawn of emergent collaboration. IEEE Engineering Management Review 34(3), 38 (2006), doi:10.1109/EMR.2006.261380
Michaelides, R., Tickle, M., Morton, S.: Online communities of practice for innovation and knowledge transfer: A case study in the UK. In: The 6th IEEE International Conference on Management of Innovation and Technology (ICMIT), Singapore, June 2-5, pp. 922–927 (2010), doi:10.1109/ICMIT.2010.5492861
Panahi, S., Watson, J., Partridge, H.: Social Media and Tacit Knowledge Sharing: Developing a Conceptual Model. In: World Academy of Science, Engineering and Technology (WASET), Paris, France, pp. 1095–1102 (2012)
Schuler, D.: Communications of the ACM 37(1) (1994), doi:10.1145/175222.175223
Szulanski, G.: Exploring internal stickiness: Impediments to the transfer of best practice within the firm. Strategic Management Journal 17(Winter special issue), 27–43 (1996) (1986-1998)
Wenger, E.C.: Communities of practice: Learning, meaning and identity. Cambridge University Press, Cambridge (1999)
Wenger, E.C., Sydner, W.M.: Communities of practice: The organizational frontier. Havard Business Review 78(1), 139–146 (2000)
Wenger, E.C., White, N., Smith, J.D.: Digital habitats: Stewarding technology for communities. CPsquare, Portland (2010)

A LCIA Model Considering Pollution Transfer Phenomena

Xi Yu[1], Aicha Sekhari[1], Antoine Nongaillard[1], Abdelaziz Bouras[1], Suiran Yu[2], and Qingyan Yang[2]

[1] University Lyon 2 Lumière, DISP laboratory, France
{xi.yu,aicha.sekhari,antoine.nongaillard, abdelaziz.bouras}@univ-lyon2.fr
[2] School of Mechanical and Power Engineering, Shanghai Jiao Tong University, China
{yqy0805,sryu}@sjtu.edu.cn

Abstract. Due to market pressure and government regulations, environmental consciousness in manufacturing is becoming increasingly important. Currently, the global environmental impact (EI) of a product is a crucial criterion to judge its environmental performance. Many models were proposed in the last three decades to evaluate the global EI of products, but none of them considers the pollution transfer phenomena (PTP) of product's material flow. PTP refers to the EIs propagate from one phase to another one caused by different processes on the product's materials in different phases. PTP may have a consequence of EIs reduce in one phase but increase in other phases. The outcome will severely influence on the global EI of a product. Based on a PCB (printed circuit board) product case study, this paper proposes a new simplified life cycle impact assessment (LCIA) model which can help enterprises evaluate the global EI of product by considering the PTP in the whole product life cycle (PLC).

Keywords: PLC, PCB, PTP, LCA, LCIA, PLM, MFA.

1 Introduction

Following the increased environmental awareness of society, legislations are published to restrict the pollution emission through the whole lifecycle of products[1], such as *waste of electrical and electronic equipment* (WEEE), *reduction of hazardous substances* in EEEs (RoHS) and *energy using products* (EuP). Many models have been proposed to assess the EIs of products in the last three decades. Among these models, LCA is more accepted in Industry because this method is a quantitative analysis method based on factual information and on models of practical processes. The importance of different lifecycle phases and environmental emissions we are concerned about can be evaluated by the judgment process of LCA [2]. The implementation of LCA in different industries has boomed since last three decades. In these studies, the EIs of a product are assessed separately at each phase of the PLC since actors at a given phase cannot get easily the product data related to other PLC phases[3; 4; 5; 6].

Material flow analysis (MFA) reveals that the materials using in one product has its own material metabolism based on two fundamental and well-established scientific

A. Bernard, L. Rivest, and D. Dutta (Eds.): PLM 2013, IFIP AICT 409, pp. 365–374, 2013.

principles: system approach and mass balance. Any changes in one phase of PLC will has some consequences in other phases [7]. Cheah and colleagues examined the impact of expanded use of aluminium in the car fleet on energy resources. Using aluminium instead of steel reduced energy consumption and EIs in the use phase hence it increased fuel efficiency by reducing the weight of the car. But this is countered by the larger energy use and more EIs in the production phase [8]. Thus, the PTPs accompany with material flow in the product should take into account when assess the global environmental emissions of products.

After this introduction, section 2 discusses several environmental assessment models. Section 3 proposes an assessment model considering the PTP through the whole PLC. Section 4 presents a case study based on a PCB product, followed by conclusions.

2 Literature Review

Over the past decades, several environmental analysis methods have been developed and utilized as following:

LCA [9] may be the most famous quantitative method for evaluating environmental requirements. This method takes into account the whole product life cycle and can help enterprises to get accurate environmental information about the product. First, LCA chooses the environmental indicators that correspond to the enterprise objectives; then it analyzes the product based on the special data inventory; finally LCA provides an environmental interpretation of the product. However, a complete, quantitative full LCA has never been accomplished since its tedious, expensive and time-consuming attributes. All LCAs conducted now are simplified some way by ignoring some phases of PLC [10]. Hence they cannot get a global environmental performance of products.

MET Matrix [11] is a qualitative model which is used to summarize the EI at each stage of the product's lifecycle. MET Matrix classifies the environmental problems into three categories: Material cycle, Energy use and Toxic emission. By analyzing the importance degree of the environmental problems at each stage of the PLC, this method can generate structured qualitative information on the environmental aspects associated with the production, use and disposal of a product. However, this method is largely based on the available knowledge, the experience of the team performing the analysis and cannot provide a quantitative result.

The ERPA matrix [12] is a tool used to estimate a product's potential improvements in environmental performance. As shown in Table 1, rows in the matrix represent the stages of the life cycle, and columns stand for environmental concerns. By evaluating each cell in the matrix, the product's total environmental responsibility (R_{erp}) is computed as the sum of the matrix element values (M_{ij}):

$$R_{erp} = \sum_i \sum_j M_{ij} \tag{1}$$

Where i represents the life cycle stage and j represents the environmental concerns fields, respectively.

Table 1. The environmentally responsible product assessment matrix

Life cycle stage	Materials choice	Energy use	Solid residues	Liquid residues	Gaseous residues
Premanufacture	1.1	1.2	1.3	1.4	1.5
Product manufacture	2.1	2.2	2.3	2.4	2.5
Product delivery	3.1	3.2	3.3	3.4	3.5
Product use	4.1	4.2	4.3	4.4	4.5
Refurbishment, recycling, disposal	5.1	5.2	5.3	5.4	5.5

In the ERPA matrix, each element is assigned a rating from 0 (highest impact) to 4 (lowest impact) according to a checklist. Hence, this method is qualitative and cannot provide accurate results of the global environmental performance of products.

The Ten Golden Rules[13] is a summary of numerous guidelines that can be found in company guidelines and in handbooks of different origins. These rules must be customized to be directly useful in product development. Meanwhile, these rules are only some common criteria to help users reduce the EI of product during the design phase. This method does not evaluate the environmental performance of products.

All of the aforementioned models either only consider one phase of PLC, or only conduct a qualitative study. The problems of evaluate global EI are: 1. the product data belongs to different actors in different phases and most of these data are business secret. It is difficult for enterprises to collect a set of complete site data; 2. the product data in different phases are very massive and hard to find out the PTP factor. So it's hard for enterprises calculate the influence effect among different phases.

3 LCIA Model Considering PTP

In order to get more accurate global EI, we proposed a simplified LCIA (Life Cycle Impact Assessment) model which considers the Pollution Transfer Phenomena (PTP) factors through the whole PLC. This model uses the concept of the MFA (Material Flow Analysis) method to analyze the most important environmental factors of products. Based on the data gathered from PLM (Product Lifecycle Management) system and general design parameters, the mass of materials in each phase of PLC can be calculated. Then, LCA method helps to evaluate the global EI of products.

MFA is an effective tool to assess the physical consequences of human activities in the field of industrial ecology, where it is used on different spatial and temporal scales[7]. So far, efforts by the MFA community have been mainly academic, but this theory proved the materials using in one product has its own material metabolism. This outcome gives a strong support to analyze the global environmental impacts of products.

PLM integrates people, data, processes and business systems, and provides a product information backbone for companies and their extended enterprise [14]. In PLM systems, the product data such as mass of materials, product parameters, assembling parameters, process parameters, etc. can be collected. On the basis of the information of product, the mass of discharge materials in each phase can be calculated. Thus, we can choose proper characterization factors to convert the mass of the discharge materials into EI results.

From the concept of MFA, the materials in products have its own material metabolism; any change in this context will have uncertain influence in terms of PLC. As shown in Figure 1 B, the actors reduced the EIs in the manufacturing phase compared with the reference design in Figure 1 A. But due to the material in one phase changed, the EIs brought by this material in other phases will be changed correspondingly. Consequently, the EIs increased in raw materials and end-of-life phases and make the global EIs of products changed unpredictably. Hence, the PTP related with material flow must be taken into account to calculate the global EIs of the product.

To get a more accurate global score of products environmental impacts, a model considering PTP which combined with the concept of LCA, PLM, and MFA is proposed as shown in Figure 2. As shown in Figure 2, by using the MFA theory to analyze the PTP of materials in the PLC, the mass of discharge materials in each PLC phase can be calculated based on the product data get from PLM. By choosing proper characterization factor, the mass of discharge materials in each phase can be converted into EIs. Then use the LCA method to calculate the EI of each phase. Finally, aggregate the EI of each phase into the global EI.

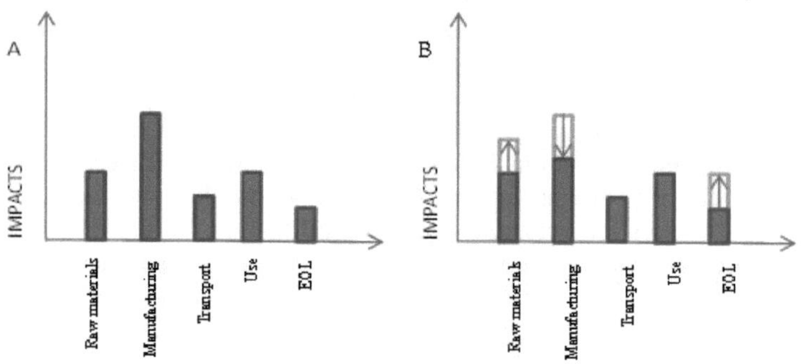

Fig. 1. Pollution transfer impacts in PLC

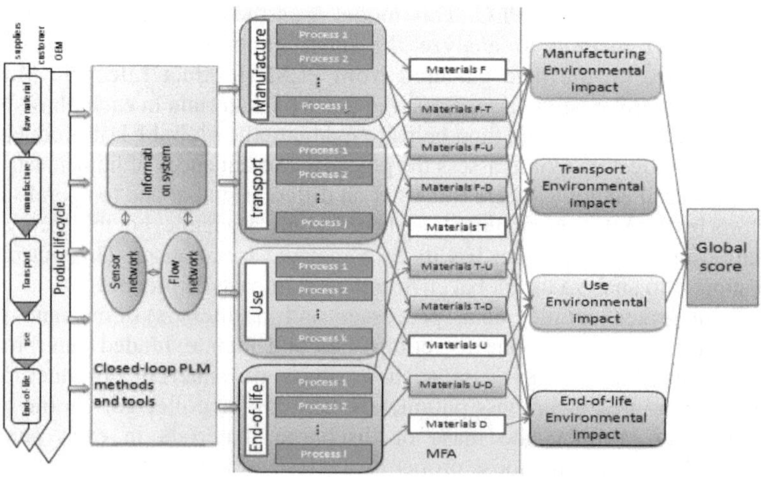

Fig. 2. The model of a product EIs through the whole PLC

From Figure 2, we can perceive there are different processes in one stage of PLC to make raw materials into a final product. To calculate the EIs of each phase, we can use the formula(2)

$$D_i = \sum p_{ij}(M_{i,k}) \quad i,k \in [1,n], j \in [1,m] \tag{2}$$

D_i denotes the mass of discharge of n different stages of PLC. At each stage, m processes exist and they will produce discharge based on the materials they dealt with. p_{ij} denotes the function in stage i and process j, which can convert the mass of materials into mass of discharge. $M_{i,k}$ denotes the mass of materials dealt in one phase. i and k represent the phase number. The materials in one phase can be divided into two parts. When $i = k$, $M_{i,k}$, represents the mass of materials only dealt in this phase. When $i \neq k$, $M_{i,k}$ represents the mass of materials dealt by phase i and phase k.

The EIs are come from the discharge materials. We can use formula (3)to calculate the environmental impacts brought by materials in one phase.

$$E_i = \sum D_i \times F_{material} \tag{3}$$

Where D_i represents the materials used in phase i .The $F_{material}$ is represent indicators for each impact category. Pennington [15] gives an example for emission data of how indicators for each impact category can be calculated from inventory data of a product using generic characterization factors shown as formula (4).

$$F_{material} = \sum_s Characterisation\ Factor(s) \times Emission\ Inventory(s) \tag{4}$$

Where the subscript s denotes the materials in the correspond category.

The broad spectrum of approaches in use today in the LCA field are CML（The Dutch Guide to Life Cycle Assessment was developed by the Leiden University Institute of Environmental Sciences）, eco-indicator 99（a project support by The Dutch Ministry of Housing, Spatial Planning and the Environment）, EDIP 97（Environmental Design of Industrial Products）, EPS 2000（Environmental Priority Strategies）, impact 2002+, and TRACI（Tool for the Reduction and Assessment of Chemical and Other Environmental Impacts） [16]. Here the most common characterization factors in each approach are listed in Table 2 to help enterprises choose more suitable method according to their practice.

When we want to get the global EI called global charge (GC) of the product, we can use the formula (5) introduced by Pennington, Potting et al. [15]

$$E_{global} = \sum E_i \tag{5}$$

Where E_{global} is the overall EI score.

Table 2. Characterization factors in different LCIA methods[16]

Impact category	Endpoint method		Midpoint method			
	Eco-indicator 99	EPS 2000	CML	EDIP 97	Impact 2002+	TRACI
Climate protection	DALYs	YOLL	GWPs	GWPs	GWPs	GWPs
Stratospheric Ozone protection	DALYs	YOLL	ODPs	ODPs	ODPs	ODPs
Acidification	PDFs	No report	APs	APs	none	APs
Smog Formation	DALYs	No report	PCOPs	PCOPs	PCOPs	PCOPs
Eutrophication	PDFs	No report	PO_4^{3-}- equivalents	NO_3^-- equivalents	none	

DALYs: disability adjusted life years; GWPs: Global Warming Potential.
ODPs: Ozone Depletion Potentials; APs: Acidification Potential
PCOPs: Photochemical ozone creation potentials; YOLL: Years of Lost Life
PDFs: Potentially Disappeared Fraction of species

4 Case Study

Nowadays, with the development of microprocessor technologies, the increasing number of electronic devices used in society [17]. The environmental pollution brought by these devices becomes more serious than before. PCBs are the foundation component of an electronic device, the environmental impact brought by PCB therefore should be studied carefully. Many literatures have already conducted to reduce the PCB's EIs [18; 19; 20]. All of them only focus on one phase of the PCB life cycle, the PTPs not be taken into account. But from these studies, the environmental emission data and formula of each process in fabrication phase is matured. Depending on these studies, users can get relatively accurate environmental emission in each process in the fabrication; the formula can be deduced in other PLC phases such as use, transportation and end-of-life.

Based on the existing studies [18; 21; 22] , the following general processes of the PCB life cycle shown in Figure 3 will be analyzed.

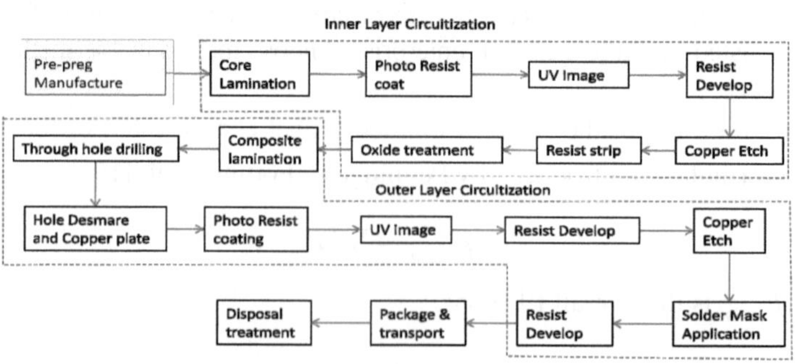

Fig. 3. Process Steps in PCB life cycle

The first step to do this case study is set the objective and scope. The manufacturing processes of PCB are complex. Enterprises use large amounts of chemicals materials generating numerous types of hazardous wastes. These wastes are potentially harmful to the environment and human health [23; 24]. The objective of this case study is to evaluate the chemical environmental emission of the PCB production. Based on the existing studies, the significant environmental emission of PCB is mostly coming from three phases: manufacture, transport, and disposal. So the model will focus on these phases.

The second step is to analyze the processes in each phase. Siddhaye, S. and P. Sheng [22] already analysed the manufacture processes of PCB and give out formulas based on general design parameters. Zhu [25] and Morris, Yuracko et al. [26] analysed the processes of transport and disposal respectively. Based on these literatures, we can deduce the formulas in each phase. For example, in the transport phase, the PCBs will be stacked and a polyethylene (PE) film will be sandwiched in every two PCBs. After this, a certain amount of PCBs will put into one boxboard. The mass of per PCB should be calculated by the follow:

$$m_{pcb} = t_{prepreg} \times \rho_{prepreg} \times A_{panel} + \sum_{layer=1}^{layer=n} t_{cu} \times \rho_{cu} \times A_{core} \times K_{cu} \quad (6)$$

Where $t_{prepreg}$ is the thickness of the substrate, $\rho_{prepreg}$ is the density of the substrate, A_{panel} is the area of the panel, $t_{cu}, \rho_{cu}, A_{core}, K_{cu}$ are the thickness of copper, density of copper, area of the core and percentage of copper in each layer respectively.

Then, let N_{pcbs} and n_{pcb} be the number of PCBs put into one boxboard and number of PCBs to be stacked respectively, w_{box} be the weight of boxboard, the mass for package one PCB is:

$$m_{package} = [(n_{pcb} + 1) / n_{pcb}] \times t_{pe} \times \rho_{pe} \times A_{panel} + w_{box} / N_{pcbs} \quad (7)$$

The modeling assumptions made are: the weight of adhesion during the manufacture is slight and not take into account.

The EI during transportation is mainly contributed by the weight of PCB and package, and the weight of one piece packaged PCB is:

$$m_{pcbpac} = m_{pcb} + m_{package} \quad (8)$$

The third step is to extract the PTP factors. After analysing the process and model the environmental emission of each process in different phase, the PTP factors should be extracted for the further assessment. Based on the formulas produced in processes analysis, we find that different phases of PCB life cycle share same factors which contribute to the environmental load of each phase. In the manufacture phase, the environmental emissions are mostly decided by the copper fraction on different layers and the area of the panel and core. In the transportation phase and disposal phase, the environmental emission is also closely related to these factors. Hence it's clear that the K_{cu}, A_{core}, A_{panel} are the PTP factors in this case.

Finally, we analyze the result of different designs. Considering the PTP factors, we propose two sets of design scheme, they are based on the data coming from a Chinese company[25]. The corresponding results are calculated using the formulas produced in process analysis. Based on the recommendation of the European Commission [27], DALY (Disability-Adjusted Life Year)is the best characterization factor to calculate the potentially harm to the environment and human health. From the characterization factor comparison in Table 2, the most suitable method is Eco-indicator 99. To get a more intuitive EI comparison of the two design schemes, we use Simapro to produce the comparison graph as shown in Figure 4, Figure 5,Figure 6.

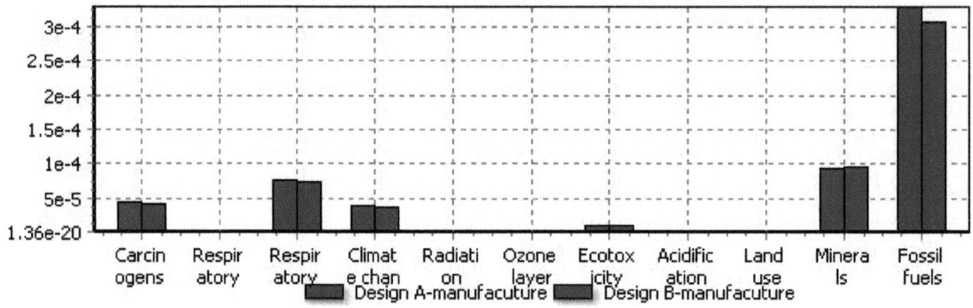

Fig. 4. EI comparison of manufacture using two methods

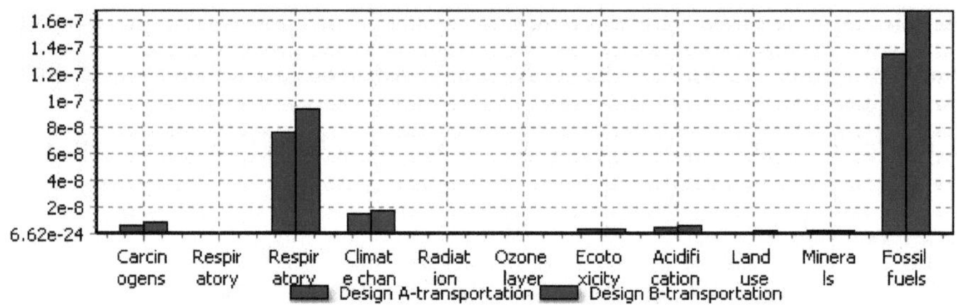

Fig. 5. EI comparison of transportation using two methods

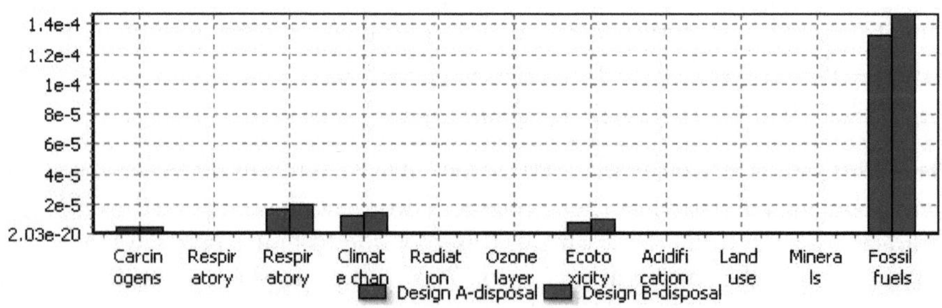

Fig. 6. EI comparison of disposal

From Figure 4, Figure 5, Figure 6, we can see that by considering the PTP in different phases, the EIs of design A in manufacture are higher than design B, but in transportation and disposal phase, the opposite effects are emerged.

5 Conclusion

This new simplified LCIA model provides an approach to help enterprises assess their products' global EI. By formulating the processes in each phase, the mass of material used in different phases can calculate based on the data get from PLM system. Depend on the formulas, the PTP factors can be abstracted and then the global EI of different designs can then be calculated. The case study using this new model shows that reduce the EIs in one phase may bring an adverse effect in other phases when we take into account the PTP factors. It also proved that by considering the PTP factors in different phases of PLC, the calculation of global EI of product will be more accurate. The model proposed in this paper will provide strong support to improve the global environmental performance of the products.

Acknowledgements. This project has been funded with support from the European Commission Project (EMA2-2010-2359) and Hubert Curien Partnership with Cai Yuanpei China program 2012-2014. This publication reflects the views only of the author, and the Commission cannot be held responsible for any use which may be made of the information contained therein.

References

1. Chung, J., Lee, H., Koh, Y., Hur, T.: Web based ecodesign supporting system for electronic products. Electronics and the Environment, 246–250 (2003)
2. Hertwich, E.G., Hammitt, J.K.: A decision-analytic framework for impact assessment part I: LCA and decision analysis. The International Journal of Life Cycle Assessment 6(1), 5–12 (2001)
3. Kuo, T.C., Huang, S.H., Zhang, H.C.: Design for manufacture and design for 'X': concepts, applications, and perspectives. Computers & Industrial Engineering 41(3), 241–260 (2001)
4. Kaebernick, H., Kara, S., Sun, M.: Sustainable product development and manufacturing by considering environmental requirements. Robotics and Computer-Integrated Manufacturing 19(6), 461–468 (2003)
5. Hauschild, M., Jeswiet, J., Alting, L.: From life cycle assessment to sustainable production: status and perspectives. CIRP Annals-Manufacturing Technology 54(2), 1–21 (2005)
6. Gehin, A., Zwolinski, P., Brissaud, D.: A tool to implement sustainable end-of-life strategies in the product development phase. Journal of Cleaner Production 16(5), 566–576 (2008)
7. Binder, C.R., Van Der Voet, E., Rosselot, K.S.: Implementing the results of material flow analysis. Journal of Industrial Ecology 13(5), 643–649 (2009)
8. Cheah, L., Heywood, J., Kirchain, R.: Aluminum stock and flows in US passenger vehicles and implications for energy use. Journal of Industrial Ecology 13(5), 718–734 (2009)
9. ISO, B.: Environmental management—life cycle assessment—principles and framework. Environmental Management 3(1) (2006)
10. Hur, T., Lee, J., Ryu, J., Kwon, E.: Simplified LCA and matrix methods in identifying the environmental aspects of a product system. Journal of Environmental Management 75(3), 229–237 (2005)

11. Brezet, H., Van Hemel, C., Böttcher, H., Clarke, R.: Ecodesign: a promising approach to sustainable production and consumption, UNEP (1997)
12. Graedel, T.E., Allenby, B.R.: Design for environment. Prentice Hall, Upper Saddle River (1996)
13. Luttropp, C., Lagerstedt, J.: EcoDesign and the Ten Golden Rules: generic advice for merging environmental aspects into product development. Journal of Cleaner Production 14(15), 1396–1408 (2006)
14. Jun, H.B., Kiritsis, D., Xirouchakis, P.: Research issues on closed-loop PLM. Computers in Industry 58(8-9), 855–868 (2007)
15. Pennington, D., Potting, J., Finnveden, G., Lindeijer, E., Jolliet, O., Rydberg, T., Rebitzer, G.: Life cycle assessment Part 2: Current impact assessment practice. Environment International 30(5), 721–739 (2004)
16. Jane, C., Gloria, T.P.: Critical analysis of the mathematical relationships and comprehensiveness of life cycle impact assessment approaches. Environmental Science & Technology 40(4), 1104–1113 (2006)
17. Suyang, G., Liu, J.: Life Cycle Assessment on Autoliv's Electronic Control Unit (2010)
18. Worhach, P., Sheng, P.: Integration of environmental factors in process modeling for printed circuit board manufacturing. I. Assembly. In: Electronics and the Environment, ISEE 1997, pp. 218–225. IEEE (1997)
19. Hertwich, E.G., Sheng, P., Koshland, C.P.: A flexible method for including environmental toxicity in DFE and LCA. In: Proceedings of the 1996 IEEE International Symposium on Electronics and the Environment, ISEE 1996, pp. 269–274. IEEE (1996)
20. Xiang, D., Mou, P., Wang, J., Duan, G., Zhang, H.C.: Printed circuit board recycling process and its environmental impact assessment. The International Journal of Advanced Manufacturing Technology 34(9), 1030–1036 (2007)
21. Kanth, R.K., Liljeberg, P., Tenhunen, H., Wan, Q., Zheng, L.: Insight into quantitative environmental emission analysis of printed circuit board. In: 2011 10th International Conference on Environment and Electrical Engineering (EEEIC), pp. 1–4. IEEE (2011)
22. Siddhaye, S., Sheng, P.: Integration of environmental factors in process modelling for printed circuit board manufacturing. II. Fabrication. In: Proceedings of the 1997 IEEE International Symposium on Electronics and the Environment, ISEE 1997, pp. 226–233. IEEE (1997)
23. Hui, I., Li, C., Lau, H.: Hierarchical environmental impact evaluation of a process in printed circuit board manufacturing. International Journal of Production Research 41(6), 1149–1165 (2003)
24. Kirsch, F.W.: Waste Minimization Assessment for Multilayered Printed Circuit Board Manufacturing (1991)
25. Zhu, G.: The study of evaluating environmental impacts in printed circuit board manufacturing, tainan, National Cheng Kung University (2001)
26. Morris, M.I., Yuracko, K.L., Govers, R.A., Maynor, D.M., Altmayer, S.: Life Cycle Analysis for Treatment and Disposal of PCB Waste at Ashtabula and Fernald, ORNL/TM-2000/254, Oak Ridge National Laboratory, Oak Ridge, TN (2000)
27. European-Commission. International Reference Life Cycle Data System (ILCD) Handbook—Recommendations for Life Cycle Impact Assessment in the European context, 1st edn. (November 2011)

Web-Based Portal for Sharing Information through CAD/PLM Software during the Eco-product Development Process

Idai Mendy Mombeshora and Elies Dekoninck

Abstract. Against the backdrop of increasing global demand for environmentally sustain-able products, the integrated software platform for Green ENgineering dESIgn and product sustainability (G.EN.ESI) project aims to develop a software platform, for use in conjunction with CAD/PLM software, which simplifies the process of integrating environmental and economic requirements into the product development process. A key component of the platform, and the main focus of this paper, is its unique web based supply chain portal that has the ability to obtain information directly from the supply chain. This paper details the work undertaken in the early stages of its development to explore possible portal architectures based on their strategic alignment with goals of firms using it. Based on research and analysis of past and existing supplier portals and data collected through an online survey and a case study, four possible architectures of the web portal were derived using scenario planning and their viability was tested using use cases and wind-tunnelling. The results suggest that although all generated scenarios are viable, the one in which multiple buyers and multiple suppliers interact with a single web portal is the most favourable. The consolidation in buyers and suppliers mitigates any bargain power related issues that might arise, while making way for the possible development of an industry wide information sharing standard for eco-design. Moving forward, the project aims to gain a better understanding of supplier collaboration in new product development through the use of the portal by exploring the nature of the information being shared, the roles that users of the portal play and any competitive conditions associated with the use of the portal.

1 Introduction

With organisations experiencing increased social and regulatory demands to behave in an environmentally conscious manner, environmental impact is fast becoming a factor considered on par with cost, functionality and value during the product development process. Against this back drop, some organisations are enhancing their competitiveness by improving their environmental performance through the mitigation of the environmental impact of their production and service activities (Bacallan, 2000). However, others view these new requirements as mandates or burdens that slow development while ramping up cost, detracting from the main business of the company. As a result, environmental aspects are often considered an afterthought, resulting in delays and added costs as changes are made after the late addition of environmental

A. Bernard, L. Rivest, and D. Dutta (Eds.): PLM 2013, IFIP AICT 409, pp. 375–384, 2013.

requirements into the development process (Handfield *et al.*, 2001). With its roots in concurrent engineering; three dimensional concurrent engineering (3DCE) holds great promise for integrating environmental considerations into the product development process. 3DCE is the notion that the simultaneous design of product, process and supply chain, through links between internal functions and participation with external partners, leads to improved operating performance (Fine, 1998). Although relatively new in practice, as companies are begin to embrace it, 3DCE appears to be a lens for demonstrating that eco-design efforts can support both traditional and environmental product development goals (Ellram *et al.*, 2008).

As the environmental performance of a product is the amalgamation of its environmental impact through all the stages of its lifecycle, from the extraction of raw materials to its end of life, it is dependent on the totality of the supply chain in both upstream and downstream directions throughout its lifecycle. During the product development process, it is necessary to have as much information as possible pertaining to the environmental performance of the various supply chain partners and the products and services they provide. With product lifecycle management (PLM) systems gaining acceptance as means for managing information about a product throughout its lifecycle (Sudarsan *et al.*, 2005), they hold the promise of seamlessly integrating and making available all of the information produced throughout all phases of a product's life cycle to everyone in an organisation and through the product network.

Set within the context of the household appliance industry and through the adoption of the 3DCE and PLM approaches, the integrated software platform for Green ENgineering dESIgn and product sustainability (G.EN.ESI) project is a European Union Seventh Framework project that aims to achieve a 30% reduction in lifecycle energy use and a 50% reduction in industrial waste in household appliances produced based on the choices made through its software platform and eco-design methodology. For the successful integration of the G.EN.ESI platform into CAD/PLM software, it is paramount to ensure that there is an accurate and reliable flow of information from various supply chain partners, including suppliers, product dismantlers and distributors, to the software. This vital flow of information from the supply chain into the design process via the G.EN.ESI platform will be realised through a unique web-based supply chain portal. Since internet communication technologies gained popularity as a means of simplifying business to business communications, supplier portals have been found to promote information sharing and coordination of operational flows (McIvor and McHugh, 2000), sup-port supplier management and create a sense of community among buyers and suppliers; while increasing the stability of relationships and suppliers' loyalty to their customers (Roberts, 1999). It is this collaborative potential within web portals that the G.EN.ESI project is looking to harness.

In this paper, the G.EN.ESI project will be presented, with particular focus on the initial steps in the development of the web portal which can be viewed as the evolution of the supply chain web portal from its traditional role as an e-procurement tool into an information sharing tool. The web portal's development will be presented after a brief discussion of information sharing and inter-organisational systems.

1.1 Importance of Inter-organisational Information Sharing during the Product Development Process

Information sharing can be applied to almost all core domains of corporate operational activities. Ranging from customer chains where information can aid in the formulation of customer experience strategies, to exchanges within the development chain where information is shared within product design and product lifecycle management activities and supply chain information exchanges that lead to greater visibility and responsiveness (Yu *et al.*, 2001). Typically, information sharing within the supply chain is associated with maximising responsiveness and efficiency while minimising cost, with the relationships formed handled by the procurement and/or logistics department; while, information sharing within the product development chain is allied with the acquisition of resources and capabilities to improve product offerings, with the collaborative relationships formed more likely to have a research and development focus.

On the one hand, there is Kanter's notion of collaboration advantage, defined as "*a significant leg up in a global economy due to a firm's well developed ability to create and sustain fruitful collaborations*" (Kanter, 1994), which is associated with the product development chain; while on the other, there is the resource-based theory view that one source of differential performance between firms is the way in which they organise exchange activity (Conner and Prahalad, 1996), which is related to the supply chain. Therefore, it would seem logical to then deduce that amalgamation of the two forms of information sharing would result in advantages gained through the unified use of the formed relationships, enriching the depth and quality of information shared via both design and supply chains. With particular focus on design chains and collaborative design, utilising supply chain information sharing relationships and methods within the product development process would offer a means of augmenting the match between product and process, which most companies accomplish through concurrent engineering, with an additional consideration of supply chain configuration.

2 The G.EN.ESI Project

Through the development of a software design tool (G.EN.ESI platform) and supporting eco-design methodology (G.EN.ESI methodology), the G.EN.ESI project aims to address the lack of easy to use and robust tools for environmental evaluation at the engineering design stage. Currently available tools are either too qualitative/subjective to be used by designers with limited experience, or too quantitative, costly and time consuming for use during the early stages of the product development process (Boks, 2006). Moreover; these tools are usually stand alone and do not allow for easy integration with traditional design tools. The shortcomings of current eco-design procedures and tools mean they fail to offer practical solutions for day-to-day use as they only achieve limited industry penetration (Lofthouse, 2006). The main objective of the project is to supply a plat-form that can be completely integrated with other main design tools, such as CAD and PLM software, which helps designers make ecological design choices without losing sight of cost and typical practicalities of industry.

The G.EN.ESI platform architecture will be based on the integration of various tools into the same structure, with the tools communicating to support the entire product design process; an example of a tool is the S-LCC analyst tool which will evaluate the whole product lifecycle. Each tool within the platform will examine design choices from a specific point of view while simultaneously possessing the ability to provide information to the designer on environmental issues. This connection between the tools will allow for an immediate check of the congruence of the choices with other key design parameters. Additionally, environmental decisions made by the designer will be supported by a case-based reasoning tool which will utilise knowledge stored from previously successful cases to suggest possible environmental improvements.

2.1 How the Supply Chain Portal Supports the G.EN.ESI Platform

A reliable input of accurate data and information is central to the success of the software platform; the platform will manage data through relational databases structured such that they align with the most common databases which support software tools used by the companies. The G.EN.ESI databases will not only inherit data from local company software tools (CAD/PLM) but will also collate data from various members of the supply chain through the use of a web-based portal. Using information that the supply base inputs into the portal, the platform tools assesses the environmental impacts and cost of various options, such as materials, components, processes etc., allowing the designer to select the most convenient in terms of environmental aspects. The use of the web portal will encourage sustainability competitiveness within industry, while stimulating eco-efficiency throughout the whole supply network.

Figure 1 shows the structure of the web portal proposed by the project and how the portal interacts with the software platform. An example of how the portal and platform interact when used by a designer is as follows: a member of the supply chain uploads information into the portal regarding a component, including weight of component, geographical location of the production plant and transport used to ship it. When the designer selects this component during the design process, the 0km tool within the platform automatically downloads all the information regarding the transport scenario from the portal. The 0km tool collates transport information relating to all the chosen components within the design, it is this information that is used as part of the environmental impact (S-LCA) and cost (S-LCC) calculation along with calculations made from other tools such as DFEE and LeanDFD. The results of these calculations are then presented to the designer.

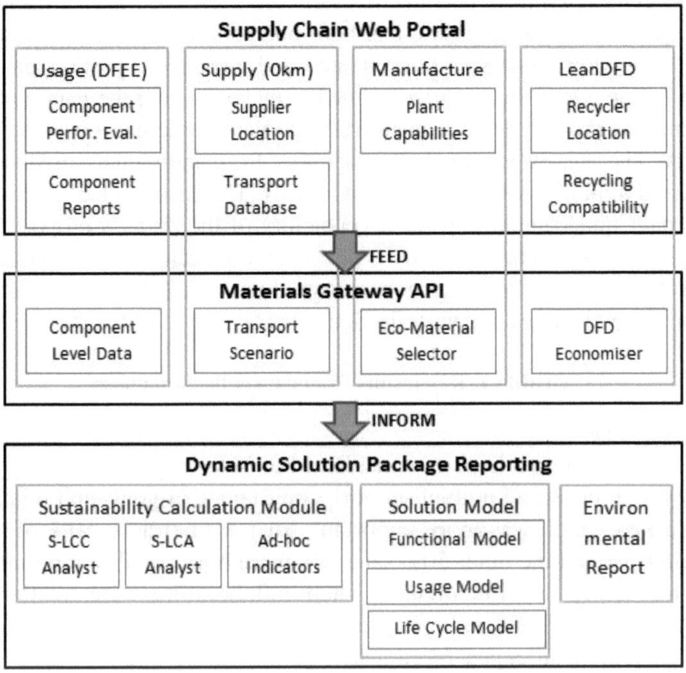

Fig. 1. Structure of the G.EN.ESI platform's web portal

3 Supply Chain Portal Development Objectives

To ensure effective deployment of the supply chain portal, it was essential at this early stage in its development to explore possible portal architectures based on the impact that the nature of shared information, who it is shared with, how it is shared and when it will be shared would have. Based on this, the following specific aims were created for this paper:

1. Explore possible portal architectures and resultant strategic scenarios for the web portal – to ensure that the G.EN.ESI web portal's functional requirements align with the strategic implications it would have on users.
2. Develop possible use cases for the web portal and use them to test the viability of the architectures and strategic scenario – to gain an understating of how the portals would perform in various situations.
3. Classify existing compliance web portals based on the developed scenarios and architecture –a way of understanding what is already available and how it relates to the proposed G.EN.ESI platform

4 Research Methodology and Results

To ensure that the architectures, scenarios and use cases developed are truly representative of what is likely to transpire in industry, it was necessary that their development was based on information gathered from potential platform users. Due to the dual nature of the collaboration requirements and to ensure that both options are sufficiently researched, a two-phase data collection process was formulated and executed. Firstly, data was collected through an online administered survey aimed at understanding the nature of supplier collaboration in new product development (SCNPD) with particular focus on the perspective of suppliers. The survey garnered 76 responses from individuals involved in SCNPD projects across a number of engineering industries. The second phase, whose aim was to acquire a better understanding of the acceptability of the portal's proposed role, the climate under with it would be used and the profile of a typical platform user, involved an in-depth case study of a G.EN.ESI project industrial partner. Table 1 summarises some key results from the two phases of data collection.

Table 1. Key results from data collection phase

Online Survey
- Most cited factors/qualities to consider when selecting a partner were trust and reliability, openness and mutual support, congruence of goals and relationship. - When asked which was more important, trust or contracts, 50% of the respondents said trust and the other 50% said they were both equally important. - Most frequently faced challenges when collaborating were relationship management, aligning goals and objectives and financial burden. - Most difficult challenges faced when collaborating were dealing with failed relationships, relationship management and aligning goals and objective - Effects of failure were relationship breakdown and end of collaborations. - Most projects only exchange information and knowledge that is essential.
Case Study
- Biggest concern with portal is the security of the information that is shared. "*I don't know if I can trust sharing information over the internet, how can you be sure that only the people you want to can see the information you upload?*" - Cited that the fear that information would get abused, used for anything that has not been agreed upon, is a concern. "*It is not like if you are not happy with what they are doing with the information you can take it back*". - "*Getting information from our suppliers is hard enough as it is, even information that they possess; they usually refer us to a data sheet on the website.*" -"*If the people we supply to asked us for the information that we would likely have to ask for from our suppliers, we would not be able to provide it.*"

5 Developing Portal Architectures and Strategic Scenarios

To determine various strategic scenarios relating to the supply chain web portal, the technique of scenario planning was used. Scenario planning is a futures technique that is used to generate different scenarios that represent possible futures associated with different trends and events to help develop policies and strategies that are robust and flexible (Schoemaker, 1995). In this case, scenario planning was undertaken to determine the following: 1) the best way to structure the supplier portal, 2) strategic implications its structure would have on buyers (firms using the G.EN.ESI platform) and suppliers (supply chain firms that upload in-formation into the portal) and 3) how the way the portal is used varies depending on the strategy implemented. The key question, central to the scenario planning, was as follows: "*what is the best and most viable way of structuring a web based supply chain portal to facilitate information sharing between firms that use the G.NE.ESI platform and members of their supply chain*?" Through the analysis of past and present web portals and insights gained from the data collection, drivers and deterrents were generated and used as the basis of the scenario generation. Some of the key driver and deterrents are listed in Table 2.

Table 2. Drivers and deterrents influencing the adoption of web portals

Drivers and Deterrents	
Impact on financial performance.	Alignment with strategic focus.
Impact on other business processes.	Buyer power vs. supplier power.
Impact on product development process.	Cost of use.
Ease of data input into portal.	Impact on reputation.
Availability of required information.	Availability of resources.

The two axis method, based on one of the approaches employed by Shell (Foresight, 2009), was then used to generate four contrasting scenarios that are related to the use of web portals by placing a major factor influencing the future of the issue on each of two axes that cross to form four quadrants. It was identified that the major factors influencing the use of the portals were related to the number of companies that would use a single portal; with Multiple Suppliers ↔ Single Supplier on one axis and Multiple Buyers ↔ Single Buyer on the other. A four scenarios diagram, with each scenario represented as a series of potential gains and barriers, was then developed; a simplified version is shown in Figure 2.

Following the scenarios development, the main actions that could be taken to manage the risks inherent in each scenario were identified. With so many firms involved with a single portal in Scenario 1, the development of robust ownership rights is a must to ensure that portal is maintained and monitored for misuse. In Scenario 2, as the buyer has access to collated information regarding a number of suppliers, there is scope for misuse, making it is essential to ensure that the buyer does not have sole responsibility of the portal. The portal should also allow suppliers to export information across multiple portals if they have multiple buyers using the G.EN.ESI platform. Scenario 3 requires a function that allows buyers to assign multiple portals to a single software platform and due to the scale of their responsibilities it is paramount to ensure supplier commitment. The main action with Scenario 4 is to ensure that both parties are fully committed and aware of the work involved if they end up associated with multiple portals; additionally, buyers should be able to assign multiple portals to a single platform and suppliers should be able to share information across multiple portals. Regardless of the scenario, it is essential to guarantee the security of information shared through the use of heightened security measures.

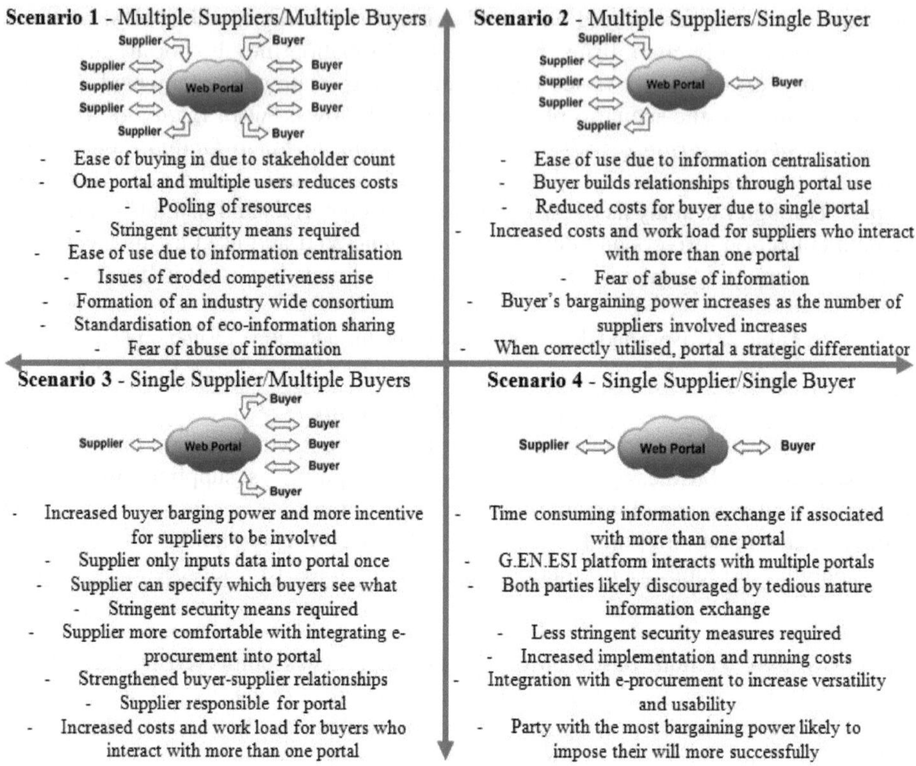

Fig. 2. Simplified four scenarios diagram

6 Strategic Scenario Viability Based on Portal Use Cases

Guided by the insights gained during the data collection phase, ten possible use cases were developed. These are possible cases that can arise when the various portal architectures, and their resultant strategic scenarios, are implemented. The list of cases was not exhaustive however; it aimed to encompass a variety of ways that the portal could be used. An example of a use case is as follows: various people from the supplying company have access to the portal. For example, designers of the components being supplied manually enter information into the web portal. There is no one that has been specifically assigned the task of regulating the way in which information is uploaded into the portal.

When set within the context of the strategic scenarios, the use cases can provide useful 'reality checks' on the scenarios, helping to consolidate the overall vision of the web portal with the way it is used and highlight potential risks and challenges. As a result, the use cases were tested against the developed scenarios by mapping them against each other in a matrix (wind-tunnelling) (Foresight, 2009). The focus was on how robust each use case is (can it be performed within the scenario) and the ease of implementation and use. Wind-tunnelling offers a way of determining the viability of the scenarios; if all use cases are robust or easy it suggests high viability, only certain use cases are robust or easy suggests medium viability and no robust or easy use cases suggests low versatility.

The results from the wind tunnelling ranked Scenario 1 as highly viable, Scenario 3 as medium-high viability and Scenarios 2 and 4 as medium viability. This suggests that within the context of the G.EN.ESI project, all the scenarios would work, with Scenario 1 being the most favourable as within it all use cases were deemed as at least possible and at most robust and easy. In the kitchen appliance manufacturing industry, which is mainly comprised of SMEs, having one portal as proposed by Scenario 1 offers significant benefits in terms of acquiring supplier buy-in. Through the use of a single portal, multiple buyers and suppliers are consolidated, mitigating any issues that might arise as a result of mismatched bargaining power that is likely to arise between individual buyers and suppliers. As more and more firms within an industry adopt the G.EN.ESI platform, it could provide a consistent method of sharing information resulting in the formation of an industry wide information sharing standard that has a particular focus of eco-design.

7 The Nature of Existing Compliance Supplier Web Portals

To put the G.EN.ESI portal into context in terms of the evolution of supply web portals, research was undertaken into existing web portals to determine their nature and the scenario which their structure would fall into.

It is undisputable that the use of web portals is on the rise as the popularity of advanced procurement increases; however, due to the difference in the nature of information being exchanged, a shift in focus from traditional procurement portals to compliance portals is required. Examples of such portals include BOMcheck (*www.bomcheck.net*), in the Scenario 1 category; Freescale (*www.freescale.com)*, in the Scenario 2 category and vendors such as Enovia (*www.3ds.com*) and Sup-plier Soft (*www.suppliersoft.com*), who offer self-service portals where suppliers get a single interface to interact with, while the deployed system depends entirely on the user and industry. These portals are generally used to exchange information including environmental compliance, conflict materials and materials compliance, amongst others. The strength of compliance portals lies in their ability to simplify and automate the process of acquiring data from different suppliers. However, their main weakness is that they require commitment from suppliers who might be reluctant to share information if they are not obliged by law to share it.

8 Conclusions and Moving Forward

The work detailed in this paper focused on the initial steps in the development of a PLM based web portal, specifically exploring possible portal architectures based on their strategic alignment with the goals of firms using it. All the work that was carried out was informed by knowledge and information gained from researching past and existing web portals, a survey into supplier collaboration projects and an in-depth case study potential G.EN.ESI platform user. Four different architectures, based on the number of companies interacting with a single portal, were generated using scenario planning and presented as a series of potential gains and barriers. Ten use cases which provided a range of possible cases that could arise within the four generated scenarios were created allowing for the viability portal architectures to be tested using the technique of wind-tunnelling. The results from the wind tunnelling ranked Scenario 1 as highly viable, Scenario 3 as medium-high viability and Scenarios 2 and 4 as medium viability. In Scenario 1, multiple buyers and multiple suppliers interact with a single web portal. The consolidation in buyers and suppliers mitigates any bargain-power related issues that might arise, while making way for the possible development of an industry wide information sharing standard. Looking in to existing portals, the presence of compliance portals highlighted that web portals are now being used as more than e-procurement tools.

Moving forward, the project aims to gain a better understanding of supplier collaboration in new product development through the use of the portal by exploring the nature of the information being shared, the roles that users of the portal play (those who initiate it vs. those who participate in it) and any competitive conditions associated with the use of the portal.

References

Bacallan, J.: Greening the Supply Chain. Business and Environment 6 (2000)

Boks, C.: The Soft Side of Eco-design. Journal of Cleaner Production 14 (2006)

Conner, K., Prahalad, C.K.: A Resource-Based Theory View of the Firm: Knowledge vs Opportunism. Organisational Science 7 (1996)

Ellram, L., Tate, W., Carter, C.: Applying 3DCE to Environmentally Responsible Manufacturing Practices. Journal of Cleaner Energy 16, 1620–1631 (2008)

Fine, C.H.: Clockspeed: Winning Industry Control in the Age of Temporary Advantage. Perseus Books, Massachusetts (1998)

Foresight, Scenario Planning. Foresight Horizon Scanning Center (2009)

Handfield, R., Melnyk, S., Calantone, R., Curkovic, S.: Integrating Environmental Concerns into the Design Process: The Gap between Theory and Practice. IEEE Transactions on Engineering Management 48, 189–208 (2001)

Kanter, R.M.: Collaborative Advantage. Harvard Business Review 72 (1994)

Lofthouse, V.: Eco-design tools for designers: Defining the requirements. Journal of Cleaner Production 14, 1386–1395 (2006)

McIvor, R., McHugh, M.: Collaborative buyer supplier relations: Implications for organization change management. Strategic Change 9, 221–236 (2000)

Roberts, B.: Web Portals pen doors to one-step services. HR Magazine 44 (1999)

Schoemaker, P.: Scenario Planning: A Tool for Strategic Thinking. Sloan Management Review, 25–40 (Winter 1995)

Sudarsan, R., Fenves, S., Sriram, R., Wang, F.: A Product Information Modelling Framework for PLM. Computer-Aided Design 37 (2005)

Yu, Z., Yan, H., Cheng, T.C.: Benefits of Information Sharing with Supply Chain Partnerships. Industrial Management and Data Systems 101 (2001)

A Meta-Model for Knowledge Representation Integrating Maturity for Decision Making in Engineering Design

Nicolas Drémont[1], Nadège Troussier[2], Robert Ian Whitfield[3], and Alex Duffy[3]

[1] Laboratoire Roberval, Université de Technologie de Compiègne, France
[2] Université de Technologie de Troyes, France
[3] DMEM, University of Strathclyde, Glasgow, UK
nicolas.dremont@utc.fr

Abstract. Computer Aided Design (CAD) and Computer Aided Engineering (CAE) models are often used during product design. Various interactions between the different models must be managed in a PLM approach for the designed system to be robust and in accordance with defined specifications. To effectively manage engineering changes on the system definition, the dependencies between the different models must be known and managed in a PLM system. A lot of data are exchanged in collaborative design and different problems must be managed in terms of data consistency. We propose a meta-model for knowledge representation integrating maturity concept to support decision making in preliminary collaborative design. A literature survey about existing knowledge models is done before presenting the proposed meta-model of knowledge.

Keywords: preliminary collaborative design, maturity, PLM, decision making, uncertainties.

1 Introduction

The design process is complex and dynamic due in part to the volume of handled data and models, the number of exchanges between the different design teams and businesses interacting. The design teams, organized in Concurrent Engineering (CE) do not wait to get the result of the later phases of the design life cycle; they anticipate them by making assumptions and by taking into consideration previous experiences and know how. In that framework, quality approaches for the control of product performance, and collaborative engineering tools to support CE and collective decision making are required.

Product development cycles, and more generally product life cycles are becoming increasingly complex. This complexity is due to several aspects. One of them is related to the different levels of representation and modeling due to the organizational and technical decomposition of the technical system, the inter-relations between different kinds of knowledge involved to anticipate the product's behavior. Another one can be associated to with the necessity to integrate different viewpoints, creating problems related to the data consistency and considering the impact of engineering

A. Bernard, L. Rivest, and D. Dutta (Eds.): PLM 2013, IFIP AICT 409, pp. 385–395, 2013.

change. It is therefore necessary to be able to qualify and quantify the data in the upstream phases of product design [1] and throughout the design process in order to help to the next step decision making [2].

In order to support decision making in early design and product's performance management, this paper proposes a meta-model for knowledge representation integrating maturity to support decision making in preliminary collaborative design. Section 2 presents an overview of the problematic of decision making in preliminary collaborative design. Section 3 presents a literature survey about knowledge meta-modeling approaches. Finally, Section 4 describes the different elements of the proposed meta-model.

2 The Decision Making in Preliminary Collaborative Design

Ullman [2] defines the decision pyramid in several levels (Data, Models, Knowledge and Decision). Decision making requires the management of data, models and knowledge, and the associated judgment on which decisions are based. In other words, data are the pyramid basis and also the basis of decision making in design (section 2.1). Moreover the collaborative aspect includes different representations of a same mechanical system, oriented with respect to the expertise domain considered. These representations are supported by knowledge and product models.

2.1 Decision Making and Lack of Knowledge

Decision making in preliminary collaborative design involves the selection of an alternative design in order to go towards the next design iteration. Several factors are considered in order to make a decision, such as market demand, design alternatives, designer's preferences and uncertainties [2]. We focus on the "uncertainties" factor because it can represent the lack of knowledge in the decision making (for epistemic uncertainties). The decision making enables us to get a new definition of the mechanical system and we assume that maturity level and uncertainties on the product design data facilitate the next design decision. Maturity level is a characteristic often used to qualify information in design [3]. It can be defined as the improvement degree through a predefined set of process domains in which all objectives of the set are completed [4].

To design a mechanical system means to integrate several technologies with strong interactions and to take into consideration different aspects such as mechanical, electronic, etc. Moreover, in a collaborative or an extended enterprise context, several people must work together in order to design efficiently a mechanical system [2]. This collaborative aspect is very important because each person has a specific point of view and way to thinking but these people must take decisions together in order to meet compromises and to be able to go to the next design iterations repeatedly until the design objectives and technical specifications are achieved.

The preliminary design in collaborative design of mechanical system provides still more difficulties because the mechanical system is being defined [3] [5] [1]. It means that uncertainties about design data and unknown data have to be considered.

2.2 Product and Knowledge Representation

Design can generate many models (geometric and simulation for example 3D geometric representations, FEA models, etc.), with respect to the behavior which is to be studied, the component and configuration of the product, as illustrated by Scheidl and Winlker [6] on a beam, where the different models are clearly in the conceptual design phase. Another reason for the model diversity is related to the complexity of actual systems being developed [7]. These systems are characterized by independent functionalities that, together, compose the product (systems of systems). Complex systems are an association of several functionalities using diverse technologies to achieve the required operation of the product. During the design phases, the models that are used aim at providing a representation of the product in terms of its physical description (geometric model) as well as behavioral description (simulation model).

Thus, the design of complex systems can necessitate a significant number of models, specific for each discipline and that require a multiple views approach. Different engineering domains require different viewpoints on the product with different levels of granularity. For instance, within an electro-mechanical product, the structural decomposition depends on the engineering domain of the expert analyzing the product: an electrical model considers the gaps between parts while mechanical analyst does not mind about these, and typically they will not use the same product decomposition [8]. In terms of data and process modeling, several product models exist to support the multiple view representation of the system and will be described Section 3, in order to support product lifecycle management and the collaborative decision making process. Moreover, in order to support knowledge mapping and to ensure consistency between different models, meta-models can be proposed using generic semantic and rich representation of concepts and relationships between them. The goal is to propose a conceptual framework that facilitates the definition of heterogeneous knowledge models integrating the maturity in order to help to the decision making.

3 Maturity, Data Qualification and Knowledge Models

3.1 Definitions

We define maturity based on the work of Beth [4], as the association of the knowledge and performance. This means that there is the judgment of an actor on information (transmitter and receiver) and the state of information from actor user of information must be taken in consideration.

Performance is the link between specification of the product and the specification achieved in the current design iteration [9]. If no specification is respected then the performance is null and if they are all achieved then the level is of 100%.

We define knowledge as a cognitive structure allowing interpreting a set of information in order to follow a reasoning in a particular situation (or context of use) and for a stated purpose [10]. The lack of knowledge, in this case, is represented by the uncertainty on parameters of the product, for example the uncertainty of the part diameter, more or less 10 millimeters. Designers and user of the parameters define this uncertainty. A type of uncertainties is interesting in this context: Epistemic: uncertainty related to a lack of knowledge or information in any phase or activity of the design process [11].

Consequently, in order to improve Computer Aided Design Software (CAD, PDM and PLM essentially), the following question addressed in this paper, is then: "How to model product information and uncertainties in collaborative preliminary design?"

To answer the question a state of the art is built on uncertainty modeling and product/knowledge models to analyze how the product models support decision making taking into account uncertainties.

3.2 Literature Survey

Table 1 is a synthesis of different qualitative and quantitative approaches allowing to qualify and quantify data uncertainty and to answer the questions identified in Section 3.1. The keypoints such as sustainability, sensitivity or collaborative dimension are presented in more detail in the following paragraphs. The product and knowledge models identified allow us to decompose, structure and take into account the different design activities of mechanical systems in order to support the product lifecycle management. However, it should be underlined that none of them considered uncertainties.

Table 1. State of art of the approaches

Uncertainties modeling		Product and knowledge models
Qualitative approaches	Quantitative app.	
Sustainability [12] Variation[13] Sensitivity[14] Completeness [15] PEPS: Precision, Accurancy, Parsimony, Specialisation [16]	Probability theory Fuzzy sets [17] Possibility theory[18] [19] Evidence theory [20] [21]	PPO: Product Process Organisation [22] KCM: Knowledge Configuration [23] CPM: Core Product Model [24] MOKA: Methods and tools Oriented to Knowledge Acquisition [25]

Qualitative approaches are based on the preliminary information concept introduced by Clark and Fujimoto [26] to allow the parallel execution of activities in the product development processes. Eppinger [27] defined the concept of preliminary information as a parameter that is in continual evolution before it achieves its final value. The status of the parameter in its evolution refers to its maturity [28].

The qualification and characterization of the model and information include several aspects: sustainability, variation, sensitivity and completeness. Information within a design office can be classified with respect to the level of sustainability [12] that is to say, the longevity of the information. A scale from "1" (Information not sustainable) to "5" (valid information for the currently used technologies) is used and refers to the information validity degree.

Sensitivity levels define the impact of change on information, according to [14] are classified along a scale from "0" corresponding to not sensitive, to "3" corresponding to sensitive.

Generally, three main categories of knowledge are distinguished in a development process: product engineering knowledge, manufacturing process knowledge and organizational knowledge. Another kind of knowledge concerns the capitalization of decision justification during the development project.

In the literature, several recent works exist, dealing with models in order to represent product, process and organization knowledge. These works are principally developed in three scientific fields: development of domain ontology in order to identify the mains concepts of a domain and the relationships between these concepts [29]; the development of projects memory that aims at achieving the traceability of the project evolution for reuse perspective [30] and finally, the development of business tools such as PDM and CAX tools in order to support the technical activities of designers [26].

The commonly accepted approach for structuring product knowledge has been through the construction of Product Models. As an example of such models, [31] translated NIST's core product model [24] and proposed an ontology for the Open Assembly Model (OAM) implementing several OWL (Ontology Web Language) capabilities. Lee [32] has developed a model for sharing product knowledge of the Beginning Of Life (BOL) on the web. Terzi [33] has proposed to use the concept of Holon for the description of product knowledge. The Holon is defined as a composition of a physical entity and all of its related information.

In parallel, the process knowledge definition is based on activity models: activities allow creation of the link between products, resources (facilities, humans...) and their characteristics (behavior, task, properties…), they structure and define the behaviour of the processes. An activity aggregates several kinds of knowledge such as sequences, functions, rules, states [34]. It concerns the process scheduling, the set of resources (human resources, machines, tools and tooling), the organization of the production unit (work centres) and the manufacturing know-how [35].

Other categories of models are developed with generic perspective in order to cover heterogeneous knowledge fields [25]. For instance, Nowak [35] have presented the architecture of a collaborative aided design framework integrating Product, Process and Organization (PPO) models for engineering improvement. The PPO information kernel stores persistent data on the interoperable files that might be reached by several external applications on the collaborative PLM system among the whole product life cycle [22]. Danesi [36] have proposed the P4LM methodology, which allows the management of Projects, Products, Processes, and Proceeds in collaborative design. It aims at allowing the integration of information coming from different partners which are involved in a PLM application. The KCM (Knowledge Configuration Model) is another example of knowledge model, which is developed with the aim to manage knowledge using configurations synchronized with expert models that enable designers to use parameters consistently in a collaborative design process [23]. The KCM approach is based on the concept of "knowledge configuration", which is a virtual object composed by a set of parameters and rules instantiated from the generic baseline and contextualized into an expert model for a specific milestone of the project in order to ensure consistency and decision making supported by all expert knowledge.

All of these models allow us to represent product or knowledge and ensure the data consistency but no one of them take in consideration uncertainties and maturity of data and mechanical systems, in order to help the decision making.

4 A Meta-Model for Knowledge Representation Integrating Maturity

4.1 The Key Factors and the Metric Allowing to Define Maturity

The presented metric allows us to evaluate the maturity of a mechanical system by calculating the maturity of each components to each iteration of design. The equation (1) presents how the maturity of a component (Ci) is defined, where 'i' is the number associated to the component. The metric evolves with each design iteration, and as a consequence each parameter is constantly updated until it meets the full technical specification of the need.

$$C_i = \frac{1}{Co_i} \times \frac{\frac{\sum_{x=1}^{n}\left[1-\left(\frac{tolerance}{value}\right)\times SusSen\right]}{n} + Perf}{2} \tag{1}$$

The factors are "n", "value", "tolerance", "SusSen", "Perf" and "Coi".

- "n" is the number of design parameters of a part (diameter, length, …)
- "value" is the nominal value of the design parameter, (diameter=25mm).
- "tolerance" is the domain of variation of the value, (diameter=25 ±5mm).
- "SusSen" represents the association of Sensitivity and Sensibility of the information. A first designer which has created this information (design parameter and tolerance) characterizes it using a sustainability level based on qualitative scale like described by Gaudin [12]. The level of sustainability is the time during which information may be considered as valid. The level of sensitivity is the impact importance of the data on the assembly. The designer qualifies the result due to a sensitivity level based on qualitative scale like described by Krishnan [14].
- "Perf" is the level of performance is defined by the percent of requirement number achieved by the end of the design iteration in comparison with the number of total requirements of the part in question. For example, if a part has three requirements and only two are achieved by the end of the design iteration, then the level of performance for this part is 66%. When 100% is achieved it means that all technical specifications of the need are completed.
- "Coi" is the level of maturity that we wish to achieve at the end of the design iteration. This is a constant that allows the adjustment of the level of maturity.

4.2 Methodology to Use the Metric

The result of the metric (level of maturity) is actualized at the end of each design iteration in order to help the decision making for the next design iteration.

The first step to build and use the metric is done by the first designer by defining the design parameters in CAD software such as CREO ® or CATIA ® More than the nominal value of the parameter, he is defining the interval of possible values ("tolerance") and the level of sustainability based on qualitative scale like the one described by Gaudin [12].

The part (with parameters, values, tolerances and level of sustainability) is integrated in a PDM system, as metadata, in order to capitalize knowledge. This will also allow us to share the information and to trace the previous information in the next design iteration.

The second point of the methodology is the definition of the level of performance for the different parts composing the system.

The third step of the proposed methodology is the simulation of the assembly behavior of parts comprising the system. The simulation of the assembly behavior allows its approval. This study is done using simulation software such as NASTRAN, SIMULIA, etc. The designer does not only simulate the behavior of the assembly but does three points:

- Adjusts the tolerances using the results of the simulation.
- Checks if the requirements are met.
- Defines the level of sensitivity of the results of calculation (design parameters including tolerances).

The level of sensitivity is the impact importance of the data on the assembly. The designer is able to qualify this result using a sensitivity level based on qualitative scale like described by Krishnan [14].

At this step, all necessary factors are defined to calculate the level of system maturity. These factors are levels of sensitivity and sustainability of information, importance of tolerances in function of the value and the level of performance. The maturity is translated as a percent of the association of these three factors taking into consideration the goals to achieve, the user experience and knowledge, and the precision of the tolerances.

This metric helps the decision making for the next design iteration by highlighting the parameters where the unknown is the most important. For example, designer could have devoted more effort to a design parameter with a low level of sustainability and a high sensitivity instead of focusing on a parameter having a high level of sustainability and lower level of sensitivity; this way it may be easier to make decision between different point of views and design activities.

4.3 Proposed Meta-Models and Models Integrating Maturity

The goal of the proposed meta-models is to provide a tool able to federate data, ensure consistency and integrate maturity in order to help to the decision making. The Data Meta-Model (DMM) generates a Data Model (DM) and the Collaboration Meta-Model (CMM) generates a Collaboration Model (CM). These Meta-Models are instances of the so-called Knowledge Meta-Model (KMM). They are described as follows:

Data's meta-modeling: the Data Meta-Model (DMM) puts the concepts allowing the representation of the business knowledge within a common and simplified semantic. In particular, it includes the parameters, their relationships and the maturity information.

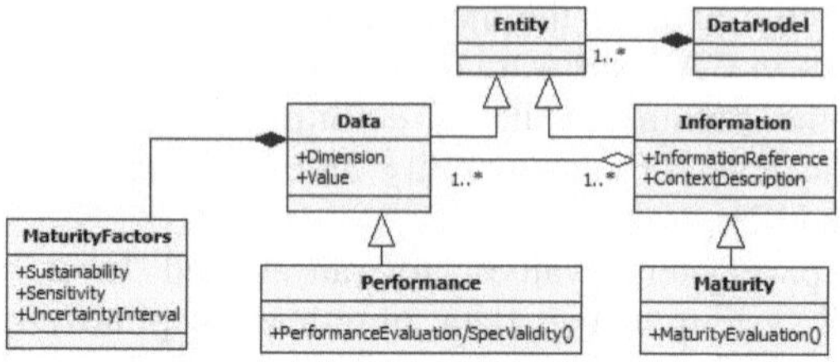

Fig. 1. DMM package description

Figure 1 details how the DMM package works. The content of the Entity class will be described later. The Data and Information classes inherit from the Entity class. For a given context of use, parameters and their values are enclosed in the Data class. MaturityFactors class composes Data class and allow the definition of the level of maturity (Maturity class). Performance class allows us to determine the level of performance based upon the SpecValidity relation. The Information class defines the knowledge configuration structure and the level of Maturity.

Collaboration meta-modelling: the Collaboration Meta-Model (CMM) (Figure 2) proposes the concepts representing the collaboration between business models in the sense of flipping from one to another, and the Specification Model. This includes inter-business parametric relationships and model transformations. The Constraint class holds the business rules. The Transformation class outlines the transformation rules, that is to say the identification elements of equivalence relationships. The SpecValidity class checks the validation of the necessary technical specifications.

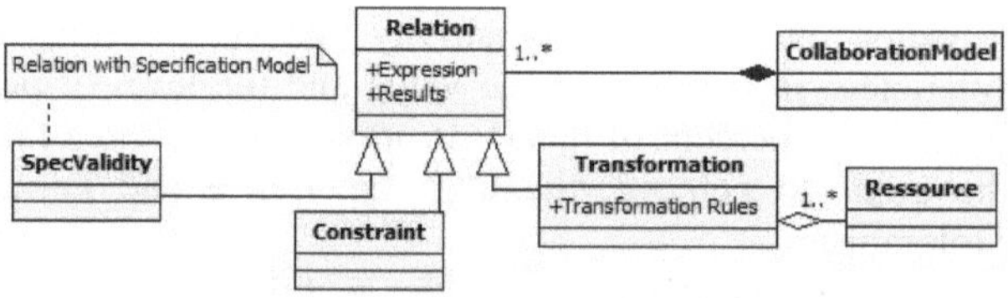

Fig. 2. CMM package description

Knowledge meta-modelling: the Knowledge Meta-Model, named KMM, is a conceptual framework allowing the creation of Knowledge Models (KM) through instantiation of the KMM. This way, the collaboration between KMM is supported. As pointed out in the previous section, there are numerous Knowledge models. Therefore, the KMM must be user-friendly and generic for the purpose of bringing consistency within one conceptual representation in order to open the possibility of combining different models and then building the most appropriate one.

The MMCore package (Meta Model Core) is the heart of the modelling approach. It contains all generic classes that are common for the different meta-models. The specific meta-model classes are then obtained by means of specification relations from the MMCore classes.

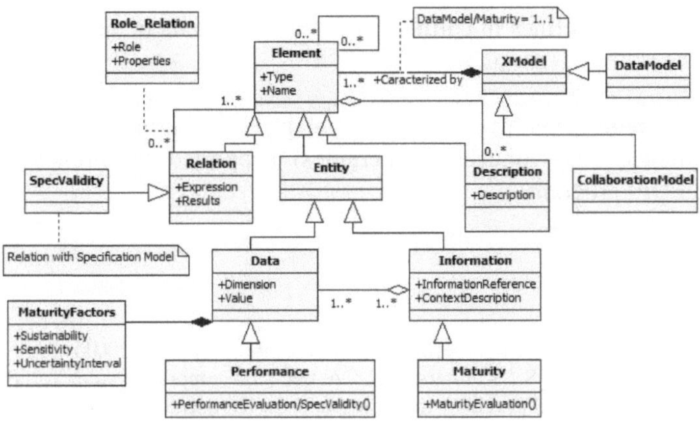

Fig. 3. MMCore package description

Figure 3 presents the UML diagram of the MMCore package. The MMCore includes six main classes:

- The Element class is the most generic level of the MMKM.
- XModel class defines the type of model (data, collaboration) linked to an element
- Description class enables the formulation of a specification as any of the quantifiable properties
- Entity class capitalizes and structures on the main data extracted from business models or from experts.
- Relation class provides a link between the components of the Entity class.
- RoleRelation class manages the relations, namely to give a direction to the relation, to handle the spread of the modifications using a tree approach instead of CSP.

5 Conclusion

In the product development project, the large variety of knowledge models identified in the literature survey pointed out the importance of robust meta-modelling approach to guarantee the coherence of the elements of heterogeneous knowledge produced during the collaborative design project. Indeed, this knowledge is generally coming from various sources, expressed with different semantics and supported in large numbers of business models.

Based on the analysis of the literature survey and the industrial experience, we have proposed in this paper a new meta-modelling approach integrating maturity that aims to help take into account the lack of knowledge (uncertainties and maturity) in decision making during preliminary design in a collaborative environment, but also to support the integration of multi-knowledge models and guarantee data consistency.

Current work consists to validate this proposal by doing an implementation of the MMK in the KCM (Knowledge Configuration Model) and by this way to validate its feasibility. Another level of validation also being established is to implement the

MMK on a use case defines in partnerships with industrials in the case of the national project ADN.

Acknowledgement: This work has been realized in partnership with the project A.D.N. (Alliance des Données Numériques) supported by French public funds through the FUI9 program.

References

1. Pahl and beitz
2. Ullman, D.G.: The Ideal Engineering Decision Support System (2001)
3. Besharati, B., Azarm, S., Kannan, P.K.: A decision support system for product design selection: A generalized purchase modeling approach. Journal: DSS 42(1), 333–350 (2006)
4. Grebici, K., Blanco, E., Rieu, D.: Framework for Managing Preliminary Information in Collaborative Design Processes. In: PLM 2005, vol. 1(1) (2005)
5. Beth, C.M., Konrad, M., Shrum, S.: CMMI. In: Guidelines for Process Integration and Product Improvement. Addison-Wesley (2007)
6. Blessing, L.T.M.: Comparison of Design Models Proposed in Prescriptive Literature. In: Perrin, J., Vinck, D. (eds.) Acts of: The Role of Design in the Shaping of Technology, COST A3/ COST A4 International Research Workshop, Lyon. Social Sciences Series, vol. 5, pp. 187–212 (1996)
7. Scheidl, Winkler: Relation between conceptual design and detail design, Mechatronics (2010)
8. Mtopi-Fotso, B., Dulmet, M., Bonjour, E.: Design of product families based on a modular architecture. In: ASMDO (2007)
9. Noel, F., Roucoules, L., Teissandier, D.: Specification of a product modelling concepts dedicating to information sharing in a collaborative design context. In: Advances in Integrated Design and Manufacturing in Mechanical Engineering, Part 1, pp. 135–146. Springer (2005)
10. Boucher, C.: Towards the competency integration in performance piloting of enterprise. Journal Européen de Systèmes automantisés 37(3), 363–390 (2003)
11. Ganascia, J.: Les sciences cognitives, éd. Flammarion (1996)
12. Thunnisen, D.P.: Propagating and Mitigating Uncertainty in the Design of Complex Multidisciplinary Systems. Phd thesis, California Ins. of Technology, Pasadena, Californie (2005)
13. Gaudin, J.: Description and modeling of information flow within an integrated design team, to define a tool of help for designer. DEA de Génie Industriel. INP Grenoble (2001)
14. Grebici, K., Ouertani, M.Z., Blanco, E., Gzara-Yesilbas, L., Rieu, D.: Conflict management in design process: focus on change impact. In: CE 2006, ICCE (2006)
15. Krishnan, V.: Managing the simultaneous execution of coupled phases in concurrent product development. IEEE Transactions on Engineering Management 43(2), 210–217 (1996)
16. Yassine, A., Falkenburg, D., Chelst, K.: Engineering design management: An information structure approach. International Journal of Production Research 37(13), 2957–2975 (1999)
17. Sebastian, P., Nadeau, J.P., Fischer, X., Chenouard, R.: Knowledge modeling in mechanical embodiment design for real time simulation and decision support. In: Proceedings of Virtual Concept 2005, Biarritz, France (2005)
18. Zadeh, L.A.: Fuzzy Sets. Information and Control 8, 338–353 (1965)

19. Zadeh, L.A.: Fuzzy Sets as a Basis for a Theory of Possibility. Fuzzy Sets and Systems 1, 3–28 (1978)
20. Du, L., Choi, K.K.: A New Fuzzy Analysis Method for Possibility-Based Design Optimization. AIAA Journal (2006)
21. Dempster, A.P.: Upper and Lower Probabilities Induced by a Multivalued Mapping. The Annals of Statistics 28, 325–339 (1967)
22. Shafer, G.: A Mathematical Theory of Evidence. Prin. Univ. Press, Princeton (1976)
23. Noël, F., Roucoules, L.: The PPO design model with respect to digital enterprise technologies among product life cycle. International Journal of Computer Integrated Manufacturing 21(2), 139–145 (2006), doi:10.1080/09511920701607782
24. Badin, J.: Using the Knowledge Configuration Model (KCModel) to manage configurated knowledge for upstream phases of the design Process. Editorial Manager(tm) for International Journal on Interactive Design and Manufacturing (IJIDeM) (2011)
25. Sudarsan, R., Fenves, S.J., Sriram, R.D., Wang, F.: A product information modelling framework for product lifecycle management. Computer-Aided Design 37(13), 1399–1411 (2005)
26. Moka user guide, deliverable du consortium MOKA, on web, `http://www.kbe.coventry.ac.uk/moka/`
27. Clark Kim, B., Fujimoto, T.: Product Development Performance. Strategy, Organization, and Management in the World Auto Industry. Harvard Business School, Boston (1991)
28. Eppinger, S.D., Krishnan, V., Whitney, D.E.: A model-based framework to overlap product development activities. Management Science 43(4) (1997)
29. Hanssen, R.W.: Reducing delivery times in engineer-to-order firms by using the concepts of concurrent engineering. In: Proceedings of the 4th International Conference on Concurrent Enterprising (ICE 1997), The University of Nottingham, October 8-10, pp. 495–498 (1997)
30. Uschold, M., King, M., Moralee, S., Zorgios, Y.: The Enterprise Ontology. The Knowledge Engineering Review 13(1), 31–89 (1998)
31. Matta, N., Corby, O., Ribière, M.: Méthodes de capitalisation de mémoire de projet. INRIA, Rapport de recherche 3819 (1999)
32. Fiorentini, X., Gambino, I., Liang, V.C., Foufou, S., Rachuri, S., Bock, C., Mani, M.: Towards an Ontology for Open Assembly model. In: International Conference on Product Lifecycle Management, PLM 2007, Stezzano, Italy, July 11-13 (2007)
33. Lee, J.H., Suh, H.W.: OWL-based product ontology architecture and representation for sharing product knowledge on a web. In: The 27th ASME International Design Engineering Technical Conferences and Computers and Information in Engineering Conference, Las Vegas, USA, September 4-7 (2007)
34. Terzi, S., Cassina, J., Panetto, H.: Development of a meta-model to foster interoperability along the product lifecycle traceability. In: 1st International Conference on Interoperability of Enterprise Software and Applications, Geneva, Switzerland (February 2005)
35. Vliegen, H.J.W., Van Mal, H.H.: The Structuring of Process Knowledge: Function, Task, Properties and State. Robotics&Computer-Integrated Manufacturing 6(2), 101–107 (1989)
36. Fortin, C., Huet, G.: Manufacturing Process Management: Iterative synchronisation of engineering data with manufacturing realities. IJPD 4(3-4), 280–295 (2007)
37. Danesi, F., Gardan, F., Gardan, Y., Reimeringer, M.: P4LM: A methodology for product lifecycle management. Computers in Industry 59(2-3), 304–317 (2008)

Towards Higher Configuration Management Maturity

Masoud Niknam and Jivka Ovtcharova

IMI, Karlsruhe Institute for Technology, Germany
masoud.niknam@kit.edu

Abstract. Configuration Management (CM) as a discipline assuring the consistency between product information with the reality all along the product lifecycle has recently been more appreciated by most industries. Although the extensive benefits of this discipline such as direct impact on increasing return on investment, lowering lifecycle costs and leadtime, are realized by most organizations, there is no specific maturity model in the field for evaluating different aspects of organizations' CM activities. Therefore, a Configuration Management Maturity Assessment framework is developed in this paper using state-of-the-art, standards and other maturity models. In order to evaluate the overall CM maturity of various industry sectors using the developed maturity model, the maturity appraisal material in the frame of a web-survey has been sent to a wide range of CM related employees in different industrial sectors. The extensive results coming out of this analysis has shown the overall competency level of various industries as well as potentials for improvement.

Keywords: Product Lifecycle Management, Configuration Management, Maturity model, Continuous Improvement, Self-assessment.

1 Introduction

Configuration management (CM) is a managerial discipline that aims at providing consistency and accuracy of product knowledge throughout its lifecycle and for the same purpose it is being used in different extents in most of the organizations. The primary objective of CM is to ensure that in all the phases of the product lifecycle, changes to product components such as requirements, design and "as-made" information for both software and hardware aspects are assessed and approved before being implemented and recorded and traced after implementation [1]. In a shorter form, CM ensures that products and facilities, including all the systems, equipment and components, are accurately described all the time [2].

It is noted by many researchers that implementing effective configuration management processes not only improves the safety in organizations, but also has direct positive impacts on return on investment, product lifecycle costs, on-time deliveries and product quality [1, 3-4]. Although the benefits of effective CM discipline in place are prominent to all professional organizations, there have not been many works to elucidate a clear roadmap to evaluate their maturity in the field, prioritize their improvement activities and implement missing elements step-by-step. Therefore, it is highly beneficial for organizations to have a framework by which they can evaluate their CM activities in order to uncover their gaps and focus on future

A. Bernard, L. Rivest, and D. Dutta (Eds.): PLM 2013, IFIP AICT 409, pp. 396–405, 2013.

improvements in a more efficient manner. This lack escalates in higher levels when organizations intend to compare their know-hows in the field with best practices in their industrial sectors.

The rest of this paper is organized in the following order. Next section gives a brief description about the nature of maturity models. Section 3 illustrates the key features of CM in standards and maturity models. Accordingly, in Section 4 the concept of CM maturity model is presented. Section 5 describes the research methodology followed for the overall industry assessment. Section 6 provides the results of the survey followed in section 7 by conclusion and overview of future work.

2 Maturity Models

Due to the high importance of continuous improvement in organizations for obtaining more competitive advantages, there are always needs for supportive tools to assess the "as-is" situation, prioritize improvement measures and control the progress of such improvements. Maturity models are the essential tools to address these issues [5, 6].

A maturity model consists of a sequence of maturity levels ranging from the very basic level to the completely mature level for each important criterion within the discipline being measured. [7,8] The main elements of maturity models according to [9], are (1) a number of maturity levels, (2) a descriptor for each level, (3) the characteristics of organizations in each maturity level, (4) a number of important dimensions of the discipline being assessed, (5) important activities under each dimension and (6) the description of the way each activity might be performed in each maturity level.

So far Configuration Management has mostly been considered as part of other subject areas and therefore has not been covered comprehensively and with sufficient level of details in maturity models [10]. Thus, the aim of this paper is to extract the primary dimensions of Configuration Management and develop a CM Maturity Model with sufficient level of detail.

For this purpose, the maturity model design framework proposed by De Bruin *et al.* [5] is chosen for developing the Configuration Management Maturity Model (Figure 1). Based on these principles, first the most important dimensions of CM and the critical activities under each dimension shall be extracted and formalized by using state-of-the-art analysis and comprehensive review of current maturity models and standards in the field. The collected information then was verified by using expert in the field feedback through a case study at CERN [11]. Subsequently, suitable maturity levels were developed based on the Idea of maturity and organizational alignment [12]. Finally the appraisal material in the frame of a web survey was developed and used.

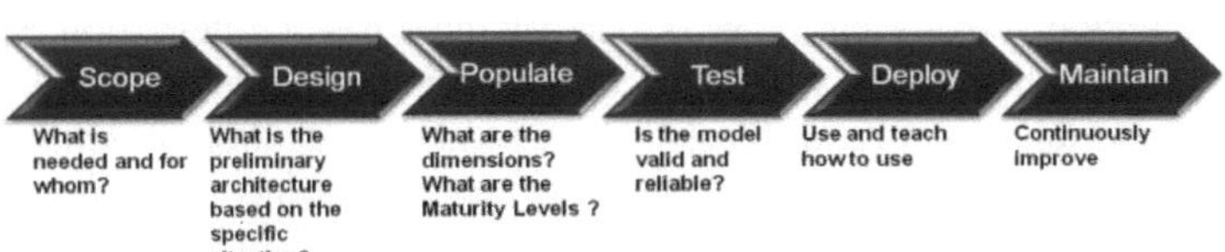

Fig. 1. Development phases of a maturity model [5]

3 CM in Maturity Models and Standards

Configuration Management has so far been mostly considered as part of other disciplines. Therefore, its coverage in other maturity models has to a high extent been limited to application of change management processes. The available Maturity Models in the field of business processes are mostly focusing on the organizational development in general and although some of them include requirements for CM, the requirements vary from model to model depending on the processes they are focused on. [10]

CMMI (Capability Maturity Model Integrated) [13], developed by Software Engineering Institute (SEI) at Carnegie Mellon University, as one of the most comprehensive maturity models, covers and evaluates organizations Configuration Management processes as one of the sixteen core functions in an organization. Here, Configuration Management is a support process that shall be followed along with some other processes for the organization to reach the second level of maturity out of five. As an example of a necessity for complementary requirements from other aspect than sole processes to this maturity model, Gupta & RAO [14] acknowledge the role of IT tools for reaching higher maturity levels in Configuration Management practices and try to find matches between the CM process areas described in the CMMI standard and IT tools for supporting those process areas.

In its proposed self assessment framework, IAEA (International Atomic Energy Agency) [2], more deeply focuses on CM discipline and defines main criteria for assessing the Configuration Management discipline in safety-critical environments based on experience and best practices gathered from different nuclear power plants. These criteria include program management, design requirements, information and change control, assessment and training.

BOOTSTRAP, a European assessment process was developed in the 1990s for assessing the capability of the European Software industry [15]. Bootstrap served as a basis for SPICE (now ISO 15504 [16]) as an overall framework for developing maturity assessment models and was later extended to include guidelines from the ISO 9000 [17]. Similar to SEI Software assessment model [18] it utilizes both Capability and Maturity levels. Configuration Management, as a support process, is a necessity for process areas to reach capability level 2. For this purpose, a CM strategy shall be developed and all process and project items shall be identified and baselined. Modifications to those items shall be controlled, recorded and reported. Finally storage, handling and delivery of the item shall be recorded.

The Project Management Maturity Model [19] developed by the US Project Management Institute (PMI) based on the Project Management Body of Knowledge (PMBOK® Guide [20]). Here, CM is part of the Project Integration Management knowledge area which mainly focuses on the integration of the different project deliverables and documents and thus it is being assessed as an individual function. In order for reaching higher levels of maturity, organizations shall practice change monitoring and control to the scope, schedule and cost and also communicate the information about changes to all stakeholders. [19]

In the American standard EIA-731.1 or Systems Engineering Capability Model, CM involves Identification, Change control, Status accounting and auditing of the product and its elements. The CM definitions here are taken from the National Consensus Standard for Configuration management, EIA- STD-649-A. [21]

ISO/IEC 12207 [22] emphasizes on the importance of defining a CM strategy and policy which shall include the authorities for decision making and change control as well as methodology and process storage to be used for the CM system. In this standard, the organizations are suggested to ensure the changes to baselines are properly identified, evaluated, approved, incorporated and verified. For further information this standard refers to more specific CM standard, ISO 10007. ISO 10007:2003 standard [23] is developed to give a better understanding of the CM subject to organizations and promote the use of CM as well as assist the organizations in applying this discipline. According to this standard, the CM process is comprised of the main five stages of planning, identification, change control, status accounting and audit. This standard provides a more detailed description of what is expected in a Configuration Management Plan. This shows the importance of having a CM strategy and policy together with a clear set of defined roadmaps and methodologies, as well as clearly defined responsibilities and authorities to be used in each process stage.

US military standard EIA-649-B [24] which replaces the old MIL-STD-973 covers Configuration Management principles and practices more comprehensively than the others. The importance of using a clear set of terminology for Configuration Management is acknowledged and followed in this standard. However, the main functions of CM are similar to the main five functions introduced in ISO 10007.

EIA-649-B proposes that implementing policies, assigning functional responsibilities, CM-related training, considering CM-tools and their necessary functionalities, establishing KPIs for CM, assuring supplier's involvement in CM activities and integrating organization wide CM processes shall be included for CM planning & Management.

Currently, the U.S. Department of Defence (DoD) is in the process of releasing a new standard for Configuration Management (MIL-STD-3046 [25]). The draft version issued for feedback collection purposes shows more or less the same level of comprehensiveness as EIA-649-B with more focus on standardization of processes. This purpose is achieved by providing standard and simplified process steps and forms for CM functions.

4 Configuration Management Maturity Model

According to the various functions and categories discussed in the previous section, the authors propose the following five primary dimensions of CM discipline and the sub-dimensions in each area for maturity assessment purposes in organizations (for further details also see [11]).(Figure 2)

Strategy & Performance	Processes	Information Technology	Organization & Value-stream	Knowledge & Support
CM strategic objective and policy	Clear processes for different org. units, projects and lifecycle phases	High level of visualization and user-friendliness corresponding all stakeholders needs	Suitable CM organization structure with respect to Org. complexity and CM needs	Standard CM terminology and knowledge support accessible by stakeholders
Deployment of CM strategy in different organization levels	Standard processes: ✓ Configuration Identification ✓ Baselining ✓ Product structure management ✓ Change evaluation, control & implementation ✓ Status Accounting ✓ Configuration Audits	Integration of CM tool with other IT systems	Defined roles and responsibilities for CM personnel	Regular CM-related training activities (processes, IT, etc)
Communication of the deployed strategy to stakeholders	Process ownership, maintenance and update based on feedbacks	Supporting the CM functionalities such as Naming, Numbering, Versioning, Workflow management, Change traceability	Cross-functional collaboration among different stakeholders for CM purposes	Accessibility and promotion of latest standards, lessons learned, best practices and internal & external benchmarks in CM field
KPIs for performance measurements	Stakeholders access to processes	Solid IT tool all over the organization for all lifecycle phases	Consideration of suppliers and subcontractors in CM activities	Support and empowerment of CM discipline by top management
Regular measurement and update of KPIs	Process customizability for different scenarios	Authorization capabilities for different CM activities	Involvement of key stakeholders in major configuration changes	Communication of CM benefits to stakeholders by top management

Fig. 2. Configuration Management primary dimensions and sub-dimensions

As one of the support disciplines in systems engineering and product lifecycle management, the extent up to which it permeate into the organization's structure and activities could represent the level of organization's maturity in this discipline. Therefore, the concept of Maturity and Organizational Alignment utilized by [12] is used for categorizing different maturity levels of organizations with respect to their CM activities. Figure 3 represents the authors' proposition for CM four maturity levels.

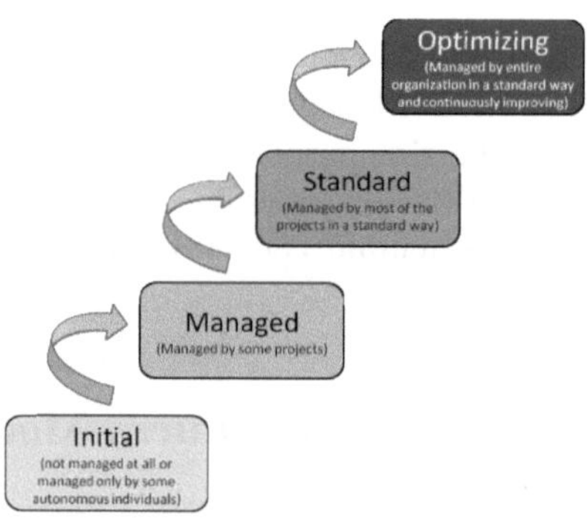

Fig. 3. Configuration Management Maturity Levels

Considering the CM maturity dimensions and sub-categories discussed in previous section, the detailed description for organizations fulfilling the requirements for each maturity level is brought below. [11]

Initial **-** In this level, there is no specific level of Configuration Management dimensions and sub-dimensions in place and people just rely on their own grasp of every situation.
Managed **-** At this level, the generic need for a formal CM discipline is still missing; however some specific methods are in place in some projects or groups.
Standard **-** At this level, due to the understood need for CM discipline, clear methods are in place as standard way of doing things in most/all projects and groups. However, such methods are not being reviewed and updated based on the benchmark results.
Optimizing **-** The Configuration Management activities and processes are regularly updated. The organization has processes for collecting feedback to improve its CM-related activities continuously.

5 Research Methodology

In order for the appraisal material to be distributed rapidly and easily to all target cases and at the same time collect as detail information as possible, online survey methodology was selected [26]. Through a partnership with CM experts from a leading consultant company in CM area, the survey went through 11 iterations for the content and 20 iterations for the visuals. For raising the quality and quantity of the answers, the survey was made available in both English and German languages. Altogether there were 53 questions in the survey which were mostly multiple-choice questions with the choices matching the maturity areas described in section 4. This was chosen to give a logical measure for the respondents for rating the maturity of their organization in the respective subject. After completion, the survey was tested by three CM professionals who were not involved in the process. The content was approved to be sufficiently covering various CM aspects and a few editorial comments were made and implemented. Afterwards, the survey link was distributed to about 150 professionals and CM-related employees from different industrial sectors. Simultaneously the link was posted on well-known online CM communities to collect data from international experts and practitioners. The survey material could be sent for further use upon contacting the authors.

6 Results

Altogether 61 complete answers were recorded of which 4 were excluded due to having lower response time than average. The analysis result of the remaining responses is clustered in the following sections.

6.1 Demographic and General

Important characteristics such as organization sizes and nature, respondents' involvement extent in CM activities, distribution of industrial sectors and level of CM application in various lifecycle phases among participants are shown in Figure 4.

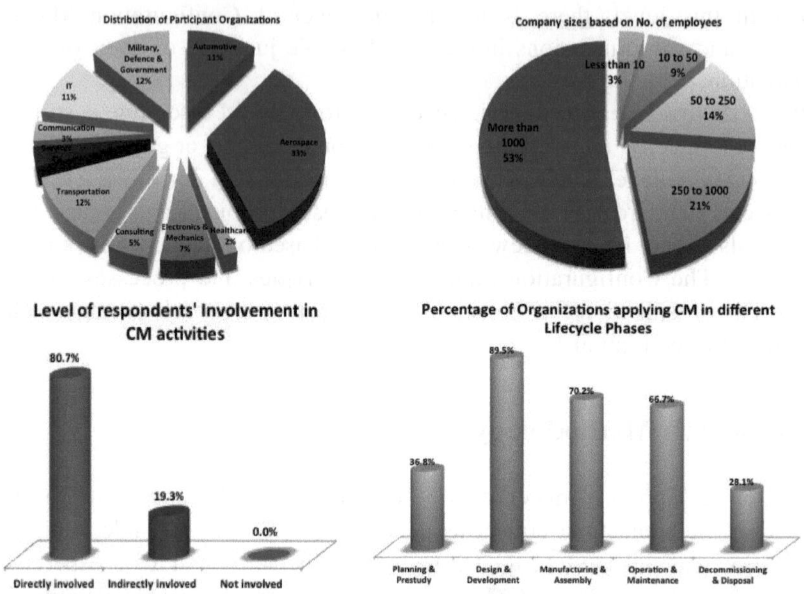

Fig. 4. Various characteristics of the survey participants and their organizations

6.2 Criteria-Based Maturity Results

The overall maturity of each dimension is calculated based on a simple weighted average formula shown below.

$$M = \frac{\sum_{k=1}^{j}(\sum_{i=1}^{4} i * xi)}{j} \tag{1}$$

Where M is the maturity in the dimension e.g. Strategy & Performance, i is the maturity level from 1 corresponding to the level initial to 4 corresponding to the level optimizing. xi is the percentage of answers in the i_{th} choice and j is the number of questions in the dimension.

For the whole Strategy & Performance dimension overall maturity observed from all responses is 2.25 which is just a bit more than managed level. This shows the need for a more advanced focus on measuring strategic performance in organizations.

In the Process dimension, the outcome maturity from the detailed questions in CM Process showed a maturity level of 2.29. This level still leaves much room for improvement of the CM processes to higher levels of Standard and Optimizing.

In the Information Technology dimension, the interesting results show that only 33 percent of the organizations use single IT systems while 16 percent don't even use an information system support for CM and about 51 percent use different CM IT systems for different projects or groups of the organization. Some organizations have introduced more than 6 different tools in this respect. More specifically for Engineering Change Management process, the support of IT systems is in a low level of managed only and considering the impact of this function needs immediate care and focus. With the overall Maturity of 2.15 in IT dimension, obviously more standardization among different groups and project teams as well as more consistency among the tools being chosen for the whole lifecycle could lead to much better results.

In Organization and Value-stream dimension, more than 60% of the respondents believe their choice of CM organization structure to a high extent does not correspond to the organization complexity and needs. As it was expected before, the maturity of organizations with respect to consideration of subcontractors' CM tasks during contract negotiations is very low (1.8) where more than 70 percent of the companies do not have an standard and consistent procedure for this matter. The overall maturity in this dimension is 2.17 with the strength of organizations being the involvement of key stakeholders in major changes.

The last dimension Knowledge & Support shows an overall maturity of 1.9 where the use of internal and external benchmarks has a maturity of as low as 1.67 which could show the lack of continuous improvement in this discipline's practices. Another interesting aspect could be the low maturity (1.81) for communication of CM benefits by management which could show the lack of support, promotion and motivation. The overall maturity of target organizations in CM discipline could be observed in Figure 5a.

6.3 Industry-Specific Maturity

In this section the maturity results of specific industries which had the most respondents are discussed and illustrated in Figure 5. In the Aerospace industry with the majority of respondents, the overall maturity level is 2.61 which compared to 1.65 in Transportation with lowest maturity is rather high. The results show that in most industries especially transportation, focusing on Information Technology, Knowledge & Support and Strategy modules could result in higher efficiency.

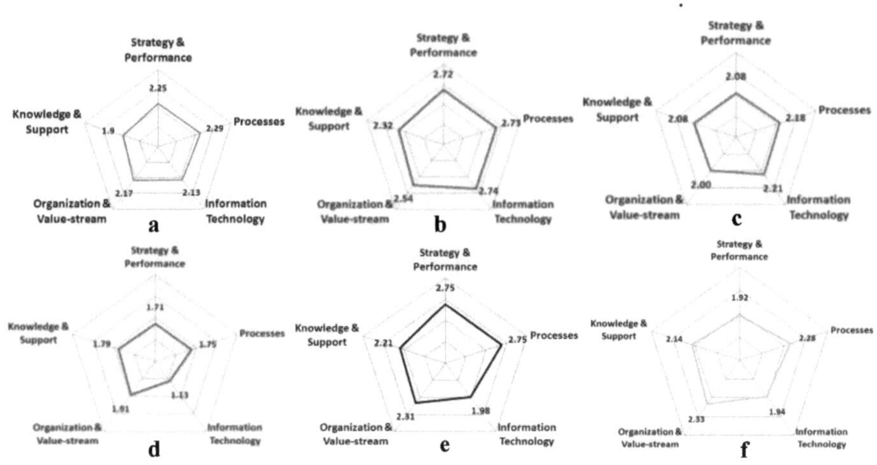

Fig. 5. CM maturity in **a)** all industries **b)** Aerospace **c)** Automotive **d)** Transportation **e)** Military & Government **f)** IT

7 Conclusion and Future Work

In this paper the key influential factors for the success of Configuration Management activities have been extracted and categorized. Configuration Management maturity model was developed and was used to identify the level of maturity and gaps in various industrial organizations. The results demonstrated a rather high potential for improvement in different aspects associated with this discipline. Considering the direct and indirect effect of CM discipline on product leadtime, cost, quality, safety, etc, filling the gap could be of high importance and benefit for all organizations.

Nature of the CM maturity model, developed in this paper, is so far descriptive in the sense that it is limited to evaluation of CM maturity level in the target organizations and identification of gaps in different areas. However, in order for the organizations to have an ideal model, next step would be to develop the model further for having prescriptive abilities and leading the organizations for filling the identified gaps in an optimized way. Also using weights for various sub-dimensions according to their importance could obviously lead to more practical results but the importance of each subject could vary in different industries. The choice of web survey was made for its suitability to industry-wide studies and its simplicity in simultaneous data collection from different organizations and in analysis of the quantitative data. However, the level of detail that could be covered in this method is as deep as the level that understanding of the questions would not be difficult. In order to have a specific case study for one organization, a more comprehensive appraisal material shall be developed for other methods such as focus group meetings and semi-structured interviews.

Acknowledgments. The authors would like to appreciate FP7 European Union Marie Curie program for providing the funding in the framework of PURESAFE project. The authors also would like to thank P3 Group for their support in data collection.

References

1. Sage, A.P., Rouse, W.B.: Handbook of Systems Engineering and Management, pp. 267–289. Jon Wiley & Sons (2011)
2. International Atomic Energy Agency, Application of Configuration Management in Nuclear Power Plants, Safety Reports Series No. 65 (2010)
3. Dvir, D., Lipovetsky, S., Shenhar, A., Tishler, A.: In search of project classification: A non-universal approach to project success factors. Research Policy 27, 915–935 (1998)
4. International Aerospace Quality Group (IAQG). Configuration Management Guidelines (2010), `http://www.sae.org/iaqg/` (accessed September 2011)
5. De Bruin, T., Rosemann, M., Freeze, R., Kulkarni, U.: Understanding the main phases of developing a maturity assessment model. In: Australasian Conference on Information Systems (ACIS), Sydney (2005)
6. Becker, J., Knackstedt, R., Pöppelbuss, J.: Developing Maturity Models for IT Management – A Procedure Model and Its Application. Business & Information Systems Engineering J. (3), 213–222 (2009)

7. Röglinger, M., Pöppelbuss, J., Becker, J.: Maturity models in business process management. Business Process Management J. 18(2), 328–346 (2012)
8. Saco, R.M.: Maturity Models: Inject New Life. Industrial Management J. 50(3), 11–16 (2008)
9. Mettler, T., Rohner, P., Winter, R.: Towards a Classification of Maturity Models in Information Systems. In: Management of the Interconnected World. Springer (2010), doi:10.1007/978-3-7908-2404-9_39
10. Hass, A.M.J.: Configuration Management Principles and Practice. Addison-Wesley Professional (2003)
11. Niknam, M., Bonnal, P., Ovtcharova, J.: Configuration Management Maturity in Scientific Facilities. To be Published in International Journal of Advanced Robotic Systems Special Issue on Telerobotics and Systems Engineering in Scientific Facilities (2013)
12. Batenburg, R., Helms, R.W., Versendaal, J.: PLM roadmap: Stepwise PLM implementation based on the concepts of maturity and alignment. Int. J. of Product Lifecycle Management 1(4), 333–351 (2006)
13. CMMI Product Team, CMMI for Development, Version 1.3 (CMU/SEI-2010-TR-033). Software Engineering Institute, Carnegie Mellon University (2010), http://www.sei.cmu.edu/library/abstracts/reports/10tr033.cfm
14. Gupta, P., Rao, D.S.: Best Practices to Achieve CMMI Level 2 Configuration Management Process Area through VSS tool. Int. J. of Computer Technology And Applications (2011)
15. Kuvaja, P., Bicego, A.: Bootstrap – A European Assessment Methodology. Software Quality Journal (3), 117–127 (1994)
16. ISO/IEC TS 15504-9:2011. International Organization for Standardization (ISO).
17. Pereira, R., Mira da Silva, M.: A Maturity Model for Implementing ITIL V3 in Practice. In: 15th IEEE International Enterprise Distributed Object Computing Conference Workshops (2011)
18. Humphrey, W.S.: Characterizing the Software Process: A Maturity Framework, Software Engineering Institute, CMU/SEI-87-TR-11, ADA182895 (1987)
19. Crawford, J.K.: Project Management Maturity Model. Taylor & Francis gr (2006)
20. PMI (Project Management Institute), A Guide to Project Management Body of Knowledge, Project Management Institute (2010)
21. Government Electronics and Information Technology Association (GEIA), Systems Engineering Capability Model (EIA-731.1), Electronic Industries Alliance, EIA (2002)
22. ISO/IEC 12207, Systems and Software Engineering – Software Life cycle Processes, Software and Systems Engineering Standards Committee, International Standard Organization (2008)
23. BS ISO 10007, Quality Management Systems – Guidelines for Configuration Management, British Standards (2003)
24. Tech. America, ANSI/EIA-649-B, Configuration Management Standard (2011)
25. Department of Defence (DoD), MIL-STD-3046, Standard for Configuration Management (2013), https://assist.dla.mil (accessed online on September 11, 2012)
26. Czaja, R., Blair, J.: Designing Surveys: A guide to divisions and procedures. Pine Forge Press (December 9, 2004)

Product Lifecycle Management: Measuring What Is Important – Product Lifecycle Implementation Maturity Model

Abram L.J. Walton[1], Cynthia L. Tomovic[2], and Michael W. Grieves[3]

[1] Florida Institute of Technology, USA
[2] Old Dominion University, USA
[3] Florida Institute of Technology, USA
awalton@fit.edu

Abstract. Industry reports that benefits of PLM are difficult to assess because the same benefit can be expressed as a function of time, cost, quality, or any combination. Based on a review of the PLM literature in an earlier study, a PLM Process Model and an initial list of PLM related metrics was generated and later confirmed through interviews with experienced PLM users. In the current study, the original PLM Process Model was refined and the list of metrics was subjected to an exploratory factor analysis in which specific metrics were found to be related to one of four factors: Inputs, Processes, Outputs, and Outcomes. Based on the results of this study, a Product Lifecycle Implementation Maturity Model was developed that serves as a program-level guide in helping to quantify PLM performance in support of meeting organizational strategic goals.

Keywords: PLM, product lifecycle management, innovation, performance measurement, metrics, maturity model.

1 Introduction

Product Lifecycle Management (PLM) is an integrated, information-driven approach comprised of people, processes/practices, and technology. It serves to integrate information across all phases of a product's lifecycle and its environment including product ideation, design, manufacturing, distribution, support, and retirement from use [1], [2]. Over the last decade, PLM has become an integral part of the global manufacturing landscape [3].

The concept of PLM emerged in the late 1990's-early 2000's. Its specific aim was to move information sharing beyond the engineering phase of a product by providing a shared platform for the creation, organization, and dissemination of product-related information across the extended enterprise [4]. In essence, PLM is to provide a holistic approach to managing product information [1], [5].

In today's marketplace, global competition is forcing manufacturing industries to reduce costs and time associated with product development, manufacturing, and mass

A. Bernard, L. Rivest, and D. Dutta (Eds.): PLM 2013, IFIP AICT 409, pp. 406–421, 2013.

customization. PLM is viewed often times as an investment in technology that supports operations and provides companies an overall competitive advantage in these areas [6, [7]. However, if companies were to view PLM as a means to achieve overarching organizational goals, rather than as simply as an investment in technology in support of operations, companies would come to appreciate PLM as an investment that improves and enhances all facets of the enterprise [8], [9], [10], [11].

As companies begin to think about implementing PLM, even in its earliest stages, they need to think about what metrics to employ when measuring the actual benefits of a PLM-driven solution [12], [13]. Building on earlier works that focused on developing a PLM Process Model and developing a list of PLM-related metrics [11], [16], [17], this paper seeks to empirically further verify the importance of the initial list of PLM-related metrics by conducting an exploratory factor analysis.

2 Significance of the Problem

Although some companies and engineering firms may posit that PLM is merely an extension of prior Product Data Management (PDM) efforts, since 2001 a number of businesses have launched new PLM initiatives based on the understanding that, if successfully implemented, PLM leads to enterprise-wide efficiencies and opportunities [11], [14]. Although founded on the main tenets of Just-in-Time (JIT) and Lean principles, PLM has a different orientation to Lean [2], [15]. According to Grieves [2], [15], PLM focuses on identifying and capturing wasted resources associated with time, energy, and materials, and the subsequent reallocation of these captured resources in support of product and process improvements and innovations that, ultimately, result in new revenue streams [11], [16], [17]. Manufacturing companies that have implemented new PLM systems and processes beyond those of traditional PDM systems and processes are reporting gains as much as: 20% increases in design productivity, 50-80% reductions in the time required to modify complex designs, 50% increases in time to explore more design options, improving the capability of conducting numeric control programming up to 10 times faster, machining up to 35% faster, 60% reductions in pallet manufacturing time, and 40% decreases in the errors found at the final assembly stage, as well as other benefits [18]. Nonetheless, even with these gains, industry continues to report that the benefits of PLM are difficult to assess because the same benefit can be expressed as a function of time, cost, quality, or a combination thereof. According to Shah and Ward [8], some of the confusion associated with PLM is due to the lack of a consistent definition as to what constitutes a PLM system. Given that this is the case, it follows then that there is also an inconsistent way to measure the impact of PLM. This lack of consistency is problematic as, according to Walton [5], unless PLM-related metrics are purposefully and strategically developed, PLM initiatives may result in nothing more than an instantiation of PDM principles.

If companies are to continue investing significant portions of their IT budgets in PLM-related technology, infrastructure, training and support, they must be able to derive valid and reliable data that measures the impact of their PLM investments [5],

[11], [16], [17]. Moreover, without being able to accurately assess the impact of PLM on the bottom line, or its direct and indirect influences on cost-savings and revenue-generation, risk mitigation strategies often employed during IT installations and upgrades may fall short of providing a holistic foundation for future PLM investments [5], [11], [16], [17]. While the more traditional performance measures of net income, operating income, and revenue, will always be relevant and important in determining the profitability and successes of an organization, new PLM-related metrics must be identified to more accurately account for the costs and potential impacts associated with PLM initiatives [19].

Shah and Ward [8] found that there is significant overlap, and yet unique differences, in performance attributes with studies associated with Lean Manufacturing when compared to PLM. According to Grieves [1], [2], these differences exist because the main tenets of a PLM system diverge from Lean by including more holistic measures of data-attributes such as data singularity, data correspondence, data cohesion, data traceability, data reflectivity, and cued availability of data. Due to these differences, companies cannot use traditional Lean manufacturing-related metrics alone when attempting to measure the impact of PLM. Rather, accurate and valid PLM-specific metrics reflective of an entire PLM system need to be developed.

3 PLM Assessment Process Model

This paper further analyzes the PLM Assessment Process Model and PLM Metrics Framework proposed and explicated by Tomovic [16], and further refined by Walton [5] (Figure 1).

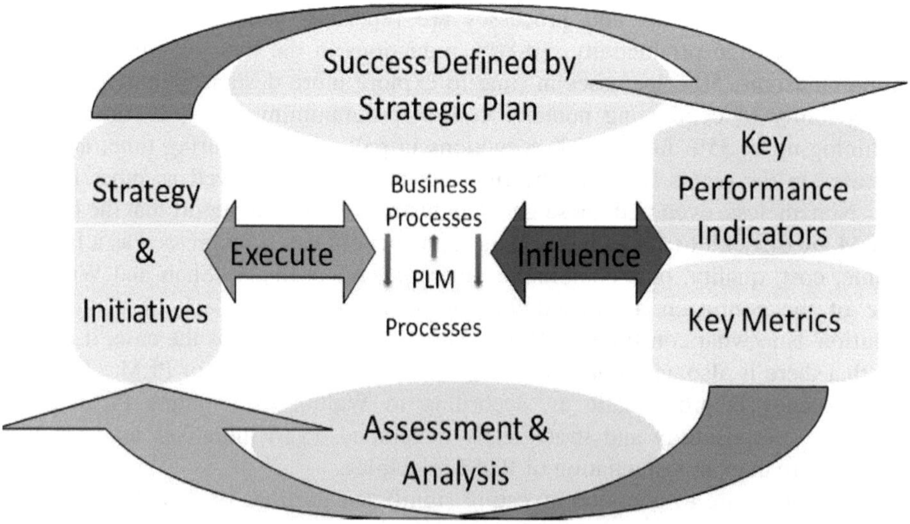

Fig. 1. PLM Assessment Process Model & Strategic Technology Road Mapping [5]

Figure 1 indicates how various processes and business functions intersect and influence an organization's strategy, outcomes, and the development of the measurement standards. Effective management of the product lifecycle assumes measurement of relevant metrics derived from business goals and objectives. Furthermore, understanding how PLM processes and systems contribute to an organization's strategic plan and initiatives, and monitoring the impact of PLM outcomes in this context, minimizes misaligned spending on PLM initiatives. The business strategy provides the organization's definition of success; it is from these definitions of success that targeted, key performance indicators and metrics are identified. Accurate collection, reporting, assessment, and analysis of these key performance indicators provide feedback in the PLM Process Model and are measured against the initial strategic goals.

Ultimately, all metrics should be tied to business objectives related to growth, revenue, and profitability; in this manner, organizations will be better able to see where money is being effectively spent to support and further justify their PLM initiative. Each organization's unique instantiation of their PLM processes ultimately determines the metrics that should be measured and impacts the execution of an organization's strategic plan; no ubiquitous and definitive set of metrics will apply to all organizations. Nonetheless, a common, core set of metrics may be identifiable, which is the focus of this study.

4 Methodology

Prior Study. In prior studies [5], [11], [16], [17], numerous PLM metric frameworks were developed based on a review of the literature, and their level of importance and priority were later confirmed through qualitative interviews and focus groups with key PLM users. This line of research sought to develop and validate key PLM metrics and then link those metrics to a framework that would assist industry in their use and interpretation of data. Metrics were defined and a web based PLM metrics survey was developed and pilot tested. During these studies, the following research objectives were met: 1) pilot tested the PLM metrics survey with an initial set of mature PLM users; 2) established and distributed an electronic version of the survey; 3) codified and analyzed preliminary data in the aggregate; 4) reviewed findings with industry-based PLM focus groups; 5) revised the PLM metrics survey, and 6) retested the survey by expanding the pool of participants.

Current Study. Expanding on the previous studies, this project worked toward the development of a program-level guide for quantifying PLM performance in support of organizational strategic goals. A PLM Implementation Maturity Model was derived and validated. The following key questions were considered: 1) What metrics are appropriate in the measurement of PLM performance? 2) What are the key features of a balanced performance measurement system? 3) How can a performance measurement system help to drive desired business and human capital results? 4) How can companies determine if a global, regional, or local approach is appropriate? and 5) What are the potential outcomes and benefits from an effective performance measurement system?

4.1 Data Collection and Development of the Instrument

In the data collection phase of this study, a mixed methods approach was employed whereby surveys and open-ended interviews were conducted with mature PLM users and focus groups to identify and examine the impact of PLM. According to the literature, when attempting to measure the impact of a phenomenon, a mixed method approach is more likely to result in more reliable data than in a single method alone [20], [21], 22].

There are multiple authors that have created, tested, and published models that delineate a suggested methodology when creating a survey instrument to be used in business and social science research [20], [23], [24]. In accordance with the suggested literature, the first step in this study was to identify key literature related to metrics for PLM. This literature supported the development of a framework in which two main tenets emerged, waste reduction and innovation [11]. Centering all metrics on these objectives led to the development of a multi-tiered metrics framework, which was used as the primary tool in the creation, and categorization of subsequent metrics.

This study extended the analysis and evaluation of the initial data set and descriptive statistics delineated in Tomovic [11], [16], [17]. The initial data collection, survey methodology, and participant recruiting methods were as follows: 1) 67 metrics were identified from the literature that measured the impact of PLM within an organization; 2) the metrics framework and initial set of 67 metrics were validated using focus groups that included key industrial representatives and practitioners; 3) the findings from the focus groups resulted in the refinement of the target areas used in the metrics framework; 4) through further analysis, interviews, and literature synthesis, a series of additional Key Performance Indicators and an additional 113 metrics were added to the overall list, totalling 180 metrics; and 5) a few select follow-up interviews were conducted with key individuals in participating firms.

Based on yet further study and practitioners' reviews, and through additional literature reviews, and interviews, the framework was used to identify an additional 170 metrics, resulting in a total of 350 PLM metrics. The resulting outcome of 350 metrics exemplified the fact that there was no consistency in the number, depth, breadth, or overall application of metrics in the PLM space. To resolve these issues, researchers then conducted focus groups and a pilot study with advisory board members from the Center for Advanced Manufacturing at a major university. Once again, concerns were addressed regarding the scope of the metrics framework, and it was refined accordingly, reducing the number of metrics to create a 'global' list of approximately 60 high-level or strategic metrics, from which the remaining metrics could be rolled-out like a multi-tiered, hierarchical dashboard.

The development of the data collection instrument for this research resulted in a web-based survey. The 65-item survey instrument was professionally designed and tested for face validity according to the methods prescribed by Borg and Gall[20].

The survey design was simplistic and straightforward. Based on the focus groups, interviews, the comprehensive design, and the all-encompassing nature of the survey questions, the survey instrument was determined to have content validity. The completed survey instrument was submitted to both academic-experts and industry-based focus groups for final pilot testing in order to ensure no topic had been neglected.

The final survey was composed of 8 high-level organizational variables and 57 PLM-specific metrics. In order to validate the PLM metrics identified and refined in steps one and two of this study, participants were asked to assess, for each survey-item, whether the metric was currently "in use"; and, to indicate whether the metric was considered important, or not, in assessing the overall impact of PLM. As delineated through clear instruction in the Metrics survey, in order for a participant to consider the metric "in use", the item had to pass the following criteria: 1) be collected at least on an annual basis; 2) be utilized by all members of top management; 3) be stored in a manner that ensures availability to numerous appropriate people in the organization; and 4) have a standard method for calculation. With regard to measuring importance, it was assumed that if the participant indicated that the item was "in use", the item was considered important. Additionally, respondents had the option of indicating that an item was either "not in use, but important:" or "not used, not important".

4.2 Participants

Various members of the research team attended several international conferences, workshops, and educational conferences, such as Partners for the Advancement of Collaborative Education (PACE) and the North American PLM Summit. At each venue potential participants were identified and subsequently contacted regarding their willingness to take the PLM metrics survey. Moreover, each participant was given the option to invite other PLM practitioners to take the survey, thus resulting in snowball sampling; often times, others included were those associated with one of the initial invitee's own organization or network affiliation, or were based on other professional contacts (e.g., professional associations, clients, etc.). The web-based survey was ultimately distributed to over 150 participants, of which 50 participants or 33% completed the survey.

5 Data Analysis

The initial analysis and descriptive statistics related to the data collected in this study was previously published [11]. Briefly, the majority of the respondents (40%) were from Aerospace and Automotive industries, with a majority of companies having implemented PLM for between 5-10 years. Furthermore, the majority of companies responding to the survey had gross sales revenue in excess of $1 billion per year.

The majority of people responding to the survey was in research and development or engineering (20%), followed by management (16.5%), and the remaining 63.5%

were comprised of individuals from marketing, sales, R&D, IT, and HR. Based on specific trade or job-related knowledge, individuals from engineering and management were probably the most appropriate to respond to the survey as Subject Matter Experts (SMEs). Descriptive statistics delineated the perceived usefulness and importance, or lack thereof, for each metric with regard to whether or not each respondent and/or his or her company employed that metric. The data analysis presented in this paper sought to extend the investigation and evaluation of the initial set of PLM-related metrics by conducting an exploratory factor analysis (EPA). The EPA allowed researchers to investigate whether or not groupings of metrics were easily developed, such that a more holistic framework could be created should a practitioner decide to employ these metrics in a meaningful way.

5.1 Exploratory Factory Analysis

An Exploratory Factor Analysis (EFA) was conducted using the software package SPSS to identify PLM-metrics related factors based on the PLM Metrics survey [25]. The extraction method used was Principal Components Analysis (PCA), which is the default method of extraction in SPSS. Several EFAs were conducted, with the final set containing four factors retained for rotation. Of the various models tested through SPSS, the four factor set was chosen to be retained because metrics used in manufacturing tend to focus on Input, Process, Output, and Outcomes, and these categories are typically normalized to enable comparisons between phases of production [26]. Regarding Input and Output metrics, they are commonly applied because they are highly specific and directly related to a specific end point in a process [27].

Input metrics assessed level of capital, labor, and time, while Process metrics assessed the extent to which the inputs are being processed and the extent to which appropriate processes were being implemented. Output metrics included the product or service delivery and implementation targets for PLM, including, for example completion performance, resource optimization, change control and change capacity, configuration management, project or product quality metrics, among others [28]. Outcome metrics assessed the changes and/or benefits resulting from PLM activities. Output metrics included such results as waste reduction, innovations and new products, continuous improvement, and sustainable green manufacturing.

The EFA did not reveal an Impact factor. Impact metrics measure long-term outcomes such as the return on investment, which many of the companies surveyed, have not yet realized to date. It is hypothesized, however, that future research will find the last few items listed in the Outcome Factor to be Impact Metrics. However, results for this study resulted in only a four-factor model.

5.2 Reliability (4-factors)

Cronbach's alpha for the study was calculated using SPSS factor structure suggested by Chelladurai [29]. Reliability of the 4-factor structure in the study ranged from .941-.953 with a mean of .978. Table 1 lists the 4 factors items included in each factor and factor alphas for the study sample (n=58).

Table 1. Scale of PLM Metrics Reliability Statistics

	Number of items	**Cronbach's Alpha on Standardized items**
Factor 1	12	.941
Factor 2	9	.904
Factor 3	16	.945
Factor 4	21	.953
Total scale	58 items	.978

5.3 Product Lifecycle Implementation Maturity Model (PLIMM)

As shown by the results in the preceeding section, many organizations in the manufacturing industry continue to face difficulties related to data and information access, and the value-measurement of their respective information systems. As a result of this study a Product Lifecycle Implementation Maturity Model was developed. The Product Lifecycle Implementation Maturity Model (PLIMM) helps organizations determine their level of maturity in terms of employing and measuring PLM. The PLIMM was based on the Capability Maturity Model (CMM) literature. According to Wang [30], CMM was originally developed to help the Department of Defense in acquiring appropriate software. The Capability Maturity Model (CMM) approach has been used successfully by many organizations as a basis for assessing relative maturity of practices in various areas, including: data management, warehousing, and governance maturities [31]. For this reason, CMM was adapted in order to create the PLIMM. Furthermore, the metrics identified in this paper and validated through the survey results were parsed into their respective categories to fit within the new PLIMM model. Although the metrics derived from this study may benefit any company wishing to better understand their successes related to PLM, not all companies have processes that are mature enough to benefit from or even provide accurate data enough to capitalize on the PLM metrics. By parsing the metrics according to a maturity model, companies can employ the framework regardless of their own current maturity level associated with their PLM processes. Therefore, even if benchmarking metrics have yet to be collected, companies can use the framework to identify the most appropriate starting point when broaching the subject of identifying and employing PLM metrics.

The PLIMM model presents the performance indicators for each level, providing a broad perspective for assessing PLM capacity. At Level 1, Inputs, the performance indicators delineate resource needs, and whether appropriate amounts of resources have been invested. Level 2, Processes, indicators determine if appropriate processes are being employed; in other words, it helps companies determine if PLM is being implemented and employed properly. Level 3, Outputs, indicators demonstrate the extent to which outputs meet customers' needs and requirements. Level 4, Outcomes, indicators demonstrate whether or not the desired results are being achieved. It is hypothesized that at the highest level, Level 5, Impact, the indicators will demonstrate success by measuring the return on a PLM investment. Table 2 illustrates the Product

Lifecycle Implementation Maturity Model. Further research is needed to confirm whether Level 5 metrics, Impact metrics, are statistically a separate factor from Level 4, Outcome metrics. Even though only a four-factor model was confirmed in this study, for illustration purposes, Level 5 metrics are included in Table 2, but technically belong to Level 4.

Table 2. Product Lifecycle Implementation Maturity Model

	Level 1	**Level 2**	**Level 3**	**Level 4**	***Hypothetical Level 5***
Metric Types	Inputs *(Have appropriate resource been invested?)*	Processes *(Have appropriate processes been implemented?)*	Outputs: *(How efficient are the processes?)*	Outcomes: *(How effective are the processes?)*	Impact *(What is the ROI?)*
Metrics	Money Time People Technology Infrastructure	Ideation Concept Development Requirements Management Design Engineering Quality Regulatory Sourcing and procurement Manufacturing and Launch Distribution Quote/order generation Field Service Dispose Reuse	Requirements-traceability Visualization Device master record control Ideas & concepts Design capture & accessibility Change control Capacity configuration management Metrics Cost of Risk Product development & prototype Resource optimization Product Quality	Generation of new business Software integration Globalization Cost performance Larger market share Cost reduction Design reuse	Waste reduction Innovation New Products New Practices New Processes Continuous improvement Sustainable Green manufacturing
Data Availability	Limited	Moderate	Moderate	Limited	Limited
Collection Difficulty	High	High	Moderate	High	Very High
Collection Automation	None	Low	Moderate	Low	Very low

5.3.1 Level 1: Input Metrics

At Level 1, Input metrics, organizations are still at a very immature level of metrics collection. At this level the focus is on measuring the extent to which appropriate resources are being invested in PLM, with broad measurement of overall success. The resource inputs driving the applicability of metrics include capital, labor, and time [11], [16], [17]. Specific metrics measuring resources are listed in Table 3.

For research purposes involving such specific and confidential information, the availability of data is limited and difficult to collect. Most organizations do not typically automate or share data collection on their investment efforts; as such information is highly confidential. In future studies, 'number of customers captured by new products' and 'total number of new customers' may be better defined as a Level 5, Impact metric.

Table 3. Input Metrics

Metric	Metric
Average cash expense cost per product/project	Average manufacturing engineering development cost per project/product
Average manufacturing capital cost per product/project	Average planning/design cash expense cost per product/project
Average manufacturing cash expense per product/project	Average planning/design cost per product/project
Average manufacturing development cost per project/product	Average planning/design development cost per product/project
Average manufacturing engineering capital cost per product/project	Number of customers captured by new products*
Average manufacturing engineering cash expense cost per product/project	Number of new customers captured by new products
Number of responses to RFP's	Cost of tool design/redesign
Total number of new customers*	

(* Potentially a Level 5 Impact metric)

5.3.2 Level 2: Process Metrics

The second level in the PLIMM is Process metrics. These metrics allow organizations to examine their procedures and then, in turn, more effectively control processes. The focus is on assessing the appropriateness of the processes being implemented within the design, build, service, and retirement/reuse/recycle phases of PLM. Table 4 lists the metrics that can be measured to determine the effectiveness of these PLM processes.

Table 4. Process Metrics

Metric	Metric
Amount of time required for manufacturing	Cost per manufacturing engineering error
Average capital cost per project/product	Cost per manufacturing error
Average development cost per project/product	Number of business processes re-engineered
Cost per planning and design errors	Number of parts re-used

5.3.3 Level 3: Output Metrics

Level 3 are the Output metrics, the focus of which is on whether the PLM process is efficient in producing products or services. At this level, data is beginning to become more accessible and organizations are beginning to automate their data collection efforts. However, collection of data on the processes is still quite difficult despite the fact that there is greater automation of data collection, which should make data more accessible. Table 5 outlines metrics that are used to measure the Output indicators. In future studies, overall revenue and market share may be better defined as a Level 5, Impact Metric.

Table 5. Output Metrics

Metric	Metric
Amount of inventory	Number of RFP's won
Amount of personnel output	Number of product prototypes built
Amount of time for break-even for new product introductions	Number of pre-production design changes
Amount of time required for manufacturing engineering	Number of suppliers meeting requirements
Amount of time required for product planning and designing	Number post-production design changes
Market share*	Overall revenue*
Number of engineering change orders	Revenue from new products less than 3 years old
Number of manufacturing engineering errors	Time to market for new products
Number of planning and design errors	Number of manufacturing errors
Time to market for product improvements	

(*Potentially a Level 5 Impact metric)

5.3.4 Level 4: Outcome Metrics

Outcome metrics help the organization determine if the production processes are effective. At this level the metrics help to determine if there are any changes and/or benefits resulting from the overarching PLM activities. The collection and reporting of effectiveness metrics are difficult to automate, thus limiting the availability of data. Performance indicators at this level focus on the extent to which procedures and controls have been integrated into the systems. Table 6 lists metrics for measuring outcomes of PLM investments. Again, based on conjecture of future studies, some of the metrics may be better thought of as Level 5, Impact Metrics.

5.3.5 Hypothetical Level 5: Impact Metrics

At hypothetical Level 5, Impact, metrics measure the impact of PLM investment by determining if there are positive changes in the manufacturing situation or other enterprise divisions. Impact metrics allow organizations to determine if there is a long-term return on their PLM investments. Metrics at this level measure such results as enterprise-wide waste reduction, innovations in new processes, practices, and products, continuous improvement, and sustainable green manufacturing [11], [16], [17]. In future studies, the metrics delineated in Table 7 will need to be confirmed as Impact metrics.

Table 6. Outcome Metrics

Metric	Metric
Hours of downtime	Number of new products
Number of processes documented in regards to the "support" of products	Number of processes documented in regards to the "disposal" of products
Amount of time to develop new ideas	Number of product recalls
Number of applications, operating systems, and DBMS integrated	Reallocation of saved manufacturing engineering processes time*
Number of collaborative research ventures	Reallocation of saved planning and designing process time*
Number of liability lawsuits	Number of simulated tests
Number of new industry initiatives supported	Number of warranty claims
Number of new product functions or features	Reallocation of saved manufacturing process time*
Number of new product ideas evaluated	Number of product failures
Number of simulated prototypes	

(*Potentially a Level 5 Impact metric)

Table 7. Hypothetical Impact Metrics

Metric	Metric
Number of customers captured by new products	Total number of new customers
Market share	Overall revenue
Reallocation of saved manufacturing process time	Reallocation of saved manufacturing engineering processes time
Reallocation of saved planning and designing process time	

6 Discussion and Implications

The purpose of this study was to further refine a PLM Assessment Model (Figure 1) and identify, develop and integrate PLM metrics into a Product Lifecycle Implementation Maturing Model (Table 2). The PLIMM framework developed supports organizations as they define PLM metrics and measure how effectively they are being implemented across the enterprise. Initially, through an iterative process of synthesizing literature, interviewing key PLM stakeholders, and applying scholarly research methods, a large number of metrics were identified. It became quickly apparent, however, that there is a myriad of overlapping metrics, many of which measure overlapping benefits. The final results of the survey produced and validated

PLM metrics that are most widely used and considered to be important to industry for measuring PLM initiatives.

A number of metrics were identified as being 'used and important' in the PLM performance measurement process. Overall revenue was considered by a significantly large proportion of the respondents as being 'used and important' as a metric. Market share and productivity were also identified as important measures. Crucial to the PLM process is time and cost measures, as evidence by the number of other metrics identified as 'used and important'.

As previously discussed, many organizations have yet to fully implement all phases of their PLM initiative, and thus the issue of return on investments remains elusive. Nonetheless, as a normal course of business, executives must justify their current and future PLM investments as a function of organizational performance, both at the tactical and strategic levels. When designing a PLM process, it is critical that organizations first consult their strategic plan and conduct a PLM benefits analysis as it relates to achieving their strategic goals. While important, defining metrics that accurately measure the impact of PLM is no easy task. The difficulty, in large part, arises from the need to filter standard business-process improvements from the overall impact of PLM on cost-savings and revenue-generation in an organization. The ultimate goal of PLM is to pay dividends through a significant return on investments and increases in innovations. However, without direct measures, most respondents do not seem to have a clear picture of whether, or how, PLM is impacting their bottom line.

As organizations continue to migrate past the more segregated Product Data Management (PDM) software and move towards more holistic and integrated PLM enterprise systems, each organization will inevitably struggle to identify the most appropriate starting point for metrics development and deployment. Thus, the Product Lifecycle Implementation Maturity Model, which integrates and categorizes metrics, may prove helpful as organizations attempt to identify the most appropriate, realistic, and feasible starting point for their metric-development initiatives.

7 Conclusions, Limitations of the Study, and Future Research

In this study, researchers extended upon earlier PLM metrics-related studies [5], [11], [16], [17], to provide program-level guidance for quantifying PLM performance in support of organizational strategic goals. In this study, an Exploratory Factor Analysis (EFA) was conducted, a complex procedure further exacerbated by the imperfections of "real world" data [26], [32], [33]. While principal components with varimax rotation and the Kaiser criterion are the norm, they are not optimal; particularly when data do not meet assumptions, as is often the case with social science and business related data [26]. The most replicable results are still obtained by using large samples [34]. Ideally, there would be at least a 5:1 subject to item ratio. The diversity in our data set was limited with the majority of participants coming from very large industries with revenue streams of over one billion dollars.

Future research initiatives could make the results more generalizable and applicable to a broader spectrum of industries; both horizontally across industry-types and vertically within various-sized organizations. Researchers for this study have already begun to identify additional participants. In future studies, not only will online surveys be conducted, but more interviews with industry executives and employees will be conducted to determine what metrics are appropriate for ongoing PLM performance measurement. Arguably, as PLM systems continue to evolve, solution providers are 'building better islands', but they are still building islands [5]. The metrics associated with each of these software islands will necessitate further investigation until at which point PLM systems evolve to a point where all systems are fully and tightly integrated, and where data flows consistently, accurately, and without error between PLM subsystems. As PLM systems continue to evolve, it is anticipated there will be a much broader spectrum of participants available for future study which will necessitate a secondary exploratory factor analysis to incorporate the new data, followed later by studies employing confirmatory factor analysis.

In future work researchers plan to test the refined PLM Assessment Process Model and the Product Lifecycle Implementation Maturing Model. Further testing will attempt to resolve the practical and theoretical issues in the implementation of the PLIMM that will support performance metrics. The literature will need to be reviewed continually, validity of metrics will need to be verified continuously, and the participant pool will need to be expanded.

Summarizing the PLIMM, at Level 1, Inputs, of the Maturity Model, companies should focus on defining and measuring inputs. At this level, the focus is on measuring the extent to which appropriate resources are being invested in the system. Companies at Level 2, Processes, should focus on process measures such as whether a process is in control or not. At this level, companies should focus on measuring features of procedures and processes. At Level 3, Outputs, companies should focus on measuring whether products and services produced are meeting performance standards for example. Companies at Level 4, Outcomes, should focus on measuring outcomes such as improvements in production processes, and capturing wasted resources, time energy, and material. The highest level, hypothetical Level 5, Impacts, concerns optimization and measuring impact and return on investment with an eye towards reallocating resources for the purpose of generating new and innovative ideas and technologies that result in new products, new markets, and impact on bottom line [35]. Defining appropriate PLM-related metrics becomes increasingly complex and difficult to collect as an organization matures in its PLM implementation. Two issues in particular are foremost: (1) the lack of pre-PLM implementation data, by which to compare post-PLM implementation data, and (2), as organizations mature in their PLM implementation, the process is exacerbated by the lack of pre-PLM benchmarks. Nonetheless, given the sizable investments that PLM requires, it is imperative that the impact of those investments be understood in the context of meeting and potentially exceeding organizational goals. Thus, preemptive attention to and inclusion of a PLIMM will aid organizations in their PLM ventures.

References

1. Grieves, M.: Product Lifecycle Management: Driving the Next Generation of Lean Thinking. The McGraw-Hill Company, Inc., New York (2006)
2. Grieves, M.: Virtually Perfect: Driving Innovative and Lean Products through Product Lifecycle Management. Space Coast Press, Cocoa Beach (2011)

3. Subrahmanian, E., Rachuri, S., Fenves, S.J., Foufou, S., Sriram, R.D.: Product Llifecycle Management Support: A Challenge in Supporting Product Design and Manufacturing in a Networked Economy. Int. J. Prod. Life Cycle Man 1, 4–25 (2004)
4. Ameril, F., Dutta, D.: Product Lifecycle Management: Closing the KnowledgeLloops. Computer-Aided Design and Applications 2, 577–590 (2005)
5. Walton, A.: Product Lifecycle Management: Strategic Technology Road Mapping. Ph.D. Dissertation, Purdue University, West Lafayette (2009)
6. Arena Solutions, Inc.: Why PLM?, http://www.arenasolutions.com/why/plm/index.html (accessed November 12, 2008)
7. Williams, A.: Cost control: Trim manufacturing costs during product design. CADalyst (2005), http://findarticles.com/p/articles/mi_m0BLL/is_5_22/ai_n15394545 (accessed January 10, 2009)
8. Shah, R., Ward, P.T.: Defining and Developing Measures of Lean Production. J. Ops. Man 25, 785–805 (2007)
9. CIMdata: PLM Benefits Appraisal Guide. CIMdata Report (July 2002), http://www.cimdata.com/publications/desc_benefits_appraisal.html (accessed January 15, 2009)
10. CIMdata: Product Lifecycle Management: Empowering the Future of Business. CIMdata Report, June 1 (2006), http://www.cimdata.com/publications/PLM_Definition_0210.pdf (accessed January 15, 2009)
11. Tomovic, C.L., Ncube, L.B., Walton, A., Grieves, M.: Development of Product Lifecycle Management Metrics: Measuring the impact of PLM. Int. J. Mfg. Tech. Man. 19(3/4), 167–179 (2010)
12. Mercer, P.: ERP #66: Implementing an Effective Global Performance Measurement System (2007), http://www.mercer.com/summary.htm?siteLanguage=100&idContent=1286845 (accessed December 12, 2008)
13. CIMdata: PLM and ERP Integration: Business Efficiency and Value. CIMdata Report (March 8, 2003), http://www.cimdata.com/publications/complimentary_white_papers.php (accessed January 15, 2009)
14. Stark, J.: Product Lifecycle Management: 21st Century Paradigm for Product Realization. Springer, London (2004)
15. Grieves, M.W.: PLM–Beyond Lean Manufacturing. Mfg Eng. 130(3), 23–25 (2003)
16. Tomovic, C., Ncube, L.B., Walton, A.: Development of Product Lifecycle Management Metrics: Measuring the Impact of PLM. Paper presented at the International Conference on Product Lifecycle Management, Beijing, China, July 9-11 (2008)
17. Tomovic, C.L., Walton, A., Ncube, L., Grieves, M., Birtles, B., Bednar, B.: Measuring the Impact of Product Lifecycle Management: Process Plan, Waste Reduction and Innovations Conceptual Frameworks, and Logic Model for Developing Metrics. In: Tomovic, M., Wang, S. (eds.) Product Realization: A Comprehensive Approach, pp. 2–4. Springer, New York (2008)
18. IBM: PLM Challenges and Benefits: Results of the IBM Online Diagnostic Tool (2004), ftp://ftp.software.ibm.com/software/plm/uk/plm_diagnostic_exec.pdf (accessed November 29, 2008)
19. Barchan, M.: Measuring Success in a Changing Environment. Strat & Leadership 27(3), 12–15 (1999)
20. Borg, W.R., Gall, M.D.: Educational Research. Longman, New York (1989)

21. Tesch, R.: Qualitative Research: Analysis Types and Software Tools, Falmer, New York (2002), http://www.bing.com/search?q=Tomovic%2C+Walton%2C+Ncube%2C+Grieves%2C+Birtles+and+Bednar&src=IE-SearchBox
22. Bourque, L.B., Fielder, E.P.: How to Conduct Self-Administered and Mail Surveys. Sage, London (1995)
23. Rea, L.M., Parker, R.A.: Designing and Conducting Survey Research: A Comprehensive Guide. Jossey-Bass, San Francisco (2007)
24. Sekaran, U.: Research Methods for Business: A Skill Building Approach. John Wiley & Sons, Inc., Hoboken (2003)
25. Velicer, W.F., Jackson, D.N.: Component Analysis Versus Common Factor Analysis: Some Issues in Selecting an Appropriate Procedure. Multivariate Behav. Res. 25(1), 1–28 (2009)
26. Costello, A.B., Osborne, J.W.: Best Practices in Exploratory Factor Analysis: Four Recommendations for Getting the Most from your Analysis. Practical Ass. Res. & Eval. 10, 1–9 (2005)
27. Committee on Metrics for Global Change Research, Climate Research Committee, National Research Council: Thinking Strategically about the Appropriate use of Metrics for the Climate Change Science Program. National Research Council of The National Academies. The National Academies Press (2005), http://books.nap.edu/openbook.php?record_id=11292&page=R1 (accessed February 14, 2009)
28. PTC: The Definition and Implementation of PLM Technologies. PTC Executive Briefing, PTC Aerospace and Defense (2004), http://www.ptc.com/WCMS/files/25853en_file1.pdf (accessed October 20, 2008)
29. Chelladurai, P., Inglis, S.E., Danylchuck, K.E.: Priorities in intercollegiate athletics: Development of a scale. Res. Quart. for Exerc. and Sport 55(1), 74–79 (1984)
30. Wang, J.: Capability Maturity Model with Information Systems Development. IS6840 Information Systems Analysis. University of Missouri at St. Louis (2003), http://www.umsl.edu/~sauter/analysis/6840./wang/IS6840FinalPaper.doc (accessed March 7, 2009)
31. Enterprise Warehousing Solutions, INC.: Implementing a Maturity Model (2008), http://www.ewsolutions.com/education/cmm-training/implement-cmm (accessed April 10, 2009)
32. Suhr, D.: Reliability, Exploratory & Confirmatory Factor Analysis for the Scale of Athletic Priorities. Paper Presented at SUGI 28 SAS Conference Proceedings: Western Users of SAS Software, San Jose, California (2002)
33. Suhr, D.D.: Exploratory or Confirmatory Factor Analysis? In: SUGI 31 SAS Conference Proceedings: Western Users of SAS Software, San Jose, California (2005)
34. Fabrigar, L.R., Wegener, D.T., MacCallum, R.C., Strahan, E.J.: Evaluating the Use of Exploratory Factor Analysis in Psychological Research. Psychol. Meth. 4(3), 272–299 (1999)
35. Chew, E., Clay, A., Hash, J., Bartol, B., Brown, A.: Guide for Developing Performance Metrics for Information Security: Recommendations of the National Institute of Standards and Technology. NIST Special Publication. 800-80(2006)

A Reverse Engineering Method for DMU Maturity Management: Use of a Functional Reeb Graph

Guillaume Herlem[1], Guillaume Ducellier[1], Pierre-Antoine Adragna[1], Alexandre Durupt[2], and Sébastien Remy[1]

[1] Université de Technologie de Troyes, Troyes, France
{guillaume.herlem,pierre_antoine.adragna, guillaume.ducellier,sebastien.remy}@utt.fr
[2] Université de Technologie de Compiègne, Compiègne, France
alexandre.durupt@utc.fr

Abstract. In a development process, Digital Mock-Up (DMU) is the referential view of the developed product, all along the product states ("as-design", "as-manufactured", etc.). In case of long lifetime products, such as boats or planes, each released product has its own DMU. During the use, maintenance operations are made. Some of the modifications are made "on field" and are not always reported to the DMU which is no longer mature. The product lifecycle is impacted and not efficient anymore. This paper focuses on a systematized methodology for checking the maturity level of a DMU by confronting it to the real product it is intended to represent. DMU inconsistencies correspond to unreported product components modifications. The first step of the process is a global comparison between the DMU and a digitization of the in-use product using the Reeb graph. The used comparison criterion is the topology. The second step is to identify the kept DMU components in the digitized dataset and thus deduce inconsistencies. That step implies a new shape descriptor combining topological and functional descriptions of a mechanical part: the Functional Reeb Graph.

Keywords: DMU, PLM, Reverse Engineering, Reeb Graph, CAD, Shape Matching.

1 Introduction

In the industry, PLM (Product Lifecycle Management) solutions are widely used for supporting product development projects. They are intended to be the answer to collaborative design and integrated engineering. It implies many actors with various kinds of expertise and often located in different geographical places. The modern way to develop a product then is in extended mode: partners share and manage design information with massive use of 3D models. The project relies on a referential representation: the **DMU** (**D**igital **M**ock-**U**p) which is basically a representation of the product **BOM** (**B**ill **o**f **M**aterials) by an assembly of CAD models. It gathers different views of the product development related to expertise domains. The DMU is intended

A. Bernard, L. Rivest, and D. Dutta (Eds.): PLM 2013, IFIP AICT 409, pp. 422–431, 2013.

to be a referential representation during the different states of the product development: "as-design", "as-manufactured", "as-used", etc. For mass consuming products (few years), a common DMU is used for all produced products. But for long lifetime products (dozens of years) such as aeronautical ones for example, each produced product has its own DMU. Even if the design or manufacturing phases are well handled, the "as-used" state can be more uncertain. In fact, unplanned maintenance activities can be made "on-field" on a long lifetime product, generating variations that are not always reported to the DMU. The PLM is no longer efficient. The inconsistency of the DMU is a problem which impacts further planned modifications: design activities based on non-up-to-date DMU data generates mistakes and additional delays caused by an a posteriori on-field data discrepancy checking.

This paper focuses on a reverse engineering approach for identifying DMU inconsistencies in a discrepancy checking context. We propose to acquire a virtual view of the in-use product and confront it to its digital representation. We present a new way to describe CAD models for identifying components in a digitized product assembly. The aim is to isolate the implied component(s) causing the maturity differential with the in-use product. The process is intended to be integrated in a CAD environment. In section 2, we briefly present related works. The proposed solution is presented in section 3. In section 4, we discuss on our solution.

2 Related Works

Our problematic is partially covered by 3 scientific research domains: (1) the global aim is to check the DMU and its level of maturity, an activity close to "discrepancy checking", (2) our approach of the problem (retrieving virtual data from a real object) is similar to "reverse engineering" approaches and (3) identifying 3D models (identifying components) in a scanned dataset is linked to "shape matching" studies.

2.1 DMU Discrepancy Checking

DMU discrepancy checking is a kind of 3D inspection which consists in con-fronting a manufactured model to its digital representation. The purposes can be multiple: checking unplanned component and validate the manufacturing as in [1] and [2] or update the design after manufacturing a physical prototype as in [3]. 3D inspection is well-covered and widely used in the industry to check mechanical parts. A 3D model is retrieved by generating surfaces on a digitized point cloud (using laser scanner for example) from a real model. Then, the 3D inspection resides in the analysis of the deviation between the original design and the captured one. DMU discrepancy checking is the application to assembly models. The recent works use other means than laser scanner like augmented reality ([2], [3]) or on-site pictures ([1]). The proposed solutions are applied to static systems like plants or piping. There is not any application on mechanical systems (with mobility and different poses between the DMU and the reality).

2.2 Reverse Engineering

Retrieving data from a real part or a product into a virtual engineering framework is known as **R**everse **E**ngineering (**RE**). The main objective is to enable redesign or new design activities based on a physical object. In the scientific literature, RE is a well-covered domain. The input data is generally a point cloud (acquired as in 3D inspection for instance). The first studies, initiated with [4], were based on a pure geometrical approach with the fitting and assembling of surfaces on the point cloud. The rebuild model is automatically generated from the point cloud and that fully-geometrical approach is well-implemented in commercial software. But the model is generally frozen and does not enable redesign activity without tedious work. Another kind of approach exists: rebuilding a model using features. Studies like [5] propose to retrieve a 3D model by fitting manufacturing features or functional features in the point cloud. The features are geometrical sets driven by parameters. The result is close to a common 3D model handled in CAD software. Thus, redesign activity is possible. For now, all those solutions have been fully-tested on single part component. A new scientific and industrial challenge is to apply them to the components assembly context in order to get a "virtual view" of an in-use product assembly.

2.3 Shape Matching

Comparing two 3D models is covered in the "shape matching" (or "shape retrieval", "shape indexing") methods. It consists in defining a (dis)similarity level between the models by comparing them using their shape signature. The most common purpose is to retrieve similar shapes in a 3D models database. And the main challenge of shape matching is to describe in a compact but highly descriptive way the shape of a 3D model. That shape signature is obtained with the use of a shape descriptor, mainly applied on the 3D model meshed surface. A shape descriptor is a 3D model discretization based on an abstraction of the model. A way to check the discrepancy between two products assembly representations is to identify common components between them. Shape descriptors have that potential possibility which has not been tested yet.

Among the different shape descriptors in the scientific literature, the **R**eeb **G**raph (**RG**) initiated in [6], is a well-covered graph-based representation with a high descriptive power and a high potential of evolution, as in [7], [8] and [9]. The generation principle is simple[1]. A scalar function is applied on each vertex of the meshed model. The vertices values are sorted into groups of same values intervals. A RG node is attributed to each group of vertices (the node is the barycenter of the mesh portion) and a RG edge connects two RG nodes if the corresponding mesh portions are connected. The RG nodes gather attributes: computed local information like surface area or curvature. The 3D models comparison is then simplified to a 1D graphs comparison. The choice of the mathematical function enables the RG to be insensible to the object orientation and pose. That property is useful four our context. Indeed, an in-use product may have a different pose and a different orientation (due to its installation, its use or its wear for example) from the setup defined in its DMU which can be arbitrary.

[1] More details on the RG generation are available in [7].

2.4 Conclusion on Related Works

In our study of the related works, we identify a shape descriptor with a high potential of application for our purpose: (1) comparing a DMU and a digitized dataset from a real product, (2) identifying DMU components in the dataset. For the first step, it can be simplified as the comparison of two 3D models, as in shape matching methods. It is possible to extract an external envelop from a DMU and mesh it. And a digitized point cloud from a real object can be easily meshed too. The comparison between two meshes is well-covered. The Reeb graph (RG) (and its extensions) is a powerful tool, suitable for the meshed assemblies' comparison. For the second step, it appears that topology (and local embedded geometrical information) is not enough. We need to retrieve components in a meshed assembly model. In terms of shape matching, it is similar to partial shape matching: the component model is here a subpart of the assembly model. And even if it can be applied to simple shapes, mechanical parts are more complex: as stated in [10], the RG of a meshed components assembly model is not the "assembly" of the RG of each component model. The contacts between part components generate undefined zones.

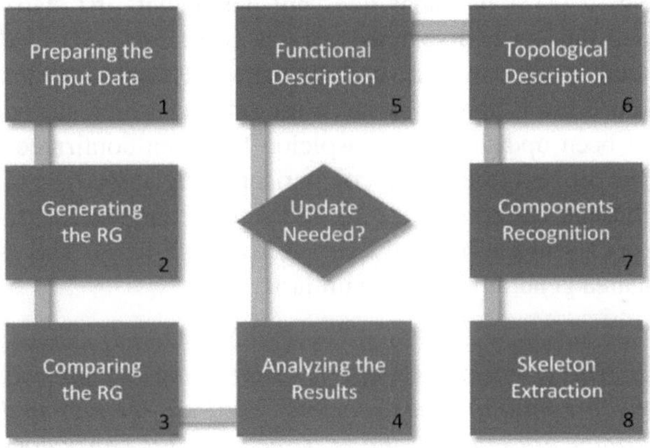

Fig. 1. This paper proposition of a reverse engineering process for DMU maturity management

3 Proposed Solution

3.1 Main Principle and DMU Inconsistencies Definition

We consider two input data:

- A point cloud digitized from the real product
- A product DMU at an unknown maturity state

For being compared on a common criterion, the shape, the two inputs are meshed giving two 3D representations of the product. We propose a process in two steps assisted by a product expert:

1. Determining the presence of at least one inconsistency,
2. If at least one inconsistency, identifying the component(s) generating that inconsistency(ies)

That steps are made of activities, numbered 1 to 4 for the first step and numbered 5 to 8 for the second step (Fig. 1).

Our proposition is, at first, to consider a product assembly as a unique 3D model. So a component modification results in a modification of the topology of the assembly model. Our contribution is to use the study of the topology variation as an indicator of the maturity state of the DMU (among other possible indicators but not presented in this paper). Thus, an inconsistency is assumed to be:

A *component* which is | *added* / *lacking* / *replaced* / *moved* | in the *real product* compared to the *DMU.*

And then, for the first step, in a global approach, we propose to use the aMRG comparison presented in [8]. Our paper does not detail that first step, as we treat the meshed DMU and the meshed scanned data as two simple 3D models. The graphs generation and comparison are the same as the aMRG solution. In this section, we consider that the process is applied to an in-use product which has been modified and its DMU has not been updated. That suspicion has been confirmed to the expert by the first step of the process (the global comparison using aMRG).

In this contribution, we present the second step of our process: the recognition of the DMU components in the meshed scan (Activities 5 to 7). The expert focuses on the meshed scan area generating the dissimilarity score.

Our process is supported by a ***CPM*** *(Core* ***P****roduct* ***M****odel) extension originally introduced in [10]. The extension is made for supporting our approach by managing the new product representation: abstractions based on topology and kinematics and used in the descriptor presented in the next section. This paper does not present the data model.*

3.2 A New CAD Model Descriptor

As stated in section 2.4, the RG is not suitable "as-is" for identifying a component in a meshed assembly. For supporting our identification purpose, we propose to derivate a new RG shape descriptor (more specific to CAD models) from a simple definition of a mechanical part:

"Functional features linked by Topological features"

In our study, we choose to restraint functional features to be the sets of geometrical elements of a part aimed to enable mobility with compliant features of another part. We only consider the functional surfaces linked to the kinematic domain. The other geometrical elements are simply considered as links between functional features, as topological features. This descriptor, the **FRG** (**F**unctional **R**eeb **G**raph), is a direct

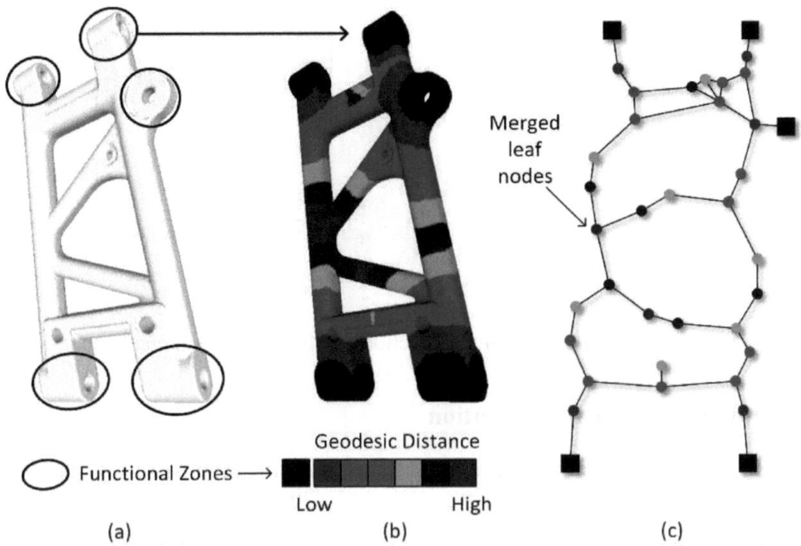

Fig. 2. The FRG generation on a lower triangle of a suspension

illustration of that basic definition. We extend the current works on the RG by a knowledge addition: the creation of a new graph node, the functional node. That node is aimed to describe the "undefined zones" detailed in [10]. In fact, in the case of a mechanical product, they are the areas corresponding to the kinematic pairs of the product. We proposed to inspire the new descriptor generation from [9]: using feature points as sources for the RG generation. In our case, the feature points are the centroids of the functional zones of a part, the functional nodes. The principle then is to link the different functional zones by travelling along the topology of the model. For that step, we use the approach of the geodesic distances computation presented in [7] and [8]. An example of the generation of an FRG on mechanical part is displayed in Fig. 2.

The computation of the FRG follows this procedure:

```
1. For each functional node (from functional zones, Fig. 2a), the geodesic distances to all the mesh vertices are computed
2. Each mesh vertex is attached to the closer functional node, giving a set of "under influence" vertices for all functional node
3. For each set of vertices:
 3.1. The vertices are sorted by group of geodesic distance intervals (Fig. 2b)
 3.2. A topological node is attributed to each group of vertices (as in [7] and [8])
 3.3. An edge links two nodes if the vertices groups are connected (as in [7] and [8])
4. The connected sets are linked by merging the corresponding leaf nodes (Fig. 2c)
```

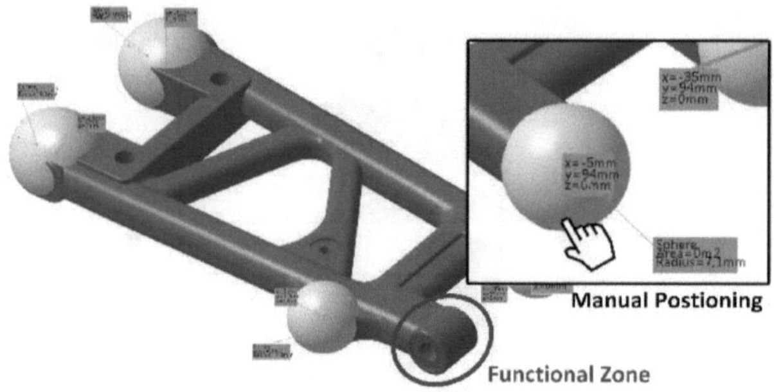

Fig. 3. The localization of the functional zones of a mechanical part

3.3 The Inconsistency Identification

This section presents the aim of the FRG: enabling the inconsistency identification (activities 5 to 8 in Fig. 1).

Functional Description (5). Using a custom user interface, the expert defines the kinematic pairs locations on his focus on the meshed scanned product. He uses enclosing spheres that can be stretched (Fig. 3). Not all the system is described. Our use case in Fig. 4 is a mechanical part of a vehicle suspension. The previous step of the process enables to locate the dissimilarity area so only that area is treated, not all the vehicle or all the chassis. From this enclosing shapes (Fig. 4a), which are the functional zones (darker mesh areas in Fig. 4b), the centroids are computed giving the functional nodes.

Topological Description (6). This activity corresponds to the FRG generation: the topological links between the functional zones are computed (Fig. 4b), generating topological nodes and edges of the FRG. The same generation as described in 3.2 is applied to the meshed assembly. The resulting FRG then is a direct assembly of the FRG of the components as they are based on the functional zones which are undefined zones with previous RG alternatives.

Components Recognition (7). When the meshed scanned assembly have been described with the FRG, an algorithm is ran to identify the DMU components that are present in the real product scan. That algorithm is similar to partial shape matching basic procedures which can be found in the scientific literature. The variation is the addition of the number of functional nodes as a primary search criterion. For that activity, we assumed that all DMU components are described with the FRG and accessible by querying a database with our graph structure. And they are retrievable under a meshed form. A list of matching results is presented to the product expert who validates the right components. The Fig. 4c illustrates the recognized lower triangle in the meshed assembly scan. Using the nodes locations, each recognized and validated component mesh is coarsely aligned in the assembly mesh and then finely fitted using best-fit algorithms. The equivalent meshed scanned portion is then suppressed (Fig. 5).

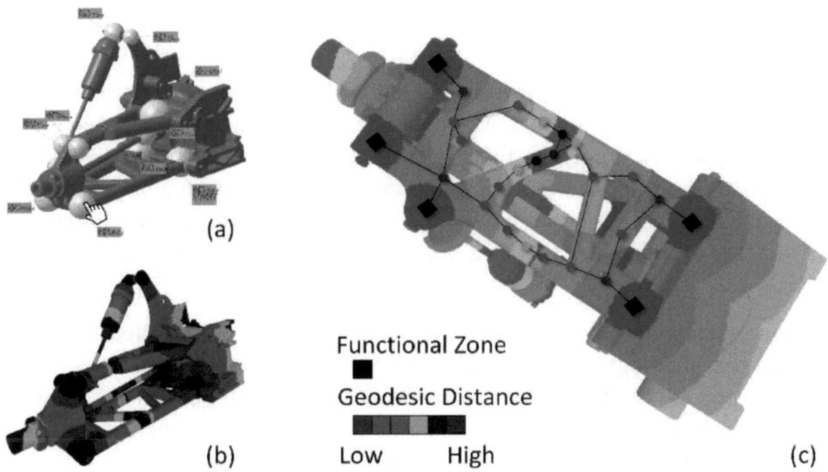

Fig. 4. The identification of the lower triangle in the meshed assembly scan using the FRG

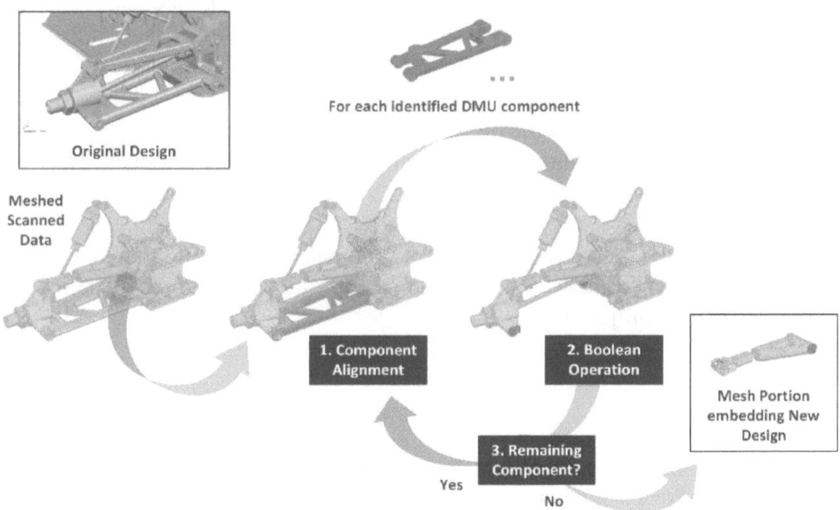

Fig. 5. The suppression of the meshed scan portions corresponding to recognized components

Skeleton Extraction (8). All the mesh areas of the identified components have been suppressed. The remaining mesh portion(s) (Fig 5) correspond to unrecognized component(s): DMU inconsistency(ies) as defined in section 3.1. The skeleton extraction from that remaining mesh is still a work in progress activity. Its aim is detailed in the further works in section 4.

4 Conclusion

This paper proposes an approach for checking DMU discrepancy. The main contribution is the development of a new CAD model descriptor based on the Reeb graph (and evolutions) shape descriptor: the Functional Reeb Graph. As a knowledge addition to the topological description, we proposed to take into account, in a basic way, the purpose of a mechanical part: the "kinematic" intent. The FRG allows identifying the inconsistencies of a product DMU as we defined them: unreported component modifications.

Discussion. The proposed process enable to isolate a partial meshed model corresponding to the unrecognized component which can be a useful basis for a reverse engineering process with a CAD commercial software. In the methodology setup resides two strong constraints: the studied system needs to be a kinematical one with a high exposition of its components and a product expert must be implied.

Further Works. The next step is to improve the information stored in the functional node. At the moment, it is only the centroid of a functional zone of a component. In the future, information on the kinematic pair the functional zone is intended to enable will be stored in the node. Further works will be on the information extraction from the isolated mesh part corresponding to the implied component. We strongly believe it is possible to store functional features and topological features directly into the nodes. The final stage of our approach will be the generation of a geometrical skeleton of the component enclosed in the remaining mesh portion of the scanned product. That skeleton will be a support for the redesign activity in a CAD environment for updating the DMU.

Acknowledgments. The study presented in this paper is possible thanks to the **E**uropean **R**egional **D**evelopment **F**und (ERDF) and the Champagne-Ardenne Region providing NUM3D equipment.

References

1. Georgel, P.F., Schroeder, P., Navab, N.: Navigation tools for viewing augmented CAD models. IEEE Computer Graphics and Applications 29(5), 65–73 (2009)
2. Kahn, S., Wuest, H., Stricker, D., Fellner, D.W.: 3D discrepancy check via augmented reality. In: 9th IEEE International Symposium on Mixed and Augmented Reality 2010: Science and Technology, ISMAR 2010, pp. 241–242. IEEE, Seoul (2010)
3. Webel, S., Becker, M., Stricker, D., Wuest, H.: Identifying differences between CAD and physical mock-ups using AR. In: Proceedings of the 6th IEEE and ACM International Symposium on Mixed and Augmented Reality, ISMAR 2007, pp. 281–282. IEEE, Nara (2007)
4. Várady, T., Martin, R.R., Cox, J.: Reverse engineering of geometric models - An introduction. CAD Computer Aided Design 29(4), 255–268 (1997)
5. Durupt, A., Remy, S., Ducellier, G.: KBRE: A knowledge based reverse engineering for mechanical components. Computer-Aided Design and Applications 7(2), 279–289 (2010)

6. Reeb, G.: Sur les points singuliers d'une forme de Pfaff complètement intégrable ou d'une fonction numérique. In: Comptes Rendus de L'Académie des Sciences, Paris, France, vol. 222, pp. 847–849 (1946)
7. Hilaga, M., Shinagawa, Y., Kohmura, T., Kunii, T.L.: Topology matching for fully automatic similarity estimation of 3D shapes. In: Proceedings of the 28th International Conference on Computer Graphics and Interactive Techniques, SIGGRAPH 2001, pp. 203–212. ACM, New York (2001)
8. Tung, T., Schmitt, F.: The augmented multiresolution Reeb graph approach for content-based retrieval of 3D shapes. International Journal of Shape Modeling 11(1), 91–120 (2005)
9. Tierny, J., Vandeborre, J.P., Daoudi, M.: Partial 3D shape retrieval by Reeb pattern unfolding. Computer Graphics Forum 28(1), 41–55 (2009)
10. Herlem, G., Adragna, P.-A., Ducellier, G., Durupt, A.: DMU Maturity Management as an Extension of the Core Product Model. Product Lifecycle Management: Towards Knowledge-Rich Enterprises 388, 192–201 (2012)

Case Study on the Relation of PLM Maturity, Architecture and Business Processes

Antti Pulkkinen, Ville Vainio, and Noora Rissanen

Department of Production Engineering, Tampere University of Technology

Abstract. A study focusing on the three factors of product lifecycle management (PLM) is being presented. The selected factors are maturity of adoption, systems' architectures and product lifecycle (PLC) related businesses. The research material comes from six globally operating companies. The applied data collection method is the synthesis of interviews, benchmarking, and peer-reviewing the case companies. The material is analyzed with the application of comparative case study method. Modern PLM systems manage the data of fixed product items and the configuration knowledge of product families. Thus, companies with the most mature PLM approach are able to enhance the product configuration oriented business processes with legacy PLM architectures. Most of the studied companies are transforming their to single source architecture. This may be a challenge for some of the businesses. Another challenge is the increasing share of service related PLC businesses, which is also supported by the most mature PLM approaches.

1 Introduction

Product lifecycle management (PLM) was being studied through the analysis of six industrial cases. The focused factors of PLM were the maturity of PLM, business types and PLM systems' architectures. Motivation was to find out the potential combinations of factors in the above. The research questions of the paper are: what kind of business processes are the main customers of PLM, how mature is the PLM approach and what kind of changes are taking place in PLM architectures of case companies?

The paper continues with literature review, which substantiates the research approach and outlines the details of the factors, which serve as a means of analysis. The research method is outlined and results presented. The conclusions summarize the findings, estimate the effects of the changes in the architectures of PLM systems and compare the aspired situation with the overall diversity of business processes taking place in the case companies.

2 Three PLM Factors: Maturity, Business and Systems Architecture

PLM is the activity of managing products effectively across their lifecycle [Stark 2004] or a strategic business approach, which applies business solutions, collaborative

A. Bernard, L. Rivest, and D. Dutta (Eds.): PLM 2013, IFIP AICT 409, pp. 432–438, 2013.

creation, management, dissemination of product definition information throughout the PLC [CIMdata 2011].

Essentially, Product Data Management (PDM) is the core activity of PLM [Stark 2004] and PDM system an essential IT platform for PLM. A PDM project is composed of two main stages [Crnkovic et al. 2003]: evaluation and deployment. As the implementing and utilizing PLM is not only a software project, we consider PLM as a continuous process that comprises of several IT-projects, as well as strategic and organizational initiatives. Generally, the productivity of PLM is a sum of the efficiency of implementation projects and effects attained by the utilization of PLM in business. Hence, we chose to assess the maturity of PLM in different cases, the type of business and the architecture and integration of PLM subsystems (CAE, PDM, etc.).

2.1 PLM Maturity

For this research, a four level PLM maturity model was put together by Vainio [2012]. It is based on the two models presented by Stark [2004] and Batenburg et al. [2006]. The five dimensions of the model characterize the state of PLM systems and organisations in a company. The synthesized model is presented in the Table 1.

Table 1. The PLM maturity definition model

	Level 0	Level 1	Level 2	Level 3
Application of PLM	Non-existent	Local initiatives exist, but there is no overall vision	Company-wide understanding of the importance of product data is taking shape	PLM is seen as a business problem spanning the whole product lifecycle
Involvement and understanding	From few to none people involved	Few people understand PLM	It is clear for everyone where the company is and where it wants to be	Widespread understanding of PLM in the company and in its extended enterprise
Organisational integration	No integration	Simple departmental integrations between some PDM tools	Integration between PDM tools and simple integrations with for example ERP	PDM tools are fully integrated and there is widespread integration with related systems such as ERP
Level of interoperability	Between individual tools only	On a departmental level	On a cross-departmental level	Across the extended enterprise
General description	There is no PLM investment and individual legacy systems are used.	PLM is realized as individual applications integrated on a departmental level. There is no overall PLM vision.	PLM is understood relatively well and integrated on a cross-departmental level	PLM is integrated across the supply chain. PLM is utilized in state-of-the-art ways, for example in a closed-loop fashion.

In the analysis, the position in the table above presents the maturity of the PLM in a company regarding the dimension of maturity.

2.2 Type of Businesses

It is important to understand the business processes, because the industrial characteristics define the context of PLM in a company. This is why we characterize the main business processes into two main areas. The case companies create and deliver value by selling and delivering:

- Tangible products in the beginning of PLC.
- Service products (operations and spare parts) in the middle of PLC.

Service business has steadily gained importance instead of the plain manufacturing of investment goods. In practice, it is important to know the share of service business in a company's turnover.

In the sales-delivery processes the products can be engineered, configured and/or assembled to order or made to stock (ETO, CTO & ATO, MTS). However, the pre-recognized sub-domain of above characterization, which is typical for Finnish industry, is partial configuration, i.e. the use of configured products as sub-elements of projects. Therefore, the kinds of product definition processes for the analysis were

1. ETO in project deliveries
2. Partial CTO in project deliveries
3. CTO in ATO
4. Fixed / Standard products / MTS

The abovementioned typology of product definition does apply to both tangible products and services. Also services can be engineered or configured to order (e.g. in the upgrading of a plant or maintenance of an investment product) or standardized (e.g. standard service programs in automotive industry).

2.3 The Architecture of PLM System

Vainio [2012] characterized the relations of PLM applications with the synthesis of two architecture integration models [Crnkovic et al. 2003, Bergsjö et al. 2006] as three major trends of integration: legacy, single source and service-oriented architecture.

Table 2. Synthesis of the architecture definitions and analysis of case PLM architectures [adapted from Vainio 2012]

	No integration	Loose integration	Full integration
Best in class	Has typically resulted in **Legacy Architecture** Case: *F→F'*	One to one *ad-hoc* integrations. Cases: *A→A'*, *B* & *C→C'*, *D*	One system as an integrator (standard integration interface). Cases: *C''*, *E''*
Peer to Peer		**Service Oriented Architecture** (SOA). Case: *B''*	
All in one			Typically **Single Source architecture**. Case: *A''*, *B'*, *D'*, *E→E'*

Table 2 illustrates which of the definitions are essentially describing the same architecture types. The synthesis is used in the analysis, which is presented also in the table (case state and transition in italics). For example, case company A will either remain to have loose integrations between best in class systems (*A→A'*) or transform to single source architecture (*A''*).

3 Research Method and Material

We applied different methods for collecting the raw data and for the analyzing of it. The data was collected with eight of structured interviews (3-4 hours) and six benchmarking sessions (six of each). The benchmarking sessions involved the participants of all the case companies. In a session the hosts presented the PLM approach of a company and answered consequent questions. The active audience (typically 15-25 PLM experts) consisted of practitioners, managers, consultants, and researchers. The benchmarking sessions gave more accurate information on the PLM in a company than the interviews.

All the sessions were recorded, notes were taken and presentation material (e.g. presentation slides) collected. The collected data was processed and reported (6 reports of 20-30 pages). Four people were involved in the processing of the material. Their expertise varied from novice in transcribing audio recordings to senior researcher correcting the reports. Finally, the reports were sent for validation and verification to the interviewees. The reports were the basis of the analysis and therefore are the essential material for this research.

The application of benchmarking was considered positive by all participants. The practitioners got the direct feedback and insight on level of PLM in all the companies. So, they could attain other experts' ideas for the benefit of their own PLM processes. For the researchers there was a large set of experience taking place in the sessions. The quality of questions was high and new issues arose in the discussion resulting with a large set of material. However, the common themes are recognizable in the material.

The cases were analyzed with the application of comparative case study method. A more detailed description on the utilization of Qualitative Comparative Analysis (QCA) by Ragin [1987] for our purposes is presented in [Rissanen et al. 2012]. In short, the essence of the method is the set of truth tables documenting the properties of the cases with Boolean logic (best illustrated with the Table 4 of the results). The tables of the cases are summed up as matrices, which are comparable to tabular formats of other fields. The combinations of tables present the properties of cases with a matrix that is conceptually close to the utilization of morphological matrices in product development [Pahl & Beitz 1996]. The combinations of case properties are similar to possible configurations in matrix based product configuration methods [e.g. Bongulielmi 2003].

4 Results and Analysis: Maturity, Processes and Architecture

We present the studied cases with figures and tables, which are based on the frame of analysis, which consists of the factors of research. Each factor is dealt separately and conclusion combines them.

The maturity of the companies is analyzed in five dimensions represented with the five directions of the Table 3. The range of maturity is according to Table 1 from level 0 to level 3. The most mature PLM approaches were recognized in cases D, A and E.

Table 3. The PLM maturity of studied companies

Maturity vs. Cases	*A*	*B*	*C*	*D*	*E*	*F*
Application of PLM	3	2	2	3	2	1
Involvement and understanding	2	1	1	3	2	1
Organisational integration	2	2	2	3	3	2
Level of interoperability	2	1	1	3	2	1
General description	**2**	**1**	**1**	**3**	**2**	**1**

In the Table 3, the sales-delivery type is according to previous combination. Many of the companies utilized configuration in ETO projects, which is visible in the table (cases A, C & D). In these cases there is an indicator (1) in the both of the rows designated for ETO and CTO.

Table 4. The type of business vs. case companies

Business vs. Cases	*A*	*B*	*C*	*D*	*E*	*F*
Sales-Delivery type	2	1	2	2	3	1
- **MTS**	0	0	1	0	0	0
- **ETO**	1	1	1	1	0	1
- **CTO**	1	0	1	1	1	0
Service business > 50%	1	0	0	1	0	0

The share of service business is higher than the 50% of turnover in two companies (A & D). The share of turnover is characterized with options ranging from less than (0) to more than (1) half of the turnover. We had more accurate data on the share of service business that could be used in fuzzy-set QCA more precisely. Actually, the row presenting sales delivery type as a whole combines the approach with a more precise manner (1 for MTS, 1 for pure ETO, 2 for CTO in ETO, 3 for pure CTO). Concerning PLM architecture the present and future dimensions were presented already in the Table 2.

5 Conclusions

According to the sample of study the sales-delivery (ETO) projects applying partial configuration are the main customers of PLM. The most mature company (at least PLM wise) is making its turnover mostly by service business. Pure project based business seem to be less mature. However, the sample is small and statistic verification is impossible with it.

It seems to be a sound strategy to approach PLM is to first systematize products and processes along with the increase of PLM awareness and the readiness of adoption in an organization. Focusing only on changing PLM architecture may lead to mismatch that lies within the compatibility of IT architecture and the diversity of product lifecycle (PLC) related business needs the companies are running.

Obviously, maturity is a matter of aligned initiatives (see Table 3). A company cannot focus the one dimension of maturity and omit the development in another. In all dimensions the most mature company appeared to be the case D, which had started its PDM/PLM process already in early 1990's. However, the PDM/PLM process of another company (case F) had begun already in the same years, but the maturity of case F was much lower. Apparently, long history of PLM does not ensure the maturity in a company. The companies that utilized configuration (in sales-delivery projects) had the higher degrees of PLM maturity.

There are some research findings that are not reported in the results of this paper. One of them is that the deployment processes are actually long chains of consecutive development projects. The consecutive projects can be considered as the reason of legacy architectures, which are comprised of several independent pieces of software integrated loosely by the companies, consultants and vendors.

Application integration is an important factor in PLM. The dominant trend seems to be the transition from legacy to single source architecture. This has advantages, such as data correctness and the ease administration of PLM systems. However, the disadvantages of the single source architecture, see e.g. Silcher et al. [2010] and Bergsjö et al. [2008], may lead to difficulties in the PLM processes of companies (especially with ETO products). The companies may not be aware or lack of trust in service oriented architecture.

Based on our study it appears to be so that the product configuration based businesses are supported quite well with legacy architecture. Moreover, the maturity analysis suggests that the dominant issues in companies are related to the management of PLM systems, which is one of the advantages of single source architecture. However, the notion that the emerging changes in PLM architectures may appear difficult to validate for some business functions. The role of PLM as the support of business processes should not be forsaken. Another future challenge is the configuration of services, such as maintenance and spare parts, in the middle of PLC. This requires the updating of PLM systems, e.g. data models. However, it opens new business opportunities instead of just relying on the limited markets of green field installations.

The applied research methods were very welcome way of collaborating between industry and academia. Especially the novel approach of benchmarking in data collection served all the participants. The analysis of the collected material appeared tedious. The crisp-set QCA seems to apply poorly to the material (see Table 3). Instead, for screening the material we used a frame consisting of three dimensions with values ranging from 0 to 3 (see e.g. Table 2, which is based on the PLM maturity dimensions). This approach could be transformed as a fuzzy-set QCA supported by a survey.

Acknowledgments. We thank all the participants of benchmarking and Finnish funding Agency for Technology and Innovation for funding the research.

References

Stark, J.: Product Lifecycle Management: 21st Century Paradigm for Product Realisation, 400 p. Springer (2004)

CIMdata. PLM Definition (WWW) (2011), `http://www.cimdata.com/plm/definition.html` (Cited September 8, 2011)

Crnkovic, I., Asklund, U., Persson Dahlqvist, A.: Implementing and Integrating Product Data Management and Software Configuration Management, 338 p. Artech House Inc., Norwood (2003)

Vainio, V.V.: Comparative research of PLM usage and architecture. M.Sc. thesis. Tampere University of Technology, p. 73 (2012), `https://wiki.tut.fi/Fudge/WebHome`

Batenburg, R., Helms, R.W., Versendaal, J.: PLM roadmap: stepwise PLM implementation based on the concepts of maturity and alignment. Int. J. Product Lifecycle Management 1(4), 333–351 (2006)

Bergsjö, D., Malmqvist, J., Ström, M.: Architectures for Mechatronic Product Data Integration in PLM Systems. In: Proceedings of Design 2006, Dubrovnik, Croatia, pp. 1065–1076 (2006)

Ragin, C.C.: The Comparative Method. Moving beyond qualitative and quantitative strategies. Univ. of California Press, Berkeley (1987)

Rissanen, N., Pulkkinen, A., Vainio, V.V.: Testing a Framework for Analyzing PLM Architecture in Global Manufacturing Companies. In: Torvinen, S., Nylund, H. (eds.) FAIM 2012: Ferry Cruise Conference, Helsinki, Stockholm, June 10-13 (2012)

Pahl, G., Beitz, W.: Engineering Design: A Systematic Approach, 2nd edn., 544 p. Springer (1996), Wallace, K. Blessing, L., Bauert, F. (trans.) ISBN: 3540199179

Bongulielmi, L.: Die Konfigurations- & Verträglichkeitsmatrix als Beitrag zur Darstellung konfigurationsrelevanter Aspekte im Produktentstehungsprozess. Zentrum für Produktentwicklung. Diss. Nr. 14904, Zürich, ETH, 218 p. (2003) ISBN: 3-18-315116-2

Bergsjö, D., Ćatić, A., Malmqvist, J.: Implementing a service-oriented PLM architecture focusing on support for engineering change management. International Journal of Product Lifecycle Management 3(4), 335–355 (2008)

Silcher, S., Minguez, J., Scheibler, T., Mitschang, B.: A Service-Based Approach for Next-Generation Product Lifecycle Management. In: International Conference on Information Reuse and Integration (IRI), Las Vegas, NV, pp. 219–224 (2010)

PLM Components Selection Based on a Maturity Assessment and AHP Methodology

Haiqing Zhang[1], Yacine Ouzrout[1], Abdelaziz Bouras[1], Antonio Mazza [2], and Matteo Mario Savino[2]

[1] DISP Laboratory, University Lumière Lyon 2, France
160 Bd de l'Université 69676 Bron Cedex
{haizhang,yacine.ouzrout,abdelaziz.bouras}@univ-lyon2.fr
[2] University of Sannio – Dept. of Engineering, Italy
Piazza Roma, 21 – 82100 Benevento
{matteo.savino,antonio.mazza}@unisannio.it

Abstract. The benefits of Product Lifecycle Management (PLM) have been noted for improving business, creating collaboration, and reducing energy and time by making transcendent decisions through the process of product life cycle. This work aims to propose a PLM Components Maturity Assessment (PCMA) model to gain comprehensive maturity results and reduce the complexity in obtaining maturity scores. According to PLM functionalities, we divide PLM into fifteen components. PLM components can be cataloged into five main fields: 'TechnoWare', 'InforWare', 'FunctionWare', 'OrgaWare', and 'SustainWare' (TIFOS Framework). With PCMA model we analyzed PLM components and proposed mature content of each dimension, obtaining specific key performance indicators for each dimension. This work has been also useful to solve decision-making issues based on AHP methodology, such as: selecting the optimal PLM components in TIFOS Framework, obtaining the components ranking weight, getting components maturity score, and comparing it with the actual situation to give constructive business suggestions. These business suggestions include strengths and weakness of PLM components and conducting selection of PLM components. Experimental studies have been conducted to verify maturity scores for each component and to achieve component-ranking weights.

Keywords: PLM Maturity Model, AHP Methodology, Key Performance Indicators, TIFOS Framework.

1 Introduction

The concepts of PLM are very extensive (Stark et al., 2011). PLM manages and accesses product information to make companies run smooth and secure. PLM guarantees persistent integrity of product definitions and related information during the life of a product. The functionalities of PLM include maintaining business processes, such as: creating, managing, disseminating, and sharing product information (Stark et al., 2011). The foundation components are used to construct

A. Bernard, L. Rivest, and D. Dutta (Eds.): PLM 2013, IFIP AICT 409, pp. 439–448, 2013.

these PLM functionalities. The integration of several components is a PLM solution. Selecting right PLM components lead to a better PLM solution, which has substantial opportunity to meet company requirements. In contrast, misuse of PLM components will cause products to malfunction or fail.

The main purpose of this work is to help companies to select the right PLM components with their different goal oriented objectives. To achieve this aim, four basic research questions need to be addressed:

1. What are the full PLM functionalities that have to be considered in relation to PLM capabilities?

2. How many components constitute these PLM functionalities?

3. How can we identify the strengths and weaknesses of PLM components?

4. Which one is the most suitable PLM component for a company?

To answer the first research question, two important literature works are presented and a new framework is proposed in section 2.1. To answer the second question, the basic literature on PLM components is presented and fifteen PLM components are proposed in section 2.3. To answer the third question, a PLM maturity model has been proposed by analyzing characters and KPIs of PLM components in section 3. To answer the fourth question, AHP (Analytic Hierarchy Process) methodology is developed in section 4. Section 5 gives the case study and section 6 concludes our work.

2 TIFOS Framework and PLM Components

2.1 TIFOS Framework

Firstly, from Sharif's perspective (Sharif, 1997), technology can be classified into four categories: TechnoWare, InforWare, HumanWare, and OrgaWare.

- TechnoWare: contains components, equipment (manual and powered), vehicles, machinery, IT and other facilities;
- InforWare: contains documents or knowledge records that reflect facts and formulas (design parameters, standards), principles of physical and social phenomena; computer software; technical information; theories and state-of-the-art knowledge for innovation;
- HumanWare: describes the skills to comprehend and use the job related components; the ability to utilize technology components; have the motivation to improve the work performance;
- OrgaWare: consists in organizational techniques, work assignments, education, and experience-based work facilitation; has the means for using and controlling factors of production, systems analysis, organization of products, processes, and components.

Secondly, from Vengugopalan et al.'s perspective (Vengugopalan et al, 2008), the functionalities of PLM are classified into four major categories based on TIFO Framework (TechnoWare, InfoWare, FunctionWare, and OrgaWare). They mixed the initial HumanWare with the OrgaWare components and added a new FunctionWare category:

- FunctionWare: depth and breadth of functionalities.

Every product life cycle is characterized by three phases: beginning of life (BOL), middle of life (MOL), and end of life (EOL). Most previous works focus on the BOL (design and manufacturing) phase (Kiritsis et al, 2010). However, in order to get tangible products, achieve top range performance, and obtain optimum product lifecycle, businesses must extend to EOL phase, which is PLM sustainability (Kiritsis et al, 2010). Next, we give the reasons why sustainability should be added into PLM functionalities.

PLM sustainability is the potential for a long-term maintenance of product lifecycle (Trotta et al, 2010). To meet the requirements of product performance, present designer decisions heavily impact upon product design (BOL phase) as well as on environmental aspects (EOL phase). To minimize efforts, time, and costs for improving product quality, businesses need sustainable, stable process management, and product development. Analysis, synthesis, evaluation and improvement of product lifecycle design, DFE (Design for Environment), TRIZ (Theory of Inventive Problem Resolution), and LCA (Life Cycle Assessment) need to be integrated and collaborated with PLM.

Based on what was mentioned above, we extend the TIFO framework into TIFOS and add a new category called SustainWare. The content of SustainWare is:

- SustainWare: reducing waste and pollution; designing eco-friendly products; using new materials and supply chain; minimizing damage to environment and human; consuming low energy.

2.2 Successful Sustainability Indicators to Obtain Sustainable PLM

In current literature studies, sustainability indicators and concepts have been studied and defined based on five dimensions: economy, ecology, society, technology, and performance management. Number these five dimensions in sequence: 1, 2, 3, etc. First, we will discuss presently acceptable and better recognized indicators for sustainable PLM.

Efforts are made by multiple organizations. An effort by the United Nations Environment Program (UNEP) and the United States nongovernmental organization called Global Reporting Initiative (GRI) (GRI, 2011) has defined more than 100 indicators and focused the first three dimensions. Other efforts by the National Institute of Standards and Technology (NIST) is the Sustainable Manufacturing Indicator Repository (SMIR) (SMIR, 2012), which defined extensively available indicator sets by using the five dimensions.

Efforts have been made by researchers to study system sustainable indicators. Laurent et al. studied the ability of carbon footprint emissions as an indicator, eager to find out the correlation between carbon footprints and other environmental impacts (Laurent et al., 2010). Fang et al. developed sustainable manufacturing metrics to measure sustainability performance in entire product lifecycle based on the first three dimensions (Fang et al., 2010). Trotta et al. analyzed important tools to formalize information and knowledge for sustainable new product development in companies (Trotta et al., 2010). We investigated the literature studies to give a list of 19 successful sustainability indicators based on four dimensions (Table 1).

Table 1. Successful sustainability indicators to obtain sustainable PLM from literature

Dimensions	Sustainability indicators	Dimensions	Sustainability indicators
Economy	Investment	Society	Labor Practices
	Economic performance		Human Rights
	Product Presence in the market		Social influence
	Green Process Design		Product Responsibility
	Green Manufacturing		Eco-design Responsibility
Ecology	Energy emissions		Innovative new materials care
	Carbon Foot Print	Technology	Life Cycle Assessment
	Waste Reduction		Design for Environment tools
	Water Usage		Zero Emissions &Waste
	Compliance		

2.3 PLM Components

Now we will define how many important components PLM has and what they are on the basis of the TIFOS framework. Stark et al. presented that PLM is a holistic approach, which contains nine PLM components: products, data, applications, processes, people, work methods, and equipment (Stark et al., 2011). Abramovici et al. defined five PLM levels; every PLM levels is described by several concrete PLM components that can have interdependencies with other components (Abramovici et al., 2012). After comprehensively analyzing PLM functionalities and reviewing the works, which have been done by the other researchers, fifteen different types of PLM components have been collected and showed in Table 2.

Table 2. TIFOS Frameworks and corresponding components

PLM Functionalities			
TIFOS Framework	Components		
TechnoWare	Techniques & Practices	PLM Softwares &Applications	Strategy &Supervision
InfoWare	Quality &Compliance Management	Business Management	Maintenance & Repair Operations Management
FunctionWare	BOM management	PDM	Financial Management
OrgaWare	People	Distributed Collaboration management	Workflow&Process Management
SustainWare	Sourcing & Supply chain Management	New Products Development &Skills	Eco-friendly &Innovation

A PLM maturity model needs to be proposed to measure the current maturity situation of each PLM component, which can help the company identify strengths and weaknesses of PLM components. Evaluation of the integration and maturity of different components is essential and advantageous. For instance, PDM (Product Data Management) maturity models (Stark, 2005) define the activities that a company needs to carry out at each stage and also defines a generic five-step process per stage; related to the as-is situation and to-be situation of the studied company. CPI (Collaborative Product Innovation) maturity model (Sharma, 2005) proposes three unique stages of CPI based on collaborative maturity. Batenburg (Batenburg, 2006) developed a PLM framework to assess and guide PLM implementations. Sääksvuori Model (Sääksvuori & Immonen, 2008) determines the maturity of a large international corporation for a corporate-wide PLM development program and develops business and PLM related issues. Other maturity models include Savino model (Savino et al, 2012) and BPMM (looy et al, 2012). But it should be mentioned that none of these maturity models have solved the following questions:

1 Complete degree of PLM areas: how many dimensions that need to be studied to cover all of the necessary PLM themes to get comprehensive results;
2 Relative importance of dimensions to the overall PLM maturity level: needed to strategize for allocation of structural weights of different dimensions based on different business needs.

Next step, we will propose a maturity model which can solve these two questions.

3 Maturity Model to Assess Maturity Level of PLM Components

This paper has considered viewpoints of different maturity models, analyzed success factors and key performance indicators of each component, then proposed a PLM Maturity Model called PLM Components Maturity Assessment (PCMA). This maturity model follows the principle structure of capability maturity model by using the same maturity levels and structured questionnaires. CMMI defined process maturity is developed incrementally from one level to the next level and it does not allow for skipping levels. This limitation of CMMI will result in misleading interpretations. This work gives detailed information of fifteen components in each maturity level in which the maturity is assessed separately, and the items of maturity descriptions are outlined in Table 3.

Table 3. PCMA Maturity Level and Corresponding Content

Maturity Levels	CMMI(Short Description)	Our Work (Items for Maturity Levels)
1 *ad-hoc*	Process unpredictable	• The activity is done with expediency • Nobody is responsible for PLM • Documentation is at the lowest point to satisfy operational needs • PLM software system and processes have deficiencies

Table 3. (*continued*)

2 *Managed*	Process reactive	• The activity is defined and managed, but it is repetitious • Documentation and record is carefully studied • Mutual actions are finished in processes and departments • No effort has been made to consider about recycling
3 *Defined*	Process proactive	• The activity is formalized and supported by standards • Documentation and record is studied and shared • Personal actions are carried out efficiently • PLM systems are easily implemented • Environmental awareness occurs
4 *Quantitatively managed*	Process measured & controlled	• Activities run smoothly • PLM systems cooperate with other enterprise systems • The products run efficiently and are effective • Progressively eliminates errors and failures
5 *optimized*	Continuous process improvement	• The activity runs optimally • PLM system helps company make improved decisions • Best practices and innovative ideas are considered

PCMA serves the goal of measuring, monitoring, and comparing PLM components in relative and absolute terms. It provides a holistic assessment for fifteen PLM components based on a comprehensive set of key performance indicators (KPI) in each maturity level. Table 4 summarizes on what needs to be accomplished for "People" dimension in each maturity level. In order to simplify assessment work, avoid missing information, and improve the measurement of progress, we propose KPIs for each dimension, develop questionnaires, and obtain maturity scores based on KPI. For example, we outline the overall KPI of "people" dimension; the maturity score range of "Level 1" is 0-1, the maturity score is 0.5 for each KPI, the maturity score of "People" dimension is the average of all KPIs' score. Similarly, we can obtain the maturity score of every dimension.

4 Selection the Optimal PLM Components Based on Company Requirements

The AHP method is a multi-criteria, multi-item decision-making technique (Carlos et al., 2008). It involves in structuring multiple criteria into a hierarchy and assessing the relative importance of these criteria, while comparing alternatives for each criterion, and obtaining an overall ranking of the alternatives. This process has been conceptualized as a hierarchical composition of 'Goals', 'Criteria', and 'Alternatives'. Selecting the optimal PLM components based on business profits can be approached by the AHP method. The objective is to choose PLM components in the TIFOS framework represented by O1 (TechnoWare), O2 (InforWare), O3 (FunctionWare),

O4 (OrgaWare) and O5 (SustainWare). The features of O1-O5 can be selected as "Criteria" in the second hierarchy. Each criterion is individually connected to the competing alternatives, which come from PLM components (T1-T15), (limited in the examples given in this paper to T9).

We first determine the priorities of each PLM component. Priorities for each criterion are calculated from their importance in reaching the goal. The priorities are then combined throughout the hierarchy to get an overall priority for each component. The component with the highest priority will be the best alternative, and the ratios of PLM components' priorities indicate their relative importance to the goal. The decision process is described in depth in Figure 1.

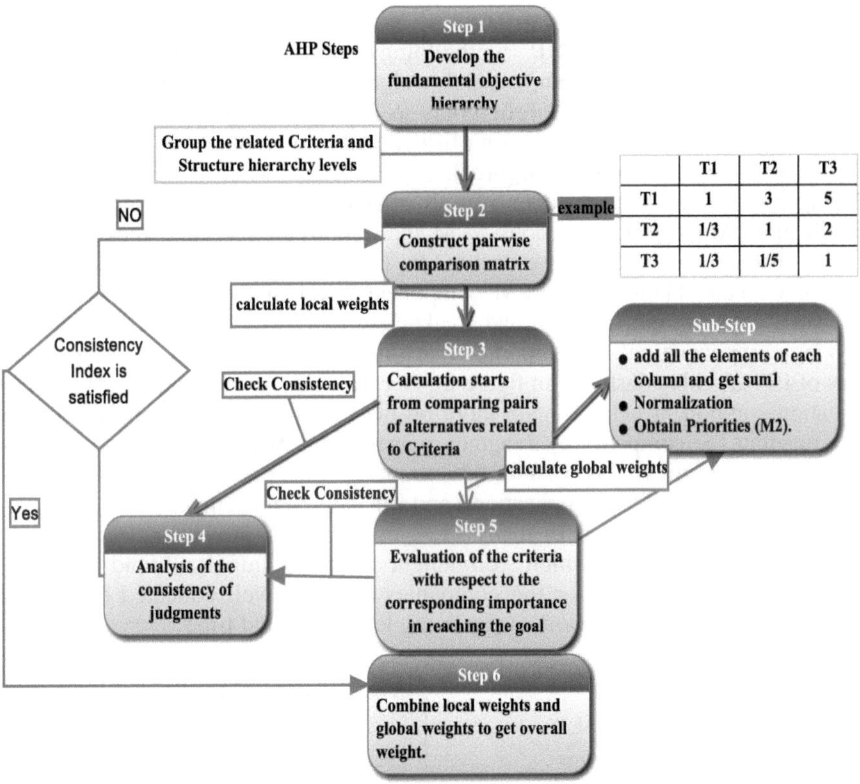

Fig. 1. AHP calculation steps

In figure 1, the equation to get overall weights (step 6) is:

$$W_j = \sum_{i=1}^{n} w_i a_{i\,j} \forall i \in (1,2,...,n) \forall j \in (1,2,...,m) \tag{1}$$

Where, W_j is the priority value of the alternative j; W_i is the priority value of criteria i; a_{ij} is the priority value of the alternative j related to criteria i. m is the number of alternatives and n is the number of criteria.

5 Case Studies

This section focuses on case studies. Two parts are studied in this section: evaluating PCMA for a particular unit to get a maturity score; and choosing the right PLM components from the defined business targets. Experimental data and important information have been collected by interviewing the managers of an Italian prefabrication company.

We calculate final maturity score per PCMA dimension by calculating the weighted sum of the KPIs in each dimension; and determine the overall PCMA maturity as the mean score of the fifteen dimensions. The result can be seen in the radar chart (figure 2) showing the level of achievement for each dimension (limited in the examples given in this paper to T6).

Our work developed AHP methodology and derived priorities of PLM components. Describe the components' weight by using the descending order in figure 3. We define business profit goals as 'Reduce time-to-market' and achieve features of it as criteria, while adopting fifteen PLM components as alternatives. PLM components' weight is shown in figure 4.

Figure 2 shows the average score over all assessments. The yellow line represents the as-is situation. Among six dimensions, PLM applications are scoring highest with 3.8, and financial management scores lowest with 1.9. The overall maturity score is 2.76. From figure 3, we can obtain which PLM component is relatively important in the TIFOS framework. Figuring out strengths and weaknesses of PLM components in figure 2 and analyzing components relative importance in figure 3; we can work out future maturity scores of PCMA (blue dash line in figure 2). According to figure 2 and figure 3, the PLM application component helps to gain more profits than the other components, therefore, recommending the company to strengthen management of this component. In figure 4, when a business profit goal is 'Reduce time-to market', the optimal PLM components that should be selected are: PLM Applications, and Business Management.

Business actions are blind to many PLM components. However, this model, it is convenient to figure out which component is more important and improve. In conclusion, it is beneficial for the companies to make well educated choices when choosing the right PLM components by using less effort and time.

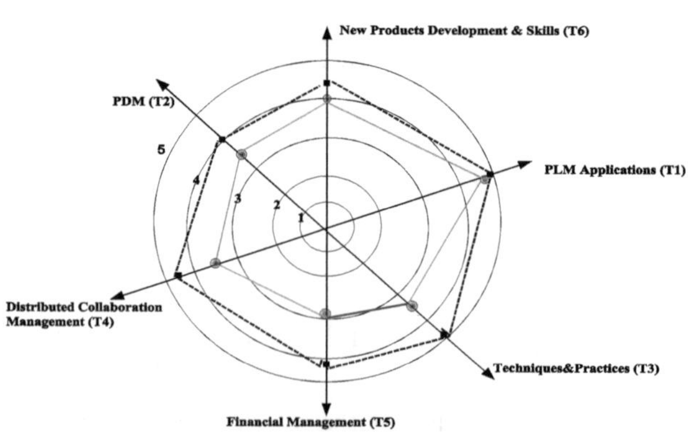

Fig. 2. PCMA Maturity Score

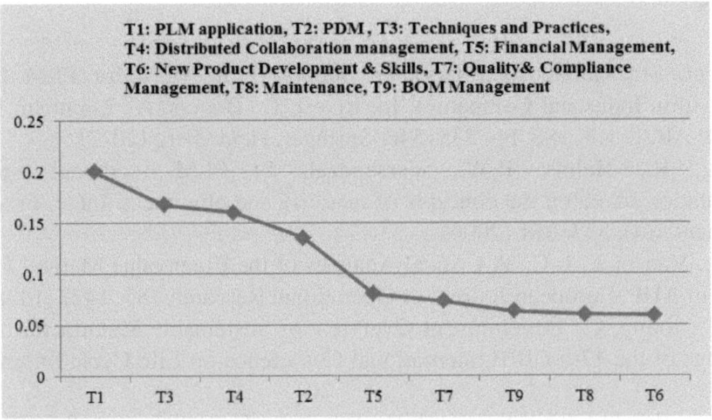

Fig. 3. PLM components' ranking and corresponding weight value

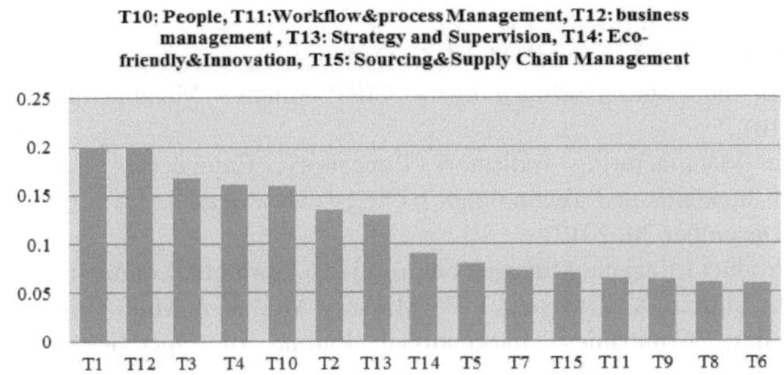

Fig. 4. PLM components' ranking based on 'Reduce time-to-market' goal

6 Conclusion and Future Work

This research work proposes an extension of the TIFO framework by adding Sustainability. This new framework, TIFOS, can cover entire functionalities of PLM and contains all PLM components. We introduced PCMA maturity model to evaluate the performance of each PLM component based on TIFOS. PCMA maturity score is given by assessing the characters and KPIs, which can entirely cover all PLM areas and reflects the strengths and weaknesses of PLM components. Then we selected optimal PLM components in TIFOS by developing AHP methodology, which is a weighting process in competing alternatives via pair-wise comparison matrices. Finally, we have done an experimental study to achieve PCMA as-is and to-be maturity scores, to select the optimal PLM components based on weight priorities.

The future work will use more realistic data to examine the effectiveness of the PCMA Model, concentrate on the consistency ratio of AHP, and test criteria and KPIs validations. Then we will develop Fuzzy AHP method to handle the uncertainty of the collected data.

References

1. Abramovici, M., Göbel, J.C.: Decision Support Framework for PLM Harmonization Projects within Industrial Companies. In: Rivest, L., Bouras, A., Louhichi, B. (eds.) PLM 2012. IFIP AICT, vol. 388, pp. 535–546. Springer, Heidelberg (2012)
2. Batenburg, R., Helms, R.W., Versendaal, J.: PLM roadmap: Stepwise PLM implementation based on the concepts of maturity and alignment. Int. J. Product Lifecycle Management 1(4), 333–351 (2006)
3. Carlos, A., Vansnick, J.-C.: A Critical Analysis of the Eigenvalue Method Used to Derive Priorities in AHP. European Journal of Operational Research 187, 1422–1428 (2008)
4. Feng, S.C., Joung, C.: Development Overview of Sustainable Manufacturing Metrics. In: Proceedings of the 17th CIRP International Conference on Life Cycle Engineering, pp. 6–12 (2010)
5. Global Reporting Initiative, Sustainability Reporting Guidelines, ver. 3.1 (2011), `http://www.globalreporting.org/` (accessed June 2, 2011)
6. Kiritsis, D., Marco, G.: Report from workshop 2: Sustainable products and production, services and management. In: IMS 2020-Proceedings from IMS 2020 Summer School on Sustainable Manufacturing (2010)
7. Laurent, A., Olsen, S.I., Hauschild, M.Z.: Carbon footprint as environmental performance indicator for the manufacturing industry. CIRP Annals - Manufacturing Technology 59, 37–40 (2010)
8. Sustainable Manufacturing Indicators Repository, Engineering Laboratory, National Institute of Standards and Technology, `http://www.mel.nist.gov/msid/SMIR/` (accessed December 20, 2012)
9. Stark, J.: Product Lifecycle Management, pp. 1–16. Springer, London (2011)
10. Savino, M., Mazza, A., Ouzrout, Y.P.: Maturity Model: A Multi-Criteria Assessment in Southern Italy Companies. International Journal of Operations and Quantitative Management 18(3), 159–180 (2012)
11. Lee, S.G., Ma, Y.S., et al.: Product lifecycle management in aviation maintenance, repair and overhaul. Computers in Industry, 296–303 (2008)
12. Stark, J.: Product Lifecycle Management -21st Century Paradigm for Product Realisation. Springer, London (2005)
13. Sharma, A.: Collaborative Product Innovation: Integrating Elements of CPI via PLM Framework. Computer-Aided Design 37(13), 1425–1434 (2005)
14. Sharif, N.: Technology Strategy in Developing Countries: Evolving from Comparative to Competitive Advantage. International Journal of Technology Management 10(10), 1–33 (1997)
15. Trotta, M.: Product Lifecycle Management: Sustainability and knowledge management as keys in a complex system of product development. Journal of Industrial Engineering and Management 3(2), 309–322 (2010)
16. Vengugopalan, S.R., et al.: Application of AHP for PLM Tools Selection. Product Lifecycle Management: Fostering the culture of innovation. In: PLM-SP4, pp. 111–125 (2008)
17. Van Looy, A., De Backer, M., Poels, G.: Towards a Decision Tool for Choosing a Business Process Maturity Model. In: Peffers, K., Rothenberger, M., Kuechler, B. (eds.) DESRIST 2012. LNCS, vol. 7286, pp. 78–87. Springer, Heidelberg (2012)

The Use of a Service Modeler Together with a PLM Software for the Management of Product-Related Services: A First Use-case-based Approach to Configure Service Components for Product-Related Services

Christian Zinke, Kyrill Meyer, Florian Golemo, and Lars-Peter Meyer

University Leipzig
zinke@informatik.uni-leipzig.de

Abstract. For most goods-producing companies the provision of product-related services is already a necessary commodity (Wildemann 2009). Such services are regarded as necessary attachment to a successful production of goods by most companies. To manage products and services, companies rely on different methods and tools that span the entire lifecycle (Sendler 2009). With the goal of raising efficiency and quality at affordable costs, those methods and tools are implemented or supported with the help of information systems such as PLM/PDM solutions. In this context, it is observed that the development and management of services, even though, they increasingly become a vital part for many companies, is neglected. Furthermore a systematic, tool-supported approach using the existing PLM/PDM-systems can be seen as problem area (Blinn et al. 2009).

The objective of our paper is to minimize problems with product related services such as fitting cost estimation, matters of quality control and communication inhouse or with the customer. Therefore, existing management approaches of service engineering (Ganz et al. 2010) need to find their implementation within PLM/PDM systems in a way, that product related services can be handled throughout the lifecycle and interrelationships between product and service (e.g. a maintenance service for a certain sold machine) can be accounted for. Our scope is the establishment of a Service Lifecycle Management for product related services. Our work is based on case study work conducted in the field of engineering that supports the problem and objective. Therefore, as results we can show the validated problem field and exemplary demonstrate with the help of the ARAS Innovator PLM solution (Aras Corporation 2012) and the Service Modeller (Klingner et al. 2011) how product related services can be developed and managed by using a service lifecycle PLM tool. The example focusses especially on the configuration of service components and how service instances can be connected to product data.

1 Objective and Domain

To manage material goods producers use methods and tools which can be summarized in its entirety as a Product-Lifecycle-Management (Sendler 2009). They

A. Bernard, L. Rivest, and D. Dutta (Eds.): PLM 2013, IFIP AICT 409, pp. 449–457, 2013.

normally include ways to manage ressources, processes and data (such as e.g. CAD). The aim is to ensure a systematic approach to reach a higheffectiveness, guarantee the quality of products and ultimately safeguard the competitiveness and profitability of the entire company.

As part of the onging developments in the markets one can recognize an upgrowing interest in product-related services during the recent years (Stille 2003). High business competition, globalization and a decreasing time-to-market present itself as a difficult situation for good-producing companies (Bruhn, Hadwich 2006). In this, product-related services become more and more a unique selling proposition (Blinn et al. 2009). At the same time it has been recognized that the support for services during the lifecycle is not at the same level as it is for material goods (Ganz et al. 2010). Even though in order to guarantee a high-quality service it is necessary to use different management methods and tools (for services). Such methods and tools are the objective of the Services Science and Service Engineering (Böttcher et al. 2011). By neglecting already existing management methods and standardized procedures (Bullinger 2006; Corsten 2007), such as provided by the Service Engineering, companies do not exploit their full potential and provide their services inefficiently in a way that may result in damage of their own interests. A systematic approach and active management (planning, monitoring and controlling) of services provides a better understanding of the benefits of solutions offered, the marketing opportunities, an adherence to quality standards and gives the ability to increase the efficiency and reduce costs (Klingner et al. 2011). A holistic and overall method to manage services is the Service-Lifecycle-Management (SLM) (Ap Verlag 2012). The SLM approach combines different management methods and tools, based on a lifecycle view. In Science and Economy, this approach is only used and explored for pure (IT-) service providers (Orr 2011) so far. The motivation of this paper is to transfer knowledge to a more general SLM approach that can also be used in other domains. We demonstrate the feasabilty in the areas of product-related services (Vargo 2011).

The paper, the approach and the use-cases are based on a qualitative study in the domain of special machinery. This domain is technology intensive, highly interactive (on the side to the customer) and very constumer specific. The following solution will show the theoretical and practical integration of a SLM and PLM/PDM system, so that product-related services can be handled throughout the lifecycle and interrelationships between product and service (e.g. a maintenance service for a certain sold machine) can be accounted for.

Therefore, we first present an integrated PSLM (product-service-lifecycle management) approach as the scientific basis for the use-case based integration of a SLM Tool ("Service Modeller") in a PLM/PDM System (Aras Innovator).

2 Scope and Technology

The scope of this paper is to establish a Service Lifecycle Management for product related services. Firstly, there is a need to describe functions that will be necessary for Service Engineering and Management. Secondly, it is neccessary to describe how these functions can be integrated with PLM/PDM solutions to form a holistic support system. First of all, we describe the Service Lifecycle Management and how we can combine PLM approaches mainly focusing on material goods.

2.1 Service and Product Lifecycle Management

A Service Lifecycle Management is a holistic management approach, which combines different methods and tools for managing services over its lifecycle. These methods are: service portfolio management, service strategy, idea management, service level management, quality management, process management, configuration management, resource management, supply chain management and customer management (see Fig. 1).

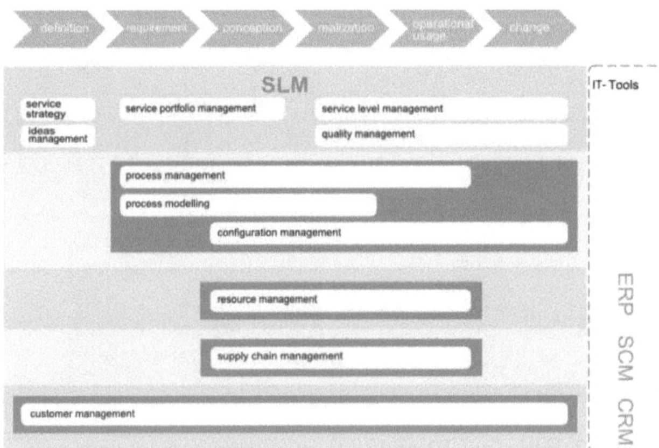

Fig. 1. SLM Methods and Tools (Meyer, 2012)

This lifecycle management approach for services will have to be used for any service delivered in relationship to a certain product. This is our theoretical framework to integrate a Service Lifecycle Management for product-related services. Combined with practical studies we identified some basic core functions for an IT-based support of these methods.

While a number of necessary functions could be identified, yet as part of this paper we will focus our discussion on the following: (F1) management of portfolio information, which means the managing of services, service components, products and product components and their access to information. Other functions identified are:

- F2: Creation and management of workflows and processes for services and service components
- F3: Management and assignment of the resources to be provided for the service and its service level
- F4: Management of customers - as contractors and access to relevant information for product and services

- F5: Managing knowledge that is formed in the processes about the whole service and access to the information during the performance
- F6: Management of departments and suppliers during the implementation and modification of products and services
- F7: Measurement and recording of parameters of individual services
- F8: Reporting
- F9: Managing Customer Feedback
- F10: Managing the lifecycle of services and possibilities for change of the parameters and components

The focused function F1 has some subfunctions, which are:

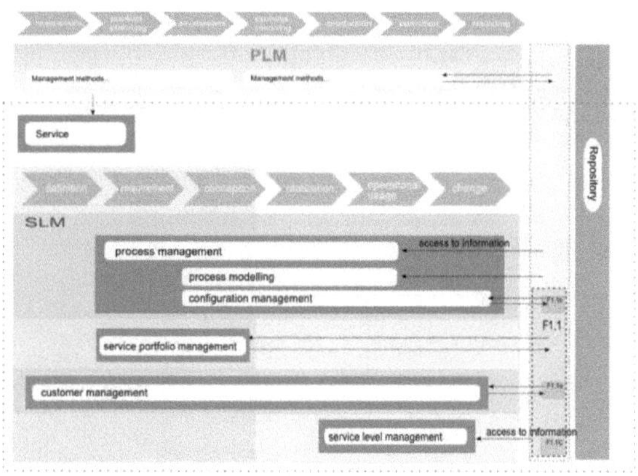

Fig. 2. Functions F1 and supported management approach

- F1.1a: Provision of services and product catalog for the customer
- F1.1b: General management of the configuration options of the service modules and the configuration selected by the customer

The management of portfolio information for services is not supported in standard PLM/PDM systems (see Fig. 2). These systems mostly focus on Bill of Material (BOM) and CAD integration. To support the portfolio and configuration management we can use the "Service Modeller". This tool and the chosen PLM/PDM system will be presented next.

2.2 Used Technology and Tools

2.2.1 Description of the Product-Lifecycle Management Tool

For our prototype solution we used the Aras Innovator, a freely available PLM system developed by the Aras Corporation (Aras Corporation 2012a). The selection of this solution is the result of a comparison of different free PLM systems, but stands as an example for any other software available in this context. The Aras PLM system consists of several open source modules build on top of the closed source Aras Enterprise

Application Framework. A major factor (A significant aspect or key factor) for our choice was the highly flexible data model and the implementation of the SOAP-Interface (Aras Corporation 2012b).

2.2.2 Description of the Service Modeller

The Service Modeller is a tool, which has been prototyped and developed at the Business Information Systems chair at the University of Leipzig. It helps with the component tree based modeling and management of complex services and service portfolios. For each service component key performance indicators can be defined and stored, which can either be dynamically calculated formulas or fixed values. In addition to that, nonfunctional attributes can be defined. While the dynamic key performance indicators helps by the evaluation of services, the nonfunctional attributes can be used for filtering or further descriptions. Finally, cardinality restrictions on the tree connectors can be used to model constraints for the component combinations (Klingner et al. 2011).

3 Results

3.1 Use Case

Our descriptions are based on case study work conducted in the field of engineering that supports the problem and objective. Thes use-case focuses on the configuration of service components and how service instances can be connected to the product data. Hereinafter a simplified example is outlined to illustrate the interaction between product and service configuration (see fig. 3).

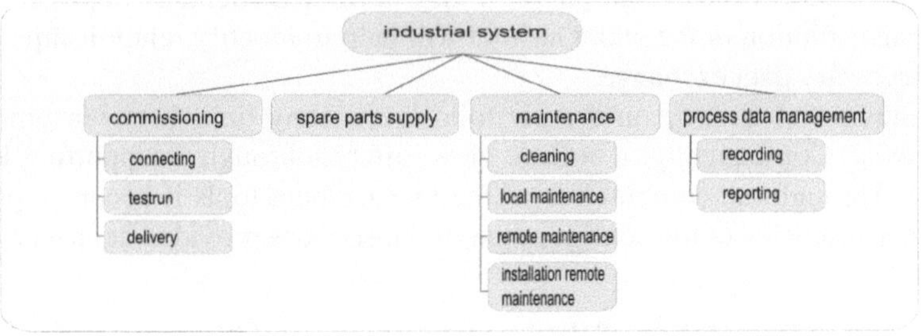

Fig. 3. (After-sales) service components

In this case, an abstract industrial system is used. For this industrial system the producer provides some (after-sales) services. In a nutshell, they can be described as: commission, spare parts supply, maintenance and process data management. To manage these services and to make it transparent for the customer, it is necessary to use a service portfolio management. This means, that single services get divided into different service components which can be managed later. The components in which the service is devided are: local maintenance, remote maintenance, cleaning and the installation of a remote maintenance. Some of the services are optional, such as the remote maintenance or the delivery.That means the service is only delivered if the customer chooses it or a component may be technically necessary. The service commissioning is divided into the components delivery, connecting (electricity or some remote connections) and test run (to test the complex system). The process data management is separated in two components: recording and reporting. Here, we see the dependency between material good and other services: a reporting service needs to store information, and this information can only be stored if the material good has components (such as sensors) to measure this information. As an overview this shows how services can be modularized and how these modules can be sold customer specific.

Many of these services cannot be regarded independently of the industrial system to which they relate. Thus, there are numerous links to various components of the system itself. To understand the correlation, it is necessary to know the product portfolio. The product data is stored in the PLM/PDM system. There we find a Bill of Material, installation layouts and technical documentations for each sold product. In our case, the Aras Innovator can store all data. Product-configuration can be done with the help of the PLM/PDM and calculations conducted afterwards, such e.g. the price and delivery time.

Certain dependencies between product components and service components will remain. Thus, in the presented case, a remote service will only be provided if the component LAN was installed. Beyond such direct dependencies, a recommender engine may hint to other helpful components. On assembly of an industrial system, the services "connection" and "test run" may be recommended to ensure a consistent performance of the system. If the customer opts for on-site maintenance (local maintenance), the vendor should recommend the product component LAN for diagnostics to lower costs for the maintenance service. If such product-service relationship is not considered as part of the design phase, it may become difficult or impossible to offer an integrated solution in the end. Our tool will help to identify relationships and manage the necessary data exchange.

This shows that already on the portfolio level many links between products and services exist. Consequently, a holistic view, offered through a supporting IT-system is crucial. Through the combination of the management tools it becomes possible to detect inconsistencies in the configuration of the services provided at an early stage.

3.2 Interface Description of the Used Tools

The Aras Innovator requires a Microsoft windows server with installed Internet Information Services (IIS). On the client side it utilizes an ActiveX component which requires the use of the Microsoft Internet Explorer. Core components of the Aras Innovator can be modified or extended by editing C# or visual basic code in the browser. The frontend modification is possible with primarily JavaScript.

As interface the Aras Innovator supports SOAP and a special .NET/COM library called IOM-API. According to the documentation both interfaces support the same functionality, the IOM is just a convenient method to handle the SOAP requests. Which data and methods are available via SOAP can be configured at the frontend.

The Service Modeller offers a SOAP interface as well and supports the retrieval of service models or service configurations. This is a static interface, thus, any modifications need programming effort. This is an important difference to the Aras Innovator.

3.3 Implementation Concept

For the integration of the service models into the PLM system we need to retrieve them from the Service Modeller and create a copy in the Aras Innovator. Furthermore, we want to facilitate the coupling of product data to services and the collection of data from specific products and service contracts.

This goal is achieved by the use of a converter. The converter enables the use of existing interfaces of both systems and can manage the data transfer. As mentioned above, the SOAP interface as well as the IOM interface would be possible with the Aras innovator. Our implementation utilizes the SOAP interfaces of the Service-Modeller and the Aras Innovator.

In this paper, we should distinguish between a product model and a product configuration. The product model contains all necessary or possible parts and configurations for a product. A product configuration is the specific configuration of a product as ordered by a specific customer. This is important, because in some scenarios the available services depend on the selection of product parts. As an example one may imagine an industrial system, delivered with an optional remote administration module. If the module is chosen by the customer, the producer may repair the system from afar. If not, an engineer has to travel there and do the maintenance manually. These services may be mapped analogously in the Service Modeller: There are service models, which define the possible services and service configurations, which select certain services from a model. Both data entities have to be saved, because depending on the product, different service models may be available, and depending on customer and product the service configuration may vary.

For the sake of integration it should be possible to connect this information. The design of the integration process is displayed in Fig. 4.

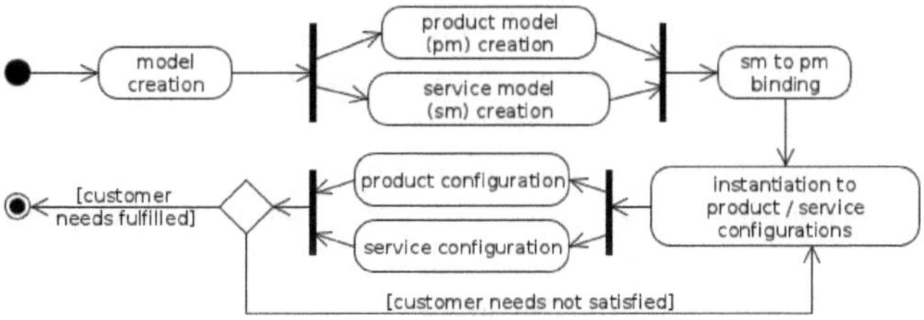

Fig. 4. The process of integration. Models are created in the Aras Innovator and in the Service Modeller independently of each other. For each product model the service models are chosen. The so created bundles may be offered to customers. As soon as a consumer is found, certain options of product and service get picked. If they are satisfying for all parties, they may be delivered. If not they must be respecified as product and service configurations.

3.4 Technical Realization

The Aras Innovator already contains the item types "part" and "product". A part in the Innovator can either be a part or a setup of different parts. For example, the part "Ford Mustang GT" consists among others of the parts "wheel" (4 pcs.), "engine" and "chassis". A wheel may consist of "tire rubber", "rim" and "screw" (4 pcs.). The item type "product" is the equivalent of the product model. All available parts and options may be saved there. For example, in the product "Ford Mustang" there may be options for "Ford Mustang GT" and "Ford Mustang GT/CS", where the last one is a variation of the first.

For the implementation a counterpart of the product configuration is necessary. It should store which variants of a certain product have been choosen by a customer. Therefore, in Aras Innovator a new item type is introduced: product configuration. For each selected product model it saves the model and the chosen options.

In the Service Modeller the required item types already exist. To be able to map them onto the Innovator, they must be created there, too. Therefore, the item types "service model", "service configuration" and "service component" must be set up whereas the latter forms models and configurations. In order to refer to each other, the following new relationships are needed: model - component, configuration - component, component - component and model - configuration. These X-Y relationships correspond to the 1:n schema, i.e. "one X can have many Y". To realize service-product mapping, the relations explained in the previous chapter have to be included, too: product - service model, product configuration - service configuration. The corresponding data model is displayed in fig. 5.

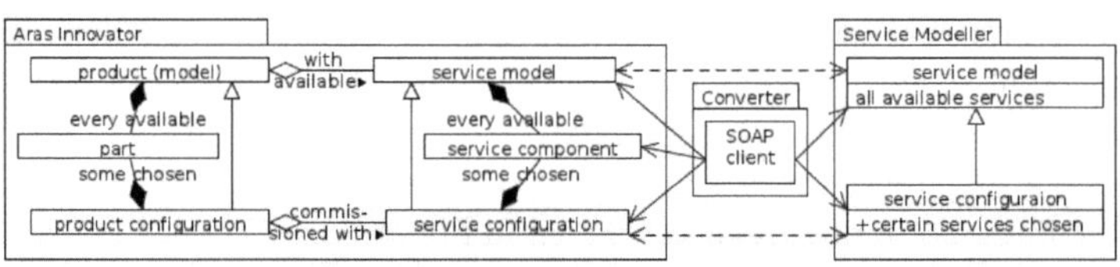

Fig. 5. Data model of the overall system of Aras Innovator, Converter and Service Modeller. The Converter accesses the SOAP-interfaces of both tools. It helps extracting service data from the Service Modeller and transforming it for Aras Innovator.

In the Aras Innovator new interfaces have to be set up for the new service item types and service relations, allowing for their creation out of other programs. As soon as these interfaces are ready, the converter may fetch the service models and configurations in certain intervals and transmit them. When this is done, the user is offered a possibility to integrate the service into the product lifecycle as described earlier.

4 Conclusion and Further Work

We have shown how product-oriented support systems (PLM/PDM) can be enriched with a service-oriented approach and its utility. The "Service Modeller" initially supports only a part of the Service Lifecycle Management, the portfolio management, mainly the componentization and configuration. In the presented scenario not only the components of service and product can be linked, but also external factors can be integrated.

We presented how an integrated service and product data management as basis of a SLM. Our demonstration is limited to the configuration and portolio managemen functions (F1). For other necessary functions it will also be required to identifiy tools and how they can interact with PLM/PDM systems.

References

Ap Verlag GmbH (2012), http://www.apverlag.de/OnlineArtikel/20081112/20081112h%20Siemens%20Service%20Lifecycle%20Management.htm. (accessed January 31, 2013)

Aras Corporation (2012a), http://www.aras.com (accessed July 24, 2012)

Aras Corporation Model-based SOA (2012b), http://www.aras.com/technology/model-based-soa.aspx. (accessed July 24, 2012)

Blinn, N., et al.: Lebenszyklusmodelle hybrider Wertschöpfung. Modellimplikationen und Fallstudie. In: Thomas, O., Loos, P., Nüttgens, M. (eds.) Hybride Wertschöpfung: Mobile Anwendungssysteme für effiziente Dienstleistungsprozesse im Technischen Kundendienst. Springer, Heidelberg (2010)

Böttcher, M., Klingner, S.: Providing a Method for Composing Modular B2B-Services. Journal of Business and Industrial Marketing 26(5), S. 320–S. 331 (2011)

Bruhn, M., Hadwich, K.: Produkt- und Servicemanagement. Vahlen, München (2006)

Bullinger, H., Scheer, J.: Service Engineering - Entwicklung und Gestaltung innovativer Dienstleistungen. 2. Aufl. Springer (2006)

Corsten, H., Gössinger, R.: Dienstleistungsmanagement.5. Aufl, München, Wien Oldenburg (2007)

Ganz, W., Bienzeisler, B.: Management hybrider Wertschöpfung - Potenziale, Perspektiven und praxisorientierte Beispiele, Fraunhofer-IAO-, Stuttgart (2010)

Klingner, S., et al.: Managing complex service portfolios: A business case from a full service provider. In: Reser 2011 Proceedings, Hamburg (2011)

Meyer, K., et al.: Produkt-Dienstleistungs-Lebenszyklus: Methoden und Funktionen für die Entwicklung und das Management produktbegleitender Dienstleistungen. In: Meyer, K., Abdelkafi, N. (eds.) Smart Services and Service Science – Proceedings of the 4th International Symposium on Services Science. Leipziger Beiträge zur Informatik, Band 36, Leipzig (2012)

Orr, A.T.: Introductiontothe ITIL servicelifecycle, 3rd edn. TSO, London (2011)

Sendler, U.: Das PLM-Kompendium Referenzbuch des Produkt-Lebenszyklus-Managements. Springer, Heidelberg (2009)

Stille, F.: Produktbegleitende Dienstleistungen gewinnen weiter an Bedeutung. Wochenbericht des DIW Nr.21/2003, pp. 336–342 (2003)

Vargo, S., Lusch, R., Hobel, C., Wieland, H.: Alternative Logiken für Dienstleistungen: von hybriden Systemen zu Serviceökosystemen. In: Spath, D., Ganz, W. (eds.) Am Puls wirtschaftlicher Entwicklung – Dienstleistungstrends, pp. 137–153. Carl Hanser Verlag, München (2011)

Wildemann, H.: Produkte und Services entwickeln und managen: Strategien, Konzepte, Methoden, 2. Aufl. TCW Transfer-Centrum, München (2009)

Agile Design Methods for Mechatronics System Integration

Matthieu Bricogne[1], Nadège Troussier[2], Louis Rivest[3], and Benoît Eynard[1]

[1] Université de Technologie de Compiègne,
Department of Mechanical Systems Engineering,
CNRS UMR7337 Roberval
Rue du Docteur Schweitzer, BP 60319
60203 Compiègne Cedex, France
{matthieu.bricogne,benoit.eynard}@utc.fr
[2] Université de Technologie de Troyes,
Institut Charles Delaunay / CREIDD
CNRS UMR6972 STMR,
12 Rue Marie Curie CS 42060
10004 Troyes Cedex, France
nadege.troussier@utt.fr
[3] École de Technologie Supérieure,
Department of Automated Manufacturing Engineering,
1100 Notre-Dame Street West
Montréal, Québec
Canada H3C 1K3
louis.rivest@etsmtl.ca

Abstract. The multi-disciplinary nature of mechatronics product significantly increases complexity of the development process. In this paper, the benefits of agile design methods are presented for multi-disciplinary system integration.

After describing a model illustrating the relation between design state, decision making and multi-domain system integration, the conventional mechatronics system design process is illustrated. The weakness of "project planned" [1] management methods and their consequences on system integration are then pointed out. Finally, a framework to provide the necessary design and decision information is proposed to make agile design methods usage possible in this context.

Keywords: Mechatronics system design, multi-domain system integration, agile design methods, design-decision-integration model, Engineering action's management system, collaboration workspaces.

1 Introduction

Products are becoming increasingly complex, integrating technologies from several fields, such as mechanical engineering, electronic or electrical engineering and software engineering. Mechanical systems developed since the 80's have thus evolved

A. Bernard, L. Rivest, and D. Dutta (Eds.): PLM 2013, IFIP AICT 409, pp. 458–470, 2013.

from electro-mechanical systems with discrete electrical and mechanical parts to integrated electronic-mechanical systems with sensors, actuators, and digital microelectronics. These integrated systems are called mechatronics systems [2].

The multi-disciplinary nature of mechatronics “not only increases the complexity of products but also makes the product development process significantly more difficult” [3]. Engineers and designers use to be educated and to work discipline-wise. Some of them could have multidisciplinary skills but “cross-functional teams consisting of experts in several domains are mandatory to develop multi-disciplinary products” [3]. Several collaboration issues appear in such teams. One of them is the fact that multi-disciplinary product development leads to inter-disciplinary problems and integration issues. They are generally difficult to anticipate, hard to detect and even more hard to solve [3]. This paper aims to present some agile design methods and to propose a framework providing the design and decision information necessary for the implementation of these methods.

This paper is divided in two main parts. The first one proposes a model to illustrate the relation between design state, decision making and multi-domain system integration. This illustrating model is used to point out the weakness of “project planned” [1] project management, generally used to support mechatronics system design process. Its consequences in term of multi-disciplines system integration are then pointed out. The second part proposes a framework to provide the necessary design and decision information to make “agile design methods” [4] usage possible. These agile design methods are presented as a multi-disciplines integration enabler.

2 Mechatronics System Multi-disciplines Integration

Multi-disciplinary mechatronics system design could lead to integration issues. In order to explain what is the impact of multi-disciplines integration on the product, the different levels of mechatronics system’ integration are presented below.

Penas et al [4] describe four different mechatronics system’ integration levels (Fig. 1). The first kind of integration is called "separated components". In this case, components are designed separately and are just incorporated in the same system thanks to cables. The second level of integration corresponds to the concept of "joined components". The mechanical component will be designed in order to place the electrical and/or the electronic components in juxtaposition with each other. Distances between components have been reduced. The third kind of integration is called "inserted": electronic components are spread out into the whole system. There is no real integration. Finally, the ultimate integration level is the "merged" components: electronic is integrated as close as possible to the mechanical and electrical components. Parts are gathered in a coherent and functional manner and mechanical parts can also be used as signal transmitter. The contributions of this integration are various:

- Physical integration: spatial and weight optimizations are provided,
- Functional integration: detection, communication, control/information processing allow the system to provide new functionalities and to be reliable.

Fig. 1. The different integration levels in mechatronics system design [5]

Multi-disciplines integration is a key objective in a mechatronics system design perspective; to point out such objective, an illustrating model is proposed in the next section. This model is used to highlight the weakness of process-planned project management, generally used to support mechatronics system design process.

3 Decision – Design – Integration Illustrating Model

3.1 Decision – Design for "Single Discipline" Product Design

During product design projects, decisions are made and design information is created. Noël et al [6] describe the product–process–organization model (PPO) model where both type of information (Decision and Design) are linked. For example, the project objectives, part of the "decision framework" [6] have a great influence on the "design framework" [6]. On the other hand, technical constraints have to be taken into consideration by project leaders, which are parts of decision framework.

Fig. 2 illustrates the kind of interdependence that could traditionally exist between design framework and decision framework. It is composed of two axes. On the "Decision" axis, several design reviews are considered as the main steps during the design project decision process. On the "Design" axis, the main steps are based on various product deliverables resulting from the different stages of design process proposed by Beitz et al [7]. The polyline illustrates the "macro" evolution of a design project and the relation that can exist between the decision and the design information. During the design reviews, the overall progress is measured. Information about the project overall progress is usually seen as limited between project reviews, due to the lack of consolidated information. This idea is represented on the graph by the dashed line between points.

3.2 Decision – Design – Integration for Multidisciplinary Product Design: Application to Mechatronics System Design

In the previous section, a model illustrating the relation between decision and design information during product design involving only one discipline has been presented.

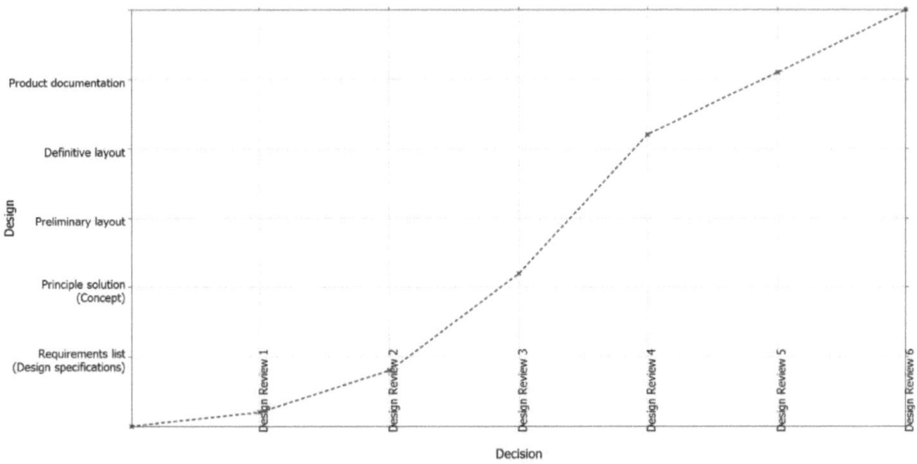

Fig. 2. Decision - Design model for "single discipline" product design

In this, section, this model will be enriched to take into consideration the multi-disciplines integration objective in the mechatronics system design context.

Project Planned Mechatronics System Design Process

Mechatronics system design is usually presented as a linear process [8]. Integration is then proposed as a specific step, in particular when the hardware part and the software part have to be integrated. Aca et al. present Product Lifecycle Management (PLM) system key benefit as its ability to facilitate the coordination of the activities among geographically distributed team members [9]. Fig. 3 illustrates how the client request is divided among the different teams (software team, electrical/electronic team and mechanical team) and how the project manager organizes the different activities. This division is often presented as a necessary method to cope with design complexity [9]. Due to this division, only few people involved on the project have a general overview on the design problems faced by the different teams. The different interfaces between the different domains are defined and ratified in the early phases. To ensure a proper integration of the different modules, these interfaces have to remain stable. That is why if a design problem occurs in a specific discipline, this problem is generally treated directly by the team concerned, even if a global solution, i.e. implicating several disciplines, could be more efficient or provides a more integrated product. This way of organising the mechatronics system design process is called in this paper "project planned" process in contrast with agile design methods which will be presented later in this paper. To illustrate the lack of this process in term of product integration, the Decision – Design – Integration model will be used in the next section.

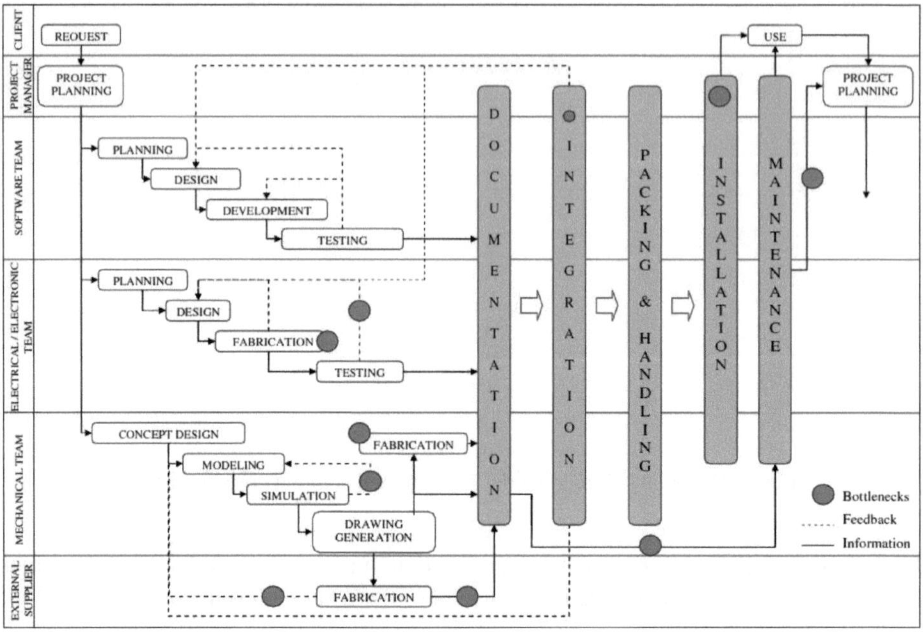

Fig. 3. Project planned mechatronics system design process [9]

Decision – Design – Integration Illustrating Project Planned Mechatronics System Design Process

As described in the previous section, project planned mechatronics system design process leads to product integration weakness. Fig. 4 illustrates the lack of this process thanks to the Decision – Design – Integration model. It points out the fact that the different teams are performing their activities independently, sharing information mainly during the different design reviews. Some of these design reviews are dedicated to system integration, generating the steps on the graph. Between these design reviews, neither precise nor consolidated information about the system to design is available. This idea is represented on the plot by the dashed straight lines.

The red (mechanical domain), the green (electrical/electronic domain) and the blue (software domain) dashed lines are independent. Every discipline is managing its own modules' design according to the requirements defined in the early phases of the project and is trying to respect the interfaces specified. As a result, the elevation on the graph is low, meaning that resulting integration is relatively poor.

In order to face this multi-discipline integration issue, agile design methods are proposed: in the next section, the general spirit of these methods is shortly described and some of their fundamental principles are presented as a key for multi-discipline integration. The Decision – Design – Integration model is finally used to illustrate the benefits of these methods in the mechatronics system design context.

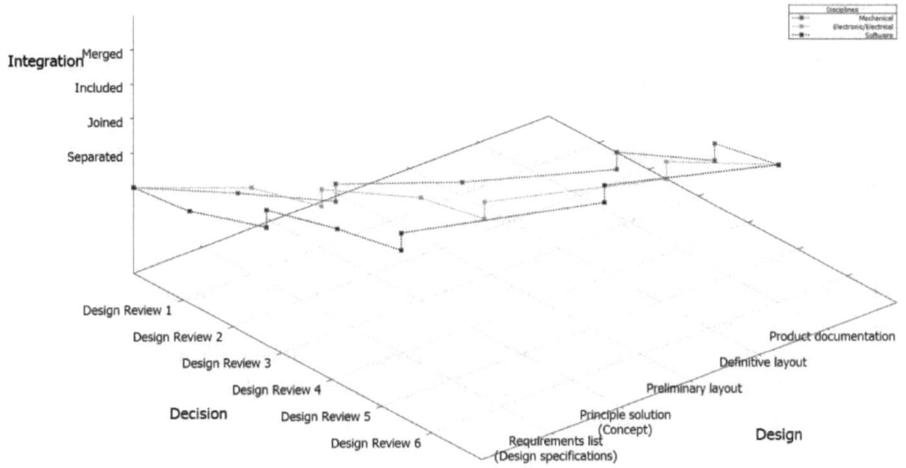

Fig. 4. Decision – Design - Integration model illustrating project planned mechatronics system design

Agile Methods for Mechatronics System Design

Agile methods are well documented for software design [1] and product manufacturing purposes [4]. However the relevance of these methods for concurrent design methods has not been so much studied. Matthews et al summarize agility benefits as "the ability to react rapidly to changes in the environment, whether expected or not" [4]. They also insist on the fact that concurrent design methods lack the ability to respond to unpredicted changes like a late customer request, a designer failure, or some other external environmental impact.

Agile design methods can be valuable for such problems, but also to support multidisciplinary system integration. With the multidisciplinary design problems that can occur, the different cross disciplines activities etc., more exchange between designers, but also a unified, up-to-date and dynamic referential to collaborate [10] are required. In this section, three agile methods concepts are considered for mechatronics system design among the twelve principles of the "Agile Manifesto"[1] which is at the base of all the agile software methods:

- The first one is related to the early, frequent and continuous deliveries. At any time, all the data concerning the mechatronics system to design have to be available for design reviews.
- The second one concerns the fact that all the requirements do not have to be frozen at the beginning of the project. Requirements can be modified or added even late in development.
- The third one relates to the fact that managers, designers, developers have to work together daily on the project. A good overview has to be shared among project team members.

The choice made by the authors about these three concepts is mainly guided by literature reviews and by the mechatronics systems design characteristics. For example, the

[1] `http://agilemanifesto.org/`

fact that mechatronics system design generally involves a great number of designers makes that it is necessary to cope with the need to adapt the agile methods to large-scale organization [11] [12]. Geographically distributed teams, or extended enterprise characteristics also implies that some of the principles are no more applicable [13] [14].

After the brief description of the three agile methods concepts considered in this paper, the expected benefits linked to their usage will be presented in the next section. To do this, the Decision – Design – Integration illustrating model is used.

Decision – Design – Integration Illustrating Agile Design Methods for Mechatronics System Design

In order to be able to contribute to effective integration during the mechatronics system design, the experts coming from the different disciplines have to frequently share information: information about the design, information about the activities, information about the design problems, etc.

Fig. 5 assumes the role of continuous information sharing for multi-disciplinary system integration. On the plot, each point corresponds to a quick review that can be performed daily by the project leaders based on the consolidated information provided to them. If inter-disciplinary problems or integration issues are detected, global solutions are provided. This ongoing project management can assist multi-discipline integration, leading to a better resulting integration. This result is illustrated on the graph by the height of the final curves' points.

In summary, this graph illustrates the need for a unique repository for all the mechatronics system data. This does not mean that no specific teams have to be created, but they have to continuously share design data into the same repository. The graph also illustrates the influence of regular project leaders' decisions, based on consolidated and dynamic indicators.

In the next section, a framework to provide such repository, in order to facilitate the multi-discipline integration, and such indicators, in order to dynamically manage the project, is presented. This framework is presented as the anchor to support agile methods for mechatronics system design.

4 A Framework to Support Agile Methods for Mechatronics System Design

As presented in the previous sections, agile methods are based on constant project reconfigurations. These reconfigurations are human decisions, but they are based on up-to-date indicators provided by the different systems supporting mechatronics system design. In this section, two main systems are presented as a framework to support agile design methods. The first one is dedicated to engineering actions management and the second one is focused on collaboration based on data exchange. The link between these two systems is finally presented.

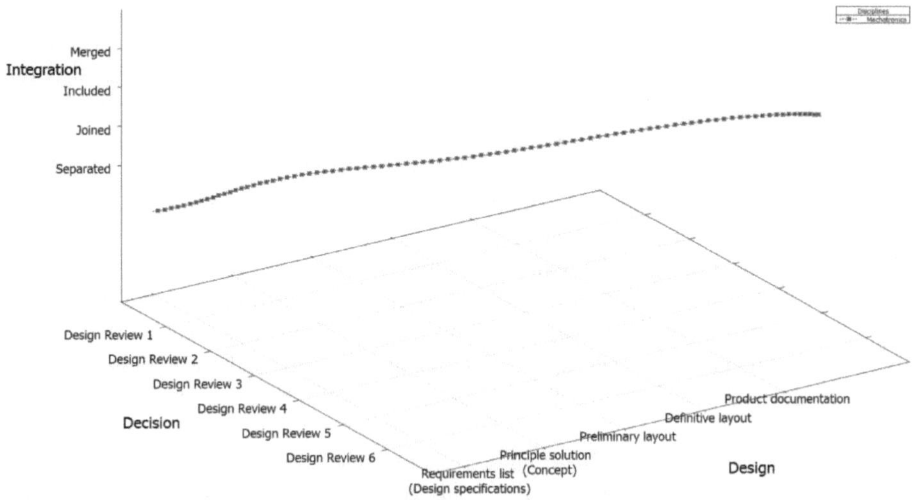

Fig. 5. Decision – Design - Integration model illustrating agile methods for mechatronics system design

4.1 Engineering Actions Management System

Engineering Action's Description

During a design project, the client requests are translated into technical requirements, driving the different design activities [9]. But other reasons influence and drive the design of a system. For example, design problems that occur are also generating specific demands and activities that are, depending on their severity, not formalized. These requests are generally informal and are considered as "daily work". The last type of activities influencing the design a system is the engineering change request/order or bug correction for software engineering. Although they have own singularities, these prescriptive and reactive activities can be managed the same way, and in the same decision support management system. Indeed, they are all called in this paper "Engineering Actions" (EA).

Engineering actions contain different information. First of all, the EA's creator has to describe the context of the demand, the system concerned, the expected result and eventually a description of the problem encountered. He also has to state on the severity of the demand. The severity can in fact be evaluated on a scale, for example from 1 to 4, thanks to the question "how will operate the system if this engineering action is not performed?". To customize this engineering actions management system to specific companies' needs, the EA can also be flagged by the creator, according to the flags available to him. When this definition stage is performed, the creator assigns the created EA to a specific person or to a domain leader if he does not know who will be in charge of it. The domain leader reads the description and, again, assigns the EA to a member of his team. During all this time, the EA's status is "Opened – Under analysis". When an engineer or a designer considers that he can play a role in the EA resolution, he changes the EA's status to "Opened – Under treatment". With the same principle, the designer will change the EA's status according to the job performed: "Opened – Solution found", "Opened – Solution in progress", "Opened – Test in progress". If he is the only actor concerned by the work to be performed, he will then deliver his modifications into the data management system and change the EA's status to "Closed – corrected". Otherwise, he could also assign the EA to another designer to perform other tasks on the same EA.

This kind of scenario could be really helpful for multi-discipline integration purpose. For example, if a mechanical part has to be modified to thermally insulate a new electronic device, a unique EA can be created. This EA is first assigned to the mechanical designer who defines a bounding box for the electronic card before transferring the EA to the electronic designer. This one design the card and transfer back the EA to the mechanical designer, specifying during the transfer the maximum temperature to respect. Finally, the mechanical designer modifies the part accordingly and closes the EA.

As showed above, this engineering actions management system differs from Product Data Management (PDM) project management modules in particular because activities are much more dynamic. When, in PDM, an activity is assigned to a person manually or because a workflow has been triggered, an EA is created by a specific person, assigned to a designer that can decide to work on the EA or to transfer it.

In this section, the EA has been described and briefly compared to traditional PDM activities management system. In the next section, the EA management system benefits for agile design methods will be presented.

Engineering Action's Management System to Support Agile Design Methods
Beyond the fact that EA allow to manage trans-disciplines activities, it also provides useful indicators on the project progress, the project maturity, the burden of the teams, etc. Project progress can be measured thanks to the number of EA representing the required functionalities still opened. For the project maturity, the EA representing the unsolved problems can be sumed up in order to determine whether the system is converging, e.g. the number of EA flagged "regression" decreases, or not. The burden of a team can be calculated thanks to the backlog of each team members, i.e. the opened EA affected to each team member.

All these calculated indicators, based on the raw indicators coming from the EA management system, are considered as a great support to decision makings. Quick review, daily meeting, executive review, standup meetings are the different terms used in the agile methods community to speak about these meetings where new priorities are defined, problems are shared, and information about one project or about the different running projects is exchanged.

In this section, the benefits of EA management system for agile design methods usage have been pointed out. This system mainly provides indicators to support decisions makings in a multi-disciplines integration purpose. In the next section, this multi-disciplines integration will still be focused thanks to simplified data exchange.

4.2 Data Exchange and Collaboration through Workspaces

The interest of a multi-disciplinary data management system has often been underlined [16]. But most of the authors continue to imagine a platform with a common interface addressing specific domain data management system, especially for hardware and software parts. Some other initiatives present the perspectives a full integrated platform [10] [17]. Whatever the solution, the workspace (WS) concept is a way of collaborating in a global environment. A WS is a set of Configuration Items (CI) with a specific version associated to each CI. A CI can be a document, an article depending on the domain involved and on the solution adopted. The only prerequisite on the nature of the CI is just that the CI has to be manageable in a version control system. For example, in the software engineering domain, a CI can be a source code file, a portion of this source code, an object class of this source code, etc. In the mechanical domain, a CI can be a parameter, a feature, a part, a product, an assembly or a set of these data.

The need for WS is linked to the fact that the design of a system generates a huge amount of data. In fact, engineers/designers are focused and interested by a subset of these data. WS allow them to be temporally insulated to be able to work on one or several engineering actions in a specific context. Insulation does not mean that they are not working under the control of the data management system. They are just not affected by the changes that can occur due to other engineering actions.

One of the major characteristic of the WS is that they have a tree structure (Fig. 6) and a "son WS" can only be composed of CI that are parts of the "parent WS".

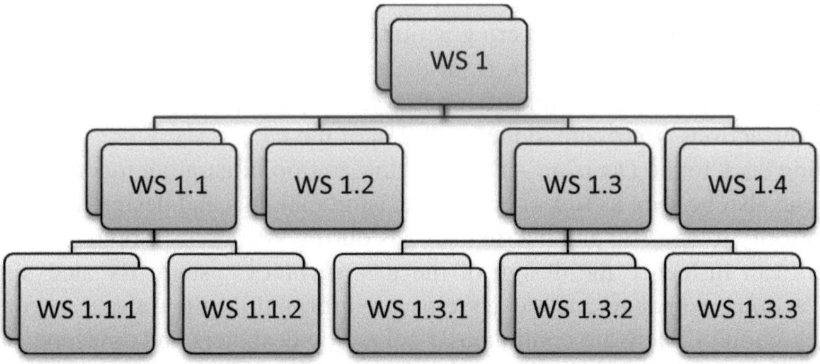

Fig. 6. Workspaces organized with a tree structure

Only workspaces located at the ends of branches are owned by the designers. The other workspaces are integration workspaces. In software engineering, in which automating testing is possible, automated or manual tests are performed in such integration workspaces.

The modifications performed by designers into their workspaces to realize an engineering action remain private until he decides to promote his modification to the parent workspace. In contrary, the fact of taking into consideration the modification performed by others from the parent workspace is called synchronization. So, the normal data exchange between two child workspaces is series of promotions followed by series synchronizations. For example, on Fig. 6 a specific version delivered in WS 1.1.1 will reach WS 1.3.2 after passing through WS 1.1, WS 1 and WS 1.3. Some other direct exchange mechanisms could also be used.

There are multiple advantages to the usage of this system in a mechatronics system design context. First, the same workspace can be composed of CI coming from different domains. For example, if a change is required on an electronic card due to a supplier change, an engineering action is created by the project leader. The electronic designer changes the layout of the device and writes a note directly in the source code to modify before transferring the engineering action to the developer. Impacts are then easier to manage. Another advantage is the fact that the same CI in different versions can exist at the same time, allowing the designers to be focused on their engineering action and to be able to delay the merging action [18].

4.3 Engineering Actions and Workspaces: A Way to Link Design and Decision Information

In the two previous sections, engineering actions management system and collaboration workspaces have been presented. They have been respectively pointed out as decision support system and data integration enabler. In order to provide a fully integrated framework, a link has to be provided between both functionalities. This connection is described in this section.

In fact, when a designer promotes his modification to the parent workspace, it is for a specific reason, described by one or several engineering actions. This means that during the promotion, the engineering action identifier has to be provided. With this information, it is possible to track from the engineering actions management system the impacted CI and their versions. In contrary, from a CI, it is possible to track which engineering actions contribute to the evolution of the CI.

Coming back to the Decision – Design – Integration illustrating model, engineering actions can also be seen as links between decision makings and design data. By giving higher priority to specific engineering actions during short design reviews, the project managers can influence the design of the mechatronics system. By analysing engineering actions exchange and tickets closure information, they also can control the way integration problem are continuously solved by designers and developers.

Fig. 7 illustrates how engineering actions can influence the curvature of the graph. On this figure, the points correspond to short design reviews, e.g. daily reviews, and engineering actions are represented thanks to labels.

In this section, a framework based on engineering actions management system and collaboration workspaces has been proposed as a support to apply agile design methods in the mechatronics system design context. This framework shall provide a great number of indicators to project leaders, but also to share more information about systems data, especially in order to improve multi-disciplinary for mechatronics system design.

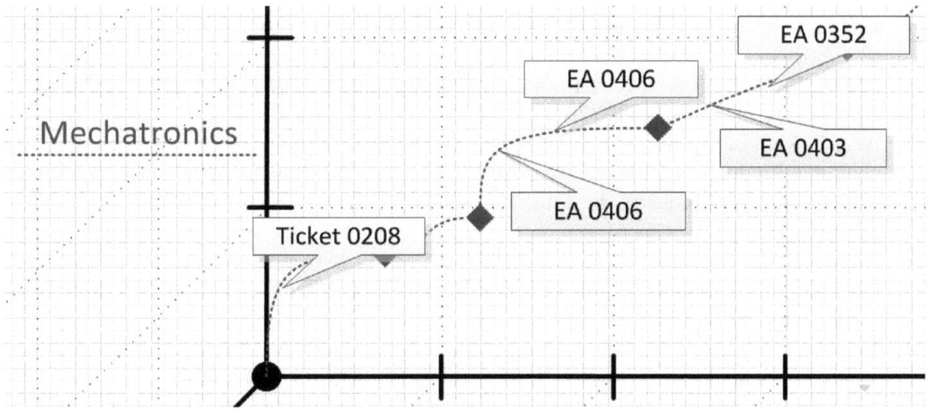

Fig. 7. Decision – Design - Integration model illustrating the tickets' role on mechatronics system integration

5 Conclusion

To design mechatronics systems, a unified, up-to-date and dynamic referential has to be provided to the project actors. The main role of this system, which could be a PLM system, is to federate design data and to assist multiple-disciplinary integration. But it could also be a support for new managing methods like agility design methods.

In this paper, a model to illustrate the benefits of agile design methods in term of multi-disciplinary integration has been suggested. A framework based on engineering actions management and collaborative workspaces to support decision processes has also been envisioned. This framework has been shortly described and future work will be focused on further framework description, its implementation and illustration on a case study in order to evaluate this proposition.

References

1. Sommerville, I.: Software Engineering, 9th edn., March 13. Addison Wesley, New York (2010)
2. Isermann, R.: Mechatronics design approach. In: The Mechatronics Handbook, pp. 2–3. CRC Press (2007)
3. Tomiyama, T., D'Amelio, V., Urbanic, J., ElMaraghy, W.: Complexity of Multi-Disciplinary Design. CIRP Annals - Manufacturing Technology 56, 185–188 (2007)
4. Matthews, P., Lomas, C., Armoutis, N.D., Maropoulos, P.G.: Foundations of an agile design methodology. International Journal of Agile Manufacturing 9, 29–38 (2006)
5. Penas, O., Plateaux, R., Choley, J.-Y., Rivière, A.: The different complex-ity levels in mechatronics design process. In: 3rd International Conference on Software, Knowledge, Information Management and Applications - SKIMA. Fes (2009)
6. Noël, F., Roucoules, L.: The PPO design model with respect to digital en-terprise technologies among product life cycle. International Journal of Computer Integrated Manufacturing 21, 139–145 (2008)

7. Beitz, W., Pahl, G., Wallace, K.: Engineering design: A systematic approach. Springer (2003)
8. Shetty, D., Kolk, R.A.: Mechatronics System Design. In: Shortt, C.M. (ed.) Mechatronics System Design: SI, pp. 1–40 (2010)
9. Aca, J., Ramos, M., Serrano, J.L., Ahuett, H., Molina, A.: Concurrent Engineering of Mechatronic Products in Virtual Enterprises: Selection and Deployment of a PLM System for the Machine Tool Industry. In: Luo, Y. (ed.) CDVE 2006. LNCS, vol. 4101, pp. 318–326. Springer, Heidelberg (2006)
10. Bricogne, M., Troussier, N., Rivest, L., Eynard, B.: PLM perspectives in mechatronics systems design. In: Advances in Production Management Systems, APMS 2010, Cernobbio, Como, Italy, pp. 1–8 (2010)
11. Kettunen, P., Laanti, M.: Combining agile software projects and large-scale organizational agility. Software Process: Improvement and Practice 13, 183–193 (2008)
12. Lindvall, M., Muthig, D., Dagnino, A., Wallin, C., Stupperich, M., Kiefer, D., May, J., Kahkonen, T.: Agile software development in large organizations. Computer 37, 26–34 (2004)
13. Sutherland, J., Viktorov, A., Blount, J., Puntikov, N.: Distributed Scrum: Agile Project Management with Outsourced Development Teams. In: 40th Annual Hawaii International Conference on System Sciences (HICSS 2007), pp. 274a–284a. IEEE (2007)
14. Smits, H., Pshigoda, G.: Implementing Scrum in a Distributed Software Development Organization. In: AGILE 2007, pp. 371–375. IEEE (2007)
15. Abrahamsson, P., Warsta, J., Siponen, M.T., Ronkainen, J.: New directions on agile methods: A comparative analysis. In: Proceedings of 25th International Conference on Software Engineering, pp. 244–254. IEEE (2003)
16. El-Khoury, J., Redell, O., Torngren, M.: A tool integration platform for multi-disciplinary development. In: 31st EUROMICRO Conference on Software Engineering and Advanced Applications, pp. 442–449. IEEE (2005)
17. Do, N., Chae, G.: A Product Data Management architecture for integrating hardware and software development. Computers in Industry 62, 854–863 (2011)
18. Bricogne, M., Rivest, L., Troussier, N., Eynard, B.: Towards PLM for mechatronics system design using concurrent software versioning principles. In: Rivest, L., Bouras, A., Louhichi, B. (eds.) PLM 2012. IFIP AICT, vol. 388, pp. 339–348. Springer, Heidelberg (2012)

Integrating User to Minimize Assembly Path Planning Time in PLM

Yu Yan, Emilie Poirson, and Fouad Bennis

LUNAM Université, IRCCYN, Ecole Centrale de Nantes, France
Yu.Yan@irccyn.ec-nantes.fr

Abstract. Assembly and disassembly verification plays an important role in Product Lifecycle Management (PLM). Mass customization and personalized production require greater agility of industrial manufacturers, and consequently the time consumed in assembly processes (which often dominates costs) is of growing importance. Narrow passages which commonly exist in assembly tasks become a bottleneck in the assembly planning process reducing the time saved by using virtual assembly. In this paper, we present a novel interactive motion planning methodology for virtual assembly and disassembly operations. In our method, user's manipulation with force feedback device in difficult scenario is liberated by relaxing collision constraints. The rough path is retracted by our random retraction method and then connected by BiRRT algorithm. For each user's operation, a path successfully passing through the narrow passage is presented, or geometrical interference information in failed case is provided for motion re-planning and design modification. Significant improvement for trajectory planning of non-convex object is observed in challenging 2D scenarios with narrow passages.

Keywords: path planning, virtual reality tools, assembly, manipulation, perception assessment.

1 Introduction

Path planning in assembly and disassembly has significant influence on many processes in product lifecycle from virtual assembly for design verification [1] to parts removal for maintainability studies [2] and robot assembly for automatic production [3], shown as Fig. 1. Assembly is capstone process in manufacturing and one of the most cost effective approaches to high production flexibility [4]. In recent decades, virtual prototyping is already widely applied in industry to lower the cost of production and shorten the production cycle time. The virtual assembly based on 3D CAD model can make the designer intuitively verify the assembly or disassembly operations. However, due to disappearance of some perceptions and shortage of human-computer interaction technology, the virtual assembly presents new challenges to the designers as well [5]. Some of the manual manipulation of 3D object in complex virtual environment is extremely difficult [1].

A. Bernard, L. Rivest, and D. Dutta (Eds.): PLM 2013, IFIP AICT 409, pp. 471–480, 2013.

Defining the assembly process as a precise description of how to move the target part gradually from its initial location to the goal location while never touching the obstacles, sampling based motion planning algorithm search a discrete path with connectivity in part's configuration space. Among this category of algorithm, Rapidly Exploring Random Trees (RRTs) have been successfully used to solve high level degree of freedom motion planning problems [6]. However, narrow passages which commonly exist in assembly tasks become a bottleneck restricting time reduction of assembly process in PLM. Despite that different heuristics have been created to improve the performance of automatic algorithms, narrow passages are still major issue for sampling based method.

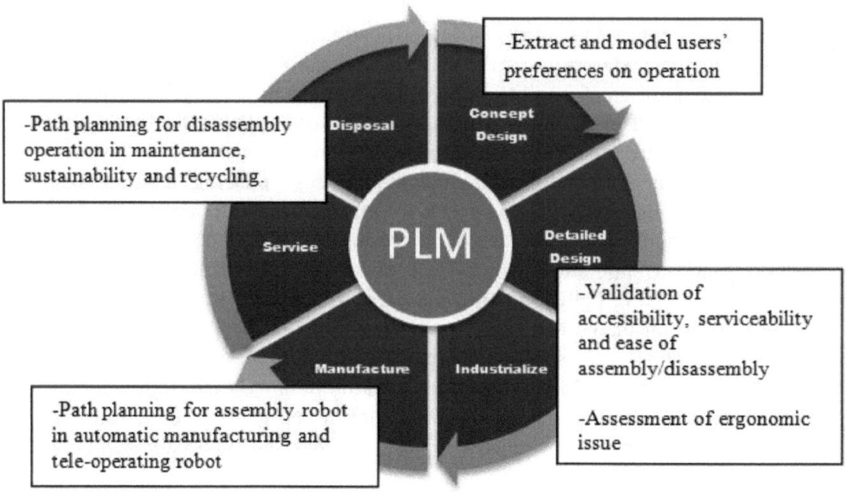

Fig. 1. Path planning for assembly/disassembly applied in product lifecycle

In contrast, humans have the abilities to globally plan motion in complex environment. Based on experience and perception to 3D environment, humans can make fast judgments and response. The skills human lack is accurate computation on geometry. Humans and computer may both encounter trouble in narrow passages. However, when relaxing collision constraints, it's easier for humans to find a solution.

Moreover, the PLM process impulses on information sharing with all the internal and external actors of companies [7]. However, the automatic algorithms cannot fulfill the gap between users, designers and assembly experts. For example, the designers have to take into account the emotion and perception evaluation of user in maintenance study. At present time, it's difficult to model humans' preferences and perceptions in assembly process, even with semantics description. In [8], authors indicated that the closed-loop PLM is more valuable when the interaction is direct between the company and the end user of product. Therefore integration of user into planning process is essential.

In this paper, we present a new interactive frame. Combined with human manipulation, retraction and RRT planners, we allow users guide the computer in difficult scenarios. Human's participations can accelerate the algorithm as well as make final path in compliance with users' operating preferences. And in reverse, the interaction process can indirectly extract the experience knowledge from assembly experts and operational preferences of end users.

The paper is organized as follows: in section 2, we provide a brief survey of related work in interactive planning. In section 3, we descript the interactive loop which integrates human manipulation, our random retraction method and BiRRT planner. Simulation results are presented and analyzed in section 4. Section 5 is dedicated to an outlook on future work and the conclusion.

2 Related Work

User's participations in motion planning process emerge in different prior works. Algorithm in [9] allow users specify some critical via configurations or sub-goals in workspace visually with haptic devices to accelerate the exploration of sampling based algorithm. However, in practical implementation, via configurations in tightly clustered environment is unlikely to be found by human.

A preliminary workspace discretization is done based on decomposition algorithm, and then a corridor between initial configuration and goal configuration is found. Harmonic functions are formulated to provide force feedback, or sampling based method explores this corridor to find a feasible path [10].

Method proposed by [11] is successfully applied to interactive motion planning for steerable needles, but difficult for non-convex assembly object. Although method proposed in [12] simultaneously allows cooperation between user and algorithm, it's still unable to tackle the situations when user and algorithm both get into trap.

As far as we observed, the existing work can neither apply to highly complex packaging scenarios in mechanical industry nor drive design for assembly processes. The proposed method integrates user to significantly reduce the assembly path planning time in different phases of product lifecycle. Based on the feedback of geometric interference information and ease of operation for inexperienced users, our method strengthens the information flow between user, designer and assembly expert.

3 Interactive Motion Planning Process

3.1 Approach Overview

The global view of our interactive assembly motion planning framework is presented in Fig. 2. The more detailed description of process is presented in Fig. 3. The path marked green is user manipulated path. This rough path is then retracted to produce seeds (marked blue) on C-contact space by our Random Retraction Method. BiRRT algorithm explores between every neighboring two seeds to find a connecting path. The algorithm either finds a solution from q_1 to q_8 shown as Fig. 3 (a), or return the nearest configuration pair (marked red) shown as Fig. 3 (b).

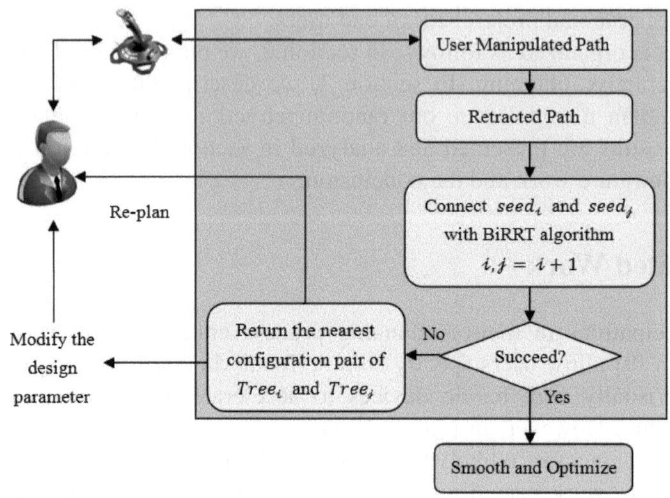

Fig. 2. Interactive motion planning process

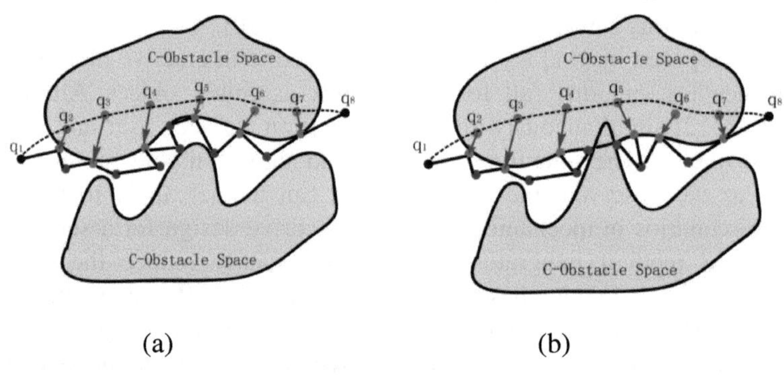

Fig. 3. Interactive planning in successful case and failed case

3.2 User Manipulation

Based on the fact that user can effectively finish the assembly task in a loose space, we firstly allow user manipulate mechanical parts with some penetration into obstacles. In this manner, user will quickly find a rough path with some configurations in-collision and close to the boundary of C-obstacle space. At the same time, the rough path satisfies user's operating habits and preference. In this process, users can choose any kind of interactive devices, no matter using cheap haptic devices or expensive movement tracking system. Moreover, we take a strategy that raise the sampling rate during capture of the human assembly process when user's operations encounter collisions more frequently and decrease it in opposite situation. This strategy will increase computational efficiency as well as guarantee a perfect description for human's operations in narrow passages.

```
Algorithm: Random Retraction Method (RRM)
  input: Path J(q1,…,qi,…,qn), Obstacles;
  for all i do
    if collision(qi) = true then
      PD = Penetration_Depth(qi,Obstacles);
      *[SLT,SLR] = initial();
      while PD > threshold(PD) do
        Drandom = Random_direction(SLT, SLR);
        qnew = Move(qi,Drandom);
        PDnew = Penetration_Depth(qnew, Obstacles);
        if PDnew < PD then
          qi = qnew;
          (SLT,SLR,PD) = (SLT*2,SLR*2,PDnew);
        else
          qnew = Move(qi,~Drandom);
          PDnew = Penetration_Depth(qnew,Obstacles);
          if PDnew < PD then
            qi = qnew;
            (SLT,SLR,PD) = (SLT*2,SLR*2,PDnew);
          else
            (SLT,SLR) = (SLT / 2,SLR / 2);
          end if
        end if
      end while
    end if
  end for
J = Smooth(J)
end
```

* SL_T Translation step length, SL_R Rotation step length.

3.3 Random Retraction Method

Due to the high computational complexity of global penetration depth, retraction based planners use simple heuristics to explore C-contact space [13]. For example, the algorithm starts from a rough solution and iteratively refines it through shrinking the obstacles and relaxing the collision constraints [1]. Algorithm proposed by [14] allows users generate path by shrinking the object, then improve user-generated path by pushing the in-collision configuration directly to collision-free.

Through defining certain types of distance metric on configuration space, retraction process can be formulated as an optimization problem. In [15], authors use geometric method simulating optimization to get the nearest collision-free configurations in

C-contact space. As the boundary of feasible solution region is the C-contact space, and the computation of C-contact space is too complex at present time. Conventional optimization algorithms are either impossible to implement or time-consuming. We provide a randomly retracting method which is based on penetration depth. Compared to pattern search optimization algorithm which uses mesh at each iteration to search a descent direction, our randomly retracting method uses random direction at each step which makes penetration depth value decrease. We also enlarge the step-length when search is successful and reduce it when search is failed. Variable step-length can effectively overcome burdensome computation of penetration depth. Our method will find a solution which is on C-contact space and near to the optimal one.

3.4 Seeds Connection

After retraction, the user manipulated path is transformed into seeds which consist of some collision-free configurations and some configurations on C-contact space. The following process is similar to multi-tree RRT. We use BiRRT algorithm [6] to connect every neighboring two seeds. Since the neighboring two seeds are close to each other, it's pretty easy for BiRRT planner to find a path between them. In case of that motion planner fails to find a solution within a limited time, we return the nearest configuration-pair in workspace. The interference information is easy to obtain through contact between the configuration-pair and obstacles. The user can make movement adjustments or modify the design size of parts according to the information.

4 Implementation and Results

The following section describes how our interactive system works for the motion planning of a non-convex part passing through a narrow passage. We also demonstrate that the interaction with user equipped by a force feedback joystick can greatly decrease the search space.

All the experiments are performed in the software platform Matlab and on a PC Dual Core, 2.4 GHz and 2 GB ram.

4.1 User Manipulation

In implementation, user manipulates the part in 2D environment with Logitech Force 3D Pro force feedback joystick. The moving object is allowed to have limited penetration into obstacles, which means that the maximum penetration is set by user and any part of the moving object is forbidden to penetrate through the obstacle. And we allow moving object have large penetration into obstacle, but only have collision with one obstacle at the same moment. User can decide the beginning and end of the motion recording time.

Collision check is realized by detecting the intersected edges between two polygons. Penetration depth is realized by calculating the area of overlap region between two polygons.

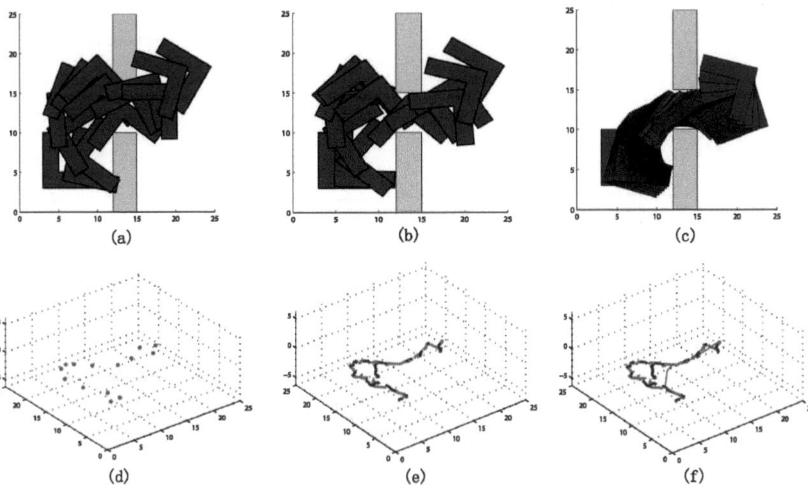

Fig. 4. Successful case for an L shape part passing through a narrow passage

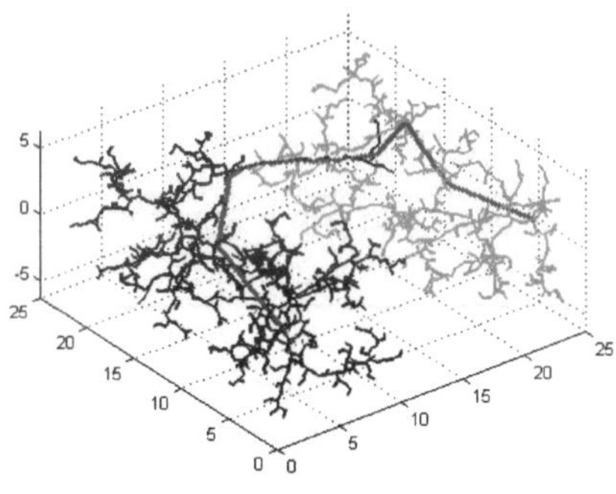

Fig. 5. Exploration trace of basic BiRRT

4.2 Results

In the situation of Fig. 4, user has to manipulate an L shape part passing through a hole of a wall in 2D environment. The moving part has three degrees of freedom. In this case, the hole is narrow enough that the planning with strict collision detection is time-consuming for both user and basic BiRRT planner. By relaxing the collision, user can quickly manipulate the part pass through the hole, as shown at Fig. 4(a). This rough path manipulated by user is then retracted as shown at Fig. 4(b) and corresponding path in configuration space shown at Fig. 4(d). As the number of configuration recorded for retraction is small, the retraction process doesn't require much time. From every neighboring two configurations of retracted path, two trees (marked green and blue) are grown by BiRRT algorithm to connect each other, as shown at Fig. 4(e).

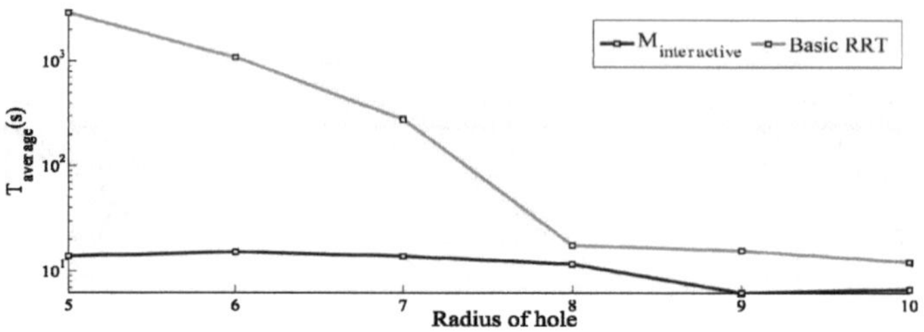

Fig. 6. Comparison between basic BiRRT and our interactive process

Table 1. Comparison between basic BiRRT and our interactive process in case of radius = 5

	$T_{all}(s)$	$T_C(s)$	$T_R(s)$	$T_S(s)$	Num_{node}	Num_R
Basic BiRRT	111.253	109.87	N/A	1.383	354	N/A
M-interactive	13.023	9.1900	1.239	2.594	93	5

$T_C = T_{Connection}, T_R = T_{Retraction}, T_S = T_{Smooth}, Num_{node} = Num_{searched}, Num_R = Num_{Retraction}$

Table 2. Comparison between basic BiRRT and our interactive process in case of different radius

	Mean					
Hole Radius	5	6	7	8	9	10
Basic BiRRT: $T(s)$	>2,901	>1,090	280.397	17.735	15.838	12.268
M-interactive: $T(s)$	13.91	15.314	13.965	11.676	6.291	6.771

A path successfully passing through the hole is found quickly by our interaction method shown at Fig. 4 (c) (f). In reason that our retraction process provides guidance to exploration of BiRRT, the number of visited configurations and tree search time of BiRRT algorithm are greatly reduced, as shown in Table 1. This result can be observed intuitively through comparison between the exploration trace of basic BiRRT algorithm in Fig. 5 and our interactive process in Fig. 4. From Table 1, we can also find how fast the random retraction process is, which only takes 1.239 seconds for 5 times retraction. We also make the comparison in cases of different radius of hole. For each radius of hole, we run both of the algorithms 5 times respectively, and take the average time. The results are demonstrated in Table 2 and Fig. 6. In challenging situation when the radius of hole is 5, the basic BiRRT will spend more than one hour to find a feasible solution. While in opposite, our method runs about 10 seconds. Moreover, in easy situations, our method also needs less time for planning. Through comparison, our interaction method appears more robust and efficient in planning motion of non-convex part in narrow passage.

In Fig. 7, the hole is designed too small for the part to pass through. However, intuitively detecting the infeasibility is difficult for user in advance of planning. In condition of relaxed collision, user can manipulate the part passing through the hole shown as Fig. 7 (b). After retraction process (shown as Fig. 7 (c) (d)) and connection process (shown as Fig. 7 (e)) of our method, the nearest configurations respectively locating at entrance and exit of the narrow hole can be returned to user, shown as Fig. 7 (f). As a result, the designer can understand the size limitations of accessibility for a product design.

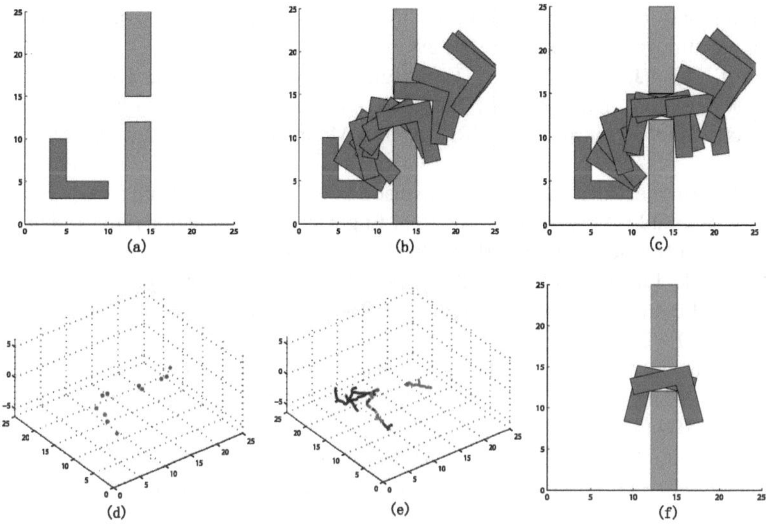

Fig. 7. Failed case for an L shape part passing through a narrow passage

5 Conclusion and Future Work

In this paper, we present an interactive path planning framework for assembly/disassembly process of PLM. Based on randomly retracting method, our method can make user and automatic planner efficiently work together to overcome narrow passages with very tight tolerances. Planning time for assembly task can be greatly reduced. Moreover, our method provides visualized geometric interference information feedback to designer, thereby facilitating designer's understanding to change and shortening design cycle time. As the generated paths comply with user's operating habits and preferences, some ergonomic issues can be quickly checked at early phase.

In future work, we will implement our interaction method in industrial cases within virtual environment. It is possible to implement different interactive device for user in virtual world such as 6dof haptic devices or motion tracking system. It is also necessary for us to make a choice on different penetration depth algorithms that can be applied to our retraction method. Although our system performs perfectly in 2D environment, it still faces some challenging issues in 3D, which includes providing deeper insights on measuring human perception in virtual assembly and facilitating user understand environment from feedback.

References

1. Ferré, E., Laumond, J.P., Arechavaleta, G., Estevès, C.: Progresses in Assembly Path Planning. In: International Conference on Product Lifecycle Management, PLM 2005, Lyon, France, pp. 373–382 (2005)
2. Santochi, M., Dini, G., Failli, F.: Computer Aided Disassembly Planning State of the Art and Perspectives. Journal of CIRP Annals-Manufacturing Technology 51(2), 507–529 (2002)
3. Kohrt, C., Stamp, R., Pipe, A.G., Kiely, J., Schiedermeier, G.: An Online Robot Trajectory Planning and Programming Support System for Industrial. Journal of Robotics and Computer-Integrated Manufacturing 29(1), 71–79 (2013)
4. Hu, S.J., Ko, J., Weyand, L., Elmaraghy, H.A., Lien, T.K., Koren, Y., Bley, H., Chryssolouris, G., Nasr, N., Shpitalni, G.: Assembly System Design and Operations for Product Variety. Journal of CIRP Annals-Manufacturing Technology 60(2), 715–733 (2011)
5. Lim, T., Ritchie, J.M., Sung, R., Kosmadoudi, Z., Liu, Y., Thin, A.G.: Haptic Virtual Reality Assembly–Moving Towards Real Engineering Applications. In: Zadeh, M.H. (ed.) Advances in Haptics. InTech (2010), doi:10.5772/8695
6. Kuffner, J.J., LaValle, S.M.: RRT-connect: An Efficient Approach to Single-Query Path Planning. In: International Conference on Robotics and Automation, ICRA 2000, vol. 2, pp. 995–1001 (2000)
7. Le Duigou, J., Bernard, A., Perry, N., Delplace, J.C.: A Constraints Driven Product Lifecycle Management Framework. In: 19th CIRP Design Conference-Competitive Design, p. 109 (2009)
8. Le Duigou, J., Bernard, A., Perry, N., Delplace, J.C.: Generic PLM System for SMEs: Application to an Equipment Manufacturer. Jounal of Product Lifecycle Management 6(1), 51–64 (2012)
9. He, X.J., Chen, Y.H.: Haptic-Aided Robot Path Planning Based on Virtual Tele-Operation. Journal of Robotics and Computer-Integrated Manufacturing 25(4-5), 792–803 (2009)
10. Vazquez, C., Rosell, J.: Haptic Guidance Based on Harmonic Functions for the Execution of Tele-operated Assembly Tasks. In: IFAC Workshop on Intelligent Assembly and Disassembly, IAD 2007, pp. 88–93 (2007)
11. Patil, S., Alterovitz, R.: Interactive Motion Planning for Steerable Needles in 3D Environments with Obstacles. In: IEEE RAS/EMBS International Conference on Biomedical Robotics and Biomechatronics, BIOROB 2010, pp. 893–899 (2010)
12. Taïx, M., Flavigné, D., Ferré, E.: Human Interaction with Motion Planning Algorithm. Journal of Intelligent & Robotic Systems 67(3-4), 285–306 (2012)
13. Rosell, J., Vázquez, C., Pérez, A., Iñiguez, P.: Motion Planning for Haptic Guidance. Journal of Intelligent & Robotic Systems 53(3), 223–245 (2008)
14. Bayazit, O.B., Song, G., Amato, N.M.: Enhancing Randomized Motion Planners: Exploring with Haptic Hints. In: International Conference on Robotics and Automation, ICRA 2000, pp. 529–536 (2000)
15. Zhang, L.J., Manocha, D.: An Efficient Retraction-based RRT Planner. In: International Conference on Robotics and Automation, ICRA 2008, pp. 3743–3750 (2008)

New Product Development Process in Fashion Industry: Empirical Investigation within Italian Companies

Elisa Soldani[1], Monica Rossi[2], Romeo Bandinelli[1], and Sergio Terzi[3]

[1] University of Florence, Department of Industrial Engineering, Florence, Italy
[2] Politecnico di Milano, Department of Economics, Management and Industrial Engineering, Milano, Italy
[3] University of Bergamo, Department of Industrial Engineering, Dalmine (BG), Italy
romeo.bandinelli@unifi.it

Abstract. This paper deals with the investigation and identification of the industrial best practices in the areas of knowledge and process management and business organization applied to design process. The results have been achieved through an empirical research carried out by the authors with the support of the Ge.Co. Observatory of Politecnico di Milano, which focus deals with the evaluation of the Product Lifecycle Management (PLM) approach within manufacturing companies. The research has been conducted with the use of a structured questionnaire distributed on a sample of Italian companies belonging to the fashion (apparel, leather and footwear) industry, carried out through face to face inter-views, according to a survey guide. The results of this study have been classified using a maturity model developed inside the Observatory, which aims to categorize these industries according to nine dimensions, grouped into three main areas: Organization, Process and Knowledge Management.

Keywords: Product Lifecycle Management, PLM, Fashion Industry, Maturity Levels.

1 Introduction

The term "fashion" is used both by practitioners and academics to generally indicate an industry which includes several sectors, from textile to clothing, from leather to knitwear, accessories, sunglasses, cosmetics and jewelry. Each of these sectors shows different characteristics and can be further divided into different competitive segments, characterized by company's dimensions, served customers and markets and applied technologies. A widely accepted classification of the fashion market has been proposed by Saviolo and Testa [1]. In their book, they classify the fashion markets using the price and the number of sold unites as variables that differentiate the type of the product, defining five main market segments: *Couture*, *Prêt-à-porter*, *Diffusion*, *Bridge* and *Mass*.

The paper will focus on companies belonging to the *semi-programmed* and *programmed* fashion (apparel/leather/footwear) group, belonging to the first two sectors identified above, the *Couture* and *Prêt-à-porter*, characterized by the

A. Bernard, L. Rivest, and D. Dutta (Eds.): PLM 2013, IFIP AICT 409, pp. 481–490, 2013.

existence of a long period (from 12 to 18 months) between the product design and the delivery of the product itself to the stores. The ability to create successful products calls for an high creativity design phase and high standards in the manufacturing process. Companies belonging to this market, in order to reduce the time to market and to increase products' variety, have to improve their flexibility, without reducing the performances in terms of delivery and quality.

The fashion value chain is a process that starts from the design phase [2][3] and ends with the products delivery process, crossing the textile/leather system, developing a culture based on integration of the supply chain through the use of Information and Communication Technology (ICT).

Considering a PLM approach, in such a system the design tools are integrated on one side with CAM tools, in order to realize prototypes, and on the other hand with CPDM (Collaborative Product Development and Management) systems, sharing drawings and technical specification of the product. 2D and 3D CAD systems are used in order to support the products engineering and the modeling. CAD systems are able to specify products' models, colors, shapes, material and many other information.

The evolution of ICTs in this area can cope with these complexities by offering software applications, including PLM. It is important to remark that markets in general, and the fashion industry in the specific, are increasingly characterized by external factors that impact directly on business. Among the most important it is possible to find quality, product complexity, the reduction of the Time to Market (TTM), etc.. As a consequence, companies know that the main critical success factors are the improvement of product quality, decreasing costs and reducing time to market. It is for this reason that the benefits of an investment, to be useful and possibly generate a profit should belong to at least one of the critical success factors. As well known, a PLM initiative has the potential to impact on all three factors required by the market.

At the same time, the companies themselves should be aware however that the PLM is an investment, that implies immediate costs and benefits which would be developed in the future. As an investment, it is necessary to justify costs that have to be supported in order to achieve the desired results. For this reason is very important to better manage the organization's PLM implementation by identifying in advance the costs and benefits. It is also important to carefully assess the scope of the project, the impact of the solution as well as about the usability of PLM itself. The results of the project derive from the definition of clear and incremental deliveries, but also realistic expectations, and involvement from the early stages, all the actors who participate in the processes involved in the PLM, and last, but not least, the identification of possible resistance to change trying to understand the reasons behind them [2].

2 Methodology and Research Question

The research question behind of this paper deals with the investigation and the identification of industrial best practices in the areas of knowledge management, process management and business organization applied to design process in the fashion Industry.

In order to achieve this result, the research has been conducted using the case studies analysis within a sample of Italian manufacturing companies belonging to the fashion Industry. Case studies have been carried out through face to face interviews, supported by a survey guide. Hereafter the questionnaire is described together with the CLIMB maturity model adopted and the variables used to describe and evaluate companies. A more comprehensive description of the CLIMB model and the methodological approach is reported in Rossi et al. [4].

2.1 The Questionnaire

As previously anticipated, the data has been collected using the case studies methodology, according to a reference framework structured in nine areas, grouped into three parts: *Organization*, *Process* and *Knowledge Management*.

The first area (*Organization*) concerns with the analysis of the behavior of people involved in daily company's activities, the second one (the *Process* perspective) investigates how NPD is performed and the third one focus on the dynamics related to the creation, sharing, representation and re-use of tacit and explicit knowledge.

These three macro-areas have been further divided into sub-areas (respectively 3, 4, and 2), defining a total of nine areas of interest, as reported in Table 1.

Table 1. Questionnaire structure

Macro Area	Area	Questions
Organization	Work Organization	1-5
	Roles and Coordination	6-9
	Skills and Competence	10-12
Process	Process Management	13-16
	Activities and Value	17-20
	Decision Making Factors	21-24
	Methods	25
Knowledge Management	Formalization	26-30
	Computerization	31-33

2.2 Analyzed Variables

In order to define the maturity of the NPD process, nine variables have been analyzed, each one corresponding to a specific section of the questionnaire:

- *Work Organization* refers to the distribution of the work between the various designers and to the task structure (innovative or routinely);
- *Roles and Coordination* analyzes the cooperation between designers, the definition of their task, the relationship with the project manager and the ability to interact with each other;

- *Skills and Competence* is the ability of company to support training and building capacity;
- *Process Management* represents the capability to lead the NPD process to the planned objectives andto evaluate possible deviations (using KPIs);
- *Activities and Value* aims to define the customer product value, how and by whom it is defined and how it is integrated into the NPD process;
- *Decision Making Factors* evaluates which elements can be considered the most important for the firm's competitiveness. They also deals with the relationship between the decision taken at the design stage and the entire product lifecycle;
- *Methods* analyzes methods, procedures and production techniques adopted by designers and project managers;
- *Formalization* analyzes how the company manages, shares and preserves the knowledge created in the design process;
- *Computerization* examines the use of software tools and their functionalities;

2.3 CLIMB Maturity Levels

The CLIMB model adopted in this paper originates from the Capability Maturity Model Integration (CMMI) [5] developed by SEI (Software Engineering Institute) in the 1990s for the software industry.

The model presents a set of recommended practices described in a set of key processes, classified in order to enhance the software development and maintenance capability. The model classifies these areas using a five levels scale:

- Initial: chaotic, ad hoc, individual heroics);
- Repeatable: the process is at least documented sufficiently;
- Defined: the process is defined/confirmed as a standard business process;
- Managed: the process is quantitatively managed;
- Optimizing: process management includes process optimization.

In this paper, in order to evaluate all the nine areas described in the previous section, they have been numerically evaluated through a % score given to the related questions. Starting from the CMMI model, five possible *Maturity Levels* have been identified (Figure 1), based on the reached % value, named CLIMB (*Chaos*, *Low*, *Intermediate*, *Mature*, *Best Practice*):

- *Chaos*: the area is usually chaotic and slightly structured;
- *Low*: the area has a simple formalization and it is barely planned and controlled;
- *Intermediate*: the area is structured and planned. Standard solutions are normally applied;
- *Mature*: the area is structured, planned, controlled and measured at its different layers, often through specific quantitative techniques;
- *Best Practice*: the organization reached all the previous stages and the area continuously improves thanks to the analysis of variance of its results. The improvement of NPD performance is reached through incremental and innovative actions.

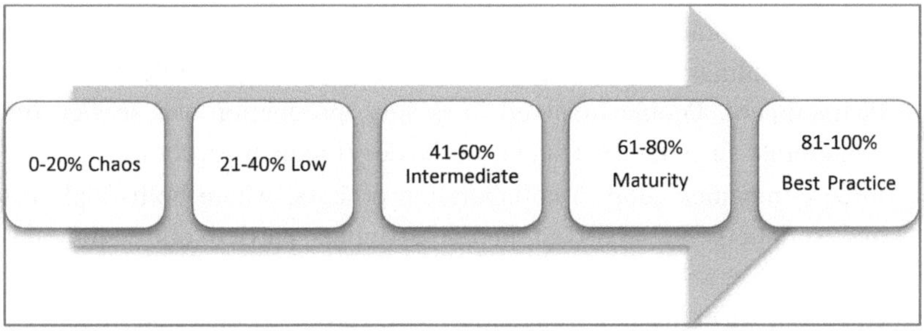

Fig. 1. Maturity level profile

3 The Sample

In this study a sample of seven fashion Italian companies have been analyzed.

Table 2. The sample

ID	Main Product	Employees	Turnover (M€)	Market	Man. Env.
A	Apparel	260	45	National	MTO
B	Apparel	5000	1300	International	ETO
C	Accessories	35	12	International	MTS
D	Apparel	900	100	International	MTO
E	Apparel & Footwear	350	286	International	MTO
F	Apparel & Activeware	200	100	International	MTO
G	Accessories & Footwear	250	150	International	MTO

The sample contains both big than small-medium firms as shown in Table 2.

Only one firm produces exclusively for the Italian national market. The rest of the sample produces for both national than international markets.

The design process takes place internally for all the interviewed companies and is localized into a single physical center. A logic of Global Product Development (GPD) has not been found in any of these industries.

The most used manufacturing environment is the Make to Order (MTO): four of the seven companies produce items starting from a catalog, which is developed twice a year. Taking into consideration the other three companies, one of them produce according to the Make to Stock (MTS) approach while the other one follows the Engineering to Order (ETO) strategy.

Focusing of the NPD process, the results shows that its structure is not uniform within the sample:

- three companies adopt a concurrent engineering process, where a multidisciplinary and multifunctional team is responsible for the product development. People involved in quality, production and service functions collaborate since the first stages of the development process;
- three companies adopt a collaborative process, where both final customers and suppliers are involved in the activities carried out within the NPD process;
- Only one firm have a sequential NPD process: different functions work sequentially, exchanging specifications and review requests.

Finally, all of the companies, except one, have both PDM/PLM and ERP systems.

4 Results

In this section, the results of the investigation on the information collected through the case studies is reported, and a possible answer to the research question is presented. The nine variables were examined and the companies positioned according to the maturity level achieved, derived from the CLIMB model previously defined.

4.1 Maturity Level of the NPD Process

The adoption of the assessment maturity model developed by the Ge.Co. Observatory permitted the representation of the results through the use of radar charts.

The maturity of NPD process in fashion industry is represented in Fig. 2. An observation of the chart shows that none of the companies belonging to this sample represents a best in class firm considering the all manufacturing industry. A first result of this research shows that fashion industry can be classified as intermediate for five variables (*decision making factors*, *methods*, *formalization*, *computerization* and *skills and competences*), while best practices can be identify in three variables (*process management*, *activities and value* and *roles and coordination*).

Because of the small number of companies interviewed, in order to validate the results presented above, the data dispersion and consequently the standard deviation have been calculated. The results are reported in Fig. 3.

The analysis of the Fig. 3 highlight that the standard deviation can be considered low only for few variables. In particular, the results regarding *Methods* and *Skill and Competence* variables cannot be considered reliable (Fig. 4, 7). On the other hand the behavior of the companies in comparison to *Roles and Coordination* and *Computerization* can be considered comparable (Fig. 4, 6).

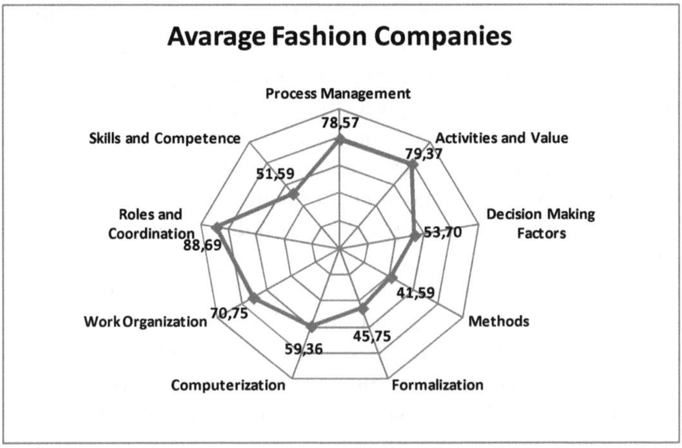

Fig. 2. Representation through a radar chart of the nine variables average score

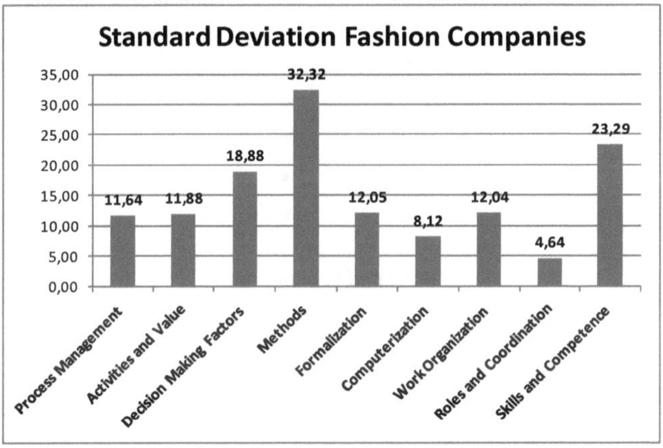

Fig. 3. Representation of the standard deviation of the nine variables

If, on one hand, *roles and coordination* seems to be well organized into fashion companies, on the other hand the research shows that *Methods* and *Formalization* are not evolved.

Focusing of the interpretation of these results, a first understanding shows that within the fashion companies roles and responsibilities are clearly defined. This is probably due the fact that the whole design process is internally performed for the totally of the sample. Moreover the geographical proximity of each actor involved in the design process could lead to the same result.

Considering the macro area Organization, the two variables present different values. The first one (*Work Organization*) (Fig. 4) achieve a *Mature* level (approximately 70%), while the second one (*Skills and Competence*) presents a lower value *(Intermediate)* and a wider data dispersion.

Process Management and *Activities and Value* standard deviation are between *Mature* and *Best Practice* (Fig. 5). Customer product value is clearly defined, starting from a market analysis. At the same time, process management is properly controlled, mainly with the use of time and cost performances indicators.

The last macro area of the questionnaire deals with the Knowledge Management topics. Within this macro area are included the variables *Formalization* and *Computerization* (Fig. 6), where fashion companies perform an Intermediate level, although all the companies belonging to the sample, except one, has adopted CAD software, PDM/PLM and ERP systems.

The low score obtained in the Formalization area can be explained by the fact that, even if PDM/PLM solution have been introduced, the exchange of information among these software is still not structured. Knowledge management tools and formal rules have not be implemented within the companies and in some cases the advantages of a full implementation of a PLM approach are not considered both a priority neither a competitive advantage for the management.

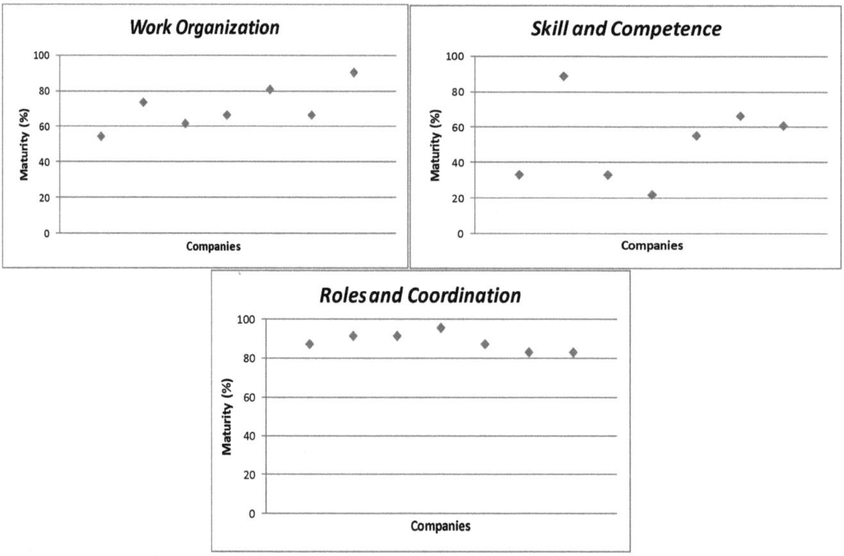

Fig. 4. Standard deviation of Work Organization, Skill and Competence and Roles and Coordination

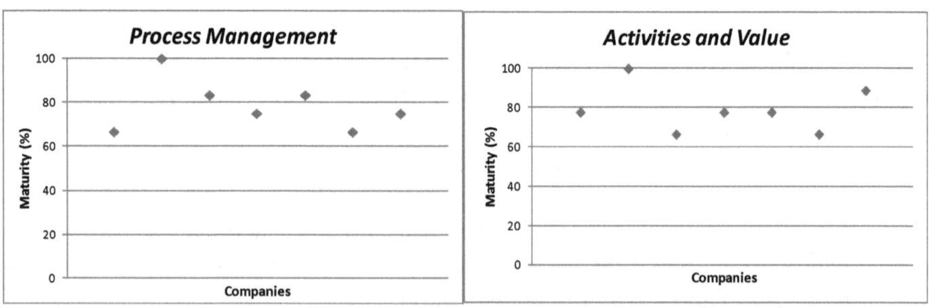

Fig. 5. Standard deviation of Process Management and Activities and Value

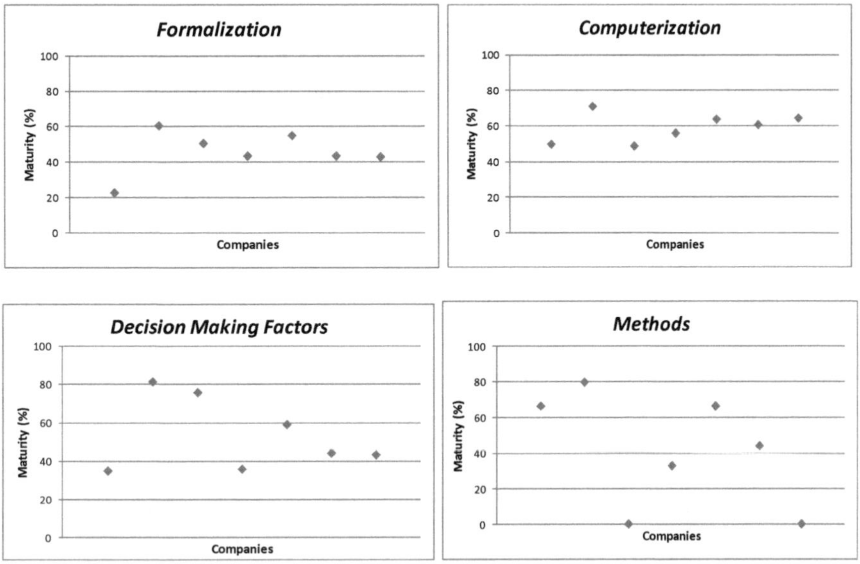

Fig. 6. Standard deviation of Formalization, Computerization, Decision Making Factors and Methods

Finally, referring to the other radar's sections (*Decision Making Factors*, *Methods* and *Skills & Competence) (Fig. 4, 6)*, the high data dispersion highlights different performances among companies.

5 Conclusions

Fashion industry is one of the most important manufacturing sector for the Italian economy. The goal of this paper was to identify and highlight the strengths and weaknesses of the NPD Process of the companies of this industry, classifying the results according to nine dimensions, grouped into three main areas: *Organization*, *Process* and *Knowledge Management.*

The outcomes of this research show that higher level of maturity is achieved in the *Organization* macro area. The majority of the companies achieve an average score which is more than 80% for *Roles and Coordination* (the standard deviation in this area can be considered low, so the behavior can be assumed the same for all the companies of the sample). Moreover, the NPD in the fashion industry is based mainly on the interaction and the exchange of information among several actors of the whole value chain. This means that the roles and responsibilities assignments across the supply chain is a very crucial aspect. Regarding the *Activities and Value*, the average score can be classified as mature: all the actors of the value chain consider the customer and the product value the focus of their activities.

Another important aspect is related to the *process management* and the flexibility of the supply chain, both in terms of independence of the design and engineering divisions than in terms of industrialization.

Last, Fig. 7 represents the average score of the lifecycle orientation of the companies. It is important to highlight that due to the high standard deviation of the obtained result, the data cannot be considered statistically reliable, and a bigger sample of companies should be analyzed.

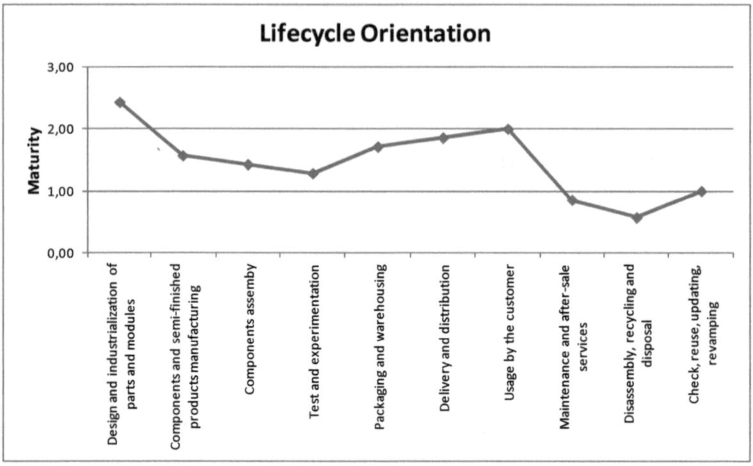

Fig. 7. Lifecycle orientation of the companies of the sample

As a future step of this research, it would be important to understand if these results represent the whole companies belonging to the fashion industry, or if a wider sample of companies could lead to different results. Moreover, a comparison among fashion industry and other manufacturing sectors would be advisable. In this study all the variables have equal weight in the definition of the radar chart. A comparison among different industries could lead to define different weights for different sectors, according to the different markets behavior.

References

1. Saviolo, S., Testa, S.: Le imprese del sistema moda - Il management al servizio della creatività, Etas Libri, Bologna (2005) (in Italian)
2. Bandinelli, R., Terzi, S.: An Exploratory Study on Product Lifecycle Management in the fashion chain – Evidences from the Italian leather luxury industry. In: Choi, T.J. (ed.) Fashion Supply Chain Management: Industry and Business Analysis, pp. 270–285. Tsan-Ming Choi, Hong Kong (2011) ISBN: 9781609607562
3. Bruce, M., Daly, L., Towers, N.: Lean or agile. A solution for supply chain management in the textile and clothing industry. International Journal of Operations and Production Management 24(2), 151–170 (2004)
4. Rossi, M., Terzi, S., Garetti, M.: Proposal of an Assessment Model for New Product Development. In: Emmanouilidis, C., Taisch, M., Kiritsis, D. (eds.) Advances in Production Management Systems. IFIP AICT, vol. 397, pp. 383–390. Springer, Heidelberg (2013)
5. Mark, P., Aulkb, P., Curtis, R., Chrissis, M.: Capability Maturity Model, Version 1.1. Software Engineering Institute (1993)

Cycle Oriented Quality Management at the Interface of Product Development and Production Planning

Jonas Koch, Josef Greitemann, Christian Plehn, and Gunther Reinhart

Institute for Machine Tools and Industrial Management (*iwb*),
Technische Universität München, Munich, Germany

Abstract. During all phases in the product life cycle quality is a key influencing factor. The earlier a high quality level reached during the product lifecycle, the lower the amount of quality deviations, required changes, and the occurrence of non-conformance costs throughout mass production. Already in the prototype phase, an efficient and effective quality control loop is an important enabler for achieving a high level of product quality. This includes a quality process and specified interfaces to product development, production planning and overall quality management. Presenting an approach for the development of such a quality control loop including interfaces to associated processes in product development, production planning and quality management as well as a first examination of affected process parts in production planning is subject of this paper.

Keywords: Product quality, quality control loop, prototype phase, ramp-up, product lifecycle, reconfiguration, manufacturing resources.

1 Introduction

1.1 Quality in Context of the Product Lifecycle

Quality is a key influencing factor on product lifecycles [1] – from the very beginning during the product development phase through the prototype phase, ramp-up (i.e. pre-series, pilot series, run-up) and mass production until product phase out (see fig. 1) [2,3]. As part of the "magic triangle of production" – costs, time and quality – quality represents one of the essential business success criteria for manufacturing companies [4].

Based on the "rule of ten", saying that costs to find and repair defects raise by the factor of ten for each level of completion (e.g. completion of development and design, completion of production planning) reached during engineering and manufacturing of a product [5,6], achieving a sufficient level of product quality in early product lifecycle phases significantly improves the subsequent occurrence of non-conformance costs during later phases such as mass-production. Non-conformance costs arise from e.g. rework due to quality deviations or necessary reconfigurations of the product or the production structure. [7,8]

Within the product lifecycle, one major phase before the start of production (SOP) is the so-called prototype phase, the direct precursor of the production ramp-up.

A. Bernard, L. Rivest, and D. Dutta (Eds.): PLM 2013, IFIP AICT 409, pp. 491–499, 2013.

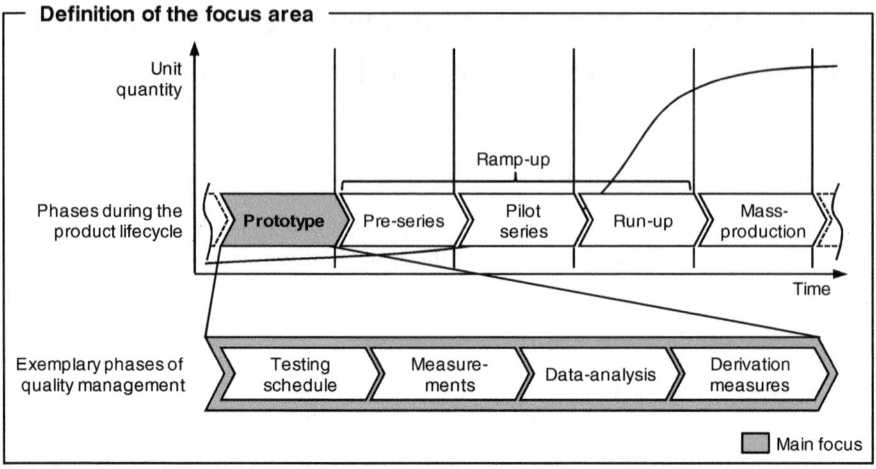

Fig. 1. Definition of the focus area [cf. 2,3]

The prototype phase is characterized by low production volumes, utilization of pre-series manufacturing resources and evaluation of process capabilities for product assembly [9]. The process capabilities are usually enhanced during the prototype phase to achieve higher levels of quality, lead time and costs which are close to those required during mass production. Comparable to the more general stage-gate-process [10], achievement of these levels marks the readiness to shift from the prototype phase to the production ramp-up phase from a manufacturing point of view [cf. 3].

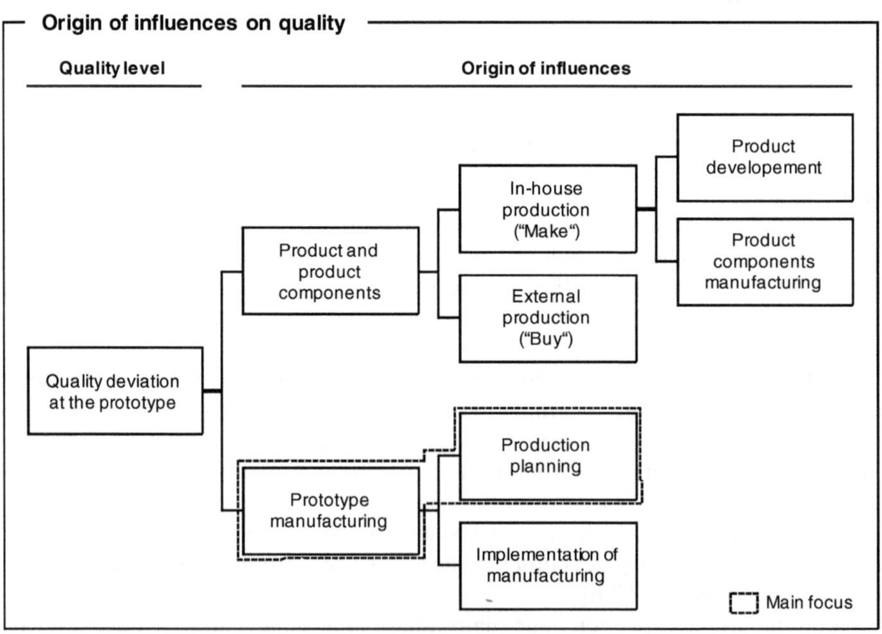

Fig. 2. Causes for quality deviations

1.2 Determination of Quality During Prototype Phase

The prototype's quality level is determined by influences related to both, product and product components as well as manufacturing, covering production structure, manufacturing resources, processes and configurations (see fig. 2) [11-13].

Product and Product Components. Influences related to product and product components result from e.g. product specifications or the quality of supplier parts. In case of product specifications not suitable for assembly or insufficient manufacturing quality of supplier parts, resulting influences show a direct negative impact on prototype quality. Controlling such influences requires a cooperative elaboration of solutions together with mainly suppliers in case of "buy-components" or with mainly product development and, if needed, manufacturing in case of "make-components". [14]

Prototype Manufacturing. Influences related to manufacturing processes and production configuration result from e.g. process planning, process requirements, process instabilities, sequence of operations or the configuration of manufacturing resources. For instance, incorrect process planning or inappropriate configurations of manufacturing resources cause negative impacts on the prototype quality. Controlling those influences requires a cooperative elaboration of measurements together with e.g. production planning or shop floor employees.[15,16]

The abovementioned influences on prototype quality manifest themselves in measurable quality deviations such as exceeded tolerances or high process variability. The occurrence of these effects determines the level of quality of prototypes as it is understood within this paper.[17] Hence, the detection and evaluation of measurable effects as well as identification and controlling of causative influences are key levers for an improved level of quality of the produced prototypes.

Besides the negative impact on prototype quality, the aforementioned influences can also delay the prototype phase, increase the required number of prototypes, cause additional effort in product development for changes and thus raise overall costs of this phase. In the worst case, consequences of quality deviations are underestimated or the quality deviations remain undetected. That can cause costly adaptations and changes of e.g. the production structure, processes or manufacturing resources during ramp-up or even mass-production phase cumulating in increased non-conformance costs. [6]

1.3 Quality Management During Prototype Phase

In order to prevent such major incidences for manufacturing companies, quality management (QM) is established as a function/department to, among others, develop, implement and improve processes for detection and evaluation of occurring quality deviations during the product lifecycle phases. This is a basis for continuous product, production and therefore quality improvements [18]. Focusing on the activities during the prototype phase and also on the interfaces to previous and subsequent phases of the product lifecycle, QM is responsible for ensuring a sufficient level of quality of prototypes. This is done by implementing adequate quality control loops and quality processes which are aligned and connected with associated processes in product development, production planning and overall QM. As mentioned above, the main task of quality processes during the prototype phase is the detection and evaluation of deviations from defined quality levels, identification of the causative influence and the consequent initiation of the development of improvement measures (see fig. 3). Depending on the respective origin of the influence, improvement measures have to be elaborated either by product development, production planning or suppliers.

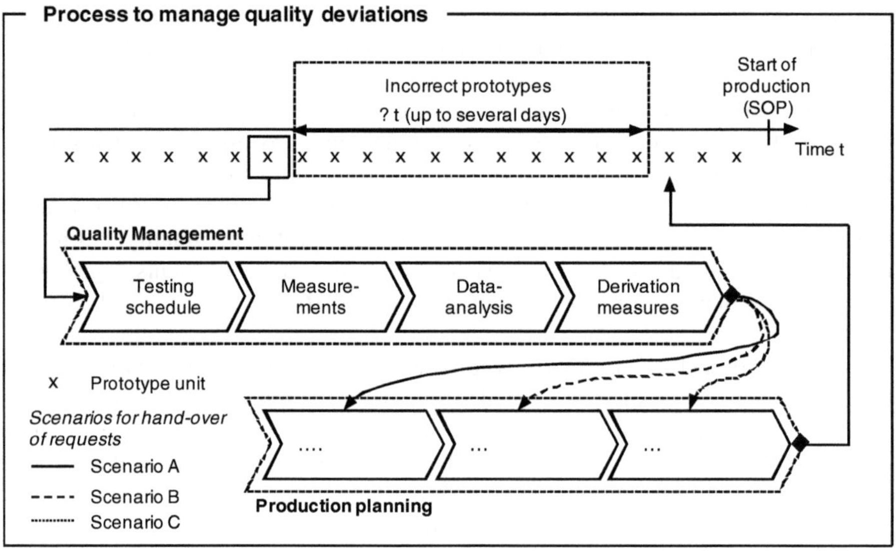

Fig. 3. Process to manage quality deviations

1.4 Problem Statement

The definition of an efficient and effective quality control loop is one of the key challenges for improving the quality level of prototypes and reducing overall non-conformance costs [cf. 19]. Such a quality control loop includes a quality process for the prototype phase with defined interfaces to associated processes, especially of production planning and product development, within the prototype phase as well as to previous and subsequent product lifecycle phases.

In this context efficient and effective mean: doing the right process activities for detecting quality deviations as well as initiating the development of measures (effective) and realizing them quickly at the right time within the prototype phase (efficient) [cf. 20].

Presenting an approach for the development of such a quality control loop including a quality process with the described interfaces to associated processes in product development, production planning and QM as well as a first examination of the affected process parts especially in production planning is subject of this paper to answer the main research question:

How should a cycle oriented QM during the prototype phase be designed leveraging and improving the interface especially to production planning?

The remainder of this article is structured as follows: Specification of the intended result of the research activities in chapter 2, followed by an explanation of the proposed scientific approach in chapter 3 and a comprehensive summary and outlook in chapter 4.

2 Indented Results of the Approach for Quality Management in the Prototype Phase

Achieving a sufficiently high prototype quality at the end of the prototype phase which is close to the required quality during mass-production is a key lever for reducing the amount of required adaptations and changes of the product as well as of production structure, processes and manufacturing resources during mass-production phase. An efficient and effective quality control loop is an important enabler for this purpose.

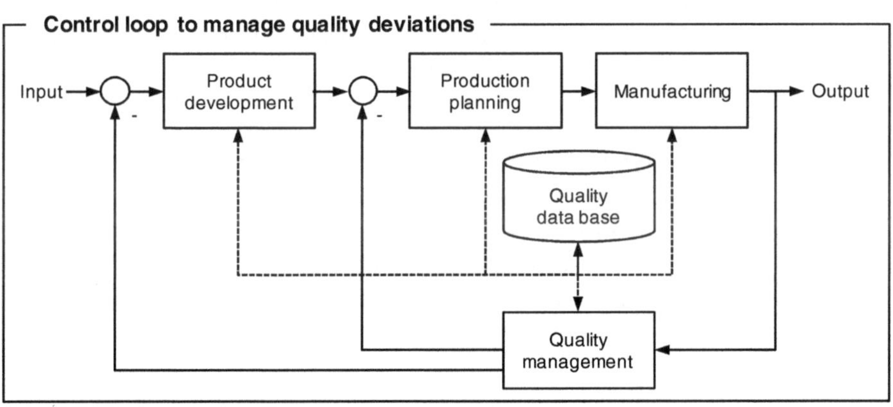

Fig. 4. Quality control loop to manage quality deviations [cf. 19]

The QM process to be developed focuses on the prototype phase while also taking the overall product lifecycle into consideration. That means, the QM process cannot be a stand-alone process but possesses distinct interfaces to production planning, product development and the overall quality management (see fig. 4). The QM process which can be understood as a cycle has to be segmented in specific phases with defined triggers for each phase, so that process activities, such as series of measurements or alignment meetings, can be clearly allocated, interfaces established and the QM cycle managed.

Within the specific phases, a deviation measurement concept has to be defined for testing of prototype quality. This concept covers not only required measurement points and frequencies but also procedures for identification and classification of deviations as well as for evaluation of potential influences and should be variable over time to meet the specific requirements of the prototype phase [cf. 3].

Based on the defined phases, triggers and the embedded deviation measurement concept, the interfaces between QM, product development and production planning act as connectors enabling an information exchange and close the quality control loop. For an efficient and effective implementation the interfaces should support a fast analysis of potential findings from deviation measurements and an aligned initiation of required measures. In practice, that could concretize e.g. in changes of product specifications or adaptations of manufacturing resources. [21]

Summarizing, the quality control loop with the QM process, the embedded deviation measurement concept and the specific interfaces provide the basis for improvements in prototype quality and later reductions of non-conformance costs during mass-production phase.

3 Scientific Approach

The definition and evaluation of a quality control loop for the prototype phase will be based on five work packages. The approach presented in this article covers the analysis of the state-of-the-art, the definition of a quality control loop and QM process based on accepted QM approaches (compare e.g. [18], a measurement concept and the elaboration of specific process interfaces (see fig. 5).

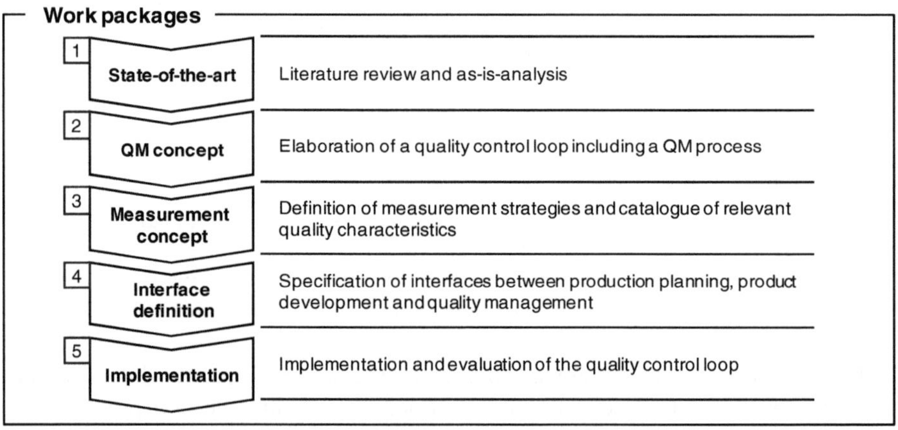

Fig. 5. Five-step-approach for the development of the quality control loop

State-of-the-Art. First, the state-of-the-art regarding product lifecycles, quality control loops, QM processes and processes for production planning with focus on interfaces to quality management will be prepared based on both, a comprehensive literature review and examples for "as-is approaches" from automotive industry.

QM Concept. Proceeding from the state-of-the-art, a general concept for a quality control loop for the prototype phase will be elaborated. This concept should comprise not only the overall description of the quality control loop but also a more detailed definition of the QM process. This requires a distinction of relevant phases within the QM process and within the quality control loop. Further, triggers for the different phases and their potential dependencies should be specified.

Measurement Concept. Third step is the definition of a deviation measurement concept as part of the QM process. This measurement concept should cover both, measurement strategies specifying when and where measurements are required and also a catalogue for measurement characteristics including e.g. measuring points, tolerances and relevance of the respective characteristic. Subsequently, this concept should be embedded in the QM process.

Interface Definition. In the following fourth step, interfaces to the processes of production planning and product development as well as the overall quality management process should be specified. That includes a detailed analysis and elaboration of potential localizations and properties of the interfaces as well as the integration of processes based on plausible scenarios. These scenarios account for the necessity of e.g. regular adaptations of manufacturing resources or processes on the one hand and "fast-track" adaptations of those on the other hand (see fig. 3). For this, process integrated approaches and methods such as design reviews or quality gates need to be considered.

Following, parts of the production planning process relevant for the interfaces should be analyzed to identify potential modifications for an adapted production planning process with respect to occurring quality deviations during the prototype phase. In addition, same has to be performed regarding product development processes, indicating an area for future research.

Implementation. In the fifth step the overall quality control loop should be implemented and evaluated. That comprises not only the practical application of the concept but also a critical concept review with regard to the defined QM process, the deviation measurement concept and the specified interfaces to product development and production planning.

4 Summary and Outlook

Product lifecycles are influenced by quality during all lifecycle phases. The earlier quality deviations are identified and the causes eliminated, the higher the positive impact on quality and potentially occurring non-conformance costs especially during mass-production. Hence, this article focuses on the analysis of quality management during the prototype phase and an approach for the development of an efficient and effective quality control loop. This includes the elaboration of a quality process with relevant interfaces to connected processes in product development, production planning and overall quality management as well as the specification of a deviation measurement concept as an embedded part of the QM process. The defined quality control loop enables an efficient and effective quality management during the prototype phase as well as connected previous and subsequent product lifecycle phases. This happens by reducing quality deviations occurring in the prototype phase and overall non-conformance costs during consecutive lifecycle phases such as the mass-production phase. Defining and establishing relevant interfaces between the quality process, the product development process or the production planning process prepares the basis for a comprehensive consideration of quality influences within production planning.

Besides quality, other influencing factors such as production quantities or manufacturing technology lifecycles impact the production planning but are rarely taken into account today [22]. Taking these often cyclic influences into consideration in the production planning process could significantly improve this process regarding required time, costs and quality. Today, existing production planning methods focus on the overall factory layout, production networks and the operative planning of the manufacturing task. However, a comprehensive planning method for the reconfiguration of manufacturing resources and the production structure involving cyclic influences such as quality, product changes or technology lifecycles is not available yet.

The approach presented in this article addresses one specific section of the aforementioned exemplary influences – quality – in relation with production planning. Next steps are the elaboration of the outlined quality control loop, the QM process, the deviation measurement concept and the required interfaces based on the proposed five-step approach (cf. chapter 3). In addition, a first examination of the affected process parts especially in production planning is to be carried out.

Future research activities will address the development and evaluation of comprehensive methods for production planning with a focus on reconfigurations of manufacturing resources and production structures, taking cyclic influences into consideration. The approach presented in this paper is a first step in this direction.

Acknowledgments. The German Research Foundation (DFG) funds this research and development project. We extend our sincere thanks to the DFG for the generous support of the work described in this paper, resulting from the subproject B5 "Design of changeable production resources" in the framework of the Collaborative Research Centre 768 "Managing cycles in innovation processes – Integrated development of product service systems based on technical products". The goal of the Collaborative Research Centre 768 is to reduce the knowledge gap regarding cycles and cyclic influences within the innovation process.

References

1. Brissaud, D., Tichkiewitch, S.: Product Models for Life-Cycle. Annals of the CIRP 50(1), 105–108 (2001)
2. Fleischer, J., Lanza, G., Ender, T.: Prozessinnovation durch prozessbasierte Qualitätsprognose im Produktionsanlauf. Zeitschrift für wirtschaftlichen Fabrikbetrieb, vol. 100. Carl Hanser, München (2005)

3. Winkler, H.: Modellierung vernetzter Wirkbeziehungen im Produktionsanlauf. Leibniz Universität Hannover, Garbsen (2007)
4. Wiendahl, H.P., Reichardt, J., Nyhuis, P.: Handbuch Fabrikplanung – Konzept, Gestaltung und Umsetzung wandlungsfähiger Produktionsstätten. Hanser, München (2009)
5. Boehm, B.W.: Software engineering economics, Englewood Cliffs, NJ. Prentice-Hall Advances in Computing Science & Technology Series (1981)
6. Clark, K.B., Fujimoto, T.: Product Development Performance. Strategy, organization and management in the world of auto industries. Harvard Business School Press, Boston (1991)
7. Feigenbaum, A.V.: Total Quality Control. McGraw-Hill, New York (1991)
8. Harrington, H.J.: Poor-Quality Cost. Society for Quality. Marcel Dekker Inc., New York (1987)
9. Nau, B.: Anlauforientierte Technologieplanung zur Auswahl von Fertigungstechnologien. RWTH Aachen, Apprimus, Aachen (2012)
10. Cooper, R.G.: Stage-gate systems: A new tool for managing new products. Business Horizons, Ontario 33 (1990)
11. Nada, O.A., ElMaraghy, H.A., ElMaraghy, W.H.: Quality Prediction in Manufacturing System Design. Journal of Manufacturing Systems 25(10), 293–314 (2006)
12. Scheer, A.W., Boczanski, M., Muth, M., Schmitz, W.G., Segelbacher, U.: Prozessorientiertes Product Lifecycle Management. Springer, Berlin (2006)
13. Schmidt, R.: The implementation of simultaneous engineering in the stage of product concept development: A process orientated improvement of quality function deployment. European Journal of Operational Research 100(10), 293–314 (1997)
14. Regius, B.: Qualität in der Produktentwicklung. Carl Hanser Verlag, München (2006)
15. Koren, Y., Heisel, U., Jovane, J., Moriwaki, T., Pritschow, G., Ulsoy, G., Van Brussel, H.: Reconfigurable Manufacturing Systems. Annals of the CIRP 48(2), 527–540 (1999)
16. Syska, A.: Produktionsmanagement. Gabler, Wiesbaden (2006)
17. Cheng, B.W., Maghsoodloo, S.: Optimization of Mechanical Assembly Tolerances by Incorporating Taguchi's Quality Loss Function. Journal of Manufacturing Systems 14(4), 264–276 (1995)
18. Hering, E., Triemel, J., Blank, H.-P.: Qualitätsmanagement für Ingenieure. Springer, Heidelberg (2003)
19. Westkämper, E.: Qualitätsmanagement in der Produktion. In: Eversheim, W., Schuh, G. (eds.) Produktion und Management: Betriebshütte. Springer, Berlin (2000)
20. Drucker, P.F.: Managing for Business Effectiveness. Harvard Business Review (1963)
21. Fricke, E., Gebhard, B., Negele, H., Igenbergs, E.: Coping with Changes: Causes, Findings, and Strategies. System Engineering 3(4), 169–179 (2000)
22. Zaeh, M.F., Reinhart, G., Karl, F., Schindler, S., Pohl, J., Rimpau, C.: Cyclic influences within the production resource planning process. Production Engineering – Research and Development 4, 309–317 (2010)

Digital Factory Assistant: Conceptual Framework and Research Propositions

Mohamed Anis Dhuieb, Florent Laroche, and Alain Bernard

LUNAM Université, Ecole Centrale de Nantes, IRCCyN UMR CNRS 6597, France
Mohamed-anis.dhuieb@irccyn.ec-nantes.fr

Abstract. Nowadays, knowledge has a major role in factory efficiency. The integration of knowledge and decision support systems in the whole factory process appears as a key for the factory of the future. The basic concept of our research work is facilitating interactions between the human being in critical working situations and information set in the factory. Our proposition is to develop a "digital factory assistant" to provide factory actors with the right information, in the right time and place. Our purpose is to build a generic factory model based on context awareness and decision support models and then create relevant information and knowledge extraction mechanisms. In this paper we discuss the conceptual architecture of the desired information system.

Keywords: Knowledge Management, PLM, Virtual Assistant, Ubiquitous computing.

1 Introduction

Industrials and researches illustrate different visions of the factory of the future. The shared aspect of these visions is providing the factory's employers with consistent IT systems to simplify and support employee's tasks.

Based on an integrated approach of material-processes-information-human being, our proposition is to develop a customable company assistant that interact with complete information set. The assistant will be inspired by knowledge based systems, contain different decision aided functionalities, and use Virtual engineering technologies techniques. This will allow extending the dimensions of Virtual Technologies models with further data sets. This assistant will assist factory's actors during engineering phases by providing them with the right information. It consists of a knowledge based system which allows the access of different knowledge resources in the factory such as Product Lifecycle management (PLM) CAx models (Computer aided Design/ Manufacturing/engineering CAD/CAE/CAM…), material flows, process chains, simulation data… [1] One of the challenges in our proposition is to select the right information from numerous sources and transforms it into useful knowledge.

The first part of the paper presents a state of the art of the evolution in digital tools in the factory. The second part deals with the human being role in the product

A. Bernard, L. Rivest, and D. Dutta (Eds.): PLM 2013, IFIP AICT 409, pp. 500–509, 2013.

lifecycle as a decision maker. Some related works are presented in the third part and the fundamentals of ARTUR project, which illustrate our vision of the factory of the future, will be explained in the third part before the conclusion.

2 Evolution of Digital Tools in Factory: Future Information Systems in Factory

Nowadays, enterprises have acquired various tools that allow them to be very confident with the products they develop. The concept of smart factories proposes them to automate and control most of their tasks [1]. Today's factory contains more and more digital tools based on ICT. The digital and virtual factory paradigm can support the design and management of a production environment by addressing various key issues like: reduction of production times and material waste thanks to the analysis of virtual mock-ups, development of a knowledge repository where people can find stored information in different versions, with both advisory role and support to the generation of new knowledge and improvement of workers efficiency and safety through training and learning on virtual production systems [2][3].

Advanced technologies such as ubiquitous computing (i), virtual engineering technologies (ii), and the concept of the Web 3.0 (iii) are supplying the factory with a new wave of intelligence:

i) Ubiquitous Computing was first introduced by Weiser in the end of 80s. It consists of a new model of interaction where the information processing is integrated in our daily life. The context-awareness is the particular aspect of ubiquitous information systems. These information systems have to anticipate the user's needs in a particular situation and act proactively to provide appropriate assistance. Many researchers describe the vision of the factory of things which adopt the basic concepts of the internet of things and implement smart objects that interact basically on semantic services integrating knowledge representations. The main goal of such propositions is to make the information available anywhere, anytime for any user based on Weiser vision of ubiquitous computing. [4][5][6][7][8][9]

ii) Virtual engineering technologies become an emerging field in industry and research. Many industrials use Virtual and Augmented Reality to make advanced simulation of their manufacturing process or for training their employees. The application fields of virtual engineering can be considered for the complete life-cycle of the product, from the earliest design stages of the products to their manufacturing, assembly, use and maintenance phases. This evolution in the field of virtual engineering reflects a real modification of our way of thinking product development. Thus, global coherency has emerged as a result of improved numerical integration and better software functionality for manufacturing preparation as well as for process simulation and part dimensional and geometrical control after manufacturing. [10][11][12][13]

iii) The Web 3.0 is the more recent technology from those mentioned previously. Mills Davis describe his vision of the web 3.0 in his industry roadmap to web 3.0: In order to connect systems, integrate information, and make processes interoperable, the first step is to integrate the knowledge about these systems, content sources, and process flows. Semantically modeled machine executable knowledge lets us connect information about people, events, locations, times, across different content sources and application processes. In Web 3.0, knowledge lives, evolves and is stored transparently. It can be used, validated, added to, and combined with other knowledge at run time by multiple systems. This enables a system to "learn" to do things that the system designer did not anticipate. This is an important shift from IT as it has been practiced until now.
The basic shift occurring in Web 3.0 is from information-centric to knowledge-centric patterns of computing. Web 3.0 encompasses a broad range of knowledge representation and reasoning capabilities including pattern detection, deep linguistics, and ontology [14] [15] [16].

In modern product development, as the complexity and variety of products increase to satisfy increasingly sophisticated customers, so does the need for knowledge and expertise for developing products. Today's knowledge-intensive product development environment requires a computational framework which effectively enables capture, representation, retrieval and reuse of product knowledge. [17][18]The factory of the future requires holistic production systems with a learning capability, based on learning effects in all stages of the process chains involved, the goal is to achieve higher production outputs by integrating knowledge modules into the engineering systems concerned [19].

As we mentioned in the introduction our proposition is to develop a customizable knowledge book called "Digital Factory Assistant". The crucial point of success of our work will be the building of a comprehensive model that represents most of the elements in the factory, seen as knowledge resources, and to guarantee the interoperability between them, but at first let's see what are the reasons that led us propose it.

3 The Human Factor in Production Systems

For an enterprise's management point of view, enterprise's managers make a significant effort to reduce the cost of non-quality (CONQ). Measuring and reporting this cost is a critical issue for any manager who aims to achieve competitiveness in today's markets [20]. Studies show that the lack of information, gaps in training, and the unavailability of documentation in production lines are the most important reasons of CONQ rising [21].

Despite the evolution of digital tools in factory as seen in the previous section, the role of the human being in product lifecycle is not insignificant. Labrousse [22] highlight the role of the human being as a decisional actor in the factory life. He makes the relation between information, knowledge, and decision: information is not easy to understand by the user, the meaning of the information can be strongly influenced by the user and the context. The knowledge is the emergence of the user and the interpreted information. In many cases elements impacting decisions are not totally mastered and suffer from incompleteness. In the process of decision making, users combine different types of data and knowledge (both tacit and explicit knowledge) available in different forms. The decision making process results in improved understanding of the problem and the process [23].

One of the solutions to reduce the cost of non-quality is developing assistant tools that help factory employees in their tasks. There are several works related to human assistance in different phases of product lifecycle. Projects deal with assistance in production phase is not very common unlike in other product lifecycle phases like design or maintenance. The next section describes few works related to the human being assistance in the factory.

4 Previous Works Relied on Human Being Assistance in Factories

Many propositions have been encountered in the literature. Despite the diversity of these projects, few of them deal with human assistance in production systems at a "machine level" where information is less available comparing to other departments in the factory. In this section, we discuss a number of works related on our work.

In a maintenance context, CARMMI model [24] provide support to operators during maintenance tasks through mixed reality providing information access from different sources. This model allows the acquisition and presentation of different data: CAx data, maintenance, and virtual data. From a decision making point of view, the big quantity of the information presented in the interface can reduce the efficiency of the operator to make the right decision. In fact, the interface contains augmented reality, visualization system, information and historical information data. The human machine interactions are not studied in this project.

A second work in the same context was presented by Toro [25]. A framework and a system implementation were developed for the exploitation of embedded knowledge in the domain of industrial maintenance. This framework uses a shared ontology designed to model and support pervasive computing applications called SOUPA. A knowledge acquisition system is also developed in this project called Experience Knowledge Structure. This system extends the functionality of SOUPA in a way that formal decision events can be suggested to the user during his work. Both of these two technologies were used to develop the UDKE system (User, Device, Knowledge, and Experience). This UDKE provide a conceptual model of a maintenance system that combines knowledge, user experience and Augmented Reality techniques. The context awareness notion was absent from this project so the possible decisions and information provided to the user were not relied to his task and did not consider his feedback.

Kwon [26] [27] has developed a framework called ubiDSS. ubiDSS is a framework of multi-agent and context-aware based proactive decision support system. The architecture of this framework is composed by a number of subsystems: context subsystem, dialogue subsystem, knowledge subsystem, model management subsystem, and a database management subsystem. Even that the application field of the ubiDSS system is far from industry, it was very important to study the interactions between the components of its framework and the models behind.

Many other propositions were encountered in the literature relied to the human being assistance in the different product lifecycle stages especially in design process. However, the application of such propositions in a production context is very rare.

5 ARTUR: A Digital Factory Assistant

5.1 Concept

Related to visions of the factory of the future, our work is to offer the factory operator with a so called "Digital Factory Assistant". Through this assistant the operator can have information from distributed knowledge resources relying in different ways of interaction in order to act upon the task that he is doing. So, the main research issue of our work is to find which information to give to the operator, where, when, and how. The basic idea is to allow each person to be able to react in given situation, mainly thanks to high speed simulation and performance evaluation models and methods. [1]

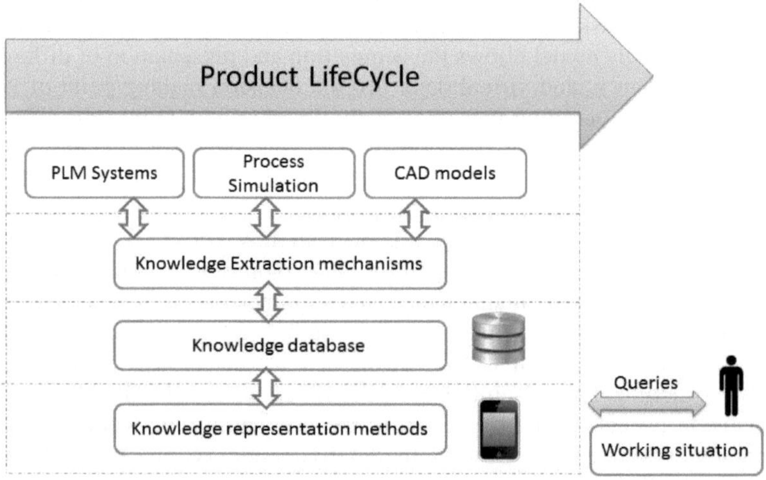

Fig. 1. Based on knowledge extraction mechanisms, knowledge will be extracted from factory information system elements compared as a lower part of an iceberg. The operator will deal only with a mobile device, compared as the top part of an iceberg, where knowledge will be deployed with intelligent navigation system [28].

Figure 1 outline the first proposition of the conceptual framework of our work in a high level. The framework will be based on three layers: the first one is related to the human-machine level, where contextual information related to user's working situation can be acquired. The second layer is related to the definition, representation, exploration, and structuring knowledge. The last layer deal with the issue of linking knowledge layer with the whole information system in the factory.

To build our "Digital Factory Assistant", we have to consider many points of view. In the following sections we will try to detail some of them.

5.2 Evaluation of Human-Machine Interactions

Interaction between the human being and the machines or environment is a topic that is often underestimated. More satisfactory relations need to take the psychological aspects into account and also improve the factory environment by controlling many factors. The relations between human beings, machines, and their environment play a central role in production systems [4].

A cognitive approach will be developed; the information quantity will be different from a beginner operator to an expert operator. With this approach, and in a context of uncertainty, the system will transfer a small amount of knowledge to a beginner user and led him, as his needs, to a larger amount of knowledge and do the opposite for a more expert user: *"smooth roads never make good drivers"*.

5.3 Knowledge Exploitation

Knowledge management aims at capturing explicit and tacit knowledge of an organization in order to facilitate the access, sharing and re-use of that knowledge [29].

Foundations of our research project relate to a new proposition for modeling and structuring information, and more generally knowledge. Consequently, dealing with the global data, information, knowledge and know-how, we will be able to contextualize reusing this knowledge in any given situation that would need this knowledge [1]. Our assistant will be based on a dynamic knowledge representation: knowledge will be presented to an operator according to some relevant information including his working situation [30] [31], the maturity level [32], and the operator experience. In a process of decision making, the actor will combine different types of data and knowledge available in various forms.

The operator will have the possibility to personalize the set of information and knowledge as his need and as his evolution on the process or the service that he works on it. An intelligent knowledge and information system will be deployed in mobile device to make the information available in any context, even in complex working situations. [22][32][33].

5.4 Ubiquitous Environment

As mentioned in the first part of this paper, our system will run in an ubiquitous environment [9]. The ubiquitous environment is now emerging as a primary driver to change the decision makers' task environment. This trend certainly has the potential to improve the decision making framework in gathering and processing decision makers' contextual data in an automated way, which intelligently extracts proactive decisions [26][27]. The context-awareness is the particular aspect of ubiquitous information systems. Dey [34] has defined the context as "any information that can be used to characterize the situation of an entity. An entity is a person, place, or object that considered relevant to the interaction between the user and the application, including the user and the applications them-selves." Humans possess a different perception of contextual information, which is mostly due to the availability of context information on different levels of granularity or abstraction [35].

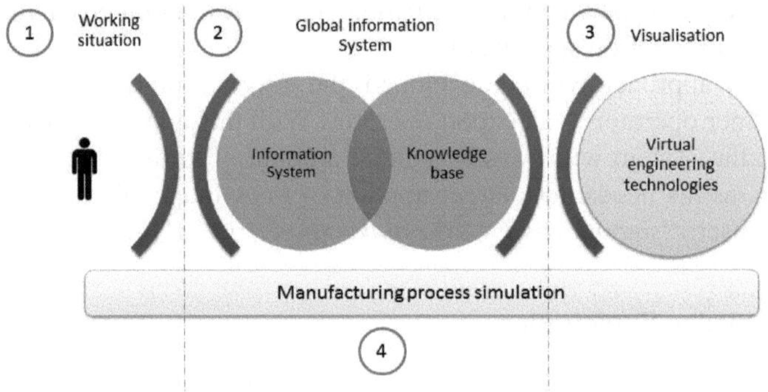

Fig. 2. Basic elements creating the ubiquitous environment

In accordance with the vision of Weiser in ubiquitous computing, our system will be based on a context aware model. The ubiquitous environment is created by the data flow coming from different resources:

- user's input dependent in his working situation (1) (this context information will act like a sensor in our model),
- the coupling of the existent information system in the factory and knowledge database (2),
- the process simulation (4) based on advanced numeric simulation technics[36],
- the extending of the virtual reality models with a further data set (3) (2).

The system will have the capability to understand the user's need by "compiling" context information and automatically "generate" the relevant information and knowledge to the user.

In addition to context awareness, reactiveness is an important requirement for a ubiquitous information environment. Proactiveness means to process information on behalf a user so an action can be taken without requiring his attention. This implies knowing what a user would want to do with the requested information, and detecting patterns for his behavior. [37] Therefore, we will define effective context information extraction techniques to identify the working situation of the operator and to determine the information set that will be presented.

5.5 Future Model Aspects

Taking into account the main aspects of our idea about the "Digital Factory assistant", our model will be based on several approaches related to enterprise, knowledge, and context modeling.

Enterprise modeling is defined by Molina [38] as the art of externalizing enterprise knowledge which adds value to the enterprise or needs to be shared. It consists of making models of the structure, behavior and organization of the enterprise. [22] A new proposition for modeling working situations will be designed. This aspect will be based on Hasan proposition [30] [31] for modeling the working situation at machine level.

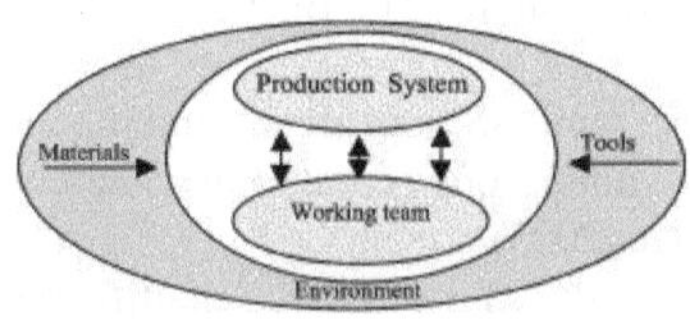

Fig. 3. Macro view of the working situation [30] [31]

A level of detail will be employed during the modeling process [13] this aspect will define the granularity of the information to be presented to the user. The desired model should be in one hand extensible to acquire more functionality and more types of data and in another hand interoperable so he can communicate and acquire knowledge and information from other existing systems in the factory.

6 Conclusion and Future Work

We believe that in the factory of the future the information and the knowledge will have more accessibility with small devices that interact with its user in an intelligent way. The main aspect for our vision is to extract the right information in the right time and give it to the right user. In a production system, the user may be faced with working situations that require him to interact with the machine in front of him by choosing the right decisions. The decisions can be a force to be applied, a position of a tool in the machine… So, to make his decision the user will need to have such propositions of what he can do or what measure he will take and, using advanced simulation technics, he can anticipate the influence of his choice. To validate all this aspects in our project ARTUR, we will be based on two use cases in aeronautic industry. Currently, we started a survey to identify the different elements that will help us to build our information model.

References

1. Laroche, F., Bordeu, F., Bernard, A., Chinesta, F.: Towards the factory of future An integrated approach of material-processes-information-human being. In: Proceedings of the 2012 Virtual Reality International Conference, p. 13. ACM (2012)

2. Smith, E.A.: The role of tacit and explicit knowledge in the workplace. Journal of Knowledge Management 5(4), 311–321 (2001)
3. Terkaj, W., Pedrielli, G., Sacco, M.: Virtual factory data model. In: Proceedings of the Second International Workshop on Searching and Integrating New Web Data Sources (VLDS 2012), Istanbul, Turkey (2012)
4. Zuehlke, D.: SmartFactory Towards a factory-of-things. Annual Reviews in Control 34(1), 129–138 (2010)
5. Stephan, P.: System architecture for using location information for process optimization within a factory of things. In: Proceedings of the 3rd International Workshop on Location and the Web, p. 6. ACM (2010)
6. Guinard, D., Trifa, V., Karnouskos, S., Spiess, P., Savio, D.: Interacting with the soa-based internet of things: Discovery, query, selection, and on-demand provisioning of web services. IEEE Transactions on Services Computing 3(3), 223–235 (2010)
7. Schmidt, A.: Context-Aware Computing: Context-Awareness, Context-Aware User Interfaces, and Implicit Interaction. In: The Encyclopedia of Human-Computer Interaction, 2nd edn. (2013)
8. Kwon, O., Yoo, K., Suh, E.: UbiDSS: a proactive intelligent decision support system as an expert system deploying ubiquitous computing technologies. Expert Systems with Applications 28(1), 149–161 (2005)
9. Weiser, M.: The computer for the 21st century. Scientific American 265(3), 94–104 (1991)
10. Bernard, A., Ammar-Khodja, S., Perry, N., Laroche, F.: Virtual engineering based on knowledge integration. Virtual and Physical Prototyping 2(3), 137–154 (2007)
11. Luna, A.S., Lopez, T., Nouviale, F., Gouranton, V., Arnaldi, B.: Collaboration et interchangeabilité entre humains réels et humains virtuels en Environnement Virtuel de Formation. AFRV, 1-8 (2012)
12. Thouvenin, I.M.: Interaction et connaissance: construction d'une expérience dans le monde virtuel (Doctoral dissertation, Université de Technologie de Compiègne) (2009)
13. Laroche, F.: Contribution à la sauvegarde des Objets techniques anciens par l'Archéologie industrielle avancée. Proposition d'un Modèle d'information de référence muséologique et d'une Méthode inter-disciplinaire pour la Capitalisation des connaissances du Patrimoine technique et industriel (Doctoral dissertation, Ecole centrale de Nantes-ECN) (2007)
14. Davis, M.: Semantic Wave 2008 Report: Industry Roadmap to Web 3.0 & Multibillion Dollar Market Opportunities. Executive Summary (2008)
15. Lai, H., Fan, Y., Xin, L., Liang, H.: The Framework of Web 3.0-Based Enterprise Knowledge Management System. In: Uden, L., Herrera, F., Bajo, J., Corchado, J.M. (eds.) 7th International Conference on KMO. AISC, vol. 172, pp. 345–351. Springer, Heidelberg (2013)
16. Hendler, J.: Web 3.0 Emerging 42(1), 111–113 (2009)
17. Ameri, F., Dutta, D.: Product lifecycle management: closing the knowledge loops. Computer-Aided Design & Applications 2(5), 577–590 (2005)
18. Sriti, M.F.: Démarche et logiciel de gestion des connaissances pour le cycle de vie des produits. PhD report, University of troyes (2008)
19. Westkämper, E., Walter, F.: EMO Hannover 2011 showcases the factory of the future: New production concepts integrate knowledge and learn from it (2011) (press release)
20. Schiffauerova, A., Thomson, V.: Managing cost of quality: insight into industry practice. The TQM Magazine 18(5), 542–550 (2006)
21. Benhabib, A., Ghomrassi, S.: Les coûts de non-qualité. Symposium International: Qualité et Maintenance au Service de l'Entreprise QUALIMA01 - Tlemcen (2004)

22. Labrousse, M.: Proposition d'un modèle conceptuel unifié pour la gestion dynamique des connaissances d'entreprise. PhD report, Ecole Centrale de Nantes (2004)
23. Bolloju, N., Khalifa, M., Turban, E.: Integrating knowledge management into enterprise environments for the next generation decision support. Decision Support Systems 33(2), 163–176 (2002)
24. Espíndola, D.B., Fumagalli, L., Garetti, M., Pereira, C.E., Botelho, S.S., Ventura Henriques, R.: A model-based approach for data integration to improve maintenance management by mixed reality. Computers in Industry (2013)
25. Toro, C., Sanín, C., Vaquero, J., Posada, J., Szczerbicki, E.: Knowledge based industrial maintenance using portable devices and augmented reality. In: Apolloni, B., Howlett, R.J., Jain, L. (eds.) KES 2007, Part I. LNCS (LNAI), vol. 4692, pp. 295–302. Springer, Heidelberg (2007)
26. Kwon, O., Yoo, K., Suh, E.: UbiDSS: a proactive intelligent decision support system as an expert system deploying ubiquitous computing technologies. Expert Systems with Applications 28(1), 149–161 (2005)
27. Kwon, O., Choi, S., Lee, H., Yoo, K.: UbiDSS: a framework of multi-agent based proactive decision support system with context-awareness. In: Proceedings of the Second IEEE Workshop on Software Technologies for Future Embedded and Ubiquitous Systems, pp. 172–174. IEEE (2004)
28. Carolan, S., Magnin, M., Evain, C., Moreau, G., Chinesta, F.: Developing models for enhanced learning in engineering. Innovative Pedagogy in Engineer Education (2012)
29. Sriti, M.F., Eynard, B., Boutinaud, F., Matta, N.: Towards a semantic-based plateform to imporove knowledge management in collaborative product development (2008)
30. Hasan, R., Bernard, A., Ciccotelli, J., Martin, P.: Integrating safety into the design process: elements and concepts relative to the working situation. Safety Science 41(2-3), 155–179 (2003)
31. Hasan, R., Bernard, A., Ciccotelli, J.: Proposal of a new design approach integrating the concept of the working situation. In: Gogu, G., Coutellier, D., Chedmail, P., Ray, P. (eds.) Recent Advances in Integrated Design and Manufacturing in Mechanical Engineering (2003)
32. Xu, Y.: Proposition d'un système intégrée de référence de connaissances pour l'évaluation de la connaissance dans le développement de produits. PhD Report. Ecole Centrale de Nantes (2010)
33. Ammar-Khodja, S.: Processus d'aide à la spécification et à la vérification d'application d'ingénierie à base de connaissances expertes. PhD Report. Ecole Centrale de Nantes (2007)
34. Dey, A.K.: Understanding and Using Context. Personal and Ubiquious Computing, 4–7 (2001)
35. Zimmermann, A., Lorenz, A., Oppermann, R.: An operational definition of context. In: Kokinov, B., Richardson, D.C., Roth-Berghofer, T.R., Vieu, L. (eds.) CONTEXT 2007. LNCS (LNAI), vol. 4635, pp. 558–571. Springer, Heidelberg (2007)
36. Chinesta, F., Leygue, A., Bognet, B., Ghnatios, C., Poulhaon, F., Bordeu, F., ... & Maison-Le-Poec, S.: First steps towards an advanced simulation of composites manufacturing by automated tape placement. International Journal of Material Forming, 1–12 (2012)
37. Van Bunningen, A.H., Feng, L., Apers, P.M.: Context for ubiquitous data management. In: International Workshop on Ubiquitous Data Management, UDM 2005, pp. 17–24. IEEE (2005)
38. Molina, A., Bell, R.: Reference models for the computer aided support of simultaneous engineering. International Journal of Computer Integrated Manufacturing 15(3), 193–213 (2002)

A Tool to Support PLM Teaching in Universities

Joel Sauza Bedolla[1], Francesco Ricci[1], Javier Martinez Gomez[1,2], and Paolo Chiabert[1]

[1] Politecnico di Torino, C.so Duca degli Abruzzi 24, Torino 10129, Italy
[2] Universidad Industrial de Santander, Calle 9 Cra.27, Bucaramanga, Colombia

Abstract. Product Lifecycle Management (PLM) is the business paradigm that companies employ as a key for success. Currently, industry needs people at working in a collaborative environment with PLM, since this is the challenge they will be facing in the global economy. At the moment this professional profile is not common in the work market and there is therefore, an educational gap. As well as technical knowledge, new engineers must be familiar with the PLM philosophy and use its tools to work effectively in collaboration with teams around the world. In order to bridge this gap, this paper presents a visualization model that gives the guidelines for a proper understanding of the CAD design activities executed in a PLM system. The proposed model, which follows the work method of a large car manufacturer, has been successfully tested and applied in a university course.

1 Introduction

Nowadays, companies operate over several continents. A designer in one country can specify a product that is then made in another and probably assembled in yet another. Furthermore, the worldwide business environment is experiencing an increase in the use of out-sourcing and sub-contracting. The globalization of markets and augmented consumer sophistication have led to a rise in the variety of products that customers demand and a consequent growth in the number of variants of any given product line that a manufacturer must supply [1]. There is also an increasing demand for outstanding functions of products at a low price [2].

Organizations communicate routinely to and from their supply chain and within their own organization. Most of the information is created, stored and shared as electronic files [3,4]. An example of this is the extensive use of CAD/CAM-systems in industry; it has become an important and widely used technology. Companies have invested large amounts in these systems and are becoming very dependent on CAD technology for the development of new products [5]. These circumstances have changed the traditional means of communication in industry in recent years.

In such a global market, PLM is the only stable channel of communication. PLM deals with the creation, modification, and exchange of product information throughout the product's lifecycle [6]. PLM is an essential tool for coping with the challenges of more demanding global competition, ever-shortening product and component lifecycles and growing customer needs [7].

A. Bernard, L. Rivest, and D. Dutta (Eds.): PLM 2013, IFIP AICT 409, pp. 510–519, 2013.

The main use of PLM include aerospace, defense, automotive, electronics/high tech, fabrication and assembly industries [8]. Most PLM knowledge is within industry and universities are now being asked to prepare future graduates with basic knowledge of PLM. The challenge for universities is to train a highly skilled pool of engineers and professionals able to work and communicate effectively in PLM systems.

Politecnico di Torino recently became aware of this situation and decided to deploy PLM theories in teaching design practices using a market leader PLM system. Proper understanding of the PLM philosophy requires awareness of the instrument (software) functionality and the methodology of use.

Torino is famous primarily for its car manufacturing industry. This industry, due to its complexity, depends almost exclusively on PLM technology. It is then extremely important to prepare the students of Automotive Engineering on the way industry works. Since the university did not have that knowledge, a collaboration agreement with FIAT FGA was established.

The course of Fundamentals of Machining Design and Drawing (FMDD) aims to provide students with basic knowledge of the technologies used in mechanical design aided systems in order to enable an efficient collaboration among designers. This course was the ideal test bench to introduce a PLM based program. This program is inspired by FIAT work method.

PLM goes beyond CAD and PDM applications and there are several examples in literature of collaborative product development curriculum [9-11]. However due to the course contents and credits, it was not possible to introduce an entire PLM approach. CAD integration in a PLM system is envisaged as the first step of an ambitious project that aims at introducing different PLM-based exercises in different courses (i.e. the clamp used in this exercise will be reused in the Manufacturing assemblies course to design a manufacturing cell).

There are several methods to represents processes. However, certain complex data, when visualized graphically, convey far more information to the reader than the raw data itself [12]. We therefore developed a formal Visualization Model (VM) of enterprise processes that offers a graphic representation of the main elements of a product lifecycle (processes, people, tools, skills and information) and makes it possible to address them on an overall level [13].

The VM proved to be an useful tool to represent industrial processes and to transfer them to PLM systems. Moreover, it was exceptionally effective as a training method for explaining the concepts of information management to persons new to this subject. We therefore decided to use the VM as a tool to explain PLM.

2 Pilot Group

Introducing a new tool, as complex as a PLM system with an integrated CAD software, in a university course without a proper testing phase would have been too risky. For this reason it was decided to try the contents with a Pilot Group. A small group of students from Automotive Engineering joined the Voluntary Educational Program (VEP) "PLM in automotive industry" to test the contents of the course and the software platform that that makes it possible to integrate machine design in a PLM framework.

At the end of the VEP course some important issues arose. The need for customization the PLM system was evident. The direct use of existing features did not guarantee the correct representation of the desired design process. Over a seven months period different modifications were made to the PLM platform at different levels (client options, site variables, access rules, server manager). Moreover, from the didactic point of view, it was recognized the need for a model that accounts for the principal concepts of PLM and serve as a guide for students.

3 Course Re-Definition

Epistemology
A packed curriculum leaves little time for students to acquire a deep understanding of the subject or to develop life-long skills such as critical thinking, problem solving, and communication [14]. This course is envisioned to encourage team work using industrial instruments that foster the learning process. Rather than depending on a teacher-centered approach, the course is based on an active process (problem solving and interaction) that relates or builds upon knowledge previously acquired by students. This constructivist learning approach increases critical thinking and active learning.

Case Study
A case study, an industrial clamp fixture (Fig. 1), was carefully chosen among other proposals. Despite a relative easy geometry it presents a good number of delicate design issues. Even though the clamp fixture is not a car component, it is employed to assemble and weld the car body elements in the production line.

Students Background
FMDD is a mandatory course of the third year at the Bachelor program of Automotive Engineering. Students have acquired, on previous courses, the basic knowledge and skills for interpreting unambiguously and correctly drawings of parts and assemblies.

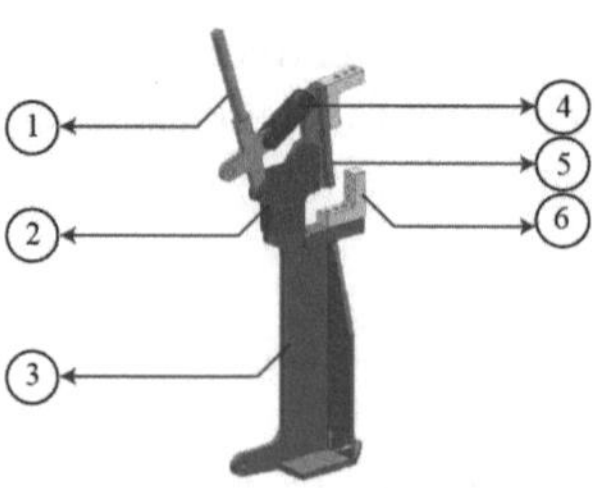

Parts description	
1	Operating lever
2	Top fixing plate
3	Support
4	Swingig transmission
5	Rotary support
6	Block fixing brackts

Fig. 1. Industrial Clamp Fixture

Situational Constraints

Automotive Engineering is an international program taught in English. It hosts 155 students (per year) from all over the world. For the year 2012, nearly 100 students were expected to attend the FMDD course.

FMDD is a 4 credit course, which means 40 hours of frontal teaching. The planned lectures were divided in 18 hours of theoretical lectures and 22 hours of training on PLM integrated CAD system.

The Mirafiori campus has three laboratories with different capacities (from 30 to 50 computer). The available software for the exercise is NX 7.5 as CAD system and Teamcenter 8.0 (TC) for Product Data Management.

Learning Objectives

The main objective of the course is to teach students how to work semi-autonomously on recurring design tasks using a PLM instrument. Students learn how to carry out a collaborative product design using an integrated work method.

In order to do this, every student first realize the clamp assembly individually and then within a 6 people team where he performs, in turn, the role of member and team-leader. Both exercises are based on the use of the same parts yet different purposes are assessed. During the single user exercise, every student is asked to design all parts of the clamp and to assemble them using standard fasteners. Efforts are focused on the CAD system while, at the same time, students acquaint confidence with the TC environment.

On the other hand, during teamwork, students reuse the parts created in the single user exercise and focus their attention on the information exchange (the main aim of a PLM system). A design error is intentionally introduced in one of the parts that has to be identified and fixed by students. Here is where the previous design knowledge is assessed and students develop the collaborative skills. In this paper only the team exercise is presented.

4 Methodological Strategy

The VM follows a Top-Down strategy, breaking down the product lifecycle to gain insight into its Process Areas (PA). Each PA characterize the aspects of product development to be covered by organizational processes and can be expressed as a workflow. Every component of the workflow is then described in a Decomposition Diagram (DD) that contains the information of who (role) is responsible of a work-product (item) generated with an activity that requires particular tools and skills. The methodology of the VM is presented in Fig. 2a.

The visual representation provided by VM makes it particularly suitable for didactic purposes. It works as an interactive guide leading the students through the principal concepts of PLM-based design.

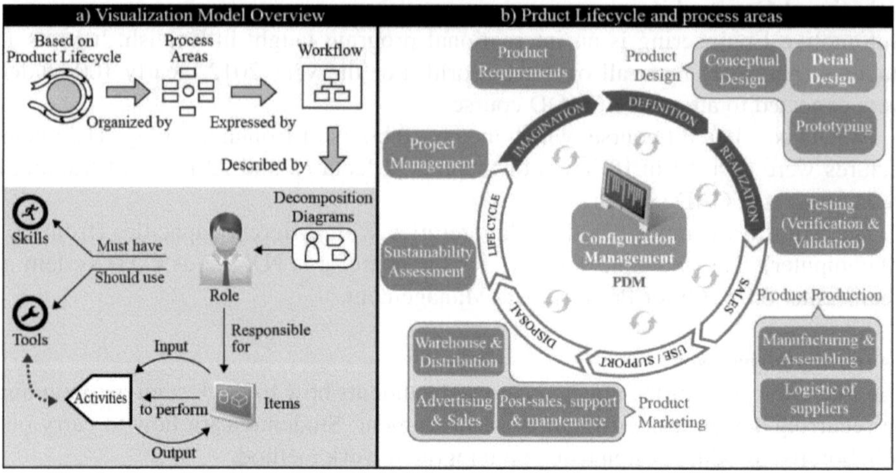

Fig. 2. a) Visualization model overview b)Product lifecycle and Process Areas

Product Lifecycle and Process Areas

The FMDD course focuses on the product design process area, with particular attention for the activities related with detail design. This implies that the process is located at the beginning of product life, during product definition phase (Fig. 2b). Being the heart of the product lifecycle, the configuration management controls all data generated during the development of any activity.

Workflow

Fig. 3 presents the team exercise workflow. The process starts with the creation of the clamp Product Structure; the product Bill of Materials (BOM). Then, every student, performing the team leader role, requires the clamp parts (task assignment) to other team members. After all parts are released, the team leader assembles the parts and releases the clamp assembly. It is the team-leader responsibility to identify the design error (intentionally introduced by the teacher) in the assembly and manage the assembly modification (change management).

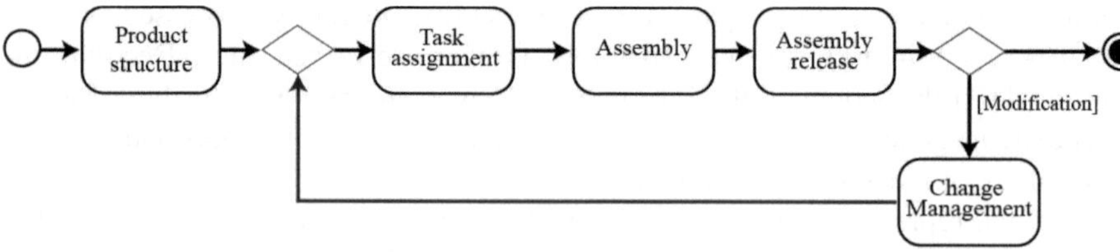

Fig. 3. Team exercise workflow

Decomposition Diagrams

The product structure is created in the structure manager of TC. However, the resulting BOM is recognized only in TC and the CAD system must be synchronized with the PDM. For this reason Fig. 5a presents two activities, the creation of the product structure and manage pending components, where issues between the instruments are solved. The process does not need any inputs to start since it is the first activity of the process. The workproduct of the activity is the Item Assembly which is composed by the 6 principal parts of the clamp.

Every student during teamwork will perform two roles: team leader and team member. As team leader the student is responsible of gathering parts from team members through the use of an automatic TC workflow (Fig. 4). As team member the student is asked to perform a component design.

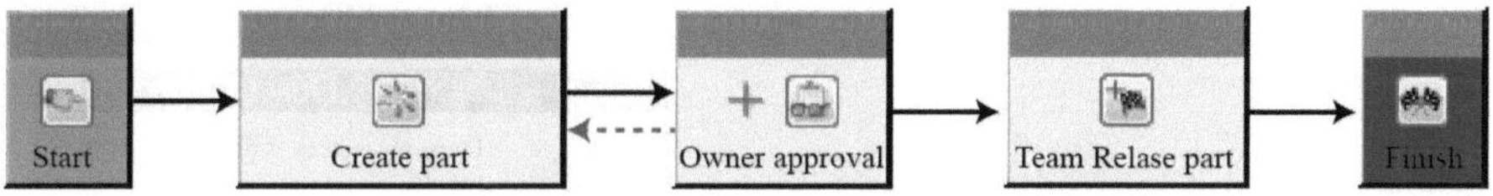

Fig. 4. Team release part TC workflow

Students exchange information following a permutation design. Every team member receives one part draft plus instructions to realize the 3D model in integrated NX. At the end of the *"workflow execution"* the part is released and accounted in the PLM system. The *"workflow assignment"* and *"workflow follow-up"* are performed by the team leader while the *"workflow execution"* is an activity allocated to team members (Fig. 5b).

The following step is to assemble the modelled parts using standard fasteners (screw, nuts and pins) previously loaded into TC. Standard fasteners are retrieved by team leader using the TC item-search function. Subsequently, team leader duplicates the necessary parts and modifies the product structure in the TC structure manager. The assembly is then constrained and finally set to a *precise* configuration. The five activities are presented in Fig. 6a. At this point the assembly is complete and can be released (Fig. 6b) using an automatic TC workflow (Team release assembly).

Once the assembly is released, the teacher alerts students that the clamp kinematic is compromised by a design error they have to fix. Team work autonomously to solve the problem. Students increase their collaboration skills and become acquainted with communication means offered by the PLM system. When the team agrees on the design change, the team leader creates a revision of the assembly and part(s) (Fig. 6c). He then coordinates the activities using the workflow of Fig. 3.

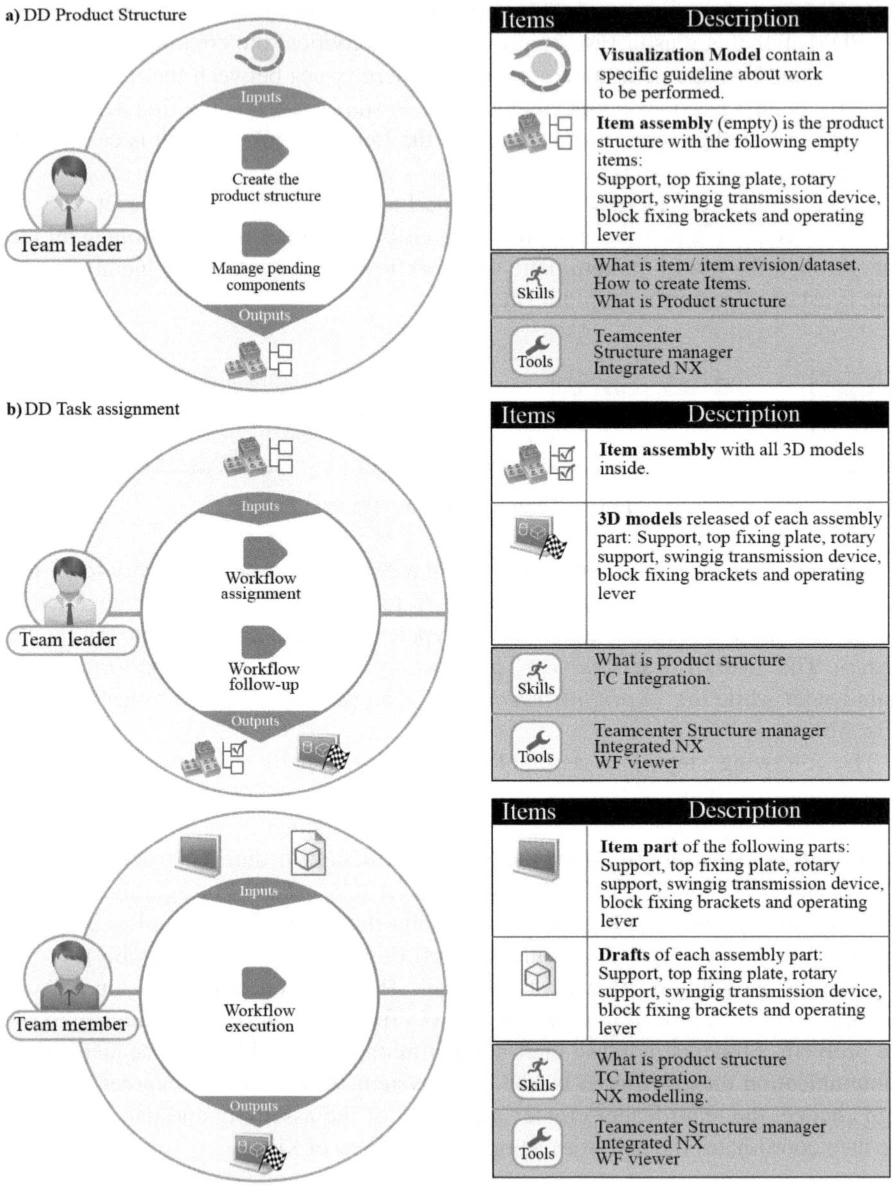

Fig. 5. Decomposition Diagrams of a)Product Structure b)Task assignment

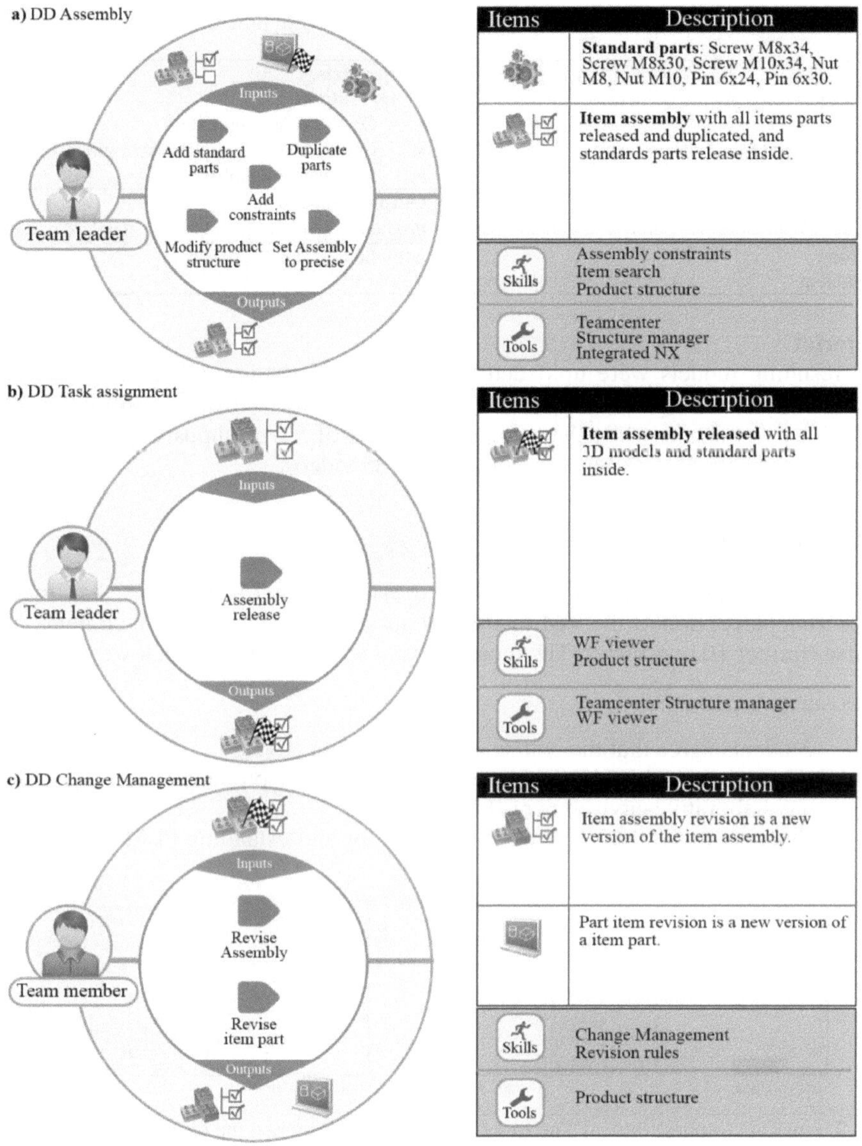

Fig. 6. Decomposition Diagrams of a)Assembly b)Task Assignment c) Change management

Activity Sheets

The model is completed with a more detailed description of the activities presented in a resume sheet. As an example, Table 1 presents the activity *"Set assembly to precise"* of the DD Assembly. At this level of detail there is a thorough description of the commands students must use in TC (or NX). It was decided to improve the clarity of instructions and repeatability of tasks by attaching videos to the VM.

Table 1. Activity sheet "Set assembly to precise"

Set assembly to precise	
Target: Set to precise the final assembly	**Operation:** • Open the Assembly item • Go to Edit→Toggle Precise/Imprecise • Save the Assembly
Input items: Product structure (Assembly + 7 standard parts)	**Output items:** Product structure (Assembly +22 standard parts)
Role: Student	**Attached information:** Video: 13_Set to precise

Material

The resulting models were uploaded to the course webpage where all students can access them. The single user VM consists of a workflow, 7 Decomposition Diagrams and 23 activity sheets while the team VM consists of 5 Decomposition Diagrams and 13 activity sheets. Both VMs are supported by 25 videos.

5 Results

At the end of the course an anonymous questionnaire (Likert scale) was used for measuring perception of the VM model (10 questions) and the general contents of the course (further 10 questions). The more relevant aspects are listed below:

- Positive Aspects
  - Students agree that the course achieved its objectives.
  - Students have a fairly clear perception of the way product design is handled in a collaborative environment (Fig. 7a).
  - Students found the VM a useful support for understanding PLM (Fig. 7b).

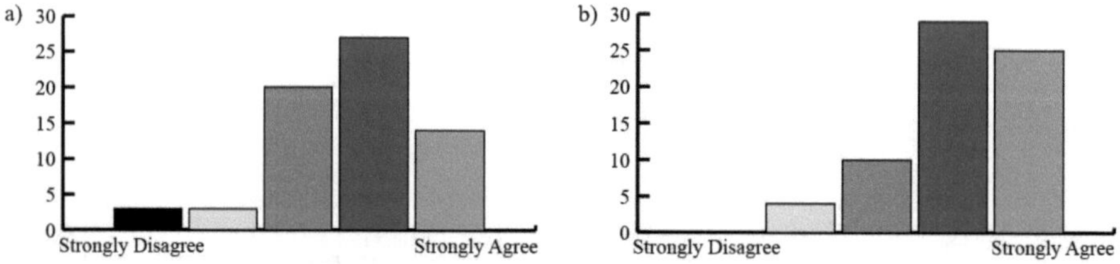

Fig. 7. Answers to questions: a) The PLM experience enlightened me on how product design is handled in a collaborative way by large companies b), I think the VM helps to understand PLM

- Negative Aspects
  - Too many interruptions due to Teamcenter crashes have been an obstacle for learning.
  - The availability of informatics laboratories for exercising was insufficient.
  - Students think that there was some inconsistency in the VM.

Several recommendations were outlined by students and are now being considering to improve next year course. Special attention has been given to Teamcenter for the several drawbacks that caused service interruption during the course. A cause-root analysis was performed and all problems were solved.

6 Conclusions

The FMDD course successfully integrated the CAD designing activity in a PLM system using a work methodology inspired by FIAT. A class of 99 students of different nationalities used the VM as a guide for its work in the PLM environment. All students successfully completed the single and team exercise. All activities were fairly clear and the use of videos as a support has simplified the explanations and reduced the misinterpretations.

The VM has proven to be an extremely effective training tool. It drove the actions of students, clarifying the activities at every step, and training them to work in a collaborative environment. Given the scarcity of PLM-specialized professionals on the work market, Politecnico di Torino is contributing to bridge the educational gap on PLM.

References

1. Swaminathan, J.M., Nitsch, T.R.: Managing Product Variety in Automobile Assembly: The Importance of the Sequencing Point. Interfaces 37(4), 324–333 (2007)
2. ISO/TC-213, Business Plan Dimensional and geometrical product specifications and verification (2004), `http://isotc213.ds.dk/213business%20plan.pdf`
3. Baldwin, A.N., Thorpe, A., Carter, C.: The use of electronic information exchange on construction alliance projects. Automation in Construction 8(6) (1999)
4. Hill, C.A., Scudder, G.D.: The use of electronic data interchange for supply chain coordination in the food industry. Journal of Operations Management 20(4) (2002)
5. Robertson, D., Allen, T.J.: CAD System Use and Engineering Performance. IEEE Transactions on Engineering Management 40(3) (1993)
6. Srinivasan, V.: An integration framework for product lifecycle management. Computer-Aided Design 43, 464–478 (2011)
7. Saaksvuori, A., Immonen, A.: Product Lifecycle Management, 3rd edn. Springer (2008)
8. CIMdata, Economic Benefits of PLM-Enabled Collaboration. CIMdata (2009)
9. Maranzana, N., Segonds, F., Lesage, F., Nelson, J.: Collaborative Design Tools: A Comparison Between Free Software and PLM Solutions in Engineering Education. In: Rivest, L., Bouras, A., Louhichi, B. (eds.) PLM 2012. IFIP AICT, vol. 388, pp. 547–558. Springer, Heidelberg (2012)
10. Segonds, F., Maranzana, N., Veron, P., Aoussat, A.: Collaborative Reverse Engineering Design Experiment Using PLM Solutions. International Journal of Engineering Education (2011)
11. Vila, C., Abellán-Nebot, J.V., Estruch, A.M., Siller, H.R.: Collaborative product development experience in a senior Integrated manufacturing course. International Journal of Engineering Education 25(5), 886–899 (2009)
12. Quatrani, T.: Visual modeling with Rational Rose, and UML. Pearson Education (2000)
13. Chiabert, P., Lombardi, F., Sauza Bedolla, J., Martinez Gomez, J.: Visualization Model for Product Lifecycle Management. Annals of Faculty Engineering Hunedoara 11(1) (2013)
14. Lujan, H.L., DiCarlo, S.E.: Too much teaching, not enough learning: what is the solution? Advances in Physiology Education 30, 17–22 (2006)

Application of PLM for Bio-Medical Imaging in Neuroscience

Marianne Allanic[1,2,3], Alexandre Durupt[1], Marc Joliot[2], Benoît Eynard[1], and Philippe Boutinaud[3]

[1] Université de Technologie de Compiègne, Department of Mechanical Systems Engineering CNRS UMR 7337 Roberval, 60200 Compigne, France
[2] UMR5296 GIN CNRS CEA Université de Bordeaux, 33000 Bordeaux, France
[3] CADeSIS, 37 rue Adam Ledoux, Bat. B, 92400 Courbevoie, France
marianne.allanic@utc.fr
http://www.plm-conference.org

Abstract. Bio-medical imaging (BMI) is currently confronted to similar issues than those of manufacturing industries twenty years ago : the growing amount of data, the heterogeneity and complexity of information coming from diverse disciplines, have to be handled by various actors belonging to different organizations. The researchers of the GIN (Neuroimaging Functional Group) laboratory study brain maps of anatomical and functional cognitive activation of hundred-subject cohorts, acquired with Magnetic Resonance Imaging (MRI). Therefore they want to manage the whole process of their research studies, from raw data to analysis results. Even if some data management systems have been developed to meet the requirements of BMI large-scale research studies, there are still many efforts to do in the integration of all the data and processes along a research study, from raw to refined data. So, the use of the Product Lifecycle Management (PLM) concepts to handle the complexity and characteristics of BMI data is proposed. A PLM neuroimaging datamodel that has been designed in collaboration between the GIN laboratory, Roberval laboratory and Cadesis company to meet the needs of the GIN, is described.

Keywords: PLM, bio-medical imaging (BMI), knowledge management, neuroscience.

1 Introduction

Bio-medical imaging (BMI) domain is currently confronted to similar issues than those of manufacturing industries twenty years ago. The inherent complexity of biological data has always challenged researchers, as they have to deal with many data sources, natures and types of processing [6]. However, with the recent technological improvements in imaging devices, but also networking and computing, the data handled by researchers has remarkably evolved. The size and amount of data have increased significantly, as huge cohorts of patients are required to

A. Bernard, L. Rivest, and D. Dutta (Eds.): PLM 2013, IFIP AICT 409, pp. 520–529, 2013.

draw strong inferences. In addition, more and more crossing analyses (eg. imaging, behavioral and genetics data together) are performed. Thus, there is a need of a unique, efficient and mature data management system.

The imaging technologies have reach a plateau which guarantee BMI data consistency at least for several years; it allows the data to be reused for longitudinal studies or any other purpose. However, costs, time and difficulty of leading BMI studies are not decreasing. So researchers would be rewarded to move toward a more synthesis-oriented research strategy: some types of studies should focus on the synthesis of previous findings [19]. Capitalizing the data among laboratories and institutions is an evident solution to get sufficient data, but it raises traceability, collaborative and confidentiality issues.

Product Lifecycle Management (PLM) software solve these issues, and permits manufacturing industry to stay efficient and competitive. Consequently, PLM systems promise to be adequate tools for the management of BMI data coming from large-scale studies that handle heterogeneous data. The data of a neuroimaging laboratory, the GIN[1], is chosen as an application; the neuroscience field is particularly active concerning imaging data management and constitutes a fertile ground for the work presented in this paper. Firstly, a state-of-the-Art of BMI efforts to design relevant data management tools is proposed. Secondly, interests of BMI field for PLM is developed. Thirdly, a proposal of a PLM neuroimaging datamodel is presented. To end with, discussion and perspectives for future work conclude this paper.

2 State-of-the-Art

2.1 BMI Data Management Tools

According to the authors of [18], the BMI scientific community must be provided with methods to query, analyze and crosslink the complex, heterogeneous and large-scale image data resources. Several sizeable database, with more or less success, show the commitment of the BMI research field.

For 15 years, the neuroimaging community has been aware of the need of neuroinformatics to advance its understanding of the brain (human and nonhuman): because of the growing amount of data to handle and the trend for collaborative studies, proper management and sharing has become crucial. Several solutions have been developed by networks of laboratories (BIRN, MRN, INCF, NIDAG[2]), aiming at designing adequate tools. In addition, projects develop their own tools, combining design of a database and large-scale imaging acquisitions: the Human Connectome Project (HCP, [16]) and the Human Brain Project (HBP, [14]) are such projects.

[1] Groupe d'Imagerie Neurofonctionnelle/ Neurofunctional Imaging Group.

[2] Biomedical Informatics Research Network `http://www.birncommunity.org/`, Mind Research Network `http://www.mrn.org/`, International Neuroinformatics Coordinating Facility `http://www.incf.org/`, Neuroimaging Data Access Group `http://www.nidag.org/`

All databases were not designed with the same purposes in mind, thus do not manage the data at the same stage of a study. A proposition of four phases of data analysis are presented in figure 1: ① study specifications (everything that define a research study and its proceedings), ② raw data (or acquired data), ③ derived data (both refined and final results), and ④ published data (peer-reviewed data recognized by the community). Neuroimaging databases can be divided in two categories; although many handle raw and processed data (phases ② and ③) accompanied by associated metadata for study management, others aim to share published results (phase ④) for future reuse:

- The first category of database permits researchers to manage locally and to share between sites and laboratories during large-scale studies. The types of handled data are demographic data in addition to imaging data. The most often used database tools by individual and collaborative projects[3] are XNAT[4] [9], LORIS [2], COINS [13] and IDA [17].
- The second category focuses on results coming from peer-reviewed published papers. Activation coordinates with associated metadata are the most frequent managed data in these databases. In some ways, published results databases, in particular BrainMap [4], supplement the literature by providing a unusual consistency of description, required for reuse: it appears that the information provided by the authors of papers to meet the requirements of such databases are sometimes more complete and precise than what is written in the original papers [3].

Nevertheless, no data management tool enables heterogeneous data management from study specifications ① to published results ④. Currently no database handles phase ①; even LORIS, which seems to be the most completed, doesn't manage it, neither published data ④. The figure 1 shows the distribution of the existing neuroimaging database tools: they all stay focused on no more than two phases. Though, neuroimaging field has now a global understanding of its acquisition and processing workflows [5], [9], [12]. Few data management tools now integrate the management of workflows (XNAT, IDA, Connectome mapping toolkit [5]) between phases ② and ③. In the figure 1, these workflows are represented by the arrow "processing".

2.2 Product Lifecycle Management and BMI

Product Lifecycle management (PLM) is summarized by [15] as a "product centric - lifecycle-oriented business model, [...] in which product data are shared among actors, processes and organizations in the different phases of the product lifecycle". Three phases define PLM [8]: the design and manufacturing phase is the Beginning-of-life (BOL), the distribution and use phase is the Middle-of-life (MOL), and the retired phase is the End-of-life (EOL). However, a common

[3] As observed in published papers.

[4] `http://xnat.org/about/xnat-implementations.php`

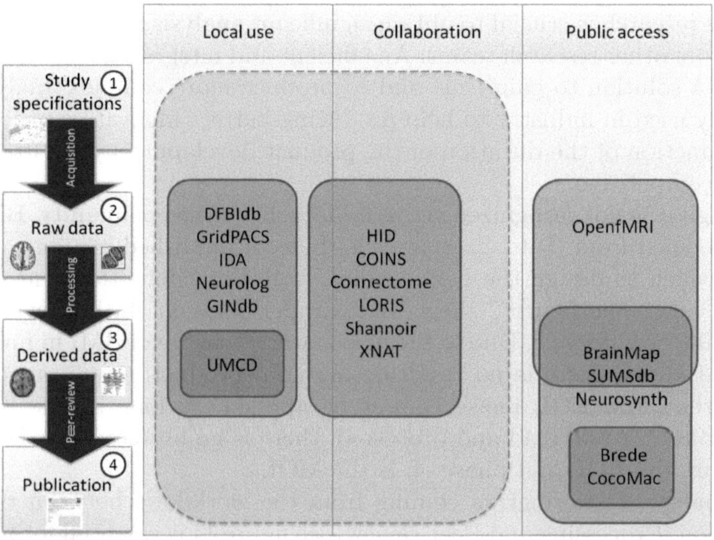

Fig. 1. Distribution of the existing neuroimaging database tools, according to our proposition of four phases of data analysis and the three level of sharing: local, collaborative and public. The area encompassed by dotted line represents the scope of our proposal in this paper.

lifecycle model cannot be applied for all the product type, depending on their complexity.

Originated from the car industry, PLM has now been widely adopted by the whole manufacturing industry world, including pharmaceutical domain, for instance the Roche[5] company. Nevertheless, PLM has not yet been widely set up in the medical field, except for prosthesis design and manufacturing: each prosthesis is one-patient customized and thus designed with BMI 3D reconstructions based on scanned images of the patient. Tornier, Groupe Lepine or Mount Kisco Medical Group [6] are example of companies using PLM to manage the lifecycle of each product, whatever the types of the documents: imaging, computer aided-design (CAD) or text.

3 PLM for BMI Data Management

3.1 Interests of BMI Field for PLM

Laboratories evolve in a competitive environment that can be compared to competitiveness in industry : researchers have to publish noteworthy papers to get

[5] `http://www.roche.fr`
[6] `http://www.tornier.com/`, `http://www.groupe-lepine.com/`, `http://www.mkmg.com/`

the financial grants that will allow them to lead the next studies. In addition, collaborative research is crucial to obtain significant analysis and to take advantage of skills from other research teams. An efficient and integrated data management system is a solution to gain time and to produce more complex analysis. PLM is precisely used in industry to help producing better (innovative products) and faster (reduction of the duration of the product development cycle) to cut costs and stay competitive.

Although it is not recognized yet as a lifecycle by the community, BMI phases can be modeled from ① to ④ as a cycle. Indeed, published results constitute a basis on which to design the next studies, from both definition and processing points of view. The figure 2 shows the parallel between BMI lifecycle and the traditional PLM lifecycle. Due to the non-material nature of BMI in fundamental research studies - there is no resulting material product, so no manufacturing phase -, the PLM EOL phase cannot be applied: as long as the images are consistent and can be read and processed, there is no obsolescence. BMI phases ① to ③ are the BOL and phase ④ is the MOL.

The quality of information coming from the workflows between two phases (Acquisition, Processing and Peer-review, see figure 1) is essential for the reusing - or repurposing - of data at any stage in a new context. This information is called provenance by the BMI community. So, reuse of previous data is an aim shared by the BMI domain and the manufacturing industry, and is one of the features of a PLM system: providing the right information at the right time and in the right context. When PLM systems matured from PDM (Product Data Management), they went from managing documents to the management of enterprise concepts ; the purpose of the work presented in this paper is to bring forward a similar kind of evolution in the BMI field.

Other disciplines, such as genetics[7] demonstrated that large-scale public sharing is a requirement for fast scientific advances in a research field [19]. Not only the PLM has not been designed for public sharing, but there are still some property rights issues or Protected Health Information (PHI) constraints that slow down data exchanges. Nonetheless, PLM is dedicated to data sharing among sites and thus can handle access restrictions needed by BMI for local and collaborative management (e.g. only a physician can access subject's individual clinical data).

An important distinction between BMI and industry is the required flexibility for BMI concerning the data model. Design and manufacturing processes and methods are mature and remain globally the same, whereas imaging computing technologies (between phases ② et ③) are continuously evolving, as well as research protocols.

3.2 PLM Features Applied to BMI

The following PLM features meet the needs of BMI data management and solve frequent issues:

[7] GenBank: `http://www.ncbi.nlm.nih.gov/genbank/`

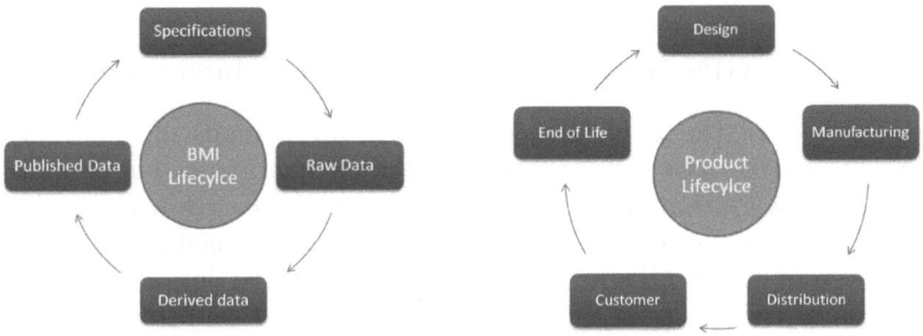

Fig. 2. Schemes of the BMI lifecycle and the traditional PLM lifecycle

- Business Object (BO) revision: keeps a track of the updates of processing definitions, computing codes...
- Workflow: notably allows the researchers to add BMI quality validation processes.
- Classification of BO: brings knowledge structuring but also flexibility to the data model, as the classification enables BOs to be associated with non-permanent attributes that can be easily defined by the users. This implies a reduction of the number of BO, and each BO represents a general concept that is robust enough to bear future changes of the data model.
- Advanced query and report generation: allows the user to run complex searches among the data and to export it for processing and analysis.
- User roles and access management: manage Protected Health Information (PHI) and property rights.

3.3 Deployment Methodology

The following methodology is proposed to deploy a PLM-based data management system to the BMI field.

The existing data management system is taken as a basis for the design of the first implementation of the PLM solution. Some end-users (key experts in neuroimaging research) are trained with the resulting tool that is provided with data. This first step is required to understand the lacks of the previous data management system and the needs of the researchers, in addition to the study of the literature. On the other hand, it allows end-users to think about their own practices and to get involved in the design process, which is important to ensure that reluctant users to new tools will use them. Specifications are written from all these feed-backs.

Then a classical AGILE methodology is deployed to manage successive design loops, from the requirement definition to the functionality test by end-users. Processing and analysis worflows will be translated into the model progressively, so that an integrated data management and analysis system will be obtained in the end.

4 Application

4.1 The BIL&GIN Dataset and GINdb Data Management System

The researchers of the GIN laboratory study brain maps of anatomical and functional cognitive activations of hundred-subject cohorts, acquired with MRI[8]. Therefore they want to manage the whole process of their research studies, from raw data to analysis results. In 2010, the laboratory designed its own data management system, called GINdb, and which is a relational database that manage metadata and paths to related files [7]. The GIN first Brain Imaging Laterality dataset (BIL&GIN1) includes 300 subjects, balanced by gender and handedness. This dataset was acquired between 2009 and 2011 and managed using GINdb [11].

However, the laboratory wants to improve its data management system, to get a more integrated environment that handle data and metadata during the whole life of a study, and that enables the data to be repurposed, e.g. for longitudinal studies.

4.2 PLM Neuroimaging Datamodel

Based on the GINdb data management tool, the litterature and interviews of key-users of the GIN, a first PLM object-oriented neuroimaging datamodel is defined. Globally, the business objects (BOs) are divided in two categories which constitute a basis for data property rights and PHI preservation :

- The BOs that can be created at any time and used for any study: unique subject in database, imaging and non-imaging exam definition, processing definition, computing tool, acquisition device, imaging template and bibliographical reference. All of these BOs are concepts and definitions that are used to justify all the data that is produced during the whole lifecycle of a study. The information resulting from the association of objects, via relations, is called provenance of data.
- The BOs that can be created only inside a study: these objects contain subject's individual context data (subject demographic and clinical information) and result data (non-imaging and imaging exam, processing) of subjects, as well as result data of groups of subjects (processing). The BO study gathers data such as ethical research comity reports and Protected Health Information (PHI) policy. Raw data is stored in a hierarchical structure of three BOs: exam (temporally uninterrupted row of acquisition), acquisition (indivisible period of data collection), and data unit (single data).

A visual summary of our proposal of a general neuroimaging data organization is given in figure 3; it highlights the category of BOs outside study (red), as well as subject's individual BOs (green) and cross subjects BOs (blue). In figure 4,

[8] Magnetic Resonance Imaging: medical imaging technique to visualize internal structures of the body.

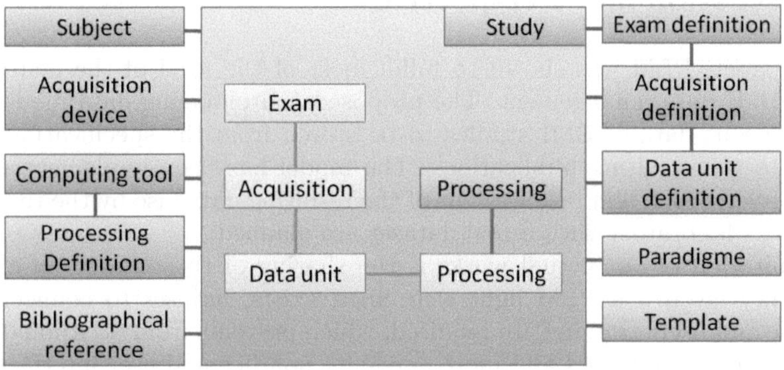

Fig. 3. Schema of the proposed neuroimaging data model. The red Business Objects (BOs) are the ones created outside a study. The other ones are created only inside a study, and can be divided in two groups: the BOs related to subject's individual data (green) and the BOs related to multi-subject's data (blue).

a simplified UML schema of the relationships between the BO that are used in figure 3 is presented with their cardinalities. This data model supports BMI data management during the four phases of the BMI lifecycle; all needed metadata and information for a potential reuse can be stored in the BOs. The concepts associated to each BO are general enough to enable any type of subject's data (e.g. imaging, genetics, behavioral...) to be managed.

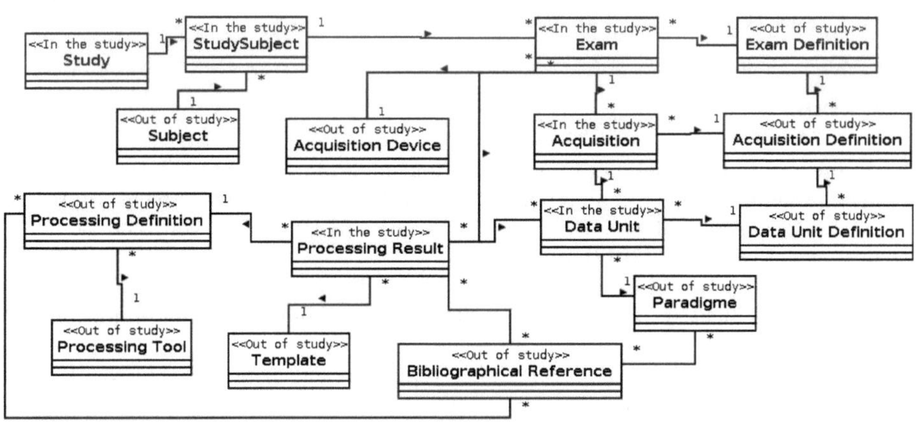

Fig. 4. Simplified UML schema of the proposed neuroimaging data model: the relationships between the Business Objects (BOs) are shown, with their cardinality. A mention is added on each BO to indicate whether it can be created inside or outside a research study. Imagery, Genetics, Processing, and Analysis BO are representing groups of BO.

5 Discussion and Perspectives

In this paper, PLM was shown to fulfill most of the need of the neuroscience field in BMI data management. The proposed neuroimaging data model allows heterogeneous data of BMI studies to be stored from the specifications of the studies to the resulting publications. The model has been implemented into a PLM software tool, and test sessions of the resulting database by the researchers of the GIN laboratory with a real dataset are planned.

A limitation of our actual works is the sharing of the data to an extended community: even if a PLM light web client exists, licenses to connect to the database and users training are required, which prevents from occasional use. So in the future, a simplified and more adequate non-licensed user interface has to be developed.

Besides, traditional PLM systems are not as flexible as required by research practices, so as a following work we will propose a semantic enrichment, based on ontology, and that will handle the management of relationships between objects [1]. As the understanding of these relationships is complex, a second point in our upcoming works will be to visualize them by graphs, in order to improve navigation as well as the visualization of data provenance in the resulting data management tool.

By all these developments for neuroscience field, we aim at achieving a BMI-dedicated module for PLM and at enhancing some PLM features as a feedback.

Acknowledgments. The authors wish to thank in particular the Association Nationale de la Recherche et de la Technologie (ANRT) for its financial support to their work (CIFRE 2012/0420).

References

1. Assouroko, I., Ducellier, G., Eynard, B., Boutinaud, P.: Semantic relationship based knowledge management and reuse in collaborative product development. In: Rivest, L., Bouras, A., Louhichi, B. (eds.) PLM 2012. IFIP AICT, vol. 388, pp. 1–13. Springer, Heidelberg (2012)
2. Das, S., Zijdenbos, A.P., Harlap, J., Vins, D., Evans, A.C.: LORIS: a web-based data management system for multi-center studies. Frontiers in Neuroinformatics 5, 37 (2011)
3. Fox, P.T., Laird, A.R., Fox, S.P., Fox, P.M., Uecker, A.M., Crank, M., Koenig, S.F., Lancaster, J.L.: BrainMap taxonomy of experimental design: description and evaluation. Human Brain Mapping 25(1), 185–198 (2005)
4. Fox, P.T., Lancaster, J.L.: Mapping context and content: the BrainMap model. Nature Reviews. Neuroscience 3(4), 319–321 (2002)
5. Gerhard, S., Daducci, A., Lemkaddem, A., Meuli, R., Thiran, J.-P., Hagmann, P.: The connectome viewer toolkit: an open source framework to manage, analyze, and visualize connectomes. Frontiers in Neuroinformatics 5, 3 (2011)
6. Goble, C., Stevens, R.: State of the nation in data integration for bioinformatics. Journal of Biomedical Informatics 41(5), 687–693 (2008)

7. Joliot, M., Delcroix, N., Zago, L., Vigneau, M., Crivello, F., Simon, G., Petit, L., Turbelin, M.R., Naveau, M., Lamberton, F., Herv, P.-Y., Jobard, G., Mellet, E., Mazoyer, B., Tzourio-Mazoyer, N.: GINdb: portable database for the storage and processing of human functional brain imaging data. In: Proceedings of the 16th Annual Meeting of the Organization for Human Brain Mapping Barcelona, Spain (2010)
8. Kiritsis, D., Bufardi, A., Xirouchakis, P.: Research issues on product lifecycle management and information tracking using smart embedded systems. Advanced Engineering Informatics 17(3-4), 189–202 (2003)
9. Marcus, D.S., Olsen, T.R., Ramaratnam, M., Buckner, R.L.: The Extensible Neuroimaging Archive Toolkit and Sharing Neuroimaging Data. Neuroinformatics, 11–34 (2007)
10. Neu, S.C., Crawford, K.L., Toga, A.W.: Practical management of heterogeneous neuroimaging metadata by global neuroimaging data repositories. Frontiers in Neuroinformatics 6, 8 (2012)
11. Petit, L., Crivello, F., Mellet, E., Jobard, G., Zago, L., Joliot, M., Mazoyer, B., Tzourio-Mazoyer, N.: BIL&GIN: a database for the study of hemispheric specialization. In: Proceedings of the 18th Annual Meeting of the Organization for Human Brain Mapping, Beijing, China (2012)
12. Poline, J.-B., Breeze, J.L., Ghosh, S., Gorgolewski, K., Halchenko, Y.O., Hanke, M., Haselgrove, C., Helmer, K.G., Keator, D.B., Marcus, D.S., Poldrack, R.A., Schwartz, Y., Ashburner, J., Kennedy, D.N.: Data sharing in neuroimaging research. Frontiers in Neuroinformatics 6, 9 (2012)
13. Scott, A., Courtney, W., Wood, D., de la Garza, R., Lane, S., King, M., Wang, R., Roberts, J., Turner, J.A., Calhoun, V.D.: COINS: An Innovative Informatics and Neuroimaging Tool Suite Built for Large Heterogeneous Datasets. Frontiers in Neuroinformatics 5, 33 (2011)
14. Shepherd, G.M., Mirsky, J.S., Healy, M.D., Singer, M.S., Skoufos, E., Hines, M.S., Nadkarni, P.M., Miller, P.L.: The Human Brain Project: neuroinformatics tools for integrating, searching and modeling multidisciplinary neuroscience data. Trends in Neurosciences 21(11), 460–496 (1998)
15. Terzi, S., Abdelaziz, B., Butta, B., Garetti, M., Kiritsis, D.: Product lifecycle management from its history to its new role. International Journal of Product Lifecycle Management 4(4), 360–389 (2010)
16. Van Essen, D.C., Ugurbil, K., Auerbach, E., Barch, D., Behrens, T.E.J., Bucholz, R., Chang, A., Chen, L., Corbetta, M., Curtiss, S.W., Della Penna, S., Feinberg, D., Glasser, M.F., Harel, N., Heath, A.C., Larson-Prior, L., Marcus, D., Michalareas, G., Moeller, S., Oostenveld, R., Petersen, S.E., Prior, F., Schlaggar, B.L., Smith, S.M., Snyder, A.Z., Xu, J., Yacoub, E.: The Human Connectome Project: a data acquisition perspective. NeuroImage 62(4), 2222–2231 (2012)
17. Van Horn, J.D., Toga, A.W.: Is it time to re-prioritize neuroimaging databases and digital repositories? NeuroImage 47(4), 1720–1734 (2009)
18. Walter, T., Shattuck, D.W., Baldock, R., Bastin, M.E., Carpenter, A.E., Duce, S., Ellenberg, J., Fraser, A., Hamilton, N., Pieper, S., Ragan, M.A., Schneider, J.E., Tomancak, P., Hériché, J.-K.: Visualization of image data from cells to organisms. Nature Methods 7(3 suppl.), S26–S41 (2010)
19. Yarkoni, T., Poldrack, R.A., Van Essen, D.C., Wager, T.D.: Cognitive neuroscience 2.0: building a cumulative science of human brain function. Trends in Cognitive Sciences 14(11), 489–496 (2010)

Proposition of Ergonomic Guidelines to Improve Usability of PLM Systems Interfaces

Perrine de Pinel[1], Nicolas Maranzana[1], Frédéric Segonds[1], Sylvain Leroux[2], and Vincent Frerebeau[3]

[1] Arts et Métiers ParisTech, LCPI,
151 bd de l'Hôpital, 75013, PARIS, France
[2] NextIS-Consulting,
18 rue Mogador, 75009 PARIS, France
[3] Vincent FREREBEAU
Independent consultant
p.depinel@gmail.com

Abstract. Evolutions of PLM systems are mainly directed towards the integration of more lifecycles stages to offer more PLM functions and information systems. At first, PLM were developed and intended only for engineers in detailed design phases. As engineers are familiar with complex and sparse interfaces, PLM software are not really ergonomic. The emerging problem in the past few years is the lack of evolution of PLM software, decreasing significantly its efficiency and utilization. But now, PLM integrate entire lifecycle of the product, so interfaces should be readjusted so that every actor, other than engineers, can easily use it.

In this paper, we assume that simplify and dynamize PLM software interfaces, by meeting usability features and user experience, make the system more interactive and coherent. In a first time, two states of art are realized. The first is about PLM evolution and web interfaces, the second about user experience and usability. A combination between agile method and user-centred design method are applied to these states of art in order to generate PLM software prototypes. Finally, user tests will be conducted on these prototypes in an incrementally and iterative way to correct and to validate them. The final target is to propose some ergonomic guidelines in order to create a generic interface adapted to several kinds of PLM software.

Keywords: Ergonomic, PLM, usability, user experience, agile method.

1 Introduction PLM and Challenge

In the earlier 2000s, PLM emerged as a solution to adapt industrial design to the demands of globalization. Indeed, as PLM addresses the entire lifecycle of the product, it has a cross-functional nature and deals closely with the way a company runs (Garetti et al., 2005).

For Amann (2002), over the past several years, PLM has emerged as a term to describe a business approach for the creation, management and use of product-associated intellectual capital and information throughout the product lifecycle.

A. Bernard, L. Rivest, and D. Dutta (Eds.): PLM 2013, IFIP AICT 409, pp. 530–539, 2013.

According to Pernelle and Lefebvre (2006), with the increasing concentration of editors and the obsession of lowering information technology costs, too few companies are aware that PLM system design has to evolve to follow user's expectations. Indeed, generic PLM methods are not adapted to the actual PDM platforms configuration causing some heterogeneity issues in the system. Other difficulties found in the PLM system design phase are the complexity and the lack of flexibility in the product models. Pernelle and Lefebvre (2006). This can be linked to the level of details of some standards (ISO 10303-1, 1994), which affects the data flowing fluidity.

These different points show the need to act on the PLM design and on its evolution through time. We intend to act along three main lines of PLM: product, processes and organization. We attempt to prove that adding innovation in PLM software design by including ergonomic and usability features can enhance user satisfaction.

2 State of Art

This state of art explains how an ergonomic approach can be integrate during the process PLM. It traces and explain the different rules attempting to improve process and interface PLM in the aim to satisfy the user.

2.1 Introduction of Concurrent Engineering and Ergonomic Approach

Introduction of concurrent engineering implies modifying design habits and requires changes in the project structure. This methodology involves different dimensions such as organizational, social, technical and economic (Bossard, 1997). In this context, it is possible to think that ergonomics can take place in this process at several levels (Fadier, 1997; Sagot, 1999).

The design process is complex and includes different cultures, actors and methods. Also, collaboration can be difficult and tensions may appear (Gronier, Sagot, 2005). A good collaboration environment requires some infrastructures such as databases, processes, and applications. This leads the company towards a common model oriented in an intuitive way that can be consulted by PLM users. With this kind of process, decisions can become more affordable and more understandable. Ergonomic approach can be considered as part of resource information and so assists the development process.

According to Kim et al. (2008), ergonomic analyses are not well managed in PLM. Indeed, they notice that the effective management of human information, along with concurrent ergonomic analysis is very important for each cycle of the product engineering in PLM. As stated Segonds et al. (2011) and Maranzana et al. (2011), PLM software evolution is still developed with a lack of maturity, of consistency, of relationship between modules.

According to Sagot (1999), integrating human factors in the design product today is an important point. Developing a multidisciplinary approach with engineering and social sciences, as ergonomics, is a huge challenge and a new way of thinking and collaborating. Nowadays, innovating in product design, it is important to meet users' needs and expectations through ergonomics.

The aim of ergonomics is to understand interactions between people and systems, define constraints of the user activities and determine the list of tasks PLM users will have to manage. Analyze the users' needs is an important first part of the approach aiming at reducing the problem scope. Therefore requirements depend on use and esteem needs. In fact, changing only one demand can have a significant impact on the system. Recommendations will help to define some guidelines to redefine the systems. They are active on the visible aspect of the interface and contribute to improve the content of the dialogue between the user and the system.

2.1.1 Ergonomics Standards

Standards are a set of rules to design and develop systems by ensuring a high level of comfort, performance, satisfaction and security when using a system. Two types exist: management process standards and standards specific to the product. The first type contains one of the most famous standards of the user-centered part design cycle, (ISO 13407, 1999). It's a guide with source information and user-centered organization principles such as: planning and management of design methods, technical aspects of human factors, usability features and general ergonomic principles. In the second type, designers can find some recommendations and the different manners of interacting when designing interfaces. For example, ISO 9241-10 (1993), the dialogue (adaptation to the task, ease of use, error tolerance...); ISO9241-13 (1998): the guidance system, etc. Usability features is an important part of the ergonomic approach and a reference in an expert evaluation of interfaces.

2.2 Human Computer Interaction and Usability Features

As stated by Juristo et al. (2007), the field of human computer interaction is often related to the usability of software systems. The authors developed a state of art in order to provide some recommendations on how to improve software system usability. Several authors refer to such recommendations named differently: design heuristics (Nielsen, 1993), usability rules (Shneiderman, 1998), usability principles (Preece et al., 1994; Constantine and Lockwood, 1999), ergonomics principles (Scapin and Bastien, 1997), usability patterns (Tidwell, 2005; Welie, 2003), etc.

According to Juristo et al., (2007), software usability is a quality attribute listed in a number of classifications (ISO 9126, 2001; Boehm, 1978). Nielsen (1993) clarifies a standard definition of usability as learnability and memorability of software system, its efficiency of use, ability to avoid and manage user errors and user satisfaction. ISO 9241-11 (1998) defines usability as ''the extent to which a product can be used by specified users to achieve specified goals with effectiveness, efficiency and satisfaction in a specific context of use''. In short, usability is also generally referred to as ''quality in use'' (ISO 14598, 1999). Many studies extol the virtues and benefits of usability (Trenner, 1998; Battey, 1999; Donahue, 2001; Griffith, 2002; Black, 2002): it improves productivity and raises team moral, reduces training and documentation costs, improves user productivity, increases e-commerce potential, etc. (Juristo et al., 2007). Usability is still insufficiently considered in most software systems (Seffah and Metzker, 2004).

Since 1990, usability inspection is the new way to evaluate user interface. According to Nielsen (1993), there are four basic ways of evaluating it: automatically (usability measured by running interface test programs), empirically (tests the interface with real users), formally (use precise models to calculate usability) and informally (based on experience of the evaluators). This kind of inspection leads us to have a large vision on the different aspects of PLM software evaluation.

Software usability is defined as an approach related to design, evaluation and use of human computer interaction, in order to optimize the compatibility between user, activity and software interfaces. Usability allows avoiding issues that could happen and tend to ensure a high performance and an ease of use. To resume, the aim is to design, correct and transform devices and software, by adapting them to human capabilities. It is important to preserve physic, mental and social aspects, preventing negative consequences during the user activities.

According to Brangier et al., (2009), scientific input of software usability can be defined in three types. Firstly, software usability defines some recommendations about style and content presented during interaction.

The goal is to guide how to design, organize and specify user's activities, taking into account human factors within the technology. Establish some rules based on experiments, methods and practices whose efficiency and effectiveness are verified. Secondly, software usability tries to specify some models of human computer interaction. It defines ways how the end users should interact with the machine and tries to identify cognitive process developed by them. It elaborates a cognitive and interactive functioning model of the user linked to the machine. Thirdly, software usability takes part of the process and methods development ensuring sensorial and cognitive compatibility and user acceptance optimizing usability features.

The aim of these three approaches is to reduce the distance between user and interfaces and to promote the user acceptance.

2.3 User's Acceptability of the System

Technological acceptability defines how users find a way to take control of a given system. It is based on how he deals and reacts to issues linked to the new technologies. To check compatibility between technical and psycho-physiologic features of the user can be interesting. For example, Shneiderman (1980) worked on compatibility between software features with the user operating mode regarding the ease of use and usability features. According to Nielsen (1993), acceptability is decomposed in many levels (Fig.1).

To design and evaluate interfaces, it can be useful to apply knowledge on cognitive, operational and social functioning.

These different ergonomic rules can be adapted to PLM software. In order to apply these recommendations in this kind of interfaces, we can use an agile software development since this approach is widely used in design engineering environments. It involves and takes into consideration the user and the client so as to adapt the development process.

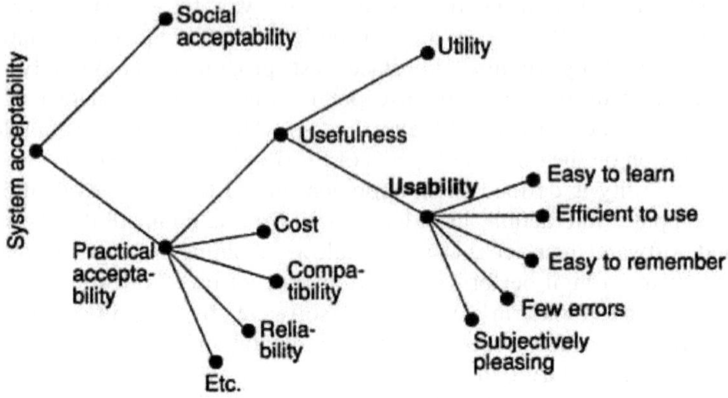

Fig. 1. System acceptability model adapted from Nielsen (1993)

3 Proposition of PLM Software Interfaces Improvement through User Centered Method and Agile Development

Losada et al., (2012) propose a guide to agile development of interactive software with a user centered driven methodology. They propose to improve the product usability by applying the maximum ergonomic recommendations and standards as possible. Even if they are different way of interaction, combining agile method with user-centered design could be a compelling approach to improve the efficiency of a PLM system. The aim is to understand the needs and tasks in order to adapt development principles by fostering individuals and interaction over process and tools and customer collaboration over contract negotiation.

Agile method objective is used to develop software in an incremental and iterative way. The main advantage is its flexibility during the development. This method is oriented on code development and ensures an adapted implementation of the functionalities. It tends to improve how software and process are developed. On the other hand, user centered design method is focused on the interaction in which the user will participate and to register the user's opinion about the application. User experience identify the expectations and cognitive brakes; study the expectations and needs; analyze user perception and analyze performance (Garett, 2002). It improve productivity and efficiency of the company by saving time, simplifying actions, and adding specific features. Both methods allow matching the users' requirement and their satisfaction while using the software.

Segonds (2011), developed a generic model based on a collaborative environment by integrating an agile development method. We base our approach on the same process by proposing a new model which describe how integrate user experience at each stage of the PLM development on the agile method. (Fig.2).We can propose the following hypothesis: Integrating User Experience and some Best Practices ergonomic during project development, facilitates the acceptance of users in the use of PLM in the company.

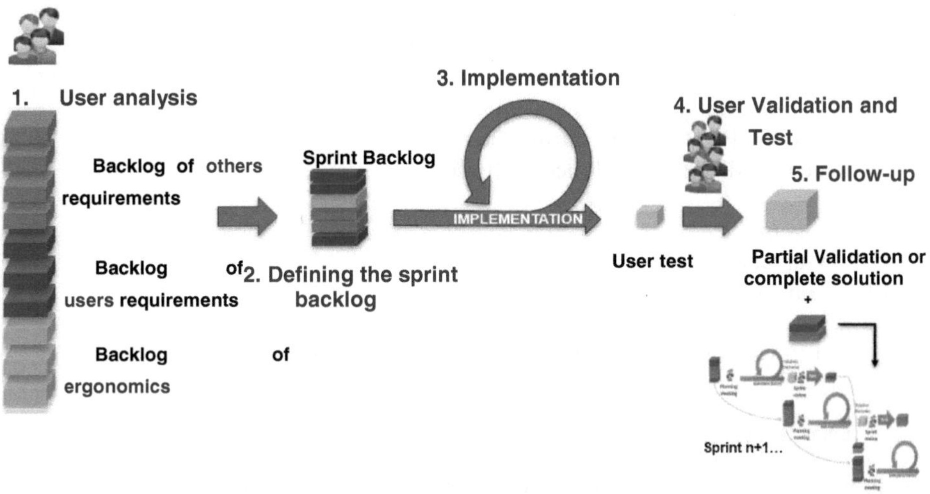

Fig. 2. PLM interface model design using a user centred method combined with agile development, adapted from Segonds and NextIS, (2011)

4 Experimental Plan

This protocol is a proposition; our hypothesis are not tested yet. Protocols below are the process we will used to answer them.

4.1 Integration of Best Practices Ergonomic User Centred

The integration of user experience in the agile model is represented by 5 steps.

1. User analysis

- To get acquainted with the project, to take account vision and objectives of the Product Owner
- Analyze the current situation, user behavior
- Define the target users and their characteristics (representative sample)
- Ensure user awareness to usability
- Identification requirements = Interview

2. Defining the sprint backlog

- Build Personas from the characteristics of users (Grudin & al. 2002)
- Write scenarios
- Design a navigation scheme based on scenarios
- Write detailed uses cases
- Prioritize uses cases with the Product Owner (P.O)

3. Implementation

- Describe the guidelines and standards for interface design
- For each use case, design a Digital Mock-Up

- Validate the mock-up developed, with users (Feedback)
- Achieve the development of the mock-up for the iteration (developers)

4. User Validation and Test
- Submit to the P.O the work during the iteration
- Validate the software developed with users

5. Follow-up
- Follow-up audit
- Change management

In order to validate our hypothesis, we establish a user test.

4.2 User Test

According to Nielsen and Laundauer (1993), 5 users can detect 75% of usability problems on an interface (Fig 3.). Each of the five users made two scenarios, one without ergonomic requirements and one with them. At the end, we compare the objective and subjective measures in order to check the productivity gain achieved with the ergonomic requirements. (Table 1).

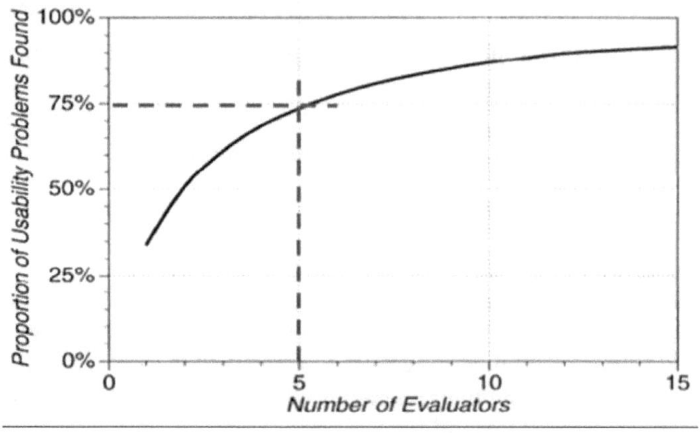

Fig. 3. Graphical representation adapted from Nielsen and Laundauer (1993)

Table 1. Table allowing to compare a scenario before and after the integration of ergonomic requirements in order to obtain objective and subjective measures

	Time to complete the scenario	The number of mouse clicks	The number of mistakes	The number of abandoned scenario	Satisfaction scale 1 to 7
Before ergonomic requirements					
After ergonomic requirements					

5 Conclusion

This article proposes to integrate an ergonomic approach to improve the usability of PLM interfaces by integrating user experience through the PLM development on the agile method. The state of art demonstrates that many problems found by PLM software users as complexity or the lack of flexibility of the system could be clearly solved by including usability features. Today, PLM systems are under-utilized and too many actors of companies do not feel concerned with this kind of software. To reduce cost, improve efficiency and delays of production were the main reasons of the creation of PLM, but current software do not meet these expectations. Pernelle, Lefebvre (2006). Our model based on the agile method integrate user experience during a project development. We suppose it is improving productivity and effectiveness by improving usability. To validate our hypothesis, we establish a user tests to validate the reliability of this model and show that involving usability features and user experience tends to promote the user acceptance on the PLM interfaces. This proposition could be beneficial to increase user's satisfaction and efficiency of the companies' production.

References

1. Amann, K.: Product Lifecycle Management: Empowering the Future of Business. CIMdata, Inc. (2002)
2. Bias, R.G., Mayhew, D.J.: Cost-Justifying Usability. An Update for the Internet Age. Elsevier (2005)
3. Bossard, P.: Origines et définition de l'ingénierie concourante. In: Bossard, P., Chanchevrier, C., Leclair, P. (eds.) Ingénierie Concourante: de la Technique au Social, Economica, Paris, ch. 1, pp. 11–28 (1997)
4. Brangier, É., Hammes-Adelé, S., Bastien, J.-M.C.: Analyse critique des approches de l'acceptation des technologies: de l'utilisabilité à la symbiose humain-technologie-organisation. Revue Européenne de Psychologie Appliquée/European Review of Applied Psychology 60(2), 129–146 (2010)

5. Donahue, G.M.: Usability and the bottom line. IEEE Software 16(1), 31–37 (2001)
6. Fadier, E.: L'intégration des facteurs humains à la conception. Phoebus, spécial sur le Facteur Humain, pp. 59–78 (1997)
7. Garetti, M., et al.: Organisational change and knowledge management in PLM implementation. International Journal of Product Lifecycle Management 1(1), 43 (2005)
8. Griffith, J.: Online transactions rise after bank redesigns for usability. The Business Journal (2002)
9. Gronier, G., Sagot, J.C.: Coopération à distance en conception de produits: analyse de l'usage d'un collecticiel. In: Battistelli, A., Depolo, M., Fraccaroli, F. (eds.) La Qualité de la vie au Travail dans les années 2000. Actes du 13ème Congrès de Psychologie du Travail et des organisations, pp. 1445–1453 (2005)
10. ISO 10303. Industrial Automation Systems and Integration - Product Data Representation and Exchange (1994)
11. ISO 13407. Human-centred design processes for interactive systems (1999)
12. ISO 9241-10. Ergonomic requirement for office work with Visual display terminal (VDTs), Part 10- Dialogue principles -First Draft International Standard (1993)
13. ISO 9241-13. Ergonomic requirements for office work with visual display terminals (VDTs) – Part 13: User guidance (1998)
14. ISO/IEC 9126. Software Product Evaluation—Quality Characteristics and Guidelines for the User, Geneva (2001)
15. ISO 9241-11. Ergonomic requirements for office work with visual display terminals (VDTs) - Part 11 Guidance on usability (1998)
16. ISO 14598. Information Technology—Software Product Evaluation, Parts, 1–5 (1999)
17. Juristo, N., Moreno, A.M., Sanchez-Segura, M.-I.: Analysing the impact of usability on software design. Journal of Systems and Software 80(9), 1506–1516 (2007)
18. Kim, G.Y., Noh, S.H., Rim, Y.H., Mun, J.H.: XML-based concurrent and integrated ergonomic analysis in PLM. The International Journal of Advanced Manufacturing Technology 39(9-10), 1045–1060 (2008)
19. Losada, B., Urretavizcaya, M., Fernández-Castro, I.: A guide to agile development of interactive software with a "User Objectives"-driven methodology. Science of Computer Programming, 1–14 (2012)
20. Maranzana, N., Segonds, F., Lesage, F., Nelson, J.: Collaborative design tools: A comparison between free software and PLM solutions in engineering education. In: Rivest, L., Bouras, A., Louhichi, B. (eds.) PLM 2012. IFIP AICT, vol. 388, pp. 547–558. Springer, Heidelberg (2012)
21. Nielsen, J., Landauer, T.K.: A mathematical model of the finding of usability problems. In: Proc. ACM INTERCHI 1993 Conf., Amsterdam, The Netherlands, April 24-29 (1993)
22. Nielsen, J.: Usability Engineering. AP Professional, Boston (1993); Perry, D., Wolf, A.: Foundations for the study of software architecture. ACM Software Engineering Notes 17(4) , 40–52
23. Pernelle, P., Lefebvre, A.: Modélisation intégrée et pérennisation des connaissances dans une approche PLM, Ingénierie de la conception et cycle de vie des produits, Traité IC2 – série Productique. Hermès Science Publications (2006)
24. Preece, J., Rogers, Y., Sharp, H., Benyon, D., Holland, S., Carey, T.: Human–Computer Interaction. Addison Wesley (1994)
25. Sagot, J.C.: Ergonomie et Conception anthropocentrée. Document pour l'Habilitation a dirigé des recherches, Institut National Polytechnique de Lorraine, INPL (1999)
26. Scapin, D.L., Bastien, J.M.C.: Ergonomic criteria for evaluating the ergonomic quality of interactive systems. Behaviour & Information Technology 16(4/5), 220–231 (1997)

27. Seffah, A., Metzker, E.: The obstacles and myths of usability and software engineering. Communications of the ACM 47(12), 71–76 (2004)
28. Segonds, F., Iraqi-Houssaini, M., Roucoules, L., Véron, P., Aoussat, A.: The use of early design tools in engineering processes: a comparative case study. International Journal of Design and Innovation Research 5(3), 61–76 (2010)
29. Segonds, F.: Contribution to the integration of a collaborative design environment in the early stages of design. PhD thesis, Arts et Métiers ParisTech (2011)
30. Shneiderman, B.: Designing the User Interface: Strategies for Effective Human–Computer Interaction, 3rd edn. Addison Wesley, Menlo Park (1998)
31. Shneiderman, B.: Software Psychology: Human Factors in Computer and Information Systems. Winthrop Publishers, Cambridge (1980)
32. Tidwell, J.: Designing Interfaces. Patterns for Effective Interaction Design. O'Reilliy, USA (2005)
33. Trenner, L., et al.: The Politics of Usability. Springer, London (1998)
34. Welie, M.: Amsterdam Collection of Patterns in User Interface Design (2003)
35. Wognum, N., Trappey, A.: PLM challenges. Advanced Engineering Informatics 22(4), 419–420 (2008)

Development of Automatic Assembly Sequence Generating System Based on the New Type of Parts Liaison Graph

Hong-Seok Park[1], Jin-Woo Park[1], Myon-Woong Park[2], and Jae-Kwan Kim[2]

[1] School of Mechanical Engineering, University of Ulsan, South Korea
[2] Korea Institute of Science and Technology, South Korea
phosk@ulsan.ac.kr

Abstract. Nowadays in order to perform assembly process planning by using CAPP (Computer Aided Process Planning), researches to generate the assembly sequence have come under constant interest by many researchers and they are devoted to optimize the assembly sequence according to the novel approach such as Genetic Algorithm and the newly biology inspired principle such as ant colony optimizing method. In this paper, the developed assembly sequence generating system analyzes the relationship between assembled parts based on surface contacting information. Moreover, this system generates the new type of parts liaison graph for the assembly sequences via analyzed information such as common area between parts, related ratio and number of the connected parts. Finally, the optimized assembly sequence is generated logically through the parts liaison graph.

Keywords: Assembly Sequence, Liaison Graph, Related Ratio, Common Area.

1 Introduction

In order to perform rapid process planning, various tools and methodologies are being used. Especially in order to achieve the automation of machining process planning, computer aided process planning (CAPP) is used by the information exchange and integration between design and machining process. And its technological level is in the maturity stage. Assembly process planning is forming 10%~30% in the whole manufacturing process and the computer aided technologies (CAx) are supporting to carry out the best assembly process plan. Nevertheless, the assembly process planning requires process planar to an enormous effort and time so far. The best assembly sequence generation for assembly process planning is an essential element because the assembly sequence concerns the correctness of process planning. Therefore, many researchers are devoted to optimize the assembly sequence by using various optimization methods.

The representation technology such as the liaison graph technique has been developed and used to represent the assembly sequence. As we know, Bourjault[1] , Homem de Mello and Sanderson[2] and De Fazio and Whitney[3] proposed the

A. Bernard, L. Rivest, and D. Dutta (Eds.): PLM 2013, IFIP AICT 409, pp. 540–549, 2013.

various graphs including precedence to generate the best assembly sequence such as relational model graph, directed graph, diamond graph, AND/OR graph and so on. From these graph techniques, hierarchical relation graph[4], skeleton graph[5] and etc. are introduced so far, however, most of the graph techniques do not generate precedence graph from the 3D CAD models automatically. It means that the precedence graph generation step using some geometry based relational model graphs is required additionally. Moreover, geometry based reasoning approach is prone to combinational explosion problem.

In order to reduce the searching space of assembly sequence planning for the complex product, the numerous intelligent algorithms have been developed and used to generate optimal assembly sequence such as genetic algorithms[6,7], artificial neural network[8], ant colony algorithm[9,10] and so on. Most of the optimization algorithms improve the processing efficiency via intelligent sequence combination. However the determination of assembly sequence depends on the initial conditions for a complex product and the influence of the parameters. According to this, part of the optimal solution often tends to converge and the sequence might be changed significantly because of the influence of parameters. In case of genetic algorithm, five stages for performing genetic algorithm can be identified: definition of genes, initial chromosomes, objective function, genetic operators and applied algorithm[11]. The parts of assembly model are considered as genes, therefore each chromosome has the feasible assembly sequences, however the initial chromosomes need to be given by the planner and not only the evaluation criteria but also the objective function for optimal sequence generation need to be set differently and variously for the assembly cases. It means that the engineering parameters such as cost, time, complexity, fits, direction, part type and so on have to be confirmed exactly to get the expected result.

This paper introduces the method of assembly sequence generation based on geometrical analyzing to overcome the shortcoming of the existing optimization methods. It means that the developed system analyzes the relationship between assembled parts based on contacting information such as common area, common volume. Furthermore, the new type of liaison graph, including the precedence between the parts is introduced to generate optimized assembly sequence. With this proposed liaison graph, the developed system generates the appropriate sequence of the product.

2 Method of Parts Relation Analyzing to Generate Assembly Sequence

2.1 Idea for Connected Condition Recognizing between Parts

The basic idea for recognizing connected condition between parts starts from combined shapes between two parts. Generally, one part has several geometric features, but not all of them are useful for assembly sequence generation. Because the assembly happens at contact surface and two parts interacting with one another, geometrical features for assembling should be defined in pairs.

This fact derives that if there are two assembled parts, contact region always exists and this contact region is always same between these two assembled parts because of matched geometric features. In other words, the contact region between two assembled parts includes the matched geometric features. Based on this reason, this paper supposes that the common area of contact region which has geometric features can derive out the precedence between the assembled parts.

2.2 Connected Parts Analyzing

This paper defines RR (Related Ratio) in order to determine the relationship between the parts. RR is classified to RR_{CAR} (Common Area Ratio) and RR_{CVR} (Common Volume Ratio). RRs between the parts can be derived as the combination of ratio for the total area(volume) and the common area(volume) of each part (Eq. 1, Eq. 2).

The common area and common area ratio can be used to recognize the precedence between the assembled parts; moreover the common volume can be used to recognize the interference fit because some designers reflect the tolerances to the 3D models directly.

$$RR_{CAR} = \left(\frac{\text{CommonArea of A\&B}}{\text{Total Area of A}} + \frac{\text{CommonArea of A\&B}}{\text{Total Area of B}} \right) \times \frac{100}{2} \quad (1)$$

$$RR_{CVR} = \left(\frac{\text{CommonVolumeof A\&B}}{\text{Total Volumeof A}} + \frac{\text{CommonVolumeof A\&B}}{\text{Total Volumeof B}} \right) \times \frac{100}{2} \quad (2)$$

If the assembly depth between the parts is increased, RR will be increased based on Eq. 1 & Eq. 2(Fig. 1). RRs need to be calculated for every part for deriving the weighting factor to draw product liaison graph.

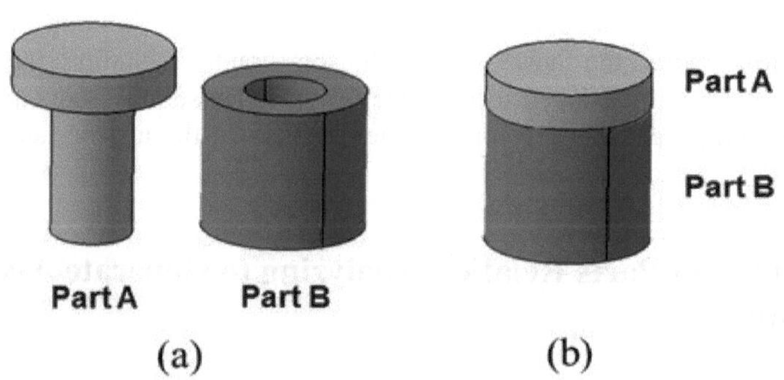

Fig. 1. Related Ratio between two parts (a) Separated case: $RR_{CAR} = 0\%$, (b) Assembled case: $RR_{CAR} = 45\%$

2.3 Calculation of Weighting Factor for Assembly Sequence

As preparation for the assembly sequence generation, the parts liaison is drawn and the liaison graph uses the weighting factors. The weighting factor is shown as Eq. 3 and it was prepared based on experiments and experiences with CA (Common Area), CV (Common Volume) and the count of connected parts of each part (n) are composed for Eq. 2.3 with RRs.

$$wf = \frac{e^{\left(\frac{\log_{RRCAR} CA + \log_{RRCVR} CV}{n}\right)}}{e^{\left(\frac{\log_{RRCAR} CA}{n}\right)} + e^{\left(\frac{\log_{RRCVR} CV}{n}\right)}} \quad (3)$$

This mathematical model considers the difficulty of assembly and the manufacturing cost indirectly. In some researches, the difficulty of assembly was derived based on log formulation [12,13] and the manufacturing cost was derived based on exponential formulation[14]. If the assembly depth is large i.e., common area and common volume is high, the assembly difficulty will be increased and the assemblability will be decreased. And if the assembly difficulty is high, the manufacturing cost will be increased. Based on this phenomenon, we use the log and exponential formulation with the RRs, CA, CV and the count of connected parts of each part. Fig. 2 shows the weighting factor variation of experiment between two parts in Fig. 1. The initial state of the experiment is the assembled condition and the final state of the experiment is the separated condition. The weighting factor was calculated during translation of part A from the initial state to the final state based on Eq. (3).

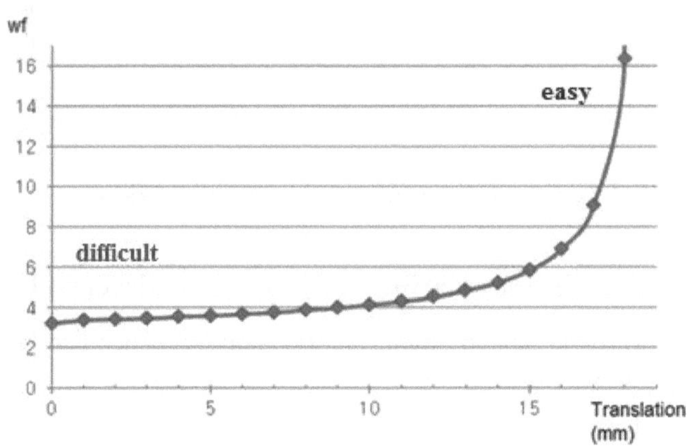

Fig. 2. Weighting factor variation during translation

As a result, if there are two cases of assembled state such as large assembly depth(difficult) and small assembly depth(easy) for the same assembly parts, normally the easy assembly will be considered priorly.

3 Parts Liaison Graph Drawing Based on Weighting Factor and Assembly Sequence Generation Based on the Graph and the Rule

3.1 Node Adding/Deleting/Combining

In order to generate the assembly sequence, the parts liaison graph needs to be drawn by using analyzed information such as connected parts list and weighting factors. The parts liaison graph is drawn based on the order of adding nodes, deleting nodes and combining nodes. The base part is selected according to the highest volume, the highest area and the largest number of connected parts.

The base part node is placed at the center and then the connected parts of the base part are placed radially around the base part node in the higher order of weighting factor. Then, the duplicated nodes that represent the same part in the upper level will be deleted. After deleting the nodes, combining step is performed to combine the same nodes at the latest level. These 3 steps will be repeated to construct the liaison graph (Fig. 3).

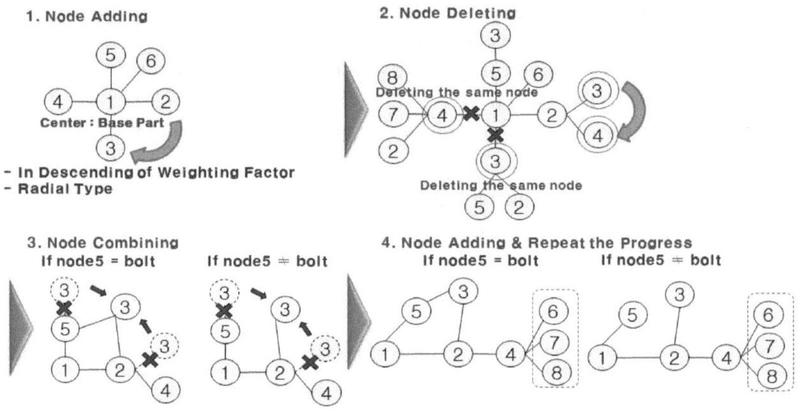

Fig. 3. Drawing Method of the Parts Liaison Graph

3.2 Rule of Assembly Sequence Generation Based on the Parts Liaison Graph

Through the drawn parts liaison graph, the assembly sequence can be generated as following summarized rules.

1. The node of base part is the start point of the assembly sequence.
2. The normal nodes of part are added to the assembly sequence after previous nodes.
3. If a node faces the branch of a road, the direction of progression is the node which has higher weighting factor.
4. The node of fastener part i.e. bolt, nut, pin, screw and washer is not added to the assembly sequence at the first progress.

5. If a node faces the branch of a road again or if the progress is stopped, the passed nodes of fastener part are added to the assembly sequence.
6. If a node is connected with three or more normal parts, they can be a sub assembly. But, the fastener connected to sub assembly will not added in sub assembly construction
7. All nodes are added once in order to configure the graph

In a sub assembly, if any fastener is connected to sub assembly and any normal part of the sub assembly, the graph doesn't show the connection of fastener with normal part of the sub assembly although this fastener is added to the sub assembly.

4 Architecture of Assembly Sequence Generating System and Its Implementation

4.1 System Architecture

The developed system architecture is shown in Fig. 4. The system architecture is configured with 4 interfaces such as the geometric data extraction, the part relation analysis, the parts liaison graph drawing, the assembly sequence generation. And several modules are consisted in each interface.

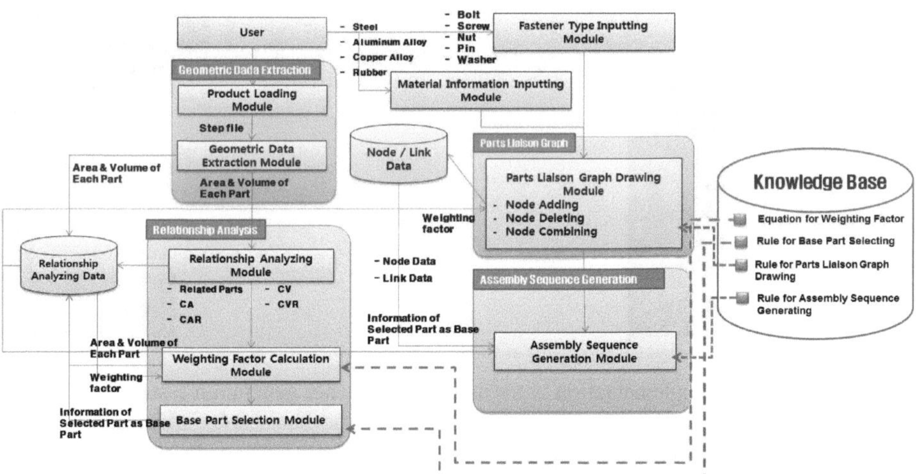

Fig. 4. Architecture of Assembly Sequence Generating System

The interface of geometric data extraction can load the product which includes the sub parts. The object file format is STEP. After loading the files, this interface collects the area and volume of each part then this information is sent to the part relation analysis interface.

The interface of part relation analysis searches connected parts of each part and this interface calculates CA, RR_{CAR}, CV, RR_{CVR} and count of connected parts. These data are transferred to the weighting factor calculation module in order to derive the weighting factors of each part. After this progress, base part will be selected.

The interface of part liaison graph drawing displays for the product on the dialog view. This interface is configured with node adding module, node deleting module and node combining module. The linked node information supports to generate assembly sequence. The drawn graph transfers the node and link information to the assembly generation interface in order to create the sequence by using knowledge-based rule.

4.2 Design of User Interface and Implementation of the System

The main user interface is shown in Fig. 5. There are 9 main parts to get result such as 1. part loading, 2. analysis of relationship between the parts, 3. selection of base part, 4. assembly sequence generation, 5. product information tree, 6. display view, 7. liaison graph display panel, 8. liaison graph drawing, 9. sequence extraction.

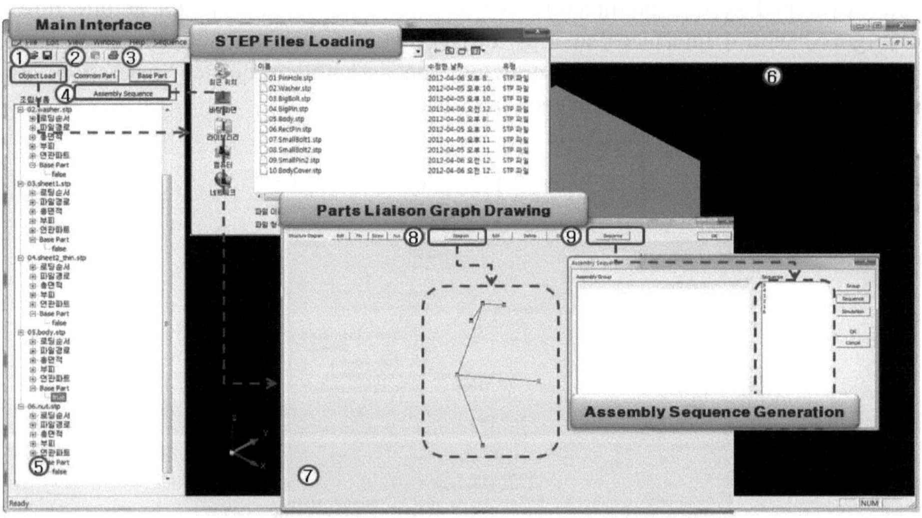

Fig. 5. Implementation of the assembly sequence generation system

User can click the part loading button to load and to display the product and then STEP files are loaded through the dialog box. After finishing the loading progress, the product is drawn at the display panel and collected data will be sent to the product information tree. If user clicks the relationship analysis button, the system analyzes and collects the whole necessary data. The color of product will be changed in analyzing progress. After completion of analysis, the system sends the message to user to notice about completion and analysis data will be sent to the information tree. Then, the system selects the base part through the base part selection button and this information will also be sent to the information tree.

The parts liaison graph can be drawn at the liaison graph display panel which is created through the button of assembly sequence generation. This dialog box has the fastener part input button, graph drawing button. User can input the information of fastener part. Furthermore, graph drawing button will draw the parts liaison graph automatically. Finally, sequence extraction button will carry out the generated assembly sequence. VC++ 8.0 (VS2005) and OpenCASCADE6.5.2. are used to implement the system.

4.3 Result of Sequence Generation

In order to evaluate the developed system, the automotive oil pump is used (Fig. 6-(a)). The oil pump has 32 parts and its exploded view is on Fig. 6-(b). The part 26 is selected as a base part. Fig. 7 shows the generated parts liaison graph of this test product. And the generated sequence based on the previous rule is "26→5→7→6→SA1→8→9→10→11→12→3→2→24→15→17→18→20→22→23→25→13→16→19→21→14→SA2". The sub assembly sequence1 is generated as "27→33→31→28" and the sub assembly sequence2 is "1→29→30→4".

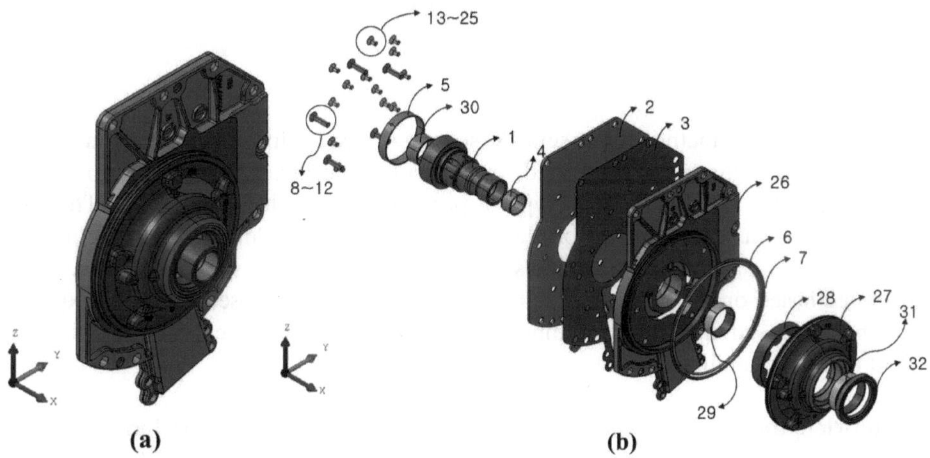

Fig. 6. Test product (a) assembled automotive oil pump product, (b) disassembled 32 parts of automotive oil pump product

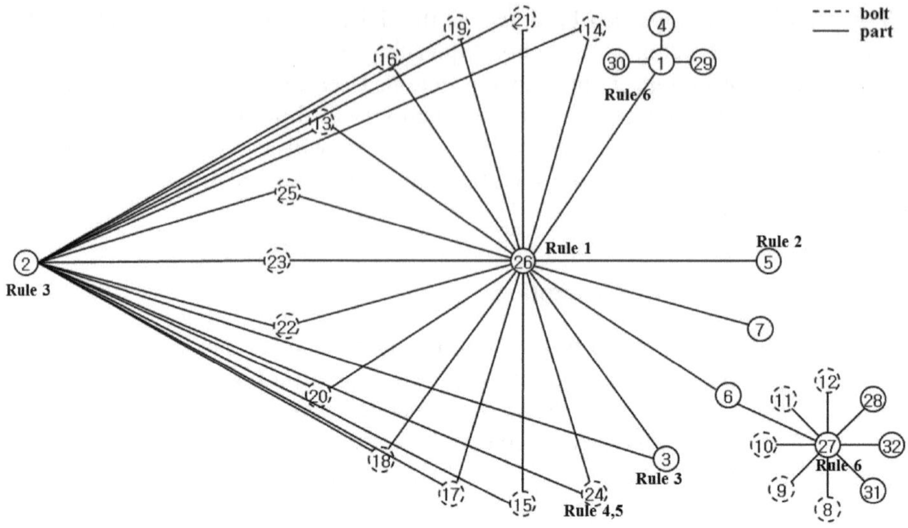

Fig. 7. Parts liaison graph of automotive oil pump product

5 Conclusion

In this paper, the method of assembly sequence generation different from several optimizing algorithm was introduced. In particular, the ideas of related ratio and the weighting factor to draw the new type of parts liaison graph were derived. The parts liaison graph was drawn based on the rules such as node adding, node deleting and node combining to display as 2D structure. Finally, the assembly sequence was generated based on the liaison graph information and the proposed rule. It is expected that the proposed method and implemented system reduce the sequence planning effort and the planning time.

Acknowledgments. This work was supported by the grant from the Industrial Core Technology Development Program (10033163) of the Ministry of Knowledge Economy of Korea.

References

1. Bourjault, A.: Computer-aided assembly process planning. Proceedings of the Institution of Mechanical Engineers, Part B: Journal of Engineering Manufacture 206(1), 61–66 (1992)
2. Homem de Mello, L., Sanderson, A.: AND/OR Graph Representation of Assembly Plans. IEEE Journal of Robotics and Automation 25(2), 188–199 (1990)
3. De Fazio, T.L., Whitney, D.E.: Simplified Generation of All Mechanical Assembly Sequences. IEEE Journal of Robotics and Automation 3(6), 640–658 (1987)

4. Niu, X., Ding, H., Xiong, Y.: A hierarchical approach to generating precedence graphs for assembly planning. International Journal of Machine Tools & Manufacture 43(14), 1473–1486 (2003)
5. Demoly, F., et al.: Geometric skeleton computation enabling concurrent product engineering and assembly sequence planning. Computer-Aided Design 43(12), 1654–1673 (2011)
6. Dini, G., et al.: Generation of optimized assembly sequences using genetic algorithms. CIRP Annals-Manufacturing Technology 48(1), 17–20 (1999)
7. Marian, R.M., Luong, L.H.S., Abhary, K.: A genetic algorithm for the optimization of assembly sequences. Computers & Industrial Engineering 50(4), 503–527 (2006)
8. Chen, W.C., et al.: A three-stage integrated approach for assembly sequence planning using neural networks. Expert Systems with Applications 34(3), 1777–1786 (2008)
9. Failli, F., Dini, G.: Ant colony systems in assembly planning: a new approach to sequence detection and optimization. In: The 2nd CIRP International Seminar on Intelligent Computation in Manufacturing Engineering, pp. 227–232 (2000)
10. Wang, J.F., Liu, L.H., Zhong, Y.F.: A novel ant colony algorithm for assembly sequence planning. The International Journal of Advanced Manufacturing Technology 48(1), 17–20 (2005)
11. Wang, L., Keshavarzmanesh, S., Feng, H.Y., Buchal, R.O.: Assembly process planning and its future in collaborative manufacturing: a review. The International Journal of Advanced Manufacturing Technology 41(1-2), 132–144 (2009)
12. Diaz-Calderon, A., Navin-Chandra, D., Khosla, P.: Measuring the difficulty of assembly tasks from tool access information. In: IEEE International Symposium on Assembly and Task Planning, pp. 1–7 (1995)
13. Park, H.S., Son, S.B.: A knowledge-based system for assembly process planning. Journal of the Korean Society of Precision Engineering 16(5), 29–39 (1999)
14. Kumar, M.S., Stalin, B.: Optimum tolerance synthesis for complex assembly with alternative process selection using Lagrange multiplier method. International Journal of Advanced Manufacturing Technology 44(3-4), 405–411 (2009)

Comparison of Configuration Rule Visualizations Methods

Anna Tidstam and Johan Malmqvist

Chalmers University of Technology, Sweden
anna.tidstam@chalmers.se

Abstract. The aim of this paper is to compare matrix- and list-based configuration rule visualization methods in order to find the effects of using a certain visualization method. Especially, the visualizations' impact on readability and how the configuration rules are authored are studied. A case study was conducted at two automotive manufacturing companies. The research method included to observe users as they were authoring configuration rules, to study the visualization methods, and to interviews users of the PDM system visualizing the configuration rules. It was found that common aim for the users is to author easy to read configuration rules, which this paper shows is highly dependent on the visualization method. The conclusion is thereby that the choice of visualization method influence how the configuration rules are authored.

Keywords: configuration rules, visualization, authoring.

1 Introduction

Configurable products are specified by a set of alternative product features. Cars are often configurable, with alternative product features including engine sizes and exterior colors. To assure that the specification of a configured product belongs to the developed product offering, there are logic expressions. An example of those logic expressions is that the *exterior color red* is not offered with *engine size 1.8 liters*. Such logic expressions are in this paper called *configuration rules* following the definitions in [1, 2]. Moreover, configuration rules validate the correctness are according to [1] rules for validating the correctness of customer orders and for guiding the actual assembly of these orders. A similar explanation is used in [2], where configuration rules are the rules for how the components can be combined to form a product. One of the main difficulties with large sets of configuration rules is the maintenance, in other words modifying the configuration rules following a product offering modification [3]. To be able to maintain the configuration rules, there is a user interface with a visualization of configuration rules. A visualization of configuration rules is a representation of configuration rules for communication of configuration rules to a user. The visualization of configuration rules is a kind of *information visualization*. The aim of information visualization is to create an effective representation of the information model and the information contained therein [4]. Effectiveness means that the user as quickly as possible gets an overview of the information. The effectiveness is challenged for the configuration rule visualization as there may be hundreds of thousands of configuration rules.

A. Bernard, L. Rivest, and D. Dutta (Eds.): PLM 2013, IFIP AICT 409, pp. 550–559, 2013.

Some researchers have studied different methods for visualization of configuration rules, for example matrices: K- and V-matrix [5], and trees: Product Family Master Plan [6] and the Variant Tree [7]. The mentioned previous research is however not empirical studies with configuration rules from the automotive industry. Earlier studies have shown benefits of matrix-based methods for configuration visualization [8]. For example, a matrix organizes data into a structured overview that is difficult to achieve with a list of text strings. The advantages and disadvantages specific to configuration rules have however not been fully studied. There is a list-based configuration rules visualization from an automotive company in [9], but unfortunately this visualization is not in detail described nor evaluated. If the configuration rules cannot be effectively visualized, an alternative approach is to change representation as for example mathematical equations on design parameters which was suggested in [9].

The authoring, i.e. the creation and modification, of configuration rules depends on the user: some users prefer a set of few but long (many product features) configuration rules, while others prefer a set of many but short (few product features) configuration rules [8]. The main aim with this paper is to compare configuration rule visualization methods in order to find the effects of using a certain visualization method, especially the impact on how the configuration rules are authored. A second aim is to find advantages and disadvantages for the visualization methods at the two automotive manufacturing companies. The following research questions have been addressed:

RQ1: What are the characteristics of the authoring methods for configuration rules that may be derived from the use of either matrix- or list-based visualization methods?

RQ2: Which visualization method is most suitable in the cases of:

(a) high number of configuration rules
(b) high number of product features in each configuration rule?

The remaining of the paper is organized as follows: In Section 2 the research method is described, Section 3 presents the results, Section 4 discusses the results and in Section 5 the conclusions are stated. Finally, in Section 6 future work is proposed.

2 Research Method

This paper studies the configuration rules visualization methods at two major European automotive manufacturing companies, henceforth called Alpha and Beta.

The research study was conducted during a 3 months stay at Beta in the team of configuration rules specialists, which was an adequate time-frame for revealing the process of authoring configuration rules as well as getting acquainted with the PDM backbone systems at Beta. During this time, several workshops were arranged with Alpha, which gave the possibility to compare both authoring and visualization methods. As seen in Fig. 1, the research process was structured into three phases: analysis, testing and evaluation. In the analysis phase, the authoring and visualization of configuration rules were described. Then in the testing phase, the configuration rules at Beta were tested with Alpha's visualization method. This comparison was later evaluated during the evaluation phase by interviewing three configuration rules specialists with various years of experience (4-30 years) at Beta.

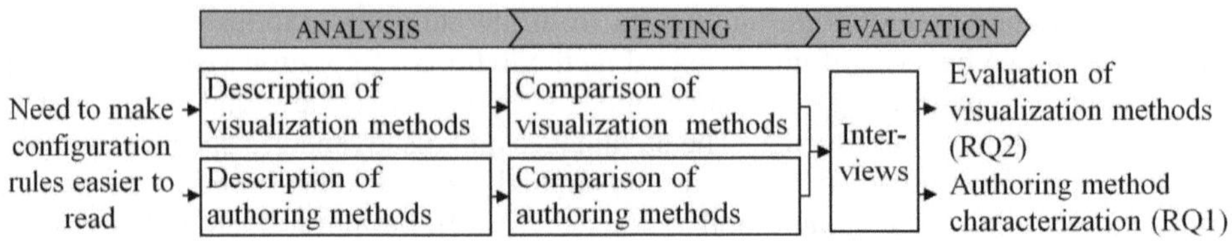

Fig. 1. Overview of applied research methods

3 Results

The result section is divided into three sections: 3.1 Analysis phase, 3.2 Testing phase and 3.3 Evaluation phase.

3.1 Analysis Phase

In this section, a use case scenario is used for describing authoring and visualization methods at Alpha and Beta. The use case describes the authoring of configuration rules for a new feature variant *a3*, e.g. *orange* exterior color. New feature variants do not have any configuration rules initially, and the use case is to author the required configuration rules. Feature variant *a3* belongs to feature family *A* (e.g. *exterior color*), which already contains the feature variants *a1* (e.g. *red*) and *a2* (e.g. *green*). Both Alpha and Beta use codes for feature families and feature variants.

Authoring and Visualizing Configuration Rules at Alpha. The purpose of this section is to show the principles for how to author configuration rules at Alpha (using their matrix-based visualization method), which is then followed by another section for Beta (using their list-based visualization method).

The authoring process at Alpha consists of three steps: Step 1 is to visualize existing configuration rules, Step 2 is to update the feature family relationship, and Step 3 is to assign configuration rule values. The authoring of configuration rules is thereby prepared in Step 1, and actually performed in Step 2 and 3.

Step 1 is to visualize the configuration rule matrix for feature family *A*, as shown in Fig. 2. The systematic configuration rule value (S) indicates that only particular combinations of feature variants are allowed. The only allowing configuration rule for *a1* is IF *a1* THEN *(m1* AND *n1)*, e.g. IF *red* THEN (*engine V6* AND *sport package*). The minus signs restrict feature variant combinations, e.g. NOT (*a1* AND *m2* AND *n1).*

Step 2 is to update, if necessary, feature family *A*'s relation, see Table 1. Feature family relations are the source data for the generation of any configuration rule matrix. In this use case scenario, it is assumed that feature family *P* is required because of the addition of feature variant *a3*.

			THEN	
		Feature families	**Feature variant combinations**	
		M	*m1*	*m2*
		N	*n1*	*n1*
	Feature family	**Feature variant**		
IF	*A*	*a1*	S	–
	A	*a2*	–	S
	A	*a3*	–	–

S = systematic and – = not allowed

Fig. 2. An example of Alpha's configuration rule matrix. This visualization is studied during the first step in authoring configuration rules at Alpha.

Table 1. Feature family *A* with its relation left) before update with *P* and right) after the update

Before update	
IF	THEN
Feature family	**Feature families**
A	*M, N*

After update	
IF	THEN
Feature family	**Feature families**
A	*M, N, P*

Step 3 is to assign configuration rule values, see Fig. 3. The new optional configuration rule value (O) for *a3* is the feature variant combination *m2* AND *n1*. Among optional configuration rule values, there is a default configuration value (D) which is the preferred feature variant combination. The configuration rule value for *a2* also needs to be updated as it is no longer the only allowed feature variant for combination *m2* AND *n1*.

			THEN			
		Feature families	**Feature variant combinations**			
		M	*m1*	*m2*	*m1*	*m2*
		N	*n1*	*n1*	*n1*	*n1*
		P	*p1*	*p1*	*p2*	*p2*
	Feature family	**Feature variant**				
IF	*A*	*a1*	S	S	–	–
	A	*a2*	–	–	D	D
	A	*a3*	–	–	O	O

S = systematic, D = default, O = optional and – = not allowed

Fig. 3. Configuration rule matrix with updated configuration rule values for feature variant *a3*, which is done during the third and last step in authoring configuration rules at Alpha

The authoring and visualization of configuration rules at Alpha have now been described, and now it will be shown hot the same operation is performed at Beta.

Authoring and Visualizing Configuration Rules at Beta. The same use case scenario is used when described in the authoring method at Beta: Step 1 is to visualize the existing configuration rules, and Step 2 is to author the configuration rules.

Step 1 in the use case is to visualize configuration rules for *a1* and *a2*, see Table 2. The purpose of Step 1 is to find frequently used feature families, for example all engine sizes can have configuration rules with gear box alternatives. The configuration rules at Beta may include both positive (AND, OR) and negative operators (NOT).

Table 2. List-based visualization of configuration rules studied for finding frequently used feature families that could be suitable to use for authoring of configuration rules for *a3*

IF	THEN
Feature variant	**Feature variant combinations**
a1	*m1* AND *n1* AND NOT(*a2*)
a2	*m2* AND *n1* AND NOT(*a1*)

Step 2 is to author the configuration rule for *a3*, see Table 3. As the customer may choose between *a2* and *a3*, also the configuration rule for *a2* has to be re-formulated. Notice that there is no difference between default and optional feature variant combinations at Beta, as this distinction is managed the separate sales system.

Table 3. List-based visualization of configuration rules with new configuration rules for *a3*, and updated configuration rule for *a2*

IF	THEN
Feature variant	**Feature variant combinations**
a1	*m1* AND *n1* AND NOT(*a2* OR *a3*)
a2	*m2* AND *n1*
a3	*m2* AND *n1*

The analysis phase is thereby ended and the next section will describe the testing phase.

3.2 Testing Phase

The purpose of the testing phase is to find relevant measures for the matrix- and the list-based visualization methods and thereby compare those using three real case examples. The real case examples were selected based on the users' at Beta interest in trying challenging examples, for instance configuration rules with extremely many configuration rules or extremely many feature variants within the configuration rules. One of the real case examples visualized with Alpha's matrix-based method is shown in Fig. 3. Two measurements have been established: a size measurement G in the growth direction (number of columns for the matrix, number of rows for the list), and a combinatory difficulty measurement C which is the number of feature variants combined in a configuration rule. The number of columns in Fig. 4 is 10, but note that the number of columns is here reduced, as for example the empty cells for the row of feature family *P* could be filled with any of *p1* or *p2*. The combinatory difficulty measurement is equal to the number of rows with feature variants in the matrix, which is 9 in Fig. 4. The number of configuration rules, could be counted as a range between 1-10, as the configuration rule values could be combined with the OR-operator.

	Feature family	THEN **Feature variant combinations**										Combinatory difficulty measurement:
	M	*m1*	*m1*	*m1*	*m1*	*m1*	*m1*	*m1*	*m1*	*m1*	*m1*	1 (*m1*)
	N	*n3*	*n3*	*n1*	*n1*	*n4*	*n4*	*n4*	*n2*	*n2*	*n2*	2 (*n1* – *n4*)
	O	*o1*	*o3*	*o2*	*o2*	*o4*	*o4*	*o4*	*o5*	*o5*	*o6*	3 (*o1* – *o6*)
	P					*p1*		*p2*	*p2*	*p1*		4 (*p1*, *p2*)
	Q					*q2*						5 (*q2*)
	R						*r1*					6 (*r1*)
	S			*s2*	*s1*							7 (*s1*, *s2*)
Feature family	**Feature variant** / *T*		*t1*		*t1*							8 (*t1*)
IF *A*	*a1*	O	O	O	O	O	O	O	O	O	O	9 (*a1*)
		1	2	3	4	5	6	7	8	9	10	

Growth measurement

S = systematic, D = default, O = optional and – = not allowed

Fig. 4. Alpha's configuration rule matrix with the measurements relevant for the tests (number of feature variants, number of feature variant combinations) marked out

The same example with Beta's original authoring of configuration rule list is shown in Fig. 5. The number of rows are 5 for measurement *G,* and the combinatory difficulty measurement *C* (number of feature variants in a configuration rule) is a range 3 to 12.

IF **Feature variant**	THEN **Feature variant combinations**	Growth measure ment	Combinatory difficulty measurement
a1	(*n1* AND *s2*) OR (*n1* AND *s1* AND *t1*) OR (*n2* AND *o5*) OR *n4* AND *p2*	1	10 (*a1*, *n1*, *s2*, *n1*, *s1*, *t1*, *n2*, *o5*, *n4*, *p2*)
a1	*n4* AND *r1*	2	3 (*a1*, *n4*, *r1*)
a1	(*n1* AND *s1* AND *t1*) OR (*n4* AND *o4*)	3	6 (*a1*, *n1*, *s1*, *t1*, *n4*, *o4*)
a1	((*n1* AND *s2*) OR (*n1* AND *s1* AND *t1*) OR (*n2* AND (*o5* OR *o6*) OR *n4*) AND *q1*) AND *p1*	4	12 (*n1*, *s2*, *n1*, *s1*, *t1*, *n2*, *o5*, *o6*, *n4*, *q1*, *p1*)
a1	*n3* AND (*o1* OR (*o3* AND *t1*))	5	5 (*n3*, *o1*, *o3*, *t1*)

Fig. 5. Beta's configuration rule list with the measurements relevant for the tests (number of configuration rules and maximal number of feature variants) are marked out

The test result summary for the three real case examples and the measurement in the growth direction (*G*) is shown in Table 4. The trend is that the number of matrix columns is higher than the list rows, which may be a disadvantage when using a matrix-based visualization method. The combinatory difficulty measurement (*C*), shown in Table 5 does not show a clear trend. The matrix-based visualization can, but not necessarily, have a combinatory difficulty within the range of the list-based visualization method. It all depends on how the configuration rules are authored and which configuration rules that are visualized together.

Table 4. Test results of measurements growth direction measurement (number of columns vs. rows) for three real case examples (A-C)

Company	Alpha (matrix-based visualization)		Beta (list-based visualization)
Growth measurement	Number of columns		Number of rows
Example A	8	is more than	4
Example B	12	is more than	9
Example C	10	is more than	5

Table 5. Test results of combinatory difficulty for three real case examples (A-C)

Company	Alpha (matrix-based visualization)		Beta (list-based visualization)
Combinatory difficulty measurement	Number of feature variants in combination		
Example A	3	is less than	max 4
Example B	41	is more than	max 34
Example C	9	is less than	max 12

3.3 Evaluation Phase

Three semi-structured interviews were held with configuration rules specialists from Beta, where they commented on the benefits and disadvantages of the matrix- and the list-based visualization method based on the real case example from the previous section. During the interviews it was found that the advantages of using the matrix-based visualization method were dominating. Arguments were that the list-based configuration rules at Beta were similar to programming with many symbols for Boolean operators and complicated use of brackets. The matrix-based visualization method does not contain any explicit Boolean algebra (signs such as OR (/), AND (,), NOT(-), AND-NOT (+-)). One quotation from an interviewee's comments is:

Our PDM system [with list-based visualization method] contains Boolean algebra which is for few people understandable, especially since we combine so many +, - and (). The matrix [without any explicit use of Boolean algebra] is in general always easier to overview and understand.

The non-specialists at Beta have great difficulties in reading the Boolean algebra in the configuration rules. This is in contrast to the non-specialists at Alpha who are competent to review the configuration rule matrixes at monthly meetings, and as well as soon there is a modification need.

4 Discussion

The main aim of this paper is to compare configuration rule visualization methods in order to find effects of how configuration rules are authored from using a certain visualization method. A second aim is to find advantages and disadvantages of the visualization methods at the two automotive manufacturing companies. The following research questions have been addressed:

RQ1: What are the characteristics of the authoring methods for configuration rules that may be derived from the use of either matrix- or list-based visualization methods?

Overall, people not familiar with the authoring of configuration rules may find it difficult to even compare the use of matrix- and list-based visualization methods. For experienced users, the probably most striking difference is that, in contrast to Beta, Alpha has a visualization method generated from feature family relations. The feature family relations are extremely important for the configuration rule matrix, as reducing the number of feature family relations is the only way users can prevent the number of matrix columns from becoming high. The user wants to have few matrix columns in order to have an easy overview configuration rule matrix. Few feature family relations give short but many configuration rules.

At Beta, it is instead the number of rows in the configuration rule lists that the users are trying to prevent from growing. That is another optimization objective, causing the configuration rules to differentiate from Alpha's configuration rules: Beta authors long but few configuration rules. The combinatorial difficulty is then higher for a list than for a matrix when the users aim for an easy to overview visualization of configuration rules.

RQ2: Which visualization method is most suitable in the cases of:
(a) high number of configuration rules
(b) high number of product feature variants in each configuration rule?

Answering RQ2a: A high number of configuration rules potentially cause the visualization of configuration rules to become, independently of the visualization method, unmanageable big. The disadvantage of the matrix-based visualization method is that the number of matrix columns can potentially grow faster than the number of rows in the list-based visualization. This was shown in the tests conducted in this paper, where all three tests examples had this behavior. When there is a high number of configuration rules to be visualized, the list-based method has the advantage there are many logical operators that could be used in order to prevent the number of rows to grow rapidly. The recommendation is therefore to use a configuration rule list when a high number of configuration rules are visualized.

Answering RQ2b: A high number of feature variants in combination causes combinatorial complexity. The benefit of the matrix-based visualization is that is does not have the OR operator; there are only the operators AND and NOT. This is a very important fact, as it is the OR operator that enables the high number of features variants in combination. Without the OR operator, the configuration rule has to be visualized using several shorter configuration rules, with lower combinatorial difficulty and thereby easier to read. Based on this discussion, the conclusion is that the matrix-based visualization method is well suited for visualizing configuration rules with a high number of feature variants in combination.

5 Conclusions

The visualization method strongly influences how the configuration rules are authored, as there are different optimization goals for readability (few matrix columns vs. few list rows) and availability of logical operators (with vs. without OR operator). There are therefore obstacles when changing visualization methods, here summarized below.

From a list-based visualization method to a matrix-based visualization: the matrix will potentially get many columns.

From a matrix-based visualization to a list-based visualization: the strength of the list is not shown until the configuration rule are reformulated with the introduction of the OR operator.

The interviewed configuration rules specialists however strongly preferred the matrix-based visualization method even when admitting the strength of the list-based visualization method. The main argument was that the matrix-based visualization kept the Boolean algebra simple as it did not allow any OR operator. With a simple Boolean algebra, the configuration rules are becoming easier-to-read for all users working with configuration rules and that would make the development of configuration rules more efficient.

6 Future Work

The three examples tested in this paper were selected on the basis of the users' wishes to test the visualization methods' strengths and weaknesses on challenging examples. Challenges in this context mean that the users had either a high number of configuration rules, or a high number of feature variants in each configuration rule. This is similar to a stress test, where a concept is tested under extreme conditions. A suitable continuation would be to build a prototype that the users could test under normal work conditions, which could capture more opinions of strengths and weaknesses of the two visualization methods.

Acknowledgements. This work was carried out at the Wingquist Laboratory VINN Excellence Centre for Efficient Product Realization at Chalmers University of Technology, supported by the Swedish Governmental Agency for Innovation Systems (VINNOVA). Further financial support was received from ProViking. For supervision during the industrial stay the first author would like to thank Hr. Eiffinger.

References

1. Barker, V.E., O'Connor, D.E.: Expert systems for configuration at Digital: XCON and beyond. Communications of the ACM 32(2), 298–318 (1989)
2. Soininen, T., Niemelä, I.: Developing a declarative rule language for applications in product configuration. In: Gupta, G. (ed.) PADL 1999. LNCS, vol. 1551, pp. 305–319. Springer, Heidelberg (1999)
3. Bachant, J., McDermott, J.: R1 revisited: Four years in the trenches. AI Magazine 5, 21–32 (1984)
4. Mackinlay, J.: Automating the design of graphical presentations of relational information. ACM Transactions on Graphics 5(2), 110–141 (1986)
5. Bongulielmi, L., Henseler, P.C., Puls, C., Meier, M.: The K- & V-Matrix-Method in Comparison with other Matrix-based Methods supporting Modular Product Family Architectures. In: Sigurjonsson, J.B. (ed.) Proceedings of NordDesign, Trondheim (2002)
6. Harlou, U.: Developing product families based on architectures – Contribution to a theory of product families, PhD thesis, Department of Mechanical Engineering, Technical University of Denmark (2006)
7. Schuh, G., Jonas, I.: Variantenreduzierung im Verbund – Praktikable Methode zum Variantenmanagement: Ein Leitfaden zur Beherrschung der Variantenvielfalt. Verbundinitiative Automobil Nordrhein-Westfalen, Düsseldorf, Germany (1997)
8. Tidstam, A., Malmqvist, J.: Authoring and Verifying Vehicle Configuration Rules. In: Proceedings of 8th International Conference on Product Lifecycle Management, Eindhoven, The Netherlands, July 11-13 (2011)
9. Hami-Nobari, S., Blessing, L.: Effect-oriented Description of Variant Rich Products. In: Proceedings to International Conference on Engineering Design (ICED 2005), Melbourne, Australia, August 15-18 (2005)

A Product Avatar for Leisure Boats Owners: Concept, Development and Findings

Karl Hribernik, Thorsten Wuest, and Klaus-Dieter Thoben

Bremer Institut für Produktion und Logistik GmbH, Hochschulring 20,
28359 Bremen, Germany
{hri,wue,tho}@biba.uni-bremen.de

Abstract. The European boat industry is suffering from a slowdown in customer demand. The manufacturers and other stakeholders are forced to think of new ways to regain competitive advantage and to attract and maintain their customers. A promising approach is to develop new services based on the collection of information throughout the product lifecycle. Different stakeholders can use the services over different channels, such as Social Network Services, by means of a Product Avatar. In this paper, a general introduction to the Product Avatar concept of providing targeted information through selected channels is given first. Next, the technical aspects regarding the implementation and integration of the required data sources are outlined briefly. A presentation of a Product Avatar prototype for a leisure boat and results of two customer acceptance surveys towards end-user acceptance is concluded by a brief discussion and interpretation of the findings and an outlook towards further research.

Keywords: PLM, Product Avatar, Closed-loop PLM, Intelligent Products, Leisure Boats, Social Network Services, Servitization.

1 Introduction

Customers increasingly expect physical products and related information of the highest quality. This brings the entire product lifecycle into focus for the manufacturer based on customer demands towards increased individualisation, customisation, sustainability, and maintainability. Accordingly, emphasis is shifting in industry towards actively managing, sharing and developing value-added services based on product lifecycle information. Intelligent Products are key to generating product data throughout the entire lifecycle. The Product Avatar is a promising approach to managing the communication, presentation and interaction with that data for all stakeholders in the lifecycle. These individualized digital counterparts of Intelligent Products can enable stakeholders to benefit from value-added services built on the lifecycle data generated by Intelligent Products.

A broad variety of usage data can be generated, stored and communicated by Intelligent Products. The availability of this item-level information creates potential benefits for processes throughout the product lifecycle. In order to make use of the

A. Bernard, L. Rivest, and D. Dutta (Eds.): PLM 2013, IFIP AICT 409, pp. 560–569, 2013.

information, its selection and presentation has to be individualized, customized and presented according to the stakeholders' requirements. Product owners have particular requirements towards Product Avatars. They need to interact with product data and services in ways that are intuitive and comfortable. Social Network Services such as Facebook are important not only for interaction with other people, but also as personal data management platforms and constitute increasingly dominant interaction and design paradigms. Thus, Social Network Services consequently need to be taken into consideration in the design of Product Avatars for consumers.

In this paper, first the Product Avatar concept is introduced as a concept for digital counterparts to represents the closed-loop lifecycle data and services of Intelligent Products towards different stakeholders involved in their lifecycle. Then, the prototypical development of a Product Avatar in a Social Network Service for leisure boat owners is described. The results of a survey for the evaluation of the prototype are presented next. The paper concludes with a summary of the findings and an outlook to future work.

2 Relevance of Product Avatars to Closed-Loop Product Lifecycle Management

This section describes the relevance of the Product Avatar concept to Closed-loop PLM. It begins by describing the perspective towards the product lifecycle adopted by the authors here. It then briefly describes Closed-loop PLM and Intelligent Products. The section concludes with a more in-depth description of the Product Avatar concept, its relevance, and finally, how Product Avatars for consumers – in the case boat owners – can benefit from being presented in Social Network Services such as Facebook.

Closed-Loop PLM and Intelligent Products

Literature broadly differentiates marketing and production engineering perspectives towards the product lifecycle [1]. The marketing perspective tends to adopt a sales-oriented view, in which the lifecycle is divided into the introduction, growth, maturity, saturation and degeneration of a product. The product seen not as a physical thing but only in terms of the degree of its economic success [2]. The scope a product refers to in this view may be a model, type or category. The production engineering perspective used here follows [3]. Here, the processes related to the development, production and distribution of the product are arranged into the beginning-of-life (BOL) phase. A product´s utilisation, service and repair are labelled middle-of-life (MOL). Reverse logistics take place in the end-of-life (EOL) phase.

Closed-loop PLM describes an approach to PLM which facilitates the closing of information loops between the individual phases of the product lifecycle [4]. It aims to achieve a pervasive availability of relevant product information at any point in the product lifecycle. Furthermore, the concept deals with closing information loops between different IT layers, from the data acquisition, through middleware and knowledge transformation layers to the business application layer. In order to do so, the concept proposes different methods of applying information technology [5], [6], [7], [8], [9]. With Closed-loop PLM, a paradigm shift from „cradle to grave" to "cradle to cradle" is put forward [10].

Closed-loop PLM relies on the pervasive availability of information throughout the product lifecycle in order to fulfil its aims. This is especially difficult in the MOL and EOL phases of the product lifecycle where, unlike in BOL processes such as design, production and sales, little data is collected in an organised manner. The "Intelligent Product" concept can support Closed-loop PLM by providing a means to collect and communicate product data throughout the entire lifecycle. "Intelligent Products" are physical products which may be transported, processed or used and which comprise the ability to act in an intelligent manner. McFarlane et al. define the Intelligent Product as *"a physical and information based representation of an item [...] which possesses a unique identification, is capable of communicating effectively with its environment, can retain or store data about itself, deploys a language to display its features, production requirements, etc., and is capable of participating in or making decisions relevant to its own destiny."* [11] The degree of intelligence an intelligent product may exhibit varies from simple data processing to complex pro-active behaviour [12]. Intelligent Products can make use e.g. of RFID, sensors and embedded computing throughout their lifecycles in order to collect data for example about their usage, service, maintenance, upgrading, decommissioning and disposal. They thus can contribute significantly to closing the information loops throughout the product lifecycle and are fundamental to a holistic implementation of Closed-loop PLM in many types of product.

The Product Avatar Concept

Closed-loop PLM and Intelligent Products together provide the conceptual and technological basis for a holistic management of item-level product information throughout the product lifecycle. The stakeholders in the product lifecycle are heterogeneous and have very different requirements towards the selection, presentation and use of product lifecycle data. They include product designers, manufacturers, sellers, maintenance staff, service providers, recycling operators and, of course, the actual owner of the product in question. Consequently, a single interface to closed-loop PLM data is not viable and a more flexible approach is required. A *Product Avatar* is a distributed approach to the interaction with and management of item-level product lifecycle information [13]. It can be understood as a *digital counterpart* or set of digital counterparts which represents the attributes and services of a physical product towards the different stakeholders involved in its lifecycle. This means a Product Avatar presents different interfaces and delivery channels depending on who uses it and how. Stakeholders such as owners, producers, designers may interact with the Product Avatar e.g. via dedicated desktop applications, web pages, or mobile "apps" tailored to their specific information, service and interaction needs. Product Avatars can also interact with other Product Avatars. This can be facilitated, for example, by means of web services, software agents, common messaging interfaces such as QMI, or a combination of these. This paper focuses on the former type of interaction between human stakeholders and Product Avatars [14].

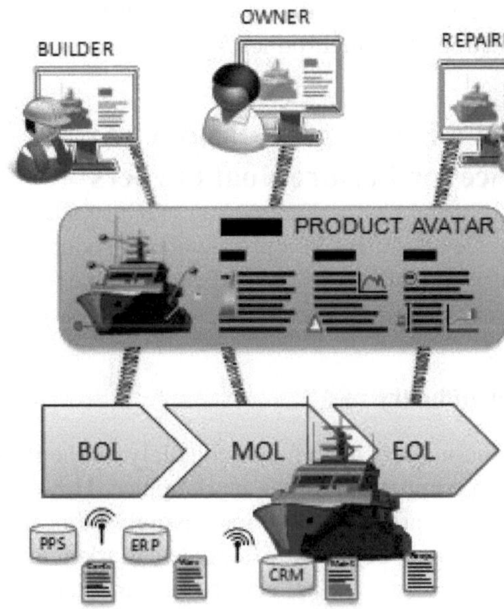

Fig. 1. Digital Representation of a Product through a Product Avatar [14]

Before the design and development of the Product Avatar for a specific intelligent product, requirements need to be elicited and analysed regarding how, over which channel, and for whom the digital counterparts need to be made available. This necessitates considering each stakeholder individually, as they each have their own individual requirements and preferences. In order to achieve a high level of acceptance for a Product Avatar with leisure boat owners, it needs to be designed taking into account interaction channels and paradigms they are already comfortable with and have come to expect. At the same time, European boat builders are seeking to expand their target market to attract the younger generations who have grown up with the Internet – the so-called "digital natives". Amongst other considerations, these two factors make Social Network Services such as Facebook an interesting channel for interacting between boat owners and Product Avatars.

Social Network Services such as Facebook boast user bases which are already familiar with their design, functionality and interaction paradigms. Furthermore, the service is an accepted communication tool, which is used anytime, anywhere via a plethora of different devices both stationary and mobile. The Product Avatar concept is, in essence, inherent to these tools – users of Social Network Services interact with "avatars" of other users as a matter of course. Thus, it seems a small step for boat owners who already actively participate in Social Network Services to also interact with their boats and the services which augment it through the same channel.

In summary, designing a Product Avatar which uses a popular Social Network Service as its interaction channel and conforms to that network's interaction paradigm promises to help users interact intuitively with it and thus enhance user acceptance, immediately leverage the user base for potential new value-added services augmenting the product, and leverage the in-built multimodality and mobility for anytime, anywhere interaction with the Product Avatar.

3 Development of a Prototypical Product Avatar in a Social Network Service for Leisure Boat Owners

This section describes the development of a prototypical Product Avatar implemented in a Social Network Service targeted at the lifecycle stakeholder group of leisure boat owners.

Use Case – Leisure Boat Industry

Up until today, leisure boat builders have focussed solely on the improvement of their products' quality to remain competitive in the marketplace. However, with the recent, drastic downturn in the boat market they are increasingly being forced to realise the need to additionally emphasize both the after-sales market and their customers' demands for products that are easy in upkeep, environmentally friendly and which offer them added-value services to enhance their boating experience. In order to fulfil these requirements, boat builders need to take concepts such as item-level and closed-loop Product Lifecycle Management (PLM) as well as Intelligent Products and Intelligent Maintenance into consideration.

In this research, boat manufacturers aim to employ Product Avatars for leisure boat owners for a number of reasons. One reason is to achieve enhanced customer relationship management and new revenue sources by enabling, for example, the boat manufacturer to provide service offers directly via the Social Network Service. Upgrades, winter storage service, maintenance and other services can be offered in this way. A further motivation is to gain access to a new market segment – spark the interest of the younger generation of "digital natives" who previously had little interest in leisure boats. Leveraging the social network – the "friends and fans" of Facebook users, for example – will also provide exposure of the products to a large number of new potential customers. Finally, boat manufacturers aim to enhance brand recognition by associating with innovative social media services.

Boat owners could integrate their product into their digital lifestyle. They could interact with their product and monitor boat functions using interfaces and technologies they already know. Checking the fuel and battery level on their boat via an app on their smartphone is a simple example. They could share their boating experiences and pictures of the places they visit or check whether their friends are at a location close by. They could also benefit from value-added services offered via the Product Avatar, for example intelligent maintenance, upgrade offers and winter storage monitoring.

Product Avatar Design

As put forward in Section 2, for the Product Avatar to be accepted by the users, in, the Product Avatar has to be tailored towards their individual requirements. For that reason, interviews with more than 100 visitors were carried out (see Table 1). Boat owners as potential buyers one were targeted in the survey. Highlights of the results show that 40% use a one or more Social Network Services. Of those 40% an overwhelming majority of 90% use Facebook. This indicates a strong preference of Facebook as the target Social Network Service for the implementation of the Product Avatar. However, a further significant result of the survey was that almost 50% of the interviewed persons expressed their concern over data security issues especially with regards to the use of Facebook as the interaction channel for the Product Avatar.

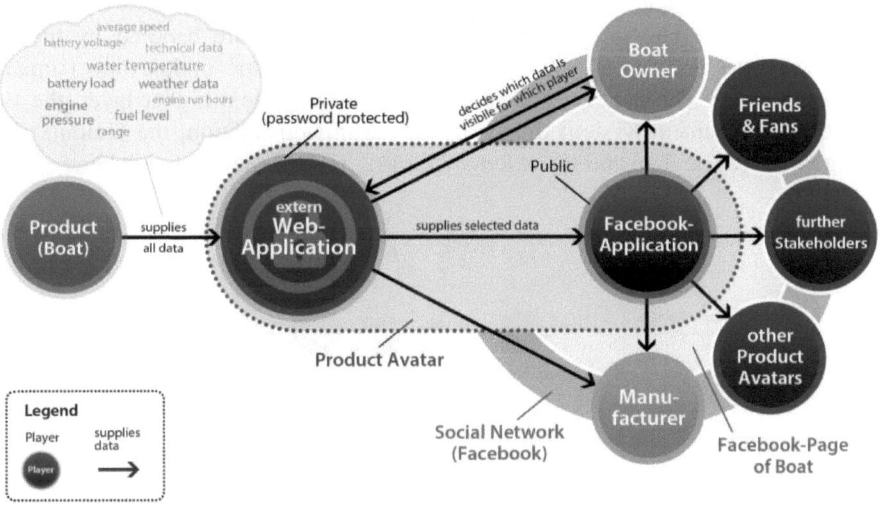

Fig. 2. Design of the Product Avatar for a Leisure Boat

This was taken into account developing the prototype Product Avatar by developing a secure and standalone web service which has most of the functionalities requested already available for the users without any connection to the Social Network Service. Fig. 2 shows the resulting Product Avatar design. It focusses on how the requirements towards data collection, data security and Facebook integration should be handled. On the left hand side, the boat generating lifecycle data can be seen. The data is fed into a standalone Product Avatar web application. The web application is password protected by the boat owner. It can be integrated into Facebook profile of the boat owner, where it can be made available to public if the owner chooses to do so. The owner can also select exactly which data should be shared via the Social Network Service. Stakeholders who can use the Product Avatar are foremost the boat owner, but also the manufacturer who can thus interact with his customer. Friends of the boat owner can also view and interact with the Product Avatar via the Social Network Service.

Closed-Loop PLM Architecture

In order to provide a technical basis for providing data to the Product Avatar, a suitable backend system is needed. Fig. 3 shows the PLM system architecture designed for the Product Avatar. The bottom layer consists of the different data sources which need to be integrated. These include on-board data sources, which can be sensors installed on the boat itself, such as slam, temperature, speed over water sensors, etc. Furthermore, existing data sources such as those connected by a NMEA 2000 bus on the boat (e.g. engine and navigation system data sources) are taken into consideration. These are connected via a gateway device which can be accessed via wireless channels such as WiFi, mobile data and satellite networks. Further data sources are the enterprise systems used by the various stakeholders. 3rd party data sources in the Web and Cloud are also taken into consideration, as well as Social Network Services. The integration of these data sources are handled by the next higher level, the middleware. For the prototype, a semantic middleware (semantic mediator) is used. The data is collected and stored in the next higher layer, the Boat Lifecycle Management System. In the prototype implementation, the Holonix iLike Intelligent Lifecycle data and Knowledge Platform is used to realise this layer.

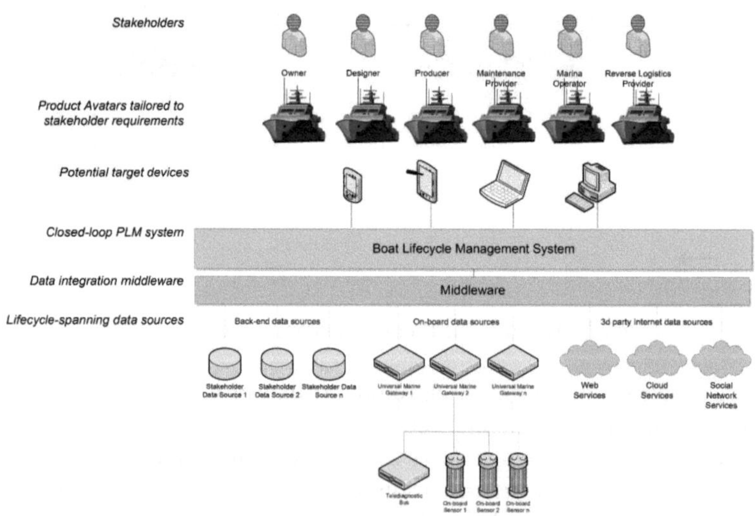

Fig. 3. PLM System Architecture

The next layer represents the potential target devices for the representation of the lifecycle data in Product Avatars. Both mobile (smartphones and tablet PCs) and stationary (laptop and desktop PCs) devices are targeted. On the layer above, different Product Avatars tailored to the needs of the stakeholders shown in the topmost layer are indicated. Depending on the needs of the stakeholders, these can take the shape of traditional, dedicated desktop applications, mobile apps, or in the case described here, a Product Avatar in a Social Network Service for the leisure boat owners.

Prototypical Product Avatar for Leisure Boat Owners

This section presents the prototypical Product Avatar for leisure boat owners which realises the design shown in Fig. 2. Fig. 4 shows a screenshot of the live Product Avatar web service[1]. After registration the user can decide what information he or she wants to have and who else can access that information. It is furthermore possible for the users to create new content, like photos or blogs, and add it to the Product Avatar connecting it to the boat.

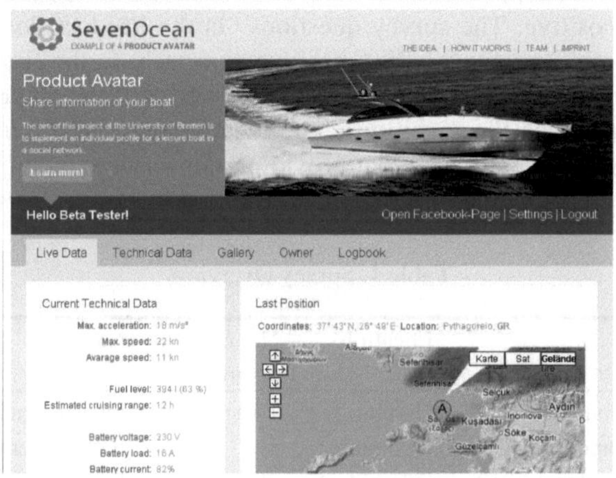

Fig. 4. Product Avatar Supplying Lifecycle Information for Registered Users

Fig. 5. Product Avatar representation via Facebook

Some social features requested by owners are only available on a Social Network Service, in this case Facebook. Thus, the Product Avatar has to be implemented there as well. The approach taken here combines both worlds by representing the stand alone web application on the Facebook wall of the Product Avatar representation.

[1] `https://prodavat.ikap-web.biba.uni-bremen.de/fb/`

This way, the user can decide specifically what information to share internally via the web service or openly via the Social Network Service (Fig. 5).

4 Evaluation

The prototypical development was evaluated in a survey carried out at the major leisure boat fair boot Düsseldorf 2013. 38 boat owners and potential buyers were interviewed. The avatar was demonstrated live on tablet PCs to the interviewed persons, who had the opportunity to use the avatar prototype. The response was overwhelmingly positive. The survey questions "Is the Product Avatar an important selling point for you?" received a 78% positive approach. In the first survey, without a practical demonstration, the same question received 83% negative responses. This result highlight indicates the viability of the idea to integrate Product Avatars with Social Network Services, and also that providing the service to compliment a leisure boat can be a significant competitive advantage to boat manufacturers.

Table 1. Survey Overview

Survey No.	Event	Location	No. of responses	Nature
1	54th Hamburg International Boat Show	Hamburg, Germany	100	Questionnaire for requirement elicitation
2	boot Düsseldorf 2013	Düsseldorf, Germany	38	Prototype presentation for evaluation purposes.

5 Conclusion and Outlook

To conclude, the approach presented to apply the developments of Facebook and its user-driven, constantly evolving information infrastructure to the Product Avatar of an Intelligent Product for consumers currently seems viable and promising. As shown in the use case, the technical realisation as part of a holistic closed-loop PLM system is feasible. The positive results of the evaluation survey indicate that integrating a Product Avatar with Social Network Services is well accepted by the target group and could constitute a significant market advantage for boat manufacturers. Future work will focus on extending the functionality of the Product Avatar to integrate service offers from the manufacturer and other stakeholders. Furthermore, push notifications from other boat lifecycle stakeholders will be integrated. The prototype will be improved to provide a fully functional pilot for select boats built by European SME boat manufacturers in the BOMA "Boat Management" project. Beyond the leisure boat sector, research needs to be conducted to investigate whether the positive reaction to the concept is isolated to the use case or transferable to other Intelligent Products.

Acknowledgement. This work has partly been funded by the European Commission through the BOMA "Boat Management" project in FP7 SME-2011-1 "Research for

SMEs". The authors gratefully acknowledge the support of the Commission and all BOMA project partners. The results presented are partly based on a student project at the University of Bremen. The authors would like to thank the participating students for their significant contributions: Anika Conrads, Erdem Galipoglu, Anna Mursinsky, Britta Pergande, Hanna Selke and Mustafa Severengiz.

References

1. Sundin, E.: Life-Cycle Perspectives of Product/Service-Systems: In Design Theory. In: Introduction to Product/Service-System Design, pp. 31–49. Springer (2009)
2. Meffert, H., Burmann, C., Kirchgeorg, M.: Marketing: Grundlagen marktorientierter Unternehmensführung Konzepte - Instrumente - Praxisbeispiele. 10. Aufl. Gabler, Wiesbaden (2008)
3. Kiritsis, D., Bufardi, A., Xirouchakis, P.: Research issues on product lifecycle management and information tracking using smart embedded systems. Advanced Engineering Informatics 17(3-4), 189–202 (2003)
4. Hong-Bae, J., Kiritsis, D., Xirouchakis, P.: Research Issues on Closed-loop PLM. Computers in Industry, 855–868 (December 2007)
5. Fleischmann, M., Bloemhof-Ruwaard, J.M., Dekker, R., van der Laan, E., van Nunen, J.A.E.E., van Wassenhove, L.: Quantitative models for reverse logistics: a review. European Journal of Operational Research 103 X(1), 1–17 (1997)
6. Hans, C., Hribernik, K.A., Thoben, K.D.: Improving reverse logistics processes using item-level product life cycle management. International Journal of Product Lifecycle Management 4(4), 338–359 (2010)
7. Jun, H.B., Kiritsis, D., Xirouchakis, P.: Research issues on closed-loop PLM. Computers in Industry 58(8-9), 855–868 (2007)
8. Kiritsis, D.: Closed-loop PLM for intelligent products in the era of the Internet of things. Computer-Aided Design 43(5), 479–501 (2011)
9. Jun, H.B., Shin, J.H., Kiritsis, D., Xirouchakis, P.: System architecture for closed-loop PLM. International Journal of Computer Integrated Manufacturing 20(7), 684–698 (2007)
10. Pokharel, S., Mutha, A.: Perspectives in reverse logistics: A review. Resources, Conservation and Recycling 53(4), 175–182 (2009)
11. McFarlane, D., Sarma, S., Chirn, J.L., Wong, C.Y., Ashton, K.: Auto ID systems and intelligent manufacturing control. Engineering Applications of Artificial Intelligence 16(4), 365–376 (2003)
12. Kärkkäinen, M., Holmström, J., Främling, K., Artto, K.: Intelligent products - a step towards a more effective project delivery chain. Computers in Industry 50(2), 141–151 (2003)
13. Hribernik, K.A., Rabe, L., Thoben, K.-D., Schumacher, J.: The product avatar as a product-instance-centric information management concept. International Journal of Product Lifecycle Management 1(4), 367–379 (2006)
14. Wuest, T., Hribernik, K., Thoben, K.-D.: Can a Product Have a Facebook? A New Perspective on Product Avatars in Product Lifecycle Management. In: Rivest, L., Bouras, A., Louhichi, B. (eds.) PLM 2012. IFIP AICT, vol. 388, pp. 400–410. Springer, Heidelberg (2012)

Experimenting New Metaphors for PDM through a Model Driven Engineering Scheme

Frédéric Noël and Mohd Azwan Azli

Univ. Grenoble Alpes, G-SCOP, France
frederic.noel@grenoble-inp.fr, mohdazwan.azli@gmail.com
http://www.g-scop.grenoble-inp.fr

Abstract. Manufacturing companies invested a lot in Product Life Management (PLM) system to save their competitiveness by a better management of their internal processes. The most deployed systems are Product Data Management tools. By deploying such systems they try to formalize complex behaviour of the company. But PLM systems did not solve complexity and new gaps must be managed. At this point, it may be interesting to investigate new ways to overpass the new complexity gap. On another hand Virtual Reality, Augmented Reality and every other Visualization and Interaction technologies are investigating more intuitive modality to interact with information, but these technologies remain quite unused for PDM applications. This paper proposes the Model Driven Engineering horizontal transformation approach to provide a systematic way to explore Virtual Reality opportunities within the PDM scope.

Keywords: PLM, PDM, Visualisation, Interaction, Complexity, Virtual Reality, Model Driven Engineering, Intuitiveness.

1 Introduction

The WP5.1 IFIP working group manifesto notes [1] that "Understanding the whole life-cycle impact of products is a critical issue in product development today". When the product development remains quite simple there is no rationale to deploy PLM. But indeed the increasing complexity of product and processes is a major trigger of technical evolution of PLM issues within industry. CAD system as many other simulation tools were a first answer to accelerate expert tasks and was a very good answer to support individual activity. But indeed as soon as more collaboration is expected, sharing information between experts became a new challenge. This step towards complexity was passed in the 80s and first Product Data Management systems appeared to answer this basic issue. It was first deployed at the service/team level where every expert has a good understanding of the colleagues activity. But complexity increased once again with both the necessity to share information at the company level, or between various stakeholders. Simultaneously, the number of actors and the number of expertises are increasing.

A. Bernard, L. Rivest, and D. Dutta (Eds.): PLM 2013, IFIP AICT 409, pp. 570–583, 2013.

PLM claims to provide an holistic view, and thus, to pass over this last complexity step. But complexity of product life management remains a challenge. Product data Management tools (PDM) are the main component of the PLM toolbox: PDM appears as not so intuitive; sometimes as complex as the problem they are expected to solve. This paper makes the assumption that every information is at the end processed by users through various metaphors (indeed mainly graphical metaphors). The complexity appearance is thus included in the proposed metaphors and may be reduced by the exploration of new visualization modalities. The aim is to propose some solutions to decrease complexity of PDM solutions by using some virtual reality opportunities.

The paper focusses first on an overall Product Data Management (PDM) description to highlight its main concepts and functions. Section 3 presents the main added value of virtual reality technologies. Virtual reality (VR) is a promising technique for many issues. It has several successful developments for the interaction with a Digital Mock Up. At last but not least, Section 4 explores how model driven engineering (MDE) [1] may provide a systematic approach to create a link between VR solutions and PLM/PDM issues. It proposes a framework where, at a first step, PDM would take benefit from virtual reality. Indeed virtual reality may provide more intuitive and natural interaction with PDM information system. It may be almost a partial solution to pass over some complexity issues.

2 Apparent Complexity of PDM Systems

2.1 Concepts of Product Data Management

Following Pal&Betz model [2] of a product manufacturing company, the product life-cycle has a main sequential stream of activities including "concept creation, creativity", "Embodiement design", "Manufacturing", "Usage and Maintenance", "Disassembly" and "Recycling". This is managed by an overall strategy and must integrate the design of the product life. Let focus on PDM systems. These systems are characteristic of complexity management since they were the first attempt to organize collaboration within a design team, providing space to share information. In the next subsections the main concepts used within PDM systems and the main functions are reminded.

A PDM system mainly provides the following concepts when looking after product definition :

An article is the major concept handled by a PDM system. It organises the product structure tree shared by every contributors to design. The tree of articles is referred as the Bill Of Material (BOM). It usually corresponds to an assembly or a single component of the product but some companies also use it as a function tree decomposition.

[1] The paper uses the horizontal translation of MDE theory and does not practise vertical translation of Model Driven Approach (MDA) (translation from PIM to PSM).

A document is a logical set of information, to identify a usual computer document (text, spreadsheet, presentation, image, etc.). The PDM document refers one or several computer files and record some meta-data (author, creation date, version, validation state, maturity, etc.). Some documents have special associated attributes or function: CAD models provide a good connection between CAD software and PDM. When the document is uploaded from the CAD software a 3D standard view may be created.

A directory is an object where designer can pack several data together. A directory may contain documents or sub-directories as on a usual computer disk, but also articles. Sub-directories create a new hierarchical view of data. Companies can decide to maintain several hierarchical view of data by sorting them respect to services (CAD service, Simulation, Manufacturing process, etc.), or to business project, or any other organization. Multi-view introduces some complexity within the analysis of the graph of information since several trees provide access to information.

A configuration is a set of article versions that identify a specific arrangement of the product. Then in the same data-base several configurations of a same product are managed. The configuration is thus a snapshot of the product definition. Several snapshots can share common parts and identify some items which are different from one configuration to another one.

A change Management item is defined to ensure the management of changes. This is a specific process where the company must capitalize problem reports, modification demands, and the management of the change process. These objects obviously refer the previous ones. Indeed a problem may occur on a specific configuration of an article and must lead to a new version of a document.

More complex meta-model could be identified if we enter into project management considerations where team, user, role, forums, authority, organisation, tasks, deliverables, milestones, etc. should be linked to this model: but the product data mainly refers about five core concepts. Figure 1 organises these concepts within a UML diagram to provide a basic vision of their relationships.

The previous concepts are tangible for end-users: at this level of analysis, a PDM system should be very simple to use by any individual person with a few professional skill. The 5 previous concepts and their relationships lead indeed to complicate models. An PDM instance is a graph of concepts instances linked by relations compatible with a UML diagram (Figure 1 is such a UML diagram). This graph is rapidly not any more understood by a human brain and appears as really complex to manage. Learning PDM usage remains non natural and practise let experts concentrate on few function to avoid the overall complexity. Next section complete this PDM description with its main functions.

2.2 Functions for Product Data Management

The main functions for PDM systems can be listed as follow:

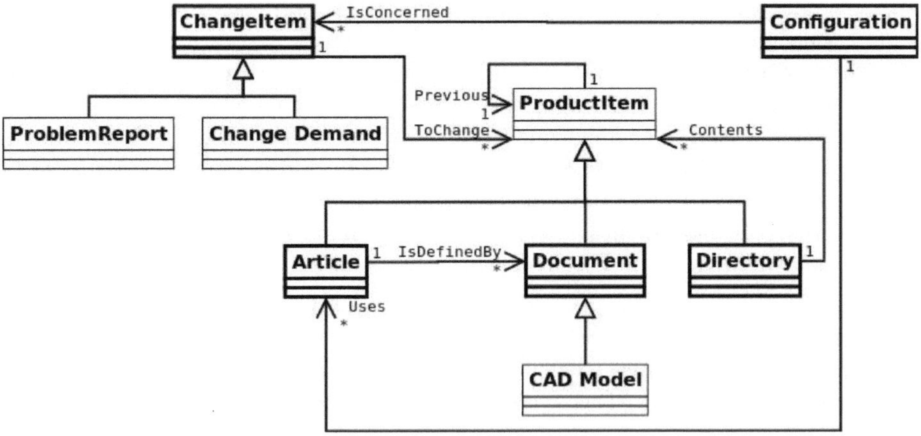

Fig. 1. A UML class diagram description of the main PDM concepts

Creation of information: these functions allow to create new parts, documents, directories, configurations and change items. Whenever a model is updated, a new version is created through a check-in process.

Right Permission Management: Most PDM systems manage the concepts of User, Group or Role which enable data protection but also work-flow management. Depending on its state, (draft, validated, etc) every item can be accessed in read or write mode by specific users or roles. When a data is shared by several users, each one can reserve the modification to himself through the check-out mechanism. Indeed processes to merge concurrent edited version of a same document [3] were poorly studied within engineering models. The reservation of data which is released by the check-in mechanism is a way to short-cut the solution.

Navigation / Search: A key feature within every PDM system helps to find information. This may be done through navigation or global search mechanisms. Indeed these functions are more complex by the existence of versions and configurations. The multi-view property for every data usually provides search output with a list of documents which looks equivalent but are indeed small variation of the same item.

Work-flow : To support work-flow management is also a real advantage of PDM systems. The main work-flow is dedicated to change management. A second one was more lately integrated with project management issues. The work-flow is another multi-view dimension which makes PDM a complex system.

Complementary functions: Many other functions are provided by PDM systems but are secondary functions:

Document pre-viewer: some specific viewers/editors can be integrated to ease the perception of the document content. Usually CAD geometric models are well supported with pre-visualization of 3D snapshot.The end-user has an overview and navigates around the object without edition facility.

Connectors: To ease interoperability with expertise tools connectors are proposed with specific software. CAD connectors are the most common practise and offer functions to directly access the PDM CAD documents from the CAD software. Check-in and check-out functions can also be integrated. At last but not least import of CAD models are available to create 3D documents or to identify the Bill of Material which is implicitly defined within the CAD system.

These functions are the main use case that can be applied by the end-user. But indeed the number of options and views that are proposed by PDM system let most end-users confused with the result of their action. Once again as for concept description, the PDM system appear a a complex system.

3 Virtual Reality for PDM

Every activity requires rendering information. Newest visualization technologies are supposed to increase the efficiency of activities. However new visualization technique does not necessarily mean a better efficiency. This article aims to explore the opportunities opened by visualization and interaction for PDM activities.

3.1 Definition of Virtual Reality

In [4] Virtual Reality is defined as *"a technical and scientific domain using computer science and behaviour interfaces for the simulation of 3D artefacts behaviour within a virtual world. The 3D artefacts interact in real time with themselves and one or more users immersed through more or less natural sensor-engine chanels"*. This definition clearly highlights the concepts which are handled through virtual reality. From a systemic point of view, the virtual reality systems is defined by:

its internal components: it may be artefacts of the virtual world. The geometric model of artefacts is a key point to identify artefacts of this world. But human user also participate to the virtual reality system. On pure virtual reality, users senses are disconnected from the real world unless mixed or augmented reality is referred.

its behaviours model the reaction of artefacts to events coming from the virtual and real world (captured with sensors) and may send feedbacks to the real world through actuators.

its functions: virtual reality enables real time interaction. That means that behaviours must be simulated in real-time or pre-simulated. The final user will accept to use virtual reality if it enables to achieve a task on a natural and efficient way.

To enable Virtual Reality usage for any use case (including PDM) expects to define the artefacts of the virtual world, the users who can be involved, their expected behaviours and a natural and efficient interaction model.

3.2 Variety of Tools and Techniques

Immersion techniques from virtual reality mainly call to mind 3D caves or head mounted devices but indeed the panel of technology is much more wide.

- In 3D caves stereoscopic views are projected on the walls of a room. The views are adapted to the tracked position of a single user.
- Head mounted devices provide a similar effect with two separated 2D displays in front of each eye.
- Holographic devices create a direct 3D perception (without glasses) which can be mixed with reality. Auto stereoscopic devices should provide the same effect on the user point of view even if technology is different with more limited 3D perception characteristics.
- Ultra-High definition (4K and 8K displays) exist in few institutes. However applications could increase more rapidly than immersion technologies. Indeed the installation of a high definition display consume less room than 3D caves. Standards are incoming and the deployment should be more rapid. Tiled displays is another way to extend the resolution and the size of the surface with respect to traditional displays [5]
- At last but not list displays on flexible material are under study and will open new opportunities[6].

Then the combinations of displays solutions make the virtual reality equipments quite complex to classify. Moreover displays are not the unique components participating to a virtual reality environment. It is clear that the perception of immersion depends on the technical environment [7]

Indeed the interaction mode is also fundamental. In most virtual cases the observer does not interact directly with virtual objects but through avatars. The avatar is handled by a deported device. The position of this visual avatar locates an indirect connection to a behaviour of the virtual scene. In few cases like with holography, the interaction with object may be direct. [8] classifies the various interaction devices respect to the following categories:

2D/3D devices: the device is considered as a 3D device whenever it manages the 3D position of an avatar.

number of degree of freedom (dof): tactile surfaces are usually plane and thus are 2 dof system even if we can imagine some 2.5 dof systems.

Haptic/Passive devices: Haptics provides feedback to the user by several metaphors.

At last some device are a combination of displays and interaction modalities. Multi-touch tables are a good example where a tactile surface is merged with the display surface.

This classification may help defining the tangibility of the virtual world [8].

3.3 Virtual Reality for Holistic PDM

A few applications of virtual reality are already used for PDM activities: to navigate in a digital mock-up, to analyse the results of a scientific simulation, to apply ergonomics analysis, to extend collaboration by improving remote presence. This applications are dedicated to design and production but only few research project is reported in the scientific literature with application for a more holistic view.

Graf et al. present several concepts to connect VR and PDM by using a software tool to navigate through the product structure using PDM information on VR [9]. The described concept covers the structure information but also all relevant PDM data and relationships between PDM objects such as articles, documents and projects. Involved designers should not be concerned about the data preparation, the creation of VR scenes in order to use VR. All product structures and part geometries in the two systems should therefore be kept up-to-date at any time. To achieve this objective, PDM system has to be a part of a PDM solution which manages all the information, required for the use of VR: it expects new metaphors for PDM.

Ralph H. Stelzer presents a process integration solution in which the VR components can be changed into basic collaboration interface of a Product Lifecycle Management (PLM) environment [10]. The connection between VR and PLM systems allow the designers to work in several VR sessions simultaneously on a product. Hence, PLM has a vital function to manage the data and to avoid conflicts during the collaboration work. This can be achieved by visualizing any information of the PLM system from a VR session. It is therefore possible to color the VR components as a function on their release status, highlight different structure allocations or view various modification states.

Hayka H. et al. present an integration solution to provide virtual reality applications with required data from heterogeneous environments such as PLM [11]. The solution uses the Gatekeeper, a Java-application that can be accessed through web service interface and communicates with other servers using web services, web protocols or ssh connections. The Gatekeeper collects data from various sources, secures the data provision and transfer and process submitted job in the background. A prototype shows that the Gatekeeper allows an easy usage of the results gathered during VR sessions and a PDM system independent usage of the data preparation methods.

Kim S. et al present MEMPHIS or Middleware for Exchanging Machinery and Product Data in Highly Immersive Systems to centralize the communication between the CAD and the VR systems via a PDM system [12]. MEMPHIS main objective is to overcome the conversion issues between the CAD and the VR systems by managing the meta data of a product and other VR related property data through Meta Data Server. The VR data, which is needed to present 3D models of future products in real time and high quality, can be produced directly from PDM systems. Thus, it reduces the repeated correction integration process between the PLM data to VR data. ManuVAR is a project that develops a prototype combining PLM, virtual reality (VR) and augmented reality (AR) and human factors (HF) methods [13]. It intends to integrate PLM and VR in a single environment.

All these studies expect a structured method to enable communication between PDM and VR. They emphasize the difficulty to manage this interoperability issue. Here it is also noted that immersion of virtual reality is mainly provided through the real perception of a third dimension not fully availale with traditional 2D displays. Then the main interest of virtual reality for PLM should be to use this third dimension to simplify the understanding of a complex set of information. [14] defines visualization as the use of interactive and computerized visual representations of abstract data to improve cognition. The final user is the main purpose of visualization to help him managing complex set of information.

In [15] authors analyse directions and metaphors to simplify complexity analyses through visualization. It proposes a model driven engineering framework to support the automatic creation of extended views in a VSML (Visualization System Modelling Language). It would provide adapted metaphors depending on the user role but also on the device and focus interest. Three main views are identified:

A tree is a hierarchical representation. On an object oriented point of view, a tree is standardized with the defintion of its root handle and for every item a method returning its childs. Each node and tree arc should be associated with attribute values that can be transformed into either, shapes, colors or pixmaps, or size, position or orientation.

A map is a reticular representation. A polyhedron visualizing a 3D shape is indeed a specific reticular representation, but every graph are included here.

A paysage , as data-scapes or data-mountains, localise information on a given surface. It expects the definition of the surface and the definition at specific location of highlited issues.

A combination of previous items : every visualization item can be locally decomposed into a smaller metaphor: it enable to combine metaphors together. It can be also processed by a distribution over a tiled environment.

On a formal way every metaphor is parametrized by a finite set of parameters. To translate a data model into these metaphors should be driven by a limited set of mechanisms. Next section proposes the base of such mechanisms and thus enables 3D perception of PLM activities. The related mechanism based on Model Driven Engineering techniques will provide transformations as described in [15] and will enable the [15] proposal by providing effective mechanisms.

4 Transformation of PDM Information into Visualization

4.1 Principle

Let suppose that we have a PDM model. Then a set of transformation rules must be defined to create potential visual metaphors and to distribute these metaphors other a set of renderers. The transformation must also identify behaviours and will lead to interactive Virtual Reality framework. This principle has been implemented through autonomous agents. Agents communicate by sharing events on

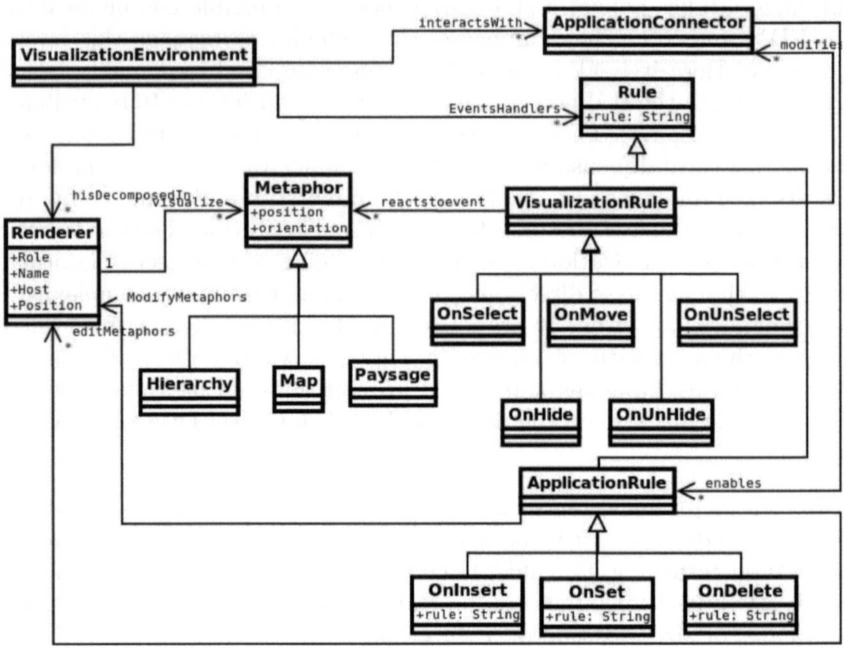

Fig. 2. Abstract description of the Visualization environment

the common model of Figure 2. As stated by this UML diagram, the visualization environment is defined by a set of renderers. These renderers can be distributed on a network by identifying the host computer and their location within the computer rendered area. Every renderer is in charge to display a metaphor. The visualization environment also controls rules in charge to manage events coming from interaction with the renderer or from the visualized information system. To ensure the link with external applications we use an application connector which is in charge to survey in real-time the events produced by the application: here the PDM Model. This connector must implement the following API:

1. `GetRootHandle()` $\mapsto$ `[ID]`: this method must return a list of unique identificators of the application items. These "root" items will play the roles of the main handles on the model issued from the application point of view. For PDM this connector method should return for example a list of the main configurations. Thus user accesses a configuration of the product potentally decomposed into several alternative configurations. Each configuration provide access to product items, but indeed this can be adapted to special requirements depending on the PDM meta-model.
2. `GetItemClassifier(ID)` $\mapsto$ `CID` : returns an identifier of the type of item identified by ID. For a specific ID the system should returns either 'Article', 'Configuration', 'Changed Demand', 'Problem Report', 'Document', 'Directory' or 'CAD Model'.

3. `GetClassifierAttributes(CID cl)` ↦ `[(name,type='Real'|'Integer'|'Boolean'|'String'])]`: a specific item associated with the classifier `CID` has a list of attributes identified by their name and their type. This method returns the list of attributes for a given classifier. For every classifier a list of attributes must be associated. For an article or document the state 'Draft', 'Proposal', 'Validated' is one of these attributes. The cost could be a second one. The right permission as 'checked in' or 'checked out' should be another one, etc.
4. `GetClassifierRelations(CID cl)` ↦ `[(name,card_{min},card_{max},RCID)]`: a specific item associated with the classifier `CID` has a list of relations with other classifiers. This method returns the list of tuples identifying the relations to a given `RCID` classifier. The relation is named and has a minimal and maximal cardinality. In the PDM case, as for attributes, every classifier has relations which are clearly identified for the PDM model on the class diagram 1. An article will have the 'IsDefined' relation associated to the classifier 'Document'.
5. `Inherits(CID cl1,CID cl2)` ↦ `boolean` : This method return True if cl1 inherits from cl2. For PDM,the class diagram 1 identifies inheritance relationships: the 'CAD Model' inherits the 'Document' class, etc.
6. `GetItemAttribute(ID,attribute)` ↦ `Real|Integer|Boolean|String`: This method return the value of an attribute from a given item.
7. `SetItemAttribute(ID,attribute,value)` : This method edits the value of an attribute from a given item.
8. `GetItemRelation(ID,relation)` ↦ `[ID]` : This method returns the list of IDs from a relation of a given item.
9. `InsertItem(ID,relation,IID)` : This method inserts a new item into a relation of a given item.
10. `DeleteItem(ID,relation,DID)` : This method removes an item from a relation of a given item.

With this API the system read from and write to any application model. It enables to connect a PDM system and to visualize everything through various metaphors. The number of events in a PDM system are important since every collaborator should edit his work whenever expected. But indeed there is no streams of modifications that need rapid updates of the visualization scene. A check-in is done once and expects a check-out almost a few second later but not at every millisecond. That means that the visualization metaphors should support a Virtual Reality environment (no real-time issue). Mainly navigation is expected.

This API provides a generic way to navigate within both :

the meta-model level since the API provides information about the classifier, their attributes and relations (including inheritance).

the model level since it provides access to items, item attributes, and relations. The `SetItemAttribute`, `InsertItem` and `DeleteItem` functions allow edition of the model.

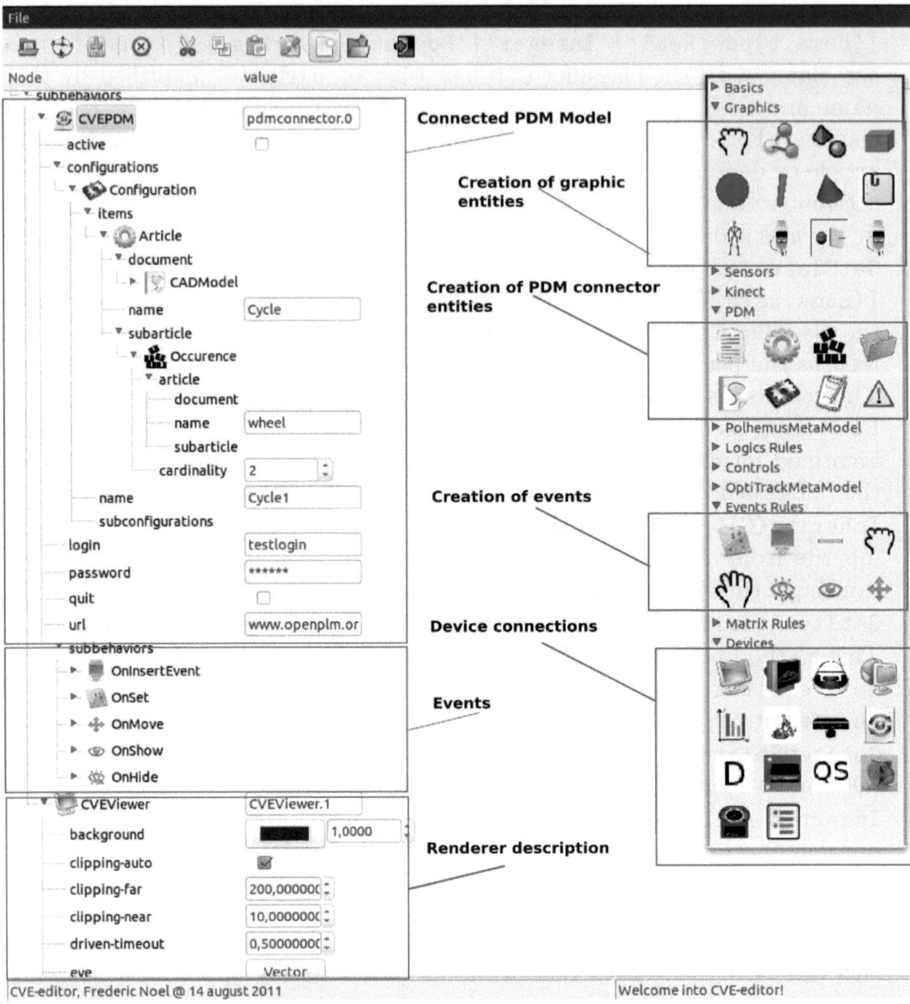

Fig. 3. Visualization Editor

By managing the meta-model and the model level, this API opens access to a Model Driven Engineering approach as discussed in the next section.

4.2 Transformation Rules

Model Driven Engineering (MDE) is based on the capacity to define transformation at the meta-model level. The current paper does not follow the usual model driven approach from computer engineering where translations are used on a vertical mode from an abstract model to a instance. This technique is usually applied for the transformation of a Platform Independent Model (PIM) into a Platform Specific Model (PSM). This paper refers to horizontal translation and synchronization rules. The rules are defined at the abstract meta-model level and should be executed at the model level. The translation concerns two different meta-models: here from the PDM meta-model to the visualization meta-model. A major challenge for visualization in Virtual reality is to apply this translations in real-time.

Then to complete the interconnection between PDM and visualization, transformation rules must be implemented. Some rules are implicit as synchronization of attributes values or relationships between items whenever the visualization expect an edition or whenever the PDM system is edited, but more complex rules require a specific development. Especially the choice of metaphors must be identified and properly linked. The rules have also the ability to define behaviour of the virtual scene since rules can react to basic events (`OnSelect`, `OnUnSelect` or `OnMove`). Moreover the connector system can be extended to connect other applications in charge of simulating some behaviours (Mechanical effects as contact, etc within the scene).

To fix ideas an example of set of rules could be used: assuming that a 3D digital mock-up is available connected with the bill of material.

1. At initialization a list of product is visualized.
2. When a product is selected its digital mock-up is visualized as a usual 3D model.
3. When a part is selected, the list of documents must appear through specific 3D representations.
4. When a document is selected, the list of versions should appear on the line normal to the surface selected point.
5. When a version is moved towards a basket 3D model, the version must be deleted.
6. etc.

A prototype environment (named "CVE") has been developed for experimentation. The system acts through autonomous agent. Every renderer or device has its own autonomy. Connected agents can be of various type: management of interactive devices (tracking system) are also developped through specific agents. This environment enables to test various metaphors for any applications (including a PDM or other PLM application). Figure 3 shows the CVE editor which supports the configuration of the visualization environment. CVE demonstrates the powerness of the system and its capacity to project any application in various visualization metaphors on distributed renderers. Events, connector to the PDM system and graphic rendering are created directly through this editor.

At the meta-model level, transformation rules can be written by the VR tool developpers in a scripted language (in CVE currently python is used). But it can be also added directly by end-users through a basic scripting language accessing the models and the meta-models through the API of the previous section. This will ensure the creation of metaphors adapted to the real expected usage of end-users. The editor of Figure 3 also supports interactive description of rules. It is a demonstration that visualisation rules could be defined by end-users with very few scripting capacity.

At the model level, when a new product is created in the PDM system (creation of an article at the highest level), a `'OnInsert'` rule is called. This rule adds an object in the related visualization renderer but also defines the type of metaphor which must be used to visualize the PDM item. When the metaphor is selected in this renderer a `'OnSelect'` rule is called: it invokes a new metaphor to display a focus on the product. This metaphor may replace the current view or be projected on any other renderer.

This environment demonstrates the capacity of Model Driven Engineering to support creation of metaphors for PDM activities enabling experimentation of new way to interact with PDM systems.

5 Conclusion

By organising visualisation as a systematic approach with a set of predefined metaphors, this paper opens new directions to visualize complex information set. It may support simplification of some views by creating unusual metaphors. 3D may be used to project things which were not thought as 3D and must not be reserved to 3D geometry visualization. The paper uses a core view of a PDM system; it proposes via a generic framework the PDM model visualization based on Model Driven Engineering transformations.

The capacity to use transformations towards Virtual Reality environments depends on the capacity of the transformations to be applied in real-time or to be prepared offline. The extension of mechanisms with interaction facility ensures a potential natural way to navigate within a virtual PDM view. The metaphors and related behaviours will have to be assessed in the context of PDM applications: the main issue is to compare intuitiveness and tangibility of every metaphor. It should lead to new metaphors for a better understanding and management of the apparent PDM complexity.

Acknowledgments. This paper was written within the scope of the VISIONAIR infrastructure project. VISIONAIR is leaded by Grenoble INP, 46 avenue Felix Viallet, F-38 031 Grenoble cedex 1, FRANCE. This project is funded by the European Commission under grant agreement 262044.

References

1. IFIP Working Group 5.1. IFIP working group 5.1 manifesto, `http://www.ifip-wg51.org/`
2. Pahl, G., Betz, W.: Engineering Design: a Systematic Approach. Springer (1996)
3. Sadeghi, M., Noël, F., Hadj-Hamou, K.: Formalization of design rules to assist conflict detection in collaborative design. International Journal of Product Development 10(1/2/3), 123–143 (2010)
4. Arnaldi, B., Fuchs, P., Tissea, J.: Tité de la réalité virtuelle, vol. 1, ch. 1. Les presses de l'école des Mines de Paris (2003)

5. Renambot, L., Rao, A., Singh, R., Jeong, B., Krishnaprasad, N., Vishwanath, V., Chandrasekhar, V., Schwarz, N., Spale, A., Zhang, C., et al.: Sage: the scalable adaptive graphics environment. In: Proceedings of WACE, vol. 9, pp. 2004–2009. Citeseer (2004)
6. Crawford, G.P.: Flexible flat panel displays. Wiley Series of Display Technologies (2005)
7. Wits, W.W., Noël, F., Masclet, C.: Exploring the potential of 3d visualization techniques for usage in collaborative design. In: 21st CIRP Design Conference, pp. 187–193 (2011)
8. Noël, F.: From integrated to intuitive design thanks to new technologies. In: MITIP 2012 (ed.) Modern Information Technology in the Innovation Processes of Industrial Enterprises, pp. 1–8, MITIP (October 2012)
9. Graf, H., Brunetti, G., Stork, A.: A methodology supporting the preparation on 3d-cad data for design reviews in vr. In: Proceedings of the International Design Conference, Design, Dubrovnik, Croatia (2002)
10. Stelzer, R.H.: Virtual reality based engineering collaboration as part of the product lifecycle management. In: Proceedings of the ASME 2010 International Design Engineering Technical Conferences & Computers and Information in Engineering Conference, Montreal, Quebec, Canada (2010)
11. Hayka, H., Langenberg, D., Stark, R., Wolter, L.: Combining heteregenous plm environments with grid computing and virtual reality applications. In: Proceedings of PLM 2010 (Bremen, Germany) (2010)
12. Kim, S., Weissmann, D.: Middleware-based integration of multiple cad and pdm systems into virtual reality environment. Computer-Aided Design and Applications 3(5), 547–556 (2006)
13. D'Cruz, M., Vink, P., Krassi, B.: Manuvar: a framework for improving manual work through virtual and augmented reality. In: Vink, P., Kantola, J. (eds.) Advances in Occupational, Social, and Organizational Ergonomics, Proceedings of the 3rd International Conference on Applied Human Factors and Ergonomics (AHFE 2010), Miami, Florida, USA, July 17-20, 10 p. CRC Press (2010) ISBN 9781439835074, ISBN-13: 978-0-9796435-4-5
14. Written, B.S., Card, S.K., Mackinlay, J.D. (eds.): Readings in information visualization: using vision to think. M. Kaufmann Publ., Cop., San Francisco (1999)
15. Bihanic, D., Polacsek, T.: Visualisation de systémes d'information complexes. Une approche par "points de vue étendus". Studia Informatica Universalis 10, 235–262 (2012)

Advanced Engineering Visualization with Standardized 3D Formats

Christian Emmer, Arnulf Fröhlich, and Josip Stjepandic

PROSTEP AG, Darmstadt, Germany
josip.stjepandic@opendesc.com

Abstract. When products are developed in 3D for the engineering applications, the data is initially stored in the native format of the used CAD software. If this 3D CAD data is to be made available to people who do not have this software, neutral 3D formats are needed. For visualization of product data in the engineering field - regardless of native CAD formats – various 3D formats are available. Among these are disclosed or standardized formats like PDF from Adobe, JT and also X3D, Collada and STEP. The choice of a format has many implications, including the options available for using the data and the resulting follow-up costs. This paper illustrates an overview of the state of development, the committees' activities, of current practical examples and gives an outlook for future developments too. The record is completed by examples from the industrial practice in the automotive industry.

Keywords: Engineering Visualization, Interoperability, Data Exchange, JT Standard, Supply Chain, Engineering Collaboration.

1 Introduction

Although the CAD translation technology has gathered a high level of maturity and robustness, there is still a strong need for further development driven by crucial business processes like digital mock-up (DMU) which is established as core validation process in the past years. Furthermore, the CAD models have already reached a level at which where they are easy to use, despite a high level of complexity behind that. Meanwhile, various 3D visualization formats have entered the market on the broad front by combining the high information content with easy handling and excellent performance. Thus, these formats can support many process chains from styling to product simulation, validation and production as well as downstream life cycle phases. By the extensive penetration of visualization formats in the market the old discussion was reopened, whether the unique format can fulfill the requirements of the engineering collaboration (internal and external). Finally, the users need the recommendation too, which format meets their needs in the best way [1], [2]. Typical use cases for functional evaluation of such formats are the viewing of engineering data, the design in context, the data exchange between partners in the supply chain, the packaging and digital mock-up (DMU), the documentation and archiving, and use

A. Bernard, L. Rivest, and D. Dutta (Eds.): PLM 2013, IFIP AICT 409, pp. 584–595, 2013.

in the portable PLM document, i.e. use of 3D and additional information in domains related to engineering (Figure 1).

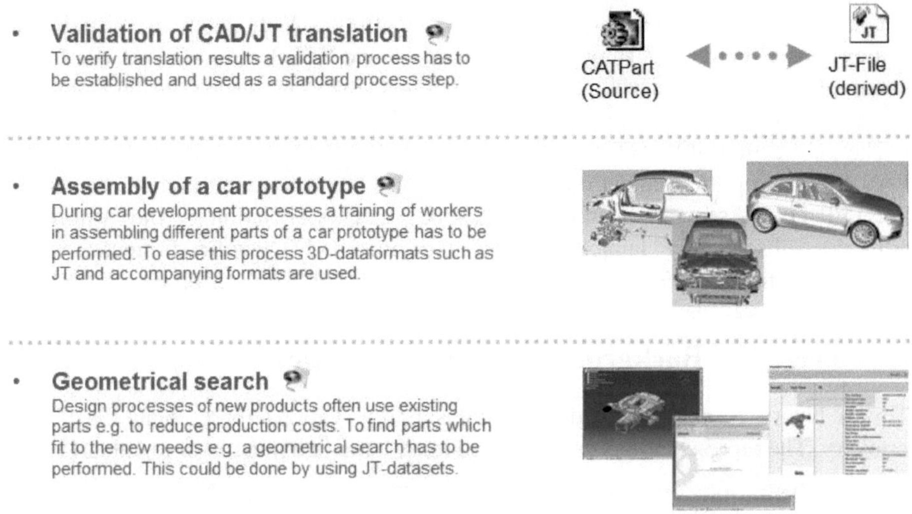

Fig. 1. Typical use cases of JT [1]

After the rough evaluation of the technical specification of the visualization formats an overall comparison can be drawn [3] (Figure 2).

Use Case	STEP	3D XML	JT	3D PDF
Viewing	●	●●	●●●	●●●
Data Exchange	●●●	●	●●	●
DMU	●	●●	●●●	●
Documentation and Archiving	●●	●	●●	●●●
Portable PLM Document	●	●	●	●●●

Legend

●●● Highly suitable

●● Well suitable

● Suitable with reservations

Fig. 2. Comparison of four visualization formats [3]

However, in the automotive and aerospace industry JT from Siemens PLM is currently under heavy investigation to apply it in downstream processes, after it was established as a leading format for the engineering visualization in many global companies [4]. For instance, there is the demand to exchange exact geometry, product data information and additional attributes. Moreover JT is also a potential data format for long-term data retention. Consequently, there is high user interest in quality and robustness of the applications, the interfaces in particular. Thus, the further explanation in this paper will be focused on JT, although other formats (STEP, 3DPDF, 3DXML) are in the different stages of standardization procedure.

Open standards enable reduction of total costs of ownership and ensure independence from specific vendors and competition. With regard to visualization data exchange there is a strong support to use JT and STEP AP 242 (ISO 10303-242) as complementing standards for lightweight visualization format for 3D industrial data as well as for product structure, meta, and kinematic data [5].

The publication of the JT specification as an ISO Publicly Available Specification (PAS 14306) laid the foundation for establishing JT as a binding process format. The ProSTEP iViP Association and the VDA (German Association of the Automotive Industry) subsequently launched three coordinated JT-specific projects: the JT Workflow Forum, the JT Implementor Forum and the JT Application Benchmark.

2 Technical Background and Standardization

JT is a binary format whose data model supports various representations of CAD geometry. The representations can be stored in a JT file individually or together [5] [6].

- **BREP (Boundary Representation):** Offers the highest level of representational precision. BREP data is compressed using different algorithms and stored without loss. In the current specification 9.5, two BREP representations are permitted: the traditional JT-BREP representation and XT-BREP, which is based on the Parasolid boundary representation and will be preferred in the further implementation of JT based software.
- **Tessellated Geometry:** A faceted representation of solids and surfaces. Different levels of detail (LOD) can be defined within a JT file. A low LOD means a lower level of precision but a smaller volume of data, while a very high LOD means an almost exact geometry but a large volume of data.
- **ULP (Ultra-Lightweight Precise):** The latest compression method is ULP. The ULP format enables a lightweight, semi-precise representation of the 3D geometry. The level of precision that ULP offers is significantly higher than for tessellated geometry while the file size is significantly smaller. The primary focus lies on providing high quality surface geometry that exhibits only minor deviations from the original BREP geometry.

JT version 8.1 has been initially published by the ISO as a publicly available specification (ISO PAS 14306). The ISO standardization process has been finished by endorsing the ISO standard (ISO 14306) in December 2012 for the recently published JT version 9.5, which has been expanded to include the specification for ULP and semantic product manufacturing information (PMI, product metadata) among other things.

Generating data in a neutral 3D format results in most use cases with a significant reduction in volume. In order to compare the file size of the 3D formats, fifteen test assemblies from different CAD systems were used to generate different 3D formats [7]. As a result, the volume of data is determined more by data content then by the format itself.

The volume of exact BREP data after conversion to JT is approximately the same as after conversion to 3D PDF. The same applies to tessellated content, where the result for both formats is about the same as for 3D XML. In the case of simplified BREP data, the volume of data for both JT and 3D PDF are approximately the same. In the case of STEP data, use of an external compression algorithm achieves a marked reduction in size. As a consequence, higher accuracy requires more storage space as a general rule.

3 Use Cases

An evaluation of the 22 use cases defined by automotive manufacturers and their suppliers indicated a particularly high priority for four use cases, which are presented below in more detail by way of example [7] (Figure 3).

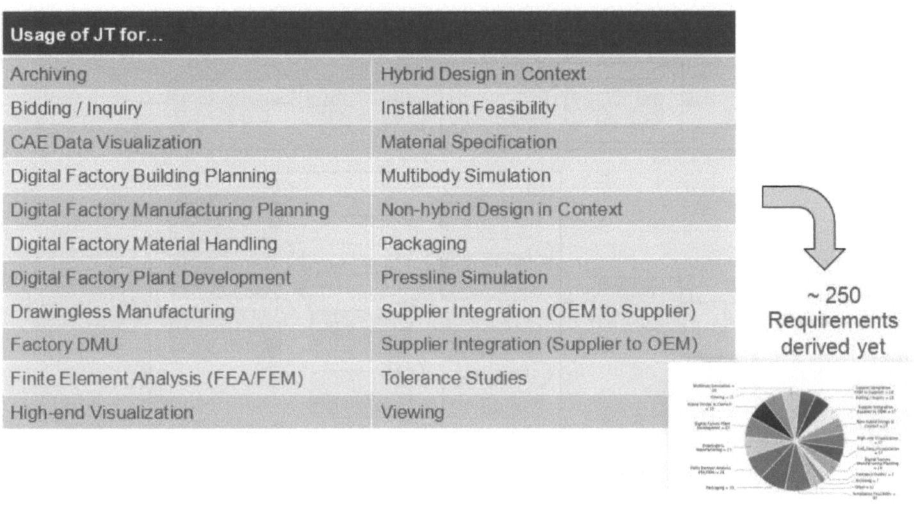

Fig. 3. Use cases for simplified formats [7]

Viewing: If the use of a CAD system is not desired, the visualization of engineering data using 3D viewers comes into play in a number of different situations: the presentation of product data, the representation of 3D models for information purposes (e.g. for a design review or marketing) and the realistic representation in virtual reality systems.

The use case can vary according to the concrete application context involved. While the simple viewing of the geometry is sufficient in many cases, in other cases metadata or high-performance viewing of huge assemblies plays a key role. The most important requirements are:

- Quality criteria for geometry accuracy must be fulfilled.
- Different level of details must be available.

- Detailed color information must be available for entire part and single geometrical features.
- Metadata like attributes must be stored.

Packaging / DMU: In digital mock-up (DMU), the spatial properties of a product are examined and checked. This can involve checking the overall geometry with regard to dimensions and shape, interference checks, collision checks for assembly and disassembly, as well as design space checks (Figure 4).

For these purposes, the geometry, product structure and metadata are displayed and analyzed in a DMU application. The result of the DMU analysis is subsequently summarized and documented in a report. The most important requirements are:

- Use of models from different source systems (multi-CAD).
- High-quality examination of large assemblies.
- Transferability of kinematics from the original model to the target model for dynamic DMU analysis.

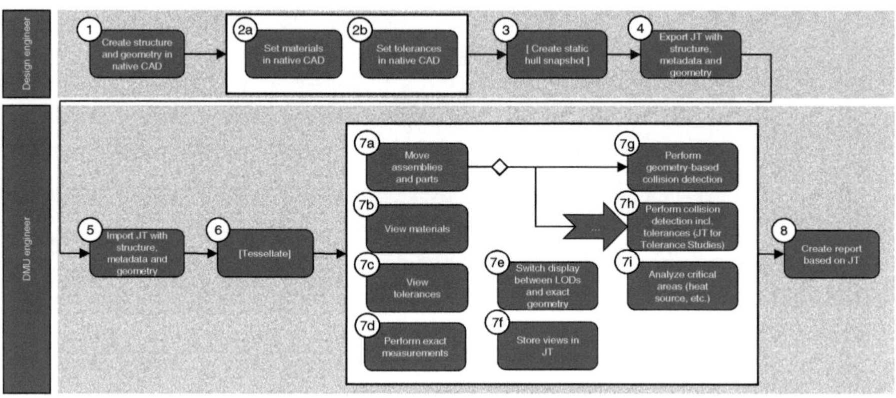

Fig. 4. Use case diagram "Packaging"

Design in Context: A typically used modeling method is the design in the context of the existing geometry. In that case existing CAD models (e.g. from previous design or from partners) are loaded into the CAD system. The design engineer then references new or existing JT-geometry to the loaded parts or assemblies. References from native CAD to JT are also in focus. These references can be between auxiliary geometry (point, axis, plane), geometrical elements such as edges, vertices or faces and exact geometrical references like curves. In the subsequent downstream processes it is required to use this assembled model as a merged single unit. Hence, the creation of technical drawings must be possible. The most important requirements are:

- Tessellated as well as exact B-Rep data must be stored.
- Links between JT and native data must be possible.
- Technical drawings must be derivable from hybrid models.

Partner Integration: The use case is divided into two sub-sections. The aim of the "OEM to Supplier" use case is to send validated JT geometry with all necessary metadata to the supplier, whereas the "Supplier to OEM" use case defines the exchange of JT files to the OEM.

Common to both sections is that the use cases provide a basis for further use cases. This means that by the Supplier or the OEM more specific use cases (viewing, design in context, etc.) will be applied subsequently. The most important requirements are:

- Quality check of JT and validation against native CAD model.
- Meta data must be contained in JT model.
- Removal of intellectual property (if necessary).

4 Evaluation and Testing

An important aspect in driving the application and development of JT is a coordinated approach between the different bodies on the one hand and a coordinated approach of the activities themselves on the other hand.

4.1 Involved Bodies

Basis for the standardization activities of JT were the enormous efforts of many international bodies. After the initial impact had been accomplished by SASIG [1], the four bodies: ProSTEP iViP Association (PSI), the German Association of the Automotive Industry (VDA), the Automotive CIO´s and the Global Automotive Advisory Group for PLM (GAAG) have played a leading role (Figure 5). Therewith ProSTEP iViP (www.prostep.org) has thoroughly pursued these activities.

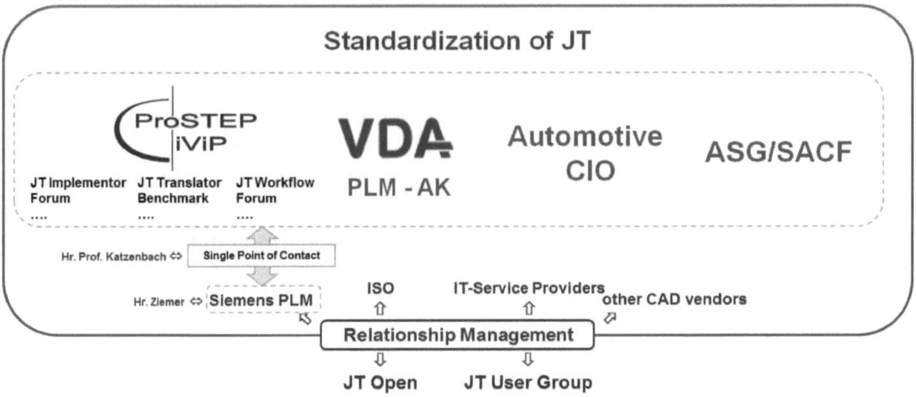

Fig. 5. International cooperation in the standardization of JT

Last but not least, the MoU (Memorandum of Understanding) between Siemens PLM und ProSTEP iViP provides the basis between both parties in the area of JT, in order to foster a common understanding of goals and measures to establish JT as a binding process format.

4.2 National and International Coordination

In 2009 the ProSTEP iViP Association, in a joint effort with the VDA (German Automotive Association), has started three different but interacting world-wide unique JT activities. Within the so-called JT Workflow Forum, Use Cases for the application of JT are specified, describing the common view from industry. The JT Implementor Forum provides support in JT translator development and maintains a platform for interoperability testing for the vendors. Within the JT Application Benchmark the requirements are comprehensively tested within neutral environment.

The project plans of these three project groups are well-harmonized, for driving the application of JT as a common effort.

JT Workflow Forum: Aim of the project is to define and prioritize key use cases and to identify relevant downstream processes for the JT based data exchange. For all use cases, requirements are collected and test criteria defined, e.g. under the aspects of exchanging of visualization data, the validation of 3D geometry, GD&T (Geometric Dimensions and Tolerances) and - last but not least - translator quality.

These tasks are supported by the Content Harmonization subgroup, which is responsible for providing a clear definition of which requirements should be satisfied by the JT format and which by STEP AP242 as backbone format.

JT Implementor Forum: Within the framework of the JT Implementor Forum Project Group, a platform for interoperability testing for the vendors is maintained. It is a forum where participating vendors can test the translators that they are developing "behind closed doors". The JT Implementor Forum is a neutral forum for software vendors, where they can perform tests in an atmosphere of mutual trust and exchange information on experience already gained.

In addition, from the vendor perspective, the activities within the JT Implementor Forum can be seen as a kind of preparation for the JT Application Benchmark.

JT Application Benchmark: Based on the recent standardization activities of JT and also STEP AP 242, it is of importance to assure data exchange quality within a neutral Benchmark and to provide support in JT translator development.

The ProSTEP iViP Association, together with the VDA PLM working group, has initiated a first JT translator benchmark in 2009. Subsequently, the second translator benchmark was conducted in 2010. The third benchmark was completed by the end of 2012. Thereby the focus will be laid on three main topics:

1. CAD to JT export, focus on LOD and PMI
2. JT viewing, focus on performance and functionality
3. Assembly conversion with STEP AP 242 XML and JT

Vendors participating in the benchmark are invited to present their latest functionalities in form of Showcases to the JT Workflow Forum members. In focus are cutting-edge solutions that demonstrate the possibilities of the JT format and applications. There are still small functional errors and therefore a need for improvement (Figure 6).

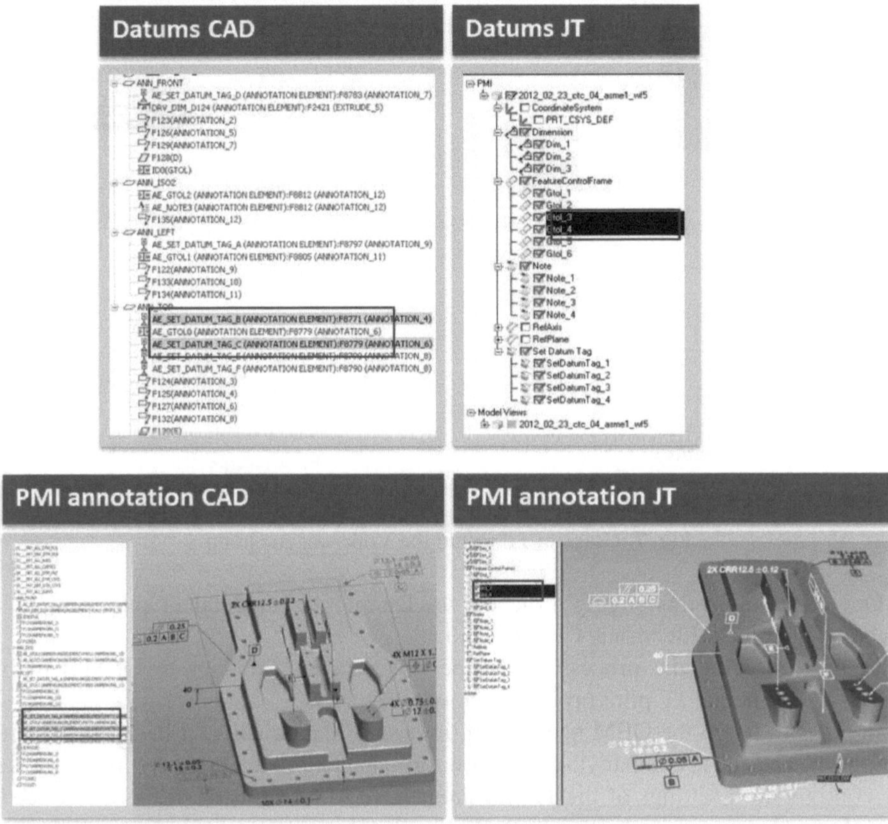

Fig. 6. Results of recent JT benchmark

5 Pilot Projects

As a further step towards the productive usage of JT in automotive downstream processes, first pilot projects are established. Volkswagen decided to use JT for internal downstream processes to eliminate the need for drawings [7] [8] (Figure 7). This application is limited to the use case "single parts" and shall be subsequently extended to the full assemblies to avoid the usage of huge JT monolithic files.

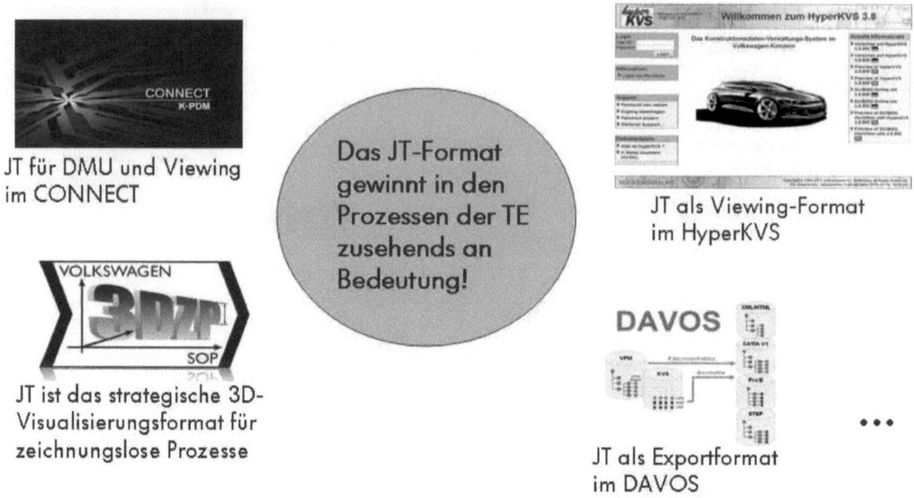

Fig. 7. Usage of JT within the Volkswagen Group

One of the most challenging project is the Daimler/Continental JT pilot project by exchanging an ESP Electronic Control Unit.

In the following the process landscape (Use Case: "Supplier to OEM") of the Daimler/Continental JT-pilot project is shown (Figure 8).

In order to fulfill the OEM needs (e. g. in case of data quality) it has to be ensured that the JT and the accompanying structure formats are created properly. In a first step the configuration settings of the JT-translator have to be adjusted to the OEM needs. Therefore, the mentioned ProSTEP iViP JT Content Harmonization workgroup (JTCH) has created a first best practice document [9]. In the second step, the OEM specific data preparation has to be done. Therefore the Daimler JT Supplier Package (JTSP) is available for all Daimler suppliers [7].

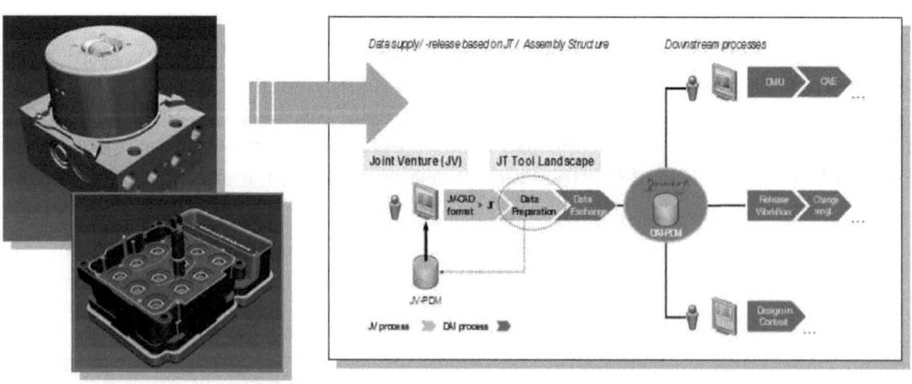

Fig. 8. Usage of JT in partner integration [7]

The Daimler JTSP offers the opportunity to edit the JT internal attributes and to prepare XML based structure formats to meet the OEM requirements. The third step in the process landscape is the data exchange to the OEM. In case of the Daimler AG the OFTP based SWAN system is used.

The final step of this process is the data import into the Daimler PDM system Smaragd. At this point in time the externally created JT datasets are released and available to all Daimler downstream processes such as Viewing, DMU or Design in Context [10].

Meanwhile the full CAD data exchange by using JT is going to be adopted as a base CAD translation technology by supplier portals like OpenDESC.com (www.opendesc.com) [11].

6 Conclusions and Outlook

This contribution addresses the state of the art activities in order to establish JT as a universal process format. Industry needs simple solutions for the efficient use of IT technology, including consistency in processes. There are strong requirements for lightweight 3D formats for the visualization and downstream processes, complementary formats in order to exchange meta data, structure data and kinematics data as well as open and standardized formats to reduce total cost of ownership and to minimize dependency of single vendors [8], [9], [10].

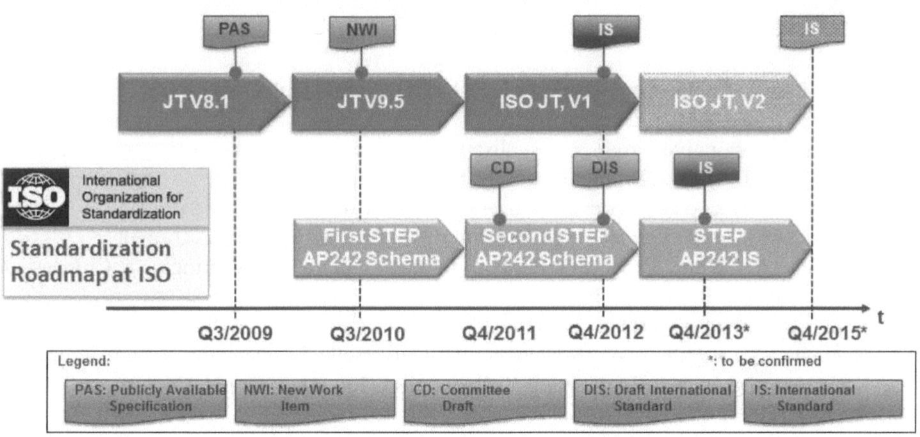

Fig. 9. The schedule of JT and STEP AP 242

After these very promising pilot projects mentioned above, the activities on the subject of lightweight visualization based on JT have already reached a good level of maturity, encouraging the wide range of companies and users, whereas it is a forthcoming task to push the integration with the accompanying format STEP AP242 (Figure 9). Although first applications creating or using STEP AP242 XML as an out- or input format are already available today, the wide usage will be announced in the

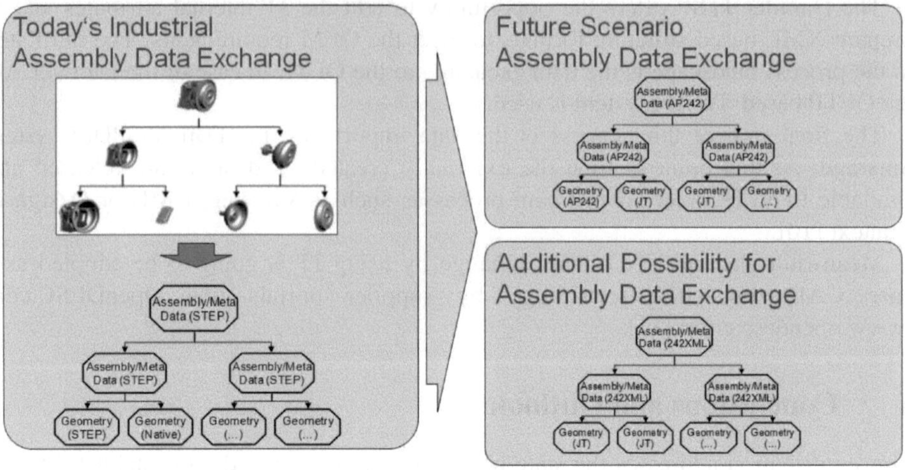

Fig. 10. Assembly data exchange with JT and STEP AP 242

next years. The future data exchange process will adopt JT as well as STEP AP242, ensuring the exchange of whole complex products at all stages of product and process development (Figure 10).

References

1. N. N.: Digital Engineering Visualization, SASIG, SASIG Guideline (2005), http://www.aiag.org/source/Orders/index.cfm?search=D-21
2. N. N.: Collaborative Product Visualisation - General issues and use case description, Frankfurt, VDA, VDA Empfehlung 4966 (2007), http://www.prostep.org/fileadmin/freie_downloads/Empfehlungen-Standards/VDA/VDA_4966_Collaborative-Product-Visualization_1.0.pdf
3. Fröhlich, A.: White Paper 3D Formats in the Field of Engineering – a Comparison, PROSTEP AG, Darmstadt, http://www.pdfgenerator3d.com/nc/en/product/white-paper.html
4. Biahmou, A., Fröhlich, A., Stjepandic, J.: Universelle Formate für Visualisierung und Konvertierung in der Engineering-Kollaboration. In: International Conference GO 3D, Rostock (2009)
5. Handschuh, S.: Wertextrahierende Nutzung von offenen leichtgewichtigen Datenformaten in automobilen Kollaborations- und Entwicklungsprozessketten, Technische Universität Kaiserslautern, PhD thesis (2011)
6. Beckers, R., Fröhlich, A., Stjepandic, J.: Anwendung und Potenziale universeller Visualisierungsformate. 9. Paderborner Workshop "Augmented & Virtual Reality in der Produktentstehung", Paderborn (2010), http://www.transmechatronic.de/uploads/tx_vitramemberadmin/literature/Anwendung_und_Potenziale_universeller_Visualisierungsformate.pdf
7. Handschuh, S., Dotzauer, R.: ProSTEP Symposium 2012: JT on the Path of Enlightenment – Report of the JT working groups, Hamburg, May 10 (2012)

8. Röhl, H., Fröhlich, A.S.: Einsatz des JT-Formates in der Digitalen Fabrik. VDI Kongress "Digitale Fabrik", Regensburg (2012)
9. ProSTEP iViP, Whitepaper Applying JT – Guidance for Using JT in Practice Version 2 (2010), http://www.prostep.org/de/mediathek/veroeffentlichungen/white-paper-studien.html
10. Handschuh, S., Dotzauer, R., Fröhlich, A.: Standardized formats for visualization - application and development of JT. In: 19th ISPE International Conference on Concurrent Engineering, Trier (2012)
11. Bondar, S., Potjewijd, L., Stjepandic, J.: Globalized OEM and Tier-1 Processes at SKF. In: 19th ISPE International Conference on Concurrent Engineering, Trier (2012)

Characteristics of Green BIM: Process and Information Management Requirements

Shalini Gandhi and Julie Rose Jupp

University of Technology, Sydney
Shalini.Gandhi@student.uts.edu.au, Julie.Jupp@uts.edu.au

Abstract. In this paper, the authors explore the characteristics and requirements of digitally supported 'green' building design. Well planned, integrated and interdisciplinary digital design practices play a vital role in the iterative processes of sustainable building design. Unlike traditional ways of working, the management of design information and process integration in green building design involves a wider range and a larger number of consultants utilizing sophisticated environmental modelling and analysis systems. To understand the complexities surrounding information management in this context, the authors focus on issues relating to: 1) information exchange and model management, and 2) multidisciplinary design process coordination. Different aspects of sustainable design modelling methodologies are explored in relation to technology requirements, information exchange, and multi-disciplinary collaboration. Finally, the literature is synthesised in a conceptual roadmap framing the key factors identified by the study.

Keywords: Building information modeling, environmental sustainable design, information management, collaboration.

1 Introduction

The construction industry has long been aware of its contribution towards CO2 emissions and is now shifting towards more sustainable design solutions. Consequently, today's AEC projects (architectural, engineering and construction) often require the use of advanced information technology (IT) to address complex building system dependencies and interdisciplinary design development processes that meet expectations of environmentally sustainable design (ESD) and the information requirements of green building. The application of building information modelling (BIM) and associated collaboration technologies (e.g., XML schemas, iCloud, etc.) represents a paradigm shift. 'Green BIM' has thus been coined to describe the convergence of two key trends, green buildings and BIM. Green BIM is emerging as a new form of project design and delivery, where industry is still trying to grasp its implications. The required level of coordination between different organisations during Green BIM design processes depends on the complexity of the building [1]. Building development projects that employ ESD strategies and target maximum GBC (green building certification) credits arguably represent a higher

A. Bernard, L. Rivest, and D. Dutta (Eds.): PLM 2013, IFIP AICT 409, pp. 596–605, 2013.

order of complexity, particularly those utilising intelligent building systems. Further, in this context, integrated design processes and accreditation procedures often increase the number of participating stakeholder organisations working in synchronous collaboration. Such projects have high levels of process, activity and task interdependencies, and consequently information exchange between collaborating design firms is arguably more complex.

Not surprisingly, the rate of adoption of BIM technologies on green building design projects has increased in recent years [2]. Properly adopted, BIM promotes buildings of higher quality, with faster project delivery and at lower cost [3]. Yet, whilst this methodology has facilitated innovations in sustainable design (see e.g., [2, 4]) and in optimising green building accreditation [5, 6] its full deployment is hindered by traditional work processes, business models, and industry fragmentation [7]. Green BIM must not only overcome the adverse effects of entrenched industry methods but also new ones such as incomplete implementations of the BIM methodology. Thus, the coordination of reciprocal design task interdependencies, the management of inter-organisational processes and the sharing of digital design information represent significant challenges [3].

This paper explores the characteristics and requirements of information management for Green BIM in a literature based study. Sect. 2 describes the main attributes of Green BIM. In Sect. 3, the paper presents the research related to information management including discipline specific modelling requirements for sustainable design and associated challenges to information exchange (Sect. 3.1), and multi-disciplinary collaboration across organisational boundaries and the challenges surrounding task interdependencies (Sect. 3.2). The authors discuss their characteristics and requirements in relation to methodologies for sustainable design modelling. In Sect. 4, the authors present the main elements of Green BIM, synthesising the literature into a conceptual roadmap that identifies the relationships between each factor. Sect. 5 provides conclusions and directions for future research.

2 What is Green BIM?

A variety of definitions of Green BIM exists in the literature, (e.g., [2, 4]). The authors define Green BIM as being based on three conceptual pillars: (1) ESD principles, (2) optimisation of GBC credits, and (3) integrated building systems and design processes supported by object-based modelling and analysis tools. The intention of ESD is to "eliminate negative environmental impact completely through skilful, sensitive design" [8]. According to its principle objectives, ESD should result in more comprehensive and assessable sustainable design solutions for the built environment. ESD methodologies target five key areas of sustainability relative to building type including 1) climate, culture and place, 2) reduction of resource consumption, 3) use of local resources, 4) efficient use of man-made systems, and 5) application of renewable energy systems. Furthermore, building systems integration is one of the main goals of ESD, and the complexity of such a task requires higher levels of process and stakeholder integration.

GBC systems such as Australia's Green Star [9] and the US LEED [10] system are generally hierarchically awarded credit-based systems assessing a range of criteria, including e.g., sustainable sites, water efficiency, energy use, and quality of atmosphere, material resources, indoor environmental quality, and innovation in design ([9, 10]). To assess these criteria during the design stages it is necessary to model, simulate and analyse the virtual building. Object oriented or component based computer aided design (CAD) assists in the generation and coordination of semantically rich building information models. BIM technologies are able to provide more accurate and reliable building data, support inter-organisational collaboration, provide simulation and analysis, and accelerate production of documentation drawings [4, 5]. Azhar *et al.* [11] shows that more than half of GBC (LEED) credits can be facilitated by BIM technologies. A virtual prototype integrated with discipline specific information models can be used to simulate ESD alternatives and optimise the final solution. In this way, BIM facilitates multidisciplinary collaborative working activities between the design team members [12]; however it can increase the complexity of information management due to the amount of information generated and the complexities surrounding interoperability and the timing of information exchange [5, 13].

Green BIM therefore requires explicit, precise information for building system integration and evaluation. Theoretically, the methodologies and technical capabilities of Green BIM should enable major improvements to both design processes and products. However there are two key challenges surrounding Green BIM: (1) the involvement of a wider diversity of the design team members from different disciplines and organisations, and (2) the high level of interdependencies between processes, activities and tasks (e.g., a change in the facade materials creates a need to change the architectural design model, the structural design model and possibly also the mechanical, electrical and hydraulic models). Sodagar and Fieldson, [14] highlight the challenges of an integrated approach to sustainable design during tentative and iterative design processes. Involvement of a wider variety of the design team participants from the early project phases also means their potential continued participation through to project delivery [15]. Figure 1 illustrates the required participation of design disciplines and the timing of their involvement in a Green BIM project.

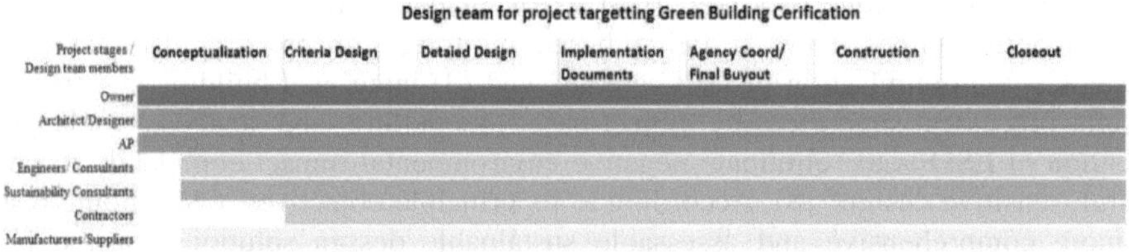

Fig. 1. Design team members in Green BIM project (Adapted from [18])

As the figure shows, Green BIM requires the involvement of the owner, architect, a variety of engineers and consultants, contractors, suppliers and manufacturers as well as an accredited professional (AP) representing the designated green certification body [10, 16, 17].

3 Characteristics and Requirements of Green BIM

The information management demands of a multidisciplinary design process cannot be managed by a single stakeholder organisation. It requires a range of design, project and IT professionals to coordinate and unify the design domains of different building systems. A comprehensive understanding of the multi-level interconnections between technologies, people, project phases, processes and systems is needed to address the (sometimes competing) requirements of Green BIM. Effective information management practices must meet the demands of the continual generation, transmission, publishing, interpreting, storing and retrieving of a wide range of building design data. Green BIM requires consideration of the policy-, process- and technology- based elements that underpin the BIM methodology [6], as well as strategies for successful information management that can support knowledge transfer and translation in multi-disciplinary ESD collaborations [18].

3.1 Information Management

The underlying requirements of information management in Green BIM projects can be seen to relate to four variables: 1) number of participants exchanging information, 2) information standards, protocols and format, 3) timeliness of information exchange, and 4) roles and responsibilities when exchanging information. In addressing policy-based information management issues, various solutions have been suggested including contractual documents, exchange protocols, modelling standards, and specification of the level of detail (LoD) in modelling (such as those found in BIM management plan templates and frameworks specifying e.g., LoD 100 to LoD 500) [19]. Interoperable file exchange schemas can partially assist with the technical difficulties surrounding compatibility (e.g., .ifc, Gbxml, .dwg, Etc.), which enables the development of an integrated data rich model.

Precise and timely information is required to overcome the adverse effects of industry fragmentation during the design process, providing accurate and coordinated 3D models for Green BIM. Tzortzopoulos-Fazenda and Cooper [20] define design management as an ill-structured process and the day-to-day operating boundaries as being imprecise. Information exchange therefore, requires well-defined standards and protocols prior to commencement of the design process. Tracing the timeliness of design information for Green BIM projects and mapping this with the capabilities and interoperability requirements of ESD technologies is essential for understanding reciprocal task interdependencies within the design team. Figure 2 presents an example of the potential information exchange and communication patterns occurring during a Green BIM project, identifying a network of task interdependencies. Green BIM is dependent on the use of digital design technologies for the purposes of both product systems integration and design process integration - such integration can be better addressed if the elements of ESD and GBC are considered in parallel. This leads to the second topic of this section: multidisciplinary collaboration – including the inter-organisational task dependencies and information modelling requirements.

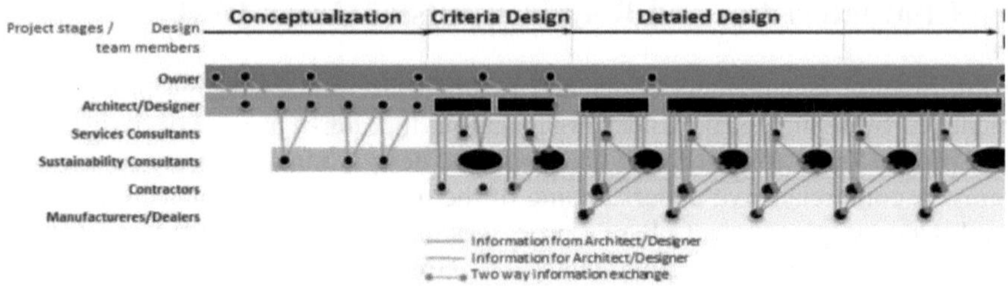

Fig. 2. Tracing task interdependencies of Green BIM

3.2 Multidisciplinary Collaboration

Design researchers have studied a range of factors responsible for the complexity surrounding multidisciplinary design collaboration. In digital design collaborations, two concerns are identified as important, namely: 1) the representation, communication and coordination of electronic information [21], and 2) differences in discipline-specific design methodologies. Undefined BIM management practices and standards can result in design team members performing functions independently of each other, and increases in levels of complexity and uncertainty. This may then negatively impact on GBC outcomes despite the time, funds and effort invested. Figure 3 provides a snapshot of the type of interactions that occur between design team members during the development of sustainable building designs. Generally to attain GBC, accreditation is based on specified criteria; to achieve the desired results from the procedure, information must be generated by a range of consultants with expertise covering e.g., water harvesting, recycle-reuse, energy analysis, sustainable material resource, day light analysis and sustainable product development. The information generated must undergo many iterations of revision depending on project requirements and design challenges. Thus, Green BIM projects with high GBC rating objectives require detailed planning during project inception.

Rohracher [22] explains that close interaction and a high level of compatibility between project participants are key necessities for ESD processes. However, a number of barriers to these necessities exist. With the high diversity of project stakeholders it is likely that individual design disciplines are located in different geographical locations and conditions. Like all projects, it may not always be possible to have close interaction with the entire project organization at any one time. In spite of the availability of advanced communication facilities, meeting agendas are difficult to define when projects are characterized by high levels of complexity, uncertainty and ambiguity. It is necessary to manage complexity and eliminate uncertainties resulting from unforeseen knock-on effects of design changes, which can also potentially identify unknown reciprocal task interdependencies [3]. Consequently, extensive resources may be required to support collaboration within Green BIM projects resulting in expensive design and development processes. In the face of complexity and rising cost, team members may revert back to traditional practices.

In Green BIM projects, successful management and coordination requires a multi-dimensional approach. However, the research literature (see Luthra[23]) reports a lack of appropriate BIM management frameworks, often resulting in the incomplete adoption of the methodology [3]. Amongst the few available solutions addressing this issue, are the AIA's [17, 18] guidelines to Integrated Project Delivery (IPD) and others such as the NATSPEC guidelines, VA BIM Guide and the AEC UK BIM Standard [17, 19, 24-27]. In other work by London *et al.* [28] a BIM process management framework is proposed, which focuses on enabling integrated design. However these frameworks fail to account for the specific technological and design process features of Green BIM. These generic frameworks ignore crucial links and interdependencies between the technical, policy and process components defining the ESD activities underpinning Green BIM.

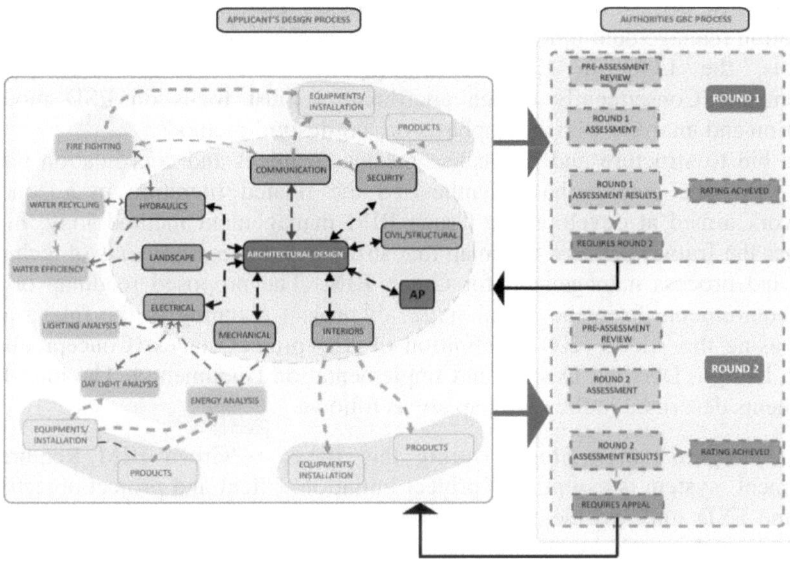

Fig. 3. Multidisciplinary design collaboration for Green Building Certification

Furthermore, in spite of the increasing interest in sustainable design and digital design practices amongst industry professionals and researchers, much attention is directed toward the development of the technical means of integration (i.e IFC-based BIM platforms, web servers for information exchange etc.) and control oriented management systems (e.g., policies, certification programs, regulations, and contract requirements). Azhar *et al.* [11] have mapped BIM capabilities with GBC requirements (in this case LEED), but fail to identify a number of Green BIM requirements including the identification of task and informational interdependencies, and the main actors responsible for generating information to meet GBC criteria.. Consequently there is a need to attend to the process dimensions of Green BIM relative to existing work on sustainable design technologies and policies. In targeting the coordination of task interdependencies along with non-linear information transfer Volker and Prins [29]show how process-based mechanisms can facilitate information management and control outputs. However there is a lack of research that integrates the process, policy and technological components of a Green BIM methodology. It is therefore necessary to analyse and amend current approaches to Green BIM projects to help achieve desired GBC credits in a more effective and efficient manner.

4 Toward a Green BIM Management Framework

The literature review highlights a lack of research into the specific modelling requirements and related challenges surrounding simulation and analysis for Green BIM and its alignment with the relatively recent introduction of GBC processes. Modelling interdependencies between building systems remain a major challenge to the coordination of design processes (e.g., water efficiency analysis requires detailed modelling of multiple building systems, including MEP services, hydraulic equipment). A Green BIM management plan that is capable of supporting the progression of ESD throughout the design stages requires further consideration of information management practices, such as the specification of information exchange protocols, the LOD in ESD modelling, and software and interoperability requirements. Consequently design coordination must focus on ESD modelling, simulation and analysis with an emphasis on 'co-design' methods.

In a bid to structure and rationalise the management and coordination issues of Green BIM, the authors have synthesised the related literature in a conceptual framework aimed at developing a Green BIM management methodology. Figure 4 describes the framework as a roadmap that structures the requirements of technology, policy and process management for Green BIM. The proposed roadmap organises these requirements from the initial stages of project planning to the final stages of design using the AIA's (2007) definition of IPD project stages (Conceptualisation, Criteria Design, Detailed Design, and Implementation Documents). The inter-linking components described in the roadmap are as follows.

1) *Conceptualisation Stage*: During this stage, a 'Green BIM Requirements Assessment' system is essential to project initiation. Client and project objectives for GBC and ESD must be identified in conjunction with the details of implementing BIM tools and processes, as well as IPD methods and contractual arrangements. Information and modelling standards, protocols, along with specification of the level of detail (LoD) throughout the design process, design team members responsible for generating information, and the ESD simulation and analysis requirements should be defined. To define these it is first necessary to identify the scope and purpose of the project before then: (a) assessing GBC criteria specifications, (b) identifying resources including key actors and assessing BIM capabilities for ESD and GBC by mapping criteria to BIM tools, and (c) assessing overall project organisation capabilities to achieve desired GBC targets. Once these requirements assessment activities have been achieved it is then possible to inform the development of IPD methods and contracts as well as provide the basis for a Green BIM methodology.

2) *Criteria Design Stage*: During this stage, it is crucial to develop the Green BIM implementation strategy; this procedure requires: (a) assessment of the feasibility of GBC/ ESD and BIM tools to achieve targeted credits, (b) identification of an ESD design activity plan that maps design participants with informational dependencies across modelling, simulation and analysis activities (e,g., water efficiency, energy efficiency, day light analysis and material resources), (c) define modelling standards and communication mediums, (d) refine information exchange protocols and assess interoperability requirements between architectural modelling and ESD team consultants before initiating the design process, and (e) map reciprocal ESD task

interdependencies between design team participants relative to GBC criteria. Thus during the Criteria Design stage, detailed process stages, stage gates and a process management matrix (describing reciprocal task interdependencies) should be developed. This will assist in mapping interdependencies between design activity plan and discipline-specific BIM technologies with emphasis on ESD methods and analysis tools. As part of this mapping process, it is also necessary to consider the interoperability requirements of each software application. Once this strategy has been developed IPD contractual arrangements can be evaluated and updated so as to ensure that the targeted GBC credits can be achieved collaboratively.

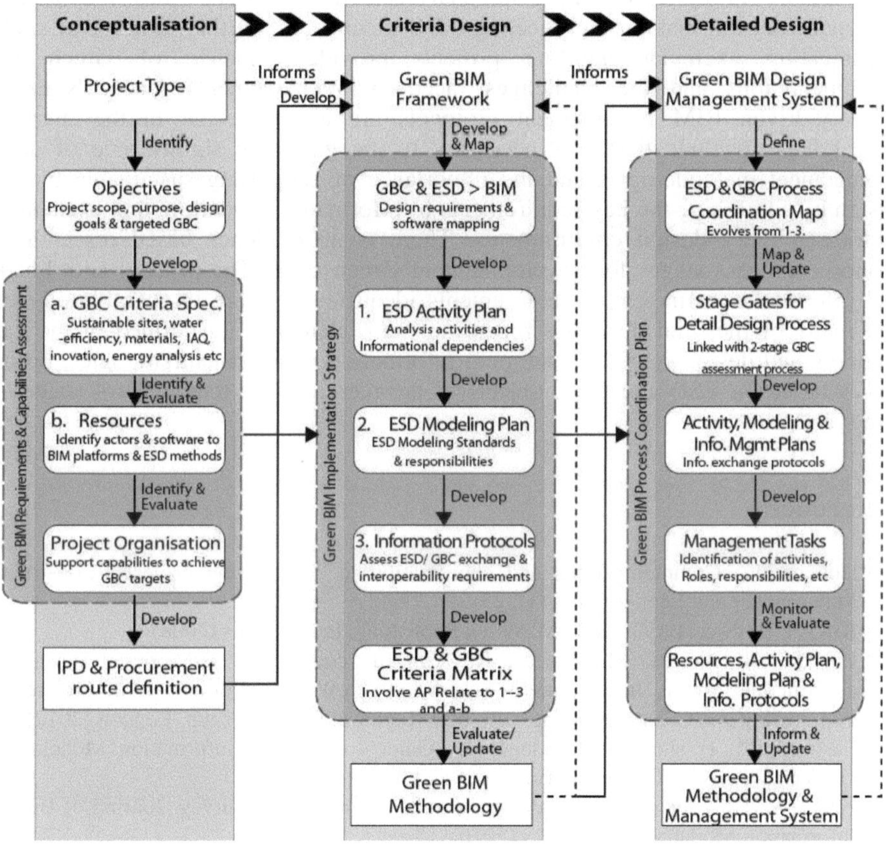

Fig. 4. Conceptual roadmap for Green BIM design management system

3) *Detailed Design Stage:* The detailed design stage must be supported by a comprehensive process coordination plan that will define a Green BIM design management approach. Prior to initiating design there is a need to prepare a design activity plan, based on process management matrix aligning ESD objectives and design tasks with information requirements and stage gates of the GBC process. To produce and implement such a plan it is necessary to: (a) update stage gates for the detailed design process (b) map stages gates to and update the design activity and modelling plans as well as information protocols, (c) develop an ESD and GBC

process coordination map, (d) define management roles and responsibilities, (d) monitor and evaluate resources, plans and protocols. These components of a Green BIM coordination plan can then be used to inform and update the overall methodology and design management system in an iterative way.

5 Conclusion

The literature reveals a number of critical elements of Green BIM encompassing technological, process and policy based attributes. Studies surrounding recent developments in digital modelling and analysis technologies show how they assist in informed decision making and meeting GBC procedures. Further, a range of studies documenting exemplar building projects provide evidence of Green BIM implementations and the challenges faced and achievements made. Numerous industry-driven BIM management protocols are also reported in the literature. Researchers conclude that it is necessary to recognise the significance of design management methodologies and the importance of supporting sustainable building design by addressing the key requirements of information modelling and exchange in multidisciplinary design environments. There is no evidence based research that proposed process stages for development of Green BIM. The process coordination and information management requirements identified here are inseparable elements and many of the vital decisions regarding these elements are defined in the early planning and design stages. Developing information management strategies, process stages based on ESD and GBC objectives are therefore pre-requisites of successful Green BIM.

References

1. Hossain, L.: Communications and coordination in construction projects. Construction Management and Economics 27(1), 25–39 (2009)
2. Kriegel, E., Nies, B.: Green BIM. Wiley Publishing, Indianapolis (2008)
3. Lavikka, R., Smeds, M., Smeds, R.: Towards coordinated BIM based design and construction process. In: Gudnason, Scherer (eds.) eWork and eBusiness in Architecture, Engineering and Construction, pp. 513–520. Taylor & Francis Group, London (2012)
4. Eastman, C., et al.: BIM Handbook: A Guide to Building Information Modeling for Owners, Managers, Designers, Engineers and Contractors (2011)
5. Azhar, S.: BIM for sustainable design: results of an industry survey. Journal of Building Information Modeling 4(1), 27–28 (2010)
6. Jupp, J., Gandhi, S.: Clarifying the role of Building Information Modelling in Green Building Certification. In: 37th Annual Conference of Australasian University Building Educators Association (AUBEA). University of New South Wales, Sydney (2012)
7. Kiviniemi, A.: The Effects of Integrated BIM in Processes and Business Models. Distributed Intelligence in Design, 123–135 (2011)
8. McLennan, J.F.: The philosophy of sustainable design: The future of architecture. Ecotone Publishing (2004)
9. GBCA. Green Building Council Australia, Certification Process (December 2010) (2012)
10. USGBC. US Green Building Council, What LEED 2011 (2011)

11. Azhar, S., et al.: Building information modeling for sustainable design and LEED® rating analysis. Automation in Construction 20(2), 217–224 (2011)
12. Succar, B.: Building information modelling framework: A research and delivery foundation for industry stakeholders. Automation in Construction 18(3), 357–375 (2009)
13. BEDP. Issues Paper: Australian Council of Built Environment Design Professions BEDP (September 2007)
14. Sodagar, B., Fieldson, R.: Towards a sustainable construction practice. Construction Information Quarterly 10(3), 101–108 (2008)
15. Häkkinen, T., Belloni, K.: Barriers and drivers for sustainable building. Building Research & Information 39(3), 239–255 (2011)
16. GBCA. Green Building Council Australia, Certification Process (December 2010)
17. AIA. Integrated Project Delivery: A Guide. version 1 (2007)
18. den Otter, A., Emmitt, S.: Design team communication and design task complexity: The preference for dialogues. Architectural Engineering and Design Management 4(2), 121–129 (2008)
19. NATSPEC. NATSPEC Construction Information – NATSPEC National BIM guide v.10 (2011)
20. Tzortzopoulos-Fazenda, P., Cooper, R.: Design management from a contractor's perspective: The need for clarity. Architectural Engineering and Design Management 3(1), 17–28 (2007)
21. Toth, B., et al.: Sky high and back again: the evolution of simulation-based design from aerospace to construction. IBPSA Australasia and AIRAH (2011)
22. Rohracher, H.: Technology Analysis and Strategic Management (2001)
23. Luthra, A.: Implementation of Building Information Modeling in Architectural Firms in India (2010)
24. ACG, A., Productivity in the buildings network: assessing the impacts of Building Information Models, report to the Built Environment Innovation and Industry Council: Sydney, Australia (2010)
25. AEC. AEC UK BIM Standard - A practical and pragmatic BIM standard for the Architectural, Engineering and Construction industry in the UK (2009)
26. NASFA, et al.: Integrated Project Delivery for Public and Private Owners (2010)
27. VABIMGuide. Department of Veterans Affairs – The VA BIM Guide, V.1.0 (2010)
28. London, K., et al.: Building information modelling project decision support framework. Association of Researchers in Construction Management, ARCOM (2008)
29. Volker, L., Prins, M.: Exploring the possibilities of correlating management with value in architectural design. In: Proceedings of CIB W096 Architectural Management. Lyngby, Denmark, pp. 8–13 (2005)

Developing a Building Information Modelling Educational Framework for the Tertiary Sector in New Zealand

Garry Miller, Shubham Sharma, Claire Donald, and Robert Amor

University of Auckland, New Zealand
g.miller@auckland.ac.nz

Abstract. Whilst Building Information Modelling (BIM) is rapidly being acknowledged as a driver for change in the Architectural, Engineering and Construction sector across the globe, the introduction of BIM into graduate and postgraduate teaching programmes in the tertiary sector in New Zealand has been minimal to date. New Zealand has an advanced albeit small economy, and whilst BIM is being deployed increasingly with effect in industry, there is no national BIM education framework and only one tertiary sector institution offers any BIM teaching in New Zealand (NZ). This paper reviews the current approaches to incorporating BIM into degree and certificate programmes in 25 leading international universities, pedagogical approaches and BIM critical success factors. A draft of a BIM educational framework for NZ is proposed based on this review. An approach for further design, development and deployment of the framework is also offered. This paper is intended to initiate debate and to start to build consensus between the academic community and industry on a national BIM educational framework for New Zealand.

Keywords: Building Information Modelling, Tertiary Education, Framework.

1 Introduction

Building Information Modelling (BIM) is "a digital representation of physical and functional characteristics of a facility. A building information model is a shared knowledge resource of information about a facility forming a reliable basis for decisions during its life-cycle; defined as existing from earliest conception to demolition" (National Institute of Building Sciences, 2007). BIM is being advocated by many as a catalyst for change, poised to reduce the industry's fragmentation and increase its efficiency by improving the communication between project teams (Succar, 2009).

BIM has been identified by the New Zealand Productivity Partnership (a partnership established between government and industry) as a new technology which integrates data and knowledge management to minimize inefficiencies and enhance the value delivered during design, build and operation (Kane, 2012). Implementation of BIM in NZ is one of four major work-streams in the Productivity Partnership's programme to deliver a productivity improvement of 20% by 2020.

A. Bernard, L. Rivest, and D. Dutta (Eds.): PLM 2013, IFIP AICT 409, pp. 606–618, 2013.

There are some early adopters of BIM in New Zealand (NZ). There is evidence that some organisations are already deriving benefits from using BIM including improved project design, co-ordination, planning, project delivery and bottom line performance improvements (Huber, 2012). However, from anecdotal evidence it would appear that organisations doing so are the larger companies with international operations, who are able to gain benefits by transferring knowledge from overseas. As such, whilst BIM has the potential to significantly improve performance of organisations, in NZ it is not widely understood nor harnessed by New Zealand industry generally. A concurrent issue is also an almost complete lack of BIM educational provision by the NZ tertiary sector institutions, which exacerbates the slow adoption of BIM. Therefore is a need in New Zealand to develop an educational framework for the tertiary sector in order to enhance knowledge and skills in the local context.

To address this challenge the University of Auckland has developed a collaborative research and educational programme for BIM issues related to the Architectural, Engineering and Construction (AEC) sector in NZ. This programme is a collaboration between several parties, including other tertiary sector organisations and industry. This paper offers a draft educational framework to initiate debate and to start to build consensus in the academic community on a national BIM educational framework for New Zealand.

2 Literature Review: Background and Contemporary Issues for New Zealand

Despite the recent global interest in BIM it is in actual fact an old idea, with origins in the 1970's (Eastman et al., 2008). It has taken almost 40 years to become the commercially attractive tool that is so widely praised today (Bernstein, 2005). Perhaps the best evidence of its potential to add value to the construction industry is its widespread uptake by countries such as (but not limited to) the United States, United Kingdom, Denmark, the Netherlands, Finland, and Australia. However, in New Zealand a recent survey found that of 417 respondents, 10% do not understand what BIM is, 60% have some understanding, a further 20% have a reasonable appreciation of BIM's potential and only a final 10% have a clear appreciation of the advantages of BIM (Huber, 2012). As such BIM is still at the development stage of the typical product life cycle in the context of NZ.

Tran et al. (2012) make a case for establishing a BIM research framework in NZ, and identify three reasons why BIM has not been widely used namely: slow uptake by companies; a lack of NZ-focused initiatives; and a lack of BIM-based building life cycle considerations. Of these three reasons the first appears to be a circular argument. The second reason is well made, and despite interest in BIM from policy makers, it would appear that there is no real appetite by political leaders to drive BIM implementation at a policy level. The third reason would appear to have some validity, but is not unique to New Zealand.

Other specific issues relating to the NZ context are the structure of NZ industry, the Canterbury post earthquake re-build, NZ regulatory issues relating to consenting processes, and the educational provisions in BIM. We discuss the structural issues and the educational provisions in more detail in the following sections.

Issues relating to BIM adoption by small to medium sized enterprises (SMEs) are particularly relevant for New Zealand. SMEs are defined in NZ as businesses that employ fewer than 20 full-time staff. More than 96% of businesses in the AEC sector are in this category (MED, 2011). Access to new technology, performance improvement approaches and training is often limited for SMEs by the lack of awareness of innovative processes, technologies and practices. This is primarily due to the costs of acquisition of new technologies and of training (Eastman and Sacks, 2008).

Furthermore, evidence is evolving from overseas that adoption of BIM models and processes by SMEs can represent a strategic driver for the performance improvement within the SME section of the AEC industry (Gledson et al., 2012, Sebastian et al., 2009). When there are early adopters within the SME community, their example helps leverage on-going introduction of BIM across industry.

Jayasena et al. (2012) and Wong et al. (2011) emphasise that for BIM expansion, we need more BIM trained professionals in the AEC industry, and that such people are very hard to find because of insufficient BIM training and education. The essential training in this regard is needed for students in tertiary educational institutes.

Gier (2007) carried out a research study in the USA to examine if BIM should be taught as a subject to construction management students. He conducted two questionnaire surveys targeted at general contractors and construction management programs. Based on the collected data, he concluded that construction management programs should teach BIM to their students.

In another study, Woo (2007) pointed out that properly structured BIM courses would provide industry-required knowledge to prepare students for successful careers in the AEC industry. Instead of teaching a separate course, he suggested restructuring existing construction courses to integrate BIM into the course content.

Whilst these studies are informative, their paradigm is from the perspective of BIM rather than from the perspective of educational design. We therefore provide a brief overview of some of the literature on educational frameworks, together with a proposed development approach in a later section of this paper.

3 Developing the Draft Educational Framework

In developing a draft educational framework for BIM we have considered a number of factors, namely:

1. Contextual issues for New Zealand;
2. Critical success factors for BIM implementation from international literature;
3. Review of existing BIM educational programmes offered by leading international universities;
4. Pedagogical approaches to the design of educational frameworks.

We have already provided an overview of context issues for New Zealand in the literature review, and the following sections of this paper consider the remaining factors before offering a draft framework.

BIM Critical Success Factors

Table 1 is a comparison of BIM success factors including enterprise resource planning, new product development and project management success factors from different authors, categorized into people, process, management and technology factors.

Table 1. BIM Critical Success Factors

BIM success factors	*Pinto et al. (1987)*	*Lester (1998)*	*Zhang (2003, 2009)*	*Autodesk (2007)*	*Staub-French et al. (2007)*	*Mom (2011)*
Process Factors	Clearly defined goals	Senior management commitment	Comprehensive survey and assessment	Sound implementation strategy	Identifying uses of 3D models and model requirements	BIM models for submittal and approval, step-by-step testing
Manage-ment factors	Competent project management	Organizational structure and processes to support venture	Efficient project management team	Assembling the right team	Developing protocol for addressing design questions	BIM standards, codes, rules and regulations
People factors	Top management support	Attract new product concepts available for development	Improve project management information system	Training for BIM	Establishing conflict resolution process	Pre-qualification of team, matching project goals with team goals
Techn-ology factors	Standard equipment, Sufficient resource allocation	Venture teams with appropriate staffing and resources	Need to embrace change and continuous improvement		Establishing drawing protocol	Technical support including training

By analyzing the table, it can be clearly seen that for process factors, most of the authors focus on a sound and clear objective or strategy by identifying the goals. On management factors, most of the authors recommend implementing in an integrated team-based approach while maintaining well-defined rules. For people factors, training and employee support as well as having the right expertise are identified as essential. Lastly, for technology factors, technical support, efficient hardware and software, sufficient resource allocation and standard equipment are considered critical factors. We believe these success factors are informative for design of a BIM educational approach.

3.1 Review of BIM Educational Programmes

We reviewed the current BIM educational programmes in the 25 leading international universities for engineering according to the Times Higher University Rankings (2012). We did keyword searches on the main website of the top 25 universities, and also specifically searched for "BIM Course Outline". The name of the BIM course, the subject level, duration of the course and teaching method were identified at both undergraduate and postgraduate levels. Also, the same approach was used to search for BIM courses for the eight universities in New Zealand in order to compare trends.

Out of all the top 25 universities in the world for engineering, 16 of them are currently teaching BIM courses as summarized in Figure 1.

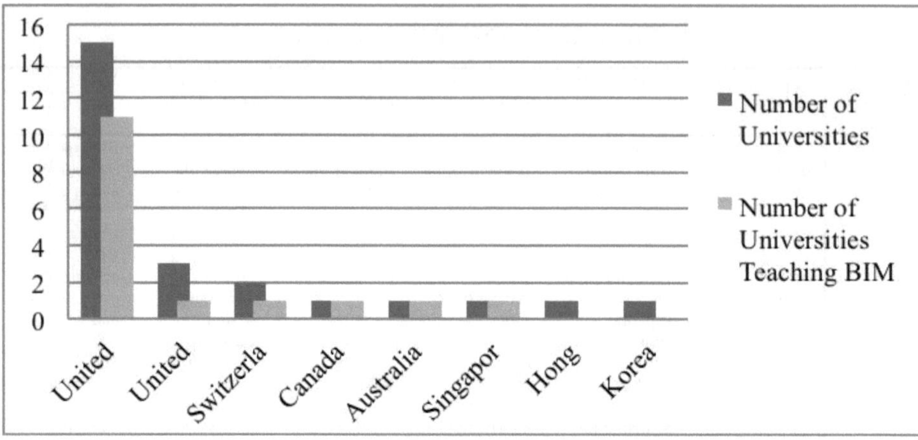

Fig. 1. BIM Education Provision in Leading Universities for Engineering

The duration of most of the courses in the universities is one semester, with 15 out of 16 having semester-long BIM courses. Also, the preferred level of teaching BIM courses is at undergraduate level, with 9 out of 16 universities teaching BIM courses at this level. Six out of 16 universities also have some BIM courses at Masters level, while only 3 universities have certificate level courses. A list of the universities and further details of their BIM course offerings are provided in the Appendix.

Of the 8 universities in New Zealand none currently have a taught course or progamme at Bachelor or Masters level in BIM. However, there is a good track record in BIM research in New Zealand, which positions universities in New Zealand well for developing research informed BIM educational programmes. Only Unitec Institute of Technology (a polytechnic) has BIM courses, which appear to be orientated towards skills development and vocational training. Therefore, there is currently a gap in the educational sector in New Zealand for providing university level education at Bachelor and taught Masters levels.

A Pedagogical Approach to the Design of a BIM Educational Framework for NZ

We propose that a starting point for designing a new educational framework for BIM in New Zealand is to conduct a comprehensive needs analysis according to the widely used ADDIE model (Analysis, Design, Development, Implementation, Evaluation) of instructional design (Dick et al., 2005). This establishes the extent and nature of the demand in the various sectors of the BIM professional community, the requirements of key stakeholders, necessary educational, technical and funding resources as well as the characteristics of the potential students. The research reported in this paper provides the basis for such a needs analysis.

The results of the completed needs analysis will inform the design of the educational framework for BIM. During this second stage we will determine the goals and intended learning outcomes for the curriculum, its structure, and plan the teaching and assessment methods. An initial set of goals and outcomes are proposed later in this paper. The central question we address during this process is: what is most important for the students to know, to be able to do, and what are the best ways for them to learn this? (Toohey, 1999).

Approaches to curriculum design at university tend to fall into five categories (Toohey, 1999): traditional, or discipline-based; performance- or systems-based; cognitive; personal relevance or experiential; and socially critical. These are not necessarily applied discretely. Indeed, we propose to combine elements from three of these categories to designing a national BIM framework: the traditional or discipline-based approach, (the BIM educational framework will be divided into topics based on the important concepts); the performance or systems-based approach, (support particular teaching and learning methods according to clear and assessable objectives) and the cognitive approach (students will be helped to develop specific intellectual abilities and conceptual structures required for problem solving across multidisciplinary domains).

Crucial to devising a successful national BIM programme for tertiary students will be applying Biggs' strategy of constructive alignment (Biggs, 1996). This involves aligning the intended learning outcomes, assessment methods and planned learning opportunities closely with one another. In addition, we will ensure that flexible e-learning opportunities are incorporated appropriately, using an integrated e-learning framework which has been successfully applied in other degree programmes (Blake and Doherty, 2008).

Currently underpinning our approach to this design are the theories of authentic learning and situated cognition (Brown et al., 1989). These place primary importance on the real-life context of learning, suggesting that for learning to be effective and meaningful, it must occur in the same context in which it will be used and applied in the future, similar to apprenticeship training. In a tertiary education context, authentic learning environments include a number of key elements proposed by Herrington, Reeves and Oliver (2010), which we would aim to incorporate in a new curriculum for BIM. These include providing authentic learning activities, access to expert performances and modeling of processes, adopting multiple roles and perspectives, collaborative construction of knowledge, and authentic assessment of learning within the tasks.

We believe that this approach will provide the sound pedagogical basis required as we move forward with the planning and development of a new BIM framework for the tertiary education sector in NZ.

4 Proposed Draft Framework

In developing a proposed educational framework for BIM in the tertiary sector for New Zealand we identified disciplines (knowledge domains) and mapped them against the NZQF. One of the challenges of devising a BIM education programme is that BIM crosses a number of traditional disciplinary boundaries. BIM certainly crosses the architectural, engineering and construction domains, and the AEC industry is often defined as a sector. However BIM is also an approach that integrates technology and software development together with business, enterprise and management. We illustrate the relationship between these sectors in a Venn Diagram in Figure 2. In devising such an integrated approach across disciplines we seek to incorporate some of the BIM critical success factors identified earlier in this paper.

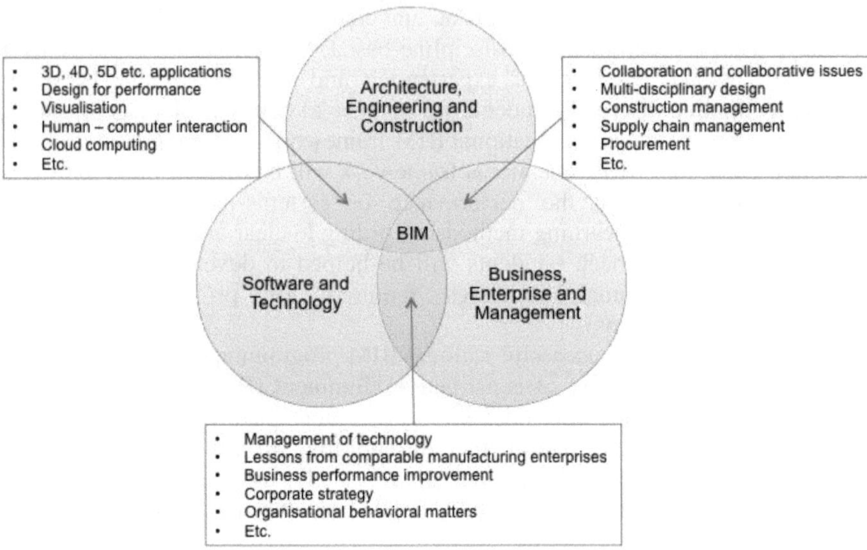

Fig. 2. Venn Diagram Showing Discipline Relationships for BIM

We also believe that an educational framework should encompass three broad types of education: vocational training / continuing professional development, degree programmes (taught), and research (including PhD programmes). The requirements in each of these are different, and so the framework needs to be designed to serve the diverse educational needs of a broad spectrum of stakeholders. Our draft framework is presented in Figure 3.

In the architectural design representation, BIM enforces a migration from two to three dimensions by creating intelligent, multi-dimensional building models. Hence, in reality BIM goes beyond simply representing the geometry of a building. As such BIM is not just a new way of drafting and is not a technique that might be taught like technical drawing. Rather it is a more fundamental approach which needs to be studied and well understood. BIM views can show and intelligently interpret the types of materials and construction details including scheduling of building elements for assembly. Through this capability BIM provides an opportunity for various users with different backgrounds to work collaboratively across traditional disciplines.

One of the debates in BIM education is the question of whether BIM should be integrated into existing curricula of architecture and engineering degrees (i.e. by integrating BIM into teaching on existing papers), or whether it should be taught as a specific topic in its own right. We take a pragmatic view that it probably needs to be a combination of both, with an incremental, organic integration into existing Bachelor level degrees probably being the more acceptable and sustainable approach. However incremental change in tertiary sector can be slow, and there is an argument to be made for an integrated degree targeted at mature students who have gained some industry experience and are seeking to gain specialized knowledge and skills in BIM. Hence we also propose an integrated postgraduate course delivered as a taught masters degree. Such a degree should cross the boundaries of traditional disciplines, and ideally should be a collaboration between faculties and even between different universities. Whilst such collaborations can be difficult to achieve in practice they are not impossible, and given that BIM typically facilitates collaboration in industry, we argue that it should do so in academia also. Development of a specialist taught Masters programme provides a possible avenue for collaboration.

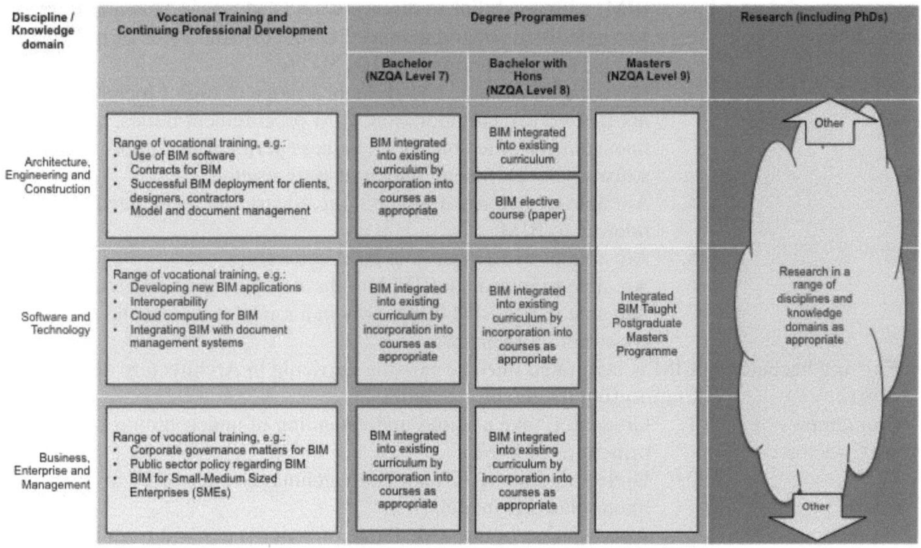

Fig. 3. Draft BIM Educational Framework for New Zealand

While it is premature to define the content of the educational programmes, goals should be identified. We have attempted to draft a set of goals and intended learning outcomes to stimulate debate. These are presented in Table 2:

Table 2. Suggested Goals for New Zealand BIM Education Framework

Element of Framework	***Goals***
National BIM Educational Framework	1. The framework is accepted by all tertiary sector organisations in NZ; 2. Universities and other tertiary sector education providers collaborate on teaching and research; 3. The New Zealand BIM educational framework is acknowledged as being world class in international comparators; 4. The BIM educational programme leads NZ industry towards the mature phase of the BIM technology lifecycle.
BIM research	1. A dynamic programme of research, extending knowledge at the most advanced level; 2. Research supported and funded by industry and public sector working in partnership with the tertiary sector; 3. Some commercialization of the best research outputs
BIM taught Masters degree	Students completing the degree: 1. Have advanced understanding of underpinning key principles of BIM, with an ability to discern what BIM can and cannot do; 2. Are able to create and manage 3D models, and some of the extension applications into 4D, 5D etc.; 3. Have the knowledge and skills in a range of topics including (but not limited to): collaboration, BIM procurement issues, management of technology, business performance improvement, software development, database systems etc.; 4. Are able to undertake research on at least one specialized topic relating to BIM; 5. Are able to use a variety of BIM software; 6. Are able to introduce BIM into their employer organisations; 7. Are able to use BIM effectively in a range of design and /or construction scenarios.
Existing bachelor degree programmes in AEC sector	BIM is integrated into the existing curricula in Architecture and Engineering degree programmes: 1. Graduates have a sound understanding of underpinning key principles of BIM; 2. Understanding of 3D modeling techniques and ability to manipulate 3D models; 3. Appreciation of the wide range of benefits derived from BIM 4. Able to use a variety of BIM software; 5. Able to use BIM effectively in a range of design and /or construction scenarios.
Vocational training and CPD education	1. An active and dynamic programme of vocational training and CPD to meet the training needs of industry; 2. Accessible and affordable training for a diverse New Zealand sector with significant portion of SMEs; 3. Awareness and knowledge at all levels of industry of benefits of BIM.

In order to measure the success of achieving the BIM educational goals we plan to implement a longitudinal study to gather data on learning outcomes and uptake of graduates being offered employment in industry in BIM related roles. In order to broaden the relevance of this research to the international community we are seeking collaborations to benchmark outcomes with the tertiary sector in other parts of the world.

5 Future Work

We outlined our planned pedagogical approach to the design of an educational framework in a previous section. To facilitate the development of the framework we will seek to establish collaboration with the other tertiary institutes in New Zealand, industry and other interested stakeholders such as professional bodies, trade associations, the Productivity Partnership, Building Research Association of New Zealand and the Ministry of Business, Innovation and Employment. There is a range of practical mechanisms we will seek to introduce including formation of an advisory group, and establishment of a funded BIM research and educational programme. An injection of funding from the public sector is needed to kick-start such a programme, as industry-led funding is unlikely to be forthcoming due to the early stage in the technology life-cycle and fragmented nature of industry in the AEC sector. An important future stage will be to derive the intended learning outcomes and align them with appropriate assessment strategies. Further research is needed to develop (or re-draft as appropriate) the learning outcomes proposed in this paper. Such research must seek to identify the particular needs of SME's. The formulation of intended learning outcomes in partnership with industry will help to ensure the educational framework meets the needs of NZ industry.

6 Conclusions

We have argued that New Zealand AEC sector is at the early development stage of BIM life-cycle, and that whilst the potential of BIM is generally recognised there are barriers to wider implementation of BIM, particularly the structure of NZ industry and the lack of BIM educational provision. Whilst the international tertiary sector has already established BIM educational courses and programmes, there is an almost complete lack of BIM educational provision at undergraduate and taught postgraduate levels in New Zealand: a deficiency that must be tackled. As a first stage in addressing this issue we have offered a draft educational framework for NZ, which seeks to incorporate disciplines across traditional boundaries, that is based on well-founded pedagogical principles, acknowledges BIM critical success factors, is informed by overseas programmes, and focused on learning outcomes. This framework is offered to initiate debate and to start to build consensus between the academic community and industry on a national BIM educational framework for New Zealand.

References

Autodesk, Transitioning to BIM (2007), http://static.ziftsolutions.com/files/8a7c9fef2693aa1e0126d28c29d806ac

Bernstein, P.: Integrated Practice: It's not just about the technology. The American Institute of Architects (2005), http://info.aia.org/aiarchitect/thisweek05/tw0930/tw0930bp_notjusttech.cfm (accessed October 31, 2012)

Biggs, J.: Enhancing teaching through constructive alignment. Higher Education 32, 347–364 (1996)

Blake, A., Doherty, I.: An Instructional Design Course for Clinical Educators: First Iteration Design Research Reflections. Journal of Learning Design 2(2), 104–115 (2008)

Brown, J., Collins, A., Duguid, P.: Situated cognition and the culture of learning. Educational Researcher 18(1), 32–42 (1989)

Dick, W., Carey, L., Carey, J.: The systematic design of instruction. Pearson (2005)

Eastman, C.M., Sacks, R.: Relative Productivity in the AEC Industries in the United States for On-Site and Off-Site Activities. Journal of Construction Engineering and Management 134, 517–526 (2008)

Eastman, C.M., Teicholz, P., Sacks, R., Liston, K.: BIM handbook: A guide to building information modeling for owners, managers, architects, engineers, contractors and fabricators. John Wiley and Sons, Hoboken (2008)

Gier, D.: Does learning building information modeling improve the plan reading skills of construction management students? (2007), http://ascpro0.ascweb.org/archives/2007/CEUE146002007.pdf

Gledson, B., Henry, D., Bleanch, P.: Does Size Matter? Experiences and Perspectives of BIM Implementation From Large and Sme Construction Contractors. In: 1st UK Academic Conference on Building Information Management (BIM), Northumbria University, Newcastle upon Tyne, UK (2012)

Herrington, J., Reeves, T., Oliver, R.: A guide to authentic learning. Routledge, New York (2010)

Huber, R.: New Zealand National BIM Survey 2012. Masterspec - Construction Information Ltd. (2012)

Jayasena, H.S., Weddikkara, C.: Building Information Modelling for Sri Lankan Construction Industry (2012), http://www.academia.edu/1772647/Building_Information_Modelling_for_Sri_Lankan_Construction_Industry

Kane, C.: Productivity Roadmap. Building and Construction Sector Productivity Partnership (2012)

Lester, D.H.: Critical success factors for new product development. Research Technology Management 41, 36–43 (1998)

Mom, M.: On Decision-making and Technology Implementing Factors for BIM Adoption (2011), http://www.academia.edu/894660/On_Decision-making_and_Technology-implementing_Factors_for_BIM_Adoption

National Institute of Building Sciences 2007, NIST, National building information modeling standard. Version 1 - Part 1: Overview, principles and methodologies (2007)

Pinto, J.K., Slevin, D.P.: Critical Factors in Successful Project Implementation. IEEE Transactions on Engineering Management EM-34, 22–27 (1987)

Sebastian, R., Haak, W., Vos, E.: BIM application for integrated design and engineering in small-scale housing development: a pilot project in The Netherlands. In: Proceedings of International Symposium CIB-W096 Future Trends in Architectural Management, Tainan, Taiwan, November 2-3 (2009)

Staub-French, S., Khanzode, A.: 3D and 4D modeling for design and construction coordination: issues and lessons learned. ITcon 12, 381–407 (2007)

Succar, B.: Building information modelling framework: A research and delivery foundation for industry stakeholders. Automation in Construction 18, 357–375 (2009)

Times Higher Education, World University Rankings (2012), http://www.timeshighereducation.co.uk/world-university-rankings/2012-13/subject-ranking/subject/engineering-and-IT (accessed December 9, 2012)

Toohey, S.: Designing Courses for Higher Education. Open University Press, Philadelphia (1999)

Tran, V., Tookey, J.E., Roberti, J.: Shaving BIM: Establishing a Framework for Future BIM Research in New Zealand. International Journal of Construction Supply Chain Management 2, 66–79 (2012)

Wong, K.A., Wong, K.F., Nadeem, A.: Building information modelling for tertiary construction education in Hong Kong. ITcon (2011)

Woo, J.H.: BIM (Building Information Modeling) and Pedagogical Challenges. In: Proceedings of the 43rd Annual Conference by Associated Schools of Construction (2007)

Zhang, L., Lee, M.K.O., Zhang, Z., Banerjee, P.: Critical success factors of enterprise resource planning systems implementation success in China. In: Proceedings of the 36th Annual Hawaii International Conference on System Sciences, 10 p. IEEE (2003)

Zhang, Y., Guangbin, W.: Cooperation between Building Information Modeling and Integrated Project Delivery Method Leads to Paradigm Shift of AEC Industry. In: Management and Service Science, September 20-22, pp. 1–4 (2009)

Appendix

#	Institution	Country	BIM course	Teaching method	Duration	Course Name	Level
1	California Institute of Technology	United States	No	-	-	-	-
2	Princeton University	United States	No	-	-	-	-
3	Massachusetts Institute of Technology	United States	Yes	Thesis, Coursework	One Semester	Computational Design Lab: Reinventing BIM	Bachelors Masters
4	University of California, Berkeley, Berkeley	United States	Yes	Coursework	One Semester	Fundamentals of Building Information Modeling, Revit, Advanced Revit	Certification
5	Stanford University, University	United States	Yes	Coursework	One Semester	Building Information Modeling	Bachelors
5	University of Cambridge	UK	Yes	Research	>One Year	Infrastructure As-Built Modeling	
7	University of California, Los Angeles	United States	Yes	Online Coursework	One Semester	Introduction to Building Information Modeling	Certification
8	ETH Zürich – Swiss Federal Institute of Technology Zürich	Switzerland	Yes	Coursework	One Semester	LowEx + Arch	Masters
9	Georgia Institute of Technology	United States	Yes	Coursework, Thesis	One Semester	BIM: Case studies, BIM for building construction	Bachelors, Masters
10	Imperial College London	UK	No	-	-	-	-
11	University of Oxford	UK	No	-	-	-	-
12	National University of Singapore	Singapore	Yes	Coursework, Workshop	One Semester	Integrated design and sustainability	Bachelors
13	University of Texas at Austin	United States	Yes	Coursework	One Semester	BIM for capital projects	Bachelors
14	École Polytechnique Fédérale de Lausanne	Switzerland	No	-	-	-	-
15	Carnegie Mellon University	United States	Yes	Coursework, Workshop	One Semester, Three days	Advanced CAD, BIM, and 3D Visualization	Masters, Research
16	North Western University	United States	Yes	Coursework	One Semester	Various 100, 200 and 400 level BIM courses	Bachelors, Masters
17	University of California, Santa Barbara	United States	No	-	-	-	-
18	Cornell University	United States	Yes	Coursework	One Semester	Introduction to Revit and BIM	Bachelors
19	University of Michigan	United States	No	-	-	-	-
20	University of Illinois at Urbana Champaign	United States	Yes	Workshop	One day	Autodesk Revit Training Workshop: BIM	Certification
21	Columbia University	United States	Yes	Coursework	One Semester	Re-Thinking BIM	Bachelors
22	University of Toronto	Canada	Yes	Coursework	One Semester	Building Information Modeling	Bachelors
23	Hong Kong University of Science and Technology	Hong Kong	No	-	-	-	-
24	Pohang University of Science and Technology	Republic of Korea	No	-	-	-	-
25	University of Melbourne	Australia	Yes	Coursework	One Semester	Construction Measurement and Estimating	Masters

Building Information Modeling (BIM) and the Construction Management Body of Knowledge

Mehmet Yalcinkaya[1] and David Arditi[2]

[1] Doctoral Student, Aalto University, Department of Structural Engineering and Building Technology, Espoo, Finland
[2] Professor, Illinois Institute of Technology, Department of Civil, Architectural and Environmental Engineering, Chicago, IL, USA
mehmet.yalcinkaya@aalto.fi,
arditi@iit.edu

Abstract. Building Information Modeling (BIM) is a process by which a digital representation of the physical and functional characteristics of a facility are built, analyzed, documented and assessed virtually, then revised iteratively until the optimal model is documented. The virtual BIM model is not only graphical design but also a virtual database which includes the management data. So the construction manager (CM) can use BIM as a real simulation of the actual project. However, there is ambiguity about the compatibility of the traditional CM duties and responsibilities and BIM.

This study looked into the construction management body of knowledge under twelve main subjects relative to the functions of BIM. It was determined that BIM is effective in the most critical phases of a project's lifecycle. The duties and responsibilities of the CM must be updated to improve CMs' efficiency in BIM-based projects.

Keywords: Building information modeling (BIM), construction manager (CM), construction management body of knowledge.

1 Introduction

Construction management involves the optimum use of available funds, the control of the scope of the work, effective project scheduling, the avoidance of delays, changes and disputes, enhancing project design and construction quality and optimum flexibility in contracting and procurement [1]. Information is of great value for the construction manager (CM). Traditionally, CMs access the necessary information via periodic meetings, blueprints, reports, and work schedules; they coordinate the construction processes with this information. However, preparing and presenting the information is time consuming and includes human factors. It can be stated that traditional methods fall short in monitoring complex construction projects. On the other hand, developments in IT allow the CM to access more accurate and current as well as visual information, which in turn allows the CM to monitor construction processes more effectively. Developments in IT have affected the CM's duties and responsibilities and therefore, are expected to change the practice of construction management too.

A. Bernard, L. Rivest, and D. Dutta (Eds.): PLM 2013, IFIP AICT 409, pp. 619–629, 2013.

IT systems used today in construction encompass all disciplines and are used to describe and document the contributions of each member of a project team [2]. The most current IT product is Building Information Modeling (BIM) which is a process by which a digital representation of the physical and functional characteristics of a facility are built, analyzed, documented, and assessed virtually, then revised iteratively until the optimal model is documented [3]. BIM is not only a 3D virtual representation of building, but also a giant database which includes significant information packages for the basic construction management practices such as estimating, scheduling, change orders, etc. So, the designer can use BIM as a real simulation of the actual project before real construction starts. However, there is ambiguity about the compatibility of the construction management body of knowledge and BIM.

Computerization has improved speed and accuracy in most construction management services. Web-based systems have improved access to information, communication between parties and overall efficiency. The basic practices of construction management involve the use of sophisticated computer tools. Budget, schedule, risks, constructability, etc. are modeled and analyzed before the execution of the actual project and tracked during the construction process on the computer screen. These computer tools allow CMs to perform their duties with great speed and accuracy. Most CMs are familiar with traditional practices that involve basic computer tools, but should they also need to get acquainted with BIM and should they explore ways to integrate BIM applications into their duties? The objective of this study is to investigate whether there is a need for updating the current construction management body of knowledge with respect to the emerging BIM technology, hence updating the CM's duties and responsibilities in response to developments in BIM.

2 Methodology

This study investigates whether the construction management body of knowledge is up to date relative to developments in BIM. The twelve subjects in the body of knowledge were extracted from the Construction Extension to *A Guide to the Project Management Body of Knowledge* [22]. A comprehensive literature review was performed to understand how BIM affects the basic functions of construction management.

3 Construction Management and BIM

3.1 Budget Management

Budget management encompasses all project-related cost aspects of CM practice [4]. The CM has the responsibility to confirm, generate, track, report, and substantiate all budgeted costs from the first estimate to the final accounting. The conceptual budget for the project, prepared by the CM before design begins, becomes the team's line-item financial guide as the design process moves toward the bidding phase. After bids are received, the amounts of accepted contractor proposals replace estimated line-item amounts and become the construction phase budget. As construction proceeds, payments to contractors, contract changes, and budgeted expenses are accounted for in detail. Every aspect of project cost is estimated as early as possible and substantiated as it occurs.

One of the important parts of budget management is cost estimating which includes the development of an estimate of the materials and other resources needed to complete the project activities. BIM models can be used for cost estimating to generate a bill of quantities. It is also possible to establish a direct link between the BIM model and the estimating software. Once a cost estimator establishes this link, changes in the BIM model are automatically propagated through the whole estimating cycle [5]. Since there are links between the BIM model and the cost estimate, the CM can get cost-related or expenditure-related evaluation for any activity. Cost budgeting includes allocating the overall cost estimate to individual work activities and controlling the cost of the changes to the project budget. BIM interconnects structural design, time, and cost effectively [6]. Alternative computer-aided methods have been developed for effective budget management. For example, Zhang et al. [7] developed a building information system that includes among other things a budget information and monitoring dimension. Hardin [8] described the use of BIM for effective budget management. Popov et al. [9] stated that cash flow can be predicted in 5D models, where the 5th dimension represents cost-related data.

3.2 Contract Management

According to Haltenhoff [4], contract management encompasses the involvement of the CM in the operational and administrative provisions of the contracts used in the project. Construction management expertise includes the recommendation of standard contract forms and the performance responsibilities to be included in contracts, but does not extend to the writing of contracts or in any way infringe upon the legal profession. This area is important because the construction management system is a unique contracting system, the success of which depends on a workable alignment of traditional contracting roles and participant responsibilities. It is the CM's responsibility to establish a contracting format for the project and see that each contractor's operational and administrative requirements are included.

AGC is the first organization that marketed contract documentation focusing on the use of BIM in a project in September 2007. The "Building Information Modeling (BIM) Addendum" of Consensus DOCS 300 "Tri-Party Collaborative Agreement" promotes an integrated process and focuses on BIM as a tool that can enable the project team. These contracts aim focus on responsible data sharing through BIM technology. AIA has also released contract language that addresses the use of BIM. AIA documents A295-2008, B195-2008 and A195-2008 require protocols for sharing, owning, and transferring data throughout a project [10]. Since BIM brings a new dimension to project delivery methods, the CM should be familiar with these new types of contract.

3.3 Decision Management

Decision management encompasses the development and handling of the interrelationships between the project and the construction team, and the relationship between the members of the construction team. It is the CM's responsibility to consistently extract decisions from the team without alienating any team members in the process. Team members must make decisions cooperatively, respecting each other's project function, expertise, and operational capacities. Decisions that become contentious must have a prescribed path for resolution.

Since BIM includes all of the design and management source data of the building, the CM can support the construction team by using BIM applications in the decision making process. Each phase of a project requires a unique decision-making process. The CM can use BIM to generate drawings, reports, design analysis, cost estimates, schedule simulation, facilities management, and ultimately enabling the building team to make informed decisions.

3.4 Information Management

Information management encompasses the collection, documentation, dissemination, safe keeping, and disposal of verbal and graphic project-related information. The team structure and the use of multiple contracts significantly increase the information available to the owner. The volume of information generated for project accountability purposes requires a multilevel, need-to-know reporting structure and an efficient information storage and retrieval system [4]. Information management can be established by setting up a communication platform such as BIM. Since BIM is a database of information, the CM can reach the digitized documents whenever needed and set up a computer-based communication system. Underwood and Isikdag [11] state that BIM acts like a shared information backbone through the lifecycle of the project. The BIM approach is essentially a conceptual way of managing project information even though the majority of construction business processes are heavily based upon traditional means of communication such as face-to-face meetings and the exchange of paper documents in the form of technical drawings, specifications and site instructions. It should be noted that the historical, industrial and market forces that perpetuate the industry's culture affect negatively the extent of adoption of IT tools like BIM [12]. Nevertheless, BIM can be used to communicate with project team members.

3.5 Material and Equipment Management

Material/equipment management encompasses all activities relating to the acquisition of materials and equipment from specification to installation and warranty. Material handling includes procurement, inventory, shop fabrication, and field servicing. The construction management delivery system facilitates direct owner purchase of materials for the project. The planning, specifying, bidding, acquisition, expediting, receiving, handling and storing of direct purchases must accurately reflect the requirements of the project schedule. Proper control and management of materials can increase productivity significantly [13]. On the other hand, the use of modern equipment impacts construction technologies and enhances the competitiveness of construction companies. Materials and equipment constitute a large portion of a project's total cost and must therefore be subject to strict control. Organizations that do not recognize the impact of various innovations in materials and equipment get forced out of the mainstream of construction activities [14].

4D and 5D BIM models can be used to analyze the time and cost impacts of the selected materials [9]. Also, Mahalingam et al. [15] state that construction planners can use 4D simulations to select the appropriate construction equipment for the project and to check the safety conditions for the movements of equipment. Currently, 4D BIM models are used to optimize site layouts [16], and improve site logistics and space work execution [17].

3.6 Project Management

Project management encompasses all of the operational aspects of project delivery, including determining, formulating, developing, installing, coordinating and administering the necessary elements from the beginning of design to the termination of the warranty period. The CM has the responsibility to coordinate the efforts of the team in achieving a common goal.

There is a growing use of BIM models to minimize the potential for design and construction errors, to identify critical space and time during construction [18], to determine the most suitable construction methods and sequence, and to monitor construction progress [19]. Russell et al. [20] discuss how visual representations and interaction technologies support a range of project management functions and enhance the understanding of project status. Song et al. [21] propose a 3D model-based project management control system that enables the CM to display a holistic picture of a project by applying the multiple project data sets to the 3D building model components [20]. Zhang et al. [7] use an integrated building information system and digital images captured on-site to semi-automate the calculation of progress measurements and project status.

3.7 Quality Management

Quality management ensures that the project will satisfy the needs for which it was undertaken. It includes all activities that determine the quality policy, objectives and responsibilities and implements them by means such as quality planning, quality assurance, quality control, and quality improvement [22]. Since the fundamental element of BIM is a 3D virtual model, the owner and the design team have a first impression of the overall project from the 3D model.

In the traditional approach, it is difficult to reconcile the different designs such as architectural vs. MEP or structural vs. MEP unless the design team is very experienced. However, BIM models allow the design team and the CM to virtually review the conflicts and resolve them during coordination meetings [23]. Therefore, the quality of the project is substantially enhanced before actual construction begins. During the construction process, quality can be controlled with traditional methods such as benchmarking the process against quality standards, but the construction process can be captured and integrated to the BIM environment too. For example, Brilakis et al. [24] experimented with automated construction site image retrieval technologies; Kim et al. [25] explored how 3D models of existing construction sites can be rapidly generated using data from laser scanners; and Akinci et al. [26]

investigated how as-built laser scan data can be used for ongoing site inspection. The captured construction processes can be used to ensure that the quality requirements of the contract are satisfied.

3.8 Resource Management

Resource management includes the selection, organization, direction and use of all project resources, both human and physical. The construction management delivery system places all consulting, design, management, contracting, and construction services in a team environment coordinated by the CM.

BIM technology is used for visualization purposes by most construction professionals. But this technology has moved far beyond its original visualization stage. Some researchers have investigated the integration of construction resource management to BIM. For example, Babic et al. [27] used BIM to link information from the enterprise resource planning (ERP) information system with the building design data, thus tracking the status of the different components of the project; and Wang et al. [28] developed a BIM-based system that integrates dynamic resource management and the decision support system.

3.9 Risk Management

Risk management encompasses the dynamic risks that are directly tied to team decisions and static risks that are simply inherent to construction. Risk management has traditionally been applied in the area of safety, cost, time, and contract management in construction projects. It can also be used in bidding policies, feasibility studies, marketability studies, performance evaluations, and contingency management [29].

The CM can use BIM to reduce safety risks and as a starting point for safety planning and communication. The utilization of BIM can result in improved occupational safety by connecting safety issues more closely to construction planning, providing more illustrative site layout and safety plans, managing and visualizing up-to date plans and site status information, as well as by supporting safety communication in various situations [30].

The CM can use BIM to reduce not only safety risks, but also the risks associated with cost and time management. For example, Zhang et al. [7] developed a building information system to address the impact of project management risks on time and cost during the construction of the superstructure of buildings.

3.10 Safety Management

Construction is one of the most hazardous industries in the world due to its unique nature including frequent work team rotations, exposure to weather conditions, and high proportions of unskilled and temporary workers [31]. Safety management includes the processes required to assure that the construction project is executed with appropriate care to prevent accidents that cause personal injury, death, or property damage. Accidents and their consequences are a major concern in the construction industry both in terms of human suffering and the direct and indirect costs to the industry.

Many researchers have addressed the lack of integration between construction and safety. Traditionally, safety is achieved through periodic meetings and training. Virtualization of the projects before the actual construction phase allows safety managers and CMs to simulate their safety precautions and identify potential safety problems. For example, Popov et al. [9] used 3D simulation to locate cranes such that their booms do not hit structures; Alshawi et al. [32] gave BIM's visualization technologies a central role in safety training; Vacharapoom and Sdhabbon [33] defined a rule-based hazard identification model using BIM to analyze and anticipate unsafe conditions; Sulavinki et al. [30] proposed BIM models to incorporate safety related activities into construction schedules; and Hu et al. [34] defined the analytical procedures based on 4D simulations to reveal potential safety threats.

3.11 Schedule Management

Construction planners typically use CPM-based networks and bar charts to describe the proposed schedule of a project. The CPM schedule does not provide any spatial information and any information about the complexities of the project components. Therefore to identify the spatial aspects of a project, planners must look at 2D drawings and conceptually associate the components with the related activities. Because CPM networks are an abstract representation of the project schedule, users need to interpret the activities to comprehend the sequence they convey [35]. The outcome could be arbitrary since different planners could have different perspectives of developing a project schedule. In addition, the current CPM methods do not allow planners to explicitly describe the constraints of a construction project, such as availability of resources, the site conditions, and the availability of capital, which are very important factors for making decisions [36]. Therefore, planners can only determine the impact factors of project scheduling in their mind, which is time consuming and frequently prone to error [37]. Besides, it is very difficult to integrate the time and cost information in the current CPM scheduling framework, one of the reasons being that schedules generated by the CPM method are activity-based, whereas in the construction process, the project is executed according to work items. The work items contain the cost and resource data of the project but are not well connected to the activities of the project schedule.

4D models integrate 3D geometry with time as the fourth dimension. Any building component in a 4D model contains geometric attributes that describe its 3D shape, as well as a time attribute that indicates the start and finish times of the construction of this element. A 4D model of a structure can therefore be used to graphically simulate the sequence of construction operations, thereby providing the operator with a virtual, visual understanding of the construction process [2]. 4D visualizations can be used by a wider variety of project participants at varying levels of skills and experience [15].

Some researchers developed integrated systems to schedule projects with basic BIM applications. For example, Dawood et al. [38] proposed a virtual construction site model to develop a decision support system for construction planning; Chau et al. [46] developed and implemented a 4D site management model for construction management; Migilinskas and Ustinovichius [39] proposed a 4D model for project life cycle management.

3.12 Value Management

Value management addresses a project's cost versus its value, and has three value components: designability, constructability, and contractibility. *Designability* relates value to overall project design. BIM models allow designers to design a building with respect to the required specifications. Having an effective knowledge about the material libraries makes the virtual model more acceptable. *Constructability* relates value to construction materials, details, means, methods, and techniques. BIM models allow the design team and the CM to virtually review the conflicts and resolve them during coordination meetings [23]. Current BIM software applications detect clashes and enhance constructability. *Contractibility* relates value to contracting options, contractual assignments, and contracting procedures. The CM is expected to extract maximum value for the owner with respect to designability, constructability and contractibility.

4 Conclusion

The future of the design and construction industry lies in the use of technology; and BIM is expected to shape this future effectively. The introduction to BIM into design and construction practice has brought along new duties and responsibilities for the CM. However, the existing CM body of knowledge is based on traditional methods despite the fact that BIM is becoming more popular. BIM is effective in every phase of a project's lifecycle as it covers several CM functions in the most critical phases. Hence, traditional CM duties and responsibilities are inadequate in handling the CM-related functions of BIM-based projects. The consequences of CMs' lack of familiarity with BIM and BIM-related tools may manifest themselves in different ways. Not taking advantage of the benefits provided by 4D and 5D BIM models reduces management efficiency and is detrimental to the overall performance of the project. Therefore CMs' duties and responsibilities must be updated to take full advantage of BIM models.

To understand what BIM brings to the table, the existing CM body of knowledge was reviewed and assessed vis-a-vis the functions of BIM. It was found that modifications are appropriate in almost all of the twelve areas of the CM body of knowledge discussed in the preceding section. For example, CMs must become familiar with tools that help the CM estimate the cost, set up a work schedule, control the cost, improve safety, and manage resources when the architect/engineer uses BIM to design a project; must adjust the organization and management of the team members to take full advantage of the communication and information exchange opportunities provided by BIM; must keep an open mind for integrated project delivery systems that make extensive use of BIM models; must rethink the necessity of constructability reviews in the face of clash detection provided by BIM; and must recognize the changes in the risk distribution that BIM brings to a regular contract.

An important outcome of this research is related to the potential of BIM to be used alongside many construction management applications. But the literature review indicates that there are differences between traditional and BIM implementation. Therefore, these findings suggest that the current construction management body of knowledge should be updated to reflect the changes caused by BIM in the current construction management duties and responsibilities.

In anticipation of BIM's takeover of design and construction activities, it would be advantageous for all parties to have a common understanding of updated CM duties and responsibilities over all phases of the construction project. Future CMs must be trained to be effective in a BIM environment. If CM education and training keeps abreast of developments such as BIM, CMs can serve the industry better.

In future research, a curriculum can be developed, refined and improved by getting and analyzing feedback from trainees and employers. Also, the effects of BIM on infrastructure projects can be evaluated in future research. It would be interesting to see whether the duties and responsibilities of CMs in BIM-based infrastructure projects are any different than in building projects.

References

1. Arditi, A., Ongkasuwan, D.: Duties and responsibilities of construction managers: perception of parties involved in construction. Journal of Construction Engineering and Management 135(12), 1370–1374 (2009)
2. Fisher, M., Kunz J.: The scope and role of information technology in construction (2004), http://cife.stanford.edu/online.publications/TR156.pdf (retrieved August 25, 2010)
3. National Institute of Building and Science (NIBS) National building information modelling standards. Facilities information council national BIM standards, Washington, DC (2007)
4. Haltenhoff, C.E.: The CM contracting system, ch. 9, pp. 128–140. Prentice Hall (1998)
5. Staub-Frenc, S., Fischer, M., Kunz, J., Paulson, B.: A generic feature driven activity-based cost estimation process. Advanced Engineering Informatics 17(1), 243–254 (2003)
6. Gabbar, H.A., Aoyama, A., Naka, Y.: Model-based computer-aided design environment for operational design. Computers and Industrial Engineering 46(3), 413–430 (2004)
7. Zhang, X., Bakis, N., Lukins, T.C., Ibrahim, Y.M., Wu, S., Kagioglu, M., Aouad, G., Kaka, A.P., Trucco, E.: Automating progress measurement of construction projects. Automation in Construction 18(3), 294–301 (2009)
8. Hardin, B.: BIM and construction management. Proven tools, methods, and workflows, pp. 176–177. Wiley Publishing Inc., Indianapolis (2009)
9. Popov, V., Juocevicius, V., Migilinskas, D., Ustinovichius, L., Mikalauskas, S.: The use of a virtual building design and construction model for developing an effective project in 5D environment. Automation in Construction 19(3), 357–367 (2010)
10. AIA, American Institute of Architects Contract documents, Integrated project delivery (IPD) family (2008), http://www.aia.org/contractdocs/AIAS076706 (retrieved August 23, 2010)
11. Underwood, J., Isikdag, U.: Handbook of Research on Building Information Modeling and Construction Informatics: Concepts and Technologies. IGI Global (2010)

12. Baldwin, A.N., Thorpe, A., Carter, C.: The use of electronic information exchange on construction alliance projects. Automation in Construction 8, 651–662 (1999)
13. Navon, R., Berkovich, O.: Development and On-Site Evaluation of an Automated Materials Management and Control Model. Journal of Construction Engineering and Management 131(12), 1328–1336 (2005)
14. Hendrickson, C.: Project management for construction, Fundamental concepts for owners, engineers, architects and builders. Prentice Hall Publishing, Pitsburg (2008)
15. Mahalingham, A., Kashyap, R., Mahajan, C.: An evaluation of the applicability of 4D CAD on construction projects. Automation in Construction 19(2), 148–159 (2010)
16. Zhang, J., Anson, M., Wang, Q.: A new 4D management approach to construction planning and site space utilization. In: 8th International Conference on Computing in Civil and Building Engineering, ASCE. Stanford University, California, pp. 14–17 (2000)
17. Akinci, B., Fischer, M., Kunz, J., Levitt, R.: Representing Work Spaces Generically in Construction Method Models. Working Paper #57. CIFE, Stanford University (2000)
18. Dawood, N., Scott, D., Sriprasert, E., Mallasi, Z.: The virtual construction site (VIRCON) tools: an industrial evaluation. Journal of Information Technology in Construction, 43–54 (2005)
19. Sriprasert, E., Dawood, N.: Genetic algorithms for multi-constraint scheduling: an application for the construction industry. In: Proceedings of CIB w78 Conference 2003, Auckland, New Zealand (2003)
20. Russel, A.D., Chiu, C.Y., Korde, T.: Visual representation of construction management data. Automation in Construction 18(8), 1045–1062 (2009)
21. Song, K., Pollalis, S.N., Pena-Mora, F.: Project dashboard: concurrent visual representation method of project metrics on 3D building models. In: ASCE International Conference on Computing in Civil Engineering, pp. 147–153. American Society of Civil Engineers, Reston (2005)
22. Project Management Institute (PMI) Construction extention to a guide to the project management body of knowledge. Project Management Institute, Newtown Square, Pennsylvania (2000)
23. Hartman, T., Gao, J., Fischer, M.: Areas of application for 3D and 4D models on construction projects. Journal of Construction Engineering and Management 134(10), 776–785 (2008)
24. Brilakis, I.K., Soibelman, L., Shinagawa, Y.: Construction site image retrieval based on material cluster recognition. Advanced Engineering Informatics 20(4), 443–452 (2006)
25. Kim, H., Haas, C.T., Rauch, A.F.: 3D image segmentation of aggregates from laser profiling. Computer Aided Civil Infrastructure Engineering 18(4), 254–263 (2003)
26. Akinci, B., Boukamp, F., Gordon, C., Huber, D., Lyons, C., Park, K.: A formalism for utilization of sensor systems and integrated project models for active construction quality control. Automation in Construction 15(2), 124–138 (2006)
27. Babic, N.C., Podbreznik, P., Rebolj, D.: Integrating resource production and construction using BIM. Automation in Construction 19(5), 539–543 (2010)
28. Wang, H.J., Zhang, J.P., Chau, K.W., Anson, M.: 4D dynamic management for construction planning and resource utilization. Automation in Construction 13(5), 575–589 (2004)
29. Han, S.H., Kim, D.Y., Kim, H., Jang, W.S.: A web-based integrated system for international project risk management. Automation in Construction 17(3), 342–356 (2008)
30. Sulavinki, K., Kahkonen, K., Makela T., Kiviniemi, M.: 4D-BIM for construction safety planning (2010), `http://www.cib2010.org/post/files/papers/1167.pdf` (retrieved August 24, 2010)

31. Jannadi, O.A., Bu-Khamsin, M.S.: Safety factors considered by industrial contractors in Saudi Arabia. Building and Environment 37(5), 539–547 (2002)
32. Alshawi, M., Goulding, J., Nadim, W.: Training and education for open building manufacturing: Closing the skills gap. ManuBuild in collaboration with VTT – Technical Research Centre of Finland, Finland (2007)
33. Vacharapoom, B., Sdhabbon, B.: An integrated safety management with construction management using 4D CAD model. Safety Science 48(3), 395–403 (2009)
34. Hu, Z., Zhang, J., Deng, Z.: Construction process simulation and safety analysis based on building information modeling and 4D technology. Tsingua Science and Technology 13, 266–272 (2008)
35. Koo, B., Fischer, M.: Feasibility study of 4D CAD in commercial construction. Journal of Construction Engineering and Management 126(4), 251–260 (2000)
36. Feng, C.W., Chen, Y.J., Huang, J.H.: Using the MD CAD model to develop the time-cost integrated schedule for construction projects. Automation in Construction 19(3), 347–356 (2010)
37. Koo, B., Fischer, M., Kunz, J.: A formal identidication and re-sequencing process of location-based scheduling and 4D CAD. Automation in Construction 16(2), 189–198 (2007)
38. Dawood, N., Akinsola, A., Hobbs, B.: Development of automated communicated of system for managing site information using internet technology. Automation in Construction 11(5), 557–572 (2002)
39. Chau, K.W., Anson, M., Zhang, J.P.: 4D dynamic construction management and visualization software: 1. Development. Automation in Construction 14(4), 512–514 (2005)
40. Migilinskas, D., Ustinovichius, L.: Computer-aided modeling, evaluation and management of construction projects according to PLM concept. In: Luo, Y. (ed.) CDVE 2006. LNCS, vol. 4101, pp. 242–250. Springer, Heidelberg (2006)

Incomplete BIM Implementation: Exploring Challenges and the Role of Product Lifecycle Management Functions

Julie Rose Jupp

University of Technology, Sydney
Julie.Jupp@uts.edu.au

Abstract. Implementing the BIM methodology relies on mastering new digital ways of working. However approaches to BIM often lack a holistic perspective that span the whole building lifecycle. The omission of Product Lifecycle Management functions in the implementation of the BIM methodology can lead to failures in delivering the benefits of BIM to operations and diminish its value to clients with large property portfolios. In an empirical study, the paper presents an investigation into the current situation of BIM using an Australian commercial property development project. It explores implications of partial implementation for the building lifecycle. Case study findings identify deficiencies in the project environment, management shortcomings associated with the specifics of client requirements, and difficulties in the transverse use of BIM and PLM platforms due to human interface problems.

Keywords: Building information modeling, product lifecycle management, multidisciplinary collaboration, operations, facilities management.

1 Introduction

Building Information Modeling (BIM) is a model-driven approach to designing, constructing, operating and maintaining buildings. The model that forms the core of the BIM approach is a shared and computable 3D model of the building that helps overcome the shortcomings of a 2D paper-based approach. BIM is therefore a methodology that facilitates multidiscipline collaboration and information management between different project stakeholders [1]. Implementing BIM relies on mastering new digital ways of working to streamline workflow and minimise task redundancies across the building lifecycle [2]. However in practice the integration and management of processes, information technologies (IT) and protocols across building lifecycle phases continues to present major challenges to its implementation.

Whilst these challenges are a complex of factors, they may stem from a lack of a holistic approach to BIM and lifecycle management during design and construction. Recent critiques of BIM highlight implementation deficiencies relative to the integration of facilities management (FM) expertise (e.g., the 'closed-loop problem', [3]), and a lack of core Product Lifecycle Management (PLM) functions during project implementation [4]. In this frame, the paper explores barriers to full BIM implementation, the implications of partial applications of the methodology, and

A. Bernard, L. Rivest, and D. Dutta (Eds.): PLM 2013, IFIP AICT 409, pp. 630–640, 2013.

examines the role PLM functions might play. A case study was conducted to identify the current situation of the use of BIM in Australian commercial property development. Findings identify deficiencies in the project environment, highlighting management shortcomings associated with the specifics of client requirements and constraints and human interface problems in the use of BIM.

The remainder of the paper is divided into four sections. Sect. 2 presents a brief review of related literature. Sect. 3 introduces the research methods and processes. Sect. 4 presents the case study and findings which are structured according to their significance relative to processes, technologies and policies. Sect. 5 concludes the paper, synthesising observations in a discussion on the nature of the challenges identified, and points to potential ways to overcome them.

2 Background

In the last five years an increasing focus on the application of BIM throughout the whole building lifecycle has emerged. The literature surveyed here reveals a growing number of studies that consider a range of building lifecycle management issues, where much of this research has sought to bridge the interface between AEC processes and operations; e.g., development of IFCs to include schemas for FM [5] and the introduction of the COBie initiative (Construction Operations Building information exchange), which allows for the exchange of IFC-based FM data [6]. Research has provided a variety of extensions of BIM technologies to support operations [7-12] and requirements management links to BIM models have been developed [13]. New uses of web technology have also been proposed to deliver building information to support FM [14], including the development BIM for FM portals to provide feedback from project stakeholders and to develop business requirements [15]. Recent studies also focus on the value of as-built datasets to FM personnel and clients [16], highlighting difficulties surrounding their creation during construction [17] and demonstrating that there are often no clear strategies for keeping the BIM model "alive" during operations [3]. Even despite a combined BIM and Integrated Project Delivery approach [18], the flow and management of information is still not fully integrated among all stakeholders [19]. This growing body of literature provides much evidence that research efforts to close the loop and develop the BIM methodology for the whole building lifecycle are increasing.

One of the main gaps identified in the literature relates to the lack of research surrounding the role of PLM in the BIM methodology. Whilst proponents of BIM assert that the methodology can be effective in process integration, knowledge transfer and information management (avoiding information losses incurred when transitioning from one team to another), a critical assumption remains that each group has the ability to "add to and reference back to all information they acquire during their period of contribution to the BIM model" [20]. Such aspirations for fully coordinated datasets and seamless information management appear to be far from reality, largely due to a lack of PLM functionality in applications of BIM. Key aspects of PLM for BIM-enabled projects include the management of processes surrounding the creation, release, change and verification of building information. For example, PLM systems typically provide for the following core functions: the management of design and process documents and models, construction and control of bill of material (product structure) records, provision of electronic file repositories, inclusion of document and model metadata, identification of model content for compliance and verification, enabling workflow and process management for approving changes, controlling multi-user secured access and data export controls.

Researchers of BIM management have tackled a variety of PLM and configuration management related issues [4]. London *et al.* [21] identify BIM management requirements that reflect core PLM functions, including data organisation, version management, release management and role/responsibility identification. BIM model servers, such as Jottne's EDM model server, are also beginning to be used in industry to gain PLM benefits, and whilst promising BIM model servers must still be integrated into a PLM environment to address change management functions [4]. Similarly, recent developments in enterprise solutions for building development, such as ArtrA Enterprise, are providing PLM functionality so as to address asset management. In a bid to integrate BIM and PLM, recent work by Reedman [4] proposes an integrated environment using the Integrated Product Model concept. The IPM concept places a "well managed digital product model" at the centre of the design and engineering process; where 'well managed' means that there are "appropriate release and change processes in place". Their approach utilises BIM to apply configuration management concepts to assure accurate documents and models "all of the time". Yet to realise the value of BIM in operations (where small information gains can result in major improvements in cost and productivity), the main building information source must be complete, error free, verified, updated and maintained, which presents significant challenges to a fragmented, low-tech industry; these challenges are explored in detail in the following case study.

3 Research Setting and Method

The research focused on a commercial high-rise project in Australia; for anonymity reasons the project shall be referred to as the 'HR Building'. The development was one of the first in Australia to implement BIM in a multidisciplinary collaboration. A case study approach was adopted [22] and data collection involved analysis of project documents (e.g. project plans, contract documents, project correspondence and reports) and semi-structured interviews with members of the project team. 18 participants were interviewed across five companies (see Table 1). Interviews took place between November 1010 and August 2011. Each interview took approximately one hour and recordings were subsequently transcribed and verified.

The semi-structured interview approach meant that a range of topics related to the research problem could be covered. Key interview questions therefore included the following two areas: (1) the drivers of and barriers to the implementation of the BIM methodology relative to the management of processes, technologies, policies and stakeholder interactions; and (2) where problems were highlighted by interviewees, their impacts on operations were explored with a specific focus on process and information management. From the data collected, workflow processes and information management were mapped, and several recurring themes were identified.

Table 1. Interviewees

Organisation	Title	# Interviewed
Developer	Project Development Manager	1
	Building Manager	1
	Facilities Manager	1
Architectural Firm	Design Technology Director	1
	Design Director	1
	Project Architect	1
	Architectural BIM Manager	1
	Architectural BIM Modeller	2
Structural Engineers	Structural Project Director	1
	Structural BIM Manager	1
Services Engineers	Services BIM Manager	1
	Services BIM Modeller	1
Construction Contractor	Project Manager	1
	Design Manager	1
	Construction BIM Manager	1
	Construction BIM Modeller	2

4 Case Study Findings

The implementation of BIM was a client requirement, mandated in the contract. A design and build procurement method was taken. Broadly, BIM was required to support design and engineering, simulation and analysis, documentation, construction and operations. Using examples from interview notes and transcripts, Sect. 4 builds a picture of the challenges encountered on the HR Building project. General findings are reported before presenting an analysis of interview responses categorised into process-, technology- and policy- based themes.

4.1 General Findings: Workflow and Management

The project commenced in 2005, and was completed in 2011. This timespan can be divided into six broad phases: 1) Stage 1 Development Application (DA); 2) Design Competition Winners Announced; 3) Stage 2 DA and Tender Documentation.; 4) Pre-construction and completion of design and construction phase services; 5) Demolition and construction commencement; and 6) Practical completion.

The creation of a collaborative federated model for construction and as-built model for FM were required by the brief. BIM management responsibilities were taken on by the architectural firm. The main architectural and structural models were complimented by intelligent information models developed by services design consultants and manufacturers. All discipline models were coordinated into a federated model for a variety of construction analysis purposes including structural, fire services, hydraulics, electrics, mechanical, interiors and manufacturer's models.

Building datasets were managed via the architectural design firm until construction where the main contractor took over responsibilities. Datasets were managed via creation, release and change processes using a central model management strategy, which was specified by the architectural firm in project planning and continued by the contractor. Verification processes beyond the use of clash detection analysis prior to construction were not continuously executed throughout construction.

The process of ensuring all facets and services of the building were resolved and coordinated ahead of a tight construction schedule presented a variety of management challenges. Critically, neither an open standard for data exchange nor an open format for FM (e.g., COBie) was utilised; consequently critical data was not captured in the as-built dataset, including some equipment lists, product data sheets, warranties, spare parts lists and preventive maintenance schedules. This information was seen by FM personnel as essential to support operations, maintenance and asset management.

On handover, the federated model could be used for FM in two basic ways, namely for creating (1) O&M manual hyperlinks, and (2) links within 2D representations of 3D component objects to some asset and technical data. Thus, the as-built model was not only incomplete, but not dynamically or intelligently mapped to the computerised maintenance management system (CMMS). The CMMS procured (by the contractor) was an open, standards-based technology which will enable the integration of the as-built model on one network providing a single user interface, local or remote accessibility and a breakdown of all building systems, including heating, ventilation, air conditioning, lighting, energy consumption, access control, video surveillance, intrusion, fire and smoke detection, electrical distribution, power quality and monitoring. Thus in contrast to the high levels of integration reached between design and engineering team members, the integration of FM requirements, knowledge and expertise was overall found to be lacking.

4.2 Process-Based Issues

Three process-related challenges to BIM implementation were identified: (1) entrenched traditional practices and lack of best practice, (2) asynchronous nature of FM knowledge integration and (3) timeliness training at hand-over.

***Entrenched Work Practices and Lack of Best Practice*:** A lack of appreciation of IT capabilities was apparent in many interviews, and in particular interviews with the main contractor. This was manifest in a level of skepticism voiced by some interviewees concerning the value of BIM; as one interviewee stated: 'Potentially and theoretically [BIM] is a great idea, but we see some issues. The whole sale speech of BIM is that it [the building design] will not change on site, because theoretically you create a virtual building. However all the clash conditions were not fully resolved by the consultants at documentation stage.' Also highlighted was a hasty close-out stage, which compromised the quality of CMMS system procured: 'An off-the-shelf solution was procured which supports neither the BIM model nor the FM team's requirements for operations and maintenance.' It was felt that the contractor didn't fully consider the requirements of an integrated BIM-FM solution. Other interviewees voiced frustrations at the level of BIM maturity within industry, particularly in relation to a lack of best practice and evidence-based research demonstrating the use of IFC schemas for FM such as COBie: 'We've found flaws in the [CMMS] system, such as missing functionalities, poor tracking and reporting mechanisms, and less than ideal integration with BIM datasets,' and 'The datasets are not in a compatible format, so we were unsure whether assets contain the required data for our systems.' Furthermore, whilst interviewees understood lifecycle management requirements, most didn't have a clear understanding of how existing approaches to PLM could support a BIM environment. A sentiment shared by most interviewees was that many PLM technologies and FM data formats, which were relatively new at the time of the project, lacked evidence-based research to support adoption decisions.

Asynchronous Nature of FM Knowledge Integration**:** It is well known that the timescale differences between design/production and operations create the 'closed loop problem', stemming from the asynchronous nature of FM knowledge integration [3]. It was confirmed that whilst BIM provided a way for FM knowledge to permeate across organisational boundaries, IT objects (and associated protocols) can be misinterpreted as they are sent from one context to another. Therefore, despite initial input from FM consultants at the outset of the project, the problem of closing the design-production-operations loop was not successfully addressed; as one interviewee put it: 'We did feel we had FM requirements covered and the specifications of the as-built model were detailed at the outset but the ball seems to have been dropped during construction.' This was also reflected in the following FM personnel statements: 'Our FM team didn't come online until just before handover, which meant our ability to influence specifications and data requirements were limited. FM seems to have dropped off what was already a long list of integration requirements'.

Timeliness of Training at Handover**:** The timeliness of FM information was therefore a common theme. Almost all interviewees believed that more FM expertise would have benefitted the creation and validation of datasets. Interviewees also believed that the continued participation of FM consultants during construction would have ensured higher levels of integration and avoided communication and training deficiencies at handover. Consequently, the FM team was largely unaware of what was contained in the as-built model: 'At hand-over when we were given the as-built model by the contractor, we didn't really know what had been modeled for our purposes. What we discovered was that there wasn't much detailed asset information.' A common frustration voiced by FM personnel concerned the timing of information exchange to begin earlier than point of hand-over so as to implement verification and training processes. Early involvement during planning and design stages as well as ongoing updates was seen as necessary to enable more efficient data sharing. The timing of these processes was seen as crucial to maximise knowledge transfer between incoming FM personnel and outgoing AEC project participants.

4.3 Technology-Based Issues

The study revealed three technology-based issues: (1) unknown FM data requirements, (2) inappropriate technologies and reluctance to use open standards for information exchange, and (3) IT skills shortages.

***Unknown FM Data Requirements*:** Interviewees raised uncertainties concerning FM data requirements and delivery of the as-built model. It was felt that this was not specified adequately. Checklists typically outlined items without specifying the level of detail of asset data required for operations: 'During construction we weren't clear on what the deliverables were in relation to FM and because we weren't clear it was difficult to provide a good brief to suppliers and manufacturers.' The challenge was seen to be a lack of FM knowledge on the type, level and format of asset data. This issue related to process-based challenges identified in Sect. 4.2 and raises the question of who is responsible for obtaining data which is accurate, complete, and in the appropriate format [16]. It also points to two significant issues: (1) the FM team didn't join the project until just before handover, and (2) the FM team's approach derived from existing organisational practices and reliant on the developer's growing centralised approach to FM across their buildings portfolio (see Sect. 4.4).

***Inappropriate Technologies or Reluctance to Use Them*:** To manage buildings through-life appropriate technologies must be utilised. It was found that required management systems, data standards (e.g., IFC) and formats (e.g., COBie) were not always available or known to users. As one interviewee indicated: 'For firms without prior experience in BIM it was a time-intensive and expensive task to integrate different software […], and some were unable to provide the required information either due to lack of IT or skills.' Project communications were controlled using an electronic document management (EDM) system. However, interviewees felt the lack of open standards in the BIM platform thwarted EDM benefits: 'The data outputs were platform specific, meeting the needs of only some design consultants. Many subcontractors did mind that we weren't using open standards since their testing couldn't be performed using our model outputs.' Open standards were not always seen as compatible, e.g., one interviewee believed their systems provided the greatest assurances in data quality and efficiency: 'We explored IFCs, and a centralised IFC server. It was thought it would require additional resources beyond the project's scope and experiments [with IFC exchange] were unsuccessful.'

***IT Skills Shortages*:** Many interviewee statements reflect a lack of training and skills, and a lack of experience in the application of BIM, as expressed by one interviewee: 'We have experienced construction professionals who know how to program and schedule a building, and our onsite managers understand the FM issues and building use […] but they can't manipulate a 4D model or lifecycle analysis models because they do not know how to use the software.' This issue combined with the tight build schedule was seen to be prohibitive to IT skills development: 'We saw the benefits of more advanced 4D and 5D modelling but incompatibilities with the skills of the team prevented this.'

4.4 Policy-Based Issues

Three key policy- or procedural-based issues were identified: (1) maturity of BIM standards and frameworks, (2) lack of verification and hand-over procedures, and (3) uncertainty in client-side FM strategy.

***Maturity of BIM Standards and Frameworks*:** Just as there are different levels of maturity in BIM capabilities across the AEC actor network (with many in the supply chain at differing points on the maturity curve), throughout the course of the seven year project, the maturity of BIM standards has rapidly developed and continues to do so. Interviewees noted the parallel development taking place in the drafting of national BIM standards by public organisations and private enterprise. In addition, project participants also noted other initiatives such as the COBie data format (piloted in 2007 and only becoming a standard in 2011 [6]) and benchmarking BIM performance tools, which were largely unknown and untested at the outset of the project in 2005.

***Lack of Verification and Hand-over Procedures*:** A common issue raised was a lack of procedures for verifying the as-built dataset. One interviewee stressed: 'There were no real verification procedures to check what's installed versus the final model." This was seen to be an industry-wide issue, where interviewees believed data verification to be a delicate problem, as it may lead to competencies being questioned. Lack of verification meant FM personnel did not have reassurance on asset data quality. An interview with the building manager highlighted concerns: 'When auditing the model, it initially looked like the data was all there, but when checking through the model it often wasn't the case.' Performance specification for digital information is a central PLM concern but may be overlooked by AEC stakeholders and unlike performance specification of physical assets, its application to digital assets is not well understood [23]. Furthermore, due to the nature of the two-stage contract, a two-part management approach ensued. The architectural organisation led BIM management protocols until construction. However these protocols during construction and in particular hand-over procedures were not fully implemented or defined: 'The project had detailed information protocols for each stage. [...] During design there were modeling specific checklists and standards to ensure each discipline was generating data as agreed. But you could say its significance petered out as we moved closer to project completion.' This breakdown was reflected in the failure to define data verification and hand-over protocols: 'By the end of construction, a 'throw-it-over the wall' attitude seemed to be emerging [...] and was compounded by the FM team not coming online until close to project completion.'

***Uncertainties in Client-Side Lifecycle Management Strategies*:** A key problem highlighted by the FM team was the client/developer's existing FM practices and their centralised approach to FM across the buildings portfolio. Any new FM strategy to be developed to incorporate the BIM model was therefore dependent on other organisational 'decision-making' factors surrounding e.g. current FM systems and methods that underpin the wider building portfolio, and existing service contractors and their own work practices. Further, it was felt that the developer needed a roadmap for a strategic FM solution for future BIM-enabled projects and would require a procedure for managing the early engagement and involvement of FM personnel in project planning. It therefore appeared that there was a lack of client-side procedures to capture digital O&M information to feed forward into future BIM-enabled developments as there was no close-out report documenting lessons learned.

5 Discussion and Conclusion

Given the fact that BIM is an interdependent network of processes, technologies and policies, which constitutes a 'methodology to manage building design and project data in digital format throughout the building's lifecycle' [24], the issues identified in Sect. 4 are linked. Connections between the challenges that lead to partial BIM implementation were mapped as shown in Table 2a, where direct (•) and indirect (○) connections and dependencies were identified.

Table 2. (a) Interdependencies between incomplete BIM implementation issues, and (b) Mapping challenges to full BIM implementation with PLM functions

		Policy-based			Technology-based			Process-based		
		Maturity of BIM standards and frameworks	Lack of verification and hand-over procedures	Uncertainties in client-side lifecycle management strategies	IT skills shortages	Inappropriate technologies and reluctance to use open standards	Unknown as-built data requirements	Timing of information and training at hand-over	Asynchronous nature of FM integration	Entrenched practices and lack of evidence-based studies
Process-based	Entrenched practices/lack of evidence	•	•	○	•	•	•	•	○	
Process-based	Asynchronous nature of FM integration	•	•	•	-	○	•	•		
Process-based	Timing of information and training	•	•	•	○	○	•			
Technology-based	Unknown as-built data requirements	•	○	○	○	○				
Technology-based	Inappropriate/reluctance to use technologies	○	•	○	•					
Technology-based	IT skills shortages	-	○	-						
Policy-based	Uncertainties in client-side lifecycle strategies	○	•							
Policy-based	Lack of verification & hand-over procedures	•								
Policy-based	Maturity of standards and frameworks									

(a)

	Opportunities to address		
Core PLM Functions	Policy-based issues	Technology-based issues	Process-based issues
Definition and management of design and process documents and models	✓	-	✓
Construction and control of bill of materials records	✓	✓	✓
Electronic file repositories	✓	-	✓
Inclusion of document and model metadata	-	✓	✓
Identification of model content for compliance & verification	✓	✓	✓
Change management workflow and approval process	✓	✓	✓
Controlling secured access & data export	✓	-	✓

(b)

The mapping reveals the interfaces that are instantiated by each connection: between individuals, teams and organisations; between required processes, information technologies and protocols; and interfaces between lifecycle stages. The complexity of managing these interfaces is vast, and the need for greater PLM functionality is highlighted. Recent approaches to integrating BIM and PLM functions can only account for some of these interfaces. Although PLM allows one to manage and exploit data whilst at the same time defining the product and processes for data development, applying PLM functions in BIM-enabled AEC projects remains problematic. However the significance of PLM is revealed in Table 2b, which maps the potential for core PLM functions to address the challenges encountered in implementing BIM (tagged as '✓'). Yet, from the case study it is apparent that the complexity and diversity of client requirements, as well as the human interface problems identified, that the transverse utilisation of a BIM-PLM solution across participating organisations would bring new implementation challenges. This is because, whilst most functional requirements of PLM applications are generic, many of the challenges faced by integrators and managers of BIM in the AEC industry arise from the specifics of unique client requirements and collaborating organisations.

This is a single study of a commercial high-rise development that implemented BIM during the relatively early years of its adoption in industry. Whilst many of the challenges identified stem from the specifics of client and organisational contexts, others are rooted in entrenched practices or result from complexity and uncertainty in collaborative project environments. The extent to which findings can be generalised and transferred to other contexts must therefore be clarified by future research.

References

1. Succar, B.: Building information modelling framework: A research and delivery foundation for industry stakeholders. Automation in Construction 18, 357–375 (2009)
2. Eastman, C., Teicholz, P., Sacks, R., Liston, K.: BIM Handbook: A Guide to Building Information Modeling, for Owners, Managers, Designers, Engineers, and Contractors. John Wiley & Sons, Hoboken (2008)
3. Anderson, A., Marsters, A., Sturts Dossick, C., Neff, G.: Construction to Operations Exchange: Challenges of Implementation COBie and BIM in a Large Owner Organization. Construction Research Congress, 15 p. Purdue University, IN (2012)
4. Reefman, R., van Nederveen, S.: A Controlled Integral Product Model (IPM®) in Building and Construction. In: Proceedings of CIB W78-W102 2011: Intl Conf., France (2012)
5. Eastman, C.M.: Building product models: Computer environments supporting design and construction. CRC Press, Boca Raton (1999)
6. East, W.E.: Construction Operation Building Information Exchange. USACE ERDC (2007)
7. Bonandrini, S., Cruz, C., Nicolle, C.: Building lifecycle management. In: Bouras, A., Gurumoorthy, B., Sudarsan, R. (eds.) Proceedings of the International Conference on Product Lifecycle Management, PLM 2005, Lyon, pp. 461–471 (2005)
8. Drogemuller, R., Schevers, H.: Sydney Opera House - FM Exemplar Project: Building Information Modelling for FM at Sydney Opera House (2006)
9. Vanlande, R., Nicolle, C., Cruz, C.: IFC and building lifecycle management. Automation in Construction 18(1), 70–78 (2008)
10. Arayici, Y., Onyenobi, T., Egbu, C.: Building information modelling (BIM) for facilities management (FM): The MediaCity case study approach. International Journal of 3-D Information Modeling (IJ3DIM) 1(1), 55–73 (2012)
11. Ebinger, M., Madritsch, T.: A Classification Framework for Facilities and Real Estate Management: The Built Environment Management Model (BEM2). Facilities 30(5/6), 1 (2012)
12. Shen, W., Hao, Q., Xue, Y.: A loosely coupled system integration approach for decision support in facility management and maintenance. Automation in Construction 25, 41–48 (2012)
13. Kiviniemi, A.: Requirements management interface to building product models (CIFE Technical Report No. 161, PhD thesis), Stanford University, Stanford, CA (2005)
14. Song, Y., Clayton, M.J., Johnson, R.E.: Anticipating reuse: Documenting buildings for operations using web technology. Automation in Construction 11(2), 185–197 (2002)
15. Jordani, D.A.: BIM and FM: The Portal to Lifecycle Facility Management. National Institute of Building Sciences and buildingSMART Alliance, Washington (2010)

16. Whyte, J., Lindkvist, C., Ibrahim, N.H.: From Projects into Operations: Lessons for Data Handover. Uni. of Reading, DIRC. Working Paper (2011), http://www.reading.ac.uk/designinnovation/for-industry/di-for-industry-workingpapers.aspx (accessed February 15, 2013)
17. Xuesong, L., Eybpoosh, M., Akinci, B.: Developing As-built Building Information Model Using Construction Process History Captured by a Laser Scanner and a Camera. Construction Research Congress (2012)
18. American Institute of Architects, Integrated Project Delivery: A Guide. CA Council (2007)
19. Glick, S., Guggemos, A.: IPD and BIM: Benefits and opportunities for regulatory agencies. In: Proc. of 45th Associated Schools of Construction National Conference, Gainesville (2009)
20. Bew, M., Underwood, J.: Delivering BIM to the UK Market. In: Underwood, J., Umit, I. (eds.) Handbook of Research on Building Information Modeling and Construction Informatics: Concepts and Technologies, pp. 30–64. IGI Global (2010)
21. London, K., Singh, V., Taylor, C., Gu, N., Brankovic, L.: Building information modelling project decision support framework. In: Dainty, A. (ed.) Proc. 24th Annual ARCOM Conference, Cardiff, UK, vol. 2, pp. 655–664. Assoc. of Researchers in Const. Mgmt (2008)
22. Yin, R.K.: Case Study Research: Design and Methods, 4th edn. Sage Pub., CA (2009)
23. East, W.E.: Performance Specification for Building Information Exchange. National Institute of Building Sciences and buildingSMART Alliance (2009)
24. Penttilä, H.: Describing the changes in architectural information technology to understand design complexity and free-form architectural expression. ITcon 11 Special Issue: The Effects of CAD on Building Form and Design Quality, 395–408 (2006)

Challenges for Integrated Design and Delivery Teams in AEC

Vishal Singh

Department of Civil and Structural Engineering, Aalto University, Finland
Vishal.Singh@aalto.fi

Abstract. This paper discusses the critical factors for managing teams for integrated design and delivery solutions (IDDS), which aims to involve BIM tools, processes and skills across different stakeholders such as architects, consultants, contractors, and suppliers through the project lifecycle. Since IDDS is a recent development, the associated teamwork factors and challenges in implementation are not currently well understood. This paper reports the findings from a research that investigates this gap and forms the basis for future research directions. The findings reported in this paper are based on focus group interviews with representatives from leading organizations in the Australian and Finnish construction sector. The critical factors for an IDDS team are examined and discussed using the construct of mental models. In particular, this research investigates the critical task, process, context, and competence factors specific to the IDDS teams.

Keywords: BIM, teamwork, mental models, integrated design and delivery solutions.

1 Introduction

The lack of integrated design and delivery across the lifecycle of multi-organizational construction projects and inefficient manpower management through the project lifecycle costs billions of dollars in waste [1]. As a result, there is a greater push for new ways of working that promote collaboration and integration across the project partners through the different phases of the project lifecycle. Accordingly, approaches such as Integrated Design Delivery Solutions (IDDS) and Integrated Project Delivery (IPD) are being developed, with greater emphasis on creating more productive environments through concurrent engineering [2], enabled by information systems, technology mediated practices, and collaborative work environments [3, 4]. This trend is based on the rationale that effective service integration and collaboration can reduce inefficiencies and waste, through reduced duplicity and rework [5, 6].

Nonetheless, full service and process integration is challenging and requires effective change management strategies [7, 8] and people engagement processes [9]. Hence, the change towards integrated design and delivery within the architecture, engineering and construction (AEC) sector is contingent on sound understanding of the teamwork and engagement processes.

A. Bernard, L. Rivest, and D. Dutta (Eds.): PLM 2013, IFIP AICT 409, pp. 641–650, 2013.

In the AEC sector, design integration requires a multiplicity of skills, knowledge and experience. Design practice requires management tools and skills besides the design skills and the domain knowledge. The performance of the collaborative design team not only depends on how the individual members perform the tasks related to their roles but also on how effectively they coordinate their tasks, roles and responsibilities with the other members of the team [2]. For collaborative teams to be efficient, team members need well developed mental models of each other and that of the task, process, context and competence of the team [10-13]. Well-developed mental models of the team members can significantly improve the cost, schedule, and quality measures, especially in complex projects [14], which is often the case with construction projects. Managing integrated construction project teams further increases the complexity as the team is expected to work concurrently across the project lifecycle. However, there is little research and understanding of the teamwork management issues within such teams, especially there is little structured breakdown of issues according to the task, process, context, competence and team factors that constitute the mental models of the members of the multi-organizational construction projects.

This paper reports on the findings from a research study aimed at identifying the critical factors affecting the formation of mental models in multi-organizational construction projects, especially in view of the IDDS objectives. In particular, we investigate the critical task, process, context and competence factors specific to the integrated design and delivery teams.

The reported findings are based on focus group interviews (FGIs) and face-to-face (FFs) interviews with representatives from Australian and Finnish AEC sector on the potential challenges to integrated design delivery practice using a collaboration platform, with Building Information Model (BIM) at the core of data exchange.

2 Background

The construction sector is known to be a slow adopter of management and technical capabilities that other industries such as manufacturing are able to integrate earlier in their practice. Among others, the structural organization of the construction sector, which is markedly different to that of the manufacturing sector, is mooted as an important factor [15]. As a result, integration of key players is considered to be important for project success. As each player pursues its own contractual objectives, it is suspected that a lack of integration and teamwork has resulted in low productivity and low innovation. Such challenges are likely to impede the IDDS initiatives envisioned by the construction industry as the design and delivery practice of the future. One of the biggest challenges for managers and organizations involved in the multi-organizational design and construction projects is to understand, and deal with, a distributed project team with diverse task, process, context, and team member mental models, resulting from the diversity in social, operational and functional backgrounds of the team members at individual as well as organizational level.

Formation of mental models has been studied across diverse domains [10, 16]. It is well established that effective teamwork requires various kinds of competencies that can be discussed in terms of the knowledge, skills and attitudes that are specific or generic to the task, and the team [17-19]. Mental models for the task, process, context, competence and the team members are critical to effective team performance [10-13]. These findings suggest that organizational contingency theories [20] also apply to formation of mental models in teams. That is, the critical parameters associated with the different mental models and their values may be specific to the project, despite generic patterns across an industry. Therefore, specific parameters and their values need to be mapped for each project, Table1.

Table 1. Mental models that team members need to develop

Mental model	Kinds of information that it requires (examples)
Task	What is the task? What comes next?
Process	How to do this?
Context	What to do in this situation?
Competence	Can we do this? Do we have the capability?
Team members	Who knows what?

Understanding the likely effects of pre-developed mental models of team members, based on their prior experience, and the impending project requirements, can improve project decision making. Such approaches have been used to form effective small project teams, where the scale of the project and the personnel data is manageable using a manual process. For example, [21] reports the use of psychometric data to consistently form high performing student design teams. However, in real world construction projects, the complexity, the number of variables, and the amount of data to analyze can be expected to be much higher. This means such approaches towards creating high performance teams cannot be adopted unless decision support systems are developed to record, manage and simulate large data sets.

This research is part of a research initiative that aims to address some of the related issues. The critical factors pertaining to teamwork in IDDS projects identified in this research will contribute towards the development of such a decision support system (DSS). The planned agent-based DSS will build on the prior research on computational modeling of project teams [22, 23].

3 Research Data Collection and Analysis

The findings reported in this paper are based on data from FGIs and FFs conducted with representatives from various stakeholder groups that typically form an IDDS team. Three FGIs were conducted in two major cities in Australia and included architects, engineers, consultants, contractors, facility managers and construction project collaboration platform service providers. Representatives from large contracting firms and government organizations, who often work as clients in construction projects also participated in the workshop. The FGI discussions revolved around the potential challenges to integrated design delivery practice using a collaboration platform, with BIM at the core of data exchange. The FGI participants were encouraged to discuss the challenges to using an integrated information system and Building Information Models for managing the information supply chain across the project lifecycle. The FGI data was complemented by twelve FFs, two in Australia and ten in Finland. The FGIs and FFs were recorded on tape and transcribed for analysis to categorize the discussions across the issues relating to task, process, context, competence and team member mental models.

Verbal protocol analysis technique was used to analyze the Australian data and identify the underlying patterns and trends across the identified themes, i.e., task, process, context, competence and team. Table 2 provides sample segments to exemplify the classification and the coding scheme. "Protocol analysis is a rigorous methodology for eliciting verbal reports of thought sequences as a valid source of data on thinking" [24].

Preliminary analysis of part of the Finnish data has been conducted, and verbal protocol analysis of the Finnish data is yet to be conducted.

Table 2. Sample coding of data to classify factors across different mental models

Segment	Task	Process	Context	Competence	Team
"Consultants and engineers tend to work in isolation..."					1
"Clash detection, ability to check dimensions, approval... all sort of things should come out of the database."		1		1	
"Important to understand what record has to be kept... Can be a photo, snapshot of what is on screen, copy of contract document ...it is not about the model, it is about how you want to maintain that record."	1				
"This is going to change the way we work. At an early stage we need a lot more communication."		1	1		

4 Research Findings

Figure 1 shows the discussion pattern in the FGIs, based on the verbal protocol analysis results. As plotted in Figure1, though the data indicate a fairly uniform distribution of issues and concerns associated with the different mental models, i.e, task, process, context, competence and team members, the apprehensions around processes, including work and business processes is relatively higher.

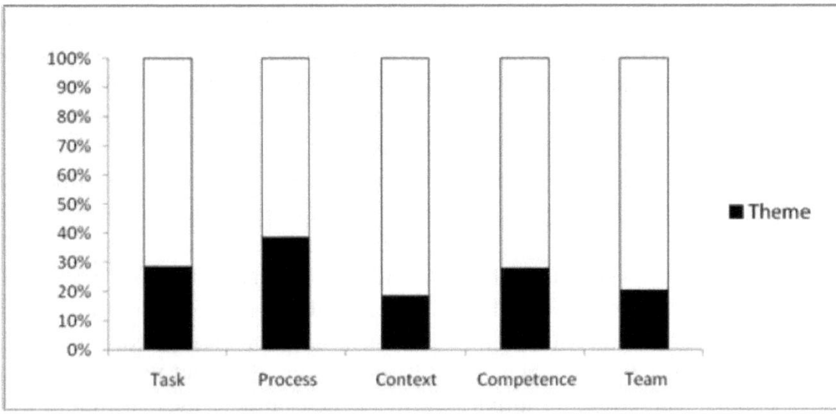

Fig. 1. Discussion pattern in FGIs reflected by % of segments dedicated to each theme (sum is greater than 100% as many issues concerned more than one theme)

The open ended discussions primarily revolved around the challenges in developing and using an integrated Building Information Model in a project, and the issues with managing the information. Discussions indicate that even at the outset of a project the different stakeholders are likely to start with conflicting mental models and apprehensions about each other's beliefs and level of engagement in the project. Following are some of the key factors associated with the task, process, context, and competence and team member mental models:

4.1 Task Mental Model

The integrated project team is expected to collectively work together in providing timely information, feedback and data through a collaborative platform to create a detailed BIM for the project, which many interviewees considered as central to the task definition in an IDDS project. Following are the critical task mental model related factor:

Purpose and Scope of the Model: Team members need a shared understanding of the purpose of BIM in the project. In some projects it might be desirable to create and use a BIM model across the entire project lifecycle while in other cases such models may only be developed for specific purposes such as simulating and planning constructability.

Level of Detail: Team members need some clarity on questions such as: How much detail is needed in the model? Which parts of the model need more details or do all parts of the model need the same level of details? How are the details at different levels of abstraction, and across the different phases of the project, to be linked and managed? Level of detail in the model is contingent on the project requirements and the purpose of the model. Clarity on the level of detail is important to determine work breakdown and planning.

Structure of the Model: The use of BIM and the task typically requires decomposition and integration of the task. That is, model development is a multi-user activity, which means the team members need to coordinate the model development activities. Hence, the team members need to understand the task breakdown structure, and how the task is shared and distributed across the team.

Purpose and the level of the model needs to be clearly stated upfront as part of the contractual agreements. Findings indicate that the different project partners may have different expectations from the purpose as well as the level of detail desired in a BIM model. For example, designers, contractors and facility managers (FM) each view the purpose of the BIM model differently, and to each of these actors, the primary role of BIM is associated with their discipline. As such, each of these models such as the design model, construction model and FM model require different types, and different levels, of details. Therefore, an initial plan is needed on how these different models can be achieved through minimal rework and duplication, and maximum reuse.

Related aspects of task or model development where shared understanding is needed include model types and sub-models, accuracy and completeness, as-built data for facilities management, and documentation and communication tasks.

4.2 Process Mental Model

The Participants identified various aspects of the collaborative process that need discussion and clarity among team members and collaborators for effective management of an integrated BIM project development. This includes agreed protocols and practices for business processes, collaboration and information exchange, and interaction with the model. Mutual agreement and processes are critical for the following:

Business Processes: IDDS and IPD approaches are yet to be embraced in the construction industry and the lack of precedence and familiarity leaves apprehensions about business models and transactions. Among other concerns, FGI participants were unclear about the fee structures in the resulting re-configured work-load distribution and information supply chain; data transfer and ownership; and liabilities and legal implications. Participants also discussed potential role for BIM service providers, model managers, application vendors, cloud computing and software licensing models, highlighting related concerns over lack of experience if any of these are to be involved in an impending construction project.

Design Review and Clash Detection: Participants acknowledged the need for agreed protocols to conduct design review using BIM models and capabilities such as clash detection. Participants reported resistance among some stakeholder groups to change design review norms that still follow traditional methods. Discussions reflect increased confidence in collocated workplaces for multi-disciplinary integration and conflict resolution such as 'Big Room' concepts.

Version Management: Discussions reveal concern towards potential conflicts that may arise from multiple files and versions of the model generated across the team and the design development phases, besides the concerns towards software versions.

Data Organization and Management: Data explosion and information overload emerged as a common concern across many participants. The need for archiving, history traceability, and data security were emphasized. Hence, a shared understanding of data management processes is needed.

4.3 Context Mental Model

Context refers to the team situation and scenarios. The discussions about the context revolved around the team's culture and practices, and what the FGI participants thought determines a team's response to known and known scenarios, including changes in tasks, processes and so on. Following were identified as the critical factors associated with context mental models:

Work Culture and Practice: Adopting IDDS approach will require adopting new work culture and news ways of working, and shifting organizational cultures towards an integrated service system.

Project Phase: Team members need to have clear understanding of their roles, responsibilities and contributions to the integrated BIM model at different phases of the project. This includes clarity on the scope of the model and its usage across the different phases of the project.

Regulations and Standards: Building regulations and standards vary across the different geographical regions, which needs alertness and clarifications, especially when working on projects or teams distributed across geographical boundaries.

Project Requirements: Team members need a shared understanding of the project requirements and the scope and level of integrated design delivery applicable to a given project. Discussions indicate the need for critical assessment of the project requirements at the outset of the project. For example, does the scale of the project justify how the team is organized for integrated design and delivery? How to monitor and measure the progress of the project? How should the team respond to the emergent and unforeseen project requirements, and what does it mean for the IDDS practice?

4.4 Competence Mental Model

Competence refers to the team's capabilities, which is either augmented or constrained by technology, which is once again related to the level of technology integration and technical competence of the team. With respect to BIM based collaboration for IDDS, competence appeared frequently in the discussions, often tied closely with team member mental models, i.e. perception of the competence of the other collaborators.

Competence of Project Partners and Their Tools: Project managers need to map the available resources and capabilities distributed across the people and tools to identify potential clashes and lack of compatibility. For example, the team may have the right tools but they may not have competent or skilled users. Teams may have competent users but they may not have the right tools. Or, teams may have competent users as well as competent tools, but the chosen tools may not necessarily be compatible, reducing the overall competence. At the same time, team members not only need to know about their competencies but they also need to know their limitations, and that of the tools being used. Issues of data format and import/ export capabilities of the software need to considered at the project planning stage itself. FGI participants also raised concerns over the other capabilities of the information systems that include security; bandwidth; server capacity; visualization capabilities; integration capabilities; querying and archiving; usability and interface.

Capabilities to Learn and Train during the Projects: How the team is organized and what knowledge management practices the team adopts, including how they use collaboration platforms and information systems, will determine how much the team members can learn during the project. Efficient teams can build on the opportunity for social learning and team building to increase competence during the project.

4.5 Team Member Mental Model

Team member mental model refers to team members' beliefs about each other, which determines how the team members interact and communicate with each other, and how they collaborate and work as a group. FGI discussions revealed a concern among the participants over the general tendency of functional groups and disciplines to work in isolation. Lack of trust in accuracy and completeness of the information and models created by members of other disciplines was a concern.

Discussions emphasized that **roles and responsibilities** need to be clearly defined, and the implications for the changing roles and responsibilities in the changing work environment needs to be communicated. Participants reported lack of clarity with changing roles and responsibilities across various dimensions such as, does the new role require new skills, or, do the changing roles and responsibilities restructure the actor network and the social ties? The discussions indicated that, in general, the team members seek answers to one common question: what is in there for me, and why should I change? That is, team members consider the effort towards the changing roles and responsibilities as an investment that must be rewarding, and there must be a return on investment. Some of the questions that individuals and firms in multi-organizational collaboration consider as part of their assessment of the return on investment include: Is it worth investing in a new technology unless the returns from the project or the alliance cover it? Is the project valuable enough to invest resources in adopting and learning new ways of working?

The task, process, context, competence and team member mental models are found to be closely interrelated, with the different issues overlapping across different mental models. For example, skills acquisition is not only about the competence but also about what the individuals think of the team, and their roles and responsibilities towards the team. Further research is needed to build on this mapping and develop a framework than can be used for computational application.

5 Conclusion

This research adopts the construct of mental models as the basis for establishing the parameters of team work, especially in context of integrated design and delivery teams in multi-organizational construction projects. Findings from the focus group interviews and face to face interviews with representatives of various stakeholder groups are analysed and categorised into issues related to task, process, context, competence and team member mental models. The empirical data suggests that there are overlaps across the different mental models and the key issues concerning efficient teamwork and project management. Among other issues it is evident that team members have a sense of measuring their investment in the project and the returns on the investment. This investment involves multiple parameters such as time, effort, money, and reputation. Further research is planned to investigate these issues and develop the framework. In particular, the primary question raised for further investigation is: what is the threshold point beyond which the critical factors combine such that investment in BIM technologies, tools, processes and skills is perceived justifiable by the different stakeholders?

References

1. ACIF - Australian Construction Industry Forum. Construction Forecasting (2010), http://www.acif.com.au/construction-forecasting/ (accessed on May 15, 2010)
2. Love, P.E.D., Gunasekaran, A., Li, H.: Concurrent engineering: a strategy for procuring construction projects. International Journal of Project Management 16(6), 375–383 (1998)
3. CIB. CIB White Paper on IDDS "Integrated Design and Delivery Solutions". CIB Publication 328 (2010) ISBN: 978-90-6363-060-7
4. AIA. Integrated Project Delivery: A Guide (2007), http://www.aia.org/contractdocs/AIAS077630 (accessed on May 15, 2010)
5. King, G., Meyer, K.: Service integration and co-ordination: A framework of approaches for the delivery of co-ordinated care to children with disabilities and their families. Child: Care, Health, and Development 32, 477–492 (2005)
6. Moore, D.R., Dainty, A.R.J.: Integrated project teams' performance in managing unexpected change events. Team Performance Management, 212–222 (1999)
7. Orlikowski, W.J., Hofman, J.D.: An Improvisational Model of Change Management: The Case of Groupware Technologies. Sloan Management Review 38(2), 11–21 (1997)
8. Nah, F.F., Lau, J.L., Kuang, J.: Critical factors for successful implementation of enterprise systems. Business Process Management Journal 7(3), 285–296 (2001)
9. Glendinning, C.: Breaking down barriers: Integrating health and care services for older people in England. Health Policy 65, 139–151 (2003)
10. Badke-Schaub, P., Neumann, A., Lauche, K., Mohammed, S.: Mental models in design teams: a valid approach to performance in design collaboration? CoDesign 3, 5–20 (2007)
11. Klimoski, R., Mohammed, S.: Team Mental Model: Construct or Metaphor? Journal of Management 20(2), 403–437 (1994)
12. Langan-Fox, J., Anglim, J., Wilson, J.R.: Mental models, team mental models, and performance: Process, development, and future directions. Human Factors in Ergonomics and Manufacturing 14(4), 331–352 (2004)

13. Lim, B.-C., Klein, K.J.: Team mental models and team performance: A field study of the effects of team mental model similarity and accuracy. Journal of Organizational Behaviour 27, 403–418 (2006)
14. Rouse, W., Cannon-Bowers, J., Salas, E.: The role of mental models in team performance in complex systems. IEEE Transactions on Systems Man and Cybernetics 22, 1296–1308 (1992)
15. Anumba, C.J., Baugh, C., Khalfan, M.M.A.: Organizational structures to support concurrent engineering in construction. Industrial Management and Data Systems 102(5), 260–270 (2002)
16. Mohammed, S., Dumville, B.C.: Team Mental Models in a Team Knowledge Framework: Expanding Theory and Measurement across Disciplinary Boundaries. Journal of Organizational Behavior 22(2), 89–106 (2001)
17. Ancona, D.G., Caldwell, D.: Improving the Performance of New Product Teams. IEEE Engineering Management Review 35(4), 45 (2007)
18. Cannon-Bowers, J.A., Salas, E.: Teamwork competencies, The interaction of team member knowledge skills and attitudes. In: O'Neil, O.F. (ed.) Workforce Readiness, Competencies and Assessment, pp. 151–174. Erlbaum, Hillsdale (1997)
19. Cohen, S.G., Bailey, D.E.: What Makes Teams Work: Group Effectiveness Research from the Shop Floor to the Executive Suite. Journal of Management 23(3), 239–290 (1997)
20. Donaldson, L.: The Contingency Theory of Organizations. Sage Publications, Thousand Oaks (2001)
21. Wilde, D.J.: Teamology: The Construction and Organization of Effective Teams. Springer (2007)
22. Kunz, J.C., Levitt, R.E., Jin, Y.: The Virtual Design Team: A Computational Simulation Model of Project Organizations. Communications of the Association for Computing Machinery 41, 84–92 (1998)
23. Singh, V.: Computational Exploration of Modes of Social Learning and Team Mental Models. PhD Thesis: Faculty of Architecture, Design and Planning, The University of Sydney, Australia (2010)
24. Ericsson, K.A.: Protocol analysis in psychology. In: Smelser, N., Baltes, P. (eds.) International Encyclopedia of the Social and Behavioral Sciences, pp. 12256–12262. Elsevier, Oxford (2001)

Systems Engineering as a First Step to Effective Use of BIM

Henk Jan Pels, Jeroen van Beek, and Ad den Otter

Eindhoven University of Technology (TU/e),
Faculty of the Built Environment,
Architectural Design Management Systems
{h.j.pels,j.p.a.v.Beek,a.f.h.j.d.otter}@tue.nl

Abstract. A Dutch AEC consulting company envisions Systems Engineering (SE) as an effective means to reduce risk in integrated AEC projects. However most of their experts doubt about the practical effectiveness. ADMS is invited to conduct a research project in order to investigate how to introduce SE in a suitable way in their practices. A research method is defined on how to assess the suitability of SE and how to enable the organization to apply it in different projects. The research shows that SE can be an effective method to reduce risk in integrated projects and helps to improves their services in this field. An instrument is developed to enable the company's consultants to apply SE effectively in Design & Build and Design, Build and Maintain-projects.

Keywords: Systems Engineering, knowledge valorization, BIM.

1 Introduction

A Dutch AEC management and consultancy office, let us call it AMCO, wants to implement Systems Engineering (SE) in their processes and asks the Architectural Design Management Systems (ADMS) professional doctorate program of TU/e to help them. ADMS is a two year postgraduate technological designers program. AMCO is active in the Dutch market for utility buildings and offers it's services in all phases from initiation to demolition. Their unique selling point is Integral Project Management (IPM).With IPM, AMCO provides the customer with an (integral) housing solution, while taking over all project risks from the customer. Currently the Dutch market moves from the conventional form, where a, where a contractor is contracted after the design is finished by the architect to Design&Build (D&B) and Design-Build-Maintain (DBM) contract forms. In such integrated contract forms, traditional project management approaches fail to manage all risks and responsibilities related to this type of projects. Especially professional public clients tend to require SE as a method to be applied in their projects. AMCO expects SE to be a method to reduce risks in such projects and thus to be able to provide better service to their customers, to increase their margins and to maintain their competitive advantage.

For ADMS, the assignment fits in their interest in implementing Building Information Modeling (BIM). BIM can be defined as "the process of creating and

A. Bernard, L. Rivest, and D. Dutta (Eds.): PLM 2013, IFIP AICT 409, pp. 651–662, 2013.

using digital models for design, construction and/or operation of projects" [Succar, 2009]. Practice shows that implementing BIM in Dutch building industry moves forward very slowly [Iliescu, 2010]. One of the reasons is that to realise the promised benefits, BIM should be embedded in adapted processes. Implementing SE tends to help resulting in the required adaptions, so implementing SE in a AEC project is a strong step towards effective use of BIM.

2 Research Approach

2.1 Research Question

For AMCO the motive for the research was to get understanding in how SE can improve their services in integrated construction projects. In this context the research goal was to develop a project independent instrument which helps to implement SE in AMCO's services in the field of D&B and DBM projects This resulted in the research question:

How can SE improve the services provided by AMCO in D&B and DBM projects in utility construction?

2.2 Method

The research is primarily focused on knowledge valorization rather than knowledge development. A large body of knowledge on SE exists and software tools to support the SE-processes are available on the market. Especially smaller AEC companies are uncertain about how to apply SE and whether implementation will be beneficial at all. The SE methodology has been extensively elaborated for complex high tech projects in e.g. aerospace and defense applications, but similar implementation of the full method in less complex projects seems a overkill to most of the experts in the AMCO organization. What they need is a clear view of the key elements of SE and a tool to guide them in the selection of what elements could be applied in what type of project. For the design of this tool a research approach in four steps was choosen, based on [Verschuren and Doorewaard, 2007]:

1. a) quick scan to establish current practices in AMCO,
   b) determine responsibilities and commitments in D&B / DBM projects.
2. a) acquire SE theoretical knowledge,
   b) analyze differences between traditional and D&B/DBM projects,
   c) analyze practical experiences,
3. diagnose possible improvements for AMCO's services in D&B/DBM projects,
4. design of a project supporting instrument.

From step 1 it appeared that the current practice in AMCO is to develop innovation as much as possible 'on the job', in order to remain focused on practice and to save costs. To make the tool acceptable in the organization a similar approach should be applied in the design. Therefore a combination of a 'science based' ([Dunbar, Romme en Starbuck, 2007]. [Romme en Endenburg, 2006], Van Aken, 2004]) and 'human centered' ([Bate and Robert, 2007], [Hatchuel, LeMasson en Weil, 2006], [Plesk, Bibby en Whitby, 2007]) approach was chosen as proposed by Pascal, Thomas and Romme, 2012. Both methods are based on the formulation of 'design principles'. Sound design is achieved by founding the design principles on organizational sciences. Practical relevance is achieved by implementing the design principles in practice according to the following steps:

- Create problem awareness,
- Develop design principles,
- Create application scenarios,
- Design and develop tangible products,
- Experiment with prototypes,
- Transformation of organization.

Data for the research was collected from literature and from several cases.

Table 1. Responsibilities and obligations according to the UAV-GC 2005 standard

client	Contractor
Obliged to timely making available of information, building area and material	Obliged to realise the work according to requirements stated in the contract, within time and budget and with good quality
Responsible for specifying a representative, consistent and unambiguous set of requirements	Obliged to Warn when inconsistencies of missing requirements are detected
Responsible for specific predescribed design or product solutions	

3 Systems Engineering and D&B/DBM projects

3.1 Responsibilities and Commitments

In Dutch AEC tradition it is common to apply certain standard conditions on project specific contracts [CROW, 2005b] in order to set rights and commitments unambiguously. The UAV-GC 2005 has been developed as a standard escecially for integrated projects [CROW, 2005a] en [CROW, 2005b]. This standard has been taken as reference in step 1b. The standard assumes only two parties in the contract: the client and the contractor. The essence of responsibilities and obligations of both parties is displayed in table 1.

3.2 Systems Engineering Backgrounds

The term Systems Engineering leaves room for different interpretations. According to the International Counsel on Systems Engineering (INCOSE) it is a term that can refer to as well a perspective, a process as a profession [INCOSE 2011]. Also the interpretation of SE can differ strongly between industry branches [Dean, Bahill en Bentz, 1997]. The USA DoD distinguishes the SE knowledge domain from SE-management. This indicates that the term SE has both a theoretical connotation as body of knowledge, and a practical connotation as management process. In this research we are primarily interested in the practical connotation. Based on the definitions of DoD and INCOSE we derived the following working definition as a practical starting point for the AEC industry sector:

> *'Systems Engineering is an interdisciplinary way of working that has been developed to design, realize and maintain, , successful housing solutions in an integral manner that probably comply to the complete set of analyzed and documented customer and user requirements.'*

SE uses a specific set of instruments and processes ([DoD, 2001], [Dean, Bahill and Bentz, 1997], [Kasser, Hitchins ad Huynh, 2009], [INCOSE 2011]). Goals, deliverables and processes are also specified as an international ISO/IEC standard [ISO/IEC, 2008]. SE has extensively been applied in aerospace, defense and telecom industry.

3.3 SE Main Characteristics

SE has extensively been applied in aerospace, defense and telecom industry. Recently also applications in road and water construction projects have been reported [Prorail and Rijkswaterstaat, 2009]. Their experience seem to be generalizable to the utility construction area. As the name does expect, systems theory is the basis of SE [Incose, 2011]. A system can be decomposed into subsystems, that may be subsystems themselves. The other way around, a system is part of a bigger system, e.g. its environment. In this environment the system performs certain functions in order to achieve specific goals and to comply with specific requirements.

SE has three essential characteristics:

1. **Requirements:** the client who commissions the system specifies goals and requirements for the system,
2. **Lifecycle approach:** the SE processes cover the complete system lifecycle including development, operation, maintenance, refurbishment and disposal. The systems design should take the requirements of all stakeholders in all phases of the lifecycle into account. Also the relationships with supporting systems and infrastructures must be considered,
3. **Verification:** in each phase of its lifecycle the system should comply to all requirements and every element of the system should refer to a requirement. This consistency should be checked and approved before the start of each following lifecycle phase.

Different sources [Dean, Bahill en Bentz, 1997; Department of Defense, 2001 and INCOSE 2011] specify their own lifecycle phasings. For the purpose of this research the following phasing was chosen, mainly based on [INCOSE, 2011]:

1. **Initiating:** identify stakeholders needs and requirements, explore ideas and technologies,
2. **Concept:** refine stakeholders needs and requirements, explore feasible concepts, propose viable solutions,
3. **Development:** refine system requirements, create solution descriptions, design the system, verify and validate the system,
4. **Production:** realise the system, inspect and verify,
5. **Utilization**, verify that it meets user requirements,
6. **Support**: keep the system operational,
7. **Retirement:** archive or demolish the system.

Each phase ends by passing a milestone, after verifying consistency of all deliverables. It is important to make a distinction between phases and activities/processes. Although activities like requirements analysis, design and construction are typical for certain phases, they may start before and continue after that phase: requirements may be changed during the development phase, certain construction activities may start already in the development phase, design activities may take place during support, when changes on the system are required.

The goal of the SE process is to transform the problems/needs of the client into a successful solution. This transformation process can be viewed from two different perspectives:

1. **Top down decomposition** from high level (system) to detailed (subsystem, component) specifications. This top down design process is mirrored in a bottom up production process. At each level of decomposition the produced/purchased component/subsystem must be verified and tested against the design specifications. This process is also known as the V-model. In building projects the realization process seems more from lowest to highest floor, but also here there are components and subsystems delivered or assembled at the construction site, that should be verified against the design.
2. **Successive transformation processes** that turn the problem into a solution. The ISO/IEC 15288:2008 standard presents an overview of these processes.

A well-considered decomposition [Dean, Bahill en Bentz, 1997] brings a number of benefits. In the first place it helps to link requirements and functions to components. Thus it can be checked whether all requirements are met and all functions and components are really required. Also it supports the specification of derived requirements and functions and to keep track of their origin. Finally the decomposition is the basis for the work breakdown structure.

SE makes a distinction between technical and management processes, that support the technical processes with planning , organization and coordination [Dean, Bahill en Bentz, 1997]. The technical processes, that are specific and characteristic for SE [INCOSE, 2011] are classified in the following types:

1. **Stakeholders requirements definition process**: transform initial needs into a complete set of requirements for all stakeholders,
2. **Requirements analysis process**: transform requirements into a technical, implementation independent view of a product that could deliver the required services,

3. **Architecture design process**: break down the system into subsystems and components, sufficiently detailed to verify the realized system,
4. **Implementation process**: realize the system components,
5. **Integration process**: asemble the components according to the architecture design
6. **Verification process**: confirm that the system is consistent with the specified design
7. **Transition process**: install the verified system together with relevant enabling system in the operational environment,
8. **Validation process**: provide objective evidence that the services provided by the system comply with the stakeholders' requirements, achieving its intended use in its intended environment,
9. **Operation process**: use the system in order to deliver its services,
10. **Maintenance process**: sustain the capability of the system to provide its services,
11. **Disposal process**: end the existence of the system.

The distinction between processes and lifecycle phases is important to enable proper control of concurrent engineering. In the traditional approach the naming of process types is often the same as the naming of lifecycle or project planning phases. This makes it impossible for planners or process designer to even think of planning activities of different phases concurrently. When designing new processes, like in this research for introducing SE, it is important to implement this distinction between process and phase –from the beginning- in the process design. Even when in the first implementation concurrent engineering is not applied, the distinction is needed to be able to implement it in later phases. Such implementation would be much more complex if the terminology of the process structure has to be changed again.

3.4 Characteristics of Consultancy Services

AMCO wants to implement SE in order to improve their services. However, their experts will only adopt SE practices if it is clear to them how SE contributes to the value of their services. AMCO provides two types of services: one is toward parties who are responsible for a housing problem, while creating housing solutions is not their core competence; the other is towards project organizations who act as contracting partner in a housing project and have no specific competence in integrated contract forms. In the first type the service is to support the client in defining their problem and taking over several risks connected to such a task. In the second type different parties have to join in one single contract in order to produce an integral answer to the contract. This requires however effective and efficient collaboration, sophisticated organization and control [Groote et al, 2001], as well as strong management of information exchange between parties [Otter and Prins, 2002]. The contracting parties are confronted with the question whether all activities needed to respond to the contract are supported by their core competences. AMCO can support them in managing the inherent risks.

Subcontracting activities brings risk, so trust is an important condition [Quinn and Hilmer, 1994]. Especially clients that do not have the technical competences to evaluate the quality of the delivered services, have a large need for insight in the process of the delivered service. Therefore strong communication, formal as well as informal [Otter and Prins, 2002], between contracting parties and the client is essential [Hatfield, 1993], especially when the contract stretches over several lifecycle phases and a large number of years. This communication can easily be disrupted by mechanisms like: selective perception, information overload, emotion and language differences [Robbing, Judge and Campbell, 2010].

3.5 SE Contribution

SE brings a uniform process structure with a strong emphasis on completeness and traceability of requirements. For the client this provides a transparent process, in which technical issues that are outside his competence, can always be traced back to requirements expressed in his own language. For the contracting parties the uniform process enables a clear and transparent assignment of responsibilities and accountabilities. The principle that released deliverables should always be proven consistent with their input requirements, enables to establish unambiguously whether the error is in the requirements or in the solution and who should have detected the inconsistency during the verification process. Thus applying SE brings extreme transparency for each party, showing his responsibilities in each specific activity and the liabilities he faces in case of errors.

4 Diagnosis of Possible Improvements

4.1 Service Toward Clients in DB/DBM Projects

Two projects have been analyzed, in order to find bottlenecks and the differences between 'traditional' (design-contract-build) projects and DB/DBM projects. For one running project participative observation techniques were applied.

The main differences detected are shown in table 2.

Table 2. Main differences for client between traditional and DB/DBM projects

aspect	traditional	DB/DBM
Requirements (1)	The whole set of requirements evolve during the whole project because of progressive insight; changed requirements are implemented directly in the current activity	Explicit release of complete requirement early in process; changes are implemented in requirements document and propagated to current input of current activity, according to strict change management
Requirements (2)	Requirements are mainly solution/technology oriented	Requirements can also be functional?/performance oriented
Influence on design	The client can proactively influence the design	Only reactive influence of the client through the processes of verification and acceptance
Communication	Intensive but ill structured communication with contracting parties	Well-structured communication process.

Observation of these differences led to the following design principle in line with the chosen design method:

- Context: housing consultants who need to make requirements specification their core competence.
- Intervention: implementing an project approach based on a Systems Engineering stakeholders requirements definition process.
- Mechanism: a systems oriented project approach that helps the customer to conceptualize and define his needs.
- Output: a representative requirements specification that maximizes the chance for a successful project result.

Following this design principle an instrument was designed that can support AMCO in its aim to provide better services. The essence of this service is securing the expectations of the client in a message that is communicable to the contracting parties. In this way the chance that the client is provided with a successful solution can be increased.

4.2 Service Toward Contracting Parties in DB/DBM Projects

In the DB/DBM situation contracters are legaly bound to the formal requirements. In the period before this research AMCO was already involved in providing services to contracting parties in DB/DBM projects. Risks and bottlenecks in these projects were analyzed and lead to an overview of main differences between 'traditional' and DB/DBM projects as displayed in table 3.

Table 3. Main difference for contracting parties between traditional and DB/DBM projects

aspect	traditional	DB/DBM
Requirements specification status	The requirements co-evolve on basis of results of the design phases.	Results of design are legally bound to the requirement specification document. Each contracting party must deploy is task strictly within the boundaries of the requirements document.
Requirements (2)	Building contractor is able to base his price offer upon a detailed design.	Price offer is based on requirements specifications?.
Test responsibility	The client is responsible for checking the quality of the project result and to organize acceptance activities.	Contractors are responsible for project result and should proactively demonstrate that the result is consistent with the client's requirements.

The observations above led to three more design principles, as shown in table 4.

Table 4. Design principles for tool for contracting parties in DB/DBM projects

aspect	Design principle 2	Design principle 3	Design principle 4
Context	consultancy for contracting parties	consultancy for contracting parties	consultancy for contracting parties
Intervention	Implement a SE based requirements ananlysis process	Implement SE based (architectural) design process	Implement a SE based verfication process
Mechanism	Prevent noise in communication process between what the client wants and how the contractor interprets this.	Explicit appoint and manage interfaces within the design process of the project	Proactive testing of partial solutions towards the client's set of requirements
Output	translation of customer need into proper bid	Optimal integration of partial solutions	Successful tranformation of the client 's needs into a satisfying solution can be secured

Using an instrument designed according to the principles in table 4, AMCO should be able to offer services that take away risk form the contracting parties by organizing and controlling a process in which the partners can concentrate primarily on contributing their core competences while the quality of the integral result is secured according to the contractual agreement.

5 Development of the Instrument

The design principles as based on theory and practice show that implementing the main SE processes, can help AMCO to improve their services. Based on the practical experiences observed in various cases during the analysis, some additional design criteria have been formulated. One of these is the observation that certain software tools are useful to support the processes. The use of a web-based Requirement Specification tool stimulates a more conscious and critical formulation of requirements'. However implementation of such a tool still raises too many questions to unconditionally stimulate broad deployment. Also the large number of relationships between system elements makes the use of a software tool beneficial, to record, manage, cluster and navigate those relationships, in order to prevent overload of information. Excel spreadsheets appear not to be the best solution for this purpose. Further a software tool can stimulate to keep the project file up-to-date. Errors in the project file may have expensive consequences in the project results. Finally better structuring and visualization of basic SE processes is important to support project managers in preparing projects since simple on-the-job introduction may cause too late implementation of verification processes.

The SE instrument, shaped as a written manual, has been developed and tested within AMCO by presenting it to five employees with experience in DB/DBM projects. They judged the instrument as complete and basically good, but still in need of more practice based examples. The content was felt to be still to theoretic. Also some improvements in readability were proposed.

6 SE and BIM

BIM is a method, based on a software tool, to organize the ACE process in a more effective and efficient way. Like SE, BIM is life cycle oriented. The BIM software enables to share an evolving 3D model between al project participants. This eliminates the overload of distributing paper copies as well as the need to mentally translate 2D drawings into 3D shapes, and thus should improve coordination between parties. Problem is that traditional distribution of tasks and responsibilities is based on the characteristics of paper communication, resulting in strong separation between partners and processes. The switch towards a shared design database implies the elimination of these separations and therefore causes uncertainty about roles, liabilities and distribution of costs and benefits. At the same time designers and managers have difficulty in understanding how using a BIM system will benefit them personally. Actually they believe that communicating immature information may cause expensive problems. Therefore they have the practice to delay finishing their design until their input has become stable and to publish their design not before they are sure it is complete and finished. Then they don't see the advantage of transforming this design into a part of the 3D digital model, over publishing it in 2D pdf format. That user requirements are strongly outdated before the design is completed, is not seen as a problem, but as a fact of life

The strong point of SE is that it shows that requirements can and must be maintained during the project and that this requires open communication between parties, especially in verification processes. When SE has been accepted in a ACE organization, then it is much easier to explain that a BIM system is much better equipped to link requirements to design choices and building components and to support verification tasks than a set of spread sheets.

Introducing SE has a much lower threshold than introducing BIM and therefore is a good first step towards BIM.

7 Conclusion

The main conclusion from this study is that SE is perceived by AEC management consultants as valuable for reducing risk in construction projects, especially in the case on integrated contracts with longer lifecycle scope. This is an important result, because, although SE is a quite well accepted as proven method in aerospace and high tech industry, in AEC it is still considered as a very novel approach.

The outcomes show that, although SE methodology has a mature body of knowledge, it still requires research to valorize this knowledge in a specific environment like AEC. The method of design principles has been proven to be very valuable in fitting new knowledge into an existing organization. In other words, it has been shown that knowing how to valorize knowledge, is a relevant piece of knowledge itself.

As a final remark it can be noted that the introduction of SE in an AEC process can be a valuable first step on the way to effective use of BIM. SE requires software support to manage the process of requirements specification, in order to keep the increasing number of requirements conceivable for the customer as well as for the contractors. Further software support is needed to manage the complexity of relationships between requirements, functions and components, in order to keep requirements traceable. In this research project it was demonstrated that good management of communication is needed. A Building Information Model is supposed to be the ultimate means of communication in a AEC project. This means that after SE has been accepted as a standard practice in daily work, it is much easier to explain the value of BIM.

References

[Aken, van, 2004] Van Aken, J.E.: Management research on the basis of the design paradigm: the quest for field-tested and grounded technological rules. Journal of Management Studies, 219–246 (2004)

[Bate and Robert, 2007] Bate, P., Robert, G.: Toward more user-centric OD: lessons from the field of experience-based design and a case study. Journal of Applied Behavioral Science, 41–66 (2007)

[CROW, 2005a] CROW, UAV-GC 2005. Model Basisovereenkomst en toelichting. Ede, CROW (2005a)

[CROW, 2005b] CROW, Toelichting bij Model Basisovereenkomst en UAV-GC 2005. Ede, CROW (2005b)

[Dean, Bahill en Bentz, 1997] Dean, F.F., Bahill, A.T., Bentz, B.: A Road Map for Implementing Systems Engineering. Albuquerque, Sandia National Laboratories (1997)

[Dunbar, Romme en Starbuck, 2007] Dunbar, R., Romme, A., Starbuck, W.: Creating better understandings of organizations while building better organizations. In: Handbook of New Approaches to Organization Studies, pp. 554–571. Sage, Los Angeles (2007)

[Hatchuel, Lemansson en Weil, 2006] Hatchuel, A., Lemasson, P., Weil, B.: Building innovation capabilities: the development of desing-oriented organizations. In: Innovation Science and Institutional Change: A Research Handbook, pp. 294–312. Oxford University Press, Oxford (2006)

[Iliescu, 2010] Iliescu, I.A.: Let's BIM, Final ICA report, Eindhoven University of Technology, Advanced Design Management System (2010)

[INCOSE 2011] INCOSE, Systems Engineering Handbook. A guide for system life cycle processes and activities. International Counsel on Systems Engineering, San Diego (2011)

[ISO/IEC, 2008] ISO/IEC, ISO/IEC 15288:2008(E). Systems and software engineering – System life cycle processes. Geneva, ISO (2008)

[Kasser, Hitchins en Huynh,2009] Kasser, J., Hitchins, D., Huynh, T.V.: Reengineering Systems Engineering. In: Proceedings of the 3rd Asia-Pacific Conference on Systems Engineering (APCOSE), Singapore (2009)

[Mintzberg, 1983] Mintzberg, H.: Structures in fives: designing effective organizations. Prentice-Hall, New Jersey (1983)

[Otter and Prins, 2002] den Otter, A.F., Prins, M.: Architectuaral design management within the digital design team. Engineering, Construction and Architectural Management (ECAM) Article, 162–173 (2002)

[Plesk, Bibby en Whitby, 2007] Plesk, P., Bibby, J., Whitby, E.: Practiacal methods for extracting explicit design rules grounded in the experience of organizational managers. Journal of Applied Behavioural Science, 153–170 (2007)

[Prorail en Rijkswaterstaat, 2009] Prorail en Rijkswaterstaat, Leidraad voor Systems Engineering binnen de GWWSector. Prorail en Rijkswaterstaat (2009)

Romme, A.G.L.: Making a difference: organization as design. Organization Science, 558–573 (2003)

Romme, A.G.L., Endenburg, G.: Construction Principles and Design Rules in the Case of Circular Design. Organization Science 17(2), 287–297 (2006)

[Succar, 2009] Succar, B.: Building Information Modelling Maturity Matrix. In: Underwood, J., Isikdag, U. (eds.) Handbook of Research on Building Information Modeling and Construction Informatics: Concept and Technologies, pp. 65–103. Information Science Publishing (2009)

[Verschuren and Doorewaard, 2007] Verschuren, P.J.M., Doorewaard, J.A.C.M.: Het ontwerpen van een onderzoek. Den Haag, Boom Lemma Uitgevers (2007)

Multidisciplinary AEC Education Utilising BIM / PLIM Tools and Processes

Jennifer A. Macdonald[1] and Marko Granroth[2]

[1] University of Technology, Sydney, Australia
[2] KTH, Stockholm, Sweden
jennifer.macdonald@uts.edu.au

Abstract. The construction industry worldwide is moving towards more collaborative working practices, aided by building information modelling (BIM) tools and processes. BIM could be more accurately described as Project Lifecycle Information Management (PLIM). Many firms are claiming to be 'doing BIM', but are just scraping the surface in terms of the benefits that can be leveraged from true integrated, collaborative design and construction. New graduates, trained in collaboration and PLIM techniques will be the best people to drive positive change, but current educational models do not tend to provide these skills. This paper describes current worldwide educational trends in collaborative multidisciplinary education, and a proposed framework to assist academics in implementing changes to AEC curricula.

Keywords: Building Information Modelling; BIM; PLIM; construction education; collaborative working; BIM education and training; Framework.

1 Introduction

Faculties of the Built Environment (including architecture, engineering and construction management) are currently facing enormous changes due to disruptive technologies and processes emerging in both the higher education sector and the wider construction industry. Governments are demanding that Universities prove their worth as education providers and research generators in order to secure further public funding. At the same time, Universities in general are also facing pressure from the "Google Generation": the rise of Massive Open Online Courses (MOOCs) and other free or low-cost courses provided over the internet means that students have more choice in their courses and may be less willing to pay high fees for traditional chalk-and-talk transmission-style classes in Universities.

Faculties are also under pressure from a construction industry that is facing disruptive changes itself, due to the ongoing global financial crisis and the introduction of new technologies and processes heralded by the "BIM revolution." The current shortage of building design professionals trained in BIM remains a barrier to universal adoption of collaborative working practices in the industry. Just as industry must undergo a paradigm shift from its old combative culture to one of integration and information sharing, so must academia. The need for a framework to

A. Bernard, L. Rivest, and D. Dutta (Eds.): PLM 2013, IFIP AICT 409, pp. 663–674, 2013.

support adoption of collaborative design and BIM education by Architecture, Engineering and Construction (AEC) schools has been stated previously [1]. A framework (called the "IMAC Framework"), to support academics in adapting their curricula to include collaborative learning and working techniques, has been developed with the aid of an OLT (Australian Office of Learning and Teaching) grant. This paper discusses current trends in multidisciplinary AEC education and the progress of the IMAC trial in three Australian partner institutions.

2 Innovation is Necessary for Survival in Industry *and* Education

The global financial crisis has driven many businesses to the wall and many of the survivors have realised they need to innovate to win further work, and to be more efficient in the way they work in order to survive. Interestingly, this trend seems most apparent in countries whose economies, and construction industries, have been hardest hit (in the US and UK in particular) and less so in better-off economies such as Australia's [2]. This effect is illustrated by Teicholz' graph [3] (Fig. 1), which shows a moderate increase in real value added per US construction employee in the years after the 2007 downturn. However, the graph also illustrates the poor performance of construction compared to the manufacturing industry over the same period (the upper line indicates manufacturing). Even without factoring in the effects of the downturn, construction productivity has declined over the past 30 years [4].

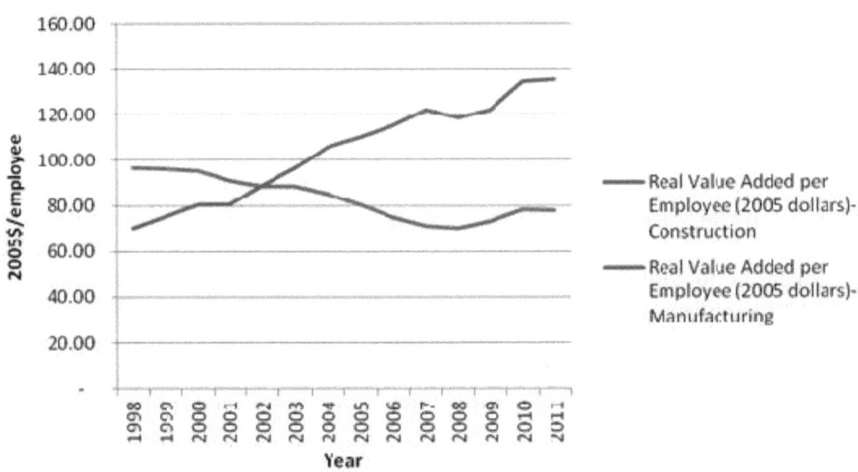

Fig. 1. Value Added per US Employee in 2005 dollars. Source: Teicholz [3]

The construction industry is extremely fragmented and lacking integration [5], [6]. Additionally, reports show that the quality of project documentation has declined over the past 20 years and that poor documentation is contributing an additional 10 to 15% to project costs. 60-90% of all variations are due to poor design and documentation

[7]. It is worth noting, here, that the introduction of computer aided drafting (CAD) tools, far from improving the quality of documentation, has actually coincided with its decline.

In an attempt to achieve greater efficiencies, and echoing earlier changes adopted by the car and manufacturing industries, the construction industry worldwide is moving towards more collaborative working practices, aided by building information modelling (BIM) tools and processes. Collaboration between multidisciplinary, trans-global AEC teams is becoming commonplace [8]. Globalisation means that consultants can work from almost anywhere in the world and building elements can be prefabricated offshore and simply assembled on site. In the future, construction workers are likely to become assembly workers as prefabrication takes over. The increasing complexity of our buildings also means that our construction professionals must collaborate at earlier stages on jobs to produce the best result for clients. However, for the industry to move wholesale into integrated, collaborative practices, a seismic change is required in its culture. The culture of the construction industry has traditionally been very pugilistic, with minimal trust between parties on projects, aided by an atmosphere of litigation and punitive contracts. This lack of trust does not encourage information sharing and collaboration. Industry needs to move from the current culture of fragmentation, litigation, mistrust and withholding of information to one of open-ness, collaboration, teamwork and trust if it really wants to maximise the potential of BIM and improve overall productivity.

The current models for teaching students of the AEC disciplines do not support the new demands from both academia and industry. However, there is also a great opportunity to rethink the way AEC courses are developed and to become more efficient in delivering them. Holland [9] describes the need for “T-shaped people” in the construction teams of the future; that is to say people who have deep knowledge of their own professional discipline, but who also have broad knowledge of the other disciplines in the team.

3 Defining BIM and PLIM

The uptake of BIM has snowballed in recent years but at the same time "BIM" has become a fashionable marketing term, promoted by software vendors. Unfortunately, these vendors have led some professionals to think that to “do BIM” they simply have to purchase a 3D-rendering software package. Some industry figures have coined the term “BIMwash” to describe the phenomenon whereby many firms are claiming to be “doing BIM” but very few are using it to its full potential and integrating with all the other construction disciplines [10].

Despite the glossy marketing materials produced by various software manufacturers, there is still no universally accepted definition for BIM. BIM is not a software product, but an approach to creating and managing information about projects. Various sources suggest that the acronym originated in the US around 2002 [11], though, as stated previously, the tools and processes and ideas have been evolving since at least the 1970s and many of the processes mimic those adopted by the car industry decades ago, such as just-in-time manufacturing (JIT). . BIM can be a noun (the building information *model*) or a verb (the modelling *process*). Additionally, the individual words making up the acronym can mean different things to different professionals:

(B) **Building** can apply to a single building envelope or the wider built environment;
(I) **Information** is really the most important part of the acronym, as the concept is all about creating and sharing quality information about a project and not losing or recreating information when moving between phases;
(M) **M** originally stood for **Modelling** or **Model** but current literature tends towards the more appropriate definition of **Management** (e.g. Race, [12]).

The major problem with the term "building information modelling" is that it is inadequate for describing the complexity involved in creating and managing information over the lifecycle of construction projects, whatever their scale. Race [12] proposes borrowing from the acronym PLM (product lifecycle management) and replacing BIM with **PLIM** (Project Lifecycle Information Management), as this is a more accurate indication of the intent to create a comprehensive package of information representing the life of a facility.

4 Overcoming the Status Quo

> *"Many academic programs still produce students who expect they will spend their careers working as heroic, solitary designers. But integrated practice is sure to stimulate a rethinking of that notion. Pedagogy must focus on teaching not only how to design and detail, but also how to engage with and lead others, and how to collaborate with the professionals they are likely to work with later."*
> Pressman [13], (p3)

Since engineering and architecture emerged as separate professional disciplines, AEC students have been educated in isolation from each other. Starzyk and McDonald [14] note that the focus of architectural education in the past was on developing individual skills such as being able to draw. Now, they state, "the importance of personal skill is yielding to the primacy of collective knowledge".

The complexity of modern building projects and technologies means that nobody can be a master of all anymore. Often the professions do not have a deep understanding of the information that each requires at different stages of a project. Time is thus wasted stripping out and even rebuilding models, when the models could have been set up more efficiently from the start of the process and unnecessary detail excluded prior to model exchange. If students are educated to work collaboratively and to learn the requirements of the other disciplines before they graduate, this level of misunderstanding is likely to be removed in future and trust improved. However, In order to bridge the disciplinary silos in industry, we need to start by breaking down the silos that exist in academia.

5 The Education vs. Training Debate

The concept of creating job-ready graduates brings to the fore the "training vs. educating" debate. Traditionally, Universities have focused on teaching theory, with many faculty members believing that it is industry's role to train incoming graduates in job-related skills. The authors have frequently heard the refrain "we're not teaching students to press buttons" being used among educators who believe that BIM is just another CAD tool. However, the uptake of BIM is facilitating process, technological, and cultural changes, and its benefits extend far beyond mere visualization: students cannot be expected to "teach themselves BIM" any more than they could be expected to "teach themselves structural engineering". BIM actually provides a great opportunity to engage students more effectively and to aid understanding of how buildings are constructed. Hardy, quoted in Deutsch [15], (p202) states:

> *"When I look at the logic of construction means and methods that BIM inherently teaches, I see the potential to educate..."*

Any major change process is likely to encounter resistance. Some of the difficulties for academia in introducing BIM may include:

1. Questions about how to fit new topics into a crowded curriculum.
2. Reluctance to change teaching habits established over many years.
3. For those who may have developed their own niche or expertise, there may be resistance to take on a new subject, about which they are not an expert, or to retrain in an area they are not familiar with.
4. As the technologies supporting BIM evolve at a rapid pace, academics who have been out of industry for some time may feel overwhelmed trying to keep abreast of them.
5. The traditional silos of architecture, engineering and construction schools can be difficult to bridge. As in industry, mistrust of the other professions also exists in academia, and questions can arise as to who is responsible for (and who will pay for) cross-disciplinary courses. *"The biggest hurdle is with true interdisciplinary efforts due to conflicting student/faculty schedules and lack of compensation for more than one faculty member involved in a course"* (Architectural Engineering Lecturer quoted in Vogt [16], p26)
6. Size of classes. Particularly in Australia, many academics face class minimum class sizes of 80 students, and the resources and time required to convert large cohort standard lecture-based courses into smaller multidisciplinary teamwork-based courses may seem an insurmountable challenge.

Motivation may also play a factor in the success of developing integrated curricula. The main motivation for industry to move towards collaborative working and the use of BIM has been pressure from major Clients and various governments, and the opportunity for improved profits and competitiveness. AEC educators are not generally subject to these same pressures. However, the construction industry has expressed a need for graduates skilled in collaborative building design and BIM. For example, BEIIC wrote to all the Deans of Australian Built Environment Faculties in June 2010 to enquire as "to what extent the universities are embracing new technologies such as BIM and equipping our future professionals with cutting edge experience." [17]. The Australian National BIM Initiative defines multi-disciplinary AEC education as one of six key areas needing support from both industry and government [18].

The AEC professional bodies are also beginning to apply pressure to academic institutions to develop integrated courses, through proposed changes to accreditation criteria. For example, the Australian Institute of Architects (AIA) and Consult Australia set up a joint BIM and IPD task force in 2012 [19], including a dedicated BIM in Education Working Group (of which the first author is a member).

6 The CODE BIM Project

The Australian Office of Learning and Teaching (OLT) has funded a project to develop a framework to assist AEC academics in introducing collaborative courses utilising BIM tools and processes. The Australian partner institutions in this project are the University of Technology, Sydney, the University of South Australia, and the University of Newcastle.

The initial stages of the project involved benchmarking current practice in academic institutions worldwide. According to Barison and Santos [20], the majority of US institutions (excepting pioneers such as Georgia Tech) began to introduce BIM in their courses from 2002, and it is a rapidly developing field. For example, Morse [21] lists eight US Academic Institutions and records survey responses from them indicating that 82% were providing formal teaching in BIM. A current web search reveals that 100% of the institutions listed by Morse now teach BIM in some of their courses, at least 17 of the 18 (94%) ABET-accredited Architectural Engineering programs in the US now offer some level of BIM instruction, and at least 9 out of the 12 ABET accredited Construction Engineering institutions offer BIM courses (75%).

To explore further the current practice and understanding of BIM and collaborative AEC education amongst AEC faculty, interviews were conducted with senior AEC academics and researchers from four leading Universities in Australia, three in the UK, one in Sweden, two in the Netherlands, one in Canada and five in the USA, over a period of two years. Some results of this study were reported previously [1]. In 2010, the first author was also involved in conducting a large on-line industry survey of AEC professionals and educators across Australia and New Zealand. The responses from the academic sector to this survey indicated that around 70% were using BIM at some level within their schools.

The most successful implementations of collaborative courses have been between Schools housed within the same financial unit (whether that is a faculty or department). For example, Penn State has implemented extremely successful capstone courses involving collaborative groups of students from its four architectural engineering disciplines, architecture and landscape architecture, as described by Solnosky *et al.* [22]. It appears that academics around the world face the same issues in relation to overcoming bureaucratic hurdles, such as which school pays for teaching of another school's students. Some schools have found that it is easier to develop collaborative courses between institutions than across faculties within their own institution. For example, the University of Southern California (USC) has run graduate-level courses with students from Virginia Tech and the University of Texas at Austin. Stanford University has collaborated with Twente University, Netherlands, to develop graduate-level courses in construction management with BIM support [23]. Other institutions have found that collaboration is easier when creating Masters-level courses, such as the Master of Design-Build program run jointly between Auburn University's Schools of Architecture and Building Science, and Salford University's Master of BIM and Integrated Design. So far, no University appears to have implemented fully collaborative courses across the three separate AEC disciplines at undergraduate level.

A striking difference observed between the US schools visited and those in Australia was typical class size. Class sizes continue to grow in Australia, boosted by the removal of government caps on entry numbers. However, staff numbers have not increased proportionally and it appears that many institutions have embraced larger and larger lecture-format classes to cope. BIM requires multidisciplinary collaboration, but it is very difficult to foster collaborative, technology-intensive teamwork in a classroom format consisting of a 3-hour weekly lecture to over 90 students. The largest multi-disciplinary class observed in the US contained 25 students, and some had as few as six.

Lectures, both physical and online, involve a transmission style of teaching that tends to focus on the lower levels of the taxonomy of learning proposed by Bloom *et al* [24]. Where small group, collaborative, problem-based learning approaches excel is in promoting the higher levels of learning in the taxonomies. Saljo [25] also defines deeper skills that students should develop, including making meaning and reinterpreting. The development of these types of skills is what Universities and other training providers should be focusing their efforts on. Transmission teaching just involves the broadcasting of data to a largely passive audience: knowledge cannot be transmitted into someone else's head.

7 The IMAC Framework

The development of the CODE BIM "IMAC" framework has been described in detail previously [26]. The framework comprises four key stages: Illustration, Manipulation, Application and Collaboration (IMAC). These stages do not necessarily always follow the years of a degree course, but can be viewed as building blocks of learning. The framework comprises two components: a benchmarking tool and a separate guide to implementation

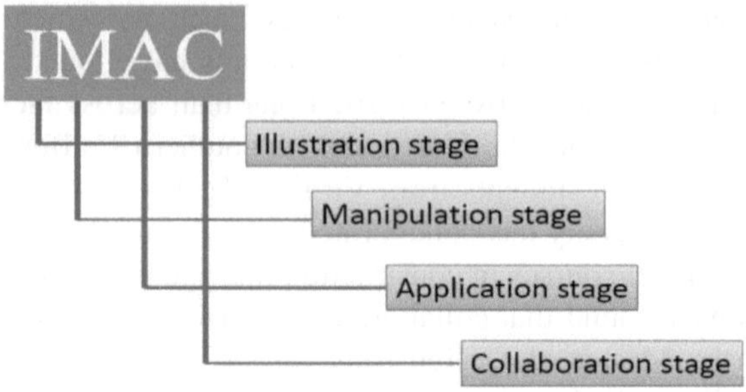

Fig. 2. The four stages making up the IMAC framework

The stages have been mapped to various levels on the taxonomy of learning proposed by Bloom *et al* [24] and expanded by Krathwohl *et al* [27]. As the IMAC framework aims to assist development of both technical (I.T and discipline-specific) and interpersonal (collaborative and teamwork) skills, it straddles the cognitive and affective domains.

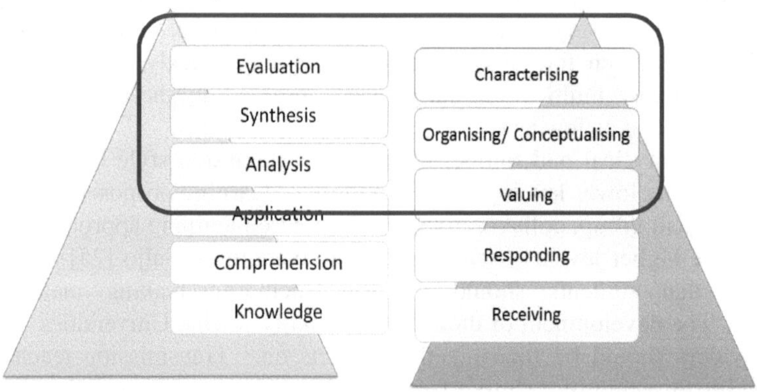

Fig. 3. Bloom's Taxonomy of Learning: Cognitive (L) and Affective (R) Domains [24],[27]

The framework does not dictate in which academic year each stage should be introduced. Students from the different AEC disciplines study courses of varying lengths and some skills are introduced earlier in some courses than others. For example, students of architecture tend to be introduced to modelling tools from first year whereas students of structural engineering might only be introduced to them in third year. It may also be possible to progress between stages within one academic year. The framework also considers suitable delivery methods at each stage, aiming to achieve deeper levels of learning as students progress through their education.

The benchmarking component of the IMAC framework has been used to benchmark existing courses at the three institutions and to plot targets for future curriculum developments. The framework recognises that the different disciplines will not be aiming to achieve full collaboration in all courses or areas – for example, architecture graduates will be expected to be able to create full BIM models from scratch whereas engineers and construction managers would usually only be expected to be able to manipulate existing models for their own analysis purposes. The framework tool thus suggests different targets (shaded, refer Fig 4) for the different discipline areas, and it is expected that these will be mapped to professional accreditation criteria as these are developed.

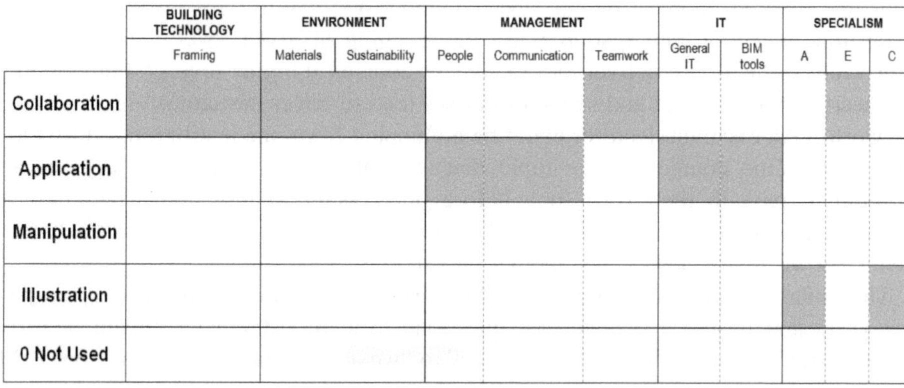

Fig. 4. IMAC chart for an Engineering Course (suggested Target Levels shaded

The project considers two separate aspects of collaboration: collaborative working and collaborative learning. Collaborative working involves student teams tackling project-based tasks that simulate the new collaborative industry working practices. In other words, they are collaborating to achieve a goal (e.g. the design of a building). By contrast, for collaborative learning it is the learning itself that is the goal. There is a large body of pedagogical research showing that students engage and learn much better through teamwork and team learning. The Stoic philosopher Seneca stated that, "by teaching we learn", and the theory that students learn more from teaching has been proven through research [28], [29]. The teacher acts more like a peer in the collaborative environment.

8 Conclusions and Some Proposals

In response to some of the questions raised earlier in this paper, integrating principles of collaboration and BIM technologies into existing classes throughout the curriculum should reduce the need to develop completely new courses. Bolt-on capstone courses, though useful as a first foray into collaborative courses, do not constitute curriculum renewal. In order to encourage true curriculum renewal, the professional bodies should update their accreditation criteria to reflect the industry need for graduates skilled in BIM and collaborative working. Accreditation criteria provide the greatest incentive for academic institutions to instigate changes to their curricula.

Ironically, the industry problem that is creating huge demand for BIM-related courses is also one that affects employers of academics: how to recruit (or train) and then retain teaching staff skilled in the areas of collaborative working and BIM technologies? This is a particularly difficult question given the high demand, and consequently high salaries, on offer in industry. Many universities are reliant on assistance from guest tutors from industry when introducing technical courses in BIM, but it would be wise for these institutions to develop strategies to capture this external knowledge and train faculty members in addition to their students. AEC education should perhaps take its cue from the construction industry by looking at ways to become more efficient and collaborative. Why, for example, should institutions not pool their resources for the teaching of lower level courses and use their valuable faculty to deliver more intensive courses at higher levels? For example, engineering mathematics and statistics classes tend to cover the same content all over the world. An excellent lecturer could be nominated from one institution to provide a definitive online course on one topic that students in all engineering courses are required to pass in their own time before progressing to more advanced in-class courses. This is not really too dissimilar to many institutions setting textbooks that have been written by academics in other universities.

The authors have attended many BIM workshops and conferences over the past few years and it seems that general questions from industry have moved on from "what is BIM and why should we adopt it?" to "we accept that we need to adopt BIM, now how do we go about doing so?" Although AEC academics (with notable exceptions) generally appear to be at the earlier stage of questioning, it is likely that they will also move towards the question of implementation, and the framework described should provide assistance in this. The future belongs to the integrators!

> *"I am looking for a lot of men who have an infinite capacity to not know what can't be done..."* [Henry Ford]

The Benchmarking component of the IMAC tool is has been trialed at the three partner institutions in the CODE BIM project and observational studies of collaborative classes developed using the tool are being carried out over the 2013 study year. It is expected that the results of the trial and classroom studies will be published towards the end of the year, as will the final CODE BIM framework tools, via the project website (www.codebim.com).

Acknowledgments. The first author acknowledges the support provided by the Office of Learning and Teaching (OLT) under OLT Priority Project Code PP10-1745, and by UTS through a Teaching Fellowship Award, which enabled research to be conducted in the overseas institutions described. Further details of the CODE BIM project can be viewed at www.codebim.com

References

1. Macdonald, J.A., Mills, J.E.: The Potential of BIM to Facilitate Collaborative AEC Education. In: Proceedings of the 118th ASEE Annual Conference, American Society of Engineering Education. Vancouver, Canada (June 2011)
2. Allen Consulting Group: Productivity in the buildings network: assessing the impacts of Building Information Models, report to the Built Environment Innovation and Industry Council, Sydney (October 2010)

3. Teicholz, P.: Labor-Productivity Declines in the Construction Industry: Causes and Remedies (Another Look). AECbytes Viewpoint (67) (March 14, 2013)
4. Teicholz, P.: Labor productivity declines in the construction industry: causes and remedies. AECbytes Viewpoint (4) (April 14, 2004)
5. NIST (National Institute of Standards and Technology), Cost Analysis of Inadequate Interoperability in the U.S. Capital Facilities Industry. NISTGCR 04-867. NIST, Gaithersburg (2004)
6. Wolstenholme: Never Waste a Good Crisis: A Review of Progress since Rethinking Construction and Thoughts for Our Future, Constructing Excellence (October 2009), http://www.constructingexcellence.org.uk/pdf/Wolstenhome_Report_Oct_2009
7. QCIF (Queensland Construction Industry Forum), Getting it Right First Time (2005)
8. O'Brien, W., Soibelman, L., Elvin, G.: Collaborative Design Proceses: An Active- and Reflective- Learning Course in Multidisciplinary Collaboration. Journal of Construction Education 8(2), 78–93 (2003)
9. Holland, R., Messner, J., Parfitt, K., Poerschke, U., Pihlak, M., Solnosky, R.: Integrated Design Courses Using BIM as the Technology Platform. In: Annual Meeting of EcoBuild America Conference, Washington, DC, December 7. National Institute of Building Sciences (2010)
10. Miller, R.: The BIM Mirage or BIMwashing, online blog entry in The Commercial Real Estate Revolution (October 2009), http://thecrerevolution.com/2009/10/the-bim-mirage-or-bimwashing/
11. Eastman, C., Teicholz, P., Sacks, R., Liston, K.: BIM Handbook: A Guide to Building Information Modeling for Owners, Managers, Designers, Engineers, and Contractors. John Wiley & Sons, Inc., New Jersey (2008)
12. Race, S.: BIM Demystified: An Architect's guide to Building Information Modelling/Management (BIM). RIBA Publishing, London (2012)
13. Pressman, A.: Integrated Practice in Perspective: A New Model for the Architectural Profession, Architectural Record (May 2007), http://archrecord.construction.com/practice/projDelivery/0705proj-3.asp
14. Starzyk, G.F., McDonald, M.: The Collaborative Dance: Only Three Steps. In: Salazar, G., Issa, R. (eds.) Proc. of the BIM-Related Academic Workshop, Washington, DC, December 7-9 (2010)
15. Deutsch, R.: BIM and Integrated Design: Strategies for Architectural Practice. John Wiley & Sons, Inc., New Jersey (2011)
16. Vogt, B.A.: Relating Building Information Modeling& Architectural Engineering Curricula, Department of Architectural Engineering, Kansas State University, MSc Thesis (2010)
17. BEIIC, Letter to all Deans of Australian Built Environment Faculties (2010) (unpublished)
18. BuildingSMART, The National BIM Initiative, Report to DIISRTe (June 2012), http://buildingsmart.org.au/nbi-folder/NationalBIMIniativeReport_6June2012.pdf
19. AIA, BIM and IPD Steering Committee. Documents produced by the four working groups (2012), http://www.bim.architecture.com.au/groups/
20. Barison, M.B., Santos, E.T.: BIM teaching strategies: an overview of the current approaches. In: Proc. of the International Conference on Computing in Civil and Building Engineering, Nottingham (2010)

21. Morse, E.J.: An Online Case Study Resource for Building nformation Modeling in College Education (Worcester Polytechnic Institute) (2009), http://www.wpi.edu/Pubs/E-project/Available/E-project-090109-010641/unrestricted/EJM-BIMinEducation.pdf
22. Solnosky, R., Parfitt, M., Holland, R.: An IPD and BIM Focused Capstone Course Based on AEC Industry Needs and Involvement. J. Prof. Issues Eng. Educ. Pract. (February 28, 2013) doi: 10.1061/(ASCE)EI.1943-5541.0000157
23. Peterson, F., Hartmann, T., et al.: Teaching construction project management with BIM support: Experience and lessons learned. Automation in Construction 20, 115–125 (2011)
24. Bloom, B.S., Englehart, M.D., Furst, E.J., Hill, W.H., Krathwohl, D.R.: The Taxonomy of Educational Objectives, The Classification of Educational Goals, Handbook I: Cognitive Domain. David McKay Company, New York (1956)
25. Säljö, R.: Learning in the learner's perspective: 1. Some common-sense conceptions. Reports from the Institute of Education, University of Gothenburg, 76 (1979)
26. Macdonald, J.A.: A framework for collaborative BIM education across the AEC disciplines. In: 37th Annual Conference of Australasian University Building Educators Association (AUBEA), Sydney, Australia, July 4-6 (2012)
27. Krathwohl, D.R., Bloom, B.S., Masia, B.B.: The Taxonomy of Educational Objectives: The Classification of Educational Goals, Handbook II: Affective Domain. David McKay Company, New York (1964)
28. Annis, L.F.: The process and effects of peer tutoring. Human Learning 2, 39–47 (1983)
29. McKeachie, W.J., Pintrich, P.R., Lin, Y.-G., Smith, D.A.F.: Teaching and Learning in the College Classroom: A Review of the Research Literature. University of Michigan, National Center for Research to Improve Postsecondary Teaching and Learning, Ann Arbor (1986)

Collaborative Engineering Paradigm Applied to the Aerospace Industry

Fernando Mas [1], José Luis Menéndez [1], Manuel Oliva [1], Alejandro Gómez [2], and José Ríos [2]

[1] AIRBUS, Av. García Morato s/n, 41011, Sevilla, Spain
fernando.mas@airbus.com
[2] Univ. Polit. Madrid, José Gutiérrez Abascal 2, 28006 Madrid, Spain
jose.rios@upm.es

Abstract. Airbus designs and industrializes aircrafts using Concurrent Engineering techniques since decades. The introduction of new PLM methods, procedures and tools, and the need to reduce time-to-market, led Airbus Military to pursue new working methods. Traditional Engineering works sequentially. Concurrent Engineering basically overlaps tasks between teams. Collaborative Engineering promotes teamwork to develop product, processes and resources from the conceptual phase to the start of the serial production. The CALIPSO-neo pilot project was launched to support the industrialization process of a medium size aerostructure. The aim is to implement the industrial Digital Mock-Up (iDMU) concept and its exploitation to create shop floor documentation. In a framework of a collaborative engineering strategy, the project is part of the efforts to deploy Digital Manufacturing as a key technology for the industrialization of aircraft assembly lines. This paper presents the context, the conceptual approach and the methodology adopted.

Keywords: collaborative engineering, industrial Digital Mock-Up, PLM systems.

1 Introduction

The design and the industrialization of aircrafts is a complex process. An aircraft like the Airbus A400M is composed of about 700.000 parts (excluding standard parts). The parts are assembled into aerostructures and major components, which are designed and manufactured in seven countries all over the world [1].

In the mid-nineties, PDM and CAD systems let Airbus to build a product Digital Mock-Up (DMU), mainly to check functional design interferences. Then the ACE (Airbus Concurrent Engineering) project [2] started to develop and deploy methods, processes and tools along all the functional design disciplines. A summary of the Airbus product DMU is presented in [3].

Since 1999, Airbus has successfully applied Concurrent Engineering to all the aircraft design programs: A380, C295, A400M, and A350. The gain is obtained mainly in the functional design area. The Industrial design activities make use of CAx tools

A. Bernard, L. Rivest, and D. Dutta (Eds.): PLM 2013, IFIP AICT 409, pp. 675–684, 2013.

in not fully integrated areas, causing interoperability issues and a lack of real influence on the functional design.

The development of computer based shared workspaces was the main aim in the early years of the Collaborative Engineering concept and product modeling, or product DMU, was the main focus [4]. Currently, Collaborative Engineering promotes to integrate design teams, both functional and industrial, to generate a unique deliverable, named industrial DMU (iDMU), integrating: product, processes and resources. It also promotes the intensive use of PLM tools to perform virtual manufacturing and support the DMU as kernel of the collaborative work [5]. The downward link with the physical manufacturing is created by feeding work instructions (WIs) to the shop floor. Since the iDMU comprises the full definition of the manufacturing activities, it can be used to generate WIs [6].

In this context, Airbus Military launched the CALIPSOneo pilot project to contribute to develop and deploy Collaborative Engineering processes and tools. The project focuses on the new A320neo Fan Cowls. The low complexity of such aerostructure, the manufacturing technologies involved and the company expertise on the design of fairings make it an excellent sample to conduct a pilot project.

2 Review of the Traditional, Concurrent and Collaborative Process

The evolution inside Airbus from Traditional Engineering to Collaborative Engineering through Concurrent Engineering is an ongoing process. The main triggers are: technological evolution of software tools, the need to short time-to-market, to reduce cost and to increase quality and the maturity of the development team.

Traditional Engineering

The Traditional Engineering approach, also known as sequential engineering, comprises the implementation of sequential tasks, often referred to as the 'over-the-wall' approach [7]. Disadvantages of this approach are extensively mentioned in the literature: focus on product functionality and drawings, lack of industrial design, problems growing at the end of the lifecycle, different teams with lack of communication between them and long time-to-market.

Concurrent Engineering

In the last decades, methodological and technological advances have significantly influenced engineering activities. Concurrent Engineering has become widely accepted. About twenty years ago, with the introduction of the emergent PLM tools, a company-wide project, ACE (Airbus Concurrent Engineering) [2] was launched. Framed within the Airbus A340-500/600 development program, it aimed to develop and deploy concurrent engineering practices and the associated PLM tools.

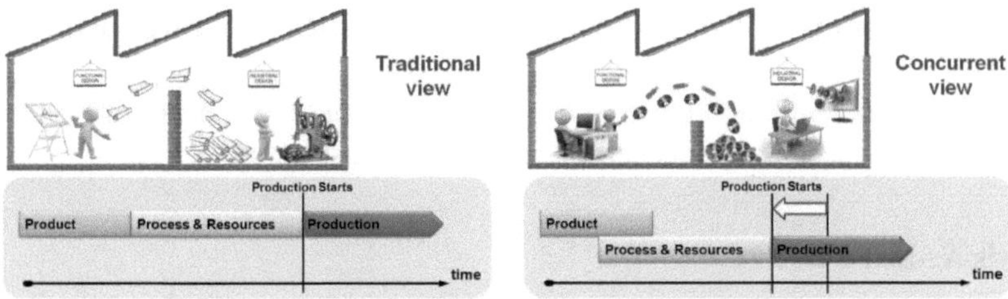

Fig. 1. Traditional view vs. Concurrent view

Currently, there are still pending issues, the wall described in Traditional Engineering still exits but it is not so high. The industrialization tasks are not as advanced as functional tasks in terms of PLM tools usage. The current deliverable is the product DMU, interoperability and working practice issues cause that compact disks or memory sticks flies over the wall instead of paper based drawings. Industrial design is not fully integrated with functional design, and it has little influence over the latter. They comprise two separate teams with dissimilar skills.

In fact, one of the most important reasons to have the wall is the certification process by the aeronautical authorities. Traditionally certification was made using the product definition, drawings, and marked the end of the aircraft design process. Concurrent Engineering still hold this idea and consider the aircraft design only as the functional design, enriched with manufacturing constrains and needs.

Collaborative Engineering

The iDMU is the key element of the Collaborative Engineering to tear down the wall between functional design and industrial design. The aim is a design process with a single team that creates a single deliverable. This approach needs new working procedures and new PLM tools. By applying virtual validation, using virtual manufacturing techniques, a further reduction of time-to-market is feasible.

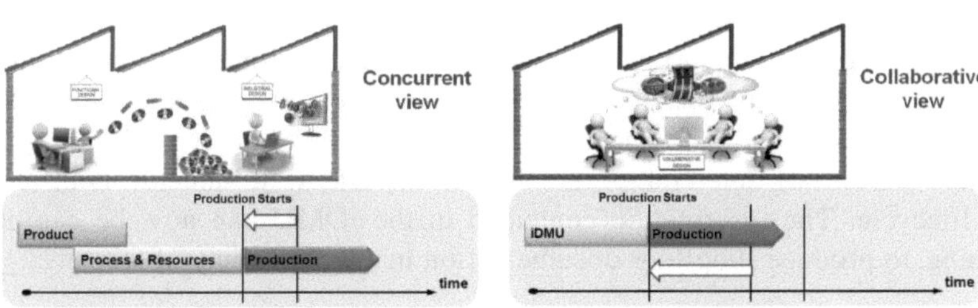

Fig. 2. Concurrent view vs. Collaborative view

3 Collaborative Engineering Airbus Military Conceptual Model

Both the functional and the industrial design areas shared the concept of Collaborative Engineering. It is seen as an answer to the current industrial challenges.

Analysis As-Is To-Be

Current or 'As Is' situation (Fig. 3) shows an optimized functional design area with a clear deliverable: the product DMU. The concurrent process closes the gap between functional design and industrial design, and feeds back functional design with manufacturing information to facilitate 'Design for Manufacturing' and 'Design for Assembly'. The functional design deliverable, the 'DMU as master', is a valuable item in the first stages of the lifecycle, but the value for the process decreases with time and most of the industrial design tasks are paper based.

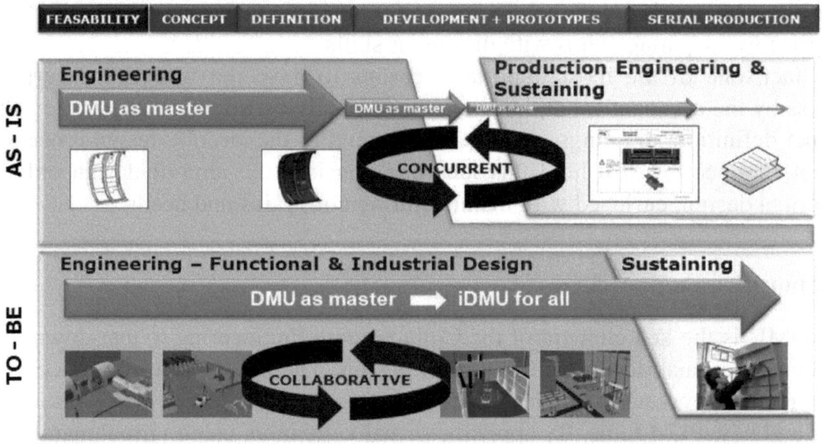

Fig. 3. Analysis 'As Is - To Be'

Future or 'To Be' situation shows an optimized functional and industrial design area with a clear deliverable: the iDMU [8]. The previous gap is eliminated by the collaborative way to build the iDMU and the virtual validation of it. The design (functional and industrial) deliverable, the 'iDMU for all', is a valuable item along the whole lifecycle. The information contained in the iDMU can now be exploited by Sustaining, to produce shopfloor documentation in a wide variety of formats.

Functional Model

Fig. 4 shows the main functions and information flow involved in the development and production of an aircraft. Management activities, box 'Manage', influence all the downstream functions.

Development activities, box 'Engineer', are controlled by the output from '*Manage*', '*Customer requirements*' and '*Industrial strategy*'. Development activities include '*Functional Design*' and '*Industrial Design*'. Both work together, as a single team, to develop product, processes and resources from the conceptual phase to the start of the serial production. The deliverable is an '*iDMU*', a complete definition and verification of the virtual manufacturing of the product [8]. All the deviations coming from the shopfloor, in terms of '*Deviations (non conformances, concessions*), are inputs to '*Engineer*', included in the '*iDMU*' and sent to '*Operation*'. The final output is an '*As built*' iDMU that fits with the real product launch by '*Operation*'.

Production activities are represented by the box 'Operation', controlled by the output from '*Manage*' and by the output from '*Engineer*' '*iDMU*'. Operation activities include 'Sustaining', which is in charge of exploit the iDMU, with the help of MES (Manufacturing Execution Systems), to launch '*Shopfloor Documents*' to '*Serial production*'. The '*Manufacturing Problems*' that can be managed without modifying the iDMU, are managed by '*Sustaining*'. Any other item affecting the iDMU is derived to '*Engineer*' as deviation. The output from '*Operation*' is the final physical product that fits 100% with the '*As built*'.

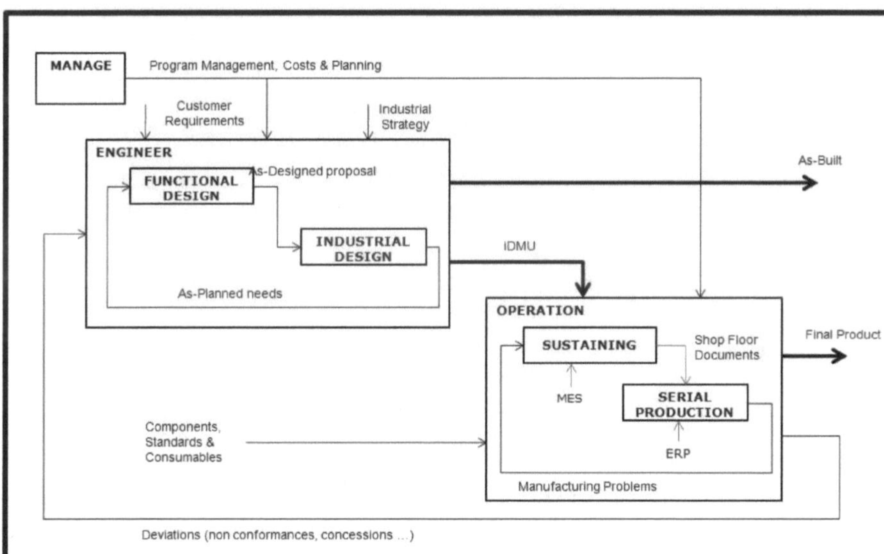

Fig. 4. Collaborative functional model

Digital MockUp (DMU) and Industrial Digital MockUp (iDMU)

Collaborative Engineering involves a lot of changes in terms of: organization, teams, relationships, skills, methods, procedures, standards, processes, tools and interfaces [4]. It is a business transformation process [5]. One of the key changes is the engineering deliverable, it comprises evolving from the 'product DMU as master' to the 'iDMU for all' (Fig. 3).

'DMU as master' is a standard inside Airbus [3]. All the information related to the functional aspects of the product is included in the product DMU, e.g. aspects like 'design in context' and clashes-free product are fully deployed. The DMU is the reference for the product functional definition, and it is built in concurrent engineering taken into account manufacturing constraints.

The 'iDMU for all' is a new concept. It is the main enabler of the Collaborative Engineering approach and provides a common virtual environment for all the aircraft development stakeholders. Functional design and industrial design are part of a single design process where they progress together and influence each other.

The iDMU collects the information related to functional design plus all the information related to industrial design: manufacturing and assembly process, associated resources, industrial means and human resources [8]. All is defined in an integrated environment, where complete and partial simulations are done continuously, and at the end of the design phase, they guarantee a validated solution. Fig. 5 shows an example of a 3D view of an iDMU.

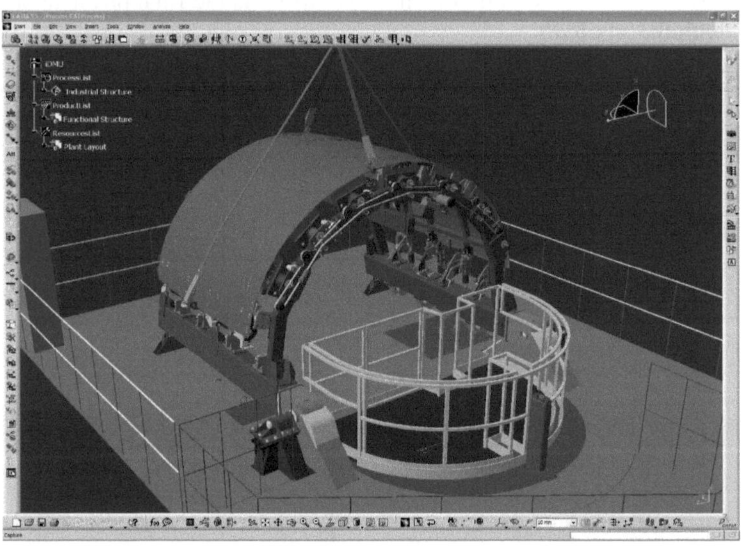

Fig. 5. Fan Cowl industrial Digital MockUp (iDMU) (Not a real iDMU due to confidentiality)

4 Collaborative Engineering Pilot Project: CALIPSOneo

CALIPSOneo is an R+D+i pilot project and it was launched early 2013 to support the development, customization and deployment of the PLM tools and processes in Airbus Military. CALIPSOneo is a joined effort that involves Engineering Companies, IT companies, PLM Vendors and Research Centers and Universities. The project runs during 2013 and the first quarter of 2014.

CALIPSOneo makes use of the newest PLM tools. It aims implementing new methods and processes needed to support a collaborative way of designing. It takes as input developments from previous projects, related to digital manufacturing techniques implementation [6, 8] and aircraft conceptual design modeling [9]. Similarly to other initiatives reported in literature [10-12], the main results will be definition and modeling of collaborative working procedures, and their implementation into collaborative software tools. The project aims to demonstrate:

- Collaborative Engineering concepts applied to aircraft design and manufacture.
- Capability to generate an iDMU and virtual validation by using it.
- Configuration based on individual specimen.
- To assess the benefits of the iDMU concept when compared to the usual practices for the industrial design.
- Availability of PLM tools to develop and deploy new capabilities.
- Capability to exploit the iDMU to produce advanced shopfloor documentation.

Fig. 6 shows the business model framework where the project is developed. It comprises the frame and conceptual model for all the project activities.

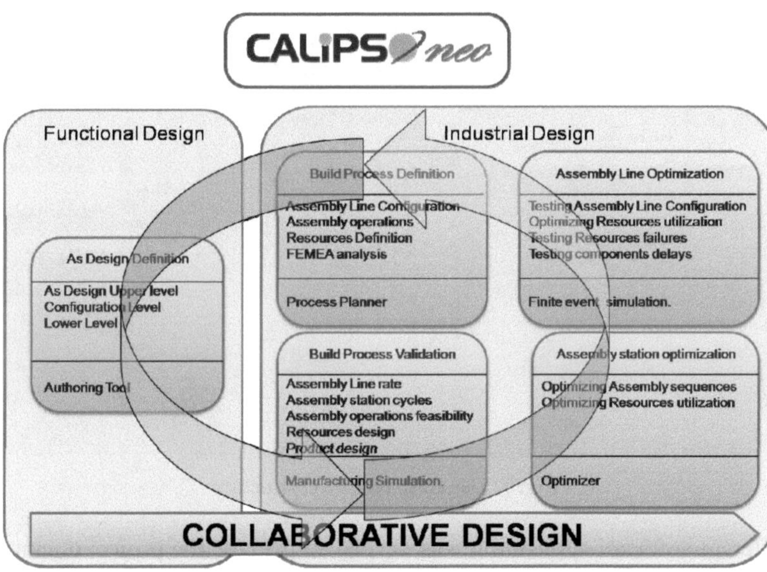

Fig. 6. CALIPSOneo functional diagram

5 Methodology

The project aims to change the current product design business process to the collaborative paradigm. To achieve it, it is proposed the use of the latest PLM tools to support the new design paradigm. As a consequence, the project required a balanced multiskilled team and a sound methodology to succeed. For that reason, a multi organization project team was created, where Dassault Systèmes, commercial PLM software provider, is the technical advisor, two university research groups are in charge of the research work and the methodological support, and two industrial partners are in charge of the development work.

For the systems development methodology, the NDT (Navigational Development Techniques) methodology was selected. NDT was developed by the IWT2 research group (University of Seville) [13]

The project was planned in two main phases, a first phase of analysis and definition and a second phase of implementation and testing of the defined solution.

The NDT methodology uses UML as the documentation technique. In the first phase, requirements defined by suitable use cases and the system data model are defined using a UML based CASE tool (Enterprise Architect). Fig. 7 illustrates a sample of the UML Use cases and data model diagrams.

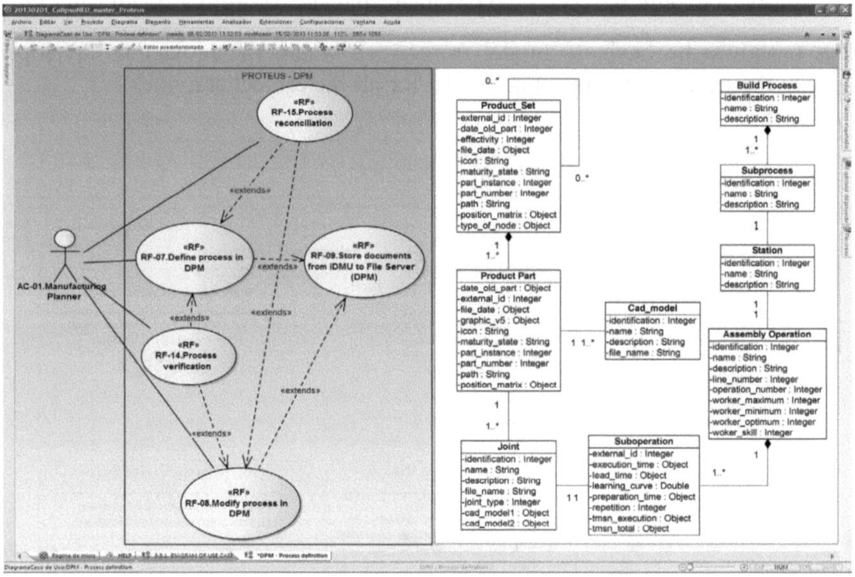

Fig. 7. Use Case & iDMU structure

A different software application was needed to manage the project documentation and to provide a collaborative environment, for this purpose a web based tool was selected: Alfresco. Alfresco provides a web environment, where all the participants can share all the documents created during the project and it also provides collaborative utilities. Alfresco allows customizing a folder structure for documents, defining review and approving workflows, establishing discussion forums for specific topics and managing the project tasks. In this way, all the documentation and task management were supported by a single tool.

6 Results and Conclusions

Collaborative Engineering is a broader approach derived from the previous Concurrent Engineering experiences. The availability of new technologies and the maturity of the teams are the key elements in the success of its industrial implementation. During the execution of the CALIPSOneo project, which is still running, several barriers were identified and have to be overcome to implement the Collaborative Engineering approach.

The first issue is the application of the Collaborative Engineering functional model from an organizational and social perspective. It demands the harmonization of the functional design area and the industrial design area, when both are assigned to different departments that are headed by different people. In addition to the organizational issue, the concept of a unique team doing all the design functions has a large set of human relationships implications. Company top management implication is a key factor. CALIPSOneo is helping to make explicit some of the benefits of the collaborative approach in the context of the Company. Extensive literature shows the expected benefits of the collaborative engineering approach, but due to the high impact of the specific organizational and social environment of each company, results must be shown in the company specific context.

The second issue is the complexity of managing a real pilot case in parallel with the development and deployment of the associated PLM tools. The PLM tools are the key enabler in creating and managing the industrial DMU (iDMU). The interoperability between the different commercial software applications and modules used in an industrial project is still an issue. Without the proper integration, the iDMU cannot be created to enable the collaborative approach. For this issue, the adopted solution was to set up a multidisciplinary working team model, where engineers, experts on the industrial design tasks, and PLM experts work altogether conducting industrial and CALIPSOneo R+D+i tasks. Engineers were trained in understanding how PLM tools could help in the industrialization design process. PLM experts were focused on developing specific utilities to facilitate the collaborative work, on customizing the PLM tools and on creating working procedures to create the iDMU.

7 Next Steps

The next step is consolidating the collaborative process, methods and the associated engineering teams and disseminating the collaborative culture inside Airbus Military and the Extended Enterprise as a standard.

Launch a new R+D+i project, as an extension to the CALIPSOneo project, to identify possible additional issues that may arise and to cover further developments associated to the complexity of larger aerostructures.

Finally, the last step would be the introduction of the collaborative process in a light or medium military transport aircraft, where the Services area will be also considered. The inclusion of MRO design in the iDMU will help to consolidate the collaborative engineering methods, processes and tools along the Company.

Acknowledgements. Authors wish to express their sincere gratitude to colleagues from Airbus Military, Universidad Politécnica de Madrid, Universidad de Sevilla and partners of CALIPSOneo project for their collaboration and contribution to the project.

References

1. Aviation News Magazine - AIRBUS A400M, http://www.aviation-news.co.uk/archive/a400m.html (retrieved in January 2013)
2. Pardessus, T.: Concurrent engineering development and practices for aircraft design at Airbus (Conference). In: Proceedings of the 24th ICAS Meeting, Yokohama (2004)
3. Garbade, R., Dolezal, W.R.: DMU at Airbus – Evolution of the Digital Mock-up (DMU) at Airbus to the Centre of Aircraft Development. In: The Future of Product Development. Proceedings of the 17th CIRP Design Conference, pp. 3–12. Springer (2007)
4. Sriram, D., Logcher, R.: The MIT Dice Project. Computer 26(1), 64–65 (1993)
5. Lu, S.C.-Y., Elmaraghy, W., Schuh, G., Wilhelm, R.: A scientific foundation of collaborative engineering. CIRP Annals - Manufacturing Technology 56(2), 605–634 (2007)
6. Mas Morate, F., Menéndez, J.L., Serván, J., Gómez, A., Ríos, J.: Aerospace Industrial Digital Mock-Up exploitation to generate assembly shop floor documentation. In: Proceedings of 29 International Manufacturing Congress, Belfast (2012)
7. Prasad, B.: Concurrent Engineering Fundamentals. Prentice-Hall PTR, New Jersey (1996)
8. Menendez, J.L., Mas Morate, F., Servan, J., Rios, J.: Virtual verification of an aircraft Final Assembly Line industrialization: an industrial case. Key Engineering Materials. Material Science and Engineering 502, 139–144 (2012)
9. Mas Morate, F., Rios, J., Menendez, J.L., Gomez, A.: A process-oriented approach to modeling the conceptual design of aircraft assembly lines. International Journal of Advanced Manufacturing Technology 62 (2012)
10. Butterfield, J., et al.: Optimization of aircraft fuselage assembly process using digital manufacturing. J. of Comput. Inf. Sci. Eng. 7, 269–275 (2007)
11. Van Wijk, D., et al.: Integrated Design and PLM Applications in Aeronautics Product Development. In: Proc. of the 19th CIRP Design Conf. Competitive Design, Cranfield University (2009)
12. Rouchon, C.: V6 deployment in new business Jet. Top 5 PLM breakthroughs. Proceedings of 3D EXPERIENCE FORUM Europe 2012, Brussels (2012)
13. García-García, J.A., Alba Ortega, M., García-Borgoñon, L., Escalona, M.J.: NDT-Suite: A Model-Based Suite for the Application of NDT. In: Brambilla, M., Tokuda, T., Tolksdorf, R. (eds.) ICWE 2012. LNCS, vol. 7387, pp. 469–472. Springer, Heidelberg (2012)

The Usage of the Standards into the Long Term Archiving and Retrieval, and the Exchange of Engineering Design Data

Frédéric Chambolle

PSA Peugeot Citroën, France
frederic.chambolle@mpsa.com

Abstract. Standards have been developed to provide means of exchange and archival of engineering design data within automotive industry. In most cases, the simple use of these standards is not enough. Indeed, the usage of such standards requires the development of recommendations and methodologies providing specific rules and processes that will guide the user on how the standard is to be used in a given context. This paper will present examples of data exchange problems with some examples of methodologies developed to solve them, and - automotive recommendations developed in several domains such as PDM data exchange, Product Data Quality, Long Term Arching and Retrieval, etc. how they are used within the industrial processes.

Keywords: Archival, Exchange, Standards, Automotive, STEP, OAIS, CAD, PLM, SASIG.

1 Introduction

The engineering development of complex products such as automotive products is made in an extended enterprise context with suppliers, but also with other car manufacturers in case of partnership projects related to the development of cars, engines, gear boxes, etc. Extended enterprise requires collaboration within a heterogeneous environment involving different actors using complex IT environments, implementing different business processes, etc.

In this context, data interoperability is a major issue. Data exchange standards are then key elements since they provide a software independent exchange solution.

Nevertheless, due to the complexity of their definition and implementation, the single usage of such standards cannot systematically lead to a successful data exchange. Software editors and automotive companies have decided to define recommendations in order to improve the technical and functional quality of data exchange. These recommendations mainly concern the domains of Computer Aided Design, Product Data Management, and Long Term Arching and Retrieval. They provide explicit and shared rules of implementation to allow a better use data exchange standards, or define processes to be applied upstream and downstream of the data exchange.

A. Bernard, L. Rivest, and D. Dutta (Eds.): PLM 2013, IFIP AICT 409, pp. 685–694, 2013.

Then, these recommendations are intended to be used and combined with the data exchange standard for a better control of the data exchange processes.

2 The Data Exchange Standards

A data exchange standard provides a means to exchange information between different IT software, in a given application context (ex : Computer Aided Design, Digital Mockup, etc.). It proposes a content that can be interpreted/decoded by any software of the concerned domain through a translation function that enables to establish a data mapping between the standard and their internal data model. A data exchange standard is also known as "neutral format".

In the engineering domain, different types of standards are used :

- **Official standard:** it is published by a standardization organization (AFNOR, ANSI, ISO),
- **Defacto standard:** it is defined by a "commercial" organization, but considered as a reference in its domain. Thus, it is used by wide population of actors of this domain,
- **Recommendation:** it is defined and published by a community of interest (SASIG, LOTAR, …). It usually defines either explicit business use cases, or mechanisms, algorithms, etc. that are not yet covered by a standard. A recommendation may become the foundation of a future standard.

Usually, for reasons of strategy and efficiency, neutral formats are opposed to native formats. The usage of native formats for data exchange has an evident interest if both partners use the same software. If not, the data exchange based on native formats requires the usage of direct translators that translate a data in an original format into the target format. A famous comparison between direct and neutral translators is presented in Fig. 1.

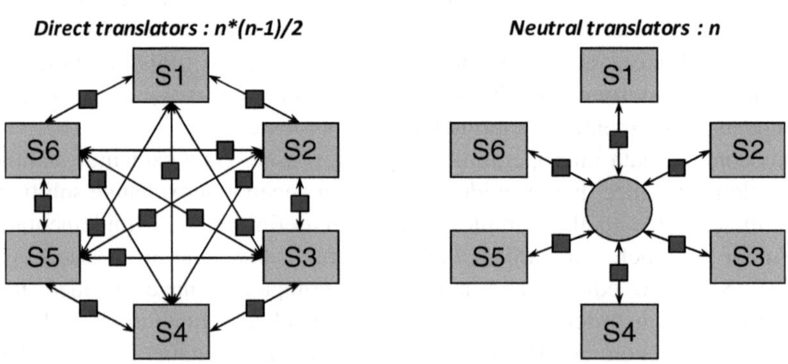

Fig. 1. Comparison amongst translators to implement in case of a direct or neutral translation strategy

The most important figure concerns the number of translators, n versus $n*(n-1)/2$, that must be implemented to enable exchange between each software.

The usage of a direct translation constraints the user to upgrade its translators every time both original and target formats evolve (see Fig. 2). This has an impact on IT maintenance costs, and the stability of the translation processes.

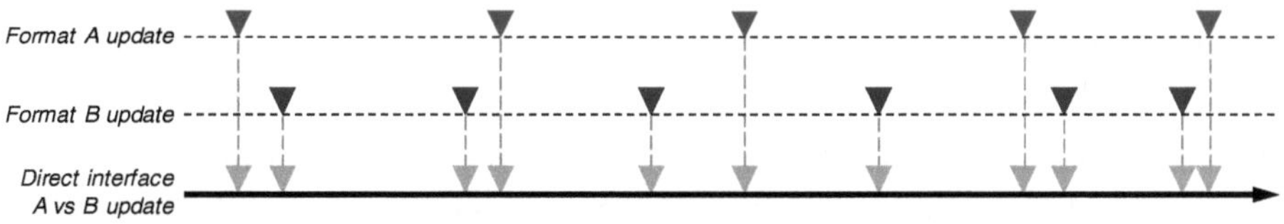

Fig. 2. Frequency of upgrades for direct translators

3 CAD Data Exchange

CAD domain is the most experienced domain in terms of data exchange. Indeed, many standards were developed since 70's in this domain (see Fig. 3).

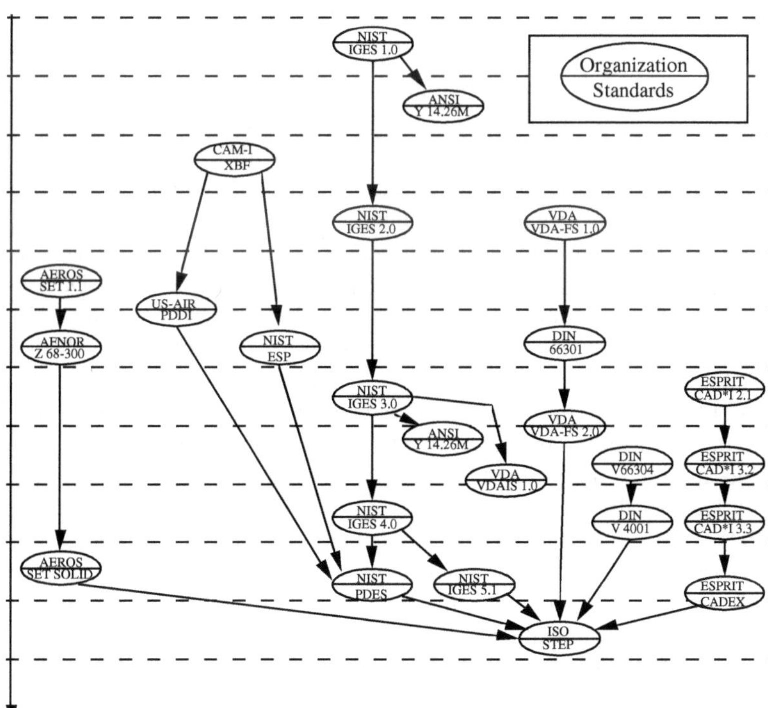

Fig. 3. History of CAD standards

The richness of the content of the standard regularly increases. This evolution is driven by the CAD functionalities increasingly advanced (Construction history, parametric design, feature based modeling, etc.).

CAD translators have now reached a good level of quality. Several reasons enabled to reach that level of maturity :

- Lessons learnt from past experiences,
- Better standards,
- Implementor Forums.

For the development of STEP related translators, the CAx Implementor Forum [10] was created in 1995 with the support of PDES Inc. and ProSTEP iViP. The objective of the forum is to accelerate CAx translator development and ensure that users' requirements are satisfied. Thus, this forum enables software editors to :

- Organize cross testing sessions (CAD Round Table),
- Synchronize functionality implementation with the user needs,
- Identify the functionalities expected for "tomorrow",
- Establish agreement through the development of Recommended Practices : define clear use cases of the STEP standards (ex : Geometric and Assembly Validation Properties, Model styling and Organization, …).

Nevertheless, even if CAD translators have reached a significant level of quality, data exchange rules needs to be implemented. This is the case in the automotive industry where each car manufacturer has developed its own CAD Data Exchange policy to be used into the data exchange processes with its suppliers. Such a policy defines CAD design rules and methodologies specific to a company, like file formats to be used, CAD model organization rules, accuracy, allowed types of entity, etc. These rules aim to optimize the integration of CAD design with processes downstream and upstream (meshing, release process, …). The CAD Data Exchange policy is a contractual document that applies in the OEM-suppliers relationship.

Most of the rules contained in this document are implemented in CAD data quality checker that is used to verify whether the CAD design rules are satisfied at any stage of the design process. This process is mainly implemented to avoid any kind of problem in the downstream processes due to a poor quality of CAD data [5].

The international automotive industry, through the international consortium SASIG [9], has decided in 2000, to develop a recommendation related to CAD data quality (PDQ). The "SASIG-PDQ" recommendation, published in 2002, defines a set of PDQ criteria used in the automotive industry. Thereafter, most of the CAD PDQ checker editors have implemented this set of criteria, and the recommendation was submitted to the ISO organization.

In terms of CAD data exchange format policy, 2 scenario need to be considered :

- **OEM-Supplier relationship** : in this case, as detailed previously, the CAD Data Exchange Policy applies. It specifies that the OEM native format (same release/version/service pack) must be used to minimize the impact of the data exchange on the data contents

- **OEM-OEM partnership** : in this case, the CAD Data Exchange Policy doesn't apply. Neutral formats are used to exchange between different CAD systems, or different releases of the same CAD system (downward compatibility no ensured). Such a scenario implies a design master to consumer relationship.

4 PDM Data Exchange

PDM domain is less mature than the CAD domain in terms of data exchange. The exchange context is then much more complex than for the CAD data. Indeed, Each company implements their own PDM/PLM system customization, often complex, that is characterized by :

- Data model : add/modify attributes or objects,
- Rules and mechanisms applicable to attribute naming and codifications,
- Reference Breakdowns (functions, components) and classifications,
- Workflows and processes,
- Terminology/Vocabulary/Language,
- Integration with other systems : Manufacturing, Planning, …

An illustration of PDM data exchange context is shown in Fig. 4 where both companies apply their own product data management rules.

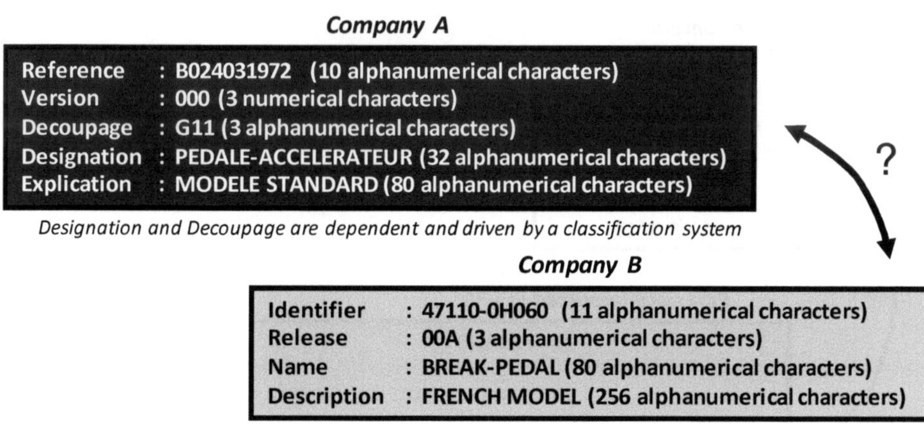

Fig. 4. Example of heterogeneous context for PDM data exchange

The usage of standards is the main way to exchange PDM data. Even if standards exist and are exhaustive, they cover a (too) wide perimeter, and their implementation remains complex. Nevertheless, data exchange solutions exist. They must be based on explicit use cases that define data exchange rules and processes, and the corresponding standard subset to be implemented.

In terms of standards, STEP provides a set of application protocols that enable to exchange PDM data (structured data). For the engineering product development, STEP AP214 [6] is the relevant standard within the automotive industry. This standard covers a very wide scope, and is on way to be replaced by the standard STEP AP242, currently under development, nevertheless a fully compatible with STEP AP214. STEP AP214 covers a wide scope [1] including in particular product management data (item, version, approval, security, effectivity, date/organization/person), item definition structure (explicit assembly), item properties, work management (project activity, change management), classification, description of products with a large number of variants (diversity description, configuration), product breakdown (components, functions), reference mechanism to external documents, and process plan (process operations). Currently, only a very limited subset for STEP AP214 is widely implemented in commercial softwares. This scope covers mainly 3D geometric representation, PMI (Product Manufacturing Information or GD&T) presentation, representation of explicit assemblies. It is estimated that it represents about 20% of the global scope of STEP AP214.

SASIG, consortium initially created to lead and support the development of the STEP AP214, has decided to develop a recommendation related to the exchange of PDM assemblies. The "SASIG-PDM Assembly Data Exchange" recommendation, published in 2003, defines how to exchange PDM assemblies with STEP AP214, with a proposal of process and STEP AP214 subset. Such a recommendation is destined to allowing assembly data exchange between PDM systems with an enriched content.

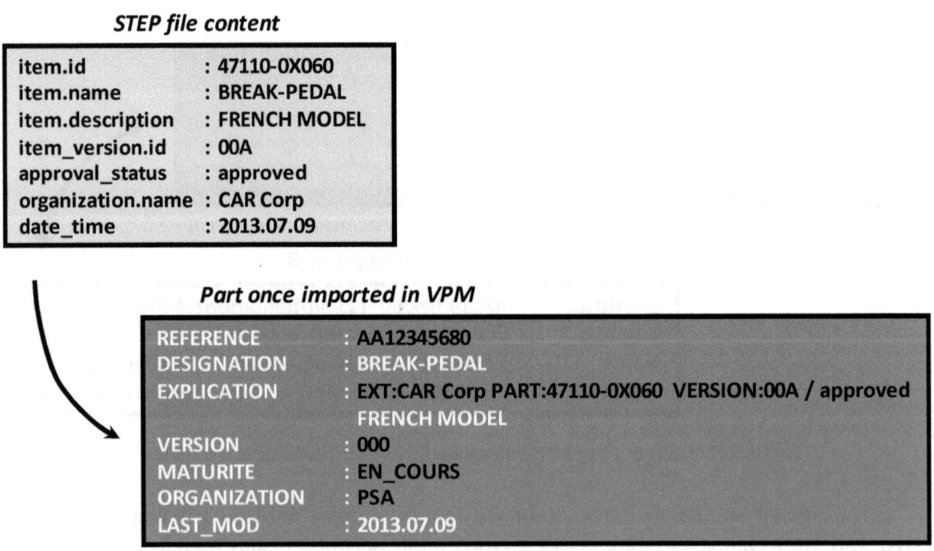

Fig. 5. Import of PDM data that are not compliant to my company codification rules

In terms of implementation, the capability to exchange with any partner is one of the success keys, whatever the used software. Indeed, a partner may have a PDM system or not, with a data exchange interface or not, but will always use a CAD system that enables to exchange 3D geometric representations and explicit assemblies in STEP format.

Thus, if we consider the export process, the experience shows that being able to export PDM data toward another PDM or CAD system enables to communicate with most of partners.

Then, if we consider the import process, generally the most complex, we need to consider 2 major cases that should enable to import any PDM data, whatever its contents :

- The partner uses the codification rules of my company. The import process should then be able to use all the attributes values provided in the exchanged package.
- The partner does not use the codification rules of my company. The import process should then create automatic values for the reference attributes (Unique identifier, Version), and the other attributes may be used as provided (see example in Fig. 5).

Once imported, depending on the business requirements, it is usually necessary to process those data in order to finalize their integration in the company IT environment (assign legacy reference, integration with other data, etc.).

5 Long Term Archival and Retrieval

For many years, the archival of engineering data has been reduced to the simple archival of drawings in the form of aperture cards or digital images. More globally, during the 2 last decades, the transition from the paper to the digital was observed within most of domains of management of product definition data. The automotive industry is now confronted with a situation, where product definition data covers a large diversity, and are managed by complex IT data structures, often with a strong adherence with solutions and their proprietary format [4]. In addition, we can observe that the required lifecycle of product definition data (more than 30 years) and the lifecycle of the used technologies (see Fig. 6) are not aligned.

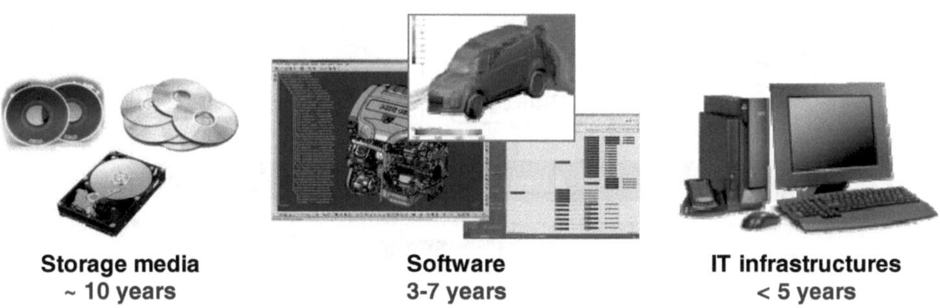

Fig. 6. Lifecycle of technologies used in the management of product definition data

The international automotive industry, following the aerospace industry [3] [8], has considered that those conditions cannot guarantee a consistent archival of its product definition data along its products lifecycle. In 2010, SASIG consortium decided to develop a set of recommendations that will guide companies to effective and efficient archival and retrieval practices. These recommendations, currently under development will include :

- A classification model of what data should be archived,
- A retention period recommendation,
- A quality assurance recommendation,
- A format recommendation,
- A LTAR process recommendation.

Data exchange standards are key elements to be considered in such recommendations. Thus, they provide a means to separate the data from their authoring softwares, and they have the biggest durability which is another important aspect in the LTAR domain [2].

At the moment, different major standards were identified by the SASIG-LTAR working group are :

- **OAIS** (ISO 14721 [7]) : The Open Archival Information System standard defines an open framework for the design and function of preservation repositories. This definition contains a reference model that defines the function, organization, and interaction of content within preservation repositories. OAIS should be considered as the basis of any archival system (see Fig. 7).

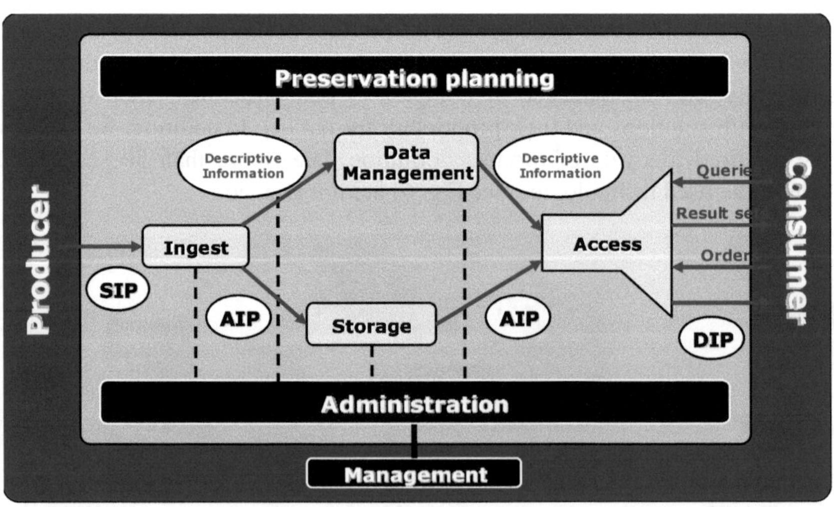

Fig. 7. OAIS Architecture

- **STEP Application Protocols** (ISO 10303) : during the period between the archival and the retrieval, it is evident that a company will update or change its softwares. If we consider an archived data, it should be readable at any time along its lifecyle, independently of the software used at this moment. Therefore, it is the typical case of an exchange where the software used to create the data is not the same than the target one. The term of "Long Term Data Exchange" can then be used. In this context, data exchange standards are the most appropriate formats, taking into account the wide scope that they address.
- **CAx-IF Recommended Practices** and **SASIG Recommendations** that provide additional processes (CAD data quality) and mechanisms (Geometric and Assembly Validation Properties, etc.) very useful in that context.

The development activities of the recommendations are going on. The Format recommendation will be published by the end of 2013, and the complete set of recommendations by end of 2014. In between, a LTAR test pilot will be developed as proof of concept, promotion support.

6 Conclusion

Standards exist but due to their complexity, they are not controlled enough. The experience shows that guidelines, such as recommended practices and recommendations, are necessary for an appropriate usage of the standards. Thus, they provide clear use cases of the standard, completed with rules and proposal of process, aligned with the user requirements, and contribute to a better understanding and usage of the standards.

Nevertheless, even if the existing guidelines deployment is successful, guidelines and implementations are still missing in many domains such as configuration management (diversity dictionary, design use cases, etc.), product data management, requirements management, engineering change management, electrical harness design, etc. The corresponding deliverables should provide important inputs in the engineering data exchange and archival domains.

References

1. Chambolle, F.: Un modèle produit piloté par les processus d'élaboration : Application au secteur automobile dans l'environnement STEP. PhD Thesis, Ecole Centrale Paris (1999)
2. Kheddouci, F.: L'archivage à long terme de la maquette numérique 3D annotée. Master Degree, Ecole de Technologie Supérieure, Université de Québec, Canada (2010)
3. Kopena, J.B., Shaffer, J., Regli, W.C.: CAD Archives based on OAIS. In: ASME 2006 International Design Engineering Technical Conferences & Computers and Information in Engineering Conference (2006)
4. Heutelbeck, D., Brunsmann, J., Wilkes, W., Hundsdörfer, A.: Motivations and Challenges for Digital Preservation in Design and Engineering. In: DP 2009, Austin, TX, USA (2009)

5. Horwood, M., Kulkarni, S.: CAD data quality. The Journal of the Institution of Engineering Designers (2005)
6. ISO 10303-214, Industrial Automation Systems and Integration - Product Data Representation and Exchange, Part 214 : Application Protocol, Core Data for Automotive Mechanical Design Processes. ISO, International Organization for Standardization, Geneva (1999)
7. ISO 14721, Space data and information transfer systems – Open archival information system Reference model. ISO, International Organization for Standardization, Geneva (2003, 2012)
8. LOTAR Project, LOng Term Archiving and Retrieval, http://www.lotar-international.org
9. SASIG, Strategic Automotive product data Standards Industry Group, http://www.sasig.com
10. CAx Implementor Forum, http://www.cax-if.org

Change Management and PLM Implementation

Kamal Cheballah[1] and Aurélie Bissay[2]

[1] Audros Technology, PLM Software editor, Lyon, France
[2] GreenLight-IT, Private research center in Informatics, Lyon, France
kcheballah@audros.fr, abissay@greenlight-it.fr

Abstract. To capitalize from the management of a company's expertise is reliant on the ability manipulate the data, information, documents, and knowledge that represent these expertise. This process is complex and so to reach this target we need to introduce new tools and methods of work to the company. These changes will face a certain amount of resistance and so attempts have been made by numerous scientific researchers, to introduce new change management methods to minimise this resistance. The classical methods of change management are a <<top-down>> approach which is not really appropriate. Our work proposes a new <<bottom-up>> approach which derives from the users instinctive ability to use certain interface elements.

Keywords: Change management, PLM implementation, AudrosBox, Collaborative features.

1 Introduction

Companies operate in an environment where it is necessary to be as competitive as possible. This race towards competitiveness can be conducted in different ways, through company strategy, its internal resources, its organization, etc. Our research focuses particularly on the organizational aspects of the company particularly through the information system. Companies' expertise Is an essential element in competitiveness. The focus is on the management of its documents, data, information, and knowledge. This management is the key point in increasing the enterprise productivity. The use of all the tools needed by the fact we need to manage these information have as a consequence a modification if working methods for the users. We contribute through our research by introducing new tools which gives a more progressive way to manage all these information, avoiding the risk of rejecting the system by users

2 Information System and Change Management

2.1 Problematic

The current situation no longer allows some companies whatever their size to manage their individual expertise. Information, data, knowledge are all principal elements of the company that need to be preserved.

A. Bernard, L. Rivest, and D. Dutta (Eds.): PLM 2013, IFIP AICT 409, pp. 695–701, 2013.

The entire expertise is often capitalized individually wick renders it impractical for the company. Furthermore its organization and its scalability is directly related to the wishes of those who want to capitalize. This leads to a bottleneck in the execution process of work done in the company. Some players are no longer able to respond to the number of inquiries needed for the execution process.

Document management systems and, PLM, responds to these needs. They aim to organize and manage information and documents within an organization. These systems implement procurement methods, Indexing, classification, management and storage, access and retrieval of data and documents. They therefore contribute to the collaborative work processes, capitalization and the exchange of information.

Management expertise leads to gains and a rapid return on investment for organizations. In this collaborative approach around a software system, it is the effective implementation of the methodology which is the source of success and not just the product which serves only to support this method. To be carried out well, this type of project requires that we dedicate a support, for implementation and training.

Despite these challenges and productivity gains, the process of implementation of a PLM solution requires time and effort to adapt the product. This ability to adapt is needed due to the fact that the expertise of every company is what makes this company unique. Capitalizing on the enterprise expertise essentially implies a unique system that comes from the adaptation of a generic PLM system.

Many PLM projects fail to achieve their goals, especially for non-technical reasons. The employees of an organization share common values, corporate culture and social benefits that can be challenged by changing the organization of the company or the introduction of a new IT tool. Change management must take into account these values and and put in place a permanent means of monitoring and identifying group apprehensions in order to, where appropriate, communicate on the stability of the values and current achievements.[1]

The results of a study [2] show that there are either difficulties or rejection in 45% of cases where PLM systems have been implemented.[3]

Beside the expense of resistance to change, one aspect to consider is the maturity of the company when putting in place and using a PLM system.

Indeed, in addition to an expensive investment, companies must have users willing to use the system. To do this results in an extremely heavy user support to make it adhere to the system, this is what is referred to hereinafter as the management of change

2.2 Change Management

Change management is a set of processes employed to ensure that significant changes are implemented in an orderly, controlled and systematic fashion to effect organizational change. It reduces failures and encourages appropriation [4] of new procedures [5]. Approaches to managing change are generally based on following items: participation, communication, and training.

According to Martin [6], change can be seen as a curve including the following steps: doubt, current situation, trigger, project, action plan.

According to Prochaska and Velicier [7], change is a process operating in cycles, with each cycle comprised of six stages of behavioural change: the pre-intention, intent, preparation, action, maintenance, resolution.

The effectiveness of the implementation of change depends on the quality of the learning process [8] introduced at both individual and team level, as well as on the interaction of both.

Finally, resistance to change is significant. Too often the weight given to the implementation of the technical objective (the software) is disproportionate compared to the effort used in deploying the methodologies of change management when available.

In fact the successfulness of the PLM implementation depends essentially on the way we conduct Change Management.

The PEGASE project (Serious Game Platform Backing and monitoring of change in SMEs / SMIs) [9] defines an environment of support for change management in industrial enterprises with an approach around the Serious Games. The purpose of this project is to develop a real Serious Game platform to help companies to effectively support their staff in adapting to the changes brought about by redesigning their information systems. Some initial actions in this platform game are driven through the integration of real scenarios in industrial processes.

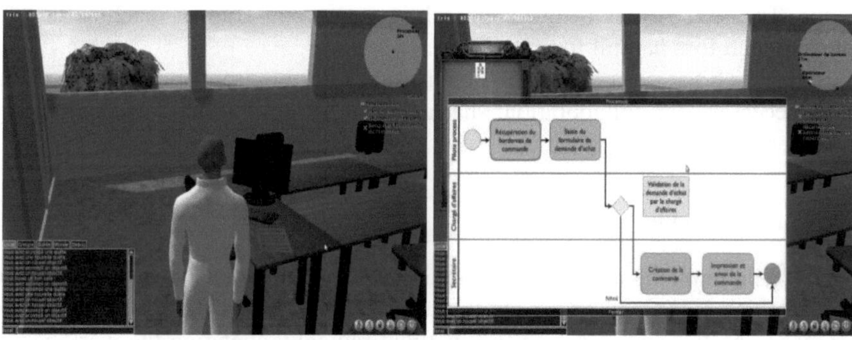

Fig. 1. Screen shot PEGASE: player interacts with its environment

Fig. 2. Screen shot PEGASE: player collects product data

This project was a success by showing that we can improve change management by using a Serious Game. However, the construction of a Serious Game is very expensive, it does not fit the limited funding of a small and medium sized company.

3 Approach to Change Management

3.1 Bottom Up Approach to Change Management

With our state of the art analysis, we find that the methods used for change management use a "top-down" approach, in the sense that they take as a starting point, the targeted system to propose methods for supporting the users. Our research introduces a « Bottom up » approach to facilitate the conduct of change. It is therefore necessary to search for elements that are widely known and accepted by the user to support this process.

Today, what we identify as a common utility in all businesses is Windows Explorer and the simple text search box.

Our initiative is thus to work on progressive methods while considering that the success of a PLM project is first and foremost a matter of the Human Machine Interface. The foundations of our approach is a common Human machine interface, simple and therefore natural for most users.

This approach focuses on users and their usual work environment, combining basic features necessary for collaboration: sharing, security, traceability, versioning, rights management.

3.2 Une Approche Évolutive

The approach implemented by our research is a comprehensive and evolutionary approach which is divided into 3 phases and smoothly brings the businesses towards better managing their capital expertise, without radically changing the work habits of the users. This methodological approach is progressive and based on what we call the « AudrosBox » approach.

The first phase, collaborative features, is a first level approach allowing for collaboration through Windows Explorer and the simple text search box. On top of these two user interface elements, we extend their functionalities by adding more sophisticated processing which offer powerful functionality for collaborative management. This approach that we call <<plug and play>> targets the fast track approach to collaborative functionalities with minimum training.

The second phase, EDM allows the user to move towards better managing the handling of such data. The use of the Audrosbox system and the habit of working in a collaborative mode induced by the first phase, usually derives from the users newely discovered and more complicated needs in terms of document management. For example when trying to figure out the percentage of copper used in the material specification document given, we will need to be able to manage attributes for each document.

The third phase, PLM-Product Lifecycle Management, allows users to integrate all of the components for these systems while maintaining a simplified Human Machine Interface. This final phase includes connectors with different CAD systems on the market, the automatic creation of documents, and the management of data dependencies (bill of material).

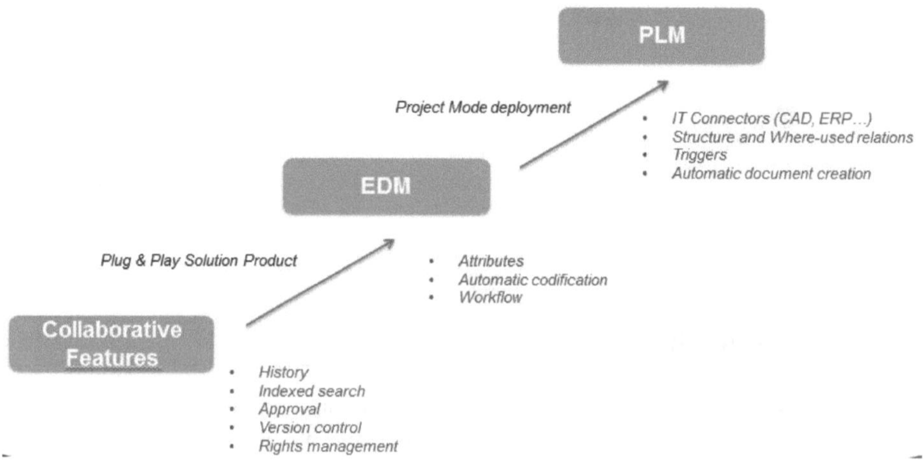

Fig. 3. Methodological approach in 3 phases

3.3 AudrosBox

Audrosbox answer to

- the collaborative management of information, mobility and right management

Audrosbox introduces four terminologies,

Repository - it is a context where all the information belongs within this context and obeys the context right managements.

Information – illustrated in the first phase as a file, is created by using instinctively the standard tools of a company.

The engine - which has the function to drive the execution of the tasks needed to make the data compliant on their arrival to the repository.

The cloud or storage space – the information in this cloud space is elected from the repository.

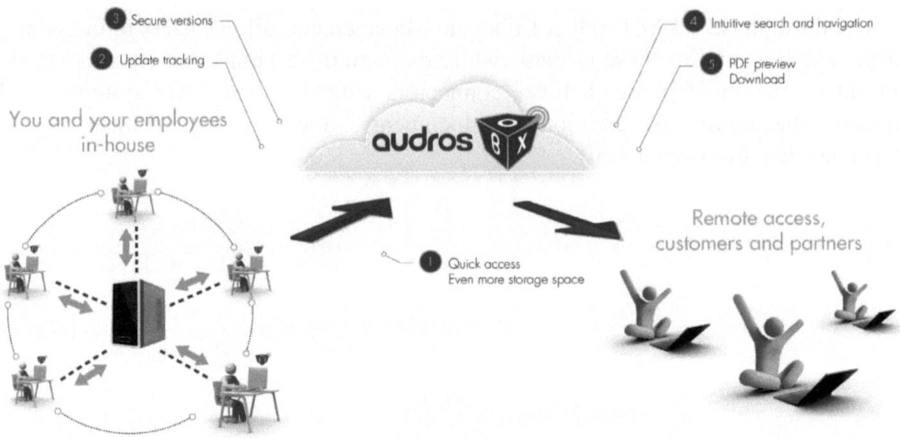

Fig. 4. Audrosbox

4 Functionnality

The system uses these methods for storing documents onto the repository.

The synchronization of the central system is done by binary comparison of the local repository regarding the same information that is on the remote repository.

The locking systems insure that no information will be updated simultaneously by different users.

The addition of attributes, the detailed business view, allows the user to benefit from the use of these attributes.

This engine allows for the atomization of tasks

5 Conclusion

These methods are very promising regarding the number of companies which decide to implement this process. In fact, due to the fast start process with minimum training, the successful introduction of the PLM system to the users can be insured.

We have discovered that we need to enhance our research by means of two topics:

- The simple text search needs to be more powerful and should not only deliver as an answer to the texts we find in the index of the documentation, but also the implementation of the semantic search should enhance this functionality.

In the 3dr phase, PLM level, it is very important to retain the malleability of the model. This is why we have begun this research

References

1. Bissay, A.: Du deployment d'un système PLM vers une integration des connaissances, Thèse de doctorat, Université Lyon 2 (2010)
2. Kadiri, S., Pernelle, P., Delattre, M., Bouras, A.: Current situation of PLM systems in SME/SMI: Survey's results and analysis. In: PLM 2009, Bath, England (2009)
3. Kadiri, S.: Management des processus collaboratifs dans les systèmes PLM, Thèse de doctorat, Université Lyon 2 (2009)
4. Gélinier, O.: Stratégies de l'entreprise et motivation des hommes, éd. d'Organisation (1990)
5. Savall, H., Zardet, V.: Ingénierie Stratégique du Roseau, Economica (1995)
6. Martin, J.: La Conduite du Changement, Université de Strasbourg (2009), http://univrcms.ustrasbg.fr/depotcel/DepotCel/514/ueop0910s1/SMQ_ConduiteChangement.ppt
7. Prochaska, J.O., Velicer, W.F.: The transtheoretical model of health behavior change. American Journal of Health Promotion (1997)
8. Argyris, C.: On Organizational learning. Blackwell Business (1992)
9. Bissay, A., Cheballah, K., Zrouki, M., Pernelle, P.: PEGASE: a platform tool to help change management support during the implementation of a PLM system in an industrial company. In: PLM 2011, Eindoven, Pays Bas (2011)

Securing Data Quality along the Supply Chain

Sergej Bondar[1], Christoph Ruppert[2], and Josip Stjepandic[1]

[1] PROSTEP AG, Darmstadt, Germany
[2] Heidelberger Druckmaschinen AG, Heidelberg, Germany
josip.stjepandic@opendesc.com

Abstract. Concurrent engineering in distributed development environments like those in the automotive industry places enormous demands on the organization of collaboration between the companies and departments involved. Efficient data communication in all phases of the product development process is a prerequisite for lean and flexible collaboration processes. Automotive suppliers that develop system components for a number of different OEMs or tier-1 suppliers face the challenge of ensuring that they make the CAD data available in the format required by their customers along with a high level of reliability and, if data translation is involved, that they take into consideration the system configuration of the respective customer. The main obstacle in this process chain is the insufficient data quality. This paper describes the approaches conducted in cooperation between the supplier portal www.opendesc.com and Heidelberger Druckmaschinen AG.

Keywords: CAD, Data Quality, Supply Chain, Engineering Collaboration, Migration.

1 Introduction

Nowadays modern manufacturing industries like the automotive are acting in the dynamic global marketplace that demands instant responses to customer requirements, short time-to-market and high flexibility in production. In the past decades the manufacturing industries were even more shifting to a distributed environment like an extended enterprise, with increasing agility. We set the customer's satisfaction on the first place in order to get the assignment against many competitors. This has caused the mass customization at high level and even more complex development, manufacturing as well as logistics processes along the manufacturing supply chain. Thus the upcoming outsourcing has derived a multi-tier supply network structure involving numerous enterprises around the globe. The product development as well takes place in global development partnerships. OEMs accomplish the development of new products at many locations in several countries across the world [1]. Furthermore, a variable number of external service providers and suppliers take part in individual projects. The most relationships in this supply network are temporary, exceed by the end of project and today's project partner can well become tomorrow's harshest competitor (Figure 1).

A. Bernard, L. Rivest, and D. Dutta (Eds.): PLM 2013, IFIP AICT 409, pp. 702–711, 2013.

The suppliers were involved in the product development as early as possible, because they mostly possess a greater depth of domain expertise for best product development. The OEM-supplier relationship is characterized by a sequential interaction, whereby the OEM gives clear product and production requirements to the supplier and the supplier delivers the product or service to the OEM. Supplier integration is a crucial method for incorporating a supplier's innovativeness in the product development process and reduces the costs and risk [2]. It also creates synergy through mutually interacting deliverables and decisions between OEM and suppliers. Both sides take advantage of each other's capability to develop the product as well as to obtain feedback from the other party to improve the product development. Due to the complex development cycle, the OEM took the lead and has begun to adopt supplier integration into its product development process. To respond to this trend, the collaboration and partnership management between the OEM and suppliers need to be continuously improved to reduce costs and time. Regarding the depth of collaboration, the integration of suppliers into the OEM process chain can be defined in many ways, depending on corresponding work package and type of collaboration [3]. To enable the success of supplier integration, this work describes how to improve the collaboration between the OEM and its suppliers, through ensuring the appropriate data quality.

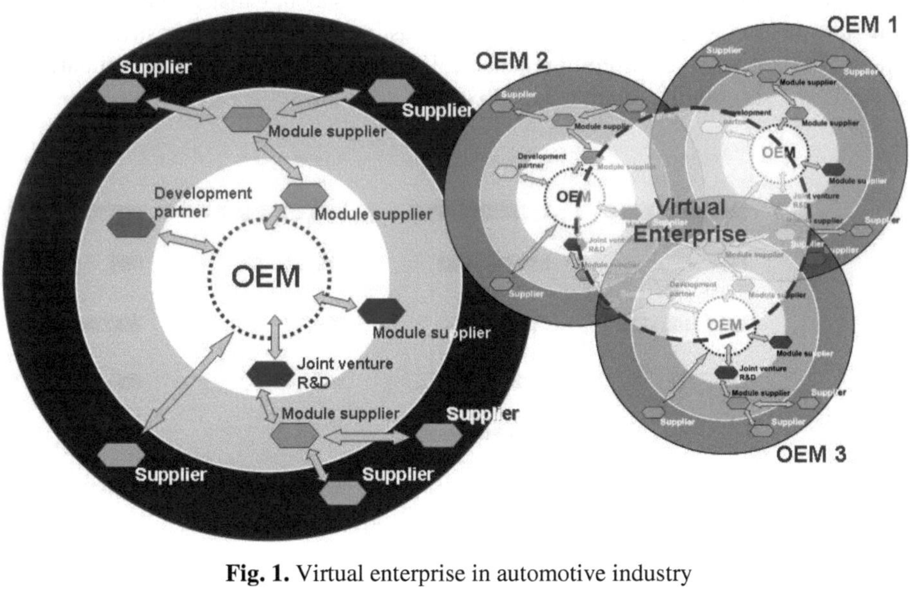

Fig. 1. Virtual enterprise in automotive industry

In the context of concurrent and collaborative engineering, the validity and consistency of product information become important. However, it is difficult for the current computer-aided systems to check the information validity and consistency because the engineers' intent is not fully represented in a consistent product model. Due to the different approaches and IT systems in the automotive OEM industry, a unified solution is not possible at this time. In particular, automotive suppliers that develop system components for a number of different OEMs or tier-1 suppliers, face the challenge of ensuring that they make the CAD data available in the format required by their customers and with a high level of reliability and, if data translation is involved, that they take the system configuration of the respective customer into consideration. Special requirements like the flexibility for further changes in business relationships and the intellectual property protection are also taken into account.

2 Cooperation Models

As the outsourcing became standard business approach in the manufacturing industries, many industry associations like the German automotive manufacturers association (VDA) accomplished the basic development work to define and classify the typical collaboration models and corresponding processes [4] (Figure 2). There are 6 supplier types defined according to the criteria: production technical integration, process integration, functional integration, and geometrical (spatial) integration of the whole product (car). Beside of the prime contractor who can be defined as a clone of the OEM without the product management, sales and marketing function, all other types of suppliers (system supplier, module supplier, component supplier, part supplier, and engineering service provider) maintain a high level of independency in their corresponding processes. Taking the fact into account that a supplier supplies many customers, who have their own, various processes and infrastructures, this creates a strong need for a comprehensive integration approach based primarily on standards and serving the relationships to all the customers.

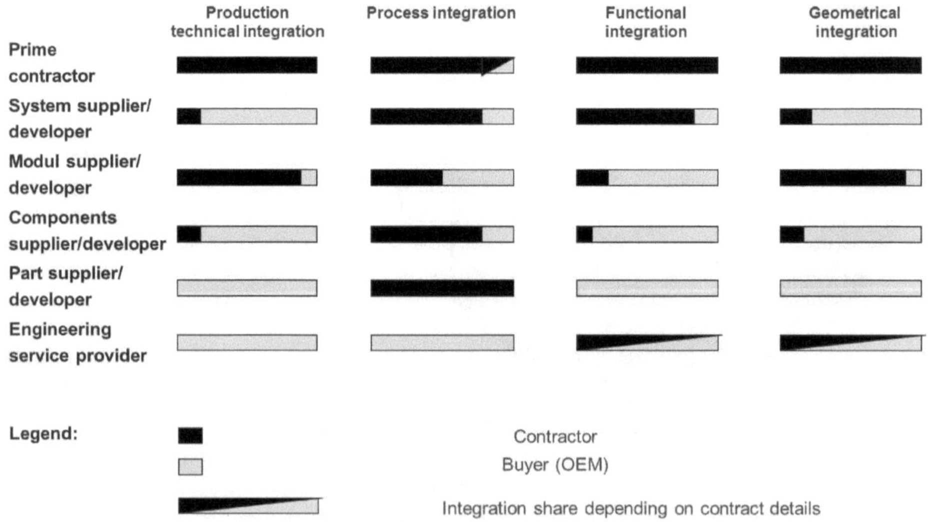

Fig. 2. Cooperation models in the automotive industry

The responsibility of suppliers to provide the suitable product documentation in each phase of product emerging process is self-evident for an OEM. Thus the supplier is forced to take the corresponding measures to adapt his data to OEM's requirements. The most important criterion is the CAD data quality as defined and required by OEM.

3 CAD Data Quality

In the product, various life-cycle quality requirements at the particular stages are defined and required. These include requirements such as the functional requirements of the product, the type of presentation form, the production requirements or the data quality in the data exchange.

Within the design and manufacturing process chains, there are different phases that shape up demands on the geometric and organizational data quality and the data size. A CAD model can both find multiple uses as well as require certain compatibility. The multiple use is mainly based on the modeling, while the compatibility refers more to the geometrical and topological characteristics. In downstream or subsequent applications, it may happen that the designer says, the CAD model would be good, while the downstream users of this CAD model in the process chain often described it as not so good or even unusable. The same situation can occur in the collaboration context.

Therefore CAD data should ensure the reusability in native CAD system, but also the derivation of the resulting geometry for downstream data processing. Although the level of detail can be low or high during a certain period, the requirements remain the same for geometry and topology.

A categorization of CAD data yields the matching of criteria and characteristics to reasonable and memorable sets of 3D CAD models. There are different approaches, such as the division into "components" or "resources" (for producing components), in various process chains (depending on the material or the manufacturing method) or in accordance with the stages of development (concept, coordination, approval, detailing, etc.). The working group of German Automotive Industry Association (VDA) recommends a two-dimensional matrix [5]. Meanwhile, these basic criteria are adopted by almost all OEMs.

Finally the term "CAD data quality" includes the fulfillment of a set of predefined criteria known as mathematical-technical and organizational. To the first set belongs the geometrical quality of CAD models and depends on fulfillment of basic accuracy criteria (coincidence, continuity), itself depending on accuracy setup of CAD system. The second set comprises the relevant rules for the structure of CAD models. Almost each large company has defined own CAD methods which include a set of prerequisites. The fulfillment of the rules is checked by special CAD checkers, which are controlled by profiles for each model purpose.

For the translation from the original into the target CAD format, direct or neutral interfaces are used. The advantage of direct interface is the higher translation speed. The neutral interfaces are more robust by using special healing algorithms for corrupt geometry and allow better logging by using neutral format like STEP and JT.

The main problem in the CAD translation is in the most cases the insufficient data quality after the translation. The requirement for the successful translation process can also be redefined as fulfillment of all relevant data quality requirements, independent of the source system and the stage of the product development process. In the context of collaboration, this requirement can be extended to a level at which the CAD conversion must successfully pass the examination with each CAD checker on the target site, independent from the source CAD system [6].

4 Solution Approach

Since the problem has been identified and analyzed, now a concept for ensuring data quality in CAD data exchange has to be developed. For this, only measures are recorded to ensure data quality, and then, finally, to apply the phase model for development of methods.

Measures to prevent loss of information can be taken by considering functional aspects, verification aspects and application aspects. The functional aspects include the division of the total amount of an element specification in compatible element subsets that are adopted in individual performance levels with their associated functional content. The verification of aspects includes procedures to verify and validate the performance of a specification.

The application aspects include specific requirements such as the implementation of a new interface. Due to the wealth and diversity of the internal data models of CAD systems a loss of information during the data exchange cannot be completely avoided. Therefore, specific agreements between data sender and receiver must contribute to minimize the loss of information in the data exchange. Appropriate checklists are required and the criteria can be derived for boundary conditions. These checklists should be created as a function of the gradual approach of the functional performance of the interface [7].

The methodological concept development can be understood as decision making process and consists of a sequence of iterative steps. These steps include extensive analytical and synthesizing activities and the appropriate documentation of the analysis and synthesis results. A methodical approach is necessary because all possible requirements have to be considered in a process. Analogous to the phases for the implementation of IT projects, the concept phase, the specification phase, and the implementation phase of development are to be introduced as part of the methodological concept development to ensure data quality,

The essential task in the concept phase is the creation of requirements profile, which includes the performance range. The requirements profile includes a checklist, or a sort of guide for meaningful modeling technique that could prevent problems in data exchange. Herein the pre-mentioned causes are considered. This checklist has been created after many investigations and has been continuously adapted to users.

Based on extensive experience, the necessary guidelines were defined similarly to the VDA recommendation 4955 [5]. Here best practices are set up or attempting to establish common guidelines that are either independent of the used CAD systems or specifically dependent on system pairing (e.g. CATIA (Creo) ➔ NX), processors and interface formats (e.g. STEP).

The implementation of design guidelines must be established by appropriate check tools. The application is done by native checking capabilities, following the progress of the design process, pointing mainly at the possible errors in data exchange, what is therefore very helpful. The final check can be done in the batch mode. The positive result is the prerequisite for the release of data exchange.

The check tools are modular. The runs by the user are executed individually or in any combination. Limits and other underlying assets for each run will be proposed through a configuration file and can be changed interactively. A selection or limitation of scope of testing is possible, but just a test of all the elements finally matters.

The logging of the test run, including indication of corrupt elements is in a log file. The respective defective items must be clearly identifiable.

Further, the display of certain entities (e.g. transferred and arrived surfaces) from the log file need to be written out after the data export to instantly identify potential losses (e.g. surface count). This required comparative studies to be made with respect to the different log files of the pertaining CAD systems and to the meaningfulness of the log files.

Finally, a figure is required, indicating the number of transferred data elements during the export of native data formats to the neutral file and potential losses as well. This is a comparison between the elements between the states "before" and "after".

The final concept is shown in Figure 3.

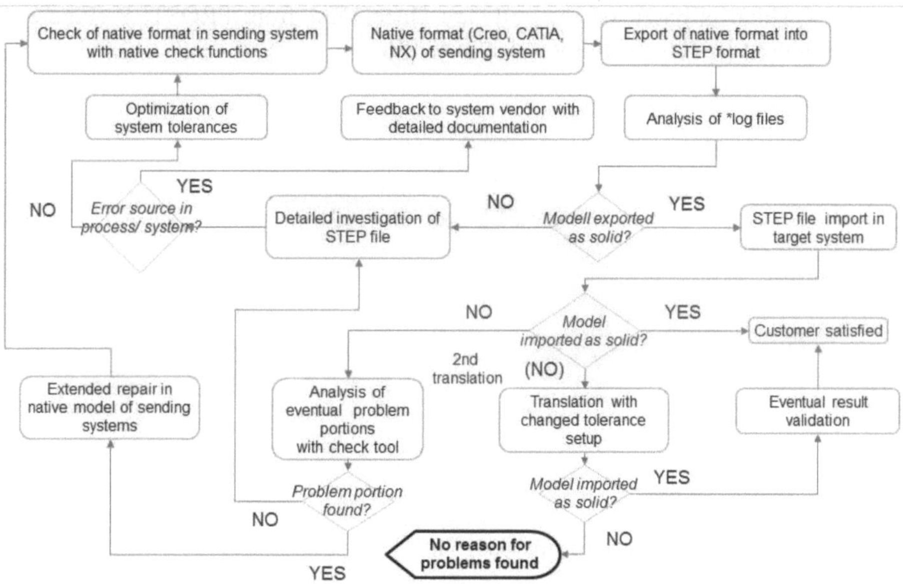

Fig. 3. Final concept for the test procedure

The validation phase is used to check and, if necessary, to improve the concept specification. It must be checked whether the developed method meets the requirements profile from the concept phase. To perform the test, it is necessary to establish criteria and procedures. Based on test criteria and methods, check tools can be developed that allow computer-aided validation. The result of the validation phase can eventually lead to the revision of the concept.

5 Validation

Validation methods target the proof of the validity of the specification and implementation. They use the methods for verification, confirming the completeness and correctness of a system with respect to a reference system, and the methods of falsification, which serve to demonstrate the faultiness of a system. For validation, test methods are used, which are employed to demonstrate conformity. For the detection of a stable behavior, one applies check methods, which are used for qualitative examination of behavior at different levels of complexity in accordance with predetermined criteria. Finally, measurement methods are used for the quantitative determination concerning the behavior of the basis of predetermined measurement criteria.

The use of validation methods is different in the different phases of the product development model. Depending on the degree of product specification model description, based on the reference model, the formal specification and the implementation, validation procedures can be used in an increasingly quantifying way. In our case, all methods have been incorporated into a fully automated workflow, which is based on the software OpenDXM from PROSTEP (Figure 4). Thus the highest level traceability is achieved [8].

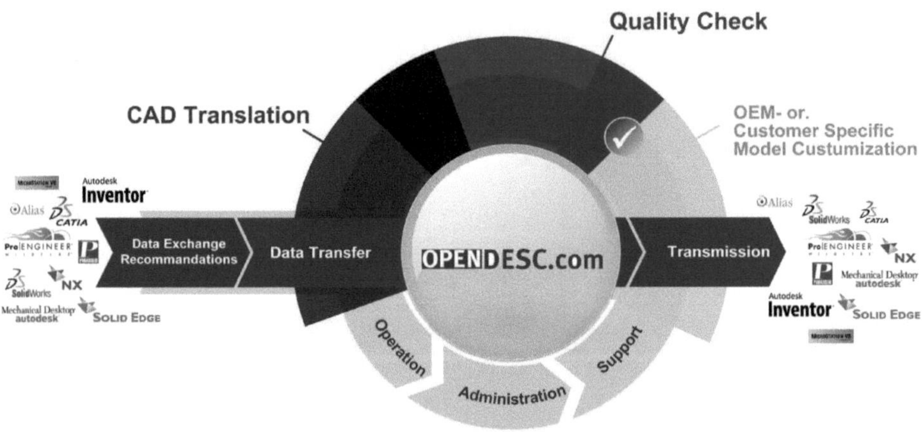

Fig. 4. CAD translation in www.opendesc.com

6 Use Case Daimler

Since Daimler has taken the decision to switch to CAD system NX of Siemens PLM instead of CATIA V5 of Dassault Systemes there is a huge change in the customer process of almost each supplier. The overall situation is shown in Figure 5. Each supplier has to serve simultaneously two target systems (CATIA for ongoing and NX for upcoming projects) with the same or similar content [9]. This procedure includes many CAD translation steps (scenarios 4 to 9) which are in principal not beneficial for good data quality. The challenge is in preserving such a level of data quality to ensure that all translating processes are successful. The data quality in CATIA is checked with QChecker again, in NX by using the newly deployed Heidelberg CAx Quality Manager (HQM).

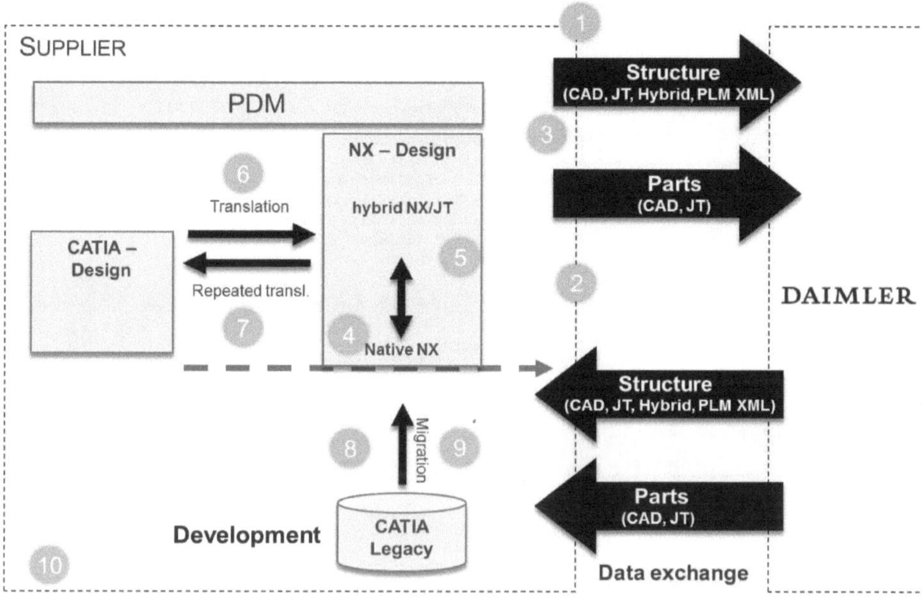

Fig. 5. The change in collaboration between Daimler and suppliers

7 Results

The procedure shown above was applied for different use cases, including different design content (powertrain, interior, electrics, chassis). Most of them were Creo data, modeled and prepared for translation to CATIA V5, as actually used in ongoing development projects at Daimler. Therefore, a good comparability between "old scenario" and "new scenario" is given.

The translators in CATIA and NX disclose the similar level of performance and robustness. The base system tolerance lies with 0,001 mm at the same level. Initially, all models can be transferred lossless without exception to CATIA and NX. However, it appears in some cases that automatic healing algorithms have slightly adjusted the geometry to satisfy the continuity condition. To what extent this would lead to further problems in further processing, could not be definitely predicted.

Further comparisons in the model properties like center of gravity, moments of inertia, as well as cloud of points were also within the allowed tolerances and showed no abnormalities.

Further investigations were accomplished with the models that once have already been converted, because that is the typical implication of complex scenario shown in Figure 5. Here occurred considerable problems and losses that had to be corrected manually. Such models generally reveal significant quality problems and should be avoided. The Heidelberg CAx Quality Manager (HQM) was very helpful to identify the problems and make a repair easier; a typical application is shown in Figure 6.

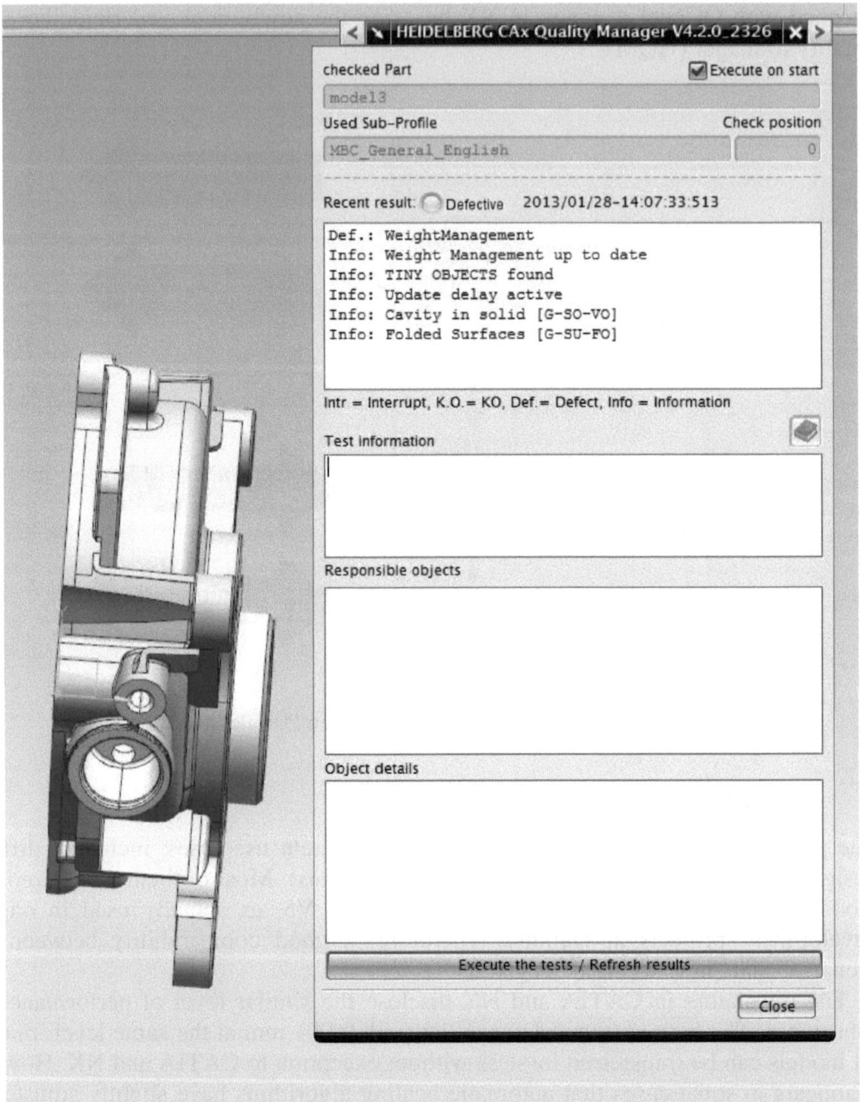

Fig. 6. Typical results in Heidelberg CAx Quality Manager

8 Conclusions and Outlook

In a dynamic collaborative environment like global automotive industry the working conditions are subject to a continuous change. Suppliers who work together with different OEMs and tier-1 suppliers have to constantly cope with new requirements relating to exchange partners, data formats, system environments to be supported, quality and security requirements, etc. If they take data communication with customers into their own hands, this means that they have to constantly adapt their data translation and exchange processes to the ever-changing requirements. This involves considerable administrative overhead in terms of time and money, which can occasionally have a negative impact on quality and adherence to deadlines. Collaboration with a competent service provider is therefore an interesting alternative, as it not only cuts costs, but also facilitates making the exchange processes uniform and ensures a higher level of reliability and traceability.

Good example for the long-term stability is the proposed approach to support the recent move of Daimler by replacing CATIA with NX. While many suppliers, which provide the data communication on their own, are forced to adapt their infrastructure, processes and methods to new environment at Daimler by spending a significant amount of money and time, the proposed solution allows to work again in the same environment by using predefined interface in the customer process like supplier portal www.opendesc.com. The check tool Heidelberg CAx Quality Manager (HQM) performs a significant contribution to successful data exchange.

The weakness of the proposed solution is the lack of solution for parametric data translation which still has to be developed.

The future development belongs the further automation of whole communication process and provision of "communication plugin" [10] for each OEM, based on recent standards (STEP AP242 and JT), in order to avoid the expensive point-to-point connection.

References

1. Stark, J.: Global Product. Strategy, Product Lifecycle Management and the Billion Customer Question. Springer, London (2007)
2. Dyer, J.H.: Collaborative advantage: winning through extended enterprise supplier networks. Oxford University Press, Oxford (2000)
3. Tang, D., Chin, K.-S.: Collaborative Supplier Integration for Product Design and Development. In: Wang, L., Nee, A.Y.C. (eds.) Collaborative Design and Planning for Digital Manufacturing, pp. 99–116. Springer, London (2009)
4. N.N: VDA Empfehlung 4961/3, Abstimmung der Datenlogistik in SE-Projekten, VDA, Frankfurt (2012)
5. N.N: VDA-Empfehlung 4955 Umfang und Qualität von CAD/CAM-Daten, Version 3, VDA, Frankfurt (2002)
6. Bondar, S., Potjewijd, L., Stjepandic, J.: Globalized OEM and Tier-1 Processes at SKF. In: Stjepandic, J., et al. (eds.) Concurrent Engineering Approaches for Sustainable Product Development in a Multi-Disciplinary Environment, pp. 789–800. Springer, London (2013)
7. Fischer, T., Martin, H.P., Endres, M., Stjepandic, J., Trinkhaus, O.: Anwendungsorientierte Optimierung des neutralen CAD-Datenaustausches mit Schwerpunkt Genauigkeit und Toleranz, VDA, Frankfurt (2000)
8. Reim, R., Cordon, P., Hund, A., Stjepandic, J.: CAD-Konvertierung: Motivation, Probleme, Lösungen, CADCAM Report, 9 (2007)
9. Wendenburg, M.: Konvertierung als Dienstleistung, CADCAM 2007, 9–10 (2007)
10. Mervyn, F., Kumar, A.S., Nee, A.Y.C.: A 'Plug-and-Play' Computing Environment for an Extended Enterprise. In: Li, W.D., et al. (eds.) Collaborative Product Design and Manufacturing Methodologies and Applications, pp. 71–91. Springer, London (2007)

Lessons Learned for Better Management of Master Geometry

Tümay Mart and Can Cangelir

Turkish Aerospace Industries Inc., Ankara, Turkey 06980
{tmart,ccangelir}@tai.com.tr

Abstract. When an aircraft is thought as a final product, it has a complex structure with numerous parts to be managed. Complexity requires multifunctional design activities, and multifunctional design needs collaborative way of working for continuous success. This cooperated approach could only be accomplished by the help of concurrent engineering techniques. Currently, several distinctive design activities are performed at digital environment of CAD tools. Position information and interrelations between parts of a product are provided by the help of associative physical CAD links. Requirement of CAD links during design activities paves the way for the usage of Master Geometry models as an official source of aircraft shape and a geometrical reference for all actors involved. Master Geometry models have to be managed in Product Lifecycle Management tools in order to provide effective implementation and usage of models from conception, through design and manufacture, to service and disposal of product. Some improper cases could be observed when a correlation is tried to be generated between Master Geometry models and 3D models of product at CAD environment. In this paper, these cases will be examined and potential solutions, which are the results of lessons learned activities, will be proposed with concrete examples.

Keywords: Master Geometry, Master Geometry Creation, Master Geometry Validation Workflow, Buffer Geometry.

1 Introduction

Concurrent engineering techniques provide collaborative strategies, which are totally focused on cost and time reduction of product development processes in parallel with improving quality level of final products. These improvements have to be seen as the key for success by all companies who want to be a leading force within their own field of industrial expertise [1]. It is mainly a question of process and way of working. For conventional method, product development processes are performed sequentially and this type of method does not answer the requirements of being a global player of challenging and competitive worldwide economy [2]. Many aerospace companies attain success only with adapting cooperated way of working strategies, due to high level competition resulting from reduced product life cycles, growing product complexity, multifunctional design activities and the need for a large number of product variants [2].

A. Bernard, L. Rivest, and D. Dutta (Eds.): PLM 2013, IFIP AICT 409, pp. 712–721, 2013.

For aerospace industry, product development processes start with works at aircraft level and iteratively continues through the level of detailed elementary parts. In another words, it could be stated that the aircraft design process is an iterative and top-down activity. When the complexity of an aircraft is taken into consideration, a final product could only be achieved by involvement of several distinctive disciplines. Additionally, there have to be continuous exchanges of information between all interested parties within a protective environment during product lifecycle. The digital environment created and leaded by concurrent engineering provides this type of collaborative work media where all the related departments can communicate with stakeholders. Integrative design environment has been a subject of intense research over the past several years. According to recent studies, NIST Core Product Model (CPM) is described as a product information-modeling framework. In CPM, a product is modeled as a triad of its function (what it is intended to do), its form (what is its shape and material) and its behavior (how it implements its function) [3]. Open Assembly Model (OAM) is defined as an extension of CPM, and OAM is used to provide a standard representation and exchange protocol for assembly and system level tolerance information [4]. Another method is The Cooperative Design Modeler (CoDeMo). CoDeMo assists the integration and the cooperation of each participant who would be an external or internal actor. It achieves, thereby, a formal network of cooperation based on the shared database, which is manipulated by the design external actors and managed by the internal actor [5,6].

In this context, Master Geometry models get on the stage as a set of 3D models, which represents a single geometrical reference database of the main aircraft geometry for all interested parties. It has to be noted that management of Master Geometry models and preserving interrelation between product and Master Geometry during product lifecycle period is important.

At following sections of this paper, three different improper incidences, which possibly could be faced with during generation, usage and management processes of Master Geometry models, will be identified and exact solutions to mentioned incidences will be proposed. Additionally, in order to provide background information about main topic, brief descriptions of product structure, product lifecycle and detailed description of creation and management of Master Geometry will be mentioned.

2 Definitions

2.1 Product Lifecycle

Product life cycle is a generic term covering all phases of acquisition, operation, and logistics support of an item, beginning with concept definition and continuing through disposal of the item [7]. As the product development activity of an aircraft proceeds, it passes through a series of reviews of increasing detail. Design reviews evaluate the technical progress toward meeting specification requirements [8]. Each review is tailored to ensure that the emerging design is ready to enter the next stage of development.

2.2 Product Structure

Product structures show component relationships and enable visualization of a product in relation to its higher and lower level components, from any level. Product structures are typically portrayed in a top-down manner starting with the end product and going down to the lowest level [9]. Product structure is a hierarchical breakdown of the product that contains 3D models and attributes of product. Attributes of product are data, which gives alpha-numeric values about part description, part number, material information, manufacturing process, version, engineering parameters etc... Product structure has to keep latest design information to prevent inconvenient design activities. It is essential to manage all involved data of product properly with up to date versions. With this purpose, Product Lifecycle Management tools are being used as a single database, which could be reached by different functional disciplines accordance with their needs.

3 Master Geometry

As mentioned previously; during product life cycle process of an aircraft, several different groups are involved in design, manufacturing and after sales service support activities. Although those groups have totally different disciplines, there has to be a strong relation between different disciplines for aircraft design. Consider a design group whose main responsibility is structural part design of the aircraft such as designing frames, ribs, spars, stringers etc. On the other, there has to be another group whose main responsibility is system design. System designers individually know the content of what needs to be generated as a system deeply and location of this system on the aircraft roughly. However, geometrical interaction between systems, absolute geometrical installation points and dimensional limitations also need to be known. This information somehow needs to be shared between different disciplines. The same situation would be observed between two different structural design groups working for different sections of the same aircraft with geometrical dependencies.

In order to make sure that design activities are performed on right location of aircraft, location information of designed parts or systems on aircraft has to be identified. Designers need design parameters or geometrical indications, which they can use as a reference point from aircraft geometry. Exact locations of all parts on final product could be provided by the help of physical CAD links. Generating links from part to part could be the first technique comes to mind. However, generating links from other parts or geometrical elements are not recommended, because of location information of common parts and geometrical elements on the aircraft could be changed due to dynamic nature of the design activity and they could not be considered as a reference point.

In this context, implementation of Master Geometry models has significant importance for aircraft development process. Master Geometry file is the collection of all primary references necessary for design of aircraft primary structure and system installation. Master Geometry models form the basis for all geometry levels of the aircraft. Thus, it has to be stated that structural parts can only be physically linked to Master Geometry features in CAD environment, since Master Geometry models are definitely controlled references. Generating links from part to part or from other geometrical elements is not recommended.

3.1 Content of Master Geometry Models

Master Geometry is a 3D CAD model, which represents the outer geometry and the elements forming the structure of the aircraft all together. This geometrical composition consists of surfaces, planes, lines and points and includes all necessary geometrical dependencies and constraints required for design of the aircraft. Following definitions show the detailed content of Master Geometry; indications e.g. planes, coordinate systems of main structural components e.g. frames, ribs, spars, cut-outs like doors or windows and the positions of main sections [10]. It has to be noted that Master Geometry is not an actual part or section that is manufactured, but it is only a conceptual part, containing a sketch or general shape of the overall design and important design parameters [10]. Following Figure 1 shows the examples of Master Geometry content.

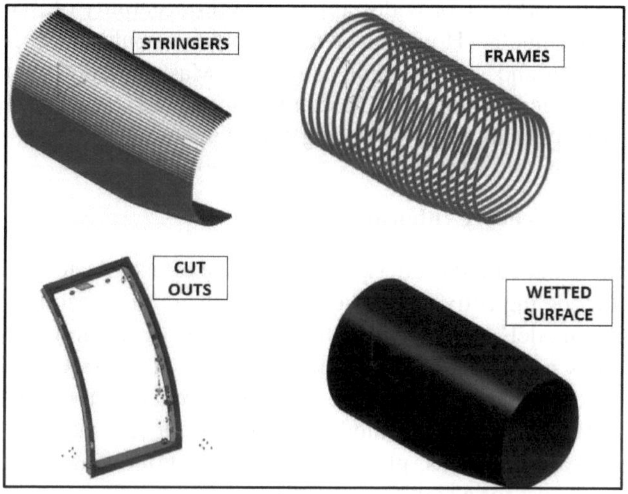

Fig. 1. Examples of Master Geometry Content

3.2 Creation of Master Geometry Models

Master Geometry creation process has to be started at conceptual design phase and mainly frozen just after the detailed design phase. However, management of the master geometry database continues for the life of the aircraft. Master Geometry models are the structural reference of the whole aircraft that contains all the external shapes of the aircraft and the main geometrical references, which could be used as a solid basis by structural designers, subcontractors, manufacturing engineers, stress engineers and aerodynamic engineers. Master Geometry models include inputs from all related disciplines especially structural design, aerodynamic, structural analysis, tool design, EMI-EMC group and system engineering. External aircraft geometry, which is an output of aerodynamic studies, could be stated as the main source for generation of Master Geometry models.

4 Management of Master Geometry

Generating Master Geometry models would be not enough for a complex product development process. Master Geometry could be evolved due to the modifications, improvements and change requests through design phases, and this evolution has to be managed within a protective and controlled environment. Thus, a special product structure, a special role and a special workflow have to be defined for Master Geometry models with the help of Product Lifecycle Management tools.

Special product structure brings hierarchical breakdown of Master Geometry models in an organizational way. Authorized role provides controlled access of creating and modifying 3D models of Master Geometry. Only the users, who have Master Geometry Specialist role, would be able to perform 3D model creation or modification tasks. Special workflow provides approval and traceability of 3D model modifications of Master Geometry. However, several problems could be observed during the 3D model generation and management periods of Master Geometry models, due to the nature of geometrical attributes of Master Geometry. Each case and potential solution will be separately analyzed at following subtitles.

4.1 Reduction of Feature Intensity

System installation and structural design groups have to use Master Geometry models during their 3D modeling activities. When the design activity becomes more detailed, Master Geometry models shall have ability to answer to requirements of all design groups. Sometimes a single Master Geometry model at aircraft level could not be used properly for detailed design activities within a dynamic environment. For a basic trainer aircraft, Master Geometry models at aircraft level includes approximately 14000 features like lines, points, planes, surfaces etc. Following Figure 2 shows the intensity of features just for a significant section of an aircraft.

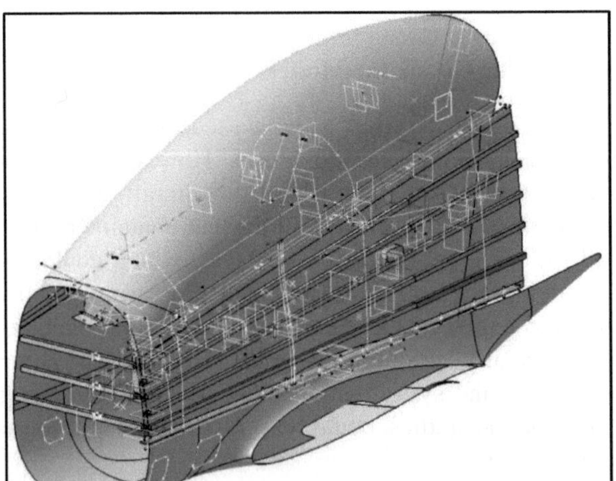

Fig. 2. Intensity of Features (lines, planes, points et.)

Using one big model for Master Geometry could be a chaos for detailed part design activities. Consider a structural designer which works on wing and totally responsible for structural parts of a definite section of the wing. When this designer tries to use Master Geometry model as a reference, he/she has to refer aircraft level model which includes all detailed geometrical information of fuselage, empennage or other major components which could be classified as out of scope according to his responsibilities. This excessive information kept in single model will causes confusion among design groups and poses as a risk for performed designs. Same situation also would be a problem for a system installation responsible.

Solution 1. If whole aircraft is being designed, the general Master Geometry shall be broken down into convenient sections, to avoid excessive information in each model and to align the Master Geometry more in line with the design and manufacture task breakdown, instead of using single model. There have to be separate Master Geometry models for structural design group and system installation group.

In order to provide better management of details and integration with design teams, Master Geometry models of structural design group shall be broken to major components, sections and ATA (Air Transport Association of America) sections sequentially. Breakdown principle totally depends on requirements of design group. For instance, there could be separate Master Geometry models for wing, fuselage, and empennage in terms of structure. Still, it can be divided into further indices if necessary. Aircraft level Master Geometry model generated for structural design includes approximately 5000 features and it is observed that the number of features included in one Master Geometry model could be reduced to 800 by splitting into further indices.

Master Geometry models of system installation group shall be derived from the Master Geometry models generated for structural design. Additionally, Master Geometry models of system installation have to be physically linked to the ones of structural design. In order to prevent excessive information in each model, system installation Master Geometry models can be split into sub-sections. There has to be a separate Master Geometry model for each system. Aircraft level Master Geometry model of system installation includes approximately 9000 features and it is observed that the number of features included in one Master Geometry model could be reduced to 250, if a separate model is created for each system. Following Figure 3 shows the reduction rates of feature intensity with approximate values of a real splitting case.

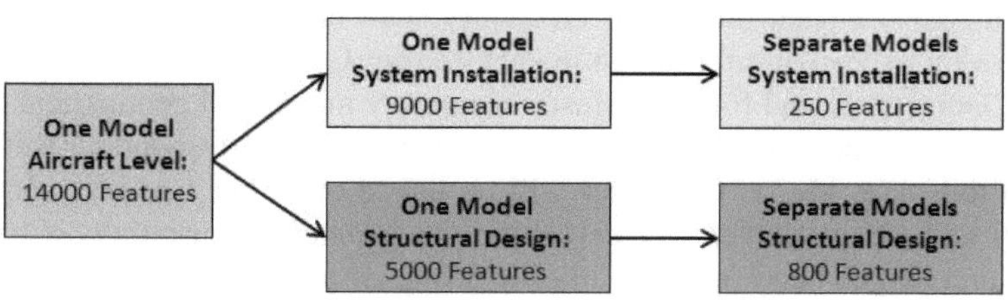

Fig. 3. Reduction of Feature Intensity

4.2 Using Buffer Geometry

As mentioned previously, all detail parts except some brackets have to be linked to Master Geometry models and Master Geometry models have to be physically linked to external aircraft geometry models at CAD environment, in order to provide association between models. This means if an external geometry model is changed, associated Master Geometry model will give link update warning, so do detail parts due to updating Master Geometry models.

For a basic trainer aircraft, there are more than 4000 detail parts. It could be estimated that updating one detail part at CAD environment takes 1 minute. Each external geometry modification causes detail part updating workload, which approximately equals to 4000 minutes for whole aircraft. Every modification of external geometry would not have an impact on detail parts. Thus, there has to be a monitoring interface between external geometry and Master Geometry models in order to prevent unnecessary updates of Master Geometry and to avoid extra workloads at detail part level.

Additionally, sometimes it is possible that external aircraft geometries could be provided by aerodynamic group as a coarse model. Coarse models include draft surfaces, lack of cut out sections of the surface etc. In this case; first of all, some arrangements and fine tunings have to be performed on models which have been directly taken from external aircraft geometry, and then these models shall be transferred to Master Geometry. These arrangements include totally CAD operations. And these all CAD operations have to be performed in order to make Master Geometry models applicable for design specifications. During detailed design phase, there will be excessive information in Master Geometry models such as initial information taken from aerodynamic group, results of CAD operations and final geometrical features intended to use as Master Geometry. When all information is kept within a same model, it would be impossible to use Master Geometry models properly.

Solution 2. If CAD operation for fine tuning of data which has been taken from external aircraft geometry is a frequent activity, there has to be a transition medium between external aircraft geometry models and Master Geometry models.

In this context, Buffer Geometry model gets on the stage as a solution. Buffer Geometry functions as a transition and monitoring model between external aircraft geometry and Master Geometry. All elements taken from the external aircraft geometry are transferred to the Master Geometry after being arranged using the Buffer Geometry. If the surfaces taken from aerodynamic engineering group have been provided as a coarse model, the Buffer Geometry shall be used to make these surfaces fine to prevent excessive information in each Master Geometry model. There shall be a Buffer Geometry model for each Master Geometry model. All geometrical elements in the Master Geometry model shall only be linked to the corresponding Buffer Geometry. In this case, Master Geometry will be linked to Buffer Geometry and Buffer Geometry will also be linked to external aircraft geometry sequentially. Changes on external aircraft geometry will directly have impact on Buffer Geometry. With the help of Buffer Geometry, only effective changes could be transferred to Master Geometry models and this way of working prevents unnecessary link updates of detail parts and provides 80% time reduction for link update task at detail part level. Following Figure 4 shows the CAD operations performed on a Buffer Geometry model.

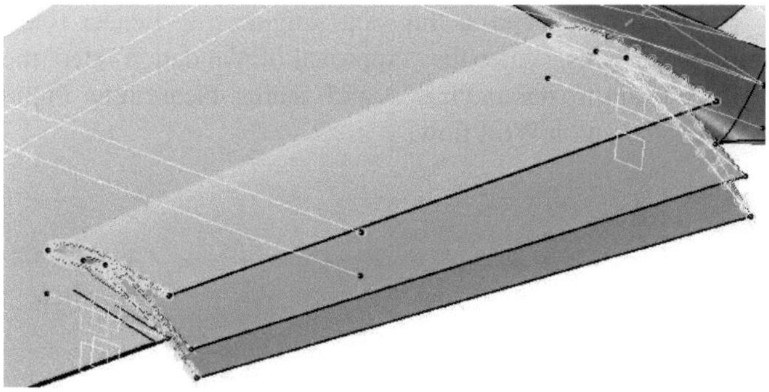

Fig. 4. Buffer Geometry (CAD arrangements and fine tunings)

4.3 Master Geometry Validation Workflow

The design data of a product has to be approved and released through workflows with revision control in order to make it applicable for stakeholders within a protective and controlled way. Same identification has to be also implemented for Master Geometry models. Consider a final product with high complexity; all parts of the product could be linked to same Master Geometry model. When this Master Geometry model could somehow up issued from Revision-A to Revision-B due to new requirements or change requests, all items which have CAD links to this Master Geometry model also have to be up issued. Otherwise, associative CAD links between parts and Master Geometry model will become broken because associative links keeps track of the file name of Master Geometry models. Updating links and up issuing of all parts will be a heavy work load for design group.

Solution 3. Giving "Released" status and issue tracking for Master Geometry models is not recommended. Because when you release an item through workflows, you have to keep track of the revision control of that item. In case of Master Geometry models; instead of using "Released" status, "Valid" status has to be used with a proper workflow.

Consider a change request has been received for an existing Master Geometry model. According to predefined rules of the Master Geometry Workflow; following steps will be performed sequentially: at first step; Master Geometry Specialist role informs and requests to rearrange the Master Geometry model in accordance with the design requirements. This first stage is "Request" step of the workflow and during this phase the data is frozen. At second step; Engineering Leader role confirms that the Master Geometry change is required and acceptable. This second stage is called "Assessment" step and at this step, Engineering Leader role can also reject the request. The data is set free from now on. At third step; Master Geometry Specialist role applies the changes to Master Geometry model. Additionally, Master Geometry Specialist starts validation request. This third stage is called "Request for Validation" step. At fourth step; Engineering Leader role confirms that the corrections and/or improvements are applied correctly. This fourth stage is called

"Approval of Validation" step and at this step, Engineering Leader role can reject the corrections and modifications. After the "Approval of Validation" step, the Master Geometry model will be again frozen and has "Valid" status. Please refer Figure 5 for details of Master Geometry Validation Workflow.

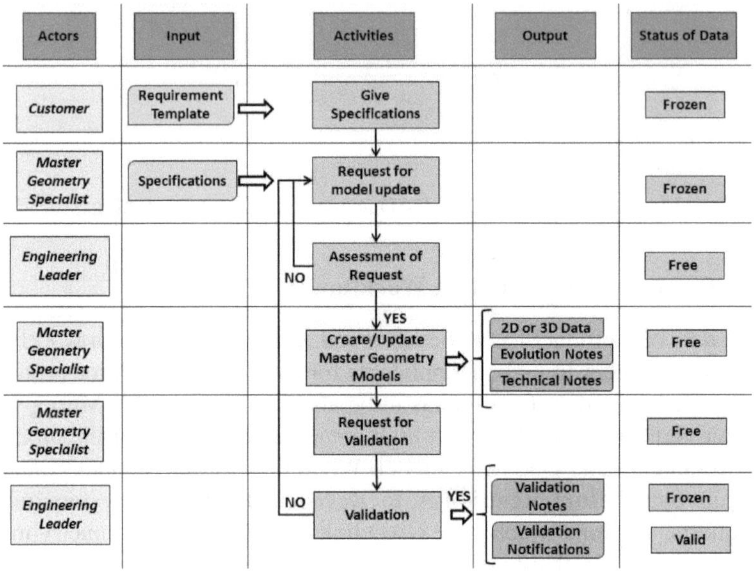

Fig. 5. Master Geometry Validation Workflow

5 Conclusion

This paper is aimed to present the importance of Master Geometry models on multi-functional design activities. Basically, interactions of structural design activity, system design activity and manufacturing process with Master Geometry models have been identified. Generic geometrical content of Master Geometry models has been also defined. In order to provide coherency between Master Geometry and other indications, brief descriptions of product structure and product life cycle are given. Afterwards, three different problems could be faced with during implementation and management period of Master Geometry has been deeply analyzed and presented with supportive convenient examples. These problems could be defined in a nutshell as follows; problem number one was about excessive content of usage single Master Geometry models during whole product development process. Problem number two was about filling out Master Geometry models with unnecessary geometrical information which makes Master Geometry models useless. And finally, problem number three was about unsuitable consequences of released status of Master Geometry models and workloads of link updates. After that, accordance with the results of lessons learned and know how activities potential solution techniques have been proposed.

Future work will concentrate on issues related to the implementation and management of Space Allocation Mock-up which is a digital mock-up made of simplified 3D solid models in CAD formats. The place of Space Allocation Mock-up design within overall aircraft development will be highlighted and the link between Space Allocation Mock-up models and Master Geometry models will be presented in details.

References

1. Hartley, J.R.: Concurrent Engineering, pp. 15–27. Productivity Press (1998)
2. Parsei, H.R., Sullivan, W.G.: Concurrent Engineering, pp. 4–19. Chapman & Hall (1993)
3. Sudarsan, R., Fenves, S.J., Sriram, R.D., Wang, F.: A product information modeling framework for product lifecycle management (2005)
4. Sudarsan, R., Young-Hyun, H., Foufou, S., Feng, S.C., Roy, U., Fujun, W., Sriram, R.D., Lyons, K.W.: A Model for Capturing Product Assembly Information. Journal of Computing and Information Science in Engineering (2005)
5. Noel, F.: A product-process-organization integrative model for collaborative design, Laboratory 3S, University of Grenoble, France (2006)
6. Lionel, R., Serge, T.: CoDE: A Cooperative Design Environment-A New Generation of CAD Systems, Domaine Universitaire (2000)
7. MIL-STD-973, Military Standard Configuration Management (1992)
8. MIL-STD-1521 B, Military Standard Technical Reviews and Audits for Systems, Equipments and Computer Software (1976)
9. EIA-649-B, National Consensus Standard for Configuration Management Department of Defence (2011)
10. Dolezal, W.: Success Factors for DMU in Complex Aerospace Product Development. Technische Universität München (2007)
11. Les, A.P.: Ten challenges in computer-aided design, Department of Computer Science and Engineering, University of South Florida (2005)

Author Index

MIX
Papier aus verantwortungsvollen Quellen
Paper from responsible sources
FSC® C105338

If you have any concerns about our products,
you can contact us on
ProductSafety@springernature.com

In case Publisher is established outside the EU,
the EU authorized representative is:
Springer Nature Customer Service Center GmbH
Europaplatz 3, 69115 Heidelberg, Germany

Printed by Libri Plureos GmbH
in Hamburg, Germany